"In its scope, structure, and sheer length, this meaty 983-page true-life epic unfolds as a sort of Beatles' *War and Peace*. . . . Spitz's genius is how he stitches together available Beatles knowledge with the artistry of a fine novelist."
—Michael Tarm, *Cincinnati Enquirer*

"Spitz has done a masterful job of focusing his kaleidoscope eyes on the greatest pop thing since Jesus."
—Richard Gehr, *Village Voice*

"Spitz knows his subject. His encyclopedic grasp pervades every page."
—Joe Selvin, *San Francisco Chronicle*

"Spitz marshals a staggering mass of research. . . . The early chapters are irresistible; they have the hypnotic effect of a film clip run backward."
—Lev Grossman, *Time*

"Spitz has performed a valuable historical service. . . . *The Beatles* respects its subjects without canonizing them. . . . Best of all, at the end of the long and winding road, it sends us back home to the music."
—David Hinckley, *New York Daily News*

"Filled with intimate scenes. . . . The first third of this opus is a treasure chest of revelation. . . . Spitz demonstrates his deep research and writing chops by transporting us to the place where it all began. . . . This book reminds us—in generous detail—that the Fab Four were just people."
—John Kehe, *Christian Science Monitor*

"A real page-turner. . . . A vibrant and exhaustive factual and emotional picture of John, Paul, George, and Ringo's early life and times. . . . It actually adds some new information—or at least a fresh analysis—to this often-told story. . . . The lads' schoolboy years are told in captivating detail. . . . Engagingly written, meticulously researched and documented, and tremendously insightful."
—*Ruminator Review*

"Fresh, terrifically entertaining. . . . Packed with details and anecdotes that bring the Fab Four to life. . . . Spitz's group portrait should now be considered the definitive Beatles biography."
—June Sawyers, *Booklist*

for
Sandy & Angie D'Amato
and Lily
And for all those whose lives are enriched
by the Beatles' music

*When the mode of the music changes,
the walls of the city shake.*
—PLATO

CONTENTS

THE BEATLES

PROLOGUE

December 27, 1960

They had begun to pour into the village of Litherland as they always did, half an hour before the doors opened. Nightcrawlers: their bodies young and liquid, legs spidering along the sidewalks, exaggerated by the blue glare of the streetlamps. This time of year, Sefton Road at 6:30 was already dark; evening pressed down early from the desolate sky, raked by gunmetal gray clouds drifting east across the river toward the stagnating city of Liverpool.

Tuesdays at Litherland's town hall were usually what promoters referred to as "soft nights"—that is, midweek affairs attracting a reasonable 600 or 700 jivers, as opposed to the weekend crush of 1,500—but tonight's shindig was billed as a Christmas dance, which accounted for the unusually large crowd. Every few minutes another double-decker bus groaned to a halt outside the hall and emptied a heaving load of teenagers onto the pavement. The crowd, moving erratically in the brittle night air, swelled like a balloon waiting for a dart.

The main attraction, ex post facto, had not yet arrived. Running customarily behind schedule, the band had left West Derby Village later than anticipated after choosing, by consensus, a playlist for that night's performance. The selection process was no mean feat, considering their repertoire of well over 150 rock 'n roll songs, from the seminal hits ("Whole Lotta Shakin' Goin' On," "What'd I Say") to pop standards ("Better Luck Next Time," "Red Sails in the Sunset") to obscure gems ("You Don't Understand Me"); each demanded brief consideration. Afterward, equipment was loaded into the old bottle green van that had been recruited for service only that morning.

The four boys, riding in the dark, grimy cargo hold like astronauts in a cramped space capsule, braced themselves with experienced hands as the old crate rattled north along the Stanley Road, past shops splashed with a waxy fluorescence. The road hugged the shoreline, where they could see harbor lights and the wharves of the distant port, then broke inland along the Leeds & Liverpool Canal. Even to a native, which they all were, it was difficult to tell where one borough ended and another began: Crosby became Kirkdale and eventually Bootle, then Litherland, their boundaries marked only by wide-mouthed intersections and the occasional shop sign incorporating a piece of local heritage into its name.

They stared silently out the back window for a while, absorbing the hallucinatory darkness. Paul McCartney and George Harrison, both prodigiously handsome, straddled two boxy amplifiers, while Pete Best, shifting and elusive, posted like a cowboy atop a bass drum case. Unspeaking also, John Lennon, who had been to Litherland twice before, rode shotgun in order to direct their driver to the proper location.

Chas Newby knew he was the odd man out. Crouched perilously on an enameled wheel arch, he regarded his mates with respectful detachment. Until a week before, nearly half a year had passed since he'd last heard them play. Those few months ago, they were like most other aspiring Liverpool bands, talented but unexceptional, performing identical cover versions of current hits that everyone else was doing. "I certainly didn't think they would make much of an impression," he says, recalling their muddy sound, their clumsy, mechanical attack, their unintentional anarchy. In fact, his former band, the Blackjacks, in which Pete Best had played, was no better or worse at entertaining the kids who followed local groups from dance club to dance club to dance club. On any given night, five bands on a bill would perform the same set of songs—the same way. Homogeneity was the criterion on which the whole scene turned.

Now suddenly everything had changed. When Chas had arrived at Pete's house in West Derby Village the week before, he was quite unprepared for the scene inside. The living room was overheated and brighter than usual. An umbrella of purple smoke hung over the coffee table, Coke bottles lay scattered like chess pieces. As Newby moved toward the couch, his eyes filled with a vision that looked like one of Rouault's Gothic monochromes: four ravenlike figures were grouped there, clad in ominous bruised leather and blackness—trousers, T-shirts, jackets, boots, a riot of black. It took him a few seconds, reading the faces of the caped quartet, to realize they belonged to Pete Best and musicians he'd previously known collectively as the Quarry Men.

The band hadn't played a date in weeks, owing to a creeping malaise that nearly rendered them extinct. Then, a week ago, four decent gigs materialized, which they'd hungrily accepted, despite one glaring obstacle: their bass player, Stuart Sutcliffe, was spending the holiday in Germany with his girlfriend.

"We need a bass player," one of the musicians complained, courting Newby.

Best nodded significantly. "Get yourself a bass and practice with us," he said. Newby was amused and touched by their invitation. His know-how extended only to rhythm guitar, but he was familiar with droning bass figures, and George Harrison, the band's true technician, volunteered to simplify it for him.

Newby borrowed a bass from his friend Tommy McGurk and agreed to an impromptu practice. They set up shop in the Bests' capacious basement—a room that moonlighted as the Casbah jive club, where kids came to hang out and dance—and ran down some songs. "The sort of music they played was fairly easy to pick up," Newby says. But the sound they made unnerved him. It was still dependent on cover versions of current hits, but unlike the reverential copies performed by all other Liverpool bands, they burst through an entirely new dimension. These songs were not meticulous imitations, there was nothing neat or controlled about them. They were fierce, rip-roaring, they had real muscle, underscored by Best's vigorous drumming—a lusty, propulsive volley that drove each song over a cliff—and the vocal acrobatics of McCartney. Newby was amazed at how Paul, especially, had transformed himself from an able crooner into a belter whose vocal range seemed to spiral off the charts. "Paul had developed this way of falsetto singing that knocked me for a loop," he says. "No one in Liverpool sang like that, like Little Richard—*no one.*"

Lennon, more than anyone, knew they had made great strides. (Years later he would acknowledge as much, saying, "We thought we were the best before anybody else had even heard us, back in Hamburg and Liverpool.") But only that August the band had left Liverpool a virtual embarrassment. Their playing was haphazard, their direction uncharted. The word around town was that their band was the worst outfit on the circuit—not even a band, if you took into account that they were unable to hold a drummer. Howie Casey, who fronted the Seniors and would one day play for Wings, says, "We sure didn't know them, and I don't think anybody else . . . knew them either." Only one bandleader of significance was able to recall a nightmarish triple bill they'd played that May at Lathom Hall, in the Liverpool suburb of Seaforth. "They were so bad," he said, "[the promoter] just shut the curtains on them!"

So it had been off to Hamburg and then, afterward, the bleak likelihood of an apprenticeship on the Liverpool docks, a clerk's position at the Cotton Exchange or British Rail, or rivet duty at one of the automobile plants sprouting in the suburbs. No doubt about it, after Germany there would be no further high life. John Lennon had been chucked out of art college for extreme indifference, a disgrace he seemed to court, as if a dark diagnosis had been confirmed. Paul McCartney had squandered his early academic promise by performing so poorly on his exams that teachers abandoned any hope that he'd advance to the university level. George Harrison, who regarded school as a terrific inconvenience, had decided to sit for exams—and failed *every one* of them. Thrilled by performing, Pete Best had drifted away from plans to attend a teachers training college. Only Stuart Sutcliffe, who was an impassioned, proven artist, had any hope of success, and his bandmates knew he would eventually forsake music to pursue his destiny as a serious painter.

But Hamburg had thrown them all a powerful curve. Something strangely significant had happened there, something intangible opened a small window of hope and gave their dreams an unpredictable new lift. Their shows took on an excitement that bordered on anarchy. Frustrated by the feeble drone that English rock 'n roll bands had settled into, they exploited their notoriety as "a gang of scruffs" and pumped up the volume. They began retooling their show to reach the audience through antics gleaned from hell-raisers like Gene Vincent and Jerry Lee Lewis. In the process, they became not only rigorously proficient onstage but immensely popular with the German nightclub crawlers.

Then, just as mercurially, it all came crashing down.

The Hamburg gig had ended in tumultuous disarray, with the boys being deported in an unbecoming fashion and shipped north again in irregular, onerous shifts. For two weeks they bummed around Liverpool, sad and aimless, avoiding one another like animals forced to share a cage in a zoo. Evidence that their dream had ended loomed starkly, and the freight of one another's company made it that much harder to bear.

It was in the midst of this deepening depression that John and Pete turned up together at the tiny Jacaranda coffee bar. They had come for a coffee and, by chance, encountered Bob Wooler, a nappy, courtly man of twenty-eight with no youth left to him aside from a passion for popular music. No one nurtured the Liverpool rock 'n roll community more ably than Wooler, a failed songwriter, until it was jerked sideways by the vise grip of Brian Epstein a few years later. He projected the dazzling eloquence of an actor and anchored his voice with a facile, flowery resonance that gave his young protégés a sense of confidence. All afternoon Lennon and Best sat sulking, ill at ease, at one of the tiny postage-stamp-size tables, surrounded by clusters of bearded university students, and whined to Wooler about their professional situation. They wanted to work again— badly. Anything would do: a show, a dance, a club date, even a party. He had to help them, he just *had* to, they insisted.

The only event of significance was the upcoming Christmas dance at Litherland Town Hall. Wooler called promoter Brian Kelly from the Jacaranda's kitchen, while Lennon and Best stood nearby, hanging on his every word. On the other end of the line, Kelly's stagy sigh leeched impatience. A cantankerous entrepreneur who was among the small band of missionaries spreading the gospel of rock 'n roll, he had heard it all before and was used to the gale force of Wooler's rhetoric when it came to plugging musicians. As far as Kelly was concerned, Wooler was trying to pick his pocket. Besides, he had already booked three bands to entertain. But Wooler was persuasive.

"They're fantastic," he assured Kelly, who deflected the compliment with a discernible grunt. "Could you possibly put them on as an extra? Like I said, they've been to Hamburg."

To punctuate this distinction, Wooler asked him for a fee of £8 for the band, an extraordinary amount for a local attraction. Kelly didn't take more than a second to respond. "Ridiculous!" Determinedly, Wooler pursued another line of argument to help further his case. "Yes, but they're professionals now," he said. This made Kelly sputter in disgust. "*Professional!* I don't give a sod about them being professional," he said.

Wooler cast an uneasy eye over his shoulder at the vigilant boys, their faces slipping in and out of the late-afternoon shadows. Hamburg had aged them, he thought. Best, the taller of the two, was bristle-haired, with a ghostly transparence in his eyes and the type of soft, matinee-idol features that could quicken a girl's pulse; Lennon, although a few inches shorter, seemed more in command by the hard glare he threw and the pitch of his face, set in an expression of thin-lipped satisfaction. And it was apparent to both of them that the conversation was not going as planned.

Momentarily distracted, Wooler threw them a swift, professional smile before returning to his sales pitch.

He and Brian Kelly went at it for another five minutes, feinting and jabbing with particulars that served their respective causes, until they had brokered an acceptable deal. Afterward, Wooler faced another uphill battle, persuading Best and Lennon to accept Kelly's £6 offer. It was considerably less than they had made overseas, nothing that would give them much incentive. But after all, it was a gig, it was another opportunity to play rock 'n roll. For the moment, they were back in business.

Past the old container dock in Bootle, Stanley Road broke up into a couple of two-lane tributaries that fed into Linacre Road. The road began a descent, and rounding a curve, they saw the town itself, stretched haggard beneath the unflattering winter light. Litherland had a great many shops, with a Methodist mission whose solid buff-and-red brick hulk was used as a mortuary during the Blitz. The floodlit Richmond sausage works sign, with its giddy neon pig marching off with a string of pork links, provided a beacon to the south; the stubby marquee outside the Regal Cinema glowed at the opposite end; the rest of the town existed obliquely behind the main road. There was no visible horizon, just block after block of wafer-thin terrace houses joined at the hip and strung together like shabby plastic beads. There had been a time when Litherland, with its rich green farms, stood proudly at the mouth of the Mersey, but the Luftwaffe had ruined its dreams. The brick-faced match works, hit by German incendiaries, remained a bombed-out blackened shell, while farther on, flattened gaps in row houses and caved-in church roofs stood as signposts to the area's tumultuous past.

Frank Garner, the band's driver (none of their families owned a car), pulled the van as close as he could to the entrance so the boys could unload their gear. In the gathering darkness, they could see a dozen or so teenagers lingering by the doors. The lack of a dense queue made the band uneasy until they realized that everyone had already gone inside to avoid the gamy stench seeping from the tannery on Field Lane, just beyond the hall.

In a scramble, they climbed out, lugging their equipment, and hurried in through an old wooden corridor cobbled to an open cloakroom that reeked of Minor's hair lacquer and disinfectant. The town council chamber and auxiliary offices, where villagers paid their bills, had been closed since 5:30, so the band wound along a hallway lined with deserted rooms to the backstage area, where Bob Wooler fussed over the evening's playlist.

Wooler was pleasantly surprised to see them. In the course of booking the date, John Lennon had bristled that the fee wasn't worth all the effort, and Wooler pleaded, "For God's sake, don't let me down." Lennon assured him they would turn up, but Wooler was skeptical.

Still, he decided to put them on at nine o'clock—the "center spot," as it was known—between the Deltones and the Searchers. "It meant that everyone would be inside the hall," Wooler recalls, "no one entering late or leaving early. For a half hour, they would have Liverpool's complete attention." Why Wooler did this remains a mystery—even to himself. Although he'd heard the band on an earlier occasion, it was only for a song before he fled to the refuge of a pub, leaving him without much of an opinion. Nor was he encouraged by their attitude. But as a victim of artistic frustration, Bob was drawn inexorably to the band's sorry predicament, especially to John's vulnerability. Wooler sensed in Lennon a person of awesome complexity and ambition; the boy seemed to emanate heat, signaling some kind of raw, restless talent. There was something there worth exploring, he concluded. "So I just trusted my instinct that they would go down in an unusual, important way."

The house was full, framed in hazy silhouette—not a fleet of drunken sailors, like in Hamburg, but local teenagers, many of whom they had gone to school with. Wooler busied himself with preparations, but between the second and third records of the intermission (there was a rule: three songs between sets, no more, to avoid the possibility of fights), he walked over to deliver some last-minute advice. "I'll announce you," he hastened to tell them, "then go straight into a number as soon as the curtain opens." He watched the recognition register on the boys' faces but noted a faint disapproval in their manner. So be it, he thought.

Out front, they could hear the overheated crowd, its attention span slipping away. The throng of teenagers wanted action. They had danced distractedly between acts; the records were no substitute for the real thing, and now, in the rambling fade, their liquid laughter and stridence signaled an excitement that sought to condense into impatience. Besides, there was a general curiosity about the next band, which had been added at the eleventh hour and was advertised as being "Direct from Hamburg." A German act. It would be interesting, from the pitch of their accents and their delivery, to see how they contrasted with the sharpness of Liverpool's top bands.

The hall was packed with teenagers, many of whom had gathered at card tables along both sidewalls to await the next act. The majority were attired in what was respectfully called "fancy dress" for what remained of the holiday festivities. The well-scrubbed boys, whose dark suits were also their school uniforms, looked stiff and self-conscious, while girls, sheathed in tight calf-length skirts and white shirts, paraded gaily to and from the up-stairs bathroom, applying last-minute retouches to their makeup. Those who danced drifted casually across the big, open dance floor, keeping an eye on the stage as the band shuffled into place behind the curtain. Promptly, amps crackled in resistance: John and George plugged into a shared Truvoice that saw them through infancy, while Paul switched on his trusty seafoam green Ampigo. The audience stirred and half turned while Bob Wooler crooned into an open mike: "And now, everybody, the band you've been waiting for. Direct from Hamburg—"

But before he got their name out, Paul McCartney jumped the gun and, in a raw, shrill burst as the curtain swung open, hollered: *"I'm gonna tell Aunt Mary / 'bout Uncle John / he said he had the mis'ry / buthegot-alotoffun . . ."*

Oh, baby! The aimless shuffle stopped dead in its tracks. The reaction of the audience was so unexpected that Wooler had failed, in the first few seconds, to take note of it. Part of the reason was the shocking explosion that shook the hall. A whomp of bass drum accompanied each quarter note beat with terrific force. The first one struck after Paul screamed, "*Tell,*" so that the charge ricocheted wildly off the walls. There was a second on *Mary,* and then another, then a terrible volley that had the familiar *bam-bam-bam* of a Messerschmitt wreaking all hell on a local target: an assault innocent of madness. The pounding came in rhythmic waves and once it started, it did not stop. There was nowhere to take cover on the open floor. All heads snapped forward and stared wild-eyed at the deafen-ing ambush. The music crashing around them was discernibly a species of rock 'n roll but played unlike they had ever heard it before. *Oh ba-by, yeahhhhhh / now ba-by, woooooo . . .* It was convulsive, ugly, frightening, and visceral in the way it touched off frenzy in the crowd.

The band's physical appearance created another commotion. For a tense moment, the crowd just stared, awestruck, trying to take in the whole disturbing scene. Four of the musicians were dressed in the black suits they'd bought at the Texas Shop in Hamburg: beautiful cracked-leather jackets with padded shoulders and artificial sheepskin lining that proved sweltering under the lights, black T-shirts, and silky skintight pants. With instruments slung low across their bodies, they looked like a teenage-rebel fantasy come to life. Nor could anyone take his eyes off the rude cowboy boots with flat, chopped heels that each man wore, especially John Lennon's, which were ornate Twin Eagles, emblazoned with birds carved on both the front and back and outlined with white stitching.

"I'd never seen any band look like this before," says Dave Foreshaw, a Liverpool promoter, who gazed on the spectacle in utter astonishment. "I thought: 'What are they? *Who* are they?'"

As if someone had flashed a prearranged cue, the entire crowd rushed the stage, pressing feverishly toward the footlights. Impetuous girls and boys alike abandoned their social proprieties to a purely emotional response. Everyone had stopped dancing; there was now a total gravitation toward the stage. Sensing that a fight had broken out, Brian Kelly rushed inside with several bouncers in tow. The promoter experienced a moment of real panic. According to Bob Wooler, "Long afterwards, [Kelly] told me they were seconds away from using brute force when he finally realized what the fuss was about."

The band, too, arrived at the same conclusion and began working the crowd into a sweat. They turned up the juice and tore into a wild jam. Drawing upon stage antics they'd devised while in Germany, they twisted and jerked their bodies with indignant energy. John and George proceeded to lunge around like snapping dogs and stomp loudly on the bandstand in time to the music. (Newby, forced to watch Harrison's hands for chord changes, joined in the fun at irregular intervals, although to his dismay, the lack of decent cowboy boots made his part in the clowning "far less effective.") "It was just so different," recalls Bill Ashton, an apprentice fitter for British Rail, who sang part-time as Billy Kramer with a band called the Coasters and had come to Litherland to size up the "foreign" competition. "To act that way onstage and make that kind of sound—I was absolutely staggered."

Like everyone else, Kramer was used to bands that patterned themselves after Cliff Richard and the Shadows, England's top rock 'n roll act and practitioners of smooth, carefully tended choreography. Up till then, everyone had followed in the Shadows' dainty footsteps. This band, however, was a beast of a different nature. According to Dave Foreshaw, "Normally, [popular Liverpool bands such as] the Remo Four or the Dominoes would come on and . . . perform in a polite, orderly way. This band's performance attacked the crowd. They [played] aggressively and with a lot less respect. They just *attacked* them!" And when John Lennon stepped to the mike and challenged the crowd to "get your knickers down!" the audience, in a state of unconscious, indiscriminate euphoria, screamed and raised their arms in delight.

Brian Kelly, especially, perceived a seismic shift in the landscape and moved fast to contain it by posting bouncers at the doors to prohibit rival promoters like Foreshaw from poaching his bounty. But it was too late for such empty measures. The house erupted in hysteria as the band concluded its half-hour set with a rousing version of "What'd I Say," in which Paul McCartney jackknifed through the crowd, whipping the kids into rapturous confrontation. Over the last wild applause, Bob Wooler managed to say, "That was fantastic, fellas," but it was doubtful anyone paid much attention to him. They were too busy trying to connect with what had just gone down on that stage, what had turned their little Christmas dance into a full-scale epiphany.

This much was inevitable: the band had somehow squeezed every nerve of the local rock 'n roll scene, and that scene would never be the same. In the wall of grinding sound and the veil of black leather, they had staked their claim to history. And in that instant, they had become the Beatles.

MERCY

[I]

Water. Those who were drawn to it—the seafarers to whom the infinitesimal lap against a bow and the white blown spray prefigured a window on the world, the merchants and craftsmen who plied goods from the North and Midlands into commercial dynasties, and the dockhands and laborers bred to keep the machinery moving—allowed the mystery of the Mersey to lay hold of their imagination. The river, with its dark, brooding magnetism, drove the city as if throughout its existence it had been waiting for a subject as pliant and as pure as these shores, those spiny timber docks, that rim of sea. This wasn't a typical Lancashire shoreline, fashioned for pleasure boats and sunbathers, but a remarkable seven-and-a-half-mile natural harbor studded with chocolate-dark rock that clung to Liverpool's lofty townscape like a dressmaker's hem. The nucleus of the dock system, with its imposing mass of antique structures—warehouses, embankments, swing bridges, overhead railways, and gates—fed a humped dense center of red brick and church spires, itself a sort of iron splash that provided a nicely supporting symmetry all around.

The people living within these confines saw the seaport as a threshold on the horizon. Beyond it, an invisible world beckoned. Not a day passed when detachments of tall-masted ships weren't diligently on the move, bound for one of the globe's imagined corners.

Liverpool considered itself "the Gateway to the British Empire" for its mastery of imperial trade. And yet to the rest of the country, especially those living in tweedy London, Liverpool was an anglicized Siberia: desolate, insular, meaningless—out of sight, out of mind. Hardworking, dressed darkly, and forgotten. The prejudice was no secret, and it made those men and women of the North fierce and intimate. People from Liverpool called themselves "Scousers," giving their common kinship an exalted magic, in much the way that Ozark Mountain dwellers are called hillbillies. The term was derived from the nautical *lobscouse,* a sailor's dish consisting of meat stewed with vegetables and a ship biscuit but revised over the years by the Irish custom of keeping a pan of scouse stew simmering on the stove all week, to which table scraps and leftovers were added as they became available. "Scousers have a fierce local patriotism," says *Mersey Beat* founder Bill Harry, who grew up in the center of town at the same time as the Beatles. "It's like belonging to your own country. A real Scouser believes he is fighting everybody else in the world, and that everyone is against him, especially Londoners. He defends this position eloquently—with his fists."

Like many seaside boys, the four young men who would form the Beatles were absurdly modest, considering the outlet water provided: "to be the best band in Liverpool" was all they ever wanted. The Mersey was their only river.

Two hundred years before the Beatles crossed the water to "take America by storm," the ships of Liverpool rode the seas in service to the upstart colonies, whose landowners coveted burly African slaves. Merseyside magnates, loathing the practice of slavery but drunk on its profits, sent "stout little ships" laden with blue and green Manchester cottons and striped loincloths called "anabasses" down the Atlantic to West Africa, where, on the swampy, malaria-ridden island of Gorée, they bartered textiles with Arab and African flesh peddlers for human cargo. This, according to ships' logs and harbor records, was the first leg of a triangular route for the so-called African trade, a twelve-month journey that required an arduous "middle passage," docking next in either Virginia or the West Indies, where cotton or sugar, respectively, was then dispatched to Liverpool.

Liverpool thrived on the backs of slaves—thrived and thickened. Historian J. A. Picton points out how new structures expressed an elaborate Grecian influence, with ornamental columns and peaked roofs, so that "everything was modeled on the Parthenon." The city's growth mushroomed dramatically, and sailors and dockworkers, trusting in the promise of wealth, came to claim it. By 1800, Liverpool had become the richest city in Britain and second only to Lyon in all of Europe. A determined new race of longshoremen scuttled along the Kings Dock's great tobacco bonded warehouse and into the mazy Duke's Warehouse terminal, where barges were unloaded as they floated through its unorthodox arched brick caverns. The sunstruck warehouses thronging Jamaica Street bulged embarrassingly with lavish cargo. New construction abounded like milkweed.

Normally, where money and success flowed, civic pride followed, but not in this case. The slave trade, made grotesque and untenable by public indignation, was finally abolished in 1807. The merchant princes conveniently converted their ships to carry produce, and for a few years prosperity endured. Eventually, however, fruit proved no match.

Their conscience was rescued by American cronies, whose unlapsing resilience defied all reason. Cultivated on plantations scattered throughout the West Indies, odd lots of silky, long staple cotton had always been mixed in with larger cargoes containing sugar, rum, tobacco, ginger, and coffee that came in exchange for slaves. Most of it was unprocessed and used for hosiery and candlewicks, but in nearby Manchester, home to an influx of textile workers who, centuries earlier, had been driven out of Flanders by the Duke of Alva, the manufacture of cloth developed at an enormous rate. By 1800, 60.3 million pounds of cotton were being imported by Great Britain, every last bit of it bound for Manchester and rerouted by dealers there to mills in southeastern Lancashire, which were working at full capacity. As England's industrial revolution exploded, so, too, did the market for textiles. And Liverpool, waiting for just such an opportunity, was ideally situated, financially and geographically, to handle the business. Cotton poured into Liverpool to such an extent that boats bottlenecked in the Narrows, an exposed channel between the city and Birkenhead, and were forced to queue, awaiting their turn to unload. Practically overnight, the stubby line of docks grew to five, pushing north along the river, while port facilities ate into the streets surrounding the harbor like sets of teeth. Banks, customhouses, mercantile exchanges, and insurance and solicitors' offices were knit into the jungled fabric of new warehouses, whose vastness, Picton writes, "surpasses the pyramid of Cheops." Three magnificent churches, constructed entirely of prefabricated iron, were built between 1812 and 1814, allowing the fortunate to give thanks for this affluence. Civic buildings, skillfully mimicking the palazzi of the Medici, provided the grandeur and versatility due a thriving commercial hub.

Cotton brought respectability to Liverpool. But the water was dominant, and while its infinite resource steered opportunity toward the seaport, it also engulfed her. From 1845 to 1849, nearly fifty thousand Irish refugees thronged into Liverpool, causing near-civic collapse. The potato famine forced entire villages from their homes and deposited wave after wave of its victims onto the Merseyside docks, dumping them there like some whaler's squalid catch waiting to be claimed. Among them were the families of John O'Leannain (their name was changed to skirt the sectarian divide) and James McCartney II. A total of 1.5 million Irish crossed, some merely stopping long enough to get a ship to America, while others, made vulnerable by sickness and sudden poverty, sought permanent residence in what was already an overpopulated boom town. In a disparaging reference that nonetheless has some truth to it, historian Quentin Hughes says that "Liverpool wound up with the dross." Entire families, whose assets were often limited to the clothes on their back, crammed into living quarters unfit for human occupancy. "Many places that had one family in residence now had . . . five families," Hughes points out, "with some living in the basement, where the floor was soil and [there was] no cross ventilation." In a hasty attempt to remedy the situation, developers relocated people in tracts of back-to-back terrace houses—dwellings backed onto each other and connected on either side, so that the only windows and ventilation were in the front. For both the townspeople and newcomers alike, Liverpool became a grim, confrontational city. The Irish were blamed for creating a raft of social problems, not the least of which were fire, mob violence, and an outbreak of cholera that ravaged the whole of downtown. Conversely, it was the public's cold insensitivity, the new arrivals argued, that fed these conditions and fears.

The McCartneys, who were handymen by trade, found temporary housing near the docks, where Joseph, Paul's grandfather, was born in 1866. The Lennons gravitated to nearby Vauxhall, a neighborhood of mostly Irish immigrants, just north of the city, on the waterfront. To John's maternal grandfather, George Earnest Stanley, the power of water was more alluring and secure than anything sheltered land could provide. Described as "a real old sea sailor" in the mold of Ishmael, he spent three-fourths of his life aboard merchant ships in service to the Crown.

There was nothing unusual about young men from the area being gone for months, sometimes years, on end. Indeed, it was often a reasonable alternative to the nimbus of misery on the streets back home. Stanley had no intention of scratching out a living in the poxy factories and slaughterhouses along the wharf. Life at sea meant fewer hardships and a chance to pursue his spiritual quest for "seeing the civilized world." Although he never rose up the chain of command, George became an accomplished sailmaker assigned to one of the first three-masted ships to sail around the world. That left little opportunity for proper courtship, but by 1885, George Stanley had met and married a twenty-two-year-old Welsh girl named Annie Jane Millward, one of three daughters from a severely strict Methodist clan whose matriarch, Mary, refused to utter a word of the devil's English. A devout churchgoer herself, with little tolerance for world-liness, Annie risked her piety by working for a common lawyer in Chester, and it was there, in the bustling old Roman seaport, that she eventually encountered George Stanley. George was "a tough character": relentless without leniency, demanding without compromise. But he was responsi-ble and well disposed to supporting a family. After watching four of her uncles die of tuberculosis contracted from milk produced on the family's dairy farm, Annie was determined, almost obsessively so, to reseed the family tree, and once married, she devoted herself almost exclusively to childbearing.

In quick succession—at least, in the timetable allowed by George's stints at sea—Annie gave birth to five children, all girls: Mary Elizabeth, called Mimi; Elizabeth, known affectionately as Betty and, later, Mater; Anne; Harriet; and the youngest, Julia, nicknamed Judy, John Lennon's mother, born in 1914.*

Conscientious husband that he was, George Stanley eventually sur-rendered to domestic reality, retiring grudgingly from sailing, and took a shoreside job with the Liverpool and Glasgow Tug Salvage Company, re-covering the scattered wreckage of submarines from treacherous ocean beds. Rather than live in Liverpool center, which was still astonishingly dangerous, the Stanleys settled in Woolton, a grassy suburb outlined by dirt roads and farms.

All five sisters grew strong and inflexibly tight in a modest row house at 9 Newcastle Road, in the district known as Penny Lane. Years later, John would say: "Those women were fantastic . . . five *strong, intelligent, beautiful* women, five sisters," as if they were a stage act: the Stanley Girls. He relished their collective spirit, and from what history has shown, they were indeed a remarkable bunch. Mimi, the eldest, assumed a matriarchal role, taking charge of her siblings in a way that eluded their abstracted mother. Mimi was grounded: a practical nurse, a lover of culture, a sharp-tongued, high-principled, duty-bound young woman who wore the kind of sensible dresses that looked as if they had been picked out for the weekly garden club meeting. "She was born with a keen sense of propriety," recalled one of her nephews. Her method was very simple: everything operated on the axis of decorum and honesty. It was all black-and-white: either you measured up or you didn't. "She had a great sense of what was right and wrong," recalls John Lennon's boyhood friend Pete Shotton.

---

* *Their first child was a boy, who died soon after birth.*

There was nothing, no situation or dilemma, that Mimi was unequipped to handle. And where the younger girls dreamed of starting families, Mimi dreamed of challenges and adventure—the kind that demanded an unusually stubborn independence. "I had no intention of getting married," she told a curious admirer, dreading the prospect of "being tied to a kitchen or a sink."

As she approached her twentieth birthday, Mimi Stanley's aspirations appeared to be right on track. Her pursuit of a respectable vocation met with early success, first as a resident nurse at a Woolton convalescent hospital and later as the private secretary to Ernest Vickers, an industrial magnate with posh residences in Manchester and Wales. Out of personal necessity, Mimi devoted herself entirely to her employer, certain that as soon as the opportunity availed itself, she would invest her savings "in a modest estate from which she could entertain scholars and dignitaries from a cross section of Liverpool society."

A confluence of events, however, placed Mimi's dream just out of reach. In the spring of 1932, when she was twenty-six years old, a short but powerfully built dairy farmer named George Smith, who lived just opposite the hospital and delivered raw milk there each morning, began courting Mimi with a vengeance. His efforts were made difficult by Mimi's frustrating indifference and her eagle-eyed father, who treated all of his daughters' suitors as adversaries. "Grandfather made it impossible for Mimi and George," according to Stanley Parkes, Mimi's nephew, who remembered watching his aunt with keen, admiring eyes. Night after night, he observed the young couple sitting in the back room at Newcastle Road, "under constant chaperone: my grandfather and grandmother always in the next room." At a ridiculously early hour, old George Stanley would barge into the parlor, shouting, "That's long enough! Away you go—*home!*" making it impossible for the relationship to develop. The courtship dragged on this way for almost seven years until, finally, George Smith delivered an ultimatum along with the milk. "Look here! I've had enough of you! Either marry me, or nothing at all!"

The marriage of such a headstrong young career woman to a relatively commonplace and unassuming man might have had more of a disruptive effect on the Stanley family were it not for another, more upheaving union among the close-knit sisters. Six months earlier, on December 3, 1938, Julia, George Stanley's favorite and most high-spirited daughter, stunned her father when she arrived home after a date with a longtime boyfriend and announced, "There! I've married him," waving a license as proof. It was only reluctantly, after her father threatened Julia with expulsion if she cohabited with a lover, that she proposed to—and married—the dapper young man with a "perfect profile" and nimble spirit named Freddie Lennon.

[II]

If John Lennon romanticized the memory of his mother, he took an altogether opposite view of his father. Freddie Lennon remained a vague shadow figure, an outcast, throughout John's life and, except for two brief appearances, had no direct influence on his son's upbringing. Aside from the resentment that lingered as a result of this circumstance, John's knowledge of his father grew fainter with every year. "I soon forgot my father," he told Hunter Davies in 1968. "It was like he was dead."

The Stanleys did a good job helping to put Freddie Lennon to rest. "They wanted nothing to do with him from the start," said his niece Leila Harvey. Julia's father considered him below their station, "certainly not middle class," and Mimi later said that "we knew he would be no use to anyone, certainly not our Julia."

Though not genteel by any stretch of the imagination, Freddie was "very intelligent . . . a clever boy," no doubt the consequence of long years spent surviving by his wits. The son of Jack Lennon, a refined British minstrel who died in 1919 when Freddie was seven, he and an elder brother, Charles, had landed in the Bluecoat Hospital, a prestigious Liverpool orphanage around the corner from Newcastle Road that prided itself on the impressive, independent-minded education provided to its young charges. There, amid a class that competed feverishly for top academic honors, Freddie earned a reputation for being happy-go-lucky. "Anywhere Freddie turned up always meant fun was about to start," said a relative. "He couldn't resist having a good time." There wasn't a room he couldn't light up with a witty remark or well-timed rejoinder. Repartee came naturally to him, carried off with such endearing joie de vivre that friends assumed he would ultimately capitalize on his personality. But he was never able to put it all together. Too frivolous to master a vocation, he bounced from office job to odd job, cadging money off friends or his eldest brother, Sydney, who worked long hours hemming pants in a tailor shop on Ranelagh Place. He spent endless nights attending any one of the city's two dozen vaudeville houses, where he was on a first-name basis with the pretty, long-legged usherettes who paraded along the aisles. At the Trocadero, a converted cinema on Camden Road, he'd often caught sight of its most beautiful attendant, a head-turner with high cheekbones and an engaging smile framed by cascading auburn hair, but he'd never actually spoken to Julia Stanley.

It wasn't until a chance meeting in Sefton Park, where he and a friend had gone one midsummer afternoon to pick up girls, that Freddie and Julia struck up a fast acquaintance. Their encounter, as Freddie related it, read like a romantic-comedy script. He was strolling jauntily along a cobblestone path, dressed in a black bowler and fingering a cigarette holder, when he came upon "this little waif" perched on a wrought-iron bench. "As I walked past her, she said, 'You look silly,'" he recalled. "I said, 'You look lovely!' and I sat down beside her." Casting him a playful sidelong glance, Julia insisted he remove his "silly hat," so, with impeccable timing, Freddie promptly flung it into the lake. It was the perfect gesture to win an invitation to go dancing and, ultimately, her heart. Julia had long been attracted to the kind of slapstick sensibility that Freddie Lennon personified. Like Freddie, "she would get a joke out of anything," recalled an adoring nephew. "If the house was burning down around Judy, she'd come out laughing and smiling—she'd make a joke of it."

Of all the Stanley sisters—all "real beauties . . . real stunners," according to a relative—only Julia knew how to exploit her precious asset. Instead of turning up her chin when a stranger gave her the once-over, Julia would flash a broad smile and wink knowingly at him. Men ogled her as often as they passed her. Only five foot two in high heels, with a full figure and large brown eyes that seemed to float in her face, Julia had an obvious, provocative beauty that exaggerated her appeal. "Judy was very feminine, she was beautiful," explained her niece, ". . . never untidy. You never saw her with her hair undone. She went to bed with makeup on so that she'd look beautiful in the morning."

But all the makeup in the world couldn't attract the right kind of man. From the time she stepped out from her family's grasp, Julia Stanley kept company with a succession of good-looking rascals with fast come-on lines and even faster escapes. Night after night, humming with energy, she made the rounds of local dance halls and breezy clubs, where the rootless crowd of dockers, soldiers, waiters, laborers, and after-hours sharks congregated. A spry dancer with a carefree sensuality, Julia found herself in great demand as a partner in the stylish jitterbug competitions that lasted into the early hours of morning. She could tell a joke as hard and bawdy as any man, which won her no shortage of admirers. And she sang—"with a voice like Vera Lynn," it was said—at the drop of a hat.

At first glance, Freddie and Julia seemed like an improbable pair, but from the moment they met they were inseparable. Both tireless dreamers, they spent long days walking around Liverpool, hatching improbable schemes. They would open a shop, a pub, a café, a club where they'd take turns performing, Julia cracking one-liners, Freddie singing and playing the banjo. He had a pretty good voice, a husky tenor, and no shortage of charisma. The legendary Satchmo was a favorite, and Freddie had Jolson down cold, with all the gesticulations. Given the chance, he could rattle off crowd-pleasers all night. *Given the chance.* But Julia's father not only disapproved of the marriage but demanded some sign of the couple's self-support. Despite Freddie's extravagant plans to perform, which earned his father-in-law's indignation, there was nothing concrete. Instead of working, he spent his afternoons taking Julia's young nephew, Stanley, for walks in the park: talking, thinking, dreaming, worrying.

Finally, Freddie escaped the dilemma by the route chosen most often by Liverpool men: he put to sea. He signed on to a ship headed toward the Mediterranean, working as a merchant navy steward. On board a succession of ocean liners, traveling between the Greek Islands, North Africa, and the West Indies, Freddie gained security, first as a bellboy and later as a headwaiter. He became a crew favorite because of his personable nature. Freddie was "a real charmer," Julia told Mimi, "a people pleaser," who never forgot a name or a passenger's favorite song. People remembered seeing him weave among tables, "with a smile that sparkled in a room." But seafaring, though pleasant, was an erratic interlude. Relatives recalled seeing Freddie back in Liverpool a few months after his first voyage, hoping without any real prospects to sail on another steamer. In the meantime, Freddie moved in with Julia's family, allegedly at George Stanley's behest, living off the fumes of his last paycheck. Calling himself by some stretch of imagination a "ship's entertainer," he auditioned for local theater managers, but without any luck. Julia urged Freddie to get something more solid, if only to appease her irascible father, but the situation became more dire by January 1940, at which time it was discovered that Julia had become pregnant.

The war arrived early on Liverpool's front doorstep. Entire neighborhoods were destroyed in the initial air strikes that pounded the city; families would wake to find their streets "just *gone,*" especially blocks in and around the Penny Lane area, where the heavy artillery, the ten-pound whistling bombs aimed at the docks, had drifted. Menlove Avenue, where

Mimi and George had bought a handsome semi-detached house, suffered tremendous damage. "There were fifty-six people blown to pieces in an air raid shelter not fifty yards from Mary's house," according to a relative, who remembered watching emergency service patrols "just burying over" the charred site. Mimi constantly grappled with a rash of incendiary bombs, those big, phosphorous flares, which fell regularly in her garden, throwing blankets over them and stamping them out.

During a succession of brutal air raids in early October 1940, the entire Stanley clan gathered nightly at Newcastle Road, determined to support one another through the terrifying uncertainty. Julia, who was almost two weeks overdue, had been ordered to hospital by her doctor, where she languished in a second-floor ward at Oxford Street Maternity Hospital. The days were long and boring, the nights even worse, a result of having the lights extinguished to avoid detection from the air. It might have helped pass the time if Julia had Freddie by her side—he would have made her laugh in that loopy, screwball way of his—but Freddie was gone, having shipped out on a troop transport earlier that month, doing his part for the war effort.

The first week in October brought an escalation of the bombing, according to newspaper accounts, wave after wave of German sorties strafing the south docks and downtown district. Still, when Mimi called the hospital on October 9, shortly after nightfall, and was told that "Mrs. Lennon has just had a boy," nothing—neither curfew nor bomb nor German technology—was going to stop her from gazing at her new nephew. Later, Mimi gave an intrepid, if somewhat suspect, account of her crosstown sprint: "I was dodging in doorways between running as fast as my legs would carry me." In the distance she could hear the thunderous echo of bombs pounding the countryside. "There was shrapnel falling and gunfire," she recalled, "and when there was a little lull I ran into the hospital ward and there was this beautiful little baby."

John Winston Lennon was a beautiful little baby, indeed. He was named after his talented grandfather in the hope that he could fulfill the Lennon legacy for stardom. (Julia offered the middle name in honor of his country's awe-inspiring leader, Winston Churchill.) His eyes were perfectly matched brown crescents set above a feminine, almost bow-shaped mouth, a pointed little nose, and the soft, dimpled chin of his father. He had his mother's fair complexion, which, later in life, made him look a shade or two paler in contrast to the other Beatles.

For the first few years of his life, Julia threw herself into motherhood, devoting all her efforts to raising her son. Freddie reappeared every now and again, but it was only for a day or two and then he was off once more, on some woolly seaborne adventure. At least money was no longer an issue: Freddie provided for his family, sending a regular check for their support, and as long as Julia and John lived at Newcastle Road, there wasn't much that lay beyond their needs.

In 1945 Julia's mother died, leaving her father, who had become "frail and old," under her uncertain care. "Mary would, on occasion, come over and help out," remembered a nephew, "but she was out working as a nurse," which left the burden of responsibility in Julia's hands. With John demanding more attention, balancing these obligations became too much for her. Julia, by her very nature, was a social creature. She needed distraction, laughs, excitement. And a fellow — "she would have always had a fellow, Judy." This had always been part of Julia's makeup, something that couldn't be denied, not even when it came to a young boy. Any sensitive child would pick up the signals, and John, who was especially perceptive, interpreted his mother's frustrations as being his fault. Reminiscences about his childhood were always filled with unconsolable guilt. It was the rejection he remembered most, the feeling that he was in the way, a source of Julia's unhappiness and Freddie's absenteeism. "The worst pain is that of not being wanted," John confessed, "of realizing your parents do not need you in the way you need them."

Julia's longing for conviviality was heightened by Liverpool's bustling nightlife, which raged almost as fiercely as the war. The city jumped to the tempo of big bands along with the guys and dolls who followed them. At the center of this scene were the all-night dance halls, where the revelry never stopped. Soldiers and civilians, wary of an uncertain future, collected under the low-slung rafters, determined to let off some steam before the full impact of the war hit.

It was probably sometime in 1942 that Julia first ventured out dancing on her own, and thereafter she stepped out frequently, first alone, then later with two neighbors whose husbands were in the service. Freddie later claimed this peccadillo was his fault, the result of a remark in a letter he sent her. "I said to her, there's a war on; go out and enjoy yourself, pet," he recalled, never realizing the extent to which she'd take him up on it.

It was only a matter of time before Julia met another man, a Welsh soldier named Taffy Williams, who was stationed in a barracks at Mossley

Hill. They hit all the pubs and dance halls that catered specially to soldiers, and Julia would often bring back from these outings a rare, precious treat—a chunk of chocolate or a sugar pastry—which she'd present to John the next morning during breakfast.

The relationship remained innocent, or at least innocent enough to escape scrutiny. Julia continued to receive regular correspondence from Freddie, which she'd read aloud to John, along with a check that underwrote her modest living expenses. John hung on every frivolous word his father wrote, then repackaged them for his cousins in the form of frothy seafaring adventures. To John, Freddie was a mysterious, romantic figure, a father of great consequence, away doing a man's work.

But, in truth, Freddie Lennon was a screwup. He constantly signed on the "wrong type" of ship, sailing as a glorified bartender or with crews that functioned as modern-day pirates. After a typical mishap in New York, he set out on the *Sammex* in February 1944, bound for the Algerian port of Bône, where he was arrested and imprisoned for "broaching the cargo," or more precisely, pilfering a bottle of contraband beer. Freddie subsequently disappeared for six months—undergoing adventures in the Dutch underground, from North Africa to Naples, he claimed—during which time his family assumed he'd deserted them.

Julia hardly needed convincing. She was living it up with Taffy Williams, and was pregnant with his child. Yet, however much she loved the soldier, she was unable—or simply unwilling—to marry him. For one thing, she was already married. And for another, there was John to worry about. Williams wasn't prepared to take on a young boy along with Julia, and abandoning John was out of the question—at least for now.

Just when it seemed that things couldn't get any worse, Freddie returned home, understandably despondent. For all of his superficiality, Freddie Lennon remained a proud man, proud enough to be wounded by an unfaithful wife. Julia treated her husband with disdain, regarding the awkward situation as if it were somehow Freddie's fault. Her personality had always been jaunty and outgoing. Now it became harsh and brittle, her words unnecessarily cruel and venomous, her mood fluctuating between irrationality and deceit. "She claimed that she was raped by a soldier," according to Freddie's brother Charles, who attempted to mediate for the couple. Ready to defend her honor, the Lennon brothers actually confronted Taffy Williams, just before Christmas 1945, but his account of the facts stood up. It was clear that Julia had been his lover for more than half a year. There was no point in pretending any longer. Freddie accepted that she was going to have another man's baby and offered to stand by her side. But there was something broken about him now.

———

Broken—but not finished. Holding Freddie Lennon together was the welfare of his son, John. Responsibility was called for now, and responsibility was neither Freddie's nor Julia's strong suit. In fact, the Lennons had courted these very circumstances by putting their own selfish interests before those of their son. Freddie leaped into action by removing John to his brother Sydney's house in the suburb of Maghull while Julia came to term. This may have been a practical, sober-minded decision, or it may have been designed to give him the opportunity to resolve his differences with Julia. It is impossible to say.

In any event, Freddie ran out of yardage. He offered to help raise the baby but was spurned. There was too much resentment, no trace of love left in Julia's heart. Besides, "she was told quite categorically by the family that this child would have to be adopted," recalled her niece. Julia's long-suffering father, indignant, refused to allow her to remain in his house. As a result, Mimi helped move her to the Elmswood Nursing Home, in Mossley Hill, where, on June 19, 1945, a girl was born, named Victoria. "She was a beautiful baby," recalled Julia's sister Anne, "but we never knew who the father was." The whole seamy affair was hushed up and was never discussed among the rest of the Stanley family. "We didn't even know that she'd had [another] baby," said Leila Harvey. Certainly, John wasn't told anything about it, much less that he had a sister. (By all accounts, he never discovered her existence.) Without further delay, the baby was taken away from Julia and given to a Norwegian Salvation Army captain, who removed the newborn to Scandinavia, which was the last anyone ever heard of her.

Freed from this latest imposition, Julia spun back into the vibrant social scene, which, by Liverpool standards, had become livelier than ever. American soldiers, stationed at a sprawling base in nearby Burtonwood, brought their irrepressible exuberance to the mix. Julia had always been a good-time girl; now, as good times became harder to afford, she sought out a sugar daddy to secure her stake. It took no longer than a few weeks for Julia to land a new suitor.

Julia and Bobby Dykins had met a year earlier, while they were involved with different partners in an ongoing double date. Dykins, whose given name was John, had been seeing Julia's neighbor Ann Stout, but there was never any doubt as to where his affections lay. He "would always wink at [Julia]," which "she enjoyed, laughing it off," as one would a playful flirtation. They met again, soon after Julia left the nursing home, and with her no longer encumbered, things turned serious right out of the box.

A Liverpool native several years Julia's senior, Dykins was a smooth, dapper Irish Catholic wine steward at the Adelphi Hotel, who was as dedicated to pursuing the high life as Julia was to living it. Bobby was "very good looking," according to those who crossed his path. A dark-skinned, wiry man who held himself erect, he was nicknamed Spiv by the Stanley kids because he reminded them so much of Arthur English, the British music hall comedian, famous for his "little pencil moustache and porkpie hat." John's memory of him wasn't as flattering, nicknaming Dykins "Twitchy" because of "a nervous cough and . . . thinning, margarine-coated hair." Few men had better access to such tightly restricted luxuries: liquor, chocolate, silks, cigarettes. "He was certainly earning good money," said Stanley Parkes, and he never failed to lavish it, along with charm, on his appreciative new woman. "He was worldly, he'd seen a lot of life . . . and he was always very open and cheerful."

Not always: Julia's family and friends remember a seismic temper that could erupt without warning. Dykins, they recalled, was moody, unpredictable, even violent when drunk and something did not please him. "He had a very short fuse. Julia knew when to get out of his way, but occasionally he would lash out and slap her." John himself remembered a time when "my mother came to see us in a black coat with her face bleeding." And there were other scattered recollections of abuse.

Still, Julia was committed to her new lover, and she and Bobby moved in together in an attempt to give their illicit affair an aura of respectability. This brought new complications to bear—especially on John. The appearance of yet another strange man in the house proved unsettling, to say nothing of the hostile flare-ups he witnessed between the adults, and he was shuttled from one sister to another while Julia devoted all her efforts to making the relationship work. This and other neglect took an early toll on John. "It confused him, and he often ran away," Mimi told an interviewer, enumerating the times she opened the door to find her distraught nephew cowering there in tears, unable to speak. More than once Mimi marched John back to Julia's, where she gave her younger sister a piece of her mind. Fuming angrily, she would shout, "Oh, for heaven's sake, Judy, *behave yourself!*" Another time, Leila Harvey recalled "being in Mimi's morning room, with John behind her in the chair, and Judy being told, 'You are not fit to have this child!'" Not only did the family "disagree with the way she was living her life," but they considered Julia "frivolous and unreliable," a woman who never took anything seriously, even when it came to mundane household chores. Relatives who visited might find her sweeping out the kitchen while wearing a pair of knickers on her head. And as for cooking, "she was absolutely crackpot," mixing ingredients like a mad scientist. "A little bit of tea went in the stew," recalled her niece. In fact, "a bit of everything went in [there]."

In June 1946 Freddie took an unexpected leave of absence from his job and returned to Liverpool to rescue John from the pressures that had been building up at home. There was no objection from Julia when he asked to visit his boy; Mimi, who was acting as John's unofficial guardian, also obliged. Father and son set off on a reunion, ostensibly for a seaside holiday in Blackpool but, as Freddie later admitted, "intending never to come back." After two weeks cruising the boardwalk, a plan materialized: they decided to emigrate to New Zealand. It seemed like the perfect place for a man like Freddie Lennon to start over, and above all, he would have John with him.

It has been said that John was delighted at the prospect of traveling with his father, although there is nothing, other than Freddie's unreliable account, that expresses such a sentiment. But in all probability, John craved a man's loving attention—to say nothing of a sailor, to say nothing of his *father*—and Freddie's dreams were always suffused with layers of romantic fantasy. How could a boy resist? What seemed to make this episode so important for John was not the relocation or the adventure of going abroad, but that he had finally gotten his father's attention. Having suffered through five years of indifference and neglect during which his parents pursued their own pleasures, that is what he wanted most.

Shortly before the long journey south, late in July 1946, Julia and Bobby Dykins appeared unexpectedly in Blackpool to take John back home to Liverpool. One can only imagine the scene this touched off. As Freddie later recounted it, an argument ensued, in which he offered to take Julia with them to New Zealand. "She said no. All she wanted was John." Freddie could not persuade her to reconsider, much less abandon her son. Sensing a standoff, he suggested that John choose between them.

It was a horrible, thoughtless decision to ask a five-year-old boy to make. And while the incident seems improbable (John never recalled it as an adult), it has an affecting, if pitiful, resonance. According to Freddie's oft-reported version: "He had to decide whether to stay with me or go with her. He said me. Julia asked again, but John still said me. Julia went out of the door and was about to go up the street when John ran after her. That was the last I saw or heard of him till I was told he'd become a Beatle."

[III]

Back in Liverpool, John Lennon soon found himself embroiled in another new melodrama, one even more traumatic and gut-wrenching than the last.

That summer, intending to give John the kind of love and stability he sorely needed, Julia organized a model of family life and enrolled him in a school near her home. But within weeks of their return, he was no longer living with her. The exact circumstances surrounding this development have been blurred by speculation and myth. There may have been some friction between Julia and Bobby Dykins that led to John's removal; perhaps the intrusion of a young boy put too much strain on their relationship. Some relatives have suggested that Julia simply wasn't up to the responsibility of full-time motherhood. Leila Harvey believed a decision "was forced" on Julia by Mimi and her tyrannical father as punishment for sinful behavior. "She wouldn't have parted with John unless she was told," Leila insisted.

None of this made any difference to John. He seemed to accept the idea that it was somehow his fault, that he was to blame for her incompetence. "My mother . . . couldn't cope with me" was the way he later explained it. Whatever the reason, at some point that August, John was sent outright to Mimi's, once and for all, where it was determined he would receive "a proper upbringing."

Mimi Smith easily made up for her sister's slack attention to raising John. Unlike Julia in every way, Mimi was a proud, no-nonsense, if "difficult," housewife with a steely determination who brought great reserves of discipline to the role of surrogate parent. "Mimi was a sensible, dignified lady . . . the absolute rock of the family," recalled a family member with a mixture of admiration and awe. Anyone who crossed her could expect to earn the full measure of her wrath—perhaps a sharp tongue-lashing or, worse, the dreaded silent treatment. Determined to "bring John up right," she had strong ideas about what was appropriate behavior that bordered on intolerance. People use words like *stubborn, impatient, authoritarian,* and *uncompromising* to describe her forceful nature. But if Mimi was a "merciless disciplinarian," as conveyed by a childhood friend of John's who knew her, she could also be an easy touch with a big heart. "She had a terrific sense of humor, which John could crack into and make her laugh in situations where she was trying to discipline him," says Pete Shotton. One minute she'd be giving John a frosty piece of her mind; the next minute "you'd find them rolling around, laughing together."

In almost no time, John settled comfortably into the Smith household. The family residence on Menlove Avenue—nicknamed Mendips, after a mountain range—was as familiar as any he'd ever known, a cozy seven-room stucco-and-brick cottage with an extra bedroom that Mimi later rented to students as a means of income after George's death. Thanks to the unobstructed expanse of a golf course across the street, sunlight filled the pleasant interior, warming an endless warren of nooks where John often curled up and paged dreamily through picture books. His bedroom was in a small but peaceful alcove over the porch, and on most mornings he was awakened early by a clatter of hoofbeats as an old dray horse made milk deliveries along the rutted road.

Aunt Mimi and Uncle George made it easy for John to feel loved there. Mimi told a close relative that she'd never wanted children, but "she *wanted* John." From the moment he arrived at Mendips, she showered him with attention. She bought him books and read him stories, especially those from a tattered, lavishly illustrated volume of *Wind in the Willows* that had been passed down from his cousin Stanley to cousin Leila and finally to John. Mimi's morning room was always filled with the sweet smells of apple tarts and crumbles, which she baked almost as capably and effortlessly as John later wrote songs. And there were always enough toys and sketch pads to entertain him. Besides, Julia visited – often, practically every day, which in some ways made it better for John, in other ways, worse.

If Mimi could at times be prickly and irascible, her moods were balanced out by her husband. Little is known about George Smith other than the sketchiest of details offered by his relatives. He was "a quiet and jolly man," as one person described him, who had left the milk trade (he operated a dairy farm and retail milk outlet with his brother Frank that spanned four generations of their prominent Woolton family) to run a small-time bookmaking business, taking bets on the gee-gees, as they called racehorses, running at the local track. (He'd let John bet on the Grand National each year, remembers a cousin.) No one was sure how Uncle George squared such activities with upright Mimi, but one thing was clear: he doted on his nephew. "Uncle George absolutely adored John," insisted another cousin who often visited Mendips. "I had no time to go playing ducks in the bath with him," Mimi sniffed, whereas "George would see him to bed with a smile most nights." Any time of the day, George might grab his nephew by the shoulder and sing out, "Give me a squeaker," which usually earned him a loud, slurpy kiss. Even though George worked nights, "he took us all to the pictures [and] to the park," recalled Leila. And on those occasions when all three cousins played outside, he allowed them to have meals in the garden shed, where they demanded to "eat just like an animal, with [their] hands."

However unlike Mimi he may have been in other respects, the two both stressed the absolute necessity, if not compulsion, for constant self-education, especially through their love of words. In the parlor, behind the couch, Mimi shelved "twenty volumes of the world's best short stories," which she claimed "John . . . read . . . over and over again," along with "most of the classics." George recited John's favorite nursery rhymes and, later, when he was old enough, taught John how to solve crossword puzzles. "Words needn't have to be taken at their face value," he explained. "They had many meanings"—valuable advice saved for later. That is not to imply, as some books claim, that John's time with Mimi was housebound. He was devoted to his cousin Stanley and remained so throughout his life. Although Stanley was seven years older than John and away most months at prep school, they enjoyed an easy, undemanding friendship that functioned on equal footing. John was sent for most vacations on a ten-hour bus ride to his cousin's home in Scotland, where the boys wandered around Loch Madie, an old anglers' haunt, and fished for trout in the icy burns. Stanley had an air rifle that fired lead pellets and he taught John how to shoot. "My mother had a .22," he recalled, "and John and I would do some target practice. We'd go out shooting rabbits . . . or [at] tin cans and bottles." If they got bored with that, as invariably happened after several hours, they'd head down to one of the five beautiful white sand beaches, where Stanley eventually taught John how to swim. The boys copied speedway riding on their bicycles, building small dirt tracks and then, recalled Leila, "peddling like hell down the straightaway before putting the bike into a slide." Afterward, they would pack picnic lunches and go to the all-day marionette shows or to the open-air baths in Blackpool. Stanley recalled "drag[ging] Leila and John to the cinema as often as three times in a day—out of one cinema and into another."

Unlike the loner persona he cultivated later on as a teenager, John Lennon's childhood seems marked by frivolity and happiness. "He was such a happy-go-lucky, good-humored, easygoing, lively lad," recalled Leila. Contrary to popular opinion, the preadolescent John Lennon wasn't an outcast. He might not have "fit in" with kids less artistically curious, as he argued incessantly with his interviewers. He might have languished "in a trance for twenty years," owing to a lack of intellectual stimulation. But he wasn't "very deprived" as a child, as Yoko Ono later tried to assert. "This image of me being the orphan is garbage," John confessed in his last published interview, "because I was well protected by my auntie and my uncle, and they looked after me very well, thanks."

He was also looked after at Quarry Bank, the state grammar school (comparable to high school) he entered in 1952, although not in the manner that one is proud of. Quickly earning the reputation as "a clown in class," he attracted the attention of Quarry Bank's stern, authoritarian masters, who prided themselves on scholarship and discipline. John, bored stiff, prized neither, flouting the rules. Not even the threats of corporal punishment fazed him. He couldn't have cared less.

Instead, the questions he grappled with later while growing up were why he was *different,* how he could cultivate the unformed ideas churning inside of him. And what, if anything, would open up the world for a well-adjusted but bored middle-class kid from suburban Liverpool? He found the answer quite by chance one night in the privacy of his bedroom as he was scanning the radio dial.

[I]

Again, luck and bliss: thanks to a confluence of geography and the cosmos, Radio Luxembourg, broadcasting at 208 on most medium-wave radio dials, had a signal that by some miracle could sprint its semidirect way to the United Kingdom. Everything depended on the fickle frontal masses that collided over the Irish Sea. "There was always a bad reception—you'd have [to put] your ear to the speaker, always fiddling with the dial," recalls one of Paul McCartney's grammar-school classmates, "but it would give you plenty to dream about." Every Saturday and Sunday night, the station's English-language service featured a playlist cobbled from a mixture of rockabilly and rhythm-and-blues hits by Bill Haley, Fats Domino, Lavern Baker, Carl Perkins, the Platters, and dozens of other American singers whose tangy delicacies served to stimulate the bland diet of Western European music. Its impact was felt most keenly in Britain, where the state-controlled radio had all the personality of an old scone. From eight o'clock to midnight, three of the boys who would later become the Beatles tuned in individually to the station's staticky signal, as prodigal deejays, in pneumatic bursts of glibness, introduced the rock 'n roll records that were climbing the American charts. No one missed the broadcast unless their parents strictly forbade it, which none fortunately did. John, Paul, and Ringo observed the radio broadcast faithfully, the way one would a religious holiday. George, who was younger and presumably asleep by eleven o'clock, got a recap of the show the following morning from his mate Arthur Kelly.

To fifteen-year-old John Lennon, the broadcast was some kind of personal blessing, like a call from a ministering spirit. He was known to "behave distractedly" around his friends hours beforehand, withdrawing like a pitcher in the midst of throwing a no-hitter. "He regarded it like scripture," says Pete Shotton, who, under penalty of best-friendship, likewise never missed a show. In the dark front bedroom of his aunt's house on Menlove Avenue, Lennon invariably sat cross-legged on the end of his bed, the ripe, impressionable student in his Fruit of the Looms, cradling a full arsenal of notetaking paraphernalia. Skillfully, with caressing finger-tips, he massaged the dial of his radio much like Willie Sutton until Jack Jackson's companionable voice crackled in the enveloping night. Sometimes he would furiously jot down lyrics to the songs, filling in his own approx-imation where he'd missed crucial words; other times, overcome by a thrilling piece of music, he would push the tablet away, lean back, close his eyes, and let himself be carried off by the voices and melodies that would have a lasting effect on his life.

"That's the music that brought me from the provinces of England to the world," John recalled later. "That's what made me what I am."

It was an unusual passion for a boy raised by archguardians who were by all accounts unmusical and by an aunt who not only disdained popular music but banished it futilely from the house. The Smiths kept an old fruitwood radiogram in the parlor of their Menlove Avenue house when John was growing up, but they rarely, if ever, burdened it with anything but one of the old 78s they'd acquired of Sir Thomas Beecham conducting Handel or Bach. The Smiths' trusty radio dial rarely strayed from the BBC's indomitable frequencies. As a result, John picked up much of what he learned from friends and, somewhat later, from his own precious transis-tor radio, which was displayed like priceless art in his bedroom.

The fresh air and easygoing lifestyle that had drawn families to Woolton from Liverpool center now drew John outside, not to escape his radio but to further connect with its transmissions. Each summer day, he'd meet up with his friends at a place they'd nicknamed "the Bank," an easy slope of grass with a view of the surrounding fields and lake, which served as their lookout in lovely Calderstones Park. No meeting time was prearranged, and none of the boys wore watches, but by eleven or twelve each morning they'd have turned up there on their bicycles—John, Pete Shotton, Len Garry, and Bill Turner. From atop the Bank, the world was theirs; they had an incom-parable vantage point and could survey the distant expanse of close-cropped lawns and magnificent gorges, where children played leisurely in unorga-nized groups and teenagers prowled the faded footpaths leading in and out of the wooded groves. The view was unobstructed, stretching far off across to the main administrative building, once an elegant Victorian mansion that now housed a café, and to the left, where boats idled on a mirror-smooth lake. Yet however much the action beckoned, the Woolton boys chose not to explore it. "We savored the pleasure of just being friends," Pete Shotton explains, with rightful significance. "Our fifteenth birthdays were approaching. We had just discovered what girls were about, and more than anything else we'd all taken an avid interest in music."

This interest was reinforced by the sudden appearance of a musical instrument, a Hohner harmonica, which had apparently been a gift from one of Aunt Mimi's student lodgers, and also by Len Garry, an easygoing, imperturbable boy who "was always singing or whistling." The boys would hunker down and burst into versions of "Bubbles" and "Cool Water," songs that fit a schoolboy's romantic vision of a real man's world. Reclining on the grass against their overturned bikes, they'd wait for the harmonica's long, slurry cue, then throw their heads back and sing: "Keep a-movin', Dan, don't you listen to him, Dan, he's a devil not a man . . ." At first, John never sang; he was too self-conscious. But as the sessions became less intimidating and more unrestrained, he was encouraged by the vigorous prompting of his friends. The boys' musical taste stretched out considerably, thanks to overworked jukeboxes at Hilda's Chip Shop and the Dutch Café, where among their many discoveries were crooners such as Johnnie Ray, Frankie Laine, and Tennessee Ernie Ford. Under the influence of the earthy, if gratuitously slick, Laine, the boys would wait until the Bank's sight lines grew clear, then burst out singing: "I'm just a-walkin' in the rain . . . ," strangling each syllable with burbles of imagined heartbreak.

Other friends may have shared their love of singing, but if they did, no one dared let on. "It wasn't manly," Pete Shotton says flatly, especially singing ballads, which did not fit the image of a typical swaggering Liverpool lad "who would just as soon fight you as look at you." That was another reason for occupying the Bank; it gave them enough high ground to practice sharp-sighted vigilance. "When one of us saw someone coming, we'd drop our heads and the harmonica would disappear."

Whatever his fears, John adored playing the harmonica and had become a familiar sight pedaling his bicycle around the streets of Woolton Village "with his trousers tucked in his socks . . . [and] the harmonica sticking out of his back pocket." Nigel Walley recalls, "It was the first indication [among our friends] of anyone having anything to do with music. Walk anywhere and you'd see [John] coming down the road—just the figure of him—and would hear that mouth organ going."

As far as a musical baptism went, John had already waded into the shallow end. He'd picked up the accordion as a child but soon grew tired of playing lightweight fare like "Greensleeves" and "Moulin Rouge." The harmonica gave him access to his own music, the songs boys his own age were listening to, a better fit for the sound he wanted. But there were limits. Harmonicas were fun, yet you couldn't play one and sing at the same time. This disturbed John, who by the year's end had shown more confidence in his voice during the sing-alongs on the Bank. He also continued to grapple with embarrassment. Looking surprisingly harried, his eyes corkscrewed tightly, he wheeled his bike closer to Pete's so that no one would overhear their conversation. "They say you're a sissy," John started, hedging, "but you're not a sissy, right? Singing's all right."

That was the way Lennon broached iffy subjects: obliquely so that he could recover, or simply retreat, from taking a compromising position. More than almost anything, John Lennon dreaded appearing weak or unmanly.

Pete learned to read his friend's ambivalence with exquisite care. Earlier the same summer, John had raised another suggestion that required careful consideration before issuing a response. The two boys had been biking around the neighborhood, when suddenly John pulled to the curb and did a subtle 180 with his eyes. Steadying his voice, he said, "Do you, uh, fancy, uh, learning to dance, Pete?" He persuaded Pete to enroll secretly with him in a "proper dancing class" held weekly at Vernon Johnson's School of Dancing, a sturdy sandstone youth center on the Allerton Road, near Penny Lane. Here, the word *proper* meant formal attire, in the style of ballroom dancing that had been a popular Liverpool pastime for as long as anyone could remember. Pete borrowed one of his elder brother Ernest's suits, which practically engulfed him in folds of spare drapery; John wore a sport coat and "proper trousers" that Aunt Mimi had bought in the hope that one day he'd wear them to regular church service. Together, they must have cut an endearing if slightly comical picture, setting out at dusk, as they did, from the corner of Menlove Avenue: two natty little men, staking their claim on grown-up society.

Earlier in the year, another schoolmate, Eric Griffiths, had tried to teach them to jive—or "kerbopping," as Pete and John called it. When it came to dancing, Griffiths was a natural. He'd picked up the steps from an elder sister who frequented local jazz clubs where resident fans seemed to dance the latest rages. After school, the boys descended on the Griffiths' house on Halewood Drive, around the corner from Mimi's, where, according to Eric, "we'd put on a few records and practice dancing. We'd jive with each other—me leading, trying to get them to do the right steps." But John, says Griffiths, "could never work out the rhythm."

"We did the steps, we were learning [how] to dance," Pete recalls. "But John was the world's worst dancer, like a stiff cardboard box." It mystified Pete why his friend wanted to torture himself this way.

One night, as soon as the music had ended and the students began to disperse, the boys wandered back to the cloakroom to retrieve their jackets, when suddenly the lights flickered off. Pete stumbled around, groping fitfully in the darkness until his arms wrapped around something soft and pleasurable; with near-flawless confidence, a girl kissed him earnestly on the mouth. The pure surprise of the embrace in such an unlikely setting could not have escaped the rascal in Pete Shotton. He'd assumed the girls who attended the classes were "modest and respectable." Eventually, to his dismay, the lights came back on. Pete glanced across the room, to where John was standing—and *grinning*—at him, another pretty, like-minded girl clamped snugly to his hip. "That's when I realized why he'd dragged me there," Shotton says.

What made the episode so memorable for Shotton was his realization that somehow John Lennon had engineered the encounter. John did not wait for situations to come to him—he created them. And never would this be more strikingly clear than in the following year.

[II]

In September, John returned for his final stint at Quarry Bank, burdened by the dismal prospect of another year in school. He remained anchored in the lowly C stream, "with the thick lads," which proved a constant source of embarrassment, but whereas in the past he had struggled to stay afloat, he no longer pretended to be interested in studying and simply gave up. The classes he was assigned to—English, history, geography, math, science, and French—held absolutely no interest for him. And phys. ed. was anathema. Rod Davis, the future Quarry Man who served as swim-team captain, persuaded John to join the school relay team, where he shined in the crawl stroke, "but eventually," reports Davis, "he just drifted off."

Ironically, the one skill that brought him such pleasure went unsupported—and John resented it. "I was obviously musical from very early,"

John recalled, "and I wonder why nobody ever did anything about it. . . ." It might have solved some basic developmental problems had a friend or teacher suggested that he transfer to the Liverpool College of Art, which offered an entry-level "junior" program to talented fourteen-year-olds (and where his future wife, Cynthia, was matriculated), but astounding though it might seem, he was unaware of its existence.

Having given up any pretense of academic pursuit, he was content to bide time. There was nothing in school, academically or extracurricularly, that captured his imagination, no teacher willing to address his obvious estrangement. Most days he sat in class, scribbling distractedly in the borders of his exercise book, making crude line drawings that expressed his contempt for society. His targets were authority figures and institutions that symbolized his own shortcomings: families were dead ends, marriages plainly unromantic, the church a font of hypocrisy; children were depicted with various deformities, teachers appeared as bumblers. As schoolmates responded to the cartoons that landed furtively on their desks, he turned up the frequency in a desperate effort to provoke a reaction.

The upshot of this attention-getting device was a compendium of drawings, accompanied by a few nonsensical stories that drew upon puns and unconventional wordplay spiked with obscenities. Some of the contents were no more than a few pages of simplistic illustrated stories designed to produce rude laughs, including a takeoff on Davy Crockett titled "The Story of Davy Crutch-Head" and sketchy marginalia. But there were also flashes of brilliance, truly inspired entries that foreshadowed the talent to come. One item in particular, "The Land of the Lunapots," written in a relaxed, colorful, pidgin Scots dialect, succeeded in blending conventional poetry with splashes of pure garbled nonsense:

> *T'was custard time and as I*
> *Snuffed at the haggis pie pie*
> *The noodles ran about my plunk*
> *Which rode my wyrtle uncle drunk*
> *T'was not the dreaded thrilling thud*
> *That made the porridge taste like mud*
> *T'was Wilburs graftiens graffen Bing*
> *That makes black pudding want to sing*
> *For them in music can be heard*
> *Like the dying cough of a humming bird*

The lowland chick astound agasted
Wonder how long it lasted
In this land of Lunapots
I who sail the earth in paper yachts.

John's body of work, eventually known in school as "The Daily Howl," was greatly influenced by John's friend and neighbor Ivan Vaughan, whose own version made its appearance in the form of a tearsheet months earlier at the Liverpool Institute of Art, where he studied classics with Paul McCartney. Ivan was a "lovely mutt of a guy," tall and gangly, whose oddball qualities made him immensely attractive; there was no menace in his eccentricity, only charm. Vaughan was always in motion, the flip side of John: vivacious, intellectual, ambitious, confident, and extremely sincere. "He was his own man, so outstandingly different [and] outrageous," says Don Andrew, a classmate of Vaughan's and later a member of Liverpool's pop band the Remo Four. "Everyone wanted to [be able to] say: 'I'm Ive's mate.'" It was Ivan who introduced John to *The Goon Show*, a half-hour potpourri of way-out humor and double-talk featuring Spike Milligan, Peter Sellers, and Harry Secombe that was broadcast weekly on the BBC's Home Service, beginning in 1951. Of all the boys John had encountered, until he met Paul McCartney (to whom he would be introduced by Ivan), Vaughan came closest to his idea of "an original."

The unlikely pair spent many evenings in Aunt Mimi's parlor, dreaming up sketches for "The Daily Howl." In typical Goon fashion, they lampooned teachers whose idiosyncrasies were ripe for exaggeration; warts, humps, gargantuan noses, claws, and assorted deformities were grafted onto caricatures that John drew with gusto. "It was so smooth and easy for him," Pete Shotton recalls. "Without it, I'm not sure what trouble he would have gotten himself into."

By January 1956, however, John had pretty much solved that riddle.

[III]

John's musical interests had remained undefined through the first half of the 1950s. He listened with captive indifference to the banal hit-parade vocalists who performed on the BBC, but there had been little, if anything, that genuinely excited him. That changed drastically in early 1956, when, with Radio Luxembourg's help, he feasted on "Shake, Rattle and Roll," by

Bill Haley, "You Don't Have to Go," by Jimmy Reed, "Such a Night," by the Drifters, Carl Perkins's "Blue Suede Shoes," and a pared-down version of "Maybelline," by Chuck Berry, who was emerging as a bona fide star. John was mesmerized by the big, aggressive beat and the tidal spill of lyrics. But like so many teenagers John's age, it was Elvis Presley who really captured his imagination.

Radio Luxembourg had played Elvis's version of "That's All Right (Mama)" sporadically—and without much fanfare—through the latter part of 1955, following it with "I Forgot to Remember to Forget" to much the same result, but it wasn't until the spring of 1956, with the debut of "Heartbreak Hotel," that an explosion was felt by teenage listeners unlike anything that had ever hit them before. "When I heard it," John recalled, "it was the end for me." "Heartbreak Hotel" set off an emotional groundswell. It is not difficult to appreciate the song's immense impact; the provocative lyric, offset by ferocious despair and Elvis's convulsive, wounded delivery, was a potent stimulus to a young English boy's awkward dreams and desires.

"Nothing really affected me until Elvis," John told Hunter Davies in 1968. It was not simply a boyish infatuation or a distraction; Elvis's music spoke to John in a way that nothing ever had before. Pete Shotton recalls discussing Elvis with John. "Heartbreak Hotel" "was the most exciting thing [we'd] ever heard." Without question, he says, "it was the spark, and then the whole world opened up for us." John bought into the whole novel package: the look, the sound, and the spirit of his performance. No one other than Paul McCartney would have a more tangible influence on John's development until he fell under the spell of Yoko Ono in 1967. "That was him," Paul has said of his own opportune discovery of Elvis Presley, "that was the guru we'd been waiting for. The Messiah had arrived."

Like an earnest disciple, John reacted with missionary devotion. The "Presley image" had already landed Merseyside, as John could see by the sprinkling of teddy boys who capered about like gargoyles at local dances. The teds had been on the fringe of British society since 1954, when a series of violent incidents involving juvenile delinquents dressed in long Edwardian jackets crept steadily into the press. The teds personified a classic example of adolescent rebellion; they drank, brawled, screwed, defied convention, and acted out by dressing like ghoulish undertakers. The uniform, in particular, drew critical attention to their rarefied ranks. Its mongrel style was adapted from a fusion of postwar London homosexuals, who wore velvet half collars on Edwardian jackets, with the biker gangs as depicted by Marlon Brando in the film *The Wild One*. A bootstring tie was added for effect, along with skintight jeans, called drainpipes or "drainies," spongy crepe-soled shoes known as "brothel creepers," muttonchop side-burns, and long hair greased liberally and combed forward to a point that bisected the middle of the forehead. Seasoned with a dose of aggressive rock 'n roll, the result was a new specimen of teenager. All it took for a middle-class kid like John to make that leap was to put on the clothes.

Shotton and Lennon began by acquiring brassy "Tony Curtises," lop-ping off shanks of each other's hair in John's bedroom one afternoon when Mimi was out of the house and then applying enough Vaseline to hold a Woody Woodpecker–shaped quiff in place. "We'd heard about [a] place [in Liverpool], which was the teds' shop," Shotton recalls, outlining their plan to mimic the elaborate wardrobe. After school, still in their school blazers, John and Pete hopped on the no. 4 bus to the city center and walked the short distance to London Road, where a "little Jewish tailor" had assem-bled a spectacular selection of these accessories. "They had the most glori-ous clothes [we'd] ever seen in our life [sic]. It was wonderful!" Within a week, John had shucked his casual chinos for a pair of bona fide drainies, trained his hair straight back, in a defiant "DA," or duck's ass, and grown bushy "sidies."

By the middle of 1956, after a volatile courtship with both Bill Haley and Elvis Presley, the UK gave birth to the first British pop event. Tommy Steele was the perfect stand-in for the American prototype, part pop idol, part show-business proxy, with an engine that ran on charisma. Unlike Presley, who had burst from obscurity on the strength of his bombshell voice and persona, Tommy Steele was the product of elaborate backstage designs. A merchant seaman born Tommy Hicks, he was "discovered" in the loosest sense of the word, singing in a Regent Street club called the Stork Room, in London. There was nothing groundbreaking about his performance, nothing particularly original or outlandish. Even his reper-toire was a mixed bag of harmless folk songs put through the metal-edged PA system and reconstituted as low-grade rock 'n roll. But it was obvious from the moment the lights hit Tommy that "he had enormous presence." He lit up the entire room. Larry Parnes, who went on to become one of the pioneer impresarios of the British pop world and who unwittingly gave the Beatles their first break, retooled Steele's image and launched his young protégé as "the British Elvis Presley," kicking off a marketing blitz that boasted a Decca recording contract, several well-placed television appear-ances, and a bit part in the mainstream movie *Kill Me Tomorrow*. Steele's first record, the absurdly titled "Rock with the Caveman," was a dismal stab at the idiom, thus alienating his intended public. Nevertheless, for two years he managed to draw the crowds that would eventually turn to harder-edged fare for sustenance. To his credit, he looked like a young boy and worked like an old hand. Eventually, Parnes yanked him from the harsh glare of rock 'n roll into a more subdued spotlight, headlining variety shows on the Moss Empire circuit, where he could cut loose, so to speak, without soiling his professional image. In the end, Steele had proved not so much untalented as too slick to be taken seriously.

John Lennon had followed—and rejected—Tommy Steele as cheap costume jewelry. Far more stimulating to him was the debut of Lonnie Donegan and the skiffle craze that exploded in mid-1956.

At first glance, Anthony James Donegan and John Lennon would hardly seem made for each other, aside from the coincidence of their birthplace in "the North." Ten years older than John, Donegan was from Glasgow, where he grew up in a world crowded with accomplished musicians, thanks to his father, who was first-chair violinist for the National Scottish Orchestra. His own talent, however, was somewhat less endowed. The stringed instruments he mastered showcased songs as opposed to scores, prompting a rift in the family orchestration. Tony left home at seventeen to undertake a vague but essential odyssey; he changed his first name to honor blues guitarist Lonnie Johnson and, after a stint in the national service, joined the Ken Colyer Band, one of the mainstays of the traditional jazz-club circuit.

When Chris Barber left Colyer's band to form a rival outfit in 1951, he created the Washboard Wonders from his rhythm section as a confection to fill intermissions. He'd play his trademark double bass (instead of using a washtub-and-broomstick contraption), accompanied by drummer Beryl Bryden on the washboard and Donegan on guitar, performing an odd assortment of American blues, spirituals, and folk songs that seemed to galvanize the mixed crowds. One of those numbers, "Rock Island Line," appeared on the Barber LP *New Orleans Joys* in 1954 and was "requested so often on radio programmes that [in 1956] it was eventually issued as a single" that climbed steadily to the top of the charts. The song itself generated excitement through its whirlwind, almost manic tempo, but it was the offhand charm of skiffle that captured the country's imagination. Rock 'n roll was too much, too fast; as perceived by most British parents, it was confrontational, rooted in social taboos such as violence and sex, and thus unacceptable as an escape. Skiffle was a compromise. It cranked up pop music's intensity level several notches, away from the torchy commiserations of "When Irish Eyes Are Smiling" and "Who's Sorry Now." But the songs' homespun familiarity, filled with the socially conscious rhetoric of the Depression era, brought a measure of respite to a culture in rapid international decline. And Lonnie Donegan was its perfect spokesman. With his scrawny body planted conspicuously center stage, Lonnie launched headlong into songs as though each was regulated by a stopwatch, galloping along whip and spur, building up kettles of speed, until it was inevitable that he either stomped on the brakes or self-destructed. His performances weren't so much musical as melodramatic.

Skiffle enthralled Liverpool audiences, not because it was new but because it was so unexpectedly familiar. In it, they heard the influence of country-and-western music, which had long enjoyed popularity among sailors and dockhands who trolled the Merseyside wharves. There was a time, right after the war, when Liverpool was regarded as "the Nashville of the North" for its rich deposit of attractions; local groups such as Hank Walters and the Dusty Road Ramblers, the Blue Mountain Boys, Johnny Good and His Country Kinfolk, and nearly forty contemporaries performed regularly throughout the 1950s, introducing the latest country rave as soon as another ship anchored in port. But while country and western had its share of admirers, it was skiffle that created a sensation.

It wasn't long before most of the 328 venues affiliated with the Liverpool Social Club Association were involved in some sort of skiffle-related show. Even restaurants and department stores got in on the action. Over the next few months, British teenagers would seize this primitive, readily accessible new sound and make it their own. Skiffle bands sprouted wherever there were people to exploit the family laundry equipment. Compared with other types of music, it was child's play. "Rock 'n roll was beyond our imagination," says Eric Griffiths, who soon after hearing Lonnie Donegan began working on his mother to buy him an inexpensive guitar. "[But] skiffle was music we could play and sound okay [doing] right away."

More than any other member of the Woolton gang, Griffiths was prepared to give this skiffle business a fair spin. He eventually acquired a practice instrument and signed up for a few lessons with a teacher in nearby Hunt's Cross who advertised in the local newspaper. Desperate for someone to share his enthusiasm and experience with, he appealed to several boys in the neighborhood, many of whom expressed curiosity, but the only one who took him up on it was John Lennon.

[IV]

Even before he got a guitar, John would pantomime playing one, striking a pose in front of his bedroom mirror and stomping determinedly across the floor until his aunt Mimi ordered him to desist. He spent endless hours lip-syncing songs on the radio, the popular ballads, like "Singing the Blues," "Little White Cloud," and "Jezebel," that clung so tenuously to the national charts, as well as occasional skiffle numbers that appeared on the BBC's playlist.

From time to time, John took the bus into Liverpool and stared longingly at the guitars in the window of Hessy's, a music store in Whitechapel that carried the city's best selection of instruments. If you bought a guitar there, John knew, Frank "Hessy" Hesselberg threw in free instruction, with classes of three or four beginners taught by his showroom manager. And yet, despite the opportunity to study with a teacher, Mimi steadfastly refused John's appeals. She wouldn't hear of it, arguing that guitar playing pertained to teddy boys and "was of no worldly use" to him.

His mother, Julia, warmed easily to the subject and was more approachable. During her daily visits to Menlove Avenue, John would bring it up at opportune times, reminding her how much she herself enjoyed playing the banjo. But Mimi's objections posed a real dilemma. She'd borne the responsibility for John, after all; Julia couldn't very well undermine her sister, not after the effort she put into raising him. "Perhaps next year," she told her son, "when you are finished with school."

This was small comfort to John, who was determined to have his way, no matter if it meant playing the sisters against each other. He came across an advertisement in *Reveille* for an inexpensive guitar that was "guaranteed not to split." All that separated him from owning it was £5 10 s., and after much cajoling on John's part, Julia relented and "lent" him the money on the condition that the instrument be delivered to her house instead of Mimi's. The steel-string guitar, a production-line Gallotone Champion, was constructed out of lacquered wide-grain maple, as opposed to the customary alpine spruce, with white piping and black trim, in a style part cowboy, part Spanish, and wholly unspectacular. Its body was significantly smaller than the arched *f*-hole models popular with most Liverpool musicians and lacked even a standard pick guard. "It was a bit crummy," John admitted in retrospect. But as guitars go, it was sturdy enough to hold a note, despite the stubborn action, and John immediately commenced to diligently wrestle with it to produce a persistent, if lacerating, sound.

It remains a mystery as to how John broke the news to his aunt, although it is reasonable to conclude that when he finally produced the guitar she sighed dramatically, as was her wont, and accepted its place in her house as fait accompli. Years later she would seize the opportunity to claim that it was she, and not in fact Julia, who bought John's first guitar, going so far as to invent a new price and provenance, but by that time the specifics were irrelevant. By that time, John and his guitar were part of history.

[I]

Some ideas seem so obvious when they are presented that you just naturally assume a proprietary right to them. That was how John Lennon felt when George Lee proposed they form a skiffle band. Lee, a fifth-year Quarry Bank student with dark, curly hair, encountered John and Eric Griffiths during their lunch hour one day in early March 1957. The three boys shared a congenial smoke out by the bike shed and "began chatting about music in earnest"—what songs they especially liked, which artists they admired, whose arrangements were most compelling.

At a point near the end of the conversation, George Lee, brimming with enthusiasm, suggested that they pursue their passion in a more active, enterprising manner. "We should start our own skiffle band!" he blurted out, as if it were a completely revolutionary idea. In fact, the phenomenon had caught fire in Liverpool months before, with new bands sighted more frequently than steamships, but it was still relatively rare at Quarry Bank. As early as February a school group had formed there called the Kingfishers, more noted for its trailblazing than its talent; otherwise, they were on virgin ground.

A skiffle band: John was intrigued, to put it mildly. It made so much sense, "he had difficulty concentrating on anything else that day." After school, he and Eric bicycled breathlessly to George Lee's house for some further discussion. "We *should* form our own band," he told Eric afterward on the sidewalk, safely out of Lee's earshot, signifying a sudden shift in personnel. By Eric's own admission, they considered George Lee "a fancy little character" who should be rejected simply "because he wasn't part of our gang." Moreover, they sensed that Lee's excitement was just a whim. "John and I took it seriously," Griffiths insists; there was no room in the picture for fence-sitters. (Undeterred, Lee eventually started a competing band, the Bluebirds.) They both had new guitars, and John began accompanying Eric to lessons in Hunt's Cross, where their painstaking teacher "aspired to make us guitarists, when all we wanted was to play a few chords and start 'blues-ing.'"

After two lessons, John had had enough. He responded wretchedly to anything structured, and guitar instruction was no exception. There were too many rules, not enough instant payoffs. Ever resourceful, Julia knew exactly how to resolve the matter. As an adequate banjo player, Griffiths says, "she retuned our guitar strings to the banjo and we decided to play, from then on, [by] using banjo chords." That meant they "tuned the bottom three strings all the same," according to Rod Davis, who over the years has mastered a number of stringed instruments, "and played banjo chords on the top four strings," which simplified the process. "It took me about two years, on and off, to be able to strum tunes without thinking," John recalled.

"John picked it up easier than me," Griffiths says. "[He] was more musical than me in terms of . . . sorting out what the chords were." Julia taught them how to play G, C, and D7, which was enough to accompany any number of popular songs. To get them started, she applied the triad to "Ain't That a Shame," Fats Domino's first hit, and demonstrated the method, singing along in a carefree, zesty voice.*

With that much under their belt, John and Eric were soon working out their own informal arrangements. After school, they met at Menlove Avenue, holed up in the parlor or upstairs in John's bedroom, where they tried learning, without much success, other rock 'n roll songs they'd heard on the radio. "We were [too] limited by the few chords [we knew]," Griffiths recalls. Normally, this would have produced divots of frustration, although in this case the boys hit on an alternative. Griffiths, who was as headstrong and only slightly less impatient than John, suggested they switch gears, perhaps try something simpler. As they soon discovered, playing "Rock Island Line" was a cinch using the three basic chords. It required little skill and few nimble changes to pull off, providing something of a confidence boost. The same went for "Pick a Bale of Cotton," "Alabamy Bound," and "Cumberland Gap." As they progressed, John and Eric responded by shuffling a selection of manageable rock 'n roll numbers into

---

* Hunter Davies maintains that the first song John learned was "That'll Be the Day"; however, since it was not recorded with the Crickets until February 1957, the premise remains highly unlikely.

their skiffle repertoire, simplifying the form of "That's All Right (Mama)" and "Mean Woman Blues" to suit their meager ability.

John threw himself into the practices, which took place daily after school, usually at Mendips or occasionally at Eric's house on Halewood Drive. He was completely uninhibited about singing, belting out each number the way he imagined an entertainer would deliver it. But John's was a provincial voice, hundreds of miles away from the urban toughness of his heroes. It was achingly beautiful and honest in a way that underscored its raw vulnerability, and yet the delivery was powerful—there was a clear quality of whimsy that shadowed each line he sang, a kind of half-cast vocal smirk juxtaposed with stinging emotion, as though it weren't enough simply to sing a lyric when you could comment on it as well. "John was a born performer," Griffiths says without equivocation. "You could sense that when he sang. It lifted him, he was energized [by it]."

Both boys soon grew dissatisfied with their after-school practice sessions. They were too confining; nor were they social, expressive, or theatrical enough. "We wanted to play to people," Griffiths says. "That was our objective from the start. It didn't matter where we performed, either, as long as we were playing in front of [an audience]." When John finally announced that it was time to assemble a band, Eric didn't so much as blink.

[II]

There were few things that Pete Shotton put beyond his best friend, but when John invited him to join a skiffle band, he was dumbfounded. They had been walking across the field out beyond Quarry Bank High School, ruminating over some musical triviality, when John confronted him with it in much the same way he asked about dancing class. "Should we start a band, then, Pete?" he asked evasively. Shotton, who hadn't a scintilla of musical ability, assumed John was making fun of him. He cursed and snapped, "I can't be bothered!" But a trace of rejection in John's face warned Pete that he'd misread the situation. Laughing to recover the bonhomie, Shotton said, "Don't be silly—I can't play anything." That was all it took to revive John. Instantly, the fantasy was rekindled. "It doesn't matter," John said encouragingly. "You can get a tea chest [washtub] or a washboard and just have a plunk-plunk. We'll sing our songs . . . like on the Bank. We can have a laugh, right? Let's have a laugh."

Upon hearing about the band, Pete's mother, Bessie, contributed a washboard she found in the shed, along with some thimbles from her sewing gear. "Mum was very supportive of this," he recalls, despite the fact that she considered "cheeky" John Lennon to be a "bad influence on her beloved son. She liked the fact we were doing something constructive . . . and the idea of her son [being] in a band was thrilling [to her]."

But Pete secretly loathed the undertaking. While he shared John's love of music and the package it came wrapped in, he "absolutely hated" the idea of participating in a band. For one thing, he was shy in front of strangers, mortified by having to stand up in public and sing, "playing this silly piece of tin." That he wasn't musical caused him to feel humiliated in front of his more talented friends; strafed by this insecurity, he was convinced, albeit wrongly, that it diminished him in their eyes. But he was John's best mate, determined to give his friend what Mimi had thus far refused to provide: encouragement, even at the expense of his own displeasure.

Shotton, in turn, persuaded another classmate and neighbor, Bill Smith, to throw in with them. Smith, like Pete, had no musical experience, which didn't detract from his eligibility; what he had was an old washtub that proved expendable and was thereby coveted by the band. By attaching a broomstick-and-rope getup to it, one could simulate a bass sound merely by leaning one way or the other, adjusting the rope's tension and plucking. Truthfully, it made no difference what note was played as long as the constant thumping provided some grave, resonant bottom—a trick that Smith, or just about anybody, could pull off.

Meanwhile, Eric Griffiths recruited Rod Davis to play banjo. The instrument was an oddity—a five-string Windsor model, unusual because it replaced the standard extra peg on the neck with a brass tube that conveyed the fifth string from the neck to the machine head, but for £5 there had been no reason for Davis to pass it up. "I took it to school [that] Monday," Davis recalls, and encountering Eric Griffiths, he exclaimed, "Eric, I got a banjo yesterday." Griffiths, who was eager to get the band under way, seized the opportunity. "Oh," he said, "do you want to be in a group?" Davis was caught off guard, not only by the invitation but by Griffith's apparent lack of interest in whether he could even play the banjo. Davis reminded his friend that he couldn't so much as finger a chord. Griffiths assured him that it wouldn't be a problem.

"Count me in," he eventually told Griffiths, and made plans to attend a practice after school, at Pete Shotton's house.

*   *   *

There were too many boys to assemble inside the Shottons' house on Vale Road, so Pete's mother sent them out back, to the garden, where an old corrugated-iron bomb shelter, exposed on one whole side, stood abandoned in the leaves. It was bitter cold in the yard, not for the fainthearted, and the four boys, bundled in sweaters, huddled under the damp metal shell with its reflected light pooled between them, hugging their shoulders and rubbing red, chafed hands in an effort to recharge their circulation.

Right away, Lennon took control of things, telling everyone where to stand, how to act, what to play—and when. There was a flow and an authority in the way he spoke that kept the others in thrall. "I remember being very impressed that John had all this in his head," says Nigel Walley, another childhood friend, who lived in a semi-detached house called Leosdene on Vale Road, halfway between Ivan Vaughan and Pete Shotton, and had stopped by "to see what all the fuss was about." Since few of the boys had ever had the chance to actually see a skiffle band in action, they were obliged by John's special knowledge, unaware that his know-how was for the most part intuitive. "He just *knew* what to do, it was right at his fingertips," Walley says. "It wasn't this concept he'd worked out; it came naturally to him. The amazing thing, too, was how effortlessly he got everyone else to follow him."

The first song they attempted to play was "Rock Island Line" (John had bought a copy of the Donegan single from old Mrs. Roberts, who owned the village record shop, opposite the baths), with John naturally taking the lead. There was never any discussion about who should sing. With his pale face lifted to the light, John barreled through the song, while his befuddled sidemen did everything they could to stay with him. Chords were jumbled unintelligibly, each instrument reeling in its own orbit. They looked clumsy, crowded under the little metal canopy, with everyone flailing away at the strings. All the boys would later agree that the sound was an unadulterated mess, but at the time no one gave it a second thought. The thrill of playing a song together—*as a band!*—overshadowed their ineptitude. They grinned at one another's beaming faces, proud and lit from within. By the end of the day, they had plowed through four folk songs, if not with measurable accomplishment, then at least brimming with determination.

Almost as vital as the music was choosing a name for the band. No one is certain who proposed calling them the Blackjacks, but it was approved unanimously and with a measure of deservedness. Eric Griffiths says, "It had the right sound for boys our age—rugged, dark, and American. We tried it on for size, and it just fit like a glove."

Successive after-school practices produced a solid, if unpolished, set of songs. The Blackjacks learned the entire Donegan songbook, including "Wabash Cannonball," "Dead or Alive," "Bring Me Little Water, Sylvie," "John Henry," "Midnight Special," "Cumberland Gap," and "Worried Man Blues." Even though John sang lead, everyone joined in the choruses. The words were so familiar that, by now, each boy had absorbed them like oxygen. When the sidemen chimed in, "*Oh, let the Midnight Special shine her light on me / Let the Midnight Special shine her ever-lovin' light on me,*" the boys puffed out their chests and sang with a faintly forbidden enchantment, their voices, once timid and off-key, rising with a greedy incandescence.

Two weeks later, the quartet discovered that another skiffle band—a group with enough of a reputation to impress the boys—was also called the Blackjacks. With no alternative other than to rename the band, they gathered at Mendips one afternoon—John, Eric, Pete, Rod, and Nigel— for "a mini-brainstorming." After a time, Pete facetiously suggested a name that apparently clicked. There was a tradition at the end of the term whereby the entire student body would stand in the auditorium and sing the school song. Everyone knew it by rote; they were forced to practice it endlessly during Prep, with Cliff Cook, a woodworking teacher, hammering it stiffly on the piano. "*Quarry men, old before our birth / Straining each muscle and sinew . . .*" The Quarry Men. John latched onto it right away, agreeing, "Yep, that sounds good, all right." But a slight smile betrayed his underlying motivation. The name was nothing if not a send-up of the school. "We'd never strained a muscle or sinew in our life at Quarry Bank," Shotton gently insists. "So Quarry Men, to me, seemed very appropriate."

[III]

Finding new, fresh material quickly became John's most pressing goal— and greatest problem. Radio was the most accessible medium, with even the BBC now acquiescing to the skiffle phenomenon, but airplay was still severely limited. Sheet music was scarce, and the cost of records was prohibitive. The only other prospect was going to a record store, where it was possible to preview one or two selections. To John, this was a font of material, and so he, Eric, and Rod joined the other fifth-term Quarry Bank students who climbed over the wall at lunchtime, bought some chips at a shop outside the school grounds, and made the hajj down Harthill Road to the roundabout at Penny Lane, where a branch of the North End Music Store (or NEMS, as it was known) serviced the small community. "You could listen to the odd record there . . . in a booth," Davis says, explaining how it was impossible to crib words under the circumstances, "but then they threw [us] out when they realized [we] weren't buying anything."

By the end of April, the momentum was broken by the defection of Bill Smith, who proved unreliable and simply stopped showing up for practice. His departure presented no serious threat to the Quarry Men. John and Pete broke into Smith's garage and "liberated" the tea-chest bass, figuring Bill wouldn't miss it much.

Smith was promptly replaced by Len Garry, the boys' singing mate from the Bank, who was now in his last year at the Liverpool Institute, in a class with his friend Ivan Vaughan and Paul McCartney. An easygoing, self-confident, and articulate Woolton lad, Len could also be indifferent to the point of distraction. But, as Griffiths recalled, "he could . . . pluck the strings of the tea chest as well as anybody. It didn't matter what [notes] he played—he was acceptable as a person."

The situation became even more exciting when Eric announced, quite unexpectedly, that he had found a drummer who might be of some use to them. A rarity in Liverpool, principally because of the cost of a set of drums, there was no greater luxury for a skiffle band. Moreover, it would provide them with an opportunity to play some rock 'n roll, which had always been John's objective. He was beside himself with anticipation.

Griffiths knew Colin Hanton from traveling home with him on the same bus. A little gamecock of a fellow with a quick grin and hair-trigger temper, Hanton commuted regularly from his job as an apprentice at Guy Rogers, an upholstery firm in Speke that operated out of an airy, modern factory that had been used by the RAF during the war to make airplane parts. The boys had exchanged nodding glances at first, in recognition of being neighbors, then fell into genial chitchat, during which, on one occasion, Hanton divulged that he played the drums. "I was very, very amateur, never a good drummer, probably because I never had lessons," admits Hanton, who beat out rhythms on the wooden furniture as if he were Sonny Liston, as opposed to Buddy Rich.

Hanton leaped at the invitation, but he knew the score. "I was [asked] to join the group simply because I had a set of drums," he says without a trace of rancor. "It didn't matter how bad I played."

Nigel Walley, who felt slightly left out of the configuration, declared himself available to be the band's manager and vowed to get the Quarry Men work. "I didn't know the first thing about managing," Walley admits now, "but no one had the slightest idea how to go about getting gigs." Walley discovered soon enough that many of the local stores in Woolton Village would accept posters, if they looked professional. "John made up a nice-looking ad in colored inks that said, 'Country-and-western, rock 'n roll, skiffle band—The Quarry Men—Open for Engagements—Please Call Nigel Walley, Tel. GAtacre 1715,'" and they convinced the manager of Mantle's record shop to place it centrally, in the window. Business cards, printed by Charles Roberts, carried basically the same legend.

Nigel's early efforts to place the Quarry Men in a paying gig proved fruitless. Still, no one more than John Lennon was convinced that fame and fortune were but a phone call away.

[IV]

The Quarry Men were too enamored of the spotlight to worry about paying gigs. The experience alone was enough to keep them turning up at practice. There were a number of places they found suitable for rehearsal. Eric Griffiths's house was usually available during the day: his father, a pilot, had been killed during the war, and his mother worked, so the place was invariably empty. On Saturday afternoons they jammed in Colin Hanton's living room, on Heyscroft Road, while his mother was out grocery shopping, or they went around the corner to Rod Davis's. Even Mimi hosted a couple of practices, minus the heavy equipment. "The tea-chest bass and my drums would have been too much for [her]," Hanton points out, so the boys limited rehearsals there to some singing, mindful to "watch [their] p's and q's."

At one time or another, John took each of the boys to Julia's house in what can only be construed as a Quarry Man rite of passage. The series of unannounced, informal visits wasn't anything like the ones they'd endured at the Griffiths' or the Hantons' or the Davises', where a rigid decorum was observed. At Julia's, the boys could be themselves, without worrying about "minding [their] manners." They could listen to records, play instruments in her parlor, make as much noise as they wanted, smoke and swear. She expected nothing of them in the way of conventional parental respect, except that they heed her wish to "just enjoy [them]selves."

Several of the boys, while completely charmed by the familiarity, didn't know what to make of her.

"Julia was unlike anyone I'd ever met before," says Rod Davis, who accompanied John to her house, alone and with the group, on several occasions. "She acted familiar in a way that was almost flirtatious, and yet there was such a clear division of standing. She was John's mum—that never strayed from anyone's mind—but her manner and the way she acted around us was more like that of a mate."

"One time," Colin Hanton recalls, "I was at Mimi's, when John developed a problem with some guitar chords, so it was off to his mum's. Julia immediately got the banjo out and showed him everything he needed to know. If one of the riffs got too complicated, she'd sing things to emphasize what she was trying to explain. I thought, 'Crikey, this is his *mother*. They're talking *music!*' It was a lot for a lad like me to digest."

John tended to forget the distance that separated his friends from Julia. He often talked Shotton and Griffiths into forsaking their school lunch for a surreptitious trip to her house. They'd stock up on chips and cigarettes, then pedal off to Blomfield Road, where they'd flop on the couch like cocker spaniels and listen to records in her sitting room. "She had loads of records—mostly her pop, not our pop," Shotton recalls. But Eric Griffiths remembers unearthing a cluster of rock 'n roll 78s there, which they devoured like sweets. "In fact, we discovered Gene Vincent there," he says with certainty. Somehow Julia had gotten her hands on an American issue of "Be-Bop-A-Lula," which the boys played endlessly until she begged them to stop. Of all the singers John had encountered, next to Elvis, Vincent came closest to possessing his ideal of a rock 'n roll voice—a deathly growl tempered with blatant sexuality and menace wrapped around an outrageous self-image. He didn't have to see Vincent to grasp the singer's penchant for black leather, fast bikes, and faster women; it was all right there, on that steamy track. Julia also introduced the boys to records by Shirley and Lee ("Let the Good Times Roll") and Charlie Gracie ("Butterfly"). It would take some time for those songs to be deciphered and inserted into the Quarry Men's repertoire to give them more of a rock 'n roll flavor, but the band's little cushion of material, largely due to Julia's bohemian taste, was already swinging in that direction.

Throughout April and the rest of May, the Quarry Men accepted any reasonable invitation to play, performing at various friends' parties. Nothing seemed to discourage the boys; sometimes, the shabbier the place, the more they were able to cut loose. Mike Rice, who was in the C stream at Quarry Bank with John, recalls, "They once came and played in our garage on Manor Way, to the annoyance of all the neighbors. The noise was such that people confronted my parents and forbid the lads from coming back."

Nigel Walley, acting as the Quarry Men's manager, sent homemade flyers to operators of the Pavilion Theatre, the Locarno Ballroom, the Rialto, and the Grafton; however, none were quick to respond. "Instead, we played the Gaumont Cinema, near Penny Lane, a couple [of] times," he recalls, where performers were treated about as respectfully as the beleaguered ushers who patrolled the aisles. "Most Saturday afternoons, they used to have a skiffle group on [during] intermission. They'd show a couple of short films, then have a break [in order] to change projectors, which is when we'd get up. The kids were never quiet; they'd sing along or stand up on their chairs. I don't know how the lads got through it; John treated it like an important gig, and incredibly no one ever complained."

Just how good—or bad—the Quarry Men were at those early gigs is difficult to gauge. Few people have any recollection of them. "We were starting to make some music that sounded good," says Pete Shotton. But Mike Rice, who watched them rehearse at Hanton's house, thinks they made a "general noise." And as chaotic as they sounded at practice, he says, they were absolutely lost onstage.

By John's own admission, the stakes grew higher in front of an audience. There was an undeniable rush to performing, "a sense that you could control a crowd's emotions with your voice." Eric Griffiths remembers admiring how comfortably John worked an audience, singing and emoting with an ease that eluded him in other social situations, how he seemed "to loosen up" in the spotlight "like a captive animal released into its natural habitat."

Encouraged by the band's progress, John was determined to test this new power under more challenging circumstances. Part of that was accomplished by entering the Quarry Men in a succession of "skiffle contests" that had become a seemingly indispensable feature of every dance hall, cabaret, and church social in Liverpool. While these shows fed the public's insatiable appetite for skiffle, the word *contest* was merely code for "no pay." Promoters had found a way, however disingenuously, of providing a rousing variety show without spending a shilling on talent. The bands played for bragging rights, or in the Quarry Men's case, the opportunity to cut their teeth and satisfy a powerful craving for the spotlight.

Toward the beginning of May, the *Liverpool Echo* began announcing auditions for a talent contest run by Carroll Levis, a corpulent Canadian impresario who was making a name in Great Britain for holding amateur shows in local theaters throughout the country. Later on, he would parlay this into a national TV spectacle and his own cottage industry on the order of *Star Search* or *Stars in Their Eyes,* but in the gloom of postwar England the stage—along with the opportunity to see some homegrown talent discovered and (hopefully) ascend to the big time—proved a tremendous draw.

In Liverpool, especially, the heritage of theater remained strong, providing the city with its chief means of entertainment. Television was in its infancy; very few people in Britain owned a TV set, and those who did watched one with a screen the size of a teacup. "People actually preferred the theater," says a Liverpudlian who remembers that period for its vibrancy of local stage shows and enthusiastic audiences. The grand Pavilion Theatre, for example, packed people into panoramas like "Bareway to the Stars," in which famous strippers, prohibited from moving (lest they be arrested) by police eager to invoke Lord Chamberlain's decency law, enacted a series of statuesque tableaux that changed in content only when the curtains were closed. There were lowbrow comedies, burlesque, any number of goofy Dracula spin-offs, topical revues. The audiences were ripe for theatrical entertainment and tapped right into Levis's brand of open talent shows, with their endless heats and face-offs.

By Liverpool standards, the Levis program was an extravaganza. There were eight acts, featuring a solid hour of old-fashioned entertainment, including Levis himself wearing a tuxedo and dickey bow. The Quarry Men turned up early that night, dressed as uniformly as their wardrobes allowed, in white shirts and dark pants. The entire band was nervous, but they plowed enviably through the allotted three-minute set that restricted them to one song, a straightforward rendition of "Worried Man Blues," to rousing applause. The last act to appear was another skiffle band, the Sunnyside Skiffle Group from North Wales, fronted by an arch four foot two comic named Nicky Cuff, who mugged shamelessly throughout the number. Rod Davis sensed right away there was trouble ahead. "They had a coach and a lot of supporters with them," he says of the competition, "plus, they really performed. The band jumped all over the stage. At one point, the bass player collapsed and played lying on his back. They created some excitement, whereas we stood in one spot, expecting people to just enjoy the music."

As it turned out, that was the least of their problems. It was determined by the promoter that there was an extra three-minute segment that needed filling at the end of the show; since the Sunnyside Skiffle Group was already onstage, they were invited to perform another number. "We felt that was a disadvantage right away," Hanton recalls. "As soon as they started the second song, John began arguing [about it backstage] with Levis. 'That's not right. You're giving them the upper hand.' We were all mad as hell." But it was too late. Levis offered a halfhearted apology but stood adamantly aside while the Welsh group put their luck to good use, turning up the heat.

When it was time to select the winner, the Quarry Men braced themselves for the audience's reaction. Levis wheeled out the Clap-o-Meter, a device that supposedly read the noise level of the applause. Every act registered scores in the high seventies and low eighties, except two. Portentously, Levis walked center stage to the microphone and announced: "This is an unusual situation, ladies and gentlemen, but we've actually got a tie." Both the Quarry Men and the Sunnyside Skiffle Group had scored an identical perfect ninety. "We're going to bring these two groups onstage again, and we'd like you all to clap for either one or the other." Each skiffle band posed proudly in the spotlight's glare, while their supporters hollered and whistled in the seats. It was a thrilling moment all around, but when the last hand subsided, the Sunnyside Skiffle Group proved victorious by a hair. "We were robbed," Hanton says, tapping into some residual anger, "and Carroll Levis knew it, too. While he was lining us up for the grand finale, he apologized, saying, 'I might have been a bit unfair there, lads, but it's too late now. Don't despair—you were quite good. Just keep at it.'"

Typically, Rod Davis managed to extract a valuable service from the disappointment. He says, "We got a lesson in showmanship. We didn't win because of the other group's antics, and that was where the germ of performing came over [us]." For John, however, the letdown was crushing. He had hoped to capitalize on a win in the talent show, wielding it as a magnet to attract work. Come the end of June, he'd be finished with Quarry Bank, shorn of his security blanket, such as it were, and forced to consider a trade. It was a destiny he pushed further and further from his mind. "I was just drifting," John acknowledged. "I wouldn't study at school, and when I was put in for nine GCEs [General Certificates of Education], I was a hopeless failure."

[V]

Despite the largely unsatisfying result of their talent competition, the Quarry Men pushed on. Nigel Walley, who had quit school at the age of fifteen to become an apprentice golf pro, came up with their "first real engagement" of note at the club where he worked. Lee Park had been founded by a collective of Liverpool's Jewish families who, having been denied membership in almost every Merseyside club, desired a social sanctuary for their community. One afternoon during a round of golf with Dr. Joseph Sytner, a member whom Walley lionized as a "great tipper," Nigel broached the subject of his alternate existence managing the Quarry Men. Sytner's son, Alan, who "was crazy for jazz" and had run two jazz clubs—the 21 Club, in Toxteth, and the West Coast, on Dale Street—was launching yet another venture that had so far attracted considerable attention in Liverpool. Called the Cavern and situated accordingly belowground in an old produce warehouse, it was modeled after Le Caveau Français Jazz Club, a Parisian haunt Alan had visited on holiday, and had been financed by the £400 inheritance he'd received on his twenty-first birthday. Since its official launch in January, the club had showcased a stellar lineup of traditional jazz bands whose fans thronged the subterranean den nightly. Nigel didn't care a whit for trad jazz, but he'd heard that Sytner filled intermissions with the Swinging Bluegenes, a "sophisticated skiffle" band that played traditional standards such as "Old Man Mose" and "Down by the Riverside" with a "jazzy rhythm section." If it wasn't too much to ask, Nigel proposed to his teemate, "Would your son give us a shot at [playing] the Cavern?"

Sytner, who knew Nigel well and liked the boy, said he would be happy to arrange something; however, first he wanted to hear the group for himself. "Can you bring them down to the golf club one night?" he asked. Nigel volunteered the Quarry Men's services for the club's upcoming social committee reception quicker than he could yell, "Fore!" Once again, no pay was involved, but Dr. Sytner said, "We'll feed and water you. The rest is up to your group." If everything came off as expected, they'd be assured of at least an audition at the exclusive Cavern.

The Quarry Men regarded the Lee Park "gig" as even more crucial than the Carroll Levis show. The audition aside, there was the matter of vindication, a chance to prove to themselves that they were worthy of commanding such a venerable audience. But the real plum was the billing: they were the evening's solo attraction, which meant they'd need to put on a full-scale show, they'd have to *entertain*.

"John reacted as though we were playing the Palladium," Shotton recalls. For him, a country club triggered images of poshly dressed socialites, standing in a haze of perfumed cigarette smoke while sipping cocktails from triangular-shaped flutes and basking in unforced elegance. He had an immediate attack of grandeur, suggesting to the others that they wear "real uniforms" out of respect for their position as headliners at such a ritzy affair. On its face it seemed absurd that a cash-poor skiffle band without much experience should worry about smartening up for a party of outcast Jews. A brief discussion ensued in which it was decided to dress respectfully but authentically: white shirts (out of respect) with black jeans (to maintain the edge). Everyone gave his consent, except for Rod Davis, whose parents found jeans repugnant and forbade him to wear them. The lads fretted over this dilemma for a moment, until finally even the upstanding Davis acknowledged the gig's importance and arranged to buy a secondhand pair from Mike Rice at the usurious price of 37 pence.

The night of the performance, the Quarry Men felt in fine form. They had arrived a few minutes before seven o'clock, while the old guard club members were finishing dinner, and were impressed with the fastidious arrangements. Says Nigel Walley: "We played in the club's downstairs lounge. They had moved all the chairs back to make it look like a music hall. A little stage had been set up, and to our surprise they'd provided a microphone, which was as scarce as money in those days. It gave John a real boost; he was chomping at the bit to get at it."

Half an hour later, the audience started filing in — and not the twenty or so punters they had expected, but seventy-five to a hundred distinguished-looking people primed with enough liquor to give the room a gentle buzz of excitement. That seemed to raise the bar a few notches. Feeling flushed, the Quarry Men scrambled to tune their equipment. (Contrary to popular myth, John was completely capable of tuning his own guitar, Eric Griffiths insists.) A minor catastrophe was averted when Rod Davis bent for his banjo, splitting the zipper on his contraband jeans, but John cleverly instructed him to lengthen his strap so the instrument would hang low enough to conceal the tear.

As for the show itself, the Quarry Men had never been better. They careened through a dozen or so songs with relative spryness, feeling only "a slight tension [from the audience] toward the odd rock 'n roll song" mixed into the skiffle-heavy selection. But nothing could dampen John's exuberance at the mike. When the spotlight fell on him, he responded like a moth to the flame. There was an unusually bluff spontaneity to his repartee, the velvet-smooth touch of a more seasoned entertainer. "John was very witty that night, throwing off one-liners and quips," says Nigel Walley, who watched bemusedly from the sidelines while the crowd struggled to muzzle their laughter at each new inventive Lennon wisecrack. "In between numbers, he [came] out with the funniest lines. Someone in the crowd would say something and John would twist it into something else. They chuckled at everything he threw at them. It was fantastic."

Despite a few off-key mishaps, the appearance was an unqualified, cracking success. "They were even nice enough to pass the hat around afterwards," Walley recalls. "We wound up with fourteen or fifteen pounds, which was a lot more than we [would] ever [get] paid in the clubs." To say nothing of its being their first paying gig!

The night also paid another dividend. As the audience dispersed, the band's potential benefactor approached, shaking outstretched hands like a politician. They could tell Dr. Sytner's reaction simply by the brilliant grin plastered on his face. He made no attempt to conceal his delight. The members, he told them, had roundly enjoyed the Quarry Men's performance. In a reception area outside the lounge he reported to Nigel that he'd "thoroughly appreciated" the band's attitude and wit as well. "That's a real professional group you've got there," he said, not mentioning a word about the Cavern or his son. Walley initially determined to bring it up but declined, thinking, "There was only so far that I could push the matter."

In the end, there was no need. Alan Sytner called Walley a week after the Lee Park show and offered the Quarry Men the opportunity to make their debut appearance at "a big-time music club." In actuality, the so-called gig was nothing more than a guest spot—they'd play what was known as the "skiffle interlude," a few songs, at most, sandwiched between the evening's two main jazz attractions—but it would be the first of many bookings that would transform the Cavern into an international mecca.

The Quarry Men managed to play only a few scattered dates before the end of the school term. No gig was too small to fill their impoverished dance card. They made appearances at the St. Barnabas Church Hall and at St. Peter's Youth Club, which were both done gratis. They were also featured performers at a Quarry Bank school dance. John became progressively more confident at introducing numbers, making humorous patter, and singing, while his sidemen did a fair job of hanging together instrumentally. The trouble was, their wiring was so agonizingly basic: three chords strummed like a baker grating apples to songs that demanded little else. John continued to play skiffle with élan, but his thoughts turned more and more to rock 'n roll. Skiffle was outlaw ballads, populist struggle, protest songs, rural blues, and folklore of the American Plains. Rock 'n roll came from the streets and "the jungle"; it had a young, aggressive energy that seemed to provoke expression in a changing world.

Throughout the spring of 1957, John binged on the bumper crop of music slowly making its way to Britain. School lunch periods were devoted exclusively to searching out new sources, and come noon each day John would break away from Quarry Bank, taking either Pete Shotton or Eric Griffiths with him as he followed up each lead like a sleuth piecing together a case. They checked out Woolworth's, W. H. Smith, several shops on the Allerton Road. His legwork eventually led to Michael Hill, a fellow classmate who, it was discovered, had "a great collection of American [rock 'n roll] records," to say nothing of the early jump and blues artists, which were a revelation. Hill lived a few blocks from school, near Penny Lane, and since his mother worked, the boys could spend an unchaperoned hour or two sampling 78s in the empty house. By some miracle, Mike Hill owned the entire Elvis Presley oeuvre, as well as singles by Hank Ballard and the Midnighters, Johnny Otis, Lloyd Price, and Fats Domino. "He also had records by the Dutch Swing Band," says Pete Shotton, "which wasn't our genre, but we . . . loved them."

One afternoon as the boys picked through a lunch of chips and cigarettes, John was struck speechless when Hill dropped the needle on a copy of Little Richard's "Long Tall Sally." As recalled later by John: "[Mike] said he's got this record . . . by somebody who was better than Elvis. When I heard it, it was so great I couldn't speak." John was beside himself, overwhelmed by Little Richard's hoarse, howling vocal accompanied by a savage boogie-woogie bass line and barrelhouse piano that never faltered from the breakaway opening until the last decisive beat. "We all looked at each other, but I didn't want to say anything against Elvis, not even in my mind. How could they be happening in my life, *both* of them? And then someone said, 'It's a nigger singing.' I didn't know Negroes sang.* So Elvis was white and Little Richard was black."

John was already feeling a little shaky about his faith in the almighty Elvis. Eric, for one, noticed that although John treasured those early hits,

---

* *This is clearly an exaggeration.*

"some things just didn't click with him." Recalling a day in 1957, on their way to afternoon classes, he says they took a hasty detour, busing into Liverpool instead to catch a matinee of *Love Me Tender.* "We sat in the cinema in Lime Street and killed ourselves laughing at [Elvis]. John thought he was ridiculous." And yet, that fiasco, an artistic misfire, seemed to take none of his enjoyment away from the music. Almost immediately the Quarry Men began practicing "Don't Be Cruel," "Heartbreak Hotel," and "All Shook Up," easy, poky versions, just shy a spark plug or two, that would satisfy the band's itch for rock 'n roll without alienating the skiffle crowd. (They also took a stab at "Slippin' and Slidin'," the flip side of "Long Tall Sally," but without much success.) "We started doing even more numbers by Elvis," says Colin Hanton, who, as a drummer, welcomed every chance to pick up the languorous beat. "The audiences were beginning to ask for it; John was feeling it. We were ready to move on."

But readiness was no substitute for talent.

The first real indication of trouble came during the band's debut at the Cavern, sometime during the late spring of 1957. The Cavern was enemy territory, as traditional a jazz club as traditional jazz could muster: restricted, segregated, as exclusive as an autopsy, it was the sanctum sanctorum of Liverpool's aficionados, with its own "would-be intellectual" clientele who were inflexible when it came to worshipping their righteous music. Inside, you were either for them or against them, and naysayers be damned. Only a year earlier, jazz pianist Steve Race, writing in his *Melody Maker* column, sounded the siren for a holy war against the heathen tongue. "Rock and roll is a monstrous threat, both to the moral acceptance and the artistic emancipation of jazz," he warned his confreres. "Let us oppose it to the end." The Cavern was the tabernacle for people who preached this absurdity like gospel.

The Quarry Men spent a fair amount of time preparing for the Cavern show, sorting through material, tightening arrangements, battling nerves as the date loomed near. Until the Quarry Men, John had little if any sense of the stability—and responsibility—that came with being in a band. Suddenly, he had the nucleus of a family, the subject for a meaningful (albeit unorthodox) education, the sneaking suspicion of pop stardom, and the attention he craved. "By this time, John thought he was Elvis Presley," says Shotton. Whereas before, disagreements would come to a point of impasse, he now began exerting his authority, demanding artistic control.

To that end, John could be cruelly dismissive. He revealed flashes of

pique at a rehearsal just prior to the Cavern date, when the band was practicing "Maggie May." Rod Davis, who applied to banjo the same kind of
aptitude he demonstrated for schoolwork, began crabbing his hand up the
instrument neck, playing intricate chord inversions he had learned from a
self-instruction book. John abruptly stopped the music. "What do you
think you're doing?" he said with a sneer. Davis tried explaining that it was
the same chords played on different frets, for effect, but John cut him off.
"You'll play the same chords as me and Griff," he insisted, glowering. A
moment followed when neither boy said anything; it was reminiscent of a
scene from an American western, when two gunslingers face off, waiting
to see who intends to draw first. Davis isn't sure whether the sound he was
making cut through the other instruments too loudly or whether John,
able to play only three chords, was jealous. But it is reasonable to assume
that John didn't like being showed up. Not this way, not in *his* band. Rod
backed down, knowing better than to confront John. At school he had
seen Lennon in action and considered him a bully, eager to prey on weaker
boys. "He was a punch-up artist . . . a pretty good scrapper, whereas I was
hopeless," Davis admits.

The friction carried into the Cavern, where the two boys argued
over the song list. At rehearsal, it was clear which way John intended to
take the band. "Elvis, Eddie Cochran, Jerry Lee Lewis—all of those
[artists' songs] were inching into our repertoire," Davis recalls. "He was
turning us into a rock 'n roll band." It wasn't that Davis necessarily objected to that direction, but as a boy who played by the rules, he thought
they'd be cutting their own throats at this juncture. "Because there was
this major confrontation between rock 'n roll and jazz, you had to be careful what you played in front of whom. There were some venues where it
didn't matter, but if you [played rock 'n roll] in a jazz club like the Cavern,
it was like going into Woolworth's and shouting: 'Marks and Spencer!' It
was a way of courting sudden death."

The only thing the boys agreed on, entering the Cavern that first time,
was what a creepy place they'd encountered. The entrance, a tiny doorway
on an otherwise deserted street of warehouses, was right out of a Vincent
Price film. There was a dismal solitude to the setting, enveloped, as it was,
in an orb of cold, misty light thrown by a solitary bulb. Had the door
creaked open to reveal a Transylvanian count, they might have run the other
way. Most of the way down the steep, dark stairway there was no clue the
passage actually led anywhere—no sound rose from the darkness, no flick-

ering light at the end of the tunnel. The only sign of life was a stench that grew fouler and muskier as they progressed downward. Eventually the stairs bottomed out into a vestibule of sorts, which emptied into the club, itself a dank cellar in three sections separated by archways. The middle section, where the stage bisected a wall, contained roughly forty chairs from which people could watch the performance. The two outer sections were reserved for dancing and milling about. The room, although ill-conceived, insufferably hot, and claustrophobic, was nevertheless, in the opinion of the Quarry Men, well suited to its purpose. The acoustics were good, and the crowd could see the stage from practically anywhere in the cellar.

John disliked jazz almost as much as he hated jazz fans. He bristled at the clubgoers that drifted in, dressed alike in their duffel coats, jeans, and baggy sweaters. "From the beginning, we started arguing onstage," recalls Davis. The band opened up with a trusty Donegan number, but then John cued the others for "Don't Be Cruel." Davis, who stood on his right, leaned over and whispered, "You can't *do* that. They'll eat you alive if you start playing rock 'n roll in the Cavern." Determined, he completely ignored Davis and launched into the song. Says Rod, "You could tell the audience was uneasy about it, but that didn't stop John. He was just going to continue and expected us to follow. I kept trying to persuade him, to no avail. He did several rock 'n roll numbers until it became clear that the powers that be were unhappy." At some point, Alan Sytner sliced through the crowd and handed John a note on which was written: "Cut out the bloody rock 'n roll." But anyone watching the slight, spectacled boy racing from song to song and drifting from one musical form to another knew he was not going to be deterred, whether by this crowd or by any other.

After the Cavern gig was over, the other members of the Quarry Men questioned whether the show had been worth the hassle. John felt they had turned a corner. The city may have been in the throes of a mad love affair with skiffle, but the natural evolution of teenagers augured a fickle heart whose beat was shifting to a more up-tempo rhythm, one in which rock 'n roll would prevail. Clearly, that seemed to be the sound calling to him.

Partly out of recognition of that change, Pete Shotton felt he was no longer equipped to remain with the band. He never liked participating to begin with, but the rigors of playing rock 'n roll demanded more than his thimbled fingers were able to contribute. The rhythm brought him into direct competition with Colin Hanton. At the Cavern, when John started to rock, Hanton occasionally hit a rim shot to sauce up the accompaniment. As Shotton recalls, "The sound of it got to me. I didn't think it [was] right. So I told him, 'Don't hit it like that, it sounds awful.'" Instead of a compliant response, Hanton instructed him to "fuck off." A few weeks later John and Pete crossed swords at a party, ostensibly over the washboard. They had played outdoors, at a birthday celebration thrown by Hanton's aunt, who lived in Toxteth. Afterward, the best mates wandered inside her house with their instruments and chugged down a few pints each. They sat there convulsed with laughter while John tossed off jokes and wisecracks at other guests' expense. Eventually, Shotton's gaze drifted toward his lap, where the washboard lay balanced on his knees. He rocked it slightly, to draw his friend's attention to it, and admitted what up till then had been tacitly unspoken between them: "I hate this, John. It's not for me." Shotton recalls being stunned by what happened next. "[John] picked up the washboard and smashed it over my head, just like that!" Pete says. "The tin part came out, and the frame was wrapped around my [shoulders]." Smirking slightly, John stared at the ridiculous scene he'd created and said, "Well, that solves *that,* then, doesn't it?"

The real focus of their tension wasn't the washboard or their friendship, however; it was the future of the Quarry Men. The band could not seem to generate momentum. Having outlived a brief honeymoon, during which John evaluated each band member and his contribution to the group, it became clear to him that, to continue at all, two elements were absolutely crucial: seriousness and ability. Shotton possessed neither quality. "It was perfectly obvious [to him] that I wasn't musical," Shotton says, "and John was taking the band seriously. [At last,] he really wanted to be a musician."

A few obligations remained, for which Pete agreed to play, including one that his mother had arranged at the St. Peter's garden fete, the most important event on Woolton's social calendar. Otherwise, the band needed simple retooling. Perhaps replacing Pete wasn't even necessary. Drums were all the percussion that was really needed, especially if the band moved further away from skiffle. But there were other cogs in the machine— namely, personality and ambition. It must have been unnervingly clear to John that he was never going anywhere with this gang.

The Quarry Men had run its course as far as a frolic was concerned. Len, Griff, Rod, even Colin—they were in it for a laugh. He couldn't blame them for that, but somehow there was more at stake now for John Lennon. And here it was unraveling, slipping away. Sacking Pete, as it were, only precipitated the obvious destiny, though it is doubtful John could see it. With some distance he might have realized that it spelled the end of his band—and signaled the beginning of another.

[I]

The Quarry Men set out in pursuit of their dream at a time when the world, especially Great Britain, seemed poised to oblige them. An enormous shift was taking place, nudged on by the climax of World War II and wrenched sideways by its aftershocks. The leitmotif of postwar life was the idea of endlessly unfolding progress. Jet plane travel idled on the horizon, as did color TV and England's first high-speed motorway. Many working-class families in urban wastelands were moved into council estates near the suburbs, or into newly created towns. And despite a 47 percent increase in the cost of living, the growth in wages nearly doubled, putting more money in people's pockets than at any time in fifty years. As Harold Macmillan, in his July 1957 speech at Bedford Market Place, enthused: "Indeed, let us be frank about it, most of our people have never had it so good."

And those who believe, as Donne contends, that all circumstance is "slave to fate" would glean further significance from the fact that John Lennon and a teenager who would become his closest friend and partner began the school year of 1957 in twin limestone buildings linked by a courtyard and located within a hundred feet of each other. "There was neither an affiliation, nor appreciable synergy, between the art college and Liverpool Institute," Quentin Hughes indicates in his sage evaluation, "but the proximity was such that they invited a certain kinship." If John's awakening to rock 'n roll and the formation of the Quarry Men was a prelude to what was to come, the arrival of the boy across the street commenced the first act of the legend. His name, of course, was Paul.

On the surface, Paul McCartney had it made. He possessed not only the most striking physical characteristics of the McCartney clan but also the expansiveness of their humor, their passion for music, and their practice of urbanity so epitomized by his uncle, the family patriarch, Jack McCartney, who was described as being "one of nature's true gentlemen." In a city of characters distinguished by dry, pithy pragmatists, Jack may have been the one Scouser who played against part. Tall, gaunt, always relentlessly debonair, he was a bon vivant and brilliant spinner of yarns in a raspy, unearthly voice that held listeners in thrall. As a deputy of the ubiquitous Liverpool Corporation, the bureaucratic rat's nest that ran the city, he feasted on its foibles like a stand-up comedian. Everybody had a smile for Jack McCartney.

Such was the role of a patriarch in a family of underprivileged Scousers who refused to be cowed by their circumstances. Jack, the eldest among the nine children of Joe and Florrie McCartney, was a man for the new age: gregarious, pleasure-seeking, and properly awestruck. All Joe McCartney's children—James (Jim), Joseph, Edith, Ann Alice, Millie, Jack, Ann, Jin, and Joe (named for an elder brother who died young)—it was noted, were "gentle, happy-go-lucky dreamers" and, fortunately, resourceful, if not simply oblivious, in their efforts to avoid the city's strong criminal undercurrent. Despite their inquisitiveness, each chose to remain Merseyside.

The McCartneys were a boisterous crew, alight with affection. In 1912, nine years after Jim's birth, Joe moved literally around the corner and resettled the family in a new, cheaply constructed terrace house at 3 Solva Street in Everton, a residential district in northeastern Liverpool, roughly three-quarters of a mile from the city center. The McCartney place, at the beginning of a narrow, cobblestone cul-de-sac, was woefully small for an ever-expanding family, but really no different from any neighbor's situation in the solid but overcrowded Irish enclave. One of the rare remaining photos of the house (it was demolished in the Liverpool Slum Clearance Program of the late 1960s) depicts a sad, deeply rutted structure stripped of any decorative amenity other than what was required to hold it together. It was a typical redbrick Victorian cereal box, with three stingy bedrooms outfitted like barracks and a front parlor whose threadbare couch was occupied in shifts to accommodate the extra-heavy traffic. The toilet—really little more than a hole, a hunch-down arrangement, below two horizontal boards—was in a shed out beyond the kitchen and was shared by two other families, the Dowds and the Simnors, with washroom facilities in even shorter supply. Each Saturday morning, all the kids grabbed towels, a washcloth, soap, and clean underwear and trooped over to the Margaret Street Baths, a public swimming pool, for their weekly scrubbing. For Jim McCartney, who had an almost feline fastidiousness about his appearance, extreme measures were required just to stay comparatively groomed.

Before the McCartneys arrived, in the early nineteenth century, Everton had been "a place to aspire to." Built on a steep natural ridge known as the Heights, it was the most elevated point in Liverpool, invigorated by the pure sea air, with views over the Mersey and Liverpool Bay across to the Welsh hills. It was, according to J. A. Picton, "a suburb of which Liverpool had cause to be proud." Compared with the unsavory city center, it was considered "a healthy place to live" and drew the wealthy upper crust of society to its lush parkland setting. Noble mansions, in tier above tier, looked out on a lovely landscape. The district's dense roster of churches spoke optimistically of its expectations: an expanse of cathedrals dotted the landscape, not the least of which was stately St. George's, the first cast-iron church in the world. But by 1860 its allure had all but evaporated. A victim in its own right of the Irish potato famine, Everton was transformed into a ghetto known as Little Dublin, the first terminal of swarming refugees, as inbred and overcrowded as Calcutta. By 1881, the onetime jeweled paradise had become the most densely populated area of the city, its patchwork fields clawed under to dower the mazy grid of roads thronged by "cottages," which sounds pastoral but is actually a euphemism for cheap terrace houses.

Jim McCartney probably had little time to submit to the temptations that were everywhere on Everton's streets. His days were devoted almost entirely to part-time work in order to compensate for his father's insufficient salary at Cope's Tobacco (Everton's largest employer, where he worked for thirty-two years as a cutter), various household chores, and the duty of watching out for six brothers and sisters who were barely of school age. With brother Jack, he attended the nearby Steers Street School, a county primary named for the city's first dock engineer, just off Everton Road. He was a decent student but "never really excelled" in any subject, and left school at fourteen, as soon as he was old enough for a regular job.

For an Irish lad in Liverpool, the priesthood was the highest work, but it was a calling from which the McCartney boys were "gratefully exempt." "Joe put all his faith in the almighty pound," says an old Everton resident, "and he raised his sons to believe employment came before godliness." Jack, who found a rock-steady, if innocuous, position with the Liverpool Corporation, offered to "inquire there" on behalf of his vivacious younger brother, but Jim had a taste for something more exciting. Eagerly and with great expectations, Jim went to work as a sample boy in the office of A. Hannay & Co., one of the myriad cotton firms servicing the Lancashire mills, where he did what salesmen referred to as "the donkey work"—running along Old Hall Street with bundles of extra-long-staple Sudanese, short-staple Indian, or strict low middling Memphis cotton earmarked for brokers or merchants in various salesrooms. He worked ten-hour days, five days a week, for less than £1, plus a bonus each Christmas that often doubled his annual salary. The duties called for neither much initiative nor imagination, but in the process, Jim soaked up the ins and outs of the business—from grading and warehousing to negotiating and bookkeeping—much of it over stand-up lunches with salesmen at the local pub.

A jovial, effusive man with a penchant for deadpan humor and the idioms of the Liverpool Irish, Jim McCartney had a streak of romanticism in him that can be traced directly to the influence of music. The house on Solva Street was flush with it; one form or another provided a constant soundtrack to the raucous family soap opera that unspooled in the overcrowded rooms. Joe loved opera and played the cumbersome E-flat double bass in the local Territorial Army band that entertained regularly in Stanley Park and at the commemorative parades that snaked along Netherfield Road so often that they seemed biweekly occurrences. When he wasn't marching, there were evening practices with his brass band at Cope's Tobacco. And Joe often played the double bass at home, hoping to encourage his children to pursue some form of music.

As it happened, none of the McCartney kids showed much interest. It wasn't until 1918, when a neighbor unloaded his fusty piano, purchased from the local NEMS store, on Joe that the gesture bore real fruit. In no time, Jim had taught himself a shorthand method of chording that allowed him to play along with popular songs of the day. He had a brittle, choppy style that suited the syncopation inherent to ragtime, whose melodies seemed to fill every dance hall and pub. Nothing made Jim feel more carefree than music, and his exposure to potent entertainers only heightened this passion. He and Jack stole off regularly to the Hippodrome and the Olympia, both ornate neighborhood theaters, to catch the latest music hall revue. Standing along the Hippy's balcony wall, the McCartney brothers enjoyed acts such as Harry Houdini, Little Tich, the Two Bobs, Charlie Chaplin, Rob Wilton, George Formby Sr., and the Great Hackenschmidt. "My father learned his music from listening to it every single night of the week, two shows every night, Sundays off," Paul recalled. Jim entertained every chance he got, playing for family gatherings and impromptu community mixers. While oppressive summer days brought Everton to an early boil, more than a dozen neighbors often congregated in the street below the McCartneys' parlor window and danced to Jim's accompaniment into the night.

Before he was twenty, Jim was already "the swingman of Solva Street," a youngster preoccupied with pop music who would stumble home from work, stay just long enough for dinner, then hit the road, looking for a jam. During the early 1920s, he fronted his own band, the Masked Melody Makers, a quintet of like-minded musicians, including his brother Jack on trombone, outfitted in "rakish" black facecloths, who played irregularly at small dance halls around Liverpool. The same configuration evolved into Jim Mac's Jazz Band, with a repertoire of ragtime standards and at least one original McCartney composition, "Eloise," a bright-eyed but unwaveringly banal ditty.

Jim McCartney's performing wound down in 1930, at precisely the same time he was promoted to the position of salesman. No longer restricted to side streets girding the Cotton Exchange, he threw himself into the friendly price wars waged with local buyers, and with his easy Scouse affability and natural charm, he quickly became a fixture in the market, "a born salesman who invited easy confidence and left an imprint of his personality on everyone he met." In his demeanor, his generosity, his plain-spokenness, his effusiveness, his intimacy, and his irrepressible wit, Jim, like Paul later on, proved an earnest, often devoted companion. People of both sexes were attracted to him. But having served such a daunting apprenticeship to an industry that rarely promoted men of working-class backgrounds, he dedicated himself single-mindedly to the job, shunning serious relationships for a period of almost ten years.

It wasn't until June 1940, during one of the increasingly frequent German air raids over Liverpool, that Jim fell in love. That night, the family had gathered at the McCartneys' new home in the suburb of leafy West Derby Village to socialize with Jim's sister Jin and her new husband, Harry Harris. There was a great deal of excitement, with whimsical toasts made in honor of the newlyweds and vain attempts at song. One of the guests, a fair, round-faced woman with unruly hair and a tender, abstracted look in her eye, gazed at the proceedings as if she belonged somewhere else. She'd arrived with the Harrises poised and gracious, but soon settled quietly in an armchair, an unseen presence.

Her name was Mary Mohin. Her voice was soft and resonant, without a trace of the guttural Scouse accent that echoed around the room. Paul would later say that she spoke "posh," which was the basic Liverpudlian knock on anyone who practiced the King's English. In Mary's case, her accent didn't sound at all pretentious, having been drawn quite naturally from the melodic Welsh and cultured university cadences of various hospital staffs on which she'd worked. It was indicative of her overall character, which is to say she was an exacting person who sought to refine her circumstances through hard work and determination. Yet at thirty-one and unmarried, Mary was no longer considered "a prime catch." At the age of fourteen, she had worked as a nurse trainee at Smithtown Road Hospital, where dormitory accommodations were provided. Afterward, she enrolled in a three-year general program at Walton Hospital, the main neurological facility serving northwestern Liverpool, rising quickly through the ranks to become a staff attendant and eventually a prestigious state-registered nurse.

Remarkably, over the next seventeen years, there were no serious suitors in her life. "Mary was so career-conscious that she didn't worry much about men," says her sister-in-law and confidante Dill Mohin. A Welsh nurse who trained with and later worked alongside Mary explains how the job extracted an enormous commitment: "We were so immersed in our work," she recalls, "no one was in any hurry to get married." But if Mary Mohin harbored any regrets or disappointment in what had been dealt her, she never let on to a soul.

Jim, at forty, had settled into what friends considered "a confirmed bachelorhood." Although he was about the same age as his father when he found a bride, he had shown no inclination toward marriage, and throughout the evening, the quiet guest who "wasn't at all musical" did nothing to alter that facade. Had the festivities progressed as a matter of course, it is likely Jim and Mary would never have seen each other again. The reality, however, was more extraordinary. About 9:30, a blast of air-raid sirens rumbled across Merseyside. The Luftwaffe had resumed its habitual sorties, attempting to knock out the strategic port. Usually, an all-clear blew within the hour, but this time emergency measures lasted all night, so the McCartneys and their guests hunkered down in the cellar until dawn.

Despite such unromantic surroundings, Jim and Mary shared enough moments to kindle serious interest. She found him "utterly charming and uncomplicated," delighted by his "considerable good humor." With his steel-blue eyes, thin hair swept back from a high forehead, trim business-man's build, and robust personality, Jim became an object of Mary's disciplined interest.

She was no doubt enamored of his openly affectionate family as well, having been deprived of similar feelings in the Mohin house. The situation there had deteriorated soon after her mother's untimely death in 1919 while giving birth to a fourth child. With her brother Wilf away in the army and two-year-old Bill in need of vigilant supervision, Mary, who was only twelve, found herself pressed into service. She looked after the family for two years and was predisposed to the maternal role until the spring of 1921, when her new stepmother, Rose, arrived. Rose was a witch, according to Bill Mohin. Elderly, embittered, reluctant to adapt, she was a scornful, iron-willed woman devoted entirely to a son and daughter from a previous marriage who'd accompanied her to Liverpool. It became instantly clear to everyone, especially Mary, that Rose had no love for domesticity, even less for sparing her new husband's children. Within a year, the women had reached a point whereby they were unable to communicate. "Mary went to nursing school because she couldn't stand being at home with her stepmother," Dill Mohin recalls. "She'd occasionally meet her father on his rounds," delivering coal by horse-drawn cart to Liverpool families. "That way, they could be together for a while. But because of Rose, she never went home again."

Jim and Mary began dating that summer, an otherwise fearful, desultory period marked by the staggered advance of war. Hardly a day passed that prevented them from enjoying each other's company. They were like a pair of mismatched bookends: Jim, frisky and unserious, a man of modest dreams; Mary, an earnest, resourceful nurse on the front lines of a dangerous world. Despite the depth of their love, it wasn't an easy business. They faced turmoil head-on as a function of the war. The government formed the Royal Cotton Commission, becoming, in essence, the central body for importing the crop—as well as its rationing—which meant that after twenty-four years at A. Hannay & Co., Jim was chucked out of work. Mary's job, too, was in turmoil, owing to the scarcity of experienced nurses at the front; rumor circulated that she faced imminent military conscription. "Medical personnel were being recruited for emergency posts as far off as Egypt and Ethiopia," says one local historian. Jim, whose age and boyhood injury exempted him from national service, feared abandonment—and worse.* At forty, he was disconsolate, afraid of drifting into uselessness.

---

* In 1912, he tumbled off a wall and punctured an eardrum.

It was the "austere side" of Jim McCartney that regained its bearings in a temporary job designed to aid and expand the war effort. Everywhere in Liverpool, businesses had hastily retooled their facilities, becoming functional military providers. The Bear Brand Stocking factory was a perfect example, abandoning production of silk tights in favor of parachutes. Clothing factories in Litherland churned out infantry uniforms, auto assembly lines built tanks, warehouses were appropriated and conveyed to the Royal Ordnance Factory, churches were converted to mortuaries. The Napier plant, which had flourished making plane parts, was commissioned by the Air Ministry to produce engines for the streamlined Typhoons that strafed enemy skies. Ungrudgingly, Jim labored there for the duration of the war, turning a lathe that made shell casings for explosives.

There were other perks that rendered his job more agreeable. To good, solid citizens like Jim McCartney who did "war work," the government made subsidized housing available. Tiny terrace dwellings, referred to as "half houses" inasmuch as they resembled sheds, were authorized on the outskirts of the city. That was all the incentive necessary to hasten Jim and Mary's plans. They had been dancing around the issue of marriage for several months, postponing decisions on the pretext of Jim's job loss or Mary's possible transfer. Finally, unwilling to wait out the war, they took out a license at Town Hall on April 8, 1941, and got married a week later at St. Swithins Chapel, in a Roman Catholic ceremony that was undoubtedly a concession to Mary's traditional Irish family.

[II]

On June 18, 1942, a boy was born in a private ward at Walton Hospital, coincidentally on the same floor where, twelve years earlier, Mary had satisfied her state registry requirements. As was customary with the practice of midwifery, no doctor was present during the delivery. Instead, Mary was attended by a team of maternity nurses, dressed in a spectrum of colored uniforms that determined their rank, most of whom the mother-to-be knew by name. Because of his volunteer service in the local war effort, Jim was detained fighting a blaze behind the Martin's Bank Building, where German bombs had incinerated a warehouse, and arrived later that night after visiting hours were over and was granted a special dispensation to see his son.

There was never any doubt what the baby would be named. With the "teardrop eyes, high forehead and raised eyebrow — the famous

McCartney eyebrow"—that were unmistakable characteristics, the first-born would be James, after his father and great-grandfather, who brought the clan to Liverpool. As no one on Jim's side had a middle name and in keeping with tradition, it was simply James McCartney IV. But before it was registered on the birth certificate, Mary, thoughtful and scrupulous as always, wondered how she would distinguish the men from each other. To solve the problem, it was decided that her son would be James Paul. Exactly when James was dropped in favor of the more familiar middle name has been a source of some speculation among family members. Some believe that during the hospital stay both parents referred to the baby as Jimmy; others swear that was never a factor. Given the circumstances, an explanation seems immaterial because by the time they brought their son home he was acknowledged only—and forevermore—as Paul.

The first few years of Paul McCartney's life were marked by a blur of consecutive moves.

It was evident from the start that Jim and Mary's flat in Anfield was hopelessly inadequate to shelter their little family. In addition, Everton was growing increasingly popular as a German bombing target, the district frequently a mottle of smoldering frames where houses once stood, the air heavy with lime from nearby mass graves where war casualties were buried. "Everton," as a longtime resident put it, "was a place to leave."

Wrapped snugly in Mary's arms, Paul adjusted to the extreme northern weather as his parents hopscotched around Liverpool, scaling each rung up the Corporation housing ladder in measured stride. Initially, they commuted by ferry, relocating in Wallasey, across the Mersey and an ostensibly safer district by comparison. Then, in 1944, after the birth of another son, Peter Michael (he, too, known by his middle name), they moved back to the mainland, to a "drab part" of the city called Knowsley Estates, whose condition was typified by its street name: Roach Avenue. The building, called Sir Thomas White Gardens, was part of a semicircular complex and decent enough, according to a relative who visited often. They "had a [ground-floor] flat in a well-built tenement, a big block of concrete with kids everywhere. But the [neighbors] were very much to be desired."

Jim, by this time, was beyond the restless stage, waiting for the Cotton Exchange to reopen. His job at Napier's was eliminated, and a temporary position with the Liverpool Corporation's sanitation department proved debilitating. Mary bore the brunt of his frustration. She returned to work part-time, in order to supplement their income—and get out of the house. Fortunately, the Corporation had been signing up state-registered nurses to canvass each district, inspecting the hygienic conditions in places where women elected to give birth at home. Such deliveries had grown common in the forties, in no small part because travel was severely restricted during the war. To meet the demand, district midwives took on great local importance, "much like the parish priest or the beat policeman." People came to her door for advice. "Is the nurse in? I need to talk to the nurse," they'd inquire, then anguish "about the sister-in-law who'd run off with the postman."

But mostly Paul watched his mother depart at all hours of the day— or night—to assist in the home delivery of babies. The usually mellow Mary switched over to automatic pilot when pressed into action. Her transformation never failed to astound Paul. Double-time, she'd inventory her equipment, checking the contents of the black leather delivery bag for thoroughness. Her cases were thrown over a bicycle, whose front and rear lights were tested, as were the batteries in her headlamp. When everything was approved for takeoff, Mary straddled the bike, threw her purse into a brown wicker basket attached to the handlebars, and sped into the dark like Bruce Wayne, often not returning home in time for sleep.

Cycling around Liverpool was no waltz in the park. The hills surrounding the McCartneys' residence were steep and unforgiving. Incredibly, Mary never surrendered to them, despite the effects of a deadly cigarette habit that left her gasping for breath. One road in particular, Fairway Street, was the steepest in all of Liverpool, but Mary routinely scaled it at all hours of the night, rain or shine.

Jim often put the boys to bed while his wife was on call, never complaining, taking great pleasure in raising his sons. During the spring, Mary would be called out nearly every night, leaving the house during dinner and not returning until after breakfast, while still finding time to lavish attention on Paul and Mike and produce "sumptuous casseroles" in her tiny kitchen.

In 1946, to everyone's great delight, cotton was returned to the private sector and Jim found his old job waiting at A. Hannay & Co. No doubt this turn of events ended a grave personal crisis. It was a relief to be back doing the work he knew and loved. But almost immediately there was evidence that the once-vital industry lay in shambles; nothing stood up to five years of bureaucratic fumbling. The boom trade, when Lancashire imported 4.5 million bales of cotton annually, had dwindled to a lowly fraction of that bounty. Mills were encouraged to close, their machinery exported, along with jobs and taxable income. As one veteran of the cotton trenches described it: "The rot had set in."

Still, Jim pushed on. The salary wasn't commensurate with his experience, but his weekly take of £6 to £10 was enough to supplement Mary's income. They'd "never be wealthy," in the estimation of a relative, "but with two wages coming in, it wasn't difficult" to make ends meet. And while not as comfortable, perhaps, as they had dreamed of becoming, the McCartneys were better off than the run of Scousers living in Liverpool center. Mary even mustered her courage and "asked [her bosses] for a move to Speke."

Lured by the prospect of wide-open space, Liverpool families had begun migrating south a few miles, to where new settlements rose from lush glades and pastures, in pursuit of the middle-class dream. But Speke was the sort of culturally deprived suburb only the British could refer to as an "estate." The area had existed since the sixteenth century as an old Elizabethan manor house that was rashly redesigned in the mid-1930s as "a new model town" for the masses. Street after street, row after row, the layout was a grid of numbing monotony superimposed on the landscape's windswept fields. There were churches, clinics, and schools, but not the pubs and little shops that encouraged social interaction. Moreover, there was no social or economic diversity: Speke functioned as a one-class town of laborers, without any middle class aside from priests and doctors.

To many people, the eight-mile distance to Liverpool center seemed "half a universe away." Cars and trains would one day bridge that gap, but when the McCartneys moved to Speke, few people in their financial bracket owned automobiles despite Ford and Vauxhall being the estate's largest employers. And the bus routes were hopeless; necessitating a devious maze of transfers, it often took an hour or more to make the fifteen-minute trip into the city. Geographically, Speke had the forlornness and seclusion of a military installation, its residents' sense of isolation—of being cut off from the rest of the city—overwhelming.

Still, there was something delicious about leaving all that inner-city congestion behind. The streets, though too close together, were spectacularly clean. Most houses had stopped burning coke and coal in favor of gas, "smokeless fuel," providing an immediate sense of wholesomeness, and as a result Mary's boys could play outside in a pillow of crisp, fresh air.

The house the McCartneys got at 72 Western Avenue on the edge of a flat, featureless field was comfortable by council standards: a living room with a generous bay window, a kitchen more spacious than Mary was accustomed to, and two snug bedrooms on a sooty lot that stood tangent to a neighboring orchard. Inside, it was roughly the same size as the flat in Everton, but thanks to the location and the promise of better things, Jim and Mary's modest Scouse sense of how much of the world they deserved to call their own was satisfied. Paul was four when they arrived, and to this inquisitive city child, Speke was a magical, imaginary kingdom—unbounded by horizons and gaping with wide-open spaces—a kingdom that was at least as enchanting and magical as those in the stories his mother read at night. In summer, the bluebells that feasted on the sandy northern soil turned the estate from an undernourished tract into a picture postcard.

Within a year, however, the Corporation moved the family to another part of Speke, in an expansion that stretched a mile farther east, on Ardwick Road. This site was even more rudimentary than the last, just neat rows of brick buildings on either side of a muddy pudding of road gouged with irrigation ditches. It had a huge view of the fields opposite the house and a wind exposure that defied insulation. Only a handful of families had moved into this section of the development, and to young Paul it seemed particularly isolated, as though "we were always on the edge of the world."

Soon after they unpacked, in early 1948, Mary began complaining to Jim about stomach pains. She had probably been experiencing discomfort, if moderately and privately, since returning to work. "Oh, I've been poorly today," she complained to a relative at tea one afternoon after a comment about her low spirits. "I had terrible indigestion." On another occasion she declined a plate of cucumber sandwiches, blaming them as the source of lingering "indigestion."

But the distress wasn't easily shrugged off. Eventually, Mary's pains grew more severe. She tired easily from bicycling and early in the day. At first it was attributed to stress caused by her erratic work schedule, which seemed logical. Hastily eaten meals and extreme lack of sleep were enough to cause anyone nagging indigestion. But in Dill Mohin's eyes, Mary hadn't looked well for a long time. "Why don't you go to the doctor?" she argued.

Mary dismissed her sister-in-law's suggestion with a wave. "Oh, you don't go to the doctor with *indigestion*, Dill," she scolded her.

"I think, for the most part, she was afraid to go, she was afraid to know," says Dill, who suspected that something more serious was involved. "I could see doubt and fear in her eyes. She was such a clever nurse, she must have known what was wrong."

Finally, Jim persuaded her to have a thorough examination. It was scheduled for a Tuesday afternoon, but as he was due in Manchester that morning, his sister-in-law accompanied Mary to Northern Hospital, where she was to undergo an upper GI series. "I left her in the waiting room," Dill recalls. "She wouldn't have me stay. 'I'll catch the bus,' she said, 'and be home in time to get the boys from school.'"

However, by the time she was released later in the day, Mary was too shaken to go straight home. She found a telephone booth on the corner, just outside the hospital, and phoned Jim's office. He could barely understand what she said through the tears. "Jim, oh, *Jim,*" she sobbed, "I've got cancer!"

"Don't move—stay where you are," he instructed her. "I'll come get you."

Within minutes, Jim had run several blocks to the telephone booth and found his wife curled up inside. It unnerved him to see her, always the unflappable nurse, in such a state of emotional distress. He was determined to console her, trying everything he knew to lessen her foreboding, but the doctor hadn't minced words. The mastitis he diagnosed was already in an advanced stage; cases like these, as she knew, were almost always fatal.

———

Practical as ever, Mary put a good face on misfortune. The diagnosis passed as something instantly forgotten, like a fascination or a mistake. She could find no incentive in it, and that challenged her, touched off her stubborn Irish defiance to seek comfort where she could find it—in her family. The boys, especially, distracted her, demanding constant supervision.

There are numerous accounts of how Jim occasionally walloped his sons when provoked—Mike McCartney even claims they were "duly bashed"—but his sister-in-law maintains they are untrue. "Jim and Mary never smacked the boys," she says. "They took them to their room and gave them a good talking-to, but they never hit them. Never." Whatever the case, Paul and Mike remained a handful.

"The McCartney boys were like a circus all on their own," says a cousin who was an occasional playmate. They were as rambunctious as any two brothers who depended on each other for entertainment. Paul, as ringmaster, set a ferocious pace for Mike, a full head shorter, who "followed him like a puppy down every street." He could read, shoot conkers and ollies (Scouser for chestnuts and marbles), swim, chew gum, and whistle. Best of all, Paul was canny; even at an early age, he could "charm the skin off a snake" just by pulling that angelic face. A fleshy, rather pretty boy with dark brown hair and huge, expressive eyes accentuated by unusually long silky lashes and a tiny rosebud mouth, he developed a smooth, winning profile that was effective in any variety of situations. In photographs taken when he was a toddler, his face is a mask of bluff innocence, the lower lip carefully retracted while his mouth betrays the flicker of a smirk. These same pictures indicate another revealing pose: puffing out his chest and folding his arms across it in an expression of utter satisfaction. It was apparent that, more than anything, Paul had a real sense of himself. Of all the kids in the neighborhood, he was the most polite and well-spoken, ingratiating, eager to please and self-deprecating, which came in handy when denying a piece of infantile mischief. Hunter Davies referred to this style of Paul's as "quiet diplomacy," but it was more like a hustle. Already a song-and-dance man, he'd perfected this little shuffle that accommodated him for years to come. "Saint" Paul and his disciple, Mike, kept Mary on her toes.

Indeed, Mary would run herself ragged trying to keep up with those boys. They were always off on a rousing bicycle adventure whose itinerary rounded downhill through the lacy arc of nearby countryside. Beyond Speke itself the topography changed and the road fed into the greenstriped fields that converged on Dungeon Lane. On those occasions when Michael was allowed to tag along, the brothers left the estate by that route and traversed the steep embankment that bordered the Mersey. From the top of the rise, they could see the entire northern coast: the unkempt sliver of beach that limned the shore to Hale Head, where an old lighthouse stood sentry to ships navigating around the yawning channel. On the Wirral side of the river, in dizzying perspective, was Ellesmere Port, glinting, turned into the wind, and beyond it the crenellated horizon of Wales, the gateway to other worlds unto themselves. A steady parade of ships wreaked havoc with the ledgy mud banks, but periodic lulls in traffic, at hours the boys knew by heart, enabled them to scramble down the forbidding incline and swim in the icy, graphite water. Other times, they bypassed the river entirely en route to Tabletop Bridge, where, lying in wait like a "super spy," they would pelt onrushing trains with turnips scavenged from an adjacent field. "This is where my love of country came from," Paul later recalled. Too young to travel long distances by himself, he would retreat to a secluded glade of the woods, entertained by a local cricket ensemble while he read book after book—a practice he repeated often over the years, albeit in cushier environs.

Even in Speke, where most families were blue-collar workers, parents chased the middle-class dream: that higher education would lead to advancement for their children. Jim and Mary were perhaps more aggressive than others in that regard. It became a passion for them, as they steered their sons toward the right venues. In addition to Stockton Wood Road Primary, not far from the house, Paul attended the Joseph Williams Primary School. Both were well regarded for their standards of academic achievement.

Jim and Mary also challenged the boys in their own ways. Jim was an armchair philosopher who rattled on incessantly about conventional "principles" such as self-respect, perseverance, a relentless work ethic, fairness. "He was a great conversationalist, very opinionated, an impassioned talker," says a nephew who recalled Jim's ritual of "matching wits" with everyone—and Paul, especially—in an effort to provoke an animated discussion. He devoured the newspaper each day, which provided fresh fodder for his observations—as well as an onslaught of information for his sons. In the evenings, with logs crackling in the fireplace, Jim would settle comfortably into an armchair in the front parlor, fold back a section of the *Liverpool Echo* or the *Express,* and scrutinize the crossword puzzle, inviting the boys to "solve clues" for him while explaining the meaning of new and uncommon words. "He was very into crosswords," Paul recalled. "'Learn crosswords, they're good for your word power.' . . . If you didn't know what a word meant or how it was spelled, my dad would say, 'Look it up.'" Mary read poetry to them and insisted that her sons cultivate an interest in books and ideas that would carry them far beyond the limitations of their parents. "Mary was very keen on the boys' schooling—*very* keen," says Dill Mohin. "She knew Paul was clever and pledged to facilitate that in any way she could. No lazy Scouse accent was permitted. To her credit, he spoke right up, articulately, without sounding precocious. The boys weren't allowed to go out to play until they'd done their [homework]," which Mary inspected as scrupulously as she did their appearance.

Despite the so-called model curriculum set by headmaster John Gore and his well-intentioned staff, Joseph Williams was a reflection of its constituency. Few students at the primary level went on to grammar school; most graduated to secondary modern schools, lingering there only until they were old enough to work. In Paul's class, out of several hundred students only ninety chose to sit the eleven-plus exam—a test to determine whether or not a student was grammar-school caliber and eligible to work toward a General Certificate of Education—and only four, one of whom was Paul McCartney, received a passing grade. The divisiveness it caused was painful. Decades later, the effect of that exam was still fresh on Paul's mind: "It was too big a cutoff. All your friends who didn't make it weren't your friends anymore."

The grammar school Paul entered in September 1953 was a shining exemplar of the British education system. Founded as "a gentleman's school" in 1825, the Liverpool Institute was a state-endowed academic facility whose ethos was geared exclusively to funneling as many of its students as possible into Oxford and Cambridge. Its Prussian curriculum was modeled on a university-type education, with streams, forms, and majors designed to maximize individual scholarship. The masters wore gowns in deference to their first-class pedigrees; an astonishing twenty of the fifty-two faculty members had Oxbridge degrees. Outstanding students were chosen as prefects in their later years. Administrators reported on the progress of standouts to sharp-eyed university dons. The whole process at the "Inny," as it was known, imitated a grand and long-standing intellectual tradition, and nothing defined it better than the august school motto: *No nobis solum set toti mundo nati*—You're born not for yourself but for the whole world.

On Monday, September 8, 1953, looking scrubbed, spruced, and more than the least bit intimidated, Paul, dressed in a navy blue blazer with a green badge over the heart, short gray trousers, a green-and-black-striped tie, and redoubtable dog's-tongue cap, stumbled off the bus from Garston and walked up Mount Street and through the wrought-iron railing that delimited the yards behind the immense school building. Like most boys who crossed the threshold, he must have been swept with thoughts of smallness. The Inny was the largest building he'd ever entered, larger even than his mother's hospital and almost as imposing as the mammoth Liverpool Cathedral, whose unfinished sandstone friezes loomed in eerie relief across the street. Nearly a thousand boys mingled in the lower yard, a sea of bodies, many of them seventeen or eighteen—grown *men!*—with serious features. "We were *eleven*," says Colin Manley, who was in Paul's class and later played guitar for the Remo Four. "They herded us into the auditorium, told us what forms we'd be split up into, what subjects we were to take, and what was expected of us. It was horrendous, really— overwhelming."

Paul, slightly awed by it all, drew languages as his area of concentration, which seemed well suited to a boy with an ear for cadences. He began in the French stream but went on to do modern languages. "The first year, I was pretty lost," he recalls. "But by the second year, I was learning Latin, Spanish, and German. At age twelve, which wasn't bad." Although

spelling wasn't a strong suit, and math even less so, he developed a particular knack for grammar and English literature, thanks in no small part to
the influence of Alan Durband. Durband, known as Dusty to friends
and colleagues, was somewhat of a celebrity at the Liverpool Institute,
having written a short script for the BBC that was aired as a popular
"morning story" on the radio. A disciple of the great literary critic F. R.
Leavis, Durband brought the old rooted classics to life, beginning with
Chaucer, which Paul read in its original Middle English, then trawled
through Shakespeare's plays. He responded strongly to the moral dilem-
mas faced by the characters, but he especially loved the way Alan Durband
pared the stories down to their most basic themes, exposing the simplicity
of it all. Indeed, Paul's grasp of Durband's lessons would be showcased in
those early Beatles lyrics, deconstructing adolescent sexuality into pure
sentiment (if not mere cliché): she loves you, I want to hold your hand, do
you want to know a secret—small signs that what lay beyond might offer
something more conceptual.

Fascinating as literature was, Paul found his firmest expression in art.
"He had a real talent when it came to drawing," remembers Don Andrew,
another future Remo Four member, who sat next to Paul in class. "It
wasn't something he learned from a book, he was self-taught, and so the
work he produced was truly imaginative." Paul had drawn for as long as he
could remember; he was "always sketching." Come vacation time, he recalls, "I always [made] my own Christmas cards," decorating them with
nervous pencil sketches overlaid with watercolor washes.

Many years later he would linger in a Long Island barn and watch his
friend Willem de Kooning "work on these massive, great canvases" that
fed Paul's own hunger to paint, but there was no such encouragement from
the masters. At the institute, students never "stayed with art" throughout
their school career; the meat-and-potatoes classes were so demanding that
there just wasn't enough time for it. But those boys who showed talent
were given the opportunity to "stay behind on a Tuesday night" for extra
art instruction. Once a week Stan Reed, the institute's resident draftsman,
conducted lessons in line and perspective drawing, as well as watercolors for
a class of ten or twelve self-motivated students. Paul, who had energy, albeit
conventional talent, flourished under Reed's practical guidance. What's
more, Reed helped Paul overcome the insecurity he had in relation to "true"
artists at the art college next door—abnegating the notion "that *they* paint,
and *we* don't." Paul took full advantage of the advice—so much so that, in
time, some students actually approached *him* for tips and technical hints.

Says Don Andrew: "I remember walking along the art room on Parents Nights, when our work was hung, and being drawn to the most outstanding piece on exhibit. It was always Paul McCartney's—he was that good."

But art wasn't the anchor of a grammar-school education, not at the Liverpool Institute. Paul described his performance as "reasonably academic," but the masters were anything but reasonable, especially not about his grades, which fell consistently—and sharply—toward the end of his third year. He knew the score: only true scholars gained admittance to university, and Paul wasn't performing to those standards. Not that it would have mattered all that much. By then, there were too many distractions, and nothing in school could compete with a force as great as rock 'n roll.

[III]

There was always some vagrant rumble of music in the McCartney house, be it from the radio, which provided a constant source of entertainment; Jim's stash of scratchy 78s, which contained an assortment of family favorites; or his repertoire of "party pieces" played to exhaustion on the piano with unflagging exuberance. Jim "had a lot of music in him," Paul was to say, and throughout this period he took great care to convey its pleasures to the boys. Paul had been raised on an elementary mix of pop music—his father's music hall standards, or what Paul referred to as "sing-along stuff," plus highlights of the big band era coupled with the dreary mainstream hits of the day, such as "Greensleeves" and "Let Me Go Lover." Aside from that fare and show tunes, there was little else that engaged him. Before 1955, if Paul wanted to hear live music, he accompanied Jim to the brass band concerts in Sefton Park, where he felt "very northern" settled on a bench, as he was, among an immense sweep of bedrock Liverpudlians, people rooted to the glorious past and proud to celebrate it in deference to the future. He had little if any sense of diversity or abundance. Music in general, to Paul, existed solely as entertainment, to be appreciated secondhand.

During Paul's early teenage years, Jim began to concentrate more on fine-tuning his sons' inner ear, identifying instruments whenever a record was played and talking in elaborate detail about chord patterns and the architecture of harmony. Piano lessons were encouraged as a matter of course; Jim knew it would give Paul the right foundation should he ever wish to play in a band. But though Jim's intentions were good, his timing was god-awful. "We made the mistake of starting [the lessons] in the summer," he soon realized, ". . . and all the kids would be knocking at the door all the time, wanting [the boys] to come out and play." Concentration was next to impossible; Paul had no discipline whatsoever, and when he struggled to practice the scales—or develop greater interest, for that matter—the lessons were dropped without fanfare.

On Paul's fourteenth birthday, Jim presented his son with a nickel-plated trumpet that had belonged to his cousin Ian Harris. There was more than a bit of family ritual in the passing of the horn. The trumpet was a real jazz musician's instrument, the choice of King Oliver, Louis Armstrong, Roy Eldridge, and Dizzy Gillespie. It didn't take a great ear to know that Paul McCartney wasn't cut from the same cloth. Though he couldn't articulate very well, he made up for it by blowing with great enthusiasm, learning how to make a big noise just by running the valves. But in truth, he had no range, no chops. He could blow his nose with more conviction.

Once again, Paul had his priorities elsewhere. Among his mounting distractions at the time was Radio Luxembourg's nighttime broadcast of American music, which he listened to in bed via an extension-cord-and-headphone device that Jim had hooked up to the radiogram in the living room. Paul considered it "a revelation," and in his enthusiasm he began to mimic the voices that wailed aross the airwaves. Whereas he'd taken only an occasional whiff of big band crooners, he inhaled the gut-wrenching rock 'n roll singers. The raw, raunchy and often ferocious intensity of Ray Charles, Ivory Joe Hunter, Hank Ballard, and Fats Domino riveted Paul; they were capable of anything, from lusty, menacing growls to lilting falsettos. Some vocal styles, like the freakish bump-and-grind vamping of Bo Diddley, were undoubtedly puzzling, while Little Richard's explosiveness and extraordinary range would ultimately feed Paul throughout his career.

Of course, Paul's itch to sing like these recording artists was next to impossible with a trumpet—the same dilemma John Lennon had faced with the harmonica. Fruitlessly, Paul pleaded with Jim to buy him a guitar. Whether money factored into the refusal that was given, it was certainly an issue for Jim; he couldn't afford to blow almost three weeks' salary on such an extravagance, especially since Paul already had a perfectly good instrument. After some wheel-spinning, Paul cleverly restructured his proposal: since the trumpet had no appeal, he sought permission to trade it for a more desirable instrument. Jim, sensing the futility of his position, finally gave in. Sometime about the end of June, just before school let out for vacation, Paul wrapped his trumpet in a cloth and took it to Rushworth and

Dreaper, one of Liverpool's leading music stores, where he exchanged it for a crudely made Zenith guitar—a henna-brown sunburst model, with *f*-holes, a cutaway tuning head, and action as high as a diving board—that was propped against one of the shelves. The salesman at Rushworth's must have struggled to conceal his delight at the deal; it wasn't every day he came by a trumpet worth five or six times the price of the £15 guitar. All the same, he had no idea how pivotal that transaction would be.

[IV]

Throughout the sweltering summer months of 1956, Paul remained cloistered indoors, the guitar monopolizing his attention in ways that made him seem preoccupied, if not obsessed. "The minute he got the guitar that was the end," his brother, Michael, told a writer in 1967. "He was lost. He didn't have time to eat or think about anything else." The lifelong romance had begun, but from the outset there were mechanical problems that tested his devotion. For instance, he struggled almost perversely to make right-handed chord patterns conform to his stubborn left-handed perspective. It was no easy feat; whatever natural instinct he relied on proved maddeningly ineffective. And he had no simple answer for it. Years before, Paul's cousin Bett Robbins, who babysat him and was also left-handed, had tried teaching him chords on her ukulele. It seemed manageable at the time; he would "have a little go" and accompany himself to a medley of wide-eyed children's songs. But a full-size guitar presented full-size problems. In most cases, a lefty would chord it as if he were right-handed or simply turn the guitar around so that the fingers were reversed. Neither method, however, met with any success. It intruded on his rhythm, his arm sawing the air clumsily in stiff, erratic curves, tripping his timing like a broken switch. At times, such lack of control felt like a physical disability. And yet, it wasn't for lack of coordination; Paul had a gift for the considerable complexities that went into making music. But like an American's spastic attempt to shift and clutch a British car, he simply couldn't discipline his hands to make the necessary moves.

Yet he would not give up. Discipline had never been Paul's strong suit, but this was something more. This was desire—and an inflexible determination. Ingeniously, Paul turned to the hardware, as opposed to merely technique, and restrung the guitar in reverse so that the thinnest, high-pitched strings were now in the bass-notes position, and vice versa. The solution was jerry-rigged and "all rather inexact," in his appraisal, but served to give him the control necessary to synchronize the rhythm with the mechanics. *Voilà!* That got him up and running almost immediately. "I learned some chords my way up," he recalled, "A, D, and E—which was all you needed in those days."

The change it caused was stunning. Since entering Liverpool Institute, Paul had been focused almost intransigently on classwork, competing con brio against students in the upper streams, with the intention that one day he would return to his alma mater, awash in prestigious degrees, and teach alongside his tweedy mentors. But now only the guitar mattered, "and so the academic things were forgotten," as Paul remembered.

Mary tried to stay after him as best she could, her ultimate goal being to groom Paul for medical school. But while Mary spared no effort to further Paul's future, her own was on the verge of unraveling. "Physically, she wasn't able to handle the load," says Dill Mohin, citing the rigors of yet another residential move designed to march the McCartneys progressively up the food chain.

This time, Mary wrangled a council house on Forthlin Road in the suburb of Allerton, not far from their previous home but as different from Speke as go-karts are from Cadillacs. Founded as a manor settlement "for families of above-modest means," Allerton had become an oasis of upward mobility on the clover-groomed pastures of South Liverpool. "I always thought of the area as being slightly posh," says a friend who visited the McCartneys often at 20 Forthlin Road. Built in the 1920s, the quaint three-bedroom cottage in the middle of a terrace row reminded people of a gingerbread house, with its stubby picture window, smokestack chimney, and high-crowned brick facade the color of gravy. Slate-roof effects had been skillfully mimicked in asphalt. A lavender hedge squatted at the bend in a narrow walk. By the time the McCartneys took over the house, in late 1955, a garden budded nicely in the front courtyard. And best of all was the price: an affordable £1 6s. a week, thanks to Mary's seniority at work.

But this move cost Mary more of her health and energy. In the spring of 1956, those bouts of "indigestion" resurfaced and the harsh reality cast a shadow over her short-lived contentment. There was no denying it this time: the cancer was back. She'd probably known it was there all along but felt too good to deal with it.

Yet, however much she suffered, Mary kept up appearances in an effort to counteract the inevitable. Work remained a perfect distraction.

When midwifery proved too debilitating—which it did often now that the cancer flared up, wiping her out most days by noon—she reclaimed her old job as a health visitor for the Liverpool Corporation, while moonlighting at a clinic in the Dingle, a working-class ghetto. She even maintained an exhaustive regimen of housework: making the beds, washing the laundry, preparing the meals, cleaning the dishes, and vacuuming the rooms. It sometimes seemed as if she were able to defiantly squeeze out the last drops of reserve energy needed to tackle yet another punishing task. But at times the symptoms were too severe to keep hidden. Occasionally, she would yelp and double over, kneading her chest until the spasms passed. One day after school, Mike encountered her in an upstairs bedroom, sobbing, a silver crucifix clutched tightly in her fist.

As the cancer spread unchecked, her stamina faded. Relatives vividly recall how Mary could barely get up the stairs to the bedroom without help. Pain and shortness of breath played havoc with her strength. In an attempt to staunch the metastasis of malignant cells, her doctor, gambling for time, ordered a mastectomy. Relatively assured of a successful outcome, Jim remained at work instead of accompanying Mary to the hospital. Once again, he asked his sister-in-law Dill Mohin to act as a chaperone, planning to visit soon after the Cotton Exchange closed. When on the morning of October, 30, 1956, Dill arrived at Forthlin Road, she found Mary scurrying around, putting the final touches on each room. Dill remembers thinking how the house looked like "a pin in paper," which was the Scouse equivalent of "impeccably tidy." The breakfast dishes were drying in the sink; wastebaskets had been emptied. Nothing was out of place. "She had all the boys' things ready for the next day," Dill recalls. "Their shirts were ironed, their underwear cleaned."

Standing back to admire her handiwork, Mary sighed and smiled sadly at her sister-in-law's disapproving scowl. "Now everything's ready for them," she said, "in case I don't come back."

By the next afternoon, her words were all too prophetic. The mastectomy had been successful—up to a point—but the cancer was entrenched; there was no hope. "We knew she was dying," Dill Mohin recalls, explaining how the family now assembled to pay their last respects. "Jim rang me up [that afternoon] and said, 'I'm bringing the boys to see you, Dill. I'm taking them in to see Mary for the last time. I've put clean shirts on them; they've got on their best clothes, their school ties. Their fingernails are clean; so are their teeth. Would you look them over for me? If they pass [inspection] with you, they're all right."

The image Mary had cultivated so carefully was intact when Paul and Mike shuffled into her hospital room just after six o'clock on October 31. They had been groomed to perfection, "two little gentlemen," and stood in sharp contrast to the "ghastly" figure of their bedridden mother that now struggled on an elbow to greet them. The operation had clearly ravaged Mary. Her usually open face was expressionless, rigid, grim; so dark were the circles under her eyes, so demonic and disfiguring, that a relative might have assumed they'd stumbled into the wrong room. Paul remembered that "there was blood on the sheets," an image that never left him.

Dill and Bill Mohin waited anxiously in the reception area "so that she would have a bit of time on her own with the boys." When they finally joined the family, however, Dill noticed with astonishment that the boys "were romping all over her." Mary, "putting on a brave face," seemed not to mind—or was too sick to object. "Oh, leave them alone," she said in response to her sister-in-law's remonstrances. "They're all right." Jim, silent as a statue, stood stonily in the corner, his eyes flushed with tears, his face so anguished, laboring—fighting hard—to maintain his composure. Inconsolability was not a part of his character. His gift had always been optimism, an extra beacon of light thrown onto the path of adversity; friends and family relied on him to pump up their spirits, and he did, too, always without a qualm. Ever the salesman, he had immense strength and the right words at hand to reverse any dark mood. And yet all of it failed him now.

That night, about 9:30, Jim arrived unannounced at the Eagle Hotel, on Paradise Street, where the Mohins were tending bar in the back room of their half-filled pub. He was physically wasted, empty. All he could manage to say was "She's gone." Mary had suffered an embolism and died shortly after the boys left.

Paul reacted to the news with misplaced alarm—it is rumored he blurted out: "What are we going to do without her money?"—but there was no misjudging the depth of his loss. It was a devastating blow. "The big shock in my teenage years," he was to say. Jim may have helped shape Paul's early attitude toward music, but no one had the impact on him that Mary did. In later years, after he was fabulously wealthy and knighted before the Queen, Paul would often talk about success in terms of his mother's encouragement "to do better" than her and Jim, to improve his circumstances. Suddenly, without her stabilizing presence, without her insight and pragmatism, he felt desperate.

For weeks afterward, Paul bumped around the house "like a lost soul," suffering the symptoms of an emotional free fall. He was aloof, unresponsive; when he spoke, it was through a smoke screen of feints and grunts. No one recalls ever seeing him sink so low. "I was determined not to let it affect me," he said. "I learned to put a shell around me at that age." For long stretches, sometimes hours, he would retreat into a cloud of silence. In all the upheaval, there was nothing, other than time, to bring him out of this depression.

To fill the gaps, Paul turned to music. He threw himself into playing the guitar, practicing chords and finger positions for hours on end, but not in any way that expressed a sense of pleasure. It was more therapeutic, a release—less musical than remedial. There was never any intention of sharing it with someone else. "He used to lock himself in the toilet and play the guitar," says Dill, who visited often in order to help Jim around the house. "It was the only place he could disengage himself from the tragedy."

Jim, who was himself heartbroken and threatening suicide, had nothing left in reserve for Paul. Dazed, in a state of emotional shock, he depended entirely on his sisters, Jin and Millie, to keep the family afloat. Millie arrived regularly to cook and help clean the house, but she was "much more straitlaced" than Jin, with an aversion "to showing her feelings" and "a very dour husband," Paul's uncle Albert, who had undergone "a bizarre personality change" in the navy that bordered on hostile. Jin Harris, on the other hand, was "the motherly aunt" whose manner was not dissimilar to that of Mary's. A big, heavy woman with a cool head and an unchecked liberal philosophy, she knew intuitively that what the McCartney boys needed more than anything else was TLC. She showered them with attention, listened dutifully to them, indulged them, held and consoled them, devoting a lot of time and energy to the healing process. "There was no one better suited to picking up the pieces in Paul's life," according to her great-niece Kate Robbins. "She lived entirely through her heart."

But Paul's and Mike's anguish spilled out in other, more detrimental ways. Paul's grades, which had already been compromised to a degree, slipped even further. Grudgingly, he put in the necessary effort—but barely. He "skivved off" classes with alarming regularity, paid little attention to homework, and basically ignored the requirements necessary to prepare him for O-level exams, which were critical to his future.

In the midst of so much emotional turbulence, Paul quickly reached out for the one lifeline that held him in thrall: rock 'n roll. Listening to it for long stretches, escaping into its defiant tone and fanciful lyrics, took him away from the painful memories. Paul loved the improvisational aspect of it, and he loved mimicking its exaggerated nuances. Thanks to his ear for languages, it was easy to pick up the subtle inflections and shadings in the performances. Buddy Holly and Elvis, Chuck Berry, and even Carl Perkins—they had the magic, all right. He wanted to sound how they sounded, look how they looked, play how they played. Stretched across his bed, he would sink into a kind of reverie, staring out the window, not looking at anything in particular, not even thinking, but lulled by the music's alchemy, hour after hour. There was nothing he could point to that supported a claim that music was anything more than a hobby, especially *this* music. His talent was at the service of some hidden energy. And yet at the center of this vortex was the desire to do something more with it. What or with whom, he wasn't sure. But he sensed it was only a matter of time until it all came together and he put his own stamp on it.

Eight months later, he met John Lennon.

[I]

The only real surprise about the 1957 St. Peter's Church garden fete was that the Quarry Men were part of it.

In the more than forty years that Woolton's villagers had celebrated an event they commonly referred to as "the Rose Queen," only marching bands had ever entertained. There was still a heroic glow, a natural emotional response, to all those ruddy-faced men in uniform playing stilted pop standards arranged as though they were meant to accompany the retreat at Dunkirk. The crowds who lined the church field each July cheered as a featured band pumped out all the good old songs, the melodies born in some distant smoke when husbands and fathers trooped off to defend the empire's honor. But something had changed. The steady song of the men in blue failed to enchant their children, whose expanding world held little glamour for tradition. Bessie Shotton, Pete's mother, convinced the church fete committee that a skiffle band would bridge the divide between young and old and proposed the Quarry Men—all but one of whom, she assured them, had been confirmed at St. Peter's—as the obvious choice.

The boys were understandably ecstatic. The garden fete (Scousers pronounced it *fate*) was "the biggest social event on the village calendar," a church fund-raiser that coincided with the feast of St. Peter, for which the entire community turned out. In addition to performing, the Quarry Men were offered another distinction: riding in the annual procession, a parade of decorative floats presenting the Rose Queen and her entourage that threaded lazily through the village streets while members of the Discoverers, as the church youth club was known, worked the pliant crowd for contributions.

The band clambered onto a flatbed truck that departed the church slightly after two o'clock on the afternoon of July 6. They were conveniently positioned at the rear end of the cavalcade, so far from the front car that they barely even heard the Band of the Cheshire Yeomanry, which led the procession. With a stretch, they could see the young queen herself, a sunstruck rosebud named Sally Wright, whose pink crinoline dress had wilted like gardenia petals in the sticky heat. Behind her, Susan Dixon, fourteen, whose reign was ending, waved at the crowd with the poise of a forty-year-old. Children in elaborate costumes, along with groups of Boy Scouts, Brownies, Girl Guides, and Cubs, perched gaily atop the floats, dangling their legs over the sides like fringe.

The Quarry Men began to play as the procession turned onto King's Drive, but it was clear from the start that even their staging was in disarray. "John packed it in straightaway," Colin Hanton explains, "because people in the crowd were only getting [to hear] a couple strums as we [went by]. He, Eric, and Len just gave up; they fenced with each other, horsing around, which left it to Rod on the banjo and me on drums, just making a noise until we got back to the [church]."

By that time, St. Peter's was engulfed with people: clusters of adults, teenage couples, and children spilled rhythmically across the narrow court-yard and beyond it onto the graveled path that separated the sanctuary from the dilapidated church hall. A smell of circus lingered in the heavy blanched air. Long tables had been set up on the grass, teetering with sand-wiches and cakes. Lemonade stands were posted at either end, diagonally across from a plywood booth where children, their bodies nicely poised in liftoff, leaned strategically over a rope in an effort to land wooden rings on the necks of milk bottles. There were literally dozens of such stalls on the field out behind the church: dart games, coin tosses, quoits, and a treasure hunt. Used books were stacked for sale, as were lacquered candy apples, handkerchiefs and scarves, even household bric-a-brac.

Legend has it that the lads, anxious about playing in front of such a fa-miliar crowd, decided to lubricate their nerves with a few hastily downed beers, but that simply isn't true. "John wasn't drinking, certainly not that day," Colin Hanton insists. None of the other musicians recall there being any alcohol, either. Eyewitnesses say that John and Pete Shotton traveled together for a while but separated when John ran into his twelve-year-old cousin, David Birch, who had come to hear him play.

Birch reported seeing John's mother and Aunt Mimi somewhere on the grounds, which, unbeknownst to the younger boy, set off an alarm. Earlier that morning Mimi had castigated John for "coming downstairs dressed like a Teddy boy," in skintight jeans and a checkered shirt, and that was one scene he preferred not to have replayed in public, if it could be avoided. Instead, the boys drifted in the opposite direction to watch a Liverpool police dog obedience display, featuring Alsatians trained to jump through fire-encrusted hoops.

About four o'clock, the band was introduced by the vicar himself, "a simple soul" of weatherproof rightness named Maurice Pryce-Jones. Though accounts differ somewhat, this appears to be what happened next: The Quarry Men played a spirited set of songs—half skiffle, half rock 'n roll—that was greeted enthusiastically by the wide-eyed youngsters who had pressed around the stage. "The singing got raunchier and raunchier," recalls someone who was standing in the crowd, "and the sound got louder and louder." John recalled: "It was the first day I did 'Be-Bop-A-Lula' live on stage," and one can only imagine how he cut loose on it. He also mangled a version of "Come Go with Me" to hilarious effect.

At some point Julia heard the music and dragged Mimi with her to investigate. John's radar picked his aunt right out of the crowd, though he misread her stunned reaction for dismay. "I couldn't take my eyes off him," she told a writer as late as 1984. "I was pleased as punch to see him up there." And yet in a different rendering, Mimi claimed she "was horrified to behold [John] standing in front of the microphone." Either way, her presence threw John slightly off balance, and aside from a little wordplay that incorporated Mimi cleverly into a lyric, he toned down the remainder of the performance.

Shortly before they were finished, both Eric Griffiths and Pete Shotton noticed Ivan Vaughan standing below them, off to the right of the stage, with another boy in tow. They were both particularly happy to see Ivy—a dear, charismatic, unflagging friend and occasional member of the Quarry Men, who stood in for Len Garry when he was unavailable to rehearse. Smiles were exchanged, and somewhere in the communication it was understood that they would all hook up with one another after the show.

Afterward, in the Scout hut, Ivan came in like a cannon. He said hello to everyone, then introduced his friend from school—Paul McCartney. Everyone glanced up from around a table, where they were having coffee, and nodded perfunctorily. Colin Hanton remembers, "I was sitting off by myself, just playing drums; a couple of older Boy Scouts were playing their bugles and just messing about. But it was clear once Ivan and Paul got around to John, there was a lot of 'checking out' being done."

Len Garry recalled: "There was a bit of a stony atmosphere at first. . . . Ivan had told John about Paul being a great guitarist, so he felt a bit threatened." And Pete Shotton noted that John, who was "notoriously wary of strangers . . . acted, at first, almost standoffish." John's eyes slit to pin Paul fast in the taupey lamplit room. McCartney, who was younger and looked it, wore an outfit that required a little getting used to: a white sport coat with an underweave of fine silvery thread that sparkled, depending upon how the light hit it. The jacket, which was meant to convey a cheeky, debonair look, seemed almost comical on Paul, whose body was helplessly plump, his moonface putty-soft and pale. He had beautiful eyes, though, like a spaniel's, and his spunk was jacked up several notches, almost to the point of being cocky for a boy who was, for all intents, on foreign turf.

Curiously, Paul had brought his guitar along with him. Sensing an opportunity, he stole the spotlight, running through a version of Eddie Cochran's "Twenty Flight Rock," complete with the sibilant rockabilly phrasing and an Elvisy catch in his throat. "He played with a cool, authoritative touch," recalls Nigel Walley. There is a tricky little downshift in the chord progression when the chorus, played in the key of G, drops in a difficult F chord, and Paul handled it effortlessly, vamping on the guitar strings with the heel of his hand. He had also succeeded in memorizing the lyrics, which was no mean feat, considering how Cochran jammed them up against one another in the galloping minute-and-three-quarters-length song. His voice almost hiccuped the chorus:

> *"So I walked one, two flight, three flight, four*
> *five, six, seven flight, eight flight more,*
> *Up on the twelfth I'm starting to sag,*
> *fifteenth before I'm ready to drag,*
> *Get to the top—I'm too tired to rock."*

"Right off, I could see John was checking this kid out," says Pete Shotton, who was standing behind John, off to the side. "Paul came on as very attractive, very loose, very easy, very confident—*wildly* confident. He played the guitar well. I could see that John was very impressed."

Paul must have picked up on it, too. He seemed to zero right in on John, whom he recognized as the band's legitimate front man. Not wanting to lose the edge, he launched into his own rendition of "Be-Bop-A-Lula." It impressed John that Paul knew all the words; John could never remember them, preferring to make up his own as the rhyme scheme required. Paul's version of the song drove harder, was sharper, bringing the tonic fifth in on cue, which the band had simply ignored. And he sang it with all the stops pulled out, belting it with complete abandon, as if he were standing in front of his bedroom mirror, without anyone else in the room. The fact that a local band and a dozen Scouts were crowded in there didn't seem to faze Paul. Conversely, the onlookers were riveted by his performance.

"It was uncanny. He could play and sing in a way that none of us could, including John," Eric Griffiths recalls. "He had such confidence, he gave a *performance*. It was so natural. We couldn't get enough of it. It was a real eye-opener."

But Paul wasn't finished yet. Knowing even then how to work an audience, he tore through a medley of Little Richard numbers—"Tutti Frutti," "Good Golly, Miss Molly," and "Long Tall Sally"—really cutting loose, howling the lyrics like a madman, scaling those treacherous vocal Alps that served as the coup de grâce.

"Afterwards," Colin Hanton says, "John and Paul circled each other like cats." Their interest in each other was deeper and more complex than it appeared to anyone watching the encounter. There was instant recognition, a chemical connection made between two boys who sensed in the other the same heartfelt commitment to this music, the same do-or-die. For all the circling, posturing, and checking out that went on, what it all came down to was love at first sight.

After listening to Paul play, John recalled, "I half thought to myself, 'He's as good as me.' Now, I thought, if I take him on, what will happen? It went through my head that I'd have to keep him in line if I let him join [the band]. But he was good, so he was worth having. He also looked like Elvis. I dug him."

Paul and Ivan left before the Quarry Men's evening "dance concert" in the church hall, playing between sets of an old-fashioned dance band. Aside from a brief electrical storm, which knocked out the lights for a while, the later show came off without a hitch. The Quarry Men packed up their gear afterward and hopped onto various buses home, except for John and Pete, who decided to walk. It was a beautiful night. The storm had drained the humidity from the air, and the boys took a shortcut along a piece of land they called "the style," a "slither of rock only as wide as a passageway" that led across the quarry into Linkstor Road.

They walked without talking most of the way. At some point during their stroll, John glanced sideways at his friend and asked, "What did you think of that kid, Paul?" Shotton was crestfallen at what he interpreted as "a danger signal," a warning that their friendship was about to face a serious challenge. "I'd watched his reaction. In his question 'What did you think of him?' he was talking about *personally*, not *musically*." Pete answered John honestly. "I liked him, actually," he said. "I thought he was really good."

Shotton realized then and there that Paul's infiltration was "a fait accompli." Even when John immediately inquired, "What do you think about him joining the band?" he knew the decision had already been made.

[II]

That summer, everything changed—the friendship, the band, and especially their lives.

At the end of July, postcards were returned containing the test scores of the General Certificate of Education Ordinary level exams that fifth formers had taken before school let out. The O levels were crucial to a student's destiny: they determined whether a sixteen-year-old was eligible to return for a sixth year, go on to higher education, or be unloaded into the workforce. "The whole point of a grammar school was to get students to do well on this examination and hopefully go on to university," says Rod Davis, who had passed his subjects with flying colors, thus designating him for Cambridge. It didn't seem to faze John that he had failed every one of them, most by just a few points below the 45 percent cutoff. He was "disappointed" in not passing art, a course that by all accounts he should have aced, but as he was to admit, "I'd given up." John refused all Mimi's suggestions for apprenticeships and jobs in the family domain.

Instead, John turned all his attention and energy to the pursuit of music. He was haunted by Paul McCartney's display of skill at the garden fete, the way he'd wielded the guitar so smoothly and with such panache, the way he'd sung all the correct words to the rock 'n roll songs. "Paul had made a huge impression on John," says Pete Shotton. "In a way, his ability underscored all John's [musical] shortcomings."

Retreating to his bedroom, John practiced the guitar for hours each day in an effort to broaden his repertoire. Painstakingly, he transposed the banjo chords he'd learned into proper guitar positions. He waited patiently for certain songs to play over Radio Luxembourg, then copied a line or two of lyrics into a notebook, satisfied that he'd made some progress until the next opportunity arose. He cherished these transcripts as though they were the Dead Sea Scrolls, he told later interviewers.

None of this, however, satisfied his desire to streamline the band. As it was, the Quarry Men were as ragtag a bunch of musicians as anyone could put together. Of the core group, only Rod Davis showed any promise, and he was committed to playing skiffle, which John was growing to detest. The rest of the lads—Griff, Len, and Colin—had no spark, as far as he was concerned. They'd served a purpose, but they'd outlived their usefulness.

John spent much time debating what to do about the situation—and Paul. "Was it better to have a guy who was better than the guy I had in?" he wondered. "To make the group stronger, or to let me be stronger?"

Ivan Vaughan solved part of the problem by simply inviting Paul McCartney to join the Quarry Men. He and Len Garry, who were class-mates of Paul's, had independently courted their friend during the last week school was in session. "John was very laid-back about it," recalls Shotton, offering no real enthusiasm other than saying, "Oh. Great." But Pete could tell that "he seemed relieved" by the development. The only foreseeable problem was that Paul was leaving immediately for Scout camp, followed by a spell at Butlins Holiday Camp in Yorkshire with his father and brother, and wasn't expected back until school started in September.

In fact, in the interim John had time to polish his technique and attend to other matters that necessitated his attention. One had to do with the gridlock on guitar that would be caused by Paul's joining the band. It was impractical for the Quarry Men to carry four guitarists, especially in light of Paul's ability. That meant either Rod or Griff would have to be sacked. "Rod took everything too seriously," says an observer who often accom-panied the band and considered Davis "a bit snobbish, too concerned with doing things by the book." On several occasions John had reprimanded him for appearing "too flash," which, in Davis's opinion, signaled that "he didn't want it to look as though I could play better than him." There had always been some friction between the boys, be it their attitude toward school or their regard of propriety in general. In any case, the choice was simple and relatively painless. Davis had gone on summer vacation to Annecy, France, and was eased out of the band by his very absence.

In the following years, while at Cambridge, Rod played banjo in a similar band that succeeded, however superficially, in making a record for Decca.* Rod mentioned this rather blithely to John when they bumped into each other crossing Clayton Square in Liverpool center in the spring of 1960. An actual record—the taste of it must have made John salivate

---

* *"Runnin' Shoes" (Decca, 45-F 11403), by the Trad Grads.*

with envy. "He asked me if I could [learn to] play drums and wanted to go to Hamburg," Rod recalls with a pang of wistfulness. As preposterous as the idea sounded at the time, it nevertheless intrigued him, even if his parents strictly forbade it. He was preparing to enter his final year at university—and besides, the band, as it was described, sounded like another of John's flaky deals. The name told Rod everything he needed to know: they were now calling themselves the Beatles.

Mimi had resigned herself to the fact that John would not, as she had hoped, return to Quarry Bank for the prestigious sixth form; John's O level results put that squarely out of consideration. And yet, she was not convinced that his situation was hopeless. He wasn't beyond redemption; he wasn't like his father. One thing was certain: Mimi wouldn't allow John to waste away in his bedroom with that guitar. Whatever the consequences of his indifference toward school, the responsibility fell to Mimi alone. She'd have to make some crucial decisions for him.

Mimi's mission was precipitated by an event that had nearly rendered her apoplectic. The first week in August, John and Nigel Walley procured railway passes to Hampshire, where they intended to enroll at a catering college. John discussed his plan with Mimi, who put her foot down. No nephew of hers was going to be a ship's steward, especially considering the deplorable precedent: Freddie Lennon wasn't her idea of a role model, not of any kind. Mortified by such a scheme, she accosted John's headmaster, William Pobjoy, and demanded that he sort something out for the boy he let slip through the cracks.

Pobjoy recommended that they reapply to Liverpool College of Art. John had gone there for an interview before receiving the O levels results but failed to impress the proper authorities. But Pobjoy's letter appealing to Headmaster Stephenson won John a reprieve. This time Mimi picked out his wardrobe and accompanied him to the school, a fortresslike building on Hope Street, next door to the Liverpool Institute. He was interviewed by Arthur Ballard, who taught painting. Even before John met him, Ballard's name struck an appropriate chord of awe. There were marvelous stories about Ballard's exploits—as a former heavyweight boxer, drinker, womanizer, vulgarian, rebel, aesthete, "soft-core" communist, and all-around provocateur at a conservative institution where the emphasis was on making art as opposed to waves. His status as a legendary teacher was due in no small part to an irresistible personality, a gritty, vaunted machismo that galvanized his lectures. And he was extraordinarily talented. No one outside of the other Beatles would take more of an interest in John's welfare until, three years later, Brian Epstein materialized.

Be that as it may, there was no immediate bond formed between John and Ballard—far from it, in fact. From that first meeting there was palpable friction between them. Ballard's brusque demeanor intimidated John, who reacted defensively. Conversely, the cheekiness and defiance that provided for John at Quarry Bank didn't cut it with Ballard; he didn't for a moment buy into the boy's indulgent attitude. "Arthur could see right through John," says a classmate who knew Ballard socially. And yet, on a deeper level, he recognized budding potential that had escaped other educators. Whether there was an artistic empathy in the haphazard line drawings or merely some dim intuition he tapped into, Ballard felt John deserved a chance and endorsed his entrance application.

Good news aside, it was no cause for celebration. When Mimi received the art college acceptance letter, John acknowledged it grudgingly. School was for grinds. "I was [going] there instead of going to work," he would admit. There was nothing anyone could teach him that wasn't better served by his wits. That much he'd learned from experience.

Through the summer, John grappled with adolescent longings. He had taken notice of Barbara Baker, a pretty, valentine-faced girl with a thick, slightly wild array of mauve-colored hair, flirtatious eyes, and a way of looking at him that suggested she had his number, which she did. In fact, she had had it from when they were both nine, at which time she pegged him as "a rather nasty little boy" who fired rubber-tipped arrows at her from a treehouse perch on Menlove Avenue. Though he saw Barbara daily, often listening to records in the parlor of Mendips, John was reluctant to introduce her as his girlfriend. "With Mimi, I was always just one of the gang," said Barbara, who sensed in John's aunt "an air of foreboding." It was evident from the way he acted that John preferred that Mimi not interfere in this new grown-up area of his life. Barb's status was more aboveboard at Julia's, where she received his mother's enthusiastic approval and felt, if not one of the family, at least "completely comfortable" in the role of girlfriend.

It wasn't just romance that had him dizzy. He was moving on to college and away from the old gang; breaching the bounds between Aunt Mimi's and Julia's house; changing his appearance to suit a restless soul; and experiencing an intense emotional awakening. In the midst of all this was the crucible of his consuming passion—music. Rock 'n roll—what precious little there was of it in Liverpool—became his dependable touchstone. The execution itself was still primitive—John had barely five chords under his belt—but its effectiveness was dead-on. It was only a matter of time before someone or something provided the proper tools.

In a manner of speaking, he could have held his breath. The last week in August, Paul McCartney returned to Liverpool, tanned and noticeably slimmer. In addition to starting school, he came back to begin a relationship he seemed destined for: hooking up with John Lennon. Their first official practice together, a Saturday afternoon get-together in Colin Hanton's living room, was more revealing than productive. Paul blew in, full of enthusiasm, ready to rock. He knew "more than a dozen songs" that the boys had been eager but unable to pull off: "Party Doll," "Honeycomb," and "Bye Bye Love," among them. John had been working on "All Shook Up," but Paul had it down cold, with all the vocal trimmings. Such an extravagant outpouring did not go unappreciated. For perhaps the first time in his life, John ceded the spotlight without putting up a struggle. In another situation, he might have misread this spectacle as a blatant power grab; anxious about losing control, sarcasm would have surfaced to mask his envy and inexperience. But he was enamored of Paul's prodigious talent, so much so that all previous reservations disappeared. Transfixed, John squatted on his haunches, squinting, close enough to study Paul's elastic hands. Despite the convoluted right-handed chording (Paul was left-handed), which gave a reverse "mirror image" to his patterns, the mechanics made perfect sense to John. "Paul taught me how to play properly," John recalled. "So I learned [the chords] upside down, and I'd go home and reverse them." Paul, he discovered, had the necessary tools to build a sturdy musical foundation. Hanton and Eric Griffiths did their best to keep up during this and subsequent sessions, but next to Paul's stylish craftsmanship, their best proved inadequate.* An instinctive musician only served to highlight their shortcomings. And in Paul, John saw something that he'd never before consciously considered, something essential that couldn't be taught or absorbed. More than his ability or his singing voice, both of which were first-rate, John admired Paul's knack for performing, his seemingly innate power to excite, to shade the music with personality. It seemed to define everything John was thinking about rock 'n roll and a way to perform.

---

* Len Garry's performance on the washtub bass required no musical accomplishment.

"From the beginning, Paul was a showman," says Pete Shotton. "He'd probably been a showman all his life."

It was rough and it was raw, but it was also one of those moments when invisible pieces of an invisible jigsaw puzzle snap together. Never in the realm of pop music would there be a more perfect or productive match—all the more timely, because individually Paul McCartney and John Lennon were headed for trouble.

[III]

On a cool September day in 1957, between classes at the Liverpool College of Art, Bill Harry was relaxing in a corner of the canteen with two friends from the school's new graphic design department. The three artistes, as they referred to themselves, were critiquing students at the other tables, conferring in urgent whispers, and growing more depressed—and scornful—by the minute. "To us, they were all dilettantes, dabblers," recalls Harry, a poor boy from a tough dockside neighborhood who believed that art students by their nature ought to be practicing bohemians. These classmates disgusted him for their anemic conformity: every one of them dressed alike, in either fawn, gray, or bottle green turtleneck sweaters and corduroy pants beneath either fawn, gray, or bottle green duffel coats. A postwar squirearchy of provincial underachievers gone back on their birthright.

Suddenly his gaze rotated toward the dark streak of a figure weaving through the tables with a violent grace. "*Bloody hell!*" Harry shouted, startling his friends from their funk. "That's a *teddy boy* there!"

All eyes noticed. John Lennon stuck out "like a sore thumb," in a baby-blue Edwardian jacket and frilly shirt with a string tie, black pegged jeans, and the kind of crepe-soled orthopedic shoes such as Frankenstein would wear. With his hair ducktailed down behind his neck and jaw-length sideburns, the jarring "ted" image emanated heat. Bill Harry wondered how a character like that had managed to slip into a toothless enclave like the art college.

It had been easy, of course—and irresistible. Unlike the procrustean law enforced at Quarry Bank, the art college had no dress code, no nervous courtesies. There were no masters prowling the halls like bounty hunters, pouncing on offenders, no detention handed out for minor infractions. All gallant pretenses were abandoned. "There was total and utter freedom," recalls a student who was enrolled in John's class, "and everyone thought it was fantastic."

But no one other than John took such sartorial liberties. There had been a clangor about him from the start, an "intimidating air" of self-parody. His appearance was "so over the top," the effect so "exaggerated and conspicuous," according to another classmate, that it seemed calculated to attract attention. "I imitated Teddy boys," John recalled, "but I was always torn between being a Teddy boy and an art student. One week I'd go to art school with my art-school scarf on and my hair down, and the next week I'd go for the leather jacket and tight jeans." Ann Mason, a student in the painting department who also happened to be in the canteen, recalls the impression John cast on the others sitting there. "He was quite a sight," she says, adding, "shocking, but also ridiculous, because he was the *only one* in a teddy boy outfit. Nobody else at college was interested in that trend. As artists, we were conceited enough to think we were before the fashion, rather than following it. [T]o those of us who weren't of his mind-set, the more *in* fashion someone tried to be, the more *out* of it they seemed. So, after the initial impact, we didn't take much notice of anybody like John."

Everyone ignored John's outlandish display—everyone, that is, except Bill Harry. "Ah—*he's* the unconventional one!" Harry recalls thinking at the time. "I've got to get to know him."

No one could have predicted a more improbable friendship: Harry, the soft-spoken little leprechaun, perpetually amused, with a tense, troubled smile, and an air of sorrowful endurance that dated from his father's early death and the abject poverty it imposed on his childhood, and Lennon, whose outbursts were barely contained, boisterous and cynical, with an indifference wrought from Aunt Mimi's pampered custody. Whereas John had bumbled through a posh grammar school, Bill fought his way, literally, through the gritty St. Vincent's Institute, where even the priests would "bang you upside the head" to make their point and where students ultimately jumped him, kicked in his appendix, and left him for dead, an incident that caused his penniless mother to transfer him to art school. Not until Bill latched onto his cousin's science-fiction books did his artistic aptitude bear fruit. Devouring them by candlelight (there was no electricity in the house), he eventually started his own science-fiction magazine, *Biped*, at the age of thirteen, working until dawn illustrating it, along with Tarzan comic books and fanzines. By the time he got to art college, his ambition was in full bloom. "They gave me a room . . . with a desk, a typewriter, and a copy machine," Harry remembers, "and I [started] a [school] magazine called *Premier.*"

More than sharing a talent for drawing, John was drawn to Harry's offbeat brand of humor, a confection of double entendres and puns that coalesced in a guerrilla satire group, the Natty Look Society, which gained notoriety by posting whimsical illustrations on the college bulletin board. From the outset, he admired John's immense reserve of raw talent and knew that for all his friend's abrasiveness, cynicism, disruptive behavior, outrageousness, and general apathy toward art, there was something wildly inventive that would eventually take root. "John had a fantastic imagination that enabled him to see things for what they really were," Harry recalls, "and then jumble them up in a hilarious, thought-provoking way. With a little luck, [I hoped] it would rub off on all of us."

Harry immediately attached himself to John and drew him into an inner circle of students with artistic and intellectual aspirations. The most appealing among them, both for his mordant wit and precocious ability with a paintbrush, was an elfin, delicately handsome boy named Stuart Sutcliffe. A year older than John, Sutcliffe had a "marvelous art portfolio" by the age of fourteen and was already "a really talented, serious painter, one of the stars at the art college." Unlike most of his classmates, he had no Scouse accent, having been born in Edinburgh and raised there on and off since childhood; nevertheless, he qualified for an art school scholarship by having lived near enough to Liverpool while his father, Charles, a navy officer, was at sea. Stuart, like John, had been shaped by a household of women and emotional disarray. "More often than not, our father was abroad," recalled Sutcliffe's sister Pauline. On those rare occasions when home, he'd take Stuart and his roommate, Rod Murray, to the pub "for a real good booze-up," after which he'd slip Stuart ten quid. "Then they wouldn't see each other again for six months," Pauline said. Their mother, Millie, worked full-time as a teacher, moonlighting as the local Labour Party officer, "which meant that Stuart was always in charge. He liked being the head of the household," Pauline remembered. And despite the encumbrance of chores, as well as a steady babysitting job for novelist Beryl Bainbridge and her husband, Austin Davis, an art school don, he still immersed himself in painting and the pursuit of romantic mysticism.

"Stuart was obsessed with Kierkegaard and mysticism," Harry says. "And together we pored over those big mysterious questions: What does the future hold? What will happen to us? How can we extend the powers of the mind, expand our consciousness?" Like most art students, they glorified the existentialists—"not so much Sartre as Françoise Sagan"—and French cinema, spending hours camped out in the dark Continental Theatre in Birkenhead, where coffee was served between features of *Bonjour Tristesse* and *Ashes and Diamonds*.

For John, the dreamy, pensive musings of Bill Harry and Stuart Sutcliffe were rich new sources to mine; but for laughs, which he craved, he turned to another art school misfit, Geoff Mohammed. If anyone was more conspicuous than John at the college, it was Mohammed, a hulking six foot three student of Indian and French-Italian extraction who drank, ranted, and blustered his way through classes without producing a scintilla of credible work. The product of a boarding school education, followed by a stint in the military police, Mohammed developed a passion for philosophy, palmistry, and jazz, the latter of which—not art—consumed his waking hours. John made no secret of the fact that he despised jazz, but he was nonetheless enamored of Geoff's defense of it. Some years before, upon learning that Humphrey Lyttelton had forsaken traditional jazz for its modern counterpart, Geoff had waited for the renowned musician backstage one night after a show and dutifully punched him in the nose. "Geoff was very unconventional, with a magpie mind and attitude," says Ann Mason, "and that made him quite unique in John's eyes." "They wanted to stand the system on its head," recalls Helen Anderson, one of John's classmates. "But, in truth, they were just fuckups."

The school instituted a "do as you please" policy, which meant that regular lectures, seminars, and workshops were scheduled but not entirely mandatory. Students worked at their own pace on a variety of projects that were presented to a tutor for evaluation every Friday afternoon. In every respect, John should have flourished in those circumstances. All those years spent under the thumb of Aunt Mimi and hostile masters, all those rules and requirements meant to stifle creativity, should have been enough to unleash his inspiration. And yet, ultimately, that was his undoing. Attitude and rebellion were essential to the creative process, but eventually he had to confront the essence of the college and produce a portfolio of art.

For John, that couldn't have been further from his reach. His lack of versatility, inexplicably overlooked by the school's admissions officers, became a tremendous handicap. Recalled his friend and classmate Jonathan Hague: "John was absolutely untalented as far as serious art went. Part of the problem was that he was incredibly lazy . . . but he was also terribly out of his depth. He had to resit the lettering course, which was the most elementary of disciplines; he made a mockery of composition and was incapable of doing a serious perspective drawing. Clearly, he was mixed up. He wanted to do well, and yet he couldn't."

Overwhelmed, John withdrew into a snug, sullen shell. "His paintings were always very thick, slapped-on things," recalls Helen Anderson, who sat next to him in the third-floor classroom redolent of oil and turpentine. "He worked very quickly and got bored in no time. It was all scrub-scrub-scrub, then he'd walk away and have a smoke or start screaming his head off, acting the goat, to make everybody around him laugh." He focused almost singularly on drawing cartoons, "endless cartoons"—distinctive "troggy-type figures" and scribble-scrabble characteristic of the technique he'd acquired from Ivan Vaughan, which were dismissed by the faculty as infantile and pointless. But the cartoons confirmed a pattern of drafting skills that were on par with the best of his lettering classmates. Bill Harry has concluded that "he was an illustrator in the mold of [Saul] Steinberg, but no one was willing to develop his talent."

Things only worsened when Sutcliffe wandered into John's life class, looking for an empty seat and easel where he could paint. Stuart was the genuine article; one only had to glance at his painting to be convinced of it. Formerly "besotted" with Cézanne and van Gogh, whose work he once emulated, Stuart had moved on—and tunneled in—experimenting with abstraction in order to develop a personal style that would carry him past the amateur level. According to Rod Murray, "he was painting like the American painters of the time—de Kooning and Rothko—although where they were nonfigurative, Stuart's work was still based on images." Helen Anderson recalls the material he turned out that year as being "very aggressive . . . with dark, moody colors, not at all the type of painting you'd expect from such a quiet fellow." Stuart's work made John feel more insecure than ever about his own skills. He tried woefully to overcome this reaction, but Stuart, whose determination and ambition were never well concealed, was a poster boy for the art college that John found so formidable. He had the glow, and it stung like hell.

Nothing quite captured John's outlook as succinctly as a scene Hague observed one afternoon in 1957, at a time when first-year students were expected to choose an area of concentration. "I remember John being dragged out of class into a passageway by a teacher in the metalwork department who was positively irate," he says. The way Hague recalls it, the man was "grilling him for making no effort at all," and John, hands dug securely into his pockets to avoid an impulsive response, was growing more distant by the moment. Slouching against the wall, he stared, unseeing, out the window, not really looking at anything but squarely off in some distant reverie, someplace silent, his own. The man lit into him unmercifully, chiding John, dredging up each shortcoming he'd observed, as though reading from a bill of particulars. Unable to stand it any longer, John lunged toward the teacher and exclaimed: "If you have to know, I don't really want to be an artist—or have *anything to do with art!*" Absolutely flabbergasted, the man replied, "Well, what do you think you'll end up doing?" glaring at this insolent young student as one would a deranged patient. John looked him straight in the eye and, with utter conviction, said, "I'm going to be a rock 'n roll singer."

[IV]

Paul's debut appearance with the Quarry Men—on October 18, 1957—was anything but auspicious. The band had been booked to entertain at a Conservative Club social held at New Clubmoor Hall, in the Norris Green section of Liverpool. Norris Green was considered "a posh neighborhood," so to mark the event, John and Paul decided on "smartening up" their look. Says Colin Hanton: "They started talking about white jackets, the idea being that we [should] *look* like a group." It sounded like a great idea; the band was all for it, a step up from "looking like a bunch of ragamuffins" onstage. But after some discussion, it was agreed that John and Paul would get the jackets, "creamy-colored, tweedy sportcoats," subsidized by the rest of the band at the rate of "half a crown a week, collected by Nigel [Walley] until the bill was paid"; the rest would wear white shirts with tassels and black piping and black bootlace ties. Whether that decision was due to the expense of new jackets or the caliber of talent, no one is certain; however, it established Lennon and McCartney as partners and the band's enduring front men.

Determined to make an impression, Paul had been boning up for the gig, "practicing relentlessly," according to a friend. For days before the show the boys tooled around Liverpool, chauffered by a well-to-do friend named Arthur Wong, in the flashy new Vauxhall he'd gotten for his seventeenth birthday. Everyone was "larking around"—smoking and wisecracking and howling at girls—except McCartney. Huddled with his guitar in the spacious backseat, oblivious to all the hijinks, Paul worked out the signature riff to "Raunchy," an instrumental single by sax virtuoso Bill Justis that was burning up the radio. "Every damn minute, he would be picking at it until we threatened to toss him *and* the guitar out of the car," recalls Charles Roberts, who had crawled decisively into the front seat to escape the torturous drone. It was unlikely that he'd finish it in time for the gig, and even less so that John would give him the opportunity for a solo. But Paul simply could not think of anything else.

On that fateful evening, halfway through the show, John introduced the newest member of the band before launching into a version of "Guitar Boogie Shuffle," which showcased Paul's deliberate pickwork. But when the time came for him to step out front, he suffered an attack of butter-fingers, missing his cue. Then, trying to catch up to the rhythm section, he pecked haphazardly at the strings, hitting clam after clam until the whole arrangement caved in like a soufflé.

"At first we were embarrassed," says Colin Hanton, "just really un-comfortable with what had happened. John insisted on a certain degree of professionalism. And now the new guy made us look worse than the ama-teurs we were."

It was all Paul could do to slink back a few steps, in an attempt to dis-appear in the narrow space between Hanton and Len Garry. John, who took great personal pride in the Quarry Men, was momentarily startled. Normally, this provoked a dagger stare of disgust—or worse. "I thought he was going to lay into him something fierce," Hanton says. But the piti-ful sight of Paul cut right through his rancor. "Paul McCartney—normally so confident, so cocky, so graceful even ill at ease that you wanted to hate him—looked so deflated. Why, John laughed so hard, he almost pissed himself."

To the band's surprise, the promoter invited them back to perform on other bills, both at New Clubmoor and Wilson Hall, in Garston. Garston was what the Woolton boys called a "no-go area," a notoriously rough council estate near the docks where the Fyffe banana boats were unloaded, and Wilson Hall was its deepest, darkest site. "You could have your ass kicked there, just for having an ass," says Mike Rice, a friend of John's from Quarry Bank who accompanied the band on two dates toward the end of 1957. Rice recalls following the lads into the band room there, where pro-moter Charlie McBain (known as Charlie Mac) gave each of them a shilling—their first official fee—which they tucked into their shoes "so they could get out without being robbed." Adding to Wilson Hall's reputa-tion was its status as a teddy boy hangout. The audience swaggered in there dressed to kill and dying to jive—followed by a good old-fashioned brawl

at the slightest provocation. You could almost set your watch by it: invariably toward the end of each evening, after a particularly overheated song, a
ring would expand around two rivals who had squared off and begun to
snap. No one needed an excuse to swing on a mate, especially if he'd
brought along a sand-filled sock for just the occasion, and rock 'n roll provided the perfect soundtrack, working the teds into a lather. "The bus station was literally across the street, and we knew the exact time the last
number sixty-six left for Woolton," recalls Eric Griffiths. "So one of us
would stand watch, with the others lined up behind him. Then, with a half
a minute to go, we'd make a run for it."

The gigs more than made up for the danger. The Quarry Men loved
playing to those packed houses, willing to take their chances with the teds
because they loved to entertain. They would finish a song, maybe play it
over again, faster and looser for effect, then tear into the next one without
waiting for applause. If things got hairy, with "blokes waiting for an excuse to thump" them, John would invariably lunge into some superfluous
riff, distracting them until the situation calmed down.

If the Quarry Men were inexperienced or self-conscious—as, by all
means, they were—they gave no sign of it. They pushed ahead, promoting
themselves for dances as if the demand—and their reputation—warranted it.
But there were better bands for any promoter who might be looking.
Nigel Walley scoured the city for fresh venues, no matter how shabby or
unprestigious the room, and chased down any source, including private
parties, that presented live acts. Occasionally Charlie McBain would call,
offering a weeknight at one of his dances, but aside from a few scattered
dates, the Quarry Men were dormant through the end of the year.

Although the band was stalled, it did nothing to brake the speed at which
John and Paul's relationship was developing. The two boys spent part of
every day together, talking about music. Often, after school or on the errant
day off, John would invite Paul back to his house, in Woolton, where they
would hole up in the tiny front bedroom, smoking and playing records.
Out from under Mimi's watchful eye, they would sit cross-legged on the
bed, running down bits of lyrics they'd memorized in an attempt to piece
together an entire song, working a new chord into their slight repertoire.
"We spent hours just listening to the stars we admired," John recalled.
"We'd sit round and look all intent and intense and then, when the record
had ended, we [sic] try and reproduce the same sort of sounds for ourselves." Paul's pet expression for it—"just bashing away"—seems appro-

priate; they found ways to play songs using what little they knew about chord structure or technique. Other days they'd meet outside the art college and take the no. 86 bus together all the way out to Forthlin Road. During the week, while Jim was away selling cotton, they had the run of the house. Alone in the sun-filled living room—John on the chintz-covered sofa, and Paul curled into an easy chair at its side—they poured out all their big dreams: the kind of band they envisioned putting together, the musical possibilities that lay in store, the great possibilities if they worked. John talked, in fact, about playing serious gigs, even making records. Anyone eavesdropping might have written off these plans as teenage fantasies. Still, other teenagers had somehow pulled it off: Gene Vincent, Buddy Holly, the Everly Brothers, Chuck Berry. Sure, they were all Americans, but that had to change *sometime.*

During their sessions, Paul shared with John the jewels from his "very diverse little record collection" and pointed him toward singers such as the Coasters and Larry Williams, the hard-pounding session piano player for Specialty Records, who may not "have [had] quite as an identifiable voice as [Little] Richard" but could rip off gems like "Short Fat Fanny" or "Bony Maronie" with the same manic pitch. John hooked right in and fed off the energy. He and Paul had remarkably similar tastes; they liked it fast, hard, and loose. Black music hit them both the same way, too, especially the wild-sounding, primitive stuff, with lyrics that crackled with innuendo: Bo Diddley, Lloyd Price, and Big Joe Turner made an impression. Later, as the Beatles, they would roll all of it into their presentation, riffing on Chuck Berry, the Miracles, Little Richard, Ray Charles, Jerry Lee Lewis—so many of the early innovators. But for now, they were just trying to take it all in.

A rhythm developed between John and Paul that got stronger and tighter. Mostly it was intuitive, unspoken. They understood each other. There were unknowns but no mysteries. "They were on the same indefinite path," says Eric Griffiths, who sensed that their bonding signaled his undoing. "Once they got together, things became serious—and fast. The band was supposed to be a laugh; now they devoted all their attention to it and in a more committed way than any of us really intended." Other Quarry Men also recognized their special rapport. In Colin Hanton's estimation: "The band quickly *became* John and Paul. It was always John and Paul, Paul and John. Even when someone didn't turn up to rehearse, John and Paul would be at it, harmonizing or arranging material, practicing, either at Auntie Mimi's or at Paul's house."

No doubt about it, they were tuned to the same groove. But aside from a musical passion and amiability, they filled enormous gaps in each other's lives. Where John was impatient and careless, Paul was a perfectionist—or, at least, appeared to be—in his methodical approach to music and the way he dealt with the world. Where John was moody and aloof, Paul was blithe and outgoing, gregarious, and irrepressibly cheerful. Where John was straightforward if brutally frank, Paul practiced diplomacy to manipulate a situation. Where John had attitude, Paul's artistic nature was a work in progress. Where John's upbringing was comfortably middle-class (according to musician Howie Casey, "the only claim he had to being a working-class hero was on sheet music"), Paul was truly blue-collar. Where John was struggling to become a musician, Paul seemed born to it.

And John gave Paul someone to look up to. Their age difference and the fact that John was in art college—a man of the world!—made John "a particularly attractive character" in Paul's eyes. There was a feral force in his manner, a sense of "fuck it all" that emanated great strength. He had a style of arrogance that dazed people and started things in motion. And he scorned any sign of fear. John's response to any tentativeness was a sneer, a sneer with humbling consequences.

John occasionally felt the need to reinforce his dominance, but he never required that Paul cede his individuality. He gave the younger boy plenty of room in which to leave his imprint. The Quarry Men would try a new song, and John would immediately seek Paul's opinion. He'd allow Paul to change keys to suit his register, propose certain variations, reconfigure arrangements. "After a while, they'd finish each other's sentences," Eric Griffiths says. "That's when we knew how strong their friendship had become. They'd grown that dependent on one another."

Dependent—and unified. They consolidated their individual strengths into a productive collaboration and grew resentful of those who questioned it. Thereafter, it was John and Paul who brought in all the new material; they assigned each musician his part, chose the songs, sequenced the sets—they literally dictated how rehearsals went down. "The rest of us hadn't a clue as far as arrangements went," Hanton says slowly. "And they seemed to have everything right there, at their fingertips, which was all right by me, because their ideas were good and I enjoyed playing with them." But the two could be unforgiving and relentless. "Say the wrong thing, contradict them, and you were frozen out. A look would pass between them, and afterwards it was as if you didn't exist."

Even in social situations, the Lennon-McCartney bond seemed well defined. The unlikely pair spent many evenings together browsing through the record stacks in the basement of NEMS, hunting for new releases that captured the aggressiveness, the intensity, and the physical tug about which they debated talmudically afterward over coffee. Occasionally, John invited Paul and his girlfriend, a Welsh nurse named Rhiannon, to double-date.

To John's further delight, he discovered that Paul was corruptible. In no time, he groomed his young cohort to shoplift cigarettes and candy, as well as stimulating in him an appetite for pranks. On one occasion that still resonates for those involved, the Quarry Men went to a party in Ford, a village on the outskirts of Liverpool, out past the Aintree Racecourse. "John and Paul were inseparable that night, like Siamese twins," says Charles Roberts, who met them en route on the upper deck of a cherry red Ripple bus. "It was like the rest of us didn't exist." They spent most of the evening talking, conducting a whispery summit in one corner, Roberts recalls. And it wasn't just music on their agenda, but mischief. "In the middle of the party they went out, ostensibly looking for a cigarette machine, and appeared some time later carrying a cocky-watchman's lamp.* The next morning, when it was time to leave, we couldn't get out of the house because [they] had put cement stolen from the roadworks into the mortise lock so the front door wouldn't open. And we had to escape through a window."

Through the rest of the year and into the brutal cold spell that blighted early February—every day that winter seemed more blustery than the last—the two boys reinforced the parameters of their friendship. After-school hours were set aside for practice and rehearsal, with weekends devoted to parties and the random gig. It left little time for studies, but then neither boy was academically motivated anyway.

Paul especially began to distinguish himself on guitar. He had a real feel for the instrument, not just for strumming it but for subtle nuances like vamping on the strings with the heel of his hand to create an organic *chukka-chukka* rhythm—inspired by listening to those high-voltage Eddie Cochran records—and accenting chords with single bass notes inserted between changes to create the kind of dramatic phrasing that became synonymous with the distinctive, undulating bass lines in his later work. John's

---

* A red lamp, with a little paraffin light inside, used by night watchmen at road-construction sites.

technique was more spontaneous, more relaxed. "He had a way of just banging out a few chords and making it sound cool," observes one of the Woolton gang. "Any song, no matter if he knew it or not—John would barrel right through it." Notes mattered less to him than feel, structure less than sound. Paul's precise efforts, on the other hand, provided a measure of syntax and kept songs from sounding too slapped together.

Sometime in late February, Paul went back to picking out the fairly uncomplicated instrumental "Raunchy," playing the melody line over and over until it was nearly note-perfect. The song, by Sun Records A&R man Bill Justis, had been one of the first pop instrumentals to smash through the Top Ten that year, and its repetitive but catchy guitar lick, supporting what was basically an alto sax showcase, made it instantly familiar—and danceable. It seemed like a natural addition to the Quarry Men's repertoire. Paul had been looking for another solo spot to redeem his fumbled debut, but there was more to it than self-esteem. He had heard another boy play it, a fifteen-year-old schoolmate whom he had befriended two years earlier, and he wanted to master it first, to maintain their friendly rivalry. He almost had it down—almost. But it wasn't quite there yet.

And not until it was dead-on would he play it for George Harrison.

[I]

Even before he met Paul McCartney, George Harrison had demonstrated that he was not to be outperformed when it came to the guitar.

One day when he was just thirteen years old, George and his best friend, Arthur Kelly, were practicing a version of "Last Train to San Fernando," a skiffle hit they'd learned from listening to a record, "just horsing around with it" up in George's bedroom, when a defining incident occurred. Because they'd only recently taken up the guitar together and had progressed at the same limping speed, Kelly says, "we could barely switch chords, let alone do anything fancy." But when they got to the middle part, where the instrumentation that filled a few bars normally eluded these novices, George lit into it as if he were Denny Wright, the riff's nimble author. "Off he goes!" Kelly remembers, feeling utterly astonished—and dazzled—as his friend galloped through the break. "We'd only heard the song two or three times, but George had somehow memorized it. He just inhaled those notes and played them back perfectly, at the same speed as on the record." He wasn't showing off; that wasn't George's style. "But from that day on," Kelly says, "I basically played rhythm and just followed George's lead."

The lead: it was an unusual role for a boy who was as unsuited to command as he was, later on, to celebrity. As a teenager, the slight, spindly George Harrison was an eerily detached, introspective boy with dark, expressive eyes, huge ears, and a mischievous smile that seized his whole face with a kind of wolfish delight. A quick grin, yes—and yet a sullen languor. Although he was by no means a loner, he was outwardly shy, and it was the kind of shyness so inhibiting that it was often misinterpreted as arrogance. He tended to disappear within himself, to give away as little as possible. Friends from the neighborhood were less eloquent, remembering him as someone who "blended in with the scenery." George was "a quieter, more taciturn kind of guy" than other blokes, according to another acquaintance, "but he was pretty tough as well." There was nothing in his development that remotely hinted at the witty, disarming Beatle whose spontaneous antics would transform press conferences into stand-up comedy.

For a man later obsessed with his own spiritual essence, it is somewhat disconcerting that young George squandered adolescence as such a blank slate. Unlike Paul's upbringing, the unworldly Harrison clan offered him little in the way of academic enrichment, nothing that would jump-start a young man's imagination. Nor did they have the kind of elitist pretensions that Mimi harbored for John. In fact, the Harrisons remained strangely indifferent to the postwar opportunities around them. Like many of the hard-nosed port people who were resettled in suburban ghettos in the 1930s, they were content just to enjoy their upgraded lifestyle—not to "rock the boat," in the wisdom of a Harrison family mantra—rather than to court intangibles and abstractions.

Like Freddie Lennon, like so many Scousers, Harry Harrison's inner compass was adjusted for water. He'd grown up around the Liverpool docks, enchanted by their gritty romance and faraway lure, and by seventeen he was already trolling the seas for the posh White Star Line, living rapturously between a series of exotic ports. But Harry's sailing experience was doomed by emotional and financial strains. To begin with, a woman had sneaked through his defenses. He met Louise French in Liverpool one evening in 1929 while she was streaking through an alleyway en route to an engagement with another friend. A plain, assertive, but engaging shopgirl given to impulse, she gamely handed her address to Harry—a perfect stranger—following a brief encounter, convinced that a sailor putting out to Africa the next day posed no threat. But a continent's separation couldn't diminish Harry's interest, and for months he inundated Louise with letters until she agreed to a proper date. He married her the next year, while on extended leave, and struggled to remain afloat—literally—for another six years. The birth of two children—named Louise and Harry, underscoring a lack of imagination—proved dispiriting to an adoring absentee father, who recognized that a sailor's take-home of "twenty-five bob [shillings] a week" was inadequate to support them. Though he had no alternative plan, by 1936, intending to alter his destiny, Harry seemed ready to come ashore.

Unfortunately, his timing couldn't have been worse. Lancashire was plagued by an economic slump that had forced thousands of Liverpudlians to go on the dole. The widening tide of the Depression had engulfed the

North. Overland work was scarce for a journeyman sailor, and Harry, who had no applicable skills aside from haircutting, which had been a hobby at sea, depended on charity to pull them through. The family moved into a modest terrace house in a South Liverpool area known as Wavertree. With Louise's meager earnings as a grocer's clerk and twenty-three shillings provided benevolently by the state, there was barely enough to cover expenses.

It took almost two years of scraping by before Harry landed a job. He began working for the Liverpool Corporation, as a streetcar conductor on the Speke-Liverpool route, when an unexpected opening for a driver vaulted him into a permanent position. He loved bus driving from the first day he slipped behind the wheel, and in thirty-one years on the job, there was never a day in which he regarded it as anything but a sacred, businesslike obligation. That meant striking an uncharacteristic facade: his long putty face was always pleasant in private, but on the bus it was expressionless, grim, like a rock. Paul McCartney, a frequent passenger on Harry's route, remembered "being a little disturbed about the hardness in his character," considering a first-name familiarity with most of the passengers and the distant way in which he treated them.

Within two years, Louise gave birth to another boy, Peter, and two years after that, on February 25, 1943, George Harold was born, completing the Harrison family portrait. George was an unnaturally beautiful child. Dark-haired and dark-eyed with skin like polished bone and a lean-jawed face that favored his father's features, he quickly developed the kind of strong, intimate armor that inures the youngest sibling to getting constantly picked on.

The Harrisons were a boisterous crew—good-natured boisterous. "They'd yell at each other and swear around the [dinner] table," recalls Arthur Kelly. There was a good deal of taunting and ridiculing one another—none of which was levied with any unpleasantness. In fact, Kelly says he was envious of their noisy rapport, the earthy way they expressed their affections. "I enjoyed being there . . . because with all the uproar they were very much a family."

And very much in need. Harry's civil-service job was as steady as a heartbeat, but money was always tight. As George later discovered, his father would never earn more than £10 a week driving a bus. In 1947, with four children to feed and clothe, there was never enough from his £6-a-week salary to provide simple luxuries like sugar and fresh fruit. Rationing put a further strain on their daily table. Even with Louise's influence at the grocer's, it was difficult enough to lay hands on butter and meat for six people without plying the black market, and that cost plenty—too much for the Harrisons. Although Harry's "overtime money and . . . winnings from snooker tournements" helped some, it didn't solve their pressing needs. They teetered precariously on the brink of debt—not crippling debt, but the kind of slow, agonizing squeeze that strangles the dreams and pleasures of poor, hardworking families. On top of everything else, they'd outgrown their accommodations; the tiny, unheated house in Wavertree was bursting at the seams, the toilet in the backyard an objectionable hazard.

All that, however, was to change overnight. Incredibly, in 1949 the Harrison family fortunes took an unexpected twist: they hit the lottery. Well, not exactly the lottery, but nearly as good: after they had been languishing for eighteen years on what everyone assumed was just a fictitious waiting list, the Liverpool Corporation drew the Harrisons' name from its deep well of housing applicants and moved them to 25 Upton Green, a spanking new council house located on an established parcel of the Speke estate, about half a mile from where Paul McCartney lived.

Their good fortune "seemed fantastic" to six-year-old George, who, as the youngest family member, had always been last in line for everything. Living in Upton Green meant some space and a chance to develop his own identity. The house, though relatively small, was comfortable by council standards and offered a boy endless opportunities for exploration. Its layout, unlike Wavertree, was circuitous, with a center hall that spilled into a front parlor and dining area without necessitating a detour through the kitchen, and four tiny upstairs bedrooms, including one all his own for George. There was even a garden in the front that opened onto a close, where he could ride his bicycle without having to dodge traffic. George couldn't have been happier. Louise Harrison was less rhapsodic, dismissing the neighborhood impudently as "a slum-clearance area," but her criticism was probably a reaction more to the melting pot of residents she encountered there—people with whom an Irish primitive like Louise had little familiarity—than to its aesthetics.

Called Geo (pronounced *Joe*) by his family, George initially seemed poised for even greater upward mobility. His term at nearby Dovedale Primary, which John Lennon had also attended, was a small triumph. He was no scholar, but he was an apt pupil with good manners and passed the eleven-plus scholarship with a solid enough margin to assure himself a coveted place in one of Liverpool's grammar schools. That was reason alone to celebrate in the Harrison family. Harry talked tirelessly about the importance of a good education and how hard work in school was the only way to escape a dreaded life of poverty and physical labor, how it would give one the chance to be somebody, a "blood," perhaps (for bluebloods, as he called them), to achieve the security he'd always longed for. But none of George's siblings had their heart set on university. Louise, though she brought home high marks, had no intention of going beyond high school. Harry Jr. and Peter were bright boys, but neither was a particularly good student; they'd gone straight into a trade. George, on the other hand, gave his father a glimmer of hope that at least one of his sons would go on to university and make something of himself.

And while part of that dream would be fulfilled in spades, it would be about as far from the halls of ivy as a boy could reasonably stray.

[II]

Within weeks of entering the Liverpool Institute, George Harrison altered the course of his trajectory—not prudently and gradually but recklessly and radically—in ways that no one could have predicted. He was marked for trouble from the start. Uncooperative, indifferent, and unmotivated in class, conspicuously immature, stubborn to the point of rebelliousness, he was adrift in a school that stressed discipline and conformity. Under guidelines that applied to all institute boys, students were required to wear black blazers, a gray or white shirt with a green-striped tie, a badge, cap, gray trousers, and black shoes. George, already testing authority, wore tight-fitting checkered shirts, inverting the tie with the wide band tucked away so that only the narrow flap hung down, black drainpipes, and—somewhat prophetically—blue suede shoes. His hair, which had grown extravagantly long—long enough for his father to label him "a refugee from a Tarzan picture"—was plastered back in a quiff with palmfuls of gel to make it behave, topped with sugar water so that it would dry like Sheetrock. Everything he did seemed calculated to attract attention. "Basically, George and I were a couple of outcasts," Arthur Kelly says. Sometimes he and Kelly simply stayed away altogether, "sagging off" school to smoke cigarettes and eat chips in a nearby cinema called the Tattler that played an endless reel of cartoons.

Eventually, they'd be hauled before Headmaster Edwards, a humorless, ruddy-faced martinet who would mete out an appropriate punishment. But oddly, none was forthcoming. What seems most probable is that the school chose not to expend the energy on such hopeless cases as these lads. Later, misplaced feelings of anger and persecution arose—George railed against "being dictated to" by authority figures and blamed "schizo-phrenic jerk[s], just out of teachers training college" for failing to stimu-late his interest—but in retrospect, Kelly realizes they'd brought it on themselves. No doubt they could have found a way, like other lackadaisi-cal classmates, to balance outside interests with a regimen of studies. But Kelly says they fell victim to extenuating circumstances: "From about the age of thirteen, all we were interested in was rock 'n roll."

Music in some form had always filled the Harrison residence. Louise loved to sing, to put it mildly. Her voice wasn't particularly melodious, but it was strong and vibrant, and her enthusiasm was infectious, even if it occa-sionally "shocked" a visitor, who recalls its "window-rattling" effect. Far be it from Harry to discourage her: when he was at sea, Harry had always brought presents for her, and one day in 1932 he arrived home with a splendid rosewood gramophone he'd picked up in the States. From that day on, "loads and loads of records"—those bulky 78 rpm "discs," as they were called, made of shellac and as fragile as an old dinner plate—blared at all hours in the parlor. Ted Heath and Hoagy Carmichael were featured regularly, but Louise's favorite was Victor Sylvester, whose big band swung with the intensity of a jungle telegraph. They had a radio, too, which Louise kept tuned to the BBC frequency, where every night, precisely at 8:10, the resident orchestra performed a tight medley of standards. Louise and Harry never missed that show. And no doubt it had a lasting effect on George, in the same way the Sunday-morning broadcast from Radio India, with its jangly sitar ragas, crept into his psyche.

As seems to be the pattern with Liverpool boys, George first connected with the ubiquitous Lonnie Donegan. That locomotive voice and the sim-plicity of skiffle "just seemed made for me," he told a biographer, recall-ing his earliest musical influence, along with Josh White and Hoagy Carmichael. Sitting in the front mezzanine of the Liverpool Empire, next to his brother Harold's girlfriend (and eventual wife), Irene, he stared trans-fixed at the Great One, who played a concert there in the fall of 1956. One can only imagine the impression it made on George. Later, fanzine writers would insist that he sat through all four of Donegan's performances, going so far as to roust the singer from his bedside and demand an autograph, but that appears to be myth. Whatever the extent of George's intentness, there remains little question of his fascination and the explosion it would touch off within him.

Not long thereafter, he bought a copy of "Rock Island Line" and invited Arthur Kelly to his house to hear it. "By the end of that afternoon, we said [to each other], 'Let's get guitars.'" George appealed to his mother, who was all for it. On this rare occasion, he had done his homework: an old Dovedale schoolmate, Raymond Hughes, was selling a three-quarter-size Egmond guitar, "a crappy old piece of junk," for the unlikely price of £3 10s., and he knew that Louise, a notoriously easy touch, had a reserve stash that would cover it. Arthur Kelly, whose family wasn't any better off than George's, talked his parents into spending the extravagant sum of £15 on a lovely lacquered studio model, with an arched top, scratch plate, and racy f-holes. Two days later, in a picture taken against the house in the Harrisons' backyard, both boys strike an age-old stance, with guitars cradled lovingly in their arms, listing slightly to the left. George is laying down an arthritic-looking C chord—one finger at a time, positioning each one precisely, the way a crane operator might plant steel girders at a construction site. His body is arched in concentration, joints and muscle taut as rubber bands. A checkered shirt is open at the collar, black jeans cinched high around his waist; otherwise, his clothes don't give an inch—they look as snug and awkward as the guitars. But his face, knit studiously in thought, conveys utter confidence.

In fact, frustrated with his inability to immediately conquer the guitar, he "put it away in the cupboard" for several months, ignoring it like another grammar-school textbook. It took a sharp nudge from overseas to jump-start his enthusiasm. Arthur Kelly's brother-in-law Red, who had been stationed in New York on business, brought home "armfuls of presents" for Kelly's sister upon his return. For Arthur, the crux of his largesse was records—not the brittle 78s, which were bountiful in Liverpool, but crystal-clear, durable 33s and 45s, virtual novelties in England, which to Kelly's young ears "sounded astounding." Most were by established crooners such as Frank Sinatra, Dean Martin, and Jackie Gleason, but among them was an EP by the curiously named Elvis Presley.

"The first track was 'Blue Suede Shoes,'" Kelly says, recalling Elvis's cover version, "and before it was over I had George on the phone."

Elvis appealed to everything smoldering in George—his ambivalence, his restlessness, and the rut of inertia from which there seemed no relief. The shock of Elvis Presley threw it all into gear: his voice juiced the circuits;

the arrangements drove his imagination wild. Suddenly, everything vague and numbing now had some relevance. George recovered his guitar from the cupboard and, with Kelly as his enthusiastic accomplice, began an odyssey that would surpass not only Elvis but all of his dreams.

———

Egged on by Kelly, George sought out someone, anyone, who could help crack the mysteries of Elvis. Their handpicked guru was "a bloke who lived round the corner" from Arthur and played the electric guitar at a local pub called the Cat. His name is lost to history; nevertheless, his role remains significant. For the princely sum of half a crown each, the man agreed—was delighted, in fact—to give George and Arthur lessons once a week, in a room directly above the pub. "He taught us a few basic root chords straightaway," Kelly recalls. "The first number we learned was 'Your Cheatin' Heart,' by Hank Williams. We hated the song but were thrilled, at least, to be changing from C to F to G7."

Soon enough, George and Arthur formed a skiffle band, the Rebels, whose name they'd "nicked off an American group."* Like most skiffle bands, it was strictly a paste-up affair—a few songs, a few chords, a few laughs. Rehearsals, for want of a better word for them, were organized in George's bedroom on Saturday mornings. "We made a tea-chest bass for Pete [Harrison] to play," Kelly says of the old washtub decorated with gnomes that was co-opted from Louise's closet, "but it didn't change the fact that we were awful."

Somehow—although no one recalls the specifics—the Rebels landed an actual gig at the local British Legion outpost, for an audience of dozy ex-servicemen. They played four or five songs, including "Cumberland Gap," their showstopper, which did exactly as was intended. "We didn't go down too well with the old punters," recalls Kelly, who, like George, was relieved when the Rebels were replaced by a magician and treated to a pint of beer as payment in full for their services. Thus ended the Rebels' illustrious, short-lived career. By now, rock 'n roll had captured George's imagination, and he threw skiffle into the rubbish bin and himself into rock with the furious energy of someone trying to escape a terrible trap. It is no coincidence that his Radio Luxembourg favorites were the exact lineup of flamethrowers that captivated John Lennon and Paul McCartney, with the exception that George was also drawn to guitarists such as Chet

---

* *Duane Eddy and the Rebels.*

Atkins and Carl Perkins, whose twangy riffs were the bedrock of rock 'n roll tradition. He paid a lot of attention to their vivid nuances, the phrasing and shading that made songs so immediately recognizable.

Restlessly, George plotted to get his hands on those records so he could learn how to play them. A part-time job as a butcher's delivery boy gave him enough pocket money to purchase the occasional 78 at Nuttle's, a nearby little electrical shop with a rack of records on the back wall, but to George's dismay their selection was pitifully small and blindingly white; the Everly Brothers, Elvis, and Bill Haley were all well stocked, but requests for Fats Domino and Ray Charles drew a blank stare. Other sources were desperately sought. One was Tony Bramwell, a lad who lived around the corner from George. Their encounters were anything but intimate. "Although George delivered meat to our house on his bicycle, I didn't really know him," Bramwell admits. "But I discovered, sometime later, that he was getting all my records from a classmate named Maurice Daniels, who was a drummer in a dance band and had borrowed them from me to rehearse with each week."

Before Brian Epstein transformed NEMS into music's mecca on the Mersey, Lewis's department store attracted all the traffic. George and Arthur were regulars at Lewis's, but not to buy records—to steal them. "I had what was called a wanker's mac," Kelly says, "a straight raincoat, allowing you to get into it through an inside pocket, and which also gave you access to your trousers." In those days, Lewis's stacked 45s on the front counter, out of the path of serious audiophiles who scorned the teenagers. "We'd stand there, and I'd start flipping through the stack, with George looking over my shoulder. When I came to a great record, I'd put it at the front [of the stack] and then lean over slightly, continuing to browse, so that George could put his hand through my raincoat, take the 45, and slip it into my pants." Kelly maintains they never shoplifted more than one or two records at a time, but over the course of several months the stash grew into a tidy little resource.

Says Colin Manley, who with George was considered the best guitar player at the Liverpool Institute: "He knew how to color a riff, which none of us even considered trying [to do] before. It was so different, so inventive—and serious. It's difficult to understand how unusual that was at the time. Most of us wanted to just play that damn instrument, but George was out to conquer it." His success as a guitarist, Manley says, was due to hours of painstaking, monotonous practice bent over the frets. "He used to come over to my house, put a record on, and we'd play a passage over and over again until we'd mastered it, wrecking my [record player] needle in the process. Another time we tried to analyze Chet Atkins's guitar playing. For hours, we sat together listening to his composition, 'Trambone,' on one of my Duane Eddy records. Later on, we learned 'The Third Man Theme' together and the [song] where he plays two separate tunes [simultaneously]. George studied guitar the way someone else would a scientific theory. And it challenged him in the same way. Whatever came later on was a direct result of his commitment to, and his preoccupation with, the guitar."

[III]

By the time he was fourteen, George's grades had plunged toward abysmal depths. He'd stopped studying altogether and concentrated solely on playing music. Only occasionally did he put in an appearance at school, and when he showed up at all, trouble followed. It came as a blessing when students got a break and rushed outside to unwind. On cue, George always made a beeline for the Smokers Corner, a well-worn patch of tundra invisible to the hawkeyed prefects, dressed in gowns with green silk braids, who patrolled the grounds like rottweilers. About ten boys, among them the institute's sorriest band of outcasts (including future Beatles road manager, Neil Aspinall), would congregate behind a brick shack where the gear for the school's Combined Cadet Force unit was kept. They'd light up contraband cigarettes and vent their collective scorn, ridiculing the platoon of uniformed students "square-bashing" about the schoolyard. Conformity offended them almost as much as the swots, or grinds, scattered around the yard on benches, grinding for an exam.

That outlook proved dicey for one of the Smokers Corner regulars. Paul McCartney considered himself a fellow traveler, a denizen of the outlaw fringe, and yet he moved so sure-footedly on the academic track. An all-out Elvis fan, Paul wore skintight pants, much like George, and combed his lovely black hair into a quiff. And although he spoke posh to a degree, his remarks were salted liberally with profanity. He was, in some ways, a bit of a double agent.

Over the years, that was to be Paul's gift. It would be easy to dismiss him as a dandy-faced naïf, but he was at the same time exceedingly shrewd. Innocent though he might look with his guileless expression and puppy-dog eyes, his lips rounded like those of an angelic choirboy, he was no angel. Not only had he won the confidence of a character like John Lennon, in the end he would outplay him.

As George recounted, "I'd met Paul on the bus, coming back from school." Paul shared George's interest in refining mechanics and technique, and the two spent afternoons practicing. But while George grappled almost entirely with execution, Paul provided interpretation. His approach was more intuitive; he could seize a few bars of music and, with a flick of the wrist or sudden burst of energy, make it his own.

Precision and expression: between them, George and Paul had hit upon the elements that distinguished their future collaboration. But almost as critical was the friendship developing between the two boys. Most institute upperclassmen never mixed with younger students, but for George, with his interest in rock 'n roll and undeniable talent, Paul felt the affection of an elder brother. He was touched by something he saw in the gangly boy. They hung around together on the weekends. He watched over George in school—Paul an effusively outgoing bloke, and George, barely fourteen and slow-talking, nipping alongside like a fawn; at lunch, Paul doled out double helpings from his outpost behind the cafeteria line; he rode the bus home with George to Allerton and dragged him along on a couple of social outings. But friends though they were, Paul had kept his business with the Quarry Men quite separate. George heard only passing remarks about the band, inasmuch as their exploits made news around school.

Toward the beginning of February, Paul mentioned to his protégé that he might want to check out the Quarry Men at a Wilson Hall gig they were playing on February 6 in Garston. It is not entirely clear how that unfolded. There are countless eyewitness versions of the historic meeting, many of which are suffused with the myopia of hindsight and self-serving glory. Everyone agrees that George turned up at Garston that night. He had traveled alone through the gray February landscape, taking the no. 66 bus from Speke. When he arrived at Wilson Hall, the dance was already in progress, and he watched the Quarry Men's raucous set from the sidelines with envy and admiration. The so-called official version of the meeting is that, afterward, George auditioned for John and the others in the tiny bandroom behind the stage, although the likelihood of that is remote. "Charlie McBain wouldn't have permitted it," says Colin Hanton of their persnickety employer. "He always had a six-to-eight-piece band onstage, and you weren't allowed to make a peep in the bandroom."

In fact, it wasn't until a month later, on March 12, that George Harrison lit the fuse that eventually shot him into orbit. At Paul's urging, he arranged to meet the band at the opening of a dingy unlicensed skiffle cellar in West Oakhill Park, which wasn't too far from city center. The Morgue, as it was aptly called, was the brainchild of a teenager teeming with outrageous theatrical flair named Alan Caldwell, who soon would change his name to Rory Storm. Caldwell raised enough money to rent the damp basement of a ramshackle Victorian house from his friend Marjorie Thompson's mother. "It was a dump, the pits," Colin Hanton recalls, "two pitch-black rooms, joined by a long corridor, with one blue bulb in the far corner." Ultraviolet skeletons had been painted on the walls as the sole concession to decoration; a wall fan pumped enough fresh air inside to keep patrons from passing out. You had to be at least fifteen years old. And in the absence of an admission charge, it was mandatory to purchase a bottle of orange juice or a Coke, which just about covered expenses.

George was friendly with Caldwell's thirteen-year-old sister, Iris, who was one of the prettiest girls in Liverpool. In fact, two weeks later, following a cruel prank that involved Caldwell announcing over the P.A. how his flat-chested sister secretly stuffed socks into her training bra, George chased the heartbroken girl down the street and gave her what amounted to first kisses for both youngsters. On opening night Iris was at her post, manning the club's makeshift cloakroom, and she waved shyly as he entered, carrying a beat-up guitar.

The front room was blindingly dark. The only way anyone could tell Caldwell was performing was by the sound of his Hofner Senator washing out of a distant corner. It took a few minutes before George found the Quarry Men, with Nigel Walley in tow, standing in the doorway to the half-empty back room. Paul made introductions, then stood back to watch how things developed. The other lads treated him indifferently at first, especially John Lennon, who seemed to look right through George. "He was a very tiny teddy boy," says Hanton, "just a schoolkid, without much to say." Finally, Paul steered everyone into the back room, where it was determined that George would play.

With very little prompting, George launched into "Guitar Boogie Shuffle," the signature tune of British dance-band virtuoso Burt Weedon, which he'd copied in exquisite detail from a record. "The lads were very impressed," recalls Eric Griffiths, for whom playing a piece like that was inconceivable. It was an elaborate song that demanded more than a bit of fancy fretwork, and George played it "right the way through," with élan, like a trouper. "I couldn't believe it," says Colin Hanton. "He played the guitar brilliantly—better than any of us handled an instrument—so I had no hang-up about inviting him to come around."

Maybe Hanton didn't, but John did. He wanted nothing to do with a mere schoolboy and told Paul so. Not one to be denied easily, Paul went into action, engineering another "chance" meeting between John and George in, of all places, the empty upper deck of a Liverpool bus. Once again, George had his guitar in tow, and this time he zipped, albeit "nervously," through a credible rendition of "Raunchy." Beaming like a shrewd politician, Paul knew he had won his argument.

Still, George's age was almost "too much" for John to get past, "Raunchy" or no "Raunchy." John admitted as much, saying, "George was just too young. . . . [He] looked even younger than Paul, and Paul looked about ten, with his baby face." That wasn't the image John wanted to project. But George was, in fact, the best musician up for grabs that John had come across, and ultimately that made Harrison irresistible. John had worked very hard picking sidemen for the Quarry Men who best showed off his talent. In no other area were his energy and willingness to do whatever was necessary to achieve a goal more evident. He'd landed the rare-as-sugar drummer, exiled his inadequate best friend, and recruited Paul McCartney, thus relinquishing some of the spotlight he'd monopolized up to now. In that sense, George Harrison was like catnip.

As for George, he felt liberated. He'd been doing his musical homework without any real payoff, no outlet in which to show what he could do; this was a chance to work with some dedicated players who shared his aims and interests. To join up with his grammar-school mentor had been a godsend, and now a character like John, as well—it was almost too good to believe. George later said, "I don't know what I felt about him when I first met him; I just thought he was O.K." But Arthur Kelly disagrees. "George idolized John from the outset," Kelly says. "We all did. He was one of those guys you couldn't take your eyes off. It was a combination of everything: his sense of humor, his attitude, the way he dressed. Even if he sat there saying nothing, you felt drawn to him." Together, John and Paul were pure magnetism; they had everything George wanted. Says Kelly, "When he met Paul and John, they were the missing links."

Not everyone in the band, however, felt as comfortable with the new configuration. Everyone knew that John had his heart set on a three-man guitar front line; in terms of skill alone, the lineup was clear. An initial re-hearsal attended by George put it right under Eric Griffiths's nose. A quiet, sensitive boy to begin with, Griff "took it badly." Afterward, he cornered Colin Hanton and expressed his uneasiness. Hanton, in his own right, wasn't blind to it. "I said to him, 'Don't feel so bad, I'm only on borrowed time, too,'" Colin recalls. "John and Paul were getting too serious about the band. Eventually they'd decide that the drummer just wasn't up to it."

John and Paul eventually forced the issue. One Saturday afternoon a rehearsal was hastily called at Paul's house, made unprecedented by Griff's conspicuous absence. They simply hadn't told him about it. "It was an aw-ful situation," Hanton admits. Forty years later, he still feels the flush of betrayal. And that wasn't the end of it. Coincidentally, Griff telephoned Paul's house while the Quarry Men were running down a number. "And they made me deal with it, then and there," Hanton recalls. "John and Paul refused to acknowledge the situation." They stayed in another room, "tin-ker[ing] on their guitars," removing themselves from the fray.

Rather than participate in the fallout, Griff honorably walked away. He'd had enough of a taste of show business, enough of a friendship riven by ambition. And, his standards being very simple, he had enough sense to know when to quit.

A similar fate would have befallen Len Garry had he not contracted tu-bercular meningitis. Confined to a ward in Fazakerley Hospital for seven months, he simply drifted away from the others—out of sight, out of mind.

Normally, as a band loses members, it snowballs into decline. But with the Quarry Men, just the opposite happened. The group, pared down to its core musicians, got very tight. Where before they had lacked a vision—a way of playing songs that brought their literal interpretations to life—there was now an unmuzzled sense of creativity. Fragments of individual passages clicked into place. Rehearsals took on a more practical impera-tive. The three future Beatles spent time retooling jagged arrangements, using what each boy brought to the equation, so that the songs acquired tension and excitement. To one observer, "it was like cracking code." Three guitarists playing with a more concentrated focus succeeded in brightening and clarifying what had been the group's increasingly shapeless sound. Old songs that had vibrated with too many possibilities evolved exponentially, with new resonance, new exuberance.

The new, improved Quarry Men reveled in the possibilities. John, Paul, George—and Colin. They were almost there.

Chapter 7 | **A Good Little Sideshow**

[I]

For almost a year after George Harrison joined the Quarry Men, living rooms and backyards were, in general, the only venues where the band played gigs. Though local dance halls and "jive hives" actively booked acts to fill the huge demand for live music, they showed little, if any, interest in hiring the boys.

The neglect stemmed from a conventional reflex that went beyond mere talent itself. Despite the shift in influence from skiffle to rock 'n roll, Liverpool still served the forces of vaudeville, and for old-school promoters who governed the scene, its proprieties could not be shouldered aside. Never mind the crazy, foolish-sounding music—*that* they could abide. But disrespect for the past—*never*. They expected the type of slick, showbiz professionalism that had graced stage shows for sixty years, and anything less, any loss of respect, would not be tolerated whatsoever. Of course, this thinking ran contrary to the whole aesthetic of rock 'n roll. The beauty of the music was that it so rudely flouted tradition. Perhaps rock critic Lester Bangs put it best when he suggested that rock was "nothing but a Wham-O toy to bash around as you please in the nursery." It sent up the whole feeble showbiz establishment in a way that was guaranteed to offend the old-timers who worshipped it. In Liverpool, the network of promoters—Brian Kelly, Charlie McBain, Vic Anton, Bill Marsden, Ralph Webster, and Doug Martin, among others—accepted the shift away from more traditional music, but only on their terms, which meant that the beat groups they hired maintained a certain stodgy decorum. Most wore matching suits, played a polished set of songs mixed with corny patter, and behaved themselves like perfect gentlemen.

All of which eluded the Quarry Men.

"John refused to behave like a trained monkey," says Nigel Walley. "He'd take a gig seriously, show up on time, and [be] ready to play, but as for someone's idea of proper behavior, he was having none of it." John wouldn't kowtow to promoters who insisted that the band present a hokey stage show. Requests to "tone down the volume" were routinely ignored.

And there were too many other acts who were willing to play by the rules. The same names kept cropping up wherever Nigel tried to land a gig. The Swinging Bluegenes blended jazz and traditional blues into a silky smooth, if innocuous, confection that went down with relative ease. The same with the Mars Bars, fronted by a Scouse sprite named Gerry Marsden, whose twinkly, eager-to-please stage persona reminded many spectators of a docile marionette and whose show packed all the punch of a pub sing-along. Slightly harder-edged, but no less parochial, were the James Boys, who later, as Kingsize Taylor and the Dominoes, became the resident, or house, band at St. Luke's Hall, in the suburb of Crosby. Eddie Miles, arguably the best guitarist in Liverpool, launched Eddie Clayton and the Clayton Squares (with his next-door neighbor, a teenager named Richard Starkey) to showcase a "down-home" style session. Cass and the Cassanovas appeared regularly in a "student joint" called the Corinthian, where Brian Casser, "an assertive, all-around showman" with a sweet, toothy image, played the type of tame set that required his drummer to use brushes. And Al Caldwell's Raging Texans, unconvincing as teenage rebels, mined the same rank showmanship that established them a year later as Rory Storm and the Hurricanes. These bands, which became the vanguard of the Merseybeat phenomenon, along with the Two Jays, the Hi Tones, and half a dozen other beat groups, developed faster, rocked respectfully, and toed the line.

Frustrated by the band's slow progress, John and Paul concentrated on practicing together every spare moment they got—and lit upon a momentous discovery. Paul, as it happened, mentioned casually that he'd written several songs, and he played John an early effort called "I Lost My Little Girl." The song is an achingly simplistic romantic ballad from the perspective of an uninitiated fourteen-year-old; nevertheless, John was, in Pete Shotton's estimation, "floored."* It is difficult to imagine that writing songs had never occurred to John, although he may have assumed that the effort was beyond him; or it is possible he just never gave it a whirl. There was little precedent for it among British teenagers. At any rate, Paul's dis-

---

* *The song was written in 1956, soon after his mother's death, although McCartney remains vague about a correlation between the two events.*

closure set the current flowing and is arguably a pivotal event in modern musical history.

A few years later, people who toured with the Beatles related countless stories about watching John and Paul bang out songs together on a crowded bus or a plane or a van or in the throes of backstage chaos—they could write anywhere and were apparently unself-conscious about it—but by that time the formula was ingrained; they were cranking them out like piecework.

In the spring of 1958, John and Paul exorcised the music that was heard—and shared—in their heads. It was a burst of pure, unconscious energy, and despite all later efforts to perpetuate it, the urgency was no longer there. As John so archly put it: "You can't be that hungry twice." They had all the tools right at hand: innocence, enthusiasm, desire, opportunity. Between them there was no shortage of imagination or energy. If they lacked anything, it was technique, the musical skills necessary to bring the kind of intricate, unconventional, even intellectual touches to their songs that marked their later work. Their talent was so natural, so unforced and kinetic, that it developed like infant speech. Perhaps they didn't understand it themselves.

That spring John and Paul gorged themselves on a bumper crop of fresh material, experimenting with lyrical harmonies and a panoply of vocal styles served by their natural abilities. Most of the treatments they tackled were copied faithfully from American records, down to the last marginal lick. Later John urged fans away from such crutches, admonishing them, "Don't copy the swimming teacher, learn how to swim," but for the time being, imitation prevailed as they jumped from one influence to another, casting around for an identity.

Initially there was an almost obsessive preoccupation with the Everly Brothers, whom the boys adopted as their "idols." They careened from one Everly hit to the next—"Cathy's Clown," "Bye Bye Love," "Wake Up Little Susie," "All I Have to Do Is Dream," "So How Come (No One Loves Me)"—including, as Paul noted, "even some of the B sides like 'So Sad (to Watch Good Love Go Bad).'" Their parts were custom-made for impersonation. "I'd be Phil and John would be Don," he explained, recalling the flights of fantasy in which they performed the songs with exaggerated emotion, trying their best to imitate the brothers' downy harmonies.

Eventually they gravitated to Buddy Holly, whose cadences bore a twangy, albeit double-tracked, similarity. After being sacked from the

Quarry Men, Griff had enlisted in the merchant marine, shipping out immediately to ports in South America and Canada. "That's where I picked up Buddy Holly," Griffiths says. "I brought his records back to Liverpool [along with Chuck Berry's "Roll Over Beethoven," "Rock and Roll Music," and "Sweet Little Sixteen"], and John and Paul would either buy them off me, or we'd swap." The attraction wasn't hard to fathom. Buddy Holly had everything they wanted, everything they'd been struggling to create musically: melodic songs; a crisp, clean sound; impeccable rhythm; unforgettable riffs; and monster appeal. His entire image was suffused with the dreamy romanticism of a small-town success story. Only twenty-two, he conveyed an Everyman presence, with his birdlike face, unfashionable horn-rimmed glasses, and a gawkiness at odds with rock 'n roll stardom. When he sang, his clear, slightly nasal alto, with a hint of the Deep South, carried a message of determination. One song, in particular—"Listen to Me"—presented an enormous challenge. "We sat around for an entire afternoon trying to decipher the lyric," recalls Arthur Kelly. "No one could figure out the line 'I will love you tenderly,' because [Holly] phrased it so awkwardly. It drove John nuts: 'What is it? What *is* it?' They went through every possible rhyme, matching it to the previous line, before hitting on the proper word." Eventually, after putting it all together, they worked up a neat little arrangement to go with the rest of Holly's vibrant repertoire.

More germane to their discovery of Buddy Holly was that he wrote his own songs. "People these days take it for granted that you do," Paul recalled, "but nobody used to then." It reinforced the capricious experiment that they'd heretofore only tiptoed around with trepidation. Buddy Holly gave them sanction—and courage. He was the whole rock 'n roll package. For John and Paul, this hit like an explosion. "John and I started to write because of Buddy Holly," said Paul.

[II]

By March 1958, songs were pouring out at an extraordinary rate. The McCartney parlor, conveniently deserted during weekdays, played host to a revolving cast of layabouts sagging off school, its frost-rimed windows pooled with condensation from the rising body heat, the wallpapered room, which was too small for the turnout, engulfed in a purple cloud of cigarette smoke. Guitars rested against the coffee table, sandwich wrappers and cups lay balled up on its surface, creating an impression that the place had been vandalized. Framed within this tableau were John and Paul, their hunched figures posed in profile on the couch—"playing into each other's noses," as John often described it—sifting through papers and notebooks fanned out on the seat cushion between them. "We kept the record player going a lot of the time, playing the latest American hits." They would begin by scrawling, "A Lennon-McCartney Original," at the top of a blank, blue-lined page, then jotting down "anything [they] came up with"— words, images, or fragments of lyrics that corresponded to one of the protean melodies that bounced back and forth like a beach ball until it was resolved. Gradually, a verse would take shape, then another; verses would get linked to a refrain, with rejected phrases blacked out or reworked, and substitutes annotated in the margins to fit a particular meter. It was an in-definite, unpredictable process; there was nothing sophisticated about it— no method to speak of, aside from studying other songs—just a general notion of where something was headed. A large measure of luck factored into it. And even then they regarded the outcome perfunctorily, like drift-wood that had washed up onshore. As John recalled, "We were just writ-ing songs a la [the] Everly Brothers, a la Buddy Holly, pop songs with no more thought to them than that—to create a sound." Constructing a great hook was their chief goal, something sly and memorable. "Lyrics didn't really count as long as we had some vague theme: 'She loves you, he loves her, and they love each other.'"

From the beginning, John tapped right into the approach that Paul first experimented with. Clearly, it presented no struggle for him. He had an innate feel for songwriting, a talent for turning a phrase inside out until it squealed. "It was great," Paul recalled, "because instead of looking into my own mind for a song, I could see John playing—as if he was holding a mirror to what I was doing."

But like all scientific processes, the payoffs were inconsistent. Their first collaborative efforts—"Too Bad About Sorrows" and "Just Fun"—lacked intensity. Burdened by lazy moon/June rhymes, there wasn't enough to res-cue either song. "In Spite of All the Danger," a sloppy doo-wop treatment that stands as the first original tune they recorded (although it wasn't re-leased until 1996), and "Like Dreamers Do," another misfire that eventually earned a cover,* were shelved for lack of enthusiasm. The first songs that showed some promise were "One After 909" and "I Call Your Name," the latter of which they wrote in April while camped out in John's bedroom.

---

* By the Applejacks, a Birmingham band, in 1964.

"One After 909" is as simple and straightforward as any song they ever wrote, and surprisingly durable for its economy. Built on a standard three-chord progression, it owes plenty to the early Chuck Berry hits, especially "Maybelline," with a chunky R&B vamp, thumping bass, and country-type licks woven into the breaks. The lyric bristles with an emotional uneasiness, full of the unfocused, adolescent frustrations a guy experiences when attempting to hook up with his girl. But unlike the classic boy-meets-girl, boy-gets-girl scenario, this one is ill fated from the start. He is certain what train she is traveling on—she's told him "the one after 909"—but to no avail. When he turns up at the station to meet her, even the location is wrong. The song had all the potential for whiny self-pity, but instead of its being cast as a lovesick plaint, an unexpected bitterness churns below the surface—"Move over once, move over twice / C'mon, baby, don't be cold as ice"—an early glimpse into John and Paul's narrative finesse.

"I Call Your Name" proved every bit as effective, but with more of the upheaval and restlessness that appear in later songs. Lyrically, the song is a trifle, no more than a verse with a whiff of a chorus, but it packs plenty of heat. Unlike in "909," the subject suffers great emotional fallout from a broken relationship, particularly at night, when, at his most vulnerable, he calls his girlfriend's name—and she's not there. There's no way he can sleep; haunted by the breakup, he feels he can't "go on." Images resonate with despair. "Don't you know I can't take it" reconciles into "I'm not gonna may-yay-yake it, I'm not that kind of man." The rhymes may scan in a rather mundane way, but the execution is extraordinary.

By the end of the school year, a respectable number of original songs had been copied into that beat-up notebook. In addition to the early Lennon-McCartney efforts, bits and pieces existed of "I'll Follow the Sun" (featured on the *Beatles for Sale* album [U.S. title: *Beatles '65*]), "Years Roll Along," and "Love Me Do," whose structure had been begun months earlier by Paul and awaited John's tinkering. There were between fifteen and twenty, in all, "most of them written under two or three hours," Paul explains, divulging a process that served the boys through nearly all their collaborations. "It was the amount of time we allotted ourselves and, in fact, it hardly ever took much longer than that." Whenever they hit a wall—blanking on a phrase, a transition, or that elusive chord change—instead of resisting or addressing it later, they pushed through until the problem was solved, or at least they could see some daylight through the snarl. Nearly always they brought a song to the point where it required some feedback. That was the main reason friends were invited to sit in on their writing sessions. "It was always good practice playing [a new song] for people," Paul recalls. "We'd kind of try it out on them."

Barbara Baker, George Harrison, Nigel Walley, and several of John's art school mates formed the audience for regular Lennon-McCartney showcases. Slouched on the furniture at Forthlin Road while John and Paul wrote, they'd look up from whatever they were doing and listen to the latest work in progress. "We'd do some good rhythm on the guitars, and we probably harmonized a little together," Paul recalled in a memoir. "For people who'd never seen anyone who could write songs before, we were probably quite a good little sideshow."

With John and Paul spurred on by such favorable reaction, nothing could keep them from pursuing their craft. School proved a nagging obstacle, the occasional stolen afternoons unsatisfying, hardly time enough to get something going before Jim arrived home from work. Weekends were reserved primarily for the band. It wasn't so much that they needed time to write as much as it was each other's company. "Something special was growing between them," says Colin Hanton, "something that went past friendship as we knew it. It was as if they drew power from each other."

Or simply comfort. Their two fates seemed strangely connected. They were the perfect foils for each other's disaffections. For Paul, who had lost his mother to an illness, and for John, whose home life was fraught with emotional confusion, their relationship created an alternate reality, free of such tensions. Certainly there was a competitive element between them, but it demanded so little in the way of compromise. And the compromise, they found, produced an aggressive inventiveness. If nothing else, that spring they established a mutual language for talking about music and dreaming about the future, a language that gave them common currency. Mostly, however, they let their guitars do the talking. No matter how anyone interpreted it, it was the way John Lennon and Paul McCartney best communicated.

To augment their time together, Paul and George began spending lunch hours with John next door, in the art college canteen. This was more problematic than it sounds. For one thing, institute students were forbidden to stray from the grounds during school hours (a minor glitch, however, to boys for whom hooky was a routine choice). For two years they'd been "sneaking out" to a fish and chips shop on Huskisson Street without incident, so an art school detour seemed of little consequence. Rather, an image problem prevailed. The last thing Paul and George wanted was to look like kids in their mentor's eyes. They craved John's camaraderie and, ultimately, his respect. And yet, walking into that building across the courtyard was a humbling experience, dressed conspicuously as they were in precious grammar-school uniforms, especially in contrast to John's black shirt and jeans. Ties got yanked off; badges were unpinned from blazers. However, there was no practical way to disguise their clothes other than keeping their macs buttoned to the neck, which they did in a desperate effort at first, until realizing it only served to draw more attention to them. And there was nothing they could do to hide their adolescence. Most of the art students had already turned eighteen, and to them, Paul and George appeared like "lovely little boys" visiting an elder brother.

To his credit, John wasn't deceived by appearances. Each day, he met his friends by the entrance, then accompanied them down a wide flight of cast-iron stairs to the crowded canteen, where they lounged across a tiny stage reserved exclusively for the annual college dress designers' show and ate the students' staple of baked beans on toast, with tea. The canteen was noisy, but its appeal was "you could smoke there," says a classmate who occasionally joined the boys for lunch. As soon as everyone got settled, John would "whip out a pack of fags" and entertain Paul and George with "stories about the art school birds he was shagging," spinning tales with about as much veracity as a fortune-teller. Eventually their attention was drawn toward "an older, ethereal, very talented painter" named Johnnie Crosby, who fashioned her appearance after Brigitte Bardot, with slinky, formfitting sweaters and "wonderful honey-blond hair piled up into a beehive," and sat alone each lunch hour at the opposite side of the stage, her long legs crossed provocatively in deference to the boys who were "swanning about and drooling over her."

"Hey, John? Have you had *her* yet?" they'd chime in a chorus of breathless anticipation. To which John would glumly snap, "No!" before amending it to "Not *yet.*"

John had no way of knowing the effect that his boasts of casual sex had on other classmates. All around him, he saw fellow students living out their bohemian fantasies. He just assumed that included sexual fulfillment. And yet, for all the free-spiritedness, the art college crowd remained frightfully inexperienced. "A student's having sex wasn't socially acceptable," says Ann Mason, who fought off escalating advances from Geoff Mohammed with game defiance. "Contraception was not easy to come by; you couldn't get it without some dispensation from the vicar that said you were getting married within the next three weeks, and even then you needed credentials proving you were worthy of family planning. Actually, I didn't know anyone at school who was having casual sex aside from the teachers—and John Lennon."

In fact, Barb Baker had resisted his constant groping for nearly a year. She was "too afraid of getting pregnant" to surrender to their lust and said that "as far as we got were kisses and cuddles." Still, they teased each other with maddening recklessness, necking and petting, until sleeping together seemed like the only recourse. Pleadingly, calculatingly, John swore his undying love, "proposing to [Barb] nearly every night." Things got so intense between them that "getting pregnant . . . no longer mattered," she said, and so in the spring of 1958 they "became each other's first [sexual] experience."*

Barb and John's romantic exploits, combined with the continuing creative outpouring, converted those lunch hours into lively, much-anticipated affairs. In the canteen, Paul and George huddled with John, their heads te-peed together, earnestly talking music and sex while art students filed past them. Consistent with George's laissez-faire attitude toward school, it was left to Paul to keep an eye on the clock, lest they miss the one o'clock class bell. Most days they made it back to the institute with seconds to spare. On other occasions, however, when intrepid conversation ruled, they forswore afternoon classes with a nonchalance that bordered on audacity.

Toward the end of the term, Paul and George began carrying their guitars with them. The institute had a long-standing practice of allowing students to occupy their own time in the classroom while teachers marked final papers and exams. Boys clustered together at desks and worked jointly on models, some drew, others read. Stirred by the rare loosening of rules, the boys felt an irrepressible itch to see how far things could be stretched. Having pushed the envelope so daringly and for so long, Paul and George rose fervently to the challenge.

Late one morning in May, students heard "the noise of an electric guitar . . . come twanging out of the music room." This was an extraordinary occurrence, inasmuch as music at the institute was largely theoretical,

---

* Despite Baker's belief, John told friends that he was initiated into sex at the age of fifteen by a cousin.

limited to the practice of notation and its analysis. Any hands-on experience consisted of mindless exercises, such as triangles being distributed so that students could tap out tinkly rhythms, which snuffed out any spark of enthusiasm. What's more, the music teacher would never have permitted such a display, being "such a right swine," as he was, a man who was known "to smack boys he accused of looking at him in an insolent manner."

And yet, the renegade sound persisted, loud and clear.

Colin Manley and Don Andrew remember being in a classroom on the first floor when the music began. Both energetic guitarists who played skiffle at the Cavern as the Remo Four, they bolted from their seats in an attempt to track the big-game sound. "It was fantastic," Manley recalls wistfully, "just wave after wave of a bluesy, instrumental thing that had us rushing up and down stairs, trying to locate its source." When they hit the third floor, the mystery was partially solved. Students were jammed into the music room, spilling out into the crowded hall. "We couldn't even get near the door," Andrew says, so reluctantly he and Manley hiked up on tiptoe, peering into the room.

They were startled to see George Harrison, a boy they regarded as "just filling in time at the school," hugging the spotlight. He was perched on a stool in front of the blackboard, with the new Hofner guitar his mother had bought at his insistence, running down a riff with an incisive, authoritative touch. George finished playing "Raunchy," which was becoming his signature number, then joined Paul in a medley of rock 'n roll songs. "They played some Little Richard, a Carl Perkins song, and maybe a couple of Chuck Berry [numbers]," Andrew recalls. Eventually a prefect turned up to move the crowd along. But the damage had been done. Rock 'n roll had invaded the institute's hallowed halls for the first time in anyone's memory.

"They began playing in the art school canteen," Bill Harry remembers, "working out new songs or playing requests." Usually a small crowd would gather to listen. Though not yet polished performers, there was an appealing quality about them, especially their voices. Helen Anderson, in particular, was touched by their flair. "With no backing to speak of, they were wonderful," she says. "They harmonized just beautifully together."

＊＊＊

But occasionally John needed breathing room. Paul and George were great sidekicks, but in his eyes they remained kids, grammar-school boys. When the weather turned warm, John organized outings to New Brighton beach with classmates his own age. Helen Anderson says, "We'd share sandwiches and a bottle of lemonade. None of us had bathing suits; we just pulled our sweaters down off our shoulders and relaxed." As always, John provided the entertainment. He'd play the guitar, often accompanied by Stuart Sutcliffe, who was learning some rock 'n roll. "If things were miserable at school," Anderson says, "I'd prod him to be funny—'Oh come on, John, give us a bit of a laugh'—at which point he'd invent lyrics to popular songs and start buffooning."

"I like New York and Jews, how about you?" he'd sing, affecting a Jolsonesque voice. "Holding rabbis in the movie show, when all the lights are low . . ."

The other students "laughed their socks off" at these "very twisted" parodies. It was a relief for most of them, considering the strained relationship that existed at college. Dedicated artists, utterly committed to their schoolwork, they liked John but resented his nonstop clowning, the senseless disruptions during class. "He made quite a few tutors look foolish," says Ann Mason.

John would have gotten the boot long before were it not for Arthur Ballard. Like John, he was a terribly tormented man. "Most people had a perilous relationship with him: the closer you got, the more difficult it was," says Helen Anderson, one of his star pupils that year. Much of that could be attributed to alcohol. His favorite watering hole was Ye Cracke, a tumbledown little public house with small drinking rooms stained brown from nicotine, around the corner from the college on Rice Street. Ballard held court there in a cubbyhole called the War Office, below a panorama of *The Death of Nelson* in which Hardy is depicted holding Nelson in his arms, oblivious to hundreds of anguished onlookers with their heads turned away—and which John Lennon retitled *Who Farted?* It was there that Ballard entertained his disciples, a small but acutely serious group of students whose perspective demanded mental exercise in addition to art. In Ballard's eyes, "John had an awful lot of intensity" but was "totally overshadowed by Sutcliffe . . . and Bill Harry," both of whom were "extremely well educated" and "very eager for information." Then, near the end of the term, an event occurred that altered their relationship. As Ballard recalled it: "I found a sketchbook in the studio. I looked through it, and it was extremely amusing—[filled with] sketches, little drawings of other students. I found it quite satirical [and asked], 'Who did this?' [The students] were loath to tell me. Eventually they said, 'It's John Lennon.' God, I was absolutely amazed! It showed so much talent."

Overwhelmed by the discovery, Ballard "recommended [to the college administration] that John do graphic art so that he could get illustration instruction." This was an extraordinary act of charity, considering that so far John had put no effort into his work. But Roy Sharpe, the "very conservative" director of the graphic art division, flatly turned down the request, a denial that was echoed by the head of the illustration department. Neither tutor wished to take on such a liability, dismissing John as a "totally disruptive" influence.

This only confirmed John's worst fears about art college. After eight uninspiring months at the school, he saw it for what it was: a treadmill, a dead end. From the outset, he'd always suspected as much. His well-regarded classmates played by the rules; they were lackeys to the system and they'd leave school with no more insight than it permitted them to have. They'd be like sheep, ordinary and unoriginal, turned out of a mold. To John, that was no more interesting than "wallpaper." Besides, few students had the talent to make their mark; they'd inevitably wind up teaching, which was a death sentence. "I was different," he protested much later. "But most of the time they were trying to beat me into being a fuckin' dentist or a teacher."

"They" were the tutors, the source of his greatest frustration. It was "they," after all, who stifled his creativity, "they" who wanted to put him in a box. "All they had was information that I didn't need," he complained, looking back on his art college nemeses. For the first—and surely not the last—time in his life, John sensed a conspiracy to handcuff and muzzle him.

It was more productive for him to reject the whole business. John may have suspected as early as the summer that his writing with Paul was the turning point. It certainly provided enough evidence of his uniqueness; it gave his special gift some place to flourish. By the end of June, John and Paul decided to put their talent to the test.

The Quarry Men were going to make a record.

[I]

In all of Liverpool, there was only one recording studio—and it wasn't much of a recording studio, at that.

Percy Phillips's "professional tape and disc recording service" was sandwiched between the family kitchen and a front parlor that functioned as an electrical goods shop, in the converted living room of a rambling, redbrick terrace house. Upstairs, Phillips's wife rented "a theatrical flat" to actors from the Liverpool Playhouse and, on occasion, would entice them into the studio to record poetry and monologues from favorite plays. But for the most part, the studio attracted school choirs and would-be singers. Phillips, a formal but snarly gentleman who'd just turned sixty, spent endless hours tucked away in the hot, airless cell, engineering sessions for the popular country-and-western singers he loved.

George first heard of the studio from Al Caldwell's guitarist, Johnny Byrne, who had recorded a version of "Butterfly" there in June of 1957. "You can't imagine how impressed he was," recalls Byrne. "He just kept staring at it, then looking at me and grinning like a fool." The next day at lunch, George dropped this soul-stirring discovery on John and Paul, and from that moment on, a record loomed as their raison d'être.

The session must have weighed heavily on the boys as they traveled up the broad, well-paved stretch of Kensington Street in a rattly tram. Even though basically an unmastered demo and not a bona fide disc, it would be a record all the same. But if they felt intimidated or unsure, no one gave any sign of it.

As arranged beforehand, they'd met outside the Hippodrome Cinema, where the no. 12 bus deposited John "Duff" Lowe, a classmate of Paul's who played a crude, honky-tonk-style piano and had been invited to sit in with the Quarry Men. Duff and the band had rehearsed a pistol-hot version of "That'll Be the Day" for the session, but as he greeted the others, debate flared up again over what to put on the flip side. A rainstorm materialized out of nowhere and sent the boys scrambling with their equipment onto another northbound bus, leaving the song selection unresolved even as they disembarked at the studio.

They couldn't have been prepared for what they found. The "studio" was even more primitive than they'd expected, "a tiny, tiny room with some basic recording equipment* shoved to one side" and a solitary microphone in the center. Percy Phillips, says Colin Hanton, "was a naffy old man, grumpy and excitable, who insisted we settle up the bill before setting up the equipment." The five boys were prepared to kick in 3s. 6d. each to cover the cost quoted over the telephone. But as they now pooled their resources, Phillips mentioned a surcharge to transfer the song from tape to record.

The plan had been to lay down a basic track, rebuilding it with as many retakes as was necessary to produce a flawless performance. But as Phillips performed a sound check, he explained that for the cut-rate price, he wasn't putting them on tape; they'd "go straight to vinyl," which meant any mistakes were permanent. This news troubled the band, which had only rehearsed one song, and even that still had its rough spots. Hastily, they tuned up and ran down the number, patching any holes as best they could, while Phillips struggled to get a level of some kind on Colin Hanton's thunderous drums. When a solution was finally worked out—John, rather ingeniously, suggested draping Hanton's scarf over the snare drum to dampen the vibration—they launched into "That'll Be the Day" with the energy of a man chasing a train.

Listening to the scratchy recording today, there is a clear sense of the band's rush to perfection. From that opening legendary riff—a series of exacting triplets that George performed with flair, having transposed it to the B-string (unaware that Buddy Holly capoed his guitar on the seventh fret and began lower)—there is an energy, a roiling exuberance, that serves them obligingly throughout the song. The style is no longer Holly's alone. There are still echoes of twangy rockabilly in the delivery, but the interplay of vocal jabs between Paul and John, who sings lead with complete, almost startling assuredness, shades the song's buoyancy with an intensity unexplored in the original. John seemed to know intuitively how to grab a listener's attention from the start, refusing to loosen his grip; the

---

* A boxy tape recorder, an MSS disc cutter, an amplifier, and a four-channel mixer.

tension he invests in the lyric never falters. And the band is right in there behind him to provide ample support. All three guitars frame the performance in a sturdy, rhythmic groove, leading to a stylish instrumental break in which George and Duff Lowe trade the solo spotlight. For a shotgun, one-take, warts-and-all performance—let alone the band's first dreamy foray into a recording studio—the Quarry Men managed to pull off a minor miracle.

When they completed the song, Percy Phillips pressed them to continue without delay: kick off the next number. For a long moment, no one responded. "Then, out of the blue," Hanton recalls, "Paul announced, 'We're going to do this new one *we've* written—"In Spite of All the Danger."' I'd never even heard the damned song and was surprised they'd actually written something." They begged for a minute to rehearse, but Phillips gruffly refused. "For seventeen and six you're not here all day," he snapped from his post behind the tape recorder, reminding them again of their frugality. "Just follow us," John advised Lowe and Hanton, who were duly perplexed.

Incredibly, the band managed to hang in there, considering its total lack of preparation, with Lowe and Hanton busking along nimbly in the background.

Overall, the Quarry Men were satisfied with the results. Their first recording session was an unalloyed triumph, a dynamic, irresistible record. Except for the hastily patched-together B-side, John, Paul, and George, et al. had accomplished the improbable: they had made a record that resonates with energy and confidence. The boys were understandably ecstatic. Percy Phillips handed them their trophy, a superfragile ten-inch shellac disc, on whose label Paul scrawled both titles and the applicable songwriting credits, after which they immediately hit the street, drunk on the exhilaration of their accomplishment.

"When we got the record, the agreement was we would have it for a week each," Paul recalled. John, Paul, and George primarily entertained their friends with it; anyone who inquired was permitted to take it home for a day or two. (Considered "the rarest record in the world," it was rediscovered by Duff Lowe in 1981 and sold to Paul McCartney for an undisclosed sum.) When it fell into Colin Hanton's hands he passed it on to his friend Charles Roberts, who worked at Littlewood's, the big football "pools" firm in the city center. "Charlie got it played daily, over the P.A. system in the staff canteen," Hanton recalls, "but apparently there were mixed feelings about it [there]."

But the desire to record was more a by-product of circumstance than a consuming passion. Performing—playing rock 'n roll—was their true love, but Nigel Walley recalls that "week after week went by without gigs, and the band really suffered by it." Occasionally they were asked to entertain at private parties, but that wasn't the same; by Paul's own admission, it wasn't much fun without a proper audience. "Girls were always there at our gigs," recalls Colin Hanton. "Even in those days we signed plenty of autographs, many of them on *thighs.*"

That certainly would *not* have occurred at the one gig of any significance they played that June, a dinner dance at St. Barnabas Hall—Barney's, the scene of so many Woolton youth dances—in Penny Lane. It was inevitable that Julia would turn up. John had desperately wanted her to hear the band for some time, but stalled until a real gig made it seem more attractive. And now, here she was at last, in a dazzling scarlet dress and "with a smile that lit up the room," standing alongside Barb Baker. Though tainted by the past, John and Julia had gravitated naturally toward each other and at this point in their lives welcomed the closeness that, by all accounts, they'd missed out on earlier. Now in her mid-forties, Julia finally had the wherewithal—the ability and enthusiasm, as well as the influence—to counsel her son, and she provided the perfect ear for John's mounting anxieties. The two spent long hours together discussing everything from school to music, subjects Mimi opined upon with inflexible certainty. For all her perceived inadequacies, Julia had a wonderful sense of dealing with teenagers.

That unseasonably warm night, the hall was filled with members of a local scooter club celebrating their annual race. Despite the otherwise private event, no one seemed put out by the arrival of two uninvited guests, especially two attractive, radiant women who, in their exalted intimacy, might have passed for mother and daughter. There was plenty of room along the edges for them to stand back and observe the show. Julia was "absolutely overwhelmed" by the sight of John cutting loose on the platform stage, a guest remembers. "She couldn't stop moving" to the music. Her entire body responded to the tempo: the points of her hips swaying in gentle seesaw waves, shoulders rocking, weight switching foot to foot. "Between numbers she was the only person who clapped every time—and loud," Colin Hanton recalls. "If that didn't get things going, she put her fingers in her teeth and whistled. She probably liked us just fine, but she would have done anything to encourage John."

Coming to the gig had been a test of sorts for Julia. She'd seemed genuinely proud of John and thrilled by his band. It was one thing to sit there politely, another thing entirely to dance and cheer like one of the gang.

And it was all the more poignant, considering she'd never see them again.

[II]

For Mimi Smith, Julia's visit to the Quarry Men gig was yet further proof of her sister's irresponsibility. Imagine sanctioning such foolishness! It was just as Mimi thought: nothing had changed since the day, almost two decades earlier, when Julia ran off with Freddie Lennon. That girl was still governed by her impulses.

Presumably, Julia described the performance for Mimi in blinding detail over tea the next afternoon. The sisters rarely missed an opportunity to spend time together each day. There was always a tug-of-war over some issue concerning John's welfare, which invariably ended with Mimi "laying down the law." Frustrated and resentful of this, Julia waged a constant battle for Mimi's approval. She implored her elder sister to make peace with Bobby Dykins. After all, he had long demonstrated that he was a decent man. It went without saying that he earned a good, honest living; no longer employed solely as a waiter, he also managed several bars around the Liverpool area and contributed generously to the family so that Julia didn't need to work. As John's cousin Stanley Parkes observed, "He was always very open and cheerful and seemed quite happy to me. [A]nd he gave Julia a good life." For all that, Mimi refused to give an inch.

Despite the sensitive situation, Julia and Mimi were unfailingly loyal to each other, and whatever the tension over John, tea at Menlove Avenue was a ritual not to be broken. Usually the sisters sat at a table in Mimi's morning room, off the kitchen, but in warmer weather they often stood in the garden and talked, sometimes lingering into the early evening. It was there that Nigel Walley found them on July 15, 1958, chatting across the garden gate. "I'd gone around to John's house to call for him," Walley remembers. "It was a beautiful summer night, just getting dark, and I thought maybe we'd do something together. But as it turned out, he was off staying at Julia's. In fact, she was in the process of leaving Mimi's to rejoin him." Gracious to a fault, Julia invited Nigel to ride along home with her, but that didn't appeal to Walley, who offered to walk her as far as the bus stop, farther down Menlove Avenue. Standing together on the sidewalk, invigorated by the delicious night air, Julia dallied, cracking joke after joke with the rhythm of a Liverpool comic. Finally, about 9:30, after the last glimmer of light had disappeared, Julia and Nigel headed toward the bus. As they got to the intersection at Vale Road, Nigel waved good night and turned toward home.

Julia decided to cross Menlove Avenue in the middle of the block. The road widened beyond that point, with two lanes of traffic on each side, separated by an old tram track thickened with hedges. When Nigel was partway up Vale Road he turned back momentarily to watch Julia dart across two lanes and disappear into the hedge. Afterward, he continued on his way. Not "five seconds later," he heard a hideous thud, followed by the screech of tires and "saw her body flying through the air." For a split second, the whole world froze. The only movement in the scene was Julia's ghostly arc, backlit by lamplight. Nigel, whose eyes followed her slow-motion trajectory in disbelief, tried to scream but "couldn't get a sound out." He felt a rush of terror. Then suddenly everything came unstuck. It wasn't until he saw her land, "almost a hundred feet from where she was hit," that he started running toward the accident.

It was clear, when Nigel finally reached Julia, what had happened. "The camber of the road runs into the hedge, right where she reemerged," he says. "If a car hugs too close . . . you can't see it, and vice versa." Nigel himself had been in countless cars that edged cautiously into the outer lane when rounding that curve. Julia, he knew, wasn't oblivious to the danger it presented, but she must have been preoccupied. An off-duty policeman, rocketing around the innocent-looking curve, hit her head-on, the right front bumper of his car flinging her skyward, like a football. It was also clear to Walley that Julia's injuries were critical. "She wasn't moving," he recalls. "I ran back to get Mimi, and we rushed to wait for the ambulance." Julia's elder sister bent mournfully over her body, "white with terror, and crying in hysterics."

———

It was just after eleven o'clock when the patrol car pulled up in front of 1 Blomfield Road. A policeman stood stiffly on the front step, his face frozen with the look of a naughty schoolboy. John and Bobby Dykins answered the door. When they heard the news, John recalled, "we both went white." Not wasting a minute, they took a taxi to Sefton General, the hospital where Julia had been taken by the ambulance, but John refused to view her body. Devastated, gripped by a suffocating melancholy, he waited in the reception area while a grief-stricken Dykins made the identification. Thoughts of the past, of his father, absent and inaccessible, mingled with thoughts of the present and future. Aside from Mimi, he was really on his own this time. "That's really fucked everything!" he thought. "I've no responsibility to anyone now."

Later that night John wandered over to Barbara Baker's house, where he had been persona non grata since the recent disclosure of their affair had resulted in Baker's parents' ending the relationship. Sensing his desperation, she defied her parents and went for a walk with him. "He didn't say anything," she remembered, as they strolled through Reynolds Park. "I didn't know [Julia had died]. He didn't tell me. We just walked and walked." It seemed odd, she thought after a while, that he didn't try to kiss her. It had been several days since they'd been alone; their impulse, when that much time had elapsed, was usually driven by desire. He seemed "physically ill." Finally, John just broke down, his body heaving uncontrollably. Barbara held him tenderly, and through a hail of tears it all came pouring out—about the accident, his heartbreak, the terror of outright abandonment. "We walked until well after midnight," Baker said, until she felt he was well enough to go home. But as he moped away, alone, down the dark ribbon of road, she knew that John Lennon had been changed forever.

———

It would seem logical that he'd bury his sorrow in the band. "Now we were both in this, both losing our mothers," Paul later wrote. "This was a bond for us, something of ours, a special thing."

In a way, Paul was right. From that day onward, he and John must have formed a mutual, unspoken acknowledgment couched in their respective sadness. Already bound by music, they were connected in more intimate, complicated ways. Neither boy was inclined to explore these emotions, and John, especially, was hard-set in denial. While he struggled with limited success to cope with his mother's death, he refused to discuss it with Paul or, for that matter, anyone else. Nigel Walley, cruelly traumatized by the accident and struggling to make sense of it on his own, was rebuffed by John in repeated attempts to discuss what had happened. "For months [afterward], John refused to speak to me," Walley says. "Inwardly, he was blaming me for the death. You know: 'if Nige hadn't walked her to the bus stop' or 'if he'd have kept her [occupied] another five minutes, it never would have happened.' Even Pete Shotton couldn't engage John on the subject, drawing only a mumbled response when he offered condolences. There was something trusting, something innocent that "went out of him forever," Shotton realized. As far as Pete was concerned, John and Julia had enjoyed "a girlfriend-boyfriend relationship. She was his buddy . . . not his mother." Though their attraction was expressly platonic, John, in essence, had lost "a mate."

For all his nurturing, Paul couldn't fill the void. John wasn't ready to accept any kind of social comforting. As John was to later remark: "I lost [my mother] twice. Once as a five-year-old when I was moved in with my auntie. And once again at fifteen [sic] when she actually, physically died." He had never felt more detached in his life, or with more need for some reinforcement. And yet, though Paul was prepared to strengthen their intimacy as friends, John wanted no part of it. He wanted to be angry for a while.

Dejected and resentful, John passed the remainder of the summer largely in solitude. For the first time in several years, he didn't go to visit his cousin Stanley in Scotland. Instead, he sulked in his room at Menlove Avenue, refusing to see visitors. When friends showed up unannounced, Mimi met them at the door with a disapproving glare and turned them away. Even Paul and George saw little of their bandleader, and on the few occasions when they lured him out to practice, there was no real enthusiasm. Songwriting especially became a struggle. The five or six tunes he and Paul managed to finish were bright, upbeat, and romantic—hardly reflective of John's dark mood, and there is no doubt as to who was chiefly responsible for them. Neither boy ever claimed there was parity in producing their material, or pretended otherwise. In the course of their extraordinary collaboration, John and Paul routinely worked alone on songs before putting their heads together. In this case, Paul provided the basic structure for "Love Me Do," a catchy and direct, albeit innocuous, song whose plodding lyric does nothing to revive the melody's stunted hook. The writing has few of the stylized nuances—the elliptical rhythmic twists and inflections—that give contour to their later songs. Paul had tinkered with "Love Me Do" for some time before bringing it respectfully to John for a polish, but it never evinced the spirit that a studio production ultimately gave it. As for "P.S. I Love You," with its playful admission of vulnerability, Paul noted: "It was pretty much mine. I don't think John had much of a hand in it."

When school started again, there was a noticeable shift in the group's balance. Creatively, physically, emotionally, John was coming apart at the seams. He had begun drinking heavily, as though determined to drown his anguish in self-abuse. Night after night, in a room at Ye Cracke, he downed beer and whiskey until he could barely stand. Straddling a low-backed chair, he plunged into soul-searching conversations with strangers, punctuating them with explosions of anxious rage. Most nights, John was "very entertaining . . . inclined to talk about the bum of a girl or tell funny stories about somebody sitting across the room." But he could very quickly turn nasty. Boundaries were drawn and redrawn without any warning. If old friends stopped by the pub, they avoided him because, sometimes, John seemed determined to drive them away, determined to abandon them as his mother had abandoned him. On one occasion, barely sober, John began egging on "some blokes . . . prancing about, doing ballet steps" in front of the old police station on Renshaw Street, when he finally pushed the wrong button and they "butted him in the face." Another time, undoubtedly drunk, he picked an unanticipated fight with his dear art school mate Jonathan Hague, for whom he had nothing but the fondest feelings. "He got my duffel coat up over my head and started flailing away," Hague remembers. "It actually didn't mean a thing to me; I was too drunk. But the next day in school, in a very shaky, frightened way, John told me that he was trying to kill the person under the coat and didn't understand the anger in him to do such a thing."

Faced with trying to keep things vital, Paul took over as "the motivator," calling rehearsals, then persuading John to attend. He even moved their location from his house in Allerton to Menlove Avenue in an effort to engage Lennon, but with little success. A friend who attended those practices observed: "John could just as easily have gone over to the golf course across the road for a walk, or gone to town." He was that uninterested. It was no different at school. John was enrolled, but in name only. He attended classes but hardly participated in any work; nothing lit a fire under him, no tutor came to his rescue.

One of the band's few joys that semester was playing at the art school dances, which were held intermittently on Friday nights in the basement canteen. Unlike the "fancy-dress dos" that marked the college's social rituals, the dances were "crowded, informal affairs, pitch-black and sweaty." For those dances, the band shelved its trusty Quarry Men moniker, probably to dissociate themselves from being identified as grammar-school boys. "They were simply [known as] 'the college band,'" says Harry. And it wasn't much of a band, at that. There was no drummer, for starters; inexplicably, Colin Hanton hadn't been summoned to play for the two initial college functions. Whether the band considered him expendable or he had fallen from their good graces remains unclear. But his relationship with the other boys, while cordial, was never that comfortable. He wasn't one of the "inner bunch," he wasn't "an anchorman," and, what's more, he had a full-time day job as an upholsterer that would always take precedence over music. In all probability, however, their distancing came down to talent: John, Paul, and George were getting better as the band grew tighter—and Colin wasn't. After a gig at the Pavilion Theatre, in Lodge Lane—where Julia Lennon had once danced professionally in a theater troupe—things went from great to gone. The management was looking for a regular band to play a half-hour set of music between each bingo session. As Nigel Walley had explained it, the residency was the Quarry Men's to lose: an entertaining show that night would seal the deal.

To everyone's great relief, the band cruised through an energetic, very satisfying set. As they were leaving the stage, the announcer wandered over and said, "That was very good. There's a pint for you at the bar, lads."

One pint, however, led to two, then three. "Aside from George," recalls Hanton, "Paul, John, and I got pretty well drunk." Slowly but steadily, they got plastered on black velvets—a bottle of Guinness mixed with a half-pint of cider. "By the time we had to go on again, we were totally out of it," George recalled. Any effort to contain the damage backfired. With the impact of yet another setback, Paul exploded. All the repressed anger—from months of not playing regularly, tiptoeing around John's depression, and putting out a cheesy, half-assed sound—pressed in on him. As they headed home, in a rage, Paul turned on Colin Hanton, whose ineffectiveness Paul blamed for dragging the band down. Hanton was a wiry, little guy, not much over five foot four, but absolutely fearless, and he refused to take crap from any slick, "mealy-mouth" grammar-school boy.

Pete Shotton, who had met the band at the hall, stepped between the fuming antagonists. He glanced furtively outside; the bus had just crossed Queen's Drive. Without taking his eyes off Paul, he said, "C'mon, Colin, this is our stop." Breathing heavily, Hanton turned and went downstairs to get his drums. Pete helped him drag the equipment home, then left, saying he'd see Colin soon, most likely at the next gig. But there was no next gig, and no phone call from any of the Quarry Men. "In fact, I never saw them again," Hanton says, "until three years later, when I turned on the telly and some bloke was going on about a band called the Beatles."

[I]

There was no eulogy for the Quarry Men—no tears shed, no post-mortem. It was never actually acknowledged by anyone that they'd disbanded. But if they weren't officially "done with," the group was none-theless in deep freeze. Without any gigs, there was nothing to keep them in action. Helplessly, they sat idle while the local rave scene grew up and around them, never reaching out an inviting hand.

Adrift, George, Paul, and John spent many nights at the Rialto, listen-ing to and studying Kingsize Taylor and the Dominoes, whose transforma-tion from catchy skiffle to a set heavily influenced by American rhythm and blues awakened the young bands in Liverpool. They also kept an eye trained on Alan Caldwell, who had emerged from his skiffly torpor with an intriguing persona to go with a flashy new sound. Jet (later, Rory) Storm and the Hurricanes were slick and soul-stirring, and they took advantage of the need for some pure entertainment in an idiom suffused with raw energy. Storm, a star athlete, was incredibly handsome and brimming with confi-dence—or at least appeared to be, with a hundred-watt smile he toggled on and off to the delight of his fans. Tall and reed-thin, with "peroxide-blond hair," he went to dancing class to refine certain theatrics and wore either gold lamé or peacock blue suits onstage as a means of commanding the spotlight. He spent hours before a show choosing a wardrobe. And if clothes didn't make the man, he simply removed them, once "stripping down to a tiny bikini string thing before prancing about to the music." A friend says, "He would do *anything* to get attention on the stage." Even a pet monkey was drafted into the act "because it had excellent pulling power." Storm's voice was flimsy at best, and Johnny Byrne, a natural lead guitarist—Ringo called him "Liverpool's Jimi Hendrix"—was deaf in one ear and played incredibly loud. But when the lights hit them and the music kicked in, there was magic in their performance. Howie Casey, who played sax for a rival band, the Seniors, and found himself frequently paired on the same bill, marveled at the Hurricanes' "big stage act." Recalling it fondly, he says, "When the lights came up, all the guitarists had a foot up on their [cream-and-red Selmer] amps, their backs turned to the audience. And when they started to play, [Caldwell] would come swinging on and they'd turn around on cue. It was very sharp, very bold. No one else, in 1958, was doing anything remotely like that." More than any movie or record, this band's stage presence left an indelible mark on the Beatles.

Everywhere the former Quarry Men looked, the rock 'n roll band-wagon was rumbling ahead, picking up steam. Teenage venues opened as fast as promoters could find vacant buildings or church halls to rent. The Dominoes and the Hurricanes worked four or five times a week, and one only had to open a newspaper to glimpse lists of regular "big beat dances" featuring young bands like Ian and the Zodiacs, Dale Roberts and the Jaywalkers, the Swinging Bluegenes, Gerry and the Pacemakers, and Cass and the Cassanovas.

Quietly, George attempted to join Storm's tony outfit, showing up at his West Oakhill Park house one afternoon in a bid to audition for the band. Vi Caldwell, a blunt, outspoken woman who steered her son's career with fastidiousness, dismissed George as if he were a child. "I told him he was too young," she reported to her son and Johnny Byrne, both of whom were having tea in the kitchen. But George's appearance there confirmed something that up till then Byrne had only suspected. He turned to Storm and said, "It seems the Quarry Men are done with."

By the end of 1958, George's itch to play was so strong that he took up with three other friends — Ken Brown, Les Stewart, and a lad known only as Skinner — in a rather pedestrian unit called the Les Stewart Quartet. Mostly, they just rehearsed together in the Lowlands, a coffee bar in a residential section of town, but eventually some work dribbled their way. Limited to the outer fringe of the rock 'n roll scene, they concentrated on gigs held at "working-men's clubs [which] never paid . . . more than ten bob" and the occasional wedding reception.

Harry and Louise continued to encourage George's musical interests, although (like most parents) they had grown leery of John Lennon's influence over their son. John had always been welcome at the Harrisons' house; Louise, especially, treated him with warmth and jollity, playing the giddy hostess and feeding him endless helpings of beans and toast, a Scouse favorite that Mimi refused to make. But as the year wore on and his behavior grew more erratic—and more terrifying—even Louise was forced to reconsider her opinion.

"By December, he was completely out of control," recalls Jonathan Hague, who continued to drink and carouse with John almost every night that fall. "We had learned to drink together, but somewhere along the way he left me in the dust." Hague attributes John's excess to rage, which crept over him unexpectedly, like the dense Liverpool fog. "He seemed to be consumed by anger at that stage. He was jealous of other students, resentful about his mother's death, and frustrated—trapped—by his situation at school. He was clearly mixed up—just lost—with no one willing or able to help him."

John always struck where he knew people would be most vulnerable, "mimicking their accents or a particular disfigurement," according to Hague. There are countless stories about how John pulled up limping alongside a cripple or insisted on shaking hands with an armless veteran. "Most of his antics were harsh—but harmless," says an art school classmate. But more than once, a sharp-eyed art student had to rescue John from an imminent beating, or buy a couple of pints for "an enraged neighbor" he'd insulted, as goodwill. Helen Anderson says that "he was embarrassingly rude to people, hurling insults at them, telling them to fuck off. It was terrible. Most of us eventually got fed up with him."

Friends looked to Paul to control the damage, but it was beyond even his know-how. When John "went off like that," Paul usually waited for the storm to pass or humored John to keep him from turning up the heat. And unbeknownst to Paul, some considered his presence in these situations more problem than solution. "It was obvious that John had big reservations about Paul, too," says Hague, who absorbed his friend's harangues during their drinking binges. "Even then, there was great jealousy there. He was all too aware of Paul's talent and wanted to be as good and grand himself. After a while, you could see it, plain as day: the subtle body language or remarks that flew between them. He wasn't about to let someone like Paul McCartney pull his strings."

In the closing days of 1958, there seemed to be few options that could save John from himself. Julia was gone; Pete Shotton was preoccupied with police cadet training; Geoff Mohammed's relationship with a cranky coed kept him on a tight leash; even Barbara Baker, his loyal moll, had thrown in the towel and taken up with another young man, to whom she would eventually get married. Everything brought the feeling of alienation into sharper focus. His friendships with Bill Harry and Stuart Sutcliffe provided a respite, although both students were committed to their art. Aside from Paul and George, there seemed to be no one to fill the encapsulating void. His entire support system was falling apart.

Then, a few days before the end of the term, Cynthia Powell walked into his life.

[II]

It had never occurred to Cynthia that the "scruffy, dangerous-looking, and totally disruptive" boy who "frightened the life out" of her at art college would end up her soul mate. John Lennon was a character out of her worst nightmares, a tatty ted, "outrageous . . . a rough sort" who flew so far below her social radar that his existence barely even registered.

They had been in class together for most of the year, but as the girl from the wrong side of the aisle, Cynthia Powell had escaped special notice. It wasn't that she was maidenly or unglamorous. But in a school filled with artsy "individuals," she toed the conventional line. Pale and painfully timid, to the point of walking half a step behind her best friend when they entered a room together, she melted into crowds like the scenery in an unfocused photograph. With her flat, Irish forehead, pleading eyes, and fine, honey-colored hair bobbed in a secretarial fashion, Cynthia saw her image as something so plain and common that it was "otherwise known as [a] mouse." She was slim and delicately shaped with good legs and a smile that puckered slightly with suggestive intimacy. But her Gainsborough beauty was a gift she ignored.

Most of the male population there had her pegged as another well-mannered "good girl," no less a *posh* good girl, from the suburbs—and rightfully so. In the evenings, when her father, Charles, arrived home from work, Cynthia would be dressed to please, with her corn-silk hair brushed extravagantly, to which she'd added a special touch like a bow or matching combs so he would "take notice," which he invariably did. Cynthia revered Charles Powell, and in her rush to build herself in his image, she adopted his best qualities: tact, graciousness, modesty, and impeccable manners.

Nothing on file explains where her attraction to John came from. As a teenager, she had always developed strong crushes on boys about whom there were unknowns but no mysteries. Anyone whom Cynthia dated was basically a well-scrubbed Catholic boy focused on the middle-class dream, his conduct always respectful and proper. Her last boyfriend, a student from the art college named Rodney Begg, did nothing to shatter that mold.

It was almost by accident that Cynthia even came into contact with John. The thirty-six students in their class had been divided arbitrarily into three groups, each of which stayed together all term for the various courses. But one afternoon a week they all met for lettering, and John, wandering in late as always, wound up at a desk directly behind her.

Art never commanded the rigors of, say, math or science—but lettering did. "It was a skill that required patience and discipline," said Cynthia, who, as an illustrator of some talent, excelled when it came to making precise measurements and drawing perfectly balanced shapes. "For John . . . [lettering] was impossible." He had neither the ability nor the temperament to pull it off. In order to distract from his inadequacy, he resorted to an old dodge as the class cutup, "making dirty smudges across his paper" and ridiculing Cynthia's "superior" finishing-school appearance. That kind of noisy attention should have been enough to drive her far off his path. But something lit a fire in her. This bad boy, whose shadowy air disrupted everything it came into contact with, had sparked a chemistry of unrest within her body that was outside the boundaries of respect.

One afternoon, when their tutor failed to show up on time, the class scrambled his Victorian oaktag letter cards to make an optometrist's eye chart, which inspired mock-examinations that led to the unmasking of Cynthia's and John's chronic—and dreaded—nearsightedness. For two teenagers who never saw eye to eye, the insecurity they shared was deliciously ironic. This kicked up a "vague friendship between them" that culminated in her cutting John curious glances during class and his addressing her broadly, and quite affectionately, thereafter as "Miss Powell."

John aroused in Cynthia a nervous corruptibility she had never acted on before. The most daring thing she had ever done was to harmlessly experiment with pale lipstick and black eyeliner, along with a splash of Hiltone hair dye intended to turn her "into [a] blond bombshell." She tried to explain away the sudden butterflies in her stomach by blaming it on a curiosity that had gotten out of hand, a fascination with the unknown. Yet for all Cynthia's weak excuses, she soon admitted being "completely out of control."

Later that December, a few days before the end of the term, an event occurred that brought some harmony to her internal disorder. Cynthia and a group of fellow students decided to celebrate the upcoming holiday by going around the corner to Ye Cracke between classes. After a lunch of sandwiches and black velvets, everyone drifted back to school, where an impromptu party was already in progress. A record player had been set up in one of the rooms. Cynthia was already quite light-headed, and when John pushed his way through the tangle of couples and asked her to dance, she fell rapturously into his arms. Over the years, both John and Cynthia loved to tell the story of how he asked her out on a date that afternoon, only to be politely rebuffed. "I'm terribly sorry, but I'm engaged to a fellow in Hoylake," Cynthia purportedly replied. To which John shot back: "I only asked you out. I didn't ask you to marry me, did I?"

No matter how later accounts differed, at the time Cynthia apparently relented. She came away from that room "madly in love," so much so, in fact, that when classes resumed that afternoon, the two of them stole off to Stuart Sutcliffe's flat, where they immediately slept together. The man from Hoylake was quickly forgotten.

For the next few weeks, John and Cynthia were just about inseparable. "He had found someone who took the edge off his anger," says Jonathan Hague. Helen Anderson, who had known Cynthia from the age of twelve, says, "Even as a child, she was easygoing and philosophical. It used to impress us how much she always reasoned things through. But when she took up with John, we were fairly flabbergasted. They were like chalk and cheese because Cyn was so serious and John acted such a buffoon. She didn't have that streak of outrageousness in her." Nor was she bohemian—or "bohernia," as John used to say. Their attraction may have "shocked" other students in their circle, but it was mostly regarded with enthusiasm and relief. Ann Mason felt that Cynthia did the whole school a favor by dating John. "When she took a shine to him, it did his confidence no end of good. And that calmed him down, letting us live and learn in peace." What Cynthia may have lacked in spirit, she made up for in her blind devotion. "John was absolutely the dominant figure in that relationship," recalls Bill Harry. "He was like most Scouse men, who demanded a subservient mate. Cynthia was a doormat. But she was very influential in keeping him under control."

"Immediately, he started a metamorphosis on her," says Helen Anderson, who watched the makeover with fascination. All of John's canvases, she says, were depictions of smoky nightclub scenes, with a ripe-figured Brigitte Bardot character planted prominently on a barstool. "She was his dream girl," and that was how he molded Cynthia. She started getting blonder, her hair grew longer, and finally she put it up, like Brigitte

Bardot. All of a sudden Cynthia became very *glamorous*—and sexy! Cynthia wasn't totally comfortable with her new guise. A friend recalls how she would duck into "the ladies' loo before lunch, get tarted up, then wait for somebody—anybody she knew—to follow into the canteen." She "didn't have a clue" about how to carry off the new image. But John wanted it that way, and she complied without argument.

As 1959 unfolded, an exhilarating burst of rock 'n roll releases made it impossible for John to ignore the stubborn, intoxicating pull of pop music. Hits of the day—now golden classics—surfaced faster than stores could stock them:* "La Bamba," "To Know Him Is to Love Him," "C'mon Everybody," "Sea of Love," "There Goes My Baby," "A Teenager in Love," "Sleep Walk," "Rockin' Robin," "Dream Lover," "Lonely Teardrops," "Sea Cruise," "Little Star," "It's Only Make Believe," "Back in the U.S.A." (the flip side was "Memphis"), and an extraordinary Ray Charles record that would emerge in the early 1960s as a trusty Beatles showstopper, "What'd I Say." Week after week the racks were filled with new offerings by Ricky Nelson, Sam Cooke, the Everly Brothers, Del Shannon, the Coasters, Connie Francis, Dee Clark, Lloyd Price, and Bobby Darin, to say nothing of another half a dozen hits courtesy of the irrepressible Elvis Presley.

And by mid-1959, England had its first true homegrown star in the genre. Cliff Richard, with his malt-shop features, perfect haircut, and gleaming smile, was Britain's answer to the likes of Elvis and Holly. He had been discovered performing at pubs around Hertfordshire and signed to EMI Records, which in August 1958 released an innocuous and stiff little single called "Schoolboy Crush." During a promotional television appearance Richard ditched his single in favor of its much hotter B-side, "Move It," which featured some furious guitar playing. A week later the record was a runaway smash.

With his band, the Shadows, Richard cast a Presley-like shadow on the landscape of British rock 'n roll. British teenagers embraced him as an identifiable voice, if not a cultural icon—proof that the empire could strike back musically when and if it wished. But in Liverpool, especially, there was a backlash against Richard's squeaky-clean appeal. Scousers considered him too much of a lightweight, his music too mainstream, too derivative. And yet, dazzled by his success, most Liverpool bands imitated Richard's every

---

* *British release dates often differ from U.S. chart appearances.*

move. They put on matching suits, practiced the rhythmic little dance steps he popularized, and cooked up an act that used guitars in its choreography, much the way the Shadows did.

From the start, John, Paul, and George were determined to distinguish themselves among the army of Shadows imitators who thronged the dance halls. They were turned off by Cliff's whole image, the way he pandered to audiences with an airbrushed suggestiveness, defusing the power of rock 'n roll. And their fiery reaction to Richard's sugarcoated pop and the lemming-like behavior of their fellow Liverpool musicians energized John, Paul, and George, reviving their desire to perform.

Liverpool's coffee-bar culture had grown up around the university and the art college as early as 1957, but it wasn't until 1959 that these places shifted into full swing. For the longest time, students frequented Streates, the Kardomah, or the Marlborough, the latter of which had special rooms set aside where they could drink on the sly and sing bawdy songs. But it was a coffee bar next door to the Marlborough, called the Jacaranda, that attracted John, Paul, and George.

The Jacaranda was the largest room of its kind, a Dickensian soot-blackened storefront set near the corner of Slater and Bold Streets, so close to the schools that one of the university clubs proposed making it an annex. Inside, the café was all studied unpretentiousness: a cluster of mismatched wooden tables surrounded by metal-legged chairs, bare brick walls painted a glossy white, and a shelf warped from the weight of the copper kettles displayed on it.

"It was like all the places we'd hung out in," recalls Beryl Williams, who with her husband, Allan, had opened the Jacaranda coffee bar in the former premises of a watch-repair shop in September 1958. Like many of Liverpool's young, working artsy set, the Williamses had spent the fifties in thrall of jazz—and bohemian culture. Hitchhiking across the Continent, they'd "lived in the cafés of France and Holland," until at the age of twenty-six, they opted to join the wave of offbeat hipsters determined to bring the counterculture to Liverpool.

Initially, the Jacaranda drew Liverpool university students, but eventually Stuart Sutcliffe and John Lennon gravitated there to discuss their work and dreams. The two would sit for hours in one of the corner booths near the window, talking earnestly about art and philosophy, while a mini–soap opera unfolded around them. It wasn't long before John brought Paul and George with him to check out the music scene downstairs. The Jac's tiny cellar had been converted from coal storage into a crude sort of cabaret, with barely enough space for a small group to perform in a corner. To create the right atmosphere, Allan Williams had booked a ragtag West Indian outfit—called, rather optimistically, the Royal Caribbean Steel Band—he'd first heard "in a Greek joint" near the art college. Almost immediately they attracted a devoted following. Jac regulars loved the metallic warble of "the big tubs" and the catchy calypsos that were de rigueur, but their awe was reserved for the band's hugely dynamic leader, a spindly, gap-toothed Trinidadian named Harold Phillips, who knew how to work a crowd.

Over the next decade, Phillips became an almost legendary figure on the streets of Liverpool. Known to everyone as Lord Woodbine, or Woody, after the cheap cigarette always pasted to his lower lip, he was a man of immense charisma, with a rich, dulcet singing voice and a talent for wielding maracas like signal flags. He worked at the American air base in nearby Burtonwood but also ran a strip club and a number of illegal honky-tonks called shabeens, the most notable of which was the Berkeley, where John Lennon occasionally slept on a cot.

Allan Williams had passed the word that local groups were welcome to play at the Jacaranda on the steel band's night off. Aside from extremely informal shindigs at the art college, John, Paul, and George had never performed as a trio, and it was unlikely they could stage a show on such little practice. Besides, even with Cynthia, John was still too troubled to give the band more time. There were days when he would stay in bed or sit forlornly at a table in one of the coffee bars, tortured by "feelings of remorse."

The inertia caught up with John in June, as another college term drew to a close. Second-year students were required to take the intermediates, a series of exams that gauged individual progress, assessed skills, and determined whether they'd graduate to another two-year program, leading to a National Diploma in Design. Everyone was required to "submit for his certificate," which meant you wrestled a folder of your work together, then sent it to a review board at the Ministry of Education for evaluation. Despite benefiting from several drawings Ann Mason offered to him, John still didn't have enough to make a folder. According to Rod Murray, "everybody chipped bits of paintings and drawings in, and they made up a folder for him."

Things only got worse when news came that he failed the lettering portion of his intermediates and would have to "resit" the course again. Naturally: the one subject he absolutely detested. It seemed like more punishment. John was clearly overwhelmed by a strong sense of failure, and his anger turned to despair. But just when it seemed that he couldn't find any outlet for his anxieties, one found him.

[I]

Over the years, John and Cynthia told many stories about George Harrison, the flap-eared little "whacker" with the slow hand and fast mouth. To George, they seemed the perfect pair, a symbol of independence. During summer vacation, he would determine their whereabouts and lock in on them like anti-aircraft artillery. "Cyn and I would be going to a coffee shop or a movie," John told an interviewer, "and George would follow us down the street two hundred yards behind." At first, they pretended not to see him. Cynthia, who was circumspect and too sweet-tempered to execute a "push-off," would mumble a tremulous appeal to John on the fifteen-year-old's behalf. "[George] would hurriedly catch up to us," she recalled, "and [ask], 'Where are you two off to? Can I come?'" More often than not, the lovebirds had plans for a movie that included some steamy necking in the dark theater—now rudely preempted. "So we would spend the lost afternoon as a jolly threesome, wondering what on earth we were going to do with ourselves."

What on earth, indeed. At the time, it never occurred to them that George would soon jump-start the band's stalled career.

It is doubtful that George even told John he was playing with anyone else. Besides, the Les Stewart Quartet was nothing to brag about. As musicians, they "didn't hold a candle to John and Paul." The upside, however, was their access to a generous rehearsal space at the Lowlands, along with an aura that netted George his first steady girlfriend, Ruth Morrison.

Unlikely as it seems, it was Ruth Morrison who brought the keys to the kingdom. One evening during a rather dispiriting coffee break at the Lowlands, she disclosed that a new coffee bar was opening farther down and across the street, in Hayman's Green, which promised to make a considerable splash. It was located in the basement of a cavernous private home that could hold more than three hundred kids, and from what Ruth had heard, there was going to be live music. Bands knew from experience that new coffee-bar owners usually gave residencies to the first group that walked in the door—self-promotion, not quality, being the foremost criterion. Without waiting for more details, the Les Stewart outfit dispatched their most presentable representative, a guitarist named Ken Brown, to make his best pitch.

The house at 8 Hayman's Green was a mini-mansion, a handsome gray Victorian structure of fifteen rooms set back from the road in a grove of tall trees. Ken was more than familiar with "the Best place," as it was known, inasmuch as the owners' son Pete was in his class at Collegiate Grammar School. It had been Pete who first proposed the idea of a club in the family's unfinished cellar and instantly won the approval of his mother, Mona, a gregarious Indian-born diva for whom drama of this type was an essential fuel. And the club would provide a suitable distraction to her faltering marriage to Johnny Best, a flamboyant Liverpool fight promoter sidelined with a heart condition.

"I went round to see her," Brown recalled, "and we helped her get the coffee bar ready, installing lighting, covering the walls with hardboard to prevent condensation, painting the place orange and black. In return Mrs. Best promised that we could play [there] when it finally opened."

In the weeks before the club opened, a steady buzz built unlike anything the West Derby Village neighborhood had ever experienced. Kids came to gape at all the work being done: lights were put in, walls were lined with timber paneling, a dark alcove was converted into a snack bar. Finally, membership cards were printed, revealing the club's alluring name: the Casbah.

The club was set to open on a Saturday night: August 29, 1959. For the Les Stewart Quartet the date was a milestone in their brief, relatively obscure existence. More than three hundred teenagers had already purchased membership cards in anticipation of the event, and the attention would catapult them into the limelight. But on the verge of celebrity, Les Stewart misinterpreted Ken Brown's hands-on role at the Casbah as a power play. The insult, as Stewart perceived it, ignited an argument between the two boys just a week or so before their debut, culminating in Stewart's refusing to play. The band folded prematurely, while George joined Ken Brown to give Mona Best the bad news.

On their way over to the club, Brown asked George if there was any way they could salvage the residency. "He said he had two mates," Brown recalled, "and went off on a bus to fetch them."

———

From the instant it opened, the Casbah was a runaway success. The kids who turned up couldn't believe their eyes. It was dazzling, hot, loud, smoky, young, private—rocking—pulsing with just the right atmosphere. Mo Best offered up "the perfect house," and the Quarry Men—John, Paul, George, and Ken Brown—brought that house down. Even without a drummer—or a P.A. system—they knocked out the rapturous crowd. Kids, standing "shoulder to shoulder," swarmed around the band, which was pressed back into a corner that had once functioned as the coal bin. It seemed inconceivable they'd ever disbanded; there wasn't so much as a wrinkle in their performance.

"Among the songs we performed [that] night," Ken Brown recalled, "were 'Long Tall Sally' . . . and 'Three Cool Cats,' which John sang rolling his eyes." The rest glided by in a fantastic blur, but it was infinitely gratifying. To be performing again, in front of such a great crowd, was so satisfying—and such a relief. Even Mo Best got more than she expected, transferring to the boys the agreed-upon Les Stewart residency that guaranteed them a princely £3 every Saturday night.

More than the music and refreshments, it was the *idea* of the Casbah that vitalized its members. There was an exclusivity about it, not in the class-restrictive rivalries that isolated—and divided—the British empire but in a celebration of togetherness. Here, belonging was really a function of age, not class or breeding or religion or wealth. Kids came to dance, to talk, and to get away from the enervating grind that had been bequeathed to them by their mostly distant parents. "None of us dreamed that we'd ever have much of anything in our lives," says Colin Manley, whose band, the Remo Four, later played at the club. "We may have still been in school at that point, but we were already in the System, our lives were pretty well preordained, which for most Liverpool kids meant no diploma, a dead-end job, a loveless marriage, too many kids, never enough money, and lots of beer to drown the burden. So a place like the Casbah was something else entirely. It was outside the System—and it was ours."

As the Quarry Men enjoyed their run, the Casbah membership spiraled into the thousands. The club became so crowded that after a while you could "just about hear the band." To cure that, John talked a short, slight guitar player named Harry into "opening for them," which was nothing more than a ruse, really, amounting to a brief two-song spot in exchange for the use of Harry's amplifier. "It was a good idea that nearly backfired," recalls George's friend Arthur Kelly. "The kid was a disaster. His party piece was a cringe-worthy version of 'Apple Blossom Time' that nearly always caused a lynching." Fortunately, before there was any time for violence, the band plugged in and shook things up with "Blue Suede Shoes" and "Johnny B. Goode" crackling through the cellar on forty watts of juice.

When the boys weren't performing, they wandered through the crowd, chatting with friends and flirting. "Girls were the main reason you joined a band," Paul says, citing a condition known to every schoolboy who ever picked up a guitar, and from the start there was never a shortage of them around. Of the many attractive girls who hung around the Casbah, one in particular caught John's eye. She was an elfin blonde with a tense, wounded look, whom he nicknamed Bubbles, for lack of a proper introduction and because it so unsuited her. In fact, all the guys had noticed her watching them. While not a beautiful girl, she was catlike and intense, in a mysterious kind of way. She also was eager to meet them. "It must have been all over my face that I fancied John," recalls Bubbles, whose real name is Dot Rhone, "but once it became clear he had a girlfriend, I lost interest." Instead, she approached Paul with game determination, pretending to be faint in order to get him outside, where they could be by themselves.

Once alone, an "immediate attraction" developed between them. Paul discovered in Dot a person who hardly fit the profile of the other girls at the Casbah. She had grown up in a better section of Liverpool called Childwall, around the corner from Brian Epstein, the Beatles' future manager. But "it might have been two different worlds," Dot says, her humble situation being anything unlike Epstein's glaringly "posh" circumstances. "I didn't have a normal childhood. My dad was an alcoholic; he never hung on to any money. And the only reason we lived in that neighborhood was because a sickly aunt left the house to my mother." A year younger than Paul, Dot had gone to Liverpool Institute High School, "the girls' school across the road from the Inny," but had left in June, taking a clerk's job at the Dale Street branch of District Bank in order to support her family. Paul, she believes, was attracted by how needy and impressionable she was, which put her under his sway; she found him "adorably handsome, opinionated," and loaded with confidence. "He came from the first family I'd ever known that cared about each other so much," Dot says. "Everyone would gather round the piano, while Jim played songs like 'You Must Have Been a Beautiful Baby,' and sometimes [he] would sing with Paul and Mike." At a deeper level, they undoubtedly recognized the loneliness in each other's lives, each absent a parent—in her case because of addiction.

Within days Paul and Dot were an item. A nearly exclusive togetherness during the week quickly became the norm, but Saturdays were reserved for the Casbah, where Dot now joined Cynthia in her new role as inconspicuous cheerleader. "It was amazing how popular the band had become—and how fast," Dot says, recalling those nights from a vaunted perspective. "Watching them, you could see how effortlessly they engaged the crowd. It was a full-blown mutual admiration society." Perhaps nobody appreciated it as much as Mona Best, who couldn't print Casbah membership cards fast enough to satisfy the demand. She was thrilled by "the fantastic scenes outside the house"—interminable queues that snaked across her front lawn, along the drive, and down Hayman's Green—to say nothing of the club fees and five-pence admission that accrued beyond her wildest expectations. On word of mouth alone, she could pack in four hundred kids before conditions reached a critical stage, when tempers flared and the crowd became uncontrollable, and with the nonstop turnover, as many as 1,300 kids passed through the club on any given Saturday night. Despite the constant crush, parents drifted unobtrusively downstairs to check out the goings-on; policemen on the beat stopped by for a Coke. And everyone had a good word for the house band, whose residency seemed destined to stretch on indefinitely.

Which is why everyone was dismayed when it all soon collapsed.

Stories abound about how the Beatles hemorrhaged money, mostly because there was so damn much of it and no one to tend the purse strings. But in the early days they could tell you where every farthing went. "They didn't have much . . . in those days," Mona Best recalled, "so they'd fight over a halfpenny."

Inconceivably, the Quarry Men blew off their gig at the Casbah over the equivalent of a whopping seventy-five cents. On the seventh Saturday night that the Quarry Men rocked the Casbah, Ken Brown, who had done a capable job of handling rhythm guitar, turned up suffering from a mighty bout of the flu. He was ordered upstairs, to the Bests' living room, where he lay slumped across a sofa for the rest of the night. The band went on without him, which didn't make a speck of difference to their performance, of course, since a fourth guitar was almost as superfluous as the fact that Ken didn't sing. But he was missed. Ken was "an immensely likeable guy," whose ongoing work around the club had endeared him to Mo Best and Pete, whom he had encouraged to learn the drums. In the spirit of appreciation, "Mo decided to pay [Ken], even though he didn't play," said Pete, who should have heeded the consequences with a keener eye.

According to an observer, John, Paul, and George "went ballistic." Since Ken hadn't played, they argued, he didn't deserve a cut, and they demanded Ken's share of the fee, which amounted to a measly fifteen shillings. It didn't matter that the three others each received the amount due them; even if Mo wouldn't fork over Ken's share, they stood opposed to *his* getting it. Nobody, they insisted, was going to get a free ride.

Mona Best was the last person who would yield to a band's demands, and there was never any effort made to appease them. Said Pete: "She kept Ken's fifteen bob and gave it to him later." When the Quarry Men found out, they decided to ankle their residency. "Right, that's it, then!" Ken Brown remembered Paul shouting before they stormed out of the club.

A few days later, as Pete Best recalled, Ken came up with a solution. They'd form their own band—the Blackjacks—which would get them "back into the business." Initially, Best balked at the offer. He had only recently taken up the drums after months of tattooing the furniture with "pencils, and later drumsticks." At the time, the most he could do was "knock beats out" on his thigh, the way successive generations of teenagers have marked time to "Wipeout." Bright, coordinated, and energetic, Pete could probably muddle his way through some standard rock 'n roll covers, but not capably enough to power a band. But as time wore on, as unexceptional bands passed through the Casbah, the idea seemed to make some sense. Rationalizing, Pete figured that it provided him with a hands-on opportunity to practice and right an unprincipled wrong at the same time, Pete still being "shocked" by the way Ken had been treated by his former bandmates. Little could he have imagined that Brown's dismissal was a mere dress rehearsal for the sacking that would haunt Pete Best for the rest of his life.

[II]

When the Liverpool College of Art reopened in September 1959, John was permitted to enroll in the painting department, working toward a National Diploma in Design, but only on a probationary basis. Having failed his intermediates, only the advocacy of Arthur Ballard allowed him to advance to a permanent area of concentration instead of having to resit the general studies program.

Having stuck his neck out for John, Ballard enlisted the help of his prodigy, Stuart Sutcliffe, to somehow inspire and motivate this problem student. "Stuart was his last hope," says Bill Harry. "[Arthur] knew if anyone could reach John, it was Stu."

Somehow, Sutcliffe hit the right note, and before long the two boys began painting together in late-afternoon sessions conducted in an empty studio on the top floor. Long after the other students had gone home, they worked furiously on technique, experimenting with free expression and a nebula of colors to generate a flow of ideas. In what was essentially a painting tutorial, Stuart introduced John to the basics of image and composition, doling out tips on how to control the brush or direct the flow of paint. Sutcliffe taught him how to grind his own paints, which oils produced the most effective mixtures, how to control and exploit the flow of emulsions. Cynthia, who sat framed by the windows, where soft, blue light filtered in off the street, remembered being "fascinated" by the way John took instruction. "Here with no one watching, no one to entertain, and no one to criticize, [he] could relax and learn," she recalled. "John was having a wonderful time, splashing bold colors across his canvas, throwing sand at it—trying out all sorts of experiments that he would have been too cautious to try in front of anyone else."

They were a breed apart, and Sutcliffe looked it, too. "Stuart wore tinted glasses in honor of his idol, Cybulski, the so-called Polish James Dean, to say nothing of his underground art heroes," Harry recalls. "[He] had a lot of innovative ideas about how to dress," said Rod Murray. "Stuart wore what we called Chelsea boots, Italian pointy-toed [shoes] with side gussets . . . and one of those old flying jackets made out of the inside of a sheep." Cynthia referred to Stuart as "a tiddler" because of his size and frail build, but it never detracted from his stature. As Rod Murray pointed out, there is a difference between being weak and being quiet. "Stuart was not an outwardly forceful personality—not insofar as John was—but he was a *very* strong character. He was small, but determined . . . a very intense person." No art student was more respected or better liked. In whatever class Stuart sat down in—painting, drawing, lifework—"a tremendous energy and intensity" filled the room. He painted with power and conviction, and John knew it. In most cases, that would have been enough to drive John into an envious rage, but Stuart didn't affect him that way. Neither his popularity nor his talent proved threatening to John's ego. He didn't flaunt his artistry or try to stick it under John's nose, and he always encouraged John without making an issue of his deficiencies. It also impressed John that, unlike so many other students he encountered, Stuart wasn't handed everything on a silver platter. He had no grant, no student subsidy. Whatever "milk money" his mother set aside for him was spent on paint. "Stuart never let on how hard he had it," says Bill Harry, "but things were really difficult for him at that time. He had practically no money, and you were only allowed a certain amount of free materials from the college. It was never enough. Canvas was expensive, so his art was done on big sheets of cheap foolscap paper; otherwise, he broke up furniture and painted on the unfinished surface. But as hard up as he was, you were always entitled to half of anything he had." That was Stuart's power: his sincerity.

"John did all the things that Stuart would have loved to have done if he had the courage," Stuart's mother, Millie, recalled. And he had the same passion for music and poetry that Stuart exhibited for art. In fact, John exuded onstage what Stuart felt like in front of an easel, something real and visceral.

By the mid-sixties, the prevailing cultural sensibility would embrace both Shakespeare and Pynchon, Rembrandt and Warhol, Beethoven and the Beatles. But in 1959, in an insular city such as Liverpool, the aesthetic took longer to gain a foothold. The incipient taste was enshrined in popularized "experimental work" such as *The Catcher in the Rye* and *The Outsider,* both of which, according to Bill Harry, "were highly regarded" by Stuart and John. Throughout the fall, the two mates were inseparable, reinforcing each other's pressing passions. And exploring the fringe. John schooled his painting mentor in all the vagaries of rock 'n roll—playing every record he could get his hands on and rhapsodizing about Elvis, Buddy, and Chuck—to which Stuart responded in kind, dragging out museum exhibition catalogues and analyzing John Bratby or Russian abstractionist Nicolas de Stael in great detail, explaining the composition of each picture. In the evenings, they would head over to Ye Cracke, tanking up on half-pints of beer, and then wind up at the Jac, drinking coffee and talking until closing time.

For John, it was an idyllic semester. He practically moved into the little Percy Street flat—"kipping in [Stuart's] room" most weekdays, much to Mimi's consternation—where there was always space to paint, play guitar, or cuddle with Cynthia. It provided a place to exchange ideas and escape the loneliness of Menlove Avenue, and Rod and Stuart were happy to have him around. When they got tired of working or just bored, a party solved the doldrums. They could always count on an interesting mix of acquaintances turning up, not just other art students but people they'd met in Ye Cracke: nurses, dockworkers, faculty—even Paul and George, whose presence confirmed their boost into John's orbit. Music was never a problem. Stuart had an old turntable, Rod a tape recorder, and with John handling music chores, enough records to go all night, which was usually the case.

By early November, however, the parties stopped as every effort was being made to accommodate Sutcliffe, who was preoccupied almost obsessively, often lapsing into long, trancelike work sessions, painting for the prestigious biennial John Moores Exhibition at Liverpool's Walker Art Gallery. Underwritten by the city's most eminent philanthropist, the show was a tour de force of local talent and eagerly anticipated throughout the year. All students at the college were encouraged to submit work, even though it was hardly ever accepted. Stuart, however, was determined to make the final cut and had been struggling with a "monumental painting"— in size alone, its eight-foot-square proportions filled the bill—that captured the impetuosity and restlessness of his generation. His progress was excruciatingly slow, but worth the effort: the canvas had "real resonance," its scrim of irregular shapes on a field of green and blue shading giving off a rhythmic, abstract energy that lent legitimacy to Stuart's mission.

The painting, which was actually done on a board, had to be assembled in two pieces and hinged because of its size. "We carried half of the painting down to the Walker Art Gallery," recalled Rod Murray, whose own entry, a piece of sculpture, had already been rejected. "Something happened, and the other half never [made it, but] the half that got carried down got into the exhibition—and got sold!" And to no less formidable a collector than the show's esteemed sponsor, the John Moores Foundation, which paid £65 for the piece.

Stuart was ecstatic. The fabled arbiter of the local art scene had reached across a vast field of inveterate talent and conferred honor on a young abstractionist. It was the ultimate endorsement. To be selected for the exhibition and achieve critical success, along with his first sale! The combination proved thrilling, to say nothing of a financial boon. "All of a sudden Stuart had some serious money," Murray said. How he spent it would be unforgettable.

[III]

John undoubtedly felt the loss of his friend's attention, but if he was stung or resentful, it didn't show. Eager to harness the progress made at the Casbah, he rechanneled his energy into the band. Paul and George shared his urge to push ahead. But in the fall of 1959, logistics presented some uncommon obstacles. Paul remained close by, at the Liverpool Institute, where he had advanced into the Remove* and joined the regular lunchtime crowd at the art college. But George, who by this time had become an integral part of the band, was unable to tag along.

At the end of the term, no doubt in response to his persistent truancy, George received a particularly dismal report showing how he'd "failed everything"—art, language, literature, math, science, even phys. ed.; attached to the bottom was a scathing rebuke by the headmaster that said: "It is very difficult to give an assessment of this boy's work—because he hasn't done any." If the comment was intended as a wake-up call, it failed. George was already thin-skinned and intellectually insecure; nothing rankled him more than authority. He was especially infuriated by criticism from a teacher—"some old fellow chundering on"—and in retaliation he quit school.

Arthur Kelly says, "His parents were fairly easygoing about it"; however, it is reasonable to assume his father's profound disappointment. Using Louise to run interference, George bumped aimlessly around the neighborhood each day, hoping to stumble into a trade. "At that stage, he didn't have any idea what he wanted to do with his life," says Kelly, who remained a close friend. Everyone weighed in with a suggestion, one more implausible than the next. Days stretched into months. Eventually, at Harry's insistence, George took the city's apprentice exam but failed. Soon afterward, a youth employment officer referred him to a window-dressing job at Blackler's, one of Liverpool's thriving department stores, which led to an apprenticeship there, at a salary of £1.50 a week. The job came as a relief, but having entered the workforce, it became impossible for George to spend his lunch hour singing.

Only rarely that fall was the band able to do something meaningful together. With their boycotting of the Casbah, few gigs provided much of a satisfying audience, or adequate money. A handful of competitions became the band's lifeline, keeping them in front of a crowd, but they were

---

* *The class immediately prior to the sixth form.*

simply going through the motions; there was nothing of substance to be gained from those opportunities.

Determined to break cleanly with the past, they entered the *Star Search* competition as Johnny and the Moondogs. Most likely they appropriated the name from Alan Freed, whose early radio broadcasts on WJW went out in syndication as *The Moondog Show*. It may also have been one of those spur-of-the-moment inspirations that took shape on the registration form. Either way, it was characteristic, just odd enough, combining the right touch of goon humor and irreverence necessary to rattle the traditionalists. "Moondogs," like "Beatles," was a bit playful, a bit absurd. It could go anywhere and not seem out of the groove.

Johnny and the Moondogs performed at the Empire on October 18, the second Sunday of the auditions. The band, "singing brilliantly," qualified for the local finals in two weeks' time and, following a weeklong elimination, snared a berth at the runoff in Manchester. A larger number of acts than expected had turned out at the Manchester Hippodrome on November 15, 1959. Registration was a daylong process. "We got there in the morning," says Ray Ennis, of the Swinging Bluegenes, "and there was a queue right around the whole place. Hundreds of kids, dragging instruments and amps. It was four o'clock before we got inside the front door."

Johnny and the Moondogs took the train from Liverpool, arriving with a small entourage of friends in the nick of time for rehearsals. "Everyone hung around backstage until the audience was admitted," recalls Arthur Kelly. "Then we all went out front in order to whistle and applaud as loud as we could so the Clap-o-Meter would hit a certain level." The band performed a delightful rendition of Buddy Holly's "Think It Over," with John handling the vocal in front of Paul and George's nicely tapered harmonies, and as they came offstage to rousing applause there was a feeling that they could win the top prize. It all depended on the finale, when each act was reintroduced for a deciding round of applause.

But as the show wore on, time weighed in against them. With the introduction of each new act, John's eyes searched out a clock over the stagehands' lit console, nervously noting the hour. The last bus and train left for Liverpool at 9:47; they had to make it or face being stranded in Manchester with less than a pound between them, which was out of the question.

At 9:20 there were still more than a dozen acts set to go on, too many to permit a reappearance. No question about it, time had run out. Their chance for a TV spot was over. As John, Paul, and George stalked out, followed by two or three long-faced friends, there was a lot of bitter grumbling, although John was unusually subdued. As they were going out the stage door, where various instruments had been stacked, John suddenly veered off from the pack. "He'd had his eye on the guitars other [performers] had left there," Kelly says, "and as we hit the exit, he just picked up a little electric cutaway number and out he went."

After two years bashing around that "old tatty piece of junk," John Lennon finally had his first electric guitar—"nicked," he later said, "so the trip wasn't a total loss."

As 1959 drew to a close, the boys spent more time with girlfriends than with one another. John and Cynthia, according to friends closest to the couple, were "besotted with each other." For his part, Paul stopped playing the field and settled down with Dot Rhone. As a couple, they had an appealingly unthreatening air. They discovered each other to be solicitous and sensual, gentle and clumsy, with Paul at times taking on a paternal and sympathetic role. Once, at a friend's house, Dot happened to mention that she'd been standing all day and he began to massage her feet, stroking them as though they were precious pets. And yet, at the time the gesture felt almost preposterous.

Eventually Paul's attention grew relentless, almost disparaging. His simple gregariousness turned uncompromising and willful. Paul was immensely charming, but there was a darker side. He had a need—Dot believes a compulsion—to control every situation. As John had done with Cynthia, he began to pick out her clothes, redesign her makeup. Dot remembers how much it pleased Paul to stand beside her and study her appearance, then, in a roundabout way, critique the way she looked—and suggest how to improve upon it. On one occasion, he insisted that she have her hair done and produced money to pay for it. Not wanting to displease him, Dot went off to the beauty parlor. "Unfortunately, they did [my hair] in a terrible-looking beehive," she says. "Paul was furious when he saw it. He told me to go home and not to call him until it grew out again."

She detected other changes in Paul that proved equally disagreeable. He had an almost stuffy, explosive air of self-importance, with his simple superiority, cool poise, and weatherproof rightness. He scorned any sign of self-confidence in her. And Dot, pricked by love, submitted. As a rule, she did not impose her will on him, certainly never when they were among friends. She would sit quietly and smile tensely for entire evenings at the Jacaranda while Paul and John discussed music. If Paul glared, she would freeze like a rabbit. "We weren't allowed to open our mouths," Dot says of her and Cynthia's attendance at these nightly discussions. "They'd talk all night, and we just listened."

One day, just before the end of the year, John announced that Stuart Sutcliffe was moving into a spacious student flat near school, where they'd have plenty of room to rehearse. Without delay, everyone decided to meet over there and check it out.

Stuart's flat was on the first floor of a Georgian-style town house called Hillary Mansions, located directly catercorner to the art college at 3 Gambier Terrace. When the guys walked in, they found a strikingly familiar student layout: a warren of sparsely furnished rooms, two "bohemian" girls—Diz Morris and Margaret Duxburry, who had moved in to help shoulder the "ridiculously expensive" £3-a-week rent—a revolving-door cast of visitors, and enough disarray to reinforce its reputation as a crash pad. But whereas Stuart's previous flat had been a cramped one-room affair, this place was rambling: a huge high-ceilinged living room warmed by a fireplace faced the front, along with a smaller bedroom, which the two girls quickly claimed. At the end of a long corridor was the kitchen, a bathroom, and an enormous back room with two walk-in closets. "Stuart had the big back room," said Rod Murray, "and we put all the easels in there." A gallery of paintings went up on the walls.

John, Paul, and George started playing in the back room almost from the day Stuart moved in. They met there each evening, after Blackler's closed, and lit into two dozen or more songs culled from an expanding repertoire of current hits. No one remembers them working on originals, although it is likely that a few were sprinkled in the mix. Nevertheless, they touched off a festive atmosphere each night, as friends poured into the flat to listen and dance. To many, it was "like a never-ending party," but almost immediately "we got complaints from above and below," Rod Murray recalled.

By then, John had more or less moved into Gambier Terrace, sharing the back room with Stuart, who was happy for the company. Although John had shown little interest in literature while at Quarry Bank, he tore greedily through Stuart's books, including Lucretius's *On the Nature of the Universe,* one of the titles with cachet that Stuart had thrust at him rather daringly one night, with the challenge to "expand his Scouser mind."

John was doing more than expanding his mind. By the end of 1959, it was evident to him that if the band were to be elevated in any meaningful way, they'd need to make adjustments. Without a bass and drums, it just wasn't rock 'n roll. They needed to revamp—or forget the whole thing.

Sometime right after Christmas, he and Stuart were meandering through the frost-rimed cemetery in the Anglican cathedral, directly across the street from Gambier Terrace. It was a favorite haunt of theirs; the boys spent hours, sometimes entire afternoons, walking around the windy, saucer-shaped slopes that hemmed the church near the front courtyard. They could see the glinting dome of the Royal Insurance Company Building in the distance, and beyond it the brooding Mersey, with a queue of boats trawling the Narrows channel.

Ordinarily, John loved to peruse the sooty headstones half-buried in the spongy ground. No matter how many he examined, there were untold more to keep him entertained. But this day, he seemed distracted. While Stuart crouched by an overgrown plot, John stared off into the landscape. Finally, haltingly, he said, "Now [that] you've got all this money, Stu, you can buy a [bass] and join our group."

It was a calculated risk in more ways than one. He certainly didn't want Stuart to feel taken advantage of. And there was a greater harmony to consider. Would he fit in with Paul and George? The fellows all got along well—as friends. That simplified their social lives, but bands had a personality all their own and required communication of an entirely different kind. Painting was one thing, but rhythm? Could Stuart pick up the beat or carry a tune? For that matter, would he be able to learn how to play the instrument? These were all questions that John had no answers to.

But Stuart took only a long moment to mull it over before responding to John's offer. "Stuart thought it was a wonderful idea," his sister Pauline remembered. "If anything, it was the image, not the music, that was attractive to him. He liked the whole [concept] of pop and Buddy Holly and Elvis—how they looked." Years before aesthetics became the cornerstone of rock 'n roll, Stuart knew that image was everything. As for the bass, Stuart decided it'd be relatively easy to learn. His mother had insisted on piano lessons, which he'd taken scrupulously since the age of nine. There was the bugle that he'd played in the Air Training Corps. And his father had "taught him a few chords on [the] guitar." The hardest part about the bass, he figured, was getting hold of one.

As it turned out, that was the least of his problems. He found a sunburst Hofner President at Hessy's Music Store that filled the bill nicely. Stories about how he turned over the entire Moores commission in exchange for the bass are legion. According to one version, his father found the guitar while snooping around Stuart's room and pitched a fit about its price. In fact, using a bit of creative financing, a monthly purchase plan was worked out with Frank Hesselberg so that only a modest £5 deposit snared him the bass.

Stuart may well have been the natural choice, but his decision to play music perplexed his fellow artists. Bill Harry, for one, remembers the irritation he felt when Stuart flashed the new bass as though exhibiting a finished oil painting. "I said to him, 'What the bloody hell are you doing?'" Harry recalls. "'You're passionate about *art,* not music!'" Stuart shook off such concern with bemused disregard. To Harry's objection, he responded soothingly: "No, it's all right. I think it's art." He had decided to dedicate himself to the band with "as much seriousness and intensity" as he approached painting. "And anyway," Stuart told him, "they're going to be the greatest. I want to be a part of it."

[I]

After Stuart joined the group, a proper name seemed more appropriate. One night in February, while sitting around the Gambier Street flat, John and Stuart brainstormed to come up with something that worked better than Johnny and the Moondogs. John later told Hunter Davies that he was "just thinking about what a good name the Crickets [Buddy Holly's band] would be for an English group, [when] the idea of beetles came into my head." It may have been no more complicated than that, or as other accounts contend, Stuart might have suggested beetles from the slang term given to biker chicks in *The Wild One*. In either event, it was John's idea to change the spelling "to make it look like beat music, just as a joke," although when they printed it on a card to show the other boys, it became Beatals.

Paul remembers being told of the name the next day, along with George, and immediately liking it. "John and Stuart came out of their flat and said, 'We've just thought of a name!'" he recalls, smiling. *The Beatals.* It had the right sound, its reference a dazzling throwback. The name was bluff and cheeky, sturdy; it possessed an easy, buoyant, ornamental quality. *The Beatals.* Yes, he thought, it would do, it would do nicely.

But names do not gigs get. Even with a conversation piece like "the Beatals," the band was still not able to compete for legitimate work. There was still the hitch with the drums, or lack thereof. And while Stuart looked swell with an electric bass slung across his body, there was the matter of actually playing it that needed to be worked out. Instead of the bass notes accenting the beat, as is the purpose, Stuart's leaden thumb thunked the chunky strings, producing little more than a steady but tedious heartbeat. There was no flourish or glide to his phrasing, just that monotonous pulse: *thunk-thunk-thunk-thunk.* Even so, John never grew discouraged. In a reversal of their painting roles, John began to fine-tune Stuart's technique, working diligently with him each evening to teach him the set of songs. The sole objective now was to get him ready to face an audience; without that, there was no point in holding everything together.

The only gig to speak of was at the end of February 1960, a short spot offered by Jim McCartney's Labour Club, which only Paul and George attended. This was a world apart from their Quarry Men gigs and certainly any they would ever play as the Beatles. But as a favor to Paul's dad, the boys pulled up stools and played "Peg o' My Heart" to the delight of two dozen, middle-aged Scousers.

It wasn't until March that the Beatals got a shove in the right direction. Early that month news rocketed through the city that Eddie Cochran and Gene Vincent would headline a show at the Liverpool Empire. The concert was a milestone for local bands, which thronged to the theater like mayflies. Here, live and in person, was confirmation of their calling—and everyone heard an identical call.

The Beatals began by rewiring the sound of the band. "They knew that to get any attention, they needed amplifiers," Bill Harry recalls. "This really hit home after the Eddie Cochran show." Up to then, they'd relied on whatever P.A. system, if any, was provided by a hall; otherwise, their increased output was a result of just strumming or singing louder. That method, however, no longer carried any weight with an audience. They wanted it loud; they wanted some juice behind the music.

But how? Amplifiers cost money. The boys were just about getting by on fumes, and everyone was already into "Hessy" for one hire-purchase loan or another. There was no way he'd float them enough for an amplifier. Frustrated and resentful of their situation, John hatched a plan. Weren't they considered the art college band? The Student Union had a discretionary fund to purchase equipment. Certainly, an amplifier was within its jurisdiction.

Both Bill Harry and Stuart Sutcliffe were members of the Student Union committee. "At the next meeting, in the library," Harry recalls, "Stuart and I proposed and seconded a motion that we use our funds to buy P.A. equipment for the art college dances." It sounded like a good idea to the other students. No one raised any opposition. *Voilà!* The Beatals had amps, and not just a tiny Truvoices, the staple of most Liverpool bands, but a professional getup, with cabinets and eighteen-inch speakers.

To show their appreciation, the band played an art college dance that same month, in the school's basement auditorium. The place was packed to capacity. Fresh from a series of midterms, students welcomed the opportunity to unwind, but there was also an air of anticipation—and great spectacle—about the musical debut of Stuart Sutcliffe. Everyone showed up, including Arthur Ballard, who told colleagues he was "troubled" by his prize student's "distraction."

Ballard had good reason to be concerned. Stuart hadn't touched a paintbrush in weeks. A usually disciplined worker, now days—even weeks—elapsed between sessions at the easel; visits to life classes, once as routine as breathing, had become increasingly erratic. It seemed to Ballard and others that Stuart had turned his back on that world. And his hands—those delicate instruments through which his expression flowed to the canvas—were in terrible shape. Bill Harry remembers encountering Stuart at the college dance, bent over his guitar in such a way as to conceal wrenching pain. "He told me, 'Oh, the skin has come off all my fingers,'" Harry recalls, having noticed blood on Stuart's hands. "He hadn't built up proper calluses. He'd plunged right in, never realizing that conditioning was necessary." Or if he had realized it, it was with the knowledge that the other boys did not want to slow their stride to wait for him.

The four boys would rehearse for hours at Gambier Terrace, really winding it up, then camp out at the Jacaranda, talking until closing time, well past one in the morning. They'd commandeer a table that would grow like dominoes as each new friend appeared, requiring additional chairs and tables. "Art students were inclined to drop in . . . and loll around a bit," says Beryl Williams, whose role fell somewhat precariously between that of den mother and disenchanted bar manager. She loved having students and musicians there, provided that they buy something to eat, which meant putting the squeeze on them every so often. Bill Harry recalls that when flush, they'd order the "student specialty—toast," which cost fourpence and a penny extra for jam. According to Allan Williams: "They'd go into a great big huddle . . . and decide if they could afford to have jam or whether it would be best to stick to toast and butter." Always a premium, jam toast was usually split five ways.

The "sort of musical revolution" Williams discovered unfolding in small local basement clubs was intriguing, inasmuch as it complemented his stake in the Jacaranda. However, it wasn't until he attended the Gene Vincent–Eddie Cochran show at the Empire that he experienced an epiphany. Sitting ringside, walled in by rows of clearly overwrought teenagers, Williams was flabbergasted. "I began to realise the implications," he recalled, taking the temperature and doing the math. Everyone was rockin' and rolling, "and I simply had to get in on it."

Williams wasted no time attaching himself to the scene. He booked Liverpool Stadium for a night in May, then traveled to London, where he sought out a meeting with no less a figure than megapromoter Larry Parnes.

Before Brian Epstein and Robert Stigwood, before the dozens of future British pop moguls who dominated the music business, Larry Parnes ruled the scene. LARRY PARNES PRESENTS toplined every bill featuring a rock 'n roll act in London. Only twenty-four years old, Parnes—or "Flash Larry," as he was known—was a modern-day Svengali. Cruising the bedrock of London coffee bars, he signed up a stable of good-looking male singers—pretty faces, actually—that he could groom into teen idols, regardless of talent, as he'd done so successfully with Tommy Steele. "In most cases, what attracted Larry was their potential to whip audiences into a frenzy," says Hal Carter, who served as Parnes's right-hand man. "But he was gay and loved pretty boys, which became his stock-in-trade."

By 1960, Parnes had a cluster of glittery stars, each with an outlandish stage name he'd created in the hope of adding that undefinable pizzazz: Marty Wilde, Vince Eager, Duffy Power, Dickie Pride, Nelson Keene, and Johnny Gentle. Recalls Carter: "Larry was on tour in New York and had heard the [Elvis] Presley tune, 'Fame and Fortune.' He immediately sent a telegram back to the office that said: CLIVE POWELL NOW GEORGIE FAME."

His most accomplished creation, however, was turning Ronnie Wycherly, an ex–tugboat hand with a sludgy Scouse accent, into pop sensation Billy Fury. Parnes had discovered the lad backstage at a Marty Wilde show in Birkenhead and "immediately fell in love." Billy had little in the way of a voice and, if it were at all possible, even less stage presence, but his "high cheekbones and restless eyes" were all Parnes needed to throw the star-making machinery into gear. He swathed the youngster in gold lamé, framed his hair in a mane of wild forelocks, brought him a riot of American hits to cover, and packaged him on the high-powered Cochran-Vincent tour that was crisscrossing the U.K. In no time, Billy Fury was being mentioned in the same heated breath as Cliff Richard.

Insecure and basically uneducated, plagued by a round, pudgy face, Parnes was "a very elegant dresser," coming, as he did, from what friends described as "a good Jewish family in the *shmatte* business." He had bronzed, olive skin and a perpetual five o'clock shadow. Williams found his manner to have "much of the smooth persuasiveness of a lawyer" and was delighted that Parnes was amenable to his pitch. For a "fee of about £500," Williams booked a show he dubbed "the Merseyside and International Beat Show." It was a rather grandiose name for a rehash of the Cochran-Vincent tour, although Parnes attached another half a dozen artists from his stable, along with local attractions Cass and the Cassanovas and Rory Storm and the Hurricanes to give it a homegrown touch. The show was scheduled for May 3, and by early April all indications were that it would sell out. Ticket sales were strong—there were six thousand seats available—and it appeared profits would exceed all projections.

Perhaps with luck running in such an unlikely surge, disaster was inevitable. On April 17, a television show Williams was half listening to was interrupted to report "the tragic death of Eddie Cochran." Cochran and Gene Vincent had been on their way to Heathrow Airport following a concert in Bristol when their speeding car blew a tire and crashed into a lamppost. Cochran died from massive head injuries; Vincent suffered a broken collarbone and was hospitalized, along with Cochran's girlfriend, Sharon Sheeley, who had been a passenger in the car. Williams couldn't believe it. "Robbed of [his] two top stars," there would be no way to recover. He flushed with guilt for even thinking that way, but he couldn't help himself.

Despondent, Williams called Larry Parnes, who commiserated. Neither man had to say what each was privately thinking: this tragedy was going to cost them a bundle. Indirectly, Parnes suggested that if Vincent were healthy, they might still be able to pull something off, but he couldn't make any promises. Days went by without word while Williams made arrangements to dissolve his obligations with stadium vendors. Rumors persisted that Vincent's condition was worse than reported and that he would return to the United States as soon as he was able to travel. Then Parnes called with an update: Vincent was okay and had agreed to do the show. To fill the gaping hole left by Eddie Cochran, they added two more of Parnes's acts to the bill—Julian X and Dean Webb—as well as local groups Derry and the Seniors, Bob Evans and the Five Shillings, Mal Perry, and Gerry and the Pacemakers. As Bill Harry recalls: "Everyone who was anyone was invited to perform."

Not quite everyone. It never even dawned on Williams to include the Beatals on the program. Without a drummer, they wouldn't stand a chance alongside other major bands. To spare the lads the embarrassment, he made sure they had good seats. In the audience. Punters. Fans. Like everyone else.

[II]

All the same, the concert prevailed as "a seminal event." It was the first time, says a local musician, "that all the Liverpool bands became aware of one another." After the stadium show, the local scene was invigorated by a sense of community. According to Adrian Barber, the Cassanovas' guitarist: "As the groups started to communicate with one another, they shared information about places to play. Phone numbers were exchanged, schedules coordinated." They flocked to one another's gigs. Since everyone played basically the same set, new songs became not only community property but currency. Bands burst out of obscurity by introducing the latest unknown American hit, then passed it around to fellow acolytes, to underscore its provenance.

By virtue of Williams's new status, the Jacaranda became headquarters to the fraternal order of Liverpool bands that emerged immediately after the Stadium show. Gathering ad hoc in the early afternoon, minutes after most had only just crawled out of bed, they would graze around tables like docile water buffalo and recharge themselves on cups of inky espresso followed by a trough of eggs, bacon, and beans on toast, animatedly rehashing the highlights of last night's gig, discussing the current hit parade, or airing the usual complaints about insulting pay and horrible work conditions.

John, Paul, and Stuart often sat on the periphery of these discussions. Socially aloof, young, and lacking credentials, they were seldom invited into the galaxy of the coffee bar's guiding stars. They seemed to be waiting for a signal, a nod of approval—from a body of peers, not gurus—that they were worthy of joining the party.

Ultimately, Brian Casser of Cass and the Cassanovas gave them that nod. Cass was the first to express, even vaguely, the possibility that the Beatals might contain a gleam of real talent. A week earlier, sitting in the Jac with some cronies, he heard them rehearse, belting out a version of "Tutti Frutti" in the basement, and was struck by the haunting falsetto delivery of Paul McCartney. "It was [the type of] voice we'd never heard before," says a musician who happened to be sitting next to Casser. "None of us sang like that; we sang full-voiced, street. This was something unique to our ears, and it got Cass's attention."

Cass told them not to test the market without a drummer and offered to help find one from among Liverpool's lean talent pool. He also cautioned them against going out with their "ridiculous" name. A band's name,

Cass believed, must focus attention on its leader, like Buddy Holly and the Crickets.

Encouraged by the interest, John listened. When Cass returned to his table he told friends that "he had convinced Lennon to call the band Long John and the Silver Beetles."

Convinced—maybe for a moment. John, after all, was practical and fired by personal ambition. If Cass could deliver a drummer, then pissing him off was not in John's best interest. But while he was willing to do almost anything to advance the cause of the band, he was not about to demean it by posing as Long John Silver. A peg-leg pirate from a children's tale? Never. He did admit to himself that Beatals gave them no handle to grab hold of. Everyone agreed it didn't look right on the page. So, for the time being, they struck a compromise, calling themselves the Silver Beetles. Apparently that was enough to satisfy Cass, and a few days later he delivered on his promise by finding them a drummer named Tommy Moore.

It is not entirely clear who Moore was. Like many musicians who hung around the scene, he was familiar to others by his face, but few had ever heard Tommy actually play. Part of the reason was his age. Already thirty-six, he was well outside the core rock 'n roll demographic—twice Paul's age—and part of another world as far as performance bands went. He also had a day job, operating a forklift at the Garston bottle works, which made him unfamiliar to the Jac's daytime crowd. Still, he had all the qualifications: he was small but stocky, with powerful, responsive wrists and impeccable timing. "Tommy Moore was a pro," says one of the Cassanovas, "what we call a session drummer today. He had played in dance bands, at social clubs. He could put the beat in the right place, and he could play anything."

It's a good thing he could. John, Paul, George, and Stuart were mildly shocked when Tommy showed up to meet them at the Gambier Terrace flat. No one had quite expected such an old guy, and they were unprepared—perhaps even a bit frustrated—by his lounge-act repertoire. Tommy had only just begun to show an interest in rock 'n roll. But during an impromptu audition, he drew knowingly on fifteen years of experience and impressed the boys with his chops and ability to play almost anything they threw at him. This was especially clear when they segued into "Cathy's Clown," with its tricky cha-cha beat, and Tommy hung right in there with them. Stripped of frills and flash, Tommy's straightforward drumming made no attempt to upstage the rest of the band. But he would do.

Sometime during the merriment following the Stadium concert, Larry Parnes had pulled Williams aside and praised his efforts, expressing admiration for the Liverpool bands. He'd been especially impressed by how tight they'd played, how professionally they'd handled themselves. Finally, he had suggested that there might be something they could do together on a few upcoming tours. That is, of course, if Williams represented these bands.

Represented. A light went off in Allan's head. Why not, indeed? With all the local bands pecking aimlessly for work, he could roll them, by contract, into a company and build his own northern talent stable, much as Parnes had done in London. The beauty of it was, it required no real investment on his part. It was what he'd counted on all along: "the crock of gold at the end of the rainbow."

With the incentive from Parnes, Allan began to consider the options. There were a number of bands he planned on approaching, all obvious choices, all part of the small but close-knit community. But for the first time, he thought about the up-and-coming groups that used the Jac's basement for rehearsal. He also began to reevaluate, in light of the potential market, the young bands to whom he had given the cold shoulder only weeks, even days, before. In a stroke of providence, his musings were interrupted by a visit from Stuart Sutcliffe.

—◆—

Stuart had been after Williams about giving the Silver Beetles a break, and as usual, Allan's responses were polite but noncommittal. But after the Stadium concert, Sutcliffe's appeals grew relentless. The band had felt humiliated watching the action from the sidelines; they were desperate to get going. "But you *must* have a drummer," Williams insisted. "If you haven't got a drummer, then you'll have to go and find one."

Still "very dubious about the group," Williams ran their name past Brian Casser, who gave him a quick thumbs-up. To Allan, Cass was "the prophet," the only forthright musician in this scene on whom he could rely.

Not a moment too soon. A day after Tommy Moore showed up, Williams received a letter from London. Inside, on a page of plush, woven-linen stock used as personal stationery by the aristocracy, was an invitation that would ultimately alter the course of popular music. It was from one of Larry Parnes's henchmen, Mark Forster, stating that both Duffy Power and Johnny Gentle had scheduled Scottish tours for June, which necessitated an urgent search for backing bands. "For these two periods, as agreed, we are willing to pay your groups £120.0d plus the fares from Liverpool," he proposed. "Should you agree to these suggestions we will arrange for both Duffy and Johnny, who incidentally is a Liverpool boy, to travel up to Liverpool to rehearse with your groups towards the end of May." Equally tantalizing was news that Larry Parnes would attend, too. Not only that, he was bringing Billy Fury with him, "as Billy will want one of these four groups for his own personal use."

Williams had initially suggested they choose from among a pool of Liverpool's best bands: Cass and the Cassanovas, Gerry and the Pacemakers, Cliff Roberts and the Rockers, and Derry and the Seniors—all of whom he'd persuaded to be represented by his new management firm, Jacaranda Enterprises. Later that day, he stopped by Gambier Terrace to deliver the news to Stuart Sutcliffe, albeit with one significant change: he intended to extend the list and include the Silver Beetles.

[III]

The audition had been scheduled for the early afternoon of May 10, 1960, at the Jacaranda, but because of severe space problems and an inescapable funky heat, it was shifted to a new location a few blocks away. Flush from his new endeavors, Allan Williams had taken a lease on two other places, the Wyvern Social Club on reedy-thin Seel Street (where the audition would be held) and another building down the block he intended to call the Maggie May, after a popular local legend.

It was one of those rare Liverpool days when the weather let up and the sky brightened. Outside, the crosscurrents triggered a strong sentimental tug: a lemony scent of blossoms and pine intermingled with the briny Mersey air. A blanket of warm escorting winds had transformed the dreary landscape from sober seaport to a true urban glen, inviting gulls and terns to kite weightlessly overhead, their tiny frames held motionless against the gentle breeze.

Inside the dark, shingled Wyvern there was the tumult of renovation, accompanied by the churning and chuffing of machinery. In its former life, the place had functioned as a workingman's drinking club, with the kind of heavy-timbered decor that made thirsty punters feel right at home; now, in need of total repair, it was undergoing an expedited face-lift so that Williams could open in time for the hearty summer crowds. He'd decided to rename it the Blue Angel and to make it an upscale cabaret. Williams envisioned opening a more sophisticated hangout, a nightclub like New

York's Copacabana or Latin Quarter, where elegance and privilege played a prominent role. Rock 'n roll was an aberration to his ears, moribund, just noise for the teenage crowd; when its novelty appeal ran out, he believed, there would always be an audience of big spenders that appreciated the standards.

Because work was ongoing in the club, the musicians set up just past the bar, on the top level, against the rear wall. The Silver Beetles arrived a few minutes after eleven o'clock, minus Tommy Moore, who was retrieving his drums from another club over on Dale Street. Howie Casey, who was already inside with the Seniors, recalls seeing them come in and noticing how dissimilar they looked from the other groups. "They blew in, rough and tumble, dressed like gangsters, in black shirts, black jeans, and two-tone shoes," he remembers. Everyone else showed up in a suit. But if the boys felt underdressed, they didn't show it. "John, Paul, George, and Stuart sat laughing together on a little bench seat along the side of the room. Everyone else was crowded on the other side, ready to play. Initially, there was a lot of chatter from among our ranks when they showed up. We didn't know [the Silver Beetles], and I don't think anybody else knew them either."

As the audition loomed near, the bands were introduced to the guests of honor—Larry Parnes and Billy Fury who "sat stone-faced" three-quarters of the way back on folding chairs. So strong was the aura of celebrity that even a solicitous John Lennon pressed Billy Fury for an autograph, which he graciously signed.

The good news was the announcement by Parnes that in addition to the Scottish tours, Fury sought a Liverpool band to back him in Blackpool for the summer season. Everyone's face lit up with expectation. The promise of a trip to Blackpool was magic in the north of England. "Just up the road," it was a magnet for Scousers on a budget, a blue-collar "holiday resort" with fairgrounds, "Kiss Me Quick" hats, and racks of naughty postcards of the kind depicting fat men riding the slogan "Haven't seen my Little Willie in years." A three-month gig there would be icing on the cake. "Most important of all," says Howie Casey, "we could justify to our families that there was money in music."

The Cassanovas were up first and were horribly off their show. The Seniors, who followed them, sounded almost hot by comparison. The band was perfectly tight and live-wire, yet vocal flaws eventually shone through and they ended up sounding shrieky and shrill, with none of the hot, honking nitro needed to kick out the jams. Gerry and the Pacemakers, on the other hand, were loaded in the vocal department but without a dynamic musical spark. And Cliff Roberts and the Rockers couldn't match the highlights on either end.

Stuart sat quietly, sketching a charcoal portrait of Larry Parnes while his mates studied the competition. All the pressure was on the other bands. They had nothing to lose. Still, they had to reconcile a larger dilemma that threatened to foil their chance of an upset: with only minutes to spare, Tommy Moore hadn't appeared. There had been no word from him—not even a call to give them an update.

By the time they were summoned to perform, the Silver Beetles could read their fate in Allan Williams's stooped shoulders. They'd never make an impression without a drummer. It was useless even to try. Desperate, John asked Johnny Hutchinson of the Cassanovas to stand in for the AWOL Moore. It was a bold move, considering Hutch's reputation. He was a spitfire: he could become an ugly customer without any provocation. As Adrian Barber notes, "Johnny did and played whatever the fuck he wanted to do and play, and that was it, brother." Most people knew to stay out of his way. But John was left no other choice. They had no drummer, and Johnny Hutch was the best in the room.

No one knows why he agreed to John's request. According to Howie Casey, "It was Johnny Hutch's [drum] kit that was there, so he reluctantly got up and played." That sounds likely enough, but no matter what the reason, it did the trick. The band launched into a relentless set that left their predecessors in the dust—four songs, all up-tempo, with John and Paul trading vocals in the seamless way that was to become their trademark. There are so many varying reports of their performance that the only thing eyewitnesses can agree upon is that they were there. Adrian Barber concedes that "they blew everyone away," while in Howie Casey's estimation, "They weren't brilliant, it sounded underrehearsed." Only a few pictures of the session exist. On viewing them, it is impossible to draw anything conclusive about their sound, but the familiar body language reveals volumes. John and Paul stand shoulder to shoulder, cocked fiercely over their guitars, feet splayed and churning, in a gritty pose that defined garage bands for years to come. They look determined, unfaltering, comfortably in the groove. George, to their left, concentrates gamely on a lick, while Stuart and Johnny Hutch filled the gaps between the rhythm.

Billy Fury heard it immediately and cued Parnes that the Silver Beetles were a natural fit. Parnes, ever cautious, remained unconvinced. "I thought the boys in front were great," he told a writer many years later. "The lead guitar and the bass, so-so." Stuart had played in "a most off-putting style," wandering toward the rear of the stage, with his back to the room either to create a bit of mystique or to conceal his lack of ability. Meanwhile, Tommy Moore stalked in, looking disheveled and breathing heavily from his sprint across town, and went straight to the drums, where he took over for Johnny Hutch. Together at last, they had time for one more song, but it was anticlimactic. Afterward, Parnes noted that the magic seemed to collapse. "It was the drummer . . . who was wrong," he'd concluded.

Given how chaotic their audition turned out, the Silver Beetles were received with surprising kindness by Parnes. They weren't perfect, by any stretch of the imagination, but there was something intriguing to work with, something that suited his artist's style. "Quite suddenly," Allan Williams recalled, "[Parnes] said he'd take the Beatles [sic] as Billy Fury's backing group—but that he only wanted four [band members]. No bass."

There are numerous accounts of what happened next, though most remain sketchy at best. According to Williams, John stepped forward like a knight-errant and turned him down cold. The message was bluntly clear: as far as the Silver Beetles were concerned, it was an all-or-nothing proposition. Stuart was a mate, a musketeer: one for all, and all for one. Parnes later said he had no recollection of this mythic showdown and insisted that Tommy Moore, not Stuart, had soured the band's chances. Instead, Parnes cast his blessing on Cass and the Cassanovas.

With sentiments running in such contrary directions, some clarity was needed. Williams and Parnes stole off to the Jacaranda, where they attempted to sort out a deal: who would play with whom and where and for how much. There were myriad configurations that might work. The bands trailed the two promoters to the tiny, deserted coffee bar and sat around tables near the door, speculating about their chances and casting glances at the two men huddled like warlords in the back. In the end, there was confusion in the cards. Parnes did a swift about-face and decided that no Liverpool band was needed to back Billy Fury. Instead, he offered the Scottish tours to Cass and the Cassanovas and the Silver Beetles, who would open for Duffy Power and Johnny Gentle, respectively.

The Silver Beetles were understandably ecstatic. In their eyes, Johnny Gentle, while hardly a household name, was an up-and-coming recording star. When Williams brought them the offer, they greeted it with jubilation, all except for Stuart, who felt he'd lost them the big-time Fury gig. Stuart's mother recalled that he apologized to John for letting the band down. "Forget it, Stu," John reportedly told him, ending any discussion of the subject. They'd been offered a legitimate tour at the astounding sum of £90 a week. For a Liverpool band, it was an unprecedented deal. Ten days on the road, most expenses paid by Parnes, playing in front of adoring audiences, hotels, girls, invaluable experience, proper exposure. An unprecedented deal from any angle.

——▬——

Crowning a burst of energy and artifice, arrangements were hastily made. George and Tommy took time off from their jobs, Paul sweet-talked his father into a holiday before the upcoming exams, while John and Stuart simply cut classes. The problem of equipment was similarly solved when they decided to "borrow" the art school P.A. All the pieces fell neatly into place. Suddenly everything seemed possible. They were actually going on the road—a road from which they would never look back.

[IV]

It began with a baby step.

Sometime after daybreak on May 20, John, Paul, George, Stuart, and Tommy assembled on a platform outside Liverpool's Lime Street Station, where the glossy black Midland "locos" sat huffing, steam rising in plumes against the sharp morning chill. The platform was a confusion of commuters, businessmen, sightseers, porters, conductors, and freight handlers in whose midst the boys stood, slightly bewildered by their role. Their gear was sprawled around them in a circle of fluent disarray. In consensus, the band had decided to travel light; few personal items infiltrated the tangle of incidental clothes jammed into old satchels. John and Stuart had brought along sketch pads, Paul a couple of books.

Before they boarded the train, the subject of names arose. *Names:* there was never any question that the band would be known as anything but the Silver Beetles; however, that did not limit them, as musicians, from adopting temporary personal stage names. Most likely the idea originated with Stuart Sutcliffe, who had a penchant for affectation and image. He decided to call himself Stuart de Stael, after his painting idol, the Russian abstract classicist. John had already rejected using a pseudonym, as did Tommy, but Paul and George were game. The two mates from Speke, stepping out, called themselves Paul Ramon and Carl Harrison (after Carl Perkins), respectively.

The train was insufferably hot and depressing, the stale air not only bone-dry but hard to breathe. There were none of the modern conveniences that cushioned rail travel between cities such as Liverpool and London. The boys surrendered to an inherent restlessness as the last ripples of civilization flattened into grim, barren tundra. Hundreds of lonely miles rolled by between Carlisle, Queensberry, Broughton, and Lanark. Only John was used to the long, desolate route that stretched for hours into the countryside, having made a similar trip each summer to visit his cousin Stanley in Edinburgh.

They landed in Glasgow a rude ten hours after leaving home, then transferred to a rugged little local line and transferred again in Central Fife as the train snaked slowly up the east coast of Scotland, past the villages and one-street towns that skirted the veiny river Clyde. Alloa was provincial, the sticks, a stagnant little industrial town at the crook of the Firth of Forth, the inlet from the North Sea that fed into Edinburgh. The tired, sallow streets, lined with thin, half-timbered houses, had been starved by the more colorful urban centers farther west that beckoned to young families. More than half of the fourteen thousand Alloans served the fringe of hosiery mills that huddled along the riverbanks; the rest, like good Scots everywhere, distilled whiskey or fished.

Parnes broke in all his acts on the Scottish dance-hall circuit, where there were more than six thousand such small venues for bands to play. It provided steady work and an opportunity to develop an act away from London's unforgiving stare. You could go on the road for months, playing one-nighters in outposts like Newcastleton, Musselburgh, Sunderland, Melrose, Stirling, and Dundee, hopscotching across the whole of northeastern Scotland, and never have to repeat a stop. For Johnny Gentle, by no means yet a star, Parnes had scheduled a seven-city tour of "border dances," social gatherings in little halls that held 200 to 300 kids who could shuttle between upstairs rooms featuring a rock 'n roll show and a downstairs auditorium where traditional bands played the Scottish reel.

Arriving in Alloa late that afternoon, weary from the trip, there was no time for the band to get acclimated to the alien surroundings. They went right to work, transferring directly to the local town hall, where they were scheduled to go on within an hour.

Gentle (born John Askew) was waiting for them in a canteen behind the stage. With his velvety black hair, eyes and cheekbones sculpted in flawless proportion, a sleepy, inviting smile, and, of course, personality on the order of Cliff Richard, he was the very model of a Larry Parnes artist.

A Liverpool dropout, he had apprenticed as a ship's carpenter on the *Rindel Pacifico,* a plush passenger steamer on the Britain–South America run, and took to entertaining folks on deck in his spare time. Parnes discovered Johnny during a layover in London in 1958 and signed him to a modest record deal with the Philips label. He made two records in quick succession—"Wendy" and "Milk from the Coconut"—and though neither struck gold, they'd mined a respectable enough audience to hold Parnes's interest.

Johnny and the Silver Beetles had half an hour to hammer out an agreeable set of songs and work out arrangements. They needed enough material for two one-hour shows, and even though the Silver Beetles had practiced Johnny's repertoire in advance, there were copious all-important details about the performance yet to solve. Johnny relied on a sleepy mix of rock 'n roll and country standards that included Jim Reeves's "He'll Have to Go," "(I Don't Know Why I Love You) But I Do," popularized by Clarence "Frogman" Henry, and the current Presley release, "I Need Your Love Tonight." A die-hard Ricky Nelson fan, he proposed they do "Be-Bop Baby" and "I Got a Feeling" but couldn't get a decent enough take of "Poor Little Fool" in time for the performance, substituting Bobby Darin's "Dream Lover," which had, at one time, been a trusty Quarry Men number. As the band worked furiously to get up to speed, a squad of stiff-backed women made haggis pies to serve during the interval.

The first set went remarkably well for an act that had just met. "The crowd was lovely," remembers Askew. "They knew who I was. And the Beatles [sic] sounded as good as any group that was thrown at me by Parnes." That said, it came as something of a surprise when, a day later, he got a phone call from a rather disgruntled Larry Parnes. "I'm thinking of sending the Beatles [sic] back to Liverpool and getting you another group up there," Askew recalls being told. "[The promoter] is not happy with them and doesn't think they're an outfit, he feels they're not together."

"They weren't the normal bunch of kids he was used to having up there," says Hal Carter. "They were flippant, cheeky northern kids who could be quite rude at times, which didn't go down [well]."

Askew practically begged Parnes to buy them more time. "They are good lads, the enthusiasm's there," he argued in their defense. "Leave it be and we'll get it right."

He was right. Soon the tour found real artistic balance. The Silver Beetles, dressed in matching black shirts, paired effortlessly with Johnny Gentle, his slick, earnest crooning and their raw, high-charged accompaniment an ideal match. The opening numbers, giving Johnny his brief star turn, were stronger than anything he'd done in the past—energetically or artistically. But once he finished and Paul rushed the mike, winding out the nearly incomprehensible opening of "Long Tall Sally," the pretense fell away: Johnny had entertained, but now it was time to rock 'n roll.

Inside those dinky, dilapidated halls, the Silver Beetles "pulled out all the stops." They pummeled those Scottish kids with forty minutes of kick-ass music that never let up for a beat. One after the next, the songs built to a furious, undisciplined pitch, rumbling, wailing, like a train through a tunnel. The kids at each show were undone by the music, practically throwing themselves around the floor. "Those two boys operated on a different frequency," Askew says of Paul and John. "I used to watch them work the crowd as though they'd been doing it all their lives—and without any effort other than their amazing talent. I'd never seen anything like it. They were so tapped into what the other was doing and could sense their partner's next move, they just read each other like a book." It was uncanny, he thought, how well they *knew* each other. "It was always Lennon and McCartney, even then. *Lennon and McCartney.* They wouldn't even look at George or Stu to determine where things were going. Everything was designed around the two of them—and the others had to catch up on their own."

Incredibly enough, the rest of the Silver Beetles never flinched. George maneuvered like a master in their long shadows to keep the rhythm more interesting than the mere slap-slap-slapping of chords. He worked intently, embroidering their strums with a plait of textured riffs and intonations that, while simple in structure, served to string the songs with bits of glorious color. "[And] Tommy Moore," says Askew, "made just enough noise to distract attention from Stuart, [who] was inept—and not needed." Almost in spite of themselves, the Silver Beetles rose mightily to steal the whole show. And the stronger they played, the more girls they attracted; the more girls they attracted, the stronger they played. Askew remembers watching a litter of sweet young "birds homing in on the stage" each night, lying in wait for the boys, as they finished their performance. "There were plenty to choose from after the gigs," he says. "They'd take them back to the hotels for all-night parties and have so much fun that I'd find them stretched out, asleep, on the stairways around dawn."

With all the tomcatting, it's a wonder they got out of some of those towns alive. The crowds that border dances attracted were notoriously tough. "All farm lads," says Hal Carter, "who'd get pissed and have a punch-up at the drop of a hat"—or the drop of a hem. "Often, if the [local] boys suspected some kind of attraction going on, they'd start a fight onstage and stop the show. However, if they were feeling charitable, they'd just whip glass ashtrays at the band to send a message."

A battered skull wasn't the only danger. In no time, the Silver Beetles learned one of the profession's dirtiest little secrets: beyond the lights and the applause, beyond the hotels and the girls, no one ever makes money on the road. Four days into the tour, in godforsaken Fraserburgh, the last scrap of land on the gusty northeast coast, their pockets were empty. John Askew had to plead with Parnes to advance them some money, which eventually arrived by courier. "But the lads were so in debt by then," he says, "they'd just spent it." Because of the penny-wise sleeping arrangements—musicians were doubled up in most cases—eager couples had to wait their turn in the hall or steal off to a dark corner. Usually, no one got to sleep before dawn, when they would simply pass out on a bed or, as Askew already observed, in a deserted stairwell.

The next day could be even rougher. One morning, after determining the roadie "was out of it," Askew loaded the band into the van and took off through the maze of rutted Highland roads. John Lennon was slumped in the navigator's seat, and not much use to Askew. "The lads were still shattered from a gig [that lasted until] one in the morning, and of course there was the bird scene afterwards that ran to five or six." Piloting on intuition, Askew panicked at a crossroads just outside Banff and, realizing—a hair too late—that he should have gone left instead of right, caromed "straight across the junction and into a little old couple" in their modest Ford.

The van took "such a smack" that John Lennon ended up crumpled under the dashboard. Tommy Moore, who was sitting behind him, flipped over the front seat and landed on top of John. Anguished by the apparent damage he caused, Askew bounded out of the car to assist the people he'd hit. "Don't worry about us," the woman said adamantly. "Take care of that boy over there."

Askew wheeled around and nearly fainted. Tommy's face was a garish mask of blood. "[It] was everywhere," Askew recalls, "mostly streaming from the drummer's mouth."

A detour to the hospital provided more encouraging news: Tommy was okay. He'd lost a tooth, with several others knocked loose, but "there was no concussion." At the worst, he was extremely shaken up. He'd never been in an accident before, and the strain of it had unnerved him. "I don't think I can play tonight," he told John Lennon, who returned to the hospital later that afternoon to collect his drummer. John did not reply for a long moment while a black rage crept across his face. "You listen to me, mate," he eventually growled. "*You're bloody playing!* Understand? What do you got—a bloody loose tooth?" He bent menacingly over Tommy, his lips twisted in a snarl, and Askew, worried that John was about to haul Tommy out of the bed by his hospital gown, edged closer in case it was necessary for him to intervene. "We need a drummer, and *you're it!* Now, let's go."

When it came to the band, you didn't demur. There was no halfway about commitment. If there was a future to playing music together, it had to start somewhere. The only way to find out was to begin playing with some consistency. And Tommy, who was fifteen years older than John, melted obediently under his smoldering glare. Wordlessly, he peeled back the covers, slipped out of bed, and got dressed for the gig.

[V]

Courtesy of the well-oiled Scottish pipeline, Allan Williams knew that this unheralded local band had held their own—and then some—with a figure like Johnny Gentle. That struck him as fortunate inasmuch as he'd brokered their inaugural appearance, and hoping to cash in on his run of luck, he swooped in with another bid of timely offers that bound band and Williams in an informal but deliberate management situation.

The most promising proposal came via Larry Parnes, who dangled the prospect of another Scottish tour, this time with one of his top dogs, Dickie Pride. It was a giant step up the same ladder that held the houndlike Johnny Gentle. But somewhere in the early stages of discussion, negotiations foundered. In rebounding from the setback, Williams stumbled into the honeypot. He managed to book the Silver Beetles for a string of dances that ran through the summer, across the Mersey, on the Wirral. The gigs, which would help establish them locally, were steady, well attended, and paid an awesome £10 per night. But they were in the worst hellholes this side of the equator—the Grosvenor Ballroom and the Neston Institute. Punch-ups were strictly kid stuff where these crowds were concerned; for dances here, you came fully armed. This was combat duty. As the Quarry Men, they had played in similarly dangerous situations, but on the Wirral they'd graduated to the big time. Come Saturday night, the Bootle teds and the Garston teds would go at it, with "flying crates and beer bottles and glasses." All it took was one misinterpreted look and—*bam!*—while the band whipped through a version of "Hully Gully." After one show, awakened by a disturbance in the middle of the night, Pauline Sutcliffe crept nervously into the bathroom, where she found her mother, Millie, laboring over Stuart's scrawny body, stretched out awkwardly in the tub. "He was injured," recalled Pauline, who stood speechless in the doorframe. "He said he'd been beaten up—'Well, you know how rough these clubs [are]. There's a lot of jealousy'—the implication being that it was some girl's boyfriend. He'd been kicked . . . and badly beaten. He had bruising on his face." Fortunately, there were no broken bones. It was reported that at another show a boy was almost kicked to death as the band continued to play.

The violence, however, seemed the least of their immediate worries. In early June the momentum of the Silver Beetles' progress was snapped by the defection of Tommy Moore, who left the band "in the lurch" following a raucous gig at the Neston Institute. It took them by complete surprise when he failed to show up for a ride they'd arranged to their next scheduled date. Four weeks of working with a capable drummer had lulled them into an unrealistic sense of security. Of course, no one imagined for a moment that Tommy was a Silver Beetle at heart. Indeed, by the end of the Johnny Gentle tour, he was barely on speaking terms with anyone. His ability, however, was undeniable. Desperate to keep the band intact, they tracked Tommy to the Garston bottling plant where he worked, in an effort to beg him to reconsider, but it was no use. The excuse he lamely offered was an unexpected transfer to the factory's night shift, but the truth was he'd just had it.

The boys were devastated. Unable to play the Wirral dances without a drummer, they agreed to provide background music at a couple of unlicensed cootch joints run by Allan Williams and Lord Woodbine. John, Paul, and George had not thought it possible to sink much lower. They'd done their share of oddball engagements in the pursuit of an appreciative audience: golf clubs, bus depots, cellars, and socials. But this was another world entirely. Where other gigs had been raucous and exhilarating, the shabeens were decadent and corrupt. There was an "anything goes" quality about them, where the very fringe of society collected like sludge in a rain puddle. They were generally small and filthy rooms, just big enough for ten or twenty men to congregate for the express purpose of drinking themselves blind. Many of the patrons were drunks, nothing more; they turned up there not out of congeniality but because the pubs were closed and there was no place else to satisfy their addiction. One of the tenements, the New Cabaret Artistes, was nothing but a cover for a grungy strip club in one of the city's worst neighborhoods. Nothing in their experience had prepared them for the likes of this. Their mission was to back "an exotic dancer" while she wound up a small crowd of randy middle-aged men. Miserable, embarrassing, presumably pathetic, and depressing—an indication of how badly their dreams had stalled.

The band tried to keep up appearances. John continued to call rehearsals at the Gambier Terrace flat and work on scraps of songs with Paul. They even retained a new drummer named Norman Chapman, whose bruising backbeat seemed tailor-made for their style of music. Only twenty, he was young enough to fit in socially, enthusiastic, and reliable, with a healthy passion for rock 'n roll. But following three promising gigs together at the volatile Grosvenor Ballroom, the band's lousy luck intervened. Chapman, to his own great surprise, was suddenly called for national service and dispatched to Africa for two years.

The sense of impotence—of being cut off from the action again—was devastating. From the weekend section of the *Liverpool Echo,* now about three pages strong, it was possible to see dozens of ads for local jive dances, and at each hall, the names, band after band—an elite corps of groups bundled together, who were cashing in on all the action. And always the same names—Gerry and the Pacemakers, Cass and the Cassanovas, Derry and the Seniors, Rory Storm and the Hurricanes, Kingsize Taylor and the Dominoes—playing in every conceivable combination. Running one's finger down each column, there was no mention of the Silver Beetles. Nothing. As far as anyone knew, they'd disbanded, they didn't exist.

This time, they needed serious help.

Of all the characters influential in the Liverpool beat scene, the Silver Beetles turned to only one—again: Allan Williams. But Williams was up to his whiskers in other problems. In mid-June, when the steel band failed to show for their regular Tuesday night performance at the Jacaranda, Allan was informed they'd done "a moonlight flit." Unbeknownst to him, the "dusky troupe," sans Lord Woodbine, crept into the basement after hours and made off with their set of tinny oil drums. Williams depended on music to attract college students to the Jacaranda, and the intensely exotic steel band gave him untold cachet. Williams's nightmare was that they'd gone over to the Royal Restaurant, whose owner, Ted Roberts, had tried repeatedly to woo them away and, when that failed, declared "war" on the Jacaranda. But, alas, it was worse than that. They were nowhere in Liverpool. Or even Great Britain, for that matter. Where in the world, he wondered, would a Caribbean steel band find favor and gainful employment?

Given any number of guesses, it is unlikely he ever would have come up with Hamburg, Germany.

Two summers before, Williams and his wife, Beryl, had befriended a fifteen-year-old hitchhiker they'd picked up on the road from Chester to Liverpool. The boy, whose name was Rudiger, was from Ahrensburg, a few miles north of Hamburg, and he beguiled them with tales of hedonistic excess surrounding the bustling German port. Rudiger—whose name they anglicized as Roger—returned to Liverpool several times the following year, always extending an invitation for Allan to "come to Germany and stay with him." Now, prompted by rumors of his steel band's new home, the opportunity presented itself.

Williams, along with the irrepressible Lord Woodbine, booked a weekend charter to Amsterdam and then connected by train to Hamburg, where he arranged to stay chez Rudiger, who was delighted to be able to reciprocate. Looking rather Mephistophelian, they set off, conspicuous in their matching top hats, with shabby suits, scruffy beards, and wild-looking hair, and chainsmoking cheap English cigarettes.

To many people, Hamburg was a terrifying place: bustling, turbulent, dirty, decadent, German—especially for Liverpudlians, whose city had been strafed by Messerschmitt bombs. But Williams basked in its seedy glow. "Hamburg fascinated me," Williams wrote in an unpublished memoir. For someone who traded in hyperbole, that was an understatement of colossal proportions. No city could have been more aptly suited for a man on the make such as Allan. All day long, he and Woody trolled the notorious St. Pauli district, pickling themselves in the endless chain of bars and wandering through the mazy arcades that featured flagrant down-and-dirty sex shows and where prostitution was hawked in roughly the same manner as schnitzel.

There was something else, too. With all the British and American servicemen stationed in Hamburg, demand for live music far exceeded the supply. Despite all future denials, Williams knew that—and he'd brought a tape along with him, showcasing three Liverpool bands, including the

Silver Beatles (they had changed the spelling in June), which he intended to play for German club owners. If he timed things right, Williams could corner the Hamburg market for British bands.

Sometime on a weekend in early July—the exact date cannot be determined, but it was a night when Lord Woodbine, exhausted, remained behind in a strip club on the Grosse Freiheit—Allan Williams wandered through the Reeperbahn, Hamburg's red-light district, taking its fidgety pulse. Stopping outside the Kaiserkeller, a three-step-down tourist club, he listened to a "dreadfully crummy" German band attempt to mug its way phonetically through a set of American rock 'n roll standards. Their delivery was awful. Seizing the opportunity, Allan pushed through the club's big glass doors and accosted the Kaiserkeller's manager, a florid-faced man with a preposterous wiglike mop of hair named Bruno Koschmider, and made his pitch. As "the manager of a very famous rock 'n roll group in England," Williams proposed to stock the Kaiserkeller with authentic British bands for the sum of £100 per week, plus expenses. It was a ridiculously large amount of money and Williams knew it, but he held his ground when Koschmider expressed interest.

With a cardsharp's sangfroid, Williams handed over the preview tape he'd made. But when the tape rolled, it contained nothing but babble; someone or something had distorted the magnetic signal rendering the performance useless.

The flush on Williams's face grew so intense that it seemed to sizzle. Skeptical, Koschmider backed away from his previous offer. He flatly refused to book a band without hearing them. Apologizing, Williams promised to send a proper tape as soon as he returned to Liverpool, but he left the Kaiserkeller sensing that he'd blown the opportunity of a lifetime.

He was wrong: that distinction would come later. Meanwhile, upon returning to Liverpool, there were more vital concerns that served to distract Allan Williams from his temporary setback.

The Seniors were waiting for him as he stumbled home from the "dirty weekend." Steady gigs were hard to come by in Liverpool, where standard practice was a sampling of itinerant one-nighters, so they insisted that Williams make good on his promise to introduce them around the London club scene. There was work in London—or "the Smoke," as it was called in the provinces—where residencies were common and house bands drew interest from talent scouts. The Seniors were sure that, given the chance, they could make a similar impression.

Howie Casey remembers his skepticism at Allan Williams's ability to come through for them. "He was always thinking on his feet, talking fast, with no real credentials, aside from his tongue." But a week later, on July 24, Williams pulled up with two cars, packed in the entire six-piece band along with all their equipment, and took off for the Smoke. "Incredibly, he drove straight to London, stopping magically on Old Compton Street, right in front of the Two I's," Casey says. The Seniors stared openmouthed at the holy shrine, "the place all the important bands in London played," which until then had existed only as a fantasy in their minds. It was the middle of the afternoon and the place was packed. Upstairs, in the café, there were rocker types hunched over a jukebox, studying the selections. A Screaming Lord Sutch record was blasting over the speakers. "We were in totally alien country," Casey recalls thinking. "Liverpool boys in a London coffee bar—to everyone there we were thick and stupid."

Williams seemed to know Tom Littlewood, who ran the place. Shifting the ever-present toothpick from one side of his mouth to the other, Littlewood herded them downstairs, where groups showcased their stuff. "We'll put you on after the next band," he promised.

The next band, as it was, proved a hokey Shadows knockoff, and the Seniors impressed with their energetic R&B set. "I thought we acquitted ourselves quite well," Casey recalls, "although we were distracted by Allan, who was standing in the audience." From the stage, they could see a slightly contorted, older-looking man trying to make contact with him, actually elbowing the crowd aside as though it were a matter of life and death. In his memoir, Williams claims disingenuously that he couldn't immediately identify the eccentric figure who practically leaped into his arms, but he would have had to have been blind not to recognize Bruno Koschmider.

In the standing of Beatle kismet, this episode ranks near the top. Koschmider, convinced by Williams's pitch that British bands would add spark to his club, had flown north to scout bands for a residency at the Kaiserkeller. "What a coincidence!" the two men exclaimed, hugging each other like long-lost cousins, but the Seniors weren't so sure. The reunion seemed almost too accidental.

Initially, Williams and Koschmider had trouble communicating; after some awkward jabbering, a Swiss waiter from the Heaven and Hell, a neighboring coffee bar, was enlisted to translate. Koschmider explained that he was seeking a replacement for Tony Sheridan, who had recently decamped to the rival Studio X. Tony Sheridan: even then the name struck a resonant chord. A guitarist of extraordinary flair, he'd backed Marty

Wilde and Vince Taylor before drawing a cult following of his own. His rave 1959 appearance on *Oh Boy!* was one of those transcendent TV moments in which an unknown performer leaps from obscurity to stardom. But Sheridan, it turned out, was a remarkable head case. Late for nearly every appearance, he often arrived without his guitar, was duly pissed, forgot words to songs, offended promoters, and simply didn't give a hoot. Eventually, television and the BBC refused to touch him. But in Hamburg, Sheridan became an overnight folk hero. "He was *the star,*" recalls a denizen of the local scene. In Hamburg it didn't matter if he got loaded before a show or mooned the audience, it didn't matter if "he went nuts onstage." The Germans "loved that kind of outrageous behavior." In Hamburg, where nothing was considered over the top, Tony Sheridan loved testing the limits. "He was unpredictable, very violent," says an observer. "He wouldn't stay on the stage [when he performed]. He'd tumble on[to] the dance floor, then roll around and put his body forward in an obscene gesture." One of the musicians who worked with him recalls a recurring stunt that had made Sheridan an instant legend on the Reeperbahn: "Tony was extremely well endowed and he wasn't adverse to displaying it to the audience. 'Hey, you fucking Germans, *check this out!*' There was always the threat of some madness."

That was a hard act to replace, but Bruno Koschmider had to fill the void somehow. At the Two I's, he'd liked what he'd seen. Derry Wilkie, a real live wire, was black. He wasn't Tony Sheridan, not by a long shot, but for the moment he was the next-best thing. Plus, the Seniors cooked. "[Koschmider] made us an offer on the spot," Howie Casey recalls. "We didn't even ask how much money we'd be paid. It didn't matter. We had a gig—great! We were going to Germany for a month." And off they went.

The Kaiserkeller was all Allan had cracked it up to be—"as big as the Rialto," thought Casey, when he and the Seniors walked in—with a decent-size stage and P.A. system, but was foreboding. Willy Limper, the club's manager, scoffed when they asked about their accommodations. "You stay here!" he declared, pointing toward the floor. Downstairs, it turned out, were two windowless rooms, with one bed, a settee, and two armchairs—*for six men!* One blanket—an old Union Jack—was provided, to be shared. No sink, no shower or bath. They could wash up in the ladies toilet, which was used by hundreds of people each night and not cleaned until the following afternoon, so "you just became funkier and funkier as time wore on."

Work began at seven o'clock, and the pace was grueling: four 45-minute sets, with fifteen minutes off for the band to tank up on free beer. The forty-five-minute blocks meant learning more material, or just stretching each song into drawn-out jams. The band also filled time with long calypso numbers whose melodies were borrowed from Lord Woodbine but whose rude lyrics were improvised on the spot. "It was all to do with 'wanking' and 'cocks,'" recalls Casey. "And, of course, we were killing ourselves laughing, thinking how amusing it was that the Germans were dancing away, digging it, without understanding a word." Not that anyone minded. "The crowds were great. When we played, they leaped on the tables, going absolutely apeshit." But they were also fickle. As soon as the set ended and the jukebox went on, the place emptied out, which meant that intermissions were eventually abolished.

It didn't matter. When the joint was rocking, there was no better place to play. But as time wore on, the once-naive Scousers began to notice another vibe in the Kaiserkeller—a core of intense, dark violence just under the glitzy surface. Willy Limper had presented himself as a dimpled, jolly old German geezer, but "a nice vicious streak" revealed the essential man. He ran Koschmider's infamous empire—a network of seedy music and strip clubs—with an iron fist that struck swiftly and without mercy. As one musician remembers observing: "When somebody didn't pay their bill, they were hauled into Willy's office so we could watch what was going on. The waiters had *koshes*"—leather saps—"and would stand in a semicircle, whacking the guy from one waiter to the next, playing tennis with him." Other times, violators were kicked senseless and then hauled into the back alley, where they were dumped, unconscious, alongside the garbage. Entertainment was merely a sideline for Koschmider. His tentacles extended to all kinds of vice—prostitution, child pornography, drugs, and protection. "Limper was the leader of his gang, and the waiters were his enforcers," says an observer.

It was a familiar showbiz story. As in Cuba and Las Vegas, entertainment provided a glamorous front for racketeers. But as Derry and the Seniors acclimated themselves to the Reeperbahn, they viewed their situation as being quite wonderful indeed. "We were in heaven," Casey says. Audiences loved them. They drank their weight in free vodka and whiskey. They discovered big department stores in Mönckebergstrasse, whose restaurants served *schwartzwalder kirschtorte*—rich cakes filled with wonderful cream that were unlike anything they'd eaten in Liverpool. And they gorged on sex. According to one of the musicians, "you had to chase and work at British girls." The minute they hit Hamburg, however, it seemed as if "girls came out of the woodwork." There was a girl for everybody, and not just edge-of-the-bed virgins, like back home. These girls were polished, stylish, smart, and fashionable. The musicians were invited to the homes of their German girlfriends, introduced to approving mothers, and then hauled upstairs to bed. The Scousers were shocked, just *shocked!* Even more so when they all got gonorrhea. "We were going to *marry* those girls," says one of the Seniors, "never realizing that Willy Limper was giving it to them, as were most of the waiters."

To each of the Seniors alike, it "was like being released into a sweet shop, a first-class orgy." So it was not surprising that after a month of pure bliss, the Seniors panicked when a letter from Allan Williams arrived, threatening to torpedo their perfect world. According to Williams, Koschmider had another club on the Grosse Freiheit that begged for another Liverpool band. That, in itself, actually seemed promising; it would be good, they thought, to have some companionship in Hamburg. But the Seniors were convinced that the group in question "would ruin the scene."

Williams's letter delivered the news: he was sending the Beatles.

[I]

It was "pissing rain" on the evening of October 1, 1960, when Rory Storm and the Hurricanes arrived in Hamburg. A slashing downpour had chased their train all the way from the Dutch border, and by the time they arrived at Steintorplatz the city lay under a seizing mist.

Germany. Enemy territory. Only fifteen years earlier, England had been at war here, set on destroying this country and the evil it represented. Conflict and hatred had been so mingled in the Scouse psyche that in contemplating this godforsaken country, one imagined storm troopers, a twisted cross, and the treachery of poxy fräulein, with their alabaster skin and scornful, froggy eyes. And now here they were, incomprehensibly enough, poised to perform, to play music on streets where *only fifteen years earlier* brothers and fathers had died.

Germany. It looked exactly as they'd pictured it: stern, mournful, impenetrable. A cloud of premature darkness pressed down against the rooftops and ghosts of fog rose from the asphalt, erasing all vanishing points so that the few stragglers who hastened along the slick streets looked as though they melted into the unseen. There was a solitude that resonated in the shadows, with its fresh scars of siege and patches of hasty restoration. Buildings were knocked cockeyed, salvaged; new towers stood out of place among ancient rubbled structures. An uneasy stir emanated from the landscape.

The Hurricanes arrived at the Kaiserkeller about 6:30 and piled out of three taxis, along with all their equipment. The street was deserted, eerie; the club shuttered and dark. The cool air drawing tight around them, they just stood there helplessly, watching the equipment get soaked. Johnny Byrne, the band's guitarist, recalls confronting Rory Storm, who seemed bemused by the predicament. "Now what are we going to do?" he asked.

Before Storm could answer, a faint rumble of music came drifting up the street. It was off in the distance, not more than a block or two away, but instantly recognizable: "Roll Over Beethoven." "God, that's strange!" Storm murmured.

Strange, indeed. There was nothing within proximity to indicate a connection to rock 'n roll. No club was open, no church hall in sight. Clumsily, they gathered up the gear and headed toward the music.

A block down the street they stopped in front of a building at 58 Grosse Freiheit that looked "like a funeral parlor." THE INDRA, a sign announced over the front door. Inside, the music rumbled away. A rush came over them—"a great rush," Byrne remembers. "Someone was giving this tune a fantastic workout."

The Indra was a strip joint, nothing more than a "small and tatty" lounge with red flock wallpaper and heavy drapes. There wasn't a soul inside, other than the band that was rehearsing explosively at the back. "We couldn't believe our eyes—or our ears," Byrne recalls. "The sound that was coming from these guys was fantastic, it was raw and exciting, just plain rocking out, and as tight as I'd heard a band play. There was something about the way they looked, too—rough, and intense, and a little bit rebellious. Not anything like we remembered them from Liverpool. Once we realized who it was, Rory and I turned to each other with this shocked look on our faces and we both kind of blurted out: 'It's the *Beatles!*'"

When Allan Williams endeavored to send another band to Hamburg in August 1960, the Beatles were probably the last group on his mind. According to several acquaintances, he offered the gig to Rory Storm and the Hurricanes, but they were adamant about finishing an engagement at Butlins Holiday Camp in Pwllheli, Wales, which ran through the summer, into September. He also got the brush-off from Gerry and the Pacemakers, who refused to quit steady day jobs for work that was short-term at best. "Allan was having plenty of trouble finding a band," says Bill Harry, "and that's how the Beatles got involved. They were really in no condition to perform"—Williams himself considered them "sort of a crappy group"— "but they courted Allan, and Stuart came on strong."

Strong—and somewhat vengeful. A few weeks earlier, Williams had participated in an intrigue whose outcome eventually cost Stuart his flat. According to roommate Rod Murray, Williams had encountered them one afternoon at Ye Cracke, trailing an entourage he introduced as "reporters from the *Empire News.*" They were in Liverpool, he explained, to do a survey on student grants, trying to discern how students lived and survived on such meager allowances. Oh-ho! That was all the boys needed to hear. Everyone had a hard-luck story he loved to tell. Stuart described how, when money ran out, they burned pieces of furniture to stay warm. Another friend, Rod Jones, complained that on weekends, he bummed meals off his relatives. Each story got better—and more outrageous—as the drinks flowed. Eventually one of the reporters said, "Come on, let's go have a look at your flat. We'll bring a couple bottles of whiskey and some beer."

On first glimpse, Gambier Terrace wasn't the hole the press expected, but by the time they got done with it, Charles Dickens would have been aghast. "They got newspapers," Bill Harry says, "crumpled them up, threw them about haphazardly. Strew empty beer bottles everywhere. Made it look a dirty mess." Stuart posed boldly in the forefront (along with John and Allan Williams) as photographers snapped away.

In fact, the reporters weren't from the *Empire News,* considered a "respectable paper" by local standards, but the scandalmongering *Sunday People,* which gave the piece a proper front-page bashing. Worse, perhaps, was the headline—THIS IS THE BEATNIK HORROR—warning that "most beatniks like dirt . . . [and] dress in filthy clothes" and bemoaning the conditions of "the decaying Gambier Terrace." That latter tidbit especially caught the attention of the building's residents association, which wasted no time in having the students evicted.

John and Stuart were livid. Williams had used them in order "to suck up to the press," and now Stuart was calling in a chit. He demanded more consideration from Williams in booking the band, specifically when it came to Hamburg. Though he remained unconvinced of the Beatles' artistic ability—"I wasn't altogether happy about their stagecraft," he wrote rather unctuously—Williams agreed to book them overseas, provided, of course, that they find a competent drummer. Williams no doubt figured that bought him precious time; in all likelihood, they'd be unable to satisfy that condition for the Hamburg gig, by which point he'd have found a more qualified band.

Now fate intervened. With their Wirral residency prematurely ended and nowhere else to play, the band bumped around town, scouting the competition. One of their stops was the Casbah, from which they had unceremoniously stomped off six months earlier. Mo greeted them warmly at the door, casting an especially heartfelt smile at George, who had remained in touch, occasionally stopping by the club with his brother Peter.

Inside, the Blackjacks were playing at one end of the complex. Sitting behind the drums was Mo's son Pete Best. As far as they could tell, he was consistent, a "real pounding rock 'n roll drummer" who lashed his foot to the bass and, in a sober, mathematical manner, spanked out four beats to the bar—which drummers call "playing fours"—instead of the usual two, which gave off "a powerful effect." He seemed to know most of the standards; his movement had a certain nice economy to it. He owned an impressive new kit and it probably also didn't hurt that he looked good. A pale, stiff boy with a dusty mop of hair, eyelids all but shuttered, and a languid, adolescent smile carved from a lower lip that was saucily retracted, girls were drawn to him in a visceral way. Later, observers labeled him "moody," but there was nothing in his personality that marked him as remotely temperamental. Rather, Pete seemed adrift and forlorn in a milieu of small-time characters and egotists—quiet, perhaps fortified to the point of indifference, dispassionate maybe, but not moody.

There are several versions of what happened next. Best told one interviewer that an offer to join the Beatles came through his mother, who pushed him toward the group. He later amended the account, saying that Paul called, dangling a job opportunity in Hamburg that would pay £15 a week. In neither version did he hesitate to accept. "I'd always liked them very much," he allowed of the Beatles. Shunning a spot at the teachers training college, he said, "I decided [instead] to persevere with the music."

John, meanwhile, had to come up with something good enough to divert Aunt Mimi's attention from a more damning piece of news. It had recently come to his attention that he would not be welcomed back to art college in the fall. Too much messy baggage had accumulated on his record, and it all finally piled up on him. "He was absent too much," says Helen Anderson. "He never produced any work. The tutors blamed him, in general, for misbehaving, disrupting classes, making trouble, and telling people to bugger off. And they eventually got fed up with it."

If Mimi found out, he'd never hear the end of it. Furthermore, it would mean having to get a job, which was anathema to John; he'd never worked a day in his life, aside from playing music for a few bob here and there. Rather than risk all that, he presented Hamburg to Mimi with inflated fringe benefits, claiming he'd earn £100 a week. A hundred pounds! It was an extraordinary figure in a country whose average weekly wage was almost half that figure, and it should have tipped her off to the bluff. Much later, Mimi told Lennon biographer Ray Coleman that she "feared the worst," which may have meant that she suspected the story all along;

but even if she had, there was nothing she could do to keep John from going. He was nineteen, of legal age and well outside his aunt's grasp.

Paul's strategy was—like Paul—more subtle and cunning. A promising if erratic student, he had another term left at the Liverpool Institute and a father for whom education was the one sure route to social betterment. For the most part, Paul had cooperated; he'd even sat his A levels in June and was awaiting the results.* But music was biting into those plans. Over Jim's objections, Paul devoted increasing amounts of time and energy to the band. "I didn't want to go back to school, or college," Paul later told Hunter Davies. Yet he knew that Jim would not tolerate idleness.

The only way around that was, of course, convincing Jim that there was opportunity in Hamburg. First, brother Mike would be needed to help promote the cause. Mike, Paul knew, would be able to soften up his father in an unassuming way. In exchange for this support, Paul promised to "buy . . . lots of things" for Mike, who worshipped his elder brother and would have done anything to help him, even without bribery. Jim was moved by his sons' eloquence, not to mention Paul's fiery intensity, and no doubt drew a parallel to his own dashed musical ambitions. Paul invited Allan Williams to the house to further plead his case. One can only imagine how Williams described Hamburg to Jim, but it can be assumed with some confidence that the promoter laid it on thick. He assured Jim that there would be no problems, that Bruno Koschmider would look after them. Somehow, Jim took his word that it would be a good place for the boys to play, and before the get-together was over Jim had given his consent.

Williams also went to bat for Stuart Sutcliffe, whose parents (incredibly) considered Williams a role model for Liverpool boys, "a respectable and kind person" just enterprising enough to combine art and commerce in a viably successful manner. Stuart, they reasoned, would do well to follow that formula. Even so, they were still fuming from the Johnny Gentle tour. Not only did they have to send Stuart money so he could get home from Scotland, but the tour had interrupted—and almost thwarted—his submission for the National Diploma in Design. As a result, Williams's sales pitch became more delicate—and somewhat misleading. "Allan didn't entirely tell [our parents] the whole truth about going to Hamburg," Pauline Sutcliffe recalled. "It was presented . . . as an interesting venture. It would be a good experience for [Stuart], being abroad and traveling. It was

---

* A few days after departing for Hamburg, the test results arrived, revealing that Paul had failed every subject but art.

very much dressed up as an interlude in his life" as opposed to a job, which they never would have permitted.

Eventually, Millie Sutcliffe relented. She was never very good at denying Stuart anything he wanted, and with the Harrisons' and the Bests' approval—both families were enthusiastic from the start—the deal was sealed.

Very quickly thereafter, the gears began to crank. Birth certificates were produced, along with passports and visas; bags and equipment were packed and properly labeled for transit. It all came together with remarkable speed. Four days later, on August 16, 1960, the Beatles left for Hamburg.

[II]

The Beatles had been out of England before—to Scotland, which they considered a pleasant enough place. But Hamburg was a different world altogether. Maybe even a different planet. The city itself was as familiar as their own modest backyards. A port with a thriving shipping trade conducted under a blanket of perpetual fog, it not only looked, felt, and smelled like Liverpool, the cafés even served a "typical" dish of gruel called *labskaus* that stood up to their brackish minced-meat stew. The sooty streets were narrow and mazy, studded with ancient crumbling cobblestones, and ran between the pitted redbrick facades of surviving neo-Gothic warehouses whose musky scents defied all insulation. The marine stench of the waterfront mingled with tangy notes of coffee, tea, tobacco, spices, even the sharp chemical trail of petroleum, and smelled much like Bootle or Garston.

They'd arrived at dusk, driving through the Mönckebergstrasse, whose wide tree-lined sidewalks were crowded with well-dressed pedestrians on their way home from work. On either side of their van, observed in dizzying perspective, the scene was surpassingly normal: couples dawdled at cafés, spun in and out of stores, stopped to peer in windows featuring lavish end-of-season sales. The Alster lakes, a glinting aqueduct speckled with rowboats and swans, shared a ledgy rise with an office complex that bisected the center of town. They passed the Rathaus, dark and ominous, where the Senate and city Parliament convened; the market square; and St. Michael's Church.

All perfectly normal, until Allan Williams swung the van around a concrete divider and into the corridors of the St. Pauli district, where they would be working.

Alas, Babylon! If ever a stage designer tried to create a set for depravity, this was it. St. Pauli rushed in on them from every direction. It resembled a carnival midway, only gaudier and more vulgar. The action was shoulder to shoulder, back-to-back: bars, nightclubs, cafés, luncheonettes, clip joints, arcades, dance halls, saloons. And lights—miles of lights—blazed with such dizzying, high-toned intensity that colors simply melted into one another. Slender girls, nude but for cowboy boots, blinked in neon above open doors. Floodlights lit the sky and arc lamps, suspended on poles, washed the street in a sublunar light that made all cars cruising by appear purple. Indifferent to time, the night seemed pushed back a few blocks. Here it was bright around the clock, a daylight for vampires.

Allan Williams knew what to expect, but he hadn't prepared the boys. Nor had he told them about the district's overriding theme, which wasn't music but sex. Its two main streets—the Grosse Freiheit and the Herbertstrasse—formed the city's infamous "mile of sin," and it was there, along with the intersecting Reeperbahn, that men flocked to behave as they might at a Roman orgy. "It was an 'anything goes' kind of place," says Adrian Barber, who turned up there later, as a member of the Big Three, but stayed to work for nearly a decade. There existed an ethos of hedonism that stretched back to the Middle Ages, when Hamburg was a member of the Hanseatic League, a free port, and therefore an essentially lawless haven—"kind of a Dodge City of the open seas," says Barber—where bad behavior was overlooked by the local authorities. Throughout history, the tradition was preserved as a foil to the rigid German culture, which was built around regimentation and power.

The place looked just right to the Beatles, who could hardly believe their eyes. It was all out there in front of them: girls prowling the streets, sitting provocatively in brothel picture windows, leaning just so against cars; music blaring from every open doorway; drunken sailors stumbling along the sidewalk, lofting steins of beer.

"That's the club!" Williams shouted, pulling to the curb outside a squat building on the Grosse Freiheit.

The Kaiserkeller, on the corner of Schmuckstrasse, was everything they imagined it would be. The club was bigger, brighter, louder, and groovier than anything they had seen before. Its decor alone left them practically speechless: a long boat-shaped bar, fishing nets stretched tautly on the ceilings, banquettes built to resemble a ship's galley, with portholes sunk into the walls and shiny brass fixtures salvaged from the port. The sweet smell of beer filled the room like a perfumed boudoir. The Kaiserkeller was posh compared with the saltcellars in Liverpool, and wired for rock 'n roll. The sound system was first-rate. And four microphones had been placed at intervals across the small stage, where Derry and the Seniors rocked the house.

Bruno Koschmider must have detected their excitement. Even so, he barely paused long enough to hear their praise before rushing them off to another club several hundred yards down the street, where the Beatles were scheduled to play.

The Indra "was depressing" by comparison. "We were crestfallen when we saw [it]," said Pete Best. It was a lounge—a girlie lounge—and deader than dead. A few bleary-eyed tourists sat glumly sipping beers. Along one side of the small rectangular room stood five spare banquettes, all empty, as were four of the six tables placed strategically on the floor. The heavy, worn red curtains and carpeting made the place seem even more shabby than it already appeared.

There was hope. It was explained through an interpreter that Koschmider planned to turn the Indra into a balls-out rock 'n roll club, optimally another Kaiserkeller. All the place needed was a hot British band to generate a buzz, and the owner had been assured that the Beatles were up to the job.

But the Beatles were as stiff as the punters who trickled into the club. Accustomed to playing a few songs to a houseful of teenagers, they were oblivious to the demands of a difficult crowd. They had no act to speak of, knew almost nothing of stagecraft, and as musicians they weren't terribly engaging. Stuart still struggled woefully to follow the melody lines, on top of which, they'd had no time to work Pete into the band. By contract, the Beatles were required to play a staggering four and a half hours each night, six hours on the weekend. "You can't imagine the work that took," says Ray Ennis, who showed up in Hamburg sometime later, with the Swinging Blue Jeans. (They had modernized the spelling of their name beginning with this gig.) "All the Liverpool bands were used to playing twenty-minute sets back home. Suddenly we had to go all night. That meant coming up with the material, not to mention the stamina."

The Beatles had material. John, Paul, and George were a walking encyclopedia of rock 'n roll songs, to say nothing of the skiffle tunes and pub standards still shuffled into their act. If necessary, they could put together an hour of material without repeating a song. But somehow it didn't click with the crowd. People would poke their heads inside the Indra doorway to check out the scene, then do a quick about-face. Certainly some blame could be laid to the place itself, which wasn't exactly inviting. But as far as creating excitement went, the Beatles weren't cutting it.

Angrily, Koschmider contacted Allan Williams and expressed his dissatisfaction. Hastily, Williams raced to Hamburg to size up the situation and run some interference. Much to his chagrin, he found Koschmider's objections justified. The Beatles were performing at the Indra in an unexceptional manner. Their sets "were . . . far too deadpan," he surmised; they just "stood still and strummed." This was a bigger problem than it had seemed. Williams had a good thing going with Koschmider. He didn't want a group like the Beatles to louse up the arrangement.

According to Williams, he gave "the boys a really rough lecture" and followed up with another visit to gauge its effect. Exasperated, he found it hadn't made the slightest impression. They were playing "almost motionless [sic]," scarcely even trying to complement the inescapable beat. It baffled him. How could they churn out manic rockers like "Roll Over Beethoven" or "Good Golly, Miss Molly" without giving it any oomph? In his interpretive study, *Tell Me Why,* Tim Riley nails it when he calls rock 'n roll "the sexiest music of all—it makes you want to *move.*" Even Williams, who had no love for the form, felt its physical tug. "C'mon, boys," he exhorted them, "make a show."

Make a show.

It was like something a teacher might say before the start of school speech day or the class play. Make a show: it sounded completely inappropriate for rock 'n roll. John couldn't stop snickering. He lurched around the stage in mock-theatrics, diving toward the mike and duck-walking like Chuck Berry or dropping into a split. Williams, who didn't realize John was taking the mickey out of him, cheered on the antics. "That's it! Make a show! Make a show!"

Koschmider, too, took up the chant, barking at the band in a kind of quasi-militaristic chant: *"Mach Schau! Mach Schau!"*

The Beatles thought that was a scream. A German shouting, *"Mach Schau!"* To them it sounded like the Goons doing a hilarious take on the Nazis—the shrill accent, the jerky hand motion, the bugged-out eyes. However frivolous, it did the trick. They had finally found the stimulus that freed their inhibitions. *"Mach Schau!"* The entire band got into the act, imitating John's happy horseplay. Paul raised his guitar, as though fencing with John, repeating this gesture until his partner responded. He made pass after pass, speeding up, slowing down. In no time, George chimed in, stamping and scrabbling his feet like a demented Cossack. Stuart, though saddled with the bass, contorted his body as though he were dodging bullets. A cyclone of rhythmic unrest swept across the Indra's stage, synced to Pete's ferocious beat.

It was the breakthrough the band had needed, and immediately they began to work these outbursts into the act. Songs were suddenly larded with physical surges and thrusts. An emphatic spin or kick accented every beat. Once agonizingly inert, the Beatles now leaped off the stage in bursts of manic exhilaration. They were in perpetual motion, and in no time they transformed their sorry sets into something primitive and exciting. And that's all it took to turn the corner. Word spread quickly around St. Pauli that the Beatles were all the rage, and crowds thronged the Indra to check out the newest British import. Imitating Derry and the Seniors' high-tension act, they'd started playing what Pete Best referred to as "powerhouse music," which was basically a selection of all-out rockers with the volume cranked up for effect (and the bass turned down for cover), underscored by a palpitating bass-drum beat and frisky stage pranks. "After a few weeks, you could barely move in the place, it was so jammed" recalls Johnny Byrne. "The heat was terrific, everyone smoked, drank. Everyone was having a blast. There was a real sense that something incredible was going down."

Watching greedily from the sidelines, Bruno Koschmider could barely contain his delight. Not only had the Beatles succeeded in drawing good crowds, they had established a direct link for audiences between the Indra and the Kaiserkeller. They'd plug Derry down the street, and crowds would gravitate to that show—and vice versa. It was impossible to go to one without being aware of the other. A Hamburg teenager who spent his weekends in St. Pauli found it "possible to pass the whole night going from the Kaiserkeller to the Indra without the need for other entertainment. . . . There was no place else in the district that offered such an exciting selection of live music."

And it was nonstop. The scene demanded it. When people strolled by, looking from place to place, their decision whether or not to go into a club was based largely on the music blaring from the doorway. There was no food served in either of the clubs. According to one frequent visitor, "Eating wasn't part of the equation. You went in there to get pissed, dance, and pick up chicks." The music had to be loud and hot; otherwise, a potential customer would continue on. That meant working at a brutal pace and pitch, sort of "a baptism by fire," according to Bill Harry. Even though there were breaks planted at forty-five-minute intervals, there was really never any letdown until well after two in the morning. And the breaks, as they discovered, were merely breathers. There was hardly enough time to recharge, no civilized place to rest. At best, the boys would sit slumped at the bar, uninterrupted by drunken patrons, sipping a fifty-pfennig beer,* or they'd run around the corner for a *frikadella*—a greasy meat-and-onion patty that they lived on for weeks on end. There was never time for a proper meal—or enough money. The prices in St. Pauli had been jacked up to fleece the tourists. "Besides," as Howie Casey recalls, "the first week you spent all your money right away and realized you couldn't afford to eat." When possible, the bands crowded into a booth at Wienerwald, a cheap deli featuring rotisserie chickens that they shared, or went to Schmu Goos on Schmuckstrasse, which was "a Chinese place that did workingman's food"; for a few pfennigs, they'd gobble down a big bowl of soup with a roll that would have to hold them for an entire day—or longer.

Adrenaline was an even bigger headache. After a long night's work jackknifing across a stage to endless wild applause, the boys were so pumped up that it usually took several hours to reach a state where they were calm enough to drift off. (That is, if they weren't hunting up a party or hanging out in an all-night bar.) Often they didn't get to sleep until four or five in the morning, and even then it was an unpleasant prospect.

Their accommodations were appalling—even worse than the Seniors'. With utter indifference, Koschmider had stashed the boys, like props, in abject old storage rooms at the back of a run-down cinema he owned at the bottom of the Grosse Freiheit. The Bambi Kino, as it was known, showed dubbed German-language two-reelers practically twenty-four hours a day, old gangster movies and westerns that were streaked and pitted from use. At one time, before the war, the place had functioned as a legitimate theater, but that time was long past, and the once-swank appointments were beat up and decrepit. Their rooms, in a corridor behind the screen, had fared no better—"filthy, dirty, and disgusting" cubicles without windows or proper beds. John, Stuart, and George shared a cell fitted with a camp bed and sofa. Farther down the hall, past the urinal and just off the fire exit, Paul and Pete had adjoining rooms—"the black holes of Calcutta," as they called them—without any lights, to say nothing of facilities or heat. "It was freezing cold in there," recalls Johnny Byrne, who visited the

---

* *Willy Limper included free drinks in their salaries, but after the first week so much vodka, whiskey, and brandy was consumed that he limited them to free beer.*

Beatles often during their stay in St. Pauli. "We'd knock for them at the side door of the Bambi Kino, and John would answer, standing there in a pair of grandad long johns and a button-down vest. It was too cold for us to hang around, just too bitter and damp, and impossible to have a conversation with the German dialogue booming from the cinema."

But the Beatles were rarely in their rooms. They spent virtually all their spare time at Bruno Koschmider's two clubs, either performing or finetuning arrangements to help tighten the act. On the face of things, this might have seemed relatively ordinary, but it was unique to the impetuous nature of a rock 'n roll band and just one of the many distinctions that contributed to the Beatles' prodigious success. Exceptionally conscientious about expanding their appeal, they worked as painstakingly as engineers, constructing a set of songs needed to engage the fitful crowds. It didn't take long for them to hit on a surefire formula: volume. It got people off. More than anyone so far, the Beatles realized that the function of a bar band wasn't to promote artistry, expand the musical genre, or even entertain. Bar bands really weren't performers in the conventional sense, but rather were agitators, and as such they had far more in common with the touts than with show business. From their opening chords, the Beatles let it rip. All-out rockers soon filled every minute of the set. Thanks to Paul's high, unyielding voice, a barn burner like "Long Tall Sally" could ignite an edgy house, with each successive number arranged to ratchet up the emotional heat. He and John combined on a steady string of rockers: "Johnny B. Goode," "Good Golly, Miss Molly," "Bony Maronie," "C'mon Everybody," "Rock and Roll Music," "Great Balls of Fire," and "Dizzy Miss Lizzy," which set a blazing pace.

Most of their songs lasted two and a half or three minutes at the most, making it possible to exhaust maybe twenty songs in a typical set. In the beginning, they often found themselves short a song at the end of a set, forcing the hasty relaunch of, say, "Johnny B. Goode." Chances are, the crowd never even noticed or, at the least, didn't mind—but it disheartened the band. They considered it a mark of amateurism, feared that it dulled their competitive edge. So even though they were already overworked, the Beatles devoted hours on end to rehearsing. Most afternoons they met at the Indra, giving the songs a real workout, packing each measure with rhythmic tension and pulling out all the stops, to ensure that the material was hot. But like the Seniors, they soon grew tired of rehearsing each afternoon, instead expanding what songs they already knew into long drawn-out jams. One night they walked up to the Kaiserkeller and watched in awe as the Seniors ate up an entire set with a vapid romp called "Rock with the Seniors," which was nothing more than a twelve-bar blues riff with shifting rhythmic patterns and no lyric to speak of; every so often, one of the musicians would shout, "Rock with the Seniors!" giving it a kind of "hey-ba-ba-re-bop" holler to hold the pudding together. "What'd I Say," more than anything else, became what Paul called their trusty "show song." Paul recalled: "We used to work the hell out of it . . . kept it going for hours and hours." And every night it took on a different shape, by either substituting their own lyrics or vamping on the bridge; it could—and often did—take off in a number of directions, perilously close to falling apart at any moment, which made it so exciting to watch. The same occurred with "Whole Lotta Shakin' Goin' On," a rollicking tour de force, which could last a good half hour. By mid-September the Beatles had turned a corner. A dancer could walk out of the Indra, go across the street for a pack of cigarettes—or a screw—and still, whenever he got back, catch the same song running.

Upon arriving in Hamburg, the Beatles felt an impulse to appear "professional," which in England meant well groomed. Eager to look the part, they had taken dress cues from the natty Johnny Gentle, who had impressed upon them the importance of "looking sharp" onstage, and in their own way the Beatles proffered a version of sartorial grace. Dressed in matching lilac-colored sport coats draped over black shirts with a silver stripe on the collar, black slacks, and clay-colored, imitation-crocodile, pointy-toed shoes, or winkle-pickers, they looked more like a Cuban nightclub act. Pete Best, who—perhaps mercifully—joined too late to benefit from the sporty makeover, came up with his own black attire and an Italian navy blue jacket, which put him in the general vicinity of their inelegance.

To their credit, the band never felt self-conscious in the suits, but after playing in them seven nights a week—sweating buckets in them, stretching them out, ripping them, *punishing* them—the inevitable happened: they began to stink and give way at the seams. In place of proper tailoring, the Beatles took them to the Indra's bathroom attendant, a stocky, sixty-year-old woman named Rosa Hoffman, known to one and all as simply "Mutti," who made emergency repairs during intermissions. But eventually that, too, proved futile, as in no time the fabric had decomposed and the matching clothes "went by the board."

New suits were out of the question. There wasn't enough money to spare and, anyway, the whole image suddenly seemed tired—especially in

Hamburg, where the dress code reached new levels of informality. Thanks to Tony Sheridan, who had always gone his own way, the Beatles were introduced to the Texas Shop, at the top of the Reeperbahn, where they found sleek black leather bomber jackets—Luftwaffe, in this case—and hand-stitched cowboy boots. It was exactly the dark, uncompromising image they'd been looking for—part rebel, part street tough, and wholly in tune with the hard-driving music they were playing. Except for Pete, who preferred to play in shirtsleeves, they each bought an outfit and wore them onstage that same night, making an immediate impression.

The new look showed the influence of the more hard-nosed American performers, Gene Vincent in particular. Moreover, their haircuts (or lack thereof) refined this image—a longer, fuller style that crept over their collars and shook loose during long, raucous jams, but not so long that it would induce hostility, let alone an uproar. The Seniors took notice of the changes but didn't know what to make of them at first. "We thought they were a pretty scruffy bunch," recalls Howie Casey, who, along with Derry Wilkie, initially rejected the Beatles' streetlike approach. But within days, the Seniors felt awkward in their "cheap, junky suits with bagged-out knees and the asses all slack," so, says Casey, "we bought jeans and stuff rather than fight what we must have known was the coming trend."

Somehow the new incarnation motivated the Beatles to play even harder, if that were even possible. They really turned it on—and up—squeezing all they could out of the two tiny Truvoices that pumped out their sound. It wasn't unusual for Pete Best to crawl into place behind his drum set, only to have John or Paul whisper, "Crank it up, Pete, we're really going for it tonight." Neighbors complained about the noise, which seemed preposterous, considering the district's reputation. But because of the Indra's secluded location, on the perimeter of the Grosse Freiheit, there were residents within earshot. Girlie shows hadn't disrupted their lives, but the din of rock 'n roll posed real problems.

Normally, Koschmider would have ignored the complaints or used his influence with the police to have them quashed. But the neighbors were mostly elderly, not the least of whom was a widow who lived upstairs and claimed that the music was making her sick. Reluctantly, Bruno ordered the Beatles to tone things down—the "most absurd request they'd ever heard." No one took it seriously enough to reduce the volume. But the requests, friendly at first, turned intense. Day after day, the police fielded increasing complaints and leaned on Koschmider to comply. Finally, Koschmider had had enough, and in one audacious stroke he closed the Indra.

Ordinarily, this would have spelled doom for the Beatles, but Koschmider wasn't about to lose his new star attraction. (Besides, they had a month left on their contract.) Instead, he offered the young Liverpudlians the opportunity to share the Kaiserkeller stage. They could alternate sets with Derry and the Seniors, who had another week left on their contract. Koschmider outlined the plan to John, hoping to convince the Beatles of its merits, but it proved an easy sell. The Kaiserkeller meant a bigger stage, better sound, wilder crowds, and, hopefully, lighter hours. As far as John and the Beatles were concerned, they were movin' on up.

In fact, it was the beginning of the end.

[III]

Dismissing Rory Storm in the early sixties was easy. Unlike the performances of Kingsize Taylor or the Big Three (the reconfigured Cassanovas, sans Cass), the Hurricanes were all flash, with none of the slashing intensity that raised the other bands' emotional stakes another notch or two. They weren't exquisitely disciplined like Gerry and the Pacemakers or rhythmically precise like Derry and the Seniors. Although Rory was dubbed "Mr. Showmanship" by local promoters, evidence suggests that his shows were forgettable, the band a muddle of instrumentation. George Harrison, writing from Hamburg, dismissed the Hurricanes in a single word: "crumby." Rory, he reported, "does a bit of dancing around but it still doesn't make up for his phoney group." ("The only person who is any good in the group," George noted, "was the drummer," a wiry, bearded lad named Ringo.)

Even so, from the moment they arrived to replace the Seniors, Rory Storm and the Hurricanes were treated like outright stars. A sign outside the Kaiserkeller heralded their engagement in large, striking letters, with a postscript — "*und* the Beatles" — buried feebly below. By all accounts, they were paid more than either the Beatles or the Seniors and were given greater flexibility. They also inherited Derry's living quarters at the side of the Kaiserkeller stage.

To the Beatles' credit, the billing mattered naught. Nor were they concerned with the material perks, content that, come what may, they could "blow these guys off the stage." They actually liked the Hurricanes, having often spent hours in Liverpool with them, hanging out, bullshitting in the Storms' — or rather, Caldwells' — crowded parlor. Stormsville (as Rory insisted on calling his home) was Liverpool Central to the local musicians. Vi Caldwell, or Ma Storm, as she called herself, kept Paul in cigarettes when he was broke, which was nearly always, and made John and George "chick butties"—chicken and butter sandwiches, a Scouser staple. George had casually dated Rory's sister, Iris, considered "the prettiest girl in the neighborhood," since 1959, and for a brief time later Paul would court her in a more serious way. Each of the Hurricanes was regarded fondly by the Beatles. Charles "Ty Brien" O'Brien and Wally "Lu Walters" Egmond, who played lead and bass, respectively, were amiable guys and a wellspring of new songs, having introduced "Fever" and "Summertime" to the communal repertoire. Johnny Byrne talked incessantly about rock 'n roll, and John, Paul, and George listened: the more obscure and esoteric the topic, the more enthusiastically they responded. They were friendly, even flattering, toward Rory; moreover, John, who relished tormenting anyone with the slightest handicap, resisted repeated opportunities to ridicule the severely stuttering Rory. In fact, the only Hurricane who eluded the young Beatles (aside from George) was Rory's drummer, the hound-faced, self-mocking jester from the Dingle named Ritchie Starkey, whom the band fondly called Ringo.

From the opening night on October 4, 1960, the two bands commandeered the Kaiserkeller stage with a red-hot, rough-and-tumble force. For more than seven uninterrupted hours, the bands churned out a string of high-octane rockers that left the capacity crowds in a sweaty, beer-soaked frenzy. "Every night was another amazing jam fest," recalls Byrne. "The music got everyone so cranked up and the whole place just shook, like Jell-O. It was a solid mass of bodies. You couldn't see through the smoke. Fights would break out on the dance floor or in the seats, and these huge glasses would be flying every which way. The bouncers all had truncheons. If there was a sailor on the floor, you'd see them lay into him, kicking him. And Koschmider would run up, screaming: 'Don't stop the music! Play on!'"

And play on they did. Every night it got louder and longer—seven o'clock in the evening until five in the morning. "Marathon sessions," as the two bands mutually termed them, with a "very friendly rivalry" serving to fatten the stakes. If Rory delivered a solid rendering of "Blue Suede Shoes," John countered with his own crack version; Wally would warble "September's Song" and Paul would squeeze the sap out of "That's When Your Heartaches Begin." One of the Hurricanes recalls how Paul threw them a curve one night by belting out "Bama Lama Bama Loo." "It was such an incredible number, it just buried us," he says. "We spent the entire next day at a record store in Hamburg trying to come up with something powerful enough to top that." There was no letup—and no downtime. If a musician needed a bathroom break or got dehydrated and stopped for a sip of water, Koschmider angrily waved him back onstage, demanding a full ensemble at all times, as stipulated in their contract. "I pay five men!" he'd shout, turning red in the face. *"Mach Schau! Mach Schau!"*

"It got very funny out there, very fast," says Johnny Byrne, who helped ignite the appreciable hijinks. "I used to egg John on and he'd swear down the mike, in English, assuming the audience couldn't understand him. He'd say, 'Go on, you fucking Krauts, you fucking ignorant German bastards!' It was all we could do not to piss ourselves." Other nights Paul performed in a bedsheet. Emboldened, George draped an old, yellowed toilet seat around his neck and goose-stepped across the boards. Word spread through Hamburg that the Beatles were *verrückt*—crazy—their shows insanely unpredictable. In a moment of typical abandon, John paraded jauntily onstage in a pair of "scabby" swimming trunks, selecting a choice moment to moon the unsuspecting audience. According to Pete Best, "There was a stunned silence, then the place erupted . . . [with] people banging bottles on the tables, jumping up and down."

Onstage, however, that was about as wild as things got. There was lots of clowning and immature antics, obnoxious jokes, the occasional outburst. A musician remembers John picking a fight with a drunken sailor who heckled him from the dance floor—"the guy tried to climb up onstage after Lennon offered to flatten his nose"—before the waiters hustled the culprit outside. For years, stories circulated about how the Beatles did horrible things while playing at the Kaiserkeller. Several scenarios were concocted by Allan Williams, who dined out for years on tart, black commentary about the boys, John in particular. But eyewitnesses indicate that wasn't the case at all. They were simply undisciplined kids away from home for the first time, engaging in as much rude behavior as they could get away with.

Of course, that was fueled in no small way by a constant liquid diet. Everywhere in Hamburg, beer flowed like water, but nowhere was it as copious and affordable as in the Kaiserkeller, where the bands drank for free. To working-class Scousers, free beer was a jackpot, "like winning the lottery." First, being paid a decent wage to play rock 'n roll, and now downing beer as a job benefit! They could hardly believe their good fortune.

Like the Seniors before them, the Beatles went on a bender from the moment they unpacked. Hardly an hour went by without a beer of some kind. Mostly, they feasted on the cheap watered-down variety, which came in little stubby bottles, and later, after one of the musicians slipped Bruno Koschmider's Danish cellarman a few extra bob, "he fixed [them] up with the good stuff." During those first weeks in Hamburg, they drank as much as quickly as possible, not believing it would last. One after the next, they downed bottles, fortifying themselves through the overheated sets. And after a series of hard, raunchy numbers, when the dance floor was jumping, club patrons would send drinks up to the stage, big trays balanced with foaming steins that the band was expected to chug. "German customers would say, 'You must drink, boys, you must finish the drink,'" Pete Best recalled, "and there'd be some sessions, especially at the weekend, when the drinks were coming up faster than our playing."

Musicians had to be careful about what and whom they refused in St. Pauli. In some cases, fear replaced common sense when they were offered yet another round of drinks, especially when it involved the club owners or their associates who were regarded—and rightly so—as violent "gangsters." Paul McCartney remembered how the mobsters "would come in late at night . . . and send a little tray of schnapps"—called *doppelkorn*— "up to the band," demanding that they drink it down straightaway. At first, the Beatles were reluctant, desperately trying to talk their way out of it without offending anyone, but it was hopeless and certainly not worth provoking a confrontation. "There were gas guns and murderers amongst us, so you weren't messing around here," McCartney recalled. "So we'd drink the schnapps and they'd occasionally send up pills."

The pills, of course, were amphetamines. They were available over the counter in the form of diet pills, called Preludin, and favored by overweight housewives, but most were repackaged for recreational use by the German underworld, which controlled the market with an iron fist. "Prellies" and Purple Hearts, another form of speed, were the drugs of choice on the Reeperbahn. Within the next three years, they would be joined by virtually the entire line of narcotics, with Hamburg eventually becoming the gateway for heroin into Russia. But during the Beatles' stay there, it was limited to speed and just about every musician put it to good use.

The Beatles had fought fatigue from the outset. Even after playing their initial marathon session, "they were so exhausted they could barely move." Beer wasn't the answer; too many drinks made the musicians feel bloated and sluggish. But a highball—a potent combo of stimulants—fired the backup jets. According to Ray Ennis, "Once you had a few beers and the odd pill, you could stay awake for days and didn't give a shit."

With little else to sustain them, the Beatles relied more and more on Preludin to maintain their stamina through the endless weeks of performances. John, already struggling with alcoholism, "gobbled them down" like candy, and George, in a long, disjointed letter to his friend Arthur Kelly reported "eating Prellie sandwiches" as a supplement to battle the twelve-hour nights. Stuart and Paul also experimented with speed, although to a somewhat lesser degree. Ever cautious, Paul determined that the quick high "was dodgy . . . you could get a little too wired on stuff like that" and managed to keep his edge sharp with only the occasional pill or two. Only Pete Best abstained, further setting his own beat apart from the rest of the band.

With speed to lube their engines, both the Beatles and the Hurricanes cranked the energy into overdrive. Songs grew more aggressive, convoluted, and unpredictable, the volume eventually peaked out, and the boys gyroscoped on and off the stage, working themselves into a frenzy and leaving everyone exhilarated—and exhausted. "We tried any number of crazy things out of boredom," Byrne says. The bands traded members; they traded repertoires; they traded instruments and even their mock-insults with the audience, eventually turning their attention to the rickety stage.

It wasn't a proper stage by any stretch of the imagination, just a few planks of warped wood supported by empty Schweppes crates. It had always slumped to one side, thanks in no small part to the forcible Seniors, who had busted through it one night shortly after the Beatles arrived in Hamburg. Bruno's promises to have it fixed rang hollow, and there things stood.

But not for long. Busting the stage was too much of a temptation. In no time, wagers were made, and a foolproof method proposed: the aptly named stomp. Using the heels of their new cowboy boots, the guitarists would mete out a savage beat to each song, torturing the planks of the stage. The Beatles tried it out first, with an extreme rendition of "Roll Over Beethoven" that was almost Russian in its execution. A friend who watched from the side of the stage recalled how when John launched into the chorus—"roll over Beethoven . . ."—Paul, George, and Stuart answered: *stomp! stomp! stomp!* Again and again, the trio converged near stage center, deemed the most fragile spot—*stomp! stomp! stomp!*—bashing the soft planks with their heels. When Rory tried leaping off the upright piano, same thing. Toward the weekend, a hairline fracture appeared in the planks. When a musician put any weight at all on them, he could see the boxes underneath and knew the end was near. Friday night, they vowed, was *it*.

When the big night arrived, the Beatles gave the stage several good beatings, but as Pete Best recalled, "it hung on and we were getting frustrated." After four sets, they gave up in disgust and went across the street for breakfast. According to Johnny Byrne, "We went on and saw it was really getting ropy. Then, about two o'clock in the morning, Rory summoned up enough energy and leaped off the piano right onto a weak spot. There was a loud crack and all the planks went up in a v shape as the center caved in. Moments later, the amplifiers toppled over and slid into the hole, along with the mikes and Ringo's cymbals."

Bruno Koschmider was furious. He came running from his office to inspect the damage, shooing Rory and the Hurricanes from the stage. One glance was all it took for him to determine that it was hopeless. Live music was replaced by a jukebox, and the Hurricanes joined the Beatles in Harold's across the street to celebrate.

All seven boys crammed into two adjoining booths, laughing and telling war stories over bowls of cornflakes and pints of freezing cold milk. A toast was in order! They were about to clink glasses when the front door burst open and Koschmider and his bouncers flew in with an all-too-familiar look on their faces. "They had their *koshes,* and they started setting about us," says Byrne, who was wedged in a booth against the wall. The boys managed to scramble up and over the tables, sending cornflakes and milk flying, but not before the thugs got in a few bruising whacks.

The next night, everyone got to the Kaiserkeller early to inspect the new stage, but to their collective dismay, not much had changed. The old stage had been repaired in the most makeshift manner, with a few new planks slapped across the crates and chairs wedged underneath to hold everything in place. Otherwise, it was even more treacherous and unstable, "like a waterbed." But to the bruised and battered Beatles, it would make no difference.

[IV]

It had never occurred to the Beatles that they might have fans. Girls were certainly no indication of their musical talent—at least, not the girls who chased them in Hamburg. Most were what Pete Best regarded as "high-class call girls," strippers or hookers who worked the district and took a fleeting fancy to young English musicians. Nor did the Kaiserkeller regulars show any real interest in the band. They either danced or talked among themselves. "Nobody really looked at the stage," recalled an observer. "The Beatles were just like background music."

In the ever-shifting bad light, it seemed unlikely that any of the Beatles noticed the trio sitting rigidly upright near the front and to the left of the stage. Each night they came into the club about nine o'clock—two extraordinary-looking young men and a woman who did everything in their power not to draw attention to themselves. Even so, they stood out like sore thumbs, dressed rather exotically as they were, in suede jackets, wool sweaters, jeans, and round-toed slippers. Although they were largely ignored by the black-leather-jacket-and-boots crowd, there was an inherent sense of danger to their presence, their fey appearance being enough of an excuse to warrant a beating from the German teds, whom they referred to as "rockers." Eventually, during a break, one of the young men approached John rather meekly and, in fractured English, introduced himself as Klaus Voormann, a Berlin-born graphic artist, pressing a crumpled record sleeve he'd designed into John's hands. John was uninterested and shunted him off on Stuart, whom he referred to somewhat backhandedly as "the artist round here."

Stuart didn't share John's reservations. In fact, Stuart had spotted all three from the stage, mistaking them for "typical bohemians." Embarrassed and flattered, he discovered them staring at him in an openly seductive manner and, in a letter to a friend, admitted an instant mutual attraction, acknowledging that it was "extremely difficult to keep my eyes off them." He'd even searched for the trio during a break, trying to make some kind of contact, but concluded that they had left before the show was over.

Introduced at last, he was "completely captivated." The three, it turned out, were former students at the Meisterschule für Mode, a kitchen sink–type art college in Hamburg not unlike the art college back in Liverpool, and had zeroed in on the lithe, theatrical Stuart as a fellow traveler. For everyone concerned, it was love at first sight. Stuart was immediately drawn to both "boys"—Voormann and Jürgen Vollmer—who, with their exquisitely handsome faces and unself-conscious flair, cast a striking presence in any crowd. The woman was in a category all to herself. At almost twenty-two, Astrid Kirchherr already had little in common with the other German fräulein who shared her blond good looks. Strong and willowy like Jean Seberg, with a wide, flat forehead and distant ice-blue eyes, she captivated men with attitude rather than beauty. "The minute she walked into a room all heads immediately turned her way," says Bill Harry, "and she was in full control of that room." Neither outwardly personable nor particularly well read, she relied more on an aura of mystery and dreamy sophistication that found a receptive audience among young, frustrated artistic misfits who sensed in her a kind of Circean eminence and for whom she became a guiding force. Gibson Kemp, who later played drums for Rory Storm and eventually married her, credits Astrid's beguiling influence to an almost innate—and wildly eccentric—visionary style. "She had a tremendous feel for shape and form," he says, an unerring eye for the aesthetic, the unconventional, even the kinky, born out of a preoccupation to model herself after avant-garde Left Bank intellectuals.

Despite the difficulties of their often impenetrable accents, the vulnerable Sutcliffe was clearly entranced. He wrote a friend immediately after meeting the trio, explaining in no uncertain terms how their energy was irresistibly addictive. "I had never met anybody like them . . . ," he gushed. "It's somehow like a dream which I'm still participating in."

The young Germans were equally in thrall of their Liverpool darling. To them, he not only looked different from the other Beatles but seemed introspective and "refined." Jürgen Vollmer recalled, "My impression was that Stuart just didn't fit in. He was strange when compared to others in that group. He wasn't [a] part of the Beatles; he was always like an outsider . . . dreaming all the time that he played wrong notes and got looks from Paul and George." The young Germans felt an immediate affinity and confessed as much. "They asked me why I was playing in a rock and roll band as I obviously wasn't the type," Stuart wrote to a friend. He also admitted being delighted that they'd pegged him as an artist (unaware that John had already tipped off Voormann to that fact):

> They could see immediately, they said . . . Here was I, feeling
> the most insipid working member of the group being told how
> much superior I looked—this along side the great Romeo John
> Lennon and his two stalwarts Paul and George—the casanovas
> [sic] of Hamburg!

The trio—whom John dubbed the "exis" as a gibe to their existentialist affectations—knew practically nothing about rock 'n roll. Like most college students, they'd been fans of traditional jazz, with a bit of Nat King Cole and the Platters sifted into the mix. They were not alone. Rock 'n roll was still an anomaly to most of Germany, whose contact with the outside world lagged in the process of being repaired. None of them had ever seen rock 'n roll performed live, ignorant of the heated excitement it inspired, its racy suggestiveness. Not knowing what to expect, they were "totally and immediately fascinated by rock. That was it [for jazz]." From that point on in their lives, rock 'n roll delivered the gospel, and the Beatles were its perfect missionaries: entertaining, sexy, unpredictable. "We were totally fans, totally in awe," Vollmer remembered. "The quality, the chemistry, the way they interrelated was . . . marvelous." After seeing them that first time, the exis were overwhelmed, perhaps none of them more so than Astrid. She said, "It was like a merry-go-round in my head. . . . They looked absolutely astonishing. . . . [M]y whole life changed in a couple minutes. All I wanted was to be with them and to know them."

Astrid's way in to the Beatles was with her camera. An enthusiastic photographer (although an assistant to a well-known fashion and product lensman, she was nothing more than an amateur enthusiast), she offered to take pictures of the band in various casual poses around Hamburg, and the Beatles eagerly accepted. To the band, this was an unprecedented offer. Even among the longer-established groups like Kingsize Taylor and the Dominoes, it was rare to receive anything more than fuzzy snapshots taken by friends. By Astrid's calling the outing "a session," it elevated the shoot to something of more consequence, to the extent that they took it very seriously.

The photographs taken that afternoon in der Dom—a municipal park close by the Reeperbahn—show no ordinary group of musicians of the type available for weddings, church fetes, and socials. On the contrary, they resonate powerfully in ways that struck down all former conceptions. Astrid, in her enthusiasm, captured the grittiness, attitude, energy, and easy confidence that distinguished the Beatles from their slick, simpering counterparts. Hardly a show band or "teddy boys," as they'd been described by previous chroniclers, they projected a cool, postured identity, and in the process established the classic iconography for rock 'n roll bands for the next forty years.

Looking at these photos nearly half a century later, it seems extraordinary how effortlessly they took to this new identity. There was no precedent for it, no mentor to teach them how or what to project. Nevertheless, the Beatles show an acute awareness for individualism and style. Historians have said they basically adapted mannerisms gleaned from *The Wild One*—more specifically, its enigmatic star, Marlon Brando—but that seems limited. In a sense, what the Beatles conveyed was evolutionary, a shaping power, extending the cultural pose of the young. In one frame, taken against an old fairgrounds wagon, their whole aura is firmly in place: strength, scorn, rebellion, danger, mystery, sex appeal—presence. The Beatles appear almost eerily detached, insouciant, perhaps even a little threatening. John and Paul already look like the modern image of rock stars, with faces as composed and striking as the chords they played on their guitars. George, a gangly stick of a kid, stares directly, defiantly, into the camera, while Pete and Stuart flank the nucleus as a pair of oddly mismatched bookends. In another, posed in an overtly arty way on the hood of a tractor, George, Stuart, and John practically assault the lens with stares of frank, consuming heat. It's an explicit look of such hip, intense power—the new face of rock 'n roll.

Intuitive, ambitious, aroused, Astrid was not about to let a treasure like the Beatles slip through her fingers. Following the session in der Dom, she drove the band (minus Pete Best, who chose not to accompany them) straight to her mother's house in the rather posh suburb of Altona, where she entertained them with afternoon tea. To a man, the Beatles were properly impressed and taken by surprise. The sight of Astrid's handsome, solid-looking house and fashionable neighborhood was totally alien to the four boys, who had seen nothing of Hamburg outside of its grungy red-light district. Flowers and shrubs hugged the front steps, with a welcoming sweep of lawn. Children raced bicycles along the freshly paved street. Cars gleamed at the curb. It was tasteful, without being what local people referred to as *spiessbürger,* or grossly bourgeois, with a curl of the lip. It reminded the band of Childwall, in Liverpool, a suburb of impeccably manicured homes and estates, housing the city's upper crust.

Impressed as they were, however, the Beatles' reaction turned unsettled when they were escorted upstairs to Astrid's attic studio. It was a sight for which they were totally unprepared. The room, which faced the back of the house, was like Satan's lair—black curtains and sheets covered the shuttered window, the furniture had been painted black to match the bedspread, a black cloth covered the mirror, with sheets of aluminum foil pasted to the walls to reflect light from the black candles that cast a somber glow. Astrid, completely blasé, attributed it to her "Cocteau phase," which seemed to satisfy her openmouthed audience and heighten their intrigue.

In fact, the room had been decorated for Klaus Voormann, who had spent much of the previous two years there as Astrid's steady lover. Now, Klaus lived in an apartment "literally around the corner," and while he and Astrid still saw each other every day, the relationship had suddenly turned platonic—and for good reason. Moments after meeting Stuart Sutcliffe, Astrid had fallen headlong and seriously in love with him. At first, it was purely physical, spurred by his "tight jeans and leather jacket," but after those first few minutes, Jürgen Vollmer said, she became "fascinated with Stuart . . . his mysterious image, his artistic ties, [and] it was more chemical than anything else."

And not at all one-sided. "[Stuart] let it be known how much he was infatuated [with her]," a friend recalls. Others have said he "was besotted" with her. Almost from the start, Stuart began hounding Astrid's inner circle for any scrap of information about her—how she thought, what she liked, who she fancied. He didn't want to alienate Klaus, who remained devotedly at her side, but there was no secret to their mutual attraction; it was unrestrained and intense, and grew increasingly more passionate with each passing day. Pete Best, who watched things unfold from atop the drum stand, viewed it "like one of those fairy stories." And to a certain extent it was, although not one blessed with a happy ending.

[V]

From the beginning, John and Paul relied heavily on early recording heroes—most notably, the Everly Brothers and Buddy Holly—to give the vocals personality, then factored in their own distinctive tonal qualities for color and shading. While both were essentially tenors, Paul's voice tended toward being smooth, upbeat, and whimsical, while John, who was more nasal, provided an essential edge, albeit jagged at times, that stirred the blend with ambiguity. One of them would tackle the lead in any given song. As the melody expanded, the other—practically waiting to pounce—chimed in with a line of harmony until their voices overlapped and interweaved. Duets, however, are unstable compounds; tensions are unavoidably created from the moment each voice splinters into harmony. But when John and Paul sang together they pulled toward the middle. They complemented each other but also, to some degree, tried to match each other without losing balance.

There was more to the Beatles' magic than John's and Paul's voices, however. George's guitar had become the anchor to the arrangements, giving them form as well as movement. The incidental fills that unspooled between melody lines drew songs together and reinforced interest where things normally fell apart. Later, George would mastermind the Beatles' magnificent leads, playing them almost like a machine, but in Hamburg his riffs were in perpetual motion, sheepdogging, keeping the wandering, sometimes capricious energy of the rhythm guitars in focus, while other times brightening their steady patterns.

As it happened, George could also sing, not quite as stylishly as John and Paul, but with consistency and fervor. He proved more than capable as a lead vocalist, handling the chores on "Young Blood," "Three Cool Cats," and occasionally "Roll Over Beethoven," on which he alternated with John. When John took the spotlight, Paul and George doubled together at another microphone, creating what one Hamburg fan called "a very charming image."

Only Stuart remained a lingering problem. Nothing had changed: he had absolutely no facility for the bass, no innate feel for music. Even the exis, his most ardent admirers, recognized his inadequacy onstage. None of the Beatles had any illusions about Stu. They knew he was inept, eternally an amateur. But something else counted for more than pure ability: he was a mate. Yet for all the friendship in the world, his welcome as a Beatle was wearing thin. The better the Beatles got, the more dissatisfied Paul became. "I was always practical, thinking our band could be great," Paul said, "but with [Stu] on bass there was always something holding us back." He considered Stuart the "weak link," too glaring an embarrassment; it reflected on all of them, not just on Stuart. It troubled John as well, but he seemed helpless—or unwilling—to do anything about it. At times, the others suggested that Stuart turn away from the audience, looking moodily over his shoulder instead, so that the misplaced fingering wasn't easily detected. But people had ears, and with the band's rapid strides, the clams he played sounded ever more pronounced.

Stuart wasn't oblivious. In a letter to his friend Sue Williams written as early as October 1960, he explained:

> I have definitely decided to pack in the band at the beginning of January . . . particularly after what I forfeited in return for a few months in a foreign country*—but my curiosity is quenched—as far as rock and roll is concerned anyway.

It might have helped had he conveyed this decision to the other Beatles. Given January as a reference, they might have played out these few months

---

* This refers to the apparent disregard of his painting and the break in formal studies.

in a wisp of lighthearted amiability, with the anticipation of a fresh start in the New Year. But if Stuart contemplated leaving, as he'd implied, he kept the news to himself, which only served to sow resentment among the once-contented Beatles.

There is no doubt his musical shortcomings cost him dearly with John. Signs of souring showed in their usually puncture-proof relationship: veiled glances at first, then eventually the unforeseen snide comment lobbed into the midst of a group conversation. With John, there was always a lot of acid-tipped barbs flying around, but now he aimed them more accurately at Stuart, who internalized them, without a word of self-defense. Wrathful, John snapped without warning. He poked fun at Stuart's gracefulness, his persona, his size, and, of course, his infatuation with Astrid. "He was always kidding, but kidding in a way that was borderline hurting," said Jürgen Vollmer. As a small, mannered young man, Stuart had endured his share of taunts, in most cases gamely defending himself against them. "But he just seemed to take it from John," recalls Bill Harry. "Stuart was no match for him."

On October 21, a new club opened around the corner on the Reeperbahn, featuring an act unaffected by competition. That illustrious bad boy, Tony Sheridan, was back in business, headlining at the Top Ten, a sensational, glitzy venue in a huge space formerly occupied by a peep show, and fronting a configuration of the Jets, his revolving-door backing band, that knocked audiences dead. The Beatles went to see him every night after their show, sometimes even slipping in during breaks, stationing themselves practically at his feet so they could pick up pointers, songs, licks, riffs, anything that punched up their act.

Not surprisingly, no one proved more influential to the Beatles during this stretch. Tony did all sorts of obscure material, from Little Richard B-sides to urban blues; he did lovely versions of Bobby Darin's "Mighty Mighty Man" and "I'll Be There" and hot-wired standards such as "When the Saints Go Marching In," "Fever," and "My Bonnie Lies Over the Ocean" until they kicked out the jams. The Beatles pinched "Besame Mucho" from him, along with Bill Haley's gasoline-powered "Skinny Minnie," the song Sheridan always closed with. Thanks to Tony they got hip to R&B gurus like Jimmy Reed, T-Bone Walker, Jimmy Witherspoon, and John Lee Hooker. He was a walking encyclopedia of important material, to say nothing of the way he handled a guitar. "I've never seen anybody equal to him," musician John Frankland says forty years later, post-Hendrix, post-Allman, post-Thompson, post-Clapton. "He was a musician's musician"—a contortionist, an elocutionist with six strings. Over the years, he'd learned how to make the guitar talk—albeit in his own oddball language. "He would play solos that ran completely off-key, but somehow he would stay within the lines," recalls Johnny Byrne, who often accompanied the Beatles to Tony's sets at the Top Ten and watched openmouthed as he ran down half a dozen songs. Unlike his sidekicks with their solid-body Fenders and fancy Ricks, Sheridan wielded a big-bellied Martin Dreadnought with an electric pickup wedged under the strings, not a flexible instrument by any stretch of the imagination, and plied it like a knife and fork. Nothing got to him, except inertia. "He'd get guitar diarrhea—he couldn't stop playing," says Gibson Kemp, who described how Tony would "play 'Skinny Minnie' as the last song on Saturday morning at six [o'clock], and he'd still be playing it at eight, as they cleaned the club."

And no one worked harder onstage. He worked his husky voice until it cracked like old plaster, worked it to the bone every night. And he put his body through the kind of physical punishment that had no precedent in this idiom. John Frankland recalls how difficult it was to appear on the same bill. "When you followed Tony onstage, the microphone would be full of snot," he says. "And where he had been standing, you'd think somebody had thrown a bottle of water because that's how much the guy sweat. He'd come offstage literally soaking wet. That's how hard he pushed—he was a *worker* extraordinaire! No one could keep up with him."

Only a year later, Liverpool bands would complain about how the Beatles set a bad example by talking among themselves and to the audience, even smoking, while they performed onstage. But that, too, can be traced to Tony Sheridan, who played by his own rules. He never shut up, keeping up a running dialogue with the fans. Or, recalls Frankland: "He'd turn around in mid-song and scream at the drummer: 'You fucking son of a bitch!' Once, for no apparent reason, I saw him whack [pianist] Roy Young with a tambourine. He didn't give a damn about the audience. Tony played for himself."

All nonsense aside, however, he was a sight to behold. There was so much to learn from the way he worked a room, so much to absorb. The Beatles and the Hurricanes sensed that from the get-go. "In the end," recalls Johnny Byrne, "we started doing sets with him—Rory would get up first, then the Beatles. It was like a crazy jam session. We weren't getting paid for it, but it didn't matter. We honestly loved it."

So did the Top Ten audience. Word spread through Hamburg that the new club had it all, and that wasn't just limited to the talent. Everything about the Top Ten was bigger, better, bolder, brassier—a fact not lost on the Beatles. "We suddenly realized [it] was a far better club than Koschmider's," recalled Pete Best. "Better clientele, plus the sound system had echo mikes, reverb and all that type of stuff." The Beatles had been slaving away under dreadful circumstances for almost four months. Now they wanted better working conditions, more money, a new stage—and after they were invited to Sheridan's cozy flat above the Top Ten, a scene of nightly wild parties, well, they wanted that, too.

The last thing Koschmider expected was a power play by this ungrateful British band. He turned the Beatles down flat, reminding them of their existing contract extension, along with a clause that forbade them from playing at another club within a five-kilometer radius without his permission. Clearly, he'd heard about the crowd-pleasing jams with Sheridan and was taking steps to prevent any more of them.

As far as Bruno was concerned, that should have been the end of it. But the Beatles, stung by his curt rebuff, approached Peter Eckhorn, the Top Ten's slick, cutthroat young owner, and inquired about the possibility of a job. Eckhorn recognized them immediately as the band that had teamed up so successfully with Tony Sheridan. No doubt he also recognized the advantage it would give him in a heated turf war with Bruno Koschmider. As it happened, the current lineup of Jets were returning to London, necessitating a new house band to back his flaky star, and Eckhorn offered them the job on the spot.

This development inflamed Koschmider, who went on the offensive. He terminated the Beatles' contract at once, invoking a clause that bound them to employment for another, final month. Fortunately, Eckhorn agreed to wait. But the interim climaxed in fiasco. For months George had been flouting a local curfew, the *Ausweiskontrolle*, that forbade minors from being out after ten o'clock at night. The band was required to make an announcement from the stage, a few minutes before the curfew went into effect, at which time police canvassed the crowd, examining passports. Ironically, the authorities never thought to check the band, and George, who was still seventeen, had skated free all these months. Suddenly, however, on the evening of November 20, he came under scrutiny. No one knew who tipped off the police, but everyone suspected it was Bruno Koschmider. At the same time it was discovered that George had no work permit. "So I had to leave [Germany]," he said. "I had to go home on my own." No grace period was extended; he was ordered to comply within twenty-four hours.

Through the early-morning hours, George worked frantically to teach John the lead guitar parts to their songs so that the Beatles could function as a quartet. Merely a capable rhythm guitarist, John didn't have the chops to pull off anything that required more intricate fretwork. Then some-one—no one is sure who—came up with a clever solution: they wouldn't need a lead playing behind Tony Sheridan. It made more sense to leave the Kaiserkeller early and take their chances with Koschmider.

Seizing a competitive advantage, Eckhorn offered the Beatles immedi-ate work along with a modest attic apartment above the Top Ten. It seemed like the perfect antidote to an otherwise deteriorating situation. Without delay, John and Stuart moved their gear in and claimed a set of bunk beds along the wall. Paul and Pete returned to the Bambi Kino to collect their things. According to accounts given by both of them, the theater was dark when they got there. There was no way to see along the hall, much less their belongings, so they stuck condoms to a nail in the concrete wall and set fire to them. "This gave us just enough light to throw our stuff into our suitcases," Pete recalled.

Sometime in the early morning of December 1, only hours after the boys had gone to bed, two plainclothes German policemen burst into the Top Ten, seeking Paul and Pete for questioning. Allowed nothing more than to dress, the boys were hustled off to the local station house, where they were grilled on their whereabouts for the past twenty-four hours. It took a bit of doing, piecing together the phrases of broken English, before the boys deduced what the problem was. Their breach of contract and sneaky departure had apparently infuriated Bruno Koschmider, who, out of revenge, accused them of "attempting to burn down the Bambi Kino." It was a ludicrous charge, yet nonetheless effective. Paul and Pete did their best to explain away the incident—to no avail. The police were not amused and decided to scare the British hooligans, transferring them to a dingy jail cell for several hours before finally deporting them.

Leaving behind their clothing and instruments, Paul and Pete arrived back in Liverpool the next day, exhausted, broke, and greatly disillusioned. John and Stuart had remained in Hamburg, but without work permits it was impossible for them to earn a living. Besides, there was no one left to play with. John stayed only long enough to cadge money for a train ticket home. Stuart, recovering from a head cold, borrowed airfare from Astrid and followed him several weeks later.

The incredible adventure was over. The Beatles had not only crept home penniless and in disgrace but had burned several important bridges back in Germany. Each had to do some fancy explaining to his parents, to whom he'd boasted about fame and riches before setting off for Hamburg. In almost every case, they left out key details about the gig's bitter resolution and avoided any speculation about their future. Perhaps more notably, they couldn't face one another. John suffered from such a hollow-eyed depression, friends remember, that after Aunt Mimi helped clean him up, he crawled into bed, locked his door, and refused most company. When he finally did appear, two weeks later, no attempt was made to reach Paul. George, too, said he "felt ashamed" and looked for work, as did Paul, who glumly took a menial job, at his father's insistence. There was little, if any, feeling of optimism. Pete and his mother worked the phone in an effort to recover the band's lost equipment—which they did—but for several weeks afterward no one touched base. It seemed pointless. They weren't saying as much, but each of the Beatles was convinced that his career in the band was over.

[1]

If the Beatles weren't the same when they returned home, neither was Liverpool. The city had drifted into a gradual but unyielding decline, and yet, the beat scene thrived like never before. Faced with such opportunity, the Beatles could hardly remain dormant for long. A week before Christmas, during another idle afternoon, Pete phoned George and suggested they comb Liverpool for potential gigs. A few days later John and Pete were reunited, meeting over coffee at their regular corner table in the Jacaranda. Still "disgruntled and very angry" over the Hamburg fiasco, armed with theories and eager to rebuild the band's stalled career, they wanted to touch base with Allan Williams on the off chance of snaring a few stray dates.

But Williams was struggling with his own set of woes. Petulantly, he told the boys that Bruno Koschmider had failed to pay him the 10 percent commission promised for booking the Beatles into the Kaiserkeller. Plus, only two weeks earlier, his latest venture, a flashy Liverpool version of the Top Ten, had met with unexpected catastrophe. Intrigued by the explosion of beat music and the popularity of local bands, he'd rented an old bottle-washing plant on the periphery of town, hired a personality named Bob Wooler to manage it, and set out to cash in on the new phenomenon with lightning speed. In no time, he and Wooler had booked an impressive lineup of top London talent to alternate with native stock, the objective being that the headliners would focus attention on—and help groom— Merseyside bands, who would inevitably sign up with a talent agency Williams was mulling. For five memorable nights the Top Ten hosted packed, enthusiastic houses, and on the sixth night the club mysteriously burned down. (Wooler, to this day, claims it "was torched.")

Williams was in no mood to throw in with the Beatles right now. As a means of shelving the subject, he introduced John and Pete to Wooler, who happened to be seated at a nearby table, licking his own wounds. Wooler had good reason to be dejected. In a span of a few days, he'd fallen from the lap of a promising future to sudden standing unemployment. Not only had Wooler resigned his "job for life" with British Transport Railways to run the now ashen club, he had tied his entire well-being to a rogue like Allan Williams, whom he suspected of hanky-panky. The earnest, high-principled Wooler had begun "drinking heavily" as a result.

The role of a pop impresario was a new one for Bob Wooler. He had spent most of his adult life in thrall of Tin Pan Alley. He had even taken a stab at songwriting, assuming the nom de plume Dave Woolander, because he was "convinced that the great songwriters were all Jewish." After several failed attempts at the craft, Wooler abandoned his dream—temporarily, at least—and turned to artist management, spending evenings promoting a skiffle band from Garston called the Kingstrums. One night at Wilson Hall in Garston, near the end of a set, Wooler overheard one of the jivers say, "The band's not bad, but—who *are* they?" Wooler stepped to the mike and "hesitantly and tremblingly" announced the Kingstrums.

Seemingly older than his twenty-eight years, Wooler looked nothing like the teds and surly scrappers who populated the dance halls. To these teenagers, he was more of a paternal figure, a slight man with a courtly, engaging demeanor, always meticulously groomed in a sport coat and tie. But the kids responded to him; in no time, they actually expected to hear Bob Wooler's rich, melodic voice whenever a local band went onstage. Even after a long day at British Rail, Wooler spent virtually every night whirling from hall to hall: the Winter Gardens Ballroom in Garston, Holly Oak at Penny Lane, Peel Hall in the Dingle, the Jive Hive and Alexandra Hall in Crosby, Lathom Hall in Seaforth, the Orrell Park Ballroom in Aintree, Blair Hall in Walton, Hambleton Hall in Huyton, the Riverpark Ballroom in Hoylake, the Plaza in St. Helen's, the Marine Club in Southport, Knotty Ash Village Hall, Litherland Town Hall, the Aintree Institute, Mossway, the David Lewis Theatre. "Long before the Cavern, these venues provided rock 'n roll havens for Liverpool's teenagers," recalls Wooler, who either bummed a ride with the bands or caught the bus and train. Usually he spent his entire night out, mixing with the kids and gabbing. When he wasn't spinning records, he solicited bookings for the groups he liked, even calling from his stodgy office at the Garston Docks. "I had a Jekyll and Hyde existence," he says, "spending days clerking behind a desk, then at night becoming the Alan Freed of Liverpool."

Wooler was also a legendary soft touch, and the Beatles seemed like such decent kids. He couldn't help himself. Working the phone in the Jacaranda kitchen, he booked them into a gig at Litherland Town Hall.

—————

There was also the Casbah. Few people had a more unsung role in the Beatles' young career than Pete's enterprising mother, Mo. "She was always there to throw us a lifeline," Pete has said over the years, and this time proved no different. Behind the dominating personality and owlish stare, beyond the keen sense for putting out fires with an appropriately leveled word, lurked a mom with a big, mushy heart. "She gave them the kind of work they couldn't get at other venues," says Bob Wooler. "Without her, it remains doubtful they would have held together so ably."

The Casbah was exactly what the Beatles needed: it was familiar, intimate, and friendly, a good springboard for diving back into the 'Pool. There was a big, boisterous local crowd, which provided the kind of delirious reaction they'd been hoping for. Of late, Mo had anticipated something special. The Seniors had played there only a week earlier and briefed her about the Beatles' transformation in Hamburg, but it was nothing she could have envisioned. The band took everyone by complete surprise, including Pete's dumbstruck mother, who watched them—wordlessly, for a change—from her post behind the refreshment counter. Their look, their sound, their poise—it was "a revelation to behold."

Word spread swiftly through Liverpool after the Beatles' Casbah and Litherland Town Hall shows. All these months, bands had presented themselves as a likely alternative to Cliff Richard and the Shadows, each in neat little suits, with neat little songs. And now this band of black-leather creatures had popped up "and had the nerve to play hard rock 'n roll." They made no concession to etiquette. "We'd been pussyfooting around . . . and the Beatles just came straight at you," said a guitarist with Rikki and the Red Streaks. Look mean, play hard—it was a revolutionary concept and contradicted everything that had gone before it.

—————

Whatever confidence the Beatles had managed to generate onstage of late was quickly dissipated in uncertainty. Stuart still hadn't returned from Hamburg. Meanwhile, offers for the band were pouring in.

What had detained Stuart for so long? Everyone knew he was dazzled by Astrid Kirchherr. He had stolen every opportunity to be with her during the Kaiserkeller gig, courting her between sets and spending nights in Altona. Leaving her seemed out of the question. But everyone was surprised—flabbergasted—when Stuart wrote home that they were engaged.

No one had seen it coming, least of all his parents, who "were utterly, *utterly* devastated" by the news. Their hopes were pinned on Stuart, the family's golden boy, for whom they had sacrificed beyond practical wisdom. This news, as they read it, wrecked everything: his art, his education, his enormous promise. He had written before Christmas to ask for their blessing, but they had a difficult time imparting it. As did George: "He didn't seem keen on the idea of me getting engaged," Stuart divulged in a letter to his sister Pauline adding that he hoped everyone would "become used to the idea" in time.

Of course, he was wrong. Upon his return in early February, Stuart's mother was still suffering from the shock, anguished that "anybody would be taking her son away" from her. And the Beatles, in their own way, proved no more receptive. They needled Stuart mercilessly about the engagement, "picking on him" for being weak, distracted, foolish, pussy-whipped. At face value, it seems absurd that a band in the grasp of hard-earned recognition should react with such vitriol toward a mate's personal happiness. There was nothing in the way Stuart presented it to them that was either glib or contentious. Yet they did care, refusing to let up even as he rejoined the Beatles fold.

Even Stuart must have realized it wasn't just about Astrid. For several months a rancorous dissension had been sowing over Stuart's ersatz role in the Beatles. Now it seemed only underscored by their success. They'd felt it sorely since returning to Liverpool, with either Paul or the Blackjacks' Chas Newby standing in for him. Wrote George: "Come home sooner. . . . It's no good with Paul playing bass, we've decided, that is if he had some kind of bass and amp to play on!"* But that was so much blather. Friendship aside, everyone knew Stuart was holding them back. Yet no one had the heart or the wherewithal to suggest that he step aside. That responsibility was John's burden, and he clearly wasn't ready—or able—to shoulder it.

Despite this growing dilemma, the Beatles clung to their ambition, working steadily, if not furiously, at the lavish number of dates available each week. They were playing somewhere almost every night, occasionally doubling up gigs and commuting between them at a dizzying, exhilarating

---

* *Without a bass at his disposal, Paul was forced to play his guitar upside down and restrung with piano wire to imitate the sound of a bass.*

pace. "For the first time people were following us around," George noticed, "coming to see us personally, not just coming to dance."

[II]

Toward the end of 1959, Alan Sytner sold the Cavern to the family accountant, a tidy thirty-two-year-old man named Ray McFall, who, like Sytner, loved jazz and had worked in the club gratis as a means of indulging his passion. Nothing really changed in the transition of ownership. Jazz still ruled supreme—McFall rather brazenly announced his intention to "put Liverpool on the map as the leading jazz center in the country outside London"—but in a gesture to diversity, he hired the Swinging Blue Jeans once a week to help lighten the frowsty atmosphere. The Blue Jeans were an anomaly: not quite jazz but not quite skiffle, either. Falling somewhere in between, they played a kind of pop-inflected swing that appeased the Cavern purists while catering to disgruntled teenagers. Soon after the Blue Jeans came aboard, McFall arranged for them to take charge of a Tuesday night showcase, when the club was normally dark. Rory Storm, Gerry and the Pacemakers, and the Searchers made initial appearances there, and while the Blue Jeans continued "doing the jazzy-type stuff," their guest artists played rock 'n roll. Normally, crusader McFall would have pulled the plug, but the accountant in him overruled his heart. Not only was the turnout a phenomenal success, but, as the Blue Jeans' Ray Ennis reports: "Tuesday's show became the most popular Cavern night of the week."

In fact, attendance for the jazz shows had fallen off to such a degree that "Ray eventually had to make the choice of switching totally over to rock 'n roll or to close the place down," Ennis recalls. McFall bit the bullet. Henceforth, from May 1960 on, the Cavern presented an array of local beat acts, reserving Thursdays—ordinarily the slowest night of the week—for the last handful of its earnest jazz disciples.

The Cavern was still a filthy, sweltering, fetid, claustrophobic little firetrap of a club. The walls and ceiling sweated absolute humidity; there was no exit aside from the main entrance, which was located three stories above the cellar and accessible only by an unlighted stone stairway. An ersatz ventilation pipe had been installed as a concession to the public health department, but as it extended only about thirty feet up a shaft between two taller buildings, it was functionally worthless. The plumbing was marginal, Victorian, a disaster. And with eight hundred to a thousand smoking, wasted teenagers sardined into a space fit for six hundred under ideal conditions, it was an accident waiting to happen. Adrian Barber puts it quite plainly when he says, "The Cavern was a shithole—but with soul. No place was more conducive to the spirit of rock 'n roll."

Barber had played there in the dying days of trad jazz, intruding on its turgidity with Cass and the Cassanovas. They were the first all-out pop band to invade its yellowed arches, not as a featured attraction with the dignity accorded a jazz outfit but as noontime bait to attract the local office staff on their lunch breaks from neighboring businesses. Ray McFall decided to revive the lunch session with rock 'n roll in the hope that it might generate a new audience.

Even so, it remained a distasteful venture. "You could see Ray putting his rubber gloves on," says Barber. "We were what he called toxic. And we were warned: 'If you make too much noise, you're out!'"

News had drifted back to Bob Wooler that something special was occurring at the Cavern, and he wandered over there during a lunchtime to see what the fuss was about. As hard as it is to believe, he'd never been there before. The whole oddness of it amused him, especially the setting—three misshapen tunnels, linked by arches, dug out from the core of Liverpool's mustiest substratum; there was a wee patch of a stage, no curtain, with kids dancing, "kicking up a storm," in between the chapel chairs that lined a vaulted middle chamber. "At first, it was difficult to breathe down there," Wooler remembers. And cranking up the heat was the Big Three, whom Wooler knew casually from gigs at the halls he'd emceed.

He watched them for a while, amazed by the vigorous scene—and despondent that he wasn't a part of it. The experience with Allan Williams and the star-crossed Top Ten still rankled him, Wooler tending to it with alcohol "because everything was going so awfully." As the Big Three came offstage, Johnny Hutch thrust a microphone at Wooler and said, "Come on, say something, Bob." Wooler, momentarily flustered, asked Hutch for a suggestion. "Tell them who's on tomorrow," the burly drummer grunted. Wooler hesitated, thinking. He'd overheard Hutch refer to the club as "the cave," so in inimitable form, Bob crooned, "Remember, all you cave dwellers, that the Cavern is the best of cellars. Tomorrow, it's Tommy and the Metronomes who will play your lunchtime session. Make sure you don't miss it."

Ray McFall, who was at the other end of the club, talking to the sound system consultants, asked: "Who was that?" "It sounds like Bob Wooler," said Charlie McBain, who knew Wooler from Wilson Hall. A few days later, on a return visit, Wooler was confronted by McFall and offered a job as the Cavern's lunchtime deejay. In no time, Wooler and the Cavern became a local institution. But it was more than spinning records and frisky announcing, which he did with great flair; Wooler was the personality the rock 'n roll scene had been waiting for, its spokesman, its guiding star. And unlike the promoters, who were strictly bottom-line men, Wooler genuinely loved the scene and its offbeat components. He wasn't tough, he wasn't commanding, but he oozed stature, and that gave him plenty of influence with his audience.

More than anything, however, Wooler had a wonderful touch. Every song benefited from a splash of his fine, flamboyant patter; every artist got the full star treatment. From noon until 12:30 Wooler played records—on a single turntable, no less, unthinkable by today's standards—that he personally collected and carried there himself in a handsome, blue wooden case made by a joiner on the Garston Docks. The band performed from 12:30 to 1:10, came off for half an hour, and went on again at 1:40 until 2:15. Wooler provided "time checks" at every interval for those who had to keep an eye on the clock; most everyone there was on a strict lunch break from their jobs, so there was much to-ing and fro-ing throughout the two-hour session.

The Beatles had gravitated to the Cavern in early February to check it out, although no one had to sell them on its virtues. A daytime gig there would be the perfect complement to their already overbooked evening schedule, but hard as they tried, it seemed impossible to break into the lineup. Mona Best had put the moves on Ray McFall without success. Even Bob Wooler, who sung their praises, got nowhere with his boss. According to Wooler, "McFall was the law unto himself and you had to go easy on him with a new act. I was constantly saying, 'The Beatles are available for lunch, Ray.' 'I've never heard of them.' I knew he had, but I played along. 'They're quite marvelous, Ray.' He'd put on that pained expression of his. Then, one day, *he* came up with the idea of booking them—all by himself."

Following Ray McFall's initiative, the Beatles debuted at the Cavern on February 21, 1961, playing a lunchtime session to a solidly packed house. Little is known about the particulars of the show aside from the fact that they got £3 for their efforts; in the months and years to come, the band played the club so often that individual details have become blurred in the retelling. But suffice it to say, their performance made an impact on the

Cavern regulars that sent the band's stock soaring smartly. While the Big Three were loud and Rory's antics entertaining, no band sang with more finesse and more style, or provided more drama in their delivery. What the Beatles had was stage presence, personality that conveyed a real intimacy with the audience. The girls there locked into it right away, and much to emphatic denials, the boys soon followed suit.

Even Ray McFall caught the vibe, sending word through Bob Wooler that the band was welcome back at the first opportunity. He had to stand in line, however. The day of their Cavern debut, for instance, they played two additional gigs—at the new Casanova Club, across town, and at the scene of their breakout, Litherland Town Hall—a situation known among the musicians as "piggybacking." Suddenly they were in great demand; work was everywhere. Each great performance led to further offers. For musicians who had been living on handouts, the goodwill of parents, and the occasional £2 gig, they were finally pulling their own financial weight. No doubt, Paul and George were outearning their fathers, and while Mimi continued to hammer John about certain failure, she couldn't have been too disapproving of his £25-per-week income. The Beatles had never strayed from their game plan to play music for a living and they never blinked in the face of serious money woes, but no one really expected it to materialize in this manner—not in Liverpool, not in such a gratifying way. Becoming a rock 'n roll star, making records, was still the ultimate goal, but for the time being there was plenty of action to groove on.

———

Both Dot Rhone and Cynthia Powell had waited enduringly for their boyfriends to return. "It was as if they'd gone off to war," Dot recalls— except that in this case, only the girls stood a chance of being wounded. During those long, lonely months, Paul and John had written faithfully, John to an almost obsessive degree, often scribbling twelve to twenty pages to Cynthia, the same simplistic pledges of love, over and over and over: "Lovely lovely lovely lovely Cyn Lovely Cyn I love lovely Cynthia Cynthia I love you You are wonderful I adore you I want you I love you I need you . . ." Of course, the Beatles reported only selective highlights from their Hamburg adventures, leaving out anything that so much as hinted at promiscuity. But the letters served their purpose and kept the relationships intact.

Presumably, Dot and Cynthia knew the score. Hamburg's earthly delights were legendary, especially now that so many musicians had returned home. Neither had any illusions about the Beatles' fidelity. As Cynthia expressed it, "John was a flirt." But it seems doubtful she understood the full extent of his exploits. "As long as they were happy, we were happy," Dot says.

Neither young woman summoned the courage to press her man about plans to go back. Getting back had become an obsession for the band, but there were so many hurdles: an outstanding charge of arson, Paul's and Pete's deportation ban, necessary work permits. One obstacle was lifted on February 25, when George turned eighteen; however, that appeared minor compared with the other snags.

One by one, those snags began to unravel. For months, Peter Eckhorn, the Top Ten's receptive owner, had appealed to the West German Immigration Office for a concession on the Beatles' status. Pete Best worked the same angle from Liverpool, papering the German consul's office with requests for visas. In the meantime, Bruno Koschmider withdrew his ridiculous arson charge against Pete and Paul and promised not to oppose their return, somehow hoping, one might presume, to engage the Beatles again.

Stuart got there first. In the bleakness of a Liverpool winter, he brightened at every thought of Astrid and in early March headed back to her without a thought to anything else. Impervious to his parents' dismay, he intended to marry Astrid. Unapologetic, he resigned from the Liverpool College of Art—a drastic, definitive move—applying to the State College of Art, nicknamed the Hochschule, Hamburg's leading conservatory. The decision practically broke his mother's heart. Forsaking his scholarship seemed like such a tragic mistake to Millie, who was also terrified for her son's safety. In January he had been beaten up again, this time more severely, fracturing his skull, following a gig at Lathom Hall.* But no matter how Millie begged him to reconsider, Stuart stood his ground.

The Beatles were somewhat less despairing. As far as performing went, they were better off without Stuart, and his absence gave them time to regroup for Hamburg without having to compensate for his unhandiness. In fact, as soon as he left, they plunged into a heated round of rehearsals, with afternoons devoted almost entirely to rejuvenating their tired repertoire. With two months at the Top Ten scheduled to begin on April 1, they were in desperate need of new material. A contract negotiated with Peter Eckhorn engaged them for seven hours a night, seven nights a week. Even at the peak of their skill, this would prove daunting. On top of that, they'd be co-

---

* *John also broke his little finger in the skirmish.*

starring with Tony Sheridan, whose song bag seemed bottomless. It was important that the Beatles hold their own.

Why didn't they simply perform the songs Paul and John had written? Even a wildcat such as Sheridan couldn't compete with the punch of original tunes. Certainly there were already several dozen Lennon-McCartney numbers polished to perfection. With a backward glance, it seems doubtful that "Love Me Do," "Please Please Me," and "P.S. I Love You" would have survived the near-convulsive pace of a Hamburg jam. Any one of them might have brought a set that included "Long Tall Sally," "Do You Want to Dance," "Roll Over Beethoven," "Whole Lotta Shakin' Goin' On," and "Money" to a screeching halt. Later, at the Cavern, when the Beatles established their quirky song sequence, they could mix and match numbers as they saw fit, but until that time they exercised good judgment in bagging their originals for the future.

No one knew better than the Beatles how to fatten their repertoire. At NEMS, they routinely scanned the new releases that were piled in a box near the cash register. Selecting a batch, they relied on the salesgirls—many of whom were budding Beatles fans—to play them while they squeezed into one of the listening booths. "We'd listen to both sides of a record, not just the 'A' side," Pete Best recalled of a process that recurred "three or four times a week." If anything caught someone's ear, he simply claimed it for a solo spot in the show. Then the clerks were enlisted to play the song two or three additional times until the band had the words and proper chord sequence down, or they "clubbed together" and bought it.

[III]

The Top Ten was a definite "step up" from the Kaiserkeller (which itself would soon close), beginning with its street-level location on the bustling Reeperbahn. It was also a step back into Germany's violent past. The *kellners* (waiters), under the brutal command of Horst Fascher (who had served in the same capacity at the Kaiserkeller), carried gas guns and "knuckledusters" in addition to the ubiquitous truncheons—and they relished using them. "If someone got out of line," a musician recalls, "the waiters simply dragged them outside in the alley . . . and pounded these people to shit." On the other hand, the Reeperbahn drew a better class of nightcrawler, if that was a reasonable consideration. Even the exis found it a sociable hangout, turning out in such numbers that rockers often formed a minority constituency. At the Top Ten, feeling more relaxed and confident, they mimicked the rockers' burly leather gear with their own take on the look: a sleek, sophisticated version in glove-soft jackets and matching pants. Stuart, of all people, strove to personify the trend. He and Astrid, lately inseparable, showed up at the Top Ten looking stunning in identical expensive licorice-stick suits that were the envy of their Liverpool friends. Certainly the Beatles approved of the style; in time, they would all buy similar getups.

Among his potential costars, there was always some trepidation about opening for Sheridan—or following him. But the Beatles looked forward to it: his shows were as riotously loose as theirs, with more energy and interaction than other bands in the district. He was restless and unpredictable, sure, but stylistically he was always moving forward, pushing, pushing, pushing to break up the monotony of the standards everyone played. Recalled Pete: "He liked us backing him . . . because of the great harmonies we used to do for him. . . . [H]e'd have three people harmonizing with him, which produced a great overall sound." Reciprocally, adding Sheridan's guitar to their lineup thrust the Beatles into instrumental overdrive. It also gave them something to shoot for. As guitarists they were good, they were very good—but musically, Sheridan was light-years ahead of them.

The only drawback was durability. With both acts onstage all night, it became impossible to maintain the sky-high energy. There were fewer opportunities for breaks, or "powsas" (pauses), as they were called; stage jams seemed to go on forever, sapping their strength. No one complained, but the cumulative effect took its toll. Spirits flagged, tempers flared. Fortunately, Sheridan came to the rescue with his bottomless stash of amphetamines. "Here's something to keep you awake," he'd offer the Beatles, doling out handfuls of Preludin with which to fortify them.

Stuart's former plans to quit the Beatles, once clear-cut and firm, seemed to have evaporated. According to his sister Pauline, "in letters from Germany, he states quite emphatically that he's improving [as a musician] . . . that his repertoire was expanding." Elsewhere, Stuart wrote about the satisfaction he derived from performing solo each night, when he came center stage to sing "Love Me Tender":

> Everybody says I sing it better than Elvis. . . . Just before I sing, I receive the best applause of the night. Minutes after I finish singing the people all look at me with sad eyes and sad looks on

> their faces. Recently, I've become very popular both with girls
> and homosexuals who tell me I'm the sweetest, most beautiful
> boy. . . . Also it appears that people refer to me as the James
> Dean of Hamburg.

Clearly he loved the spotlight, just as he was conflicted about leaving the band. Appearing on that stage provided a release, emotionally and artistically. It made no demands on him, unlike a canvas—or Astrid, for that matter. Meanwhile, the others rode him mercilessly—about his appearance, his size, his dependence on Astrid, anything that crossed their minds. Stuart had always been the butt of some rude "mickey-taking," as the Scousers called it, but as the gulf between the boys widened, the ragging turned nasty, with an edge of abusiveness. Hardly a night went by that John didn't turn on Stuart, needling him, severely berating some aspect of his fragile character. As Stuart ventured further from the band, it was harder to regard him as one of the gang. As he withdrew from the pack, moving into Astrid's house seemed like the final straw.

Over the years, the Beatles faced many tough judgment calls that fared as high drama in their overall saga, each one handled definitively but carelessly (in fact, badly), ending with their inevitable split. The first—dismissing Allan Williams—was only a prelude.

Williams had never formally served as the Beatles' manager—or anybody else's. Says his first wife, Beryl, "It was loose and always rather benevolent. There was a day-to-day routine he went through: 'Oh, here's a letter. Let us send a group to Hamburg—or the south of France. Which group is available? Oh, *you* can go.' He never really referred to himself as anyone's manager." But for almost a year, he'd exclusively booked the Beatles' Liverpool gigs and not only introduced them to the exotica of Hamburg but actually took them there by hand. A business card that read THE BEATLES / SOLE DIRECTION: A. WILLIAMS was passed to promoters when they inquired whom to contact for bookings, leaving no uncertainty about his intent. And if there were doubts, it was settled by the 10 percent commission he collected—and they paid without any coercion—from their wages.

But the way they saw it, Williams had played no role whatsoever in their engagement at the Top Ten, despite the fact he had issued a contract for it. Pete Best arranged the booking himself, and upon the Beatles' arrival in Hamburg it was decided that paying a cut of their fee was unwarranted.

Shortly thereafter, most likely at John's urging, Stuart informed Williams by letter that the Beatles had no intention of paying his commission. Their refusal was based on the pretext that an extraordinary income tax was being deducted from their Top Ten earnings, leaving them no cushion with expenses from their weekly draw, but that was clearly an excuse. Dismissing the seriousness of its contents ("[It] struck me as being completely unfair," Williams recalled), he wrote back, explaining that all workers had tax withheld from their income, and if they hadn't before, then they were extremely lucky.

It made no difference to the Beatles. Stuart's follow-up letter instructed Williams that the band was taking a hard line. There would be no commission: that much was final.

Later, Williams would claim that "he wasn't disappointed" by their decision. There were other bands, better bands, worth his attention and expertise. At the time, however, he angrily banned them from setting foot in the Blue Angel and warned of repercussions.

In Hamburg, far away from the storm's epicenter, his threats hardly seemed worth taking seriously. Their shows with Tony Sheridan were models of the smoldering rock 'n roll rave-up power extravaganzas that stretched on for hours at a clip. As a performer, Sheridan was as electrifying as ever, but with the Beatles at his back, his act leaped into the stratosphere. "It was loud," recalled a regular who marveled at the intensity level. The sound they put out was "amazing, unlike anything Hamburg ever heard before—or since."

This was an entirely new experience for them, being the center of attention, the talk of the town. And it allowed them to experiment with new roles and identities that were far beyond Liverpool's grasp. Of all the Beatles, Stuart was the one who proved most open to new experiences. The first to don a leather suit, he made use of flamboyant clothes and accessories to transform himself. Part of this enthusiasm stemmed from Astrid's fascination with clothing and image. Her sense of drama was beguiling. None of the Beatles pushed the envelope further than Stuart, and when he showed up at the Top Ten one night sporting a flashy new haircut, it set off a bomb in the Hamburg music world that resonated for years to come. The style was a takeoff on the exis' "French" cut, combed long and splayed across the forehead in a soft, sculpted fringe. "Astrid had styled it," said

Jürgen Vollmer, who wore his hair in a similar fashion. To the Germans, the look was nothing extraordinary. "In my art school . . . all the boys used to have this haircut," Astrid acknowledged sometime later. While dating Klaus Voormann, she had urged him to cut his hair that way, to please her aesthetically, as well as to show his dedication; with Stuart's accession, it became his dutiful rite of passage.

There is no clear way of knowing how the other Beatles responded in truth to Stuart's deviant hairstyle. Out of ignorance—or envy—they lashed out defensively, pelting Stuart with an arsenal of childish taunts. But two days later a hesitant George followed suit, brushing his pompadour into an informal shaggy mop, and, like that, the mold for the Beatle haircut was indelibly cast.

The Beatles' first few weeks back in Hamburg had been another lusty fun-filled adventure, but things took a sedate turn when Cynthia and Dot showed up to visit. As expected, they appeared in Hamburg like misplaced, long-lost relatives, and John and Paul were almost immediately swallowed up in their girlfriends' needy demands.

A noticeable gulf formed between them from the very start of their reunion. Cynthia got off the train in Hamburg and noticed a shift in the boys' personalities. "The pills and booze they had been stuffing into themselves had heightened their senses beyond our reason, and they overwhelmed us with their nonstop chat and frenzied excitement." The amphetamine rush had caught the girls off guard, but after "two weeks in Hamburg," she noted, "we were all on them."

There were other changes, too, changes that proved more heart-warming and encouraging. From the moment Dot rushed into Paul's arms, she noticed that "he seemed more grown-up . . . more confident." She could tell right off that "he loved being in Hamburg, he was so excited about all it had to offer."

And though no one said as much aloud, the prospect of marriage was on everyone's mind. Cynthia and Dot certainly discussed it with breathless enchantment, and if letters home were any indication of John's true feelings, he was similarly marriage-minded. And yet there were lingering questions, not the least of which was their age. Also, the band was on the verge of something important; everyone could feel it. The vacation in Hamburg was the first measure of how the girls would take to the Beatles' expanding success. This was the world they'd all left home in pursuit of.

As it turned out, the reunion with the girls was a glorious one. John and Paul, enormously attentive, romanced them with Hamburg proper by day and St. Pauli by night. "We did a lot of sightseeing," Dot recalls of her "idyllic time" with Paul. "There was a boat tour of Hamburg harbor and visits to churches." John took Cynthia to more familiar turf, the port, where they clutched hands and watched ferries scuttling the waves around the Elbe's endless basins. And when the sights became burdensome, everyone shopped. After embracing Hamburg's everyday charms, each girl was treated to a glimpse of kinky street life, taken for a stroll along the Herbertstrasse in an attempt to shock them silly, which amused the boys.

The seedy sideshow produced the desired effect, but the girls were more shocked and initially speechless when Astrid Kirchherr appeared. They had been hearing endlessly about her since the Beatles' brief homestand—Astrid's beauty, style, sophistication, sexiness, and, on top of everything, her extraordinary photographs. Astrid, Astrid, Astrid: she seemed like a dream girl to her Liverpool counterparts, gifted and impossibly gorgeous—not to mention an A-number-one threat. "She sounded as though she could run rings around me in every way," Cynthia recalled in a 1978 memoir. Astrid and John gobbled Prellies together and gossiped like magpies; they even occasionally held hands. Of course, few women could have satisfied John's Brigitte Bardot fantasy more ably than Astrid. Like the art college beauty Johnnie Crosby, she was a blond, slim-hipped, heat-seeking woman oozing mystique. But as far as is known, John's relationship with Astrid never got more physical than a brotherly hug. It wasn't that he didn't lust after her—he did, most likely in a big way, too. But she was Stuart's girl, so that's where it began and ended. And as it happened, the girls hit it off, which was fortunate since it had been arranged that Cynthia would board with Astrid, while Paul and Dot bunked on a houseboat owned by Rosa Hoffman, the Kaiserkeller bathroom attendant who, like Horst Fascher, had decamped to the Top Ten.

Even though she "felt uncomfortable around the boys," with "no self-confidence" to ground her, the Hamburg nights were filled with a devil-may-care vitality that Dot had never experienced before. "Everyone was so alive," she remembers, "so full of hope." But despite the esprit, she detected cracks in the facade. "You could see it if you just watched Pete Best," she says. "He was very quiet in those situations, unable to join in the conversation with the other guys. He was never fast enough for their comments. John and Paul were fierce, and George was no threat to them." But Pete was not the main issue. "Even though the girls loved Pete, Paul wasn't really jealous of him. But he hated Stu." In fact, everything Stuart did now seemed to enrage him. And after years of excusing this travesty, suffering Stuart's arrogance and capitulating to John's apologies—still, Paul was forced to swallow his anger. It wasn't just the music and the hair and the clothes. "It's true that Paul had his eye on Stu's bass," Dot says, "but, in fact, he was jealous of Stu, especially of Stu's friendship with John." What's more, Stuart flaunted it. Time and again, he put it under Paul's nose and gave it a scornful swish.

Dot must have sensed things were coming to a head, because the next night, while she and Cynthia were "dollying up" at Astrid's house, the phone rang. It was Stuart, convulsed by a white rage, sounding completely irrational. When he learned that Dot was there, "he insisted that Astrid toss me out," Dot recalls. Astrid calmed him down enough to determine what had happened: Paul and Stuart had finally had it out, not in private but onstage in the middle of a set, in full view of an astonished German audience.

They had been backing Tony Sheridan for the nine o'clock set. Paul, at the piano, where he had recently been pounding out guitar chords with innate flair, was muttering to himself, vexed by the enormity of Stuart's mistakes. At some point he let go with an utterly outrageous comment about Astrid that hit a nerve. Stuart dropped the bass in the middle of the song, lunged at Paul, and caught him "with such a wallop that it knocked him off his stool." The fight, which had been brewing for months, was wild and fierce. Stuart and Paul rolled around on the floor, punching and stomping each other, while the other Beatles and Sheridan soldiered on. "They beat the shit out of each other," says an observer, and thrashed about until the song ended, when John, George, and Pete finally pried them apart.

Nothing was settled by the fight, but as Pete Best interpreted it: "It was the beginning of the end of Stu as a Beatle." Sutcliffe realized the situation was untenable. There was no place for him on that stage anymore; Paul—and even John, by his neutrality—had made that absolutely clear. Stuart moped around for a few days, disillusioned with the band and with himself. The constant insults, the humiliation—he'd had enough. There were more important things than playing with the Beatles. He had barely touched a paintbrush in months. That alone struck him as absurd. He'd made a horrendous mistake in ignoring his art for so long and needed to reclaim that part of his life.

Despite the consequence of Stuart's decision, there was no formal resignation. Later that week he simply turned up at the Top Ten and told the others he was through with the band. It was all very matter-of-fact, devoid of lingering resentment or even drama. If any of the Beatles were surprised, no one let it show, nor did anyone try to discourage Stuart from leaving. Stuart, for his part, couldn't have been more accommodating. In a magnanimous gesture, he even handed his bass over to Paul in an acknowledgment of proper succession, but as Paul pointed out, "he was only lending it to me, so he didn't want me to change the strings around."[*]

[IV]

The departure of Stuart Sutcliffe coincided with the end of Cynthia and Dot's Hamburg vacation, unburdening the band of any external distractions. The girls' brief stay vibrated with many good feelings. Dot, especially, was given an unexpected boost when Paul presented her with a gift—a gold band—as a keepsake from Hamburg. The seriousness of the present caught everyone off guard. Dot remembers staring at it, unable to grasp its significance. *A wedding band!* She was speechless. Finally, Paul suggested smoothly that she try it on. "Turns out, it was an engagement ring," Dot recalls. "He told me that in Germany you buy a ring that looks like a wedding band and, for the engagement [period], you put it on your left hand. When you get married you just change it to your right."

Married: this was the first that she'd heard as much from Paul. All this time, she "felt [she] was never good enough for him," and here he was in love with her. "I was thrilled," Dot says. Paul had everything she secretly desired. He was charming, talented, as good-looking as any movie star, and from a solid, loving family. Dot made no secret of her happiness when she returned to Liverpool in May, moving out of her parents' house and into a flat, in anticipation of Paul's return.

Behind their pronouncements and gestures of love, the Beatles' front men had more practical matters on their minds. Music remained the top priority. Now that their stage shows were sharp, next on the agenda was making a record.

The route to the recording studio in the early sixties was mazy and exclusive. Unlike the opportunities in America, where A&R scouts practically herded singing groups off the street corners and into the studio, European

---

[*] *Paul was left-handed, Stuart right-handed.*

openings were scarce. A scant four labels operated in all of England, each with one meager recording facility to its name. There were only a handful of independents on the order of Sun, J&M, Chess, Radio Recorders, or Atlantic, and none as exquisitely appointed or technically proficient. Although any yabbo with £5 could cut a disc at the HMV store in London, conditions there were less than primitive and not unlike the Quarry Men's experience at Percy Phillips's studio. Bands weren't simply discovered and recorded in England; they underwent a long, involved process that meandered through interviews, courtships, showcases, auditions, rehearsals, teas, and finally the rare, exalted session. The Beatles were well aware of that; moreover, they knew that the inside track was clubby and that most opportunities fell to London bands or twinky acts like Cliff Richard, who'd showcased at Two I's. Provincial rock 'n roll bands were regarded "like lepers."

It was only a matter of time, however, before word of their talent spread past the ghetto of St. Pauli and into the stiff-necked musical establishment. Tommy Kent, a German rock 'n roll star on the magnitude of Billy Fury, was the first local celebrity to "discover" the Beatles. "He said we were the best group he'd ever heard," Paul wrote to a friend in Liverpool, quoting the highlight of a backstage visit. It sounded, to be sure, like extravagant praise, but Kent's enthusiasm was apparently sincere. Following a repeat visit to the Top Ten, he alerted Bert Kaempfert, a popular German bandleader whose company had struck a recent production deal with Polydor Records, a subsidiary label of mighty Deutsche Grammophon. Kaempfert was no ordinary kappellmeister. A handsome, charismatic composer and popular recording artist, he spent the postwar years stringing together an impressive array of instrumental hits, including "Wonderland by Night" and "Strangers in the Night," and as an icon-turned-entrepreneur, he began building a small but accomplished pop talent roster.

Tommy Kent urged Kaempfert to go see the Beatles after his visit to the Top Ten. Kaempfert's response was polite but noncommittal. He was more focused on Tony Sheridan, whose talent he recognized the minute he saw it. A performer such as Sheridan would add panache to his roster; the energy he put out would create its own demand. He offered Sheridan a recording contract, which included the Beatles as his backing band. The Beatles were stunned and overjoyed by the offer. Unable to restrain themselves, they scrawled their signatures on an undated contract written completely in German whose only copy was given to Kaempfert. The terms were simple: they'd be paid a total of DM 300 per person—comparable to a week's wages at the Top Ten—which precluded them from a share of future royalties; moreover, the contract would be in effect from July 1961 until July 1962, with an option—Kaempfert's—for a year's extension.

It was a sticky piece of business, a kind of take-it-or-leave-it offer in the spirit of deals signed by doo-wop groups in the early fifties. Even among London musicians it was rare to receive anything more than a standard flat fee for studio work. It remains doubtful that they had legal counsel or that the terms were even explained to them. Not that it would have mattered. To their grand satisfaction, the boys felt: "What the hell, we're recording!" A dream had come true: the Beatles were finally making records.

But they were records in name only—and not even in their name. As a concession to German slang, in which the word *peedles* skewed as "tiny dicks," the band appeared as the Beat Brothers, the collective name used for all of Sheridan's backing groups between 1961 and 1965. Otherwise, they performed a lineup of songs similar to the one played on the Top Ten stage six times a night, seven nights a week.

Kaempfert must have planned on a set that strove to rock out without offending his loyal mainstream audience. Why else would it have been weighted with souped-up standards like "My Bonnie" and "[When] The Saints [Go Marching In]"? Even the Beatles' showcase—"Ain't She Sweet"—was a retread of the old music hall number.* As novices, the Beatles were too impressionable and excited to stage a protest, but Tony Sheridan, arguably no greenhorn, merely followed orders. Although it seems thoroughly out of character, it is reasonable to assume he viewed the session as a comeback opportunity and chose not to make waves. Kaempfert and his staff worked briskly and diligently, seldom requiring more than two takes on any song. Each track rolled out with Germanic precision, and along with George's instrumental debut on the self-penned "Cry for a Shadow," the whole session went down without so much as a hiccup. For a single release, "My Bonnie" sounded like the obvious choice, but it would be up to the suits at Polydor to make that decision. Convinced that the sound "represented something new" and unusual, the engineers and technicians left the session feeling upbeat about their work.

No one felt the flush more acutely than the Beatles. Not even guarded restraint from an experienced hand like Kaempfert put a damper on their sanguine outlook. However naively, they regarded the session as their big break, the break that would lead to inevitable stardom. It didn't matter

---

* On a different occasion, they recorded "Sweet Georgia Brown."

that the release was still a ways off or that the spotlight, if it shone, would fall on Tony Sheridan.

In fact, the Beatles wouldn't even be around to partake in the launch. Less than a week after the session, their engagement at the Top Ten concluded and, like it or not, they were on their way back to Liverpool.

[I]

On a hazy Saturday evening in September 1961, Bob Wooler climbed aboard the 500 Limited bus bound for Liverpool center and spied a familiar face. George Harrison was seated about halfway back, steadying a cardboard envelope on his knees. As Wooler settled in next to him, George slipped a record sleeve from the package in one neat motion. "Look at this. I've just received it today," he gushed, fingering it as one might a precious heirloom. Wooler examined the single: a near-mint copy of "My Bonnie" by Tony Sheridan and the Beat Brothers.* So, it was finally released, Wooler mused. The band had jabbered about nothing else since returning from Hamburg, to the point that Wooler actually dreaded its arrival. Nevertheless, he was impressed, seeing it in the flesh. "Up until then, none of the Merseyside bands had made a record," he recalls, "so it was quite an achievement."

Determined to make an event of it, he begged George for the record. "Let me play it tonight," he cajoled, but George squirmed reluctantly. The copy had just arrived from Hamburg,** and the other Beatles had yet to see it. With uncharacteristic aggressiveness, Wooler dismissed the argument with a wave. "They'll have plenty of time for that," he said. "Anyway, we're all [appearing] at Hambleton Hall tomorrow night, at which time I'll return it." He also schemed to borrow it for lunchtime sessions at the Cavern, which the Beatles now headlined almost exclusively.

Like others on the scene, Wooler sensed a breakthrough in the making and wanted to capitalize on it. "The local pop scene," as he saw it, "was

---

* *The German version, subtitled "Mein Herz ist bei dir nur"; the British version wasn't released until January 5, 1962.*
** *Stuart, who had remained in Germany, sent it to George.*

ready for a star." Rock 'n roll was no longer simply a weekend dessert in Liverpool; it had become part of the essential daily diet, with lunchtime and evening shows a staple of everyday life. You could almost set your watch by it, a rhythm to the musical intervals that dovetailed with meals, commuting, work, and sleep. No one looked to the States or even to London for the latest hot sound. Why bother? Liverpool had everything they needed.

And it was the Beatles who defined the scene—maybe too much for its own good, Wooler thought. "The Beatles were difficult," he recalls, "and so unprofessional onstage—smoking, swearing, eating, talking with one another. They considered themselves lords unto themselves." One day, the Beatles played the Cavern wearing jeans. Jeans spelled trouble; anyone wearing them was turned away at the door. In no time, the band had attracted the attention of Ray McFall, who demanded that Wooler discipline the Beatles. During a break Wooler reluctantly delivered Ray's message in the bandroom. "Go and tell him to get fucking well stuffed!" John snapped. From opposite angles, Paul and George converged, launching similar tirades. Wooler backed out of the room to symphonic abuse. Lords unto themselves.

The scene had somehow bought into the Beatles' cheek. Their whole renegade attitude had caught on, and not only with fellow musicians. With rock 'n roll, as with nothing else in their lives, the fans cared as much about the attitude as the music. They were looking for a mind-set, a way of looking at things that pressed past the music itself into issues of identity—personality, looks, character, and originality. While stars such as Elvis and Buddy Holly had given them the music and the look, attitude remained uncultivated. Teddy boys had come the closest to defining a cultural outlook, but they proved too extreme. The Beatles, on the other hand, managed to push the envelope without hurting anyone. Violence wasn't part of their agenda. Their music was loud, in-your-face loud, their stage presence disorderly and impolite. Anyone who disapproved could "get fucking well stuffed," but that was the extent of their defiance. They were rebels, not anarchists.

And yet Wooler was determined to hasten their stardom, no matter how rudely they treated him. He plugged their record relentlessly—at dozens of dance halls on the weekends, numerous times a day at the crowded Cavern, to anyone, in fact, who would listen—even though it wasn't available anywhere in the United Kingdom. "Buy the record, folks," he'd implore. "Make sure you ask for it at your favorite record shop. If they don't have it, insist that they order it, and make sure that they get it for you." But local retailers, who concentrated on sturdy sellers like Anthony Newley, Perry Como, Nat King Cole, and instrumentalists, had no interest. According to Wooler, "There was only one record store that took any interest in it and that was . . . [the NEMS] shop in Whitechapel." North End Music Stores had a record department that was unmatched for its eclectic selection of music, thanks largely to the exuberance of its demanding manager, a tightly strung aesthete named Brian Epstein. The well-born son of retail magnates from the upper crust of Liverpool's Jewish community, Brian had little in common with the teenage riffraff who infested his store like crows. Although only six years older than John Lennon, Brian comported himself in a way that bespoke a man in his contented forties. And not out of some sort of pretense: he belonged to that segment of his generation which subscribed to refinement and discipline and maintained its manners during the periodic upheavals of rebellion. Raised as a gentleman, he wore immaculately tailored suits, spoke the King's English with a crisp, polished clip, and led conversations with his chin raised to convey the superiority he keenly felt among commoners.*

Indulging an alliance of passions, his adolescent heart beat furiously for all things musical, except rock 'n roll, which he abhorred. He was a connoisseur of serious music, spanning theater, opera, and symphony—an erudite, cultured, and opinionated enthusiast who "lived for Beethoven, Mozart, Haydn, and Sibelius." Although as a child Brian apparently showed little interest in playing an instrument, he had a box at the Liverpool Philharmonic from the age of twelve, and soon after acquired a collection of the Brandenburg Concertos, whose score he knew by heart.

Rock 'n roll had begun to ring up substantial sales for NEMS, making it a genre he could no longer afford to ignore. But as a listener, he wouldn't give it the time of day. "The closest Brian ever got to rock 'n roll was 'Volare,'" recalls Peter Brown, a friend and protégé who oversaw the NEMS shop on Great Charlotte Street.

He was born on September 19, 1934, during the denouement of a crisp Yom Kippur afternoon while his father and uncle davened, as ploddingly as they polished furniture, in the crowded sanctuary of the Green Park Drive Synagogue, not too far from their homes. The Epsteins were lions of Liverpool's resurgent Jewish community: merchants, philanthropists, pil-

---

* In a datebook he carried at the age of fifteen, under "Personal Memoranda," the only entry (aside from his address and birth date) is "hat size," under which he scrawled: "7⅛."

lars of society, a long way up the ladder from their hardscrabble beginnings. In fact, Brian's paternal grandfather, a furniture maker named Isaac, an émigré from the village of Hodan, Lithuania, arrived in England in the wave of immigration of the 1890s at the age of eighteen, with nothing except for the provisions of his trade and the forbearance of his wife, Diana. From the beginning, Isaac proved extremely talented, and there was plenty of work to keep him busy. Isaac offered customers a selection of his own handcrafted staples along with varied consignment pieces, and after a decade of struggle and sacrifice, he succeeded in opening a modest furniture shop that offered easy credit to families, and thus rather quickly attracted a solid clientele.

Isaac's third child, Harry, an equally enterprising but very affable man, had hardly finished school before joining his father's business on Walton Road, in the north end of the city. Renamed I. Epstein & Sons, it featured showrooms of well-crafted goods ranging from bassinets to bedroom suites and served families of all social and economic strata. Harry and his brother, Leslie, watched their father with curious, admiring eyes. Restlessly, they expanded into an adjacent shop (North End Music Stores) and then another and another, the unfolding empire consolidated under the catchy NEMS logo. More than anyone, Harry recognized the opportunity for growth, diversifying the company with home furnishings and appliances.

It took a momentous marriage to solidify NEMS' primacy. Queenie Hyman (the nickname was given to her as a child, being that Malka, her given name, was the Hebrew word for *queen*),* although eleven years Harry's junior, was his partner in every respect—a capricious but capable wife born of aristocratic self-possession, whose family owned the highly esteemed Sheffield Veneering Company in the heart of the Midlands. A slim, dark-haired beauty, Queenie was educated at a Catholic boarding school, to which she applied herself with ungrudging tenacity; she had no intention of letting down in front of non-Jews. Among her firmest convictions, along with her fierce Jewish faith, was the treachery of Gentiles, most of whom she viewed as closet anti-Semites. It was a prejudice, however irrational, that remained with Queenie throughout her life—and that was subsequently passed down to Brian—despite the unshakable power of Liverpool's Jewish community, the oldest, most unified, and prosperous of its kind outside of London.

---

* On Brian's birth certificate, her name was listed as "Minnie Epstein formerly Hyman."

Unquestionably, Queenie filled the empty spaces in Harry's life. She ran an orderly and immaculate house, cultivated a social circle from among Liverpool's most prominent Jewish families, and was an instinctive hostess who entertained with grand style and élan. "She knew what it meant to be a lady," says a longtime friend of the family. What's more, Queenie loved culture. She filled the living room with beautifully bound books and china figurines. A profusion of tasteful if innocuous art landscaped the walls. And she nurtured a passion for fine music, becoming an influential theater and symphony patron, amassing a library of records that was even more voluminous and diverse than that of her own parents. To accommodate her grandiose designs, the Epsteins built their dream house in 1934, the year following their marriage. It was a comfortable eleven-room stone residence, with a vaulted entrance, five high-ceilinged bedrooms, and a magnificent alcoved parlor in back, well situated on a lovely wooded property in Childwall, one of the suburbs undergoing rapid upscaling.

While Brian was still very young, Queenie began indoctrinating him in the things that captivated her most, playing him scores of gorgeous music—from concertos by Tchaikovsky, Mendelssohn, and Bach—as he lay in his crib. "She put so much emotion into his fairy tales that you thought she was auditioning for the West End," says a neighbor. "And by the time Brian was five, he could recite a favorite story giving it the same dramatic emphasis as Queenie."

Normal child play didn't seem to interest him. He wasn't particularly athletic or sports-minded, like other boys his age; there was no fascination with dinosaurs, tree forts, or family pets. He rarely played with his brother, Clive, who was almost two years younger. Brian was happiest, his relatives say, when among adults, having adult discussions. To an unnatural degree, he kept up with community chatter—what families argued about, who wasn't on speaking terms, how people were managing personal crises. His aunt Stella recalls that when she babysat for her nephew, Brian would often ask after her friends, an expression of the most profound interest pasted on his tiny face. "Tell me, Auntie," he would inquire, gazing at her earnestly, "how is Mrs. Abromowitz? What's become of lovely Mrs. Shapiro's son, Harold?" Listening to Brian, Stella thought, "he sounded like a little old man."

But the little boy in him was frighteningly neglected, an oversight that was devastating to Brian's development. "Queenie treated him as an equal," says Rex Makin, a solicitor who lived next door and represented the Epsteins, and later Brian, in a professional capacity. "And this, among other things, made him a very volatile person. He was subject to terrific mood swings, no doubt, to a great degree, because of frustration."

To make matters worse, the physical geography of Brian's life was every bit as unstable as the treacherous emotional terrain. The outbreak of war in Europe in 1940, exacerbated by Germany's relentless bombardment of England, sent northerners scrambling to provide security for their families in areas deemed unlikely targets for bombs. Most Scousers remained rooted at the mercy of the unpredictable nightly air raids, but anyone with the resources escaped the harsh realities of war. The Epsteins were only one of hundreds of families who fled Liverpool for relative safety, moving in with relatives in Southport, just thirty miles up the Lancashire coast but a world apart. On the one hand, the move brought them immediate and effective security, but for Brian the sudden change proved a catastrophic force in his development.

Unlike Liverpool, where he participated in his parents' active social life and accompanied them to the city's finest restaurants, Southport was sleepy and unsophisticated—a fringe of tiny, cramped homes bordering the sea. It was the most unlikely place in the world for a boy in love with all the symbols of society.

Upon returning home, in 1945, Brian was disoriented, in more ways than one. He was already "one of those out-of-sorts boys who never quite fit," and his grades, which were notably inconsistent, slipped even further. He ping-ponged from school to school, angry and unmotivated, unable to focus on his studies or to make friends. Two schools in Southport dismissed him for laziness and poor performance. A residency at Liverpool College ended shortly in his expulsion, along with a stinging censure from the headmaster, branding him a "problem child." The next stop, at a coeducational prep school, proved even more disastrous—and ever brief. Brian lasted a only month, blaming his strident failure to conform on antiSemitism. That may indeed have contributed to his discomfort (owing to a strong residue of postwar resentment in the North), but in fact it was only a smoke screen for a deepening alienation of a much darker and devious nature.

"It was at this school . . . that I can first remember my feeling for other male persons and a longing for a close and intimate friend," Brian confessed in the pages of a private handwritten journal. As he had grown up in genteel surroundings and under Queenie's indulgent spell, there was nothing in the way of stimuli to test the inchoate feelings that had always eluded him. Now, undercurrents of homosexuality welled to the surface, coinciding with his own intensifying adolescence. He found it difficult to disguise his preference for other boys. The facade of "normalcy" began to crumble, replaced by fears of inadequacy and dread. No doubt he was unprepared for a confrontation of this sort. Certainly there were no role models to admire, no peers from whom to seek counsel. For a boy who had always been pampered and provided for, he was wildly unsuited to handle such a complicated matter. "Indeed," he later admitted, "no one had explained to me the facts of life."

While Brian struggled to cope with the nature of his sexuality, his parents, oblivious to any emotional turmoil, continued shipping him around to a string of less-than-illustrious boarding schools. He spent short, ineffectual terms at "benevolent academies" such as Beaconsfield and Clayesmore, and finally two years at the trivial Wrekin College, in Shropshire, where, out of resignation, despair, or simply an effort to fit in, he joined the track team—called the Colts—to uniformly disastrous results. In a diary entry that year he wrote: "I tried very hard. But did not succeed. I think I was rather insignificant."

As he approached his sixteenth birthday, Brian sent a long, unflinching letter to Harry, describing his frustration and alienation at school. He poured out his heart, confiding his lack of interest in academics and, in an unexpected turn of events, announcing his intention to become a dress designer and the wish to train in London. A portfolio of eight drawings, each on an individual piece of lined notebook paper, was attached as evidence of his potential—fashionably drawn evening dresses in the style of Chanel, crisply tailored, with asymmetrical collars and calf-length hems. If one overlooks the informal presentation, the drawings themselves display a real gift: a fine precision of line and sensitivity to shape, rhythm, and detail. Harry, a relative recalls, "went up the pole." In all the years, through the fitful cycle of schools, Brian had barely acknowledged his interest in drawing, much less fashion. The whole proposal sounded so outrageous, so confounding. Harry, after all, expected his son to follow him into the family business, not undertake some poncey scheme designing dresses.

Instead of writing back, Harry and Queenie turned up at Wrekin a week later to lay down the law: it "was impossible" to give Brian's request their blessing. Furthermore, "it would be stupid," they advised, "to give up going into the family business and [the] security [that provided]."

Predictably, Brian was incensed. "In a rage of temper," he threatened to leave school at the end of term, when he turned sixteen. A furious argument ensued, in which his parents demanded that he stay and sit exams, but he refused to listen. "I was stubborn," Brian admitted later, after dropping out of school, but by that time he realized his obstinacy and its steep price. Without a high school diploma or any visible means of support, the path of his destiny became narrowly clear. A month later, following a summer of unfolding depression, he surrendered to fate and reluctantly "reported for duty" at the family furniture store in Liverpool.

Much to Brian's surprise, the furniture trade wasn't the living hell he'd imagined it to be. Seeing an opportunity to perform a task without fumbling—an opportunity, moreover, to win some respect from a much-esteemed man like his father—he seized it with the unmitigated energy of someone on a mission. At the family shop, he could reinvent himself in the image of a young, savvy salesman. As such, he threw himself into the job, bringing more excitement to it than perhaps was called for. He took "a keen interest in display work and interior decoration" that often strayed beyond the scope of necessity. The window sets he redressed were stagy and eye-catching, though somewhat radical and unnerving to the shop's provincial customers. His grandfather Isaac was neither amused nor tolerant of his grandson's verve. He demanded that Brian toe the line—*his* line—and when this met with sulky disapproval, Brian was apprenticed to a rival firm across town.

When he returned to NEMS six months later, it was a gracious, more cooperative Brian Epstein, licked into shape perhaps, but no less ambitious. Not only did he seem to understand his role, he appeared to grow into it—and with appreciable delight. Brian learned how to interact with people in such a way that, while often obsequious and subtle, conveyed the impression of immense refinement. He conducted himself with courtly authority. Even when he helped someone, he assumed a dignified air that placed customers twenty years his senior in a position of subordinacy. Much of that force of personality can be ascribed to heritage. Brian never forgot what class he came from—and how it ennobled him. There is a saying that every Englishman knows his place, and if he forgets, there is always someone there to remind him. Brian Epstein knew his place, and he knew how to remind people of its power.

In December 1952, on the cusp of a new year and all that it promised, Brian was drafted, as a clerk, into the Royal Army Service Corps and eventually posted to the Regent's Park barracks in London. It was a shock of immense consequences. Overnight, every personal stride he'd made came undone. From the very start, military life was an evolving disaster. The charmed life of a privileged furniture heir, concerned only with the expedience of sales and service, had not given Brian the tools that soldiering required. He had learned to conduct himself with authority, not subservience. But military discipline was the least of Brian's troubles. For years Brian had been able to deny—or suppress—what he called his "latent homosexuality." There was nothing in his pervading attitude that compelled him to either acknowledge or act on it. Or perhaps he'd become adept at masking his indecisiveness as indifference. Once in the army, however, it all rushed to the fore. "Within the first few weeks," he wrote, "I met all sorts of young men who little by little revealed the strange homosexual life in London. [And] I became aware of homosexuals wherever I went."

Oddly, this realization made Brian more alone and "confused" than ever. Having no one with whom he could share his feelings or even glean the facts of life—*his* life—he became unnaturally high-strung, panicked. His fellow cadets must have sussed out his secret, inasmuch as they ostracized him from their inner circle. Officers, he recalled, "mercilessly" picked on him. Depressed, fretful, insecure, Brian must have radiated weakness. About the same time, he was robbed on a midnight train from Liverpool, an obvious target for bullies and predators.

In his autobiography, Brian invents a dramatic version of his subsequent premature discharge from the army. He claims to have returned to base one night in a fancy car and dressed in a three-piece suit, whereupon the guards mistook him for an officer. In the fading light, they threw him a crisp salute, for which he was remanded to solitary confinement.

Such was the story he decided to tell in 1964, when homosexuality was still a criminal act. In fact, his discharge was a much simpler affair. Sometime before the first of the year, he plunged into a deep depression that left him all but immobilized. Fearing a breakdown, army psychiatrists began delving into Brian's past and, when they hit upon the source of his disorder, recommended early discharge, which was issued "on medical grounds."

Brian was understandably relieved. He was no longer a misfit in uniform. Finally, he could get back to Liverpool and concentrate on his career. His old job at NEMS was waiting for him; in his absence, brother Clive had joined the firm.

Once back in Liverpool, Brian was no longer able to ignore his adult feelings. Without a great deal of caution, he plunged into the shadow world of "homosexual life and its various rendezvous." It must have been a lonely, frightening experience, not at all like today's accommodating scene, with its sense of community and support groups. The conditions in Liverpool were absolutely degrading, giving rise to solitary, clandestine assignations in seedy haunts that, however intimate or satisfying, he was unable to reconcile. "My life became a succession of mental illnesses and sordid unhappy events," he concluded in a haze of confusion.

At twenty-one, he was appointed a director of NEMS, but even an endorsement of that magnitude failed to bring some clarity to his life. He lived in terror that someone would discover his dark secret, that it would embarrass—even destroy—his family. By September 1956, that pressure became too much for Brian to bear. Without any warning, he packed, gave notice at work, and left home for an extended visit to London. He'd arranged to meet a friend there for the pursuit of undisclosed leisure, but before the first day was out a familiar incident recurred. He was robbed again; this time, all his personal effects were stolen—his passport, birth certificate, checkbook, wristwatch, all the money he'd brought with him. Afraid to tell his parents the truth, he wangled a job as a department-store clerk until he earned enough to cover a ticket back to Liverpool. He intended to stay only long enough to grab some clothes and cash a few checks, but he was made so distraught by the experience that he suffered a near-physical collapse.

It was during subsequent treatment by the family psychiatrist, he recalled, that "I confessed everything to my doctor." It all came pouring out—the robberies, the homosexuality, the sordid trysts, the self-loathing. To alleviate the crushing anxiety, the doctor suggested to Brian's parents that he leave Liverpool as soon as possible. In the course of analysis, it was discovered that Brian yearned to be an actor. His parents, who considered the acting profession barely a notch above window dressing, were in no mood to oblige. But now, with the doctor as his advocate, Harry and Queenie allowed him—quite reluctantly—to audition for a place in the Royal Academy of Dramatic Arts.

Incredible as it may seem, Brian impressed the school's no-nonsense director, John Fernald, who admitted him for the forthcoming term, in the late fall of 1956. Peter O'Toole, Albert Finney, and Susannah York had graduated just ahead of Brian and won instant recognition. His own class boasted a galaxy of young meteors whose names would light up the West End's marquees in a few years. Brian was mesmerized by the energy of the work, but by the spring of 1957, the gilt had worn off the novelty. "The narcissism . . . and the detachment of the actor from other people" left him cold. Besides, instructors had marked him as "a second male lead" with little chance—or talent enough—for greater stardom. Still, he might have stayed on at RADA and graduated had not the edge of self-destruction prevailed, rerouting the course of his life.

Loneliness was partly to blame. Stranded in London between semesters, Brian found part-time work at a bookshop, but there was no one around with whom he could spend those difficult chunks of downtime. On the evening of April 17 he took in a play at the Arts Theatre Club, then stopped for coffee at a nearby bar. Depressed, he took the tube home to Swiss Cottage. It was late, approaching midnight. Coming out of the station, Brian stopped in a public lavatory, where he encountered a tough-looking young man framed in the doorway. They gave each other the once-over. Something unspoken passed between them. They played cat and mouse for five minutes along a deserted stretch of Finchley Road while Brian worked up the nerve to make a move. Another man appeared out of the darkness. Two of them! He hadn't anticipated that kind of situation. Brian's "mind went in great fear"; he began sweating profusely. Frantically, he paused in front of a drugstore window for—what? To allow his suitors an opportunity to introduce themselves? To brush up casually against them? He wasn't sure. It was their move, but when it finally came, it wasn't the move Brian expected. They were undercover cops. "[And] after a few minutes," he recalled, "they arrested me for 'persistently importuning.'" Miraculously, a family solicitor helped bury the arrest and quietly return Brian to Liverpool, where he slipped into a routine of work and seclusion. A few months later another disturbance occurred that in many ways mirrored the London incident. This time, he got involved with an ex-guardsman named Billy Connolly, who was on probation for his involvement in the death of a friend. An encounter between them on the docks turned violent. In the course of it, Brian was badly beaten and his expensive watch stolen.

The plot got complicated a few days later when Connolly called, demanding money in exchange for the watch—and his silence. Brian confided in his solicitor, who promptly marched him around to see detectives at the Dale Street station house. "They arranged for a drop," the lawyer recalls. "The man was to call at Brian's shop at a certain time for the watch to be redeemed and the money handed over." It all came off like a charm; Connolly was apprehended, "proper restitution was made." But it was customary, when a person was robbed in this manner, to protect his identity in the press by providing a generic alias, "Mr. X." And while Brian's anonymity was preserved, enough people knew the details so that the unfortunate label dogged him for years to come.

The only positive—and, to Brian, heartening—thing to come out of this was the support of his family. There has always been speculation about whether they knew he was gay. It was never acknowledged by either Harry or Queenie, but, in fact, both these episodes left no doubt of their awareness. There had been shame aplenty to warrant their rancor, even estrangement. And yet, readily enough, they rallied to his side. Harry, especially, found compassion for his son. Those close to the family felt that "he was oblivious" to Brian's homosexuality or that he chose to ignore it rather than confront a subject outside his grasp. And yet, it was Harry who steadfastly came to his son's emotional rescue, Harry who supported Brian through each successive mess.

What's more, it was Harry who now decided that Brian needed some kind of stabilizing influence to ensure against his son's further unhappiness. Brian was already beating himself up over the Mr. X affair. To keep his son's spirits up, Harry suggested expanding the small record department they'd opened in the Great Charlotte Street store and letting Brian manage it in any way he saw fit. Clive, in turn, would take over the appliance department, thereby establishing a clear division of responsibility.

The result was an unqualified success. In no time, Brian built the record department from a nook in the ground floor into a solid, full-scale enterprise that challenged NEMS' much larger and more well established competitors. It wasn't location or floor space or special pricing that did the trick as much as it was Brian's wide-eyed ambition. Instead of stocking a selection of current hits and staples, as was the custom among Liverpool's retailers, he resolved to carry *every record in print* on demand, so as not to have to special-order one when a customer requested an obscure title. That meant keeping a huge inventory on hand, as well as a system for constantly updating it. Had he bothered to run this scheme past Harry, it is likely to have been dismissed as too speculative or grandiose. But as he was promised free rein—and seeing as his parents were reluctant to dampen his happiness—no effort was made to check the hasty growth, and as a result, the department expanded and flourished.

More important, Brian seemed to thrive in his new role. No one worked harder or showed more determination. Every minute of his day was given over to the demands of his precious record department. He ordered every record himself, stayed in contact with the major distributors in Manchester, trained and supervised the young staff, and handled the books. Along with Peter Brown, he even worked the counter on a regular basis. John Lennon's boyhood friend Mike Rice, who worked at Martin's Bank, where NEMS had its account, recalls how Brian was always at the store, always working no matter what the time of day. "My girlfriend and I would usually stay late in Liverpool, and walking past NEMS, we always saw him slaving away. It became a joke between us. We'd phone each other late at night and say, 'I've just been past the record store and—*he's still there!*'"

By the end of 1960, NEMS had become "the most important record outlet in Liverpool, if not the whole North of England." Teenagers thronged the three stores each day to stay in the swing of things. Says Brown: "There was really no radio [for them] to listen to; the BBC didn't play rock 'n roll and Radio Luxembourg was spotty. So, if these kids wanted to hear new music, they had to come in[to NEMS] and listen to it."

Promoters were encouraged to put up posters in the stores, while NEMS always handled tickets to local events and sponsored transportation. For a teenager in Liverpool, NEMS was the pipeline for reliable information. Someone hanging out there always knew what was going on. And if all else failed, you could always go there to pick up a copy of *Mersey Beat.*

Mersey Beat was the brainchild of John's art school mate Bill Harry, who'd been pasting up magazines since he was old enough to hold a pencil. Frank Hesselberg commissioned him to start a newsletter reporting on the local club scene, which they called *Frank Comments.* It folded after a few issues, but Harry wasn't deterred. He made further half-baked attempts with *Storyville* and *52nd Street,* to keep tabs on the jazz movement, but with dwindling financial support, they both lapsed into a precipitate decline.

He scrounged up another £50 from a friend and persuaded his girlfriend, Virginia, to leave her accounting job at Woolworth's. Together, they rented attic space in a building on Renshaw Street, near the art college, and with a single Olivetti typewriter began compiling material for the first issue. *Mersey Beat,* which made its debut on July 6, 1961, broke no new ground as far as appearances went, looking too much like a dense student newspaper. But its copy leaped over a cliff. No one in the North had devoted more than a line or two to rock 'n roll, and here was a whole magazine full of the stuff. A grainy picture of Gene Vincent grinning graced the cover, along with an article about "Swinging Cilla," a local, throaty-voiced girl named Cilla White who sang on and off with the Dominoes, Hurricanes, and the Big Three.* And most peculiar, and perhaps just the irreverent edge Harry was striving for, a disjointed piece of nonsense called "Being a Short Diversion on the Dubious Origins of Beatles" as "Translated from the John Lennon."

Harry cranked out a print run of five thousand and hit the streets running. Most newsagents and bookshops agreed to sell his funky rag, but only one or two copies each. (He split the cover price – threepence a copy—with the retailer.) At the Whitechapel branch of NEMS, Harry asked to see the manager and was shown directly into Brian Epstein's office. "He looked extremely smart, was very polite, talked posh—everything about him was precise and impressive," Harry recalls. "Straightaway, he agreed to take a dozen copies of [*Mersey Beat*]."

Brian was waiting when Harry returned the next week to collect the receipts. "I can't understand it," he told Bill, pointing to the empty paper bin near the counter. "They sold out in a day. Next time, I'll take twelve dozen copies." Harry was stunned, but not as much as Brian was when the second issue sold out. Harry arrived at NEMS at noon with the next allotment and kids were queued up, waiting for it. He had a phenomenon on his hands.

"The next week," Harry recalls, "[Brian] invited me upstairs to his office and offered me a sherry. I thought: how civilized of him." Civilized indeed, but with an underlying purpose. "He wanted to know all about what was happening—who was buying the newspaper and what the music scene was like in Liverpool." The front page was devoted to a breaking story: BEATLES SIGN RECORDING CONTRACT! accompanied by an Astrid Kirchherr photograph of the band. "This is actually in *Liverpool*?" Brian marveled, thumbing through *Mersey Beat*. "Who are all these groups?" He couldn't get over it.

When the third issue appeared, it carried a new column—"Record Releases by Brian Epstein of NEMS"—that flaunted his newly acquired enlightenment about Liverpool's beat music scene, gleaned almost verbatim from the pages of *Mersey Beat*. Eventually, he got around to the question that would change everything. Sitting owl-eyed across from Bill Harry, he held up a page of *Mersey Beat* and wondered: "What about these Beatles?"

---

* According to Harry, on the eve of publication he couldn't remember her last name. "I thought, 'It's a color,' and I just put Black. After it appeared, she told me, 'It's Cilla White, but I like what you put. I'm going to keep it.'"

*   *   *

What about these Beatles?

Legend has it that Brian stumbled inadvertently over the Beatles when folk hero Raymond Jones confronted him at the NEMS counter sometime on October 28, 1961, and demanded a copy of "My Bonnie." In his autobiography, Brian wrote: "The name 'Beatle' meant nothing to me. . . . I had never [before] given a thought to any of the Liverpool beat groups then up and coming [sic] in the cellar clubs." It made for nice copy later, when the press began to call, but as far as the truth went, it was hogwash.

Epstein knew all about the Beatles from his careful scrutiny of *Mersey Beat,* and what that didn't tell him, Billy Harry did. What's more, there were posters plastered everywhere around NEMS announcing various Beatles appearances. "He would have had to have been blind—or ignorant—not to have noticed their name," Harry contends. Besides, his salesgirls knew the Beatles and made a fuss over them when they came into the store.

A month or two later, interrupting a routine inventory at NEMS, Brian confronted an unsuspecting Alistair Taylor. "Do you remember that record by a band called the Beatles?" he asked out of the blue. Taylor had, indeed; "My Bonnie" enjoyed an embarrassment of sales and was constantly on reorder. "They're playing at this place called the Cavern. We ought to go see them."

Without further delay, Brian phoned Bill Harry at the *Mersey Beat* office. "The Beatles are at the Cavern," he said. "Could you arrange for me to go and see them?"

What an odd request, Harry mused. No one needed help getting into the Cavern, especially for a lunchtime session; all you had to do was stand in line and pay the shilling. But he recognized Brian's appetite for protocol. A call to Ray McFall, placed by an intermediary such as Bill, would set Brian apart from the hoi polloi. With his perfectly sculpted hair, his blue, pin-striped suit furling like drapery, and of course a black, calf-skinned briefcase clutched rather powerfully in his hand, he'd stride into the club as if he owned the place.

Any suspicions Harry had about Brian Epstein's motives were no longer in doubt.

[II]

In early October, shortly before John's twenty-first birthday, he had received a £100 gift from his aunt Elizabeth (whom John called Mater) in Scotland and had taken off with Paul for a spontaneous two-week jaunt. A letter from Stuart had indicated that their exi buddy Jürgen Vollmer now lived in Paris, working as an assistant to photographer William Klein. When John and Paul turned up unannounced outside his tiny hotel on the rue de Beaune, Vollmer was thrilled to see them, delighted that they had come, as they'd explained, to hang out and soak up whatever it was that made him unique. One of those idiosyncrasies was his groovy clothing. Even in Hamburg, they'd known of Vollmer's frequent excursions to the Paris flea markets, where he put together that wardrobe. Now, they encountered him wearing bell-bottoms a good five years before the rest of the world would catch the trend. That look wouldn't fly in Liverpool, where sailors were derided unmercifully for their flared legs. But the Beatles bought corduroy jackets, wide-striped "grandfather" shirts, and the sleeveless sweaters that were staples of the Left Bank exis.

"I showed them all the places where I hung out with the artistic crowd," Vollmer remembered. They couldn't take their eyes off these people, who seemed so exotic and fascinating, even more so than the colorful Hamburg natives. Finally, after a few days on the prowl, John and Paul asked for a special favor. "We want our hair like you have it," they said.

In a room at the back of the Hôtel de Beaune, John and Paul sat patiently, nervously, on an unmade bed while Jürgen took a pair of scissors to their greasy manes. According to Vollmer, "I cut their hair [so that it was] more to the side, [although] forward nevertheless, until it looked like mine." Hardly bowl-shaped, it was sleek and soft-looking, swept to one side, with the hint of a tail that bounced delicately on their shoulders. The Beatles had always possessed half of the equation. Now the whole package was in place.

No one was more surprised than Alistair Taylor when Brian invited him to see the Beatles at the Cavern. He'd been in that dungeon before — "dozens of times" — when it was a jazz club. "We both detested pop music," Taylor recalls. "The music was totally alien to us. Even though we'd sold all those records [of "My Bonnie"], neither of us played it, nor particularly liked it."

Brian had no idea how to get to the Cavern, even though it was two hundred yards from NEMS. And once inside, he was awestruck. "It was nothing like what we'd expected," Taylor remembers. "The place was packed and steam was rolling down the walls. The music was so loud, we couldn't hear ourselves think." Both men were uncomfortable in ways that had nothing to do with the physical surroundings. "We were way out of our element. We were both in suits and ties, everyone was staring at us. We were very self-conscious."

To make themselves less conspicuous, Brian and Alistair took seats near the back. Both men sat stiffly, with their hands folded across their chests. And the band—why, they were shocking, disgraceful. "They could barely play," Taylor says, "and they were deafening and *so* unprofessional— laughing with the girls, smoking onstage, and sipping from Cokes during their act. But *absolutely magic!* The vibe they generated was just unbeliev- able." Halfway through the set, he glanced over at Brian and noticed they both were doing the same thing: tapping their hands on their legs.

Afterward, the Beatles disappeared into "a broom cupboard" at the side of the stage. Brian looked reassuringly at Alistair. "Well, that's it," he said. "We'll go have some lunch now. But . . . let's just go and say hello to them."

As Epstein and Taylor made their way to the front, Bob Wooler an- nounced their presence and asked the kids to give them a hand. Wooler didn't know Brian, other than having seen him "hovering around the counter at NEMS," but he sensed this Cavern appearance was something sig- nificant. Only a few days before, while negotiating a fee for the Beatles with promoter Brian Kelly, Wooler got a taste of the band's surging popu- larity. Discussing a contract, Kelly had grumbled bitterly about paying their £10 7s. fee. "Then, I'm sorry to have to tell you this, Brian, but they want double that from now on. I've been told they're going for fifteen pounds." Kelly was irate. "I'm not going to pay those fuckers fifteen pounds!" he screamed. "They're not worth it." Wooler disagreed: "You've *got* to book them, Brian, and you'll have to pay them what they want." And Kelly did.

No one so much as got up to greet Epstein when he edged inside the bandroom. They knew who he was, however, having drawn his ire on sev- eral occasions for loitering in NEMS' listening booths. George decided to give him a friendly tweak. "And what brings Mr. Epstein here?" he asked, smirking and thickening his Scouse accent.

Brian didn't notice—or wouldn't give George the satisfaction. Flashing his tightest, most professional smile, he replied: "We just popped in to say hello. I enjoyed your performance." He introduced Alistair, who nodded stiffly. "Well done, then. Good-bye." And they left.

Neither Brian nor Alistair said a word to each other all the way to Peacock's, in Hackins Hey. Both men were puzzling over the bizarre experience, and besides, their ears were pounding: neither of them could hear. The restaurant was crowded. It was a businessman's hangout and a welcome sight; it went without saying, they felt more comfortable around people who looked and acted their age. After being seated and ordering drinks, Brian asked Alistair for his opinion. Taylor, a notorious yes-man, was honest. He thought the Beatles were "absolutely awful," but admitted there was something "remarkable" about them, something he couldn't quite put into words.

Brian's reaction made Alistair uncomfortable. "He stared at me for the longest time, with a tight little smile on his lips," Taylor remembers. "It seemed like he was going to burst. Finally, he blurted out: 'I think they're tremendous!'"

Taylor found this admission "very odd." Brian wasn't at all the kind of person who showed emotion in front of the help, especially over something as superficial as a rock 'n roll band. It wouldn't be the proper thing to do. But as they talked more about the Beatles—and that was the only thing they discussed throughout lunch—a consensus arose that the band, and even pop music in general, had something extraordinary to offer, something they'd overlooked before and that now demanded their involvement. "We laughed at how both of us had been converted—like *that*—to the pop world," Taylor recalls. It felt refreshing, they admitted, to have been among kids who were intoxicated by music. And all that power and excitement—while neither man professed to understand it, they'd been nonetheless moved.

They were still laughing and a bit flushed from drink when Brian called for the check. Then, out of nowhere, he grabbed Alistair by the arm and said, "Do you think I should manage them?"

[I]

As word spread about the Beatles, Liverpool's music-minded teenagers reached for their own piece of the rock, with new bands forming at the rate of three or four a week. The Cavern, always besieged by hopefuls, was suddenly awash with young, mop-topped rockers angling for a showcase in the dark, dingy, sweaty-hot cellar. On any given day, Ray McFall was inundated by bands with the most "delicious-sounding" names: Wump and His Werbles, the Kruzads, Gerry Bach and the Beathovens, Liam and the Invaders, Abraham and His Lot, Ray Satan and the Devils, San Quentin and the Rock Pounders, Rip Van Winkle and the Rip-It-Ups, Dean Stacey and the Dominators, the Big Three, the L'il Three, the Four Just Men, Eddy Falcon and the Vampires, Danny and the Hi-Cats, Dino and the Wild Fires . . .

Rummaging through the pages of *Mersey Beat* revealed a similar euphonious constituency: Ian and the Zodiacs, Karl Terry and the Cruisers, Pete Picasso and the Rock Sculptors *(really!),* Steve and the Syndicate, Dee Fenton and the Silhouettes, Ken Dallas and the Silhouettes, the Spidermen, the Cyclones, the Undertakers, Nero and the Gladiators, Alby and the Sorrals, the Press Gang, the Pressmen, Earl Preston and the TTs, the Morockans, Eddie Dean and the Onlookers, the Landslides . . .

Slightly over three hundred rock 'n roll bands combed the city for gigs, more than three times the number of the previous winter, before the Beatles' phenomenal debut at Litherland Town Hall. Every lunchtime was a picnic, every night another party. It didn't matter how professional you sounded or how nimbly you handled a riff as long as the audience was happy. (And that didn't take much.) Bands played what they wanted; shared material, equipment, and personnel; referred one another to gigs; passed lazy afternoons talking shop. Neither jealousies nor egos interfered with the spirit of friendly competition. A few star attractions seemed to have cornered the market on paying gigs, but anyone who showed talent was welcomed into the fold. The sense of community was that strong.

But all that was about to change.

For Brian Epstein, putting the Beatles out of his mind should have been easy. He already had enough on his plate at NEMS. Harry had ceded almost all responsibility to his capable sons. The three record departments were booming. Conceivably, there was incentive enough to open more NEMS stores, perhaps a string of them across the North of England and beyond. Brian was sitting on a potential retail empire. All he had to do was concentrate on the work.

But that had become next to impossible. According to Alistair Taylor, Brian was "besotted" the minute he saw the Beatles. He couldn't stay away from them. At lunchtime, instead of joining his father and brother at a restaurant, as had been their daily custom, Brian pulled off his tie and headed straight for the Cavern. He'd stand by himself at the back of the cellar, underneath the middle archway, starry-eyed, clearly entranced by the performance. The whole atmosphere captivated him. It wasn't just opportunity knocking, the chance to cash in on a phenomenon. To a young man who had been struggling his entire life to fit in, tormented by insecurity and shame, this was Shangri-la. Here, you could be whatever you wished, you could act on your impulses, be as reckless as your heart desired. Brian may not have looked or dressed like these kids, but he responded to the turbulence, the sexual tension, and uninhibitedness of their scene. He wasn't an outcast here. Here, he was the great Oz.

And, of course, from the outset he had been attracted to rough trade — tough, rugged young men of a lower class than his who were a threat to degrade and inflict harm on him. He'd seen guys like this all his life around the docks, fancied them from afar. Clad in cheap skintight leather suits, ruggedly built, marginally educated, foul-mouthed, completely disrespectful, and bashing away at their instruments — the Beatles revved his engine like nothing he'd experienced. "John, especially," says Peter Brown, who was acquainted with Brian's tastes and was also gay. "John wasn't a pretty boy, he had a good look, and a general fuck-you attitude, which was a turn-on. Once Brian saw John, there was no turning away." Bob Wooler would never forget the manner in which Brian presented himself to the band, "with all the pride of a peacock but the nervousness of a sparrow." Eventually, Brian invited the Beatles to his office at the Whitechapel branch of NEMS "for a chat," as he put it. For the record, he would "never know what made [him] say to this eccentric group of boys that [he] thought a further meeting might be helpful to them." But whatever he might—or might not—have intended, the Beatles took him seriously.

On December 3, 1961, Brian paced anxiously around the ground floor of NEMS. The store, closed every Wednesday afternoon for inventory, was dark and shuttered; unpacked cartons of records littered the aisles, and as Brian waded among them, poking the contents here and there, he made cursory marks on an order form clamped in a plastic clipboard.

As the prearranged time drew near, then passed, he grew increasingly irritated. His face tightened into a scowl. A deep flush rose in his cheeks, and his lips pressed so tightly together that they almost disappeared inside his mouth. It began to look as if the Beatles were standing him up.

As he would come to learn, the Beatles were always late—always. They rarely paid any attention to time, even in the case of a performance. Even on this day, they'd stopped off for a few pints of brown mix—mild and brown ales—at the Grapes, a pub on Mathew Street across from the Cavern.

Bob Wooler picked up on Brian's irritation immediately as he "rattled on the glass" to announce their arrival. The Beatles had asked Wooler to attend in order to "offer [them] a view of Epstein," but why and for what purpose he could not even begin to guess. A moment later Wooler was to feel greater discomfort. John handled the introductions, and when he got to Wooler, he said, "This is me dad." The usually loquacious Wooler was struck speechless as Brian extended a hand. "I thought, 'Christ, I'm only ten years older than him!'" Wooler felt an urge to correct John's bluff, but no explanation was necessary as Brian and the Beatles burst out laughing. And Wooler, baring his teeth at John, laughed loudest of all.

Another awkward moment ensued when Brian realized that Paul wasn't among them. He flashed anger at George's explanation that Paul was in the midst of taking a bath, but it evaporated when John stepped in fast to express the band's appreciation for the way NEMS was selling their record. "My Bonnie" proved to be the icebreaker, especially when Brian reported strong sales, along with his intention to order another hundred copies. "Apparently quite a number of people want it," he said, flattering them.

Normally, Brian was a persuasive salesman and took exactly the right approach in marketing appliances and records. Much of that he owed to his acting experience: the ability to deliver lines effectively and convince an audience of his credibility. Customers always gave him their full attention; he enjoyed a certain comfort level with them. But with the Beatles, he wasn't so sure, and it showed. He was nervous in presenting his credentials, his timing was off. As Pete Best put it, "he was picking his words very carefully as to how he could sell himself to us," dancing around the subject with no apparent purpose.

Finally, he cut to the chase. "So, tell me," Brian asked casually, "do you have a manager?" The question hung in the air for a moment before someone replied that, at this time, they did not. Brian nodded appreciably. "It seems to me that with everything going on, someone ought to be looking after you." And that was all he said about it. He let it sink in, without proposing any arrangement or admitting his interest in the role. "He was noncommittal," Wooler recalls, "but he gave every impression—and we rightfully concluded—that he was intrigued." Nothing more was discussed, but Brian promised that he'd be in touch with them again soon and took Pete Best's phone number as a contact.

The prospect of a well-connected manager fascinated the Beatles, who were impressed by the come-on of money and power. "Certainly there were several things in his favor," Pete Best recalled, citing the irresistible booty: suit, shiny shoes, watch, briefcase, big office, car. This guy had what they wanted for themselves—along with the voice to keep them in line. That voice, simple as it may seem, was his biggest asset. Brian spoke with what Scousers called "a BBC accent," the grand, mannered command of language that lads from the Beatles' end of the social spectrum mistook for high education and breeding. John described it in wide-eyed detail to Cynthia, who recalled how "they were delighted that a proper businessman was actually interested in taking them on." John told his girlfriend that he felt "the man from NEMS," as he called Brian, had limitless influence. Above everything else, as Cynthia noted, John thought "[Brian] had class."

Indeed, to these city kids of modest aims and British ceilings, Brian Epstein had it all. He was so widely traveled and cultured, so sophisticated in dress and taste, that he seemed more worldly than all the others who previously had gotten involved with the Beatles' business affairs. That image made all the difference to Paul, who, of all the Beatles, aspired most to such pretensions. Paul, says Dot Rhone, "was more ambitious than John, and he got caught up in the picture of success Brian painted." From the start, as she watched Paul cozy up to Brian, "Paul wanted badly to impress him," Dot says. "Eventually, he hoped, it would give him an advantage over John."

To decide how to proceed, each of the Beatles appealed to his parents for advice. Most, like Mona Best, concluded that "Brian Epstein could be good" for them in the long run, although Jim McCartney, while certainly impressed by Brian's credentials, cautioned Paul specifically against the wiles of "a Jewboy." Only Aunt Mimi refused to give her blessing. She had nothing against Brian personally. His charm was considerable and his manners beyond reproach. Her only concern, however, was John's welfare. Brian might present an appealing strategy for the Beatles, but Mimi was convinced that a rich man like him had nothing at stake. "The novelty" would eventually wear off, she presumed, and he'd be "finished with them in two months and gone on to something else." But on October 9 John had turned twenty-one, placing him legally outside the clutches of his aunt's guardianship. Not that it would have made any difference. John wouldn't have let Mimi interfere with this opportunity. His mind was already made up; he knew what he was going to do. So did the rest of the Beatles. This was the chance they'd been waiting for—the chance to move beyond cellars and jive halls into the spotlight. And without any hesitation, they jumped at it.

[II]

For Brian Epstein, the offer was a gigantic leap of faith. Since their meeting at NEMS, he'd made some inquiries about the Beatles and the answers he'd gotten were not exactly confidence builders. The first person he went to see was Bob Wooler, who danced around questions about their reliability. "They were as unruly a bunch as I'd ever come across," Wooler says, "and I doubted Brian Epstein could tame them." Wooler refused to knock the Beatles, but he wouldn't vouch for them, either, and his silence on the matter must have been deafening.

Allan Williams, to no one's surprise, wasn't any more reassuring. As far as management went, he considered the Beatles free agents but dismissed them as "thieves" and "a right load of layabouts" for stiffing him and swore angrily when it came to their honor. "I wouldn't touch 'em with a fucking barge pole," he cautioned Brian.

A fucking barge pole. The words rang hollow in Brian's ears as he ran the proposition past Peter Brown, a blunt, slightly arrogant young man who, like Brian, could also be self-impressed and haughty. Peter could be relied on to give it to him straight. More important, he knew how to handle Brian. From their first meeting, at a birthday party for a mutual acquaintance, "there was an immediate bond of liking similar things." Both men adored going to the theater, listening to classical music and modern jazz, savoring long, chatty meals, and bargain hunting for antiques. Both ran record shops (Brown managed the counter in Lewis's Department Store). Both had perfect taste in clothes. Both affected an elegance and style that placed them above others in their circle. Years later Brown would enjoy the same compatible relationship with Andrew Lloyd Webber, who bore a striking resemblance to Brian. But, essentially, both men were lonely, desperately lonely, which ran counter to their sociable natures.

Brown, in particular, was consumed by loneliness that came from living a lie. At first, after leaving the air force, he found a reasonably credible niche in the company of a new set of straight—and mostly Jewish—Liverpool friends. "Presumably I looked as if I were a perfectly normal heterosexual guy—which I wasn't," Brown says in retrospect, "and I did nothing, such as it were, to dispel that useful notion." When he met Brian Epstein, in 1960, Brown recognized someone much like himself, "a very unhappy man" who sought to mask the depression he suffered with a fresh coat of "social aplomb."

In Brown, Brian had found a friend who shared not only his vital interests but his enthusiasm for record sales. Peter's work at Lewis's had not gone unnoticed. The department store, directly opposite Brian's Great Charlotte Street shop, was NEMS' closest competitor, in large part because of Brown's nose for sniffing out potential hits. As Brian undoubtedly knew, it would be better for business if Peter worked for NEMS, so he dangled a tempting offer that promised Brown a management position at twice his current salary. When Brian kicked in a commission on top of salary, Peter Brown gave Lewis's two weeks' notice. "Money was the deciding factor," he says, "but there was another important consideration. I sensed that Brian and I were going to have some fun."

A few weeks before Christmas in 1961, Brian invited Peter to dinner at the Corn Market, a splendid seafood restaurant near the Pier Head. The two men had been working furiously in preparation for the approaching holiday and, as a result, had spent little leisure time in each other's company. They finished aperitifs in silence. "He just sat there," Brown remembers.

"I could tell he was working up to something important." Finally he said, "You know that group, the Beatles? I'm going to sign them to be their manager."

Brown was speechless but managed to blurt out a single word. "Why?" he gasped. In an effort to enlighten Brown, they passed on dessert in order to make the evening show at the Cavern. Peter had never been there before and was aghast at the sight of the place. "It was incredibly foul," he recalls, "just a horrid little place. And I didn't think the Beatles were anything special. No matter how brightly Brian painted it, I certainly had no enthusiasm whatsoever for what he intended to do."

Rex Makin came to almost the same conclusion. Brian had gone to see the lawyer for advice. Maintaining that "he'd discovered a gold mine in the Beatles," he wanted a management contract drawn "so it was absolutely unbreakable." But a business contract seemed like a waste of his time, and Makin, a smug, scornful man, dismissed Brian. "Get yourself a standard contract in any stationery store. Bring it to me and I'll have a look at it," he suggested, figuring it was "the last he'd hear of this nonsense from Brian Epstein." In fact, Brian—in all his inexperience—did precisely what Makin recommended: a generic form contract, bought at a stationery shop, became the basis for his future partnership.

Peter Brown and now Rex Makin—two men whose opinions Brian trusted—had greeted his intention to manage the Beatles with barely restrained skepticism. And Harry and Queenie were also bewildered. "Harry was indignant, just furious. He'd put so much faith in Brian, and now—*this!* Another harebrained scheme. The bottom line was that the family would suffer, and NEMS along with it." Brian's attempt to calm his father proved futile. Flustered, he assured Harry that "the Beatles would be bigger than Elvis Presley." But if Queenie wasn't any more optimistic, neither would she take a dim view of Brian's "project." She treated it like the musing of a gifted genius, one of his "artistic things." Where was the harm in it? she chided Harry. Besides, she knew how stubborn Brian was. No one could talk him out of something once he was fixated on it.

Fortunately, there was no skepticism whatsoever on the Beatles' part. Each of them felt that if a breakthrough were to come, it would take someone with money and power to boost them to another level of success. Their next meeting with Brian Epstein sealed the deal. With the band's endorsement and probably at Bob Wooler's urging, John informed him that the Beatles were ready to accept his offer. Various accounts record John as either saying, "Okay, you're on . . . we're in business," or tossing off, "Right, then, Brian—manage us." But while reports may vary, nothing was lost in the translation. By the end of 1961, riding the crest of local popularity, the Beatles, with Brian Epstein in their corner, were ready to take on all comers.

Stuart wasn't expected to return from Hamburg before the summer; he had talked about spending the winter in Germany, reassuring his family that art school—in this case, a German art school—was foremost on his agenda. But as the holiday season drew near, homesickness soured his creative juices and forced an interruption to his studies that only a Liverpool visit was certain to cure. There were also his feelings for Astrid to consider. In anticipation of their eventual marriage, she was eager—and growing impatient—to meet Stuart's family. A trip home for the holidays would serve both purposes.

Perhaps no one looked forward to it as much as John and George. Both Beatles had kept up a fairly steady correspondence with Stuart and noticed a bewildering emotional change in his most recent letters. The tone he used in them was not one that the friends were used to hearing when they'd hung out together in Hamburg. They ran on for ten or fifteen handwritten pages at a clip, loose, blustering, hypersensitive affairs, in which he'd begun to ramble incoherently. Music journalist Ray Coleman, who was given a rare look at the letters, wrote it off to "a restlessness about life," but the agitation mortared between the lines revealed a consuming madness. It set off a lot of signals in Liverpool, and not just to his Beatle mates, who knew Stuart best. His letters home were "clearly distressed— bizarre and disturbed," recalled his sister Pauline. "By now, [my mother] took the view that it was [related to] drugs, lifestyle—being up all night painting." That, and being abroad: Millie remained vehemently opposed to her son's engagement to Astrid, and anything she could use to reinforce its harmful effect was additional ammunition.

The appearance of both Stuart and Astrid, however, caught everyone unawares. No sooner had the couple arrived in Liverpool than attitudes began to reverse course without warning. Most responsible for this change of heart was Astrid Kirchherr, who surprised everyone by remaking her arty image. Although her bohemian reputation preceded her, the sight of this naturally beautiful and elegant young woman wasn't at all what anyone expected. Gone were the black turtleneck sweaters, slinky leather pants, and pointy-toed slippers that identified her exi mind-set. In their place was a round-necked cashmere tunic over a beautifully tailored skirt, opaque stockings, and calfskin Italian pumps that provided a subtle lift of grandeur. "We were quite stunned by her," Pauline Sutcliffe remembered. "She was like nothing we had ever seen before—ever." Astrid arrived at the Sutcliffes' house in Aigburth with only a single long-stemmed orchid in her hand, which she presented with great ceremony to a speechless Millie. "You can't imagine the impact that had on my mother," Pauline said. "We didn't see orchids every day in Liverpool." And Stuart's father "was utterly enamored [of] her."

In Liverpool, people turned and stared at Astrid as they had stared at her in Hamburg, and for the time being her appearance distracted all eyes from Stuart. But it wasn't that long before he drew stares, too—although not under the same glowing conditions. "Stuart looked absolutely godawful," Bill Harry recalls. "It was almost scary seeing what had become of him. He was pale and withered and complained about headaches, severe headaches that would almost cripple him."

The Sutcliffe family knew all about the headaches. Stuart had written to them from Hamburg that he'd been afflicted with migraines and flashes of extreme pain. They came without warning and could disappear in an instant or linger for several hours. Jarred by this news, his mother demanded he see a doctor but was told that "there was no supporting evidence that anything was wrong with him."*

Despite his grave appearance now, all Stuart wanted to talk about was his art, which he had resumed with new fervor. A grant had come through from the German government that reduced his English stipend to chump change, and he was elated about his development under mentor Eduardo Paolozzi, the Scottish abstractionist who held a chair at the Meisterschule. It was Paolozzi, in fact, who had derided Stuart's commitment and issued the ultimatum: music or art—"but not both." And it was Paolozzi who rekindled Stuart's most enduring passion once he dispensed with the Beatles.** Germany had been good to Stuart in so many different ways, and now, with Astrid to care for him, he was not only painting again but writing stories and poems.

---

* His Liverpool College of Art roommate, Rod Murray, recalled how Stuart had occasional severe headaches while enrolled at school. "Stuart fell over from time to time. We thought he just has a bad sense of balance."
** Interestingly, Paolozzi attempted to convert Stuart into a sculptor, and they undertook several welding projects together.

The Beatles were genuinely happy to see Stuart. There were no hard feelings over his departure from the band—only relief, on both sides—and even Paul seemed to forget past grievances during their reunion at Ye Cracke. It was apparent from the conversation that Stuart had become very much at peace with his newfound life in Germany. Music was behind him now (although he would later occasionally sit in with local bands). The Beatles were his mates, and he remained their undying fan. But as mates, they'd revealed themselves in ways that had demonstrated frightening judgment. He warned his sister to exercise the "good sense to keep away from the Beatles because they're a bad lot, completely lacking in moral fiber."

[III]

From the start, the would-be dress designer and store-window stylist marked the Beatles for a makeover, an effort to present them properly and "to smarten them up" for discriminating audiences. Leather and jeans were fine for the Cavern, Brian argued, but the gatekeepers of the entertainment establishment they hoped to conquer would never look twice at them.

He was horribly wrong, of course—and horribly right. To Brian, Elvis may have been the epitome, but not the *old* Elvis, with his greasy hair, swivel hips, and sharkskin snarl. No, since Elvis had been discharged from the army, he'd turned over a new leaf. The *new* Elvis, in his toned-down civilian apparel, resembled Cliff Richard, of all people, and had waded so far into the mainstream that for the next ten years he'd languish as a Las Vegas act.

But that suited Brian just fine. What did he know of Eddie Cochran, Chuck Berry, or Jerry Lee Lewis? He may have sold their records at NEMS, but that didn't make them household names. The real stars, to Brian, weren't rock 'n rollers but pop stars: Ricky Nelson, Connie Francis, Pat Boone, Bobby Darin, Neil Sedaka, performers who understood the conventions of show business and were willing to adapt their images—and music—accordingly. They'd wind up with longevity.

For almost a month now, Brian had watched the Beatles' performance with rising disappointment. His eye was drawn to their reckless behavior onstage, and not just the smoking and drinking, which were bad enough, but the way they sequenced a set of songs. Anyone who yelled out a request was granted his wish, even in the middle of another song. Often they'd just stop dead and launch into something else. There was no rhyme or reason to what they played and, therefore, no logical pacing. Having gone to drama school, Brian appreciated the beauty of building an act, controlling the ebb and flow of material, working the crowd toward a rousing climax. In the Beatles' case, that meant getting from "Hippy Hippy Shake" to "What'd I Say" and, later, "Twist and Shout," which always brought down the house. Too often, however, they got lost in between and blew the pay-off. Not only amateurish, he maintained, but self-defeating.

This was a brave tack for a new manager with no points in the plus column, and even braver because, as the Beatles saw it, whatever they were doing seemed to be working onstage. The kids loved them, no matter what they did. Besides, real rock 'n roll wasn't orderly, it wasn't slick. Perhaps Brian didn't appreciate that.

In a similar situation, John might have told a critic to fuck off, especially someone so glaringly "one of *them.*" But Brian's outright admiration and straight speaking enabled him to make a convincing case, and when he spoke that way the Beatles listened. He insisted on some ground rules. From now on, eating onstage was out; so was smoking and punching one another, cursing, chatting up girls, taking requests, and sleeping. Lateness would no longer be tolerated. Brian expected everyone to show up on time and be ready to play, and he promised to print up a weekly list of gigs, along with addresses and fees, and provide copies for each of the Beatles in advance. To ensure there would be no slipups, he liaised with Pete's mate Neil Aspinall, who was acting as driver and roadie for the band. In addition to the above, the Beatles were required to post their set lists before-hand and—this provoked heated debate—bow after each number. And not just a casual nod—a big, choreographed bow, which, by a silent count, was delivered smartly and on cue.

"Brian believed that would be very good for us," Paul explained, "and I was also a great believer in that." Bowing made sense, he reasoned, be-cause it showed some polish on the Beatles' part. It set them apart from the other bands. Later on, he would convince the others of the wisdom in wearing suits—and courting the press. "Paul was Mr. Show Business," says Bill Harry. "Everything he did was calculated to promote the group." John, on the other hand, greeted each concession, each nod to conformity, with unmasked hostility. He hated pandering, no matter how advanta-geous it might seem, and made no bones about it. When he felt threatened by Paul, he lashed out viciously—not necessarily at the target of his anger, nor with regard for the consequences—until the rage subsided.

That was the intricate nature of the band. It put Paul and John at cross-purposes, terrific cross-purposes, that would grow in intensity over the years. Passing was the perfect harmony that marked their songwriting relationship. In its place was a distinction so contrary, a conflict so profound, that the friction it produced built up an armor. Both men schemed aggressively to impose their vision on the Beatles. Always there was Paul's need to smooth the rough edges and John's need to rough them up. Somehow, it drove them to fertile middle ground. But the constant compromise was ultimately a debilitating position, and the balance on both sides could not be sustained forever.

The last two months of 1961 made enormous demands on the Beatles' time. They were booked solid, six days a week, two—and occasionally three—shows a day. They played civil-service clubs, jive halls, charity shows, and guest nights; they continued appearing at the low-paying Cavern lunchtime sessions; they even put in time at the Casbah, which still drew modest crowds to Pete's basement. Restless and itching to push beyond Liverpool, hoping to attract big-time attention, they accepted a booking in the South floated by a wily, energetic promoter named Sam Leach. Aldershot was an army-barracks town about thirty miles outside of London with "a nice old ballroom suited to hold three hundred people." But when they got there, they found neither a single London agent in the house nor much of a crowd to speak of; only a dozen or so uninterested people showed up. The Beatles went through the motions anyway, then wound down the night dancing with one another and playing Ping-Pong.

On the way back to Liverpool, tired and depressed, the band put Leach from their minds and struck up a familiar refrain that had carried them through the doldrums in Hamburg. Affecting the accent of an American announcer, John would blare: "Where are we going, boys?"

"To the top, Johnny! To the top!" they'd answer in unison.

"And where is the top?" he persisted.

"The toppermost of the poppermost!"

The toppermost of the poppermost. Convinced that they were on the right track, the Beatles saw only one barrier remaining between them and the possibility of real stardom: a recording contract with a major label. It was their ticket out of the provinces, and it was so close, they believed, they could almost taste it.

[1]

For a man who prized great recordings and traded in the hits of the day, it seems odd that Brian Epstein had never set foot inside of a record company. There had never before been incentive—nor, for that matter, invitation—for a representative of NEMS to go to the source. To a record company, NEMS was merely another of its accounts, and while it was a luminous one—the North Star, so to speak, in the galaxy of provincial retail outlets—all business with merchants was conducted through distributors located in Manchester. The London offices—the labels themselves—were reserved for the *talent,* a word construed to describe not only singers and musicians but also the A&R staff, producers, publicists, and marketing flacks.

Tony Barrow was hardly older than twenty when Brian Epstein strode into his office. A graduate of the Merchant Taylors' School just outside of Liverpool, in Crosby, he went into the record business in 1957 at the unlikely age of seventeen, writing a review column that appeared weekly in the *Echo.* Pop music was a complete mystery to the newspaper's editors in those days; the idiom and its slang weren't serious enough to warrant their hard-hitting brand of journalism. Barrow not only spoke the language, he could write pretty decent copy. But while the *Echo* deeded precious space to "a schoolboy," it refused to admit as much in print, insisting instead that his column appear under the nom de plume "Disker."

In one of those wonderful ironies that cater to legend, Disker became Brian Epstein's oracle. Each week, before placing the NEMS record order, Brian consulted the column for tips about upcoming releases, and thanks to the generosity of Disker's insight, he cashed in on many a hit that might otherwise have slipped past him. Disker was his trusty link to the trade, and therefore it was to the visionary Disker he wrote in December 1961 about his exciting new venture. "I have this fabulous group called the Beatles," the letter began. "Will you write about them in the *Echo*?"

By this time, Barrow had moved to London, where he was working for Decca, churning out sleeve copy for the backside of album covers. "I was still writing the Disker column," he recalls, "and was offended by Brian's misconception of it. 'Don't you read the column?' I wrote back rather stiffly. 'I don't write about local bands.'" Dismissively, he referred Brian to another *Echo* columnist—a lackluster "diarist," or feature writer, named, quite coincidentally, George Harrison—but doubted that anything would come of it. Still, he ended his response on an upbeat note: "Keep me posted, because the moment they've got a record, I'll certainly do something on it."

A week later Brian turned up in London on the doorstep of his one and only Decca contact. He had come on short notice, he explained, to pick Tony Barrow's brain and to wade ever so gently into the deep waters of the record business.

Decca Records, located in a stately stone mansion just off the Albert Embankment across from the Tate Gallery, presented an imposing image of a multinational company. But if Brian imagined partaking in the hushed tones of business conducted at high-polished board tables under glittering chandeliers, he was sorely mistaken. Barrow was stationed in a rather depressing annex across a side road, overlooking the backyard of a fire station. The office was a shabby, paneled cubicle of a room with a few posters on the wall, a double desk he shared with an Indian typist, and a tiny window through which they watched the neighboring firemen practice running out their hoses. It was difficult for Brian to find a seat in the clutter. Everywhere there were boxes surrounded by massive piles of unfolded, unlaminated record sleeves, called "flats "—mostly overruns of *South Pacific*, which had been Decca's biggest seller for years, and the latest Elvis Presley release, whose sales were in free fall and which, as a result, they had in excess.

Brian launched into his sales pitch about the Beatles, tossing out his "bigger than Elvis" knuckleball. Such hyperbole was still a novelty in the record business, but even so, Barrow couldn't have been less interested. He was, however, charmed by Brian himself, whom he typed as "instantly impressive" and not at all "like the typical agent of the era." It was essentially painless to indulge the "charismatic" man sitting across the desk from him for a few minutes.

Brian opened his briefcase and produced an acetate of the band. "I put it on the player," Barrow recalls, "and heard the very exciting atmosphere of the Cavern—lots of screaming, chanting, and a steady *bunk-bunk-bunk* in the background, with a few errant falsetto notes mixed in—and that was about it." Voices were impossible to decipher, to say nothing of songs.

Brian apologized for the awful quality. "I've taken it from the sound-track of a Grenada television documentary about the Cavern," he explained disingenuously. (It wasn't until 1966, when Paul McCartney asked Barrow to hold up a cheap tape-recorder microphone to the loudspeakers, during the Beatles' final concert at Candlestick Park, that Brian admitted he'd used the same technique to make the acetate.) Not that better sound would have made any difference. If Brian had brought something special, Barrow would have run it across to the A&R department, but from all evidence so far, the Beatles had nothing going for them.

As Brian was packing up to leave, he said, "Well, I'm in the midst [of] trying to arrange an audition with Decca." Barrow asked who was acting as his go-between and Epstein mentioned Selecta, the local Decca distribution company in the Northwest. Barrow waited until Brian had left, then called Sidney Beecher-Stevens, who ran the label's sales department, and described his meeting with the record-shop owner. "Epstein . . . Epstein . . . ?" Beecher-Stevens wracked his brain for a connection. "Sorry, never heard of him. They must be pretty small." When Barrow explained that it was NEMS, he could hear the huff on the other end of the phone. "Oh, they're one of our biggest customers! Yes, *yes,* the band *has* to have an audition."

A week later, just days before Christmas, Mike Smith, one of Decca's young "bright lights," turned up in Liverpool to catch the Beatles at the Cavern. Right off the bat, Brian was "very taken" with Smith, who wasn't at all the kind of record-label hotshot he'd expected. A tall, slim East Londoner with slicked-back black hair, Mike was outgoing and polite and didn't lord his position over them. Moreover, Brian could tell from observing Mike that "he liked the boys." He didn't stiffen up or attempt to remain poker-faced at their show; his expression flashed excitement from ear to ear. It hit all the right notes.

After a rousing lunchtime session, Mike went across Mathew Street to the Grapes, where he and the Beatles hoisted a few pints and promised to meet up again for the evening performance. Then Brian and Alistair Taylor took him out to eat at Peacock's, in order to gauge the extent of his interest. "Right," Smith said without any ado, "we've got to have them down for a bash in the studio at once. Let's see what they can do."

That was all Brian needed to hear. Alistair Taylor would never forget how his boss's face turned beet-red. "He was barely able to contain his excitement—and it bled right through any presumption of coolness. We dropped Mike off at the Adelphi Hotel, then went straight back to Peacock's and had a few too many gin and tonics to celebrate. Brian was in a splendid mood. He felt this was it. This was the break that would vindicate him."

If Brian needed any vindication, it was not so much for his taking up with the Beatles as it was for the unlikely time he'd scheduled their Decca audition—January 1, 1962, a day not suitable even for singing in the shower. As a result, New Year's Eve parties were out of the question; both John and Paul had been looking forward to celebrating with their girls, Cynthia and Dot, with whom things were growing progressively serious, but the appointment required they travel to London that night, a long, difficult trip that was discouraging from the get-go. Dot Rhone recalls the boys' "ill humor" at what should have otherwise been an extremely joyous occasion for the Beatles. They celebrated the New Year over drinks early that afternoon and were on the road to London well before nightfall.

It had already begun snowing before they left Liverpool. Neil Aspinall drove the old Commer van through the wintry squall, an unsteady ride under optimal circumstances, with the four Beatles crammed clumsily in the back among the stack of loose, shifting equipment. The roads, dusted with fresh powder, wound circuitously south. Crawling and lurching along what was then the major motor route—the ponderous A5—they often spent long, frustrating stretches stuck behind long-distance trucks that heaved like elephants up the hillside to Carthage. At Birmingham, where the roads zigzagged through isolated farmland, they went east, following lonely roads that were rutted and in this weather largely impassable—not even divided highways—and then down, down, down through the outskirts to London.

The trip took nine hours. The Beatles were cold and grumpy upon their arrival at a hotel in Russell Square, and when someone suggested that they hoist a few in relief, there wasn't a man among them who was inclined to protest.

It was late when they got to bed—and "very late" the next morning when they arrived at Decca Studios, in the north of London. Brian, who had come down by train on his own, was pacing figure eights in the corridor, furious with them. "He was frothing at the mouth," Pete Best recalled. "I'd never seen him as angry as that." John, in defiance, told him to "bugger off." To make matters worse, Mike Smith hadn't arrived. He'd been out late at a party and wandered in at a leisurely pace, a good hour late, which only wound up Epstein into a tighter knot.

Everyone was on edge. The guys were sleepy, hungover, nervous. To make matters worse, the studios were "freezing cold"; they hadn't been used between Christmas and New Year. The Beatles, "ill at ease," were left bumping about, waiting for a skeleton crew to set up inside the control booth.

History has held Brian Epstein largely responsible for the selection of songs performed at the audition. "[He] believed that the way to impress Mike Smith was not by John and Paul's original songs," Philip Norman concludes in *Shout!*, "but by their imaginative, sometimes eccentric arrangements of standards." In cloudy hindsight, even John blamed Brian for picking "all these weird novelty things" that were "O.K. for the lads at the Cavern . . . but don't mean a thing when you do them cold in a recording studio for people who don't know the group." To some extent, this is true. The standards no doubt pleased Brian, who regarded them as legitimate crowd-pleasers, but while he may have weighed in with his opinion, the decision of what to play was left entirely to the Beatles.

In fact, they'd taken a cue from Mike Smith, who encouraged the band to "play the whole spectrum of music" he'd heard at the Cavern. "We thought hard about the material we were going to play at the audition," recalled Pete. And even though in hindsight Paul dismissed it as a "fairly silly repertoire," the set they chose was significant principally because it indicated the band's versatility and was an accurate cross section of their material.

The flip side was a lack of consistency. The fifteen songs wander from genre to genre, like a minstrel looking for a crowd. "Till There Was You," "The Sheik of Araby," "September in the Rain," and "Besame Mucho" were the kind of corny, melodramatic standards that young British bands continued to sprinkle throughout their sets as concessions to the naysayers of rock 'n roll; eight other songs covered an array of pop records they'd been performing over the years—"Crying, Waiting, Hoping," "Memphis," "Money," "Searchin'," "Sure to Fall," "Three Cool Cats," "To Know Her Is to Love Her," and "Take Good Care of My Baby," the latter of which had just been a number one hit for Bobby Vee and was included late in the process at George's insistence; and finally there were three Lennon-McCartney originals: "Hello Little Girl," one of their earliest compositions, "Like Dreamers Do" (which incidentally would reach the charts in 1964 on a record by the Applejacks that was produced by Mike Smith), and the future Cilla Black hit "Love of the Loved."

The songs hardly mattered, however; their performance was flat across the board. There is none of the spark, the exuberant personality, that characterize all future Beatles recordings. In fact, the soaring vocals so familiar to generations of fans sound halting in some places, too deliberate in others. Paul certainly was off his game; he repeatedly reached for notes that were well within his range and experienced some fluttering in his voice that sounded like nerves. John lost his way momentarily in the middle of "Memphis." And Pete's leaden drumming produced the same expression in every song, be it a ballad or an all-out rocker.

John knew right off that the performance was not up to par. While he held his tongue at the time, he later confided to a friend that their style was cramped by too many "pretty" numbers. "We should have rocked like mad in there and shown what we're like when we're roused."

Nevertheless, optimism ran high. The band felt their work had been "productive." And as far as they could tell, Mike Smith seemed elated. He flashed them a rousing thumbs-up sign from the control booth and, afterward, threw them an unexpected compliment. "Can't see any problems — you should record," he imparted. "I'll let you know in a couple of weeks."

"You should record!" The three magic words hung in the air for everyone to savor. The Beatles practically floated out of the studio on a cushion of pure exhilaration. Over a celebratory lunch, hosted by their new and ecstatic manager, the Liverpudlians toasted the New Year and all its promise in grand tradition. Brian surprised them by ordering a bottle of wine, a touch that, in most of their families, was reserved for funerals. Clinking glasses, they howled with delight over the prospect of a brilliant future. "What a great way to start 1962," someone proposed at an opportune moment, "right from day one. Here were go!"

[II]

Immediately after returning from London, there was good news — and bad.

On January 4, *Mersey Beat* announced the results of its first popularity poll and, to no one's surprise, the Beatles came out on top of the list.

"No doubt about it, they were the best group in Liverpool," says the paper's editor—and the band's longtime friend—Bill Harry. But the contest hadn't come off as squarely as anticipated. Rory Storm and the Hurricanes actually got more votes, but whether out of fairness, loyalty, or good judgment, Harry had doctored the final results when, during the tally, he suspected Rory had filled out hundreds of his own ballots. Little did he know that the Beatles had done the same thing. In any case, it was official: their supremacy was announced in bold type just inches below *Mersey Beat*'s innocuous banner. And the next day it was rubber-stamped by the release of "My Bonnie," at long last, on Polydor's English label.

Brian had spent almost two weeks trying to force a proper release. Alistair Taylor overheard the effort that went into it as he passed his office four or five times a day and heard Brian frantically pleading the band's case. "He was always on the phone to Polydor, insisting, 'Something is happening here! [NEMS has] to import this on your German label, which is ridiculous. You ought to have a listen.' At first, they just told him to get knotted, but after so much persistence they finally gave in."

On January 5 the record arrived and the Beatles were now—officially—recording stars. Immediately, Brian shot off copies of "My Bonnie"—now correctly labeled by "Tony Sheridan *and the Beatles*"—to all the London record labels, requesting an audition for the band. Meanwhile, his tiny Whitechapel office, once devoted entirely to updating the NEMS stock, had been converted into Beatles Central, his own role now suggestive of a full-time press agent. "It became hard, right off the bat, for Brian to juggle his growing responsibilities," says Peter Brown, who often picked up the slack out of consideration for his friend. By now, Brian was more interested in artist management than retailing. As the Beatles required more attention, he began to offload NEMS business matters to assistants and other underlings—or just ignore them, the effect of which was not lost on the exacting Harry Epstein. "Whatever you do," Brian pleaded with Alistair Taylor, "don't tell Daddy about any of this. If he comes in, just make up some story."

The instructions Brian had given the Beatles about arriving at a show on time, not smoking or swearing onstage, doing tightly programmed sets, and bowing were having a residual effect on their image. He could see it, even at the Cavern, where they fought the grungy ambience. They were making strides, but there was a long way to go yet. Lunchtime shows were still too disorganized. Guitarist Colin Manley, who had hung on to his day job, used to take an extended lunch hour in order to catch their act and re-members marveling at the "anarchy" that rumbled through their set. "Nine times out of ten, when they kicked off the show, George hadn't even ar-rived. He'd have been out late the night before or his bus wasn't on time. Occasionally, I'd have to get up and play a couple songs until he showed. And if Lennon broke a string, he'd have Paul do a song while he put on a new one, going *dwoiiiiinnng dwoiiiiinnng* [winding the string] right through the vocals. Nothing they did was polished."

And attitude was a tough nut to crack. Onstage, the Beatles continued to take requests shouted from the audience, acknowledging them with a rude remark designed to get a laugh. Sometimes, however, it got out of control. John, more than anyone, had trouble knowing where to draw the line, often saying things just to be contrary. When he was in a foul mood—or drunk—he could terrorize people with a cutting remark, abusing fans ver-bally. "Shut yer fucking yap!" It wasn't unusual for him to unleash a string of obscenities at a visitor to the Cavern or snarl at a backstage guest, then dedicate a song to his victim.

Brian was smart enough to realize that John couldn't be tamed. In that respect, he avoided issuing ultimatums that might provoke a confronta-tion. But he tried to head off certain situations before they backfired. One thing particularly troubling was John's trail of personal effects. They were littered across the city—letters, articles, poems, notebooks, drawings, and pictures in which he'd held nothing back. He may have been a loose can-non onstage, but many of these items weren't fit for public consumption. The most incriminating stuff was a packet of "rude photos" from Hamburg he'd given to Bill Harry for use in upcoming issues of *Mersey Beat*. Nothing that was scandalous, but rather off-color: pictures of Paul in the bathroom, John with a toilet seat around his neck. Not long after Brian got involved with the band, Bill Harry recalls, "John rushed into the office and said, 'Brian insists I've got to get them back—the pictures, everything you've got. I must take it all with me now.' It wasn't enough to change their image; he was getting rid of the evidence as well."

Another lingering sore spot remained the girlfriends. Brian considered it unprofessional that Cynthia Powell and Dot Rhone turned up at each gig, and he was aghast, not to mention annoyed, when each time, inevitably, they got up together to dance. It was too distracting for the boys. Performing was work, he argued, not a social outing. What's more, the presence of steady girlfriends might turn off the female fans who entertained fantasies about their favorite Beatle (to say nothing of Brian's own fantasies). A new decree was handed down: Cyn and Dot were no longer welcome—no longer *allowed*—at Beatles shows. John and Paul were instructed to inform their respective girlfriends.

Dot, already insecure and self-contained, was crestfallen when Paul delivered the news. "It seemed cruel and unnecessary," she says. "We always stayed out of their way, never interfered in anything they did." On more than one occasion, she recalls, they arrived at a show with the boys, were deposited in a corner, and ignored until it was time to leave. That was all right by them. Even after gigs, at the Jacaranda or one of their other haunts, they sat for hours, just listening to the boys talk among themselves, absolutely silent. They never, except on rare occasions, contributed to the conversation. "We were completely subservient." Their reward was simply going to the gigs—watching their boyfriends play and basking in the glow.

Dot had already gone against her better judgment, "stealing Preludin and Purple Hearts for the band" from her new job, working at a pharmacy. But disobeying Paul's wishes was out of the question. Cynthia, on the other hand, learned how to blend into the crowd. At shows, John would stash her in a seat at the back of the hall, where she watched like any other punter.

———

The events of January 1962 had convinced the Beatles that their attention should be focused solely on their careers.

They began by finally signing an official management contract with Brian, which had been in the works for over a month.* It was a modified boilerplate agreement, tying the four musicians to Epstein for a period of six years and at a rate of 20 percent of their earnings. Brian had originally asked for 25 percent, a sum refused by the Beatles, who considered it too exorbitant a chunk. He accepted the lower figure without further negotiation, perhaps owing to an unexpected savings of 2.5 percent. A month earlier, overcome with gratitude by Alistair Taylor's noble allegiance, he offered the loyal record salesman what amounted to a finder's fee, 2.5 percent of the Beatles, which Taylor had politely—but foolishly—declined.

At the signing, Brian repeated his foremost goal: to nail down a legitimate recording contract for the Beatles. Even before the Decca session, as early as December 7, 1961, he had been in touch with labels, submitting "My Bonnie" in lieu of an audition. Upbeat and sturdy, the record cut the

---

* *Oddly enough, Brian never put his signature to the contract.*

right groove, but it was basically a Tony Sheridan showcase; it gave even professional ears too little to go on as far as the Beatles were concerned. To Brian's disappointment, the A&R managers didn't take long to underscore that point. On the fourteenth, he received the band's first rejection from no less a tone-setter than EMI, the titan of British labels. "Whilst we appreciate the talents of this group," wrote Ron White, the company's general manager, "we feel that we have sufficient groups of this type at the present time under contract and that it would not be advisable for us to sign any further contract of this nature. . . ." While not a stinging rebuke—the kind that dismisses a band as a pack of hopeless amateurs—it certainly wasn't the endorsement they were looking for.

Meanwhile, Decca wasn't exactly beating down the door. The Beatles hadn't heard from Mike Smith following their seemingly triumphant New Year's Day audition and assumed he was deluged with work as a result of the long holiday season. In fact, Smith had made up his mind to sign the Beatles while they were still in the studio, but he had to run it by his boss.

Unfortunately, Decca's A&R chief was in New York on business and didn't return until the middle of the month.

The role of tastemaker was an unlikely one for Dick Rowe. Like his father and grandfather before him, he had spent most of his life as a stockbroker in service to Decca's chairman, Sir Edward Lewis. The sole pleasure in a livelihood otherwise tedious and unfulfilling was his "amazing record collection," most of whose gems had actually been obtained through the black market. Word of his unconventional musical knowledge spread through the firm, and Sir Edward staggered an unsuspecting Rowe by asking him to run Decca.

Rowe rose rapidly through the A&R department, serving as one of Decca's early in-house producers. By the mid-1950s, he had assembled an impressive roster of pop artists, gleaned from his opportune signing of Tommy Steele. Anthony Newley, Billy Fury, and Marty Wilde all reaped glory from Rowe's workmanlike productions, as, later, would Van Morrison ("Here Comes the Night") and Englebert Humperdinck ("Release Me"). He worked with dozens of significant acts, including the Rolling Stones, over his career. Nevertheless, he would always be linked, albeit ignominiously, for his mishandling of the Beatles.

At the time, the thorn in Rowe's side was Decca's budget, the subject of his recent meetings in the States. A&R expenditures, he noted, were in danger of exploding. So when Mike Smith bounded into his office that

Monday morning, delirious with enthusiasm for two new groups he just had to sign, Rowe tightened the company belt. "No, Mike, it's impossible," he told him. "They can't both be sensational. You choose the one that you think is right."

Rowe's generosity was actually self-serving. He'd listened to both auditions—the Beatles and Brian Poole and the Tremeloes—on his own and agreed with Smith's eventual choice. The nod went to the Tremeloes, hands down. Their audition was better, they had that identifiable "Decca sound," and perhaps most significant, they lived in Mike Smith's neighborhood in Dagenham, which put them a neat twenty minutes from the studio, as opposed to their northern counterparts. "Liverpool could have been in Greenland to us then," Rowe recalled years later.

Decca held off on giving Epstein the news. The company had never dealt in this manner with one of its retail accounts, especially one with billings as significant as NEMS'. Lest it risk injuring a profitable relationship, Decca decided to string him along for a while, in the hope that he'd either lose interest in this hobby or just go away.

Despite the delay, Brian allowed himself a cautious confidence. The Beatles had done their part, they'd delivered a respectable demo, and with NEMS' influence firmly behind them, there was every reason to expect a deal to materialize. It was only a matter of time, he reasoned. And yet, a creeping frustration began to take hold. "He had very substantial accounts with these companies and yet he couldn't seem to pull any strings," Peter Brown recalls. It was this lack of respect that stung the most. For Brian, it meant one thing: humiliation, a reaction that resonated back to his school days and the army. "He was furious. He thought he was being treated like everybody else and felt he deserved more attention."

With EMI out of the picture and Decca mysteriously on hold, Brian turned up the heat at the two other major English labels, Pye and Philips. He began commuting to London in earnest, dropping off copies of the Decca audition tape at whatever office he could squeeze a foot in the door. Alistair Taylor had connections at Pye and, with some gentle arm-twisting, got the Beatles' tape to Les Cox, the label's head of A&R. Cox and Tony Hatch, one of Pye's in-house producers, gave it a cursory listen and "thought it was awful." Still, Taylor urged them to see the band perform. But nothing doing. As far as London was concerned, Liverpool was off the musical radar screen.

After Pye's rejection of the Beatles, Philips also passed, leaving few options remaining for a deal. It would be another year before the influence of independent labels, so prevalent in the United States, surfaced in Great Britain. For the time being, there were only the four majors—EMI, Decca, Pye, and Philips—with which to do business in London, as well as EMI's two subsidiaries, Columbia and HMV, which had also passed.

By February, Brian's anxiety had reached a critical stage. He continued to reassure the Beatles that their recording career was inevitable, but to friends he admitted that it was beginning to look bleak. "It appears that we are cursed as far as record companies are concerned," he complained bitterly to Peter Brown. "Either that, or [the labels] are just too tone-deaf to recognize a hit group—in which case we are definitely doomed."

Decca especially perplexed him. Mike Smith had shown such optimism and seemed to enjoy the Beatles' company. A deal there seemed like a fait accompli. Now, he sensed they were giving him the brush-off.

Exasperated, Brian tried to force Decca's hand. After leaving a string of curt messages with the receptionist, he finally heard from Dick Rowe on February 1. Rowe apologized for the delay in returning Brian's calls and confessed embarrassment. The Beatles, he reported, failed to stir much enthusiasm at the label. "The people at Decca didn't like the boys' sound," he explained. More to the point: "Groups with guitars are on the way out." To make such a claim credible, he pointed to the new crop of vocalists now popular in the States—Bobby Vee, Frankie Avalon, Bobby Rydell, Bobby Darin, Dion. "Besides, they sound too much like the Shadows."

Even to a square like Brian, this argument rang false. Desperate to salvage a deal, he begged Rowe for a few minutes of his time and arranged to meet him the following week at Decca's offices in London.

In the meantime, Rowe decided to safeguard himself against the likelihood of an unreasonable Brian Epstein: he'd audition the Beatles himself. Without telling anyone, Rowe took the train to Liverpool on Saturday, February 3, with the intention of catching the band at the Cavern. His objective was simple: he'd get a good look at this group, without any buildup or hype. That way, no one would be able to claim that Decca hadn't jumped through hoops for Epstein.

It was "pissing with rain" when he arrived in Liverpool, the city besieged by a typical winter storm, the kind whose blustery winds and rawness bit through every stitch of one's clothing deep into the skin. Rowe's mood was as foul as the weather by the time he stepped out in front of the

Cavern. One glance at the scene churned up further shudders of indignation. Mathew Street was straight out of Dickens: remote, squalid, creepy. The entrance to the Cavern was packed with kids forcing their way like animals into the tiny club. Standing alone in the dark, shivering in the downpour, Rowe smoked a cigarette and weighed his options. "You couldn't get in, and what with the rain outside, I was getting drenched," he recalled. "I thought, 'Oh sod it,' and I walked away."

Thus, Rowe let the most popular band in history slip through his fingers.

To insulate himself against the Beatles' headstrong manager, Rowe had recruited Sidney Beecher-Stevens to join them for lunch in a private dining room at Decca House, where, without beating around the bush, he delivered a polite but final rejection. Brian seethed with indignation. It was clear the end had come; the expectations fanned by the productive recording session were dashed. Brian was convinced that he and the Beatles had been slighted and strung along by Decca. At one point during lunch, voices were raised. Struggling to recover his composure, Brian announced quite pompously that they were making the mistake of their careers. Now Rowe had heard enough. He had been listening to this babble about "the Beatles' potential" for over an hour. Through clenched teeth, he offered Brian a piece of advice: "You have a good record business in Liverpool, Mr. Epstein. Stick to that."

Brian left Decca House "completely shattered." He had failed to deliver what he had promised. Even more unsettling was the absence of options. He was out of places to shop the Beatles. Against the backdrop of failure, Brian reached out to a London acquaintance for some constructive advice. The previous year he had gone to a retail record management seminar in Hamburg, where he'd hit it off with a young man named Bob Boast. At first, they seemed like an improbable pair, but the more the two men talked, the more a rapport developed between them. They both liked the same kind of music, were devoted to their jobs, and possessed the same direct, earnest attitude toward record sales. Boast managed the tony HMV record store, and Brian dropped in on him as a measure of last resort.

Boast listened to the Beatles' Decca tapes without much enthusiasm. There was no way he could help, other than to suggest that Brian convert several of the songs to discs, which, in the future, would allow A&R men to hear only the highlights, the killer songs, without having to wade through everything else. Right away, that suggestion made excellent sense. One flight above the record store was a studio where acetates could be cut while Brian waited. This, too, proved providential, inasmuch as Jim Foy, the engineer on duty, happened to listen and liked what he heard. When Brian bragged that his favorite songs were written by the Beatles themselves, Foy introduced him to Sid Coleman, the general manager of Ardmore & Beechwood, who expressed interest in acquiring the publishing rights. The offer was significant principally because it corroborated Brian's impression of the Beatles as viable talents. It was not, he recognized, the kind of deal dangled to many groups without a record in the marketplace. Intrigued, Brian promised to explore it, but at the moment, he explained, a recording contract was more crucial to his agenda. Coleman, eager to pursue matters, volunteered to help. No extraordinary effort was necessary, he assured Brian—everything was all in the family; HMV and Ardmore & Beechwood happened to share the same corporate parent, EMI. "Now, who hasn't [already] got a group in EMI?" he speculated aloud, running his finger down a list of company telephone extensions. "Let me see, Norrie's got the Shadows. . . ." On and on Coleman went, puzzling over a chore in which he seemed to match the entire roster to their respective in-house producers. The label and its affiliates were inundated with pop acts whose lineups bore too close a resemblance to the Beatles. None of the producers on the list were likely to take on a project that duplicated an act already under contract, and each had his own respectable share.

Except for one.

Coleman's finger lingered over the name, a wild card, and not even that—more like a shot in the dark. He must have felt uneasy at the prospect of taking such a shot; it had "misfire" written all over it. No doubt he deliberated over how Brian Epstein would react at the end of yet another hopeless audition. It would be easy to judge Coleman's assistance as inappropriate, a waste of time. He was savvy enough to know that if there was any value in these Beatles, such a miscue might scare off Epstein or, worse, steer him to a competitor. Still, it seemed like the only alternative. There was no one else at the label likely to give him the time of day. So, without any more debate, Coleman picked up the phone and called George Martin.

[III]

Even before he had become famous, George Martin had the aura. He was a tall man, well over six feet, with a fine head of thick, wavy, swept-back hair and dramatic features: a wide, helmet-shaped forehead; long, sloping jawline; liquid blue eyes; and an afterglow of masculine beauty that filled out and crystallized with age. He also conducted himself with such natural deference that every gesture seemed informed by a graciousness and decency beyond him. Nevertheless, for all Martin's personal poetry, at EMI he was something of a joke.

From the moment he arrived at the record company, in 1950, George answered his EMI telephone with the punch line: Parlophone. The label, once a vital German imprint, had dwindled in stature to the extent that it existed primarily as a repository for EMI's most insignificant acts. In a company loaded with up-and-coming stars, Parlophone was lit by baroque ensembles, light orchestras, dance bands, and obscure music hall luminaries whose commercial prospects were as dim as their material. HMV and Columbia got the heavy hitters licensed from their American affiliates; even when EMI bought Capitol Records in 1956, its artists landed everywhere but Parlophone, which was insular and self-contained. "It was the bastard child of the recording industry," says a musician familiar with the scene, "kept locked away in the clock tower and treated with disdain."

Martin inherited Parlophone's reins in 1955 and, for a brief period, continued along much in the same timeworn tradition, flogging such pedestrian artists as Jimmy Shand, Jim Dale, Humphrey Lyttelton, Ron Goodwin, and "a lot of traditional Scottish bands that actually sold themselves." With the upswing of pop, it became increasingly clear that if Parlophone was ever to be productive again—and not just productive, but vital—Martin would have "to do something" bold to forge a distinct and profitable identity using material that fell "between the cracks" at other labels, or risk increased alienation from within the corporate hierarchy.

Most A&R men would have studied the competition and staked a similar claim. But for whatever reason, George Martin demurred. He had spent most of his life in thrall of serious music—and serious musicians. He had studied piano and oboe in earnest at London's Guildhall School of Music, idolized Rachmaninoff and Ravel, swooned over Cole Porter, befriended Sidney Torch and Johnny Dankworth. Clearly, pop music was out of his register.

Rather than leap the scales, Martin pitched a note no one else had struck and one loaded with gold. Comedy was enormously popular in England and relatively cheap to record; there were no musicians to pay, no arrangements to write, no copyrights to secure. Of course, comedy didn't present the creative challenge of a Mozart serenade. Nor was it studded with finely crafted highlights like the intricate phrasing of a Dankworth Seven record or the lushly produced orchestrations of Eve Boswell. But the payoffs were handsome. Martin scored a smash with *At the Drop of a Hat,* a two-man show starring Michael Flanders and Donald Swann, which sold steadily for more than twenty-five years. That was followed by the hugely innovative, and every bit as lucrative, *Beyond the Fringe.* It's irreverent cast—Jonathan Miller, Peter Cook, and Dudley Moore—cracked the whole silly scene open, sparking a "satirical movement" among the highbrow university crowd. They also gave George Martin purchase on a genre that rang up untold sales points at EMI.

If the Fringe gang gave Martin cachet, Peter Sellers put him over the top. Sellers was a comic phenomenon—a mimic and impressionist and master of the ad-lib, the verbal grenade which had taken on a cultural but dubious significance. Young people especially, such as John Lennon, considered Sellers an icon because of his brilliant eccentricity and outrageous offbeat humor. And somehow George Martin managed to capture all of that on tape. Martin and Sellers made a series of records over the years— some alone, others with Spike Milligan, even ensemble pieces with the entire Goon squad (Spike Milligan and Harry Secombe)—that transformed Parlophone's position at EMI. "We had gone from being known as a sad little company to making a mint of money," says Ron Richards, Parlophone's "song plugger" at the time.

But while providing the label with substantial security, comedy alone wasn't enough to satisfy Martin. He was a musician; it was in his blood. And though there were some marginal contemporary singers on the roster, what Martin lusted after, what he determined would raise Parlophone's jokey image, was a legitimate pop act, the same kind of hit pop act that fueled every other label in the marketplace. The closest it had come was a single called "Who Could Be Bluer," by Jerry Lordan, who went on to write the Shadows' biggest hits. It bulleted to the Top Ten for a week or two, whetting Parlophone's appetite for pop. But when it came down to the nitty-gritty, Lordan wasn't a rallying force; he was too sedate to cause much of a sensation. And Shane Fenton, whose voice was "so soft the engineers had enormous difficulty getting it on tape," eventually "ran out of steam."

Ron Richards says, "George was desperate to get something off the ground in the pop department." It "humiliated him" the way Parlophone got upstaged by its sister labels, so much so that when Sid Coleman phoned about a promising group he'd heard—so promising, in fact, that they'd already been turned down by EMI—Martin agreed to book a meeting on Tuesday, February 13, 1962, with their manager, Brian Epstein.

Each time Brian returned empty-handed from London, the Beatles had listened without grumbling. But with the passes piling up, the Beatles' patience had worn thin. Only a few weeks before, Brian had assured them that the Decca deal was all but cinched. Now, over a long, tense dinner, he scrambled to account for its startling demise, stuttering over the details like a deeply rutted record. At one point in the strained encounter, John, still smarting about the audition tape repertoire, warned him "not to be so clever." The silence that followed was brittle. The hostility in the exchange was impossible to ignore. Brian sat there, looking awkward and embarrassed, until finally John, having made his point, snapped: "Right. Try Embassy." That had broken the ice. Embassy was Woolworth's in-house label, devoted to novelty and children's records. Everyone, including Brian, appreciated the absurdity of his remark and especially how deftly John had wielded it as a tension breaker.

Nevertheless, the incident brought to the surface the resentment that was brewing. The Beatles felt they had done their share; in addition to jacking up their show several notches, they had reshaped their act to suit Brian's specifications. It was his turn to be tested. They expected some results.

Brian reminded them about an upcoming audition in Manchester for the BBC dance show *Teenager's Turn* and several other promotions that carried his imprimatur. Most were harmless schemes designed to boost the band's image, but one, at a club in Southport, stirred some dormant internal strife. Ron Appleby, who promoted the show, recalled an incident that would soon have far-reaching repercussions. "Brian Epstein decided that everyone who came into the dance before eight [o'clock] would be given a photograph of the Beatles." It was a nice incentive, although an unusual practice for a Liverpool dance, and it went over in a big way before taking an unforeseen turn. "The girls were ripping up the photograph and sticking the picture of Pete Best onto their jumpers."

No one, especially Pete, had counted on that happening. He was "embarrassed" by the attention, but it wasn't an isolated incident. "Almost since he joined the band, Pete was the most popular Beatle," says Bill Harry, expressing a view shared by many early fans. "He was certainly the best-looking among them, and the girls used to go bananas over him." This phenomenon was nothing new. Best had immense stage presence. Unlike the other Beatles, who mugged shamelessly for the girls, Pete, unsmiling, ignored the crowd, attacking the drums with his long muscular arms, which only heightened his mystique.

One can only imagine how much resentment and envy that stirred, especially in Paul, who was sensitive to being upstaged. He'd already gotten bent out of shape by the way Stuart Sutcliffe used to steal the limelight. Now suddenly Pete was crawling up his back. "If one of the others got more applause, Paul would notice and be on him like lightning," recalls Bob Wooler, whose own behavior did nothing to tone down the jealousy. Wooler had worked out a little rap he delivered at the end of a band's set to introduce individual musicians. A poster for *The Outlaw* he'd seen described Jane Russell as being "mean, moody, and magnificent," which Wooler borrowed and applied to Pete Best. "He was the only Beatle I mentioned by name every time, and it sparked enmity between them—especially with McCartney."

Every day at the Cavern, whether intentionally or not, Wooler twisted the knife. "And on the drums, our very own Jeff Chandler," he'd intone over an orgasm of shrieks. "Mean, moody, and magnificent . . . *Mr. Pete Best!*" Paul would seethe as he listened to the swell of female approval, although he didn't need a cheering section to know that he was being overshadowed. To him, the implications were all too clear: if this was allowed to continue unchecked, Pete would wind up the Beatles' heartthrob. "That had always been Paul's role," says Bill Harry. "He always promoted the girl fans. He'd stop and talk to them, take their requests, be friendly. Now, unintentionally, Pete had cut into his territory."

Paul must have known it wouldn't be difficult to rally the other Beatles against Pete. Privately, they all grumbled their discontent about the way he murdered the backbeat. He was too much of what drummers call "a bricklayer" to suit their interests, too hamfisted, an unimaginative musician. What's more, he was always the odd man out. Whenever the band went out together after a gig, Pete either clammed up or left early. In a spirit that demanded the battle cry "All for one and one for all," it made him seem aloof and distant.

For the time being, however, Paul kept any resentment to himself. This was a fight that, for a lot of reasons, didn't seem worth picking. The Beatles were on a roll; it would have been foolish to upset the momentum. And as they knew only too well, drummers—no matter how detached or heavy-handed—were still at a premium in Liverpool.

On February 5 Pete called in sick a few hours before a prearranged gig at the Cavern. His timing couldn't have been worse. Not only were the Beatles due to play a lunchtime session, but they were also booked for an evening performance at the Kingsway Club, in Southport, where their fee had swollen to £18. No one wanted to give that up; they'd take too great a hit. A few phone calls later, the Beatles determined that their buddies, the Hurricanes, happened to have a rare day off and were willing to loan out their drummer—Ringo Starr.

For Pete Best, it was the beginning of the end.

———

On February 13, in a desperate last-ditch attempt to make good, Brian doubled back to London for his interview with George Martin. Although officially a label chief, Martin preferred a more relaxed approach in his dealings with hopeful, young managers, most of whom consulted him with great humility.

Brian was leaving nothing to chance as he strode into the Parlophone office on Manchester Square all charged up about the Beatles. He turned up the juice, describing the band as "brilliant" and proclaiming, in no uncertain terms, that "they were going to conquer the world." That took real nerve, inasmuch as Sid Coleman had already explained to Martin how the Beatles had "been completely rejected by everybody, absolutely everybody in the country." Brian may have suspected as much. Nevertheless, he plowed ahead in a manner Martin interpreted as "blind faith," painting Liverpool as an untapped rock 'n roll mecca in which these Beatles reigned supreme. Martin, who thought he "had seen it all before," found it gallingly outrageous when Brian fell back on an old drama-school trick. "He . . . expressed surprise that I hadn't heard of [the Beatles]," Martin wrote in his autobiography. Brian arched an eyebrow, leaned back presumptuously, and donned a look of disbelief. It was a desperate tactic, and one that might have earned him the boot from a busier record executive, but Martin was charmed by such "unswerving devotion. . . . I kind of inwardly laughed" and forgave Brian for what he recognized as "a big hype."

One thing Brian couldn't hustle, however, was Martin's ears. It didn't take them long into a preview of the Decca tapes to determine that the Beatles weren't worth more effort. Martin considered them to be "a rather unpromising group," with tired material. Even the original songs, which Epstein had gone on about quite glowingly, were "very mediocre" in his opinion. But something in the vocalists' delivery raised his antennae a few inches. Paul's voice proved rather enjoyable, and "a certain roughness"— obviously John's contribution—pleased him.

When the tape ended, Martin had to decide: bite or pass. It was too difficult. He remained on the fence; there wasn't enough to go on—either way. Issuing a pass would have been simple enough, but what if he was wrong? What if there was more to this backwater band than a surface listen allowed? It wouldn't serve him to make a snap decision. "You know, I really can't judge it, on what you're playing me here," he recalled telling Brian. "It's *interesting,* but I can't offer you any kind of deal on this basis. I must see them and meet them. Bring them down to London and I'll work with them in the studio."

Another audition. Brian tried not to let his disappointment show. He had hoped to return to Liverpool with more positive news, but this slim overture would have to do. Unfortunately, it meant replaying the trip they had made to Decca, which had been hard on everyone involved, as well as his underwriting it, picking up hotels and expenses to the tune of several hundred pounds.

Money, however, was never an issue. According to Alistair Taylor, "Brian's investment in the band had become quite substantial, without much return. In fact, it was growing more uncertain that he would ever recoup money from the Beatles." But if he was having second thoughts about this undertaking, he never said so, and he certainly never complained. "Brian was too captivated by the whole experience, too into it," says Peter Brown. He was caught up in what he perceived to be the exciting world of show business. And, as those close to him realized, he was drawn into the fantasy of rock 'n roll, intent on exploring its shadowy, rebellious, slightly amoral demimonde. By February, he was taking amphetamines. Initially, he blamed it on the gigs—it was the only way he could stay up that late— and to some extent that is true. But the crazy nights out with the Beatles, the pressures at NEMS, the anxieties of London, the desires he may have felt—the roller coaster of highs and lows—all required some form of self-abuse. Preludin was the easy answer. They were in plentiful supply, and the Beatles took them. It was a subtle, if reckless, way for him to fit in. "Brian didn't want to go to gigs dressed as Mr. Epstein from NEMS," says Peter Brown. "He didn't want to look like a prick in a suit, so he put on a turtleneck and a leather jacket to seem more like the boys." Bill Harry even recalls him at the Cavern one night, "with his hair combed forward, looking completely ridiculous." He was experimenting, looking for ways to square himself with the Beatles, to square himself with himself.

One thing he refused to share, however, was his sexual identity. The subject had never come up and Brian was loath to raise it. The military discharge, the brush with the police—not to mention the stigma attached to such unspeakable behavior—had already shaken his trust in confiding in anyone who wasn't like-minded. There is no telling how he thought the Beatles would deal with the truth, but he was unsure enough not to try it out on them. In any case, they suspected as much from the start. "We'd heard Brian was queer," Paul recalled, although this remark is disingenuous, at best. As Peter Brown recalls, the Beatles were never confused about Brian's homosexuality. "They always knew he was a queen from the other side of the tracks. It was something they would tease him about."

John could be especially tough on Brian, if not downright cruel. One night during the disc interlude at the Cavern, Brian stopped backstage, as he often did, to visit with the band. Instantly, Bob Wooler knew rough weather was brewing by the tart look on John's face and the way he was slumped in his seat. It was a comportment the deejay recognized all too well, an ornery prestrike effect, forewarning that someone, unexpectedly, was about to get the royal treatment. The cloud burst, Wooler recalls, when John crooked one side of his mouth to reflect aloud: "I see that new Dirk Bogarde film is at the Odeon." More than an observation, it was a cue for someone else in the room to respond: "Which one is that?" To which John replied: "*Victim*. It's all about those fucking queers."

But however hypocritical it sounds, while the Beatles entertained themselves regularly at Brian's expense, they wouldn't permit it from outsiders— ever. Ian Sharp, one of John's art school chums, found out the hard way when he made an off-color remark about Brian during an afternoon bull session at the Kardomah Café. "Within forty-eight hours" Sharp had a letter from Brian's solicitors demanding a formal apology. Frightened by its implications, Sharp shot back a response full of regret and penitence, thinking that was the end of the matter. But there was one final condition.

"I was told by Paul, consequently, that I was never to make any contact with [the Beatles] at all." It was punctuated by "Sorry about that, mate. See you." Much to Sharp's surprise, the Beatles were faithful to the letter of Brian's wish. Except for a wave when they passed in a car, he says, "that was the very last time I saw them."

[I]

With recording efforts at a standstill and the Beatles breathing down his neck, Brian Epstein gained something of a reprieve when the band left Liverpool in April for a third extended appearance in Hamburg. The Beatles were just as eager to leave as Brian was to be free of them for a while. "The Beatles were home in Hamburg," says Adrian Barber. "It was their town." Plus it would be great to see old friends: the exis, Tony Sheridan, Stu and Astrid, the ceaseless flow of musicians that funneled through neighboring clubs. Hamburg would help take their minds off the sorry state of affairs back home.

Brian had considered sending them overland with Neil Aspinall in the van, but as their departure loomed, he surprised the band with plane tickets, paid for out of his own pocket. The Beatles were clearly excited. Among them, only Paul had flown before. There was a sense of adventure from the get-go, but in more appreciable terms, it was reassuring that Brian had elevated their status, that they were to be treated more respectfully than in the past, in a manner befitting true *artistes*.

And yet, for all Brian's attempts at accommodating them, the Beatles could not ward off misfortune. An omen presented itself when George came down with the measles, forcing him to miss the scheduled flight from Manchester. The rest of the band left without him. Clearing Customs in Hamburg, they charged through the airport, spotting Astrid Kirchherr across the hall. It was hard to miss her; she was majestic, a full sail in black linen. John, pulled into her orbit, windmilled his arms comically in greeting.

"Where's Stu?" everyone wanted to know.

Her face was blank, still. Noting the guarded blur of her gaze, John asked, "Oh, what's the matter?"

"Stuart died, John. He's gone."

The room went silent, out of focus. A vacuum gathered around them, beyond the uproar, the announcements, the multitudes hurrying past. Paul and Pete stumbled backward on their heels; unable to check their emotions, they caved in to the grief. John, seemingly impervious, had been dealt a sideways blow. He didn't know how to process this news. Death: it took everything he loved—Uncle George, Julia, now Stuart. His grief was numbing. Nothing registered. Later, myth would have it that he "burst into laughter," but laughter was beyond him. It was enough that he gave voice to a single word: "How?"

Astrid was forthcoming with details. Since their return from Liverpool, Stuart's headaches had increased in intensity. They struck like electrical storms, sudden and scary, without warning. It was like "a bomb going off in his head." There were times, she said, that he lapsed into such black swoons that nothing she did could dislodge him from the excruciating pain. It paralyzed him to the point of crippling agony. In a letter to his mother, he expressed the fear that "he was going blind." There had been spells when he couldn't see, couldn't think. Creatively, physically, emotionally, Stuart was falling apart. The fancy clothes and sunglasses couldn't conceal his haggard face, his sunken eyes, or his ghastly pallor. His nerves were shot. He couldn't function in school; his work suffered. Once, he keeled over in class, which alarmed the other students, particularly because he was helpless during these attacks. Astrid was limited in her capacity to sit with him, reduced to stroking a hand or shoulder while he suffered wave after wave of pain. She spent many afternoons that way, with Stuart's head cradled in her lap, scared for his safety. Other times, she struggled to hold him down, often with her mother's help, to keep him from endangering himself.

Finally, in order to keep a close eye on him, Astrid insisted that he move into her house. She and her mother dressed up the attic so that it functioned as both a bedroom and an art studio, where Stuart could paint, but that, too, had its drawbacks. According to one account, he'd blacked out and fallen down a flight of stairs. What's more, it was cold upstairs; he was constantly shivering.

On April 10, a day before the Beatles left for Hamburg, Astrid was summoned home from work by her mother. Stuart was convulsed with pain, she said, and needed immediate attention. "He has to go to the hospital right now." There was an adamant alarm in her voice; Astrid reacted to it as she might to an air-raid signal, with fear condensing into swift, definite action. An ambulance was already waiting, and without a word, Astrid leaped into the back a moment before it sped away from the curb.

Stuart was inside, curled up into a ball. Somehow Astrid managed to bundle his frail, dishrag body into her arms, and it was there, pressed against her, that Stuart died—of a brain aneurism or other disorder, it would never be certain—before they ever reached the hospital.

The Beatles were stunned, confused. No one that close in age had died so tragically. It was "a real shock," especially for John, who "looked up to Stu" on so many levels.

But the Beatles were determined to open in Hamburg on schedule. Even Astrid insisted that they go on the next night, promising to be in the audience, as Stu would have wanted it.*

———

The Grosse Freiheit had changed remarkably in the six months since the Beatles had left Hamburg as a versatile but struggling rock 'n roll band. It was still sleazy, still an outpost devoted to the kind of wanton, vulgar behavior that demanded a rock 'n roll soundtrack. Nightclubs still provided the biggest take, and the most opulent of these was the Star-Club, set to open its doors with a bill called the "Rock 'n Twist Parade" headed by the Beatles.** Its owner was a former pig farmer from Munich named Manfred Weissleder, who had risen to prominence by building the most efficient—and most fearsome—organization in Hamburg and eliminating the competition, one by one, so that by the spring of 1962 "without [his] approval you did not work on the Grosse Freiheit." Weissleder, who stood over six foot seven and "spoke English with a typical German World War II accent," and his partner, a "ruthless" pit bull named Paul Mueller, passed themselves off as impresarios, but their business was prostitution. Under various fronts and guises, they ran sixteen strip bars in the district—the Rote Katz, or Red Cat, among the largest—and a string of three hundred young girls recruited from across Eastern Europe and as far off as Mongolia.

The Star-Club was on the site of an old cinema, "an immense, cavernous rock 'n roll cathedral," decked out in plush carpeting, an expanse of dark, polished wood, and, around the perimeter, a grouping of taupe-colored upholstered settees where people lounged between numbers, sipping from stubby bottles of local beer and plying the aggressive pickup scene. Sweating, wandering through a cloud of dense cigarette smoke, around-the-clock revelers explored the many levels of a hedonistic universe.

---

* She eventually showed up there two weeks later.
** The rest of the bill featured Tex Roberg, Roy Young, the Bachelors, and the Graduates.

The floors were diverse planets, each with its own stellar personality: music and dancing downstairs, a small "twistin' base" situated in an overhanging U-shaped balcony, a strip joint—the Erotic Film Night Club—above that, featuring movable, transparent panels that beheld a cinematic smorgasbord of sexual perversion, an old projection room with a sliding peephole that served as Manfred Weissleder's private lair.

The Beatles took one look at the Star-Club and saw paradise. It seemed tailored to showcase their music, "the first real theatrical setting [they'd] ever seen devoted to rock 'n roll." The stage was huge, with a spangled backdrop of the Manhattan skyline suspended from struts and lit from behind by a rotating light box. There were enough microphones for a symphony orchestra, and a full arsenal of extraordinary American gear (the amplifiers were all Fenders, which the Beatles had only heard of, never seen). Paul's eyes bugged out at the equipment specially installed for his use: a Fender Bassman head and two 15-inch speakers in an open-backed cabinet. Even the spotlights were clever: the electrician had coupled car headlights to a twelve-volt transformer and strung them along the front of the balcony. No expense had been spared. "There was a fucking curtain, brother!" recalls a duly impressed Liverpool musician. "We'd never seen one before and didn't know what to do with it, so for the first few days everyone kept pushing the button, making it go back and forth."

To keep the place operating efficiently, Weissleder had hired Horst Fascher as his chief of security. Fascher, a short, fair-haired man known for eerie politeness, had performed similar duties as enforcer at the Kaiserkeller and the Top Ten, which made him something of a fearsome legend on the Grosse Freiheit. "The beatings he gave to people were unbelievable!" says a musician with awe nearly forty years later. "He'd absolutely batter someone until they were senseless. In some of the fights I saw, his men hit guys with wooden chairs, barstools—hit them five or six times over the head, with blood pouring out. They could have easily killed someone, but it never seemed to bother Horst. He'd just throw the person outside and leave him." Rumor had it that the missing three fingers on his right hand had been cut off by gangsters.

The musicians, especially the Beatles, loved Fascher. He doted on them like a favorite uncle, practicing his precious English, which he spoke in clipped, precise tones, and chauffeuring them around town in his prized gleaming-white 1957 Chevy convertible. But there were other advantages to his stewardship. "Horst made sure we were protected," says the Merseybeats' Tony Crane. Every musician was provided with an artful Star-Club badge—gold typescript on a pin featuring a prominent blue star—which "gave [them] immunity" anywhere in the district. "Horst warned us never to go out without it," recalls Ray Ennis. "We knew that no one would bother us as long as we had it on—and no one ever did." Liverpool groups could abandon the old, naturally honed fears that stalked them back home. It was a relief not to have to fight their way out of a gig after work, or constantly worry that equipment would be nicked. Out of appreciation, they put up a sign backstage, renaming the club "Manfred's Home for Itinerant Scousers."

The opening of the Star-Club on April 13, 1962, was an unmitigated sensation. The dance floor was packed, according to Don Arden, the London promoter who held a small interest in the place, with "roughly 850 to 1,000 people, depending on how we wanted to shift the tables around and lie to the police about capacity." And the Beatles kicked out the jams. George had arrived on time, chaperoned from Liverpool by Brian Epstein, and he seemed fully recovered, ready to play. Except for the wall-to-wall crowd that made it difficult to see the band and "got too rowdy and aggressive at times," Weissleder had pulled off something of a coup: overnight, he had knocked the Top Ten off its enviable perch. Thereafter, all Liverpool bands played the Star-Club, "a step up" on the German rock 'n roll circuit, while the Top Ten relied on booking Scottish bands, a factor that eventually doomed it to oblivion.

During the next few weeks, Gerry and the Pacemakers, Kingsize Taylor and the Dominoes, the Big Three, Cliff Bennett and the Rebel Rousers, the Swinging Blue Jeans, and the Searchers all joined the Beatles at intervals during their triumphant residency. It was, from beginning to end, a Liverpool phenomenon. There was no mistaking that a distinctive sound was developing: chord patterns that repeated in their repertoires, a penchant for exquisitely modulated phrasing and sudden downshifting into minor chords, deliberate Everly Brothers references in the harmonies, ways of punctuating lyrics with dynamics, all of it creating a unique, idiosyncratic pop style. It would be another year before those features coalesced and became identified the world over as the Liverpool or Mersey sound, but the essential aspects of it were already in place.

In the almost two months the Beatles were in Hamburg, their sets bulged with new songs: the soulful "If You Gotta Make a Fool of Somebody," Ritchie Barrett's "Some Other Guy," a trio of Shirelles' songs— "Will You Love Me Tomorrow," "Mama Said," and "Baby It's You"—plus crowd-pleasers like "You've Really Got a Hold on Me," "Nobody But

You," "Please Mr. Postman," and "Mr. Moonlight." To spotlight Pete, they incorporated "Boys" and "The Peppermint Twist" into the repertoire, and for George a pair of Goffin-King songs—"Don't Ever Change" and "Sharing You"—as well as "Devil in Her Heart," which was unearthed from a single by a little-known girl group, the Donays.

From the outset, the Beatles had a great ear. They could listen to something that was either raw or somehow never got off the ground and know instantly how to breathe new life into it. Such was the case in early 1962 when they stumbled across records by an American R&B singer named Arthur Alexander, one of the pioneers of the Muscle Shoals soul sound. Only one of his songs, "You Better Move On" (covered by the Rolling Stones in 1964) managed to nick the *Billboard* charts, but there was something powerful about his material that captured the Beatles' imagination: it was direct, heartfelt and earnest, infused with great melodies. "We wanted to [sound] like Arthur Alexander," Paul reflected in 1987. And for a while his songs dominated their nightly sets—lean, soulful versions of "Soldier of Love," "A Shot of Rhythm and Blues," and "Anna (Go to Him)," the latter of which was recorded for their first album.

With the new songs came a new round of drugs, for the Beatles and the other Liverpool bands. Combined with ridiculous quantities of beer, the speed produced harrowing exploits of drunkenness—smashing guitars onstage, driving insanely, fighting, terrorizing women, behaving rudely at boisterous parties. To keep it all from collapsing necessitated more and more speed. Conveniently, there was no shortage of suppliers right on the premises. Mutti, who followed Horst Fascher to the Star-Club, doled out pills from her stall outside the toilets. Otherwise, Tony Sheridan functioned as the Johnny Appleseed of uppers. He had a bottomless supply, which flowed generously from band to band. When a musician voiced a concern about supply, one of the resident gangsters proudly and swaggeringly drove him out to a farm in the Hamburg countryside. As the eyewitness recalls it: "He opened the barn door and there was the trailer of a semi, with its doors flung open and a cascade of boxes and bottles stretching from the back of the truck to the barn door. He'd hijacked the entire supply of amphetamines for northern Germany for a year—just so they could furnish them to us for free." The craziness that a beer-and-Prellie binge brought on was neither accidental nor arbitrary. The Big Three's Adrian Barber remembers that Manfred Weissleder deliberately promoted both substances to musicians, not for profits from the drug trade, per se, but because "it kept us stoned and dependent."

Deliberate or not, John Lennon managed to fuel his rage in a stupor of uncontrolled intoxication. He'd begun blowing off steam in Hamburg from the moment the Beatles arrived, drinking steadily. At an early-morning party following their opening shows, he doused an annoyed Brian Epstein with warm beer. That established a pattern for the next seven weeks. No one complained when John showed up drunk onstage or played in animal skins or "foamed at the mouth" following a "Prellie sandwich," but it had a cumulative effect. Gradually, the antics grew wilder and more destructive. John began to pick fights he couldn't win, storming friends in a hail of insults. He told Adrian Barber that "all people [were] basically shit" and deserved abuse. It seemed that anyone who crossed his path was fair game. Gerry Marsden recalled how one night, without any provocation, John crowned a fellow with a bottle during a friendly card game and got a beating in return. The guy "knocked hell" out of John. "And all of us just stood there and let him do it." He had it coming, they agreed, and got what he deserved.

John's spring was filled with similar binges and brawls. It became "a trend [for musicians] to bounce around and do inexplicable, outrageous things," but John took on audiences without regard for the consequences. One night he danced up to the microphone and announced: "Hey, remember the war? Well, we fuckin' won!" Then, grabbing his crotch, he screamed, "Sieg heil *this!*" In case that hadn't gotten their attention, he dropped his pants and pranced across the stage in his underwear.

Friends from Liverpool, who were used to John's belligerence, thought he'd gone "a little bit mad." John, in a harsher self-evaluation, later insisted he was "*out of my fucking mind.*" But the anger and self-hatred were the result of something much more rational. Wounded by the real world, he preferred to face it drunk. Drinking was an excuse, a way to bury the pain of Stu's death. Drunk, he wouldn't have to deal with the loss or his unresolved feelings.

If the other Beatles were concerned, they did nothing to intercede. As far as anyone could tell, they never acknowledged that John was out of control, never suggested he take it down a notch or two. It may have seemed perfectly normal to three twenty-year-olds that a comrade would blow off steam in a place like the Grosse Freiheit. Liverpool lads were known to "let loose like maniacs." And it wasn't too far afield from John's usual hostile behavior—only more pronounced and enduring than before.

Part of it, no doubt, could be traced to frustration. It was a word he grappled with repeatedly in later recollections of Hamburg—frustration over the Decca rejection, over the Beatles' image, over their lack of a topflight drummer, over an indefinite future. Now, news from Cynthia added to his frustration. She had moved into a one-room flat, a "shabby little . . . bedsit" with a shared bath, in a terrace house near Penny Lane, where John looked forward to setting up permanent residence with her following the band's return to Liverpool. (This, despite the fact that John had begun a torrid relationship with Bettina Derlin, one of the Star-Club's raunchier bartenders.) Until then, however, Cynthia had invited Dot Rhone to keep her company there. Instead of applauding her self-sufficiency, John dashed off a letter to Cynthia, barely disguising his displeasure. He urged her to "find another flat" for Dot so that it wouldn't infringe on their privacy. He viewed Dot, who was even more fragile and insecure than he was, as a threat to their relationship. "Imagine having her there all the time when we were in bed—and imagine Paul coming all the time—and especially when I wasn't there. I'd hate the idea."

Aside from music, Cynthia was the one bright spot in John's life. Now, too, those sands had begun to shift, and everything under their feet started to give way.

[II]

By the beginning of May, Brian Epstein was desperate. He had run out of options as far as record-company contacts were concerned and dreaded facing the Beatles empty-handed when they returned home in a few weeks. "The pressure was really getting to him," recalls Alistair Taylor. "He'd grown increasingly distraught." With his back to the wall, Brian relented and went back to see George Martin about his open-ended offer to audition the Beatles.

It seemed like an exercise in futility, but Brian put on his most charming face for the meeting, determined to win the producer's friendship as well as his support. Apparently, the approach paid off. During their amiable meeting at EMI Studios on the morning of May 9, Martin not only honored his offer for an audition but proposed issuing a recording contract for the Beatles before even meeting them. It was an extraordinary development and, no doubt, one that Brian hadn't anticipated. He must have been astonished, not to mention giddy with excitement.

And yet, while the gesture appeared magnanimous, it was little more than an insurance policy for Martin, should the Beatles live up to expectations. The contract, in effect, guaranteed the band nothing, least of all a recording session. Instead, by signing it, the Beatles gave EMI a lock on their services *if* the audition showed promise, at which time Martin only had to countersign the document for it to be binding. Otherwise, it would be worthless.

Brian, who surely recognized the drawbacks, responded quickly, believing that any contract was better than nothing at this point. So, on May 9, 1962, he arranged an audition date for a few days after the Beatles returned from Hamburg, then rushed off to the nearest post office to telephone his parents and wire two cables. The first was to the Beatles in Hamburg—an incisive announcement that set the tone for everything that eventually happened. It read:

CONGRATULATIONS BOYS. EMI REQUEST RECORDING SESSION. PLEASE REHEARSE NEW MATERIAL.

A second message, delivered to the *Mersey Beat* offices the same day, said:

HAVE SECURED CONTRACT FOR BEATLES TO RECORDED [SIC] FOR EMI ON PARLAPHONE [SIC] LABEL. 1ST RECORDING DATE SET FOR JUNE 6TH.

It was a stunning piece of news. None of the Beatles had been forewarned of new developments on that front, and only George had held out hope for such an outcome. By way of celebration, they clapped one another on the back and reprised a popular chant:

"Where are we going, lads?"

"To the toppermost, Johnny!"

"And where is that?"

"The toppermost of the poppermost!"

They had lusted after this for so long that, finally in hand, it hardly seemed real.

While the Beatles had rescued John from a murky home life, nothing had rescued Cynthia Powell from hers. In February Cynthia's mother had emigrated unexpectedly to Canada, renting out the family house and leaving her daughter, who was only nineteen, to her own devices. Unable to make ends meet while continuing her art studies, Cynthia bounced from place to place like a foster child, surviving a disastrous, short-lived stint as one of Mimi's boarders, followed by a month with her aunt Tess, commuting from the remote Wirral peninsula, interspersed with nights on the couch of her friend Phyllis McKenzie.

By late spring, the turmoil of Cynthia's life had reached an unprecedented pitch. John was gone, her mother situated halfway across the world. Rather than resuming classes at art school, she now taught all day at a high school in darkest Garston, where the kids were such savages that it was said "they played tick* with hatchets." A feeling of "isolation" began to take hold. To complicate matters, Cynthia's "money had run out," forcing her to accept public assistance. Despite finding her own flat, she felt vulnerable, desperate. Convinced that control was slipping from her grasp, Cynthia began to worry herself sick—literally. In the mornings she woke up feeling nauseous, lethargic; it took an effort just to get out of bed. When her "period got later and later," the wild card fell.

Cynthia feared the worst: she was pregnant. At a hastily arranged exam, the doctor confirmed it, delivering a stern lecture on responsibility and birth control. "The horror of it was almost too great to take in," she recalled. Afterward, Phyllis McKenzie attempted to console her, but there was more: on the way to the examination, Cynthia tore open an envelope from art school that had arrived in the morning post to discover that she'd failed her exams. Bursting with shame, she admitted to Phyllis that the situation had gotten beyond her.

With her mother gone and John in Hamburg, the only person Cyn could discuss things with was Dot Rhone. The girls had grown inseparable since the Beatles had left. Both naive, both insecure, both overshadowed by manipulative boyfriends who exploited their naïveté and insecurity, they clung to each other like two orphans. Neither girl had much of a life outside her relationship; they were as needy as nestlings—John and Paul provided everything that had been missing from their lives. Now, alone all these weeks, there was a sense of real intimacy between them. They spent most nights scraping together "crummy" meals, then stretched across Cynthia's bed until late, smoking and giggling about the boys. Unexpectedly, in May the flat next to Cynthia's became vacant. Dot says, "I couldn't afford it, but Paul volunteered to pay the rent." She moved in the next day. Like Cynthia, Dot flirted with fantasies of Paul returning, making a home with her, and eventually proposing marriage. The whole setup seemed ideal: the two Beatles living next door to each other, their girlfriends best of pals.

---

* A form of tag.

When Cynthia became pregnant, Dot naturally came to the rescue. "She was so scared," Dot remembers. "She wanted to marry John—very definitely—it just wasn't the right time. She realized they weren't ready for it, but there was no other solution."

Against the rise of irrational fear, Dot tried to calm her friend, offering copious emotional support. She knew better than to treat Cynthia's pregnancy with neglect. Certain precautions had to be taken, sensible diets observed. Dutifully, Dot tended to Cynthia, reassuring her that everything would turn out all right. She filled the nights with advice and companionship, even rehearsing ways with Cynthia of how to break the news to John. When that moment finally came, however, it was more difficult than either of them had anticipated.

On June 2 the Beatles returned to Liverpool amid a torrent of expectation. *Mersey Beat* stirred up excitement about their homecoming, which caused a great tidal wave of joy in the hearts of faithful fans. There was even an "official fan club" that beat the drum in the clubs. Word buzzed through the city that "the Beatles [were] back." There was a clamor to see what innovations Hamburg had handed them, what breakthroughs they'd made, what new goodies they brought home.

Brian met the boys at the airport and suggested an impromptu meal to celebrate, but everyone was eager to get home.

John, especially, wanted to see Cynthia and their new flat. He made a beeline to the dreary building and took the stairs "two at a time," bursting into the room with flowers, food, and a rakish smile. The silence that followed was painfully awkward. Cynthia decided not to beat around the bush. John hadn't been in the flat more than a moment or two when she blurted out the news.

Pregnant: it must have felt like an ambush to John, who initially had trouble digesting its meaning. Frozen in place, he stared at her, dazed, unable to fire off a customary glib remark. "As the words sunk in I saw the color literally drain from his cheeks," Cynthia recounted. "He went white." She did her best to put an ironic spin on it, but John's disappointment was impossible to ignore.

His concern went straight to the Beatles. "I thought it would be good-bye to the group . . . ," John admitted later, when the shock had worn off. After all the hard work, the years of endless garbage gigs and enduring disappointment, the idyll was shattered. Just like that, just when a breakthrough seemed inevitable. Now it appeared that fate had dealt him a timely blow, and blowing it big-time would surely be his fate.

Resignedly, he proposed they do the right thing and get married.

For a short time, Cynthia remained hopeful. There was plenty of Beatles business to distract John from this latest blow. It's unclear whether he even confided in Paul, who always showed pragmatism in such matters. "John didn't share much with anybody," recalls Bill Harry. "He was more comfortable playing the loner. He seemed very secretive, as though he were unwilling to trust people—or unsure how to go about it."

Despite such emotional upheaval, the Beatles were distanced from it somewhat by their audition, which raced up blindly on June 6, 1962, only four days after their return from Hamburg. Dazed and punished by exhaustion from the seven-week bacchanal, the Beatles were cautiously optimistic about their chances with George Martin, believing, as Brian himself wished, that the contract provided by the label led directly to a recording session. Still, the grim specter of Decca hung over them: nothing could be taken for granted anymore, especially by Brian, who implied that this "was [their] last chance" as far as record companies went.

If kismet was any indication, then they were already in a hole. The studio Brian directed them to proved nearly impossible to find. For more than half an hour, Neil Aspinall steered the van, loaded with the Beatles and their equipment, haltingly through the sleepy north London suburb of St. John's Wood, searching for the entrance to EMI Studios. Somehow, they wound up in an upscale residential area whose weave of streets held extravagant Edwardian mansions set off by ample lawns, lilac hedges, and bushes trimmed to the flatness of tables. "Where's the recording studio?" the Beatles jabbered impatiently as the van slowed in front of 3 Abbey Road, at the intersection where it meets Grove End. Neil checked the location against the address he'd been given. It matched, but the place seemed utterly wrong. "It's a house!" Pete Best recalled saying, staring at the squat two-story structure surrounded by a fenced-off wall. There was no sign, nothing official that announced EMI's proprietary claim. "This has got to be it," Neil concluded, pulling into a forecourt behind the gates. But as they unloaded the van, a fissure of uncertainty took hold. "What *is* this place?" they wondered. "Where's [George Martin] going to record us?"

Their noisy fluster was no coincidence. Abbey Road wasn't meant to look like a recording complex, much less *a facility* like EMI's other studios at Hayes, which adjoined its record factories. It had originated in 1831 as a nine-bedroom residence, with five reception rooms, servants' quarters, and a wine cellar, before being converted in 1928 into the world's first "purpose- [or custom-] built" studio. For all the building's unpretentiousness, much of the modern technology found in the more imposing high-tech studios was first designed by EMI engineers in one of its boxy, low-ceilinged rooms. The fundamentals of stereo were developed here, as were moving-coil microphones, large-valve tape recorders, and an amusing battery of sound effects that gained industrywide use throughout the war years and beyond. None of that, however, would have impressed the apprehensive Beatles, who were growing increasingly anxious to make their own mark.

Be that as it may, they were momentarily awed, entering the building and "stepping into . . . another world." The scope of the interior plainly unnerved them. "Coming into Abbey Road for the first time . . . we thought, 'This is a small place,'" Paul recalled, "but it just kept going on and on." The homespun facade, as it turned out, was just for show. The place was immense. Like a Chinese puzzle box, a block of buildings had been erected, one behind the other, in what was formerly the garden, with corridors leading off at right angles to more studios and offices. Lugging their equipment like porters, the Beatles struggled to maintain their composure. It was awesome. And the library *stillness* inside was terrifying.

Brian came rushing up to meet them as they trundled inside. Laughing, probably relieved that they'd turned up within a reasonable time frame, he attempted to answer their scattershot questions while herding them toward Studio Three, the "corner suite," which had been reserved for their test. There was a feverish excitement in the air, and as two EMI assistants accompanied the band down the hall, the Beatles established a kind of frisky onstage rapport, joking and "firing [off] quick one-liners" at one another to take the edge off their nerves. "We were nervous," Pete Best acknowledged. "We were feeling the old butterflies." Still, defensively, they threw up a clownish smoke screen so as not to let on about their fears. "We were arrogant, cocky. You know: *We're the Beatles*. We weren't about to let anything show."

All that changed, however, when they pushed through the doors to Studio Three. "Look at the size of this place!" they beamed to one another, thinking it resembled "a football pitch." The room was wide and airy, with a faint hospital-like smell. Errant wires snaked along the floor, and there were some chairs stacked routinely in one corner and a sound booth off to the side; otherwise, it was empty of the sound paraphernalia they had seen at Decca or even the Polydor sessions with Tony Sheridan.

While they set up, George Martin wasn't anywhere to be seen. The Beatles were talked through the technical process by Ron Richards, another Parlophone producer, who brought along a couple of sound engineers to check out the band's meager equipment. Eventually, the boys were escorted downstairs to the canteen, where Martin sat having tea. In his subsequent revisions of their meeting, Martin liked to skip directly to the session, where "it was love at first sight." No doubt he was drawn to them in some instinctive way, charmed by their personalities, cowed by the length of their hair (which he considered "shocking"). But in fact, the introductions were more businesslike than romantic. It all boiled down to this: he wanted to hear what they could do. Then he would evaluate their potential and determine the next move.

In the meantime, the Beatles spent all afternoon running material for Ron Richards. They had polished a set of thirty-two songs that Brian had selected from their prodigious repertoire, and barely stopping to catch a breath between numbers, they breezed through them all, as though they were playing a breakneck lunchtime session at the Cavern. Richards says that he took an immediate liking to the boys themselves but "wasn't terribly impressed" with what he heard. Their songs bored him, and their musicianship was "adequate" at best. If it were up to him, Richards says, "I probably wouldn't have signed the Beatles."

Fortunately, it wasn't his call. Martin had instructed Ron only to put them at ease and find two or three songs that might be suitable for a record. Right off the bat, Richards chose "Please Please Me," which the band had started performing at the Star-Club. But the song was too slow and plaintive—John had patterned it after Roy Orbison's "Only the Lonely"—with a repetitive guitar phrase that drove Richards nuts. "They had a riff going"—the two instrumental bars that prefigure "Last night I said these words to my girl"—"all the way through," he recalls. It was overkill, an amateur's mistake. Politely, Ron suggested that George "just play it in the gaps," which immediately refocused and energized the song. He also liked the starkly primitive "Love Me Do," cowritten by John and Paul when they were still Quarry Men, for the way they spun out "so plee-ee-ee-ese—love me do" at the end of each verse.

After sifting through the band's material, Richards decided to break for dinner before recording four songs—the two aforementioned Lennon-

McCartney originals, along with another, "Ask Me Why," and the old Latin chestnut "Besame Mucho," which the Beatles had learned from a Coasters single.

As an audition, the session brought mixed results. Ron Richards thought that "they handled themselves pretty well in the studio" but heard nothing that excited him. His engineer, Norman Smith, agreed. "They didn't impress me at all," he recalled. George Martin shared their reservations when he listened to a playback of the tape at the end of the session. While he quite enjoyed the Beatles' voices, it was the material that troubled him most. "Besame Mucho" spoke for itself—it was a slippery little retread— but their original songs just didn't cut it. "They were rotten composers," Martin thought at the time. "Their own stuff wasn't any good."

After the playback, Martin and Norman Smith rather mercilessly critiqued the tape. The fury of their response surprised the Beatles, who listened, crestfallen, as the two men "laid into them for about an hour and . . . were pretty forthright" about their performance. They went over everything, from the lack of "suitable material" to "embellish[ing] the sound" to their presence, which had somehow, incredibly, disappointed the record men. Despite laying things bare, however, they decided to hold back one criticism. Ron Richards had complained privately to Martin that "the drummer was no good and needed to be changed." They'd labored in vain over the beat, trying to bring Pete up to speed. Richards coaxed him through the session, clapping out a fairly straightforward bass drum pattern—*boomp bah-boomp / boomp bah-boomp*—which he exhorted Pete to play with his left foot. "I thought it moved the song along better," Richards recalls, "but he just couldn't do it." All Pete could do was play "fours": *boom— boom—boom—boom*. If they intended to record this group properly, "he'd have to go," Richards told Martin, who promised to have a word about it with Brian Epstein. But even without dredging up this fault, the producer's overall response had been brutal. He'd given them a real raking-over. When the final blow had been delivered, there was a long, anxious silence. Almost apologetically, Martin asked the Beatles if there was anything *they* didn't like. After a well-timed beat, George Harrison sneered: "I don't like your tie."

The room went silent. For a split second, nobody breathed. A line had been crossed. Martin fixed George with a stern look, not certain what tack to take with this boy, when he noticed the flicker of a smile at the corner of George's mouth. A joke! He'd been making a joke! What a perfect ice-breaker. Martin's grin flashed approval ear to ear.

As Norman Smith recalled: "That was the turning point." The band clicked into Beatles mode, cutting up and peppering them with wordplay and double-talk in a manner reminiscent of the Goons. "During that one conversation, we realized they were something special." It was exhilarating stuff. The three of them—Pete never uttered a word—worked off one another like comic pros. Martin and Smith laughed so hard that tears soaked the inside collars of their shirts. "We've got to sign them for their wit," Smith told Martin after the band had packed up. Martin promised to think about it—but he'd already made up his mind. The Beatles were a go.

The Beatles returned to Liverpool feeling reasonably optimistic. Martin had promised to see them again soon, and he'd given Brian encouragement that a proper recording session lay ahead. A pledge that he'd look for material for the band seemed proof enough of Martin's interest. Suddenly everything seemed to be breaking the Beatles' way.

But there were unforeseen complications. For one thing, the Beatles had contracted gonorrhea in Hamburg. There was so much sex on the fly that it seemed almost quid pro quo that they would eventually have gotten it for their efforts. Now, however, it was Brian's problem—to help them and hush it up. Brian had asked his solicitor, Rex Makin, to refer the band to a venereologist, and the lawyer urged discretion. By that time, John and Cynthia had taken out a marriage license, and gonorrhea was prima facie evidence of adultery and automatic grounds for divorce. Also, if John passed the clap on to Cyn, she could dissolve their relationship and lay claim to his earnings. It was an unlikely scenario, but Brian wasn't taking any chances. Makin, who handled his share of dicey matrimonial cases, had a team of what he called "tame venereologists" on file who treated such cases with extreme confidentiality.

All things considered, this situation paled in contrast to the problem that soon confronted Paul. One evening shortly after returning from London, he picked up Dot, who had spent the afternoon being examined by a girlfriend's doctor. In the damp spring night, he took one look at Dot's face and knew. He leaned against her and whispered: "You're going to have a baby." Dot could only hang her tiny shoulders and nod, trying not to drown in despair.

Wordlessly, they drove out to the Mersey ferry and rode the choppy river in darkness, searching for answers. They held each other, reassured but suspicious. Cruel hours passed. Neither was prepared to tell the other exactly what they were feeling. "[Paul] was trying to be good about it," Dot recalls, "but he was scared. At first, he said we shouldn't get married, we were too young. I *wanted* to get married, but I couldn't tell him that." Against all impulses, she had already made an appointment with a local adoption agency. He hushed her lips with two fingers: no. That wasn't the right way. There was honor to think about—his and hers.

Clutching each other, they went off to face the music. Together, they confessed to Jim McCartney, who, to their surprise, "was delighted." They should have this baby, Jim urged, irrespective of the fact that Paul wasn't ready and Dot even less so; she was only eighteen. Jim loved kids. Besides, since Mary's death, he was lonely.

It was settled: Paul and Dot would get married before the momentous event, after which they'd move in with Jim. Paul would be the second of the Beatles to settle down: Lennon and McCartney, as it should be. Before there was any more discussion, Paul marched down to City Hall and took out a marriage license. Dot already wore the gold band he'd given her in Hamburg.

If only Paul had wanted to get married.

———

Between the Parlophone audition, on June 6, and another rock 'n roll extravaganza set for the Tower Ballroom on June 21, Brian booked the Beatles into an unrelenting twelve-performance marathon at the Cavern, kicked off by a "Beatles Welcome Home Show" that squeezed nine hundred screaming fans into that foul, cramped cellar. They did two sets daily for six days, back-to-back, broken up only by a stray appearance on a BBC radio program broadcast from Manchester.

All of this was carefully coordinated by Brian, whose meager NEMS office, above the record shop in Whitechapel, became "the Eppy-center" of a fringe operation devoted almost entirely to his management business. Suddenly the roster doubled as he took on Gerry and the Pacemakers, and the staff expanded—and expanded again.

Everyone was crammed into an orderly two-room suite. Brian was tucked away behind a glass-walled office, beyond which sat two young women who typed contracts, wage slips, and letters to promoters confirming various dates. Brian, driven himself, worked them like slaves. "He was very meticulous about how things were handled," says Frieda Kelly Norris, who was sixteen when she joined the firm. "If you made any kind of mistake, his face would get flushed until he lost it completely and came down hard on you." Letters were fired off in every available spare moment, and "he couldn't wait" to see it on paper. He got very angry if they weren't ready for his signature after what seemed like an unreasonable interval. After he dictated one—or sometimes a string of them, in a rapid, staccato style, stopping repeatedly mid-sentence to change direction—it was scrutinized for form, and God help the typist who let an error slip through. "Once, I transcribed a very long letter and took it in to him to be signed," recalls Frieda Kelly. On inspection, Brian found a spelling mistake and, sputtering with fury, flung it back on her desk to be retyped. In the next draft, she left out a comma. "Now, all I had to do was insert it at the end of the line, where it belonged, but he inked around the entire paragraph so that it couldn't be corrected, forcing me to type it over again."

Style was supreme—and diligence. It infuriated Brian if the staff wasn't constantly busy. "Sometimes, I'd move papers from one side of my desk to the other, just to avoid his scorn," says Beryl Adams, his earliest assistant. "If I stopped to blow my nose, he'd appear over my shoulder, staring hard at me until it was clear I'd gone back to work." If anyone got done with her assigned tasks, which wasn't at all likely, there was plenty of fan-club material to keep her occupied.

Even before the group's first recording session, the Beatles Fan Club had swung into full flower. A teenager named Roberta Brown, who followed the Beatles from gig to gig, had started it in 1961 as a means to ingratiate herself with the band. Each month Bobbie sent out a chatty mimeographed newsletter to mostly local girls who paid the five-shilling dues and wrote in periodically requesting intimate information about the lads—"the color of their eyes and hair, their height, their ideal girl, car, and food [in that order], and also their upcoming appearances." This was a small, passionate group—perhaps thirty-five or forty in number. But by mid-1962, the mail descended on her home in bulging sacks, and as each day passed, the demand on her time—and the drain on her bank account—seemed more daunting.

Frieda Kelly had pitched in to help before she went to work at NEMS, then persuaded Brian to get involved. This opportunity, as he read it, was a blessing. It gave him a pipeline directly to hard-core Beatle fans that he could flush with propaganda. "He said that if we gave him the postal orders, he would pay our bills for the postage and stationery," she says. As a businessman, Brian recognized the value of a loyal consumer base.

He also knew how to motivate people. "We'd talk in his office every afternoon, at teatime," Bob Wooler recalls. "He usually kept a bottle of brandy there. If we were in a real drinking mood—in other words, gin—we'd meet at the Beehive, in Paradise Street, just so he could keep me up-to-date." Every move the Beatles made was reported back to Wooler so he could cajole their fans and keep the home fires burning. It was a tactic Colonel Parker had employed while Elvis was in the army, studied with envy and admiration by Brian. "Sometimes he'd rub his hands. *Oh, great news, Bob, great news. They're going to do a BBC radio broadcast in Manchester. Do you think you could organize a coach trip from the Cavern?*" As incentive, Brian offered to pay for the whole thing.

The Manchester show would be a turning point. Brian had talked the Beatles into riding the bus home. It was a gracious gesture to their fans who had clapped like crazy during the band's performance. Inside the Playhouse Theatre, the Beatles had played their hearts out. The response was phenomenal, better than anyone had anticipated. Afterward, as they made their way out, a crowd had gathered in the parking lot, not a big crowd but a spirited one intent on getting a closer look at these long-haired rock 'n rollers from Liverpool. The Beatles had to push their way through a gauntlet in order to board the bus. Bill Harry, who accompanied the band from backstage, recalls: "It was an amazing scene. The Beatles managed to climb into the coach, but the girls were mobbing Pete and he couldn't get on." Everyone on the bus had to wait—and watch. John, Paul, and George watched expressionlessly in the dark. Few friends who observed them realized what this grave demeanor concealed—how, in fact, it was a mask worn to conceal a bitter dissatisfaction. So hard were the lines of their lips and the set of their jaws that they might have been statues for a garden display. Outwardly, their composure never cracked, but inwardly they smoldered as Neil Aspinall extricated his friend from the crowd's adoring grip. The Beatles never said a word—it was Jim McCartney, of all people, who angrily accosted Pete and accused him of trying to upstage the others—but they had already made up their minds to make sure that it never happened again.

[I]

In the dawning days of the Mersey sound, before packaged tours kept bands booked for months on end, a summerlong gig at Butlins was regarded as either Fat City or the Gulag. Few getaways were as popular as the institutionalized "holiday camps" scattered around Great Britain in rather modest and unassuming locales. Vacation retreats in Skegness, Pwllheli (Wales), Clacton, Blackpool, Filey, and Bognor Regis provided sanctuary for thousands of young working families on a budget for whom two weeks of regulated social activity and nightly entertainment was the perfect interlude to a fearsome fifty-week grind. Work and play: you could load up the car, drive a few hours through countryside as uncompromisingly beautiful and familiar as the backyard, and arrive in a walled-in oasis shimmering in the heat, where kids and adults romped side by side.

Catering to the masses, the Butlins camps were governed by vox populi, and by 1960 it was clear that rock 'n roll had crystallized as a mainstream trend. Up-and-coming groups were awarded summer residencies at each Butlins satellite: Cliff Richard at Clacton, Clay Nicholls and the Blue Flames at Filey, and the Trebletones at Bognor Regis. For £16 a week—a cushy *twenty-hour* week—plus room, board, and flocks of adoring birds, it was a steady, much-sought-after gig.

The Beatles, however, avoided Butlins like church. Disdainful of organized functions and the camps' loutish appeal, John, who was inexorably middle class, refused to apply there for work. The whole concept of "chalet"—or barracks—living and uniformed perky "redcoats" who herded guests from activity to activity revolted him, and he waxed eloquent on it, despite (or perhaps because of) the fact that Paul's family had spent many happy summers at Butlins. Johnny Byrne recalls how John wasted no opportunity to trash Butlins. "He told us it reminded him of a German concentration camp," Byrne says.

Liverpool's representative at Butlins was Rory Storm and the Hurricanes. In 1960, billed as Jet Storm, they spent two fun-packed months at Pwllheli, opening for the blustery Blackjacks. After the headliners departed early, Storm swiped Rory Blackwell's first name and suggested his sidemen change theirs as well to spice up the band's "boring" image. Just as the aggressively offbeat Lord Sutch had given his Savages appropriate stage names, Storm imposed a Wild West theme, so Johnny Byrne became Johnny Guitar, Charlie O'Brien metamorphosed as Ty Brien (after Ty Hardin, the star of TV's *Bronco*), and Wally Egmond adopted the name Lu Walters, which, for all its commonness, sounded to Scousers like a chaw-spittin' desperado. The only group member who balked at the hijinks was the drummer.

Ritchie Starkey's tenure as a teddy boy gave him the requisite aura: flamboyant clothes, an exquisitely chiseled beard, swaths of silver streaked through his lank hair, and status as one of the city's fleetest dancers. His twelve-cylinder, red-and-white Standard Vanguard (for which he had no license) sealed the spectacular image. Although disenchanted with the idea of stage names, Ritchie was a team player and for a while consented, begrudgingly, to let Storm introduce him as "Rings," in deference to his penchant for flashy jewelry. There was an effort to amend it to Johnny Ringo, after the mythical gunslinger; however, that fizzled when it was determined that the Colts' singer had already staked a claim to it. Still, Rory was nothing but persevering. When Rory grabbed a ten-minute break in the middle of a set, his illustrious drummer took over the spotlight. "Ritch wasn't that interested," recalls Byrne. "He didn't want to sing. But we'd bring the drums forward, which kind of amazed the crowd—you'd never see a drummer singing—and he'd do three numbers: 'Alley-Oop,' 'Matchbox,' and 'Boys,' the B-side of a Shirelles record we dug up." In no time, he grew into the role; its blinding attraction energized him. "And eventually Rory began introducing the break, saying: 'All right folks—it's *Ringo Star-Time!*'"

Ringo: it had a nice theatricality—not too tricky, not too serious. It synchronized awkwardly with Starkey, but "Starr was a natural," the drummer recalled. "It made sense to me, and I liked it." *Ringo Starr*. It rolled right off the tongue. What's more, it looked great emblazoned on his bass drum. While the others struggled to establish their new names, Ringo seemed born to it.

But his style wasn't limited by name alone. Ringo had chops. "He was an excellent drummer and had a good feel," says Adrian Barber, with whom Ringo occasionally gigged. It was an opinion that resonated throughout the Merseyside club scene. He was very popular with musicians, in general because of his personality, but particularly because he wasn't a showboat: he established a nice groove that managed to serve the songs without taking anything away from them. His ego never got in the way. Of all the drummers in Liverpool, where the pecking order was so clearly established, bands ranked Ringo among the best. And by the summer of 1962, he figured in many of their plans.

One band in particular.

The Beatles had more than an inkling that they were only one man away from being great. As musicians, they had developed immeasurably over the years together, and it was impossible not to hear exactly how far they had come. They had gotten progressively better—and not just better, but accomplished, versatile. There was a cleverness about their playing, an ingenuity that took routine lines of music and gave them a sharp, inventive twist. A lot of it happened without a great deal of forethought. They'd hit a chord, either experimentally or by accident, and bells would go off. Some of it was innate. Paul picked up instruments the way some people pick up new languages; he had the ear for it, with all the proper accents in place. And George, especially, seemed consumed with fundamentals and technique. Both handled guitars with stunning self-assuredness and possessed the power to make their instruments hum like Maseratis. John had everything else: the right sensibility and taste. And it all fit together in a stylized groove.

And then there was the matter of ambition. "There was a feeling we all had, built into us all, that something was going to happen," George recalled in his memoirs. Who else would have presumed to write their own songs? Or team up so audaciously with a manager? Ambition. It was never more apparent than in their long-range outlook: none of them had anything to fall back on. Their peers all had day jobs; the Beatles had never even thought seriously about punching a clock. It was only ever music, only the band, *only the Beatles.* There were no other options. This was their life's work.

If perfectionism was one objective, continuity was another. Neither John nor Paul wanted to rock the boat, so it was George who ultimately was "responsible for stirring things up." As a perfectionist, it bugged him that the drum patterns remained so static. *Thunk-thunk-thunk-thunk! Thunk-thunk-thunk-thunk!* They provided no contrast to the music, no matter what was being played.

Paul's own deep passion for drumming had never been concealed. He'd long had a trap set at home, which he mastered as he did all the other instruments in the band. And during jam sessions at the Blue Angel, with Gerry Marsden and Wally Shepherd, he "always made for the drums." Earl Preston's drummer, Ritchie Galvin, recalled encountering Paul and Pete huddled at the Mandolin Club one afternoon in 1962 after a lunchtime session at the Cavern. "Paul was showing Pete the drum pattern that he wanted on a particular song," Galvin remembered. "Pete tried to do it, but he didn't get it."

And by now it was no secret that the other Beatles resented Mona Best. The band had used her house as its unofficial headquarters since 1960, camping in the Bests' upstairs Oriental living room between gigs and using her phone to confirm dates; as a result, they suffered her persistent interruptions—and opinions. "Mona was an attractive, strong, very forceful woman, in the tradition of John's aunt Mimi," says Bill Harry, who admired her. "She ran the Casbah with an iron fist, and she tried to run the Beatles with the same vigor." Radio personality Spencer Leigh shared Harry's regard for Mona but wrote that "she could also be a harridan." "If she said it was Sunday when it was Tuesday," one musician relented, "you'd say it was Sunday too." Her high-handedness seemed particularly accentuated when the Beatles were there holding court. She came to view herself as their adviser, their patron, and the Beatles, who were fiercely independent, to say nothing of chauvinistic, "didn't want her interference." Only one person dreaded her more, and that was Brian Epstein. She was the bane of his existence, always on his back, always haranguing him, demeaning his position, challenging his authority, belittling him. In self-defense, he referred to her impersonally, as *that woman,* never by name.

Aside from a two-month stint with Tony Sheridan, Ringo had been with the Hurricanes for four years, but rumors abounded that he was again up for grabs. Kingsize Taylor's band, on tour in Hamburg, was losing its drummer, Dave Lovelady, who was due back at school in September to finish his degree in architecture. "Teddy wrote to Ringo to ask him if he'd take my place," Lovelady recalled. A decent raise was proposed: £5 a week more than the £15 Rory was paying him. A 35 percent hike was nothing to sneeze at. "[Ringo] wrote back to say that he would [do it,] and he gave Rory Storm his notice."

But Ringo and Johnny Byrne were tight. They had shared a camp chalet at Pwllheli for two years running, and this summer at Skegness, on the east coast of England, arrangements remained the same. Truthfully, their chalet was an awful hole—a shabby little room so primitive that it had no electricity aside from a solitary bulb hanging by a frayed cord. But otherwise, "the lifestyle," as Byrne says, "was ideal." There was a snazzy new performing center, the Rock 'n Calypso Ballroom, with energetic crowds and "an electric-type atmosphere" that recharged itself every night. The boys would get up late and go for a swim or a horseback ride. Johnny and Ringo, in particular, enjoyed some lazy roller-skating in the afternoons, then came back for "a lie-in." If they behaved, Rory's sister, Iris, who worked in the camp dance troupe, brought some of her friends around. Recalled Johnny, "We had food, money in our pockets. We weren't getting our hands dirty. And *the girls!* We did quite well with them at Butlins. There were different campers every week, so nothing ever got messy. After all, they were the main reason we'd gotten into rock 'n roll—the money and the girls. What else was there? Well, maybe the music."

Ringo remembered the scene was "fabulous . . . the best place we could have been." And his years with the Hurricanes were loaded with similar memories. "But Ringo was like all of us," according to Byrne, "ruthless. You had to be to stay on top. Rory was that way; I was, too. And the Beatles were the most ruthless of all. No one was going to stand in the way of success."

On the morning of August 15, 1962, Johnny and Ringo had slept late after having been up "until nearly dawn" the night before following a raucous show and its vital cool-down. Two weeks earlier Johnny and Ringo had been unceremoniously "put off" the Butlins grounds for "security purposes." At two in the morning, after yet another uproarious show, the boys had been caught "committing the cardinal sin" of playing music in their chalet. The two young girls lounging there, however innocently, didn't help matters.

So as not to jeopardize the gig, the two boys had rented a trailer, laying out a precious £2 per week, and parked it rather presumptuously opposite the Butlins front gates. "Ringo had one end, I had the other," Byrne recalled. They decorated it with posters of American rock 'n roll artists and brought the record player out of hiding. Johnny brewed coffee; Ringo heated "tins of beans," which before would have tipped them to "the camp Gestapo." And it was there, on that Wednesday morning in August, just after ten o'clock, they were so rudely awakened by a knock.

Drowsily, Byrne answered the door. "It was John and Paul," Johnny recalls vividly. "As soon as I saw them, I knew what they wanted. They wanted Ringo." Apparently they'd been driving since dawn, roaring along the narrow highways toward Wales, around the sprawl of Manchester and Sheffield, then winding, with slow progress that continued mile after mile, through Wragby, Horncastle, and Spilsby, traveling even narrower roads that took a good five hours to negotiate. Byrne invited the two Beatles inside, but he grew increasingly distraught at the sight of them. He loved Rory Storm and the music they'd made together, and this development had disaster written all over it. As Johnny rubbed his eyes, sinking into the dull reality of the situation, John Lennon confirmed his worst suspicions. "Pete Best is leaving [the band]," John stated, "and we want Ringo to join." Everyone stood there awkwardly, embarrassed, as Johnny and Ringo got dressed. "Let's find Rory," they suggested, and set off for their leader's chalet.

It took more than two hours to locate Storm. He'd been in the coffee shop having breakfast and had sunk into a tranquil reverie. He was thinking, planning new routines, sending out discouraging vibes to any friendly camper who might otherwise intrude, so much so that he missed hearing the repeated announcements blaring over the camp's P.A. system: "*Would Rory Storm report to Reception. Rory Storm—please report to Reception.*"

When he finally arrived, Johnny, Ringo, John, and Paul were already deep into discussions about an exit strategy and timing. The Beatles were pressuring Ringo to leave immediately with them. They had a gig that night at the Cavern and planned to introduce him as their new mate. The whole situation caught Rory totally off guard. "He was angry," Byrne recalls. "We'd had no warning. Ringo had been with us for four years. We were in the middle of a season-long gig, doing two shows a day—and suddenly your drummer's going on you." Pinched by longtime pals. Still, even the ambitious Rory recognized a golden opportunity when he heard one. The Beatles were offering Ringo a king's ransom: £25 a week! As Byrne says, "They were also waving a recording contract around, which was a big thing in 1962. Nobody was queuing up to sign us. If they had come to me and said, 'George is leaving and we want you to replace him,' I wouldn't have thought about it for very long." The same went for Rory; a pragmatist at heart, he refused to stand in Ringo's way. Yes, he was annoyed, but he also knew the score. "You should go," Rory told him with a shrug of inevitability.

But not so fast. Rory insisted that Ringo finish out the week: two more nights. If Ringo left them cold, they'd likely lose a week's wages, which would sour everything. Ringo, who "was embarrassed" by the state of affairs, agreed. And reluctantly, so did John and Paul before they headed back to Liverpool—empty-handed but content. They got what they had come for, a drummer and, ultimately, a legacy.

Forevermore, the Beatles would be John, Paul, George, and Ringo.

[II]

The Beatles played a routine show that evening at the Cavern. While they were thrashing away onstage, Brian sauntered into the bandroom, where Bob Wooler was enjoying a sly nip, and asked: "Is it possible for us to talk later?" The men agreed to meet at the Old Dive, one of the furtive late-night pubs on Williamson Square, where anyone demanding entrance was required to knock three times at the window, Prohibition-style, and ask for "Joe."

Sometime after eleven o'clock, Bob found Brian in the back room, hunched over a bottle of gin. "He was terribly upset," Wooler recalls. And he wasted no time in delivering the news: Pete was being sacked. Moreover, the other Beatles had insisted that it was Brian's duty, as their manager, to "do the dirty work." Desperate to get it over with, he'd already made an appointment to meet Pete at NEMS the next morning for the showdown.

Wooler was stunned. "*Why?*" he wondered aloud.

Brian ignored the question. "How do you think the fans will react?" he asked.

Wooler was frank. "They're not going to like this at all. Pete's very popular."

Following Wednesday night's gig at the Cavern, Pete made arrangements to have Neil Aspinall drive the Beatles to Thursday's gig at the tony Riverpark Ballroom, the first of four weekly performances there that would run through the end of September. As was usual, Pete scheduled convenient pickup times with each of the guys so that he could coordinate it with Neil. When he got to John, however, there was some hesitation. Pete thought that "his face looked scared" and was confused when John told him not to worry about it, "he would go on his own." That didn't make sense. The Beatles always traveled together to gigs, especially when they went someplace so distant. Moreover, John didn't drive. But to each his own, Pete decided. He certainly wasn't going to lose any sleep over it.

On the morning of August 16, a typical summer day in the muggiest part of England, Neil Aspinall drove Pete to NEMS and dropped him off at the curb in Whitechapel, outside the busy shop. Pete went upstairs alone. There, he "found Brian in a very uneasy mood," straining for meaningless pleasantries and chitchat. This wasn't the usual rule. Brian normally got right down to business, but this time he "hedged a little," and although the manager's smile never wavered, there was not only nervousness behind it but fear. He was delaying the inevitable, trying to build up some nerve. Finally, he just blurted it out: "Pete, I have some bad news for you. The boys want you out, and it's already been arranged that Ringo will join the band on Saturday."

Pete stared dazedly at Brian. The news knocked him sideways. He was "in a state of shock." After a short but numb swoon, he managed only one word, mumbling, "Why?"

Rather than tap-dance, Brian told him the truth: the other Beatles didn't think he was a good enough drummer. And neither did George Martin, who had decided to sign the band to Parlophone. The Beatles had known this for two weeks and had kept it from Pete. Brian could be shrill and irrational at times, a bully with a knack for delivering a vicious tongue-lashing, for picking apart his victim for sport, but he was also a master of tact, appealing to people's most unresolved feelings, expressing sympathetic concern, and deploying great reserves of compassion when the situation demanded it—and this was one of those situations. There was no ruthlessness to it, he assured Pete in as soothing a voice as was possible. It was a business decision. "The lads don't want you in the group anymore."

It's unlikely that any of Brian's finesse had a consoling effect on Pete. It hit him so suddenly, caught him so seriously off guard, Pete recalled, that "my mind was in a turmoil." All that time he'd put in with the Beatles, their would-be friendship, the dreams. Now, for *this* to happen—on the eve of a record deal. He considered it a "stab in the back." Partly to defuse Pete's rage and partly to remain in the boy's good graces, Brian offered to form another group around Pete.

Somehow, as Pete stalked out of the office, Brian found the nerve to ask him to play the three remaining gigs before Ringo joined the Beatles on Saturday. And somehow Pete, insanely, agreed. If Brian believed him, it was because there was never any doubt in his mind, or anyone else's, that Pete was an honorable guy. But like his drumming, the agony became too overpowering. The promise rang hollow; it was nothing more than an exit line.

———

Pete's face, pale, downcast, alerted Neil Aspinall to the fact that something had gone wrong. "What's happened?" he asked.

Pete barked back: "They've kicked me out!"

Neil, skimming the spaces between what he heard and guessed, suggested they go someplace to talk. The Grapes, opposite the Cavern, was nearby, and the two boys dug in there to drink and sulk.

Pete was stunned and demoralized, not just by the dismissal but by the cutthroat way in which it had been handled. Where were the Beatles? he wanted to know. Why hadn't they been men enough to tell him themselves? A confrontation would have made it easier to accept. This way just "disgusted" him. Neil agreed, vowing to quit his job as road manager in protest over Pete's treatment. Neil's loyalty to Pete was complicated. The dark, handsome Aspinall, just turned twenty-one, was a different type of "guest" or "lodger" in the Bests' house than history has recorded. Throughout his residency there, he'd been having an affair with Mona Best, well into her forties. By the end of 1961, she was pregnant, and the birth of a son, born on July 21, 1962, less than a month before Pete's dismissal, was registered as Vincent Roag Best despite—or maybe to blur—the fact that Neil Aspinall was his father.* Neil and Pete were like brothers—now perhaps more. It was all Pete could do to talk him out of quitting that night.

Pete promised Brian that he would finish out the week, but by the time he got home the absurdity of that idea loomed large. "I'm not going to the gig," he told Neil. "I couldn't play with them, knowing that this has happened and I'm out." Later he would admit: "Once I was home at Hayman's Green, I broke down and wept."

[III]

Pete's fate mattered naught to Ringo Starr. "I never felt sorry, for [him]," Ringo admitted much later, dismissing the entire matter by saying: "I was not involved. Besides, I felt I was a much better drummer than he was."

---

* The birth certificate, registered on August 31, 1962, records the boy's name as Vincent Rogue Best, listing Mona and John Best as parents.

Unlike Pete, he would be considered by many to be the Luckiest Man Alive. But Ringo Starr began life battling more adversity than Job.

The saga of Ringo's personal history—more like a Dickensian chronicle of misfortune—is one of the erratic tragic chapters in the glittering Beatles legacy. In contrast to the others, who were middle- (John) or working-class (Paul and George), Ringo was "ordinary, poor," a hardship case. "He was not a barefoot, ragged child," recalls Marie Maguire Crawford, a neighbor who doubled as his surrogate sister, "but like all of the families who lived in the Dingle, he was part of an ongoing struggle to survive."

The Dingle, which was christened by immigrant settlers after the arcadian glade in Ireland, bore little resemblance to its romantic namesake. One of the oldest inner-city districts in Liverpool, it was grim and "really rough," the very edge of civilization, and housed the "artisan working class"—a miscellany of carpenters, plumbers, joiners, and "others with a trade," who became as tightly intertwined as the terrace houses. Sixty families, a mixed bag of Irish and Welsh, were often jammed shoulder to shoulder on a short, sooty Dingle street, each clinging to its tiny stake, impervious to the vagaries of fate. There was nothing grandiose about their provisions: generally, a poorly ventilated, postage-stamp-size house patched together by crumbling plaster walls, with a rear door that opened onto an outhouse. Parents shooed their children to the embrace of nearby Prince's Park, on which it is said New York's Central Park planners had based their design. "Most of us were brought up there," recalls Marie Maguire Crawford. "People lit coal fires, and so the green parks became our lungs."

When Richard Starkey, Ringo's father, married Elsie Gleave in 1936, he followed the Dingle tradition and set up house a scant hundred yards from where he was raised. The Starkeys moved into an unusually roomy—Ringo recalled it as being "palatial"—three-bedroom terrace house at 9 Madryn Street, a narrow artery lined with humble plane trees (a species known to every local schoolchild who recited: "The plane trees / kind to the poor, dull city") and grids of discolored, cracked pavement. Richard's parents, John and Annie, lived nearby at number 59, just as later his sister, Nancy, would move into number 21, following her marriage to Tony Christian. The Starkey houses might well have been interchangeable in the way the occupants shuffled back and forth between them all day long.

Richard and Elsie had met at Cooper's, one of Liverpool's larger commercial bakeries, where he worked near the ovens, methodically icing cakes. To him, Elsie was "the cherry on top," an attractive, risible woman, with lovely, big, clear eyes and a wonderful singing voice. She had been raised in neighboring Toxteth Park, the youngest of fourteen children, and at an early age was bundled off to her grandmother's, where she spent most of a happy, if somewhat alienated, childhood. Elsie Gleave learned early that a woman should be self-sufficient, that independence meant getting a job, that spare time was devoted to the piano, and that evenings were for going out on the town. "Dancing feet," she would say, needed a regular workout.

Indeed, dancing was her only salvation from the hardscrabble Dingle life, and the fleet-footed Richard Starkey, who liked swing and seemed born to perform it, proved a kindred spirit. Most of the time, Elsie and Richard joined the crowds at Reece's, a cafeteria-style restaurant where some of the strongest dancers capered into the early dawn hours. It was a raucous, ebullient scene. Vendors circled through the hall dispensing cheap, red wine they called plunk from jugs, and when Elsie felt especially gay, she would say, "Make it a big one—a plunk plunk."

For three years, the Starkeys were a fixture on the ballroom circuit, but eventually Elsie's thirst grew parched for other desires. Working-class tradition dictated that newlyweds have a baby within a year of marriage— if not sooner. Elsie tried everything necessary to conceive, but without results. "Elsie was nervous that she'd never have a child," recalls Marie Maguire Crawford. "She never asked for much, but that was all she really wanted."

Just when Elsie got accustomed to the idea that children might not be in the cards, she became pregnant and gave birth to a son, named Richard after his father, on July 7, 1940. There was much celebration on sleepy Madryn Street, whose houses were unusually dormant thanks to the escalating war with Germany. Relatives stopped by at all hours to gaze upon the baby "with the big, soulful eyes," who everyone agreed was the "spitting image of his mum." He had his mother's long face and sensuous mouth, to say nothing of the thick, dark hair that would serve him handily twenty years hence. Ritchie, as he was called, bore hardly any resemblance to his father, who was "quite a handsome man, with curly hair and a thin, narrow smile." This was Elsie's boy, from head to toe, and she doted upon him to the point of preoccupation.

Richard Sr.—subsequently renamed Big Ritchie, to his great amusement—wasn't used to sharing the spotlight. It didn't suit his large personality, an ego that had blossomed under Elsie's absorption. He was ill-prepared for fatherhood and even less willing to sacrifice for it, especially those wonderful nights on the town, which had dwindled to an occasional pub crawl. It wasn't just the dancing that captivated Richard. "He liked going out," says a Dingle acquaintance, and enjoyed the whole process, which began with getting dressed up and extended to the quick stares he drew as "one of the smartest," best-groomed men on the scene. Those looks hadn't impressed him so much during Elsie's constant companionship, but on his own they began to take a toll.

Within months after Little Ritchie's birth, things started to unravel for the Starkeys. Richard, supplanted by his son, withdrew further and further from the family. His attention began to drift. With most able-bodied men off fighting the war, this sharpie with a hot smile and the latest moves became a hot commodity at the dance halls, where lonely wives often congregated to escape an empty house. His nights on the town became more and more frequent, sometimes stretching on for days. No matter how Elsie pleaded, "he just put on his suit and went." Sometimes, to avoid making a scene, he didn't even bother coming home from work, instead heading straight to a pub and then off somewhere crowded, wherever the action happened to be.

Elsie Starkey didn't surrender her husband without a fight, but by 1943 she realized it was a battle she was going to lose and consented, rather agreeably, when a separation was proposed. Richard moved out of the house, and in no time—no more than a year at the most—they were divorced. Some stories claim that Starkey left Liverpool and went to sea with one of the luxury passenger liners that berthed in Liverpool; some that he remarried and settled "over the water," in the Wirral. But in all likelihood, he remained close to his work. Throughout the war, with staples growing ever more scarce, he supplied his parents with "bags of icing sugar," which they, in turn, distributed to families on Madryn Street.

For his part, Ringo, who says he has "no real memories of dad," always knew how to reach him, if he wanted to: his grandparents, John and Annie, remained just a few doors up the street and, to their credit, never stopped treating Elsie and Little Ritchie as members of their immediate family. But Ringo never made any attempt to locate his father. Elsie "filled me up with all the things about him," he recalled, poisoning the waters, while Richard drifted in and out of the picture maybe five times in as many years, never making an attempt to care for, or even get to know, his son.

Elsie was resourceful enough to pull through. Richard provided support, but only a paltry thirty shillings a week, so she took a number of menial jobs, doing mostly housework—scrubbing floors and laundry—until discovering her calling as a barmaid. Pub work was easy to come by and the hours were suitable; she could work as much or as little as she wanted. Elsie, a gregarious woman by nature, enjoyed pubs and the people who came to them. There was a sense of community inside—it felt familiar to her, much the way it felt on Madryn Street—and for the next twelve years she was a well-liked fixture in some of Liverpool's best public houses, beginning at the Wellington, in Garston, and concluding at Yates's Wine Lodge, in city center, near Marks & Spencer.

No matter how much Elsie made, however, there wasn't enough to cover the house on Madryn Street. While living in a three-up, three-down was comfortable, it was too big—and certainly extravagant—for just her and Ritchie. This was the situation she described to her friends Muriel and Jack Patterson one night as they sat outside on the sidewalk, getting some air. The Pattersons, who lived just behind Elsie, on Admiral Grove, grappled with their own housing problems. With three children, their two-bedroom terrace house was bursting at the seams; the trouble was, the housing market was tight; there were no bigger places available. It's not clear who came up with the idea to swap houses, but before the night was out both families agreed it posed the perfect solution: the Pattersons reaped more space, Elsie got rent relief, whereas no one was forced to leave the neighborhood. A week later Elsie packed up the house and paid the Maguire boys to carry her belongings around the block. It was no more difficult than that.

Like most congested inner-city ghettos, the Dingle was dangerous terrain. There was a homey, community character to it, but under the gauzy facade lay an atmosphere bleak and treacherous. Any street was relatively safe—as long as you lived on it. Stray fifty yards in any direction, however, and your safety came to an abrupt end. The friendly faces gave way to glares and tough talk. Bullies, looking for a fight, made it impossible for anyone to walk away. Even Ringo, who always counted the Dingle as home, never underestimated its reputation for violence. As Ringo recalled: "You kept your head down, your eyes open, and you didn't get in anybody's way." Or else.

As a result, Ritchie, like other Dingle boys, quickly developed intuitive street smarts. But that was small comfort to a mother who was off working during the day. "Elsie was always terrified that something dreadful would happen to him," says Marie Maguire Crawford. "With Richard gone, Ritchie was her 'all,' as she called him, and as a result, she made sure there was always an extra set of eyes watching him."

His grandparents did what they could to help out. Of the immediate family, John and Annie Starkey gave Ritchie the attention he craved. They "fussed over" him almost every morning. Then, about noon, Marie would collect Ritchie and bring him down the street to her house so that her mother could look after him until Elsie returned. Ritchie's joyous hours with Marie offset the traumatic uprooting he experienced by being shuffled from house to house. A pale, fair-haired little girl who was "born responsible," Marie was put "in charge" of entertaining him. They spent most nice days outside in Prince's Park or went roller-skating on High Park Street, whose surface was freshly paved and icy slick. As the days grew warmer, they crept "further and further afield." Mrs. Maguire made sure they always had enough money to come home on the tram, but as it usually got spent on ice cream, Marie, who was four years older, often had to carry Ritchie back in her arms.

"Ritchie and I would play for hours on our own," Marie recalls. They might camp out at Elsie's piano and "belt away," harmonizing to "You Are My Sunshine," "Where Are You All," "Bobby Shaftoe," and "There'll Always Be an England." There were movies—children's matinees at the Gaumont, or the Mayfair or the Rivoli in Aigburth Road—followed by a greasy treat at Eric's Chip Shop. Or they'd simply walk. Liverpool was a great walking city in the days before two-car families and congested highways. Afterward, Marie would dutifully bathe him in a tin tub in front of a fire in the back room.

All this attention eased Elsie's fears, but there was nothing that could safeguard Ritchie from the chance grip of illness. A few days before his seventh birthday, on July 3, 1947, Ritchie complained about an upset stomach, and later sharp pains in his side. Elsie fretted at dinnertime about what to do. Calling the doctor seemed like a fairly extreme step for a case of what she assumed was indigestion. But by bedtime, as the pains persisted and his temperature soared, she sent for an ambulance and bundled him off to Children's Hospital. It was a "straightforward appendicitis, a little slit and it was out." But in the aftermath, Ritchie developed peritonitis, the deadly inflammation of the membrane lining the abdomen, and lapsed into a coma. For three days, it was touch and go. Elsie, who had for years watched her son make the most out of life, was told by his doctors to prepare for the worst. Ritchie's condition deteriorated, so much so that on July 7, Marie's mother, Annie, accompanied Elsie to his hospital room, where both women resigned themselves to say their good-byes. As it turned out, Ritchie opened his eyes a few times—the first encouraging sign, they were told to great relief.

Ritchie "was very lucky to survive" the ordeal, which necessitated a long rehabilitation in a crowded hospital ward. As late as December, six months after being admitted, Ritchie was restless to go home. Convinced that his symptoms had more or less improved, the doctors planned to release him in time to spend Christmas with his family. But a relapse a week or two before the holidays forced him back to bed, where he remained, barely mobile, for another six months.

Back on Admiral Grove, Ritchie's efforts to reintegrate at school were quickly undermined by his well-meaning but overprotective mother. Elsie, who "doted on him and was very lenient" to begin with, allowed him to sit out the rest of the year—for "convalescing"—which put him so far behind in his academic development that it became impossible for him to catch up. Now in the fourth grade, he couldn't read or write; math was like a foreign language he didn't speak. No one seemed to take an interest in tutoring him. School became a great and terrifying burden—he felt ostracized there—making it easier to simply stay away. So, each morning, after wedging a stack of books under his arm and saying good-bye to Elsie, he'd detour into the park and kill time, bumping around with other truants until it was time to return home.

All of this made Ritchie something of an outcast in his neighborhood. Families in the Dingle may have been dirt-poor and largely uneducated, but they placed a serious emphasis on self-improvement.

Until almost the end of his twelfth year, at his mother's prodding, Ritchie was tutored by Marie Maguire in an effort to teach him the basics and to help him function. Twice a week Marie supervised classes at a table in the back room of Admiral Grove, where Ritchie, who resented such regimentation and attended against his will, struggled over the simple exercises—"the cat sat on the mat"—found in the little brown-backed editions of *Chambers Primary Readers.* Despite his intense objections, however, the results proved encouraging. "He made incredible progress," Marie recalls. "It seemed like we were *that* close to bringing him up to proper school standards when he got sick again."

It was a disastrous setback. This time, it was tuberculosis, and it came as no real surprise, considering the epidemic that raged through the filthy Dingle streets; everywhere one turned, people wheezed or hacked or coughed into their fists. Kids, especially, were susceptible, their tender immune systems unable to stand up to the infection.

This time, Elsie wasted no time in getting him to the hospital. Ritchie spent the first few days at Children's, undergoing tests and observation, after which he was transferred to Royal Liverpool Children's Hospital, in Heswall, on the Wirral peninsula. "It was a huge old sanitarium off the main road, leading to the Welsh coast," a frequent visitor recalls, "providing a much less polluted atmosphere, so the kids could begin to breathe in good health again." The vaulted wards were packed with children in various stages of the disease, and most of them, terrified by the strangers in white coats who performed a battery of nonstop tests and treatments, cried and hollered throughout the beginning weeks of their long confinements.

A veteran of hospitals, Ritchie wasn't fazed by the medical staff. He understood the procedure and swung right into the routine, making instant friends with the nurses who provided various therapies and, whenever possible, supervised classes throughout the day. Normally intimidated and socially awkward, Ritchie thrived. "He was like the mayor of the ward," says a visitor, who marveled at the easy self-confidence he demonstrated. There were plenty of playmates to choose from, and girls in the next room. Over the weeks, then months, they organized games and informal social gatherings to help the kids pass the time. To keep their minds occupied, a wide assortment of therapeutic activities disguised as recreation helped spur recovery. Ritchie taught himself to weave and knit, but it was nothing compared with an activity that would ultimately change his life.

In a move intended to stimulate motor activity and soothe enduring bouts of anguish, young patients were encouraged to join the hospital band. Inside the ward, "instruments" were distributed so that participants, even those without a whiff of musical experience, could play along with pre-recorded songs. You didn't need chops to handle a triangle or tambourine or cymbal or any of the percussion instruments that made up the hospital band. Improvisation and free expression ensured that everyone participated. Ritchie played the drums, using "cotton bobbins to hit on the cabinet next to the bed." It made a flat, dull sound, but there was an energy unleashed in his execution, an instinct for the intricate rhythms and dynamics that were essential to keeping a beat. Good coordination also allowed Ritchie control over these seemingly simple but exacting mechanics. There was something familiar in the process, a natural feel to the way he held his hands, the impact of the sticks on the wooden surface, and the colorful patterns that emerged. He didn't just make noise; there was more to it than that, there was a complex range of sounds he could produce just by experimenting with his wrists. The more he played, the more he discovered — about cadence, syncopation, movement, drive, precision, none of which he could articulate, of course, or even attribute to traditional technique. But that didn't interfere with his intense enjoyment. For him, the drumming process was organic. He relied on the pure kinetics of it, letting the energy take over. And somewhere in the thick of things, he'd stumbled on true love.

"That was all he talked about, so much interest in the drums," recalls Marie Maguire Crawford, who on a subsequent visit brought him a copy of "Bedtime for Drums," a rather flashy, if overwrought, solo recording by veteran swingman Alyn Ainsworth. "Someday, I'm going to play just like that," he bragged after listening to the record over and over again.

Following his recovery from tuberculosis, Ritchie returned home to the Dingle in the late fall of 1953, having "grown into a young man, but much frailer than other boys his age and somewhat disoriented." Behind him was the painful memory of his debilitating illness; ahead, the dim prospect of returning to school, where he'd fallen even further behind. Another year of absence had left him woefully ill prepared; he was hopelessly lost in class, unfairly ostracized. As a result, "he played on his illness to avoid school," says a friend, hatching a dozen excuses not to attend. Ultimately, he never went back to school, staying home instead, languishing in the back room of Admiral Grove, listening to music and rapping along on "biscuit tins" with a pair of sticks. There was also a new development there that knocked him slightly more off his stride: another man had become a fixture in what had always been a strong, matriarchal household.

For the past few years, Elsie had been dating Harry Graves, an unusually warm and even-tempered ex-Londoner who had "come to Liverpool for a change of air" when his first marriage had "gone wrong." A conspicuous presence at the little gatherings that were customary in the Dingle homes, Harry was a gamer with a lovely voice who never hesitated to break into "Star Dust" or "That Old Black Magic"—his so-called party pieces— whenever someone was seated at a piano. In fact, Harry had been roaming the periphery for some time, dating Ritchie's widowed aunt, Edie Starkey, while Elsie was romantically involved with a local man named Joe Taylor. For some time, the couples had been eyeing each other's partners, trying to devise a way to make their restless feelings known. Finally, one night it all came tumbling out—everyone confessed—and without any awkwardness, they coordinated "a swap," whereby both half-baked relationships now fell neatly into place.

Ritchie was drawn to Harry the moment he laid eyes on him. "He was a really sweet guy," Ringo remembered, ruggedly handsome, with elfin eyes and an easy, engaging smile that hid a pent-up melancholy. As a painter at the American army base in nearby Burtonwood, Harry had access to all the luxuries that captivated poor Scouser boys brought up on wartime rationing: comic books and American magazines, exotic chewing gum, toys, and, every Valentine's Day, big red hearts stuffed with rare, scrumptious candy. Best of all, music was an essential part of his makeup. Having grown up around London, where he ferreted out live music, Harry had acquired a consuming passion for big bands and their vocalists—Dinah Shore, Sarah Vaughan, and Billy Daniels, among his favorites—whose records he collected and played incessantly for Ritchie.

Much like Paul's father, Harry helped introduce Ritchie to the intricacies of popular music, pointing out how the classic stylists expressed themselves and why their music had the power to touch listeners. The new wave of lowbrow pop singers such as Frankie Laine, Johnnie Ray, and Eddie Fisher had not yet managed to claim the airwaves, though they were clearly on the horizon. In the meantime, Harry taught Ritchie to appreciate the old crooners and the relationship between their voices and the instruments. In countless interviews after the Beatles became famous, Ringo would always insist he had had no formal musical training, but the shaping of his ear—this introduction to sophisticated syncopated rhythms, along with the ability to identify a scattering of tempos—provided a root foundation that forged his talent in ways no formal training could duplicate.

Harry was also the perfect answer for an emotionally needy adolescent who'd somehow coasted through a broken home and two life-threatening illnesses. As a role model, he was a world apart from the absentee Richard Sr., exuding understanding, reassurance, and unerring commitment to the strictures of a conventional family life. Harry bent over backward to connect with Elsie's son, and Ritchie quickly succumbed to the favor of his "great gentleness." Whatever misgivings he may have had about his mother's remarriage, in April 1954, they were quickly erased by Harry's abiding—some might say blind—support for Ritchie's scattered pursuits.

Indeed, from the day he quit school until his break with Rory Storm, Ritchie Starkey's experience in the workforce was an unfolding disaster. Having grown up free of any real discipline or accountability, he had learned indifference, not ambition. He took a job at British Rail for the uniform, "because they give you suits." Unable to pass the physical, Ritchie was eventually laid off and forced onto the dole until he signed on as a waiter, serving drinks on a day boat from Liverpool to North Wales. It was light, agreeable work that appealed to his happy-go-lucky nature and ostensibly served as an apprenticeship, a jumping-off point to his dream job, working at sea on a succession of international luxury liners. Unfortunately, reality got in the way. With the effects of war still prominent on every street, it was the responsibility of all able-bodied British men, if called, to do active duty in the armed forces. Ritchie, fresh from a hospital lie-in, was unnaturally "terrified" that he'd be drafted. Had he stopped to consider his pathology, of course, he'd have known there was no way the army would induct such a run-down specimen. Nevertheless, he immediately set about ensuring that the possibility would not occur. For starters, that meant quitting his job on the day boat. If he was fit for seafaring work, he believed, it remained likely that before very long he'd attract the navy's interest. Instead, he cast about for some kind of engineering work, based on a rumor that the armed services weren't taking apprentices that year.

Fortunately, Harry had a contact at Henry Hunt & Sons, a gymnastic-equipment company in the south end of Liverpool, and in the summer of 1956 Ritchie began working there as an apprentice fitter. It was steady, if unstimulating, work, just a short daily commute from Admiral Grove. At first, Ritchie was "the altar boy," dispatched "to fill the glue pots and to fetch chips during the breaks." There wasn't much else for him to do all day long. "But it was a great gang of people," recalls Roy Trafford, a gangly dropout from Toxteth, who worked side by side with Ritchie as an apprentice joiner and, in no time, became his closest friend. "Eventually, we were taught to finish the wooden parts—all the balancing beams for the gymnasium bars. There was only thirty-eight and six in our pay packets—no more than a handout—but at the time the money was secondary. We were learning a trade, which was more than most guys in our situation, and as we well knew, it was considered a job for life."

It wasn't long before the boys discovered a shared love of music. The two of them would spend dinner breaks at Hunt's in the downstairs shaving shed, earnestly talking about trad jazz and blues while their coworkers rummaged through brown-bag lunches. Trafford's conversation was filled with the snappy jargon of skiffle, which he'd gravitated to via weekly guitar lessons. Stirred by the spontaneity and directness of it, Ritchie became an ardent fan, and before long they began "working some songs in the cellar" during lunch. "I played guitar, and [Ritchie] just made a noise on a box," Trafford recalls. "Sometimes, he just slapped a biscuit tin with some keys, or banged on the backs of chairs." It was a strictly rudimentary but joyous affair. Eventually, Ritch invited his neighbor and workmate, Eddie Miles, to sit in, and a little band began to take shape.

Eddie, with his bird's-eye maple Hofner cutaway and its homemade pickups, was something of a guitar dynamo in Liverpool. He had a vigorous, impatient way of strumming that went wildly astray; strings snapped like rubber bands as he picked at simple leads. When, instead of polishing off phrases, he bulldozed straight through mistakes, it gave songs a loose but heated energy that was like nothing else they'd ever heard. A twelve-bar break would become a tangle of chords and flourishes. A traditional folk song would be transformed into a jazzy Big Bill Broonzy–like interplay of whoops and hollers. Eddie impressed the boys with his flamboyant ability, to say nothing of his enthusiasm, and over the next few months they developed a band around him.

What began as the Eddie Miles Band soon evolved into Eddie Clayton and the Clayton Squares, named after a landmark in downtown Liverpool. It had a revolving-door cast of anywhere from five to seven musicians, all of whom (aside from Eddie, of course) were interchangeable. At Ritchie's insistence, they featured him on percussion. When the accompaniment kicked in behind Eddie, Ritchie tucked an old washboard under his arm, leaned back at a slight angle, and raked thimbles across the bevels— slashing at them, really—to produce a driving, clattering sound. On skiffle standards such as "Walking Cane" and "Rock Island Line," he could rap out a beat at a reasonably steady clip. It was still fairly unsophisticated, but he didn't care—and neither did anybody else. He was in his element.

When they put down their instruments (never for long), it was usually to dance. "We really loved the whole idea of dancing and wanted to learn properly," remembers Trafford, who, on more than one occasion, dragged Ritchie to Skellen's Dance School on the corner of Lark Lane for lessons. Later, they tried another dance school on Aigburth Road, where Ritchie was partnered with a policeman—"a bloody big fella, about six-two"— resolved to teach him the waltz. It was a short-lived disaster, but enough of an introduction to the basics for them to eventually end up dancing rather capably at the Winter Gardens, the Rialto, and Wilson Hall.

Every Friday they would "meander around town," beginning at the pub where Elsie worked "for a couple of freebies, a few large whites to give us the glow." After that, they stopped at the Lisbon Pub on Victoria Street to meet friends, retank the engines, and then head over to the Cavern, where trad jazz still ruled. "We loved trad jazz," says Trafford, "almost as much as we loved to dress up." The boys always went out "immaculately groomed." Like twins, they wore matching outfits purchased at Yaffe's: black-and-gray-striped jackets, crepe trousers with red-and-black half-inch stripes, a red-and-black-striped shirt, studded belts, and string ties from the haberdashery counter at Woolworth's. Their overcoats came from Eric's, the Quarry Men's local tailor. "I got a black one and Ritch's was blue," recalls Trafford. "We thought we were the bee's knees." To complete the effect, they plastered down their hair with gobs of brilliantine, which melted in their hands, then "went hard like a helmet" in the cold night air.

That Christmas of 1957, Harry presented Ritchie with a secondhand drum set he'd found in a shop near his old home in Romford. It was just a snare with plastic heads and a big old bass, "like a Salvation Army drum," that bore the marks of past ownership. There was also a cymbal, a big garbage can lid with nicks and dings on it, that made a clangorous sound. At the time, it was merely something durable, something that he could pound on to keep him engaged, but the gift enthralled Ritchie—and changed his life.

Before, they had only played at being a band, but now with a drummer, the Eddie Clayton group powered its way into the world of small-time show business. Drums set them apart from the hundreds of other amateur bands vying for precious stage time. The boys, having sharpened their act, began hustling for gigs on the skiffle circuit and, in no time, won a number of impressive bookings that gave them a definite glow. The pay was pitifully small—"just buttons"—but they kept regularly engaged.

Nevertheless, before too long skiffle ran out of steam. Unable to compete with the visceral kick of rock 'n roll, its practitioners defected en masse, trading in their washboards and tea chests for instruments that sizzled with electricity. Ritchie continued to play behind Eddie Clayton but moonlighted with other bands as well. One of the best-known local skiffle groups making the transition to rock was Al Caldwell's Texans, who were desperate to snag a sideman with his own drum kit. "We knew him pretty well. He'd gotten a snare drum, a high hat, and a cymbal by then," Johnny Byrne recalls. "When we told him we were going into rock 'n roll full-tilt, he said he was interested." With Ritchie keeping the beat, they reemerged in the clubs in November 1958 as the Raging Texans, and shortly thereafter as Jet Storm and the Raging Texans, and finally Rory Storm and the Hurricanes, a name that might easily have rolled off the Larry Parnes assembly line of stars. Ritchie borrowed £46 from his grandfather to buy an Ajax drum kit with "lapped" pigskin instead of plastic heads, designed to resemble the pricey Ludwigs favored by professional drummers.

Formerly a diehard blues fan (he even considered emigrating to Texas so he could "live with Lightnin' Hopkins"), Ritchie was lit up by rock 'n roll. He spent all his spare time gorging on it, listening to Radio Luxembourg's staticky broadcasts, and on Sundays religiously tuning in to Alan Freed. As a drummer, he played along with whatever came over the airwaves, beating time to one song after the next, even running through the commercial breaks.

Almost immediately, the simple rat-a-tat-tat patterns evolved into ever more complicated, exuberant wrist work. This would eventually help set him apart from drummers like Pete Best and Johnny Hutch. Everyone else at the time was emulating the bangers who relied on bruising upper-arm strength to power an arrangement, but Ritchie developed a discipline for playing shuffle rhythms that made the drums a more integral part of songs. He could punctuate what the other instruments were doing musically instead of just keeping strict time. Largely unschooled as a drummer—he claimed he "had about three lessons" as a beginner—he only knew how to play by ear. But however he approached the drums, no matter how reflexive or improvisational, the patterns he played were distinguished by an overriding degree of control. Perhaps, barring other explanation, this was an outgrowth of his unusually broad musical tastes. Whereas other teenagers jumped right into bands from a steady diet of uptempo pop, Ritchie was influenced by exacting country artists and modern jazz exponents such as Chico Hamilton and Yusef Lateef, who relied heavily on their knowledge of composition. Intuitively—and beyond explanation—he captured an energy and ease of expression that eluded other young drummers trying to find the right groove.

Alone in the Dingle, Ritchie had been a distant, almost maddeningly backward introvert. As part of the Hurricanes, he developed "a bubble of personality." Playing with the band seemed to invest him with confidence, the attention and exposure acting like a spark plug, stimulating an ego and identity that, up to then, had gone largely uncultivated. Onstage, he located a hidden charm—grinning earnestly at girls; casting enigmatic, brooding stares into the dark distance, playing with his eyes closed and head tilted to one side, trancelike, as though listening to the drum's inner beat; making lunges and parries at the cymbals. Ritchie savored the glow, and Rory, "who liked to take care of the other guys in the band," made sure he shared the spotlight. Now, under Rory's tutelage, he began creating a role for himself that reached beyond the act. Ritchie had experimented with images that he used to offset his inadequacies; now he streaked his hair silver and dressed up in a long duster and cowboy hat. The teddy boy outfit he had shared with Roy Trafford disappeared for good late that year, but he began wearing rings, not just one but many, simultaneously, an affectation that arose from his mother's passion for flashy jewelry. Elsie bought him several tawdry costume pieces studded with cut-glass "gems," which he wore along with a man's signet ring that had belonged to Grandpa Starkey. "He always loved his rings," recalls Marie Maguire Crawford. "It was a kind of attention-getter—something flashy to offset the idea that he was sickly and not well educated, perhaps distancing him from the Dingle."

Inspired by his popularity with the Hurricanes, Ritchie immersed himself in the company of adoring young women who began following bands from gig to gig. Illness had wreaked havoc on Ritchie's shaky self-confidence, but the band offset all that and, before long, he had two serious girlfriends, Pat Davies, a schoolmate of Cilla Black's, and later a Jacaranda waitress named Geraldine McGovern, to whom he eventually became engaged. But a band was no place to nurture a relationship. Besides, Gerri was Catholic—a fact that never sat well with Elsie, who "was nominally of the Orange lodge" and, with a few drinks under her belt, would break into "The Sash My Father Wore" as a swipe at her "sworn enemy."

Ultimately, Ritchie carved out a niche as a free agent. Like many teenagers who grow up in a ghetto, he was in a terrible rush to move onward—and upward. Dingle boys were drilled to place security above all else. The Ritchie Starkey who had never amounted to much at school and seemed doomed to the family fate of being yet another in a long line of menial laborers and soldiers was determined "to say [he] was actually *something*," a professional, as opposed to a working stiff. Working at Hunt's, with its boisterous crew, rustling of machinery, and long silences interrupted occasionally by the camaraderie of Roy Trafford and Eddie Miles, was deathly dull, but it provided both security and self-esteem.

Still, Ritchie wanted more—he wanted fulfillment—and the only way to get it was through music. And a choice would have to be made.

———

Sometime that spring of 1962, Rory and the Hurricanes learned they'd been hired for the summer residency at Butlins in Wales. Throughout April and May, Ritchie remained undecided whether to accept, furiously turning over in his mind the impact of such a move. "It was a difficult decision for him," recalls Johnny Byrne, who himself reluctantly ditched a good job as an invoice clerk at the Cotton Exchange to go. "Ringo never counted on music interrupting his apprenticeship, but Rory painted a picture of it that was impossible to ignore."

One can only imagine how tempting he made it sound. Ritchie accepted the offer and announced his decision shortly thereafter at a family gathering. To his aunts and uncles, he was foolishly risking a solid future on such an ill-considered scheme. But playing with the Hurricanes had shown him that nothing—and no one—could compete with the thrill of the stage. Even his mother's objections fell on deaf ears.

Somehow, decisions like this one always proved clear-cut for Ringo. He never doubted that leaving Hunt's and joining Rory Storm and the Hurricanes was a worthwhile opportunity, just as he later left Rory in 1962 to play in Hamburg with Tony Sheridan, and just as, later that year, he rejected Kingsize Taylor's offer to become a member of an outstanding outfit like the Dominoes. When the Beatles made their play, Ringo hesitated only long enough to discuss it with Roy Trafford, who encouraged him to move on—and up—with a better band. "Why not?" Roy recalls telling his mate. "You've got nothing to lose."

For the Beatles, the significance of a first-class drummer was essential to their survival. "Our career was on the line," Paul recalled, and the band knew that the only surefire way of taking it to the next level was by adding a world-beater to the mix. It was evident they'd found their man from the moment that Ringo took over the beat. Immediately they recaptured a spark that had eluded them for so long. The energy, the cleverness, the right groove—the *magic*—breezed back into their overall sound. At last, after six years, stardom seemed possible to the Beatles.

[I]

Ringo's Liverpool debut on August 19, 1962, did nothing to tickle the ears of the pop music world or rocket the Beatles to stardom. Only later, in retrospect, would it achieve mythic status. No one was affected by the situation more than Ringo. He'd heard the fan outcry in the days leading up to the Cavern gig. The dance halls and cafés had been full of it—and the schools, too, where there was a wave of adulation for Pete. Even in the record shops there was constant debate and grumbling. An hour before going on, Ringo ducked into the White Star for a remedial pint and collapsed at a table with the Blue Jeans. *They* knew he was "petrified." Even his appearance—a little goatee and straight, slicked-back hair—bespoke an uneasiness, like someone who was one step ahead of the law. "We felt sorry for him because he was so nervous," Ray Ennis recalls.

Most of those who attended the show shared Colin Manley's reaction: "I felt sorry for the lads. The crowd was so worked up over Pete's sacking that no one would let them play." "From the time the doors opened," Wooler recalled, "the crowd was chanting, 'Pete forever. Ringo—*never!'* We were prepared for a disturbance." And from the moment the Beatles took the stage, angry shouts punctuated the music: *"Where's Pete?" "Traitors!" "We want Pete!"* Others supported the change. Eventually, both factions began jawing at each other, glaring, pointing fingers. *"Up with Ringo!" "Pete is Best!"* Ringo, half-obscured behind the drums, grew "extremely more nervous" with each outburst.

Be that as it may, none of the other Beatles seemed to notice. And considering the circumstances, Ringo held his own. He adapted perfectly to the Beatles' raw, assertive style, powering up the tempo without letting it drown out the key ensemble energy. Probably nobody appreciated that more than Paul, whose lovely bass runs had been strangled by Pete's heavy hand, whereas Ringo complemented them, giving Paul a "very solid beat" to work with. "Ringo didn't try and direct the beat," says Adrian Barber, "but you could always rely on it." He brought order to an otherwise fitful rhythm section; there was an economy to his playing that kept the drums from running away with the beat. During one particularly tense moment onstage George warned some hecklers to "shut yer yaps." Later, when he stepped out of the bandroom into a crowded dark passage, someone lurched forward and head-butted him under the eye, giving him a tremendous shiner. George took it in stride, but Brian Epstein, worked up to a near-hysterical pitch, ordered the Cavern's heavyweight doorman, Paddy Delaney, to escort the band upstairs to safety.

That week in 1962 also marked upheaval in the Beatles' personal lives. Without much warning, Paul ended his two-and-a-half-year relationship with Dot Rhone. It came as a shock, inasmuch as "it had all been settled," according to Dot, that they "were going to get married and [she] was going to move in with [the McCartneys]." She already had the ring, the gold band from Hamburg; he'd taken out a marriage license. Paul's aunt Jin had even given Dot a crash course in "domestic lessons," explaining how to make the bed, do the laundry, shop for groceries, prepare dinner. But in July, with her pregnancy only three months along, Dot miscarried. The tragedy brought to the surface problems that had been brewing for half a year. Now there was no baby—and considerably less of Paul. All through the spring she'd felt "his feelings cool off." With him suddenly free of obligation, it was only a matter of time before they turned bitterly frigid, and a few weeks later he announced that it was over between them.

The split came at an awkward time. Four days after Ringo's Cavern debut, John and Cynthia got married in a civil ceremony at the stern worn-brick registry office on Mount Pleasant. It was, in the words of Cynthia, "a bizarre affair," not only because of its dreary ambience but also for the fact that it was carried out on a shoestring and without any foreseeable plan. No photographer took pictures; no flowers arrived for the bride. Fortunately, Brian sent a car for Cynthia, who'd spent the morning smartening herself in a purple-and-white-check suit over the white blouse Astrid Kirchherr had given her. It had rained steadily since dawn, and the weather wreaked havoc on the bride, especially her hair, which she had done up in intricate French plaits. Aside from Brian, Cynthia's brother Tony and his wife, Marjorie, only the Beatles, in matching black suits, attended (but not Ringo, who "was never even told" about it). Predictably, John's aunt Mimi refused to attend. John had waited until the last minute to spring the news on her, seeking to obtain at least the appearance of understanding, then suffered her outrage.

John was sober—he was not about to risk the wrath of his fetching wife-to-be—but he might as well have drank, considering the attack of giggles that ruffled through the ceremony. No one, aside from the Puritan Brian, could keep a straight face. The registrar, a twitchy, provincial man with florid cheeks and bloodshot eyes, fought a conspiracy of jackhammers from a construction site just outside the building. Every time he posed a question to either John or Cynthia, the drills rattled back, drowning them out, until the preposterous circumstances proved too hilarious to contain.

After Brian treated everyone to a celebratory lunch—at Reece's, co-incidentally, the same place John's parents, as well as Ringo's, celebrated after their respective weddings—he presented the bride and groom with an extraordinary gift: the keys to his secret furnished flat on Falkner Street, a few bocks from the art college. It was a modest little place, with one bedroom and a small walled-in garden, that he used occasionally as "a fucking pad" but primarily as a place to crash after late-night gigs so that he could sleep until noon and avoid his parents. In any event, it was a godsend to John and Cynthia, who wanted desperately—who needed desperately—to live on their own. After lunch, they moved their things into the flat, which was already decorated by Brian's graceful hand. Cynthia's mother, who had visited but returned to Canada a few days before the wedding, bought them a secondhand red rug, matching lamps, and a miscellany of cookware. And even Mimi, who everyone predicted would come around in time, provided a coffee table with a hammered-copper top.

To John and Cynthia it was a vaunted refuge, a jewel box of their own, where they could settle down to married life. But as friends came and went unannounced and the tidings gradually wore down on their first day together, that life slipped back into familiar routine. "We actually did a gig that night," George recalled, noting how it put the final twist on an otherwise surreal day. The Beatles sped off to Chester, where not a word of John's marriage was mentioned, while Cynthia stayed home, alone, to unpack. Amid crates of clothes and pooled belongings, thinking about life with a musician, Cynthia formulated a theory she kept to herself. "I was the only one thinking about the future," she remembered musing, ". . . because I knew what I was in for."

[II]

Many wonderful performing groups promptly fell apart in the studio. Making a record was an exacting process, not at all the loose, spontaneous joyride that galvanized a band onstage. The atmosphere, as a rule, was predominantly tense. Artists were contractually required to record three songs in as many hours. There was no audience to play off of, no outside energy or stimulus; it all took place in a vacuum, under the hard gaze of a demanding producer—Bruce Welch of the Shadows likened the role to that of God—which many artists found too "intimidating." As a creative experience, recording was plodding and intricate, especially at Abbey Road, where much of the process was reduced to a technical exercise. There was a "very strong engineering discipline" observed at the studio, prescribed times for recording, even a strict dress code among the ranks of personnel. "We all wore white lab coats when we worked," recalls longtime Abbey Road technician Alan Brown—"we," in this case, being anyone relegated to the control booths. Apprentices wore brown coats, the cleaning staff blue; only balance engineers were permitted to remove their jackets, and then only while setting up equipment. It was a finely drawn tradition; every aspect was scrutinized from above. According to Geoff Emerick, who engineered many of the Beatles' sessions, "You had to polish your shoes, [be]cause if management saw you with dirty shoes, you were in trouble." Most work was conducted in a rather austere bubble of silence. There was "a right time to speak to artists, and a right time *not* to." Above all else, as every British subject was aware, you "had to know your place."

Fortunately, the Beatles let it all roll off their backs. They took naturally to the studio environment, oblivious to most of the guidelines that kept the staff on edge. Of course, this wasn't their first session; nevertheless, its significance was deeply felt, so they showed up on time for their 2:30 P.M. rehearsal. They even wore the suits they had broken out for John's wedding.

"They didn't seem at all nervous," says Ron Richards, who conducted the three-hour rehearsal on September 4, in Studio Three. "They already knew their way around and had done enough work on their own so that we didn't have to sit and arrange every note for them." Richards, who shunned that kind of hand-holding, was a good match for the Beatles. He worked very fast and knew his way around pop music to such an extent that he covered for his "blissfully unaware" boss. Later, Richards would strike gold on his own, producing the Hollies, so it is no surprise that with the Beatles he focused on their vocal blend and harmonies. "It was obvious, right away, that they had their own *sound*. At that time, few groups came in with anything unique or identifiable, but the way they sang and played set them immediately apart." Norman Smith, who engineered the session, heard it, too, and decided to capture as much of it as he could by opening the microphones and letting the sound bleed so that it took on more of a live—that is, less slickly produced—quality. It was a risky move coming out of such a steady, well-grounded program, but ultimately it showed off the Beatles in a way that best suited them.

That afternoon the Beatles rehearsed six songs, from which they selected two to record later that evening—"Love Me Do" and the catchy but lightweight "How Do You Do It," a song Martin had selected for them, certain it would be a hit. "Love Me Do" was a concession to the band, who practically begged Martin to consider their own material. Up until then, most British pop groups recorded what was put in front of them by their producers—songs written by polished professionals that reflected an overall image the label had in mind for them. Parlophone's view of the Beatles was as performers, not songwriters. Besides, George Martin so far hadn't heard "any evidence of what was to come in the way of songwriting." Of their demos, the only songs that stood out were "P.S. I Love You"* and possibly "Love Me Do." "I thought it might have made a good 'B' side," Martin recalled, referring to "Love Me Do," but he wasn't giving them any more than that.

Martin was determined that the Beatles' first single would be "How Do You Do It." It had formula written all over it and was, indeed, the kind of song that might have passed muster with Cliff Richard and the Shadows, who remained the industry standard. But the Beatles had shied away from the Shadows' image since they first formed the band. Yes, they'd modeled themselves on more refined vocalists like the Everly Brothers, Bobby Vee, and Roy Orbison, but other influences, as well as their own developing sound, had sharpened their edge—and their perspective. Recording a song like "How Do You Do It" ran contrary to everything they stood for. The song embarrassed them. Demoralized, they complained to Brian Epstein and asked him to intercede with Martin on their behalf. But Brian didn't want to make waves. "Do it!" he insisted. "It doesn't matter if you don't like it. Do it!"

---

* *Ron Richards rejected "P.S. I Love You" because there was another record in the charts with that title, published by Campbell, Connelly, his former employer.*

Martin recorded the song with them later that evening, along with "Love Me Do," which required fifteen takes and was pressed onto an acetate for the producer's review. Much to his credit—and displaying a quality that marked his entire relationship with the Beatles—Martin kept an open mind. The Beatles were dead set against releasing "How Do You Do It." They argued: "We just don't want this kind of song. It's a different thing we're going for . . . something new." Their vehemence forced Martin to reconsider "Love Me Do," and after listening to it again, he agreed to see it their way—for now.

As it turned out, Ringo was the problem. The next day Martin and Ron Richards listened repeatedly to the acetate and determined from the playback that it lacked drive. Paul has since observed that "Ringo at that point was not *that* steady on time," and to Norman Smith's ear, "he didn't have quite enough push." The drums were too muddy, not as precise as the situation demanded. "Ringo had a lot more zest to his drumming than Pete," Richards recalls, "and I knew he'd be able to handle recording—in time. But we had a record to make and I needed someone who could deliver exactly what the song required on every take."

That afternoon Martin and Richards walked down Oxford Street, discussing how to handle it. Richards had already put in a call to Kenny Clair, "probably the top session drummer at the time . . . who was a brilliant player and could do anything." His background was big band, as opposed to rock 'n roll, but as far as recording went, he would solve their immediate problem. Martin, however, was already thinking ahead. The Beatles had put a bug into his ear about image, and he was concerned that the first record should lay it all on the line. "He knew how important it was to establish their identity," Richards says, "so we kept walking and talked about what to call them—Paul McCartney and the Beatles, or John Lennon and the Beatles." Martin felt they needed a leader out front, like Cliff and the Shadows. Paul could handle that; he was "the pretty boy" and more outgoing, whereas "John was the down-to-earth type" and the sharp wit. That could also work to the band's advantage, they decided. It was a tough choice. Paul . . . John? John . . . Paul? "It went on like that, back and forth, as we continued along Oxford Street," Richards says. Nothing emerged from their various proposed scenarios to sway things one way or the other. Each boy had enough star power to carry the group. And yet, a move like that might serve to fracture the beautiful balance they seemed to have found. The band's personality was pretty much intact—and a very important part of their appeal. There were no apparent power struggles. Besides, Martin mused, maybe the Beatles were right. Maybe this was something new and different that didn't fall into the same tired mold. "And when we got to the end, we knew it was perfect the way it was."

A week later, on September 11, the Beatles returned to Abbey Road and recorded another version of "Love Me Do." Ringo was stunned and "devastated" upon learning that a session drummer had been brought in to replace him. Kenny Clair was unavailable, but Ron Richards had booked another big band veteran, thirty-two-year-old Andy White, who performed with Vic Lewis's orchestra and had worked on numerous Parlophone sessions. "I knew he could play the beat I was looking for," says Richards, who invited Ringo to join him upstairs in the sound booth during the session.

Ringo was not pacified. When Richards asked him to play tambourine and maracas on the track, he complied "but he was not pleased." The song was hardly what anyone would consider difficult. There was no tricky time signature, no intricate pattern. "It didn't call for any drumnastics," as Bob Wooler assessed it, nothing Ringo couldn't handle in his sleep. Still, he stepped aside, silently seething, and let the trained ears prevail.

The result was a success. The Beatles cut "Love Me Do," featuring a nifty harmonica riff by John, and its flip side, "P.S. I Love You," in a little under two hours, with Ron Richards at the helm. George Martin, who had been preoccupied with his secretary, returned at the end of the session while the band was lumbering through a version of "Please Please Me." From what he could hear, it still lacked conviction. The song was slow—Martin called it "much too dreary"—patterned, as it was, on Roy Orbison's haunting delivery of "Only the Lonely." John tinkered with the vocal, roughing it up a bit, making it more bluesy and aggressive, but no matter what they tried, it never got off the ground. Most producers would have ditched the song at that point and instructed the band to move on. And perhaps if Richards had continued as point man, that might have been its fate. But Martin heard whatever it was that inspired the Beatles to pursue the song in the first place. In fact, it was "obvious" to him how to rescue "Please Please Me." Rather than cast it aside, he suggested they pick up the tempo and "work out some tight harmonies." They could "have another go at it" the next time they were in the studio.

September was particularly hot that year. Thanks to the North Atlantic Drift and its entourage of warm winds, the normally pleasant nights remained uncomfortably sticky throughout the month. Clumps of soggy

Irish moss, garbage, and dead fish collected in oily pools around the docks, cooking during the day and unleashing a black, marshy stench that by nightfall closed around one's mouth and tasted of the ripe sea. Few places in Liverpool enjoyed the luxury of air-conditioning. The Cavern, especially, was a sweatbox, and by eight o'clock, with two hundred teenagers whipping themselves into a frenzy in the smoke-filled, airless cellar, body heat vaporized on the ceiling and streamed down the walls until the floors were puddled in slime. Every so often a wilted dancer would keel over, sometimes unnoticed until the music stopped, and have to be carried up the stairs, to recover in the street. Or tempers would overheat, with the inevitable punch-up that would follow. How the club avoided an outbreak of malaria is anyone's guess.

Somehow, the Beatles never complained. Not even when Brian demanded they wear the new mohair suits he'd picked out to spruce up their "undesirable" image. All his energies went into grooming the Beatles for stardom, and now with a record coming out and the need to "open doors" in places that frowned on black leather, he decided they should dress for success, even at the Cavern, where the attire that September was decidedly receding. Later, John would mark the suits as a turning point in the band's eventual climb, noting that from the moment they put them on, they'd more or less sold out to the showbiz establishment. He'd blame the outfits on Paul, who, he said, caved in all too willingly to that kind of pretense, but at the time, all of the Beatles complied—and quite "gladly," as George noted—believing in the long run that it would broaden their appeal.

To the Beatles' fans, suits were a very big deal—leather jackets, black T-shirts, and dark jeans had been their trademark. Brian had tipped off Bob Wooler about the new outfits, and the exuberant disc jockey played it for all it was worth. "Hey, listen, Cavernites," he teased a lunchtime crowd on the day of their forthcoming show, "the next time the Beatles appear on this stage they'll be wearing their *brand-new suits.* Now, this is going to be a *revelation!* We've never seen them in suits before, so be sure to be here for the unveiling." Even Wooler admits that "there was a touch of the Barnum and Bailey in this," but it was too good to resist. Even Ray McFall, the Cavern's huffy owner, caught the fever and ordered the ceiling covered in a new coat of white emulsion paint to celebrate the momentous event.

That night happened to be a scorcher. It had rained earlier in the day, and moisture hung in the thick air like clotted cream, none of which deterred an overly large crowd from descending into the Cavern right on schedule. It seemed like "an extra two hundred kids turned out" to check out the young emperors' new clothes—and they weren't disappointed. The Beatles looked resplendent and, in their manager's eyes, finally like proper entertainers. They "actually glowed" as they took the stage, slightly embarrassed in front of the hometown crowd, but not enough to diminish their obvious pride. Unfortunately, that mood didn't last very long. No one had taken into account what heat did to new paint, and as the temperature climbed, water condensed on the ceiling and ultimately the emulsion dripped, splattering their new clothes.

It was Brian, not the Beatles, who emerged from the episode enraged. Convinced that the Liverpool scene was run with the maximum ineptitude, he began to see catastrophe in every piece of business outside of his control. The only solution was to take matters into his own hands, beginning with the release of "Love Me Do," which would not, under any circumstances, be left to chance. Thanks to NEMS, Brian had an insider's knowledge of how record companies operated. Most threw a dozen new records out there each week in the hope that one of them caught fire. The Beatles weren't a priority of EMI's, but they were *his* priority. And he intended to do everything in his power to ensure that they got the best shot.

First on Brian's crowded agenda was publicity. Drawing on the previous contacts he had made, Brian touched base once again with Tony Barrow, who was still working for Decca, and notified him that the Beatles' debut record would finally appear in a month. "He'd been picking my brains on the phone from Liverpool for almost a year," Barrow recalls, "relying on my relationships with guys at *NME* [*New Musical Express*] and *Melody Maker.*" Now Brian wanted Barrow to work for him, doing independent PR from behind his desk, of all things, at a rival record label. On the face of it, the proposal appeared dicey, but Barrow replied that he saw no conflict as long as it didn't require him to pound the pavement at the music trades. To avoid the appearance of impropriety, Barrow enlisted Andrew Loog Oldham, a "flamboyant" eighteen-year-old hustler "with an attitude," to cover the press while he concentrated on writing releases. "I put together the original press manual on the Beatles, along with some biography on each of them that Brian intended to send out to the media," says Barrow.

The stuff Barrow turned out was dry as toast, rewrites of the fluff spun out by the girls who ran the Beatles Fan Club. ("John . . . likes the colour black, steak and chips and jelly . . . and dislikes—thick heads and traditional jazz." "Paul . . . favours black polo necked sweaters, suits, leather and suede." "George . . . enjoys egg and chips, Carl Perkins and Eartha Kitt, and wants nothing more than to retire with lots of money.") Brian wasn't fooled. "He suggested the whole thing be written with more of an edge," Barrow says, "harder, more colorful, punchier stuff about each boy." To draw attention to the unusual spelling of the band's name, he insisted they include an apocryphal story of John's about an odd man descending with a flaming pie delivering the news that they shall forevermore be Beatles—*with an a.* "Then he pushed me to do a review of the record, right up front in the press kit, under the name Disker of the *Liverpool Echo.*" Initially, Barrow refused on the grounds that it smelled bad, not to mention the vaguest whiff of dishonesty, but for enough money, it was easy to rationalize. Says Barrow: "I was a hack being paid a fee to do some writing. And, after all, I *was* impressed with 'Love Me Do.'" Eventually, Brian decided to blanket the media with these press kits to supplement EMI's beleaguered in-house staff.

The next challenge was airplay. "It was a hell of a job trying to get 'Love Me Do' on the radio," recalls Ron Richards, who moonlighted as Parlophone's promotion man. "At that time, there weren't many programs on the BBC where you could get a pop record played." The most obvious show was a Sunday morning countdown of the charts, one of the top-rated shows, which all labels courted. Richards was friendly with its producer, Ron Belchier, who promised to give the Beatles a special listen. But when Richards called back for a reaction, he was told, "No, they're too amateurish for me." Richards was understandably dejected. He knew that without significant BBC airplay, the Beatles didn't stand a chance. There was no other reasonable way to effect a breakout (or to launch them).

The disappointment must have been evident in his voice, because Belchier took pity and recommended that Ron try a new show—its name long since forgotten—that the Beeb was starting on Saturday mornings to showcase young groups. Richards immediately sent over a demo (the label misidentified Paul's writing credit as McArtney, which was corrected on the eventual release) and won a precious slot in the rotation. "They promised to play it," he remembers, "and it felt like we'd won the lottery."

But they still had to convince Radio Luxembourg. It was the only station that played pop nonstop, with a signal beamed directly into London's teenage market. To ply goodwill, EMI flew its tastemakers to Luxembourg twice a year, in order to wine and dine the station's deejays and play the new lineup. "Then, we came back [to the U.K.]," scoffs a promo man, "and they forgot about our records and played somebody else's."

When "Love Me Do" appeared, on October 5, it received only scant attention on the station. For one thing, there was too much competition from abroad: "Sheila," by Tommy Roe; Little Eva's "The Loco-Motion" (which had been cowritten by Carole King, whose own single, "It Might as Well Rain Until September," was running up the charts); Gene Pitney's "Only Love Can Break a Heart"; the 4 Seasons' debut smash, "Sherry"; "Let's Dance," by Chris Montez; as well as new records by Elvis, Ray Charles, Neil Sedaka, and Del Shannon. But while "Love Me Do" had a nice little pop groove to it, reinforced by John's portentous bluesy harmonica intro (fashioned after the one Delbert McClinton played on "Hey! Baby"), its stripped-down lyric and molasses-paced beat, which quite needlessly jolts to a standstill at the end of the break, failed to convey the bold energy the Beatles personally felt toward rock 'n roll. It didn't give disk jockeys anything to sink their teeth into. There was the flood of competing British releases to consider, which left hardly any opening for new artists, much less the Beatles. Even Parlophone was chagrined by the apparent lack of effort coming from its parent, EMI, and further annoyed by the meager two thousand records that were initially issued, the standard pressing at the time for new, unproven artists. Despite its seeming lack of interest, however, EMI did buy time for the Beatles to appear on the October 12 segment of Radio Luxembourg's *The Friday Spectacular*, a kind of live studio party that featured new releases, which it hoped would at least stir some interest in the record.

For a time it appeared to be an uphill battle. Tony Barrow played "Love Me Do" for London's top deejay, Jimmy Saville—later an intimate friend of the Beatles, but back then a force to reckon with—who was "unimpressed." The same response occurred when the boys polled around for reaction on their own. Dot Rhone, who had rented the basement flat below John and Cynthia, recalls being invited upstairs one night in early October and being asked by John to phone Radio Luxembourg to request "Love Me Do." Dot didn't mind doing the favor. John had shown enormous sympathy following her breakup with Paul, going so far as to give her the rent sometimes when she was short. There was no problem getting a deejay on the phone, nor responding that it was "fantastic" when he asked her personal opinion of the song. But her heart skipped when, out of the blue, the deejay confessed he "wasn't at all that thrilled with it." It startled Dot, and it must have shown on her face, because as soon as she hung up, John sneered: "He didn't like it, did he?"

Nevertheless, the record flew out of the stores in Liverpool, especially at NEMS, where it was promoted as though Elvis had put in a personal appearance there. Hundreds were sold in the week following its release, though there was no danger of its ever going out of stock. "Love Me Do" reached a respectable if unspectacular number on the British charts, thanks, in large part, to those heavy sales in the North. "Brian bought boxes and boxes of 'Love Me Do,'" recalls Alistair Taylor. "Later, when it came onto the charts, he bought several thousand more, hoping to push it higher and draw more attention to it, but after a while we realized that it could only go so far."

The Beatles, however, were headed to the toppermost of the poppermost.

[III]

With hardly any time to catch their breath, the Beatles kept another appointment at Abbey Road, on November 26, to undertake a follow-up to "Love Me Do." Despite the fact that the record had stalled, there wasn't much financially at stake from the label's standpoint. "EMI never gave us any budget," says Ron Richards. "We'd decide to record an artist and simply set up studio time." Nevertheless, George Martin preferred to oversee the session himself. Initially, the label chief may have shown ambivalent faith in the Beatles, but he had seen and heard enough to fire up his optimism. What's more, he suspected the label had a real shot at breaking this band, especially considering a secret weapon: "How Do You Do It." Martin remained convinced that the song was a hit; after the Beatles retooled their previous version, he believed, they could ride its coattails to stardom.

But once inside the studio, the band almost immediately began hustling Martin to record a song of their own. Exasperated, Martin grew peevish with their defiance and snapped: "When you can write material as good as this, then I'll record it."

Such a rebuke would have silenced most bands, but the Beatles saw it as an opportunity. They reminded Martin about "Please Please Me," a version of which was already in the can. "We've revamped it," they explained, angling for a chance to convince him of its merits. Gradually, their persistence and endearing Scouse charm wore down Martin's defenses, and once more, to his credit, the producer relented.

Without hesitation, they ran through a take of the song that incorporated all of Martin's suggestions. It was no longer dreary or overblown; the Roy Orbison influence had been carefully pared away. In fact, it bore hardly any resemblance to the demo they had cut with Ron Richards eight weeks earlier. Martin "knew right away" he had something special on his hands, but he checked his enthusiasm, suggesting instead that they give it a try together to see what turned up. It was a huge concession. It meant he was once more shelving "How Do You Do It" to take a flier on an unpolished Lennon and McCartney song.

"Please Please Me" may have been unpolished, but not unexceptional. Only a sigh longer than two minutes, it rocked the lofty studio like a small explosion, its beat unleashed to startling intensity: a bass throbbing faster than an accelerated heartbeat, a cascading harmonica riff as joyful as birdsong, a lead vocal that drives like a sports car with a hole in its muffler, harmonies that soar and clutch each other for dear life, a convulsion of "c'mons" that churns up tension and desire. Throughout, the song sends spikes of exclamation and falsetto raging through the lyric. Not since Little Richard had vocals raged so viscerally in a pop song.

"Please Please Me" was the world's real introduction to the Beatles. It was a stark concentration of the band's emerging sound—catchy melodies, clever lyrics, seamless three-part harmonies, nimble instrumentation, and dynamic chords dropped into patterns that transformed a tired form. John's vocal is about as raw and rough-edged as anything to come out of the British pop scene—and distinctive. He makes no effort to sound boyish or cute; there is an aggression in his voice, a tenacity loaded with innuendo that digs right into the suggestive lyric. Paul's bass lines are already synthesizing elements of a dramatic style, accenting the standard runs with sudden shifts of phrasing and hiccups that later revolutionized the form. The way his bass and George's guitar recoil from the four "c'mons" sounds almost as if they are being jerked away from the melody. And Ringo forever dispels any notion of his ineffectiveness in the recording process by providing a precise, sharply dealt backbeat, which cuts loose at the end of the song, with a crisp, machine-gun burst of percussion.

Critics tend to credit "I Saw Her Standing There" and "All My Loving" with setting off the initial blast of Beatlemania, but "Please Please Me" was the spark that lit its fuse. It was a rejection of all the sugarcoated pop that had clogged the British charts for more than five years. In its place, the Beatles had assembled fragments of their favorite American hits, borrowing from the Everly Brothers, Eddie Cochran, and Buddy Holly, and given the resulting mosaic a bold personal touch.

One can only imagine what George Martin felt when listening to the playback. A man schooled in the formalities of classical music, it must have rattled his bones to hear the track he had just produced. It was so far outside the parameters of his own taste, not to mention what colleagues considered to be well beyond his grasp. Martin was an old-school music man.

He believed in good, carefully structured songwriting, tight arrangements, very controlled orchestration, and pitch-perfect acoustics—all of which resonated in the cracks of "Please Please Me," but with a remarkable new vibrancy. "Please Please Me" rocked! Martin knew it the moment he heard the tape. Grinning, he looked up over the console and exclaimed: "Gentlemen, you've just made your first number one record."

Yet the Beatles didn't feel like stars. In part, of course, this was because they were virtually unknown outside of Liverpool. The surrounding cities— places like Manchester, Leeds, Sheffield, and Birmingham—nurtured their own hometown pop heroes who had built a loyal following in much the same way the Beatles had done at the Cavern. Promoting a Liverpool band in Manchester was like asking the United fans there to root for the Anfield soccer team. Even the French could expect to be shown more courtesy. If "Love Me Do" managed to explode, then the Beatles could march through distant clubs on their own terms; but until that happened, they were more or less restricted to playing gigs closer to home.

Still, there were plenty to go around, and throughout the fall of 1962 Brian made sure their collective dance card was filled. He worked furiously to keep them busy and in front of as many kids as possible, believing that exposure, more than anything, would contribute to their success. "He spent all day on the phone, booking the gigs himself," says Frieda Kelly, whose desk sat in an alcove outside Brian's office door. "The second he hung up on one person, he was already dialing another." Often, unable to endure an indecisive promoter, he toggled between two lines, juggling dates and deals like a harried stockbroker. "He was a very impatient man. Everything had to be done by his clock. And if he didn't get the answer he wanted, he pushed harder and harder."

And more steadily. There weren't enough hours in the day; there weren't enough days in the week. As time wore on, Brian devoted only cursory attention to NEMS, laying off most of the administrative responsibilities onto his brother, Clive. Even when the store closed at midday on Wednesdays, he stayed rooted to his desk, his assistants working the phones and typewriters, going at a breakneck pace. No one took time off.

Because he remained so insecure, Brian often accepted offers for the band that fell way beneath their current stature—ridiculous gigs at cinemas, floral halls, and jive hives—to keep up the appearance of surplus bookings. These were interspersed with enough big shows to keep the money respectable, but eventually Brian sought a bigger share of the pie.

Ballrooms and arenas guaranteed larger paydays, which gave him another idea about upping the ante.

In preparation, he met promoter Sam Leach at the Kardomah Café and proposed what he thought was an intriguing deal. The objective, he explained, was to book the Beatles onto shows headlined by established stars; that way, he could command a larger fee and, at the same time, link the Beatles to popular recording artists. All he needed was the proper venue. Locally, there was only the Tower Ballroom, a massive hall that Leach had locked up under contract every weekend throughout the year. "I will book big names and we'll do it together," Brian said. "How does that sound?"

To most ears, it would have sounded crazy. But Leach was thinking ahead. Convinced that the Beatles were on the verge of stardom, he thought: "If I do this, we might do other things together." Secretly, he'd always wanted to manage the Beatles; perhaps this would lead to some kind of co-operative arrangement. Besides, he'd started a little independent label, Troubadour Records, which in June 1961 had released a single by Gerry and the Pacemakers; even though the Beatles already had a Parlophone contract, their record might bomb and he could wind up holding an option on their next effort. So instead of dismissing Brian's offer out of hand, Sam said: "All right then, Brian. I'll do it. Fifty-fifty."

It was more than gracious, but Brian balked. Dismissively, he explained, as if lecturing an employee: "That would be impossible. I'm in [business] with Clive, who is a part of NEMS. We'll have to share a third each." Leach, predictably, refused to budge, at which point Brian stood up to leave. "You've made a very big mistake," he warned, his voice barely above a whisper.

Leach went directly to John, who wrenched a few leftover dates out of Brian. But, as usual, financial hijinks followed. "Sam had a habit of not paying groups," says Bob Wooler. "There was always an excuse. But he'd charm them, [saying]: 'I'll book you next time, and you can rest assured there will be a double fee.'"

Brian had heard that one once too often and finally pulled the plug minutes before the Beatles were due to go onstage at the Tower. "This meant war," Leach recalled. "The Beatles were now finished there, and without them, so was I. That forced me to book bigger attractions to compensate." Desperate, Leach called Don Arden, a notoriously hard-assed promoter who toured fading American stars around Europe, and begged for one of his Little Richard dates. Banking on big advance ticket sales, he promised Arden £350, "to be paid in cash before [Little Richard] goes on." Arden promised to shoot off a contract, but before he could get it in the mail, Brian Epstein offered £500. Money, money, money—Arden couldn't resist. Meanwhile, Leach had papered Liverpool with advertisements for the show: SAM PRESENTS LITTLE RICHARD AT THE TOWER! "Even before the Beatles exploded, Brian viewed himself as an impresario," says Peter Brown. "There was always that infatuation with *presenting* someone, and with concerts he could do it in an area that expanded his control and influence."

As Brian saw it, the local concert business seemed rightfully his. He understood its simple mechanics, had the financial wherewithal to promote successful shows, knew the bands, knew whose records sold, had ties to the press. And he viewed Liverpool's existing gang of promoters with undisguised scorn.

No longer was Brian Epstein seeking cover in the shadows. Now he was vying to take over the scene. The soft-spoken record-shop owner who pleaded rock 'n roll ignorance was gone. That persona had been replaced by a vigorous, opinionated businessman who began to view himself as a power broker.

Brian printed posters and hiked ticket prices to an "unheard-of twelve and six," according to Sam Leach, to ensure a tidy profit. In fact, the show was so successful that he took another date, this time at the classy Empire Theatre, on Sunday, October 28, for which he doubled the advertising budget. And in every case the Beatles' name appeared in the same type size—and was given the same prominence—as Little Richard's. Fans, watching in awe, concluded that "the Beatles had really hit the big time." Sitting in the audience that evening, Frieda Kelly says she grew melancholy. "When I saw them on the stage of the Empire, I knew they were no longer ours."

———

Immediately following the Little Richard shows, the entire entourage left for Hamburg, where the Beatles fulfilled an outstanding obligation at their old haunt, the Star-Club. When they returned, on November 14, things cranked into high gear. Without time to recharge, the band made a beeline for London, where two days later they performed for another intimate audience of teenagers on a show that went out over Radio Luxembourg. Tony Barrow, who had never seen them perform, marveled at the spell they seemed to cast over the room at EMI headquarters. Standing near the side of a makeshift stage, in an office that had been specially converted to simulate a club atmosphere, he was unprepared for the audience reaction as the Beatles were introduced.

Muriel Young, the show's host, announced: "I'm going to bring on a new band now who've just got their first record into the charts, and their names are John, Paul . . ."

"Immediately," Barrow recalls, "the kids started screaming." This caught him by surprise. "I'd never experienced anything like it before. The Beatles, at this time, were basically unknown. But if this bunch of kids in London had gotten as far as finding out the individual band members' names, then it was a phenomenon of some kind, which, to me, was extremely significant."

What provoked such a reaction? It is difficult to say. "Love Me Do" had received only scant airplay so far, not enough to spark a popular groundswell. Barrow suspects the APPLAUSE! sign had little to do with it, either, judging from the look on the kids' faces. "They were genuinely excited," he says. "They knew the song; they knew about the band. It had to be spontaneous, to some extent. But if you ask me, that special Beatles mystique was already at work." At the time, such a phenomenon was unknown, even puzzling. This was London, after all, not the provinces. Bands didn't simply wander into the city and take it by storm. But the jungle drums were already beating through cultural channels. Word of mouth traveled from town to town, from city to city, via teenagers who had seen the Beatles on the cinema circuit.

"Everyone had said, 'You'll never make [it], coming from Liverpool,'" Paul remembered. When, in late 1962, Bill Harry wrote an article about the vibrant Liverpool music scene in *Mersey Beat*, beseeching record-company moguls in London to "take a look up North," not a single A&R man responded.

Others knew the score. Alistair Taylor, who left NEMS that November to work in London for Pye Records, knew from the moment Brian signed the Beatles that they were his ticket south. Says Tony Bramwell, then a NEMS office boy, "No one ever mentioned London, but it was understood we'd eventually be going there. Brian had a plan; he wanted to be Larry Parnes and swim in a big pond." Everything would be in-house: "His own press officer, booking agent, television liaison—we'd all be under his thumb," says Tony Barrow. "It was unheard-of."

Brian certainly made no secret of his intention to dismiss the publishing firm Ardmore & Beechwood, who, according to George Martin, "did virtually nothing about getting ["Love Me Do"] played." It incensed Brian that their professional managers, or song pluggers, couldn't point to five or ten outlets they'd helped persuade to play the Beatles. Not even a single ad was placed by them in any of the music papers. Why should he add another Lennon-McCartney song to their catalogue? He could have done as well with "Love Me Do" on his own, without giving away the publisher's share of the royalties.

George Martin provided the names of three alternatives—all of whom, he promised, "won't rip you off." The first one Brian went to see on the list was Dick James.

Calling Dick James a publisher was like calling Brian an impresario. A former big band singer with a gregarious, music hall personality and ever-present smile, James, who was forty-four, had been in business for himself for only a year, and with very little to show for it. There were no major hits in his portfolio and only a handful of potential standouts. But what he lacked in assets, he made up for in connections. Although James was no longer a performer, he claimed a wide network of show-business friends left over from his moderately successful run as a recording artist. In the mid-1950s, he'd enjoyed a string of popular hits—most notably "Tenderly" and the theme song to TV's *Robin Hood,* both of which had been produced by George Martin. Dick and George had stayed in touch throughout the years. James had spent a decade toiling for various London music publishers, resolutely sending their demos to Parlophone for Martin's consideration. "How Do You Do It" represented his biggest break to date, and he was crestfallen when he learned the Beatles had rejected it.

James, whose cubbyhole office was on Charing Cross Road in the heart of London's music district, hadn't been floored by the impact of "Love Me Do." Though it placed at forty-nine on the *Record Mirror* Top 100 chart, he considered the tune nothing more than "a riff" and consequently had no expectations as far as any other songs written by the northern writers who were responsible for it. Still, he was curious to hear what appealed to an act that had the nerve to reject his own hottest prospect.

As luck would have it, Brian had brought along an acetate of "Please Please Me," and as soon as James heard it he knew: it was *better* than "How Do You Do It." Infinitely better—a smash. Without hesitating, he offered to publish it. Two months earlier Brian might have jumped at the chance, but with each successive professional experience, he grew more skeptical and restrained. What, he demanded bluntly, did Dick James intend to bring to the table? How would he contribute to the record's promotion?

As the story goes, James swallowed his answer. Instead, he immediately picked up the phone and called Philip Jones, who produced a new prime-time television show called *Thank Your Lucky Stars.* Giving the performance of his career, Dick James instructed Jones to listen to "a guaranteed future hit," then held the receiver up to a speaker blaring "Please Please Me." Incredibly enough, Jones heard enough to interest him and, with the publisher urging him on, agreed to present the Beatles on an upcoming show.

Brian Epstein was stunned. Next to *Juke Box Jury*, this was the most influential spot on television that a recording artist could hope for. It meant national exposure, something EMI hadn't produced with all its supposed firepower. Nothing like this had been offered to him before.

Brian and Dick James did everything but jump into each others' arms. The wily James had already formulated a deal. Instead of the usual song-by-song arrangement favored by many British publishers—including EMI's deal with the Beatles—James had something novel up his sleeve. According to George Martin, "Dick said, 'Why don't we sign . . . their future writing to a company which the Beatles would partly own?'" On the surface, it seemed like a magnanimous—and radical—offer. Most publishers got 50 percent of an artist's performance royalties in addition to a cut of the sheet-music sales. ("By today's terms," Martin says, "if you accepted that, you'd be considered an idiot.") James suggested creating a separate company—Northern Songs—that would publish all Lennon-McCartney songs and be administered by Dick James Music. Of this new venture, royalties would be split evenly (instead of James taking the standard 100 percent of the publishing rights and 50 percent of the writers' royalties), albeit with a 10 percent fee taken *off the top* by Dick James Music. "Brian thought it was wonderful," Martin recalled. And without hesitation, he recommended it to John and Paul.

Forty years later, Paul McCartney, in nearly every reminiscence, goes out of his way to curse the Northern Songs pact as "a slave deal"—and worse. He believes they were bamboozled out of the rights to their songs and, ultimately, untold millions of dollars, saying: "Dick James's entire empire was built on our backs." But at the time, it must have sounded like a sweetheart of an offer. When they were asked if they wanted to read the agreement, John and Paul declined. It called for Northern Songs to acquire Lenmac Enterprises, a holding company set up in April by Brian that owned fifty-nine Lennon-McCartney songs. Under the terms of the agreement, John and Paul were obligated to write only six songs per year for the next four years. During that time, however, they would add an extraordinary hundred new copyrights to the catalogue, each one a classic that would never again be under their control.

[I]

Only days after the release of their latest single, the Beatles viewed their Saturday, January 19, 1963, appearance on *Thank Your Lucky Stars* as a major plug for "Please Please Me." (At the afternoon rehearsal they learned that the spots were all "mimed" to records, which allowed them to more or less walk through the two-minute segment.) The audience was completely unprepared for what they saw. Gliding eerily across the screen were four extraordinary-looking boys, grinning at one another with goofy joy from beneath mops of unhumanly long hair and behaving like cuddly wind-up toys—heads bobbing on an invisible spring, shoulders seesawing to the beat, bodies jerking back and forth—in a manner reminiscent of a *Carry On* gang send-up. No one had ever seen hair that long—or that shape—before. Was it some kind of a joke? And their suits broke all the rules; they were smart and relaxed, with a nod to the tradition of good English tailoring, but also a wink in the way they were buttoned to the neck.

Once viewers got past the window dressing, the music knocked them out cold. Hearing "Please Please Me" had the same effect as being thrown into an icy shower. After sitting through thirty-eight minutes of warm, sudsy pop, this bracing rock 'n roll song cut right to the bone. The intro alone hit a nerve. The tone of it was powerful, unrelenting. *Listen to this:* "Last night I said these words to m-y-y-y- g-i-r-r-r-l . . ." *Harmonies!* Gorgeous three-part vocals, followed by a dramatic explosion of ascending guitar chords. "Please *pleeeeeease* me, wo-yeah, like I please . . ." And that finish—five sharp, emphatically executed chords wrapped up in a sustained burst of drumbeats—left the whole thing vibrating with uncommon energy.

A bomb had gone off. British rock 'n roll had arrived.

In the next three years, the Beatles would be joined by the Olympian forces of British rock: the Rolling Stones, the Kinks, the Who, the Yardbirds, the Animals, the Moody Blues, the Hollies, Van Morrison, Manfred Mann, and Traffic, as well as virtually the entire Merseybeat roster—all of them swept in on the vast tide of musicians and personalities that transformed the popular culture. Plenty of others contributed to the exuberant groundswell, from artists (Hockney) to critics (Tynan) to photographers (Bailey) to designers (Quant) to writers (Fleming), but none of them caused such a stir as did the Beatles; none was as personable or as newsworthy; none was so innocent that every exploit, every record seemed genuinely fresh and unspoiled by creeping commercialism. "To those of us in England who lived for the next great American single," says journalist Ray Connolly, "it seemed like the Beatles were the promise we'd been waiting for all our lives."

Unlike "Love Me Do," which had scrounged for random airplay, "Please Please Me" echoed everywhere. Radio Luxembourg had added it right out of the box, and not the occasional spotty play they begrudged to borderline new releases but the kind of all-out saturation that indicated a smash. The same happened at the BBC, where it immediately cracked the teenage playlists, then crept ever so gently into the "light programming" shows. Critics—including some who had found fault with "Love Me Do"—raved. By the end of the month, a year after being told the Beatles were inappropriate for radio, Brian was fielding offers from a variety of producers for appearances on such important shows as *The Friday Spectacular, People and Places, Saturday Club, The Talent Spot,* and *Here We Go.*

The mood in the overcrowded headquarters of NEMS was irrepressibly upbeat. Since the beginning of the year, the management end of the business had taken on a momentum of its own, sustained mostly by the Beatles but intensified by some fresh roster moves Brian had made, as well as others in the works. Plans were now under way for the release of Gerry and the Pacemakers' first record—the resurrected "How Do You Do It," produced by George Martin—which was scheduled for the end of January. And sensing some ground gained at EMI, Brian also signed the Big Three, in the hope of grooming them for a session with one of the company's labels. "Things were going so well," recalls Tony Bramwell, "that he started believing he had the magic touch."

Indeed, Brian so enjoyed the deal-making aspect that he decided to develop another artist almost from scratch. Since the end of the previous year, he'd had his eye on a shy, plump-faced boy with unobvious good looks named Billy Ashton. Ashton's voice was as thin as watered-down soup, he moved awkwardly onstage, and those loud, black-and-pink suits he favored didn't fool anyone. But Brian, according to Alistair Taylor, "probably fancied the lad" and was full of his own "star-making" potential. "Brian knew Billy couldn't sing," says Taylor, but he wouldn't allow a little thing like that to get in the way, "because [Billy] had the right image; he was a good-looking, clean-cut, impressionable young lad who could *approximately* sing, which would more than do."

Decades later, Billy Kramer (Brian changed his name, thinking Ashton "too posh") would be asked to account for Brian Epstein's interest in his career. Shrugging, he says, "I was just a wild card," meaning an inconsequential component. "It could have been anybody, when you think about it."

[II]

Up until a year earlier, Brian Epstein's only experience with rock 'n roll had been ordering records to stock the bins at his father's store. Now he had to organize—relying mostly on his imagination—a full-blown management company substantial in size and complicated in detail. The duties were no longer limited to penciling in local club appearances but now involved recording dates, radio appearances, press interviews, label and contract negotiations, transportation, overnight accommodations, and fan mail. There were fees to be collected, weekly salaries paid (each of the Beatles received a paycheck of £50 every Friday), schedules coordinated, equipment purchased, wardrobe fitted. And Brian handled everything himself—every phone call, every booking, every piece of mail, every arrangement: every decision. There were assistants to do the legwork, but the responsibility was entirely his.

It was a demanding but manageable workload that Brian had undertaken. But with the success of "Please Please Me," all hell broke loose. Sales were strong, stronger than anything EMI had expected, requiring repeated pressings to satisfy demand. And in Liverpool the impact was explosive. Now every time the band came in to see Brian, be it for routine business or to root through stacks of fan mail, extreme measures had to be taken to provide for their safety. "Whenever word spread that the boys were inside, kids started coming around the shop, blocking the doors so the ordinary customers couldn't get in," Frieda Kelly remembers. After so many years of complete informality, it seemed downright unfriendly, if not hostile, to suddenly throw up barriers. Eventually, Norris explains, the hard-core fans refused to leave NEMS until the Beatles came downstairs, so Brian would send the boys out the second-floor fire escape, onto the roof, where a cast-iron ladder lowered them to safety on busy Whitechapel.

Harry Epstein wasn't pleased. His business—Liverpool's foremost appliance store—had become a hangout for crowds of Beatles fans that often snowballed into thirty or forty kids. More and more, when Harry returned from lunch with Clive they had to fight their way inside. Brian did his best to propose remedies—"I'll ask Bob Wooler to have a word with the kids," he promised—but the inconvenience grew only worse. Harry put his foot down: Brian had to look for another place to conduct his new venture.

It couldn't have come at a worse time. The Beatles were set to embark on their first major tour—dead-last on a six-act bill headlined by Helen Shapiro, the teenage pop sensation who reigned as Britain's Sweetheart. A poised, showbiz-style belter with a megawatt personality, often described by friends as "a pint-sized Ethel Merman" (although Teresa Brewer was probably more apropos), Shapiro had racked up several middle-of-the-road hits and a following that was rock-solid in the provinces. The Beatles were "elated" to appear on the bill. In their book, Helen Shapiro was a star, even though she sang what John openly referred to as "mush."

"The Beatles made little or no impression on the first few nights of the tour," singer Kenny Lynch, one of the other performers, recalled years later. "They played their hearts out, like everyone else, but it would have taken a blowtorch to get those audiences to warm to us." The response in Bradford, and again in Doncaster, reflected the brutal chill gripping England, especially in the Northeast, where the flatlands, naked and defenseless, were hammered by howling North Sea winds. There was little cheer in the lonely towns around Yorkshire that winter. Blizzards—one right after another—had ripped across the country, isolating villages and their people from one another, and a fresh covering of snow, layered in strata on the pitted roads, swept down from Scotland, keeping many of the faithful fans away. The Beatles appear not to have minded the inconvenience. Even the shabby accommodations—fifteen-shilling guesthouses, some of which "looked like something out of Vincent Price's cellar"—failed to dampen their spirits. As John noted, they were happy "just to get out of Liverpool and [to] break new ground." Those dire jive-hall gigs, the endless lunchtime sessions, even Hamburg, where they were regarded as stars—all had run their course, and the Beatles, bored and restless, aspired to new challenges, no matter the Siberian conditions.

By the time they reached Carlisle, the ice had thawed. At the ABC Cinema, a grand, slightly tattered, old picture palace where they were booked to play two shows, the seats were packed with kids who had been shut inside all month. Besides the insurgent relief they felt, there was palpable anticipation in the room. "Please Please Me" was proving an efficient calling card. The record—along with fairly heavy buzz dispatched by favorable disc jockeys—had sparked serious interest in the Beatles, and fans scattered among the crowd began to react with tremendous enthusiasm. Gordon Sampson, covering the show for *NME,* found the behavior incredible. A buildup for the Beatles erupted from the moment the houselights went down, as "the audience repeatedly called for them while other artists were performing." The response was unprecedented.

That night the Beatles were fourth on the bill, following three professionally tight but insipid acts. Kenny Lynch was on right before them. Before he left the stage, a murmur was rippling through the hall. "It was clear from the middle of my set," Lynch recalls, "that [the] audience was waiting for them." Lynch remained onstage while his backing band unplugged their instruments and fled, then looked into the wings for his cue. John and George, standing practically on top of each other, waggled the necks of their guitars. Lynch put the microphone to his lips and said, "And now . . ." But the rest of it was drowned out by an uproar as the Beatles bounded onto the stage.

Looking back over the Beatles' set, the repertoire seems unexceptional. They opened with a jaunty cover version of "Chains," then more covers— "Keep Your Hands Off My Baby" and "A Taste of Honey"—which provided a comfort zone for the audience who expected as much, no more and no less, from young British bands. But the Beatles' showmanship, that mix of aggression coupled with those dazzling, seductive smiles they'd hit upon at the Cavern and perfected in Hamburg, scored instantly with the kids. And it was in sharp contrast to the canned arrangements pumped out by the previous bands. By the time they launched into "Please Please Me"—jacking up the excitement with that raucous harmonica-bass intro and shaking their heads in unison—the place just went wild.

"I think the Beatles shook those crowds up, even scared them a little," says Kenny Lynch, who watched every set from the cinema wings. "They were so different, so tight, so confident, really playing their hearts out. It was like no experience those kids ever had before. Every girl thought they were singing straight to her, every boy saw himself standing in their place.

"It all changed from that night. We took a break a day or two later, before the next leg of the tour, but when we went back out on the road you could tell the whole balance had shifted, because all anyone wanted to hear was the Beatles."

The next day, instead of accompanying the coach tour to Peterborough, the Beatles traveled by van to London, where, on Monday, February 11, they were expected at Abbey Road. Just before the tour began, George Martin had contacted Brian Epstein about plans to schedule another recording session, this time for an album to be released sometime that spring. Martin was determined to capitalize on the success of the first two singles. "Please Please Me" had shot to number five on the charts, and conventional wisdom dictated that an album sold best shortly after a single broke into the Top Twenty, which is when most kids would decide to buy it. That meant working fast to get an album into the stores before the record peaked.

It also left little time to come up with a concept. For a while, George Martin toyed with the idea of recording a live album. He'd been captivated by the raw energy of the Beatles' Cavern performances and thought that if there was somehow a way to duplicate the magic of it—if he could sneak the outside world into the party for a night—then the songs would take care of themselves. That sounded good in theory, but it soon became evident to him that the logistics for such a session made the reality impossible. This wasn't like recording the cast album for *Beyond the Fringe*, when his producer sat under a stage for three nights, operating a tape recorder. Acoustically, the Cavern was a nightmare, all cement-and-brick entrails, with nothing to absorb the reverberation. They'd never be able to control sound levels or get any kind of balance there. And how would they mix those gorgeous harmonies? Or cover up the inevitable clams? It was more practical, Martin decided, to work in a controlled environment.

Instead, Martin prepared a list of fourteen songs—highlights gleaned from the Cavern sessions—and suggested that the Beatles run down all of them when they got to the studio. To fill the album, they needed ten songs in addition to the two singles and their B-sides, and from their repertoire Martin had selected mostly covers—some pop hits, a few rock 'n roll gems, a schmaltzy ballad or two—along with a number of Lennon-McCartney songs to show off their originality. The entire album had to be cut in a day-long, ten-hour session.

To complicate matters, sessions ran "strictly to time" at Abbey Road, which meant working from ten o'clock in the morning until one; taking an hour off for lunch; returning to the studio from two until five (with a tea break at 3:45); followed by an evening session from seven until ten, when the studio closed.

It didn't help matters that John had arrived sick. He had developed a cold during the Helen Shapiro tour that was festering in his chest by the time they arrived in London. "[His] voice was pretty shot," recalled engineer Norman Smith, who glowered at the tin of Zubes throat lozenges and cartons of cigarettes the boys stockpiled on the piano. As it was, Smith had his hands full trying, as Martin requested, to capture "the sound of the Beatles singing and playing as [if] they'd [be] perform[ing] on stage." Earlier in the week they'd decided to lay down the rhythm tracks first, before adding any vocals, in order to imitate the atmospherics of live sound, and as such, Smith allowed the brown coats extra time that morning to double-check the configuration of the patch bays on the recording console.

In the meantime, George Martin ran over the song list with the Beatles to make sure they were all on the same page. Paul seemed adamant about recording "Falling in Love Again," the overstylized Marlene Dietrich torch song, and it took some time for Martin, who considered the number "corny," to talk him out of it. The same for "Besame Mucho," which the Beatles had performed regularly since 1960. As a ballad, it meant more to them, Paul argued, than "A Taste of Honey," which Martin preferred, but the producer stood his ground, insisting that he knew what would sound best on tape and asking them to trust his judgment. Ordinarily, the Beatles might have resisted. If anything, they were confident about their choice of material and stood up for their choices when they believed they were right, but neither John nor Paul pressed the point.

All their attention was focused on the original songs, which Martin had shuffled evenly into the album sequence. The singles—"Love Me Do" and "Please Please Me," along with their B-sides—were a lock, but since the last string of Cavern dates John and Paul had been writing steadily, just churning out songs, and some seemed to warrant strong consideration. Huddled in a corner of the big studio while technicians swarmed around, the boys picked up guitars and launched into three of them for Martin: "Misery," "There's a Place," and "17," the latter two which they had finished some time before.

When they were done, there was no doubt that all three should be recorded. These numbers were more fully developed than their predecessors, more well crafted and rhythmically textured, allowing for dramatic shifts in the melodies with transitions suited to all sorts of imaginative orchestration. Martin was duly impressed; the boys seemed to get better each time they walked through the door.

The first session started about twenty minutes late, with the Beatles getting right to work on the newest songs. They cut "There's a Place" (the title pinched from *West Side Story*) first thing that morning, a stirring, melodic tune that showed off the lushness of their interlocking harmonies, singing it again and again—ten takes in all—until everyone was satisfied with the result. From the beginning, it was clear that John's voice was ragged, tearing at the seams. As the opening word uncoils—"There-re-re-re's"—he struggles to stay with Paul, almost growling the bottom part of the duet while the low, sepulchral phrase threads its uneasy approach. Once aloft, however, there is a sweet synthesis of their voices, as beautiful as they ever sound on record, climaxing with a powerful, dramatic finish riding over John's haunting harmonica.

With enough time left before lunch, they recorded "17," a number the Beatles had been performing to great acclaim since Hamburg. It was a breathless, all-out rocker whose opening lines—"She was just seventeen, and she'd never been a beauty queen"—Paul had written down in the van one night in 1962 on his way home from a gig. The melody and the first stanza came right away, but by the next afternoon, when he showed it to John, both boys agreed that the second line was "useless." Sitting on the living-room floor at Paul's house, with a Liverpool Institute notebook open at their feet, they ran through the alphabet looking for acceptable rhymes. It's a tribute to their cleverness, and perhaps a prophetic gesture toward the blasé shorthand of disaffected youth, that they went for a complete throwaway: "You know what I mean." What cheek! And yet, how effective. It said it all, without really saying a thing.

"She was just seventeen, you know what I mean" eventually became the cornerstone of this album, certainly the heart of the song, which they retitled "I Saw Her Standing There." Nothing the Beatles had done so far packed more excitement into a number. From the opening bar, when Paul counts off the time, the song takes off, fairly well soars, with all the spark and spirit of a rave-up. Clearly, they put everything they had into it—raspy, suggestive vocals; twangy, rhythmic guitars; syncopated handclaps; falsetto *ooooh*s; and a galloping bass line that Paul claimed to have lifted, almost note for note, from Chuck Berry's album cut "I'm Talking About You." For two minutes and fifty-five seconds, the Beatles find the groove and never let go.

When they were done, George Martin called for a lunch break, inviting the band to join him, Norman Smith, and the second engineer, Richard Langham, "for a pie and a pint" at the Heroes of Alma pub around the corner from the studio. The Beatles were visibly tired and in need of a break—besides touring, they'd traveled hours to get to the session and had worked under extreme pressure since their arrival—but they passed on the offer in order to continue rehearsing the material.

After lunch the producers returned to find the Beatles still at it. "We couldn't believe it," Richard Langham later told chronologist Mark Lewisohn. "We had never seen a group work right through their lunch break before." Sometime during that stretch, they had traipsed down to the studio canteen and bought containers of milk on the premise that it would soothe their ragged voices. Milk was hardly an elixir—the relief it brought was temporary and produced a phlegmy wheeze—but as the afternoon session began, John swigged often from the wax containers stacked by the steps of the control room. His voice gained a brief reprieve while Paul sang lead on "A Taste of Honey," followed by "Do You Want to Know a Secret," a lilting, innocent confession of adolescent love that John had written, based on the tune of "I'm Wishing" from Disney's *Snow White and the Seven Dwarfs,* as a vehicle to showcase George's vocal debut.

No doubt George wasn't the same intuitive stylist as his bandmates, nor in their rarefied category. But while his voice wasn't yet cultivated or as confident as John's or Paul's, neither was it feeble or ineffective. His rendition of "Do You Want to Know a Secret" (which Paul considered a "hack song") may not have been as exciting as some of the other tracks, but it was entirely capable, even charming. And there was nothing to disassociate it from the overall Beatles sound; it caused no disruption to the flow of the album that might prove jarring or out of place.

After the Beatles came back from a tea and dinner break, Paul stumbled through thirteen takes of "Hold Me Tight," a song he'd written that they were still on the fence about. (It was eventually left off the album.) Five songs remained—a sizable workload by any reasonable standard, especially with three hours left on the studio clock. But these were songs the Beatles could—and occasionally did—play in their sleep: "Anna," "Boys," "Chains," "Baby It's You," and one more to be chosen from their trusty playlist. Since the concept had been to simulate a Cavern gig, the boys determined to let it rip.

"They just put their heads down and played" was how Brian explained it to a friend. And when they did, as George Martin predicted, echoes of Garston, Litherland, Mathew Street, and Hamburg flooded the studio. The infectious excitement and the raw and ragged beat, all the ingredients vital to a live Beatles show, come right through. In the scheme of things, the covers are the least interesting aspect of the Beatles' remarkable output. But they cook with the true spirit of the band, from the distinctive American influence to the energy and power of the beat.

The four songs required only four or five takes each, with the first take, in most cases, enough to do the trick. By ten o'clock, they had finished. Abbey Road was packing up for the night; technicians switched off the equipment and looped miles of extension cables over their arms, musicians said good night at the door, lights were dimmed. There was still a great deal that might be done with the evening, but the Beatles were spent, physically and emotionally. Over the years there were places they'd played longer and harder, but never with as much on the line. They'd put everything they had into the session. George Martin was understandably ecstatic, but wouldn't it be perfect, he speculated, if they wrapped the whole project that night? The album was still one song short. The way they'd smoked through the others, it would take only another half an hour or so to cut a final track.

If he expected reluctance on the Beatles' part, there was none forthcoming. At this point in the game, they were willing to do whatever Martin asked, so they followed him downstairs to the canteen, where, over coffee, they sorted through songs, looking for a killer finale. The way Norman Smith recalled it, "someone suggested they do 'Twist and Shout,'" a staple of their shows throughout the past year. It was a kick-ass song, an early teen anthem, usually wound out into an extended jam, that never failed to jack up an audience. But it required a tremendous vocal performance, pushing every line to the limit of the register. "A real larynx-tearer," as George Martin would later refer to it. And it was John's song to carry. Was he up to it? No one, including John, was sure. If his voice was shot that morning, it was certainly worse for all the wear now. He'd been burdening it all day, straining and draining it like a car running on fumes. There was enough left, he insisted, though admittedly his voice felt "like sandpaper" when he swallowed.

Everyone knew they'd have to get it on the first take—the band, the engineer, everyone had to do his job, without a missed note or a glitch. There would be nothing left of John's voice after that.

The band returned to the studio and tuned up while Brian and the production staff climbed the stairs to the control booth. It was cold and stale-smelling in the room: lived in. The air inside seemed thicker, sad, vaguely intimate. In the vast paneled space, ceilinged with fluorescent lamps, the light cast a calm and creamy umbrella over the boys, who went about their work like seasoned professionals. It took some concentration to pull the guitars together, which the Beatles wrote off to fatigue. Their fingers grew impatient. Coaxing, *dwoing*-ing the strings, the instruments eventually complied under protest. Not more than ten minutes passed until Martin, invisible behind the glass booth, signaled that they were ready.

John tore open a wax carton and gargled noisily with milk. He'd played most of the day in a rumpled suit, but sometime after dinner the jacket was removed and two fingers yanked down the tie. Now, without a word, he stripped off his shirt. He draped it over a bench, then walked over to the mike and nodded to the others: good to go.

It is obvious from the very first notes that John was straining for control. "Shake it up bay-be-eee . . ." was more of a shriek than singing. There was nothing left of his voice. It was bone-dry, stripped bare, with all the resonance husked from the tone, and the sound it made was like an angry, hoarse-voiced fan screeching at a football match. Between clamped jaws, contorting his face, he croaked, *"Twist and shout."* He had been struggling all day to reach notes, but this was different, this hurt. And it was painful to listen to. Still, John held nothing in reserve. Trancelike, as the band rocked harder, building excitement with their impetuous energy, the struggle grew more intense. "C'mon, and twist a little closer" broke up into an agonizing, demonic rasp, until on the last refrain the tortured throatiness strangled every word before Paul, in admiration, shouted, *"Hey,"* celebrating, as they miraculously crossed the finish line.

John was wasted, near collapse, but the others already knew what he was about to find out from a playback: that for all its hairiness, "Twist and Shout" is a masterpiece—imperfect but no less masterful, with all the rough edges exposed to underscore its power. It is raw, explosive. The sound of ravaged lassitude, of everything coming apart, only complements the spirit of a tumultuous live performance. In the booth, there was jubilation. George Martin and his crew knew they had "got it in one," and as he and

The ten-year-old John Lennon in 1951, standing outside Mendips, his aunt Mimi's home in Woolton.

PHOTO: TOM HANLEY
CAMERA PRESS (TEXT &
ILLUSTRATIONS) LONDON

Paul's fifth-form class at Liverpool Institute, c. 1955.

MIRRORPIX

Arthur Kelly and George Harrison (age twelve), just days after George got his first guitar.

One of the earliest photos of John, taken in May 1948, a few weeks after he entered Dovedale Primary School in Allerton.

The Quarry Men perform at the Woolton church fete, July 8, 1957. The photo was taken fifteen minutes before John Lennon was introduced to Paul McCartney. From left to right: Eric Griffiths, Rod Davis, John, Pete Shotton, Len Garry.

LONDON FEATURES
INTERNATIONAL

One of the Beatles' awkward Hamburg stage arrangements, with Paul stationed at the piano while Stuart anchored the bass, 1960.

K & K STUDIOS/REDFERNS

John, pre-Beatles haircut, captured in a beautiful but eerie profile by Astrid Kirchherr, with the ghostly image of Stuart in the background. Hamburg, 1960.

ASTRID KERCHHERR/REDFERNS

George Harrison in a young, and ultimately underage, portrait during the Beatles' first residency in Hamburg, 1960.

Paul was also photographed with a ghostly image of Stuart in the background. Perhaps Astrid had already sensed his early exit from the Beatles — and all of their lives.

*The Beatles performing with mentor Tony Sheridan
(right), onstage at the Top Ten Club in Hamburg, 1961.*
PHOTO: ELLEN PIEL

*The Beatles, photographed by Astrid Kirchherr in der
Dom, a municipal park near the Reeperbahn, following
one of their all-night blowouts onstage, 1960.*
ASTRID KERCHHERR/REDFERNS

*George and Stuart,
who became good
friends, sharing a
quiet and thoughtful
musical interlude
onstage in Hamburg,
1960.*
PETER BRUCHMANN/
REDFERNS

*The Beatles as they appeared in Liverpool
in 1961, after returning from Hamburg
with those shocking leather jackets.*
K&K STUDIOS/REDFERNS

One of the last concerts before the madness set in.
© Hulton-Deutsch Collection/CORBIS

The classic Cavern stage shot, under the club's distinct brick archway.
Michael Ward/Rex Features

The gang celebrating Paul's birthday: that's Arthur Kelly with a date (left), Gerry Marsden (middle), George Harrison and Pattie Boyd (smoking).

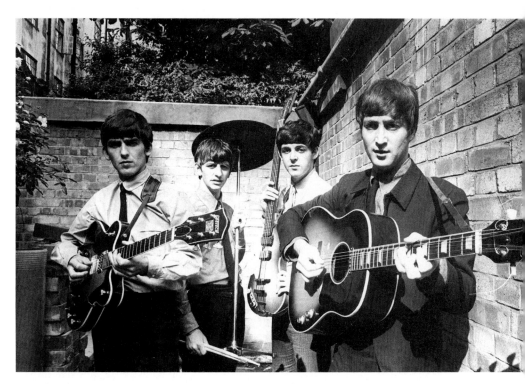

The Beatles posing in the backyard of one of their houses, 1964.

Brian Epstein in 1964, caught sitting alone and ignored at the Cavern, where he first discovered the Beatles.

The Beatles in 1963, performing live at an EMI reception launching their first album.

The Beatles in December 1964, performing in silly costumes on one of the myriad BBC-TV musical shows, which they hated doing.
MIRRORPIX

The Beatles carefully groomed their image, working on those iconic hairdos before going onstage in 1964.
PHOTO: TERENCE SPENCER
CAMERA PRESS LONDON

Paul and John backstage at East Ham in 1963, perusing reviews of their shows. The Beatles avidly read all press reports of their exploits.

PHOTO: JANE BOWN
CAMERA PRESS LONDON

Brian Epstein (standing, center) surrounded by his budding NEMS roster: the Beatles, Gerry and the Pacemakers, and Billy J. Kramer with the Dakotas, 1964.

MIRRORPIX

Ringo and John reminisce with Astrid Kirchherr en route from Munich before the Beatles' triumphant return to Hamburg in 1964.
MAX SCHELER/REDFERNS

The Beatles read one of Don Short's daily articles about them in the Mirror.
MIRRORPIX

Ringo at home with his mother, Elsie, and his stepfather,
Harry, before the release of the Beatles' third album in 1964.
MAX SCHELER/K&K/REDFERNS

The classic stage routine, with the entire sound
output coming from those puny amps.
MIRRORPIX

The Beatles took New York by storm in February 1964, initiated by their rousing press conference moments after arriving at JFK. That is NEMS press officer Brian Sommerville to their left.

MIRRORPIX

The Beatles' first appearance on The Ed Sullivan Show *in February 1964.*

During rehearsals at the Sullivan show in February 1964, the Beatles give Ed an impromptu guitar lesson.

the others later claimed, they reveled in it. The Beatles had their first album, and as John so eloquently put it, they were "dead chuffed."

[III]

But there was no rest for the weary. For the next ten days the Beatles humped around the country playing one-nighters on a route that often seemed designed by Jackson Pollock. After tearing out of London, they drove straight to Yorkshire, then east to Hull, stopping in Liverpool on February 14 long enough to play a Valentine's Day dance.

It was a riotous homecoming, with almost two thousand of the faithful jamming into the Locarno Ballroom, where an agitated disc jockey repeatedly admonished the crowd "to give the boys some air." The Beatles were no longer the loutish, chain-smoking, largely unprofessional—shameless—band that had haunted local jive hives months before. They took the stage like stars and launched into a set that had been shaped and refined to make the most of their new success. Kinder, gentler, even their look had improved; it was more tailored, their Beatles haircuts stylishly groomed, and at key points during songs, when they sensed the audience was in their thrall, George, Paul, and John, on cue, would hit a falsetto *oooo-o-o* and shake their heads in unison, inciting an ecstatic response. This was a trick they had practiced on tour, and when it worked onstage they grinned broadly, beaming, as though delighted by the adulation. Screams ripped through the seams of each song: rapturous approval and vows of love mixed with general hysteria, amplified tenfold since their last appearance. For some friends, the scene held great significance. Colin Manley, the Remo Four's guitarist, recalls how he had stopped by the Locarno to say hello to George and felt humbled by the Beatles' aura. "Just a few weeks before they'd been nothing more than mates, one of us," he recalls, "but it was clear that night they'd become stars."

But becoming stars didn't mean star treatment. A week later the Beatles played an uproarious show at the Cavern, drawing the biggest queue that anyone could remember since the place had opened. Their sets ran long, instigated by delirious pleas for encores. As a result, it wasn't until after eleven o'clock that they could break free of the club. Immediately afterward, they piled into the van and headed south to London, Neil Aspinall pitching down road after narrow road, mile after mile, against swirling winds and in almost total darkness, while the Beatles, slumped against one another in the back, stole whatever shut-eye the potholes permitted. Just before dawn, they crept into London, grabbed some breakfast, then wandered around the shops to kill a few hours, before turning up at the Playhouse Theatre for a BBC television taping. Afterward, they darted out the door and spun back on the same roads. All for a four-minute spot.

There were times during the zigzag around the nation that the Beatles grumbled—grumbled *mightily*—about the brutal grind. How much would this really boost record sales? Why couldn't it have been scheduled more conveniently? Was Brian driving them too hard? In the space of ten days, they'd come off a difficult tour, cut an album, played ten shows, and pulled off a day trip to London, with a solid block of eight days still ahead of them. The great distances they covered on the lousy British roads wore them out. "There was only a small piece of motorway in those days, so we'd be on the A5 for hours," Ringo recalled. The roads killed them; the roads—and the lousy British weather. "Some nights it was so foggy that we'd be doing one mile an hour, but we'd still keep going."

Going—and grumbling. But after the grumbling came the work. Exhausted though the Beatles might have been, they never passed up an opportunity of any kind to promote themselves. A workingman's club, a talent show, a dance, a radio plug—no appearance was too small for the Beatles. Drive all night to a gig, shake hands with a distributor, sign autographs at a record shop, they did everything—*everything*—necessary to get their name around, to win fans, to succeed. There was a feeling shared among the band that if they kept at it, the dream would come true. And every so often there was a payoff, an incentive that let them know they were on the right track, that it mattered, that it wasn't for naught.

The record deal was just such a reward, and it had kept them going for quite a long time. But it was nothing compared with the news Brian delivered the following week, while the Beatles played a club date in Manchester. "Please Please Me" had not only hit the charts, it had shot straight to number one.

— —

Number one! As much as the news thrilled them, they had to hear it for themselves.

The Beatles remained skeptical. The *NME* Top Thirty cast them in a tie for the top spot, sharing honors with Frank Ifield's dirgelike cover of "The Wayward Wind," an American hit. Paul took a lot of grief over this distinction. Since breaking up with Dot Rhone, he'd been dating Iris Caldwell, Rory Storm's ravishingly beautiful sister, who, as everyone in Liverpool knew, was two-timing him—with Frank Ifield. There was no denying that it irked Paul. He "was berserk over [Iris]," says a friend who knew them, and her affair with Ifield really set Paul's teeth on edge, especially after Iris reported playing "Please Please Me" for Ifield and "he just burst out laughing." Another incident at a concert intensified the rivalry. Paul, for some twisted reason, insisted on taking Iris to see Ifield perform at the Liverpool Empire. It seemed harmless enough at the time. Iris "knew Frank was practically blind," and with her trademark long hair twisted in a bun, it seemed unlikely he would ever spot her in a dark, crowded audience. From their seats in the second row, Iris and Paul held hands, enjoying their little shenanigans. But near the end of the show, Ifield strode downstage and put his boot up on the footlights. "I'd like to sing a song that's a great favorite of mine," he announced, then rather suddenly pointed directly at Paul. "It's called '*He'll* Have to Go.'" Now their paths had crossed again: *tied for Iris's affections, tied for number one.* If that didn't take the cake! *Disc,* on the other hand, showed the Beatles holding down the number one position all by themselves.

There was only one clear way to sort out the accuracy.

On Sunday, February 23, the Beatles rejoined the Helen Shapiro tour, which was appearing at the Grenada, in Mansfield. The next day, before leaving for Coventry, Kenny Lynch invited Paul, George, and John to accompany him in a car he'd borrowed rather than take the bus. No one had to twist the boys' arms. The bus was "a drag." Besides, the scenes Lynch made were a hoot, usually culminating in some kinky backstage grope with a couple of birds.

The Beatles, sans Ringo, piled into Kenny's car—John holding the seat for Paul and George, which signaled he'd be riding shotgun. "It was a beautiful afternoon," Lynch recalls. "Clear but with a cold, blustery wind. We were all happy to see each other and exchange recording war stories." For Kenny, the layoff marked a milestone of a different sort; while the Beatles were making their album, he had rushed off to record "Misery," making him the first artist to cover one of their songs. It was a dubious distinction from the Beatles' point of view, inasmuch as they loathed Kenny's interpretation. But on this day their only concern was determining if "Please Please Me" was number one.

"We were following the coach," Lynch remembers, "so we wouldn't get lost." But in Coventry, they pulled off the road, into a car park just behind the Lucien Theatre, to listen to a Sunday-afternoon radio show that counted down the charts. Waiting on edge, shivering in the unheated car, everyone lit cigarettes against the uneasiness, hope, and excitement that had been building up over the past two days. "It was a pretty intense moment. They knew [the record] would be pretty high because it was selling like hotcakes." Kenny noticed that John, Paul, and George were "stern-faced" as they stared at the radio in the dashboard, waiting for the news. Finally, at about 3:30, the BBC disc jockey announced: "This week, at number two, Frank Ifield and 'The Wayward Wind' . . ."

Before the opening bars even filtered over the airwaves, a cheer went up in the car. It was official. How the music magazines broke it down was beside the point. In England the BBC had the final word on the chart rankings, and by its count, Frank Ifield was number two.

"Where are we going, Johnny?" the Beatles had asked repeatedly throughout 1961 and 1962. "To the toppermost of the poppermost," John had promised. Now, only a year later, they had reached the summit.

MANIA

[I]

For the Beatles, everything changed with their leap to the top of the charts. They were no longer just a local act, not even a northern act. Once their record hit number one, they were lofted into a larger orbit that identified them as "Parlophone Recording Stars" or, perhaps somewhat prematurely, "Britain's top vocal-instrumental group." "Please Please Me" had extended their popularity far beyond the Cavern walls and far beyond the Mersey banks, establishing them as something of a national phenomenon. By the second half of the Helen Shapiro tour, everywhere the Beatles played, ear-splitting screams broke out at the mere mention of their names. The minute the lights went down, the crowd went crazy. And after each act finished its set, the theaters shook with kids hollering, *"We want the Beatles! We want the Beatles!"*

The Beatles got a charge out of it, playing off the energy with increasing confidence, but it wreaked havoc with the tour. The show had been constructed so that each act was assured of its own twenty-minute set, giving Helen half an hour to close the performance. That had worked for a while, but as each day passed, as audiences grew more familiar with "Please Please Me," as word of the Beatles spread from town to town, "all the people coming to the show were just waiting for the Beatles" and it often took several minutes to restore order between sets.

During those first few months in the spotlight, the Beatles regarded the mayhem as a novelty—and a boost to their spirits. Most of the days were interminably long and insufferably boring, with hours spent cooped up on the bus followed by ridiculous hours of downtime. In the northern towns, they'd "have a walk through the streets and visit a greasy spoon for some lunch." Afterward, if there was time, they would go shopping. Then, about four o'clock, before the first show, says Kenny Lynch, "we'd have a bacon sarnie and a mug of tea in the closest café to the theater."

The tea came in handy. John, for one, couldn't function without it. His voice had never fully recovered from the bashing he'd given it recording "Twist and Shout," and as a result, the live shows did a number on his vocal chords. On long bus trips, he'd sweet-talk the driver into stopping whenever possible so he could tank up on something warm. And "in the dressing-rooms," observed Ray Coleman, who covered the Beatles for *Melody Maker*, "Lennon was addicted to tea." His hand was constantly wrapped around a steam-capped paper cup, convenient to sip from or to warm his fingers. The conditions in most theaters were impoverished, the backstage comforts less than meager, the heat often nonexistent. If the Beatles had envisioned a world of glamour and luxury as rock 'n roll stars, this tour brought them back to earth with a thud.

As dreary as the theaters were, their accommodations were often worse—the guesthouses they stayed in run-down, staffed with local help who regarded them as nothing more than riffraff. All-night service stations were the restaurant of choice for most package-tour units, with a heaping portion of starchy beans on toast and chips a safe enough bet to see them through until the next opportunity arose to eat something.

Touring was hard work—and worse. "It was always a bore," Ringo recalled. At least when they were on the bus, there were plenty of diversions. A card game was usually in progress among facing rows of seats. There were invariably conversations about the previous night's show and its aftermath, with bloated conquests bandied about like fish stories. Each day, the boys plowed through newspapers, searching for their names. Once, in a Yorkshire town, they found an article hailing them as "a band in the American Negro blues tradition," in which they reveled and quoted from ad nauseam. For a change of scenery, John read avant-garde poetry, along with a volume of Spike Milligan's verse to lighten the mood. Everyone wrote home, with dreamy postcards sent to their girls.

In the highs and lows of those journeys, however, John and Paul always made time to work on some music. "They wrote every day on the coach, like clockwork," says Kenny Lynch. At some point John or Paul would catch the other's eye, then they would get up nonchalantly, work their way to the back of the bus, take out their guitars, and get down to business. "It was always the same routine: one would play, and the other would be writing down lyrics and chord changes." They were in their own private world back there, absorbed by the instant gratification of the work and adept at blocking out distractions. Every so often Kenny would lean over the seat in front of them and attempt to offer a line or critique the work. "Fuck off! Turn around!" they replied — and they meant it.

On the bus, they began to explore new ground. The steadying success of the collaboration encouraged them to experiment with different chord combinations, concentrating more on the choruses — or what they called "the middle eight" — to give the songs a fuller, more accomplished sound.

The effects of this creative experimentation began to show up immediately. A real breakthrough came on February 28, as the bus rolled south along roads from York to Shrewsbury. To fulfill an urgent request from George Martin for a follow-up single to "Please Please Me," John and Paul spread out across the backseat and worked on several ideas. One, finished a few days earlier, was "Thank You Little Girl."* The song still needed tinkering, but as they played around with it, other themes emerged and they went off on a tangent, leaving the song behind. In an interview with columnist Alan Smith, John recalled how after a while they were just "fooling around" on the guitar. "Then we began to get a good melody line, and we really started to work on it."

The new tune came quickly. Working in the key of C, they sketched out a verse using a standard four-chord progression. But when it came time to construct the middle eight, Paul accidentally hit a G-minor and felt something shift. "It went to a surprising place," he explained.

Once they had the melody, the words just tumbled out. It was John who came up with the basic premise. As he recalled it: "Paul and I had been talking about one of the letters in [*NME*'s] 'From You to Us' column." Up to that point, all their songs exploited pronouns in the title as a way of making them "very direct and personal." That way, Paul thought, "people can identify . . . with it." This time around, they'd finally hit the mother lode: me and you, together, in the same phrase.

"From Me to You" was finished before they even crossed the Shrewsbury town line. As soon as the ink was dry on the last "to you," the Beatles knew they had another smash.

— — —

The Beatles cut their new single five days later, sandwiched between a show in St. Helens and a radio appearance in Manchester. The session, which ran from 2:30 until 10:00 P.M. at Abbey Road, went as smoothly as

---

* Later shortened to "Thank You Girl."

the last. As uncertain as he still was about rock 'n roll, George Martin was amazed by the quality of the song—and that John and Paul kept writing obvious winners. He'd never experienced anything like it before, and the prospect that they were *real,* as opposed to one-shot wonders, gave him chills.

They rehearsed the number once or twice while Norman Smith worked in the booth to get a balance on the mikes. George's guitar intro'ed the song with a lick that mimicked the opening line. But something about it didn't work for the producer. Martin pulled up a stool and listened to them play it again. There, right at the top: it was unexciting, slack. Why not sing the intro? he suggested. Just as George played it: "Da da da da da dum dum da . . ."

Sing it? What an odd approach. No rock 'n roll artist in their memory had ever sung an opening lick, but it never occurred to the Beatles—nor would they have *dared*—to argue with Martin. Martin was known for creating an atmosphere in which recording artists felt comfortable to express their feelings. But there was a clear, almost palpable distinction between them, based largely on roles of authority. To working-class Liverpool lads, inadequate by nature in London, in the Smoke, Martin's refined social graces and perfect diction drew a line. It put him in a position of command, of authority, and while their relationship was harmonious, it was an uneasy alliance. If he wanted them to sing it, they'd give it a try. Besides, after an initial pass at it, they heard the difference: it was dynamic, it drove them into the song. "In a way, this made them aware of George's enormous musical sense," says Ron Richards, who listened to the result sometime later that week and "wasn't at all surprised" by how well it turned out. "The Beatles had marvelous ears when it came to writing and arranging their material, but George had real taste—and an innate sense of what worked."

━━━

From the moment they were signed, the Beatles regarded the States as the Promised Land. That isn't to say they weren't pleased with recent developments. In fact, they were thrilled by the opportunity to make the kind of records they were making and tickled by the possibility of getting airplay in London. But it was America—home of Chuck, Buddy, Elvis, Gene, Richard, and Phil and Don—on which they ultimately set their sights. America had the aura; it would legitimize them in a way that no one from England had yet experienced.

Brian shared their dream and persisted in his belief that an American tour should happen without delay. He had first brought it to EMI's attention after "Love Me Do" cracked the charts, but the brass couldn't promise anything other than that they would try to find a suitable outlet. Now, with "Please Please Me" at number one and the third single in the can, he stepped up his efforts, pestering George Martin to get something done.

The stumbling block seemed to be Capitol Records, which, according to its president, Alan Livingston, had the right of first refusal on EMI products in the States. EMI had bought Capitol in the late 1950s, cashing in almost immediately in Europe with Frank Sinatra, Johnny Mercer, and Nat King Cole. "The idea was that [Capitol] would also be useful for launching EMI's roster in the USA," says Roland Rennie, who had come up through the ranks of the British organization and functioned as its chief traffic coordinator, fighting to get product released overseas, and vice versa. "But the Capitol Tower in Hollywood was very much its own master. They called all the shots—and they frankly refused to put out any of our records." Every two weeks EMI sent packages to Capitol, stuffed with their latest releases, and within days always got back the same terse response: Not suitable for the U.S. market. "They turned everything down."

Most parent companies would simply demand that their subsidiaries follow orders, but EMI took a very hands-off position with Capitol. Its lawyers had warned that such interference might summon up antitrust litigation, which, Rennie says, "put the fear of God in the British." EMI never said so much as peep to Capitol about its A&R responsibilities. "Think of that," he muses, "not a word—they only *owned* it."

In America, Alan Livingston claims he "didn't even hear the first Beatles record"—it was just one more bloodless import that Capitol chucked on the overflowing slush pile. Earlier, he had appointed a producer named David Dexter to screen every EMI artist that was sent to Capitol for consideration. And according to Dexter, the Beatles were "nothing." According to his Capitol colleagues, Dexter was "a jazz man . . . who couldn't see [sic] pop records." Out of "courtesy," Alan Livingston says, they would occasionally put out an English artist to satisfy the parent company, but it was merely a gesture, never bearing any fruit.

That left matters in the hands of Leonard G. Wood, known to everyone as L.G., who was EMI's managing director and "very sympathetic" toward the company's growing "American problem." Rennie had first brought the Beatles to Wood's attention in late 1962, after George Martin had turned up the heat. "He was polite but noncommittal, warning me again about this antitrust business," Rennie remembers. But there was another course of action that Wood recommended he explore. A year earlier, frustrated by Capitol's rigid resistance toward EMI releases, he commandeered a Capitol employee named Joe Zerger and set up a company in America—the absurdly important-sounding Transglobal Music—which was to lease EMI's repertoire throughout the States once Capitol had turned it down.

Zerger, whose heart wasn't in it, "didn't do anything much," says Rennie. But his partner was a young man named Paul Marshall, a dapper, dynamic, raspy-voiced lawyer with a passion for music and a finely tuned ear for quality. Behind a perfectly coiffed head of cotton-white hair and a blinding smile lurked an impetuous deal maker. Marshall had placed dozens of foreign masters with independent labels and undertook EMI's offer as a personal challenge.

Having listened to a few dozen EMI releases, Marshall was determined to push the record business in a radically new direction. He chose a handful of those records he considered American in spirit, and in early January 1963, with Roland Rennie replacing Joe Zerger, Marshall set out to find British artists a home for their music in the New World. Coincidentally, the first record he put his hands on was by a group called the Beatles.

———

Marshall could not, he felt, make hay at Capitol Records. "I wasn't going to call [Dave] Dexter back," he recalls. "He'd already said no to Len Wood." So, without any hesitation, Marshall scratched Capitol off the list of prospective labels. Instead, he sent copies of "Love Me Do" and "Please Please Me" to Jerry Wexler at Atlantic Records. Atlantic was enjoying a blistering hot streak, churning out hit after hit by Ray Charles, the Coasters, Ben E. King, the Drifters, Solomon Burke, and Bobby Darin. The label was the most successful independent of its kind—and it abounded in cachet. But after a week—and then *two*—without return calls from Wexler, Marshall began to grow impatient. He called Noreen Woods, who was Wexler's and Ahmet Ertegun's joint secretary, for Jerry's response and got an evasive reply. Which meant that Wexler "was probably too distracted" and hadn't gotten around to listening to it yet. The next time Marshall called for an answer, Woods informed him: "I haven't got one. Jerry says, 'If you can't wait—then go ahead.'" And Marshall couldn't wait.

Cursing his luck, Marshall decided to go for broke and hastened to send the Beatles' material out en masse—to Columbia, RCA, London, Mercury,

United Artists, all the major New York labels. That way, it eliminated the weeks of waiting between submissions. By the middle of January, however, he had come up empty-handed. No one expressed interest in the Beatles, even at a bargain-basement royalty rate. Perhaps this was related in some way to the cold winds blowing from the north: Capitol's Canadian affiliate label had put out both singles on the heels of their British releases and, according to its Canadian A&R rep, they "fell right to the bottom." With the majors impassive, Marshall merely turned his sights to the independents. The most attractive outlet was Vee-Jay Records, a reservoir of fresh waters from which Marshall had drunk long and greedily in the past. Its owners were a married couple named Vivian and James Bracken, who owned bars on the South Side of Chicago and had scored over the years with a roster of classy R&B artists such as Jimmy Reed and the Dells. In the past two years alone, they'd put together an incredible string of crossover hits that included "Raindrops," by Dee Clark, "Duke of Earl," by Gene Chandler, and a million-seller by Jerry Butler called "He Will Break Your Heart." They also feasted on a string of hits by another of Marshall's clients, Frankie Valli and the 4 Seasons, with "Sherry," "Big Girls Don't Cry," and "Walk Like a Man" winning the trifecta for Vee-Jay in 1962 and early 1963.

On January 25, 1963, *NME* broke the story that Vee-Jay had signed the Beatles, in a deal that had been brokered in London the previous Monday. The band might still be considered a bunch of Johnny-come-latelies from the provinces, but in the world of rock 'n roll, where merely being British doomed an artist to provincialism, an American release gave them admittance to a select circle.

According to Roland Rennie and others, EMI sent the Beatles' tapes to Chicago, where they were to be pressed for a timely Vee-Jay release. Shortly before their arrival, the record company's president, Ewart Abner (who would one day head Motown), went to Las Vegas with a Scandinavian distributor to celebrate Abner's fortieth birthday. During the second weekend of festivities, the distributor uncharacteristically placed a call to Paul Marshall at his home. Marshall immediately heard the alarm in the man's voice. He said, "I carried [Ewart] away from the tables an hour ago. But he's back at the tables. Watch out, Paul." By the time Marshall could leap into action, however, it was too late. Not only had he gambled away the money earmarked to pay for the hotel rooms, but with it went a sizable chunk of Vee-Jay's operating expenses. "[The company] was blown by Abner in Vegas," Marshall recalls. "Two weekends—done."

[II]

For the Beatles and Brian Epstein, the next few months were a blur of intense activity, so much so that they were blissfully ignorant of the problems at Vee-Jay. The Helen Shapiro tour had alerted promoter Arthur Howes to the Beatles' soaring popularity, and without wasting a beat, he negotiated a deal for them to segue into another tour—opening for teen idols Tommy Roe and Chris Montez—beginning on March 9, a few days after the Shapiro gig ended. Then, in the February 8 issue of *NME,* an article appeared under the banner BEATLES HEAD PACKAGE SHOW, announcing plans for the band to headline "a nationwide package tour" in May, with "a U.S. artist" who was "being sought to share top billing with them." Booking another tour—their third in a row—looked like a bad move on Brian's part; between all the recording sessions, the songwriting, and endless months of performing, the Beatles appeared to be driven to the point of exhaustion. But a small follow-up in *Melody Maker,* which revealed their costar to be none other than Roy Orbison, made an apparent miscue seem like a perfectly calculated move.* Orbison already had a mystique about him. An early crony of Buddy Holly's in Texas, he'd recorded his own songs, among which "Only the Lonely," "Running Scared," "Crying," and "Dream Baby" became instant classics. He'd written "Claudette" and "All I Have to Do Is Dream" for the Everly Brothers, and fans were awestruck by his incredible vocal range, clocked somewhere around E above high C—territory frequented by Enrico Caruso. The Beatles loved him and he had another hit—the intensely soulful "In Dreams"— currently clawing its way up the British charts. Three weeks on the road with him would be a treat for the Beatles. Besides, their stamina was hardly in question, not after Hamburg, not after all those marathon jams. If problems arose, there was always speed to fall back on, to which, according to his biographer, Orbison was also "devoted."

To accommodate his growing roster, which included Gerry and the Pacemakers, Billy J. Kramer with the Dakotas, and the Big Three—and to mollify his growing-angrier-by-the-day father—Brian leased office space in a stately old building on Moorfields Avenue. A stone staircase swept up to the second floor, where letters painted on a glass door announced the new headquarters of NEMS ENTERPRISES. Brian's private office was the fo-

---

* *The scheduled headliner was originally Duane Eddy, who bowed out for contractual reasons.*

cal point. "Eppy's Epitorium," as it was called—although never within his earshot—was a bright, airy room, with an enormous teak desk, a tufted black-leather chair, and a "posh," hand-knotted Abyssinian carpet that looked large enough to land a plane on. Waterford crystal tumblers were arranged on a silver tray atop a credenza, and above that, the room's only other decoration: a huge picture of the Beatles with Little Richard taken at the 1962 Tower Ballroom show. The most memorable effect, however, was a traffic signal positioned just outside the door. Frieda Kelly recalls how everyone who worked at NEMS kept one eye peeled on those lights, which Brian controlled like the Great Oz. They all lived in dread of having to cross Brian's threshold, even on green. He was too unpredictable, too quick to "jump down [their] throats." With green, at least, the odds edged slightly in your favor. "No way you'd enter on red," Frieda says. "Amber was touch and go—you'd take a chance if you were brave enough." Only the Beatles, who were impetuous drivers in their own right, barreled straight through that signal, no matter what color was lit.

But the Beatles were seldom in town anymore. They came home as often as humanly possible, for a day at the most, then they were off again, to play a gig or to plug their latest record on one of the myriad radio shows that Brian managed to line up on an appallingly regular basis. Through the spring of 1963 the Beatles phenomenon steadily built momentum. With their records leading the way and the music press dewy-eyed with fascination— their sharp, cheeky banter made good copy—the Beatles single-handedly spurred interest in the Merseyside rock 'n roll scene. When John claimed that "there are three groups in Liverpool for every top Yank act," even his fans rolled their eyes. But the comment also raised eyebrows. Chris Roberts, writing in *Melody Maker*, explained how a hastily arranged trip to Liverpool—a place so alien to him, it might as well have been Zanzibar—made a believer out of him. Breathlessly, he described a music "scene that could only find its counterpart in the USA" and concluded that the "Beat City," a nickname appropriate in every respect, qualified as "Britain's Nashville." The sheer number of clubs, dances, and groups made his head spin. "You say London's got it all?" he speculated, but the question was gratuitous—readers already knew the score. Truly, there was something incredible going on up in Liverpool, and across Britain, kids beat the jungle drums.

Throughout the end of February and most of March, the Beatles still managed to get home, although more and more on an irregular basis. All of them needed to reconnect with their families—and vice versa. If to the fans, the Beatles were the young heartthrobs taking the country by storm, there were four loving families left behind, a collection of common, unpretentious Scousers, not all of whom understood what all the fuss was about and whose sons—not one of them yet twenty-two years old—were especially missed.

For Elsie Graves, the Beatles' success was a particularly difficult burden. The way she doted on Ritchie, her only child, touched friends, who felt as though she "idolized him." Theirs wasn't just a conventional mother-son relationship. They were friends as well, having been through so much together. Now, with the Beatles, everything had changed. "Elsie felt they were taking him away from her," says Marie Crawford, "and that terrified her." Even the unexpected perks, like money and popularity, failed to appease her. "Of all the parents, she found it quite difficult to cope," remembers Frieda Kelly, who visited Elsie every Wednesday on her half day off from NEMS. "She could have done without any of the success. Elsie would have preferred Ritchie to be ordinary, to live down the road with four children she could visit every day."

It was easier for Paul and George. Both the Harrisons and Jim McCartney "were thrilled" by what was happening to the Beatles. Friends close to Louise Harrison recall how much pleasure she got from George's new success. "She followed the Beatles as avidly as any of their fans," says Arthur Kelly, who received regular updates from the Harrisons. It was the same at Forthlin Road, where fans who turned up at the door were treated to tea and biscuits. "Jim was probably the Beatles' biggest fan," recalls Bill Harry, who frequently ran into Paul's father on his rounds through the city. "He was so proud of what was happening," remembers Shelagh Johnson, a local girl and, later, director of the Beatles Museum. "Outwardly, all his attention occasionally embarrassed Paul, but I think secretly Paul loved it and enjoyed coming home."

Only John was anxious about being away. Cynthia's pregnancy, nearing term, had encountered some unforeseen bumps. Scarcely two months along, she began "showing blood," at which point, as a precautionary measure, the doctor confined her to bed. This only served to alarm the naturally timid Cynthia, who was on her own and scared. With John on tour and her mother in Canada, she was happy when Paul's old girlfriend, Dot Rhone, moved into the "dank, awful basement" flat just below them on

Falkner Street. "Once I arrived, Cynthia seemed to be fine," Dot recalls. "It upset her that John wasn't around, but she got used to it after a while."

Even when John managed to get home, the atmosphere bristled with tension. Flush with excitement from another triumph with the Beatles, he'd bound in unannounced to find Cynthia—languorously pregnant—like an anchor, a jolt of reality. For John, the situation was too emotionally charged—and confusing. "There were a lot of fights," says Dot. "He would drink an awful lot—just get drunk and mean. And then he'd say such awful things to Cyn. He was so moody. One moment he could be so funny and wonderful, and the next—so damn cruel." Having grown up around an alcoholic father, Rhone recognized the symptoms that ignited his rage. "John told me that there had never been a day in his life when he didn't feel he needed some kind of drug," Dot recalls.

The prospect of fatherhood made John increasingly resentful and merely turned up the heat in an already smoldering domestic cauldron. Falling into black moods, he'd storm out of the flat, claiming to need cigarettes, and just disappear. Instead of blowing off steam and returning, he'd spend late evenings at the Jacaranda or drinking at the Blue Angel. Paddy Delaney, the Cavern's bouncer, remembered encountering him there sometime in late February, grafted to the bar, where they "drank whiskey after whiskey" until well after four in the morning.

That spring friends often saw John wandering from club to club in the company of Ida "Stevie" Holly, a tall, "spunky" seventeen-year-old with jet-black hair to the middle of her back. According to reports, they'd been hanging out together, on and off, for a period of several months. "We presumed he'd broken up with Cynthia and had got a new girlfriend," says Bill Harry, who, like most of the old crowd, was unaware that Cynthia was pregnant, let alone that she and John were married. Harry and his girlfriend, Virginia, who would eventually become his wife, remembers barging into the Blue Angel one night in March and finding John and Stevie at the bar "all over each other, like a couple of wildcats." Tactfully, the Harrys avoided them, scooting downstairs before they were seen. Virginia was already in enough trouble with John, who had lent her a pile of notebooks filled with the poems he'd written. During *Mersey Beat*'s move from their tiny attic office to larger space on a lower floor, she'd absentmindedly "thrown them in the bin." A few weeks earlier they'd run into John—again at the Blue Angel—and Bill insisted that Virginia confess. "I crept over and admitted what I'd done with his poems," she recalls, "and he just started *sobbing*."

Stevie Holly had been with him that night, too. And there were other nights at the Cavern. And afternoons, strolling lazily through the Walker Art Gallery. Even *with the Beatles.* "He had no shame," Bill Harry says in a voice flattened by scorn. "He acted as if he were still a bachelor—even after the baby came."

In the first hours of April 8, Cynthia, who had been staying at Aunt Mimi's house with her friend Phyllis McKenzie, was rushed by ambulance to Sefton General Hospital, where just after 6 A.M.* she gave birth to a six-pound, eight-ounce boy. Had it been a girl, she was to be called Julia, after John's mother. For the birth certificate, however, Cynthia confidently recorded his name as John Charles Julian Lennon.

John, out of town with the Beatles, phoned the next day, "triumphant at the news that it was a boy," but, ironically it was Mimi who saw Julian first. No one had expected Mimi to rush to the hospital. Relations between the women had always been frosty, and a month of living together had left them straining for ways to remain courteous, then civil. Why Mimi urged Cynthia to move into Mendips was anyone's guess. Far from comforting Cynthia, whose condition had admittedly made her "over-sensitive," Mimi was her old supercilious self, "moody and sharp-tongued" toward her rabbity niece-in-law. Even though they attempted to steer clear of each other, there was always some explosive, petty incident that set Mimi off, with her carping about Cynthia's "willfulness" or the way she left the kitchen a mess. Some people felt as though Mimi got "a perverse pleasure" from the situation, as though it were retribution for the shotgun marriage and the "terrible scenes" that preceded it. Their relationship had deteriorated to the point where, according to a published report, Mimi "didn't even emerge from upstairs" when Cynthia, doubled over with labor pains, was loaded into the ambulance.

John turned up two days later, on April 10, fresh from taping an appearance on one of the popular new BBC rave-ups, *The 625 Show,* followed by a party in a London suburb at the home of the Shadows' guitarist, Bruce Welch, where the Beatles first met Cliff Richard. Conveniently, the Beatles were slated to play three dates in and around Liverpool that week. Julian and Cynthia were still in the hospital so that the doctors could keep an eye

---

* *Over the years, Cynthia has provided various times for Julian's birth—at 6:00 A.M. and at 7:45.*

on the baby, who was born weak and jaundiced as a result of the umbilical cord being wrapped around his neck.

According to various accounts Cynthia gave over the years, John behaved like any other new father. No one was more elated—or proud—than the demonstrative Beatle. He bounced Julian around like a football, gloating at his son's wan, wrinkled face. "Who's going to be a famous little rocker like his Dad then?" she quoted him as crowing. The baby was either "bloody marvelous" or "a miracle" in his eyes. In every retelling, Cynthia polished the story to portray John as a devoted dad. But no matter what kind of shine she put on it, Cynthia must have known—or, at least, had a sinking sense of—the truth.

Like Cynthia, the baby tightened the chains around John. Especially now, with the long struggle to stardom finally within reach. The tiny margin separating the Beatles from their ultimate goal required his undivided attention; the Big Party lay just over the next rise—John was sure of it. There was nothing left in the tank to give a wife and child.

It had been hard enough keeping Cynthia hidden in the shadows. Brian had insisted that John keep the marriage a secret to avoid diminishing his popularity with the fans. "It was a calculated judgment on [Brian's] part that pop stars oughtn't to have partners," remembers Tony Barrow.* That was the rationale, at least, and apparently John was content to abide by it. And the exuberant success was all about freedom—freedom to pick and choose among the flock of available birds and his choice of crazy scenes, the freedom to experiment, to live it up. With no wife to his credit—at least, not in any published account—John could behave as most rock 'n roll stars did on the road.

Cynthia may have suppressed this latest slight in order to give herself hope, but she had turned a blind eye toward John's indiscretions too many times not to know what was going on. The stories that drifted back from Hamburg had upset her until she learned to block them out. And those times at the Cavern, when John disappeared for a few hours—she'd seen the way those girls had looked at him onstage and knew the score. Even in the hospital, she recognized the familiar signs: John "was beginning to feel trapped."

Bill Harry, like Cynthia, had been awakened to John's freewheeling behavior. He spent several late nights at the Blue Angel, drinking with the Beatles, while they were back in Liverpool. It was especially gratifying for

---

* *Cynthia's name does not appear in Brian's autobiography,* A Cellarful of Noise.

Harry to reconnect with his old art school mate and to hear the latest fabulous adventures involving the Beatles and John's life. "But he never talked
about Julian or being a proud father," says Harry. "Julian was never mentioned. As far as John was concerned, it was as if Cynthia or Julian didn't
exist."

[III]

What did exist for John was the new world taking shape around him—a
world that increasingly involved success. "Once the Beatles hit the pop
charts, we all envied what they had—and wanted it for ourselves," says
Johnny Byrne. "Guys like Gerry [Marsden] and Billy J. [Kramer] rode the
Beatles' coattails for a while. But for the rest of us, who never made it out
of the clubs, a kind of resentment took hold." The Big Three, who were
more exciting, couldn't write their own material; Kingsize Taylor and the
Dominoes stayed too long in Hamburg, playing bars and getting shitfaced;
Rory Storm and the Hurricanes lacked the ambition—and the talent. But
after the Beatles, returning from the Tommy Roe–Chris Montez tour,
caught the national ear in a big way, the resentment directed toward them
at home diminished as a result of the enormous groundswell that was created and the power it conferred.

If there was one spark responsible, it was the release of "From Me to You,"
on April 11. Initially, the record got mixed reviews from the music papers.
The *NME* critic noted that it had "plenty of sparkle" but got in his licks,
concluding: "I don't rate the tune as being anything like as good as on the
last two discs from the group." And Ray Coleman, writing in *Melody
Maker,* expressed his disappointment in the "so-so melody" and questioned whether "if this average song was done by a less prominent group,"
it would have the same impact.

Nevertheless, the impact was stunning. Instead of building steady,
solid momentum, as was usual with a potential hit record, "From Me to
You" "came crashing" into the charts at the number six position—a first
for a British pop group. "From Me to You" flew out of the stores. In the
first week alone, sales hit 200,000 copies, outselling the entire issue of
"Please Please Me." A keen witness on the scene observed: "By now, the
Beatle legend was beginning to grow. . . . It was becoming clear that they

were something rather special." Actually, that was putting it mildly. All of London, it seemed, had their name on its lips. *The Beatles!* What was it with this funny-sounding—funny-*looking*—group? And where was this great music coming from?

With few exceptions, the critics caught the drift. "The Beatles could take it to the Americans," argued a writer from *Melody Maker* after watching them snatch the stage out from under Chris Montez and Tommy Roe in East Ham. That, in itself, was a remarkable observation, if very un-British. And it was picked up in *NME,* which led its story with a note on the trend. "Latest visitors from America . . . were given scream-filled receptions," wrote columnist Andy Gray. "But the Beatles stole top honours for entertainment and audience reaction."

The Beatles could take it to the Americans.

Amazing! Even though Beatlemania was still á good year off, the tremors were already being felt. There was something quintessentially British about these uncompromising musicians, these charismatic, cheeky, shaggy-haired Scousers from the uncultured North, taking the larger cities by storm but still living in Liverpool, mostly with their parents, where they worked overtime to hone the emerging "Liverpool sound." Suddenly their beleaguered northern city had become exotic, chic. Suddenly the real Brits weren't sophisticated Londoners but those with caustic accents who worked in the trenches. Suddenly teenagers across the kingdom made a pilgrimage to the Cavern. Suddenly the North was known as "home of the Beatles." Suddenly Liverpool was on the map. It was "Music City," "the Nashville of the North," even *"Nashpool."* And if anyone needed further evidence, they had only to glance at the charts, where suddenly Gerry and the Pacemakers had themselves trudged their way to *number one* with "How Do You Do It." A single group from Liverpool was uncommon enough, but two groups—it was revolutionary! And to make sense of it all, you only had to point to the Beatles.

Unfazed by the outbreak of attention, they plowed through critical appearances on national television, promoting "From Me to You" without pause, including, of all things, the BBC Jazz 'n' Pop Festival in the venerable Royal Albert Hall. (The show was broadcast simultaneously as part of the BBC's *Light Programme.*) They acted so loose and behaved so playfully during rehearsal, impervious to tradition or other stars on the bill, that the show's producer, Terry Henebery, bristled. "A couple of records in the charts," he fumed, "and they think they can do exactly what they like."

He wasn't the only one discomfited by the Beatles' outsize personalities. Right off the bat, the show's promoters were forced to deal with the feverish wave of anticipation the Beatles inspired. The dense crowd that had packed the stalls arrived in a bubble of highly charged expectation. A diaphanous buzz punctuated by whistles filled the upper reaches of the cavernous space. This wasn't the usual contingent that bought tickets to the frequent package shows and sat politely through each performance. These were pumped-up teenagers—most of them girls—in every manner of emotional thrall, behaving rather curiously, as if they all knew one another. "They acted that way because they had one thing in common," says Tony Barrow, who wasn't in the theater that night. "They were Beatles fans."

Writer and scenemaker George Melly later admitted that even he wasn't prepared for the reception that crowd gave the Beatles. "It was my chore to announce them," he recalled, "and the moment I went on I was met by a solid wall of screams. In the end I just gestured into the stairwell, mouthed 'the Beatles' and walked off. The screams lasted right through their act." And through Del Shannon's as well. Cries of *"We want the Beatles! We want the Beatles!"* repeatedly interrupted his set, forcing an awkward, abruptly shortened performance.*

Success at the Albert Hall was no mean feat for any new band on the scene, but the sensation the Beatles caused, marked by the screams and rampant hysteria, heightened its subsequent impact. Their new single rather rudely evicted Gerry Marsden from his perch atop the charts, and their just-released album, *Please Please Me,* shot to the number two position, breathing down the neck of current top dog, Cliff Richard. After years of working on the entertainment fringe, and only months after being rejected by all major labels, the band was besieged with offers pouring into the NEMS office. The Beatles were wanted on the *NME* poll winners' concert at Wembley's Empire Pool, the self-styled "highlight of the pop music year." There was an invitation for them to appear on an all-Liverpool version of *Thank Your Lucky Stars,* which was accepted. A top-of-the-bill appearance on *Saturday Club* caught their fancy. And from Paris came an offer for them to headline an eleven-day run at the Olympia Theater. Within a relatively short time, the Beatles had moved from the fringes to ground zero of the increasingly fertile British rock 'n roll community.

The attention left the Beatles in such a state of euphoria that they refused another lucrative offer to join yet a fourth package tour that would

---

* To his credit, however, Shannon became the first American to cover a Beatles record, cutting "From Me to You" the moment he arrived back in the States.

leave from London at the end of April. They were exhausted from the months of touring, let alone the spinning of their four heads. Records . . . tours . . . television interviews . . . screams . . . money . . . fame . . . It was too much to absorb at once. They had worked so hard for this—and for so long. And yet, they were running too hard, worn out. There was an urgent need for some breathing room. Fast.

Earlier in the year Brian had set aside a block of time at the end of April, specifically for a vacation, and recommended the Beatles get away, too: visit a place where they could unload all the incremental tension that had accumulated during the past year—and where nobody knew who they were. At the same time, Brian mentioned to John that he was going to Spain during the hiatus and invited him to go along.

It is not known what prompted Brian to make such a bold—and potentially dangerous—offer. So far, all his experiences with the Beatles had been strictly professional, and to a large extent protective, leading observers to view their relationship "more like that of a father and his sons" than manager and artist. Only once had Brian stepped over a line, and even then it was more a matter of appearances than of any intent.

It had occurred on an afternoon almost a year earlier, in Liverpool, after a lunch session at the Cavern. Headed toward his car, Brian offered George Harrison a lift home and somehow they wound up driving through the leafy environs of Childwall. This, in and of itself, wasn't unusual. Childwall, where Brian grew up, was en route to Speke, and George thought nothing more of it when his manager stopped to show him around the lovely house at Queen's Drive. According to an account that George later gave Bob Wooler, it was an entirely innocent gesture. Proud of the estate and aware of the impression it was making on this council-house lad, Brian glided rather imperiously through the lavishly appointed rooms, annotating as though a curator at Versailles. It was only when his brother, Clive, showed up unexpectedly that anything untoward was insinuated. "Clive took one look at the scene and exploded," says Wooler. "The family anguished over Brian's vulnerability, and here he was, alone in an empty house, with this quite adorable boy." With George standing there, smoking a cigarette, befuddled by the commotion, screaming broke out as the brothers, their faces white with fury, disappeared behind closed doors to hurl and deny accusations.

Afterward, in the car, Brian was visibly "flustered." The remainder of the drive to Speke was uncomfortable, silent. It still wasn't clear to George what had occurred. The whole baffling incident seemed to have come out of—and to—nothing, and George, who had never seen Brian so debased, couldn't think of anything to say. Finally, he broke the awkward silence. "Clive's younger than you, isn't he?" George wondered. Brian, seized with self-loathing, could only nod. "Well, he shouldn't talk to you like that."

George's naïveté served to shade the undertones and rescue Brian from complete humiliation. But with John, it was another matter altogether. Lennon was catnip; no young man could have filled Brian's sexual fantasies more perfectly. Like other encounters Epstein had responded to, John was young, studly, foul-mouthed, dangerous, alternately caring and cruel—and off-limits. For two years Brian had pushed all lascivious thoughts of John as far out of his mind as humanly possible. But it was difficult. He was always around, spotlighted onstage, standing splay-legged with the guitar, or lounging in dressing rooms. (Or sulking, which proved to be another turn-on.) That John sensed this and teased, perhaps even tormented, Brian is undeniable. His attentions, according to Paul, may have been intended to flatter Brian and assert his power, but it had a pitiable effect. It was a constant temptation—all those longings and forbidden looks, the persistent infatuation—but through it all Brian remained creditably aloof.

It was only a matter of time, however, before the desperate fantasy that had first drawn Brian to the Beatles proved too overwhelming. There is no record of what emboldened him to act on it—whether it was that he'd become successful in his own right, that he was feeling more confident, or that he was just reckless. Certainly, his relationship with John had changed. But since the beginning of the year, he'd begun to construct in his imagination the plans for an inevitable liaison. He just had to bide his time.

Finally, after the Beatles announced they'd be spending the break at a beach house belonging to Klaus Voormann's parents, in the Canary Islands, Brian made his move. It must have taken all of his courage to pop the question. The recruiting phase, in fact, lasted several weeks. In between shows, he would entertain John on end with amiable stories about several enchanting visits to Spain: witnessing his first bullfight at a time when few gringos ventured into the arena; eating paella at midnight from a *paellera* the size of a Ford, hopping from café to café and from nightclub to nightclub where the energy seemed to run on a different—furious—current. As nonchalantly as possible, he described his romance with the mysterious country and wondered if John might want to consider coming along. Whether there was any discussion up front about accommodations is unknown. Certainly John recognized Brian's attraction to him. "He was in love with me," John later admitted, with characteristic bluntness.

How John responded to this brazen offer is not recorded, except that he said yes. Doubly surprising, perhaps, is that he didn't cancel the trip, following, as it did, so closely on the heels of Julian's birth. According to an account that Cynthia later gave, while she was still recovering in the hospital John told her about the planned trip and "wanted to know if [she] objected" to his going. The news, she recalled, hit her "like a bolt out of the blue," which must be a terrific understatement in light of the circumstances. After all, John had been gone throughout her pregnancy and was absent for Julian's birth. She'd half expected him to pitch in and help out now that he was back. If the Beatles had obligations, that was one thing. But a *vacation* wasn't anything she'd contemplated—or understood. Cynthia tried to maintain her composure in the face of such gall. She was "hurt," to say nothing of envious. And even John knew "what a bastard [he] was," while acknowledging he "wasn't going to break the holiday for a baby."

On April 28, George, Paul, and Ringo shuttled to the striking black-sand beaches of Tenerife, which provided some welcome relaxation but little comfort. The Voormanns' tiny cottage, like most of those that dotted the hillside, was an amusing, rustic affair, without electricity, that overlooked the festive coast, where the last ripples of tidewater spilled into the Atlantic Ocean. From each window was a Matisse-like view of paradise. The land sweeping down to the sea radiated a dizzying canvas of color: patches of blue and yellow foxglove bloomed in the chalky brush, pale pink finches and red admiral butterflies rustled among natural tones of saffron and berries and olives and flax. Orange groves lined the ridges above the town. The light on the land was so strong, the colors so intense, that the scenery often resembled a montage of overexposed snapshots.

Embracing the torrid island stillness, though without much forethought, the trio of Beatles "stayed in the sun too long and got incredibly sunburnt." With Klaus, they tooled around the briny port in his Austin Healy Sprite and drove up the jagged mountain slopes to Teide Peak, an idle volcano, where they explored the craterlike rim that George likened to "the surface of the moon." Local teenagers had no idea who they were— or knew their records. It came as no small relief that they could blend in with other vacationers. Every day after lunch, when the sun was at its highest, the Beatles would change into their suits and join the resident sunbirds at the beach for a swim. Occasionally Paul would drift off by himself, notebook in hand, to find a quiet place in which to work on an unfinished lyric. He'd spend hours nesting in the sand, gazing intently at a slightly crumpled page while all around him bathers screamed and splashed in the rugged surf. Despite bouts of sunstroke and a swimming mishap in which Paul nearly drowned in the swift current, the boys considered the getaway "a real good holiday"; nevertheless, they were eager to get back to the music—and to John.

If only they suspected what he was up to.

The friends who knew John best—who knew how single-minded he was, how "nothing would stand in his way of stardom, not friendship, not love, absolutely nothing"—had felt upon hearing of his vacation with Brian, as Paul had, that John was "a smart cookie . . . [who] saw his opportunity to impress upon Mr. Epstein who was the boss of his group." In 1963 very few straight men in their twenties would have gone away with a homosexual, no matter how much influence he might wield. None of that fazed John. An hour after the other Beatles left for Tenerife, he and Brian boarded a plane for Barcelona, "the Paris of Spain," where they checked into a suite at the Manila Hotel. Brian had been there before. In November 1960 he kicked off his lifelong love affair with Spain from a room in this "superb" hotel with its view of the eastern hills. "Where else may I have a gin and guests in my room at 4:00 A.M.?" he wrote in his journal the next day. There is evidence to indicate that Brian entertained a series of men in his room, although in typical fashion, he "behaved foolishly and irresponsibly," and things eventually turned rough. "Last night I suffered, for I was robbed and it was not pleasant. In many ways fortunate [sic], for in England I would not have been left so lightly."

With John in tow, everything was straightforward and aboveboard. The two spent several days shopping and sightseeing along the historic cobblestone promenades that twined through the city center. John was particularly delighted by the ornate Gaudi architecture, those inventive distortions incorporated into the medieval skyline, which no doubt appealed to his wacky aesthetic. In the late afternoons they dug in at a café in the Ramblas, Barcelona's most famous promenade, where they could watch the smartly dressed Catalans nose around the stalls and kiosks heaped with books, flowers, and even pets. Then, after a few drinks, they took dinner at one of the stylish local restaurants that Brian knew or toured the nightclubs in search of entertainment.

A few days later, on the recommendation of a friend, Brian rented a car and drove south along the coastal roads that led to Torremolinos and Sitges, on the Costa Brava. Between the heat, the beach, and the familiarity that had been developing since they left Liverpool, souls were bared. Sitting around the outdoor seaside cafés, wandering along the spit of sandy coastline—walking and talking without any inhibitions—Brian and John shared intimate information about themselves, much of it long-suppressed and often traumatic memories of their past, their fears, their frustrations. One can only imagine the loose range of subjects they covered: John's fractured boyhood, his absent father, Julia's tragic death, his sudden marriage and fatherhood, perhaps his rivalry with Paul, money, the allure—and pitfalls—of fame.

Sexuality. John was almost as unsparing about gays as he was about cripples and the retarded. "My God, how he ranted about 'fucking queers' and 'fucking fags!'" says Bob Wooler, who was privy to many of John's backstage outbursts. "He was very outspoken, indifferent to anyone's feelings. He didn't give a shite about anyone, really—but he was especially intolerant of gays." But there is every reason to believe that as they became more relaxed, John was drawn further and further into Brian's guarded confidence. Gradually, Brian unburdened himself of the decisive role homosexuality played in his life, its captive grip and stigma. Certainly he explained its permissive appeal. It must have surprised both men how easy it was to talk so openly about this thorny emotional issue, how therapeutic, in light of their often complicated relationship. No doubt John encouraged the direction of the conversation, but Brian did most of the talking, regaling John with details about the life, sometimes with rapturous descriptions of encounters and taboos. In the provocative Spanish sun, Brian became bold enough to behave with John as he might naturally around other gay men, pointing out "all the boys" he found attractive, even daring to act on his desires. "I watched Brian picking up boys," John recalled, "and I liked playing it a bit faggy—it's enjoyable."

In all the months that they had worked together, through all the conferences and interaction, there was never an instance in which John felt either uncomfortable or threatened by Brian's attention. There was plenty of talk about it; plenty of jokes flew among friends. But for all of the clear signals, no line was ever crossed.

Until Spain. Something happened while Brian and John were in Sitges. In the privacy of their room, after an evening of drinking and sporting about, Brian initiated something that led to physical contact. The extent of their intimacy was never discussed, and all secret details died with the two men. Only John ever spoke of it, and then only cryptically, in an attempt to explain away the incident. "It was almost a love affair," he conceded, "but not quite. It was not consummated. But it was a pretty intense relationship."

Love affair . . . pretty intense . . . relationship . . . These phrases provide enough clues to paint a pretty persuasive picture. And yet if John participated in some sort of a homosexual act, it follows that he played a passive role, allowing Brian an opportunity to probe his fantasies. A lot has been written about their impromptu seaside getaway, most of it imagined by a battery of creative historians. Several insist that Brian and John cruised the bars for unattached young men, even engaging rather impetuously in experimental sex. Albert Goldman is most emphatic: "[John] and Brian had sex," he declares in *The Lives of John Lennon.* Pete Shotton, in his footloose memoir, claims that John told him: "I let [Brian] toss me off." And in *The Love You Make,* Peter Brown and his coauthor, Steven Gaines, go so far as to construct an intimate bedroom scene, complete with cartoonish, overheated dialogue, in which "John lay there, tentative and still, and Brian fulfilled the fantasies he was so sure would bring him contentment. . . ." As far as it is known, the issue of homosexuality never surfaced again in John's life. Curiosity may well have gotten the better of him in Spain. He may have been experimenting, nothing more—or just in an extremely vulnerable state. It had been less than a month since Julian's birth; John not only felt trapped in marriage but did not want to deal with being a father. It stands to reason that his dalliance with Brian was impulsive, more of a reaction to his situation than from any emotional attraction. Away from home, in a beautiful resort with a man—certainly a father figure—who was devoted to taking care of him, John was relaxed and open enough to let it happen unconditionally.

Still, it set a dangerous precedent. Brian came away from the vacation brimming with exhilaration, overjoyed that John had opened up to him and poised for something more. He told friends that their time together had been "something to build on" in the months ahead. The other Beatles were aware that something consensual had gone on between John and Brian. In retrospect, Paul referred to it as "the homosexual thing" and suggested that it was John's way of exercising power over their manager. But if power was part of John's strategy, he was also exercising it over Paul. More influence with Brian also meant more control of Paul—and ultimately of the Beatles. It was a currency he would collect for the rest of his life.

[I]

It was at this pivotal moment that the Beatles influenced an event that was to shape the pop music scene for decades to come.

The day after returning from vacation—before hitting the road again, with Roy Orbison—a promoter enlisted George Harrison to judge a talent show, the Lancashire and Cheshire Beat Group Contest, at Liverpool's Philharmonic Hall. It was one of many such shows that summer designed to flush promising young talent out into the open. Thanks to the Beatles' riotous success, record labels were hot on the prowl for amateur jive bands, and local contests like this one provided excellent showcases throughout Britain. Liverpool proved especially attractive to high-ranking A&R men, convinced that the local water supply had been spiked with something, some rare gene-smashing agent that produced a mongrel breed of rock 'n roll act geared to make young girls swoon.

Anyone who could carry a tune turned out for the contest. The prize was the brass ring: a contract with Decca Records. And on hand to present it to the winner, none other than "the man who turned down the Beatles," Decca's president, Dick Rowe.

Rowe and his aides arrived at Lime Street Station as dusk fell on May 10, to be greeted by the ever-gracious Brian Epstein, who guided them past the Adelphi Hotel and up the hill to Hope Street, where a crowd thronged the Philharmonic steps. Inside, Rowe somehow got seated next to George, of all people, and as the show wore on, the two men chatted amiably about the music business. "I . . . told him how I'd really had my backside kicked over turning the Beatles down," Rowe recalled years later, and as it was water under the bridge, George laughed it off good-naturedly.

Flashing a winning smile, Rowe prodded George to point out the groups he considered the most talented of the lot. George did not reply for a long moment, waiting for a wave of applause to die down. Then he said: "As a matter of fact, we heard a great group down in London called the Rolling Stones. They're almost as good as our Roadrunners." Rowe instantly lost interest in what was happening onstage, and less than halfway through the contest he got up and left without saying good-bye. He took the next train back to London, picked up his wife, and drove directly to see the band that had captured George's attention.

The Rolling Stones. It was only a month earlier that the Beatles had first laid eyes on them. Following the taping of *Thank Your Lucky Stars,* an experimental filmmaker and part-time jazz promoter named Giorgio Gomelsky had approached the Beatles in Twickenham, with the intention of making a documentary film about them. Brian, who was already fantasizing about Hollywood, gave him a polite brush-off. Nevertheless, Gomelsky invited the boys to hear a great "full-bodied R&B" band playing at the Crawdaddy Club, which he ran in a room behind the Station Hotel in Richmond, later that night.

Although largely ignored by the trad-jazz-obsessed Soho "mods" who flocked to the Flamingo, the Crawdaddy Club was one of the linchpins of the rapidly changing pop music scene. It still catered to the stalwarts each Monday with Johnny Dankworth's cool quintet, but on Sundays it featured the Dave Hunt Band, fronted by their wild-ass singer, Ray Davies. Gradually, however, R&B muscled its way in, led there by a rash of white British teenagers whose sole ambition was to imitate urban American Negro blues heroes. Georgie Fame, John Mayall, Herbie Goins, and Chris Farlowe were among the small group of British missionaries who had already brought the new gospel to the London club scene. Hip to the trend, Gomelsky booked the ragtag Stones in February for the relatively generous fee of £1 per musician and watched jubilantly as they proceeded to set the Crawdaddy on fire.

The Beatles had been hearing the buzz for some time. After dinner Neil Aspinall drove them to the club, only three miles from the TV studio, where they quite unexpectedly came upon a tumultuous scene. The place was mobbed with a wild and woolly bunch, mostly art students from the Kingston College of Technology. "It was a real rave," George remembered. The audience shouted across the din and screamed and danced on tables. At one end of the room, a cluster of couples demonstrated the Shake, which was catching on all over the country. Many of the kids stripped off their shirts to compensate for the almost palpable wall of heat. The Beatles heard right away what a "great sound" the band was making. "The beat the Stones laid down was so solid it shook off the walls and seemed to move right inside your head."

Led by the talented but unstable Brian Jones, whose intensity generated a potent charisma, the Rolling Stones pumped out ambitious versions of grassroots R&B. They bounced effortlessly between Bo Diddley, Billy Boy Arnold, Muddy Waters, and Jimmy Reed classics, backlit by dueling red and blue spotlights that seemed to accent the appropriate mood. The Beatles, dressed in identical knee-length suede coats, stood in the back of the club for the remainder of the set, grooving on the vibe. There was, according to Ringo, an instant attraction. "Keith and Brian—wow!" he recalled years later. "They just had *presence*." Moreover, those two had chops: both boys did nothing all day but sit around a grubby, infested flat, working on riffs and alternating on leads until they could intuit what the other was about to do. John, Paul, and George certainly identified with that. Mick Jagger, the vocalist, seemed more than stylish playing the maracas. Everything sounded just right, and John couldn't help feeling that they were "doing things a little bit more radical" than the Beatles.

Later that night, as the two bands talked until dawn, none of the musicians could have dreamed of the incredible fame that awaited them or the cultural revolution brewing in Britain. But there were already signs of a musical undertow that was pulling uniquely talented and expressive youths into the onrushing tide of change.

In London even the most die-hard mods—next-generation beatniks who took their name from *modernist* and were devoted to modern jazz and existentialism—were clambering aboard the rock 'n roll bandwagon, stumbling from scruffy basement clubs under the influence of R&B. They gorged on Sartre, Magritte, Buñuel, and Man Ray during the day, but at night, in sweaty clubs like the Flamingo and the Scene, the intellectualism gave way to John Lee Hooker, Johnny "Guitar" Watson, and Solomon Burke. Besides the Beatles and eventually the Stones, inroads were being made by the Yardbirds (featuring Eric Clapton), the Pretty Things, Long John Baldry, and Zoot Money, among others. And everywhere the momentum was building. By mid-1963, caught up in the red-hot flush of the nascent underground club life, these and other artists had begun to reverse the force of colonial rock 'n roll in Great Britain.

Despite the impact of Merseyside bands and the movement's roots in a working-class sensibility, London still remained ground zero in terms of an exciting creative base. Bands were forced to rely on the record companies, whose magnetic force drew talent south to the capital, not only from Liverpool, Manchester, and Leeds but from across the country. If you wanted to be a rock 'n roller, there was only one place to be, where it was all happening—London.

Brian had already gleaned as much from his endless excursions there. The combination of business contacts, abundant culture, wonderful restaurants, and especially anonymity—the ability for him to live however he pleased—was a powerful incentive to spur a move south. In such an unrestrained, stimulating environment, Brian could easily flourish. But he feared that such a move would distance him from the honeypot—from Liverpool—which to date was the source of all his "artistes." There were still plenty of young Merseyside acts that were ripe for the picking, but knowing how Scousers frowned on pretense, he suspected a London address might well scare them off. Meanwhile, his absence would allow others—outsiders—to horn in on the action, which would be a major tactical error. Thus, he decided to begin laying the foundation for a London-based firm, a company that would handle everything in-house—personal management, booking agency, public relations, the works—whose operation he would guide from afar.

On May 1, 1963, Tony Barrow opened Brian Epstein's first London office, a seedy little one-and-a-half-room affair above a pornographic bookshop on Monmouth Street. Its previous tenant, Joe "Mr. Piano" Henderson, had been a colleague of Dick James, and the space impressed Barrow as "a cozy little setup, complete with casting couch and subdued lighting." The largest of the rooms showcased a superb custom-made desk, with a cocktail cabinet built into the front of it, stocked with hand-cut crystal and a soda siphon. On Brian's instructions, Barrow installed cheap draw blinds and half a dozen plastic potted plants, which he spaced along the windowsills; by the building's entrance, he nailed up a plaque that read: NEMS ENTERPRISES—PRESS OFFICE—UPSTAIRS.

The place was in full swing by the time Brian arrived back from holiday, on May 10. "From Me to You" was holding strong at number one; Billy J. had his cover of "Do You Want to Know a Secret" right behind it, at number two; "How Do You Do It" was sliding off the charts, but Gerry and the Pacemakers had a bang-up follow-up, "I Like It," all ready to go. Barrow had never seen such a run of luck, and it was all due to the Beatles. The fan mail alone presented a somewhat alarming body of evidence, further proof of what lay ahead. Complete strangers wrote to thank the Beatles for their music and to pledge undying loyalty, thousands of letters pouring in every week—bundles, cartons, sacks of it, including autograph requests, love letters, stuffed animals, pictures, and extremely intimate queries. "They wanted to know the ins and outs of a dog's dinner," recalls Frieda Kelly.

The Beatles also got mail at their homes, the addresses no secret to a determined fan. Most of the parents handled it with facility—and delight. "Louise Harrison was *excellent*," Frieda Kelly remembers. "She answered every letter—by *hand!* I'd supply her with a five hundred-pack of handout photographs, envelopes, compliment slips, stamps, or she'd bring the whole load back completed and I'd frank it."

Jim McCartney, too, attacked Paul's stacks of letters with the dedication of a press agent. He and Mike diligently sorted through the exuberant requests, providing whatever they could in terms of a "personal" response from Paul. Occasionally, on his daily trek to the Pegasus Pub, Jim dropped off excess bundles of fan mail with Shelagh Johnson, a local schoolgirl who volunteered to help out. When the volume got unwieldy, Johnson recalls, she enlisted a girlfriend, Pat Riley, to help collect the fan mail at Forthlin Road.

From John, on the other hand, there was rarely any effort. Cynthia, already overburdened, was practically cross-eyed from caring for her new son, and Mimi dismissed fan mail as "utter nonsense," discarding most if it with the trash. Humble, unassuming Ringo had other fish to fry. When it came to the mail, he was predictably befuddled. As Frieda Kelly recalls: "Ritchie came in [the office] one day and asked politely if I would do his mail. I told him he must be joking. 'Get your mum and dad to do it. All the other parents do.' But he just stood there pathetically and said, 'Me mum doesn't know what to put. Anyway, I don't get a lot.' I felt so sorry for him, so I said, 'All right, bring it in, but just this once.' The next day he came in with one of those small poly bags that tights come in—that was all his mail, stuffed inside. Paul got two feet of mail, but Ritchie only had that small sack, with ten letters in it."

As an emergency measure, Tony Barrow stemmed the flow of mail to Kelly by splitting the fan club—which had already grown to forty thousand members in England alone—in two: a northern division, which Frieda relocated to the NEMS office in Liverpool, and a southern division housed at Monmouth Street. Barrow also invented a national secretary, "Anne Collingham," to act as a diversion and to whom fans could write. "It was actually an act of mercy," he recalls. "An outfit of northern teenagers was shouldering responsibilities better suited to a multinational corporation.

We were flying by the seat of our pants, and it was all I could do to keep things afloat—until we could figure out what came next."

To everyone's surprise, it was the press that turned up. Pop music was still an anomaly to the London newspaper establishment, which shunned any coverage of the scene. Even the show-business editors remained skeptical that pop stars had worthwhile appeal or that readers would care about this feeble and superficial genre. Tony Barrow, to his credit, didn't flinch from the task. But instead of knocking his head against the wall trying to pitch uninterested London papers, he relied on his strength in the provinces, where support was fairly strong. "Few record companies ever dealt with anything called the *Sheffield Star* or the *Birmingham Post* or the *Manchester [Evening] News* or the *Liverpool Echo*," Barrow recalls. "I'd put the four of them on the phone to these provincial editors—one right after the next," says Barrow, "and the lads just came *alive*. They were such naturals." Most subjects they dealt with were as dry as British toast, but again and again the Beatles fired off perfect ad-libs, playing off one another, cutting up. Their timing was absolutely remarkable. If Tony hadn't known better, he'd have thought it was rehearsed.

Right off the bat, Paul took charge of an interview's ebb and flow. A slick and tactful diplomat, he knew instinctively just how to deal with every journalist, turning on the charm, humility, wit, sincerity, deference, enthusiasm, flattery—whatever the situation called for. A note strategically placed by the phone allowed Paul to address a reporter by name, as if they were old chums. For instance, to a question about tour dates, he'd respond, "I'm glad you brought that up, *Graham*" or "*Russell*" or "*Dibbs*" or "*Monty.*" If the interview was with a paper from, say, Wolverhampton, Paul might mention how much he liked the town gardens or another of its prized attractions. Listening to him pour it on, one could swear he had been there only yesterday. He was as smooth as silk. And he came loaded with statistics; without the luxury of notes, he rattled off the group's chart listings and upcoming tour dates with pinpoint accuracy.

When he was satisfied that the reporter had been properly softened up, Paul passed the phone to the other Beatles, who did their respective parts: Ringo shared his feelings about joining the band in midstream, George talked music, and John provided color, offering witty recollections about life on the road.

The role of media darlings was a new one for the Beatles. Like most teenage bands, they had spent most of their professional life onstage, bashing out rock 'n roll songs. In front of an audience, they were extroverts, exuding confidence and control. No one said anything about being articulate—or quotable. This was quite a departure for four young, unworldly, largely unsophisticated Scousers, but they rose to the occasion with remarkable flair.

Such finesse made Barrow's job that much easier. All he had to do was to ply the Beatles with cigarettes and "tumblers of scotch and Coke," both of which they consumed with almost superhuman appetites. "I thought I was the world's worst chain-smoker until I went to work with this lot!" Tony marveled. They went through hundreds of cigarettes each day, lighting new ones off the smoldering end of the last. Ashtrays overflowed with stubby butts; smoke as thick as marmalade filled the room. And he learned to top up their tumblers "without waiting for the broad hints."

In those days, before rock 'n rollers were regarded—or regarded themselves—as "serious musicians," most interview questions were barely a notch above inane. Reporters asked the Beatles about their families and their favorite foods; whether they preferred blondes, brunettes, or redheads; what they planned to do after music ran its course. With the Beatles, nothing was off-limits—except for questions about John's marriage.

Cynthia paid dearly for this. Forced to deny her marriage—even her name—to anyone who asked, she skulked around Liverpool as a sort of nonperson, leading what she referred to as an "undercover existence." Out of necessity as well as obedience, she kept a low profile, never wore a wedding band, walked her son at odd hours, rarely attended gigs. When John showed up at home, they carefully avoided going out together in public.

"For up to eighteen months after the birth of Julian Lennon, we were denying that John was married, let alone that he had a son," recalls Tony Barrow. At first, the press was totally indifferent—and stupefyingly compliant. At the time, if a personality asked reporters politely not to reveal a personal matter, *they didn't reveal it!* A wanton tabloid mentality had not yet wracked the British press; journalists weren't obsessed with exposing an icon's private life, nor was there an audience slavering for it. Nothing better demonstrates the cozy relationship between the Beatles and the press than an interview that Judith Simons, of the *Daily Express,* conducted with the boys later that fall. "We still can't mention your marriage, can we, John?" she inquired as a matter of record. As the band undoubtedly knew, the request for her silence would be readily granted.

There were some who didn't know, but they too were easily dealt with. One journalist visiting NEMS "browsed through the pile of NEMS singles beside the office stereo and eventually reached the Beatles' *Please Please Me* album." On the back sleeve, beside John Lennon's name and after the words *rhythm guitar,* someone had penned in the word *married.* Barrow instantly recognized the handwriting as John's. He needed to think fast. Married? It must have been one of the flighty typists, he speculated aloud, who fantasized about marrying John and, well, wrote it as some ludicrous form of wish fulfillment. Preposterously, the writer bought the whole story and moved on to examine other records in the stack.

[II]

Throughout May and early June, the Beatles appeared on the air with astounding frequency—just about every five days—which practically made them a household name in the country. Nothing mattered as much to them as being as successful as the pop stars—such as Del Shannon and Roy Orbison—with whom they performed. But the momentum of their acclaim seemed to stop at the British shores. Their first U.S. release, "Please Please Me," had gone nowhere. Even by Paul's account, it was "a flop." Vee-Jay's perfunctory efforts at promotion produced more frustration than airplay. Now there were indications from abroad that "From Me to You" might fare the same. It was issued by Vee-Jay on May 27, 1963, and picked up glowing reviews in the music trades (*Cash Box* pounced on it as its "Pick of the Week"), but the Ewart Abner Las Vegas fiasco had drained the record company of funds, leaving it empty-handed as far as promotion went.

In the meantime, the Beatles continued to reap the profits of their runaway British success—though nowhere as much as their label.

About the time "Please Please Me" had hit number one, George Martin began to feel guilty that he'd hornswoggled the Beatles. Brian had been so desperate when he first came to Parlophone that he would have taken anything in exchange for a contract. At the end of the Beatles' first full year, should EMI deem to pick up their option, they were contractually guaranteed a 25 percent raise that would kick in at the start of each successive option year. That might have seemed generous on paper, but at a quarter of a penny per disc, it was worse than beggarly, considering this was a group larding EMI's vaults. Martin knew it; he thought "it was patently unfair." So as option time approached, he talked to L. G. Wood about doubling the Beatles' royalty immediately. Wood approved, provided that the Beatles agreed to another five-year option—at which point Martin balked. "No, you don't understand," he explained, "I don't want to ask for anything [in return]." He wanted to give it to the Beatles unconditionally, to reward them for their dramatic success.

Little did Martin realize what a tempest he'd uncorked. Although dependent on recording artists, EMI operated much like the Crown, gazing down on its subjects like a benevolent patron while tolerating no impertinence. The company functioned with royal prerogative; what it gave artists wasn't negotiable, especially on the whim of an employee. *Raising the royalty rate without getting something in return? Unthinkable!* In EMI's eyes, George Martin had committed an act of effrontery so egregious as to be unpardonable. "From that moment on, I was considered a traitor within EMI," Martin recalled. But in the end, Martin's determined efforts made a difference. The day after "From Me to You" was released in America, Parlophone exercised its option, extending the Beatles' contract for another year, and increased the group's royalty from one penny to two pennies.

Along with every rapid-fire achievement, the new contract gave the Beatles definite cause to celebrate. But there wasn't a moment to spare: every day was booked with a concert, a TV appearance, or some long-standing PR obligation that could not be broken. Finally, on June 18, 1963, following a few scheduled dates in the North, the Beatles pulled the plug and threw a party on the occasion of Paul's twenty-first birthday. It was originally going to be held in the garden at Forthlin Road, but because of the Beatles' sweeping success—and the threat of huge crowds of slightly hysterical fans determined to crash the gates—it was rerouted to Paul's aunt Jin Harris's house, across the Mersey in Huyton, where a lovely back garden assured them of privacy.

It was the perfect night for a party: fair and balmy. Summer was coming on strong and the trees surrounding the property were dubbed in a new patchy growth of green. The brilliant northern sky was filled with almost as many stars as had arrived bearing gifts: Gerry Marsden, Billy J. Kramer, the Fourmost, random members of the Merseybeats, the Searchers, the Remo Four, and the Hurricanes, and perhaps starriest of all—the Shadows, all the way from London, sans Cliff Richard, who was off making a movie. Brian arrived alone, as did Bob Wooler, and other old Liverpool chums showed up. The guests pressed under a large striped tent filled with food and flowers, and spilled out onto the lawn. Glasses clinked, toasts were made, and the babble of conversation was especially joyful and raucous.

As the night wore on, it was clear that John was descending into a black funk that radiated hostility. Perhaps all the attention focused on Paul was more than he could tolerate. In the past John never fared well for long when not reaping his share of the spotlight. He'd consumed a staggering amount of alcohol, gulping down drink after drink, and he wove through the midst of the crowd, getting continuously drunker and meaner, his vocabulary sinking deeper into obscenity.

Sometime after ten o'clock Pete Shotton went in search of the bathroom while John plunged back into the crowd. John, who remembered being "out of my mind with drink," elbowed past Bob Wooler, who was also "sinking a fair bit of booze." For all his cozy rapport with the bands, Wooler could also be remarkably glib. Bill Harry says, "Bob has a sarcastic note in his voice that often rubs people the wrong way, and the way he talked to John that night set John off."

There are various accounts of exactly what was said, but no one disagrees that Wooler made a snide reference to John's vacation with Brian Epstein—something on the order of "Oh, John and Brian's just come back from their honeymoon in Spain."* Impulsively, without warning, John leaped on Wooler, beating him viciously with "tightly closed fists." When that didn't do enough damage, he grabbed a garden shovel that was left in the yard and whacked Bob once or twice with the handle. According to one observer, "Bob was holding his hands to his face and John was kicking all the skin off his fingers." In a more lucid moment, John recalled: "I was beating the shit out of him, hitting him with a big stick, and for the first time I thought, 'I can kill this guy.'"

It took two big men—the Fourmost's bass player, Billy Hatton, and Billy J. Kramer, who had just arrived late, on the heels of a gig—to haul John off Wooler and hold him down. "He was completely out of it," Kramer recalls, "like someone who'd gone mad." Pete Shotton returned in time to drag John away, into the garden, while others called an ambulance for the injured and badly shaken Wooler. (Wooler suffered a broken nose, a cracked collarbone, and three broken ribs.)

Before long, however, John went on another drunken rampage. While

---

* John's recollection was that Wooler said, "Come on, John, tell me about you and Brian—we all know."

Cynthia watched in horror, he accosted a girl and grabbed her by the breast, refusing to let go. Once again Billy J. stepped in, pulling them apart. According to Kramer: "He was flailing his arms, screaming, 'You're *nothing*, Kramer—you're *fuck-all! We're* the greatest band.' And he was getting aggressive. So I showed him my fist and said, 'I'll fucking KO you if you don't shut up.'"

Kramer, who was a much bigger man than John, hustled him out to the curb, where he endeavored to subdue John and calm down Cynthia, who "was freaking out," until a taxi arrived to take them home.

Before the dust even settled, Bob Wooler made a beeline for Rex Makin's office. "He arrived with a black eye and a swollen nose," Makin recalls, "and instructed me to claim damages from Lennon." Normally, a situation like this put a lawyer in an awkward position. As Brian's—and thereby John's—solicitor, it presented a clear conflict of interest. But the ever-resourceful Makin wasn't troubled by such issues. "I merely rang Brian up and I acted for everybody," he says smugly. "For my trouble," says Wooler, "I got two hundred pounds and a rather halfhearted apology from John."

A few days after the party, Tony Barrow received a call from Don Short, the pesky entertainment flack for the *Daily Mirror,* who was nosing around about a punch-up involving the Beatles. Barrow did everything he could to play it down, but when other papers also got wind of it, he was forced to make a statement. "I first called John in Liverpool to get his side of the story," Barrow recalls, "but he was absolutely belligerent. His response was 'So fucking what? That bastard called me a bloody queer. He got what he deserved.'" Barrow would learn to endure these passing storms, but at the time he sensed a professional disaster looming and moved to head it off. On his instructions, John was ordered away from the phone, while Barrow, fielding all calls, "put a mighty big spin" on the incident. The *Mirror* went to press on June 21 with an eye-catching headline splashed across the back page: BEATLE IN BRAWL—SORRY I SOCKED YOU:

Guitarist John Lennon, twenty-two-year-old leader of the Beatles pop group, said last night: "Why did I have to go and punch my best friend? I was so high I didn't realize what I was doing." Then he sent off a telegram apologizing to twenty-nine-year-old Liverpool rock show compère and disc jockey Bob Wooler . . . who said: "I don't know why he did it. I have been a friend of the Beatles for a long time. I have often compèred shows where they have appeared. I am terribly upset about this, physically as well as mentally."

John Lennon said: "Bob is the last person in the world I would want to have a fight with. I can only hope he realizes that I was too far gone to know what I was doing."

In fact, neither Wooler nor John ever spoke for the record. The quotes in the copy were the handiwork of Tony Barrow. For better or worse, the Beatles had finally bagged their first national press article.

[III]

Only hours after Paul's birthday party, the Beatles returned to the road for the busy summer season ahead, "racing up and down the country," playing a solid block of one-nighters. Delirious Beatles fans carried on with an intensity never before experienced. They wanted more than music. They wanted contact with the Beatles, wanted to get at them, touch them. Fans thrashed themselves into a frenzy, screamed and cried uncontrollably, leaped from balconies onto the stage, threw themselves in front of the group's van — and worse. In the North, a reporter watched nervously as "girls were plucked from the front row in a state of collapse." The next week a group of teenage boys suffered dehydration after hiding in a hotel room for seven hours just to shake their heroes' hands.

Even the Beatles weren't safe from the mayhem. Fans ripped at their clothes for souvenirs, stripped antennae and mirrors from their cars, hurled precious gifts at them. In Blackpool on July 21, prior to a Sunday afternoon concert at the Queen's Theatre, police abandoned their efforts to disperse a mob of "nearly five thousand fans" thronging the stage door and wisely decided to detour the Beatles' arrival. The boys had to climb a scaffolding in a nearby yard and cross the roofs of adjoining buildings until they could be lowered into a ceiling loft above the stage.

It was becoming evident to keen observers that these demonstrations of adulation transcended mere popularity and stardom. Roy Orbison was popular, Cliff Richard was a full-fledged star, but neither encountered the manic emotional display, the tearing passion, that surrounded the Beatles.

This was something more. It was hard for people to put a finger on it. The hysteria was primitive and overtly sexual. Certainly there had been some of the same response to Elvis, and before him, Johnnie Ray and Frank Sinatra, but nothing so aggressive, nothing that ranged to this extreme. Publicly, the Beatles laughed it off, but it was no joking matter. Their homes were invaded, their privacy shattered. Everywhere they went, either alone or with family and friends, fans accosted them "like persistent termites," demanding autographs and pictures. "There was no longer any question of the Beatles appearing in a club or, indeed, anywhere in direct contact with their public," writes George Melly in *Revolt Into Style*. "They had become a four-headed Orpheus. They would have been torn to pieces by the teenage Furies."

While everyone debated the merits of the phenomenon, one aspect went unchallenged: the Beatles had set the stagnant British music scene on fire. Kids across the country were totally caught up in the excitement, gobbling up records and concert tickets at an unprecedented clip. Rock 'n roll—*British* rock 'n roll—became the major topic of conversation: who was coming out with a new record, what they sounded like, where they were playing, how hot they looked. Everyone wanted to be up-to-date, on top of the scene. Meanwhile, the American stars who had dominated for years began fading from the fore. Del Shannon, Roy Orbison, Buddy Holly, and Elvis continued to sell, but nowhere near as strongly as their British counterparts. "Wave the Union Jack!" *New Musical Express* advocated in a July issue, noting that "not a single American record has topped the Charts this . . . year—something which has never happened before in the 11 years since the top table was introduced!"

The record labels tore through the clubs in Liverpool, signing everyone in sight, and the subsequent proliferation of releases was dizzying indeed. In a span of two months, Decca announced singles by the Dennisons ("Come On Be My Girl"), Beryl Marsden ("I Know"), and Lee Curtis and the All Stars ("Let's Stomp"), featuring Pete Best on drums; Pye issued Johnny Sandon and the Remo Four ("Lies"), the Searchers ("Sweets for My Sweet"), and the Undertakers ("Everybody Loves a Lover"); Fontana released Earl Preston and the TTs ("I Know Something"), Howie Casey and the Seniors ("The Boll Weevil Song"), and the Merseybeats ("It's Love That Really Counts"); HMV put out the first Swinging Blue Jeans record ("Too Late Now"); and Oriole released a single by Faron's Flamingoes ("See If She Cares"), signed Rory Storm and the Hurricanes to a contract, and, in case anyone missed the point, prepared two compilation albums titled *This Is Merseybeat,* volumes one and two, featuring sixteen northern rock 'n roll bands.

In June Polydor began releasing sides from the 1961 sessions with Tony Sheridan in Hamburg—only this time crediting the band as the Beatles, as opposed to the original Beat Boys. It was inevitable that the session would come back to haunt them, but not even the Beatles expected it to crack the charts, which it did immediately following its debut. "It's terrible," John complained to a reporter for *Melody Maker,* objecting to the quality of the record and the circumstances of its release, but both refused to go away. EMI was particularly stung by the situation. After finally breaking the Beatles, it seemed unjust that a competing disc would surface to confuse record buyers.

To staunch a potential backlash, EMI countered by issuing an EP—or extended-play single—with "Twist and Shout," "A Taste of Honey," "Do You Want to Know a Secret," and "There's a Place." No one had an inkling if such a concept would meet with enthusiasm, considering that all four songs were already on the *Please Please Me* album. But it hit the stores on July 15 and by the end of the weekend had sold an astonishing 150,000 copies, with back orders for 40,000 more. Come August, it became the first EP ever to enter the Top Ten.

Dozens of dates were booked in East Kent and Bournemouth through the summer, interspersed with tours of Jersey and Wales. Meanwhile, John and Paul were busy writing "Bad to Me" for Billy J. Kramer, as well as "Hello Little Girl" for the Fourmost, another NEMS act, which George Martin agreed to produce for Parlophone. Brian also signed a rambunctious teenager named Tommy Quigley who had been working an act locally with his twin sister, Pat. Following a welcome Parnesian name change to Quickly, a recording deal was arranged with a subsidiary of Pye on the basis of John and Paul's anteing up an appropriate smash, and within a few weeks "Tip of My Tongue" was released as a single.

All the while, George Martin was pressing for another Beatles single to preserve the headlong run at the charts. A song begun in Newcastle in the afterglow of a late-June gig seemed as if it might fit the bill. Riding in the back of a poorly lit van, Paul had sketched out a lyric fragment that showed early promise. It was modeled on an "answering song," according to Paul, who recalled hearing a Bobby Rydell record that put the form to clever use. A chorus of girls would sing, "Go, Bobby, go, everything's cool," while Rydell shot back, "We all go to a swingin' school." The way Paul envisioned it for the Beatles, he'd sing, "She loves you," whereby the band would respond, *"Yeah . . . yeah . . . yeah,"* offering a nonsensical but effective hook. He subsequently ran it by John, who decided that the answering business was a "crummy idea" but the lyric was worth exploring. They went back to their room at the Turk's Hotel, whipped out their guitars, and in a few hours' time had the bones of the song in place.

"She Loves You" was finished the next evening, during a rare day off in Liverpool. The boys worked intently in the tiny dining nook at Forthlin Road while Paul's father sat not five feet away, chain-smoking and watching TV. His presence, the competing noise, didn't matter—nothing could interrupt Paul and John's concentration. They wrote with a sense of mission, replacing wobbly phrases, playing lines over and over, refining the way things scanned, until they'd gotten it right. And when they were done, they knew they had a hit on their hands. The song has a tremendous, explosive kind of energy that bursts from the opening notes and culminates in a beautiful split of harmony in the parcel of *yeahs*. George Martin listened to a rundown of it in the studio on July 1 and thought it was "brilliant . . . one of the most vital [songs] the Beatles had written so far."

The band polished the song over the next few days, teaching George Harrison a third harmony to fatten the effect. Back in the studio, with Martin perched on a wooden stool in front of the piano, they belted it out, following an arrangement John and Paul had concocted on their guitars. Engineer Norman Smith, who was standing over the mixer, did a double-take as they turned up the juice. Earlier he had spotted the lyrics on the music stand and felt his heart sink. As he later relayed to Mark Lewisohn: "'She loves you, yeah, yeah, yeah, she loves you, yeah, yeah, yeah, she loves you, yeah, yeah, yeah, yeah.' I thought[,] Oh my God, what a lyric! This is going to be one that I *do not* like."

In fact, there was something for everyone in the lyric, though nothing grabbed listeners as much as the performance. The Beatles sing "She Loves You" with such conviction and with such energy that for the brief time it lasts—considerably less than two and a half minutes—they create a groove that is not only completely irresistible but also quintessential. What the Beatles built into the song provided, for them, a perfect, lasting image: the *yeah-yeah-yeahs* and the falsetto *ooooos* (when performing this, they shook their heads in unison, setting off rapturous shrieks from the fans) became iconic symbols. No matter how their music evolved, no matter how they experimented with complex musical textures and electronics, it is hard to think of the Beatles today without visualizing them as four grinning mop tops positioned in that classic stage pose—the guitars riding high on their chests, drumsticks rhythmically pummeling the cymbals—singing, "And you know you should be glad: *oooooooo,*" with a decisive shake of their beautiful hair. Nothing identifies them more vividly.

———

When the second Vee-Jay single, "From Me to You," was released, American disc jockeys ignored it completely—a silence even more devastating than scorn. "No one played it; they thought it was a dud," says Paul Marshall, who brokered the deal. Now, with a third record due out, Marshall went back to Capitol Records. Capitol usually offered a song and dance to soften the rejection of an English act, but this time the pass was brutally direct. Dave Dexter proclaimed the Beatles "stone-cold dead in the U.S. marketplace." Capitol wasn't interested in the slightest—not now, not in the foreseeable future.

Without even Vee-Jay as a backup (the label was reorganizing in the wake of its economic bungle), the Beatles were without hope of an American release. In the meantime, Roland Rennie approached an acquaintance named Bernie Binnick, who owned a small Philadelphia label, Swan Records. Swan, which had cobbled together a few hits with teen star Freddy Cannon, didn't even register on *Billboard*'s national radar screen. But Rennie was desperate, and the price was right—"They didn't pay anything to license it," he recalls. "They just guaranteed to put the bloody thing out, as a favor to us"—which, though less than idyllic, at least assured the Beatles that "She Loves You" would get a fighting chance.

Days before "She Loves You" was due to be released, NME calculated that three Liverpool groups—the Beatles, Gerry and the Pacemakers, and Billy J. Kramer with the Dakotas—were responsible for sales amounting to more than 2.5 million records. Numbers like that left the Beatles dazed, in a state of euphoria. Only nine months before, they were still hustling for £10 gigs in Liverpool, hoping against all odds just to *make* a record. "Sometimes, you know, I feel as if there's nothing I'd like better than to get back to the kind of thing we were doing a year ago," Paul mused in the midst of the hot summer tour. "Just playing the Cavern and some of the other places around Liverpool. I suppose the rest of the lads feel that way at times, too. You feel as if you'd like to turn back the clock." If that was even remotely feasible before, all bets were off the moment "She Loves You" hit the airwaves.

Unlike any of the band's previous records, "She Loves You" touched off a nationwide reaction the press immediately dubbed "Beatles fever." Before the record was even released, Parlophone had advance orders for "a staggering 235,000" copies—figures "so enormous" that even EMI was impressed. No act in corporate memory had ever spurred such demand. And suddenly everything the Beatles did resonated with meaning. Both music papers—*Melody Maker* and *NME*—interviewed them ceaselessly, hanging on every word, as did a dozen or more radio personalities on Britain's top-rated shows. The Beatles, eager to please, did their part. They responded perceptively and with unguarded enthusiasm, supplying insights on everything from the details of their early career to their most personal habits. But mostly their conversations were filled with the chatter of young men awestruck by the general good luck that had befallen them. Beyond the burdens of touring and songwriting, Paul mooned about go-karting, Ringo discussed his special knack for dancing and dreams of one day opening a string of ladies' hairdressing salons, John fantasized about writing books before tackling a West End musical, and George confessed to sloth, admitting that his idea of "the life" wasn't so much about fame as it was "sitting round a big fire with [his] slippers on and watching the telly." Intuitive, inventive, and taken with the sound of their own voices, the Beatles developed a penchant for delivering folksy generalities that helped create accessible images of familiarity. "I'm not really interested in sport . . . except for swimming," Paul told a reporter. "But that's the thing these hot days, isn't it? It really cools you off."

The first two weeks of September were as much a whirlwind as anything the Beatles had ever experienced. From London, where they prerecorded sessions for an upcoming BBC radio special called *Pop Go the Beatles,* the path zigzagged aimlessly between mid-size cities, from Worcester to Taunton and then Luton, hitting converted cinemas along the Gaumont and Odeon chains. Then they played the ABC Theatre in Blackpool for the second time in little more than a month before turning around and heading right back to London.

Brian had managed to slip in a few midday sessions at Abbey Road studios so the Beatles could make headway on their second album. Previously, they'd recorded a slew of standout covers—"You've Really Got a Hold on Me," "Money," "Devil in Her Heart," "Till There Was You," "Roll Over Beethoven," and "Please Mr. Postman," songs they'd been playing for years—along with two exciting Lennon-McCartney originals, "It Won't Be Long" and "All My Loving," the latter of which Paul had written on a piano immediately before a gig at a Moss Empire theater. Now they were set to round things off a bit, with the first song ever written by George, "Don't Bother Me," and two numbers originally earmarked for Ringo—"Little Child" and "I Wanna Be Your Man."

Things were kept "fairly simple" for Ringo. By design, he had to sing from behind the drums, so the overall arrangement couldn't be too demanding. Besides, Ringo "didn't have a large vocal range," Paul recalled, to say nothing of his concentration. "If he couldn't mentally picture [the song], you were in trouble." But neither Paul nor John was deterred by Ringo's shortcomings. He was too likable, too amusing, not at all self-indulgent, and he appreciated their efforts on his behalf. These latest songs were a further indication of their affection for Ringo—their commitment to giving him more of the spotlight—though at the last minute John claimed the vocal on "Little Child" for himself and they fairly gave away "I Wanna Be Your Man" to the Rolling Stones.

On September 10, John and Paul encountered publicist Andrew Oldham in London's West End. The boys had been on the way to Dick James's office, window-shopping on Jermyn Street in an area overrun with music stores that Paul referred to as their "Mecca," when a taxi drew up carrying the Rolling Stones' snarky manager.* Oldham was on his way to Studio 51 in Soho, where the Stones were rehearsing, and he invited the two Beatles to attend. During the cab ride over, he casually let drop that the Stones were looking for a follow-up to their first single—a half-assed cover of Chuck Berry's "Come On"—and wondered if they had any suggestions. Left unsaid, but certainly understood, was the preference for a Lennon-McCartney number.

Not more than a few minutes later, Paul recalled telling Mick, "Well, Ringo's got this track on our album, but it won't be a single and it might suit you guys." John didn't flinch. He regarded "I Wanna Be Your Man" as "a throwaway," but even at that point it was still basically a work in progress. Paul had come up with a lick—"I want to be your lover, baby, I want to be your man"—and little more. They played what they had for the Stones—John used Keith's guitar and Paul turned Bill Wyman's bass upside down—

---

* In various memoirs, Paul insists that it was Mick Jagger and Keith Richards, but accounts by John, Oldham, and members of the Stones prove otherwise.

who were immediately intrigued. The song had their name written all over it, a stylish, bluesy vamp they could "Diddley up" when it came time to put their stamp on it. John recalled: "So Paul and I just went off in the corner of the room and finished the song while we were all still there, talking."

The donation was both friendly and strategic. For John and Paul, songs were like currency. Every solid cover boosted their fame and fortune and allowed them to reap the benefits and lay back a little when their own singles began the slow slide down the polls. On almost any given week, one could flip through the pages of *Melody Maker* or *New Musical Express* and discover ads for records by, say, Tommy Quickly that carried the tagline: "Another Smash Hit from the Sensational Song Writing Team John Lennon and Paul McCartney." Or an item that announced NEWLEY WAXES BEATLES' TUNE. After a stunning string of Beatles hits, Beatles songs became a sort of status symbol.

Of course, the more famous the Beatles became, the more other bands greedily sought out Lennon-McCartney songs. Whereas John, Paul, and George once raked record stacks for undiscovered gems by Barrett Strong, James Ray, or Arthur Alexander, now mavericks combed the Beatles' singles for B-sides they could hijack. Friends, eager to ride their coattails, routinely asked for spare songs, to the point where John and Paul grew guarded about their former generosity. Billy Kramer recalls an occasion in Bournemouth when he overheard John working on an early version of "I Want to Hold Your Hand." "Can I have that song?" Kramer asked, having instantly recognized its potential, to which John shook his head emphatically and replied, "No, we're going to do that ourselves."

On September 15, 1963, the Stones opened for the Beatles at the Great Pop Prom at London's Royal Albert Hall. The show was a milestone of sorts for both bands. An upscale benefit for the Printers' Pension Corporation, the theater hosted a formally dressed crowd of donors drawn from the upper crust of British society. Everyone was on his best behavior: the Beatles, gentlemen to the core, wore their fancy mohair suits, and the ever-scruffy Stones showed up in dark trousers, pale blue shirts with ties, and dark blue leather waistcoats that made them look like waiters from Le Caprice.

But when it came to music, no one held anything back. The Stones did what the Stones do best—they blew out the walls in a torrent of blues-inspired mayhem. As one reviewer recalled, "their act [was] fast, wound-up, explosive." And the Beatles brought down the house. "The Royal Albert Hall fairly shook on its foundations," reported a cultural magazine that covered the gig. Nothing remained intact once the bands took the stage, least of all the dignity of the fancy-dress crowd, which lost control of themselves, whistling and screaming like giddy teenagers.

It was the first of many such extraordinary events that would be repeated during the coming years. "We were like kings of the jungle then," John remembered, seeing tony London at his feet. The scene dwarfed any dream they'd had in their heads all these years. Paul was especially impressed by the magnificence—and the glory. Before the show, the two bands were herded up a wide set of marble stairs at the back of the hall, facing Prince Consort Road, for a photo op. In the late afternoon, with sunlight sifting in through the mullioned windows, Paul remembers looking over at the others, beaming in their smart, stylish clothes, and thinking, "This is it! London! The Albert Hall!" Years later he would admit to the thrill it gave him, standing there with the other boys, the world seemingly at their fingertips. "We felt like gods!" he said. "We felt like fucking gods!"

Little did he realize that this was just the beginning.

Chapter 23 | **So This Is Beatlemania**

[I]

No television show in Great Britain was more popular—or selective—than *Val Parnell's Sunday Night at the London Palladium*. It was an institution: practically every set in the country was tuned to it each Sunday night as the top English stars and visiting American performers took part in the prestigious but corny variety show that aired live from the Argyll Street theater. Every major celebrity eventually put in an appearance: Judy Garland, Frank Sinatra, Laurence Olivier, Elizabeth Taylor, Nat King Cole—*Cliff Richard*. If, to Americans, the pinnacle of success was playing Carnegie Hall, its British equivalent was the Palladium, "home of the stars." In Ringo's estimation, "there was nothing bigger in the world than making it to the Palladium." He'd always dreamed about it as a boy. It was the yardstick for success. "My mum, Annie, always used to tease Ritchie— 'See you on the *Palladium'*—when he was a boy, just practicing," recalls Marie Crawford. "You'd always hear a parent say that as a joke, knowing their child had about as good a chance of getting there as winning the football pools."

Now the Beatles could claim top prize: the toppermost of the poppermost. And even though they were doing only four numbers*—songs they could have played in their sleep—tradition demanded they participate in an all-day rehearsal.

Fans had begun gathering outside just after their arrival at the theater on Sunday, October 13, 1963. By late afternoon, the situation outside the stage door intensified to the point that it attracted Brian's attention. There were a hundred or so kids milling about there—more than the Beatles

---

* *The set included "From Me to You," "I'll Get You," "She Loves You," and "Twist and Shout."*

could safely deal with. Rehearsal was drawing to an end, and the boys had a three-hour window before they were due back at the theater. Brian consulted with Neil Aspinall and Tony Barrow to coordinate a departure. "We were talking about various decoy routes," Barrow recalls. "Should they go this way or that way, up over the roof. And we finally decided that with the kids hanging around the stage door, we should just go out the front entrance and get into the car."

Neil pulled an Austin Princess around to Argyll Street and waited for the Beatles by the curb. It was a few minutes after five o'clock. The street lay in dusky shadows, and from the look of things, they were in good shape to make a clean getaway. There was a clear path to the entrance, no one in sight. "What we hadn't counted on," says Barrow, "were the kids who'd been keeping their eyes on the car." At exactly the moment the Beatles broke through the doors, fans—"hordes of kids"—converged from everywhere, and "it all happened at once." An incredible roar went up, and not merely any roar but an ear-splitting blast of exultation, mixed with surprise, rapture, awe, and abandon. It was pandemonium on the sidewalk. Pushing and shoving broke out as the crowd moved en masse toward the agile, galloping quartet. The Beatles ran headlong through a gauntlet of grabby hands, diving for cover through the hastily opened car doors, as security guards moved quickly to hold back the crowd.

The scene on the street caught the press napping, but in ten minutes every city desk in London went on alert, cranking up the machinery to cover a story that would take on a life of its own.

———

The papers knew exactly what to call it. BEATLEMANIA! screamed the front-page banner of the *Daily Mirror*. Headlines didn't come any more eye-catching than that. Every paper carried photographs of a dark street scene that resembled a flash siege, with a police cordon struggling to hold off a mob of screaming girls. Tipped off about crowds following the rehearsal, photographers had raced to the scene, hoping to salvage a story after the show. What they encountered, however, was better than anything they could have wished for. Where earlier there had been two hundred girls outside the Palladium, by show's end there were two thousand strong, all of them overcome with frenetic Beatles rapture. Like the reporters among them, they had heard about the earlier frenzy and used it as a model to express their emotional release, so by nightfall the screaming and sobbing seemed like the accepted way to react. According to eyewitness accounts in the *Daily Herald,* "screaming girls launched themselves against the police—sending helmets flying and constables reeling." It was complete bedlam, abandoned only after the Beatles dove down the theater steps and into a car, with most girls giving chase as it sped off along Oxford Street.

"It was *exactly* the story we'd been waiting for," says Don Short, who covered "the whole spectrum of show business" for the *Mirror.* "Up until that time, I'd merely go around to Claridge's or the Savoy and interview Sammy Davis Jr. one week, Andy Williams the next, but the Beatles had all this drama swirling around them—and they were sexy, a very sexy story."

Britain's papers had discovered sex earlier that spring, when they began tracking a colorful rumor that John Profumo, the secretary of state of war, had engaged in a sexual liaison with a young call girl named Christine Keeler. Word had it that he'd met her in 1961 during a weekend social at Cliveden, Lord Astor's estate, where she was staying with her friend Dr. Stephen Ward. To make matters worse, there were also reports of Keeler's involvement with a man named Eugene Ivanov, a Russian naval attaché and reported KGB agent, possibly compromising state secrets. At first no paper dared run any part of the story, fearing the harsh slap of England's libel laws. By June, however, Profumo had admitted to committing an "impropriety," and the gloves came off. London's dailies feasted on the scandal, rolling out new installments, morning, noon, and night, as if they were segments of an ongoing soap opera.

Profumo was must reading because it exposed the rank hypocrisy of members of the establishment, but nothing seemed hotter, more sensational, or sleazier than the ongoing case in Edinburgh, detailing the voracious sexual appetite of the Duchess of Argyll, whose husband was suing her for divorce. Cabinet ministers, lords, dukes, duchesses—everyone, it seemed, wanted to get in on the act, and the news media accommodated them. Another cabinet minister was caught—*supposedly*—having oral sex with a prostitute in Richmond Park. And eight high court judges *supposedly* engaged in an orgy, leading Prime Minister Harold Macmillan to exclaim, "One, perhaps, two, conceivably. But eight—I just can't believe it."

But the newspapers did. Rather, they believed it sold copies—and they were right. Sex and innuendo had awakened a sleeping readership, and the dailies, particularly the tabloids, marketed them with skill. And Britain was ready for it. Repressive Victorian morality, so long the badge of proper society, was growing rapidly passé. The postwar wave of upper-class promiscuity and "considerable sexual license" had finally swept through the lower orders, who were itching for a piece of the action. Sex was no longer an indulgence only for the rich; it was a pastime as accessible to commoners as a pint at the pub. "The popular morality is now a wasteland," declared Professor George Carstairs in his Reith Lectures that year. "A new concept is emerging, of sexual relationships as a source of pleasure." Newspapers certainly saw the future as clearly. "On the island where the subject has long been taboo in polite society," wrote a *Times* (London) columnist, "sex has exploded into the national consciousness and national headlines." Beatlemania was the icing on the cake.

Two days after 15 million viewers got a look at them on *Sunday Night at the London Palladium,* and only one day after the bold headlines, it was announced that a secret deal had been struck back in August for the Beatles to appear before the Queen Mother and Princess Margaret at the annual Royal Variety Performance in November. This was no small development. A command performance was a considerable honor—and a considerable boost. It lifted Beatlemania out of local cinemas and thrust it center stage, giving it the Queen's blessing. It also legitimized it for the "serious" press. Two days later the so-called prestigious writers, those whose names distinguished general-feature stories and had so far expressed a total lack of interest, came courting: Derek Jewel from the *Sunday Times,* Vincent Mulchrone from the *Daily Mail,* Judith Simons from the *Daily Express,* Peter Woods from the BBC's *Radio Newsreel,* the *Mail*'s Linda Lee-Potter—there were too many to count—all demanding interviews with the Beatles. It had taken Barrow months just to get these journalists on the phone, he says. The next day they began bombarding his office line regularly, begging for leads, thanks largely to the response of their page-one stories. "All over Britain, there have been incredible scenes as stampeding fans have battled for [Beatles] tickets," wrote *Melody Maker,* which catalogued the incidents in a column titled "This Week's Beatlemania." "Girls have fainted. Police have had to control queue crowds. Fans have been camping out overnight days before tickets [go] on sale." Crowds in Birmingham jostled with police outside the ABC-TV studios, where the boys were taping a segment of *Thank Your Lucky Stars.* "At Leicester," it was reported, "hundreds slept in the streets throughout the night, waiting for box-offices to open" for an upcoming Beatles show. The city of Carlisle experienced a "midnight panic" when six hundred fans crashed police lines outside the ABC Cinema, necessitating emergency first-aid crews. More girls "fainted—and got hurt" buying tickets in Hull. In Portsmouth and

Bristol, anxious promoters, alarmed by what they read in the papers and saw on TV, turned to the police for help, calling in "every burly and able-bodied man on the staff to keep order." And that was only a warm-up. "Thousands of girls battled with police" in Huddlesfield, a town in Yorkshire, when "a stampede broke out," injuring sixty "screaming teenage fans." The story broke as front-page news in *Sunday People:*

> When the box office opened a mass of youngsters surged forward, breaking the cordon of forty policemen. . . . In the rush, many of the fans were crushed against the cinema walls and shop doorways. Ambulance men who had been on duty all night were kept busy pulling them out, carrying out other fans who had fainted, and taking them into the cinema foyer, which served as a casualty station.

There seemed no limit to the wild scenes. The riots during Bill Haley concerts seven years earlier were basically the handiwork of teddy boys, who used the music as a soundtrack for their ongoing punch-ups. But the Beatles had touched off what appeared to be a mass swoon. Girls of all classes were caught up in the screaming, love pledging, sobbing, hair pulling, and fainting that accompanied each show.

Fortunately, from October 24 through the end of the month, the band began a weeklong tour of Sweden, which temporarily removed them from the public eye. But upon their return, on the morning of October 31, hundreds, perhaps even "thousands[,] of screaming fans" thronged the terraced roof of the Queen's Building at Heathrow Airport, which ignited the hysteria anew.

By coincidence, "the commotion" caught the eye of American TV impresario and gossip journalist Ed Sullivan, who was arriving in London with his wife, Sylvia, at precisely the same time, to scout talent for future shows. Sullivan, intrigued, corralled a few giggling fans and asked if they knew whether a celebrity was arriving. Was it a member of the royal family? he demanded. The girls just laughed and sashayed away. After an airport official told him it was the Beatles, Sullivan dutifully wrote down the name and instructed his son-in-law, producer Bob Precht, to find out what he could about them.

It didn't take Sullivan long to learn that a phenomenon was streaking through all of England, and he moved to position himself for an American scoop. That meant striking a quick deal with Brian Epstein. Sullivan had some idea of what it would take to land a pop act on the brink of stardom. He'd paid Elvis Presley a staggering $50,000 for three appearances in 1956. What, almost eight years later, could the Beatles possibly command? To Sullivan it was clear that though they were still basically a foreign sensation, it was only a matter of time before their popularity spread to the States. An exclusive would mean offering Epstein enough to keep competitors at bay.

The Beatles had always refused to consider an American visit until they meant something abroad; otherwise, it could prove too humiliating an experience. The boys were all too aware of how American audiences regarded British acts. John was especially sensitive to reports that Cliff Richard, a longtime megastar, had "died"—meaning bombed—on an American tour. "He was fourteenth on the bill with Frankie Avalon," John huffed, with some exaggeration.

But Brian Epstein had an instinct—a good instinct—for timing. Not only did he feel the moment was right, he knew—he seemed to know instinctively—how to synchronize it.

One stroke of chronology was already in place. While the boys were in Sweden, Brian had concluded negotiations with United Artists for a feature-length movie to star the Beatles. For a few months other film studios had been dangling offers without any concrete idea of what they wanted to make. This frightened the Beatles, who were dead set against being packaged in a kind of standard ensemble jukebox movie, like *Rock Around the Clock* or *The Girl Can't Help It.* John, who was especially cautious about their image, told *Melody Maker:* "We prefer to wait until we find a film with a good plot that will hold the interest of the teenagers." (Much later, in blunt terms, he said, "We didn't want to make a fuckin' shitty pop movie.") But UA already had a producer in tow—a jovial American expat named Walter Shenson—who'd cast Peter Sellers in *The Mouse That Roared,* which had served to establish the comedian outside England. That scored points right off the bat with John. Shenson recalled that during his first meeting with the Beatles, in one of the empty offices at Abbey Road, John, acting as spokesman for the group, confronted him immediately about the type of film he intended to make. "Oh, I don't know," Shenson told him, shrugging, "but it should be a comedy." The Beatles cut knowing glances at one another before John said, "Okay, you can be the producer." It was as simple as that.

And Shenson was immediately captivated by their vivid personalities and the kind of zany scene that swirled about them. "I really found myself in the middle of a Marx Brothers movie," he recalls. "And they were awfully sweet." To Shenson, the Beatles embodied the beguiling blend of natural humor and wholesomeness that the classic movie comedians exhibit. He realized he was "onto something very special, on the level of a Keaton or a Fields." If he played his cards right, Shenson believed, his little low-budget picture had the potential to be something more—much more.

UA's guarantee up front of a *worldwide* release seemed like a princely—even absurd—offer. Shenson himself had asked UA boss Bud Ornstein, "You mean those kids with long hair? What do you want to make a movie with them for?" Without skipping a beat, Ornstein roared: "For the soundtrack album." Somehow, UA had determined that those rights had been withheld from EMI in the Beatles' recording contract—withheld, or overlooked—and could be worth a fortune, many times over the film's £200,000 production budget.

Very quickly, Shenson brought Richard Lester, his director on *The Mouse on the Moon,** into the deal. Lester, the irascible scion of a middle-class Philadelphia family, was another expat looking to quit his job grinding out commercials and make his mark in motion pictures. He had worked with the Goons and shared Shenson's love for their kind of goofy British humor, which seemed to make him a natural choice. "I'll do it for *nothing!*" Lester volunteered. This comment amused Shenson, who was grappling at the time with a shoestring budget. "Don't worry about that, Dick," he told him, "we're *all* going to do it for nothing."

United Artists was prepared to pay the Beatles a small salary plus 25 percent of the movie's net. On October 29, they met in Bud Ornstein's apartment to hammer out a deal. "We laid out the terms," Shenson says, "which gave us the Beatles' services for three pictures, along with the soundtracks for each." That seemed fair all around, nor did anyone object to a £25,000 fee for Brian and the four boys. But then Brian tipped his chin toward Ornstein, put on his most pugnacious game face, and said, "We're not going to take less than seven and a half percent."

A deathly silence fell over the room. According to Shenson, "We just couldn't believe it! It didn't make any sense." Only much later did he realize Brian's mistake. "He was talking percentages of *record albums*," Shenson says, "[in] which, if you get a couple of pennies, you make a lot of money." Just like that, Brian had let the steam out of his trousers. If the

---

* *A paper-thin sequel to* The Mouse That Roared, *sans Peter Sellers, which had not yet been released.*

man wanted seven and a half points, UA was certainly willing to sign off on a deal—right away. Both parties left that afternoon happy with the agreement.

If only someone had bothered to run it by the Beatles.

It was Paul who first had misgivings, not about money and not about terms. "He wanted to see a script," recalls Shenson. Actually, his concerns had less to do with substance than with romance. Earlier in the summer Paul had begun seeing a precocious seventeen-year-old actress named Jane Asher, who was wise to the vagaries of show business. She'd been acting since the age of seven, on stage, screen, and television, and urged Paul to approve a script before committing to any deal. "She was absolutely right," Shenson says today. "Who makes a film without looking at the script?"

Once it was announced that the Beatles were going to make a movie, the producers were inundated with interest from agents and writers who proposed "the most banal nonsense," in Shenson's estimation, "just silly stuff, not even close." No one had the slightest idea how to use the Beatles without treating them trivially, like cartoon characters. Finally, someone— and Shenson believes it was one of the Beatles*—suggested they contact Alun Owen, a Liverpool playwright, to kick around some ideas.

Shenson was appalled. He was familiar with Owen's work, gritty working-class dramas à la Clifford Odets, John Osborne, and Arnold Wesker, in what was known as the kitchen-sink school of writing. More recently, his plays had been adapted for television, and while Shenson was impressed with them, he was more concerned by their stunning lack of humor and bleakness. Out of curiosity, he screened Owen's *No Trams to Lime Street* and considered it "pretty heavy going." Shenson had only the bare bones of a concept in mind. "I think it should be an exaggerated day-in-the-life of the Beatles," he told Owen, and suggested the playwright meet the boys in Dublin on October 7, where they were doing two shows at the Adelphi Cinema.

In the meantime, the Beatles prepared for their performance in front of the Queen. "They were nervous," says Tony Barrow, "fairly overawed by such an important audience." Although they had basically just a short four-song spot, all of England would be watching, to say nothing of the figure who, next to God, was the most awesome symbol of the empire.** None of which deterred John. "All day long he was practicing a line he

---

* John told Jann Wenner, "And Brian came up with Allen [sic] Owen."
** The show itself was taped and seen on television the following week.

planned to deliver that night," Barrow recalls. When it came time to introduce "Twist and Shout," John explained, he intended to say, "For our last number, I'd like to ask your help. The people in the cheaper seats, clap your hands, and the rest of you, if you'd just rattle your fucking jewelry." Brian nearly burst a blood vessel. He begged—*ordered*—John to behave himself, to think of how much this meant to the Beatles. And their families! Everyone's reputation, he warned, was riding on it. Still, John gave him no satisfaction. It was evident to those watching Brian throughout the performance, flushed and sweating buckets, sitting in the second row of the front circle, that he was unsure just how far John would actually go. Friends recall Brian gripping the wooden armrests, his knuckles white with fear, as John introduced their rousing showstopper with the rehearsed remark, then relaxing as it played as written—but without the expletive. "You could almost hear him exhale," says Barrow, who was circling through the Prince of Wales Theatre on a roving ticket.

The next day the press leaped on the line, as it was repeated everywhere with the humility of an outrageous anecdote. It wasn't disrespectful (although originally intended as such) or scandalous (much to John's chagrin), but it certainly wasn't anything one expected to hear out of a loyal British subject. When the papers hit the newsstands, all the focus was on the Beatles instead of the royalty among the audience. The headline across the *Daily Express*—BEATLES ROCK THE ROYALS—was par for the course. The talk around town was comparable: in London, only John Lennon could upstage the Queen.

[II]

Another stroke on the clock was beginning to tick off.

By the end of the summer of 1963, the Beatles and their manager had grown weary of dragging themselves back and forth between Liverpool and London, sometimes two or three times a week. The grueling trip had convinced Brian that the Beatles needed to be rescued from the road—at least from unnecessary travel—and its impermanence. None of the boys had a place of his own. One might say they still lived with their parents, but even that was inexact. The two or three nights a month they touched down in Liverpool gave them no more sense of a nest than a layover at another guesthouse. Interaction with families and friends was becoming awkward. And with the constant invasion of fans, as Ringo noted, "it was impossible to go home." Even John, whose wife and son remained Merseyside, lived more or less out of a suitcase, in a low-priced bedsit in Hoylake.

As a remedy, Brian rented the Beatles an unfurnished flat in London, to use as a base when they were in the city on business or playing nearby. The little place, on Green Street, was frightfully sparse—no furniture to speak of, just three bedrooms with nothing more than single beds and lamps. A tortured hi-fi in one corner played a never-ending selection of loud music. "Overflowing ashtrays and record jackets [were] strewn over the floor." It was everything they could do to make it seem habitable, congregating in George and Ringo's room, endlessly smoking cigarettes and talking into the night. But if there was a bleakness about it, Ringo and George didn't seem to mind. As George recalled, "It was such a buzz because we'd been brought up in little two-up two-down houses in Liverpool, and now to have a posh flat in Mayfair, and with a bathroom each, it was great." To suggest that it resembled anything close to home, however, was way off track. "There was no homeliness [sic] about it at all," according to Paul, who got stuck with the closet-size room in the back. "There was nobody's touch. I hated it." Despite its austerity, the Beatles made no effort to improve the lonely space—they never so much as bought a kettle for afternoon tea.

On those rare days when they weren't jammed up with interviews and gigs, the Beatles used their spare time to explore the city streets. It was not yet the Happening it would become, not yet even swinging London; that was still a year off. But the momentum was clearly building. The "obligatory period of post-war austerity" gave rise to radical social changes and a generation waiting to break loose—and to experiment. London was where the action was, and it was in the throes of a youthful renaissance that sought to take the starch out of the Union Jack.

In fact, the transformation was already under way. The postwar generation—those specifically of the Beatles' age, just becoming adults—was coming into its own, and slowly but surely taking over the city. There was already a young presence visible on the streets. London, being the Continent's port o' call for American culture, had it all: record labels, bookshops, art galleries, clubs, cafés—a whole smorgasbord of attractions operating outside the bounds of traditional society. Disenchantment with the mainstream reverberated through these ranks; a new wave of political and philosophical thinking began to take hold. Traffic pulsed through the gaudy boutiques that had sprung up on Carnaby Street, where mods kitted up in dazzling hues launched a provocative new clothes conscious-ness. Artists, writers, musicians, poets, painters, activists: dreamers. "So many factors commingled to produce the cultural earthquakes," writes Jonathon Green in his introduction to *Days in the Life.* And now the Beatles lived on the fault line.

———

But they couldn't live in London as the Beatles: one for all and all for one. London wasn't Hamburg, where nothing mattered and no one seemed to care. A crash pad was all right for George and Ringo, but John, for one, had a family to think about. Eventually he moved with Cynthia and Julian into a tiny fifth-floor maisonette at 13 Emperor's Gate, Kensington, di-rectly above the one occupied by Bob Freeman, who had photographed the Beatles for their album covers.

Paul laid claim to John's empty room, but shortly thereafter he, too, decided to split away from the group's flat. Aside from disliking the place, he'd become increasingly involved with Jane Asher and her personal life. More and more often, after a hectic day conducting Beatles business, Paul would make a beeline for her family's town house on Wimpole Street. From there, he and Jane disappeared into the glare of brightly lit streets, where they reaped the benefits of London's nightlife. Throughout the fall of 1963, they spun madly from the West End to Covent Gardens to the National Theatre to the Royal Albert Hall to the Establishment Club, to anywhere there was something of cultural interest going on. Plays, exhibi-tions, concerts, parties, one after another—there was never a dull moment. Late at night, when the crowds thinned out, they would idle down Cork Street, browsing in the windows of the high-end galleries where Hoppers, Giacomettis, and Man Rays were displayed like the crown jewels, sharing their firsthand judgments and educating their eyes. They were also fre-quent guests of artistic royalty: Maggie Smith, Harold Pinter, Jill Bennett, Arnold Wesker, John Mortimer, Kenneth Tynan. Jane, it seemed, knew just about everybody, and just about everybody was fascinated by the Beatle on her arm.

This was quite an education for a working-class boy from Liverpool. Paul may have felt occasional twinges of insecurity concerning his low-brow northern identity, but it did nothing to curtail his eagerness to par-ticipate in the scene. "It seemed great to me," he told his biographer, Barry Miles. "I was very young and energetic and eager to experience all these great thrills that London had to offer." In the midst of so many prominent wits and garrulous conversationalists, Paul attempted to hold his own, reining in the lazy Scouse accent in favor of the more refined diction his mother had drilled into him. Although by no means an intellectual—he called his smarts "an intuitive brightness"—Paul had an acute sense of people, a knack for engaging an audience, and a musician's ear for timing. He always had a good story about some aspect of Beatlemania. His was a world completely alien to the tweedy London social set, almost as alien, in fact, as the world of Liverpool and the North. This was the kind of information that only recently had begun to fascinate Londoners, not only for the richness of the settings but also because these worlds were converging in a way that had become relevant to popular culture. Besides, when Paul found himself in over his head, he simply turned on the charm, which never failed to dazzle.

Paul wasted no time anguishing about his circumstances. "Coming in from the provinces to the center—isn't that what cities are all about?" he argued. "Aren't cities made up of ants, the outside ants attracted to the Queen's lair? It seems to me that's what it is." It mattered little that he knew practically nothing of London when he arrived. After several trips around the fashionable arts circuit, his creative instincts had been aroused. This recherché existence was an extension of everything that had brought him this far, all that contributed to his nature as a Beatle. Few men of his background ever got the opportunity to be part of this—and even fewer got an entrée to it from a more alluring benefactress than Jane Asher.

Friends describe Jane Asher as "your typical girl next door," but that holds true only if you live next door to the Muses. She was all of seventeen when Paul first met her and already a fixture in the London acting community. Most young girls who debuted onscreen at the age of five would have gladly settled for the life of an ingenue, but Jane Asher was thwarted by beauty and sophistication. "Every man who ever met Jane fancied her," Alistair Taylor recalls. She was slim-waisted and sylphlike (barely topping Paul's shoulders), enormously striking, with delicate features and a pale, creamy complexion framed—to Paul's surprise when introduced backstage at the Royal Albert Hall concert—by a mane of brilliant scarlet hair. "We'd thought she was blonde," Paul recalled, "because we had only ever seen her on black-and-white telly doing *Juke Box Jury,* but she turned out to be a redhead."*

---

* She appeared regularly on the television show.

Bearing as well as beauty impressed. After an adolescence of auditions and finishing school, Jane developed enormous poise accentuated by a lithe theatricality that made her gestalt seem somehow too perfect, as though it were a facade. When she spoke, her resonant, stage-trained voice, refined without a trace of pretentiousness, commanded the kind of attention that stopped conversations cold. And yet she was not at all self-absorbed, but rather of innate dignity. Like Paul, Jane had the aura. "She was smart and sexy," recalls Peter Brown, "one of the most charming young women I ever met."

The middle one of three gifted children, Jane was an unconventional mix of gentility and eccentricity. Her father, Richard, a psychiatrist and incorrigible kook, nervously cranked a coffee grinder while his patients poured out their hearts during analysis; her mother, Margaret, a tall, auburn-haired—"dominant"—woman of noble Cornish heritage, operated a music conservatory out of their eighteenth-century home—she had taught the oboe to no less a prodigy than George Martin—and groomed her children for stardom. It was in this latter pursuit that the family shone. Over and above Jane's accomplishments, her brother, Peter, a rather serious jazz musician, amassed credits in a number of secondary film and radio roles, while her younger sister, Claire, appeared regularly as an actress on the radio soap opera *Mrs. Dale's Diary.* For Jane, being courted by a Beatle made perfect sense. It gave her another strong foothold in the creative community but was also offbeat enough to remain consistent with the family personality.

At once, Paul and Jane were desirable. "There was something about seeing them together that was magical," says Tony Barrow. "With those two gorgeous faces and all that incredible charisma, they looked like a couple of Greek gods." Everywhere the couple went, people gravitated to them. They attracted a circle of friends from among London's grooviest and most free-spirited. "Both of them came with plenty of their own flash," says John Dunbar, who lived around the corner from the Ashers and was one of London's leading young scenemakers.

And they were inseparable. Friends began saying that you were as likely to see Paul with Jane as with John. They spent every night "out and about" on the town and then, afterward, talking or necking in the Ashers' downy parlor. If it got too late, Paul would simply sack out in the little music room on the top floor of the town house, next to Peter's bedroom, where a guest bunk was always made up. Even without the personal touches, it sure beat the dormitory-like Green Street, which was becoming more objectionable to him with each passing day.

Nothing could have satisfied Paul's fantasies of a family more fittingly than the Ashers. They were so well educated and widely traveled, so sophisticated in their tastes, be it the books they voraciously consumed or the exquisitely prepared food served at mealtimes. From their intense, if fitful, table conversations, Paul realized he didn't know as much about the arts as he thought. (Or much else, for that matter.) Their facility with words was extraordinary; it fascinated and humbled him. Everything they had bespoke elegance and fine choice. "It was really like culture shock," he recalled.

It was even more unforeseen when in November Jane suggested that he move permanently into the Ashers' magnificent town house; if he liked, the attic room was available, along with auxiliary membership in the family. The magnanimity of it must have shocked Paul, who had been living out of a suitcase—or in a filthy van—for so long that it was hard for him to remember the last time he had had his own room. To say nothing of a girlfriend living only one floor below. It was not an invitation that required much deliberation. "For a young guy who likes his home comforts," he noted, it was a dream come true.

But it was only a part of the dream. By November, America arrived. Brian had spent months laying plans to take the Colonies back for his boys. Armed with an arsenal of star-making weapons—including the movie contract, merchandising offers, a potential booking on Ed Sullivan's show, an extraordinary new single, a most impressive packet of press clippings, and a good deal of outrage—he arranged several meetings in New York, between November 5 and 13, that were necessary for an eventual launch. The trip was also timed to introduce Billy J. Kramer to executives at Liberty Records, which had taken a U.S. option on the young NEMS star.

Still, nothing illustrated the challenge as sharply as the cocktail party thrown in Brian's honor upon his arrival in New York. The party was part of the strategy hatched by Walter Hofer, a homespun but canny music lawyer who exercised his talents on NEMS' behalf in the United States.* Hofer figured that people who met Brian face-to-face would be impressed by the same elegance and determination that he'd noticed when Dick James had introduced them in 1962. So he telephoned every VIP in his

---

* Through Hofer, Brian had set up an American corporation, Beatles USA Ltd.

Rolodex, inviting them to his home in the Beresford, one of New York's most swank addresses, at Central Park West and Eighty-first Street. "I invited the whole industry," Hofer recalled, all the label bigwigs, important promoters, independent promo guys, the trade press, every major deejay. Some of music's "most prominent names," the heavy hitters, adorned the guest list. And nobody came.

Canvassing a sampling of record stores along Broadway was as discouraging to Brian as the reception at Hofer's. Not a glimmer about the Beatles surfaced anywhere. It was as if they didn't exist. And it wasn't just the absence of the Beatles that amazed him. Aside from Anthony Newley—and you had to really search to find Anthony Newley—there wasn't a single record by Billy Fury, Johnny Kidd, or Cliff and the Shadows. When he called Capitol Records to confirm his appointment to discuss the Beatles, a secretary asked him: "Are they affiliated with a label?"

Despite the chill, Brian attended to his appointments, many of which had been hurriedly set up during the week of the Royal Variety Performance. The most pressing one, at the outset, was the ongoing negotiation with Ed Sullivan. A notoriously prickly veteran of the New York show-business scene, Sullivan knew little about talent itself. He was impressed by a performer's ability as far as any stage act went, but his experience as a gossip columnist lent itself more to recognizing tips and hot stories than substance. So when it came to the Beatles, Sullivan was more enthused, he later said, that they were "a good TV attraction, and also a great news story." On a hunch, he offered Brian what was then a fairly extravagant deal for the Beatles: three appearances on his show, at a fee of $4,500 each, "plus five round-trip airline tickets and all their expenses for room and board while in America."

Brian seized a rare opportunity to capitalize on this generosity and, thus, went for broke, offering the impresario a chance to get in on the ground floor, so to speak, with Gerry and the Pacemakers. There was an unwritten rule that you didn't hustle Ed Sullivan. But Brian was "so charming, and so convincing" that Sullivan booked the Pacemakers for a guest spot on his March 15 show, which was certainly a coup.

The next play was at Capitol Records, where Brian was determined to storm the enemy gates. None of the American A&R staff wanted to be told how to conduct their business, especially by Brits, with their posh accents and stiff-necked etiquette. Nothing significant had ever broken out of the U.K., and if any of them dared admit their true feelings, nothing ever would.

Brian's contact at Capitol was a man by the curious name of Brown

Meggs, who ran the label's East Coast pop department. Under normal circumstances, Meggs probably would have made himself unavailable to a
manager without portfolio, but unbeknownst to Brian, L. G. Wood had
paved the way. Earlier that fall, he had sent Roland Rennie to "visit" Meggs,
along with a letter of introduction from Sir Joseph Lockwood, EMI's formidable chairman whose phone extension happened to be 4-6-3, or GOD.
Rennie insists it was nothing more than a friendly chat "to get over this
hurdle with the Beatles." But he also acknowledges that subtle "pressures
were put on" Capitol to get on the stick. Incredibly, it made not a lick of
difference: Dave Dexter used the occasion to issue another pass.

As a result, Len Wood himself flew to the States, a visit comparable
in frequency to that of the pope. Wood had already summoned Alan
Livingston to a meeting in New York. Livingston, a permanently tanned,
smooth-talking, Hollywood-style protégé of Frank Sinatra, was the president of Capitol Records and on the board of EMI. More attuned to image
than music, he operated Capitol in the manner of an old-style movie studio
mogul, surrounding himself with talented A&R men whose decisions he
either rubber-stamped or rejected. The prerogative — backed by Capitol's
considerable muscle — gave Livingston substantial clout in the music business. So strong was his autonomy, in fact, that it was unthinkable that anyone would, or even could, make demands on him. "But L.G. wasn't asking
anymore," says Paul Marshall, referring to the Beatles' forthcoming single.
"He told Alan, 'You *must* take it.'"

Must: Livingston was surprised by the ultimatum. Capitol and EMI
had never before operated on those terms. Each was supposed to have "the
right of first refusal" on the other's product, nothing more. And he was
surprised by Wood's demeanor, by the vehemence in the voice of this otherwise imperturbable Englishman. L.G. was, in fact, so agitated that he refused to leave it alone until Livingston agreed to put the record out.

Years later Livingston would tell a significantly different story.
According to a 1997 interview with the BBC, he insisted that Capitol's decision to release the Beatles was his idea. After a surprise visit from Brian
Epstein, he recalled: "I . . . took the record home to my wife . . . and said,
'You know, I think that this group, they'll change the whole music business if it happens.'" It was a ridiculous claim, considering the paper trail of
rejections from his office as well as other substantiated accounts. Capitol
had done everything possible to avoid the Beatles. But shoved against the
wall by its British masters, it no longer had a choice.

Fortunately, in this case, Capitol was handed a lulu of a record that launched the new group—and the label—into the stratosphere.

The record Brian delivered to Brown Meggs was "I Want to Hold Your Hand," the Beatles' most inspired production yet, the apotheosis of the bust-out "Merseybeat" sound that took all its most harmonious elements, the guitar-oriented riffs and vocal harmonies, and condensed them into a two-and-a-half-minute rave-up that fairly jumped off the grooves. From the unsparing two-chord intro, there was no letting up. "*Oh yeah, I'll tell you something . . .*" The energy was impossible to let go of. Part easygoing pop, part joyous rocker, part roller-coaster ride, it came at the listener from every angle, with rhythmic jerks and handclaps and inadvertent detours from the standard four-chord structure. As if the overheated arrangement wasn't tantalizing enough, the Beatles' performance was extraordinary, from John and Paul's slashing harmonies to Paul's sudden full-octave leap into falsetto, capped off by stirring confessions—"*I can't hide, I can't hide*"—that seem to gain in fervor each time they are sung. If the suits at Capitol were duly affected by the record, they never let on. But no doubt about it: "I Want to Hold Your Hand" was like no record they'd ever heard.

If Capitol was required to release the Beatles in America, then at least this was a record it could get behind. But according to Livingston, they wouldn't press more than an initial run of 5,000 copies, standard for any new artist. Shortsightedly, Capitol had neglected to keep an eye on the numbers in Great Britain, where EMI had received an unheard-of advance order for 700,000 copies of "I Want to Hold Your Hand" only three days after dealers there were notified of it. Even at Capitol, an artist with a strong track record could count on an advance of only 25,000 copies, 50,000 at the most. There was also an advance order for 265,000 copies of the Beatles' second album, *With the Beatles,* a figure that would have staggered any American label. But for the time being, Capitol ignored these numbers, preferring to eye with disdain the millstone that had been looped around its neck.

Sid Bernstein made up in spades for Capitol's stunning lack of enthusiasm. He was the original Charlie Hustle, and he was convinced of the Beatles' greatness before he ever heard them sing a note. The son of a Harlem tailor, Bernstein stumbled into the music business while still a journalism student at Columbia University, managing a neighborhood ballroom in Brooklyn that showcased the great Latin bands. In those days mambo was the province of not only Puerto Ricans but also Jews, both of whom shared the dance floor, and Bernstein acquired a passion for it through such leading lights as Ralph Font, Tito Rodríguez, Marcelino Guera, Tito Puente, and Esy Morales, the latter of whom Bernstein left the ballroom to manage.

Bernstein traveled the turbulent mambo circuit for two years, until the thirty-five-year-old Morales's untimely death. He came to the agency business booking Latin, jazz, and R&B acts in the 1950s before gravitating into the teen stars department at General Artists Corporation on the strength of his relationship with Judy Garland and Tony Bennett. Bobby Darin, Bobby Rydell, Dion, and Chubby Checker were a far cry from those mellifluent heights, but that never diminished Bernstein's drive, and he flogged the agency's pop roster like a team of prized stallions.

In his spare time, he began attending evening courses at the New School, in Greenwich Village, one of which was a lecture on Western civilization given by the noted analyst Max Lerner. Lerner required that each student read a British newspaper once a week to gain insight into the English form of government. "After a while," Bernstein recalled, "I started to see in the slim entertainment pages the name 'Beatles' popping up," first in small print, then in headlines. "And then the word 'Beatlemania' appeared."

Instinct convinced Bernstein that he should jump on this before someone else in America caught wind of it, so he attempted to interest GAC's agents in taking on this new group. Nothing doing. "They thought the name was crazy and gave me every excuse for not letting me go over to see them." Instead, he made private inquiries about the Beatles, eventually tracking them to Brian Epstein. It must have been child's play to tantalize Brian with lavish name-dropping and hype. "I hit him with my experience," Bernstein recalled. "Tony Bennett at Carnegie Hall, Judy Garland at Carnegie Hall." The names and that place were all the pitch he needed for Bernstein to "sell him on [the Beatles] doing Carnegie Hall" in early 1964. "So we made a deal on the phone for sixty-five hundred bucks for two shows."

From various angles, the deal was either brilliant or utterly foolish. This wasn't agency money or part of a promoter's discretionary fund. Bernstein had reached into his own pocket to book no less a venue than Carnegie Hall for a group that had no hit record and no following in America. Who would come to see them? How would he create any interest?

At their first meeting in New York, Brian brought the answers with him. Capitol, he revealed, had agreed to release "I Want to Hold Your Hand" in January. Since Bernstein had booked Carnegie Hall for Wednesday, February 12—weekends were reserved for the symphony—it gave them a good month to build word of mouth. Then Brian dropped the clincher: two appearances on *The Ed Sullivan Show*. When Bernstein heard that, he said, "I knew I was home because, in those days, when you appeared twice on Sullivan you were a star."

And then, out of nowhere, Capitol announced that it intended to put an astounding $40,000 into promoting the Beatles' new record. The sudden reversal in outlook would never be explained, but to Bernstein, it was the telltale sign that a new star had been discovered.

[III]

Even without Brian at the controls, the Beatles remained constantly on the go. Appearing in a package of endless one-nighters—five weeks of sold-out one-night stands—they racked up miles, difficult miles, hopscotching between towns and cities where fresh outbreaks of Beatlemania were reported like the flu. But as Beatlemania grew more intense, life on the road became ever more precarious, and once-precious downtime left them preoccupied with the planning of safety and escape routes.

"Girls are fainting in the streets," reported *Melody Maker* just prior to the tour. "Scores are injured in the crushes." Many locales attempted to head off such mayhem by having convoys of police cars liaise with the Beatles on the outskirts of town for an escort to the theater. Outside Birmingham, news of "rampaging fans" forced the Beatles to exchange clothes with the police in order to disguise themselves so they could enter. "Getting them inside," according to the music magazine, "was like a military operation."

Sometimes getting them out was an even hairier proposition. In Sunderland the Beatles were led like escaping refugees through a narrow, pitch-dark backstage corridor that deposited them into an adjoining firehouse. One by one, they slid down the pole, then waited while a decoy engine lured waiting fans into a wild-goose chase through the deserted town. Of course, there was another side to all of this. Before one show, in East Ham, George Martin arrived backstage quite jauntily to announce that "'I Want to Hold Your Hand' had cleared a million [advance orders] before release." It was incredible news, a first for the British music industry, and the Beatles were suitably thrilled.

During the show, as was now always the case, an exit strategy began to unfold. All plans focused on the getaway car, a gleaming black Austin Princess idling by the stage door. The Princess was considered sort of a down-market limo. "I assumed they'd have either a Daimler, a Bentley, or a Rolls-Royce," Alistair Taylor recalls. Mal Evans, a big, bearlike but scatterbrained ex-Cavern bouncer who had been hired in August to assist Neil Aspinall and act as a bodyguard for the boys, detected Alistair's disapproval and explained. They'd tested all the available limos, he said, and found that the Princess had doors that opened wider to accommodate diving in.

While half a dozen questions flashed through Taylor's head, he was pushed bodily into the car, which was already rolling forward. Up ahead, "a cordon of law enforcement officers held back a sea of screaming heads." A police car fell in alongside, with its blue light flashing.

Suddenly the car jerked forward, then skidded to a stop in front of two innocuous-looking doors behind the theater. They were flung open and four blurs burst from its dark mouth: Paul first, John right behind him, followed by George and Ringo. Each Beatle dove headfirst into the backseat of the Princess—except for Ringo, who fell on his face, with his feet in the gutter.

"Rich, Rich, *come on*, man!"

"I've got me fooking foot stuck," Ringo wailed.

Before anyone responded, the three Beatles wriggled out of the car, picked up Ringo as if he were luggage, and threw him into the back. Reaching behind him, Alistair slammed the door shut and Mal sped away.

"So, this is Beatlemania," Alistair mused. He couldn't believe the rush as the police line broke a split second after the car squeaked through and kids, hundreds of kids, swarmed through. "We screamed into central London with the blue lights flashing, running every traffic light," he recalls. "It was just like the Queen coming—only it was four Liverpool musicians. If that didn't beat all."

On the morning of November 22, expectation surged through Merseyside about the group's second album, *With the Beatles,* due to arrive in local stores later that afternoon. Information had been leaked about the selection of fourteen songs, but there was an air of intense heat surrounding the project that refused to let up until it was actually in people's hands. All the clubs were full of talk about it, and the music papers had already issued encomiums. *Melody Maker,* in a forum with three top disc jockeys, touted it as "a great album . . . that puts the Beatles unmistakably at the top of the beat tree," while Alan Smith, writing in *NME,* called it "a knockout," predicting it would top the charts for a record-setting eight weeks. "Most of the material on *With the Beatles* is wild and up-tempo," Smith revealed, while citing "All My Loving" as the album's true "highlight."

"The second album was slightly better than the first," George said, "inasmuch as we spent more time on it, and there were more original songs." Seven Lennon-McCartney numbers—half the songs—were featured among the lineup. Following the same effective balance as on their first album, mixing originals with American covers, the Beatles ripped through a stingy thirty-three and a half minutes of music that put the excitement back into Top 40 pop. There was nothing timid or bottled up about the performances on this album, from the blazing attention-grabber "It Won't Be Long" to the very last beat of "Money."

In between, "All I've Got to Do" cha-cha'ed in and out of a brooding but affectionate melody that took its cues from the kind of primitive urban R&B sound that was popular in New York. It was influenced, John recalled, by his attempt to write a Smokey Robinson–type song, but it is closer in style to the Shirelles' "Baby It's You" and early Drifters records. If "All I've Got to Do" comes off as restlessly dark and moody, the album's spirit jerks back and forth along a fragile emotional line. The fans couldn't have asked for a more exuberant teenybop anthem than "All My Loving," which became somewhat of an instant Beatles classic. To them, its sunny simplicity, with those chirpy vocals, galloping guitar triplets, and irresistible hooks, perfectly exemplified the developing "Beatles sound." And the cover of "Please Mr. Postman" is whipped with such slap-bang ferocity that the interpretation goes a long way toward overtaking the Marvelettes' version.

"We were all very interested in American music, much more so than in British," Paul later admitted. That deep-felt debt to classic rock 'n roll brought them back once more to "Roll Over Beethoven." From the band's earliest efforts, Chuck Berry songs had been a staple of their repertoire. John always considered Berry "one of the all-time great poets, a rock poet" as much as anybody (including Bob Dylan), and addressed his admiration directly when he said, "I've loved everything he's done, ever." George's vocal and guitar solos pay tribute to Berry's handiwork. He didn't try to embellish or outstrip the original — he turbocharged it with an undercurrent of handclaps accenting the beat.

If anything stuck out as being awkward or out of place, it was Paul's delivery of "Till There Was You," an overly pretty ballad from *The Music Man,* which was performed in such a precious way that, according to George, Paul "sounded like a woman." Songs like this one, along with "A Taste of Honey" and "Besame Mucho," can easily be seen as the Beatles' response to George Martin's and Brian Epstein's request that they broaden their image and appeal with a selection of pop standards. Such material had always been part of the Beatles' standard sets, even in Hamburg and at the Cavern, where audiences could either slow dance, light up cigarettes, or, if they grew too bored, visit the loo. But on an album of rock 'n roll songs, it proved too conspicuous. Such indulgence didn't harm their credibility, but it did nothing to further the Beatles along the path they had marked out for themselves.

Besides, there was too much other territory for them to explore. Paul, who wrote "Hold Me Tight" at Forthlin Road while he and John were still teenagers, refers to it as "a failed attempt at a single which then became an acceptable album filler," but since their Cavern days it had been shaped and reshaped, most recently with a quirky middle eight, that eliminated its flatness and cranked up fresh interest. Even "I Wanna Be Your Man," given a surly, suggestive reading by the Rolling Stones, sounds more intimate under Ringo's chummy vocal. And "Money," a barn burner left over from Hamburg, put the torch to all the assembly-line Liverpool covers, the repetitious rave-ups blaring out of every club within ten miles of Clayton Square, and transformed the song into something else entirely. This version pulled the song off the stage and thrust it into the garage, where the Beatles roughed it up and gave it a new potency that had eluded it before.

Among the elements that lifted this album above its predecessor are the innovative double-tracking — a process that allowed the Beatles to layer vocals and rhythm tracks rather than recording everything live, in one take — and its unique cover, an ethereal, grim-faced, black-and-white portrait that conjures up a striking, if disturbing, image of the boys. Nervous that EMI might pressure them into using the same kind of uninspired group shot as on *Please Please Me,* they enlisted Robert Freeman to come up with something "artistic," something bold. "We showed him the pictures Astrid and Jurgen [sic] had taken in Hamburg and said, 'Can't you do it like this?'" George recalled. Freeman posed the Beatles against the velvet curtains of a hotel dining room in Bournemouth, using mostly natural light that seeped in through an enormous window along one side of the wall. It was a stunning departure from the usual upbeat, glossy sleeves on which labels exclusively relied. Given the circumstances, EMI's reaction was inevitable. They hated the concept, calling it "shockingly humorless," and threatened to pull the cover for something more "happy" and less "grim." Brian, too, was less than enthusiastic. "He was convinced it would damage their image," Tony Barrow recalls, "but the boys put their feet down."

When the album finally appeared, it was clear that the cover was every bit as alluring as they had hoped. Stores were besieged with jacked-up Beatles fans throughout the afternoon of November 22. Peter Brown, who was managing the NEMS record department in Brian's absence, recalls being unprepared for the runaway demand. "I'd never seen anything like it," he says. "No record in my experience had ever caused this kind of frenzy. There were hundreds of kids trying to get into the store; a crowd had gathered on the street. Police showed up to keep things under control. Our cashiers were so overwhelmed that everyone, myself included, worked the counter until the store closed."

This scene wasn't restricted to Liverpool. All over Great Britain, teenagers mobbed the local record stores to get their hands on copies of *With the Beatles.* If a cult of personality had surrounded the group, there was now also a retail phenomenon to go with it. On that first day alone, an impressive 530,000 copies of the album were sold, along with another 200,000 more singles of "She Loves You," which had pushed beyond the vaunted million mark. No album had ever aroused this much interest. It was generally acknowledged by record companies that teenagers bought singles and, occasionally, the rare album; right up to the release of *With the Beatles,* EMI was still unsure if a market for it would materialize. Now all that had changed.

EMI couldn't afford to let a slipup burst the bubble, but neither did it want to interfere with the fantastic flow of sales. *Please Please Me* was still selling like hotcakes, too, and by the end of sales on November 22, it was keeping pace alongside *With the Beatles.* Two albums by the same artist on the British charts was rare indeed; the last time it had happened was in 1960, with Elvis Presley. But by that evening, *NME* decided that the sales situation was so unique that it launched the new album into the Top Thirty at the number fifteen position.*

---

* *The all-time entry record was set by Frank Sinatra's 1956 album,* Songs for Swingin' Lovers, *which popped onto the charts at number twelve.*

These facts and figures dominated the conversation on a DC-3 over-run with Beatles fans as it took off from Speke Airport en route to Hamburg that same afternoon. The Cavern sponsored the chartered excursion to co-incide with the release of the new Beatles album and about thirty teenagers signed on, along with Allan Williams, Bob Wooler, Bill Harry, and other supporting cast members associated with the Beatles' rise in Liverpool. Everyone spent the flight time singing the songs on *With the Beatles*— songs they knew by heart from the gigs—and swooning over the dramatic events of the past few months. At the moment, everything else seemed unimportant. The boys had come not only so far but so fast: from the side streets of Liverpool to the royal roads of London, where the Queen herself had crossed their path. Only a year before, they had alternated between a basement club and the back of a creaky van, with nothing more than a substandard demo tape and the fierce, unquenchable dream to make records, to be rock 'n roll stars. Now they were poised again to build upon that dream, and the entire country's attention had swung toward Liverpool. It was a fairy tale come true, and the fans aboard the flight—those who had been there all along, who *had known* from the beginning—were so giddy that at even 25,000 feet up in the air they seemed only a stone's throw from the stars.

When the plane touched down in Hamburg, not only was there no carpet, there was no move initiated to help them disembark. "We stood on that tarmac for what seemed like an eternity, waiting for a coach to take us to the Star-Club," Wooler remembers. The usual busyness that hastens an airport seemed eerily stalled; aside from a few planes landing in the distance, it was as quiet as a car parking lot outside church services. The passengers began to grow edgy, then irritable. Finally, an official pulled up in a car and bumbled around them in a fluster. "Oh, terrible, *terrible* news about JFK," he said, all aquiver. The American president had been shot—he was dead; the world was in mourning. "You'll find most of the Reeperbahn closed, as I'm sure you've closed your Cavern tonight."

But from the Grosse Freiheit, the American tragedy and its reverberations seemed as far away as the banks of the Mersey. The seedier bars— those where even cataclysmic events took a backseat to debauchery—ran at full tilt, dispensing fantastic quantities of alcohol to the teenagers and chaperones alike, all of whom held on to the Beatles like a life raft against such terrible tides. For three days and nights, they drank themselves silly, putting the real world and its problems out of their mind. Although history may have turned a wicked corner, there were glimmers of "hope and consolation" to be found in the Beatles' music. Of course, it was only the beginning of a generation's dependency on rock 'n roll as an escape from the harsh changes that rocked the world at large. For the next six years—and beyond—music and other intoxicants would be liberating forces, the kind of distractions that helped kids avoid the wicked corners. On the way back to Liverpool, Wooler says, "we were so diminished by our indulgences that when the pilot delivered the news about the murder of Lee Harvey Oswald, many of us, sitting there like zombies, were unable to open our eyes."

By the last week in November, "She Loves You" returned to the top spot on the *Record Retailer* chart, along with word that the band's next single, "I Want to Hold Your Hand," had more than a million advance orders. The next week "She Loves You" held its position, while "I Want to Hold Your Hand" was number three, Billy J. Kramer with the Dakotas' version of "I'll Keep You Satisfied," written by John and Paul, hovered at number six, and "I Wanna Be Your Man" by the Rolling Stones entered at number thirty. *NME*'s album chart was even more rewarding, listing *With the Beatles* and *Please Please Me* as vying for the very top, with three EPs—*Twist and Shout, The Beatles Hits,* and *Beatles No. 1*—padding close behind. The dominance was unprecedented. In a single outburst, the Beatles had hijacked the charts.

Finally America took notice. In mid-November all three U.S. networks sent film crews to the Winter Gardens Theatre in Bournemouth in an attempt to report on the Beatles phenomenon. The clips they sent back received only scattered coverage, but one viewer's impression touched off a storm of unexpected interest. A teenager named Marsha Albert was so intrigued by the music that she wrote a letter to her local deejay, at WWDC in Washington, D.C., asking to hear something by the Beatles. That station in particular was a curious place to handle such a request; it played "a real mixed bag" of pop standards, catering to a devoted Frank Sinatra–Nat King Cole audience, with only the occasional rock 'n roll song slipping onto the playlist. But the disc jockey, a genial straight arrow named Carroll James, hunted down an import copy of "I Want to Hold Your Hand" and invited Marsha Albert to introduce it on the air.

On December 17, 1963, she read a few lines of copy that James had scrawled on the back of a traffic report, then launched the Beatles into the American airwaves for the first time ever. When it was over, James invited the audience to pass on their opinion of the record. As he recalled it, "the switchboard just went totally wild." Every line lit up. Completely unprepared for such a reaction, James "played it again in the next hour, which is something I'd never ever done before." He continued programming "I Want to Hold Your Hand" every night that week, fading in the middle of the song and interjecting, "A WDDC exclusive!" in order to prevent WPGC, the area's main teen station, from taping it.

The circumstances at WDDC sounded an alarm at Capitol Records, which was planning to release the single in late January. Eventually, after days of memos flying back and forth, Capitol decided to move up the American release of "I Want to Hold Your Hand" to December 27. It would not arrive in time for Christmas, but the Beatles didn't care. It was the best gift they could have asked for that holiday season, and at long last it was under the tree.

———

After "I Want to Hold Your Hand" struck gold, Beatles Fan Club membership was no longer just an indulgence of former Cavern groupies. Applications poured in from all over the country, more than even a sophisticated mail-order company could handle. "There came a time when we had a backlog of many thousands of unopened mailbags, each one containing hundreds of applications, accompanied by money orders for membership," recalls Barrow, who'd been awakened to the danger of their negligence. "Goodness knows how many mailbags were stolen from the rickety staircase leading to the office above the dirty bookstore."

Complaints followed, and it wasn't long before the media, especially the tabloids, picked up the story. What happened, reporters wondered, to all the money sent to the Beatles? How did they intend to placate thousands of unhappy teenagers?

Faced with a public relations catastrophe, Epstein directed Tony Barrow to run damage control and propose a solution. Barrow decided to get everyone immediately onto a mailing list and appease those who were slighted by giving them something special for Christmas. But what? All the standard options—key chains, bracelets, T-shirts—took too much of a bite out of the NEMS budget. It had to be something, Brian insisted, "that only cost a few pence to produce." Finally, when it looked all but hopeless, Barrow struck gold. Paging through *Reader's Digest*, he came across something called a flexi-disk—a plastic record the size of a seven-inch forty-five but played at the speed of a thirty-three. The magazine used it quite cleverly, to preview selections from its record club. "My idea was to get out a humorous message from the Beatles to their fans, giving them something that was totally exclusive—and *free*. I ran it by the lads, who loved the idea and were eager to do their share."

Portions of the record were leaked to the press, which called it "the craziest Xmas greeting of all [time]." Following a loosely scripted sketch that skipped around for roughly five minutes, it delivered more of the "likable, crazy" Scouse-inspired zaniness fans had come to expect from the Beatles. Each musician delivered a personal greeting (in which more than a few of the band's devotees detected John's handprint) loaded with puns and loony wordplay. There were parodies of Christmas carols. Everyone sang a few bars of his favorite, the most bizarre rendition, perhaps, being Ringo's "Buddy Greco-style version" of "Good King Wenceslas," after which George deadpans: "Thank you, Ringo—we'll phone you."

At times the band responded to fans directly. "Somebody asked us if we still like jelly babies," Paul mentioned, referring to a comment John had made during an interview earlier that year in which he expressed fondness for the candies. Back then, John had joked that George had eaten his supply. "The next day," John recalled, "I started getting jelly babies with a note saying, 'Don't give George any.' And George got some saying, 'Here's some for you, George; you don't need John's.' And then it went mad." From that day on, whenever the Beatles took to the stage, a hailstorm of jelly babies pelted them from the seats—whole bags and occasionally even boxes were lobbed—with fans often winging them sidearm from overhanging balconies. Eventually it resembled a combat zone, with candy projectiles ricocheting off guitars and cymbals, once even cutting John above the eye. For the first time, Ringo said, "it felt dangerous" onstage. "Anyway, we've gone *right off* jelly babies!" Paul avowed on the flexidisk, hoping that put an end to the gesture.

To preserve the edge of lunacy that was interrupted with words of sincere thanks, the Beatles signed off with another parody, "Ricky the Red Nosed Ringo," which collapsed into uncontrollable laughter before regrouping for a final inspirational message.

The result was a resounding success. Long-neglected fan-club members, delighted by the record, were content with what all fans ultimately want—to have something that nobody else can get their hands on, something personal that was in short supply. With the exception of a few disgruntled parents, no one registered so much as a complaint over the way in which membership was handled. And if some head case wanted to make trouble, Barrow had the power to launch the ultimate defensive weapon: a personal phone call from one of the boys. "In that respect, we never had to worry," he says, "because we knew the effect something like that had."

———

None of the Beatles liked how success had reshaped their appearance. The way Paul saw it, they were way off their stride, still "on the cusp of show-biz." And John, who made no bones about regretting their phony clean-cut image, bristled when a fan described the Beatles' music as "genuine." Sentiments like that were already becoming a liability to the boys, who felt the edge they'd honed in Liverpool and Hamburg eroding even further.

The latest bit of puffery was the *Beatles Christmas Show*, which, since its announcement in September, had taken on a life of its own. Conceived primarily as "a resident show"—that is, a show where the Beatles would remain situated at one location over a period of weeks—it relied on the old-fashioned British tradition of incorporating comedy, music, and pantomime toned down to attract a family audience.

Theatrical production in London was a closed shop: a small, inbred clique of sharp, cunning, and ruthless deal-brokers governed by impresario Lew Grade and his brother Bernie Delfont. Details of every major production in the city eventually crossed their desks. Most legitimate theaters fell under the Grades' grudging jurisdiction, as did actors and agencies, with an industry's fortunes tied to their discretionary nod. Outsiders were looked upon as cockroaches.

The Grades were interested only in what they could control, and, in fact, they'd already approached Brian with an offer to absorb NEMS into their kingdom. Delfont suggested he accept the princely sum of £150,000 in exchange for half equity in the company. Brian was tempted. He had taken on a good deal more than he was rightfully equipped to handle, and the strain was beginning to "drive him crackers." But when he sounded out the Beatles, they disapproved in four-part harmony. "They said they would rather break up than leave me," Brian reported, somewhat self-servingly, to a friend. Then, in a more forthright account, he added: "John told me to 'fuck off,' which was *very* moving."

Whatever the case, it was clear that moving NEMS to London was long overdue. With Brian away so much of the time, the Liverpool office had fallen into a long decline, its day-to-day operation, according to Alistair Taylor, "a shambles, just chaos." There was no one with authority to call the shots. And the office manager, Barry Leonard, proved incapable of picking up the slack. In the meantime, Brian toured office buildings in London, finding affordable space on the fifth floor of Sutherland House, at 4–5 Argyll Street. For the most part it was unfinished, a loftlike open-floor plan that was considered "quite revolutionary" for the time, with two enclosed offices and the rest partitioned off in a maze of impersonal cubicles. "They weren't terribly good offices," says Taylor, but the location was ideal, right next door to the Palladium. According to Tony Barrow, "[Brian] loved the idea that on the other side of those walls, Judy Garland might be rehearsing."

In any event, Brian dreaded returning to Liverpool. As far as talent went, the cupboard was bare; the best local bands were already on the NEMS roster. And there was a strange, lingering local resentment. Part of it had to do with the perception that Brian had drained the city of its best bands without any regard for their fans. John had felt it even before the Merseyside musical explosion. "When I left Liverpool with the group," he recalled, "a lot of Liverpool people dropped us and said, 'Now you've let us down.'" It was an understandable reaction.

Brian, always an outsider but not one with a gift of assimilation, didn't help. The last time Brian returned to NEMS from London he "showed up at the office in a brand-new Jaguar XK-E," recalls Frieda Kelly, who watched him pull up from the window. It was a sight to behold, especially in Liverpool, whose factories mass-produced budget-priced Fords and Z-cars. In a way, the Jaguar only confirmed what everyone suspected: that NEMS was rolling in money, growing beyond all expectations. But it also embarrassed the Scousers, who considered such extravagance vulgar.

An hour later Billy Hatton, the Fourmost's bass player, showed up bearing gifts. His mother operated a kiosk in Moorfields, from which he'd lifted a box of ice pops for the NEMS' staff. "Have you seen Eppy's car?" he asked, with a snickering grin. "Who threw acid all over it?" Kelly, who was talking to a friend at the time, remembers laughing at Billy's sick sense of humor. "Then we realized he wasn't kidding," she says. "Everyone rushed outside, and sure enough, it was true. What a mess. All the paint had bubbled and began peeling back. It was destroyed."

The next morning Brian announced the firm was moving to London.

———

The *Beatles Christmas Show* was the first item launched from NEMS' new London office. Brian was determined to pull out all the stops and had enlisted help from an old-line variety agent, Joe Collins, whose daughters,

Joan and Jackie, happened to be Beatles fans. Collins hooked him up with Peter Yolland, who specialized in producing Christmas pantomimes in major provincial cities across Great Britain.

"My idea was to make the Beatles do things they had never done before," says Yolland. As far as the music went, he'd leave that up to the individual acts, but during the course of the evening he intended to present them in sketches designed around the age-old pantomime form, with the dramatization of a fairy tale followed by broad comedy and a script full of topical references that encouraged audience participation. As stories went, it was predictably hokey: at the top, the heroine, Ermyntrude, gets thrown out of the house because she's had a baby; abandoned and alone, she falls into the clutches of a mustachioed villain, Sir John Jasper (played rather villainously by John Lennon, in a top hat and brandishing a whip), who ties her to the railroad tracks, only to be rescued in the nick of time by Valiant Paul the Signalman. There was never a question that the "leggy lovely" in white headscarf and fishnet thighs would be played *en travestie* by anyone other than George; as the youngest Beatle, the time-honored role of panto boy fell naturally to him. That left a hole for Ringo. After some deliberation, he was cast as Fairy Snow, a derelict elf in head-to-toe black, who leaped around the stage, sprinkling white confetti over the other Beatles.

Today, it would be hard to imagine any men of comparable age, much less rock 'n roll stars, submitting to such drivel. But the Beatles did— "quite willingly and without resentment," says Yolland, who rehearsed the boys under the most congenial of circumstances. No one complained or balked at a procedure, not even George, in perpetual embarrassment over the woman's getup he was forced to wear.

The Beatles' spot—a nine-song mini-set—came near the end of the top-heavy two-hour show. Up first were the rest of the NEMS artists, performing medleys of their hits intermingled with Christmas songs, in a footloose, music-hall-style revue. Most of those who attended couldn't have cared less about its technical flourishes. All the work that went into the staging meant nothing to the mostly female fans, whose only aim was to gaze upon their heartthrobs—gaze with tear-rimmed, tormented eyes, hands clutched arthritically at the sides of their faces, mouths twisted in anguished, blood-curdling screams that fluctuated in waves, as if induced by jolts from electric-shock paddles. Ex–Quarry Man Nigel Walley, now the golf pro at Wrotham Heath in Kent, also fought his way inside the Astoria to catch a glimpse of his old mates. For weeks afterward, Walley says, he was haunted by those scenes. "I used to wake up in the middle of the night, thinking I must have dreamed it all."

Backstage, the police had their own nightmares to contend with. Getaways had been blueprinted and rehearsed with split-second precision. The size and layout of the Astoria, with its twenty-seven exits, left myriad options. (The police telephoned the producers ten minutes before the end of every show with the details for that night's route.) Perhaps the greatest safeguard was the mandatory playing of "God Save the Queen" at the evening's conclusion. During those two and a half minutes, the audience remained standing at attention, virtual captives, while the Beatles, escorted by an usher wielding a flashlight, fled through one of the cobwebbed underpassages.

"They're not *listening* to anything," John complained bitterly about the Beatles' ecstatic audiences. "All they're doing is going mad." The futility of it gnawed at him. Somewhere along the way, the music had taken a backseat to the act, the act of *being* the Beatles. The success it brought, however, didn't diminish John's discontent, and he hated himself for encouraging it. Pete Shotton saw that the annoyance was taking its toll. John was feeling trapped in his new celebrity, playing a role that he didn't relish; week by week, feeling more like a fraud, more like a phony. Says Shotton: "He very quickly realized that . . . he was getting cut off from the world— and that it was [only] going to get worse. He realized very early on that this was the penalty."

But there were the perks as well.

[I]

As sunlight struck the silvery wings outside the starboard windows of Pan Am Flight 101, shooting splinters of light across the interior cabin, three of the Beatles huddled at a window to size up the view as the plane banked sharply over the eastern shore of Long Island. In the first-class compartment, John sat rigidly behind the others, holding Cynthia's moist hand and staring at the back of the seat in front of him. He'd grown subdued during the last, final hour, his face closed over with something a traveling companion read as "doubt." Initially, John had "been over the moon at the prospect" of the visit—paying homage in the land of his fore-fathers: Chuck, Elvis, and Buddy. But as the reality of it drew near, he became convinced of certain failure.

That morning a crowd of four thousand fans had swarmed Heathrow to see the boys off as Beatles music "boom[ed] out over the public address system." It had been a heartening sight as they emerged on the airport tar-mac, grinning and handsome in the new pleated mohair suits that Dougie Millings had made in London from a series of Paul's sketches. Thanks to some last-minute choreography staged by Brian Epstein, they stopped in their tracks less than halfway to the plane, then turned and waved in uni-son, gazing up at the terraced observation deck draped with banners wish-ing them well and jammed with cheering, screaming teenagers hanging precariously over the rails. The Beatles laughed and shouted back at them, caught up in the spirit. It was impossible not to feel the excitement, their loyal fans solidly behind them, rooting for them, proud that the Beatles were taking it to the States. There was "nothing like it in the world," ac-cording to Paul.

"In Liverpool, when you stood on the edge of the water you knew the next place was America," John said much later, but the romance of the States had been with him since childhood. To that restless, rebellious Woolton boy "with a mess of ideas rattling around his head," everything that spoke to him was out there, somewhere over the western horizon—in America. Brando, the Beat poets, rock 'n roll: he'd long since fallen under their spell. But with America now only minutes away, it may have been too much for John to deal with.

He took a deep breath, an uneasy look crossing his ruggedly handsome face, and glanced around at the cabin full of reporters, photographers, friends, and hangers-on who had attached themselves to the Beatles' entourage: the ever-chummy Maureen Cleave of the *Evening Standard,* who'd emerged in recent weeks as the boys' pet flack; Harry Benson, the pesky *Daily Express* photographer, a talented man although something of a nuisance, to whom Pan Am had reluctantly given permission to shoot pictures exclusively throughout the flight; George Harrison, the *Liverpool Echo*'s unlikely-named columnist, who for years had stubbornly refused to write a word about the Beatles; and Phil Spector, as high-strung as a Pomeranian, and as paranoid, who booked himself on the same flight as the Beatles because, as George recalled, "he thought we were winners and he wouldn't crash."

Brian, as smooth as a diplomat, had stashed the bulk of the entourage in the 707's economy cabin, where the less genteel couldn't badger the Beatles. George, especially, wanted to be left alone; he'd been fighting off some queasiness that the boys initially dismissed as butterflies but was developing rather progressively as a case of the flu. Moreover, there were too many stowaways aboard, British manufacturers who had booked seats on Flight 101 in order to corner the Beatles with far-fetched pitches. Since just after takeoff, they'd been dispatching a stewardess to first class every few minutes, to display various products and ask for endorsements. It never failed to amaze the boys what they came up with. All kinds of cheap junk were already being produced to cash in on their name: night-lights, clocks, sweaters, pillows, scarves, pens, bracelets, games, any number of Beatles wigs, which had become a silly rage. And now here was the chance for even more.

When they were passed to him, John regarded each item as he might a dirty sock, holding it by the edge with two fingers. That stuff had never interested him much, although he had some vague appreciation for the income it produced. From time to time Brian took pains to reassure the

Beatles that nothing would be licensed that might embarrass them. Besides, all John could focus on at the moment was the next ten days in New York—and not being embarrassed by *that*. "Going to the States was a big step," Ringo admitted. The prospect of it, the significance, had made him "a bit sick," too, although by the time they were descending into New York, Ringo was in full party mode. Paul was also overheard confiding in Phil Spector about his own misgivings, although they were soon interrupted by word from the cockpit. As Paul remembered it: "The pilot had rang ahead and said, 'Tell the boys there's a big crowd waiting for them.'"

As the plane taxied toward the gate, the Beatles scrambled over one another to get a better view of the scene unfolding outside at the terminal. Everywhere they looked it was wall-to-wall kids. Shouts—whoops and cheers—erupted inside the plane, and for the first time since London John's face broke into a beautiful grin. "Just look at that!" one of them whispered hoarsely, his voice fighting the collision of relief and delight. American fans had been gathering there since early morning, whipped up by New York's most famous radio deejays broadcasting live from the airport. All day they had been urging listeners to head there, playing Beatles records every few minutes and offering prizes: Beatles wigs, sweatshirts, and photographs. As a result, it was a bigger crowd than Kennedy International Airport had ever experienced. "Not even for kings or queens," according to an official at the gate. The *New York Times* reported that "three thousand teenagers stood four deep on the upper arcade of the International Arrivals Building . . . girls, girls and more girls." From the plane, you could see them jumping up and down, percolating, much in the manner of their British counterparts. Police, using every bit of available muscle, leaned their shoulders into barricades, fighting to hold the kids in check, but as the plane shut off its engines it looked like a losing battle. Every so often a nervy girl threw herself over the thicket of navy blue uniforms like a running back against a goal-line stand, only to be pushed back behind the uprights. One older bystander suffered a mild heart attack, and according to the *Daily News*, "some punches were exchanged as the fans fought for better views."

As the boys stood by the aircraft door, grinning and gaping at the crowd, waving at random, a radio commentator breathlessly struggled to give an account of their expressions: "As far as I can tell, the four Beatles are standing at the door of the aircraft almost certainly completely and utterly in shock. No one, I mean *no one*, has ever seen or even remotely suspected anything like this before!"

"We had heard that our records were selling well in America," George recalled somewhat disingenuously (sales had hit 2.6 million singles in roughly two and a half weeks), "but it wasn't until we stepped off the plane . . . that we understood what was going on. Seeing thousands of kids there to meet us made us realize just how popular we were there." The Beatles were beside themselves with joy.

For security purposes, the Beatles circumvented Customs on their way to a press conference in the ground-floor lounge of Pan Am's Arrivals building. More than two hundred reporters and photographers were crammed into the room, jostling for position and firing questions even as the boys were led through the door wearing identical dark overcoats and carrying flight bags.

Commandeering a microphone, Brian Sommerville, the band's new press officer, attempted to broker peace by initiating an orderly hands-up policy for questions, but it was to no avail. Minutes flew by as tempers grew more heated and voices snarled. Neither side was about to give the other any satisfaction. "All right then. *Shut up!*" he barked. "Just shut up!"

"Yeah, yeah, everybody just *sharrup*," said John, the first official words from a Beatle on American soil.

A stunned press gallery fell silent, then broke into applause. Just like that, the Beatles had snatched the upper hand from the hard-core pack of reporters and never really gave it back. Whatever the press expected from these boys, they were completely unprepared for what they were about to get.

"Will you sing something for us?" a reporter shouted over the racket.

"*No!*" all four Beatles shouted in unison.

"We need money first," John shot back. The impertinence of it sent approving snickers through the crowd.

George was asked about the group's ambition, and without missing a beat, he said, "To come to America."

"What about you, Ringo? What do you think of Beethoven?"

"I love him," he said, "especially his poems."

"Are you for real?"

"Come and have a feel."

"Some of your detractors allege that you are bald and those haircuts are wigs. Is that true, John?"

"Oh, we're all bald—yeah. And I'm deaf and dumb, too."

"What about the movement in Detroit to stamp out the Beatles?"

Unruffled, Paul smiled and said, "We have two answers to the Detroit students who want to stamp us out. We've a campaign of our own to stamp out Detroit." That drew appreciative laughter, distracting attention from his "second answer," which, though never stated, was implicit.

There were the usual questions about their hair, the origin of the band's name, and how long they felt the phenomenon would last, all of which the boys handled with off-the-cuff wit and flair. The New York press corps, which had expected awkward, faltering teenagers, was delighted; the Beatles were irresistible, they made great copy. Paul, who still had the mike, couldn't resist one last crack. "We have a message," he announced, grinning, as the room suddenly fell silent, notebooks poised, cameras pointed. "Our message is: buy more Beatles records!" That did it! Everyone in the room broke out laughing at what the *New York Times* dubbed the "contagious . . . Beatle wit." According to its reporter on the scene: "Photographers forgot about pictures they wanted to take. The show was on and the Beatle boys loved it."

As the press conference broke up, George spotted an elfin man with a pencil-thin, crooked grin wearing a brightly patterned madras sport coat and straw boater squeezed into the front row of reporters. "Hey, I dig your hat," he said. "Yeah, right, you can have it," the man said, flicking it off with a thumb.

Even without the hat, Murray Kaufman had a prepossessing demeanor that compelled attention. Physically, he was slight, but a streak of brashness and self-importance added to his stature. He had that frantic New York aura about him, a real live wire, with a penetrating crinkly-eyed stare that served a multitude of emotional purposes. As "Murray the K," he was a well-known radio personality, handling the prime-time evening show, from six o'clock until ten each night, on WINS, a top pop station. His voice reached from one end of New York to the other and deep into Connecticut and New Jersey, a seemingly endless spray of magpie chatter as it spun circuitous webs around the pop hits of the day, light news, commercials, and marginalia, all thickened by a style that Murray referred to as "my shtick."

And right now Murray was positively glowing with excitement. The Beatles had "done a number on [him]," taken him by surprise. He couldn't get over their collective sense of humor and the way they'd handled the hard-boiled press corps. It was a welcome turn of events, considering he had come to the airport against his will. At the end of January, Murray had been in Florida, on a vacation that was supposed to extend to the end of February. That was where Joel Chaseman, WINS's program director, found him and ordered him back to New York. "The Beatles are coming," Chaseman told him. In October a copy of "She Loves You" had crossed Kaufman's desk, and thanks to some strong-arming by Swan Records' promotion man, Murray entered it in the "Swingin' Soiree," his nightly record-review roundup. Incredible as it seems, the Beatles came in third—a distant third. Even so, Murray was determined to give them a shot. "I played their record for about two and a half weeks," he recalled, "and nothing. No reaction." There was no way he intended to interrupt his vacation for the Beatles, and he told Chaseman as much. "Then he sort of insisted and put my job on the line."

Murray had been waiting for an opening since the press conference swung into gear, and now he got one from George big enough to drive his massive personality through. "Who *are* you?" George wanted to know.

"I'm Murray the K," Kaufman shouted back, giving it that special seductive twist.

George grinned wolfishly. "Hey, this is Murray the K," he announced, calling over the other Beatles. The Beatles loved disc jockeys, especially those who played their records. Murray immediately went into his "rap," a long-winded self-promotion that inflated his hipness and influence, and for twenty minutes he had the very hot, exclusive Beatles virtually to himself. They even invited him back to their hotel for a party that would serve as Murray's scoop.

But first they had to escape. As Nora Ephron reported in the *New York Post,* "the Beatles were lifted bodily by two policemen each, and each young man was placed and locked in his own Cadillac limousine." A handful of girls actually threw themselves at the Cadillacs, she wrote, "and were led, briefly sobbing, from the parking lot." Securely inside the cars, each of the Beatles watched the familiar scene unfold outside, albeit this time with a stunned fascination. The whirlwind at Kennedy had happened without any warning whatsoever; not even Brian had prepared them for such a reception. "I remember . . . getting into the limo and putting on the radio," Paul recalled, "and hearing a running commentary on *us:* 'They have just left the airport and are coming towards New York City. . . .' It was like a dream. The greatest fantasy ever."

[II]

It came as quite a shock to officials at the posh Plaza Hotel, just off the southeastern edge of Central Park, when it was discovered that several guests, Mr. J. Lennon, Mr. P. McCartney, Mr. G. Harrison, and Mr. R. Starkey—all holding reservations booked routinely under their own names—were, in fact, those same Beatles splashed across the news. And by the time they found out, it was too late to do anything about it.

The boys checked in a little after four o'clock, and from then on the hotel fell under siege. Hundreds of fans showed up simultaneously, causing gridlock. A throng of girls clogged the cut-through between Fifty-eighth and Fifty-ninth Streets that doubled as the Plaza's entrance; others swarmed over the fountain and statue in the tiny arcade along Fifth Avenue or took up position on the sidewalk adjoining the park. It had taken some quick work to move the kids off the front steps and secure the side doors. Those found wandering the halls were also ejected. Before long there were dozens of blue police barricades in place and horse patrols circling the block.

A special detail of guards was also stationed outside the elevators and stairwells on the Plaza's highest floors. The Beatles shared a gorgeous ten-room suite on the twelfth floor, at the back of the hotel, along with Neil and Mal, while Brian stayed down the hall. Exhausted from their flight, the boys just vegged out that first night, watching themselves on television and listening to the radio. "We wanted to hear the music," John recalled. "We were so overawed by American radio."

Unlike in the U.K., New York was covered by a web of independent airwaves. Show formats were insanely flexible, disc jockeys basically playing whatever interested them. All those songs the Beatles had been dying to hear, the obscure hits by their American R&B heroes that the BBC ignored, were finally within earshot. All they had to do was pick up the phone and ask for them—which is exactly what they did all night long. "We phoned every radio [station] in town," John explained, "saying, 'Will you play the Ronettes'" or Marvin Gaye or Smokey Robinson or the Shirelles? Mostly, however, they besieged Murray the K with requests until the excitable jock jokingly complained to listeners: "This is the Beatles' station! They've taken over! They're telling *us* what to play." Then, coining a phrase that he would exploit for the rest of his life, Murray said, "One more week of this, and I'm going to become the fifth Beatle." *The fifth Beatle!* It was an ingenious claim that might have earned the boys' scorn under routine circumstances, but not now. They were having too much fun and let it slide. Besides, they were amused by Murray. "[He] was as mad as a hatter, a fabulous guy . . . [who] knew his music," according to Ringo. And as Paul quickly concluded: "[He] was the man most onto the Beatle[s'] case." From the minute they hit town, Murray functioned as their personal promo man, playing their records repeatedly and doing his number, his shtick.

The next morning, when George's temperature nudged past 102, Jules Gordon, the hotel doctor, was finally summoned. George was ordered to bed, with Neil Aspinall standing in for him at rehearsals for *The Ed Sullivan Show*.

In the meantime, the Beatles entertained a suite full of local press, who conducted what seemed like interminable interviews, one right after another, and shot hundreds of rolls of film. Throughout the day their sitting room was filled with reporters who asked the dopiest questions. "What is your favorite food?" "What does your haircut mean?" "What do you think of American girls?" "How long do you think all this will last?" Incredibly, anyone able to present somewhat professional-looking credentials gained entrance, so that *LIFE* shared the same couch with *Tiger Beat*, the *New Yorker* with the *New York Post*, and Cousin Brucie with Norman Cousins. To make matters worse, Albert and David Maysles wandered freely around the suite, shooting footage for a Grenada TV documentary. The BBC's Malcolm Davis made himself at home; Jack Hutton, *Melody Maker*'s editor, came in with rival *NME* columnist Chris Hutchins. It was a free-for-all. The Beatles did their best to get through it without incident, putting on a show for the cameras, but it was clear as time wore on that they chafed under the intrusion.

Once word got out that the Beatles were at the Plaza, every hustler and promoter angled to get Brian on the line. It was impossible for him to field these calls, yet inexpedient to entrust them to the overloaded hotel switchboard. The hawkeyed Walter Hofer, who stood by to offer advice, wasn't about to answer phones. After complaining about the situation to a Capitol A&R rep, the record company, apparently to ingratiate itself, quickly came up with a solution. Someone in the West Coast office knew a classy English woman in New York who could serve as Brian's secretary while he was in the States.

Much like Brian, Wendy Hanson was from the North, Yorkshire, a posh-spoken girl from "a rather nouveau-riche family"; and much like Brian, she was slavishly proper, sharp-tongued, and meticulous about her appearance. If she seemed self-reliant to a fault, it was because she'd had lots of practice. After her parents died tragically young, Hanson took an *au pair* job in the States, where she met a number of important figures in the classical music field, perhaps none more impressive than Leopold Stokowski, for whom she worked as a secretary, and later Gian Carlo Menotti, who eventually hired her as his personal assistant. Menotti, as it happened, was off in Italy, which left Wendy free to work for Brian, and she set about this mission with a remarkable show of efficiency. "He was in a terrible state when I walked in there," she recalled. "There was a queue of people in the hall, many of whom had been waiting for hours and all of whom he seemed to be trying to avoid. Some were hucksters; others were demanding the return of signed documents. There were record-company executives, television commentators, promoters, friends."

One of the first visitors admitted was a blustery Englishman named Nicky Byrne. A small-time hustler who "trolled with a bunch of characters" nicknamed the Kings Road Rats, Byrne had never dedicated himself to anything long enough to put his name on it. Over the years he had worked in music publishing, designed clothes, staged theater productions, run a nightclub, the Condor, in London—he even tried his hand at marriage— none of which succeeded in holding his interest. What Byrne wanted most, what he had his heart set on, was making a big score.

As Byrne recalled it, he was "sitting around doing nothing for half of [19]63," when several of his mates began tying up rights to all sorts of Beatles merchandise. David Jacobs, the slightly daft celebrity lawyer who represented NEMS, had let them sweet-talk him out of several exclusive contracts for Beatles dolls, lockets, stationery, wigs, songbooks, photos, badges, calendars, sweaters, figurines, scrapbooks. A sculptor in London advertised wall-size panels of the Beatles carved in relief, which was "useful as a thermometer, too." There were Beatles bubble bath and Beatles wallpaper. Most of these products weren't even licensed by NEMS.

From what Byrne could see, they hadn't even begun to scratch the surface of this phenomenon. "Brian's made a terrible mess out of this," Jacobs groaned during his initial meeting with Byrne. That was all Nicky needed to hear. Dazzling the lawyer with an infusion of names and numbers—real or fictitious, it is impossible to say—he spun out a plan to blanket the world in Beatles products and basically walked out with the promise of worldwide rights, excluding the U.K. Jacobs was so uninterested in the whole matter that he instructed Byrne to have his own contract drawn up, stating the terms that were desirable.

On December 4, a contract was delivered to Jacobs's office. "We left it blank about the percentages," Byrne recalled, noting that he was prepared to accept a small, but reasonable, royalty for his efforts. "So, what are you going to pay the Beatles?" Jacobs wondered. Byrne gulped hard and said, "Oh, look, just put in ten percent." It was a ridiculous response, the first thing that popped into his head; 75 or 80 percent was a more realistic figure. Byrne fought to swallow a shit-eating grin as he watched Jacobs fill in the blank as instructed: *10 percent.* Byrne suspected that Epstein would fire this lawyer's ass over such a miscue, "but to my utter amazement it came back signed—the whole thing. They'd initialed in the right places, they'd read the contract. They *couldn't wait* to get somebody else to do this, because they were in a mess themselves."

By the time Brian arrived in New York, however, he realized what a monstrous mistake he'd made. Apparently Nicky Byrne had done a bang-up job, opening a Fifth Avenue office under the corporate name Seltaeb—*Beatles* spelled backward—and licensing North American companies to manufacture every kind of Beatles paraphernalia. The *Wall Street Journal* predicted: "U.S. teen-agers [sic] in the next 12 months are going to spend $50 million on Beatle [sic] wigs, Beatle dolls, Beatle egg cups and Beatle T-shirts, sweatshirts and narrow-legged pants." Another story outlining Nicky's handiwork, in the *New York Times,* reported that Reliance Manufacturing Company, whose factories were "smoking night and day to meet . . . demand" had already sold "Beatle [sic] merchandise valued at . . . more than $2.5 million retail," with plans in the works to produce dozens of new products. The Lowell Toy Company was "turning out Beatle [sic] wigs at the rate of 15,000 a day." Sheridan Clothes claimed to be "a month behind on orders for Beatle-type suits." Bobblehead dolls, along with other games, were soon to be introduced by Remco Industries. And all these articles referred to the mastermind behind the project: Nicky Byrne.

Nicky Byrne. Nicky Byrne. Nicky Byrne. Every time Brian read that name, it drove a spike into his heart. One thing was certain: Brian had botched this deal something fierce. "Seltaeb was . . . in a business that I felt they knew very little about," Walter Hofer explained. There was "a great deal of money" at stake, millions and millions of dollars, and he'd given away 90 percent of it just like that, and to a total stranger. Brian had never even met Nicky Byrne until that Friday night at the Plaza, when he arrived unannounced at the Beatles' suite with a sackful of gifts—"all sorts of gear we could manufacture," Byrne recalled. Negotiations with Byrne to revise the deal promptly began.

Meanwhile, the Beatles, sans George, posed for photographers at the boathouse in Central Park, then rode north in a couple of limousines donated by CBS for an impromptu tour of Harlem, where John instructed the driver to "cruise past the Apollo Theater." Forecasters had been predicting a major snowstorm, and breath rings froze on the tinted windows where all three boys pressed their faces against the glass. They gazed out at the jumble of blighted brownstones and bodegas with their crumbling wrought-iron balconies strung across the facades like tatty jewelry. The busy, narrow streets were a confusion of mongrel cars parked bumper to bumper, and everywhere there were people jostling on the sidewalk, spilling from stores and jackknifing through traffic at a dizzying speed. Suddenly the car turned onto a wide, fidgety boulevard—125th Street—and the Apollo rose up like a neon-and-concrete castle. TONIGHT—THE MARVELOUS MARVELETTES! read the marquee. *De-liveh de-letteh, de-sooneh, de-betteh:* the girls themselves! The proximity of it made the Beatles catch their breath with wonder.

There were more sites the Beatles wanted to visit—among them the specialty record shops that beckoned from every corner, but as it was, they barely made it back in time for the first round of *Ed Sullivan* rehearsals.

Afterward, Brown Meggs showed up with a group of Capitol Records execs—the surest sign there had been a breakthrough. Capitol found itself in an awkward position, having repeatedly rejected the Beatles. Now not only were they Capitol's star attraction, their records causing gridlock on the U.S. charts, but the label's pressing plants were so overburdened by the unprecedented demand that RCA Victor had been hired to press Beatles records as well.

Meggs extended greetings from Alan Livingston, who was en route to New York with two gold records for them, and from Brian Wilson, currently in the studio working on a new single with the Beach Boys. Otherwise, Meggs put himself entirely at the Beatles' disposal. Anywhere the boys wanted to go, anything they wanted to do, could be arranged. He was there to show them a good time, beginning with a sightseeing tour around Manhattan—stopping outside the United Nations and the Empire State Building—followed by dinner at "21," where Ringo ordered a bottle of "vintage Coca-Cola."

When they returned to the Plaza, however, it was inevitable there would be no peace. Edwin Newman and John Chancellor were waiting in the hall with their network camera crews, Tom Wolfe was taking notes for an impressionistic article in *Esquire,* and their suite was overrun with visitors, all entertained by Cynthia Lennon and George's sister, Louise, who had to fight her way through security to visit her brother. To make matters worse, that notorious motormouth Murray the K barged in, trailing the Ronettes, to stage a remote broadcast from George's sickbed.

By that time, Murray's shtick was beginning to wear increasingly thin. It seemed like every time they turned around, he was there, hogging the spotlight, "asking dumb questions and making bad jokes about their hair." The Ronettes, on the other hand, were a sight for sore eyes. They'd hooked up with the Beatles in London during a January promotional tour with the Rolling Stones and spent a string of evenings in each other's company, eating, smoking, dancing, and talking about everything from American rhythm and blues to the burden of fame. The boys found the Ronettes as fascinating as they were attractive, as the girls spun out outrageous backstage tales of working rock 'n roll revues at the Brooklyn Fox with the likes of Ben E. King, Frankie Lymon, Stevie Wonder, and the Impressions. Music aside, John and George quickly developed serious crushes on Ronnie Bennett and her sister, Estelle, who were both knockouts as well as first-rate singers. They'd gone on a series of double dates that crackled with sexual innuendo, but despite some feverish late-night necking, the couples remained platonic. Both girls had steady boyfriends in the States—Ronnie, especially, was devoted to her Svengali, Phil Spector, whom she would eventually marry—which precluded any serious involvement. And, of course, John already *was* married, not that that stood in his way of having some fun.

Meanwhile, the girls had brought along a copy of their latest single, "Baby, I Love You," which the Beatles already had in the suite. "There were portable record players in every room, and 45 rpm records scattered everywhere around the floor," Ronnie recalled. "The Beatles had every record you could think of up there, including a few that hadn't even come out in the stores yet." The sound of a mob drifted up from the street below, there were guards posted outside their door, cranks calling every few seconds. Ronnie was struck by the contrast to those idyllic few weeks in London. For all the apparent triumphs that winter, she came to the painful realization that "the Beatles really were like prisoners."

It was almost a relief to get down to work on Sunday. Feeling nauseous and unsteady, George arrived at Studio 50 along with the other Beatles for an afternoon dress rehearsal. A troop of mounted policeman patrolled

Seventh Avenue in front of the theater, where two hundred fans had gathered, hoping to talk their way inside. There was no chance of that, with all the 728 tickets spoken for long in advance. Normally, a sound check and run-through was staged in front of an empty house, but Sullivan had talked Brian into filming the dress camera rehearsal as an extra performance that would air a week after the boys' departure, so the audience was already in their seats before the Beatles arrived.

The boys got comfortable backstage in the well-upholstered dressing room, drinking tea and listening to their transistor radios, each tuned to a different Top 40 station. They were unusually relaxed, even for the Beatles—reading fan mail, clowning, almost oblivious to the fact that they were making their American debut. A stack of telegrams lay unopened on a ledge by the mirror. One, marked URGENT in red pen and addressed to each of the Beatles individually, caught Paul's attention, and as he read it his face corkscrewed into a mad grin.

"It's from Elvis!" he shouted to the others.

John looked up blank-faced. "Elvis who?" he asked.

Paul ignored him and read the cable's contents aloud. "'CONGRATULATIONS ON YOUR APPEARANCE ON THE ED SULLIVAN SHOW AND YOUR VISIT TO AMERICA. WE HOPE YOUR ENGAGEMENT WILL BE A SUCCESSFUL ONE AND YOUR VISIT PLEASANT. GIVE OUR BEST TO ED SULLIVAN.'" He looked up, beaming. "Signed, Elvis and the Colonel."

The filming came off without a hitch. Standing near the wings, before a closed curtain—his trademark—Sullivan in his role as emcee portentously thanked "these youngsters from Liverpool" for their exemplary conduct while in America and appreciated how they would "leave an imprint on everyone over here who's met them." Before he could get another word out, the high-pitched screams started.

The curtain opened as the spotlights snapped on. Opening with "Twist and Shout," the Beatles stood center stage and belted out a tame but rock-solid version against a backdrop of pastel-colored modular designs. It provided a good contrast to their dark mohair suits and blinding smiles, turned up a few watts higher than usual as a hedge against unfamiliarity. If there was any concern about the impression they'd make, however, it was scrapped before the first "c'mon baby." Every time they grinned, converged on a mike, or—especially—shook their heads, propelling those famous haircuts, the largely female audience screamed its approval. And before anyone had a chance to cool down, the band launched into "Please Please Me," followed by "I Want to Hold Your Hand."

Few had known what to expect. Until that moment, all that Americans had really seen of the Beatles were scattered newspaper photographs, depicting them in a crowd or mugging for publicity stills. A Beatles performance was something else entirely, and the power of it, the emotional charge they sent through the audience, moved teenagers in ways they'd never been moved before. For starters, there was the charisma, that boyish charm, which the Beatles (especially Paul) had perfected as an art form. Several times during the set, Paul stared directly into the camera—or, as a viewer might interpret it, directly at *her*—opened up his face, and projected, literally, the most innocent, adorable eyeful that American girls had ever witnessed. Hearts melted in an instant when he flipped that particular switch. John was more coy in how he went about it, but he also knew the right moment to flash a winning grin. From time to time he'd glance side-long at Paul, then turn it on, just for a few seconds, until he'd produced the desired effect. Nor were George and Ringo wholly innocent of striking a theatrical pose, displaying an innate sense of timing when it came to raising an antic squeal.

So, too, did they flaunt their musical skill. At a time when few rock 'n roll acts got a shot on TV, those with the opportunity rarely appeared with a band. Networks favored young pop singers who performed their hits in front of a studio orchestra. It was rare they were allowed to bring their own musicians. For one thing, most teenage bands couldn't cut it as pros, and unlike playing a concert hall, where horrible acoustics masked most slipups, TV was unforgiving; for another, a four-piece guitar band usually sounded thin and tinny on TV. Even self-contained bands such as Buddy Holly and the Crickets or Little Stevie Wonder adjusted their act to work with a canned ensemble that included horns and strings. On a show like *Bandstand,* where groups lip-synced to their records, there was no live music at all. Therefore, seeing the Beatles perform by themselves, working, so to speak, without a net, was a fairly eye-opening experience. And how those boys could play! This wasn't just a hunk strumming chords, like Ricky Nelson. This was a batch of boys as nimble as they were energetic, spanking their guitars and executing tasty licks and fills seamlessly. It would be a mistake to overlook the sexual heat they delivered.

Unfortunately, CBS had been unprepared to deal with miking a proper rock 'n roll band. "We weren't happy with the . . . appearance," said Paul, "because one of the mikes weren't [sic] working." John's vocals sounded washed-out and occasionally lost, all the more infuriating because they'd worked painstakingly on sound during rehearsals. Throughout it all, the Beatles themselves had consulted with Sullivan's technicians, running back and forth to the control booth after each take. "Finally," George recalled, "when they got a balance between the instruments and the vocals, they marked the boards by the controls, and then everyone broke for lunch. Then, when we came back to tape the show, the cleaners had been round and had polished all the marks off the board."

It was no better that night when the Beatles returned to Studio 50 for the live broadcast of *The Ed Sullivan Show*. This time, the crowd outside had tripled in size, giving the place the jacked-up feeling of a Broadway opening. There were flowers in the dressing room and visiting dignitaries, including Dizzy Gillespie, who was playing around the corner at Birdland and "just stopped by to get a look at them," and Carroll James, the plucky disc jockey from Washington, D.C. When Leonard Bernstein, an acquaintance of Wendy Hanson's, swept in with his daughters, George was in the midst of "having a row" over the sound with Bob Precht, Ed Sullivan's son-in-law, who produced the show. Bernstein babbled on endlessly about Washington, D.C., and about how when he was there "he sung rounds with Jackie at breakfast." One could tell from the look in their eyes that the Beatles had no idea who he was or what he was talking about. (A "round" to an English working-class lad meant a piece of buttered bread, and as for Jackie, they were completely stumped.) John turned to Wendy Hanson and said, "Look, love, we haven't known you long and we like you very much—but could you keep Sidney Bernstein's family out of this room?"

Outside, the corridor was crowded with other acts and technicians making their way backstage. Whether intentionally or not, Sullivan's show that night was top-heavy with British acts, including the vaudevillian banjo player Tessie O'Shea and the cast of *Oliver!*, a West End smash that had recently opened on Broadway, written coincidentally enough by Lionel Bart, who was quite friendly with Brian Epstein.

At the very top of the show, Sullivan lumbered onstage and wasted no time in introducing the boys. "Now, yesterday and today, our theater's been jammed with newsmen and press from all over the world, and these veterans agree with me that the city's never witnessed the excitement stirred by these youngsters from Liverpool who call themselves the Beatles." A smattering of screams ripped through the audience. "Now, tonight, you're gonna twice be entertained by them, right now and later. Ladies and gentlemen—*the Beatles!*"

If the Beatles seemed daunted by the prospect of a live American television audience, it did not show. They stood confidently center stage when the cameras hit them and launched right into a loose, if unimaginative and tightly controlled, version of "All My Loving." Paul sang it note-perfect, with all the raw edges polished off, as though he'd decided to whitewash it for a more general listening crowd. With effortless determination, George twanged a florid country-and-western riff during the instrumental break, throwing a nice light on his skill. But John's feeble mike left his voice muted and indistinct, especially with George doubling at Paul's side for the harmonies. Then, after taking a gracious bow amid energetic applause, Paul soloed on "Till There Was You." It was a curious choice, considering the song's saccharine, almost tranquilized, romanticism, as if the objective were to downplay the Beatles' rock 'n roll roots. There had been so much to-do made over their hair and the mania. A lot of Americans who'd tuned in out of curiosity already had their backs up, anticipating something menacing or vulgar. The song seemed to demonstrate how harmless it all was—and Paul sang it so sweetly, oozing sincerity. How could hard-nosed parents continue to disapprove?

But even the Beatles must have felt the inertia it created. The second it was finished, right after George's little cha-cha flourish on guitar, Paul jerked sideways on a heel and whipped his finger around a few times to launch Ringo into gear. A clatter of drums exploded into "She Loves You," and when they hit the *"woooos"* at the end of the chorus, Paul and John exaggerated the shake of their heads, which triggered shrieks of delirium from the new fans. This, girls got especially caught up in. During the song, those at home were given a special introduction to the band, with the names of each Beatle superimposed over a lingering close-up; John came last, and below his name an unexpected postscript: "Sorry, girls, he's married"—at last a formal acknowledgment of the Beatle's well-rooted heartthrob status.

When the Beatles returned at the end of the show, the audience was ready for them. Both "I Saw Her Standing There" and "I Want to Hold Your Hand" delivered on the promise of something thrilling. The boys rocked out, giving it the old high-octane treatment, and as the camera cut to the crowd, there were glimpses of budding Beatlemania churning in the seats. Girls were ecstatic, flustered, their faces frozen in rapturous glee. Yet by British standards, it still was a pretty tepid affair. Reports of "crazy girls, who were going bananas . . . screaming, tearing out their hair," were grossly exaggerated. No one fainted or leaped toward the stage. For that matter, no one even left her seat. A kinescope of the event reveals a fairly well-disciplined group of kids—screaming, yes, at times bouncing up and down, but never on the verge of pandemonium.

The mad rush took place in living rooms. The viewing audience was estimated at 74 million—a record, according to the A. C. Nielsen Company, whose survey revealed that 58 percent of all homes with televisions were tuned to *Ed Sullivan*. But over breakfast the next morning, with newspapers strewn across the table, the tone of the reviews showed markedly in the Beatles' furrowed faces. The *New York Times'* TV critic, Jack Gould, dismissed the Beatles as nothing more than "a fad" while giving them credit for a "bemused awareness" that acknowledged their complicity in the clever affair. "Televised Beatlemania," Gould wrote, "appeared to be a fine mass placebo," and he summed up the performance itself as a "sedate anticlimax" to all the hype New York had withstood since the Beatles hit town. Unsure of how to critique the finer points of their musicianship, he deferred to a more learned colleague, who analyzed their vocals as one might a Gregorian chant, citing the Beatles' tendency to create "false modal frames . . . suggesting the Mixylydian mode." The other reviews were less convoluted, although similar in opinion. The *Washington Post* thought they "seemed downright conservative . . . asexual and homely." And *Newsweek* was scathing in its overall appraisal of the Beatles:

> Visually they are a nightmare: tight, dandified Edwardian beat-
> nik suits and great pudding-bowls of hair. Musically they are a
> near disaster, guitars and drums slamming out a merciless beat
> that does away with secondary rhythms, harmony and melody.
> Their lyrics (punctuated by nutty shouts of yeah, yeah, yeah!)
> are a catastrophe, a preposterous farrago of Valentine-card ro-
> mantic sentiments.

The *Herald Tribune* carried the story on its front page under the puzzling headline BEATLES BOMB ON TV. Its columnist pointedly decried what he heard as the absence of talent in their performance, calling it "a magic act that owed less to Britain than to Barnum." The Beatles "apparently could not carry a tune across the Atlantic," he wrote, rating them as "75 percent publicity, 20 percent haircut, and 5 percent lilting lament."

If it bothered the Beatles that the reviews were largely hostile, they refused to let it show, other than a mention by George who felt the *Tribune's* crack about Barnum was "fucking soft." After all, they'd gotten what they wanted: the largest American TV audience in history. "If everybody really liked us, it would be a bore," John told a reporter. "It doesn't give any edge to it if everybody just falls flat on their face saying, 'You're great.'"

Privately, Brian fumed. Damning the reviews as a "vicious attack," he peevishly demanded cancellation of the remainder of interviews on the schedule as retribution, though Brian Sommerville eventually talked him out of it. But by the time he chaperoned the boys to a press conference in the Plaza's Baroque Room that morning, his irritation with the reporters burned clearly on his face. To an official from Capitol Records who was observing the scene, the manager was a changed person. "Before Epstein came here he had ice-water in his veins," he said. "Now it's turned to vinegar."

For their part, the Beatles handled the press with complete poise. Ostensibly, the conference was called to announce their three-film deal with United Artists, but the boys, as usual, played it strictly for laughs. John drew chuckles first, revealing that his choice for a leading lady was Brigitte Bardot. How about you, Ringo? someone called out. "I don't mind meself," he said, "as long as it's not Sophia Loren. She's so tall, I'd have to climb a ladder to kiss her!" The reporters tried in vain to get Brian involved, but he declined, redirecting their attention to the four boys. When confronted with the charge of creating "false modal frames," John grinned and said, "We're gonna see a doctor about that." A woman on the other side of the room asked George which of them was sexiest. "Our manager, Brian Epstein," he fired back, which failed to placate her. "Who chooses your clothes?" she persisted. "We choose our own," John said. "Who chooses yours?" Refusing to be intimidated, she replied, "My husband. Now tell me, are there any subjects you prefer not to discuss?" John leaned close to the microphone and without missing a beat said, "Yes, your husband." The room erupted in appreciative laughter.

It went on like that, back and forth, for nearly three hours, with a volley of one-liners that befitted a Friars Club roast. The Beatles seemed able to handle anything thrown at them, never remotely becoming rattled by the barrage of caustic questions. The result was a public relations sensation. Over Brian's mild objections, the Beatles continued to charm a professional lynch mob that had come to bury them. Not one word was said about the crummy reviews, nor was another bad word written. By the time Alan Livingston interrupted the questioning to present them with two gold records, the Beatles had climbed back into America's good graces.

[III]

On Tuesday, February 11, the Beatles and what seemed like most of the New York press corps left for Washington, D.C., where the boys were to give their first live stage show in America. It had been snowing heavily for several hours, and plans to fly were scrapped at the last minute in favor of a private sleeping car that Brian Sommerville had chartered expressly for the trip. The train had nothing on the limos and luxury planes they'd grown used to, not even on the Liverpool-to-London express. It was a dingy, malodorous cubicle, yellow from cigarette smoke and cramped with rows of dilapidated leather seats blistered by springs. None of that, however, seemed to dampen the festive spirit. Grateful to escape the confinement of their hotel room, the Beatles were at their uproarious best. John and Paul fluttered about the train, chatting with passengers and mugging for the press. George, still recovering from his illness, climbed up into a luggage rack, where he managed to take a catnap. And Ringo, juiced by the unstoppable scene, swept out the car with a broom before grabbing half a dozen camera cases from photographers, then strolled up and down the aisle, shouting, "Exclusive! *LIFE* magazine! Exclusive! I am a camera!"

It was their last chance to unwind before a tumultuous—and rather nightmarish—evening that started the minute they reached Washington. Word had leaked that the Beatles were arriving by rail, and an estimated three thousand kids, spurred on by local disc jockeys, jammed the platform when the train pulled into Union Station. A giant banner dangled above the crowd: WWDC WELCOMES THE BEATLES. Flashbulbs exploded ceaselessly, reporters converged on the train, pushing, shoving. There was complete chaos, with fans and press battling fiercely for position. The police, befuddled by the melee, stood uncertainly on the sidelines as Paul led the others out of the wheezing car. Somehow the Beatles fought their way through the crowd and into two waiting limos that skidded along the slushy streets past the capital's illuminated landmarks. The sky over the city held an immense and shifting light, reflecting off the monuments, pale as pieces of a child's board game. "Just like in the movies," Ringo muttered as the scenery whipped by. To their right, in roughly the direction of the Potomac, they passed a mansion that looked like the White House. Or maybe not. While they debated the accuracy of the discovery, the cars pulled up short in front of an enormous concrete building.

The Washington Coliseum was the biggest venue they'd ever played, a crusty old 18,000-seat downtown arena that catered mostly to ice hockey and boxing events. Brian hadn't quite prepared them for the size of the place, nor had he warned them about the uncustomary staging. It had been set up like a boxing match, which meant they'd be playing on a platform in the round, a layout that required moving their equipment every few songs.

Three opening acts warmed up the crowd—a British group called the Caravelles, their old friend Tommy Roe from the first U.K. tour, and the Chiffons.* The Beatles' plans to watch the girls' set were scrapped when Murray the K showed up unannounced and determined to broadcast his show from their dressing room. It came almost as a relief when it was time for them to play.

In most theaters-in-the-round, performers enter through tunnels situated under the floor, but because of the mechanics of the ice rink, there was no way to get the Beatles onstage without marching them through the audience. So Harry Lynn, the promoter, sent out three disc jockeys in Beatles wigs to distract the crowd, while the boys, flanked by forty ushers, charged up the aisle to a deafening blast of screams. A blinding explosion of flashbulbs blanketed the arena in light. Then another wave of screams, louder and more unruly, echoed off the walls. "The reaction was so overwhelming," Paul gushed breathlessly minutes after the show, calling it "the most tremendous reception I have ever heard in my life."

From the moment they hit the stage, the Beatles knew this would be no ordinary show. The atmosphere was electric and vaguely dangerous, with a fight-crowd current that harkened back to places like Wilson Hall in Garston. Fearlessly, they huddled together on a postage-stamp-size stage, with fans spilling right over the edges onto it. It was like "an obstacle course," between the tangle of arms reaching toward them and the cables snaked across the floor. Ringo teetered precariously atop a circular skirted platform that, under ideal circumstances, was supposed to have functioned as a turntable for his drum kit. The amps, perched on stands, threatened to topple under the slightest provocation.

"Good evening, Washington!" Paul screamed into a mike, giving the other guys time to plug in and catch their breath.

A camera crew was filming the show for a future closed-circuit broadcast, and from the opening bars of "Roll Over Beethoven" the audience— mostly teenagers—"went berserk." Several dozen police lining the stage

---

* In 1986 a court decided that George's 1970 solo hit "My Sweet Lord" infringed the copyright of the Chiffons' "He's So Fine" and awarded Bright Tunes $587,000 in a judgment against George.

"eyed the audience uneasily," then leaped into action, tackling fans who tried to vault toward the band. "All the Beatlemania ingredients are here in Washington," reported *NME*, including, the paper noted, "the throwing of jelly beans"—not the soft, squishy jelly babies, as was the custom back home, but their American cousins, with a hard outer shell. "That night, we were absolutely pelted by the fucking things," George recalled. "To make matters worse, we were on a circular stage, so they hit us from all sides . . . waves of rock-hard little bullets raining down on you from the sky." It made "the ring-side seem like Omaha Beach," according to a journalist covering the show. "Every now and again, one would hit a string on my guitar and plonk off a bad note as I was trying to play," George said.

In the long run, it didn't make a lick of difference to the quality of the show. The Beatles' performance that night was lit by something special from within. They played with a ripping, amphetamine intensity last glimpsed in Hamburg that went far beyond their usual slick, tightly con-trolled set. "Ringo, in particular, played like a madman," writes Albert Goldman, "revealing a fire that nobody had ever glimpsed before beneath his workmanlike surface." It was less a put-down of Ringo's ability than a revelation of the implicit power contained in his solid backbeat. Something primitive had taken hold of him that converted every thrust, every blow, into energy. Ringo's arms flailed feverishly and his head shook with a de-monic pendulation, making him seem at times almost spastic, at others dynamic and Herculean. It didn't even matter that "the acoustics were ter-rible" or that the equipment had to be hastily rearranged after every song. Incredibly, it never interrupted the flow or the tension gripping the arena. By the finale, a fantastic sweat-stained rendition of "Long Tall Sally," the capacity crowd was on its feet, screaming uncontrollably in one mad, sus-tained roar.

Afterward, the Beatles were dizzy from exhaustion—and exhilaration. Ringo, especially, was in thrall of the fans. "They could have ripped me apart and I wouldn't have cared," he related backstage, drenched in sweat. "What an audience! I could have played for them all night." As it was, the entire act lasted a mere twenty-eight minutes.

The Beatles didn't stick around for any last-minute backslaps. Instead, they were whisked a few miles east to the British embassy, where a "cham-pagne party and masked charity ball" was held ostensibly in their honor. This was precisely the kind of function they routinely avoided, full of stuffed shirts and other genteel functionaries who regarded the Beatles as a novelty. The embassy was packed with well-dressed British diplomats and their families for whom the Beatles provided a much-needed glimmer of home pride. Lavish trays of food stretched from one side of the ballroom to the other. And as the boys made their entrance down a grand swan-shaped staircase to the rotunda, it seemed as though the entire floor of dancers swirled around them in greeting. It was a lovely gesture. The British ambassador, Sir David Ormsby-Gore, proved gracious and hospitable, even chuckling when Ringo, who looked him up and down, asked: "So, what do you do?"

But, after all, it was an embassy party, a very la-di-da affair and not at all the kind of crowd that appealed to the boys. They had been told it would be "a quiet little party" for the overworked embassy staff, but as it turned out, the building was packed with an obnoxious, aggressive mob — the "full quota of chinless wonders," as George Martin described them. "People were touching us when we walked past," John recalled, none too pleased by the situation. It seemed, in Ringo's estimation, as if the Beatles were on exhibit, "like something in a zoo." Paul did his best to "exchange pleasantries" with the guests, but that became too much even for him. When a "slightly drunk woman" wrapped her arms around him and demanded to know his name, Paul responded, "Roger. Roger McClusky the Fifth," before ducking out from under her clutches.

That night it was Ringo who, in a mock Etonian accent, managed to talk John out of making a scene while announcing the winners of the embassy raffle, daring the recipients to exchange their signed copies of *Meet the Beatles* "for a Frank Sinatra." But as the raffle presentation wound down, a debutante snuck up behind Ringo and lopped off a hank of his hair with nail scissors. That did it. Ringo swung around and said, "What the hell do you think you are doing?" He was furious, totally out of character. "This lot here are terrifying — much worse than the kids," he fumed. John started for the door, swearing under his breath, with Ringo right behind him, calling for a cab. It was all they could do not to make a scene. "They were very sad," recalled photographer Harry Benson, who was part of the Beatles' entourage. "They looked as if they wanted to cry. John, in particular. They weren't pugnacious. They were humiliated."

All of the Beatles felt the same way. They knew how the social set regarded them — four yobbos from Liverpool who'd gotten lucky — how people like that were slumming in their presence. *People like that.* The boys had played along, acquiescing for Brian Epstein even when they dreaded attending such functions. It was part of the game, they decided, though not fully understanding the rules. But that night had finished it.

Yobbos they might be, but that didn't render them insensitive. It didn't matter what Brian thought it might do for their career. They wouldn't play that part of the game again, not with *people like that,* not ever.

The next day most of the entourage flew back to New York, while the Beatles and a handful of selected journalists returned on the train. What should have been a relaxed trip up the East Coast turned out to be another long ordeal. The nuisance and scrutiny of clicking cameras acted like a magnifying lens, focusing the anxiety and resentment of the previous night to an incendiary point. George Martin described the experience as "some giant three-ring circus from which there was no let-up." John, still seething, attempted to bury his nose in a book but was hounded relentlessly by photographers to "be a good sport." It was as shabby as he'd ever been treated. "The only place we ever got any peace," George recalled, "was when we got in the suite and locked ourselves in the bathroom. The bathroom was about the only place you could have any peace."

There was the usual mob scene at Pennsylvania Station when the train arrived in New York. In an effort to clear crowds from in front of the Plaza, the police on detail outside the hotel had announced that the Beatles were going straight from the train to Carnegie Hall. As a result, thousands of fans jammed the upper waiting area, with the overflow milling through the lower concourse and scattered along the platforms. In no time it became a perilous scene. The transit police force was unprepared to handle such an enormous crowd and panicked when a mad rush of kids broke through a line of barricades to greet the arriving train.

Unbeknownst to the fans, however, the Beatles' car had been detached from the train and diverted to an isolated platform at the opposite end of the station, where security guards planned to evacuate them by private elevator. Yet, resourceful kids had already anticipated that, too, and in the end the boys merely charged up the stairs and jumped into a taxi idling on Seventh Avenue.

The Beatles appeared twice that evening at Carnegie Hall, lounging between shows in an elegantly appointed green room that had provided sanctuary to such icons as Tchaikovsky, Ravel, and Judy Garland. If the Beatles felt awed by the august surroundings, it didn't show. To them, it wasn't a shrine but "simply another theater, like the Albert Hall or the Finsbury Park Astoria." They were totally relaxed, chain-smoking American cigarettes, not at all intimidated about performing at the most prestigious and legendary concert hall in America, if not the world. Nor were they fazed by the extraordinary circumstances that marked the occasion. Until that night, no rock 'n roll act had ever set foot on the Carnegie Hall stage, which was governed like a prize duchy by a bluenosed board of directors. Even a bid by Elvis Presley had been rejected. Sid Bernstein claimed that he convinced the board that an appearance by the Beatles would go toward promoting international relations, but it seems more likely that he misrepresented them as a folk group.

Considering the historic importance of the concert, however, Capitol had every intention of recording it for a future release. By February 3, a deal had been struck, with George Martin on hand to guide the production in tandem with Capitol's East Coast A&R man, Voyle Gilmore. Carnegie Hall granted permission in exchange for a trivial $600 fee. There remained only one hurdle: the American Federation of Musicians registered an objection over the proposed use of nonunion personnel on the session; in essence, they refused to allow George Martin to work in the States. Capitol promptly offered to pay his membership dues or do whatever was required to solve the problem, but the union held firm, claiming it would set an irreversible precedent. Without Martin, the Beatles wouldn't participate, ultimately killing any possibility for a live album.

In the long run, it was just as well. There was no way for them to connect through the impenetrable wall of screaming that went up the moment they took to the stage. "Yells and shouts rose to an absolutely ear-shattering volume," wrote Jack Hutton, the editor for *Melody Maker,* who reduced the crowd's reaction to a single word: "bedlam." No one could hear a word they sang, not that it seemed to matter to the young fans. Kids tore up and down the aisles, threw stuffed animals and handfuls of jelly beans. It was a free-for-all; there was no shape or purpose to the adulation. "A move by any Beatle in any direction induced renewed and more piercing cries." In Washington the Beatles had worked the crowd like politicians, but here in New York they remained aloof, frustrated by the audience's apparent refusal to listen. Although they remained earnest, if workmanlike, through the opening numbers, John's impatience finally broke through after the seventh song, when he stepped forward, "looked the audience sternly in the mouth and yelled, 'Shut up!'" The indifference to the music became, apparently, too much to bear. After a meteoric appearance, lasting only thirty-four minutes, the Beatles dropped their instruments and headed for the wings.

The critics treated the show less as a concert than a skirmish. None of the dailies devoted so much as a paragraph to the quality of the performance. The coverage focused entirely on audience reaction, which had mystified the forum of middle-aged reviewers whose experience with delirious behavior was limited to bravos at the opera. The *New York Times* paid only backhanded respect to the Beatles' "thumping, twanging rhythms" and referred obliquely to a number as "a ballad of tender intent"; otherwise, its verdict on the music, including the hits, was nonexistent. Only the weekly *New Yorker* weighed in with an opinion that gave no more than the slenderest support to their talent: "They are worth listening to," its intrepid reporter conceded, "even if they aren't as good as the Everly Brothers, which they really aren't."

The reviews, though condescending, were generally overlooked by the Beatles, who came to view the New York entertainment establishment as largely ignorant of what they were all about. More conspicuous, perhaps, was the absence of their peers, the local cadre of pop-music stars, none of whom made an effort to meet them during their stay. Where was Gene Pitney or Dion and the Belmonts or Lesley Gore or Frankie Valli? Where was Chubby Checker or the Singing Nun, for that matter? At a ceremony for ASCAP's fiftieth anniversary, held at City Hall the day after the Carnegie shows, the geriatric songwriters seemed to go out of their way to distance themselves from these budding British upstarts. "I hear they write their own music," one elderly songwriter insinuated, to which Dorothy Fields (the author of "I Can't Give You Anything But Love") replied: "If you can call it writing."

The best was yet to come. The next day the Beatles left for Miami, to appear on another *Ed Sullivan Show,* broadcast live from Florida. "Miami was like paradise," Paul recalled, dazzled by the difference between a tropical sun-drenched beachfront vista and New York. "The place itself is a bit like Blackpool, only with sunshine," they wrote to friends not long after the trip. Gazing like "real tourists" at the palm trees and local "bathing beauties," the Beatles landed at the Deauville Hotel—nicknamed "Beatle Central" by the press—where they immediately hit the beaches running. Unlike at the Plaza, where they'd basically been shut-ins, there was plenty of opportunity to soak in the sights. Several times a day the boys would slip into their "cozzies," as Scousers called bathing suits, and head outside, wandering along the shore and chatting with people their own age. "It was a big time for us," Paul recalled, "and there were all these lovely, gorgeous, tanned girls. We did a photo session by the beach and immediately asked them out." The freedom they experienced there was a slender relief. Each time, the Beatles ventured farther and farther, gamboling in the bracing

Atlantic surf, waterskiing, and tooling around on powerboats that skipped the waves at unbelievable speeds. As for nighttime entertainment, it was a movable feast, with the boys flitting from one club to another. Comedian Don Rickles was hurling insults in the Deauville's buttoned-down lounge, the Supremes were appearing around the corner at another beachfront hotel, and the Coasters, their longtime "heroes" (Ringo considered them "rock 'n roll gods"), were the featured attraction at a local joint called the Mau Mau Lounge. "[Miami] was just about the most brilliant place I'd ever been to," declared Ringo, who favored nightspots farther inland, at the open-air drive-in theaters that drew young crowds.

But the relaxed, unfettered lifestyle didn't last long. Within days the fans became a nuisance, and the Beatles left the Deauville—stashed in the back of a refrigerated butcher's truck—relocating to a private estate on Star Island, borrowed from one of the local Capitol Records affiliates. The owners had left the place well provisioned. There was a pool in the backyard, an armed guard on the premises, and a yacht at their disposal, a gorgeous sixty-footer called *The Southern Trail,* courtesy of manufacturing tycoon Bernard Castro. On the rare days when nothing was scheduled, the boys lounged in picture-perfect, sunny, eighty-five-degree weather, but it was a busman's holiday. Brian, who prized publicity, kept the Beatles tirelessly in the public eye. Even while they sunbathed, *LIFE* and the *Saturday Evening Post* conducted interviews poolside, interspersed with phone interviews to important disc jockeys, such as one with *Bandstand*'s Dick Clark, during which they gratefully acknowledged their reception in the States.

The Beatles had reason to be grateful. By February 15, just two and a half weeks after its release and three weeks since their *Ed Sullivan* debut, *Meet the Beatles* claimed the top spot on *Billboard*'s album chart, establishing them across the country as an unqualified pop sensation. As for their singles, the Beatles practically owned the Hot 100: "I Want to Hold Your Hand" was number one, "She Loves You" number two, "Please Please Me" number twenty-nine, "I Saw Her Standing There" number thirty-five, and "My Bonnie" number fifty-four. Columnist Nat Hentoff reported that a spokesman for the U.S. Treasury Department had made the Beatles "an economic issue," due to what he called "a gold drain" resulting from their record sales and personal appearances. When a skeptical reporter speculated in a column as to whether the Beatles' longevity would last through the month, a colleague pointed out that their ratings for the second *Ed Sullivan Show* had doubled, and at that rate, there weren't enough people left in the United States to cover the third appearance.

Now everybody wanted to see the Beatles, as if they gave off some special juju, as if they would make everything all right, which, in a sense, they actually did. The Sullivan audience was filled with celebrities eager to lay eyes on the Beatles, among them boxing legends Joe Louis and Sonny Liston, who was scheduled to fight Cassius Clay the next week for the heavyweight title. Lest their presence be perceived as a show of favoritism, Paul felt compelled to predict that Clay would win the bout, which prompted an invitation from publicist Harry Conrad to meet the young boxer during a workout at his Fifth Street Gym.

The Beatles had never been fight fans. They'd showed no interest in it while in Liverpool, even though Pete Best's father, Johnny, promoted major boxing events at the stadium. But now they carved out precious time to stage a meeting with Cassius Clay. Why, suddenly, had that become a priority? According to George: "It was a big publicity thing. It was all part of being a Beatle, really, just getting lugged around and thrust into rooms full of press men taking pictures and asking questions." It was no secret that Clay had upended the boxing world with his flamboyant personality. An incorrigible motormouth "who could talk at the rate of three hundred new words a minute," he constantly played to the cameras, boasting comically and spouting silly strings of verse. No one as of yet had a real grip on his potential in the ring, but he'd impressed most critics as a first-rate entertainer. In that respect it seemed fitting that the greatest entertainers of the moment should veer into each other's orbit.

Yet suffice it to say, the dingy, smoke-filled gym he inhabited was thrown by the invasion of four shaggy-haired boys wearing skintight pants and white terry-cloth jackets. "Get a load of them Beatles. They look like girls," grunted a ringside tough smoking a "fat cigar." The Beatles, for their part, were feeling no more well disposed, bummed by the imposition and resentful of being kept waiting fifteen minutes for Clay to appear. "Where the fuck's Clay?" Ringo asked no one in particular, clearly annoyed by the delay. Next it was John's turn to grumble with a diva's indulgence. "Let's get the fuck out of here," he told the others. But two Florida state troopers blocked the door until their host arrived.

If the boys entertained thoughts about bolting, they evaporated the second Cassius Clay—the Louisville Lip—strode through the door. "Hello there, Beatles!" he roared, walloping them with his charm. (Clay, according to Harry Conrad, "didn't know who they were.") "We ought to do some road show together. We'll get rich." He was a fireball, a spirit, beautiful indeed, stamped for greatness and unspoiled by celebrity. The Beatles took an immediate liking to him, rolling right into the campy floor show that he staged with flair. He "insisted on having fun while he trained." Luring them into the ring, he shouted, "Get down, you little worms," to which the boys dropped on their backs. Then John instructed him to stand over them "with his gloved hand in a victory pose," instructions Clay obediently followed. No one needed much coaxing. They were all, Beatles and boxer alike, consummate showmen; they knew their roles, hit all their cues. For an encore, Clay grabbed Ringo, hoisted him above his head, and swirled him around like a pinwheel—*whoosh-whoosh-whoosh-whoosh-whoosh*—the way Popeye dispensed with his foes.

The spectators and court jesters hollered and pounded their fists in approval; the cornerman, Drew "Bundini" Brown, mock-pleaded for the skinny drummer's life; and forward stepped Clay to deliver a few lines with great profundity:

> "*When Sonny Liston picks up*
> *the papers and sees,*
> *That the Beatles came to see me,*
> *He will get angry and I'll knock him out in three.*"

It wasn't exactly Byronic, though it delighted the authors of "Love, love me do / you know I love you." For the Beatles, who were fast on the way to becoming cultural icons, the twenty-two-year-old Clay was something of a soul mate. "He had the whole crazy scene under his thumb," they were said to have told Brian. Glib and graceful, he was larger than life *on his own terms,* without all the bullshit. They left the gym a short time later "with great reluctance." "Clay mesmerized them," recalled photographer Harry Benson. But what captivated and moved them was not Clay's charisma; it was his power. Clay looked beautiful, but he also punched like a sledgehammer. The Beatles knew that if Brian had his way, pretty and cute would be all that mattered. Still, the image they had cultivated, although it annoyed them, remained useful and, at the moment, afforded them something of a franchise.

Perhaps no one appreciated this more than John Lennon. Later that day, when photographer Dezo Hoffman snapped a few candid shots of the boys waterskiing, John went ballistic. Image-conscious to the nines, he suspected that the pictures, in which his hair had been swept back off his forehead, would make him—a *Beatle*—appear bald. Instead of reasoning with Hoffman, John laced into him, berating the genial Czech in front of a flock of lackeys. One witness recalled how Hoffman stood clutching the camera to his chest as if somehow it might help shield an indiscreet blow. "Vied you do that?" he asked in his accented English. "You'll look good."

"I'll look like shit," John replied. "Everyone will recognize that it's me."

[I]

The Beatles were dressed exactly as they had been two weeks earlier, although now the same dark suits were rumpled slightly from an eight-hour flight. As they came through the airliner's forward door, they stood on the same platform, offering the same wandlike wave to the same monster crowd, except that in place of the 4,000 screaming, well-behaved teenagers, there were now "8,000 to 12,000" who, at the sight of their heroes, went on a rampage through Heathrow Airport, bending steel crash barriers and demolishing car roofs as if they were made of tinfoil. Forty girls fainted, bouquets of flowers were trampled, bins overturned, and the banners— WELCOME HOME BEATLES—shredded in the mad scramble to reach the boys.

The Beatles were back in the land of jelly babies.

If the fans' behavior distressed the Beatles, they refused to let it show as they were herded into the crowded Kingsford-Smith Suite at the terminal to face the homeland press. More than one reporter remarked at the civil disorder on the tarmac in terms that encouraged the Beatles to distance themselves from the hooligans, but the boys knew better than to buy into that business. Instead, they saluted the crowd as "healthy and British and lads and mates and friends."

The Beatles defused any potential controversy with their now-expected witty one-liners, stumbling only when it came to the news that while they were overseas, the prime minister, Sir Alec Douglas-Home, named the Beatles as his "secret weapon" in diplomatic relations with the Americans. It actually "flattered" the boys that the PM knew their names. "The thing is, I don't get the bit where [he] said, 'Earning all these dollars for Britain,'" George said with a shrug, paraphrasing the item. He would learn the hard way—and before long write a song about it he called "Taxman."

As it turned out, it was impossible to put a real dollar value on their worth to Great Britain. No one knew about the $253,000 check from Capitol Records in Brian's pocket—the Beatles' share of royalties so far—but it was hot news that the *Barclays Bank Review* had declared them an "invisible export," estimating their overseas record sales at something over $7 million. But there was no clear picture of what the Beatles actually brought in. Aside from records and performances, merchandising remained a vast gray area. The Seltaeb compact was practically minting money—published reports put it somewhere around $50 million—but who knew how much of that would ever find its way back to the source. Income from the enormous number of bootleg products was impossible to peg.

Their cultural impact, however, was easier to calculate. If the Beatles had left London as explorers to the New World, they returned as conquering heroes. No other British pop star had ever scored so strongly in America. Now, practically overnight, the whole scene cracked wide open. The pop music pipeline that until their appearance had flowed one way—from America to Great Britain—suddenly reversed direction. The U.S. market was flooded with singles by topflight British acts, from the Dave Clark Five to Dusty Springfield to the Yardbirds to the Searchers, none of whom imitated American rock so much as adapted it in ways that brought new energy to the form. For the first time in the history of the English charts, British records occupied the top fourteen places. The days of second billing and second-class citizenship for British rock 'n roll seemed over. "With this transition," wrote pop music historian Greg Shaw, "British rock became real."

The day after their return, the Beatles headed straight back to work, taping a segment of the TV variety series *Big Night Out*, in which they performed three comedy sketches as well as five songs, then huddling with Walter Shenson to iron out a few details for their upcoming film. Ringo, feeling dispensable, managed to disappear for a day, flying home to Liverpool to visit his folks and keep a date with Maureen Cox, a Liverpool girlfriend to whom he was engaged.

The next morning, Tuesday, February 25—George's twenty-first birthday—the boys checked into the Abbey Road studio to work on songs for a new album. They could hardly wait to get started. Since the beginning of the year, they had barely played a note that wasn't drowned out by screams and, as musicians, they had become clearly frustrated by the emptiness of it.

This time—for the first time—the scale of the work had changed. Instead of balancing six or eight original songs with a smattering of well-known American covers, practically all the selections were to be Lennon-McCartney compositions. Most of the numbers were slated for the movie soundtrack, requiring immediate attention so they could be synced to some specific action on the screen, or vice versa; the rest, for the tie-in album, weren't as urgent.

John and Paul had written steadily over the past few months, so material wasn't going to be a problem. They had a ton of songs to choose from and, said Paul, "we knew they were good." A version of "Can't Buy Me Love" was already in the can, but a lyric change was needed and the Beatles redid the vocals. They sketched out three songs the first day, one of which— "You Can't Do That"—was pretty much completed before lunch. John had written most of the hard-nosed rocker, with Paul contributing the tart B7 chord that electrifies the bridge. The vocal, however, gives the song its most cutting edge. John delivers a stinging emotional attack in the form of a reprimand, practically spitting out the warning "because I *told you before*," while Ringo reinforces it by punching out the beat.

If there was one highlight, it was Paul's reading of "And I Love Her," a lushly melodic ballad that he'd written on the piano at Jane Asher's house. Paul's gift for immediacy had never been sharper. The plaintive lyric is simple and direct, the feeling achingly poignant. From the opening notes, his voice expresses an honesty that wrings the heart out of every word. "It was the first ballad I impressed myself with," Paul recalled, pointing to the "nice chords" and the "imagery" as its irresistible assets. There is real power in the song, but after two takes the Beatles couldn't find the right way to harness it. Dick James, who was visiting the studio, felt the song was "just too repetitive" and during a tape change he mentioned as much to George Martin. Apparently Martin agreed because he called for a short recess and left the control room briefly to discuss it with the band.

James claims that Martin suggested they write a middle eight to break up the repetitious verses. "I think it was John who shouted, 'OK, let's have a tea break,' and John and Paul went to the piano and, while Mal Evans was getting tea and some sandwiches, the boys worked at the piano," he said. "Within half an hour they wrote . . . a very constructive middle to a very commercial song." Paul, on the other hand, maintained that John "probably helped" on some minor adjustments, but otherwise, "the middle eight is mine. . . . I wrote this on my own." No matter which account is accurate, the arrangement still lacked the right touch, and they abandoned the song for another day.

The same fate befell "I Should Have Known Better," which was temporarily scrapped after three wasted takes. The Beatles were frazzled, wiped out from jet lag and the endless work, and after seven hours of recording, they succumbed to a case of terminal giggles. It was all they could do to get through one complete take. No one even felt like celebrating George's birthday, least of all George, who was "tired and depressed" from the brutal grind. Grudgingly, he'd devoted an hour that morning to posing for pictures as a favor to the press. (The *Daily Express* made George's birthday front-page news.) There were over fifteen thousand cards waiting for him, along with four postal hampers stuffed with presents from fans, none of which he had the energy to open. Dick James had given him a pair of gold cuff links, and from Brian, a gorgeous Rolex that George wore throughout his life. But what he prized more than anything was sleep, precious sleep.

Two days later another productive session yielded two more songs: "Tell Me Why" and "If I Fell." Just before the lunch break, they ran right through "Tell Me Why," a spirited, up-tempo number that John later described as mimicking "a black New York girl-group song," nailing it in eight takes. "If I Fell" proved more elusive. It was John's first attempt at a ballad, wrapped in a snug, intertwining harmony that is easily one of the most beautiful and appealing duets the Beatles ever performed. John and Paul opted to record it together, on a single microphone, which only served to intensify their delivery. The symmetry of their voices is perfect; they come to the center with such precision that it is often hard to tell who is singing which part. It sounds easy—but isn't. The way John structured it demanded chord changes on almost every note of the verse—"dripping with chords," as Paul explained to a reporter—and it took them fifteen takes to get it right.

The album was beginning to take shape. A Sunday session was highly unusual, but since the Beatles were to begin work on their film the next day, Martin suggested they grab a few hours in the studio to keep up the flow. The Beatles worked only the morning session, until breaking for lunch. Still, they managed to lay down three tracks in three hours: a retooling of "I Call Your Name," written originally for Billy J. Kramer as a B-side to "Bad to Me"; a tear-ass version of "Long Tall Sally" that was captured in one live take; and "I'm Happy Just to Dance with You," a "bit of a formula song" that Paul and John had cobbled together for George.

"The Beatles didn't get totally immersed in record production until later on, when they stopped touring," recalled George Martin. But they were no longer intimidated by the recording process, getting it right in the first few takes—or else. Most rock 'n roll groups were still expected to complete an entire album in a day, but for the Beatles that pressure had been eliminated thanks to their huge success. As a result, they could work at their own pace. "We don't stop until we're confident there is no possibility of further improvement," Martin explained. With time to spare— and the advancement of the four-track system—they had the luxury of recording the rhythm tracks and the vocals separately, instead of all at once. Another factor was George Martin's extraordinary confidence in their ability. It was impossible for Martin to ignore the Beatles' instincts, and he gave them considerable leeway to explore new techniques. In songs like "You Can't Do That" and "I Should Have Known Better," George had begun to experiment with a twelve-string Rickenbacker 360 he'd bought in New York, an instrument so new that there were only two in existence. Offbeat percussion flourishes were introduced in the form of cowbells and bongos. The Beatles were quickly fascinated with the mysteries of overdubbing and double-tracking. Contrary to what they originally feared, the studio didn't restrict their songs; it opened up a world of options that gave the songs freedom and new color.

The world of film, however, was alien and precarious.

The Beatles began production on their as-yet-untitled movie on Monday, March 2, in London. Early that morning, a good-size crowd had gathered along Platform Five at Paddington Station, from where the cast and crew were scheduled to depart for six days of shooting aboard a slow-moving British Rail car that would shuttle between various locations in the West Country.

Awkward introductions were made in haste. The Beatles met several of their costars, including Wilfrid Brambell, John Junkin, and Norman Rossington, then joined Actors' Equity at the behest of a union official who painstakingly wrote out four membership cards amid the pushing and shoving on the platform. Director Richard Lester, who stood on the periphery, held his breath as he watched the scene unfold. The first day of a movie was always a bit ticklish, but this one was riddled with uncertainty. The Beatles seemed perfectly comfortable performing onstage, but as Lester realized, film was an altogether different medium, requiring a different set of skills. He had no idea if they could deliver lines without appearing and sounding foolish. Those Scouse accents were nothing to sneeze at. Should they consider a dialogue coach? Or subtitles? Damned if he knew. The plan was to keep everything simple—no tricky monologues, no long-winded speeches. The way the script was constructed, "they spoke in sentences of five or six words each," recalled Alun Owen, who scaled down his original talky screenplay to a collage of manageable sound bites. "The director knew we couldn't act, and we knew," John admitted. "So he had to try almost to catch us off guard." It was a gamble from the start. But, as Walter Shenson notes, "the Beatles fell right into it, they were naturals. And the script was so good, it sounded like they were making it up as they went along."

Owen had done his homework. As promised, he kept the story achingly simple. The Beatles would play the Beatles and do what Beatles normally did—minus the smoking, drinking, swearing, and sex. Geoffrey Stokes, in the essential history *Rock of Ages,* summarizes the movie as a "high-speed pseudodocumentary posing the sole question: will the lads make it through a typical day of press conferences, fan pursuit, encounters with disapproving elders, manic playfulness and occasional self-doubt in time to play a concert for their adoring fans?" From spending only two days with them in Dublin, Owen had managed to pin down the nature of the Beatles' camaraderie, all the nuances and the special give-and-take that insiders found so "disarming and refreshing." It was all there, Paul recalled, the "little jokes, the sarcasm, the humor, John's wit, Ringo's laconic manner; each of our different ways. The film manages to capture our characters quite well." But the goal was not accuracy. "We *were* like that," John explained—when it was advantageous to be cute and lovable. But overall, he saw it as "a comic-strip version of what was going on" in their lives. The few scenes that dramatize the constant scrutiny they were under are but a shadow of the real thing; according to John, "the pressure was far heavier than that."

The work itself was more demanding than they'd expected. For one thing, they had to report for costume and makeup at six o'clock in the morning, which meant getting up at five—an ungodly hour for most people but especially for a Beatle. Moreover, they were seriously out of their element. Learning lines was an uphill battle on top of everything else that was going on in their lives. Victor Spinetti, another of their costars, observed how "the lads never touched the script." In fact, they "frantically" gave it a once-over in the car each morning on their way to the studio, then simply winged it. "You never knew what they were going to say or do." "We'd make things up because of our being so comfortable with each other," recalled Ringo. Some real gems came out of their mouths, the same kind of spontaneous witty stuff that dazzled at their press conferences, but for a seasoned film crew it was a hair-raising way to work. To counteract the Beatles' lack of preparation, Dick Lester kept five cameras running, even after a scene technically ended. "Dick just went on shooting," Spinetti recalled, "shooting everything. . . . [H]e just pointed the cameras at them and let them go. . . . And I just used to keep going. . . . [W]hen he caught them actually talking amongst themselves, it was just magical."

The magic was everywhere, it seemed. Yet the Beatles were still skeptical, still unsure of how long it would last. They remained convinced, to a man, that it might all end suddenly tomorrow, so despite the grind of making a movie, to say nothing of its potential upside, they turned up the heat, working simultaneously on a slew of other projects, pushing harder, persevering, to keep the fantasy alive.

[II]

The most dependable resource, the one that offered the most immediate response, was music. During the last week in February, Columbia Records released "A World Without Love," by Peter and Gordon, most of which Paul had written when he was sixteen and recently salvaged for a Billy J. Kramer session. True to form, Billy J. rejected it as being "too soft." A few weeks later Paul made a few minor changes to the lyric and gave the song instead to Peter Asher, Jane's brother, as a favor to help launch his singing career. "A World Without Love" *was* soft, a delicate harmonic soufflé in the style of "I'll Follow the Sun," lacking the more wiry sophistication of the Beatles' recent releases. It would have never made the cut for their current session, but Peter and his boarding-school mate, Gordon Waller, sang it with a pleasant laid-back yearning that transformed the song into a perfectly acceptable pop hit.

At the Ashers', Paul and Peter had grown accustomed to hanging out when the Beatles were in town. Though entirely different in nature—unlike Paul, Peter was serious and self-involved, with rust-red hair, black horn-rimmed glasses, and an imperiously arched eyebrow that made him look slightly peevish—they established a comfortable, unforced rapport, the perfect antidote to the Beatles' incestuous relationship. "I could talk to him about anything," Paul recalled, pointing to the merits of their unique living arrangement. The boys had an almost comic claim on the house's attic floor: it was an obstacle course littered with guitars, records, books, tape recorders, phonographs, suitcases, and other "bric-a-brac in a jumble" that resembled a typical college dorm. "Their bedrooms were next door to each other," John Dunbar recalls, "so it was kind of a boy's scene upstairs. They would sit there for hours, discussing art and music, endlessly playing the latest records. It was where the rest of us went to hear new music—and to groove."

The place always seemed filled with inherently restless young men who fancied themselves amateur intellectuals, smoking, discussing poetry and politics, paging through magazines, and trading harsh criticism of the establishment. Often Paul would just listen, amazed by the ideas flying around that room. The cool, intellectual agility, while raw and shapeless, was still formidable, providing a glimpse of the future. Many students who congregated at the Ashers' house were refugees from universities and art schools, "the laboratories" for the emerging sixties culture, where being hip and aggressively clever were as crucial to success as pure artistry. And many, though in denial, were patently upper-class. But if Paul felt the wide gap in their background and education, he was never made to feel inadequate. "Somehow it wasn't to do with which area you were from," Paul realized, "it was more just a level of thinking." To that extent, Paul was learning to hold his own. Besides, he was a Beatle, and they envied his enormous success, to say nothing of his talent, along with the freedom it brought him.

While Peter and Gordon promoted "A World Without Love," the Beatles prepared to release their own new single, which had already attracted an inordinate amount of buzz. EMI had wasted no time—or expense—beating the drums for "Can't Buy Me Love," which the label fully expected to break all existing sales records. In the United States, Capitol already had advance orders for 1.7 million copies, allowing it to be issued as a gold record, an unprecedented feat. The British trades were giddy with excitement. "Well, here it is!" Derek Johnson panted in his windy *NME* review. "A pounding, vibrating, fast-medium twister in the r-and-b mould, with a fascinating trembling effect in the middle eight"—he's referring to the instrumental break, actually, in which George's double-tracked guitar solo produces a riveting echo—"it's not so strong melodically as their last two discs—but there's rather more accent on beat."

Though the review made no strides in the advancement of rock criticism, it gave the record a commendable launch. It also helped distract from the pack of would-be marauders who were pecking at the kingdom walls. Competitors were flooding the market with anything that might capitalize on the Beatles' success. All along, there had been scores of singles that made no pretensions as to their agenda: "My Boyfriend Got a Beatle Haircut," "Yes, You Can Hold My Hand," "Beatle Fever," "The Beatle Dance," "The Boy with the Beatle Hair," "Beatle Mania in the U.S.A." (by the Liverpools, no less), "We Love You Beatles"—there were too many to keep track of. A start-up label, Top Six, announced that its debut album would provide a full menu of Beatles covers, coincidentally entitled *Beatlemania*. Another new label, Dial, was banking on a group called the Grasshoppers. Even Decca, at the behest of onetime Beatles producer Mike Smith, recognized the value of ancestry by signing a band called the All-Stars to be led by Pete Best. To their credit, the Beatles wasted not so much as a glance on any of these coattail surfers, their evil eyes trained on more unbenign targets that threatened to cut into their royalties.

Vee-Jay Records had become an irksome problem. The bankrupt Chicago label had revived itself on the back of its two monster Beatles smashes. As far as the boys cared, that was fair and square. Vee-Jay had licensed "Please Please Me" and "Do You Want to Know a Secret" in good faith and were entitled to the windfall they eventually produced. But the label had gotten greedy. The original demo tape submitted two years earlier had other material on it, and despite repeated requests by Roland Rennie for its return, Vee-Jay, under new leadership, claimed that it was nowhere to be found. But Vee-Jay promptly issued the extraneous songs on an album titled *Introducing the Beatles* that sprinted up the charts at a remarkable pace.* Brian pleaded with EMI to protect the Beatles' position, and in February a New York federal court awarded Capitol a temporary injunction against Vee-Jay to halt distribution of the album. But that only succeeded in sidetracking the renegade label.

The sessions in Hamburg also continued to haunt them. Polydor Records had licensed the masters for "My Bonnie" and "When the Saints Go Marching In" to MGM in the States. Now, attempting to parlay that success, the labels were releasing "Cry for a Shadow," the instrumental George had patched together in 1961, to coincide with the release of "Can't Buy Me Love." And Sheridan, who had since joined Bobby Patrick's Big

---

* *The songs included "I Saw Her Standing There," "Misery," "Anna," "Chains," "Boys," "Love Me Do," "P.S. I Love You," "A Taste of Honey," "There's a Place," and "Twist and Shout."*

Six, announced that they intended to record a song called "Tell Me If You Can" that he'd cowritten with Paul in Germany.

"Brian didn't get very good deals on anything," George argued later, with the benefit of hindsight, but at the time the abundance and grandeur of the deals themselves kept the Beatles from articulating their fears. Anyone who wanted a pound of their flesh, John joked, should get in line; with four of them in the picture, there was plenty to go around. Even if John could bring himself to laugh about it, there was a growing suspicion among them that Brian "wasn't astute enough" to handle the heavy traffic. The EMI record royalty, the Dick James publishing deal, the Seltaeb merchandising agreement, the UA movie contract, even their road shows with promoter Arthur Howes—Paul took to calling them "long-term slave contracts"—were grotesquely inadequate.

No sooner had Brian returned to London than his New York agent, GAC, cabled with news that offers—"spectacular offers"—were pouring in from American promoters, requiring an immediate answer from the Beatles. "We had fifty times as many offers as we could handle," Norman Weiss, their U.S. agent, revealed, and he urged Brian to immediately set aside dates for a major U.S. tour. And the money was staggering for a pop group: a minimum guarantee of $20,000 up front against as much as 80 percent of the gate. Absolutely no one received that much for a single performance, not even Frank Sinatra. The handful of entertainers who could even get close to that amount had been icons for fifteen or twenty years—Bob Hope, Jerry Lewis, Judy Garland.

This was completely new territory. The string of eligible arenas in America, those with seating capacities of 7,000 to 20,000, had never presented rock 'n roll shows before. They were primarily sports facilities or convention halls, deviating from the schedule once a year when the circus came to town. Among the cast of possible promoters, few had experience staging any type of show. Five years later a network of rock impresarios would establish itself, with a dominant promoter in almost every major city, but in 1964 none existed. Presenting the Beatles required that a local promoter handle tickets, publicity, staging, security ("no fewer than one hundred uniformed police officers"), sound (including "a hi-fidelity sound system . . . and a first-class sound engineer"), and hospitality ("clean and adequate dressing room facilities . . . [and] two seven-passenger Cadillac limousines, air-conditioned if possible"). Who knew how to pull that all together?

There were already ominous signs. It was inevitable that competition would eventually loosen their vise grip on the charts, and, sure enough, groups such as the Dave Clark Five, Herman's Hermits, the Animals, and Freddy and the Dreamers edged above them periodically in swings that were treated as certain downfall. When the Beatles toppled out of the number one spot, however briefly, it was *front-page news.* The dailies suggested that their popularity had peaked. "Are the Beatles finished?" a tabloid wondered. Rumors circulated that John was leaving the band, and even though he dismissed it as "foolish gossip," the speculation persisted. Harder to dismiss was the cold reception given to the closed-circuit film of the Beatles' Washington, D.C., concert. Not only was the turnout conspicuously flat, but the deal structure was such a mess that determining what royalties were owed the Beatles became next to impossible.

In late March John's book, *In His Own Write,* was published by Jonathan Cape and sold forty thousand copies on the first day of its release. It wasn't creative writing in the literary sense: the text was woefully slight, a mere seventy-eight pages, the format haphazard, the syntax clumsy and fragmented—all quirks that normally earned terse rejection slips from publishers. It looked nothing like a regular book with its crude, "scrappy" line drawings and chicken-scratch marginalia. "There's nothing deep in it," John insisted, "it's just meant to be funny." If anything, it was a descendant of "The Daily Howl" that he had passed around at Quarry Bank and was later serialized in *Mersey Beat,* studded with the puns and nonsensical wordplay he called "gobbledegook," along with a generous dose of sick humor. But it possessed an undeniable power. It had a rude, freewheeling irreverence that thumbed its nose at literary pretension, all of which appealed to the emerging "alternative" culture. It seemed to confirm what commentators had been saying about the rumblings of a "cultural earthquake" and a new, anything-goes permissiveness. And if John lacked the craftsmanship of a traditional author, there were pillars of the establishment ready to explain and defend his book. The BBC called it "a laugh a minute," and no less an institution than the *Times Literary Supplement* extolled it as being "worth the attention of anyone who fears for the impoverishment of the English language and the English imagination."

In fact, the Beatles were now welcome at several doors where, until only recently, they were scorned as riffraff. The Variety Club, that snooty, old-line showbiz establishment, named them "Show Business Personalities of 1963" in an awards ceremony at the Dorchester Hotel presided over by prime minister hopeful Harold Wilson. Then, on March 23 they received the prestigious Carl-Alan award from Prince Philip in a ceremony at London's Empire Ballroom, before accepting five Ivor Novello Awards for "outstanding contributions to British music."

Awards. Awards. Awards. Everything was finally breaking their way. Record sales were astronomical; at one point in April the Beatles had fourteen singles on *Billboard*'s Hot 100 chart, a feat not so much unparalleled as obscene. A world tour had been set, beginning June 4 in Scandinavia, continuing through Hong Kong and Australia, and culminating in a late-summer tour of North America. And the film was moving forward at a fairly painless clip. There were just a few more weeks of shooting before the Beatles scattered for vacation.

No one had any forewarning when, in April, Freddie Lennon finally turned up. The Beatles were in the midst of shooting a difficult scene at the Scala Theatre, a gorgeous old vaudeville house in Soho, which had been spruced up by Dick Lester's set designers for the movie's live concert performance. Everyone at NEMS was posted there, because of the swarm of fans blocking the streets and trying to get inside, so no one stopped the grizzled old man who hobbled into the Argyll Street office. "I'm John Lennon's father," he told the receptionist, who reacted as one might to the reappearance of Anastasia.

John had told people he was an orphan. Shaken, the receptionist passed the news to a secretary, who immediately located Brian Epstein. "Brian went into a panic," according to Brian Sommerville. He sent a car for John without any explanation.

It seems doubtful that John recognized his father on first sight. He had seen Freddie Lennon only twice in his entire life, and not since 1945, just after his fifth birthday, at a seaside retreat in Brighton. Now Freddie was sitting across the desk in Brian's private office, a stooped-over, toothless sea dog with smoke-gray hair slicked back in the style of a faded sharpie.

"I stuck out my hand to shake his," Freddie remembered, "but John just growled at me and said suspiciously, 'What do you want?'" Brian felt the hostility immediately and endeavored to subdue John, instructing him: "You can't turn your back on your family, no matter what they've done."

It helped defuse the situation temporarily. Still, John wasn't particularly sympathetic toward the broken-down man and the timing of his visit. "He turned up after I was famous," complained John, who remained "furious" at Freddie for abandoning him as a child. "He knew where I was all my life—I'd lived in the same house in the same place for most of my childhood, and he knew where."

It may have crushed John to grow up without a father, but it took no effort for him to cut short Freddie's visit and ultimately order him from Brian's office. Whatever reasons had rendered his father no longer incommunicado, it was more convenient for John that Freddie remain at large.

Because the set was basically closed to the media, there was an intensified hunger for stories about the boys. Usually during these crunch periods, the Beatles were made available to do some small, meaningless interview specifically aimed at keeping the newshounds at bay, but with the lockdown on the set, it seemed that they'd dropped out of sight. Some reporters, like the *Mirror*'s Don Short, simply decided to take things into their own hands. Up until that time, there was an unwritten policy between the press and NEMS that designated the Beatles' private lives as being off-limits. "It was casting a sprat to catch a mackerel," Short says of the unique accommodation. "We gave up the small, personal stories to land the big one. If something dicey came up, we just put a wrap on it. It was easy, considering the tremendous access we were given, and it also gave the Beatles a built-in sense of security." With the boys suddenly absent from the scene, however, all bets were off. There was too much pressure, Short says, to keep their name in the paper and for rival journalists to "stay ahead of the pack."

He finally got the break he'd been waiting for. A few days before Easter, Short was passing through a nightclub when a breathless source tipped him off that two of the Beatles were about to fly north on a weekend holiday, one of them with *a new girlfriend* in tow. That was all he needed to hear. Bolting from the club, Short made a beeline for the *Mirror*'s offices and spent a few hours on the phone, calling every aviation contact he knew who might have information on the Beatles' whereabouts. It didn't take long for him to pick up their scent. "They'd gone by private plane from one of the airports [outside London]," he discovered—John with Cynthia, and George with Pattie Boyd, a beautiful young model who had a bit part in the movie. Now that was a scoop! According to Short's source, there was a reservation in their names at Dromoland Castle, in a remote corner of western Ireland, which is where he wound up, flying puddle jumpers, late that same night.

"They had checked in under assumed names," Short recalls, "so the hotel denied they were there. So I actually climbed up the outside of the hotel, with a bottle of scotch in my pocket." Oblivious to the danger or, by this time, merely irrational, he leapfrogged from balcony to balcony, peering into open windows in search of his prey. Finally, after half an hour, he struck gold. "There was John and George, with the two girls, having dinner on the floor, on a huge rug, and I burst in through the window." They couldn't believe their eyes. The Beatles were so astounded by Short's appearance, to say nothing of his nerve, that they welcomed him in, ordered extra food, drank his scotch (as well as a few bottles held in reserve), and gave him an exclusive story.

Don Short wasted no time in breaking the news. Pattie Boyd was a very slim, angelic-looking young woman, pleasant and unpretentious, with a style that was as natural as it was alluring. In a genuinely matter-of-fact way, she seemed to be a reference point for all the bold new fashion that was percolating in London—what Mary Quant called "the total look": chic and funky clothes, shaggy haircut, sexy miniskirt, pale "dolly-bird" makeup, antique jewelry. "Whenever fashions changed Patti [sic] was in there first with all the right gear looking beautiful as ever," Cynthia wrote in one of her memoirs. Much later, Twiggy admitted that she based her look on Pattie, who never begrudged anyone her personal beauty tips. "Pattie always managed to look fabulous with very little effort," Peter Brown remembers. "George wrote 'Something in the Way You Move [sic]' about her; Eric [Clapton] wrote 'Darling, You Look Wonderful [sic] Tonight' about her. That's Pattie—she is *that* person."

As a favor, Richard Lester had cast her as an extra in the movie, along with her younger sister, Jenny, knowing they would dress up the scenery around the Beatles.* According to several friends, Pattie not only had an eye on George, she been following his career from a distance from the start. He picked up the signals on the very first day of production, during a scene in which she appeared as an immodest schoolgirl. "When we started filming, I could feel George looking at me," she recalled, "and I was a bit embarrassed." It might have been less awkward had she not been "semi-engaged" to a boyfriend, Eric Swayne, with whom she'd been living for two years. At the time, Swayne said he felt "confident about [his] relationship with her," but within a week Pattie and George were making their own plans.

Don Short wanted a photo to go with his story, which, "in those days," he says, "was taboo. You never published a picture of a Beatle with his spouse or girlfriend. But suddenly none of us cared anymore." Short had flown in a photographer expressly to get the prize shot, but by the next morning the hotel was crawling with other press. Word had leaked out about George's new romance, which put a premature end to the vaca-

---

* *Donovan, who was in love with Jenny, wrote "Jennifer Juniper" about her.*

tion. Reporters, determined to identify the young woman, had all the exits covered. It got so bad, the couples became prisoners of their room. Eventually John and George went downstairs to check out, acting as decoys so the girls could sneak away unnoticed. "In the end, Cyn and I had to dress as [chamber]maids," Pattie told Hunter Davies. "They took us out a back way, put us in a laundry basket, and we were driven to the airport in a laundry van."

The women were, in fact, only one small cloudburst in the mammoth typhoon of press that surged through the spring of 1964. Everyone followed the Beatles like a favorite soap opera. Not a day went by that didn't offer ample stories about their exploits, even if they were only vague speculation. Papers reported on where they were last seen and with whom, how they were dressed, what they had for dinner, when they went home (and with whom). The gloves had come off; all angles were now fair game.

[III]

To Ringo, the movies were magic and the experience of making one even more marvelous, indescribable. Years later he could still say: "It was all so romantic, with the lights and coming to work in the limo." And UA, which never even saw a synopsis of the script, had been viewing each day's rushes with mounting excitement. What had begun as a quickie, low-budget exploitation feature riding on the Beatles' fleeting fame now looked more and more like a quirky little gem. The Beatles were *funny*. They were naturals in front of the camera and "made it seem as if the picture was ad-libbed or improvised." What's more, its style was so distinctive: shot in black and white, using mostly handheld cameras to capture the energy of a documentary film, and chock-full of sequences that were as outrageous as they were innovative.

For convenience, on the set, everyone had been calling it *The Beatles Movie* until something more suitable came along. There are several "official" versions of how the title was finally arrived at. What they all agree on is that it occurred during a lunch break at Twickenham Studios, where either Paul remarked to Bud Ornstein—or John to Walter Shenson—"There was something Ringo said the other day . . . ," at which point, the two Beatles recounted their drummer's penchant for "abusing the English language." "Ringo would always say grammatically incorrect phrases and we'd all laugh," George recalled. One that sprang easily to mind had popped out at the Heathrow press conference, when Ringo described having his hair cut at the British embassy soiree. "I was just talking, having an interview . . . and then 'snip' . . . Well, what can you say? Tomorrow never knows." *Tomorrow never knows!* The Beatles cut wicked glances at one another when that gem fell out. And John promptly wrote it down, to use in one of his stories and, later, songs. There was another malapropism—or "Ringosim," as John called them—that had already appeared in John's book, *In His Own Write*: "He'd had a hard day's night that day." One of the boys entertained the lunch gathering with details of its origin, following a grueling late-night gig, but they were already one step ahead of him. "We've just got our title!" one of the producers exclaimed.

But only half the battle had been won. What Shenson knew, and what the studio had pointedly reminded him, was that a musical with a new title needed a title song. He despaired about burdening John and Paul with it. They'd already been pushed to the wall, filming all day while looping at night to replace lines that were lost to extraneous noise. Sometimes he knew they'd finish work well after ten o'clock, rush off to attend a cocktail party or do a late press interview over dinner, then head out to various clubs until nearly dawn before being dragged from their beds an hour or two later for makeup. It was a brutal, seven-day routine that more than qualified the film's new title, so it took some temerity to ask for any more of them.

It was at a looping session, as Shenson remembers it, that he finally made his plea. He pulled John aside during a coffee break and broached it without beating around the bush. "I'm afraid we're going to need a song called 'A Hard Day's Night,' something up-tempo that can be played over the main titles." They had already shot the opening scene at Marylebone Station, in which a throng of half-crazed girls chase the Beatles onto a train. If the song was as impetuous as the on-screen action, it would establish the perfect mood. Driving back into London from the studio, he recalls, John brooded, chain-smoking sullenly, no doubt in response to the annoying request.

The next morning on the set, the assistant producer paged Shenson and told him: "John Lennon wants to see you in his dressing room." The producer went through every imaginable scenario, wondering how he'd respond to the young man's irritation. "He and Paul were standing there, with their guitars slung over their shoulders," Shenson recalls. "John fiddled with a matchbook cover on which were scrawled the lyrics to a song—'A Hard Day's Night'—which they played and sang to perfection.

This was ten hours after I'd asked for a song." When they'd finished, John glanced at the producer and said, "Okay, that's it, right?" It was all Shenson could do to feebly mutter, "Right." "Good," John said, "now don't bother us about songs anymore."

"A Hard Day's Night" was recorded the next day, on April 16, and from the extraordinary opening chord, it was evident that once again the Beatles had raised the bar for all of pop songwriting. The "strident" chord is a powerful attention-grabber—a G7, with an added ninth and a sus-pended fourth, so unique that it is considered neither major nor minor—that hangs in the air with disturbing inevitability. How George came up with it remains a mystery to this day; he never discussed it, even though the chord has become as identifiable as the song that follows. As it uncoils, there is nothing left to chance. The energy it delivers is explosive, full of fireworks—"It's been a *haaaard daaaays* night . . . "—and musically as daring, with a vocal track that gathers so much steam that the middle eight (sung by Paul, John explained, "because I couldn't reach the notes") comes as almost a relief.

While the Beatles wrapped up work on *A Hard Day's Night,* as the movie was now readily being called, Brian left for the Devon coast, where he planned to begin work on an autobiography that had been commissioned by a small London publisher. Derek Taylor, the trusted *Daily Express* re-porter who'd been handpicked to ghostwrite the book, joined him in a sumptuous suite at the Imperial Hotel, in Torquay, for a weekend of pro-tracted interviews that would hopefully serve as the foundation for the work. Like Brian, Taylor was from an affluent Liverpool suburb, the el-dest son of a gregarious Welsh ex-officer and a sickly housewife who, at some point, relinquished all hope that Derek would pursue a respectable career "in the world of commerce." Taylor was everything a banker wasn't: effusive, generous, entertaining, impractical, and wonderfully glib. "There are only a few journalists like Derek, who are a joy to listen to in the pub," recalls Tony Barrow, who, though often at loggerheads with his "inscrutable" colleague, found him equally mesmerizing. "He had such an amazing way with words. He wrote and spoke beautiful prose. And he made rapport an art form I've never seen duplicated." Taylor could also be, like Brian, cyn-ical and obstinate. Having recently moved from covering comedians to pop music, he concluded that the Beatles "painted a new rainbow right across the world, with crocks of gold at each end, and then some," which ultimately beckoned him to their doorstep. His several meetings with the boys cultivated a remarkable rapport. Of all the journalists they encountered, and perhaps ever would encounter, Taylor's dervish intellect brought him closest to being a trusted confidant. "He's one of those people that clicks as soon as you meet him," John remarked that same month. There was no doubt: he was on their wavelength.

Trust. Brian needed to confide in his cowriter. Two days into their amiable "fact-gathering expedition," Brian poured large gin and tonics to facilitate a tricky exchange. He wondered aloud (although not too loud) if Taylor had heard rumors that he, Brian, "was queer." Derek may not have known about this dark secret in early 1964, but he no doubt sensed the underlying torment and vulnerability. The always eloquent Taylor became tongue-tied, stammering as Brian admitted: "I *am* homosexual and have known it all my adult life and there's nothing I can do about it." This was a startling confession, not so much for the context in which it was conveyed as for the information it carried. In Britain, laws still regarded homosexuality as a punishable offense, thereby casting its current pop icons in a web of deceit. Its disclosure was fraught with danger. Brian was mortified that it would bring harm to the Beatles, but he found it just as offensive to fabricate a personal—and absurd—romantic past.

Fortunately, Taylor was a sympathetic figure, completely at ease in a world from which most straight men felt alienated. The secret, he assured Brian, was safe with him. Besides, Taylor knew how to handle it with discretion so there would be no awkward references to women in the book. Not only was Brian relieved, he felt unthreatened, even secure in Derek's degree of understanding. Several soul-searching conversations with Taylor were Brian's first opportunity to explore territory that had previously been forbidden with a straight colleague. At breakfast the next day, he felt comfortable enough to share the details of a drunken late-night date that had culminated in rough sex. This was all so fantastic to Taylor, who managed to maintain a straight face throughout. Brian's entire life, it seemed, was suffused with the contingencies of indulgence and risk. Soon after he and Taylor went out together for some serious drinking and gambling, Brian arrived at a decision. "I would like you to become my personal assistant," he proposed, "and come to work at NEMS in London, in the office next to mine."

It was an inspired idea. Taylor had great antennae, which made him sensitive to Brian's volatile moods. No one was more compatible or eager to please; he mixed as easily with the Beatles as he did with the press, and he made friends easily. "The entire office took to him thirty seconds after he walked in," says Tony Bramwell. Everyone at NEMS already knew him as a northerner, their own kind. There was never any question he'd function as Brian's eyes and ears.

A rough draft of the autobiography was finished in slightly under two weeks, a thin, abstracted affair that Taylor facetiously referred to as "a potboiler." He considered it "ridiculous" to write the autobiography of someone who was not yet thirty years old, and felt constrained by the material, much of which was an acknowledged whitewash. When it came time to title the book, Derek drew a blank. Instead, Brian sounded out his friends, hoping to come up with something catchy. "Why don't you call it *Queer Jew*?" John suggested, within earshot of the other Beatles and some guests. To appease John, Brian made a show of chuckling at the needling abuse. Some part of him probably even *liked* being humiliated by John—after all, it was part of his dark nature. But after the book was submitted as *A Cellarful of Noise,* he was visibly wounded each time John referred to it as *A Cellarful of Boys.*

"My early days at NEMS resembled nothing so much as a crazy bazaar," Taylor recalled. "There were dozens, hundreds of visitors, all with pressing needs. . . . Epstein demanded all my time and all my energy." Brian put him through one wringer after the next, threatening to sack Derek at the first sign of a slip. "The heat was immediately on." But as it happened, it was only an appetizer.

[I]

The usual shock wave shuddered through Copenhagen Airport as the Beatles' plane approached from the north. More than two thousand kids had been waiting since dawn for the boys to arrive, and as the plane broke through the clouds there was the kind of chain reaction that had at one time put a smile on Dr. Teller's face. There was a deafening roar; bodies collided. Then all hell broke loose on the ground as the cabin door popped open and out bounded the Beatles: John, Paul, George, and Jimmy.

Say what?

There had been no time to warn the crowd that Ringo wasn't aboard. Only a day earlier, on the morning of June 3, he'd collapsed during a particularly stressful photo session for the *Saturday Evening Post.* Despite a blissful three-week vacation with Paul in the Virgin Islands, he'd been experiencing spells of fatigue, which were blamed on the drastic change in climates. His throat was especially sore, owing, Ringo was certain, to his excessive smoking habit. Although stricken by waves of dizziness, he'd soldiered through a June 1 and 2 recording session, as well as several telephone interviews with British teen magazines. But during the photo session he suddenly sank to his knees, and Neil, who "didn't like it one bit," rushed him to University College Hospital, where it was diagnosed he'd scored a double whammy of laryngitis and pharyngitis.

Back at Abbey Road studios, Brian, Derek, George Martin, and the rest of the Beatles debated how to handle the situation. It seemed pointless to continue without their drummer, the boys argued. "Imagine, the Beatles without Ringo!" George scoffed. The tour, as he saw it, should be postponed immediately. "Brian argued with us for more than an hour to change our minds about abandoning the tour," Paul recalled, "pleading that thousands of Dutch and Australian fans had already bought tickets, and that it would be cruel to disappoint them."

According to George, they were "bullied by Brian Epstein and George Martin into accepting the situation that [they] had to go." But how? Who would supply the right beat? Pete Best? Not a chance, according to John, who explained to a reporter: "It might have looked as if we were taking him back. Not good for him." Martin ran through his Rolodex of drummers, pulling the names of those he deemed adequate, with emphasis on a chap named Jimmy Nicol. In Martin's estimation, not only did Nicol have great hands, but it so happened that he looked the part as well. Nicol was twenty-four, from the East End of London, with the kind of round, cherubic face that would have suited any Scouser. He'd put in time drumming with Georgie Fame and, aside from a decent amount of session work, fronted a band called Jimmy Nicol and the Shub Dubs that had a minor hit single with "Humpity-Dumpity."

There are various versions as to what happened next, and over the years Nicol has related them in any number of ways, but his assertion that "I nearly shit in me pants" seems utterly reliable.

———

After three months paired off with the girlfriends and wife, the Beatles hit the road like prisoners on furlough. The moment they touched down in Denmark the scene was swarming with girls: young and older girls, blondes and raven-haired beauties, full-breasted and elfin girls, hookers and virgins. The most beautiful creatures in the world paraded through the Beatles' set of suites seemingly without end and without restriction. The rate of turnover was breathtaking, as was the boys' endurance. It was party time, day and night, and as the newcomer, Jimmy Nicol viewed it with incredulity. He had never witnessed such an extravagance of "mischief and carrying-on. I thought I could drink and lay women with the best of them until I met up with these guys," he admitted.

"Wherever we went, there was always a whole scene," John recollected, calling it "*Satyricon*" as a frame of reference, "with four musicians going through it.... When we hit a town, we hit it—we were not pissing about.... We were the Caesars."

In Copenhagen, where they broke the ice, John especially uncoiled, drinking so much, according to an observer, that "his head was a balloon"; he was nearly unrecognizable onstage, sweating and bloated. Then in Amsterdam the next day, he struck out for the city's notorious red-light district, trolling through brothels at an impressive breakneck clip, enlisting the services of a police escort to avert possible scandal. There seemed to be no limit to John's binges of alcohol and sex—nor reason that adequately explained them. His marriage to Cynthia, after all, provided a source of security as well as comfort. They'd enjoyed "the most relaxing and happy holiday" in Tahiti with George and Pattie, mulling over plans to find the house of their dreams upon his return. It seemed almost irrational that he threw himself into these scenes with such self-destructive determination. Friends close to the Lennons at the time insist that their relationship was mutually gratifying and harmonious. Cynthia herself refers to that period as "happy families time for all concerned." Perhaps the debauchery was just general therapy for John's troubled soul, a form of emotional decompression. Maybe it was a way of asserting his independence—or merely blowing off steam. God knows, Beatlemania was a pressure cooker— "like being in the eye of a hurricane," as John put it. Whatever the reason, he and the other Beatles plunged ahead on an excursion of drinking and screwing that rivaled the frenzy at their concerts.

Somehow, Jimmy Nicol took it all in stride. "He played well," Paul admitted with customary graciousness. There were no slipups, barring the odd, tricky count that only Ringo would have anticipated; there were no star trips or ugly scenes. George had been right to object that it wasn't the Beatles without "the Four Fabs," as he called them, but not even the fans seemed to mind the last-minute replacement. Wherever they went, the Beatles were welcomed like conquering heroes. Their arrival in Amsterdam was greeted by an elaborate motorcycle escort that wound through the city, flanked by auxiliary units of police and the civil guard. The next morning a glass-topped boat collected the Beatles from a ledge outside their hotel for a ten-mile trip through the Amstel Canal. "We passed at least 100,000 cheering people who lined the streets on each side of the water to wave, and sometimes almost touch, the Beatles as they passed," Andy Gray wrote with breathless exaggeration in an edition of the *NME*. "Six police boats accompanied us on the water and they were kept busy, picking up dozens of boys who swam to the boat, some climbing on to shake the Beatles' hands." Fans leaped from canal bridges as the boat passed underneath.

But sometimes the vibe turned rude and unpredictable. For example, that same night before the concert, the mayor of Blokker, the Dutch suburb where the old arena was located, approached George in the dressing room with a key to the city. "Fuck off, yer bald owd crip!" George snapped, oversaturated by the parade of grinning well-wishers.

Every city, every situation, brought out people who wanted to, in some way, touch them—and wanted to be touched back. *Insisted* on it: promoters demanded that the Beatles meet their families and friends; security men demanded autographs; the hotel manager, driver, waiter, chambermaid, reporter, nurse, newspaper vendor, flight attendant, everyone they came into contact with at every hour of the day, demanded a piece of the boys. And the *fans*—everywhere they went, fans expected, demanded, some sort of personal response: sign this, wave, say hello, touch me, heal me, call me, kiss me, fuck me. And they stopped at nothing: invading the Beatles' suites, throwing themselves in front of their cars, jumping from balconies, stalking wives, girlfriends, family members, *pets!* In Copenhagen a reporter from the *Express* admonished Paul for his seemingly callous disregard of a telegram that read: CHILD DYING IN THIS FAMILY, TWO DAYS TO LIVE. PLEASE CALL. CHILD IS MARY SUE." Paul was convinced that it was a hoax, and if not, then a tragedy that was beyond his mortal powers. The world was filled with such tragedies, he argued. Were the Beatles expected to alleviate each one? To prove his point, he instructed Derek Taylor to place a call to the sputtering Mary Sue, who, as it so happened, was in tiptop health and not at all embarrassed.

There were other obligations, too—press conferences, civic receptions, charity balls, processions, literary luncheons, awards ceremonies, record-shop appearances, social engagements . . . it was unrelenting. On the Beatles' sixteen-hour flight from London to Hong Kong, there were "welcomes" planned at every refueling stop—in Zurich, Beirut, Karachi, Calcutta, and Bangkok. Far from being honored, the Beatles felt abused. Over Derek Taylor's objections, they refused to get off the plane anywhere other than Bangkok, fueling their dark mood with a steady diet of stimulants. "We'd been sitting on the floor, drinking and taking Preludins for about thirty hours [sic]," George recalled. Then, arriving in Kowloon, exhausted and grimy, they were expected to judge the finals of the Miss Hong Kong beauty pageant.

In Australia five thousand fans staged a vigil in a torrential rainstorm when the Beatles' 707 descended into Sydney. Fierce crosswinds tugged perilously at the plane, raindrops heavy as hail slashed at the cockpit windows and drummed on the roof, making the landing on the puddled tarmac a nail-biter—none of which deterred local officials, who put the boys "on the back of a flat-bed truck so the crowd could see them." Their skeletal umbrellas were useless, and the dye in the new capes they had had made in Hong Kong ran, turning their skin a cadaverous blue.

Two days later, on June 12, in Adelaide, the numbers got crazy. In gorgeous weather, the Beatles were loaded into a Ford convertible and paraded along a nine-mile stretch of the Anzac Highway lined by 250,000 people, almost half the city's population. Over a policeman's objections, the Beatles crawled up to perch on the car's trunk in what George later referred to as "the J. F. Kennedy position." It was an incredible sight from that viewpoint, sending a "shock," especially to John, who admitted that it dawned on him "you might get shot." An additional thirty thousand more fans crammed into the square outside the gates of Town Hall for the official greeting by Adelaide's Lord Mayor, several stories above the gathering. "It was like a heroes' welcome," said Paul, who leaned way out on the balcony and flashed the crowd the old reliable thumbs-up, not realizing Australians regarded it like being given the finger.

The scene, sans the thumbs, was repeated in Melbourne, where, despite "a bitterly cold day, some 250,000 people lined the route from the airport to the [Beatles'] hotel." According to the *New York Times*, it was "nearly twice as many as turned out to see Queen Elizabeth and Prince Philip" the previous year. Ringo had arrived earlier that morning with Brian Epstein on a "horrendous" thirty-hour flight from London through Los Angeles, made tolerable by a running poker game with Vivien Leigh and Horst Buchholz. Ringo assured an attentive press corps waiting at Essendon Airport that he felt refreshed and recharged, although doctors warned that his tonsils would eventually have to come out. Otherwise, he expressed relief to be out of the hospital, the scene of so many childhood setbacks, relief to be in Australia, relief to be back in the mix—and ready to rock 'n roll.

In fact, the rocking started even before his reunion with the Beatles, when Ringo's car was surrounded outside the Southern Cross Hotel by an estimated three thousand fans. A moment of real panic ensued while officials decided how to deal with the boisterous crowd. Everywhere Ringo looked, kids were pressed up against the windows, screaming and pounding on the doors, clambering over the hood. It was "a madness we had not seen in Adelaide," observed Derek Taylor, who watched "the melée" develop from an overhanging balcony. Usually there was a contingency plan to avoid such an encounter, but for some unknown reason, it had been abandoned en route. Impractical as it might seem, they decided to go in through the front entrance. A police inspector built like a bulldozer slung Ringo over his shoulder and, charging, made a beeline for the hotel. A hotel official leading the charge stumbled in the fray—which sent an errant body block into the police inspector. In a flash, everyone went down like tenpins. Ringo was knocked to the ground and engulfed by the crowd. By the time he was rescued from the throng, he was scuffed and badly shaken.

Later, when the other Beatles arrived, the crowd in the street had swelled to an estimated twenty thousand, some of whom were whipped up in a terrific heat. Others, many of them young girls who had been waiting since dawn, suffered from hunger and exhaustion. The police force, which had been monitoring the situation nervously, called in the army and navy to help maintain order, but it was short-lived. By late afternoon, with chants of *"We want the Beatles!"* ringing through the square, the shaken troops, now four hundred strong, felt control slipping from their grasp. They didn't know where to look first: at the barricades being crushed, the girls fainting out of sight, the hooligans stomping in the roofs of cars or pushing through their lines. A fourteen-year-old "screamed so hard she burst a blood-vessel in her throat." It was "frightening, chaotic, and rather inhuman," according to a trooper on horseback. Their most pressing concern was the hotel's plate-glass windows bowing perilously against the violent crush of bodies. They threatened to explode in a cluster of razor-sharp shards at any moment. Ambulances screamed in the distance, preparing for the worst; a detachment of mounted infantry swung into position.

Just when it all seemed hopeless, at the point when one more thrashing body would undoubtedly deliver the coup de grâce, a roar went up that seemed to suck all the kids away from the hotel. *Look! Up in the air—it's a bird, it's a plane* . . . Suddenly, all five Beatles appeared on the first-floor balcony in hopes of defusing the situation. Another roar went up, this one even more deafening than the first, as John put a finger across his upper lip, threw the Nazi salute, and goose-stepped jauntily across the platform, screaming, *"Sieg heil! Sieg heil!"*

If this is how Australia was, what would America be like? There, Beatles fever was running at an all-time scalding high. Public demand seemed insatiable. In Chicago eighteen thousand tickets were sold before a single ad appeared; two thousand fans stormed Maple Leaf Gardens in Toronto, scooping up every available seat; the entire block of twelve thousand tickets for Philadelphia's Convention Hall was gone in "70 hectic minutes"; for all twenty-seven concert dates—the same thing. American deejays kept cranking up the heat.

Before that, however, there was unfinished business back home. The buzz was particularly loud concerning a swarm of notable challengers, such as the Rolling Stones, the Kinks, Manfred Mann, the Yardbirds, Them, the Dave Clark Five, and the Zombies. The Beatles were especially concerned by news that they'd been knocked from the chart's top spot by a single called "House of the Rising Sun." What was this cheeky record? they wanted to know. And who were these predators calling themselves Animals? It was time to find out.

The Beatles arrived back in London, determined to attack it all at once—but first they had a date at the movies.

The premiere of *A Hard Day's Night* wasn't expected to be normal, even by movie-gala standards. By 7:30, an hour before curtain, the streets around Piccadilly Circus were jammed by a crowd of twelve thousand fans jockeying to get a glimpse of the stars. Inside the London Pavilion, the Beatles, dressed in stiffly pressed tuxedos and glossy patent-leather shoes, stood in the midst of their families and the posh crowd. Joining them were Princess Margaret and the Earl of Snowden. Earlier that day the band had watched a run-through of the film at a private screening, with Brian, Derek, and Walter Shenson, who insists they "behaved like delighted little kids" watching themselves romp across the screen. Slouched down in the stalls, with their feet up on the backs of the seats in front of them, they wolfed down popcorn and howled like hyenas or groaned with embarrassment, depending upon the scene. Shenson, hunkered in the balcony, was confident that they had a monster hit on their hands.

With few exceptions, the critics agreed that *A Hard Day's Night* was a winner. *The Times* called it "off-beat" and an "exercise in anarchy" with a spontaneity exceptional in British films. In the *Daily Express*, critic Leonard Mosley struck the same euphoric tone, calling it "delightfully loony" and adding "there hasn't been anything like it since the Marx Brothers in the '30s." Later, Bosley Crowther, whose opinion in the *New York Times* was read like scripture, praised it as "a whale of a comedy" that "had so much good humor going for it that it is awfully hard to resist . . . with such a dazzling use of the camera that it tickles the intellect and electrifies the nerves."

The Beatles preened unflinchingly in the afterglow. "I dug *A Hard Day's Night*," John said initially. "We knew it was better than other rock movies," though "not as good as James Bond," he relented. Later, in a puff of vengefulness, he backpedaled, saying, "By the end of the film we didn't know what had happened and we hated it." But by then it didn't matter. On July 8 the movie opened to critical success and amazing business. The next morning there were lines around the block. United Artists blanketed

Britain "with a record 160 prints of the picture" and was bragging to reporters that it "would gross at least a million pounds in Britain alone,"
which wasn't bad, considering the film cost less than a quarter of a million
pounds to make. Publicly, the Beatles acted indifferent to the success. Still,
at every opportunity, they cruised past the Pavilion to check on the length
of the queues. Chris Hutchins, who accompanied them on just such a
junket, remembered their delight at the lines snaking around the theater.
"That's the stuff!" he recalled John shouting from the backseat of a car a
few days after the premiere. "A couple of hundred more for the sevens-
and-sixes* and we'll all be rich!"

That smugness was nowhere to be seen two days later for the northern
premiere of the film. On July 10 the Beatles arrived in Liverpool aboard a
capacity-filled Britannia turboprop, but they might as well have flown in
on their own buoyancy for all the butterflies in their stomachs. "It was extraordinary to see how very nervous the Beatles were," recalled BBC deejay David Jacobs, a member of the London entourage that accompanied
the boys north. "They were absolutely terrified [of going back]." Ringo
acknowledged: "[Friends] kept coming down to London, saying, 'You're
finished in Liverpool.'"

Outwardly, Paul scoffed at the "one or two little rumors," as well as
the hyperbole from routine "detractors," but whatever tension he may
have experienced was complicated by another development. A few months
earlier Paul had settled a paternity claim with a young Liverpool woman,
paying her $14,000 in exchange for her silence and the repudiation of all
claims against him. Everyone assumed that the problem had gone away,
but on the morning of the Beatles' triumphant homecoming it seemed to
have ghosted in from the cold. The night before, the girl's disgruntled uncle papered Liverpool with thirty thousand leaflets baring the gory details
of the alleged paternity. He had been thorough, too, hitting every public
telephone kiosk in the center of Liverpool as well as the Press Club in Bold
Street, where he was sure reporters would feast on the incriminating facts.
Brian's attempts to head it off proved too little, too late. Unable to face the
inevitable tempest, he dispatched Derek Taylor in his place to warn Paul,
who, to Taylor's disbelief, seemed callously unconcerned by the news,
shrugging "with astonishing nonchalance" and mumbling, "OK." How

---

* Seven shillings and sixpence (now 37.5 pence), the price of a good seat at the cinema.

Paul kept his composure was beyond all explanation. Was he that insensitive to the predicament? Did hubris blind him to the possible backlash? It's impossible to know. Whatever his intention, astonishingly the approach paid off, without a word of the accusation finding its way into print.

"Being local heroes made us nervous," John admitted. The prospect of facing family, friends, and fans—and not just any fans but *the* fans, their "own people," as Paul called them—was nerve-racking. No one knew what to expect. It didn't help matters that as the airplane descended, the once-familiar landscape appeared strange and forbidding. "Miles away from Speke Airport . . . we saw them," David Jacobs remembered, "thousands upon thousands of what looked like black currants packing the route to Liverpool." The entire city had turned out to greet them! They hadn't been forgotten—or worse, written off—after all. A wave of relief swept through the cabin, followed by childlike glee: *"Look! Over there! By the Ford factory . . . by the freight yard . . . by the bus depot . . ."* They were incredibly moved by the sight. People—*Scousers*—everywhere. And as they disembarked, a massive crowd surged forward—cheering deliriously, shouting their names. Two hundred thousand people crowded the square outside Town Hall. From the balcony high above the city, the Beatles could make out all the familiar old haunts: the movie theaters and chip joints, the institute and the art college, Gambier Terrace and Ye Old Cracke, Hessey's, the original NEMS storefront, the Kardomah and the Jacaranda and the Cavern, and, across the docks, the river Mersey, dark and brooding in the enveloping dusk. "Did you ever imagine that this day was coming?" a reporter asked Paul, who for once was caught without a slick, ready-made comeback. "Never like this," he answered haltingly. "We never imagined, you know, we'd come back to this."

For his part, John could not resist the knife. "You want to get some teeth for these people who are cheering us," John advised the Lord Mayor, who seemed befuddled by the outrageous remark. (Little did he realize the extent of the Beatles' worldly exposure, having witnessed firsthand the superiority of other cultures' hygiene. The contrast, glaring in front of them now, with rows of "gap-toothed grins," was shocking.) King for a day—and fortified by pills—John wasn't about to let it rest. "What's the matter," John persisted, "can't you spare the money?" Then, without any forewarning, he strode to the front of the balcony, put a finger across his upper lip, and threw the Nazi salute to the unsuspecting crowd.

That evening more than six thousand congregated outside the Odeon Cinema, the scene of countless teenage trysts, for the invitation-only screening of *A Hard Day's Night,* and more than fifteen hundred formed a queue around the block for its official public premiere, at 10:30 the next morning. No longer enchanted with their "awkward" acting turns, the Beatles waved under the marquee but refused to sit through another performance. As soon as the houselights dimmed, they ducked out a side door, went straight to the airport, and caught a 1:30 A.M. flight back to London.

The Beatles had been in London only intermittently since returning from Australia, and there wasn't much time left—a couple of weeks, at most—before the start of their American tour. As the next departure loomed, personal obligations requiring their attention piled up.

John, in particular, needed to rescue his family from their impossible housing situation. The tiny flat in Emperor's Gate was under constant siege by fans who were staked out at the entrance for what seemed like twenty-four hours a day. Though security now accompanied John at all times, Cynthia was repeatedly confronted by "really weird characters . . . hovering around the flat, sitting on the stairs directly outside the door." It was like a human obstacle course just trying to get in and out of the place, all the more threatening when Cynthia had Julian in tow. There were times, she said, when anyone could accost them. "We had no protection from nutcases when John was away," she bemoaned.

There wasn't a moment of privacy to be had in that place. A friend who visited for a weekend recalled: "People were ringing the phone all the time. John would answer . . . and disguise his voice. 'I'm sorry, John's not here.' 'But we seen him come in.' 'Well, he must have gone out the back door.' *'There is no back door!'* It was amusing at first, but it just went on and on; it never ended."

Finally, it became too much of a nuisance and John put his foot down: they were moving, he announced, instructing Cynthia to begin house-hunting at once. One of the Beatles' corporate accountants, who happened to live in nearby Weybridge, invited them to tea in between house inspections—and the rest was kismet. The neighborhood seemed perfectly suited to John and Cynthia's needs: it was tranquil and undisturbed without being secluded, with a whiff of exclusivity—Cynthia called the area "select"—that befitted a young celebrity. It took them about twenty minutes to locate a comparable house for sale: a twenty-seven-room timbered mock-Tudor mansion at the top of a leafy rise in the ultraposh enclave of St. George's Hill Estate. The sprawling three-acre property, about twenty miles southwest of London, was called Kenwood and belonged to an

American woman who was asking £40,000. John bought it on the spot, despite its needing a good deal of work.

With the Beatles set to tour in three weeks, the task of preparing the house fell entirely in Cynthia's lap. John, inundated by obligations, couldn't be distracted; though his thoughts inevitably drifted to his family, the band's dance card was booked solid by back-to-back TV appearances and one-nighters in an effort to strengthen the franchise before leaving the country. At the BBC's Paris Studio, they taped another episode of *From Us to You*, their fourth in the hokey music series, then swept out to Blackpool, scene of so many riotous Beatles shows, for an ABC-TV special and a concert at the Opera House. On what should have been a rare day off, John and Paul crashed a Cilla Black recording session, where their old Cavern mate was cutting "It's for You," a single they'd written especially for her. There was a fund-raiser at the Grosvenor House for the British Olympic team, a visit to Madam Tussaud's to check out their likenesses, and a breathless two-day excursion to Stockholm, all interspersed with a dozen or more interviews with local flacks to promote the release of the *A Hard Day's Night* soundtrack. "They were the hardest-working entertainers I ever met," recalls a fellow musician.

Between it all, Brian had coaxed the Beatles into attending a revue at the London Palladium to benefit the Theatrical Charities Appeals Council. The postmidnight show, on July 23, indicated just how far they'd risen in the London entertainment caste system. Billed as "The Night of 100 Stars," it was a red-hot who's who of establishment showbiz celebrities led by Laurence Olivier, Buddy Greco, Shirley Bassey, Harry Secombe, and Marlene Dietrich and fanned by rumors that Frank Sinatra, in town to promote *Robin and the Seven Hoods*, would most likely attend.

The Beatles endeavored to put their best faces on the event, but as the night wore on, as one old hoofer after another plodded across the Palladium stage, lines of boredom and outright scorn began to show through the facade. The revue was *unending*. To relieve the boredom, the Beatles began downing flutes of champagne, a drink for which they were particularly unsuited. Sitting around small, dimly lit cocktail tables at the back of the stage, they smoked to neutralize their discomfort while the resentment and disdain slowly bubbled toward the surface. The set of their mouths was impossibly lipless, grim, giving their faces the same anesthetized cast as their wax effigies in Madam Tusaaud's. Ever resourceful, Mal Evans found an old wooden oar backstage and began using it to shuttle whiskey and

Cokes to the boys onstage. That immediately did the trick. "By the time we were getting drunk, we'd become fed up with all that bullshit showbiz nonsense anyway!" George recalled.

The final outrage came when a disturbance ruffled from the wings, and the frail, insectlike figure of Judy Garland wandered into the spotlight. It seemed impossible, like a mirage. Only two weeks earlier she'd suffered a nervous collapse in Hong Kong, and a few days after that she checked into a London hospital with mysterious "cuts" on her arms. The mere sight of her alone—alive—brought down the house. The audience leaped to its feet, cheering and whistling, shouting, *"Sing, Judy, sing!"* "Do 'Over the Rainbow!'" Shaking her head, she waved humbly and began to back away from the footlights, but when the orchestra broke into the inimitable introduction, Garland regaled them with the song.

It was too much for John. Drunk and indignant, everything about the "star turn" reeked of stagy pathos. Several times during her rendition, he cupped his hands around his mouth and let out a string of obscenities. "Aw, *fuck off,* Sophie!" he hollered, thrashing about in his chair and waving her toward the wings. Finally, mercifully, the song and an encore ended, and the other stars, "very edgy and nervous," massed around Garland, ostensibly to congratulate her but no doubt to keep the Beatles away.

For Brian, it was ghastly, a nightmare, not only because of the boys' disturbing behavior but also for the humiliation it had caused him. In his book, Garland "was the epitome of great talent," everything he'd always loved about theater and the musical stage. It put him in a precarious position, now that the Beatles' hostility betrayed their anti-establishment sentiments, especially since he'd invited Garland to a party at his flat in their honor.

The party was supposed to be "a send-off for the boys," and as Brian envisioned it, "nothing less than spectacular." Two hundred invitations had been sent out to London's most eligible young scenemakers, among them Russ Conway, Dusty Springfield, Mary Quant, Lionel Bart, Alma Cogan, Cilla Black, Gerry and the Pacemakers, the Stones, the Searchers, George Martin, most of EMI's top brass, the city's most important disc jockeys, and, as a concession to the public, a handful of Beatles-friendly press. Everything had to be on a grand scale; no expense was to be spared. He hired Ken Partridge, a fancy interior decorator, to stage a setting lavish enough to rival the coronation; John Edgington and his craftsmen to install a breathtaking tented rooftop retreat with an inlaid dance floor and French windows overlooking all of Hyde Park; and Mr. Copple of Covent

Gardens, the exclusive society caterer, whose menus were legendary for their sumptuousness.

But as the plans knitted together, an indistinct cloud drifted ominously over the preparations. It hadn't taken Partridge long to determine that Brian was no ordinary client. After a string of casual evenings in the manager's company, he concluded that much about the party was a placebo to mask the desolation and torment that churned inside the Beatles' manager. The demons that weighed on him in Liverpool had turned inward again. "He tried hard to conceal the pain, but it had marked him like a beacon," recalls Partridge.

That summer the two men ate dinner together almost every night, table-hopping among the city's smartest restaurants. In gilded seclusion at the Coup de France, La Caprice, or the Connaught, caught up in the flow of alcohol and anxiety, Brian revealed "how empty his life had become and how increasingly lost he felt." There was nothing to enjoy from all the money and opportunity. With his leprechaun charm, Partridge tried to shift the small talk onto a less-burdensome track, but Brian was inconsolable. He never discussed the Beatles or any of his other successes; it was as if they didn't exist. Instead, he sulked, chafed, brooded, drank to excess, and wandered out looking, for all his sophistication, like an uneasy guest in an unaccommodating city.

"When we finished dinner, around eight-thirty, he'd always leave the Rolls [-Royce] in St. Ann's Church car park, in the middle of Soho," recalls Partridge. Across the road was the Golden Lion pub, a famous pickup place for "tuffy numbers"—guardsmen and rent boys—available at the crook of an eyebrow. "He was very well known in that pub," says Partridge, who would watch as Brian, angry and excited, disappeared hurriedly inside. "Otherwise, if he didn't find anything in the Lion, he would drive up and down the Mall—the great road up from Buckingham Palace, where all the state occasions took place. You could find a boy on just about every bench there. He'd pick them up and take them back to his flat. And the next day he'd tell me these lurid stories. There were terrifying beatings—and robberies."

Even before the summer, friends noticed Brian slipping into depressions marked by episodes of irrational and self-destructive behavior. He had always been excitable, with volatile mood swings that terrified his employees, but had never given anyone cause to think it was anything more serious. Now, it seemed, these swings grew fiercer and more erratic. Charming and sensitive when in control, he turned cold and nasty at the least excuse of pique. Simple conversations often exploded into unprovoked violence. Emotional rages erupted with unprecedented ferocity, followed by silent, subversive bouts of self-loathing that could stretch on for hours in the privacy of his locked bedroom.

Peter Brown and Brian had spent part of May together, following the *feria* in Seville among a crowd of *aficións* that included Ken Tynan and Orson Welles. There, Brown noticed Brian's growing dependence on pills, amphetamines, that he buffered with excessive quantities of alcohol in an attempt to offset the highs with lows. "It had a disastrous effect on him. It accelerated the mood swings. He was really the sweetest, most sensitive man, but he became belligerent in the blink of an eye. And the worst part was that nobody understood where it came from."

"He was always putting pills into his mouth, thinking we wouldn't notice," Billy J. Kramer recalls, demonstrating how Brian would cover his mouth with a hand and pretend to cough while slipping his other hand stealthily between his fingers and lips. It seemed like acceptable behavior for a rock 'n roll idol. But realizing his manager "got fucked up," Kramer says, "was pretty alarming."

A quick trip to Roehampton, a posh sanitarium, in early August did little to relieve the stress. The same for an "all-boys party" in Montpelier Square with footmen in full costume and powdered wigs who attended to the guests' every kinky whim. "Brian was far too uptight to enjoy himself," recalls one of the attendees. Everything seemed to convey the same fretful sensation. Then, only hours before the rooftop party, his mother, Queenie, showed up unannounced and insisted that all the red wallpaper and carnations be removed immediately as a hedge against some macabre superstition.

Later, as the party flowed along, everyone seemed to agree that "Brian was the picture of self-assurance." Dressed in an exquisite pin-striped suit and a pale blue shirt with stiff white collar and cuffs—"like a French diplomat"—he stood apart from the crowd, "beaming" in a daze, his chin tilted up at an angle like a Greco-Roman statue throughout the affair. When anyone tried to engage him in conversation, he stared past them, over their shoulders, gazing adoringly at John and Cynthia, Paul and Jane, George and Pattie, or Ringo and Maureen as they jostled their way through the crowd. Even Garland's unexpected arrival in the middle of dinner didn't seem to ruffle the facade. Anytime there was the least bit of excitement, Brian relied on the unfailing tactic. It was a simple enough solution, solving every immediate problem, but guests must have wondered how long he had had that cough.

[II]

The lure of America had once involved a fear of the unknown, but when the Beatles returned on August 18, there were no longer surprises. Their records were, according to a midwestern newspaper, "on jukeboxes in a hundred thousand joints and drugstores" (Capitol had flooded the market with an unprecedented 2 million copies of their brand-new album), airplay was nonstop to the point of punishment, *A Hard Day's Night* flickered across a mind-boggling five hundred screens, newspapers boosted circulation on their mop-haired images. Everywhere the boys went—or were rumored to be—crowds amassed in staggering numbers: three thousand, eight thousand, fifteen thousand, twenty thousand, *more.* If the Beatles themselves were still oblivious to the extent of America's infatuation with them, Neil Aspinall's perspective was somewhat more informed. "America was now very aware of the Beatles," he said, "and things were crazy."

Crazy: it was a word occurring with disturbing frequency in descriptions of the shifting American scene. There was a feeling in the States that the blissful self-contained provincialism of the Eisenhower era was in rocky disarray, with forces working to destabilize it on myriad fronts. Young people were struggling—often chaotically—to find a means of self-expression. The seething civil rights movement, galvanized by a minister named Martin Luther King Jr., had strafed the status quo, as northern college students poured into the South, committed to actively dismantling segregation. The threat of thermonuclear war and talk of a widening "missile gap" aroused interest in pacifism, while the escalation of America's military involvement in Southeast Asia heightened opposition to the draft and touched off demonstrations as well as a crusade against violence in particular and authority in general. And changing attitudes toward sexuality jump-started a raucous debate concerning public values and private moral choices.

Everything seemed connected to a growing disenchantment with the establishment and was set, coincidentally, to a soundtrack by the Beatles. As journalist Salley Rayl has concluded, with their music and appearance, the boys served as hip role models for a restless generation of Americans grappling with questions of individual freedom and rebellion. Their hair, especially, pissed off adults, she writes, "and now it was perceived to be threatening the very fabric of American society. It was a sign of degeneration. And it was intolerable. Furthermore the Beatles had an irreverent attitude, part wit and part cheeky disrespect, that questioned rigid, uptight American values."

Crazy, indeed. In all the blind spots surrounding these issues, the Beatles were a visible target. Parents quickly put them in their crosshairs for contributing to teenage delinquency; right-wing evangelists accused them as being conspirators in a "Communist . . . pact"; psychologists couldn't resist analyzing them as perpetrators of "mass hypnosis [and] contagious hysteria," all in a rabbity effort to explain away the upheaval.

There was no precedent for the kind of mayhem the Beatles provoked. In Los Angeles, where the boys had cleared Customs, the terminal's rotunda had to be cleared when the LAPD quickly lost control of the situation. "It scares you," a lieutenant on duty admitted to Jack Smith, covering the arrival for the *Los Angeles Times.* "It's just beyond me. I've *never* seen anything like this."

In San Francisco, too, the festivities turned grim and dangerous. All traffic leading to and from the airport ground to a standstill. Fans dangled over the freeway overpasses as the limousine crawled past, waving banners and throwing things at the car. "I saw two girls fall to their knees at the roadside," recalled *NME*'s feature columnist, Chris Hutchins, "biting their hands to stem the ecstasy of seeing the foursome." At another intersection he watched, horrified, as "two motorcyclists collided in the commotion." At the new Hilton, where the Beatles were booked into the fifteenth-floor penthouse, crowds throttled all entrances and disabled the elevators. Management had assured Brian's henchmen that there was no access from the roof, but according to Walter Hofer: "No sooner had the Beatles moved into their suite than people [were] coming down from the roof on sheets." One person who witnessed the scene described it as "total madness." Even the cavernous Cow Palace, whose security forces had sparkled two weeks earlier during Barry Goldwater's nomination as the Republican candidate for president, was a shambles. "Security was just awful," recalls Larry Kane, Philadelphia's longtime TV news anchor who covered the tour as a twenty-one-year-old greenhorn. "They never anticipated this kind of a problem. Certainly, the cops had never experienced anything like it. There wasn't enough manpower, very makeshift security." NEMS actually had the foresight to hire members of the Stanford football team as reinforcements around the stage, but even they were no match for the fans.

The usual number of girls fainted. Kids who flung themselves at the Beatles were turned back with unflinching firmness. Fortunately, there were no serious injuries. "But at one point," Kane remembers, "a Beatles button came flying out of the crowd and hit Lennon—and cut him. And he was scared." After the show Brian rushed the Beatles backstage to a trailer behind the arena, where a doctor was summoned to examine John. Kane, who watched from a corner of the room, remembers thinking: "It wasn't a wound—but it was a wake-up call."

The scene was the same everywhere. In Las Vegas "exasperated sheriff's deputies" brought in police dogs to quell the "shrieking mob." Mounted police first circled, then stormed the crowd in Vancouver. In Seattle the Beatles were "pinned in their dressing room for 59 minutes" before being rescued by a cordon of "Navy sailors who bent but didn't break." Jelly beans sailed at the stage from every conceivable angle. Nothing and no one, it seemed, was off-limits to attack. Journalist Art Schreiber recalls how, in Chicago, "somebody let go with a frozen T-bone [steak] from the balcony and it damn near took McCartney's head off, landing with a big thud on the stage."

The shows were patched together with no real concern for a cohesive structure. A package of four warm-up acts was the result of a shotgun marriage of rootless GAC artists. Bill Black's Combo, a "dull-sounding big beat rock ensemble," opened the bill and provided backing for the others, including the Exciters, still riding the crest of their 1962 Top 40 hit, "Tell Him"; the husky-voiced Jackie DeShannon, who wrote "Needles and Pins" for the Beatles' Liverpool mates the Searchers; and the Righteous Brothers, a few years shy of real blue-eyed-soul fame but already something of a legend on the California club circuit.

As for the shows themselves, lasting a scant thirty-one minutes, they were like sitting inside a funnel cloud. The four Beatles would rush onstage unannounced, clutching their instruments like body armor while flashbulbs exploded around them in a hail of blinding white light. Most of the kids unleashed another burst of "screaming, weeping ecstasy," keeping it up relentlessly throughout the entire performance. A solid wall of decibel-shattering sound shook the seats and floorboards, rumbling through the darkness, wave after wave of it, in a convulsion of rocking, rolling thunder. "It felt like an earthquake," recalls an astonished eyewitness who would remember the experience for the rest of his life. "It would start at one end [of the arena] and continue to the other. It was incredible to do nothing but stand there, letting it wash right over you."

Bill Medley, a member of the Righteous Brothers, recalls "feeling terrible" for the Beatles. "They were real players and singers, doing songs they'd written themselves" he says, "and yet they weren't being heard beyond the first or second row. I remember standing by the stage and thinking: 'this can't be any fun for them.'"* But, in fact, it was fun, John insisted, explaining, "we don't want [the fans] quiet." Like most rock musicians, he fed off the screams and could tease them from the audience at will. So when things got dull, as they invariably did from night to night, John merely had to shake his head or grin at the crowd to set off another explosion. Let them raise a little hell, he decided. Scream, cry, bring down the house. John meant it when he said: "I like a riot."

In many cities, the entourage went straight to the airport and headed to the next stop on the tour as a way of avoiding the crazy crowd scenes. For convenience and safety, GAC had chartered a plane for the duration, a twin-engine turboprop Electra owned by an outfit out of Fort Worth, Texas, called American Flyers Airlines, which "vibrated like crazy and made such a helluva lot of noise," recalls a passenger on the tour, "that you couldn't hear yourself think."** Still, it made road life easier for the Beatles, not having to be pestered by fans and autograph seekers every time they were in transit. The cabin crew was great, the boys could move about undisturbed to their heart's content, and there was room enough aboard to carry everyone connected with the tour.

There was a tiny lounge in the back of the plane where, whenever they got bored, the boys would congregate with several reporters always milling about, usually drinking and comparing notes. It was an uneasy standoff at first, with both groups eyeing each other like the opposition, but after a while, the ice began to thaw. "After a few days of circling, you could finally sit down with them," recalls a journalist. "They had to see you for a while to get to know you." Eventually Paul and Ringo conducted an ongoing poker game with a revolving cast of hard-core news guys, while John and George hustled Art Schreiber in many a "cutthroat game" of Monopoly. "Lennon was a fiend, and extremely competitive," Schreiber remembers. "He got so keyed up over the damn game, he had to stand up to roll the

---

* In fact, it wasn't any fun for the Righteous Brothers, who begged off the tour after the eighth city and were replaced by Clarence "Frogman" Henry.
** Two years later the plane and many of the same crew members crashed in Kansas, killing ninety-five people.

dice." And he stayed at it, racking up properties and plastic hotels until he was satisfied that he'd prevail. "I'd be falling asleep, and John would be tugging at me, saying, 'Art, Art, hey, man, it's your turn.' 'God, John, let me go to bed—*please.*' Then we'd get to the next city and I'd no sooner get into my room [than] the phone would ring. 'Come on up,' John would insist. 'We've got to play!' And we'd literally quit the games when the sun was coming up."

Through Schreiber, an older Cleveland-based radio news director who doubled as a national correspondent for Westinghouse stations, John got an unfiltered education in everything from the U.S. presidency to the upturn of violence in the streets. "We talked a lot about American politics and the racial divide," recalls Schreiber, who had marched from Selma to Montgomery with Martin Luther King Jr. and across Mississippi with James Meredith, as well as traveled closely with the candidates on the Kennedy campaign. "Lennon couldn't get enough of it; he was fascinated. I tried to familiarize him with the segregation in the South, about how blacks moved north to avoid discrimination and go where jobs were available, but that there was as much segregation in the North, only in a different way."

Prior to the start of the tour, Brian had forbade them to comment on topical issues. It wasn't appropriate, he felt, for pop stars to air particular opinions inasmuch as it might alienate—or as George put it, "rattle"—a segment of their audience, especially over a hot potato like Vietnam. "We were being asked about it all the time and it was silly," said John. "We had to pretend to be like in the old days when artists weren't meant to say anything about anything." But the Beatles weren't about to be silenced—especially George and John, both of whom in a relatively short amount of time became consumed by social and political issues. "We couldn't help ourselves. . . . We spoke our minds after that: 'We don't like it, we don't agree with it, we think it is wrong.'"

Still, even an insignificant incident could put a torch to their careers. John got a taste of it in Las Vegas, after two thrilling shows at the Convention Center. Two young twin girls—perhaps no more than fourteen years old—managed to talk their way into the Beatles' suite at the Sahara and fell asleep in his room at an extremely indelicate hour. As Derek Taylor maintained, "It was all perfectly respectable," but, of course, he was being paid to call it respectable. No matter what, it didn't look good. John was a married man after all. And it looked even worse when the girls' mother showed up in the lobby, concerned that her daughters were still somewhere upstairs with the Beatles.

"Mal knocked on my door about two-thirty in the morning," remembers Larry Kane, "and he told me there was a problem. 'Put on a jacket and tie,' he said. 'We need a clean-cut-looking suit with an authoritative voice.'" Kane, having joined the tour only two days earlier, did as he was asked and followed the roadie back to the Beatles' suite, where he understood John's dilemma at a glance. Kane was dispatched to the lobby, where he found the girls' mother waiting, and charmed her into believing that "Mr. Lennon [had] been spending some time with [her] young ladies, signing autographs." John and Derek were so "badly shaken" by the experience that they had consulted a lawyer by the time they reached Los Angeles.

Perhaps in response, the Beatles steered clear of rabid female fans in Seattle, secluding themselves instead in a suite at the Edgewater Hotel on Elliott Bay, where they dropped fishing lines from their window and idled away the downtime. Officials had taken extraordinary precautions to ensure they wouldn't be disturbed. A makeshift barricade constructed out of plywood and razor wire had been positioned around the hotel to discourage fans from storming the entrance, in conjunction with a Coast Guard detail patrolling the immediate bay area, but despite these extreme measures, a number of stowaways still managed to breach security. Girls were eventually discovered hiding in a restroom, another in a closet, and several under beds. Later the Beatles learned about a plan by the hotel's housekeeping staff to sell the sheets and shag carpeting from their rooms to a local promotional firm, which offended their sensibilities enough to sabotage the scheme by urinating on everything in sight.

In Vancouver, at Empire Stadium, police security was unprepared for the "explosive situation" that erupted on the field, as five thousand kids rushed the stage "to jam up against . . . four crush barriers" separating them from the Beatles. In the process, kids got trampled and had to be rescued from the melee. Even the Beatles had to intervene. "If you don't stop, we're going to have to leave," Paul warned the audience halfway through the show, but it had little effect on the situation. "These people have lost all ability to think," complained a greatly agitated police inspector as he surveyed the scene, trying to redirect his men. *Variety* reported that "some 160 females, mainly in the 10 to 16 year age brackets, required medical attention." Others were treated backstage or at a nearby hospital for broken ribs and legs, heat prostration, hysteria and "overexcitement," along with an assortment of cuts and bruises.

"It was pretty scary just about everywhere we went," recalls Chris Hutchins, who never strayed far from the Beatles' long shadows. "Even those of us who had experienced Beatlemania in the U.K. were amazed at the disorder lurching around those shows in 'sixty-four." Hutchens himself got a taste of the danger in Denver when the car he was riding in was mistaken for the Beatles' and wound up being "badly damaged" by fans outside the Brown Palace Hotel. In New York the situation grew more serious during a security lapse at Forest Hills Tennis Stadium. "Dozens of fans stormed [the] stage," he reported in *NME,* "and at one point Ringo was knocked off his stool by [an] overenthusiastic girl who had leaped over steel-helmeted police kneeling in front of the stage."

But that was only the tip of the iceberg. In Boston on September 12, a series of ferocious fistfights erupted on the sidewalk outside the Garden, followed by a wave of pushing and shoving during which two glass doors to the building were smashed and several gates overturned. Cops immediately converged from all sides, with a mounted police team stampeding through the mob and knocking young fans indiscriminately to the ground. "The police were truly awful," recalled Derek Taylor in his memoir of the tour.

Boston was only a warm-up for Cleveland. A force of five hundred uniformed police circulated through Public Hall, clamoring roughly for order by knocking their nightsticks on chairs. They kept a lid on things while the opening acts were on, but as soon as the Beatles hit the stage, all civility broke down. Jelly beans, toys, and much heavier objects were launched at the band's heads. Then, in the middle of "All My Loving," the audience rose as one and stood on their seats as a swarm of teenage girls "surged toward the stage in a spontaneous banzai charge," as one reporter called it. A cordon of forty cops tried to hold back the girls but eventually collapsed against the attack, "as did a brass railing . . . bolted to the floor which was ripped out" in the ensuing scuffle.

Instead of regrouping to restore order, the officer in charge, Deputy Inspector Carl Bare, charged onto the stage and attempted to stop the music. At first the Beatles ignored him, continuing to play. Undaunted, Bare elbowed Paul aside and commandeered the mike. "Sit down, sit down— this show is over!" he bellowed. When the Beatles refused to respond, the battle line was drawn. Bare advanced on John, who squibbed away, mocking the policeman with a little dance and making a face. A "hurricane of boos" flooded the arena. Another policeman, Inspector Michael Blackwell, joined Bare onstage and waved the Beatles into the wings. Predictably, the boys refused to yield, but Blackwell, known locally as Iron Mike, grabbed George by the elbow and steered him forcefully off the stage, at which point the rest of the Beatles reluctantly followed.

Art Schreiber, who was standing in the wings, grew terrified by the crowd's response. "It touched off a kind of screaming I'd never heard before," he recalls, "a violent, angry, bone-chilling roar that somehow demanded a comparable reaction." He could see packs of kids roaming aimlessly, menacingly, around the dark hall, pursued by wary policemen. Several windows were shattered as disgruntled fans tried to reach the backstage area through an adjoining building.

Calm prevailed thanks to the extraordinary efforts of Derek Taylor. Sensing a disaster in the making, he volunteered to go onstage and plead with the audience for order in return for twenty minutes of additional showtime. The police were reluctant to accept at first, as were the Beatles, who had already changed out of their stage clothes and were relishing an early escape. Much like a cagy U.N. negotiator, Taylor swung between both camps in an attempt to broker an agreement, and in the end, the show went on.

In Los Angeles on August 23, the Beatles played to a worshipful crowd of almost nineteen thousand at the Hollywood Bowl, the gilded open-air amphitheater at the foot of the Hollywood Hills. Behind them, reaching into the spectacular starlit sky, another ten or fifteen thousand gate-crashers were massed in the sparsely populated woodlands. John swung his head around reflexively, like a child discovering new scenery, taking in the unexpected guests. "Welcome to you in the trees!" he shouted, as the other Beatles plugged in. It was "a gorgeous California night, just magnificent" and moistly warm, with incomparable hibiscus-scented breezes. A lot of importance had been placed on this gig, what with the celebrity-studded crowd and Capitol Records headquartered a few miles away, and the band fed on it to get wired.

George Martin had arranged with Capitol Records to record the evening's concert in the hope that it would serve as an interim release, and so the clamshell stage was cluttered with booms and cables. Live albums were still something of an anomaly in the rock 'n roll business, but Martin, who'd struck gold with the *Beyond the Fringe* soundtrack, felt that Beatles fans would support such an effort if it captured the excitement the boys put out onstage. "They were great as a live band," he observed, having seen them dozens of times. But from the moment the tape rolled, there was no containing the screaming. Martin worked frantically with Capitol's crew, struggling to filter out the noise, but the VU meters were hopelessly red-lined throughout the Beatles' set. "It was like putting a microphone at the tail of a 747 jet," he said. "It was one continual screaming sound, and it was very difficult to get a good recording."

Still, while the *Los Angeles Times* critic claimed that "not much of the mop-haired quartet's singing could be heard" over the shrieking, the crowd was comparatively low-key for a Beatles concert. "It was almost too well behaved," John told KRLA's Jim Steck over lunch the next afternoon. For a change, he said, the Beatles could actually *hear* what they were playing, which, coupled with the lush surroundings, made the show the highlight of the tour.

Afterward, the boys were feted until nearly dawn by about thirty of the city's "best-looking" starlets, including *the Mod Squad*'s Peggy Lipton and Joan Baez, who were shipped up to the gated mansion the Beatles were renting on St. Pierre Road in a neighborhood known as Hidden Hills. In an unprecedented move, the traveling press corps was also invited, as were wives and girlfriends and a few local deejays. Ray Hildebrand and Jill Jackson, who performed as Paul and Paula, showed up as someone's guests, along with Billy Preston, whom the Beatles had first met in Liverpool and later at the Star-Club during his tenure in Little Richard's band. It was a cozy little crowd, "very casual," recalls a guest. The boys, lounging in the living room, introduced the newcomers to their friends on the tour, and as the evening stretched on and the Beatles dropped their guard, the party developed into a predictably wild scene. Guests enjoyed the general run of the house, including the pool and the bedrooms, where the action was in full swing.

Brian, who had been looking forward to enjoying L.A. nightlife, had actually turned in early and was asleep in his sprawling pink and green suite at the Beverly Hills Hotel in anticipation of two important events scheduled for the next day. He'd arranged to have lunch in the Polo Lounge at noon on August 24 with Colonel Tom Parker, Elvis's wily old mentor, so they could check each other out and compare notes on managing their two rock phenomena. Then, later, with the Beatles in tow, he would head to a charity garden party in Brentwood to benefit the Hemophilia Foundation hosted by Capitol Records' president Alan Livingston, whose wife, actress Nancy Olson, was on the foundation's board.

At the party Livingston went to great lengths to accommodate the Beatles, who, after being cold-shouldered by the label, had rocketed Capitol's profits into the stratosphere. No expense had been spared to stage a Hollywood-style spectacular. A festive striped tent had been set up in the spacious backyard, where vendors dispensed soft ice cream and lemonade to a litter of gorgeously groomed children. There were pony rides and games. Security was unparalleled, befitting a presidential visit, with a fully armed riot squad stashed in the garage, just in case. The guest list was a who's who of local dignitaries, complete with a selection of handpicked celebrities, each of whom was required by the hosts to bring a child: Edward G. Robinson had in tow his granddaughter, Francesa; Lloyd Bridges, his son Jeff; Rita Hayworth, her daughter, Princess Yasmin Khan; Donald O'Connor, his son, Freddy, and daughter, Alicia; Jack Palance, his daughter, Holly; Eva Marie Saint, her son, Darrell, and daughter, Laurie; Barbara Rush, her son, Christopher; Jeanne Martin brought five of Dean's children a few feet in front of Jerry Lewis, who bolted as soon as he saw them, leaving his son, Gary, behind rather than risk an encounter with his estranged partner.

If the Beatles were at all starstruck, they didn't show it. Longtime movie fans, they always enjoyed meeting their screen heroes, but the turnout at the party seemed on the slim side, rather far from the hip. "We saw a couple of film stars," John relented, but added: "We were expecting to see more." Then an invitation arrived that absolved the anemic turnout.

Burt Lancaster was screening the new Peter Sellers movie, *A Shot in the Dark,* at his Bel-Air estate and thought the Beatles might get a kick out of joining him. Was that *the* Burt Lancaster, they asked Derek—*the man* with all the teeth? Ringo was absolutely beside himself. A stone cowboy freak, he'd seen Lancaster in *Gunfight at the O.K. Corral, Apache, The Kentuckian,* and *Vera Cruz* the moment they were released and had the actor's persona, with the leer and cobra smile, down pat. Burt Lancaster! Sure, they'd watch a movie with him. They'd shop for groceries with him, if that was the offer.

Lancaster's pad, in George's opinion, "was a very expensive, impressive Hollywood home," with a sunken Olympic-size pool buried in a grotto of lighted waterfalls and lagoons with a tributary that fed directly into a bedroom—you could just swim right in—and a panoramic view of West Los Angeles that seemed lifted from a movie backdrop. But it wasn't nearly as impressive as Lancaster himself, a bronzed god "about eight feet tall" whose aura probably set off car alarms up and down the hills. Ringo, who came dressed in western-style gear, with a holster and toy guns strapped around his waist, drew on their host as he lumbered through the door. "Hold 'em up there now, Burt—this town ain't big enough for the two of us," he drawled. It was the equivalent of some goofball meeting the Beatles and bleating, "Yeah, yeah, yeah." But Lancaster played along, flashing his dazzling grin and going for an imaginary weapon. "What have you got there?" he frowned at Ringo's plastic gun. "Kids' stuff." The Beatles were in heaven.

The next day, during a fatiguing heat wave, more stars—and more guns—continued to show up, beginning right after lunch when Colonel Parker arrived in a station wagon loaded with presents for the Beatles. A huge box carried to the patio spilled over with rhinestone-studded leather belts and holsters with each of the boys' names engraved on the back and "From Elvis and the Colonel" burned inside. The Beatles expressed their thanks, but that was as far as they were willing to go. There was something slightly off base, something condescending about the spirit of the gift-giving that registered on the boys' shit detectors. "Bang, bang," Paul dead-panned, aiming his gun at the Colonel, who was sitting across the table from him. Ominously, John pointed a gun at his own head and mimicked Paul—*"bang!"*—as George grumbled: "I wish we had real guns." It cast an awkward hush over the table, broken finally by the Colonel's twangy appeal to "have fun, fellas," before hightailing it out of their compound.

Soon afterward, Bobby Darin and Sandra Dee stopped by to pay their respects, followed by Jayne Mansfield, a tough little number who had "ha-rangued and hassled" Derek Taylor for days in an attempt to have her picture taken with the Beatles. Brian had laid down the law about using the Beatles in photo ops: it was *out of the question,* especially with cheesy celebrities, but Derek occasionally made exceptions. Mansfield wasn't to be one of them. Having gotten the tactful Lancashire brush-off, she finally showed up at the house, "adamant about meeting them." She refused to take no for an answer. It set up an awkward situation, awkward for its exchange in front of the boys and awkward because of its inexcusably harsh pitch, but in the clamorous give-and-take, Mansfield's suggestion that everyone meet at the Whiskey-A-Go-Go seemed like a solution they could live with—anything, as long as it removed her from their doorstep.

Truth be told, the Beatles were itching to get out, tired of being cooped up and handled, eager to sample L.A. nightlife without being on a leash. John, Neil, and Derek had actually gone clothes shopping at Beau Gentry earlier in the day and were encouraged by the fact that no one had accosted them. Maybe, Derek concluded, they could survive an outing to the Whiskey. Brian wouldn't approve, but he had disappeared again, leaving Derek in charge.

Calls were made to the club, whose press agent guaranteed the Beatles "absolute privacy." Johnny Rivers was playing, and George and Ringo set out at 10:30 in a white Cadillac convertible, while John followed in a police car with Mansfield and a few guys from the press corps, leaving Paul curled up in a hammock. "It was bad from the get-go," recalls Larry Kane, who had squeezed into the backseat before Derek could give him the boot. "Before anyone knew what was happening, John grabbed Mansfield and they started making out like mad. It was almost obscene the way they went at it like that, right there in front of us."

It was evident from the moment they pulled into the Whiskey's parking lot on Sunset Boulevard that "Beatlemania [was] in full frenzy, the owners having broadcast [the] visit all over town." Somehow, John elbowed his way inside the jam-packed club, where a banquette had been reserved, but George and Ringo had to be literally lifted and passed over the crowd to keep them from being trampled. Instantly "the whole of Hollywood paparazzi descended," George remembered. Photographers zeroed right in on the money shot: busty Jayne Mansfield sandwiched between three-quarters of the Beatles. Wordlessly, the boys let them do their bit, withstanding an explosion of flashbulbs. It was over soon enough—except that Robert Flora, a stringer for UPI, refused to cut the Beatles any slack. "He just kept snapping pictures of them with one of those old-fashioned box cameras that flashed real big," says Larry Kane, "and they wanted to be left alone." After a suitable grace period, George warned Flora "to get lost," which worked for about a minute. Soon he drifted back, peppering the table with flashes. "Will you just move him?" John asked a bouncer diplomatically, waving Flora aside. "Tell him to drop his camera, come over and join the table. Anything, *but stop flashing.*"

But as the bouncer turned around, Flora reached over his biceps and boldly fired off another shot at the table. "Get the fuck out of here!" George roared to a stunned entourage. Jumping halfway to his feet, he snatched up his glass—a half-drained scotch and Coke—and hurled its contents at the camera. The drink missed its mark and hit actress Mamie Van Doren instead, who was making her way over to the table.

The next day, predictably, the incident was splashed across the front page of the *Herald Examiner*, along with "photos by Bob Flora" of the entire drink-throwing fiasco. One of the pictures shows George clearly in action, establishing a new public image to contradict that of the so-called quiet Beatle. (In Baltimore, two weeks later, he would reinforce this side of him by booting a local photographer in the ass.) "That was horrendous," admitted George, who regarded the skirmish as a lapse in judgment. The Beatles had always worked so hard to keep from losing control like that in public, from embarrassing themselves in front of fans. But it also underscored how much things had altered since they'd hit the road back in June. In fact, the whole gestalt of Beatlemania had radically changed. The fans were becoming more aggressive, the situations more dire, the press more unforgiving, the future more uncertain. From now on, the way the Beatles interacted with *anyone* had to be carefully refocused. One thing was for sure: venturing out in public was no longer a smart or safe bet. As Derek Taylor recalled: "When in future days someone would say—and someone often did say it—'You guys never go *out* anywhere. Don't you ever feel shut in?' we would recall the time we went night-clubbing [sic] with Jayne Mansfield and sigh."

[III]

The American tour dragged on through most of September, with little variation in its madcap routine. The cities sped by in a blur: Denver, Cincinnati, New York, Atlantic City, Philadelphia, Indianapolis, Milwaukee, Chicago, Detroit . . . Everywhere they went, there were greater displays of mayhem, the fans ever more determined to cross the Beatles' path. Their schemes got more inventive—and more preposterous, too—as the tour progressed and gathered steam. In Indianapolis a college student posed as a room-service waiter at the Speedway Motor Inn in order to collect their autographs. That stunt was clever enough to amuse the boys. But at the old Muhlbach Hotel in Kansas City, a mother got stuck crawling through the air-conditioning ducts trying to locate the Beatles' suite.

Mothers! They put their daughters to shame when it came to the nightly groupie scene. There was always an abundance of gorgeous young women willing to do anything—and to anyone—in order to meet one of the Beatles. But the mothers were even more determined to score one of the boys. "Older women would come up to us all the time and say, 'I want to meet the Beatles,'" recalls a journalist who traveled with the entourage. "I'd say, 'I can't do that.' And they'd say, 'No, you don't understand. I want to make them happy.'"

The variety of women that paraded through the Beatles' rooms was extraordinary for its range and magnitude. "After most shows, you couldn't get into their suite without wading through the crush of available girls," Wendy Hanson recalled. "It resembled the waiting room of a busy doctor's office. Derek or Neil would poke his head through the door and say, 'Next,' until, one by one, they'd work their way through the entire group." Invariably, when Neil confronted a promoter about arrangements following a show, he'd be waved off in mid-sentence—"Don't worry, that's all been taken care of"—which usually meant that hookers were waiting in their dressing room. "The Beatles *hated* that," says Tony Barrow, who encountered it on subsequent tours. "The promoters used to think they were being terribly helpful, but those girls were gotten rid of as fast as the Beatles could get rid of them."

Most of the time. But in Atlantic City, at a motel party following the concert at Convention Hall, the girls on call were too spectacular to resist. John, especially, couldn't take his eyes off a slim and flashy young blonde who "reminded him of Brigitte Bardot." And again, in Dallas, when bunnies from a private club showed up, the boys yielded to temptation. This time it was Paul who fancied a tall blond cowgirl standing somewhat behind the others. Art Schreiber, who happened to be passing through the suite, was startled when Paul motioned with his chin and whispered, "I like that one. Can you get her for me?" Answered Schreiber: "Listen, pal, I'm no fucking pimp. I'm a reporter."

———

The Beatles were in dire need of a substitute distraction when the tour mercifully rolled into New York. "This is it! *This* is what it's all about!" Paul gushed, as their car emerged from the Midtown Tunnel slightly before four on the morning of August 28. They had been flying since midnight, having taken off directly after the last show in Cincinnati, where the temperature onstage peaked at a torturous 115 degrees. Exhausted though they might have been, the city hit them like a handful of amphetamines. New York, New York: it was a sight for sore eyes—and a jolt to weary senses.

John immediately ordered their driver to scan the local radio stations and, sure enough, it was just the same as the last time they'd arrived. Their songs reverberated right across the AM dial. A thrill like that never wore off!

"This is it!" Paul said again to no particular response, though everyone nodded in unison.

The Plaza Hotel now knew what to expect and refused to have the Beatles back, so at Ed Sullivan's suggestion, they'd shifted headquarters to the Delmonico Hotel, a dowdy high-rise on the corner of Fifty-ninth

Street and Park Avenue, where Sullivan lived year-round and could vouch for their welfare. But when their limo pulled up to the entrance canopy and they got out, about eighty teenage girls broke through police barricades. The boys knew how to slip unscathed through these type of crowds, but a plucky fifteen-year-old named Angie McGowan, who lived just a few blocks south, pounced on a startled Ringo, ripping the St. Christopher's medal from a chain around his neck. In the havoc she also shredded his shirt, according to an account in the *New York World-Telegram*, "then retired triumphantly into the crowd."

New York, New York: double trouble, but alluring as ever. Two sold-out shows at the Forest Hills Tennis Stadium drew nearly thirty thousand teenagers to what Robert Shelton, the *New York Times* pop music critic, labeled "a screaming success." Shelton, partial to Greenwich Village folksingers, warned: "[The Beatles] have created a monster in their audience. If they have concern for anything but the money they are earning, they had better concern themselves with controlling their audiences before this contrived hysteria reaches uncontrollable proportions." It was a ridiculous admonition. No one was going to control Beatlemania, much less tame the defiant monster. The Beatles, more than anyone, had transformed the rock show from a conventional performance into a bash to blow off some steam. The audience was asserting itself without even realizing what it was doing. The feeling generated at the Beatles shows bordered on spiritual anarchy, and being nothing short of exhilarating, nothing was going to stop it. In under a year, the Beatles had redefined the experience in terms of sheer numbers, money, and energy. No one, not even Elvis, had that great of an impact all at once. A whole new chapter of musical prophecy was being written.

It was inevitable that Dylan would show up. While the Beatles had linked themselves musically to Elvis, it was Dylan with whom they would reshape their generation.

Paul had discovered him first, buying the *Freewheelin'* album before they'd left for Paris at the beginning of the year. That record hit the turntable the moment the Beatles settled into their suite at the George V. "And for the rest of our three weeks in Paris we didn't stop playing it," John recalled. In fact, George considered the experience "one of the most memorable things of the trip," alleviating the irritation of being cooped up in their rooms.

One can only imagine the impact that Dylan's music had on the boys. The album itself was the first of many watersheds in his long career. That sure command of language might have drifted by unnoticed were it the work of an older, more experienced interpreter, but from a twenty-two-year-old folksinger, this articulation of self-expression had major resonance. There was plenty to chew on, from the sentimental arguments made in "Blowin' in the Wind" to the lovesick bitterness of "Don't Think Twice, It's All Right" to the barbed topicality of "Masters of War" and especially the verbal whiplashing given to "A Hard Rain's A-Gonna Fall." "I'm sure this kind of thing found its way into our music, and into our lyrics, and influenced whom we were interested in," Paul explained many years afterward. "Vocally and poetically Dylan was a huge influence." Certainly, in addition to the obvious effect it had on his language and style, Dylan's lyrics served to turn John inward as a songwriter. From that point on, he said, "I'd started thinking about my own emotions. . . . Instead of projecting myself into a situation, I would try to express what I felt about myself."

The revelation was not merely a self-conscious one. In ten years, no other artist, not even one as inventive as the Beatles, had been able to cultivate rock's literary essence. Paul Simon, one of the more articulate young songwriters to tap into that reservoir, understood just how liberating Dylan's contributions actually were. "He made us feel at a certain time that it was good to be smart, to be observant, that it was good to have a social conscience."

There is no way of knowing how, or even if, this posed a threat to the Beatles. But John responded to the challenge much as Simon described it, probably because he was better equipped. The older John got, the more experience he acquired and discoveries he made, the less songs about holding hands and sharing secrets kept him engaged. As a songwriter, his perspective had expanded, and he was trying to break out of the mold. In Dylan, John had finally found what was, for him, a new direction. It is no coincidence that John began writing "I'm a Loser" while still in Paris. The song is clearly his attempt at constructing an early self-portrait, with its revealing soft focus on relationships and fame. "I think it was Dylan who helped me realize that," John concluded, "not by any discussion or anything, but by hearing his work." John reveled in the new possibilities of substance and character that might free his imagination from the mush he worked on with Paul.

Dylan caught up with the Beatles in their suite at the Delmonico about an hour after their first Forest Hills concert. It was a particularly maddening night. They were in the midst of having dinner with Brian, Neil, and Mal when he arrived with his road manager, Victor Maimudes, and *New York Post* columnist Al Aronowitz, who had coordinated the get-together as a favor to the boys. Of their initial introduction, John commented: "When I met Dylan I was quite dumbfounded," but within minutes he managed to get over any initial shock. Dylan was eccentric and intense but cool, very cool, in a way that only another pop phenom could appreciate. There was the usual checking-out process, followed by awkward stabs at conversation, until ultimately everyone discovered that they spoke the same language.

It didn't take long before someone retrieved the communal pillbox from John's leather bag and Drinamyls and Preludins were offered like after-dinner mints to the edgy guests. The Beatles downed a handful on most nights of the tour as a way of staying up—and *up*—when their bodies ached for sleep. But Dylan took one look at the assortment of gaily colored pills and shook his head. "How about something a little more organic?" he suggested. "Something green . . . marijuana."

The Beatles recoiled. They were scotch and Coke men, chain-smokers. Granted, there were the pills, but they served a purpose other than getting stoned.

"We've never really smoked marijuana before," Brian interjected, sensing the boys' immediate discomfort. This, unbeknownst to him, wasn't entirely true. "We first got marijuana from an older drummer with another group in Liverpool," George recalled. Besides, an acquaintance had shared a joint with the Beatles at the Star-Club in Hamburg, but it was what Neil called "just the sticks," which probably meant a deposit of stems mixed with dried oregano or some such filler.

"But what about your song—the one about getting high?" Dylan wondered. In his inimitable rasp, he sang: "'And when I touch you, I get high, I get high . . .'"

"Those aren't the words," John said stone-faced. "It's 'I can't hide, I can't hide.'"

No matter. Rolling "a skinny American joint," Dylan handed it to John, who gave it a dubious look and passed it on to Ringo, dubbing him "my official taster." Ringo was no blushing maiden. Without a word, he retreated to a back room sealed with rolled towels—there was a battalion of New York City policemen on a security detail in the hall—and smoked it down to his fingertips. A few minutes later he emerged with a twisted grin plastered on his face. As Paul recounted the experience, "We said,

'How is it?' He said, 'The ceiling's coming down on me.' And we went, Wow! Leaped up, 'God, got to do this!' So we ran into the back room— first John, then me and George, then Brian."

The effect it had on the boys was spectacular. "We were just legless, aching from laughter," George told Derek Taylor, who joined them later on in the suite. Paul greeted Taylor by gathering him up in an immense bear hug and revealing "he'd been up there," pointing to the ceiling, and Brian pressed his P.A. to smoke some weed, which he politely declined. The pot had loosened up Brian to a degree that was truly emancipating. He became entranced by his reflection in the mirror. After a moment or two he stood back, then pointed to himself, and blurted out: *"Jew!"* to everyone's hilarity. Paul noted how that was the first time Brian had ever referred to himself as a Jew. "It may not seem the least bit significant to anyone else," he admitted, "but in our circle, it was very liberating." And a sign to those not red-eyed of Brian's deep self-loathing.

Meanwhile, Paul entertained his own moments of mind-blowing significance. For a period of time he frantically crisscrossed the suite in search of pencil and paper to capture the profundities that were leapfrogging around his brain. "Get it down, Mal, get it down!" he implored his faithful roadie, appointing the also significantly stoned Evans his trusty Boswell. Exasperated, Paul scratched out his own cogent musings on a slip of paper, which Mal obediently stashed away for safekeeping, or at least until the next morning, when Paul read its contents aloud to the other Beatles. It said: "There are seven levels," nothing more, which amused everyone to no end.

An unusually gregarious Dylan was delighted by the Beatles' curiosity and readiness to experiment. They got right into the groove, which relaxed the recalcitrant bard, who lit joint after joint, fanning the fateful flame. "He kept answering our phone, saying, 'This is Beatlemania here,'" John recalled. But it was something much more than that, something as close to a cultural milestone as could be determined by academics and savants. "We were smoking dope, drinking wine and generally being rock 'n rollers, and having a laugh, you know, and surrealism. It was party time."

That it was: *party time.* And nothing would ever be the same again.

[I]

*W*hen *do you think the bubble will burst?*

It was astounding how many times the Beatles could be asked that question—and in how many myriad ways. The American press had pounded them with it, tossing it out like a beach ball at every opportunity. "I'll probably open my own hair salon," Ringo predicted in dead earnest. Paul supposed he'd fancy teaching. And as for John and George—they hadn't a clue. The future: what twenty-one-year-old boy even thought further than two days ahead?

How long do you expect Beatlemania to last?

"Till death do us part," John muttered through tightly clenched teeth. And what about his ambition, that is, after the bubble burst? "Count the money."

For all the pissing and moaning about the shelf life of pop stardom, the Beatles were, by all accounts, rock-solid. They'd banked a record $1 million-plus from the American tour (including an astonishing $150,000 for a single show in Kansas City), which seemed a mere pittance in light of the $5.8 million in U.S. rentals for *A Hard Day's Night*. Record sales were soaring, with no apparent letdown. By October 1964, EMI had shipped an estimated 10 million Beatles discs—a staggering number, just mind-boggling—accounting for the company's 80 percent surge in pretax profits. (Capitol followed suit, announcing a 17 percent sales rise "largely due to Beatle [sic] records.") When Elvis was awarded his second gold single (for sales of more than 500,000 units) it was seen as an unsurpassable record, and now the Beatles owned three, with numbers four and five within reach. The *Daily Mail* put their earnings from abroad at $56 million—this at a time when a Cadillac cost $3,600.

Only the year before, according to his autobiography, Brian had considered accepting £150,000 for a 50 percent share in the Beatles. *Variety* also reported that he was actively pursuing the sale of a quarter interest in the Beatles for $4 million, as a tax hedge. Now he turned down $10 million from an American syndicate to buy the Beatles, convinced he'd only scratched the surface of the rockpile.

Still, Brian was all too aware of how abruptly the wheel of celebrity turned, and he therefore wasted no time in planning for the future. There were promises of half a dozen TV and radio appearances, the most important being the American variety show *Shindig!*, which agreed to film a special segment around them originating from London. Another holiday pantomime (still three months off and already sold out for its entire run) began production, along with a new Christmas flexi-disk for their sixty-five thousand fan club members. And by the end of October, they had also concluded plans for their next movie—"this one in color . . . and with a much stronger plot line," according to Walter Shenson.

The most anticipated project, of course, was a new album for Parlophone; the recording sessions kicked off less than a week after the Beatles returned from abroad. It seemed ridiculous to try to squeeze it in so quickly, on top of their other obligations, but EMI had made clear that they "need[ed] another album" out by mid-November, in time for the holiday market, and the Beatles, still ever its faithful subjects, were programmed to comply.

John and Paul had been writing steadily—together and apart—throughout their travels, with about eight songs in good enough shape to record right away. But it had not been a breeze, unlike the previous records. They'd struggled through what John described as "a lousy period," a time when everything they came up with sounded trite, even flat. There were even hints that the album might have to be put off until the material was up to snuff; but before anyone panicked, they'd finally pounded out a few gems that had the earmarks of their very best work. "Basically," Paul explained, they set out to re-create their "stage show, with some new songs" as a bridge to the creative territory they were exploring.

The Beatles' drift away from the simplest pop forms, which had begun under Buddy Holly's influence, had accelerated under Dylan's. Even relatively recent hits like "Can't Buy Me Love" and "P.S. I Love You" no longer played the predominant role in their prodigal repertoire. Like John, Paul needed something new. There was no challenge anymore to churning out fare-thee-well lyrics—"the moon and June stuff," as Paul disdained it—in a neat two-and-a-half-minute frame. If anything, the seven months of constant travel and fame had given them more perspective on the structure of songwriting, confidently testing new chords and progressions, to say nothing of language, every time they buckled down. "We got more and more free to get into ourselves," Paul explained. "And I think also John and I wanted to do something bluesy, a bit darker, more grown-up. Rather than just straight pop."

This he said in describing the basis for "Baby's in Black," a pretentious, image-laden song that eventually made the cut, but it could serve as well for their entire approach. John's and Paul's fascination with Dylanesque touches—and to some extent the Stones' foray into R&B—cast an edgy enthusiasm over their latest efforts. There is a definite bridge here to their later albums, discernible in songs such as "I'm a Loser," whose melodic pattern would resonate exactly a year later in the ebb and flow of "Norwegian Wood." The same with "No Reply," with its painful scenes of rejection and humiliation. John called it his "version of 'Silhouettes,'" the 1957 doo-wop hit by the Rays, which had been a staple on his turntable in Menlove Avenue. "I had that image of walking down the street and seeing [a girl] silhouetted on the window and not answering the phone," he recalled. And while it reworked a long-established theme, its plaintiveness ran against the light current of familiar Beatles songs.

In this burst of daring songs that kicked off *Beatles for Sale,* along with the lush but anxiety-ridden "Every Little Thing," John and Paul continued to grapple with the prospect of evolving without alienating. Experimentation and growth had become something of a professional obsession, but it would have been counterproductive, they realized, to do a complete about-face. Just as they'd felt initially that "From Me to You" was "too way out," there was a suspicion that the audience "[wouldn't] know quite what to make" of the intensely charged imagery, even though its authors considered it "cool." They were still making a conscious effort not to deviate too much from the fold, to take creative baby steps as opposed to the proverbial flying leap.

The end of October was a particularly harried period when the Beatles most felt the squeeze. A number of the original songs were actually written on the spot—that is, in the studio—which broke every rule in the book. "No one was allowed to record like that," recalls Tony Crane, of the Merseybeats. "Even when we had a song in the Top Five, we were given three hours at most to record an A-side, and if at the end of that time we still weren't satisfied, it still went out as a single." But the Beatles swept that old tradition right out the studio door. Paul and John had always loved improvising, but up until now it had been done at Paul's house, in hotel rooms, in the back of vans. Now they took it a step further. "The ideas were there for a first verse, or a chorus," Ringo explained, "but it could be changed by the writers as we were doing it, or if anyone had a good idea."

Still, material for this album was at a premium. At a loss, they dredged up "I'll Follow the Sun," left over from the Forthlin Road period and four or five covers they'd "played live so often," according to George, "that we only had to get a sound on them and do them."

Through it all, John and Paul continued to write, with blocks of time devoted to working in their comfort zone: eyeball-to-eyeball. There was always a room available at Abbey Road studios where they could steal a few minutes to bash around ideas. There was also the tiny music salon below the Ashers' flat, when it wasn't booked for lessons. Otherwise, Paul ran his new forest green Aston Martin DB out to Kenwood, where John was spending most of his spare time since returning from the States, and they'd spread out in a little mess of an attic room overlooking the garden to "kick things around" for two or three hours.

Occasionally, when Paul was preoccupied, he arranged to be driven out to John's in order to spend the travel time writing or just reading the newspaper. One day, just as the limo was turning into the driveway, Paul put down his paper and, more out of politeness than real interest, asked the chauffeur how he'd been. The driver gazed in his rearview mirror and shook his head. "Oh, working hard," he replied with an emphatic huff, "working eight days a week." A bell went off in Paul's head. *Eight days a week!* "It was like a little blessing from the gods," Paul recalled. No sooner had John answered his door than Paul dropped this little nugget into his hands. "Well, I've got the title," he insisted, and blurted it out. John, normally as competitive as an insurance salesman, knew when to hop on the bus. They practically dashed upstairs and began spitting out lyrics, just "filling it in from the title," as Paul remembered it. Bam, bam, bam.

Much later John dismissed "Eight Days a Week," saying it "was never a good song," but at the time they wrote it there was no hesitation as to whether it would fit into their recording plans. An obvious crowd-pleaser, "Eight Days a Week" contains all the drive and spunk of their previous hits, its exuberant spirit punctuated by explosive guitar fanfare, joyous handclaps, and an unforgettable hook — "a typical happy John-and-Paul song," as Derek Johnson, writing in *NME*, described it. And each pop hit they offered carved out space for more radical exploration.

John and Paul had written "I Feel Fine" in the studio as one of the last songs for the new album. John had pinched the nifty guitar lick from the 1961 Bobby Parker single, "Watch Your Step," which he admitted was one of his favorite records. "I told [the other Beatles] I'd write a song specially for the riff," he explained to *NME*'s Chris Hutchins, and not more than a few hours later he and Paul had knocked it out.

Convinced it was "lousy," they cut "I Feel Fine" almost as an afterthought and were delighted by the result: it "sounded like an 'A' side" from the very first playback. *NME* called "I Feel Fine" "a real gas . . . a happy-go-lucky mid-tempo swinger [with] a tremendous rhythm and a really catchy melody." Hardly insightful (there was no one in Britain writing sophisticated pop criticism at the time), but at least it was headed in the right direction, hitting all the essential elements. One aspect the reviewer seized on—but couldn't easily articulate—was the "startling, reverberating opening" for which there was no real precedent.

It was the result of a happy accident. The Beatles had finished recording a decent take of the song and were eager to hear the playback. "We were just about to walk away," Paul remembered, "when John leaned his guitar against the amp." It was an acoustic Gibson sunburst fitted with a pickup to give it a brighter sound. There wasn't very much juice in the line, but the proximity of guitar and amp produced an electrical spike that sent distortion echoing through the studio.

For the Beatles, discovering feedback was like hitting a gusher. No one had ever considered using a sound effect before. Certainly they'd used handclaps and cowbells to enhance rhythm tracks, but nothing strictly technical, aside from double-tracking. "Can we have that on the record?" Paul remembered asking George Martin. No problem. They re-created the accident. Each time, they seemed to get more control over the sound: if they regulated the volume, the report would roar in key; cranking it up produced pure noise; by moving the guitar to and fro they could stretch the tone to their liking. They learned about electronics: how pickups function like microphones, the way distorting a frequency feeds it back into itself so that the same sound loops and spirals out of control. Lowering the volume requires pinpoint accuracy but produces a sharper, more resonant sound. Each new finding gave them incentive to tinker.

In a year, the Beatles would almost single-handedly reinvent the way music was recorded, but for now they were content to revel in their discovery. So much so that later that same session, while demo'ing a take of "Everybody's Trying to Be My Baby," they drowned George's vocal under a torrent of tape delay, creating an eerie echo effect that makes it sound as if he were singing inside of a steel drum.

While John later boasted that "I Feel Fine" contained "the first feedback on any record," there was nothing about its use that sent producers running to their consoles. The sound was already as familiar as tape hiss. What it lacked was the synthesis of imagination and experience—a way of weaving it into the densening web of a song, using each new color and shade to conceptualize the arrangement and engulf the listener in an unpredictable experience. In the fall of 1965 the Beatles eventually put it all together. Like everything else they'd done, it was the result of exploring the past and using those early pop influences to go their own way. As John described it, "We finally took over the studio."

———

With the album all but spoken for, the "autumn tour" of Britain seemed like a vacation. Booked back in December, before all hell broke loose, the luxuries were few and the chaos next to nothing. There were no fifteen-thousand-seat arenas, no hotel stampedes, no planes to catch. It was a good old-fashioned string of one-nighters through the endless British countryside, stopping at cities whose names and landmarks were as familiar as the nightly set of songs. Bradford, Leicester, Birmingham, Ardwick . . . the Beatles had covered these lonely roads repeatedly on their way up the rock 'n roll food chain, when it was exciting just to blow into the next town. They knew every turnoff and railroad crossing, every road stop, which stores had fresh cheese sandwiches on the counter or hot tea ready, the distance between filling stations and B and Bs. In the rural corners of the country, where endless stretches of miles were as bleak and isolated as the Gulag, they recognized the shortcuts and detours, the points where the roads were too narrow to get around the flatbed carts filled with hay or produce that inched their way along.

Brighton, Exeter, Plymouth, Bournemouth . . . How many times over the years the Beatles had been to Bournemouth! Playing the Winter Gardens and the Gaumont Cinema again and again until, unconsciously, they sensed the pulse of the audience. That was their kind of crowd, a bunch of impetuous shit-kickers, harkening back to the wild scenes at Garston and Litherland. Small and rough, no doubt about it, but welcome.

[II]

The Beatles never questioned the way Brian conducted business. The boys were stars and millionaires: all their wildest dreams had come true. Even later, when they suspected the worst—that "all the deals were bad," as George overstated it—there was no attempt to second-guess Brian's authority. No one wanted to derail the runaway train.

As a result, the Beatles had no indication at this time of how badly they'd been fleeced. Not about the shameful royalty rate with EMI, nor about the bargain-basement fees they received on the British package tours. At some point John and Paul would grow heartsick over their publishing arrangement, discovering that they simply gave away 50 percent of their rights—millions of pounds—to Dick James Music, but that was still several years off. There was the early closed-circuit concert fiasco, the ridiculous payout from United Artists. They got ripped off right and left.

There was other carelessness. NEMS' finances in America were particularly a mess. The proceeds from the last tour had been frozen by the Internal Revenue Service until it was satisfied that proper taxes were paid. That left the Beatles completely out-of-pocket for their five weeks of work. Moreover, during most of the tour Brian had effectively isolated himself from the outside world—there were strings of days when he simply disappeared—to the point that scores of producers and entrepreneurs bearing lucrative proposals, proposals the Beatles *should* have accepted, were unable to contact him. The number of important deals he let slip through his fingers is scandalous.

There was also the lingering suspicion that money was being squandered. The stories about the lifestyle Seltaeb's Nicky Byrne led must have made it seem that way. He lived regally and traveled in fast, flashy company. When the *Wall Street Journal* piggybacked a piece on Byrne with the next wave of Beatles merchandising deals, it sounded a thunderclap in the offices on Argyll Street. Those deals, the *Journal* reported, were worth anywhere from $40 to $70 million. Simple arithmetic clued in Brian as to the enormity of his blunder. His deal with Seltaeb had been for a measly 10 percent of the profits.

In August, Brian managed to renegotiate the deal, bringing the Beatles' cut up from 10 to 46 percent, but even that seemed insufficient. All Nicky Byrne was doing, it seemed, was issuing licenses—and reaping a fortune.

Offended, Brian decided to take matters into his own hands. Convinced that the operation was "a major ripoff" and that "Seltaeb was not accounting properly," he summarily canceled Seltaeb's authority to represent the Beatles abroad. He then instructed David Jacobs's office in London to begin issuing its own licenses directly to American manufacturers and, thus, collect identical fees. As soon as American companies got wind of the conflicting agreements, all bets were off. J. C. Penney and Woolworth's didn't waste a moment canceling $78 million worth of orders, which triggered a lawsuit by Nicky Byrne against Brian and Walter Hofer, seeking $5,168,000 in damages.

It took nearly three years to settle the suit, untangling thirty-nine separate claims against NEMS and a $22 million claim for damages, which eventually broke Nicky Byrne and rent the merchandising deal asunder. "The reality is that the Beatles never saw a penny out of the merchandising," says Nat Weiss, the avuncular divorce lawyer Brian befriended in New York who subsequently took over their American affairs. "Tens of millions of dollars went down the drain because of the way the whole thing was mishandled. Even after the judgment was vacated, you could smell the smoke from the ashes, that's how badly they had been burned."

Despite Brian's fumbling, the whole of London moved to the beat of the swinging Beatles soundtrack. Almost everyone credited them with the new and buoyant spirit that now seemed to seep into all phases of ordinary city life. The semimythical concept of "Swinging London" had not quite emerged—in fact, the term wasn't coined until April 1966*—but you could already feel its essence in the air. When Harold Wilson upset the Conservative political establishment and returned Labour to office for the first time since 1951, it signaled "a [new] kind of freedom around which hadn't been there before." Total dependence on American culture began losing ground to new, homegrown forms of expression that sparked a revolution in the arts and seemed to undermine traditional attitudes. This energy was already at work on the walls of London's galleries, where British pop art was in its earliest stages of experimentation. Several recent graduates of the Royal College of Art—including Peter Blake, Richard Smith, and David Hockney—were being exhibited all over the place, with a legion of talented young painters beginning to prowl the trail they had blazed. Fashion had been transformed by the cheeky insolence of clothing designer John Stephen, whose boutique turned a seedy lane in Soho called

---

* It was the creation of a team of American journalists for a Time magazine cover story, "You Can Walk Across It on the Grass," April 15, 1966.

Carnaby Street into "a Mecca for the Mods." As one convert recalls: "I can remember going down Carnaby Street in 1964 and feeling like my humdrum life was being reoutfitted. I'd never seen anything quite like it. There were so many different things you could wear—red corduroy trousers, green corduroy trousers, flowery shirts, polka dots everywhere. Before that, all we had were gray and brown."

The airwaves were still governed by the BBC's despotic monopoly over what was suitable for transmission, but beginning that Easter, a fleet of "pirate" radio ships moored offshore to the east of Essex or Kent, just outside the twelve-mile international-waters limit, and began broadcasting rock 'n roll on its own terms. Radio Caroline, and later Radio London, showcased the latest records, describing what was fashionable and delivering a new language, sprinkled with words like *fab* and *gear* and *dig*. British kids of every class could agree, in the abstract at least, that music cut through all the bullshit and eloquently expressed all the feelings—frustration, fear, rage, and passion—they'd suppressed for so long.

The Beatles managed to sit comfortably on the fringe of this cultural revolution, having already contributed quite substantially to it. It went without saying that they rejuvenated, if not reinvented, the local beat scene. Their clothes dominated teenage fashion with round-necked jackets and high-heeled boots. And they appeared daring and anarchic thanks to the cut of their long hair. "I can't overpitch this," writes journalist Nik Cohn in his treatise on fashion, *Today There Are No Gentlemen,* "the Beatles changed everything. Before them, all teenage life and, therefore, fashion, existed in spasms; after them, it was an entity, a separate society."

But the more the Beatles bathed in the limelight, the less they seemed willing to make a defiant splash. Considering that they had already scraped through the turbulent club scene, resigned themselves to the indignities of Hamburg, trudged cross-country in a circuit of endless one-nighters, overcome the age-old prejudice against northerners, conquered America, and captured the hearts of "ordinary blokes," it was all they could do to enjoy their fresh success. The Beatles weren't interested in upheaval. They wanted to make records, not statements. There was too much at stake, too much fever and magic, to antagonize their largely mainstream audience, leaving the extreme rule-breaking to newcomers like the Stones and the Who, both of whom were willing to be outrageous and risk everything for maximum impact.

The Beatles were the aristocracy of the new pop establishment, or "popocracy," as George Melly has called it. As such, there was no need for them to play the clubs. The nucleus of the pop elite required an exclusive place of their own where they could languish in the aura, preen, indulge themselves, and behave as only the famously hip knew how. For the Beatles, that place was the Ad Lib, a discotheque just off Leicester Square in the penthouse of what had been an unsuccessful jet-setter nightclub called Wips. Upstairs it had the perfect ambience: dark as a bank vault and mirrored from floor to ceiling, with alcoves and banquettes situated around a tiny dance floor, where fashionable young couples danced agilely to deafening music—good music, nonstop R&B—and stared at their own reflection. John and Ringo hung out there first, attracting members of the emerging pop establishment: rock groups and their managers, models and their photographers, young actors, boutique owners, groupies, columnists, and dandies of all stripes.

Every night, the band arrived—usually separately—about ten o'clock and held court at a banquette opposite the stage. Over the course of several hours (and more than several scotch and Cokes), they attracted an incongruous mix of awestruck young musicians who would crowd in around the table to compare notes while others stopped by briefly to pay their respects and buy the Beatles another round of drinks. The Stones usually turned up with an entourage, as did the Hollies, the Moody Blues, the Yardbirds, John Mayall, the Searchers, Georgie Fame—just about anybody who was making waves in the Beatles' wake. "It was a shouty, lively scene," Paul recalled. "Lots of silly things happened there." Silly things— away from prying eyes. For all that was unique about the club, for all its cachet, and all the words spent analyzing its contribution to the cultural boom, Paul offered a take on the Ad Lib that was probably closest to capturing its barroom spirit: "It was the pub, that's what it really was."

When a more intimate social scene was sought, the Beatles turned up at the frequent parties given by the West End's self-proclaimed "golden boy," Lionel Bart. One of Brian Epstein's buddies, Bart was one of the most prolific songwriters in London, already several years and a good dozen hits ahead of his beat-oriented protégés, having crossed back and forth over stylistic lines as often as a couturier. He'd discovered Tommy Steele *and* Cliff Richard, and wrote each of their debut hits, before really striking it rich with *Oliver!,* which was still packing theaters in London and New York.

As the owner of a rococo turn-of-the-century mansion on Seymour Walk, nicknamed the Fun Palace by its faithful, Bart played the Pearl Mesta role that suited his sprightly personality. His parties became instant legends as much for their self-indulgent behavior as for their stellar guest lists: Anthony Newley, Leslie Bricusse, Noël Coward, Richard Harris, Peter O'Toole, Brendan Behan, and David Bailey, each of whom brought someone equally alluring. "Michael Caine and Terence Stamp came for breakfast every morning," Bart recalls. "My next-door neighbor, Francis Bacon, showed up regularly. Peter Blake and Lucian Freud were longtime friends. And a typical party would also draw Princess Margaret, the Duke and Duchess of Bickford, the Rolling Stones, Cassius Clay—there could be six hundred people there from all walks of life."

At Bart's, John amused himself by being devious and petulant. "He liked to be outrageous—he liked to wind people up," provoking them into a confrontation. Most nights, he got stoned in the spacious Gothic toilet. Since returning from the States, John had become more and more devoted to the giddy pleasures of pot, smoking it intermittently throughout the day, from the time he got up until he collapsed from exhaustion. Then he curled up on a couch, brooding and sending out the kind of barbed-wire vibes that discouraged idle chitchat, let alone anything close to intimacy. Guests avoided him, knowing how lethal the combination of sycophants and drugs (and/or alcohol) could be for John. Of course, the more distant he became, the more the guests ignored him and the harder he had to strike out to draw enough attention. No one was immune. "Everyone who came in was a potential target," says a frequent guest. When Brian's favorite, Judy Garland, arrived on Sid Luft's arm one night, John berated her indiscriminately, implying that she was a hack and introducing her as "Judy Garbage." On another occasion, feeling "particularly wicked," he lashed out at an actor's German girlfriend, blaming her parents for killing 6 million Jews, until the poor girl fled in terror. Other times he was content to pick on Brian, embarrassing him about his sexuality—"If he pretended to be straight, for instance," says Bart, "John wouldn't let him get away with it"—in front of as many people as he could attract.

John's behavior was nothing new. It was the usual outlet for a lifetime of anger, anger at being given up by his mother and her subsequent death, anger at his father for abandoning him without a fair chance, anger at all the parochial teachers who demanded he conform, anger at Brian for tidying up the Beatles' jagged image ("I've sold myself to the devil," he complained to Tony Sheridan), and anger at trusted friends like Stu Sutcliffe, who died without warning, and now even Paul, who continuously upstaged him.

Lately, however, it was the inflexibility of his marriage to Cynthia, not his past, that piqued his darkest and most bilious moods. Cynthia had virtually abandoned her artistic aspirations, dedicating all her personal energy to intensifying her husband's star power. John couldn't help but bask in that glow. And on those occasions, he found the marriage safe and convenient, especially following a string of long gigs. But there were as many times—during those long intervals between tours—when the marriage felt confining and oppressive.

"Cynthia wanted to settle John down, pipe and slippers" according to Paul—a decision that, to his mind, spelled imminent disaster. "The minute she said that to me I thought, Kiss of Death, I know my mate and that is not what he wants." For another, they'd been cooped up rather annoyingly in the attic apartment of their new posh home while a team of local contractors gave the living quarters a thorough makeover. It had been hard enough living with Cynthia and Julian in the Emperor's Gate flat, but in the attic—and miles from nowhere—the situation groaned under the strain. To make matters worse, Cynthia's mother, Lillian Powell, recently returned from Canada, had moved in while John was on tour and now all of them squeezed into the accommodations like rabbits in a hutch. There wasn't an ounce of love lost between John and Mrs. Powell, a spiteful, insufferable woman who had never forgiven him for impregnating her daughter and fulminated against her son-in-law every chance she got.

"It was catastrophic for Cynthia," says Tony Bramwell, who made regular excursions to the house, delivering papers and other packages from NEMS. "She was stranded out there, with John in London or on the road most of the time." Incredibly, neither Cynthia nor John knew how to drive. They had bought a new Rolls-Royce that sat in the garage until a chauffeur was eventually hired, but even then, with few friends and a young son to take care of, any attempt to steal time away from home was futile. "I would frequently spend weeks of being virtually housebound by duties to child and staff," Cynthia complained in a memoir. Even when John was around, he usually slept until one or two, then took off for London, rarely coming home until the early hours of the morning, often stoned and drunk. Cynthia had learned to endure his new love of pot, which she viewed as being "relatively harmless" compared with alcohol, but despite the hip and social aspect of getting stoned, it was never something they would share. Alas, marijuana only made Cynthia "sick and sleepy," further distancing them in their eroding relationship.

Meanwhile, the other Beatles—all bachelors—seemed to be having the time of their lives. Ringo's relationship with Maureen Cox inched decisively toward the altar, although while she remained stashed conveniently in Liverpool, Ringo tooled around London with fashion model Vicky Hodge on his arm. The same occurred with George and Pattie Boyd. "George was the worst runaround of the bunch," says Peter Brown, voicing an opinion heard frequently. "He had lots of girlfriends. Lots."

Paul's situation was apparently even more enviable. With Jane Asher by his side, Paul claimed one of the most beautiful and classiest girlfriends on the scene. But he was shockingly cavalier about his intentions. "Freedom and independence" was the creed Paul lived by, and as far as Jane was concerned—well, she could like it or lump it. As far as Paul cared, he "wasn't married to Jane"; nothing else mattered as long as she understood he was "pretty free" to see whom he liked, which constituted, in his words, "a perfectly sensible relationship." Even while he lived with the Ashers, Paul admitted: "I got around quite a lot of girls. I felt that was okay, I was a young bachelor, I didn't feel ashamed of it in any way." To John, this arrangement was most extraordinary, if not the least bit galling. "He was well jealous of [it]," Paul recalled, "because at this time he couldn't do that, he was married with Cynthia and with a lot of energy bursting to get out. He'd tried to give Cynthia the traditional thing, but you kind of knew he couldn't. There were cracks appearing but he could only paste them over by staying at home and getting very wrecked."

Paul, on the other hand, lived between the cracks. Beatlemania was rampant in London, yet for some inexplicable reason he was free to move about with little regard for the usual encroachments. Throughout the end of 1964 and well into the New Year, Paul became a habitué of London nightlife, aggressively cultivating an image as a young man of substance. Each night, after the Beatles' business ended, he hit the streets like a tornado, picking up energy as he spun from theater to theater, nightspot to nightspot, often ending the whirlwind spree at one of the posh gambling clubs in Mayfair. Paul loved the upscale atmosphere almost as much as the recognition, both intoxicants to an ambitious young man only two years removed from a Liverpool council estate via Hamburg. There was a wide-eyed fascination as once-closed doors were flung open to him. "Right this way, Mr. McCartney." "Our best table, Mr. McCartney." "It's on the house, Mr. McCartney." *Mr.* McCartney! He could barely contain his joy over the classy ring to it.

Paul always aspired to tastes he perceived as having "class." Respect was class, fine art was class, French dining was class. Social status especially provided class, which he solicited in earnest through his ties to the Ashers. Whether it meant courting intellects such as Harold Pinter and, fearlessly, Bertrand Russell—Paul professed to be "very impressed by . . . the clarity of his thinking"—or having his cigarette lit by the maître d' at an exclusive joint like Annabel's, acquiring class became his overriding mandate. Now, with Jane's stabilizing influence, Paul staged an assault on legitimate theater, exposing himself to the best the West End had to offer, as well as maintaining a steady diet of repertory at the National. Jane herself was deeply immersed in the process of building a distinguished theatrical career. This pleased Paul no end. It was classy in and of itself and provided the perfect contrast to his celebrated splash. Besides, it kept Jane busy while he spread his wings on those nights he wished to fly solo, the upwardly mobile young bachelor haunting such tony nightspots as the Saddle Room, the Talk of the Town, the Astor, and other swish clubs where a "rubbing-up" occurred with famous and recognizable figures. Not that they intimidated Paul, who put his own Beatlesque spin on the situation: "They were on the way out," he concluded, "[and] we were on the way in."

[III]

But the social scene, for all its glamour and appeal, took a toll on their work. The critical reaction to the Beatles' second annual Christmas show had been less than enthusiastic. Even though its staging was more visually elaborate and the Beatles played their usually thrilling set of songs in a cocoon of screaming, nothing could excuse what some viewed as "the feebleness of the show as a whole." Despite deliriously happy audiences, the Beatles couldn't disguise their discomfort. "Obviously this show has its weaknesses," Paul conceded, but most reviewers had taken a harder look. In *NME,* Chris Hutchins echoed the consensus that the Beatles appeared "bored" and seemed to sleepwalk through the skits. "In the second sketch," he wrote, "these top world entertainers neither move, nor speak, nor sing. They're cast as waxwork dummies!"

Much the same could be said of their second film, *Help!* Unlike the groundbreaking *A Hard Day's Night,* which boiled over with reflexive wit and gave insight into the Beatles' lifestyle, *Help!* was a patchwork of generic wisecracks that sounded flat and artificial. The script, originally entitled *Eight Arms to Hold You,* about the possession of a ring with mysterious powers and those vying for control of it, had been tailored especially for Peter Sellers, who rejected it in favor of an equally frivolous picture called *What's New Pussycat?* Rewritten in ten days as a Beatles vehicle, the story took on a fractured, fairy-tale silliness from which it never recovered. No one was really happy with the script, least of all the Beatles, who called it "a mad story" as a cover for what they were saying in private.

Not that they could recall much from the shoot. They had packed ample reserves of pot to get them through the process. The Beatles were so stoned, so distracted, they couldn't remember lines. Brian's effort to contain the damage went for naught. Even though, as John revealed, they were "smoking marijuana for breakfast," mornings seemed to be the only time scenes got completed. By noon they were out of their gourds. "Dick Lester knew that very little would get done after lunch," Ringo recalled. "In the afternoon, we very seldom got past the first line of the script."

The only one of the Beatles who capitalized on the opportunity was Ringo, the unwitting star of *Help!* A lifelong movie fan, Ringo projected a vulnerability and unaffected appeal that had come across in *A Hard Day's Night* and now blossomed in *Help!* He'd always been the Beatles' unofficial mascot of sorts, the runt of the litter, less handsome and sophisticated than Paul, John, and George and, as such, often a lightning rod for their comic relief. There was also no other band that would have given him the visibility or highlighted his versatility, and by the time they blazed through the States, their intuition had paid off. "In a poll taken at Carnegie Hall," Nora Ephron wrote in her *New York Post* column, "Ringo received the most applause, screams, and gasps from the audience." "I Love Ringo" badges outsold all their other merchandise. The same proved true wherever the Beatles went. "In the States, I know I went over well," Ringo admitted in a moment of pardonable pride. "It knocked me out to see and hear the kids waving for me. I'd made it as a personality."

While Ringo would never be the Beatles' central attraction, in *Help!* he certainly made his presence felt. Perhaps part of the transformation was due to Ringo's feeling more settled. Two weeks before filming started, during a day off in London, he had married his eighteen-year-old girlfriend, Mary "Maureen" Cox, in an early-morning ceremony at Caxton Hall, a registry office near Ringo and George's Montagu Square flat. Everyone, especially George, expressed how "amazed" he was at the suddenness of it. It was a hasty, intimate affair, designed to provide the utmost privacy; even the other Beatles learned of it only a day in advance. Besides the couple's parents, very few people were invited. George arrived by bicycle, followed by John, who complained that Ringo had forgotten to buy them appropriate boutonnieres ("We were going to wear radishes actually," he told a reporter), and Brian, who served as the best man. (Paul, on holiday at a

Tunisian villa, learned of the wedding hours afterward, from an international operator who delivered a telegram from Brian that read, RICH WED EARLY THIS MORNING.) Everyone had been sworn to absolute secrecy.

There were plenty of reasons for that. "Maureen hated the spotlight and was worried that fans might disrupt things," says Roy Trafford, Ringo's boyhood friend, who was excluded from the event as a security precaution. "We went to the Ad Lib, and in the ladies' room Maureen confessed how hard everything was for her," Marie Crawford recalls. "Fans would scratch and spit at her all the time, and call her names. Why, the moment we walked in there, everyone stopped talking." But there was more to Maureen's discomfort than the harassment. "I recognized that weekend that Maureen was pregnant," Crawford says. "She was very sick in the mornings and was beginning to show."

In spite of everything, Ringo was excited to tie the knot. "He's the marrying kind," John explained after the news hit the papers, "a sort of family man," which was true enough. Only a few months earlier, Ringo had told a reporter: "No matter what the consequences, I don't want to remain single all my life. I want to get married some day and I don't plan to wait too long about it. I'm 23 now and that can seem pretty old when you look out every night and see an audience full of 13- and 14-year-old girls."

Ringo's celebrity meant something for the success of *Help!,* but in the end, it was the music that saved their hides. John and Paul had written a splendid collection of songs for the soundtrack. Gone are the standard progressions, rheumy lyrics, and simplistic arrangements. Structurally, the songs still abound with gorgeous, supple melodies complemented by sudden downshifts of chords and wiry guitar licks, interwoven with the sensuous three-part harmonies identified with the Beatles sound. But the creative momentum of the previous year, buttressed by marijuana and a powerful Dylan influence, had broadened the Beatles' perspective, giving them a new palette of ideas to draw from and explore.

In the weeks during their Christmas show, John and Paul had sketched out most of the material that would provide the soundtrack. John's music room in the new house—always littered with toys, hundreds of records, and "twelve guitars"—was suddenly ankle-deep in sheets of sloppy, pencil-smudged, nearly illegible lyric fragments, the terminally foul air severely polluted by a dense cloud of cigarette and marijuana smoke, aided and abetted by overflowing ashtrays and half a dozen half-filled teacups abandoned in the squalor. A pair of Brunell tape recorders (John claimed he "had about ten . . . all linked up") lay within arm's reach of the red couch, both of them overheated—practically cooking—from being left on for days, one or the other always frozen on PAUSE as though waiting for someone to finish his thought. Mostly John and Paul ignored the machines, preferring to jot ideas on paper that they ripped profligately from spiral-bound tablets like traders in the futures market. Sometimes words or phrases they'd considered perfect were rudely scratched out in favor of an alternative with a more wry twist to it. Almost every line of every verse was reworked several times. They spit words out quickly, not self-consciously, sometimes both of them talking over each other, testing rhymes and expressions and inflections in the outpour. Things sometimes got lost in the exuberant flow, but that had always been the way they worked best. "We made a game of it," Paul recalls. "John and I wrote songs within two or three hours—our 'time allotted.' It hardly ever took much longer than that." Or else they lost interest and moved on.

Almost immediately they struck on a tone that distinguishes these songs from their previous output. "Ticket to Ride," released as a single in advance of the movie, sounds like nothing a rock 'n roll band had ever produced. The entire character of the song is a drastic departure, with its reflective lyrics and tense, irregular patterns that make more demands on a listener. "It was a slightly new sound at the time," John said, upgrading "slightly new" to "pretty fucking heavy" in practically the next breath. Despite the hard language, no one disagreed with his opinion. His chafing vocals swerve around the rambling guitar lick and devious drum fluctuations that play havoc with the tempo, driving it to a playful, if inscrutable, ending. There is no bouncy middle eight, no obvious chorus. In "Ticket to Ride," John gives voice to self-pitying romantic disappointment, stripped of all adolescent pretensions and reduced to the bitter aftertaste that clings to rejection. "Resentfulness, or love, or hate—it's apparent in all work," he explained years later, during a particularly abrasive critique. "It's just harder to see when it's written in gobbledygook."

"Ticket to Ride" is hardly gobbledegook, and not at all the self-penned effort for which John eventually took credit. In a hasty reflection, he reduced Paul's contribution to "the way Ringo played the drums." However, Paul later argued: "We sat down and wrote it together. . . . [W]e sat down and worked on that song for a full three-hour songwriting session, and at the end of it all we had all the words, we had the harmonies, and we had all the little bits."

That wasn't always the way John and Paul wrote songs. "John and I don't work on the Rodgers and Hart pattern, one doing music and one doing lyrics," Paul explained in an uncharacteristic footnote about their creative process. "He writes a whole song on his own, or I write a whole song on my own, or if we do a song together either he might do the words and I the music, or the other way round."

Aside from "Help!" and "You're Going to Lose That Girl," which were near-perfect collaborations, the rest of the material fell somewhere within that boundless range. John brought in most of "It's Only Love" and "You've Got to Hide Your Love Away," while Paul contributed "Another Girl," which he wrote in Tunisia, and "The Night Before"—a mixed bag in the absolute sense. The one thing they have in common was that they are all Lennon-McCartney compositions. In the almost eight years of the partnership, it had seemed fruitless to try to reconcile their different styles—John's jagged emotional urgency, Paul's giddy romanticism; John's uncompromising, stripped-down homage to rock 'n roll, Paul's "lyrical melodies dressed in clever harmonic frameworks"; John "impatient," Paul "real optimistic"—because, in the larger picture, they merged seamlessly into the universally recognized Beatles sound. It serves no purpose trying to dissect the songs to determine who contributed what.

But energy and tone reveal their own clues. The influences for "You've Got to Hide Your Love Away" did not go unnoticed. According to Paul, the song "is just basically John doing Dylan." And the lyrics could never have come from McCartney.

Success begat insecurity—the greater the Beatles' popularity, the more threatened and anxious John had become, not only from his part in the band's snowballing commercialism but over his appearance and his song-writing as well. Weight, too, had become a nagging problem—John had gotten "plump," according to a friend—and he was demoralized and depressed by worsening vision. "He was paranoid about being short-sighted," George recalled, "and we'd have to take him into a club and lead him to his seat, so that he could go in without his glasses on and look cool."

Like Paul.

He was getting tired of hearing Paul described as "the handsome Beatle" or "the cute Beatle," tired of seeing Paul charm the media, posing as the band's spokesperson, voicing opinions he didn't share. Never had John seen anyone turn on the gas like that; throw the spotlight on him and he popped off like a parrot on speed. "He's a good P.R. man, Paul," John said, only half seriously. "He's about the best in the world, probably, he really does a job." Even as a rock 'n roller, Paul continued to court the kind of establishment approval that offended John. Paul was slick, as slick as they came—"He could charm the Queen's profile off a shiny shilling," says Bob Wooler and not at all kindly—and it stuck in John's craw. Paul still deferred to John, but skillfully. He knew how to play the angles, which is what it took to humor a cranky hothead like John. Paul could dance archly around his partner's subtle moods, but on tiptoe, always ready to concede center stage rather than risk confrontation.

"We were different. We were older," John believed. "We knew each other on all kinds of levels that we didn't when we were teenagers." Amenities were sacrificed in the transition. Gone was the extraordinary bond that had distinguished the first years of their partnership. In its place was a creative tension, an emotional chess game of sorts, whose pieces were toggled back and forth over squares of mutable interest, that seemed to satisfy each of their impulses to lead—and be led.

John plowed the tremendous emotional upheaval into his songs. He said "Help!" grew out of one of the "deep depressions" he went through, during which he fought the desire "to jump out the window." Clearly, he wasn't speaking literally; the people closest to John never recall any suicidal tendencies. But dissatisfied with the direction the Beatles were taking, coupled with his appearance and dispiriting marriage, he was left feeling despondent and "hopeless" during the writing. "I was fat and depressed and I *was* crying out for 'Help,'" John insisted later on, drawing that conclusion after years of psychotherapy. "He was feeling a bit constricted by the Beatle thing," Paul observed, although that impression, too, might only have become clarified over the years, with distance and more insight. George insisted that John developed that theory "retrospectively." At the time he began writing "Help!" it was fashioned as a work for hire upon learning from Dick Lester that it would be the movie's new title. Paul was summoned to Kenwood especially "to complete it," he recalled, which they did without delay, nailing it in one productive two-hour session in the upstairs music room.

[IV]

The Beatles spent the first half of 1965 in an exaggerated vacuum, ping-ponging between movie studio and recording studio. Socializing was out of the question. Aside from a brief holiday abroad the last week in May, Brian filled all their spare time with "non-stop" frivolous radio and TV appearances to plug the latest single, "Ticket to Ride," and to boost anticipation for the forthcoming film. Otherwise, there was precious little contact with the outside world.

In early May, during a break at Twickenham Studios, Brian showed up in a dither and assembled the Beatles in a dressing room. He behaved "rather secretively," according to Paul, who was more than used to Brian's affectations, but he sensed that something extraordinary was in the offing. "I've got some news for you," Brian announced with great theatricality, "the Prime Minister and the Queen have awarded you an M.B.E."

If Brian expected whoops of jubilation, he must have been roundly disappointed. None of the boys had any idea what he was talking about. M.B.E.: it might have been a sports car, for all they knew. Or better: a tax exemption. (George later joked that it stood for "*Mr. Brian Epstein.*") As mostly working-class lads from Liverpool, they had little insight into the proprieties surrounding titled Britons. In 1965, with the aristocracy still in high esteem, such honors seemed inaccessible and distant, if not other-worldly, to most commoners. And the Beatles, as famous and widely loved as they were, were still—in their own minds and English culture—as common as crumpets. They were clearly "astonished."

What they discovered was this: under a charter signed in 1917, King George V and his successors were empowered to recognize distinguished service to Crown and country through a clutch of five honorary awards. The highest rank was Knight or Dame Grand Cross (G.B.E.), then Knight or Dame Commander (K.B.E. or D.B.E.), followed by Commanders (C.B.E.) and Officers (O.B.E), before Members of the Most Excellent Order of the British Empire (M.B.E.). "The M.B.E., barely a notch above 'Guv,' is the sort of perk given out to senior hospital staff, school headmasters, and local government factotums," says a cultural historian, "but hardly the creme de la creme of U.K. social hierarchies." Still, it was coveted by recipients as a toehold to a knighthood—or at least as a license to dream—and for a while it was awarded sparingly, for acts of heroism in the war.

By the time the Beatles were considered, however, M.B.E.s were handed out as routinely as souvenir lapel pins. They were awarded twice annually—on the New Year and the Queen's birthday, in June—and each list of recipients submitted by the prime minister's office numbered in the thousands. "I think a grateful government must have given us the M.B.E. for all the taxes we paid," John joked, which wasn't that far off the mark. Harold Wilson told the press that he intended to use the honors list to encourage exporters, and while he personally admired the Beatles (he was originally, after all, their M.P. from Liverpool, Huyton), the award was for the "great commercial advantage in dollar earnings to this country" from the sale of 115 million records. Despite some initial concern from staff, Wilson dismissed all worry that the Queen would disapprove. It was "doubtful if Queen Elizabeth [had] time to read through all the 2,000 or so names and citations on the list, nor [was] it likely she would ever object to any of them," the press concluded.

"I was embarrassed," John said, recalling his initial reaction. "We all met and agreed it was daft." Jokes flew about the Queen's soundness of mind. Since it was policy to assure the palace that the award would be accepted in advance of a formal announcement, the Beatles took a consensus and agreed: "Let's not."

Eventually, Brian convinced them otherwise, but that didn't so much resolve their indecision as take it public. Opinion on the street was clearly divided on whether the Beatles were worthy of such an honor. The press was especially critical, taking an edge that dripped with contempt. "It seems that the road from rebellion to respectability is much shorter than it used to be," the *Sun* editorialized. Another caption referred to the musicians as "Sir George, Sir John, Sir Paul, and Sir Ringo," sounding a note of mockery. But the most vehement dissent came from an unexpected friend, Donald Zec, the *Mirror*'s entertainment columnist, who was said to be "irate" over the selection. "In the name of all that's sane if not sacred, isn't pinning a royal medal onto four Beatles jackets just too much?" he wondered. "What about the Dave Clark Five, the Bachelors, the Animals, and the Rolling Stones?" Only the *Daily Telegraph* struck a deferential tone, arguing that the honor was not sufficient enough and suggesting a "more generous award," such as a knighthood.

In the days that followed, controversy turned to vehement protest, as decorated M.B.E.s, furious over the Beatles' appointment, began firing off angry letters to the palace—and the press. "I am so disgusted with the Beatles being given this award that I am considering sending mine back," threatened George Read, an elderly Coast Guardsman decorated for bravery. Colonel George Wagg didn't wait. The aging war veteran returned twelve of his medals, quit the Labour Party, and took it out of his will, while another disgruntled war hero, Paul Pearson, returned his M.B.E. to the Queen, complaining that "its meaning seems to be worthless." And a former member of Canada's House of Commons, Hector Dupuis, shipped his medal back with a note denouncing the "superior authority's wish to honor sorry fellows with whom I have no desire whatever to be associated."

In the midst of the M.B.E. ruckus, the Beatles continued to record, padding their new *Help!* soundtrack with enough material for it to pass as an album. On the afternoon of June 15, Paul took center stage in Studio Two at Abbey Road and ran through what he considered to be "a strange uptempo thing" called "I've Just Seen a Face," which he wrote in the Ashers' music room at Wimpole Street. Originally titled "Auntie Gin's Theme," it was intended for the film but ultimately omitted, since it was still unfinished at the start of production. As Paul performed it now, however, it was all right there, right where he wanted it, a juggernaut of simple, streamlined lyrics that didn't flow so much as barrel along breathlessly, picking up steam—"dragging you forward," as he described the feeling—with each successive line. He'd sung it slower at one time, and with less of a country-and-western feel, but there wasn't a note out of place in the playback, leading him to feel "quite pleased with [the result]."

There was plenty of time left before the dinner break to lay down another track, and without much preparation, Paul led the Beatles into the frenzied, all-out rock assault, "I'm Down," intended as the B-side of the "Help!" single. Paul had mimicked Little Richard often over the years, belting out near-flawless covers of "Good Golly, Miss Molly," "Lucille," and "Long Tall Sally," but the spitfire intensity of "I'm Down" drove the style way over the top. It was inconceivable that a skinny white boy could make that kind of sound. With little rehearsal other than a brief run-through, Paul threw his head back and let loose with what a critic described as a "larynx-tearing, cord-shredding" vocal that nearly cut his boyhood idol for its ferocity. It was a frightening performance. There are moments during the song when it sounds as though Paul has lost all control of the vocal; he just keeps pressing, pressing, veering close to the point where the vocal exceeds the boiling point and dissolves into noise. Close—but not quite, thanks to the tightly contained boundaries set by Ringo's backbeat.

A light rain fell during the dinner break. The Beatles had run around the corner to a familiar coffee shop, where they spent slightly more than an hour scarfing down sandwiches, smoking, and exchanging personal news, probably about Paul's recent purchase of a house near Abbey Road. For most of the time they pointedly avoided talking about the session, which had gone as well as anyone expected. The songs they'd done that afternoon were certainly up to par and suitably polished—an accomplishment that must have given them satisfaction—even though they'd broken no new ground.

There were still a pair of additional tracks to record—"It's Only Love," which John and Paul had written as a throwaway for George, and

Ringo's party piece, a send-up of Johnny Russell's "Act Naturally"*—but Paul was eager to try something first. Tuning a Spanish-style acoustic guitar, he dragged a barstool to the middle of the cavernous studio and sat slope-shouldered over the wide walnut neck, tickling the strings, limbering up, while the engineers, Norman Smith and Phil McDonald, adjusted two mikes to suit George Martin's instructions. Curiously, the other Beatles stood around, smoking, attentive but uninvolved. There had been some early discussion about their roles in the forthcoming recording, but as plans progressed they'd decided to stay on the sidelines until Paul went through a take or two by himself, "as simply as possible."

To make Paul more comfortable, Martin had the studio lights dimmed to a shade resembling candlelight and moved the other Beatles out of his sight line before retreating with the engineers into the overhead control booth. There was a short last-minute lull while Smith spun dials to get a proper balance. When he finally flashed the thumbs-up, Paul stabbed out his cigarette in an ashtray, cleared his throat, and delivered a "remarkably controlled" take of a ballad that would become the most recorded song of all time.

━━ ━━

"Yesterday" had been rattling around Paul's head for nearly two years, since he "woke up one morning with the tune," tumbled out of bed, and before even washing his face ran through it at the upright piano propped against the wall by the window in his room. What was the source of his inspiration? The question gnawed at him for weeks afterward. Had it come in a dream, as he initially suspected? Was it something he'd heard that his subconscious refused to let go of? Paul hadn't the foggiest. The chords just kept coming, one after another, falling neatly into place. The melody sounded familiar, to say nothing of cozy, like one of the old standards that his father used to pound out after dinner at Forthlin Road, and while the overall impression it left was "very nice" indeed, Paul convinced himself the tune was "a nick," something he'd lifted.

And what a tragedy, too. The melody is gorgeous, with an effortless, natural flow that brings its evocative sound together. One chord doesn't so much suggest the next as dictate the progression, leaving no other option lest it collapse like a sand castle in a puff of mediocrity. From the beginning, Paul felt "it was all there . . . like an egg being laid . . . not a crack or

---

* Ringo had already recorded "If You've Got Trouble," which John and Paul had written for him, but it was scrapped after several unsuccessful takes.

a flaw in it." The melody haunted him. "It was fairly mystical," he explained. He couldn't let go of it.

Encouragement came from an array of trusted friends and sources. Lionel Bart remembers Paul turning up on his doorstep in late 1963 with the tune still fresh in his mind, wondering for all the world where he'd "pinched" it from. "He hummed it several times," Bart says, "and I couldn't place it. It sounded completely legitimate, wonderfully crafted." Bart was unsurprised by its sweep or maturity. "I recognized that in anything he wrote there was a musical signature, the kind of signature you find with Cole Porter and George Gershwin. In that respect, Paul's fingerprints were all over the score for 'Yesterday,' and I told him that night that he was onto something important."

Even with Bart's blessing, Paul was still dubious. "This one, I was convinced, was just something I'd heard before," he said, and continued seeking opinions in an attempt to prove it. But everywhere he turned, the trail went cold. No one recognized it, nor could they point to so much as a measure that resembled another song. Both John and George Martin pronounced it "original." And British chanteuse Alma Cogan, Paul's one-stop music source, expressed interest in recording it herself.

Legend has it that while he was playing the song on Cogan's piano, Alma's mother swept through the parlor wondering if "anyone want[ed] some scrambled eggs." Without missing a beat, Paul improvised a lyric for his new melody: "Scrambled eggs . . . oh my, baby, how I love your legs . . ." If his goal was to elicit laughter from the small audience, he was not disappointed—but it came at a cost. The words scanned the meter perfectly. Too perfectly, in fact: for more than a year he was unable to shake those awful lines.

"Scrambled Eggs" became Paul's nagging burden. Every day, every week, for a year and a half—without fail—he tinkered with it: massaging the chords, putting "the middle in it," playing with the pulse. Rhyme schemes were tested and discarded in search of a word or two that would give the song its identity. Colloquial expressions were picked over for a hook, even old standbys like "let it be," which was a favorite of his father's, enjoyed a brief tenure. No good—the right phrase, the one that would unlock the song and provide the way in, eluded him. This was an anomaly: rhymes, phrases—these were things Paul rattled off in his sleep, as a reflex. He had a rare talent for turning an unforgettable phrase: "P.S. I Love You," "Do You Want to Know a Secret," "Can't Buy Me Love" . . . It didn't figure that he'd go cold with a winner like this.

Lennon and McCartney had put songs aside before and come back to them; others they'd abandoned altogether. But this one—this one was different. Paul knew the melody was exquisite; it enchanted him. Frustrated, he finally ran it by John, who had nothing to offer. John thought the song was "lovely," but not in his jurisdiction. Besides, he'd heard it so often that he wanted nothing to do with it.

Nothing was settled on May 27, 1965, when Paul and Jane left for a two-week vacation at guitarist Bruce Welch's villa on the southeast coast of Portugal. The minute they touched down in Lisbon the words began to flow. It was a five-hour drive from the airport to the Gulf of Cádiz, along roads hewn from mountainous cliffs nearly the whole way. Brian had hired a chauffeured car for the trip, and the handsome young couple piled in the back, surrendering themselves to the dreadful drive south to Albufeira. "Jane was sleeping but I couldn't," Paul told a friend. The scenery was lackluster, monotonous, and before long he was at it again—running down "Scrambled Eggs," picking it apart, covering old ground. But as the car edged around Grândola onto the barren E1, the stumbling blocks began to give way. "I remember mulling over the tune . . . and suddenly getting these little one-word openings to the verse." *Da-da-da . . . yes-ter-day . . . sud-den-ly . . . fun-il-ly . . . mer-il-ly . . .* Somehow, the intimate drive with Jane had summoned up feelings of a different sort, of melancholy and solitude. Indecision had crept into the lyric's emotional complexion. No sooner was the foundation in place than the rhymes began to connect, blend, and serve one another. "'Yesterday'—that's good," he decided. "'All my troubles seemed so far away.'"

The minute they arrived in Albufeira, Paul put it to the test. Bruce Welch was waiting in the entrance to greet his guests and he remembered how eager Paul was to play the song for him. "He said straightaway, 'Have you got a guitar?'" Welch recalled. "I could see he had been writing lyrics on the way [from the airport]; he had the paper in his hand as he arrived." There was an old, abused Martin in the lounge, which Paul flipped upside down, enabling him to chord it with his right hand, then without hesitation, he strummed through the song.

As soon as he was halfway through the verse, Welch realized how far behind the curve he'd just fallen. This wasn't some three-chord rocker like the ones groups churned out over cigarettes and beer. From Elvis to the Shadows to the Beatles, the pop hits had always followed the same general form. It was easy to jump in almost anywhere and flog the big standard progressions that gave the music its intensity. Now, however, within a few sketchy lines, Paul had advanced the pop form with an inventiveness free of gimmickry, making it lyrical and vivid in ways he'd never imagined. "I didn't know those passing chords he had put into the progression," Welch admitted. But its sophisticated structure was the least of his fascination with it. It was the intangible quality of it that overwhelmed him and led Welch to say: "I knew it was magic."

The song was *exactly right* by the time he returned to London, on June 11. (Even so, Paul was demoralized by the tone of George Martin's initial reaction to the lyric. "I objected to it actually," Martin recalled, convinced that it would confuse anyone familiar with the Jerome Kern–Otto Harbach standard "Yesterdays.") "We tried ways of doing it with John on organ but it sounded weird," Paul recalled, "and in the end I was told to do it as a solo." But listening to the playback, Martin had other ideas. "What about having a string accompaniment, you know, fairly tastefully done?" he asked. Paul cringed at the suggestion, conjuring up strains of "Mantovani" and similar "syrupy stuff." That wasn't at all his style, but he agreed to at least try a string quartet.

"We spent an afternoon mapping it out," Martin recalled, devising cello and violin lines to complement the melody. Actually, arranging it wasn't that tough of a job. "Yesterday" lent itself majestically to the silken weft of strings, and the two men—Paul humming parts, searching for notes on the piano, with George Martin translating them into notation—created the quintessential "blue"-sounding accompaniment that underscores the record.*

The entire string overdub took less than three hours to complete. Martin booked four musicians from the orchestra of *Top of the Pops*—session players he'd worked with on a regular basis—and walked them through the parts. After the first take, Paul pulled Martin aside and complained about the heavy shading of vibrato the string quartet had added to fatten the sound. "It sounded a little too gypsy-like for me," Paul recalled. Normally, he took Martin's opinions to heart, appreciating the producer's vast musical training, but this time Paul stuck to his guns—every last shiver of vibrato had to go—convinced, and rightfully so, that the outcome "sounded stronger."

The only thing left to decide was the awkward question of billing.

---

* *"Blue" notes were John and Paul's shorthand for sounds that fell somewhere between two notes, often the result of a minor note played against a major.*

"Yesterday" may have evolved under the group banner, but it was by no means a *Beatles* record. Not only had Paul written it entirely himself, there wasn't another member of the Beatles on it. The implications were clear. It would be difficult for EMI in good conscience to put it out as anything but a Paul McCartney single. That wouldn't sit well at all with John, Martin knew, whose ego was in fragile enough shape without shifting more attention toward Paul. Still, Martin took that suggestion to Brian Epstein, arguing that the performance on "Yesterday" warranted a solo release. Brian, to his credit, wouldn't hear of it. He was adamant: "No, whatever we do we are not splitting up the Beatles."

But in a way, the bubble was already beginning to burst.

[I]

The Beatles had undergone quite a change since their first trip to New York in early 1964, when they sprang up like clothespin cutouts on the stage of *The Ed Sullivan Show*. Outwardly, they remained the same lovable mop tops, their smiles as familiar and flashy as the grille on a late-model Jaguar, their extreme hairdos every bit as symbolic as the Queen's crown. Privately, however, they were in transition. If, with *Beatles for Sale*, the band had reached the limits of the conventional three-minute song, then certainly *Help!* had spun them down paths into uncharted territory. Though they still cursed, drank, and fucked their way around the globe, there was something about the way they comported themselves that was sensible and precise. But the generation gap was widening, and with it came rising expectations and a feeling that they could no longer afford to play the charming but cheeky lads.

To keep ahead of the curve, the Beatles had relied on pot, a magic key to unlocking inhibitions and abandon. That was fine for an appetizer, but everything—especially the music—was changing so fast, and with it, their impulse to experiment. Together, the Beatles had crept into a darkened box at the Albert Hall in May to catch Dylan's riveting performance and left speechless, in awe. He seemed so intense, so emotionally *out there*, expressing himself at enormous risk. How did he manage to work from inside like that, to set himself free and arrive at that remarkable place? What enabled such a release?

John and George found part of the answer quite by accident one night while they were at a dinner party at the Victorian flat of a prominent dentist on the Edgware Road. The evening had peculiar, almost sinister overtones that made them uneasy from the get-go. Both Beatles had heard stories about the dentist's notorious dark side, about the kinky scenes that he staged and his appetite for orgies. Though that hadn't stopped the boys from bringing along Cynthia and Pattie, their radar was tuned rather high from the moment they walked through the door.

Nothing out of the ordinary cropped up until after dinner, when the Beatles prepared to leave. According to George, their gregarious host insisted they remain for coffee, during which he watched them soberly, silently, smiling, smoking, taking an inordinate interest in the girls. Afterward, he huddled in a corner, talking animatedly with John.

"We've had LSD," John finally revealed to George in a bone-dry voice. The acid had been slipped into their coffee on sugar cubes and might have been an after-dinner cordial, for all George knew.

It meant nothing to George, who was determined to leave. "I seem to recall that I'd heard vaguely about it," he remembered, "but I didn't really know what it was, and we didn't know we were taking it." Virtually nothing had been written about the cryptically named drug; there was no buzz about it on the street. So little was known about LSD, in fact, that it wasn't even illegal. This acid, however, had a distinguished provenance, having been supplied to the dentist by the manager of the Playboy Club, who, in turn, had gotten it from Michael Hollingshead, the man responsible for turning on Timothy Leary. Which meant that it was pure—and potent.

John was livid. He had not come to dinner to be dosed by a virtual stranger. Mumbling good-byes, they grabbed the girls and bolted, speeding toward the Pickwick, a London nightclub, with the dentist in hot pursuit. For a few minutes everything was fine. They got seated and ordered drinks, squinting in the low light to identify the faces of other musicians who waved to get their attention. "Suddenly I felt the most incredible feeling come over me," George remembered. "It was something like a very concentrated version of the best feeling I'd ever had in my whole life." He was overcome with love—hot, feathery, dizzying love. The others must have felt it, too. John, especially, had a grotesque grin plastered across his face that looked as if it belonged on a marionette. Streaks of blazing light burrowed behind the rainbow rims of their eyelids, trembling; something had altered the tone of their bodies. The sensations held them captive. It is uncertain how long they sat there like that. No one recalls seeing the performance, but at some point they got up to leave and realized, in a panic, that the club was empty, the waiters busily placing chairs atop the barren tables.

Someone—it is not certain who—mentioned the Ad Lib, which was within walking distance, just a few blocks north. That seemed to make sense—that is, until they got outside, where the gnarled skew of lights and jangly sounds bombarded them. If their eyes could be believed, the sky was velvet, opaque, the buildings rimmed with jewels. The act of walking became overlaid with intervals of clumsiness and the need to vent anxiety. Everyone was "cackling" like hyenas. Pattie Boyd, normally a picture of cool poise, came undone in the garish neon nightscape. She cowered, trapped in the glare of blinking lights and the sound of car horns swelling and roaring around Leicester Square. Even with the others' reassuring companionship, the acid flung her into fitful emotional states that alternated between dread and agitation. Later, "half crazy," she threatened to break a store window until George dragged her away. "We didn't know what was going on and [thought] we were going crackers," John explained. "It was insane going around London on it."

Beyond insane. A tiny red light in the elevator to the Ad Lib touched off a folie à quatre in which they imagined flames shooting up into the air-conditioned car. Said John, "We were all screaming, 'aaaaaaagh,' all hot and hysterical." Ringo, who was waiting for them upstairs in the crowded discotheque, recalled how they tumbled out of the elevator, shouting: *The lift's on fire!*

The bizarre hallucinations continued until dawn, nightmare flashes interspersed with periods of sublime intimacy, laughter, and intense creativity; objects took on a fun-house distortion that exaggerated their appeal. John, enraptured by the experience, summed up the extremes by saying: "It was just terrifying—but it was fantastic." It wasn't anything like the fluttery highs they got from speed or pot. The LSD possessed an undeniable power—a *spiritual* power—that forced them to look inside themselves. Indeed, it seemed to offer everything John had been searching for in his music, writing, and art. And none of the Beatles was more receptive to LSD's spiritual potential than George Harrison. From that very first trip, he felt "a light bulb" go on in his head that blazed the way to enlightenment. Years of misfit indifference to school and the alienation it generated had left him immature and callow. Even the cheeky facade that served as George's personality in the Beatles collapsed behind the scenes in the auras of Lennon and McCartney, exposing the gawky, awestricken boy who used to trail behind his mentors in Liverpool. Having always competed for their favored attention, he had learned to fit in, not stand out. Feelings of inferiority persisted, reinforced in part by his age, John's and Paul's intimidating talent, and the lingering ambivalence of their companionship.

It was this sense of alienation as much as his interest in music that made George so susceptible to guiding spirits. In the Bahamas during the filming of *Help!*, he heard the siren song of the sitar and came under the influence of Swami Vishnu-devananda, who introduced him to hatha yoga and Eastern religions. Later in life he would become vegetarian, consult an astrologer, and devote himself to Transcendental Meditation before embracing traditional Christianity. Like many others who flirted with mysticism, it gave him a sense of authority and confidence. But with LSD, George stepped out—and into the cosmic consciousness.

"Turn off your mind, relax, and float downstream": it would eventually become the mantra of every seeker of enlightenment for whom experimentation and self-discovery were the portals to the new age. But in July 1965, after their first unwitting trip, the two Beatles were too shook up by the experience to storm those precarious gates. There was "too much to sort out," George said, too much of an emotional upheaval. It would take another six weeks before they got up the nerve to take a second trip. In the meantime, they spread the gospel, cornering anyone who would listen to the fantastic tale. There was a fish-story extravagance to the retelling of the Great Acid Experience. "Each time they recounted it," says a Beatles intimate, "the hallucinations got wilder and more incredible. They introduced marvelous visions and rainbow-colored submarines and all kinds of crazy stuff." Friends and musicians were held in thrall by the shifting pool of details, and some, no doubt, felt inclined, or even pressure, to dive into the deep end, including the one companion for whom it would have disastrous effects.

[II]

From the moment George and John sang the praises of LSD, Brian Epstein had made up his mind to take it. Friends remember that he had been trying for some time to find a buffer for his snowballing unhappiness. For all his outward poise, Brian seldom spent a waking moment without being medicated to some extent. Amphetamines had served him ably through the tension-filled days—a blast of speed to keep him *up*—followed by a capful of Seconals washed down by brandy before bedtime to ensure a soft landing. Even so, he took great pains to maintain a respectable front. Few people—not even the Beatles, at this point—were privy to his indulgence. At a party with "some kids" arranged by Nat Weiss, Brian chattered, clowned, danced, and played disc jockey—long after everyone had passed out. "The next morning, when we woke up, he'd be refreshed, making notes," Weiss recalls. It wasn't until sometime later that he discovered Brian's secret. "He had suits made with little pockets on the inside, with pills tucked into each of them, which he popped like candy. And he told me that this was what kept him going." Amphetamines and pot: he had a person come by the house each week to roll thin little joints that he'd stash in a cigarette case, behind the Dunhills.

As the summer heated up and the demons became intolerable, Brian moved from the designer flat in William Mews to considerably more glamorous quarters in a Belgravia town house on Chapel Street that he decorated from top to bottom with the sleek white furniture that was all the rage that season. Together with his longtime Liverpool friend Peter Brown, who had moved to London in May to lend a hand around the office, Brian got everything situated and resumed a frantic social pace: drinking, carousing, dinner parties, anonymous sex, and nightly drug-taking until he passed out in the early hours of morning.

The drugs fortified him for the social scene, but there was still a key element missing. Nothing satisfied Brian unless some kind of risk was involved. "He loved the danger, no matter what the cost," says Ken Partridge, "whether it was bringing home a guardsman who would rough him up for twenty quid or dropping a bundle at a joint on Curzon Street." The Curzon House, behind the Hilton Hotel, was only one of the posh clubs that played host to Brian's rampant gambling habit. "He was a heavy gambler," says Terry Doran, a boyhood friend who had come to London in the recent wave of migration that brought northerners to the Smoke. Doran, who spent a great deal of time bouncing around the clubs, would encounter Brian late at night during his own furtive escapades. "In Liverpool, he gambled at the Rembrandt and a couple of other places, losing more often than not. The dough wasn't very much—maybe fifty or a hundred quid. But in London it started to get serious." Doran, who came from a dirt-poor family, watched in horror one night as Brian placed an £8,500 bet at the White Elephant. Toting Francis Bacon along as a guest, he went to the Clermont and promptly lost a cool £10,000. Another time Nat Weiss "watched him drop $17,000 in one quick moment." In fact, if he happened to hit a jackpot, he wouldn't even bother to pick it up. Paul recalled running into Brian at the Curzon House, his jaw "grinding away" on pills, when his money had run out—but not his determination. "I remember Brian putting his Dunhill lighter on a bet—'That's a hundred pounds'—and he'd lose it all."

Throughout the summer of 1965, Brian continued to pick up rugged hustlers or other undesirable characters and take them back to Chapel

Street for a night of forbidden excess. Lionel Bart remembers the time he hired a muscle-bound guardsman to abuse him—"the guy asked Brian what he had in mind and was told, 'Whatever you like, as long you don't break anything.'" Brian would show up at the office sporting "great purple bruises" or a black eye. One morning Ken Partridge was met at the door by Joanne Newfield, Brian's young personal secretary, who wore a look of shocked distress. Between clenched teeth, she warned him, "You're not going to believe this," and ushered him into the living room. A few weeks earlier, Partridge had overseen the installation of a magnificent Crowders oak staircase that led from the entrance hall up to Brian's study. "And when I walked in there, the whole staircase was piled up on the floor like matchwood," Partridge recalls. "He told me he'd picked up two guardsmen at the [Golden] Lion but, after a drink, decided that he only wanted one of them. So, on the staircase, they beat the shit out of each other—and then out of Brian."

Another night, remembers Terry Doran, "he came back with some hunk that he was totally infatuated with, who then proceeded to rob him. But he enjoyed it—he really enjoyed getting robbed." Doran recalls how the same person "took him off" again and again, as if it were a sport, a perverse sport. "George Harrison bought Brian a beautiful watch for his birthday—a really extravagant piece of jewelry, more expensive than a Dunhill. A month or so later he took this guy back to Chapel Street, and the guy robbed it. So Brian had to buy another one, because he didn't want George to know what had happened to it."

Between all this, business continued. In early 1965 Brian arranged to meet with Vic Lewis, the celebrated big-band leader whose agency now booked American acts throughout the U.K. Lewis was "a fantastic character," according to people who knew him, "a cricket-loving, jazz-loving hypochondriac." A short man—under five foot eight—he "looked very much like a Persian carpet salesman," with the manner to match. "There wasn't a day he wasn't ill," says a colleague. "But it was never anything that normal people had. One day he'd say, 'I don't know what it is, but my *hair* hurts.' Another day, his *tongue* wouldn't feel right."

Lewis controlled GAC's substantial roster of stars for the U.K. territory, but even more important was his marked foothold in the London entertainment establishment. "Norman Weiss [GAC's president] rang Brian and advised him to buy me out—which he did—at which point he suggested that I run *his* agency," Lewis recalls. NEMS absorbed all Vic Lewis's acts, among them Andy Williams, Johnny Mathis, Mel Tormé, Sarah

Vaughan, David Rose, Percy Faith, Anita O'Day, Tony Bennett, Henry Mancini, Herb Alpert, and Nelson Riddle. The ink wasn't even dry on the deal when comedian Allen Sherman turned up for a concert tour, and after that, an appearance by the great Groucho Marx. A few months later they "took on" the Moody Blues, who "were crumbling at the time," according to Tony Bramwell, but remained a fairly important name on the scene. There was also a new kid, an American expat who was still pretty raw, by the name of Jimi Hendrix.

"With Vic, NEMS really picked up steam," says Bramwell, "and within a year we were the biggest entertainment agency in the world." That was, of course, an exaggeration, but NEMS had certainly leapfrogged into the major leagues. "Instantly, it gave them size and an international reputation," says Don Black, who came aboard as part of the Vic Lewis deal. The gifted Black, who had already written a string of hit songs and would later win an Oscar for "Born Free," had a special place on the staff inasmuch as he personally managed the career of Matt Monro, "the English Frank Sinatra." The connection paid off handsomely, too: George Martin, Monro's producer, gave the vocalist first dibs on covering "Yesterday," which shot to the top of the charts.

"The office was growing, the joint was jumping," recalls Black, who moved into a cubicle down the hall from Brian. A skeleton staff had been cached during the launch of Beatlemania, but now NEMS scrambled to recruit talented folks who could handle the serious flow of work. Wendy Hanson had been hired in New York as a favor to Capitol Records, and she had steered Brian through one crisis after another. Geoffrey Ellis, the starchy ex-Oxford lawyer who had known Brian from Liverpool, was prevailed upon to "run the office." Along with Alistair Taylor and Tony Barrow, Brian formed the nucleus of a staff necessary to oversee the expanded organizational effort: capable, serious-minded managers whose experience would ensure growth and efficiency. Even Peter Brown, whose as-yet-undefined position rendered him more of "a glorified office boy," proved skillful at handling many aspects of the business—to say nothing of those surrounding Brian's personal life, which, frankly, not many other people would have wished to handle.

Of course, it was still the Beatles that everyone desired. On a particularly busy evening when phones were ringing off the hook, Black remembers picking up a call from the producer of *The Lucy Show* in New York, who'd been trying desperately to reach Brian. She explained how they were preparing to film a segment in London. If the logistics could be worked out, Lucille Ball wanted to walk down Piccadilly, do a double-take, and see the Beatles standing on the corner. It would be only a ten-second shot, for which the network was willing to pay $100,000. But Brian wanted nothing to do with it. Furthermore, he warned Black *never* to interrupt him with such a ridiculous request.

It seemed like madness at the time, but Brian was right. Everyone wanted some time with the Beatles—ten seconds, thirty, a minute and a half, *just an hour or two*. The office was inundated with calls like that every day, and not just three or four good offers but sometimes twenty or fifty. The Lord Mayor of Birmingham needed their support for a favorite charity, David Frost requested an interview, *Sunday Night at the London Palladium* would settle for a walk-on—"they won't have to say a word"— two minutes with the P.M. to discuss communications, a scene in some Hollywood movie, backup vocals for the Animals, their own TV special . . . it never ended. As heartless as it sounds, it seemed there were more dying children with a last request for one of the Beatles to bid them farewell than there were healthy ones. And each request drew the same cold response: no! Not on any condition. *Nada. Non. Nein.*

They'd already been through this with the cripples. At the outset of Beatlemania, handicapped or deformed children were wheeled into the theaters and placed along the front, at the foot of the stage, before each performance as a goodwill measure. "We were only trying to play rock 'n roll and they'd be wheeling them in, not just in wheelchairs but sometimes in oxygen tents," recalled George. "We'd come out of the bandroom to go to the stage and we'd be fighting our way through all these poor unfortunate people." To make matters worse, they were the only part of the audience the Beatles could see from the stage, and the distraction was unimaginable. John would gaze down at a child whose drool hung in a solid string from mouth to lap, and he'd pfumpf a line. Spastics trying to clap would accidentally smack themselves in the face. Epileptics would have seizures in the middle of songs. "You felt like you were at the shrine at Lourdes," says Nat Weiss. Even after the shows, it never let up. "Crippled people were constantly being brought backstage to be touched by a Beatle," remembered Ringo. Parents would traipse into the dressing room with terribly deformed children who had no idea where they were or who they were looking at, and then *the parents would leave.* "They'd go off for tea or whatever, and they would leave [the kids] behind."

Fed up with the continued imposition, John took to doing "spastic impersonations" while onstage. According to Paul, "he had a habit of putting a clear plastic bag on his foot with a couple of rubber bands" and stumbling around in a circle, until Brian had seen enough. "Finally, he took it upon himself to say 'no' to every request by the parents of these kids and even to the hospital wards," says Nat Weiss. "It was depressing the Beatles, and he couldn't expose them to it any longer."

Nada. Non. Nein.

Early in July, after looking over their schedule, Brian announced to the press that contrary to the group's usual practice, the Beatles would not be doing any radio or TV appearances to promote their new record. He was imposing a media blackout, although he didn't call it that, and to underscore his point, he canceled their appearances on *Ready, Steady, Go!,* on *Top of the Pops,* and on *Thank Your Lucky Stars,* substituting, in lieu of the boys, a rather feeble clip of the Beatles lip-syncing to "Help!"

The very next day, predictably, the tabloids made headlines out of the announcement, overshadowing an Australian initiative in Vietnam, and fans across Great Britain reached for their pens and fired off angry letters to local editors, damning the Beatles as insensitive prima donnas. "These lads have become far too big for their boots," wrote Anne Laury of Harrogate, "and it's time the fans paid them back and quit forking out their hard-earned pocket money to buy their records." Another disappointed teenager complained, "I used to be one of the Beatles' biggest fans . . . BUT I'm beginning to wonder. . . ." An *NME* poll of its readers revealed that a majority of fans felt cheated, accusing the Beatles of "taking a leaf from Mr. Presley's book." Still, Brian stood firm, and just in case that wasn't crystal-clear, NEMS dashed off a press release emphasizing that the Beatles would "definitely not tour Britain" for the remainder of the year.

The strategy behind this maneuver was entirely pragmatic. Brian had no intention of alienating anyone; he had argued with the Beatles for years about staying accessible to the fans. But John's second book of nonsense, *A Spaniard in the Works,* was published in early July, earning mostly puzzled, if not outright negative, reviews, and soon after that *Help!* took a beating from the once-adoring critics, with *NME* calling it "100 minutes of nonsense" and, worse, "unfunny." Part of the backlash, Brian was convinced, arose from the Beatles' being everywhere at once—in print, on record, in the news, on the telly, in the movies. "It was saturation point," John agreed. "You couldn't walk down a street without having us staring at you." It stood to reason that when the press finally got good and bored with singing the band's praise, they'd amuse themselves by taking pot-shots. Making the Beatles scarce took them out of the critical crosshairs. It would offset the constant glare of exposure, giving them distance and creating demand. "We need less exposure, not more," George said. "It's been Beatles, Beatles, Beatles."

Whether George realized it or not, the audience wasn't tired of the Beatles as much as grown weary of the Beatles' glossy personae. While "the Beatles had inspired an upheaval in pop music, mores, fashion, hairstyles, and manners," as Robert Shelton wrote, a new attitude was developing among rock 'n roll partisans that had no musical antecedent and distanced itself from the tame protopop that, up to now, had sustained the form. Its enthusiasts, who defined themselves culturally instead of by age, offered a tough, toothier alternative—*rock,* as opposed to rock 'n roll—steeped in gritty urban blues, art school romanticism, and folk music's outsider intellectualism. A trend emerged, inspiring songs with more meaningful lyrics intent on saying something about reality, conformity, and injustice.

The spectacle of four irrepressible woolly-jumpered lads shaking their hair and trilling, *"Oooooooooo,"* was inadequate for the emerging rock culture, and the Beatles knew it. "Things were changing," Paul realized. "The direction was moving away from the poppy stuff, like 'Thank You Girl,' 'From Me to You,' and 'She Loves You.'" Shrewdly, the Beatles anticipated the need to move with it.

All of that, however, took a backseat to the upcoming American tour.

By the end of the first week in August, the preparations were all but complete. The bags were packed, the wives and girlfriends provided for. John and Paul spent one of their last days in London producing a cover of "You've Got to Hide Your Love Away" for the Silkie, a quartet of long-faced Hull University students that Brian had signed to NEMS; otherwise, most of the last-minute arrangements focused not on music but on real estate. Ringo and Maureen closed a deal on a small but graceful estate, Sunny Heights, literally around the corner from John and Cynthia's place in Weybridge. With a baby on the way and the ongoing harassment from fans, they felt it was easier to live in the suburbs. Paul didn't share their concerns and was about to be ensconced in his handsome, newly renovated three-story Regency house on Cavendish Avenue, near Abbey Road. George had already moved into a modest California-style bungalow in Esher, about twenty miles south of the city. And in one final and overdue act of generosity, John bought Aunt Mimi an ivy-covered cottage in Poole, set in a loose cluster of houses just off the dunes, with a long front porch and a bay window that gave a huge, breathtaking view of the English Channel.

Finally, on the morning of August 13, as a heat wave swept in and scorched the streets with ribbons of heat, the Beatles and their entourage piled into the first-class cabin of a Pan Am Clipper and took off into the desolate white sky, leaving the last traces of innocence behind.

[III]

No sooner had the Beatles touched down in New York than the shift in the scene was evident. Music was everywhere; it seemed to have taken over the streets. They not only heard the new groove on the radio but could *see* it in the styles as well as the manner in which the kids carried themselves. Everywhere they turned there was a residue of the cultural fallout. The airwaves were awash in popular records by the Byrds, Sonny and Cher, Jody Miller, the Turtles, the Dixie Cups, and Bob Dylan. "The Eve of Destruction" belabored the stinging social message by whining, "This whole crazy world is just too frustratin'." Even the Righteous Brothers, their throwaway opening act from the last U.S. tour, had hijacked the Top Ten with the symphonic tearjearker "Unchained Melody," and as the Beatles' caravan of limos plodded like circus elephants into the city, everyone inside remarked how cool and sexy the Brothers' last hit, "You've Lost That Lovin' Feelin'," had turned out. Little did they know that, at that very moment, Mick Jagger was aboard the luxury yacht *Princess* moored in the Hudson River, dancing on deck to a test pressing he'd been given of the new Bob Dylan single, "Like a Rolling Stone."

The scene had shifted slightly downtown and farther west, to the Warwick Hotel at Fifty-fourth Street and Sixth Avenue, but gone was the "happy hysteria" evident during the Beatles' previous visits. This crowd was determined—ferocious. About fifteen hundred strong, they confounded the more than one hundred "tense and red-faced" cops who were brought in to provide security at the hotel, breaking through barricades and storming police lines. Everywhere one looked there were scuffles, aggression, and discord, not only between female fans and the police but also with malevolent construction workers who egged on the violence from atop nearby scaffolding.

Gone was the innocence that had accompanied the previous tour. There was no official greeting at the airport, no prearranged waving to the fans; despite a heavy turnout at Kennedy Airport, the boys remained completely out of sight throughout the arrival process. Later, at the requisite press conference, they showed none of the staccato wit that paced earlier performances. Their answers came fast, to be sure, but were strained and with a contemptuous edge, indicating how bored they had become with the "farcical affairs." Even the hotel situation grew strange. Outside of a few scheduled appearances, the Beatles remained locked in the Governor's Suite on the thirty-third floor. There was no sneaking off to a restaurant or club, none of the easy socializing with deejays and the press. Part of this turnabout might be ascribed to drugs; the Beatles didn't mind drinking scotch and Cokes or cursing in front of journalists, but smoking dope was too dicey. Or they'd simply had it with the barrage of inane questions.

The only visitors to the suite were other performers, some old friends reasserting old claims, with new acquaintances scrambling for a place in the entourage. Frank Sinatra, who once derided the Beatles as "unfit to sing in public," sent a valet bearing an invitation to a private party. (The Beatles politely declined.) Bob Dylan and Del Shannon arrived early, to much hurrahs, followed by the Supremes, who were treated to "the coolest reception [they'd] ever received." The girls showed up alone, without their handlers, looking like porcelain figurines, outfitted in precious day dresses accented with hats, gloves, costume jewelry, and little fur wraps. One can only imagine the impression this made on the Beatles, considering they were stoned and behaving in an excessively silly manner. "We felt we had interrupted something," recalled Mary Wilson, who couldn't fathom what the boys kept laughing about and left in a flash with Florence and Diana.

Ronnie Spector wasn't "so square," like the Supremes, but even she "sensed that something strange was in the air" since the Ronettes' last visit in 1964. Sometime after she arrived, Spector recalled, John steered her into one of the bedrooms, where a handpicked audience was packed along the walls watching a young girl have "sex every which way" with "one of the guys in the Beatles entourage." Then, in another bedroom, with liquor and a magnificent view to embolden him, John tried to talk her into a more intimate scene.

The atmosphere surrounding the Beatles was turning cruel and pitiless. Instead of reshaping their image, they were sharpening it in ways that offered no identifiable quality. Most everyone who came into contact with them could feel it. Larry Kane, the young Miami newscaster who had accompanied the previous tour, rejoined them in New York and was startled by the edge of detachment that had crept over the entourage. "It was alarming how hard-shelled everyone had become," Kane says. "There was a kind of Us and Them mentality to protect against the outside world." The Beatles had always been circumspect, even distrustful, toward outsiders. "Now, there was an ambiguousness about everything, a way in which they kept you off balance. One moment they could be playful or attentive; if they were in a bad mood, however, they might try to intimidate you—or simply freeze you out. You never knew what to expect. And I got the sense that they liked it that way."

Not liked—but needed. The demands on the Beatles were extraordinary, the characters and situations growing less distinguishable. More so than ever, they had no idea what they were getting themselves into.

On Saturday, August 14, they taped their third—and final—appearance on *The Ed Sullivan Show*. Chris Hutchins remembers sitting in the studio audience next to Cilla Black, who was also on the bill, and marveling at how hard the boys worked to put their set across. "Four hours of constant rehearsals," according to Hutchins. "Six songs, no break, just total dedication." Getting an adequate sound balance was further complicated by a solo spot featuring Paul playing an acoustic version of "Yesterday." But though the configuration was highly irregular, the performance otherwise came off without a hitch.

As the sun went down, the Beatles boarded a helicopter on the East River, bound for Shea Stadium, in Flushing, New York. It was a clear, sumptuous night, and as the aircraft lifted up, the jagged silhouette of the city, tinted by speckled neon light, resembled a vaulted jewel box. The Beatles, looking gaunt-faced and anxious, barely glanced at the scenery. They actually loved New York—George called it "one of the most amazing cities in the world"—but between the helicopter, which they dreaded, and the destination, which seemed unreal, it was all they could do to keep their food down.

A 56,000-seat horseshoe where the perennially crummy Mets played baseball, Shea Stadium was bathed in a halo of opalescent light and looked more like a stage prop from eight thousand feet up. "For the boys," recalls Barrow, "seeing the stadium was an absolute high. They were awestruck, *gobsmacked,* as the Liverpool expression goes." No band had ever played to an audience so large. The show was already in progress, featuring an interminable number of opening acts, with King Curtis's glorious backup band pounding away against the tsunami of screams. The pilot switched on a two-way radio so his passengers could monitor the sound onstage. As he swung over the parking lot, a deejay preempted the stadium P.A. system, shouting: "You hear that up there? Listen . . . *it's the Beatles!* They're *here!*" The sky lit up as thousands of flashbulbs exploded. "It was terrifying at first when we saw the crowds," said George, "but I don't think I ever felt so exhilarated in all my life." Geoffrey Ellis, who sat bewildered in the cockpit, sweating in a crisp blue suit and tie, didn't know what to make of the whole crazy scene. "I was caught up in the extraordinary fantasy," he recalled, "that all those kids . . . kept looking up to the heavens as though God was descending to the earth."

It was too dangerous to land the helicopter on the baseball field, so it was diverted to a macadam strip near the old World's Fair site, where the Beatles were transferred into armored cars. "It [was] organized like a military operation," according to photographer Bob Whitaker. Every aspect of the arrival was timed to split-second precision in order to elude canny fans.

Ed Sullivan, who was filming the concert for a TV special, paced anxiously in the Mets' dugout as the boys and Brian arrived. A little of the terror showed when the actual size of the place hit them. It was huge—ridiculous, John said. As the Beatles looked at the stands from the dugout they fell back in laughter. Everywhere they looked were kids—wall-to-wall kids. "It seemed like millions of people," Paul recalled, "but we were ready for it."

As the Beatles charged from the dugout to the stage situated over second base, "mass hysteria" broke out. More than fifty thousand kids jumped to their feet and screamed, wept, thrashed, and contorted themselves in a tableau that, to some, must have personified pure bedlam. "Their immature lungs produced a sound so staggering, so massive, so shrill and sustained that it quickly crossed the line from enthusiasm into hysteria and was soon in the area of the classic Greek meaning of the word pandemonium—the region of all demons," wrote the stunned reporter for the *New York Times.* Another compared the roar to "a dozen jets taking off." Mick Jagger, who, along with Keith Richards, was watching from a seat behind the first-base dugout, was visibly shaken by the crowd's behavior. "It's frightening," he told a companion.

All of this without a note of any music.

More than fifty 100-watt amplifiers had been set up along the base paths of the diamond, but they were no match for the wall of piercing sound that blared from the stands. The fans drowned out all the singing and most of the music. All that could be heard above the roar was "the pulsation of the electric guitars and thump of drums," and even then only sporadically. The Beatles played their standard half-hour set—"not a minute more, not a minute less," as Brian mandated it—but conditions on the stage never improved. "It was ridiculous!" John remarked of the experience. "We couldn't hear ourselves sing." During two numbers, he wasn't even sure what key they were in. And later, after watching the replay on TV, he noted: "You can see it in the film, George and I aren't even bothering playing half the chords, and we were just messing about."

Measured by dollars and cents, however, the show was a runaway success. *Variety* reported that the Beatles "shattered all existing . . . box office records, with a one-night gross of $304,000"—the Beatles cleared $180,000, or as the *New York Journal-American* calculated it, "$100 a second"—and took a giant step toward reshaping the concert business. For promoters everywhere, the Shea Stadium concert was a major breakthrough. It freed them from the constraints imposed by a gym or cinema, thus turning a pop performance into an event.

The Beatles bonanza continued its late-summer push across North America, rekindling the excitement in cities such as Toronto, Atlanta, Houston, Chicago, and Minneapolis. In each location, the usual concert halls had been usurped by open-air stadiums and arenas, with scenes of screaming and hysteria replayed like half-hour sitcoms. Aside from a minor skirmish in Houston, when unruly fans swarmed the plane, climbed on the wings, and banged on the windows—"It happens every time we come to Texas, we nearly get killed," John quipped—the spirit in the chartered tour plane was constantly convivial, marred only by mechanical problems as the plane descended into Portland.

Some of the Beach Boys were planning to visit backstage between shows in Portland, a visit everyone in the entourage looked forward to. Larry Kane, who was sitting over the left wing, remembers eavesdropping on a conversation between John and George that touched on their curiosity about Brian Wilson, when he happened to glance out the window. "Flames were shooting out of one of the engines in the rear," Kane recalls. Trying not to attract undue attention, he headed into the cockpit and notified the pilot, who voiced the exact sentiment that Kane was feeling: "*Oh, shit!*" This was more than anyone had bargained for. The inevitable black smoke finally alerted other passengers, who rushed to the windows. "John totally freaked. He went to the emergency door and attempted to open it. We were about eight thousand feet up and it took several of us to pull him away. Then George totally freaked." No doubt he and the others flashed

Buddy Holly. It turned grim in the cabin as the pilot struggled to maintain control of the plane. John took a seat next to Paul, both of whom "sat silently, with fixed, serious expressions," as the airport loomed into view. They could make out the outline of workers foaming the runway and fire engines speeding alongside. Ringo, "pale-faced," asked a reporter what to do in case they crashed, but an answer seemed entirely too ridiculous for words.

Thankfully, the plane, billowing smoke, bellied through the sea of white lather, stopping safely half a mile from the terminal. When the thrum of turboprops ground to a halt, there was a long, anxious silence. It was broken by the sound of a seat back groaning as John sprang to his feet. Cupping his hands around his mouth, he announced: "Beatles, women, and children first!"

When the Beatles arrived in Los Angeles two days later, still reeling from the emergency landing, they finally got what they coveted most: peace and quiet. There were two sold-out shows at the Hollywood Bowl flanked by a tantalizing four-day layover, and rather than confining them to a hotel suite, Brian had rented a luxurious horseshoe-shaped house on stilts on a secluded road in Benedict Canyon, off Mulholland Drive. It had everything they wanted—gourmet cooks, a staff of maids, an imposing gatehouse, an Olympic-size swimming pool, an intimate movie theater, lush bougainvillea-scented gardens. Better yet, there was no entourage, no meddlesome press, no annoying deejays, no Brian, no record-company flacks. And best of all, no fans. Thanks to the rugged terrain, there was a sheer drop from the pool right down the hillside, studded with bracken, cacti, and boulder-size rubble.

During those lazy days, under picture-postcard skies, the Beatles lounged by the pool, pulling on "the fattest joints" anyone had ever rolled and gorging themselves on a round-the-clock buffet to stem the "munchies." John and Mal swam with cigarettes in their mouths, seeing who could keep them lit the longest. Paul strummed idly on an acoustic guitar, while Ringo, and later John, sorted through a selection of casual sports clothes that had been sent over by a Hollywood boutique. At night they crowded into the screening room for a preview of *What's New Pussycat?*

Throughout the next day, celebrities arrived to pay their respects—Eleanor Bron, the actress who costarred in *Help!*, Joan Baez, Peter Fonda, and half the Byrds, along with a few delectable birds on loan from the

Playboy Mansion, invited to cheer up the boys. At Tony Barrow's urging, the press also attended (as a gesture of goodwill) but were heavily chaperoned lest they come upon one of the Beatles unawares.

As it happened, there was something they wanted to hide. John and George had been waiting for the perfect opportunity to take another acid trip and decided that this setting was ideally suited. Their objective was to initiate Paul and Ringo because, as George explained, after the tripping, "we couldn't relate to them anymore." The experience had changed their outlook, if not their lives, and inasmuch as the Beatles were a cliquish family with a unique vision, it was essential to get everyone, especially their mates, on the same page. "We got some [acid] in New York; it was on sugar cubes wrapped in tinfoil and we'd been carrying these all through the tour until we got to L.A."

Paul, cautious as ever, wanted nothing to do with it. But Ringo was game, as was Neil, who had Paul's share, with enough left over for Roger McGuinn, David Crosby, and Peter Fonda. "We were all ripped on LSD," recalls Fonda, who joined the guests around the pool, while Paul worked in his usual capacity "to keep everything calm and level."

By midday, the hills opposite the house were ringed with teenagers who screamed and shouted any time so much as a maid walked across the deck. Several kids actually attempted to climb the steep slope to the house but were intercepted by security guards who helped them to safety rather than letting them risk a fall going back down the hill. To make matters worse, three girls had rented a helicopter and buzzed the house, flying so low that the water in the swimming pool rippled. "The Beatles actually enjoyed the ingenuity of it," says Tony Barrow, "and they grinned and posed for the girls, who leaned dangerously out of the helicopter, taking pictures and waving." Only George's feathers were ruffled. He had been splashing around in the pool, zoned out of his skull and grooving on the "great feeling," but when the girls flew overhead, he retreated to a chaise longue between McGuinn and Fonda, where he sank into a deep funk. "He said, 'You know, man, I feel like I'm gonna die,'" remembers Fonda, who tried to assure George that LSD occasionally triggered strange reactions that needed to be ignored. The two men "bounced that around for a while," until Fonda sensed a real panic building and decided to tackle the feeling head-on. "Well, look," he confided to George, "I know what it's like to be dead, man." And he explained how in 1950, at the age of ten, he accidentally shot himself while playing with an old pistol and lost so much blood that his heart stopped three times. "The thing is, I almost died. And I'm not dead. I'm here, I'm alive. It's okay, George—everything's gonna be all right."

John, who had been passing by and overheard only a fragment of the conversation, leaned reproachfully over the recliner. "What do you mean, you know what it's like to be dead?"

Fonda, more than "a bit wasted," stared blankly at him. "I know what it's like to be dead."

"Who put all that shit in your head?" John snarled.

The two Beatles watched half fascinated, half horrified, as Fonda lifted his shirt to display the blotchy wound. "I know what it's like to be dead," he repeated, which, by this time, began to gnaw on George as well.

Weirdness abounded in Los Angeles. First, the police refused to cooperate with the Beatles, saying that "they could not be responsible for their security." Then Phil Spector invited them to his mansion and did a number with drugs and guns. Both circumstances produced some awkward moments for the boys, but nothing that would compete with their visit with Elvis.

For over a year Brian and Colonel Parker had been attempting to arrange a summit between their two megastars, with only egos—massive egos—standing in the way. "Keen to preserve their artists' prestige," neither manager wanted to blink first when it came to deciding who would accept the other's invitation. But in the end, the Beatles conceded, agreeing to pay their respects to the King.

Elvis had just returned from Honolulu, where he'd been filming *Blue Hawaii,* and was holed up with the Memphis Mafia at a rented house in Bel-Air. When the Beatles arrived, sometime after ten o'clock on August 27, they were "laughing . . . all in hysterics," partly from nerves, which they all suffered, and partly from the joints they'd shared in the car. The house was unusually big and ornate—"like a nightclub," John thought. Inside, Elvis was posed regally on a huge horseshoe-shaped couch, the King, larger than life in a flame red blouse beneath a tight-fitting black jacket and black slacks. A big arm was thrown around his queen-in-waiting, Priscilla Beaulieu, and on either side, his loyal squires: Joe Esposito, Marty Lacker, Billy Smith, Jerry Schilling, Alan Fortas, and Sonny West.

Perhaps more than anyone else, John was shaken by the sight of his boyhood idol. Before he'd gotten a guitar, before skiffle, before Paul, George, and Stu jump-started his own pop odyssey, John had heard "Heartbreak Hotel" and knew "it was the end for me." Now, John resorted to buffoonery, acting and jabbering as if he were Inspector Clouseau.

"Oh, zere you are!" he clowned, peering absentmindedly at his host over his glasses.

The other Beatles were speechless, gazing around at the Vegas-like setup of pool tables, craps tables, and roulette wheels crowding the den. A well-stocked jukebox stood purring in the corner. The room was bathed in red and blue light, which gave it the appearance of a cheesy after-hours club. No one knew what to do, or say. After a brief, embarrassing silence, Elvis summoned them to sit down beside him but grew weary of the Beatles' vacant stares—"It was hero worship of a high degree," Paul admitted—and started clicking nervously through the channels of a wall-size TV set.

"If you guys are just gonna sit there and stare at me, I'm goin' to bed," Elvis huffed, tossing the remote control on the coffee table. Turning to his girlfriend, he said, "Let's call it a night, right, 'Cilla? I didn't mean for this to be like the subjects calling on the King. I just thought we'd sit and talk about music and jam a little."

"That'd be great," Paul said, suggesting they try a song by "the other Cilla"—Cilla Black—at which point guitars and a white piano were produced, along with ample drink. "We all plugged in whatever was around, and we played and sang . . . 'You're My World,'" John recalled. Unwinding gradually, they segued into a few Presley barn burners—"That's All Right (Mama)" and "Blue Suede Shoes," with Elvis carrying the melody and Paul vamping on the piano—before finishing with "I Feel Fine."

By now John had slipped from feather to thistle. "Zis is ze way it zhould be," he mimicked, "ze szmall homely gazering wiz a few friends and a leetle music." Chris Hutchins, who recollected the visit in his 1994 chronicle, *Elvis Meets the Beatles,* writes that beyond the faux French accent, John chided Elvis rudely—and in front of his pals, no less—about his lack of chops, the post-army soft-core singles, and string of cornball movies. "I might just get around to cuttin' a few sides and knockin' you off the top," Presley said with a shrug, feeling hard-pressed to respond. Nobody could dispel the "uncomfortable undertones . . . and superficial cheerfulness" that punctuated the evening until sometime after two, when the Beatles finally departed.

"Sanks for ze music," John said in parting, then bellowed: "Long live the King!"

The next day the hungry pool of reporters covering the tour pounced on the story of the historic meeting, which had been press-managed— and largely fabricated to suit both managers—by Tony Barrow. Every journalist was supplied with a generous sampling of quotes from each of the Beatles, who fairly tripped over one another in the rush to praise their idol. Only in private would John admit what he really felt. "It was a load of rubbish," he concluded. "It was just like meeting Englebert Humperdinck."

After the Beatles' final performance—at the Cow Palace in San Francisco, on August 31, 1965—everyone was ready to head home.

The pitch of the crowd in San Francisco was a bit too "wild," even for the Beatles, who thought they had seen it all. Before the show, Wendy Hanson had been bitten by a fan who trampled on the hood of her car. Hearing about the incident made John "nervous." Superstitious by nature, he took every chance event as an omen, and when he walked onstage to discover the guitars out of tune, it set off all kinds of alarms. Paul had much the same reaction when he saw "the dreadful crush of fans up against the stage." A massive stampede of teenagers had broken through the barricades and surged forward, wave after wave attempting to vault the stage, only to be turned back by a detachment of stagehands. "Calm down!" Paul screamed at them. "Things are getting dangerous." But to no avail. One kid leaped over the amplifiers and snatched the cap off John's head before swan-diving into the audience. A security guard was knocked cold by a Coke bottle and more than two hundred fans fainted. Paul even stopped the show midway through so that police could rescue a pregnant woman who was being trampled. "At one point I glanced down and saw Joan Baez trying to pull kids to their feet and bring them around with smelling salts," recalls Tony Barrow, who says he feared for his life. Eventually the Beatles had seen enough and bolted, leaving Ringo to deliver a fitting postmortem. "We survived," he told an interviewer. "That's the important thing, wouldn't you say?"

[IV]

By the fall of 1965, the Beatles had drawn a deep collective breath. The luxury of six weeks off allowed each of the boys to catch up with his personal life and to step out of the all-consuming glare that had highlighted one of the most productive seasons of their career. In a reversal of the pattern that had governed their lives, the break gave them time to settle into new homes, see friends, and *sleep*. Beatlemania raged on without them. *Help!* kept them on the radio and in front of packed, delirious audiences, while Paul's single of "Yesterday," released only in America, captured the top spot on *Bilboard*'s Hot 100 for four weeks running, spawning a cascade of competent if uninspired covers by Marianne Faithfull, Tony Bennett, Sarah Vaughan, and Andy Williams. The only commotion during the rare hiatus was caused by Ringo Starr when, on September 13, Maureen gave birth to a boy—"a little smasher," as Ringo dubbed him—at Queen Charlotte's Maternity Hospital, whom they whimsically named Zak. "I won't let Zak be a drummer!" Ringo vowed to reporters outside the delivery room, but whether he realized it or not, the matter was out of his hands, and if he didn't realize it, most of the grinning press corps did.

In the meantime, October 12 loomed as the kickoff for recording a new album at the Abbey Road studios. EMI insisted on the date so that there would be new Beatles product available for the coming holiday season. The only song ready was "Wait," which they had completed while in the Bahamas and recorded for the *Help!* soundtrack. Otherwise, John and Paul "had to force themselves to come up with a dozen new songs" in a little more than two weeks, which seemed like an impossible feat, even for such naturals.

One thing was certain: this record wasn't going to sound like anything they'd ever done before. There was too much going on in the rock music scene, too much creativity in the air. Paul spoke for the others when he complained of "being bored by doing the same thing." Lyrics like "Can't Buy Me Love" and "Do You Want to Know a Secret" no longer seemed relevant. The Beatles had moved on emotionally, preoccupied with inner thoughts and feelings that gradually shaped their adult lives. "You can't be singing 15-year-old songs at 20 because you don't think 15-year-old thoughts at 20," Paul explained. "We were expanding in all areas of our lives," Ringo recalled, "opening up to a lot of different attitudes." And they'd moved on artistically. "We were suddenly hearing sounds that we weren't able to hear before," George observed. They were all still influenced tremendously by American R&B—although gravitating toward Stax and Motown artists as opposed to Little Richard and Chuck Berry—but other forms and diverse sources that had constantly swirled around them finally began to coalesce. Certainly jazz patterns and country licks had always figured in Beatles songs, to say nothing of the music hall influence still prevalent in every aspect of their careers. It had taken time, however, for them to learn how to put it all together.

As Paul well knew, in his capacity as a keen listener of pop radio, the summer of 1965 had already produced a rich vein of exceptional hit singles analogous for their offbeat originality and authentic voice. Dylan had started the ball rolling, not only with "Like a Rolling Stone" but also the Byrds' cover of "Mr. Tambourine Man," which bounced the process into another lyrical dimension. The Animals were offering their bluesy melo-drama, "We Gotta Get Out of This Place," followed by the Who's an-themic "My Generation," Unit 4 + 2's "Concrete and Clay," and the Yardbirds' "For Your Love." One can only imagine the bruising body heat created by the Stones' one-two punch of "The Last Time" and "Satisfaction." By contrast, the Beach Boys' "California Girls" seemed like the perfect pop confection to counterbalance the scorching imagery.

The competition, such as it was, turned out to be all the incentive John and Paul needed. Throughout the beginning of October, the songs ripped off their guitars, one right after another, and each as different and revolutionary as the last. If anything, the short two-week schedule seemed to sharpen their focus on the task of transforming and shading the Beatles' tone.

In "Norwegian Wood," which John had begun in February while ski-ing in St. Moritz, they gave a moody, vaguely Oriental voice to a furtive adult relationship. There was nothing predictable about "Norwegian Wood," neither in its lyric—"a very bitter little story," as George Martin referred to it—nor in its delivery. John claimed he based the narrative on an extramarital affair he was having—insiders say with the journalist Maureen Cleave—and that it was "my song completely," meaning the en-tire composition. Decades later Paul would take issue with that account, raking it from top to bottom, beginning with the fanciful title, which he said was nothing more than an inside joke about the cheap pine walls in Peter Asher's bedroom. "[John] had this first stanza," Paul recalled, but really only the first line and nothing else, as far as he could remember, ex-cept perhaps the underlying tune. There was in fact no indication that John had anything more than a general idea of where they were headed. But no matter: once a song was begun, no conceit could stop their momentum. Everything just poured out, the character of the girl or "bird," her rejec-tion of the lover along with his due penance—"to sleep in the bath"—and the extreme revenge he exacts the next morning, after "this bird has flown." The way Paul recollected it, they wrote most of the song together in a sin-gle afternoon, finishing it during a productive session at Weybridge.

John's house was also the scene for "Drive My Car," which Paul called "one of the stickiest" they struggled through in the writing process. Paul had sketched out a rough outline for the song on his way there from London. When he arrived, the tune was already set in his head but "the lyrics were disastrous," he admitted, "and I knew it." *Baby, you can buy me golden rings.* John called it "crap" and dismissed it as "too soft." Besides, it wouldn't scan. And the longer they played with and reworked it, the more entrenched the phrase became, much like the "scrambled eggs" impasse with "Yesterday." Pass after pass turned up the same problem. When the lyric threatened to block the entire session, John and Paul discussed throwing in the towel. Instead, they went to have tea, still unresolved: a great sassy melody with nothing to hang on it. When they returned to the attic half an hour later, they took another swing at it and replaced the central theme with an idea John suggested: *drive my car*—perhaps, as Paul implied, to ply the old blues euphemism for sex, perhaps because it just sounded good. "Baby, you can drive my car." An entire narrative flowed from it, rich with imagery and innuendo. It came alive in the studio, it just took off, with a flirtatious piano riff and a skintight backbeat, underscored by a soulful bass and guitar motif, "like the line from 'Respect,' by Otis Redding," George recalled, which further emphasizes the song's raunchy feel.

In the days that followed, a set of songs evolved that grappled with a new form: the act of self-exploration and confessional lyrics. John felt especially compelled to explore through his music the emotional upheaval that was churning in his life. His dilemma basically focused on propriety: could he get away with writing emotionally charged lyrics streaked with imagery that revealed dark truths? How much did the Beatles' fans want to know about intensely personal issues? And how much was he willing to share with them?

To sidestep these questions, John initially resorted to third-person narratives, a tactic most prevalent in the seminal "Nowhere Man." He'd begun it after a late drug-ridden night of clubhopping, arriving back at Kenwood higher than a kite. Collapsing on a couch in the attic, he said he "spent five hours that morning trying to write a song that was meaningful and good," until he finally gave up and dozed off. At some point John apparently blinked awake with a concept: "I thought of myself as a Nowhere Man sitting in this Nowhere Land," after which the words and music came—"the whole damn thing"—in a rush. Paul showed up sometime later and helped polish off the rough edges, admittedly a bit uneasy over the blatant personal slant of the lyric. "I think . . . it was about the state of his marriage," Paul surmised, aware that John had grown bored with Cynthia, frustrated by her timidity and aversion to drugs. A reflective, "dirge-like" song, "Nowhere Man" is steeped in dense harmonic pathos, the two voices intertwining, almost wearily so, around a tent pole of melancholy. The same can be said of "Girl," John's fantasy of "*that* girl—the one that a lot of us were looking for," he opined—although it is more wistful than melancholy. One of the last songs recorded for the album, "Run for Your Life" was stripped to its essential acoustic core, with some help from George's lovely guitar counterpoint as well as the control booth.

No production tricks were necessary for "In My Life," in which John even abandoned the coy third-person smoke screen for a straight biographical approach. It was the first time he consciously put the "literary part of [himself] into the lyric." And unlike "Norwegian Wood," nothing is jumbled by abstraction. As it was originally conceived, "In My Life" was a magnificent piece of songwriting, influenced by all the beloved sites from John's Liverpool childhood: Menlove Avenue, Penny Lane, Strawberry Fields, the tram sheds (or bus depot). "I had a complete set of lyrics after struggling with a journalistic version of a trip from home to downtown on a bus naming every sight," he recalled. But by the time he was finished, the structure bored him. It was too much of a travelogue, too nostalgic and sentimental. Practically none of it survived the makeover that followed. Once Paul took a crack at it, the places John identified were gone, replaced by two stanzas in which he only alluded to them and meditated on his past.

The song that resulted is a standout among innumerable gems, not only on the album but among all Lennon-McCartney compositions. It would be hard to point to a more gorgeous melody, distinct and unforgettable; in the hours John and Paul spent shaping it, each chord, each stroke, added new layers of color. None of their lyrics are as restrained—or more poignant. Proudly, John claimed authorship of the song throughout his life, and "In My Life" certainly has his stamp on it; few songs reveal his romantic sensibility more clearly. But Paul has maintained that while the "original inspiration," the "template," was John's, by the time they got done reworking it, "filling out the rest of the verses," only "very few lines" remained. According to Paul, they rewrote all but the opening lines, with Paul alone "writing the whole melody" based on a Smokey Robinson motif, "with the minors and little harmonies" lifted from Miracles records.

In fact, you can see their discrete fingerprints at various places in the material. Together, John and Paul polished off "The Word," "You Won't

See Me," and "What Goes On" in quick succession. "I'm Looking Through You" took its inspiration from Paul's relationship with Jane Asher, which had scrabbled onto an uneasy plateau. "They were like two speeding trains," observes John Dunbar, a scenemaker and fantastic character in the British underground, "running on opposite tracks. Paul liked having Jane on his arm—when it suited him. But you could see he was gradually losing patience." And interest. Jane wasn't marriage-minded—not yet, at least—and Paul didn't "feel comfortable" settling down with her. Besides, there was definitely some friction as a result of their respective careers. "Jane's star was rising," says Tony Barrow, "and Paul didn't like being upstaged." She refused to take a supporting role to the Beatles. "There was a time when he might have preferred that she play the housewife role, and that was never going to happen. Jane loved acting and Jane loved Paul, but she wasn't about to give one up for the other." Paul admitted "being disillusioned over her commitment" to the theater and reacting petulantly: "I can see through your facade—I'm looking through you."

The tune brought John and Paul a step closer to finishing, but they were still a song or two short. The Beatles were determined to load up the album with an unheard-of fourteen cuts.* "It's a question of value for money more than anything else," Paul explained in a year-end wrap-up with the *Herald Tribune*. "We want to do what *we* would have liked when we were record-buyers ourselves." It was a gracious gesture, but not without disadvantages. They were pretty much tapped out from the rigorous grind. Neither of the boys felt much like going back to the drawing board.

But they had to. "D'you remember that French thing you used to do at Mitchell's parties?" John asked Paul, referring to the all-night "bohemian" bashes they attended at the flat of Austin Mitchell, one of the tutors at the art college in Liverpool. Paul knew exactly what he was talking about: a precious, "rather French" instrumental he'd spun using a Chet Atkins–type fingerpicking technique. "Well, that's a good tune. You should do something with that."

Indeed. Paul had been noodling with a lyric built around the name Michelle and thought it might match up with the melody. To give it the musical lilt that the name seemed to suggest, he decided to weave in a few French phrases as an accent. *Michelle . . . ma belle.* It so happened he was spending the weekend with his old Liverpool mate, Ivan Vaughan, whose

---

* *On the American version, Capitol whittled the selections down to ten tracks, thus maximizing profits but substantially changing the character of the album.*

wife, Janet, taught French at a primary school and, at his urging, she helped fill in the rest of the expressions. By the time he played it for John, the song was pretty much fleshed out but still lacked a middle eight. "I had been listening to Nina Simone [doing] 'I Put a Spell on You,'" John recalled. "There was a line in it that went: 'I love *you*, I love *you*, I love *you*.'" Changing the emphasis to *love*, he "add[ed] a little bluesy edge" to the mix and they'd bagged another one.

They were almost ready—except for one not-so-minor detail. George Martin had been with EMI for fourteen years, ten of them as head of Parlophone, and after a feeble contract negotiation in 1963, he was still earning less than £70 a week. All his requests for a commission against sales were rejected out of hand—an outcome made all the more incredible considering his monumental effort in breaking seven or eight NEMS acts, to say nothing of the Beatles. "I was in the studio twenty-four hours a day," Martin argued. "You know, you don't [spend] thirty-seven weeks out of fifty-two at number one without working quite hard."

Even so, a commission was unheard-of. Producers and A&R men were company drones, ciphers, lacking any residual perks—not even a car or a negligible Christmas bonus. Martin, who not only brought in tens of millions of pounds, reversing EMI's flat earnings, but was largely responsible for thrusting the label into the rock 'n roll era, surely deserved at least the same kind of compensation as company sales reps, a reward for his extraordinary success—or so he thought.

EMI balked until the summer of 1964, when Martin notified the label that he would not be renewing his contract at the end of its current term. Len Wood attempted to broker a new deal, but each proposal he made was more preposterous, more arrogant—and ultimately more insulting—than the last. When, at their final meeting, Wood, sitting ramrod-stiff and imperious behind a polished yacht-size desk, proposed a deal by which Martin would be forced to reimburse EMI for departmental costs out of his profit, the producer yanked the plug. "Thank you, very much," George informed him. "I'm leaving."

Martin decided to start an independent production company—a revolutionary concept, "a shock to the recording industry," *NME* conceded—that would lease its staff's services to the labels for a respectable fee against royalties. Not only that, but he was taking a couple of EMI's young front-line producers, Ron Richards and John Burgess, as well as Decca's Peter Sullivan, along with him. That gave them—or A.I.R. (Associated Independent Recording), as it was to be called—an artist base that included Adam Faith, Manfred Mann, Cilla Black, Tom Jones, Peter and Gordon, the Hollies, Gerry and the Pacemakers, Matt Monro, Freddy and the Dreamers, Billy J. Kramer, P. J. Proby, Lulu, the Fourmost, and, of course, the Beatles.

Without waiting for the details of Martin's future role to be sorted out, the Beatles began working on the new album, entering a period during which their efforts together once again produced a groundbreaking style that would change the course of popular music. "For the first time we began to think of albums as art on their own, as complete entities," Martin explained. That sounded suspiciously highfalutin, as unnecessary floss for rock 'n roll, but in no way did it seem to hamstring the recording process. In the sessions that followed, the Beatles, along with their faithful producer, struck a groove that had never been mined before, in which the sound, the way a song was approached and recorded, played as important a part as the music itself. The composition turned more experimental. "The studio itself was full of instruments: pedal harmoniums, tack pianos, a celeste, and a Hammond organ," George remembered. "That's why we used all those different sounds on our records—because they were *there.*"

Harrison had already become fascinated, if not yet proficient, with the sitar, an Indian lute popularized by Wendy Hanson's friend Ravi Shankar, and he worked out a subtle arrangement that helped dramatize "Norwegian Wood." In retrospect, it seems like a minor piece of musical construction, adding a string accompaniment, but that sitar managed to turn more than one head inside out. As far as Ringo was concerned, it was "a mind-blower," a change of direction, if not a reshaping of the band's attitude. "We were all open to anything when George introduced the sitar," he said. From then on, "you could walk in with anything as long as it was going to make a musical note."

Such experiments were hastened by Martin. "He'd come up with amazing technical things, slowing down the piano and things like that," John recalled. "They were incredibly inquisitive about the recording process," Martin recalled. "They wanted to know what they could do that people hadn't [already] done." A guideline was immediately established: no idea, however vague or outlandish, was too risky or off-limits. Martin knew better than to dismiss their penchant for experimentation. For every trial concept that crashed and burned, there were four that not only took off but soared.

When it came to musical terminology, however, they couldn't speak the language. Not only didn't any of the Beatles have formal training, none could read a note. To stem the lack of communication, they developed a rapport with the eloquent Martin that facilitated discussions about music free of theory-loaded jargon. "Give it some color here," they might suggest. "Make it punchier." On one number, "In My Life," which required an instrumental bridge between the verses, John's instruction got whittled down to "play it like Bach." Exchanges like that galvanized Martin, who took up each of their abstract ideas as a challenge.

Play it like Bach. That one especially intrigued him. They needed to fill about twelve bars with a piano solo that would lend the song a classical feel. Martin felt he could swing it. Not a pianist by training, he could still manage a fairly decent passage that would approximate "something baroque-sounding," as John expressed it. "I quickly wrote out a Bach two-part invention [for piano]," he recalled, " but it was too fast for me to play. So I lowered the speed of the tape to half speed . . . and then speeded it up [on playback]," an engineering trick that allowed him to simulate an Elizabethan-style harpsichord. Another time, he wove a few sheets of newspaper through the strings of the piano "to make it sound different." He wrote the middle figure of "Michelle" as well, taking the song's basic chord structure and inverting it as an instrumental that he played in a duet with John against George's guitar solo. Martin called these departures "just manipulations of the resources we had at the time," but that would be akin to playing Hamlet just by putting on the clothes. Resources take resourceful people to manipulate them, and the Beatles, with George Martin's able assistance, injected originality and daring into the mix that hinted at the great artistic recordings to come.

"This was the departure record," Ringo said. By any name, it was a masterpiece. The Beatles had already settled on a concept for the cover: it would be a fashionable photograph of the band from among those taken by Bob Freeman in the garden of John's house in Weybridge. They'd worn new suede outfits for the occasion along with a new look: mannered, self-assured, candid. Freeman had shot more than a dozen rolls of film at the session, necessitating a consultation with the Beatles in order to choose the right photo. Everyone assembled in the parlor of a London flat one night to view the proof sheets that Freeman had converted to slides. "Whilst projecting [them] onto an album-sized piece of white cardboard, Bob inadvertently tilted the card backwards," Paul remembered. "The effect was to stretch the perspective and elongate the faces." What a groovy effect! It reminded them of hallucinations during an acid trip, where everything was out of whack. Was it possible to print the photo that way? they wondered. Freeman's response—a resounding "yes!"—triggered some discussion about an American blues artist's reaction to the Rolling Stones. "Well, you know they're good," he'd commented, "but it's plastic soul." *Plastic soul!* What a hoot, they thought. It had a clever ring to it, and it was irreverent. A potential album title? Very close. But Freeman's elasticized photo stretched the phrase in another direction, which everyone felt hit the mark. The name of the album, they agreed, would be *Rubber Soul.*

MASTERY

[I]

"*R*ubber Soul broke everything open," says Steve Winwood. "It crossed music into a whole new dimension and was responsible for kicking off the sixties rock era as we know it." Almost everyone echoed his belief that the Beatles had "raised the bar" in a way that made musicians reconsider how they wrote and recorded songs. *Newsweek,* a scant two years after tweaking the Beatles' haircuts and improbable talent, reversed itself, calling them the "Bards of Pop" and their songs "as brilliantly original as any written today." And the *New York Times,* whose grouchy critic, Jack Gould, had famously referred to the Beatles as "a fine mass placebo" and their act as "dated stuff," delivered a glowing tribute in a five-page Sunday magazine article under the friendlier byline of Maureen Cleave.

Rock 'n roll had always been an easy beat to peg—and disdain—but the Beatles, as one classical convert noted, had succeeded in "push[ing] the music into more conventional modes," especially with *Rubber Soul,* in which they were able to blend "gospel, country music, baroque counterpoint and even French popular ballads into a style that is wholly their own."

On December 17, 1965, a handful of Sinatra protégés, along with Cilla Black, Esther Phillips, Henry Mancini, Marianne Faithfull, Ella Fitzgerald, and a seriously stoned Peter Sellers, paid tribute to the Beatles in a television extravaganza titled *The Music of Lennon and McCartney.* Even John and Paul put in an appearance to plug their new single, "Day Tripper" and "We Can Work It Out," which, in an extraordinary occurrence, were both being marketed as A-sides. As expected, the show touched off an explosion of interest by entertainers to cover their songs, with everyone from Ray Charles to Count Basie sifting through the Northern Songs catalogue. By mid-1966, an astounding eighty-eight Lennon-McCartney songs had been recorded in over 2,900 versions. Gershwin finally had competition.

While the cover versions multiplied and the critics traded accolades, the Beatles themselves scattered like errant billiard balls, disappearing into various pockets of London that catered to their precious anonymity. The Lennons, the Starkeys, and George and Pattie conveniently lived in neighboring communities, less than a ten-minute drive apart, and although their individual interests took them on different courses, their bond to the larger family remained very much intact. The Beatles continued to have "a strong hold on each other," as Ringo recalled. Even though they had worked together nearly every day over the past eight years, there was an attachment, a real devotion, that was indelibly drawn. They still socialized and took vacations together; Christmas was usually an extensive group affair.

But as tributaries of the Thames threatened to freeze early in an unusually cold winter, John, George, and Ringo clung dearly to their neighboring homes in Surrey, with Paul camped out in the Ashers' Wimpole Street attic. Welcome was the cancellation of a British tour in the spring (in fact, they would never tour Britain again), but Brian refused to rule out a short, last-minute sprint around the aging cinema circuit. Nevertheless, the Beatles finally found themselves with valuable time on their hands.

John, who was becoming politicized by fractious world events, took the opportunity to catch up on the news, which he devoured ravenously, scouring "all the daily newspapers published in Great Britain" as well as watching endless hours of daytime television coverage on the set in a tiny morning room at the back of the house. The intensifying civil rights movement, America's involvement in Southeast Asia, and the allure of psychedelics were all issues that captivated him. At night, he languished in front of episodes of *The Power Game, Danger Man,* and *The Rat Catchers.* Work on a new book was postponed in favor of television—"it's supposed to be out this month but I've only done one page!" he boasted.

Ringo spent ample time doting on his family. "Nothing made him happier than sitting at the kitchen table, eating Corn Flakes, with Maureen and Zak," says Ken Partridge, who helped design Sunny Heights (which included a private club over the garage, complete with a mirrored bar, pool table, jukebox, and, reverently, a portrait of John and Paul). Otherwise, Ringo had developed a passion for fine photography, thanks to a fancy Nikon and an above-average eye, and wasted no opportunity to record "all the important events in his [son's] life." Ringo had no other grand visions. While he loved material wealth and was a rich man despite his fractional share of the Beatles' profits, his dreams, like those of many hardworking Scouse men, were incongruously modest. A house in the country was more than he'd ever expected from life. Having a good job—*a very good job*—and an adoring family was enough to seal his contentment, and aside from a few material indulgences, he refrained from the temptation to set his sights higher.

Taking the opposite view, Paul tore around London gorging himself on culture, as if he had only a short time left to live. "People are saying things and painting things and writing things and composing things that are great," he breathlessly told a reporter. "I *must* know what people are doing." To facilitate his acculturation, Paul took piano lessons from a teacher at the Guildhall School of Music, George Martin's alma mater, studying composers Karlheinz Stockhausen and Luciano Berio, and read avant-garde poetry, which he plucked from the cluttered stalls at Better Books. "It was a very free, formless time for me," he recalled. Most evenings, he capered about town in the company of John Dunbar and his wife, Marianne Faithfull, or turned up at Barry and Sue Miles's bohemian flat, curling up amid the clutter on their unusually hard chaise longue, to get "wrecked" and discuss "all these crazy ideas" about life and art while listening to jazz. Robert Fraser became his art guru, and through him Paul met Andy Warhol, Claes Oldenburg, and Jim Dine, as well as arty filmmakers such as Michelangelo Antonioni, who was in the midst of shooting *Blow-Up*. Surrounded by the *right* people, Paul delighted in those circumstances where his celebrity mattered naught.

George publicly surfaced from his romantic interlude with Indian music—"Sometimes before I go to sleep," he fantasized, "I think what it would be like to be inside Ravi's sitar"—in mid-January to announce that he'd married Pattie Boyd. The wedding itself came as no surprise; Beatles fans had been expecting it for months. But the timing of it, on January 21, while John and Ringo were vacationing in Trinidad, caught most friends unaware. He and Pattie gave their families only a few days' notice to join them in a quiet ceremony at the Leatherhead and Esher registry, in Epsom, near his home, with Paul and Brian serving as best men. George was now the third of the Beatles to be "taken out of circulation" (if in name only), and he was quick to underscore the onus it placed on the single-minded Paul. "Now he's the only Beatle left. . . . He won't get a moment's peace."

But Paul had something else on his mind. He and John finished "Paperback Writer" and "Rain," as well as "Here, There and Everywhere," which they'd originally blocked out in Austria, during the filming of *Help!* And during his final days as a lodger at the Ashers' flat, before moving to St.

John's Wood, Paul began an ambitious new song. On those dismally gray afternoons when Margaret Asher wasn't giving oboe lessons, Paul used to disappear into the cluttered, low-ceilinged basement music room to, as he so blithely put it, "have a fiddle around." There, hunched over the rugged upright piano, he produced an achingly haunting line of melody while vamping on an E minor chord. "Ola Na Tungee / Blowing his mind in the dark / With a pipeful of clay" were the lyrics that Donovan recalled hearing when Paul showed up at his flat to jam a few days later. The words were meaningless, just filler or suitable phrases to push him through the composing process. "Often you just block songs out and words just come into your mind," Paul explained much later. They became "insinuated into your consciousness . . . and when they do it's hard to get rid of them." But not long afterward, the lyric had evolved as "Dazzie-de-da-zu / Picks up the rice in the church where a wedding has been." *Picks up the rice in the church . . .* Paul remembered how "those words just fell out"; it was one of those accidents, those magical moments that had befallen him over the years, seemingly immaterial at first, "but they started to set the tone of it all."

Dazzie-de-da-zu officially became Eleanor Rigby in March. Paul says he borrowed the first name from Eleanor Bron, their comely *Help!* costar, with whom "John had a fling," and grafted it onto Rigby, the name of an old shop, Rigby & Amp, in the Bristol dock area that he'd stumbled over during a visit to see Jane perform at the Old Vic. It was so deliciously "ordinary": *Eleanor Rigby.* He had no trouble envisioning someone by that name picking up rice in a church, waiting by a window, dying alone. And those images helped him "piece all the ideas together"—the melody and the chords, everything—before taking the nearly finished song to John for a polish.

John had also been busy sketching songs, working late afternoons in the small smoke-filled music room at the top of his house. There, despite Julian's interruptions and his growing estrangement from Cynthia, he eschewed the artsy, Dylan-inspired epics like "Norwegian Wood" and "In My Life" and concentrated instead on producing a number of simpler, more hummable songs. There wasn't much left to do on "She Said She Said," which had been inspired by Peter Fonda's hallucinating poolside rambling and pretty much fleshed out in Los Angeles (except for the title, which materialized during the recording session). But he'd gotten a head start on two well-put songs: the pithy, rhythmic "And Your Bird Can Sing," with its exuberant guitar riff, and "Doctor Robert," which was "a joke," according to John, lambasting the socially prominent clientele who got scrip for casual drug use from a chichi New York internist. Without any consensus—or deadline—a new album was percolating.

[II]

The Beatles had always gone all out to make great-sounding songs; now it was time, they decided, to make great-sounding records. If you listened to American records, they argued, there was a natural brilliance to them, an *excitement* emanating from the technical side that made the performances pop. Even on 45s, the bass sound was thick and rich, the trebles clear as crystal. "The Americans seemed to be ahead of us in those days," admitted Norman Smith, the Beatles' crackerjack engineer. And it frustrated the Beatles no end. They had impeccable ears; they could hear the difference.

Listening, however, wasn't going to help matters. Abbey Road was still in the Dark Ages as far as technical practices were concerned. The four-track machines used to record every artist—from the London Phil-harmonic to Herman's Hermits—were regarded as dinosaurs elsewhere in the world. Microphone setups were outmoded. Engineers were advised against getting creative—executives called it *tampering*—with the equip-ment. There were still regulations, overseen by a tyrannical studio author-ity, about how bright the sound could be. "The Beatles . . . were screaming for more sophisticated equipment, more flexible equipment, that could give better definition," Smith explained.

No one, however, was holding his breath. If their request for a better atmosphere in the studio was any indication, they were in for a long haul. "What EMI did for them was to put in special lighting," George Martin re-called, laughing, ". . . [which amounted to] three fluorescent tubes—one white, one red, and one blue." What about Memphis? someone suggested. Those relentless, hard-driving rhythm sections, the punchy horns, that uninhibited, gospel-inspired groove recently reborn as *soul*—the high-voltage energy that came through on Bobby Bland's and Otis Redding's records under the auspices of Booker T and the MG's—all that plus a *real* studio. Without even discussing it with George Martin, the Beatles dis-patched Brian Epstein to Memphis, Tennessee, the last week in March to "look over the recording studios" there and to cut a deal with guitarist Steve Cropper to produce the sessions. George and John were especially excited to relocate overseas. "It'll shake up everything," George insisted. "You don't grow as a band unless you shake things up, you know."

But getting a fair shake in the States came at too high a price. For all Cropper's attempts to accommodate them, it remained too much of a gamble. "They wanted a fantastic amount of money to use the facilities there," Paul recalled, and he suspected that it had nothing to do with overhead and everything to do with the Beatles. "They were obviously trying to take us for a ride." With that, the Beatles immediately booked time to record at Abbey Road.

The first song they recorded, on April 6, 1966, established the pace for everything that was to come. Just after 8 P.M. the Beatles, along with their trusty acolytes Neil Aspinall and Mal Evans, George Martin, and a new, embarrassingly young engineer named Geoff Emerick who had been promoted to replace Norman Smith (otherwise engaged with his new discovery, Pink Floyd), assembled in Studio Three at Abbey Road to begin work on a song with the mysteriously obscure title of "Mark 1." The time of the session itself was quite extraordinary. Studio discipline dictated that all evening sessions end at ten o'clock, thanks to a long-standing ordinance by the local council that imposed a midnight curfew on recording in what was primarily a residential area. The rule was strictly observed for twenty-five years—that is, until the Beatles shoved it out the door. According to Vera Samwell, who booked the four studios, "the Beatles just recorded whenever they wanted to. They went into the studios and didn't come out until they'd finished and nobody ever had the nerve to ask them to leave." So the session that night ran—officially—from seven to ten, but as the clock struck twelve, and then one, the Beatles continued to work.

From the beginning, John's fertile imagination had conceptualized "Mark 1" in a special way. Paul recalled that the seed for it germinated on an afternoon in early March, when he and John visited the newly opened Indica Bookshop, ostensibly to encourage a few sales. John requested a book by an author whose name he pronounced as "Nitz Ga," and only after a long, ineffectual search did Barry Miles finally turn up *The Portable Nietzsche.* In the interim, John browsed the stalls and pounced on a copy of *The Psychedelic Experience,* by Dr. Timothy Leary. Opening the book, he read: "Whenever in doubt, turn off your mind, relax, float downstream." In fact, Leary had pinched most of that directly from *The Tibetan Book of the Dead,* which, in turn, gave John license to help himself to the lines. *Turn off your mind, relax, and float downstream.* It was an irresistible mantra—for so many different reasons. Rushing home, John dropped acid according to Leary's instructions. "I did it just like he said in the book," John recalled. Almost immediately, the words came: inscrutable strings of words started threading around ever more gauzy abstractions. *Lay down all thoughts, surrender to the void . . . That you may see the meaning of within . . .* It was an acid freak's bonanza!

He played a verse of it for Paul a few days later during a meeting at Brian Epstein's flat. Incredibly, it "was all on the chord of C," according to Paul. Somehow, John had stripped the music to its most basic structure, the level at which melody and rhythm contract to an unmodulated drone, in the fashion of Indian music. He had bored into the pores of the song until it vibrated with clarity. Paul was intrigued but wondered how George Martin would deal with it, especially considering their reputation for churning out melodic three- and four-chord hits. To his credit, Martin "didn't flinch at all when John played it to him," Paul recalled. "He just said, 'Hmmm, I see, yes. Hmm hmm.'" Martin, from Paul's standpoint, thought it was "rather interesting."

Interesting—but unfinished. The lyric was as stark as the melody: only one verse in length. "We worked very hard to stretch it into two verses," Paul explained. "We wracked our brains but couldn't come up with any more words because we felt it already said everything we wanted to say in the two verses." Nor did the structure allow for a middle eight. At that length, the track would come in at just over a minute. They had to find a way to make it longer while still preserving its originality.

It was Paul who came up with a solution: tape loops. From his growing infatuation with Stockhausen, especially *Gesang der Jünglinge,* a composition that fused vocal and electronically produced notes, he'd discovered a process of recording whereby if he removed the erase head from a tape recorder and replaced it with a loop of tape, he could play a short phrase or sound that would ultimately saturate itself. As George Martin described it: "It went round and round and overdubbed itself until the point of saturation, and that made a funny sound." Martin said recording technicians called it musique concrète, or reinforced music. There were infinite combinations of sounds that could be produced by this method, from which Paul made a number of "little symphonies." He demonstrated it for the others in the studio, encouraging George and Ringo to make loops as well. Then, Martin "listen[ed] to them at various speeds, backwards and forwards," in order to integrate them into the recording.

Meanwhile, John discussed several ideas for the vocal with his producer, each one a conceit of his overactive imagination. "He wanted his voice to sound like the Dalai Lama chanting from a hilltop," Martin recalled. Most producers would have dismissed such a cheeky idea out of hand, but Martin, a wise and patient man, gave the Beatles enormous lee-way. Their ideas might sound like gibberish *initially*, but he recognized that because of their lack of formal musical training, they often only needed someone to "translate" what they meant, to express it in terms that made sense to structured technicians, and in that respect Martin viewed his role as "the official interpreter." In any case, he struggled to create some kind of a Tibetan influence or effect in the studio, realizing that ordinary echo or reverb wouldn't do the trick. Recording out of doors was also out of the question; there was no way to contain or control the sound. And John's suggestion—that "we suspend him from a rope in the middle of the studio ceiling, put a mike in the middle of the floor, give him a push, and he'd sing as he went around and around," according to Geoff Emerick—was met with a meaningful, albeit barely tolerant smile. (When pressed by John, they were always said to be "looking into it," Emerick recalled.)

It was the nineteen-year-old Emerick who eventually came up with an inventive solution. He suggested putting John's voice through a Leslie speaker and re-recording it as it came back out. To a straitlaced, formalis-tic EMI technician, this sounded about as nutty as suspending John from a rope, but the more Martin thought about it, the more he saw its possibili-ties. A Leslie was a speaker with variable rotating baffles that was usually paired with a Hammond console organ. "By putting his voice through that and then recording it again, you got a kind of intermittent vibrato effect," Martin explained. It was a revolutionary idea—but considered taboo at Abbey Road, where engineers were discouraged from "playing about with microphones."

With Martin's "support and approval," Emerick happily rigged the mikes for the Leslie. ("It meant actually breaking into the circuitry," Emerick recalled.) The rest was a matter of simply forcing John's vocals through the vibrato, much like vegetables through a ricer. "I remember the surprise on our faces when the voice came out of the speaker," Emerick said. "It was just one of sheer amazement." The Beatles were beside them-selves with glee. Stoned—which they were most of the time in the studio—the experiments became part prank, part innovation. In that kind of dreamy, altered—*impractical*—state, the possibilities were limitless. Recording be-came no longer just another way of putting out songs, but a new way of creating them.

Of course, once the Beatles got their hands on the controls, they found it impossible to leave them alone. "The group encouraged us to break the rules," Geoff Emerick recalled. "It was implanted . . . that every instrument should sound unlike itself." As well as each of the Beatles. John flirted with the idea of having "thousands of monks chanting" in the background of "Mark I," a prospect about as likely as booking the Dalai Lama as a sideman. A way to simulate it, however, was to double-track John's voice—that is, to re-record John singing a duplicate vocal and superimpose it over the original as a way of thickening the texture—but the sound was severely limited by the lack of available tracks. Besides, John dreaded redoing a vocal—he absolutely *hated* it.

In a rather magnanimous gesture, Ken Townsend, the studio's manager of technical operations, decided to tackle the problem himself. He went home that night, amid much grousing and chin-rubbing, and came up with a solution that would forever change the state of recording. Hunched over a cannibalized tape recorder, he concluded that if you took the signals off both the recording and the playback heads and delayed them, it produced two sound images instead of the usual one. Moreover, he discovered that by varying speed and frequencies, you could make adjustments to deliver a desired effect. Artificial double-tracking—or ADT, as it became known—revolutionized not only the recording process but the way in which vocals were subsequently heard. Eventually every artist and producer put it to good use on sessions. What's more, it opened the frontiers of experimentation to all sorts of electronic recording devices.

John was especially "knocked out" by the sound. It shaved hours, maybe days, off the recording process, let alone the annoying inconvenience of having to sing vocal take after vocal take. *Tell me again what it is?* John wondered. *How does it work?* "Well, John," Martin replied earnestly, seizing the opportunity to have some fun at his artist's expense, "it's a double-bifurcated sploshing flange." *A sploshing flange!* According to Martin, John knew he was putting him on, but from that point on, the technique known throughout the recording industry as flanging was practiced.

After sampling the wattage behind the spooky-sounding "Mark I," which they eventually retitled "Tomorrow Never Knows," it was virtually inevitable that the Beatles would want to tinker in some way with every new song. A good case in point was the subsequent session for "Got to Get You into My Life," which had begun, according to studio notes, as "a very acoustic number." Paul had not composed it in a romantic gist, as the lyric might indicate, but ironically as an ode to drugs. "It was a song about pot actually," he admitted—not about acid, as John later suspected (Paul hadn't taken acid yet)—written to a great extent after Bob Dylan turned on the Beatles in New York. At first, the Beatles recorded it as a standard rhythm track, with George Martin sitting in on the organ. In the initial eight takes done over two days (April 6 and 7), familiar Beatlesque backing vocals—John and George repeating "I need your love" behind the refrain—were still discernible beneath the layers of overdubs. But nearly a month and a half later, they were scrapped for an entire brass section—two trumpets and three saxophones—to give the song "a definite jazz feel." Everyone felt they were on the right track. The horns managed to open up and brighten the song in tantalizing ways. It was clear upon playback, however, that the jazz feel was way too precious, too sedate; the song didn't rock enough. Moreover, the horns didn't scream like those on American records. Once Geoff Emerick reevaluated the setup, he hit on a method designed to sharpen the arrangement. Instead of recording the brass in the standard way, by placing the horns a polite six feet away from the mikes, he sandwiched the works—bringing "the mikes . . . right down in the bells of the instruments"—which fairly electrified the track, giving it liftoff. Then, to launch it into orbit, they overdubbed an additional three trumpets in the coda to match the intensity of Paul's vocal ad-libs, sealing in a blazing pop R&B feel.

In the sessions that followed, covering "And Your Bird Can Sing" and "Doctor Robert," the Beatles reverted to fairly straightforward recording techniques. On "Paperback Writer," which John and Paul composed in an epistolary construction, they relied on a "heavier," rock 'n roll sound utilizing "a guitar lick on a fuzzy, loud guitar," as John recalled, but otherwise kept it fairly straight. The only special effect employed was to tweak the bass by using a loudspeaker as a microphone so that the throbbing sound practically jumped off the grooves.

"Rain," however, was a whole other issue. As far as the writing went, it was "a co-effort," according to Paul's account, but they ran into problems the minute it was brought into the studio. No matter how the Beatles ran it down, they "couldn't get a backing track" to work. They couldn't find a groove; there was just no punch to it. At some point in the proceedings, they remembered how full and meaty certain instruments sounded when they were slowed down. Drums especially took on serious weight, providing "a big, ponderous, thunderous backing" like "a giant's footstep." That gave them another idea. If they played the rhythm track faster than normal and then slowed it down on playback, it thickened the whole texture of the song. They used the same effect for John's sleepy vocal. But even that didn't satisfy the Beatles' thirst for experimentation.

No one is certain exactly whose idea it was to run the tape backward. John claimed it was accidental, following an extremely late night at Abbey Road. The Beatles were halfway through work on "Rain," according to George, who recalled how each of them took home a rough mix of the song on a reference tape *tails out*, which meant that the engineer had not rewound it on the tiny four-inch spools before handing it to them. Apparently, John had forgotten that by the time his smoke-filled car pulled into Kenwood. "I got home from the studio and I was stoned out of my mind on marijuana," he recalled. Just in case he wasn't wrecked enough, however, he lit up another fat joint before threading the tape onto his recorder, tails out, and played it—*backward.* In the confusion, John must have experienced a whopper of a paranoid flash; the sound was unlike anything he'd ever heard before, a piercing *scronnnch whuppp-whuppp-whuppp* bisected by shreds of keening feedback. By John's account, it sparked an epiphany. "I ran in the next day and said, 'I know what to do with it, I know. . . . Listen to this!'"

Perhaps. George Martin, however, always maintained that the effect at the end of "Rain" was his idea. "The Beatles weren't quite sure what to do at that point," he recalled. "While they were out having a break one evening, I lifted off a bit of John's voice. [I] put it onto a bit of tape and turned it around and shoved it back in—slid it around until it was in the right position. . . . And I played it to John when they came back."

There is probably some truth to both accounts because of the intense collaboration that paced the recording of the album. It's entirely likely that John conjured the effect, and every bit as likely that Martin perfected it. What is indisputable is that the excitement was contagious. Everyone in the studio reveled in the process, running instrument and vocal tapes in myriad directions. They used it on "Taxman" and throughout George's guitar solo on "I'm Only Sleeping." There is even some reverse backing on "She Said She Said." At some point, however, it had gotten out of hand. "And that was awful," Martin recalled, "because everything we did after that was backwards. Every guitar solo was backwards, and they tried to think backwards in writing."

Backward or forward, the work was producing amazing results. There was a sense of real adventure—and real accomplishment—in the studio. Ideas were ricocheting off the walls, the boys were playing way over their heads. "We were really starting to find ourselves in the studio," Ringo observed. Some of the residual magic he attributed to drugs, which "were kicking in a little more heavily," but even with the added chemical stimulation, the Beatles' focus remained razor-sharp. "We were really hard workers . . . we worked like dogs to get it right."

———

While the Beatles thrived in the sanctuary of the studio, other events continued to build on their astounding legacy. A month or so after they began work on their next album, Capitol Records issued a self-styled Beatles album titled *Yesterday . . . and Today* that featured a hodgepodge of songs left off the American abridged versions of *Help!* and *Rubber Soul,* along with the singles "Paperback Writer" and "Rain" and three tracks raided from the *Revolver* sessions. It was an odious but common enough practice; Capitol had done it intermittently as a way of customizing the Beatles catalogue—getting an extra album or two out of a popular band by packaging leftovers and material in the vault under an innocuous title. And even though the Beatles complained about it, the royalty windfall from its sales served to mitigate their grievances.

At Capitol's request, the Beatles were to supply a cover for the LP. Specifically, the label asked for a standard picture of the band, encouraging them to use something from an old Bob Freeman session, but the prospect of another posed portrait, like *Beatles for Sale* or even *Rubber Soul,* didn't appeal to them at all. "We [wanted] to do something different," John recalled. They had felt constrained by the boring composition of the previous covers and, as early as February, discussed several other options for *Revolver,* including the use of negative imagery and religious iconography. Now, with a smaller American release, it would give them a chance to test some of the more extreme ideas that had been kicking around.

Brian put them in touch with an Australian photographer named Bob Whitaker, who "was a bit of a surrealist," according to John, and admired the imagery of Dalí disciple Merit Oppenheimer and German artist Hans Bellmer, author of the controversial book *Die Puppe,* which contained pictures of bizarrely dismembered toy dolls. Whitaker inveigled the Beatles with a concept that would depict how "he, as an outsider, viewed the world's perception of the Fab Four." Even though the album was called *Yesterday . . . and Today,* he proposed they subtitle it *A Somnambulant Adventure* so that they could place past and present within the context of mortality.

If this was all a bit of pseudophilosophical bullshit, it nonetheless appealed to the Beatles' sense of the avant-garde, as well as to their pot-indulged fantasies. Meanwhile, it would help put an end to the Beatles' in-nocent image. "We were supposed to be sort of angels," bemoaned John, who "wanted to show that we were aware of life."

Even so, the Beatles didn't know what to expect when, on March 25, they arrived at Whitaker's rented studio on the Vale, in a fashionable area of Chelsea. The props they saw that day were mostly remnants collected from a butcher shop and doll factory: pungent sausage links, a grotesque pig's head, joints of raw meat, white smocks, dismembered dolls with dis-torted faces, and numerous lifelike glass eyes. Working quickly to oblige the Beatles' notoriously short attention span, Whitaker whipped through several outlandish setups. He photographed John, Paul, George, and Ringo holding a string of sausages in front of a young girl; John clutching a card-board box, with the number 2,000,000 written on it, over Ringo's head; George banging carpenter's nails into John's head. He then dressed the Beatles in the butcher's smocks, positioned them on a bench, and arranged the meat on their laps, draping an extra joint carefully over John's shoul-der. The poses felt "gross . . . and stupid" at first. No one had any idea what the imagery was supposed to reflect. Eventually, however, the Beatles "got into it," smirking like schoolboys when Whitaker placed four decap-itated dolls in between each of them and handed them the heads.

The infamous "butcher cover" was delivered to Capitol the following week, where it quickly landed on the desk of label president Alan Living-ston. Inundated by objections from his staff, he immediately called Brian Epstein and demanded an explanation. "It's their comment on war," he was told, an interpretation that was as facetious as it was unsupportable. Paul has admitted that "we thought it was stunning and shocking, but we didn't see all the connotations." Livingston doubted he could put out the cover, and Brian promised he would ask the Beatles to reconsider. The next day, however, he indignantly "came back and said: 'They absolutely insist that's what they want.'"

Over the years, Livingston had put his foot down when artists became unreasonable — there was no upside to placating their outlandish demands — but he couldn't afford any kind of confrontation with a group like the Beatles. Going against all instincts, he ordered the cover into production and shipped out several hundred advance copies to his national sales force. "Word came back very fast that the dealers would not touch it," Living-ston recalled. "They would not put the album in their stores."

Unfortunately for Capitol, about half a million copies of the cover had already been printed, which forced the expensive process of unpacking cartons of records and replacing the sleeve. Meanwhile, on June 14, the label's press manager issued a letter stating that "the album cover is being discarded." It included a disclaimer from Livingston: "The original cover, created in England, was intended as 'Pop Art' satire. However, a sampling of opinion in the United States indicates that the cover design is subject to misinterpretation. For this reason, and to avoid any possible controversy or undeserved harm to the Beatles' image or reputation, Capitol has chosen to withdraw the LP and substitute a more generally acceptable design."

The Beatles were predictably up in arms over the recall. It wasn't the picture so much as the way Capitol had caved in to so-called public opinion that offended their sense of fair play. "I especially pushed for it to be an album cover, just to break the image," John insisted. He was sick and tired of the Beatles' constantly being held up as altar boys in contrast to the scruffy Rolling Stones. It wasn't an accurate comparison—and it needed correcting. The butcher sleeve headed in the right direction. Paul agreed: "We weren't against a little shock now and then; it was part of our make-up."

But the Beatles knew the importance of picking their battles. Their recording contract was coming up for renewal, and instead of granting worldwide rights to EMI again, Brian wanted to negotiate directly with Capitol for the United States, where he was sure to get a substantial signing bonus and a larger royalty. In fact, he made no secret of the fact that he was already putting out feelers to other American labels. Nat Weiss had introduced Brian to Atlantic Records' Ahmet Ertegun and Jerry Wexler, both of whom "he greatly respected." They'd also visited Columbia and seen Clive Davis, who "thought the Beatles had peaked and wasn't prepared to give them a large offer." RCA salivated at the prospect of pairing them with Elvis, but when Rocco Laginestra tried to impress Brian by presenting a copy of *Chet Atkins Picks the Beatles,* any deal was as good as dead. ("They are cabbage salesmen, not record people," he told Weiss.) There were still barrels of money to be made in America, that was for sure. Was it really worth jeopardizing that over the butcher cover? He put this to the Beatles, who clearly understood the implications, which is why they quietly agreed to substitute another Whitaker photograph—what John referred to as an "awful-looking picture of us looking just as deadbeat but supposed to be a happy-go-lucky foursome"—of the band posed alongside a steamer trunk.

There were, of course, other things the Beatles earmarked as worth fighting for. For one thing, they absolutely dreaded being dragged around the

British cinema circuit on another scattershot package tour. There was some sense, they agreed, to remaining barricaded behind dingy hotel-room doors when playing before a paying crowd of fifty thousand fans, but not for an audience of six or nine hundred. They agreed to appear at the annual *NME* poll-winners' show, on May 1, but it was to be their last-ever British concert performance. That wasn't the only setback. As late as December 1965, the Beatles were still turning up regularly for every light-weight TV and radio appearance. But since January, they'd refused all media requests aside from a live spot on *Top of the Pops* on June 16 (*Melody Maker* reported that they'd "succumbed to pressure from fans"). Recording occupied most all of their time; otherwise, the excuse they gave was lame: "It was too much trouble to go and fight our way through all the screaming hordes of people to mime the latest single." The truth was, it was becoming harder to reproduce onstage the kind of effects-laden music they were creating in the studio. Foot pedals for guitars were still a few years off, there were no remote sound-mixing boards, no faders, no monitors. Their new songs, like "Eleanor Rigby" and "Tomorrow Never Knows," contained crucial sounds that could be made only in the studio. It'd take a pretty substantial horn section to pull off "Got to Get You into My Life."

A *Melody Maker* poll reflected the residual impact this had on the Beatles' popularity by a tabulation showing that 80 percent of respondents were greatly disappointed by the band's dearth of personal appearances, with only slightly less declaring that Beatlemania had passed its peak. But the Beatles couldn't have cared less. "Musically, we're only just starting," George told a reporter. "We've realized for ourselves that as far as recording is concerned most of the things that recording men have said were impossible for 39 years are in fact very possible."

Brian had promised them that he'd find an alternative method to publicize the "Paperback Writer"/"Rain" single, but EMI wasn't helpful. Any shortcuts would be frowned upon, he was warned.

No one recalls who came up with the solution, but sometime in early May they decided to make amusing promotional films of both songs—lipsynced versions set to comical scenarios, not unlike those in *A Hard Day's Night*—which would be sent out in place of live performances. The whole thing, shot in half a day (by director Michael Lindsay-Hogg), cost a mere couple of thousand pounds. Their old exi pal Klaus Voormann was hired to organize the whole affair in the lovely manicured gardens behind Chiswick House, in West London, and a new medium was miraculously born. "I don't think we even thought of calling them 'videos,'" Ringo speculated, but videos indeed they were—the first of their kind, and eighteen years ahead of their explosion on the forefront of pop culture.

[III]

On June 16, 1966, Vic Lewis, NEMS' swashbuckling booking agent, took off from Heathrow Airport for the Far East, intent on making final arrangements for the Beatles' upcoming visit to Tokyo and Manila in early July. Under normal circumstances, Brian Epstein would have tended to this himself. "But by 1966," Tony Barrow writes in an unpublished memoir, "his alarming ill health and his time-consuming personal struggle with debilitating drugs, drink and sex problems led him to devote substantially less attention to the essential details of his artists' management and concert promotion companies."

As much as he tried to hide it, Brian was a physical and emotional mess. Manic depression had thrust its grip on his already volatile personality, accelerating the severe mood swings he experienced randomly throughout the day. "And the drugs made things much worse," says Peter Brown. "The more the drugs took hold, the worse his condition became." Drugs had become one of the central focuses of Brian's life—uppers and Tuinal—mixed with plenty of alcohol. And now a new vice to grapple with: John "Diz" Gillespie, a slightly built, baby-faced aspiring actor from Ohio, in his mid-twenties, who had a prodigious capacity for meting out both love and violence. To a manic-depressive masochist, the combination hit the trifecta.

Diz, in Nat Weiss's estimation, amounted to nothing more than "a garden-variety hustler." Weiss first encountered the boy when the Beatles played Shea Stadium and claims he "knew exactly what he was" the moment he laid eyes on him. "Diz was a predator," he says, and what he wanted was money. For a while, Brian bankrolled his phantom acting career, signing Diz to an artist's contract with NEMS and authorizing a modest weekly stipend. But when that didn't pan out, there were arguments and violence. Fistfights were a common enough occurrence. Valuable antique vases would be heaved against the wall or mirrors shattered during late-night assaults. "I went over [to Brian's flat] one morning and found the glass-top coffee table smashed to smithereens and five dozen tulips strewn all over," Ken Partridge recalls. "Diz had beaten Brian up and stolen his records, although Brian rather enjoyed it in a funny sort of way."

In New York, Diz demanded three thousand dollars from Nat Weiss, ostensibly to buy a car, although the lawyer suspected that it was going for drugs. Weiss wrote him a check but warned: "If you show up again after I give it to you, I *promise* you I have friends who will deal with you."

Threats meant nothing. Diz showed up—only in London next time, where he was received by the lovesick Brian as the "sweetest, most special plaything, the object of my dreams." Almost immediately, however, they reverted to their old pattern, taking obscene handfuls of drugs and beating the shit out of each other. Peter Brown outlines an explosive incident in his book, *The Love You Make,* when Brian ordered Diz out of his house, at which point, he said, "Diz raced to the kitchen, grabbed the largest knife he could find, and held it to Brian's jugular vein while extracting an additional sum of money from Brian's wallet."

By the end of May and the beginning of June, the Beatles were busy putting the finishing touches on their new album, which was perceived among them as defining "a new British sound," if not a brilliant leap forward.

"Taxman" was finally behind them. The scathing satire, with the slurry, psychedelic edge, is the strongest of a record three George Harrison compositions that made the final cut, and an extraordinary contribution to the album's aesthetic sensibility. Among the Beatles, true genius radiated from the Lennon and McCartney nexus, but "Taxman" is a huge achievement. It is wry, witty, caustic, and concentrated, with "sharp, incisive jolts of energy" that burst from the song's offbeat "studio-*verité*" introduction: wandering notes, a cough, a false count. What a delightful surprise!

Like many topical lyrics, "Taxman" sprang from the anger and disillusionment that followed a meeting with Bryce Hammer, the Beatles' accountants, weeks before the session began. "I had discovered I was paying a huge amount of money to the taxman," complained George. Paul recalled George's "righteous indignation" in those business meetings. "Well, I don't want to *pay* tax," he'd fume. "It's not *fair.*"

George's response would open the album. Everything is taxable according to his account: the street, your seat, the heat, and your feet. No matter what you do or how much you have—*pay up and shut up.* And it doesn't stop there. After you are dead, he advises listeners, be sure "to declare the pennies on your eyes." "Taxman" is as sly and critical as anything Dylan was writing. Of course, John had helped; he said he "threw in a few one-liners to help the song along." And Paul doubled on guitars, playing looping bass lines and delivering the song's signature savage guitar solo.

But as far as first-rate songwriting went, with "Taxman" George had finally arrived.

Earlier that month "Eleanor Rigby" had been given the full symphonic treatment, courtesy of a lush arrangement by George Martin—and inspired by Bernard Herrmann's score for *Fahrenheit 451*—that featured a double string quartet: four violins, two violas, and two cellos. This prompted Paul to lend a similar flourish to "For No One." The song is an elegant ballad about a crumbling relationship built atop a descending bass line that he'd written in the bathroom of a Swiss chalet in March.

The Beatles let their hair down for one of the album's final tracks. On "Yellow Submarine" they gave a blunt comic edge to a children's song Paul had brought in by layering it with gentle wisecracks and sound effects from their boyhood iconography. Studio Two was in complete disarray as the four Beatles, along with Neil, Mal, and a full battalion of Abbey Road irregulars, ransacked the trap room, a small equipment closet just inside the door, where a trove of noisemaking effects was conveniently stashed. The vast wooden floor was suddenly littered with "chains, ship's bells, hand bells from wartime, tap dancing mats, whistles, hooters, wind machines, thunderstorm machines"—every oddity they could lay their hands on. A cash register (the one eventually used to ring up Pink Floyd's "Money") was dragged out, along with several buckets, a set of bar glasses, even an old metal bath that was promptly filled with water.

"They had a whole crowd of people to do the effects," recalled Geoff Emerick, who crisscrossed the studio like a jittery football player, attempting to properly mike the gadgets. Brian Jones, Marianne Faithfull, and Pattie Harrison were recruited to rattle and clink various hardware. The Beatles' chauffeur, Alf Bicknell, swirled chains through the bath, engineers John Skinner and Terry Condon made whooshing noises. Ringo handled the vocals with his typical deadpan panache, and with George Martin at the controls, it was all very reminiscent of the goofy Spike Milligan sessions he'd produced in an earlier age. Everyone laughed and hooted as the tape captured the hijinks. At some point after hours of overdubs, Mal Evans strapped on a bass drum and, bashing away, led a conga line around the cluttered studio while the ensemble chanted the memorable refrain: "We all live in a yellow submarine. . . ." It was party time in Studio Two.

Oddly enough, by the time the Beatles set out for a three-date concert tour of Germany on June 23, the LP still wasn't titled. There were plenty of plausible candidates, however. Originally, everyone got behind calling it *Abracadabra* until Neil discovered another album with the same name. Lounging around a fifth-floor suite in the Bayerischer Hof in Munich, following a rather rusty opening concert at the Circus-Krone-Bau, other titles were proposed—and discarded: *Pendulums; Fat Man and Bobby;* and *After Geography,* Ringo's send-up of the Stones' recent album, *Aftermath.* George's tape of the album, which blared in the background, didn't inspire much. "Let's just call it *Rock 'n Roll Hits of '66,*" Paul suggested, getting prickly. "That'll solve it." But, of course, that only drew groans. John came up with *Beatles on Safari,* and Paul offered *Magic Circle,* which John tweaked and twisted into *Four Sides of the Circle.* Later, *Revolver* seemed to fall out of the sky. Paul put it up for consideration, and it was an immediate hit. *Revolver.*

It seemed fitting that the Beatles pondered album titles in Germany. Two days later they were due in Hamburg, scene of their emergence—officially—as the Beatles. It had been only four years since their last show at the Star-Club, four years since they went from being the amphetamine-stoked resident band in a Reeperbahn rathole to millionaire Members of the British Empire and a worldwide phenomenon. Four years: in that brief span they'd collected nineteen number one hits and six gold albums; they'd made two box-office smashes, become virtuosos, and played in front of more people than any other act in the history of show business.

The late-night train ride from Essen to Hamburg on June 25 was especially poignant. In the suite of smoky coach cars, Tony Barrow played host to several dozen press and members of the entourage who partied noisily until dawn. But up ahead, in a private compartment, the mood was warm, sentimental. There were only eight people in the luxurious velvet-draped car, the same one that had transported Queen Elizabeth and the royal party through Germany months before, and the significance was lost on no one. Throughout the five-hour journey, the little company cut appreciative glances at one another: the four Beatles, Neil Aspinall, Mal Evans, Brian Epstein, and Peter Brown. "We all knew each other from way back in Liverpool," recalls Brown, "and we didn't have to prove anything to each other. It was relaxing, fun. There was a lot of comfort, all of us sitting there like that, together, in peace."

Essen had been neither comfortable nor peaceful. "At Essen, the brutality started to show itself," *Melody Maker*'s Alan Walsh reported. "At each concert over-enthusiastic fans were dragged outside and on several occasions were beaten-up by bouncers who apparently seemed to enjoy it." Boys, *thugs*—not the usual gaggle of teenage girls—behaved like disembodied spirits, screaming, singing along, jerking their bodies back and forth, and fighting among themselves. Hordes of brutal-looking, jack-booted police, with loaded Lugers strapped to their hips, moved in with "huge, muzzled dogs at their heels," trying to move the crowd back. And it got uglier outside.

Nevertheless, for the first few shows the Beatles played, the country cast its inimitable spell, with the sets a core of old up-tempo rockers powered by the atomic beat. It was almost as if they could hear Bruno Koschmider demanding: *"Mach schau, mach schau!"* and responded, as they had years earlier, with exaggerated body language.

Every one of them was looking forward to arriving in Hamburg. So much had changed since their stay there as penniless wannabes; they were "still just the boys," as Paul insisted much later, but "[they'd] got famous in the meantime." Bettina Derlin, the Star-Club's buxom bartender, pushed through a cordon of police at Hamburg's railway station to greet the Beatles' train. What a blast from the past! John, who'd always fancied the girl, couldn't get óver her moxie. "How about Bettina being on the station [platform] at seven o'clock this morning!" he marveled when the touring party arrived at the Schloss Hotel in nearby Tremsbuttel later that day. But the procession of familiar faces didn't stop there. "[A] lot of old ghosts materialized out of the woodwork," George remembered (although there were several—the pimps and pill pushers—he admitted, who remained better off buried). The backstage area at Ernst-Merck-Halle, where the Beatles played two concerts, resembled an old school reunion. Bettina was there, this time with an old girlfriend of Paul's in tow. Horst Fascher bared his lethal grin. Bert Kaempfert swept in with his family, and as the boys spotted him John broke into a creaky rendition of "Strangers in the Night." It was old home night for the Beatles. But no "ghost" hit them as powerfully as when Astrid Kirchherr walked through the door.

Astrid—Stu's girl, his *wife.* Their German muse. Astrid Kirchherr— soon to be Mrs. Gibson Kemp, having become engaged to Ringo's young replacement in Rory Storm's band. And, of course, she looked absolutely ravishing, just as they remembered her.

It was hard for the Beatles to tear themselves away from her. She was someone from their past whom they'd loved and who'd never tried to capitalize on or abuse their friendship—a rarity, it seemed, these days. Moreover, she'd brought John a sheaf of letters that he'd written to Stuart Sutcliffe in 1961 and 1962—"the best present I've had in years," he told

Astrid, meaning it—and the effect of holding them again made his hands tremble. Occasions like these were too few and far between on their round-the-world odyssey as the Beatles. They helped remind these four boys every now and then that they were real people, with real needs.

Signs of strain showed at their press conference just before the Hamburg shows. In place of their trademark Scouse wit, the Beatles snapped and snarled at the German media, who fired a barrage of unusually inane questions at them. "What kind of questions are these?" John fumed after a reporter commented on Ringo's complexion. "Come on, are there any members of the press here?" Later, while Paul attempted to respond to a question about his dreams during sleep, John interrupted: "What do you think we are? What do *you* dream of? *Fuckin' hell!*" All these infantile questions—"Do you wear long pants in the wintertime?" or "Do you polish your MBE medal?"—he could bear no longer. If the press was going to act like idiots, he'd respond as he pleased. No one said he had to behave like a trained seal—and he wouldn't. Not John Lennon.

No, he'd had it with the media and their "soft questions." And he'd had it with Brian's restrictions about saying what was on his mind. They might have been okay for one of Larry Parnes's teenage attractions, they may have once even served a purpose for the struggling young Beatles, but John was twenty-five years old and had a mind of his own. If Paul wanted to play by the rules, that was his prerogative. John had decided that he wasn't going to keep his mouth shut.

In fact, he'd already started speaking his mind. In March the *London Evening Standard* published an interview he'd done with Maureen Cleave, in which John had said:

> "Christianity will go. It will vanish and shrink. I needn't argue about that. I'm right and will be proved right. We're more popular than Jesus now. I don't know which will go first—rock 'n roll or Christianity. Jesus was all right, but his disciples were thick and ordinary. It's them twisting it that ruins it for me."

The article was picked up on April 13 by the *San Francisco Chronicle* but didn't merit an editorial response. After all, no one put much stock in anything that a rock star said.

In April, during a typically banal interview with *Disc,* John and the reporter did the usual dance for half an hour, waltzing around a dozen polite questions about the Beatles' upcoming recording session and touring, when

John suddenly turned the conversation toward politics and the elections later that week. "The trouble with government as it is, is that it doesn't represent the people. It controls them." Uh-oh, the reporter thought. Topics like these, he knew, were strictly off-limits. But John persisted. "All they seem to want to do—the people who run the country—is keep themselves in power and stop us [from] knowing what's going on." John railed against "the system" and chastised people for not knowing "the difference between political propaganda and the truth."

Clearly John was feeling his oats. He had cut himself loose from the limiting orbit of Beatlemania. And, for the time being at least, he was flying solo.

[IV]

Flying was part of the Beatles' job description, and on June 27 they were back in the air, flying from Heathrow this time, en route to Tokyo. No one was looking forward to what John described as "a forty-seven hour flight." And though it was an exaggeration, he wasn't too far off the mark. Somewhere over the Atlantic Ocean, the pilots sent back word of a fierce storm raging in the China Sea, necessitating their being grounded in Anchorage, Alaska, until the danger passed.

Nearly twenty hours later the Beatles landed at Tokyo's Haneda Airport in the middle of the night to find that the storm may have passed—but not the danger. Inside the well-lit terminal—long after the last passengers had straggled off to their planes—the exhausted touring party was diverted once more, into a VIP lounge this time, by a plainclothes police commissioner who warned them about threats issued by a cult of Japanese students determined to staunch the plague of Western culture. "As far as these hooligans were concerned," recalls Vic Lewis, "allowing the Beatles inside the Budokan, where no Westerner had ever set foot, was offensive, an insult to the great warriors of Japan. If they played there, it was said, they would not leave Tokyo alive."

There was beginning to be an air of ritual about these episodes. George Harrison had been forewarned about going to Germany. It was the same thing: "You won't live beyond the next month." And a steady stream of letters flowed into NEMS brandishing similar threats. "Don't ever set foot in B——, or else." "Ringo's a dead man." Clear-eyed observers saw these threats for what they were: the saber rattling of delusional crackpots.

"We always had to deal with these nuts," says Peter Brown. "There was no alternative. I don't think we took it that seriously." But the Japanese authorities did.

As a result, the Beatles were herded through Customs and into two decrepit limousines surrounded by an armed motorcycle escort for the solemn drive into Tokyo. Fans lined the highway on either side, waving furiously at the motorcade, but no one was permitted beyond a reasonable point. Security was even tighter at the Tokyo Hilton, which "was turned into an armed camp." The Beatles' quarters, a rambling warren of rooms in the Presidential Suite, only pushed them deeper into despair. "All the other bedrooms adjoining them and on the floors below were allocated for the police—just in case," says Vic Lewis. "Aside from going to the gigs, no one was permitted to leave their rooms."

"We were locked up in the hotel for a long time," recalled Paul, "with various merchants coming around and showing us ivory and various gifts." Shopping binges consumed much of the Beatles' uneventful stay in Tokyo. During the morning hours, their suite resembled a veritable bazaar, with wares laid out splendidly on downy tufts of black velvet and brocade. Everything they could wish for was available: pearls, beads, jewels, jade, netsuke, snuff boxes, watches, fans, alabaster, lacquered objects, kites, gold jewelry, incense holders. The Beatles, lounging in ceremonial silk kimonos, picked through yards of expensive items, selecting presents for their families and themselves. They were also presented with geishas to amuse them. "They spent ten minutes with the girls," Vic Lewis recalls, "then told us, 'Get rid of them.'"

The Beatles were irritable and growing increasingly restless. "It was their first time in the Far East," says Peter Brown, "and they'd been looking forward to going out. They resented being cooped up like zoo animals. It was more difficult than usual." Especially with Brian and Brown in a suite at the opposite end of the floor, entertaining American and Japanese boys they'd picked up at the pool and in various bars. On several occasions Paul and Mal disguised themselves and tried to leave the hotel, as did John and Neil, but each time they were thwarted by security. Finally, says Brown, a government functionary came to remind Brian that millions of yen were being spent on army and police protection and that it was "dishonorable" for the Beatles not to cooperate, which triggered a promise that "it wouldn't happen again."

The concert, by contrast, was almost an intrusion. The Beatles grudgingly put on their new stage outfits—"yellow shirts and natty bottle-green suits," according to Paul—and proceeded to the Budokan, which was "like a military maneuver." Everything had been timed to the second: how and when they departed, where they sat in each vehicle. A convoy of bullet-proof cars spirited them from the hotel, past the Dau, which was opposite the Hilton, and onto the deserted motorway—deserted *at rush hour.* "The drive was absolutely eerie," recalls Vic Lewis. "We had to go under about twenty bridges, which is where all the police stood, with guns." Fans were kept in penlike structures at specific points along the route and under armed guard. Throughout the trip the Beatles were mostly silent, gazing out at the scenery, trying to get a feeling for where they were. Everything looked so different—and strange. It was unlike anything they'd experienced over the years.

The concerts were just as remarkable, with none of the hysteria or even screaming that was the hallmark of Beatlemania. "The audience was very subdued," Ringo recalled. The unsuspecting Beatles found they could actually *hear* themselves play! "There were one or two screamers," according to an account, "but for the most part the teenaged boys and girls sat politely in their seats and applauded enthusiastically after each number." The politeness was due in no small part to the cultural ethos of Japan, as well as the three thousand cops stationed conspicuously in the arena—one for every three kids who'd bought a ticket to the show.

Afterward, marijuana was consumed; *Revolver* once again set the appropriate mood, as a single bulb cast a soft spell across the suite. Numbed by the dope and the music, the Beatles took out brushes and paper and, like a clan of art school kids, painted. Thirty years later Bob Whitaker, who photographed them, would recall the wonder and satisfaction the Beatles shared as they painted together until well after three in the morning. "I couldn't believe what I was seeing," he said. "I'd never seen them calmer, happier, more contented with themselves than at this time."

———

It began to unravel, however, the moment they touched down in Manila.

On the afternoon of Sunday, July 3, 1966, the Beatles deplaned to startling news: "You're being put onto a boat." Vic Lewis had arranged for the Cathay Pacific aircraft to unload its passengers at a remote end of the runway and then return empty to the gate while the Beatles made a clean getaway. As the Beatles attempted to reclaim their briefcases, an armed guard waved them rudely away. "Leave those bags there! Get in this car!" he demanded, herding them toward a limo that had edged around the plane. The Beatles glanced meaningfully at Neil, who eyed the isolated luggage with trepidation. "Those little briefcases had the marijuana in them," he recalled. Normally, they were regarded as "diplomatic bags" and waved through Customs without inspection, but from the get-go there was nothing normal about this arrival. As the Beatles, separated from their crew, reluctantly got in the car and pulled away, George looked out the back window and felt his heart sink. "Our bags were on the runway," he recalled, "and I was thinking, 'This is it—we're going to get busted.'"

That would have been too easy.

The boat, a large, luxurious vessel, belonged to a local newspaper magnate. It was hot and humid—pushing a hundred degrees. There were more than a dozen short, squat cops on deck, grinning like gargoyles. And, perhaps worse, for the first time in the Beatles' career, neither Neil, Mal, nor Brian was at their side to direct and guide them through the process. "We were all sweating and frightened," recalled George, who collapsed next to his bandmates in one of the woven beach chairs along the starboard rail.

Brian showed up two hours later. Livid, he placed a call to Vic Lewis at the Manila Hotel. "You fucking idiot!" Brian raged. "What is this dirty place? We're on a boat stuck miles away, nobody can get anything." Lewis tried to defuse the situation. Everything they could possibly want was on that yacht, even a nice little collection of prostitutes. According to Tony Barrow, the Beatles manager throttled the phone and screamed: "We're not staying one minute longer on this bloody boat. The boys are fed up. There's absolutely nothing to do, and we want to come ashore at once." When Lewis reminded him that their hotel suite was presently occupied by General Douglas MacArthur, Brian snapped: "I don't care! Pull your weight and get us in."

Security was tight, as always; a quarter of Manila's police force "had been detailed for Beatles duty between the Sunday afternoon of [their] arrival and the Tuesday of [their] scheduled departure." In between, there were two shows at the local stadium with an expected sellout of more than eighty thousand fans. Meanwhile, a note attached to the itinerary indicated that they were to "call in on" First Lady Imelda Marcos at eleven o'clock on Monday morning, "before proceeding on from the Malacanang Palace to the stadium for the first concert."

Tony Barrow thinks it was "unlikely" that Brian Epstein noticed the appointment, although Peter Brown has a distinct recollection that an invitation to the palace came while they were still in Japan, to which Brian responded, "Regret," meaning: decline it. Certainly everyone had missed the story in the *Manila Sunday Times* about the impending palace visit.

> President Marcos, the First Lady, and the three young Beatles fans in the family have been invited as guests of honor at the concerts. The Beatles plan to personally follow up the invitation during a courtesy call on Mrs. Imelda Marcos at Malacanang Palace tomorrow [Monday] morning at eleven o'clock.

Even if they had seen it, it wouldn't have made much difference. "Since the British embassy fiasco, the policy was *never* to go to those things," says Peter Brown.

Early the next morning Vic Lewis and Tony Barrow were awakened by sharp raps on the door of their suite. Two grim-looking men, a general and a commander of the Philippine army, both in crisply starched full-dress uniforms, saluted and introduced themselves as the official reception committee from the palace. They'd come to make final arrangements for the Beatles' visit, they explained, which had been expanded to include a luncheon hosted by the First Lady to which two hundred children had been invited.

Lewis, still in his pajamas, seemed baffled by this information. He apologized and explained that there must have been a misunderstanding. No one had told him anything about a presidential visit. Besides, he said, the Beatles were otherwise engaged, although he promised, out of courtesy to Mrs. Marcos, to inform Brian Epstein of their request. "This is not a request," they insisted.

Lewis jumped into clothes and located Brian in the hotel coffee shop, where he was having breakfast with Peter Brown. "We'll do nothing of the sort," he coolly informed Vic. "We're not going to go." Lewis begged him to reconsider and implied that he might run it by the boys himself. A deep crimson pool tided into Brian's cheeks. "Don't you *dare* go over my head to the boys. I'm telling you *we're not going.*"

"Well," Lewis responded portentously, "I can assure you we're going to have a lot of trouble if you don't."

The trouble started, as Vic predicted it would, later that morning. First, Brian took an agitated call from the British ambassador to the Philippines, urging him to keep the palace appointment "in the interest of diplomacy." Brian remained adamant. Moreover, he refused to wake the Beatles to tell them they had to go to a party. "It's just not feasible," he said, washing his hands of the matter.

Unbeknownst to him, Paul and Neil had already gone out earlier that morning to take pictures in and around the city. The rest of the Beatles slept until about one o'clock, had their breakfast, and played a rousing if fairly standard afternoon show to an enthusiastic audience of 35,000 Filipinos under a blistering sun. As always, there was no cultural barrier when it came to Beatlemania. Back at the hotel before the evening show, Tony Barrow and Peter Brown gathered in Brian's suite to have drinks and watch coverage of the concert on the evening news. Every channel featured scenes depicting delirious local teenagers swooning over the Beatles. But on Channel 5, one of the country's major networks, an extended report ran footage from the palace in which friends of the First Family and their children filed into the grand reception room earlier that day. "The children began to arrive at ten," said the accompanying voice-over. "They waited until after two. . . . At noon, the First Lady decided properly and wisely not to wait any longer. 'The children have all the time in the world, but we are busy,' she said. The place cards for the Beatles at the lunch table were removed." The spin they put on it implied that the Beatles in all their rudeness had insulted President and Mrs. Marcos.

Brian faced Peter Brown, wearing a look of feline infallibility. "Well, we were fucking *right* not to do that," he said. But Tony Barrow, who understood the implications, shook his head grimly. This wasn't Los Angeles or even France, where the government shrugged off such proper nonsense. A misunderstanding like this, he thought, could flare up into a touchy international incident. To run damage control, he persuaded Brian to issue a hastily written apology and arranged for a Channel 5 remote crew to tape an interview in the hotel suite. Brian, for his part, was contrite. In his most gracious, upper-crust voice, he professed complete ignorance about the invitation and praised the Marcoses, but when it was broadcast an hour later, Brian's appearance was obliterated by static interference. "That's when we started to get very nervous," recalls Peter Brown.

The uneasiness turned to panic after the evening show at the stadium. Suddenly the Beatles' police escort disappeared, and when their car pulled up to the hotel gates, it was clear they had been locked out. As if on cue, several dozen "organized troublemakers" converged on the car, banging on the windows and rocking the vehicles. Menacing epithets were shouted in several languages. Leaning forward, Vic Lewis instructed the driver: "Drive on! Go through the people and smash the gates down!" Which is exactly what they did. As the cars raced to the entrance, doors flew open and everyone ran into the hotel—two steps ahead of the angry throng.

A short while later an official visited the hotel, demanding payment of local taxes. Lewis brought out the contract to verify that the promoter, Ramon Ramos, was responsible for the tax, but it was brushed aside. "Your fee is taxed as earnings regardless of any other contracts," he was told. Until all taxes were paid, no one from the Beatles party would be permitted to leave the country.

When he left, Lewis found Tony Barrow and said, "We've got to get out of here—now." He went straight to the phone and called the front desk for help with collecting the luggage but was told none would be forthcoming. "The whole hotel is going on strike," the manager told him. "They think you've insulted President Marcos."

The Beatles had already gotten a taste of the situation. The hotel staff refused to provide them with room service and their phones had been shut off. Paul had seen the newspaper headlines—BEATLES SNUB PRESIDENT—but didn't connect the events. The story went on to claim that the Beatles had "spit in the eyes of the first family," which, of course, wasn't true—no one had told *them* anything about the visit. "Oh, dear!" he thought. "We'll just say we're sorry." But then "things started to get really weird," as Ringo recalled. He and John were sitting around in their bathrobes, watching television, when one of the roadies stalked in. "Come on! Get out of bed! Get packed—we're getting out of here."

Vic Lewis, Tony Barrow, and the two roadies grabbed most of the baggage and headed to the airport. They hoped to have everything settled for a quick getaway by the time the Beatles arrived. Everyone else met in Brian's suite and began to make their way downstairs. The main elevators had been turned off, which meant taking the service lift. But even though the halls were dark, they weren't empty. "The passageway was lined with hotel staff who shouted at us in Spanish and English," recalls Peter Brown, trailing a few steps behind the Beatles. "It was very, very frightening." When they arrived downstairs, it was impossible to check out. The lobby was deserted; there was no security in sight. Even their cars were gone.

"Nobody would give us a ride," George recalled. "There was nothing available." Someone—no one is sure who—managed to corral a Town Car and all seven of them squeezed inside. But the airport route was sabotaged. Soldiers, stationed at intersections, kept directing the car onto ramps that led in circles. Finally they took a back road and arrived half an hour later. Rushing inside the airport, they discovered that the terminal was totally deserted. "The atmosphere was scary," Tony Barrow remembered, "as if a bomb was due to go off." Even the individual airline desks were empty. The second the Beatles hit the escalators, the electricity was mysteriously shut off. "We were shitting ourselves by this time," says Peter Brown. "There was no one to help us, no one to tell us where to go."

Barrow and Vic Lewis, who had gone ahead of the party, were carrying everyone's flight tickets and documents. "Meanwhile," recalls Vic Lewis, "I was in with KLM, pleading for them to hold the flight, which was coming in from Seoul and going on to Delhi." The passengers had already boarded the aircraft; the plane was an hour late for takeoff. "I rang through to the pilot and was pleading with him. '*Please,* hold on. This is going to be an international situation. *Please . . .*'"

"Mr. Lewis, I want to help," the captain told him, "but if we don't leave soon, we won't get our clearance."

"*Please . . .*"

Outside, Lewis and Barrow could see their worst nightmare unfold. On the tarmac, a crowd of two hundred Filipino men, many in military uniform, had gathered, waving pistols or clutching sawed-off clubs. "I didn't fancy the chances of the Beatles, without police protection, getting through to the airport unhurt," Barrow recalled. Lewis confirmed his fears. "I really felt the boys could be killed," he says.

The Beatles, meanwhile, made their way through the terminal as little bands of the demonstrators appeared. "We were all carrying amplifiers and suitcases," George remembered, "nobody was helping us to do anything—but the mania was going on, with people trying to grab us, and other people trying to hit us." Check-in lasted forever, it seemed. Eventually everyone was herded into KLM's departure lounge, a double-story glass-enclosed room with a mezzanine, where "an abusive crowd and police with guns had also gathered."

It was impossible to tell the MPs from the thugs. Customs officials indiscriminately shoved bodies from one side of the room to the other. "Get over there!" they ordered the Beatles, following it with a hard hand to their backs. Of course, once they stumbled to the other side of the room, another cop would shove them back again. "No! Get over there!" It was like a game of Ping-Pong, a vicious game, using the Beatles and their mates as equipment. According to Ringo, "they started spitting at us, spitting *on* us." It was complete chaos.

"When they started on us at the airport, I was petrified," John recalled. One of the policemen got in his face and yelled: "You treat like ordinary passenger! Ordinary passenger!" It occurred to John that ordinary passengers didn't get kicked, but knowing what was good for him, he kept his mouth shut. Instead, he and the rest of the Beatles darted toward a group of nuns and monks huddled by an alcove, hoping that would discourage the thugs. Meanwhile, Mal fell and was kicked repeatedly in the ribs, along with Alf Bicknell, who was severely beaten.

After about fifteen minutes everyone was allowed to run across the tarmac to the plane. "I was the last to go," recalls Vic Lewis, "and I remember putting a hand on my back, thinking that's where the bullet was going to hit." The terrified Beatles climbed the stairs into the cabin. It was hot, well over ninety degrees, and they were dripping with perspiration—but relieved. Then two Philippine military officers stiffly came aboard. Scanning the passengers, they announced: "Mr. Barrow and Mr. Evans, we need you to come back into the departure office." The cabin went silent. Tony, sitting in the back of the first-class compartment, grimaced. Mal struggled to his feet and walked unsteadily toward the exit. As he passed George Harrison, he stopped and tearfully whispered, "Tell Lil I love her."

Tony and Mal were detained for another half an hour. In a typical bureaucratic snafu, their papers hadn't been processed with the others when they arrived from Tokyo; their passports hadn't been stamped. After they handed over their passports, duly stamped, they were free to leave.

Once the plane was safely in the air, the Beatles were unusually subdued. Sitting across the aisle from one another, sweating in the painfully sticky cabin, they calmed themselves, smoking cigarettes against the tension, while the anger and resentment that had been simmering over the past few days finally boiled over. The boys quickly developed a need to lay blame for the debacle. It "was Brian's cock-up," they decided. He'd obviously handled that invitation business badly, either ignoring it or misleading the authorities—or *them.* Whatever the reasons, it mustn't ever happen again, they agreed. Even if it meant having someone double-check his arrangements.

Brian, stewing quietly a row in front of the Beatles, couldn't help but overhear the intensity of their complaints. And they were right, after all; he was their manager and ultimately responsible for their welfare. But to hear them go on like that, expressing their dissatisfaction with him, was brutal. Agonizing, he clutched the armrests with both hands and stared out the window. Peter Brown, who was in the seat next to him, noticed that Brian was "seizing with tension, and it was not just the Philippines." Then, a little after five o'clock, when the pillow of thick clouds absorbed the last rays of sunlight, Vic Lewis leaned across Brown and gently shook

Brian's shoulder. "I'm sorry this happened," he said. Brian took no notice of the agent; he was already on the edge. Brown shook his head ominously and said, "Another time, Vic." But Lewis refused to take the hint. "No, you don't understand," he insisted, "it shouldn't have happened like this. But I hope you got the money." Several times throughout the ostensible apology, Brian muttered to Brown through clenched teeth: "Get him away from me, *get him away!*" Lewis was concerned—and rightly so—about a paper bag containing the box-office receipts, roughly $17,000 in cash, that were due the Beatles from the Manilla dates. "Go away, Vic," Brown said, pushing Lewis's hand away. Lewis stared murderously at Brown, deciding whether to hit him. All this trouble was *their* fault, he fumed; the least they could do was account for the money. Finally, Brian blew a gasket. "*You turn to me at a time like this and talk about—money?*" he screamed. A spray of saliva splattered Lewis's cheek. That had done it. Vic reached for Brian's collar; Brian tried to slap his hand away. Before anyone landed a punch, Neil Aspinall was out of his seat and between the two men.

It was finally clear: touring was a nightmare, it wasn't about performing anymore. "It was just sort of a freak show," John complained. "The Beatles *were* the show and the music had nothing to do with it."

———

From the moment they landed in India, so George could buy a decent sitar, the Beatles discussed among themselves the feasibility of not touring. Ever. "Who fucking needs this?" was an oft-heard lament. They were tired of simply going through the motions, tired of acting like the "four wax-work dummies" John thought promoters could "send out . . . [to] satisfy the crowds." George had already intimated as much to a reporter back in June. "I've increasingly become aware that there are other things in life than being a Beatle," he observed. "I prefer to be out of the public eye anyway." And after Shea, John had never hid his contempt for stadiums filled with screaming thirteen-year-old girls. Now there was impetus to take a harder stand. "And they decided then and there," Neil recalled, "that they weren't going to do America the next year."

The finality of the Beatles' decision unnerved Brian. "It wasn't like the boys to be so uncompromising with him," says Tony Barrow. "They usually ran things like this past him, to hear his input." Peter Brown, who thought it was still all in the talking phase, saw Brian afterward "completely distraught and inconsolable." He remembered thinking, "He's blowing this all out of proportion."

By the time they boarded the plane back to London, Brian's mood had grown "very dark," according to Brown, "sinking into a hideous funk." To make matters worse, the flight was awful. Several of the Beatles got food poisoning. Everyone had been so careful about what they ate while in India that they dove into the beef Stroganoff served after takeoff, which did the real damage. John and Ringo took turns throwing up, and Brian got hives. It was a long flight, and everyone was "very disgruntled, very unhappy."

To Brian, it was clear from what he overheard that the end had come; that after four years of success and prosperity, his position was redundant; that the Beatles had precipitously cut him loose. "He was distraught about what he'd do if they stopped touring," says Brown, who sat beside Brian throughout the trip. "'There's no *place* for me,' he kept saying. I finally got impatient with him. He was just being a drama queen. There was so much other business for him to tend to, but it didn't register."

By the time they neared their destination, Brian was reeling from nerves and alcohol. His effort to contain the anxiety had backfired. A wave of manic depression swept over him that manifested itself like a shock. Slack, almost catatonic, he was consumed by the repressed anger. He was "so sick, so shaky," that the airline radioed ahead for an ambulance to meet the plane.

Whatever happened, he begged Peter Brown not to send him to a hospital or an asylum; that would have been too much of a humiliation with the Beatles looking on. Instead, they transferred Brian to a limo headed to Portmerion, an eccentric little beach resort in northern Wales run by two "campy, upper-class guys" that served as a "weekend getaway" for the Liverpool gay community. Bertrand Russell lived down the hill, it had wonderful food. An extravagance of gently wooded walkways wound through the Victorian-style countryside. To Brian, it felt "rather chic and sophisticated," the perfect place for him to contemplate the future and to mend. The hotel manifest said he would be there for a month, but that was really only for show. "Brian never stayed *anywhere* for a month," Brown explains. Even ten days of rest, however, would do wonders for his badly rattled equilibrium.

But on the fourth day, just as he had settled in comfortably, the operator put through a call from Wendy Hanson, at NEMS in London. There was a story circulating in an American magazine, she said, about John and some comments he'd made about Christianity. "You'd better get on top of this," she warned him. The shit had hit the fan.

[I]

Christianity will go. It will vanish and shrink. . . ." The words sounded vaguely familiar to Brian as Wendy Hanson read him a telex that had come over the wire from America. "We're more popular than Jesus now."

Once he had heard the whole thing, straining through the crackles of provincial static, the source grew clearer, the March interview John had given to the Beatles' longtime press groupie, Maureen Cleave. But it was more than an old story, Wendy explained. The night before, on July 31, Nat Weiss had gotten a call about six o'clock in the evening, informing him that Beatles records were being burned in Birmingham, Alabama. A few calls later he had determined that the makings of a firestorm had been ignited. Some of John's comments to Cleave had been syndicated in *Datebook*, a cheesy American teen magazine, and sensationalized by some slippery editing. A headline slashed across the cover shouted, JOHN LENNON SAYS: "BEATLES MORE POPULAR THAN JESUS," and inside, CHRISTIANITY WILL GO! The reaction was swift and predictable. Southern fundamentalists went apeshit over the remarks, labeling them blasphemous. A pair of Bible-thumping disc jockeys at WAQY immediately banned the playing of all Beatles records and sponsored a community bonfire fueled by the offending LPs for August 19 "to show them they cannot get away with this sort of thing." Once the wire services picked up the story, similar "Beatle Burnings" and boycotts spread to other, mostly hardscrabble communities.

It would come to be a personal joke among the Beatles that in order to burn their albums, one first had to buy them, "so it's no sweat off us, mate, burn 'em if you like." And at the outset, the religious backlash seemed absurd. KZEE, in Weatherford, Texas, "damned their songs 'eternally'"; in Reno, KCBN broadcast an anti-Beatles editorial every hour; WAYX, in

Waycross, Georgia, burned its entire stock of Beatles records; a Baptist minister in Cleveland threatened to revoke the membership of anyone in the congregation who played Beatles records; South Carolina's Grand Dragon of the Ku Klux Klan nailed several Beatles albums to a cross and set it aflame. Boycotts were announced by radio stations in Ashland and Hopkinsville, Kentucky; Dayton, Bryan, and Akron, Ohio; Dublin, Georgia; Jackson, Mississippi; Barnwell, South Carolina; and Corning, New York, "joining stations," the *New York Times* reported, "in Massachusetts, Connecticut, Michigan, and other states" that bought into the controversy. "We were being told" through operatives in New York, says Tony Barrow, "that there were now religious zealots who were actually threatening to assassinate John Lennon if the Beatles came to Memphis," one of the scheduled stops on the upcoming American tour.

The Beatles, according to Paul, "didn't really take it too seriously at all," and he, particularly, wrote off the excitement to "hysterical low-grade American thinking." Brian dissembled to the press, calling it "a storm in a teacup," but beneath the icy elegance he was "deeply disturbed" by the implications and decided that a trip to the States was in order.

Nat Weiss met Brian at the airport in New York. "The moment he got in the car, he asked: 'How much will it cost to cancel the tour?'" Weiss's estimation of a million dollars didn't faze Brian. "Okay," he said, "I'll pay it." Then, in the next voice and despite the tension, he got down to vital concerns. "Are there any boys around?" he asked.

For the next two days Brian ran damage control from an office in the Paramount Building, on Broadway. Nat prepared the underlying strategy: John's statements, as reported in *Datebook,* "were taken completely out of context." Most people, he argued, ignored that John was saying "We are more *popular* than Jesus," not "We are *more important . . .*" "He did not mean to boast about the Beatles' fame," Maureen Cleave insisted in a carefully scripted response. "John was certainly not comparing the Beatles to Christ. He was simply observing that, so weak was the state of Christianity, the Beatles was, to many people, better known." It was highly unusual for any reporter to issue such a ringing defense of the subject of his or her story, especially going so far as to interpret his remarks. Cleave also appeared on a number of radio shows to discuss her viewpoint, at which point Brian "request[ed] emphatically no [further] comment from her." But whatever the official reason, whatever the excuse, the situation remained volatile. Radio stations, especially in the South and the West, "were having a field day," as George later recalled. Not that John cared. "I'd forgotten [all about it]," he said upon later reflection. "It was that unimportant—it had been and gone." But once he had a chance to "reread the whole article," his tune changed. "Tell them to get stuffed. I've got nothing to apologize for," John snarled. As far as canceling the tour, that was fine with him. "I'd rather that than have to get up and lie. What I said stands."

Nevertheless, Brian succeeded in persuading John of the need to shape a public statement. "It went back and forth for two days," Nat Weiss recalls. The two men wrangled over every word until both John and Brian were satisfied that all sides were well served. John would apologize, but he refused to eat shit. Brian would do that for him.

The next day Brian booked a suite at New York's Americana Hotel and summoned the world press to a hastily convened news conference. It was a typically staged Epstein affair: drinks and hors d'oeuvres were served, after which he read the following statement:

> The quote which John Lennon made to a London columnist
> nearly three months ago has been quoted and represented en-
> tirely out of context. Lennon is deeply interested in religion. . . .
> What he said and meant was that he was astonished that in the
> last fifty years the Church of England, and therefore Christ, had
> suffered a decline in interest. He did not mean to boast about the
> Beatles' fame. He meant to point out that the Beatles' effect ap-
> peared to be, to him, a more immediate one upon certain of the
> younger generation.

To many beat reporters who listened, this sounded like a fairly liberal rewrite of John's remarks. (Brian had called it "a clarification.") Yet at the same time, it served to mollify them. Most of the papers that covered the event treated it like a news item, without comment. But it was clear to everyone, including Brian, that it wasn't the last word on this subject—not by a long shot.

The press conference coincided with the release of two new Beatles records, and the music, as always, managed to work its essential magic. On roughly five thousand radio stations on August 5—that is, the stations that were *playing*, as opposed to *burning*, Beatles records—the single "Yellow Submarine" and "Eleanor Rigby" received its first airplay. What an earful of music on two sides of a single disc—from the ridiculous to the sublime! When the reviews hit the trades, it was clear the record was every bit as audacious—and intricate—as its makers had intended. More and more often, the critics just threw up their hands. "One thing seems certain to me— you'll soon be singing about a 'Yellow Submarine,'" hedged Alan Evans in an issue of *NME.* "It should be a household favorite soon." Otherwise, Evans couldn't get a handle on "Eleanor Rigby," writing it off as "a folksy ballad sung with very clear diction by Paul McCartney."

About *Revolver,* which was released the same day, they were less ecstatic, even somewhat baffled by the music's ample complexities. "The new Beatles' album, *Revolver,* certainly has new sounds and new ideas, and should cause plenty of argument among fans as to whether it is as good as or better than previous efforts," wrote *NME.* Songs like "Tomorrow Never Knows" perplexed critics. They appreciated its message to turn off your mind, relax, and float downstream. "But how can you relax with the electronic outer-space noises, often sounding like seagulls?" they wondered. "Even John's voice is weirdly fractured and given a faraway sound." And no one predicted the album's powerful resonance, that it would be considered an artistic breakthrough, or that thirty years later, when *Mojo* magazine compiled "The 100 Greatest Albums Ever Made," its readers would rank *Revolver* number one, hands down. "From the day it came out, it changed the way everyone else made records," Geoff Emerick reminisced in that celebrated issue. "No one had ever heard anything like that before."

And though they may have been ahead of the curve, the Beatles were not alone. Every week articles filled the pages of *Billboard, NME,* and *Melody Maker* with the incredible stuff that was pouring out of new groups. Two weeks before the Beatles' American tour opened, the Lovin' Spoonful soared to the top of the pop charts with the harder-edged "Summer in the City," displacing "Wild Thing," by the Troggs. The Beach Boys put out the legendary *Pet Sounds* about the same time Bob Dylan released *Blonde on Blonde.* "Mother's Little Helper" and "Paint It Black" certified the Stones' outlaw status. The daring "Eight Miles High" launched the Byrds into outer space. The Holland-Dozier-Holland assembly line continued cranking out sweet soul classics. Tim Hardin made his enviable debut, along with albums by Quicksilver Messenger Service, the Mamas and the Papas, Simon and Garfunkel, Laura Nyro, the Mothers of Invention, and the Velvet Underground, each one as original and eclectic as the next. Ultimately, however, it was the Beatles that provided the most uncompromising, even disruptive, listening experience. *Q* would eventually refer to

Revolver as a "scaling of new musical peaks . . . a quantum leap forward" for a band of beloved pop heroes. But corresponding as it did with John's controversial comments, it also represented entry into a dark, ruthless cross-current destined to reroute the Beatles as cultural reactionaries. *Image,* which had always defined the Beatles, now daunted those fans who were unprepared for a transition. "We're not trying to pass off as kids," John insisted. "We have been Beatles as best we ever will be—those four jolly lads. But we're not those people anymore." There was no point in keeping up the pose as those wacky teenage idols, not when they'd evolved into the kind of men and musicians who produced a document as riveting as *Revolver.* As individuals, John, Paul, George, and Ringo were growing up; as the Beatles, they were beginning to grow apart.

[II]

By the time John was ready to leave for the States, he was fuming. He had glanced at the first reports of the backlash with mild amusement. Then his anger grew steadily as demands for an apology mounted until, by departure, he was incensed. He told Brian that not only did he refuse to apologize for his statement but he had no intention of saying anything to the press—about Christianity, or music, or *anything.* Brian wouldn't hear of it. There was too much at stake, the tour being the least of his worries. His offer to let any promoter out of his contract was unanimously declined. *But* he admonished John about mucking up several pending deals that could have far-reaching economic consequences. The Beatles' record deal, for instance; they were in the throes of renegotiating a contract with EMI and Capitol, one that would finally bring them deserved riches. And songwriters' royalties from dozens of potential new covers. (*NME* reported there were already nine shipped as of the week of *Revolver*'s release.) It wasn't just his own hide on the line, either. There were three other Beatles, Brian reminded John, and dozens of people whose personal well-being rested on their fortunes. "And so Brian . . . kept asking him to say something," recalled Ringo, "and in the end, John realized that he'd have to go out and do it."

The plan was to face the press before the first performance in Chicago, on the evening of August 11. Everyone was staying in the Astor Towers, on the twenty-seventh floor, and the three major American television networks had already set up cameras in the corridor and were delivering pithy commentaries. Meanwhile, John was summoned for a last-minute briefing. "We were nervous that he was going to wiseguy it up," says Tony Barrow. They were sitting in the dimly lit solitude of Brian's spacious lounge, John and Brian on the settee, Barrow cross-legged across the glass-and-steel coffee table. After drinks were served, Brian said, "Look, you do realize the implications of this, don't you? You can't go out there with a few one-liners. It's not a joke, and it's not just you getting yourself off the hook. Either we have to get positive press out of this or the tour is going to be called off. We're not talking, John, about you rescuing your own reputation; we're talking about you saving the group's tour." Pausing for dramatic impact, Brian admitted that he "feared the Beatles might be assassinated during the tour."

After gently putting his glass down on the coffee table, John burst into tears. His head bowed, body racked with sobs, John pleaded for some guidance. "I'll do anything," he said. "Anything. Whatever you say I should do, I'll have to say . . . I didn't mean to cause all of this."

He sat there for a while, until he was composed. Then, with Brian and Tony at his side, the three other Beatles trailing, John marched across the hall into Barrow's suite, where about thirty members of the media were waiting to hear his side of things.

The press conference, long a frisky Beatles performance, was an unusually somber affair. The rest of the band "stood solemnly" behind a table where John sat, clutching his hands to keep them from trembling. His torso twitched nervously, awkwardly, in his seat. Paul, at his side through many scrapes, had "never seen John so nervous." It was as if it were the first time he'd faced the press.

Leaning into a microphone, John looked a wreck. "If I'd have said, 'Television is more popular than Jesus,' I might have got away with it," he said haltingly. "I'm sorry I opened my mouth. I just happened to be talking to a friend and I used the word 'Beatles' as a remote thing—'Beatles,' like other people see us. I said they are having more influence on kids and things than anything else, including Jesus. I said it in that way, which was the wrong way. I'm not anti-God, anti-Christ, or antireligion. I was not knocking it. I was not saying we are greater or better. I think it's a bit silly. If they don't like us, why don't they just not buy the records?"

Wait a minute! Despite the fact that John spoke willingly and unaffectedly, there seemed to be some skirting of the central issue. It sounded to most of the journalists like an explanation, as opposed to an apology.

"Some teenagers have repeated your statements—'I like the Beatles more than Jesus Christ,'" a reporter interrupted. "What do you think about this?"

John paused thoughtfully before answering. "Well, originally I pointed out that fact in reference to England. That we meant more to kids than Jesus did, or religion at that time. I wasn't knocking it or putting it down. . . . I just said what I said and it was wrong." *That sounds more like it.* "Or it was taken wrong." *Uh-oh.* "And now it's all this." *Hmmm . . .*

"But are you prepared to apologize?" a broadcaster asked.

John tried to explain himself again. And again. The dance went around and around without end, each partner circling, stumbling, stepping on toes. Exasperated, exhausted—the Beatles had just come off a twelve-hour flight—he finally let it boil over. "I wasn't saying what they're saying I was saying," he said, glowering. "I'm sorry I said it—really. I never meant it to be a lousy antireligious thing. I apologize if that will make you happy. I still don't know quite what I've done. I've tried to tell you what I did do, but if you want me to apologize, if that will make you happy, then—okay, I'm sorry."

There was a long, indulgent pause, broken when a mincing voice from the back broke through the silence: "Okay, can you just actually say to the camera how sorry you are?" At which point the Beatles glanced at one another and cut wry little smiles. It was just as they figured: the press hadn't been listening for the past twenty minutes. Everything was for show. The press was "quite prepared to let the Lennon affair die a natural death" to preserve the spirit of Beatlemania.

Over the Beatles' objections, the tour had been set back in April, with the rundown of opening acts changing again and again in the intervening months. Only the Ronettes had always been part of the package; even though they hadn't had a hit in two years, the Beatles loved the girls' sassy stage personae and wanted them aboard for window dressing as much as anything else. They also added Bobby Hebb, a songwriter from Nashville, whose smash hit, "Sunny," was a fixture at the top of the summer charts; the Remains, a group of students on leave from Boston University, to provide backup; and the Cyrkle. Nat Weiss had discovered the latter playing covers in a bar while walking along the Boardwalk in Atlantic City. On June 6 he and Brian had formed a company called Nemperor Artists, designed specifically to look after the Beatles' affairs but also as a subsidiary to manage American acts, and the Cyrkle, at Nat's urging, became their first signing.

Inside the International Amphitheater, whose location next door to the Chicago stockyards provided a malodorous bouquet, the crowd of mostly screaming teenage girls staged a replay of all the mayhem that had marked the Beatles' previous tours. It was the same everywhere: Detroit, Cleveland, Washington, Philadelphia—the fans played the familiar roles required of them. But in almost every case, the threat of violence was felt. In Cleveland, especially, where an outbreak on the 1964 tour had interrupted the show, there was a repeat performance when three thousand fans rained out of the stands at Municipal Stadium and made a beeline for the stage. The police and Mal Evans valiantly defended the stage, swatting away marauding fans while the Beatles soldiered on, bashing through "Day Tripper." But at a certain point, as Barrow's assistant Bess Coleman observed in *Teen Life,* they were "given the order: *Run for your lives!* And, did they run!" The boys dropped their instruments mid-song and took off for a trailer stationed behind the home-plate stands, dragging along the frazzled Coleman.

"By the time we got to Memphis, there was a very serious feeling," recalls Tony Barrow. "It was the first Deep South date we played," and there was a strong rumor that something truly violent could happen. According to Nat Weiss, "Brian was very nervous" about Memphis. "He was convinced some nut was going to take a shot at John." Indeed, there had been discussions with his GAC agents about pulling out of the date rather than invite disaster, but ultimately—and without much discussion—the Beatles insisted on appearing. "If we cancel one, you might as well cancel all of them," Paul told him.

But the constant buildup of tension eventually dented their bravado. One of the backup musicians remembered that "the flight from Boston to Memphis was quieter than usual." The Beatles sat together on the crowded charter, staring out the windows, not talking much. John wore a troubled look as the plane made its slow descent into Memphis. "So this is where all the Christians come from," he said to Paul, slouched grim-faced in the aisle seat next to him. Paul had nothing left to counterbalance John's ominous mood. "You're a very controversial person," he muttered, devoid of the usual cheery note. Only George managed to crack the despair as they taxied to a stop. "Send John out first," he quipped. "He's the one they want."

The situation took a sinister turn the minute they hit the ground. Security was heavier than usual, a condition meant to be reassuring, but everyone was filled with unavoidable foreboding nevertheless. Instead of the usual transfer by limo, the Beatles were loaded into the back of a specially armored minivan while everyone else wordlessly boarded a bus for the trip to the arena. "Driving into Memphis from the airport, we had to lie down, because they thought snipers might shoot us," remembers the Remains' drummer, N. D. Smart. The brave few who dared peep out the windows saw protesters along the route, waving signs—and fists. "I will never forget . . . we pulled in there in the coach," Paul later said, "and there was this little blond-haired kid, he could have been no older than eleven or twelve, who barely came up to the window, screaming at me through the plate glass, banging the window with such vehemence." Intuitively, Paul knew the kid was harmless, although he had his doubts about the hooded Ku Klux Klansmen that roamed the grounds of the Mid-South Coliseum.

But the first show went off like any other. Despite pockets of empty seats, there was the typical pandemonium, plenty of crying and screaming; girls littered the stage with stuffed animals and gifts, among cruder types of debris. "The Beatles smiled through it all," said a review in the *Commercial Appeal.* "It appeared to be just the type of unrestrained welcome they are used to."

Understandably, their mood improved between shows. "Everyone started to relax," recalled an observer. Backstage, the band ate a roast beef dinner and talked amiably with reporters crammed into the cluttered room. They took some good-natured ribbing over an ad for the show that Mal found in a local newspaper. "Go to church on Sunday," it said, "*but* see THE BEATLES Friday!"

By the second show, at eight, the Beatles had good reason to be elated. The arena was packed this time, with more than twelve thousand delirious "crew-cut kids" determined to rip the stuffing out of the Old South. It was a right rebel rave-up until midway through the third song, "If I Needed Someone," when a shot rang out. Epstein and Barrow, standing at the side of the stage, jumped, banging into each other—then crouched. "I was convinced . . . it was a shot," Barrow recalls. Paul and George jerked sideways toward John, who was straddling the mike. Later, Paul explained to *Teen-Set*'s editor how "when he heard [the blast] his heart stopped, but he realized he was still standing and didn't feel anything. He looked at John and saw that he was still standing, so they all kept right on playing."

Kids. Two teenagers had lobbed a cherry bomb from the upper balcony.

The Beatles fought back with abandon. Their playing was unusually sharp, full of snap and bite, and for a moment they gave it all they had. But the fix was in. When a string of firecrackers popped and spit a few minutes later, it brought them crashing back to earth. It wasn't the music fans wanted, they realized, but *the show*—and not just what was going on on-stage, but the whole crazy atmosphere. That's what they had come for: the mayhem, the hair shaking, the *yeah, yeah, yeah*.

Of all the Beatles, only Paul was inclined to play along. Paul loved the showbiz aspect of Beatlemania, to say nothing of the acclaim. The times he spent on the road—engaging the fans, jawing with reporters, mugging for photographers, and winding up the crowds—were among the highlights of his life. Lionel Bart, who saw him often during this time, called him a born crowd-pleaser and presumed that he'd eventually find his place on main-stream stages like those at the Palladium. "It was clear from the start that show business ran deep in Paul's veins and he was committed to a lifetime on the stage." But the other three were disgusted. George especially had had his fill. Ren Grevatt, *Melody Maker*'s American stringer, had been watching throughout the tour how the whole grind weighed on the Beatles' personalities. "I've noticed that George Harrison is getting deeper and deeper every day and will probably end up being a bald recluse monk," he observed in an unusually frank column. "He's trying to figure out life, but don't let this sound mocking—he is very serious."

What Grevatt mistook for seriousness, however, was a malaise that deepened with every passing day. George was fed up with the grim, chaotic life of the Beatles. In discussions with friends, he talked of feeling "wasted" and virtually "imprisoned" by the constraints of Beatlemania. The touring and its effluvia had beat him up, physically and emotionally. "It had been four years of legging around in a screaming mania," he grumbled. Endless performances—"about 1,400 live shows," by George's count—had left him bored and dispirited. It was all he could do to get up for the thirty-minute appearance.

"Nobody was listening at the shows," complained Ringo, who said he "was fed up playing" in such a haphazard manner. Bashing along to "She's a Woman" and "I Feel Fine" day in and day out wasn't his idea of drum-ming. It was impossible for him to hear what the others were doing on-stage, forcing him to play to their body language. There was no percentage in it. Conditions were so pitiful that during many songs Ringo's drums would slide around the platform, requiring him to get up and move them back into place. Ringo had always been a sport; he'd always done whatever was asked of him, whatever was best for the band. He'd played the role that was required of him—the role of a lifetime. But his heart wasn't in it anymore.

And to John, the whole scene was a dreadful experience. "I didn't want to tour again," he said, "especially after having been accused of crucifying Jesus . . . and having to stand with the Klan outside and firecrackers going on inside." Creatively, physically, emotionally, he had had it with playing those kinds of gigs. Beatlemania represented everything he detested—the phoniness of the band's image, their lack of progress as musicians, the degree to which he'd sold out. He felt "the music was dead" long before the Beatles ever hit the States, which meant that *he* felt dead for more time than was tolerable for anyone with his instincts. "I couldn't take any more," he said.

A series of accidents, incompetences, and circumstances, including a pair of back-to-back dates in Cincinnati and St. Louis, underscored the Beatles' distaste for the road. Cincinnati was a disaster. It rained before showtime as the Beatles arrived at Crosley Field, but with a ballpark full of sodden fans determined to see their idols, the boys seemed inclined to appear. A canvas canopy hung over the stage. "They'd brought in the electricity," George recalled, "but the stage was soaking and we would have been electrocuted." "It was really scary," recalls Nat Weiss. "The crowd kept screaming, '*We want the Beatles!*' and Paul grew so upset at the prospect of going out there that he got sick. The strain was too great. And he threw up in the dressing room." Eventually, Brian called off the show—"the only gig we ever missed," George pointed out—but managed to reorganize the schedule so that they could play at noon the next day before flying out to do an evening show in Missouri.

Meanwhile, the weather followed them to St. Louis, where a gleaming new Busch Stadium wilted under a stinging drizzle. Only "a couple bits of corrugated iron" were propped above the bandstand positioned over second base, and the slipshod setup reminded Paul of "a mud hut in the middle of somewhere." "There were sparks flying all over the place," according to Ed Freeman, who handled sound for the tour. "I remember that every time Paul bumped into the mike, which was almost every beat, there were sparks." Mal had rigged an outlet with a waterproof power cord and instructed Freeman "to pull it whenever the first person on stage collapsed from any electric shock."

After the show, during a frantic and extremely narrow escape in the airless container of a chrome-paneled truck, all the damage and indignities finally caught up with the Beatles. "We were sliding around trying to hold onto something," Paul recalled, "and at that moment everyone" decided they'd had enough of touring. There was no point in pretending anymore — performing had become too much of a liability. Even Paul admitted he'd had enough; the touring, to him, "had become spiritually rather empty." The Beatles would make more than enough money from continued record sales, as well as other projects that came through the pipeline. Besides, attendance at the shows had been falling off steadily. Only two or three concerts on the American tour had been sellouts, and though no one ever mentioned as much, several promoters failed to make back their investment. It seemed useless to wait until the Beatles — *live* and *in person* — became a disposable commodity. It was easier to walk away before anyone took notice.

———

"We didn't make a formal announcement that we were going to stop touring," Ringo recalled. Nevertheless, the matter was settled between them. The August 29 concert in San Francisco would be their last. There would be no more Beatles shows, no more participation in the tumult of Beatlemania. From now on, they would exist solely in the studio as a band that made records.

It's uncertain if any of them brought Brian in on the decision. Convinced that he'd try to talk them out of it, increasingly distrustful of his ripening psychosis, they most likely kept its finality among themselves, at least for the time being.

By Los Angeles, still reeling from the Philippines fiasco and subsequent Jesus uproar, Brian was a bundle of raw nerves. On August 27 Nat Weiss arrived in their pink-tinged bungalow at the Beverly Hills Hotel and immediately sensed another personality shift, this time into rapture. "Good news," Brian said, beaming with an unnatural intensity, "Diz is here, in L.A." Protesting, Nat warned Brian away from the hustler, but any concern was waved off. "No, no," Brian insisted. "He's different — he's so sweet. You'll see."

It didn't take long for Weiss's worst fears to materialize. Diz and Brian spent the day sunning themselves by the pool. At some point late that afternoon, Brian unloaded a bombshell. "I have an important announcement," he said, fluttering his hands like a magician. "Tomorrow night is the Beatles' last concert ever, and I want the two of you to be my guest." All kinds of arrangements were discussed about flying everyone to San

Francisco for the farewell show, then Diz excused himself for another engagement. "[Brian and I] went out to dinner," Nat recalls, "and when we came back, our briefcases were gone." Along with Diz.

There have been various accounts concerning the contents of those briefcases. Nat says: "I didn't have anything in mine. Brian had about ten thousand dollars in cash along with papers and a bottle of Seconal." By Peter Brown's calculation, however, the missing cash amounted to $20,000 in addition to "half a dozen or so billets-doux containing explicit references to [Brian's] conquests, along with Polaroid photographs of his young friends."

Brian forbade Nat from reporting Diz to the police, arguing that it would lead to a scandal. For a modicum of cash—no more, really, than he might drop on a hand of baccarat—and whatever else was in those briefcases, he'd spare the Beatles any more unwarranted publicity. But while the Beatles flew north, Brian remained in L.A. and sank into "a suicidal depression" that scoured new depths of self-loathing.

The Beatles gave their farewell performance at Candlestick Park the next night, with Brian Epstein nowhere to be seen.

Candlestick Park was a notoriously windswept arena, with its outfield facing out onto San Francisco Bay, but that Monday night, on August 29, gusts whipped through the stands with an almost biblical vengeance. Banners strung around the stadium flapped ferociously against the squall and drafts picked up great clouds of dust and blew them volcanically across the infield. "It was not the sort of night you'd like to turn out for an outdoor concert," notes Tony Barrow, and, indeed, the stands were only half filled, with 25,000 die-hard Beatles fans huddled against the squall.

Their anticipation, however, rivaled baseball crowds twice the size. Fans recalled "being jolted from head to toe" by the prospect that the Beatles would appear. Mimi Fariña, who sat behind the third-base dugout with her sister, Joan Baez, described the fan response as "sounding like clouds bursting." There was an air of exhilarating suspense, she recalled. "Things were popping."

The performance itself was nothing extraordinary. The Beatles sang eleven songs—the same eleven "totally familiar studio recorded versions" they'd been singing for four years, with one or two exceptions—using precisely the same patter, the same tired jokes. (Thirty years later Tony Barrow listened to a tape of the *NME* concert at Wembley Stadium, one of the Beatles' earliest concerts, followed by a recording of Candlestick Park, and was surprised to discover that "John and Paul say exactly the same thing between songs four years apart.") It was one of their shortest shows, seconds shy of thirty minutes, and "perhaps the least inspired," recalls Barrow. "The boys were very tired indeed and couldn't wait to get that last show over." John, who referred to it afterward as "a puppet show," had nothing left in his tank. He didn't hesitate for a moment when it came to leading the charge off the field and disappearing with the others into a waiting armored truck. A great release washed over him as the van kicked up dust speeding toward the right-field bullpen, toward the end of Beatlemania—toward liberation, at last.

George also sighed and settled into the momentous finale. "I was thinking, 'This is going to be such a relief—not to have to go through this madness anymore,'" he recalled. There was an air of subtle, rarefied elation to it that he expressed as their plane took off for Los Angeles. Sinking into the seat next to Tony Barrow, George closed his eyes, smiled, and said: "Right—that's it. I'm not a Beatle anymore."

[III]

Not being a Beatle anymore brought the Beatles no instant peace. Instead of the kind of quiet interlude they had hoped for, the whole world took up their case, talking obsessively about the Beatles and pondering their future. Were they finished? "Is Beatlemania Dead?" *Time* wondered. Derek Taylor, writing in *Melody Maker*, could only speculate about their uncertain future. He'd visited with the Beatles during their recent stay in Los Angeles, where he'd found a similar position press-managing the Byrds, but even after a playful night spent passing joints back and forth, he'd come no closer to resolving their murky agenda. Still, their "impact . . . and mythology," the *Sunday Times* said, was too potent to diminish the boys' overall importance. "In a business where today's smash-hit is tomorrow's stinker, the Beatle sound will almost certainly survive as the echo of an era." Certainly *Revolver* had defied all predictions and won vast popular acclaim. It sold millions of units while giving fans and musicians alike something extraordinary to shoot for.

In July, Dick Lester approached John about taking a minor role in his new movie, a satirical antiwar comedy called *How I Won the War*. John not only agreed but promised to cut his famous hair to a length befitting a proper English soldier. It was by no means the first time John had acted.

From the moment he slung on a guitar, greased his hair back like Elvis, or decked himself out in black leather and high-heeled boots, John had been playing various parts that appealed to his sense of character. Even as one of the Beatles, he'd assumed an exaggerated role, playing to the crowd and mugging for the cameras. "It makes perfect sense," Paul said of his collaborator's sideline. "He's really only ever wanted to be James Dean or Marlon Brando."

But working as a supporting actor proved excruciatingly boring. In Germany and then southern Spain, where most of the action was filmed, John spent much of the time "hanging around," waiting for his scenes to be called. "He loathed the endless waiting in the desert," according to Ray Coleman, ". . . and learning lines, however short, drained his patience." Several weeks lapsed as John bumped from location to location, struggling to occupy himself against stretches of insufferable downtime. At first, long strolls with Cynthia along the sun-drenched Gulf of Almería proved distracting, but the charm wore off soon enough. "It was pretty damn boring to me," John recalled. "I didn't find it at all very fulfilling."

Between the rigors of acting and confronting the unknown, John withdrew deeper into himself, smoking fistfuls of Spanish dope and languishing on the beach, shielded from the stargazers by his war-torn acoustic guitar. Music would provide for him. It always had. Nothing offered the kind of comfort as the sanctuary of a song. "He used to sit cross-legged on the beach or on the bed, working out a melody," recalled Michael Crawford, who costarred in the film and shared a beach house with John in Spain. It was there, Crawford said, "I heard him playing the same bar over and over again until he got the right sequence." *Living is easy with eyes closed, misunderstanding all you see . . .* The tune had a dreamy, languid feel to it, "conjuring up a hazy impressionistic dreamworld," as George Martin later described it. Crawford, hearing the song at irregular intervals, was struck by its enigmatic beauty—the interplay of pot and nostalgic detail that John labored over in the lyric—and suggested leaving it alone. "Really, it's good," he told John. "I wouldn't mess with it."

"Strawberry Fields Forever" allowed John to wrestle with a confessional song as confused and dramatic as his emotions. "[It] was psychoanalysis set to music," he reasoned later, after having spent years on the therapist's couch. For years he had been sugarcoating his imagery, reluctant, except in a few notable cases, to reveal himself personally in a song. It was easy, with Paul as his sidekick, to keep the lyrics unspecific and upbeat. But with *Rubber Soul* and *Revolver,* John had turned a corner on his craft. He finally sensed the true scope of his potential—a gift he'd suspected all along—and realized that to make the leap to great songwriting, he would have to open up his heart.

"Strawberry Fields Forever" lifted everything onto the next level. For inspiration, John took himself back to Woolton, the scene of his favorite childhood escapades, where he spent blissful summer mornings in the company of Nigel Walley, Ivan Vaughan, and Pete Shotton playing in Calderstones Park. Strawberry Field wasn't a patch of land but, as John pointed out, the name of "an old Victorian house converted for Salvation Army orphans," near the entrance to the park. "It [provided] an escape for John," Paul remembered, musing on his own memories of the place. "There was a wall you could bunk over and it had a rather wild garden, it wasn't manicured at all, so it was easy to hide in." Aunt Mimi told Albert Goldman: "There was something about the place that always fascinated John. He could see it from his window, and he loved going to the garden party they had each year. He used to hear the Salvation Army band, and he would pull me along, saying, 'Hurry up, Mimi—we're going to be late.'"

All these memories came flooding back as John amused himself in Spain, sifting through the scrapbook of his less-than-idyllic childhood. "I took the name"—Strawberry Fields*—"as an image," John explained, and he used it as inspiration to express his seriously conflicted feelings about growing up and self-awareness. Instead of rhymes and wordplay, John poured strings of surreal images into the verses to bring his emotional world alive.

During September 1966 Paul was also abroad, in France. For a change of scenery, Paul, who loved to drive, decided to take the sightseer's route from Paris through the Loire Valley, stopping off at the grand châteaux of Chambord and Chenonceaux that bordered the country roads, before heading west to Bordeaux. His intention had been to "travel incognito, disguised so that he would not be recognized," or at least appearing as inconspicuous as any young man could while crisscrossing rural France in a sleek dark green Aston Martin DB5. It would be an ideal opportunity, he thought, "to ease the pressure . . . [a]nd retaste anonymity." Slicking his hair back with Vaseline and gluing a stage-prop Vandyke to his chin, Paul managed to walk freely around the quaint ancient villages, browsing in the

---

* *John took poetic license, adding the extra s to the name.*

little shops and dining *al fresco* at neighborhood cafés, at home in a world from which the Beatles had been excluded. Freed from the glare of megacelebrity, he settled into a blissful routine. A few hours each day were spent essentially cloistered in a hotel room, writing furiously in a journal and "thinking all sorts of artistic thoughts." In the late afternoons, with sun bathing the streets in soft, even light, Paul shot reel after reel of 8 mm film, experimenting with quirky, whimsical images: a cross leaning in a cemetery, horizons tilting at crazy angles, a Ferris wheel in full spin, a gendarme directing traffic. Movies had such seductive energy; Paul found them a particularly exhilarating way of expressing himself. The whole experience brought him back down to earth: "I was a lonely little poet on the road with my car."

But once up in the air again, Paul McCartney, lonely little poet, changed back into Superbeatle. He met Mal Evans in Bordeaux, then flew off to Kenya for a two-week safari. On the plane ride home from Nairobi, on November 19, Paul began formulating an idea for a new Beatles album. Less about music, it was more a premise: if *he* could disguise himself on vacation and travel about unnoticed, then why not all the Beatles? They hated being the Fab Four, a nickname that had become synonymous with the trappings of Beatlemania. "I thought, 'Let's not be ourselves. Let's develop alter egos so we're not having to project an image which we know.'" They could "put some distance between the Beatles and the public," take on the personae of another, fictional band.

Paul and Mal kicked around the idea during the in-flight meal. At first they played with names for a band, mimicking the variety of groups that were just coming into vogue: the Bonzo Dog Doo-Dah Band, Big Brother and the Holding Company, Lothar and the Hand People. Mal, distracted, picked up the little corrugated packets of paper marked "S" and "P," asking Paul what the initials stood for. "Salt and Pepper," he responded. "Sergeant Pepper."

By the time the plane touched down at Heathrow, the entire concept was in place.

—— ▲ ——

As always, Paul's enthusiasm was complicated by the ambivalence of the other Beatles. It was hard for them to grasp the uniqueness of what he envisioned. An album *made* by the Beatles—but *not* the Beatles. Would it be Beatles music? they wondered. Then again, what *was* Beatles music these days? "We would be Sgt. Pepper's band, and for the whole of the album we'd pretend to be someone else," Paul explained. Pretend! *Pretend* was one of those words that always raised a red flag; the whole thing sounded like a gimmick. Besides, everyone's head was in a different place.

George was especially skeptical. "I had gone through so many trips of my own," he recalled, "and I was growing out of that kind of thing." In fact, of all the Beatles, no one was undergoing as much change, with as much boundless and exciting speed. The skinny, pale boy with big ears and no ambition, the dropout burdened with intellectual insecurity, who used to follow half a block behind John Lennon, had developed into a grimly optimistic, pensive young man clamoring for "the meaning of it all." LSD had jolted George awake. Tripping had given him enlightenment; it altered his consciousness and put him on the path to self-realization. "Spirituality," George was starting to believe, was what he needed. "You've got to be connected spiritually if you hope to achieve anything in this world," he wrote to Arthur Kelly soon after the Beatles had stopped touring.

In fact, George had been dancing around the fringes of spirituality for some time. As early as Speke, when he experienced frightening flashes of "divine awareness," during which a "feeling would begin to vibrate right through [him] . . . so fast it was mind-boggling," he had begun struggling with the concept of a greater power. Before his twenty-first birthday on the set of *Help!*, in the Bahamas, when he heard the trancelike call of Indian music—the same day, coincidentally, that Swami Vishnu-devananda gave him a copy of *The Complete Illustrated Book of Yoga*—George had already been exposed to Eastern and mystical philosophies. Now when George spoke, the ideas flowed effortlessly—about the doctrines of rebirth and reincarnation, serenity and self-fulfillment, as well as pacifism, which had padded to the forefront of the Beatles' interests.

With John in Spain—along with Ringo, who claimed he "hung out with him [on the movie set] because he was lonely"—and Paul off in France, George and Pattie made an unprecedented trip to Bombay, where they were guests of the legendary sitar virtuoso Ravi Shankar. "The first time I heard Indian music," George recalled in 1967, "I felt as though I knew it. It was everything, everything I could think of. It was like every music I had ever heard, but twenty times better than everything all put together. It was just so strong, so overwhelmingly positive, it buzzed me right out of my brain." George had first met Shankar in June, at Peter Sellers's house, at which time "he offered to give me some instruction on the basics of sitar." There was challenge enough, he soon discovered, in "how to sit and hold the sitar," which was murder on the hips. As he watched Shankar—actually playing the complicated instrument—deep in concentration but in perfect form and control, George must have felt overwhelmed by the extreme discipline involved. Even after a few cursory passes at it, he had difficulty achieving a proper tone. In India, however, George presented himself as a student, Shankar's "disciple," for intensive training, most of which was conducted by the master's protégé, Shambu Das.

The instruction drew George more deeply into his teacher's professional and personal life. Often after a long day of lessons—"Sometimes [George] would play up to eight hours a day," Das recalled—Shankar would conduct him on enlightening visits to local temples or they'd meander through the maze of dusty streets, teeming with humanity and exotic musky scents, discussing the mystical enthusiasms necessary for "harmonizing with a greater power." Although a fastidious performer who aggressively pursued a demanding concert schedule, Ravi implored George to "expand his consciousness." They read books "by various holy men and swamis and mystics," practiced meditation and yoga, and listened to music in the evenings. Gradually, but not often, they approached the study of Hinduism in a manner that was more philosophical than religious. The trip to India, ostensibly a musical pilgrimage, had served as a turning point for George. "Ravi and the sitar were excuses," he came to realize. "Although they were a very important part of it, it was a search for a spiritual connection."

It was in this keen, highly tuned state, clearly pulsing with enlightenment, that George returned to London on October 22. He quickly transformed his Esher bungalow, filling it with brightly colored Indian artifacts and repositioning the furniture for maximum sunlight and serenity. Long, flowing robes replaced his customary T-shirts and jeans. When Donovan, another lotus-eater, arrived at Esher for a weeklong visit, they smoked hash, critiqued each other's lyrics, and engaged in many dreamy, abstract discussions about life that lasted late into the night. The Scottish folksinger was mesmerized listening to George, who was as much a rascal as he, "speak with such confidence about truth and self-fulfillment." He was no longer the cheeky little whacker, as Aunt Mimi had dubbed him, who would take the mickey out of others in order to amuse John and Paul. In a long, thoughtful evaluation, he acknowledged "the trip to India had really opened me up.... I'd been let out of the confines of the group." The

Beatles would always define him as a musician, but out of the limelight, George was ready to be his own man. Consumed with the burden of a developing identity, he even grew a mustache to assert his individuality.

Identity. Identity. Identity.

When he heard Paul's proposal—that the Beatles take on alter egos—it sounded "mad," as though they were somehow drifting into old, uncomfortable territory. George assumed they had been moving away from such silliness. Now, from what he could tell, "it felt like going backwards."

———

For Brian Epstein, backward or forward didn't seem to make much of a difference. *Down* was the direction he seemed directly headed. Since returning from America, his life had tilted on its side like a listing ship and now it felt as if he were sinking, drowning, and no one was there to rescue him.

To make matters worse: Diz was blackmailing him. A letter arrived at the Nemperor office in New York demanding money—$10,000 in cash—in exchange for Brian's papers and those compromising photographs. Right off the bat, Brian decided to pay up. Grievously holed up in his bone-white Chapel Street flat, he considered it "blood money," necessary to ending the hideous affair. There was no point in stirring up more trouble. "Don't do anything else about it," he instructed Nat Weiss by telephone. But Weiss's briefcase was part of the hustler's ransom, "and on that basis," Nat says, "I called a lawyer named Bob Fitzpatrick, and we had [Diz] arrested." Some of the money was recovered, along with the letters, but the photographs, the most damning material, had vanished. "And that's what ultimately sent Brian into a suicidal depression."

Those photographs haunted him, not so much for what they contained but for how they'd be used. Brian knew they'd turn up again—it was only a matter of time—and dreaded that somehow it would embarrass the Beatles. For days—weeks—he moped around the house, often not getting up until the late afternoon and then not even changing out of his pajamas. Even as the Beatles' EMI contract was being renegotiated, Brian was lurching about the rooms "just indulging himself," drinking cognac, popping pills, and sliding deeper into his depression. To Peter Brown, who had moved into the flat at the suggestion of Brian's doctor, he poured out his agony in bursts of "morbid," often incoherent tirades. Brown tried to comfort his friend but sensed the futility of it all. "Nothing I said or did seemed to help," Peter recalls. "He was miserable. A *lot*. But he was such a drama queen. I assumed this was more of the same exaggerated behavior that would spend itself, like a passing storm."

The collapse, when it eventually came, caught Brown off guard.

One evening in late September, after an informal dinner in his pajamas, Brian disappeared into his room. "I stayed in the library watching television," recalls Brown, "and when he didn't come back, I thought, 'That's strange—he'd been home asleep all day, until almost after I'd got back from the office. He *can't* have gone back to bed.'" Peter stopped to have a look in on Brian on his way upstairs, "and I couldn't rouse him—he was out cold." Finding him in this condition was nothing extraordinary. But the way Brian's body was positioned looked unnatural—sprawled and twisted in a way that couldn't be explained by dissipation.

Brown slapped him and threw some water in his face: nothing happened. The slack limbs had no elasticity. From what he could tell, Brian was breathing, but barely. Peter ran to call the servants, Antonio and Maria Garcia, who lived in the basement, but thought better of it. "They would have freaked out and left," he says. Instead, he picked up the phone and called Norman Cowan, the eccentric, shamefully indulgent doctor they shared. Cowan, who was on call in a London suburb, insisted that Brian be taken to the nearest hospital. St. George's was just around the corner, but Brown balked. "The hospitals always had someone on staff who reported to the press immediately," he recalls, "and we would have been in the tabloids the next morning." Recklessly, Peter decided to wait—half an hour, at least—for Cowan to arrive. Then, with the help of Bryan Barrett, the house chauffeur, they bundled Brian's body in a blanket and rushed him back to Cowan's private hospital, in Richmond, where his stomach was pumped.

When Brian regained consciousness, he was, Brown says, apologetic and referred to the episode as "a foolish accident." But when Brown got back to Chapel Street the next day, he found a note on Brian's night table, next to an empty vial of Nembutal. Written in Brian's familiar script, it said: "I can't deal with this anymore. It's beyond me, and I just can't go on." There was a codicil attached, in which he left his estate to Queenie and his brother, Clive, with other belongings to be distributed among Brown, Geoffrey Ellis, and Nat Weiss.

Brian's desperate act shocked his closest friends. Throughout the tour, his erratic behavior and manic depression had stirred up sympathy and concern. But in the many years they'd known him, even grown accus-

tomed to the emotional jags of his "torturous life," there was never any indication that he intended to kill himself. Certainly there had been irrational
talk, even some low-grade drama. "But none of us, however shortsighted,
suspected he was suicidal," says Nat Weiss.

At Peter Brown's insistence, Brian spent two weeks "drying out" in
the Priory, a spalike sanitorium in Roehampton that catered to well-to-do
patients with embarrassing personal problems. But once back in London,
Brian slipped back into a disturbing groove paced by indulgence and self-
destructive behavior.

While he'd all but neglected the affairs of his other artists, it seemed
that for the Beatles there was always enough juice. The deal Brian had recently struck with Capitol had been renegotiated for a hefty 10 percent royalty, with built-in escalators that could rocket the Beatles' share to an
unheard-of 17 percent. According to Weiss, "Brian was never a great push-
them-to-the-wall businessman." But he'd toughened up for Alan Livingston, and when Capitol announced plans, prematurely, to put out a *Best of
the Beatles* package, Brian gave the label president a terrible tongue-lashing,
threatening to bolt for a competitor unless the album was shelved. But otherwise, the stairs were steep, and Brian stumbling.

In late 1965 Brian had called Ken Partridge and asked him to rush
around to the NEMS office to see something "fabulous" he'd just acquired.
Brian was waiting in his car when Partridge arrived, and after a brief enigmatic exchange, they drove to the West End, pulling to the curb in front of
a once-stately but now rather dowdy building on Shaftesbury Avenue.
"I've just bought this from Bernard Delfont," Brian announced grandly,
gesturing outside. Partridge gazed up at the Saville Theatre, then back at
Brian, and exclaimed, "You must be *mad!*" In Partridge's opinion, "it was
the worst theater in London—a real pup—dirty, filthy, dilapidated, with
row after row of broken seats." Delfont and his brother Lew Grade had
tried in vain to fill the 1,200-seat theater. How did Brian expect to succeed
with it?

For Brian, the Saville was a second chance at a theater career, an opportunity to replay his botched season at the Royal Academy of Dramatic
Arts, albeit on a grander, more legendary stage, and at his own whim. "He
wanted to be Ziegfeld," says Don Black, who admired Brian's spunk. "The
theater was a perfect foray." And he had the acts to fill it.

But the first season was an unqualified disaster. A "terrible" musical
about Houdini that Brian produced set the tone for much of the woolly,
lightweight fare that would thin out the more discerning audiences. "He

also put on several revues that didn't work," recalls Ken Partridge. Tony Bramwell, who took over running the Saville Theatre, says they were forced to reshuffle the repertory, mixing in rock 'n roll with a variety of legitimate productions. "During the week, we had Gilbert and Sullivan or Shakespeare, switching to rock concerts every Sunday night: *Brian Epstein Presents.*" The name, however, was the only association Brian maintained with the shows. The fact was he had already lost interest in the theater, other than the weekly parties at his flat in honor of the Saville's current attraction. In early November, Brian sent out invitations for a reception with the Who. George and Ringo planned to attend; Paul, still in Africa on safari with Mal and Jane Asher, wired his regrets. John and Cynthia had only just returned to London, suffering from travel fatigue and an ominous melancholy. Friends described John's mood as "tense" and "bitter." "There was so much going on in his head that he couldn't get on top of," recalls John Dunbar. The future of the Beatles had arrived at a strange point; his marriage, long plagued by lethargy, waded into decline. Still, after weeks trapped on a film set, with his hair swept back and wearing distinctive granny glasses, John stood eager to accept. But two days before Brian's shindig at the Chapel Street flat, he was steered to an exhibit at Dunbar's Indica Gallery.

[IV]

In the ten months since the Indica had been open, both the bookshop and gallery had developed a tidy following, catering to the alternative literary and artistic movement—the emerging counterculture—that craved anything avant-garde. Upstairs, its bowed shelves were crammed with American independent-press imports, interspersed with magazines, beat poetry, and a hodgepodge of philosophy, while the gallery space in the basement hosted conceptual installations. There was nothing quite like it in London. The long-haired young crowd that milled through Mason's Yard lavished upon it immediate cachet, as did William Burroughs, a widely recognized habitué who lived nearby, on Duke Street. "There were all those Chelsea people," says another regular, "and they suddenly appeared." Inevitably, the Indica, along with its next-door neighbor, the Scotch of St. James, became the epicenter of all that was hip and cool.

If there was one theme that ran through the gallery, that extended the Indica's reputation as a countercultural force, it was *radical*—anything that smashed the formal categories of art. Whether it meant exhibiting Gustav Metzger's autodestructive monuments that disappeared before your eyes, Christo's wrapped objets d'art, or the environmental art of Stuart Brisley, in which the artist performed within the piece, resisting traditional form and structure became the Indica's overriding mandate. "We never had a painting as such in the place," recalled John Dunbar, who commissioned each show. Exhibits were chosen without regard for commercial return—to "liberate art as a commodity," says Dunbar.

It was in that liberated, happily stoned spirit that Dunbar underwrote an exhibit with an elfin Japanese event-art practitioner named Yoko Ono. He had heard about her breakthrough show in Trafalgar Square, during which she lunged about inside a black bag, and thought it was "a hoot, exactly the kind of thing that would bring us notoriety." Besides, she and her husband, Tony Cox, had become part of the Indica's "clubby atmosphere." Dunbar liked to support familiar artists and provide a space where they could be shown.

The opening of *Unfinished Paintings and Objects* on November 10, 1966, created a strong buzz among the city's curious trendsetters. Dunbar expected a hearty opening-night crowd, and subsequently he enticed John to a private preview—"a real happening," he called it—on November 9, "to ensure that he wasn't harassed." Attracting a celebrity of John's magnitude, he knew, would boost the Indica's crowd—word of a Beatle's interest would spread like wildfire—and so he "laid it on pretty thick," implying that part of the exhibit, "fun and games inside a bag," could lead to, well . . . anything, anything at all. "I thought, 'Hmm,' you know, 'sex,'" John recalled, misunderstanding, just as Dunbar had intended. But John had other reasons for going. Even though he'd been home for only two days, he was already bored out of his skull, ready for anything that might spark a little excitement.

Certainly, John and Cyn had little more than familiarity left to give each other. There was Julian, of course, but John was hardly an attentive father. He left the parenting to his wife, along with most other household responsibilities. Days went by in which they barely exchanged five words between them, even when living—or rather, coexisting—under the same roof. John was aloof, uncooperative, disappearing into the music room for hours on end or staring hypnotically at the television until he passed out from fatigue. Paul, who seldom saw John during this time, remembered encountering him once in London and asking what he'd been up to. "Well, watching telly, smoking pot," John replied.

In the chauffeured Mini Cooper on the way to the Indica, the weeks of boredom and frustration—the dormant Beatles, the unfulfilling movie role, the resentment of Paul, the stultifying marriage, the creeping inertia—caught up with him. "I was in a highly unshaved and tatty state," John recalled in an interview. "I was up three nights . . . tripping. I was stoned." When they pulled up to the curb outside Mason's Yard, he'd practically lost his nerve. Les Anthony, who'd been John's driver for two years, said they sat in the car for "some time"—perhaps as much as half an hour—while John debated whether to go inside. "I'm not ready yet," he agonized every few minutes. "Let's just sit here. Let's see what happens." Anthony thought the wavering was a by-product of the drugs, but more probably, like most of John's indecision, it was the result of insecurity. All this time, he'd had the Beatles to cover his anxieties. Yes, he wanted to be the leader, but there was safety in numbers. He wasn't *good* on his own. Besides, he dismissed a lot of gallery art as "bullshit and phony." The longer he sat there, the more he resented coming. But there he was, and, well, fuck it. In he went.

Recalls Dunbar, "When he came in, it was like the parting of the Red Sea. Everyone who was there, some of the staff and a few friends, just stepped aside and gave him space." Apparently convinced that John was a potential collector with deep pockets, Dunbar was "flittering around like crazy," and John went stiff from the star treatment. Protectively, he buried himself in the exhibition's attractive catalogue. "*. . . mirror to see your behind . . . sky T.V. . . . eternal time clock . . . bag wear . . . Painting to hammer a nail . . . Painting to let the light go through . . . Crying machine . . .*" "Is this stuff for real?" he wanted to know. The descriptions sounded like a put-on. "*Danger box: machine that you will never come back the same from (we cannot guarantee your safety in its use) . . . Underwear to make you high, for women, description upon request . . .*" "I wasn't quite sure what it was about. I knew there was some sort of con game going on somewhere." Then one of the exhibits caught his eye and he moved in for a closer look. On a shelf, he stared at several nails atop a Plexiglas stand and, next to that, an apple—it looked real, as far as he could tell, and quite ordinary—with a little table card that said: APPLE. "This is a joke, this is pretty funny," he thought. "I was beginning to see the humor of it." When he asked Dunbar for the price of the apple, he was told: £200. *Oh-ho!* Definitely a joke. The dry, almost inadvertent sense of humor appealed to John, who was encouraged to see the rest of the show in the downstairs gallery.

There, John's mood brightened. All sorts of contraptions, connected by gangplanks, beams, and ladders, were spread across the brightly lit basement, where a few "scruffy people" were putting the finishing touches on the installation. As he stood there, taking it all in, Dunbar excused himself to confer with the staff. When he returned, a slip of a young Asian woman was by his side, prim, in a black leotard and pale as porridge. In her tension of small bones, she resembled a serious small-faced animal. "Hey, man," Dunbar said, "allow me to introduce Yoko Ono."

Yoko Ono: was that a put-on, too? She had amazing presence, John thought; he could feel it surge through the room. There was something about her, something strange and exceptional, that was overpowering. John glanced around shyly, buying time to recover his composure. "Well, what's the event?" he wondered, obviously flustered.

Instead of answering, this little sphinxlike woman merely handed him a card, which John turned over in his hands a few times. There was nothing on it except a single word: BREATHE. "You mean, like this?" John asked, panting like a winded terrier. That was it, yes, that's what she'd intended. Yes . . . *breathe*. John liked that; it was part of the joke.

Increasingly, Yoko relaxed as John responded—perfectly—to her approach. Too many people dismissed her work as outrageous, beyond weird; they got angry instead of locating the humor in it. But this guy— Yoko claimed, hard as it seems to believe, that she neither knew John's name nor recognized him—seemed to get what she was about, or at least he was willing to play along, which was just as favorable.

Leading him to a ladder, she suggested that he climb to the top to view a ceiling painting. "It looked like a black canvas with a chain with a spyglass hanging on the end of it," he recalled. What did she expect him to make of that? "You take a magnifying glass and you look at it," Yoko explained, motioning him toward the rungs. John wasn't so sure he wanted to play anymore. He dreaded climbing the ladder and confronting some cynical witticism, some goof. Still, Yoko coaxed him upward, and with mounting trepidation, he held the magnifying glass up to the canvas and squinted. A smile spread instantly across John's face. Painted on the canvas was a single word: YES.

As soon as he'd climbed down, John asked to see more. There was a piece of plasterboard, a wall, that was painted eggshell white. A small sign invited visitors to hammer a nail into its surface. Trouble was, the show's opening was still a night off and Yoko understandably wanted it to remain unspoiled. "I argued strongly in favor of Lennon's hammering in the first nail," Dunbar remembers. "He had a lot of loot—chances are, he would buy the damn thing." Yoko's eyes flashed anger. Why let this guy ruin her pristine exhibit? She pulled Dunbar aside and they huddled for several minutes, going at it like cats and dogs. In all likelihood, Dunbar identified John and enticed her with a potential sale, because she eventually relented and said, "Okay, you can hammer a nail in for five shillings." That was all John needed to hear. Grinning, he responded, "I'll give you an imaginary five shillings if you let me hammer in an imaginary nail." Beautiful: pure Lennon. And Yoko loved it. "My God," she thought, "he's playing the same game I'm playing."

During the weeks after meeting Yoko, John spent more time than ever locked behind the door of his music room on the top floor of Kenwood. His drug-taking and depression dragged on ceaselessly, without regard for days or nights. Time passed in a vague blur, during which he leafed through magazines or one of the handsome volumes of impressionist art that were stacked next to the couch, rarely picking up a guitar other than to move it out of the way. Occasionally Terry Doran turned up and managed to coax John to the Scotch or the Bag o' Nails, but their outings routinely ended back at the house, to refuel. "John was a fun drug-taker—serious fun," Doran recalls. "We'd come home late from a nightclub . . . and go up to his attic and dose ourselves silly."

With no new songs in the hopper and nothing to inspire him, John rarely involved himself with music. Surprisingly, the Beatles seemed content to forfeit the robust Christmas sales platform that had, for several years running, been their exclusive province. The spotlight that season fell instead on Cream, the "first high-voltage superblues group," who had emerged from a crowded pack of newcomers to dazzle audiences with their formidable accompaniment. Along with Jimi Hendrix, who was competing for that share of the rock, their virtuoso lineup—Eric Clapton, Jack Bruce, and Ginger Baker—expanded and transformed the dynamics of rock, with inventive, heavily syncopated riffs and ferocious jams. (NEMS was booking Cream and Hendrix with what seemed like a vengeance across the U.K.) Everywhere around them were other alluring acts pushing boldly into the Beatles' firmament: the Easybeats, the Spencer Davis Group, Brian Auger and the Trinity, the Move, Donovan, the Four Tops—*the Monkees.* If the proliferation of bands didn't ruffle the Beatles, then surely popular response did. "Show business will vibrate with the sensational news that the Beatles have been outvoted by the Beach Boys as the World's Outstanding Vocal Group," *NME* announced in its annual poll results. ("We're all four fans of the Beach Boys," Ringo confessed, ". . . maybe *we* voted for them.") More irritating, perhaps, was the report that John had ceded his Best British Vocal Personality crown to Cliff Richard.

Normally, the Beatles would have ignored such nonsense, but with the fitful shape of their career and contract renewal in play, they grew sensitive to the pessimism imparted by the mercurial media. They still felt compelled to deny rumors that jealousy had driven a wedge between them ("This idea of jealousy is in other people's brain," Ringo insisted. "We all work for each other's success."), that they were splitting up (pure "rubbish," according to Paul), or that, despite earlier reports, they were planning to tour again in the spring. They also expressed "outrage" about a front-page "exclusive" in the *Sunday Telegraph* that they were dismissing Brian Epstein and that "two of the Beatles had approached an American"—Allen Klein, who represented the Rolling Stones—"concerning their future management." From every perspective, it seemed as though the Beatles were in free fall.

"I think we were itching to get going," Paul recalled of the days leading up to the session. The Beatles always thrived in the studio. But unlike their previous sessions, Paul hadn't written anything with John to prepare for it. There had been no time, little if any communication between them. As far as anyone knew, they were coming in cold.

Of course, John had "Strawberry Fields Forever" on the drawing board. On the evening of November 24—a blustery Thursday—the Beatles, all of whom now sported identical handlebar mustaches, regrouped in Studio Two, the enormous, slightly down-at-the-heels room that had functioned so often as their creative laboratory. John, who appeared spidery and gaunt, wasted no time previewing his song for Martin on an acoustic guitar. This version of it, sung so haltingly and in a voice barely above a hush, was dramatic indeed in the stillness of the studio, and so was John's determination to convey what he felt, to honor the starry images of his Woolton childhood. Martin listened—sitting erect, arms folded across his chest, legs crossed—as impassively as possible, but his ears burned with excitement. "It was absolutely lovely," he raved, convinced that the song was a masterpiece. "I was spellbound. I was in love." There was a poignancy, an intimacy that he hadn't expected to hear. "He had broken through into different territory, to a place I did not recognize from his past songs. . . . It was dreamlike without being fey, weird without being pretentious." The gently eloquent delivery, accented in acid-tinged shades of surreal, fragmented imagery, produced a stunning accomplishment. Martin cursed himself for not running a tape.

It was exactly the springboard the Beatles needed. "Strawberry Fields Forever," which took over forty-five hours to record, spanning nearly a month, sparked an explosively productive period during which Paul and John collaborated on nine of the twelve songs that eventually made the cut. Not every song, of course, warranted their equal contribution. As had been the case since before *Help!*, writing had become more of an individual process—Ringo estimated the apportionment at "about 80% separately written songs"—with the respective partner brought in at the last minute to provide a middle eight or a polish. But they continued, as always, to influence each other.

Coincidentally or not, Paul also seized on Woolton as inspiration for his next song. John's fond reference to Strawberry Field must have touched off a flashback that mixed nostalgia and personal mythology in a dreamlike style. George Martin credited the "coincidence" more to the wages of "creative rivalry," but whatever the moving spirit—Paul would only say that John and he "were often answering each other's songs"—it didn't take him long to single out Penny Lane, the terminal where Paul changed buses on his route from Allerton to visit any of his more centrally located Liverpool friends. "John and I would often meet at Penny Lane" on their way to center city or a gig, he recalled. And while the bus shelter "in the middle of the roundabout" at Smithdown Place wasn't the most scenic spot, its euphonious name struck the perfect note. Penny Lane: Paul incorporated all the associations he had with it—Bioletti's barber shop, with its photo spread of haircuts in the window; the British Legionnaire who sold poppies for a shilling; the fire station; St. Barnabus Church, where, for a short time, he was a choirboy. The song took form in a brief two-hour burst. Most of it came in his new upstairs music room, at a small upright piano "painted in an exploding psychedelic rainbow" pattern and positioned just beneath the picture window so that it overlooked the front yard onto Cavendish Avenue. The first two verses, which "practically wrote themselves," set a true-to-life scene, with the whole drama of the neighborhood unfolding, as it might at the beginning of a 1940s movie or "more like a play," as Paul has said. An entire cast of characters leap into action "beneath the blue suburban skies," much as they do in "Eleanor Rigby." From the beginning, however, Paul's intent was to look at Penny Lane in a special way. "The lyrics were all based on real things," he recalled, but distorted, "a little more surreal . . . twisting it to a slightly more artsy angle" to incorporate "all the trippy little ideas that we were trying to get into."

Paul's experiments with the recording of it, however, showcase little of the hallucinatory effects that range throughout "Strawberry Fields Forever." The style of "Penny Lane" is beautifully structured, saturated in rhythmic cadences, rambling like a no. 16 bus to the tram sheds. Paul narrates the action with bluff familiarity, becoming someone who has committed a childhood scene to memory and yearns to share it with a visitor as a way, perhaps, of making it come alive again.

The result was all the Beatles could have wished. To Brian's insistence that they release a single early in 1967 came back assurances that they had a killer in the can—three songs that George Martin considered "a small collection of gems": "Strawberry Fields Forever," "Penny Lane," and the durable "When I'm Sixty-four," a "rooty-tooty variety style" song, according to Paul, that he had written when he was sixteen and that the Beatles performed at the Cavern during punch-ups and power failures. "I decided to give [Brian] a super-strong combination," Martin said, "a double-punch that could not fail, an unbeatable linking of two all-time great songs: 'Strawberry Fields Forever' and 'Penny Lane.'"

But fail it did. Not, as a matter of fact, in a commercial sense; the single, which was released on February 17, 1967, sold upward of 2.5 million copies. But it broke what Martin called "the roll"—the Beatles' unprecedented achievement of twelve straight number one singles—failing to hit the top spot on the British charts. The outcome was so unexpected, so astounding, that the immediate cause was eclipsed by the end result. In fact, the Beatles' single outsold its competitor—"Release Me," by Englebert Humperdinck—by almost two to one. But in the curious mathematics of the pop charts, sales figures of the double-sided hit were being counted separately, as two singles, so that one side canceled out the other, giving Humperdinck firm grasp of the top spot.

The Beatles, to their credit, seemed amused by the curious turn of events, and only George went on to say that it was "a bit of a shock being Number Two." Neither Paul nor John gave it much thought. The concept of A- and B-sides, and even singles, was, in Ringo's words, "an old trap" they'd do best to avoid. This time around, the Beatles' sensitive ears had heard rock 'n roll in a different way. "Strawberry Fields Forever" and "Penny Lane" reveled in the possibilities of complexity and sophistication. The band's progress on this single, their experimentation with overdubs and exotic instruments, was unlike anything ever produced, and it affected different listeners in as many different ways. It was clear from initial reviews that there was no middle ground. The sinuous melodies and rhythmic devices puzzled *NME*'s Derek Johnson. "Quite honestly," he admitted, "I don't know what to make of it." On the other side of the world, however, there was nothing but enthusiasm for the record. The critics at *Time* cast their usual reservations to the wind, lavishing extravagant praise on the single, which they considered nothing short of an artistic breakthrough. From the earliest singles right through to the present, they wrote, "the Beatles have developed into the single most creative force in pop music. Wherever they go, the pack follows. And where they have gone in recent months, not even their most ardent supporters would ever have dreamed of. They have bridged the heretofore impassable gap between rock and classical, mixing elements of Bach, Oriental and electronic music with vintage twang to achieve the most compellingly original sounds ever heard in pop music."

No matter how "artistic" or "complex" the songs, when played they became instantly hummable melodies. Every so often—unavoidably—a recognizable riff or backbeat would cut through the atmospheric production to remind people that beneath this new psychedelic guise and ultrahip pretension, the Beatles remained rock 'n rollers at heart. But being a rock 'n roller no longer meant what it had. "The people who have bought our records in the past must realize that we couldn't go on making the same type forever," John explained. "We must change, and I believe those people know this."

If they didn't, they were about to find out.

[I]

Though die-hard Beatles fans anticipated something exceptional from their heroes, no one, not even other musicians, was prepared for the sound of *Sgt. Pepper's Lonely Hearts Club Band.* The music sounded unlike anything the Beatles had ever done before. Even the structure of the album was unconventional: it was *conceptual,* a kaleidoscope of interconnecting songs without the standard three-second break between tracks.

What to make of it? Especially considering the tumultuous state of popular music at the time. As EMI and Capitol prepared to release the latest Beatles opus, competing forces vied for the ears of the disenchanted — and divided — young audience. Top 40 pop, like its consumer base, had been rocked by tremors of social and cultural upheaval. A good portion of its listeners — specifically, those teenagers affected by the outburst of creative energy that embraced poetry, drugs, anti-establishment politics, and a general alternative lifestyle — no longer related to the bloodless, derivative pop music that was passed off as rock 'n roll. It didn't speak to their groovy new way of life; it no longer resonated. Radio stations continued to play the slickly polished toe-tappers and ballads that dominated the charts, but a darker, more sensual strain of music — turned-on music, for want of a better term ("cheerful music for dope smokers," as one critic called it), and very early acid rock — began to creep onto playlists. It was music for "serious" rock fans, and it raised the level of artistry that fans expected from the records they bought.

Groups like the Doors and those psychedelic boogie bands that were emerging out of San Francisco put listeners on notice that rock music was growing up. Within the next few years, they would be joined by virtually the entire sixties rock pantheon: Pink Floyd, Janis Joplin, Traffic, Jethro Tull, Sly and the Family Stone, the Band, the Chambers Brothers, Ten Years

After, the Jefferson Airplane, Elton John, Credence Clearwater Revival, the Allman Brothers, Joni Mitchell, Led Zeppelin, as well as the entire Motown and Stax/Volt rosters—all of them swept in in the aftermath of the British invasion and subsequent demise of the Brill Building factory sound. "To those of us making music for a living," said Pete Townshend, "it seemed like, finally, rock 'n roll had found a perfect groove." Pop playlists began mixing more progressive "album cuts" with singles, so that songs such as "Windy," "Happy Together," and "Somethin' Stupid" were programmed with "For What It's Worth" and "A Whiter Shade of Pale."

As all participants scrambled for a piece of the rock, the Beatles watched impassively from the sidelines. Throughout the first four months of 1967, they remained secluded in Abbey Road, working steadily, fussily, on the new album. Never had they enjoyed such a luxury of time to record. In the past there had always been a deadline looming, always a last-minute crunch to write enough material and get it down before the next tour began. For four years EMI had cracked the whip to ensure that the Beatles released four singles and two albums a year—an output unthinkable by today's standards. But now, at last, they had time, precious time. No deadlines, no tours, no commitments—no *nothing*.

The studio, always off-limits to outsiders, erupted under a crossfire of loud, jangly, exotic—indescribable—sounds competing like car horns at rush hour. George Martin considered it the Beatles' "playground," but a laboratory was more like it. No song was safe. Ideas that once might have been polished off in a day or two were turned inside out, upside down, to see what might happen. They pounced on "every trick brought out of the bag," according to George Martin. At any time, a "final take" consigned to the can might attract someone's attention and be reworked entirely the next day. At home following a long night's work, when a well-deserved joint unleashed some profound, spacey insight, John, Paul, or George might listen to an acetate of the day's work, pick up a guitar, and bang out a riff that sent everyone back to the drawing board. Instead of learning a new song and recording it, as was customary, there was more a tendency to let it develop organically, idea by idea, overdub by overdub.

The effects of this technique began to pay off immediately. By the middle of January, when they began work on the epic "A Day in the Life," in essence the first entirely new piece for the album,* the Beatles were able

---

* *"Strawberry Fields Forever" and "Penny Lane," originally intended for the album, were left off, following EMI's practice, when they were chosen as the double-sided single.*

to build the song's magnificent production, take by take and layer by layer, at their leisure, from the ground up.

They began on January 19 with a simple, two-track rendition, laying down the basic rhythm—Paul on piano, Ringo on bongos, and George on maracas—accompanied by John's despairing, spectral vocal saturated in echo "because he wanted to sound like Elvis Presley on 'Heartbreak Hotel.'" The middle section had yet to be written, so an arbitrary twenty-four bars were left blank, each counted down aloud by Mal Evans, who indicated the end by setting off a noisy alarm clock that was eventually put to good use.

Even in the early run-through, the song showed unmistakable brilliance. The gorgeous melody, as stark as it is soulful, stands as one of the Beatles' finest accomplishments. John's "dry, deadpan voice" aches with disbelief as he comments on both tragic and inane news items that defy common logic. The lyric came, he maintained, during a stretch at the piano, with the January 17 edition of the *Daily Mail* propped open on the music stand in front of him. "I noticed two stories," he explained. "One was about the Guinness heir"—Tara Browne, a friend of Paul's—"who killed himself in a car.* That was the main headline story. . . . On the next page was a story about four thousand potholes in the streets of Blackburn, Lancashire, that needed to be filled."** Paul's contribution, he said, was "the beautiful little lick 'I'd love to turn you on'" that had been "floating around" unused.

Or so John claimed. Like all Beatles' recollections, parts of that account were, indeed, accurate, while other parts improved with age. In fact, John was inspired by the newspaper inasmuch as he set out to write a lyric based on actual events. But when he arrived at Paul's house to work on the song, only the first four lines existed, along with a bit of the second verse and the melody. "The verse about the politician blowing his mind out in a car we wrote together," Paul recalled. As far as he could remember, there was no discussion about Tara Browne. "The 'blew his mind' was purely a drug reference, nothing to do with a car crash."

They spent the next few hours constructing the rest of the song, filling in "funny . . . little references" and adapting the Blackburn potholes story

---

* On December 18, 1966, Browne ran his Lotus Elan sports car through a red light in Earls Court, smashing into a van and killing himself.
** "There are 4,000 holes in the road in Blackburn, Lancashire, or one twenty-sixth of a hole per person, according to a council survey." "The Holes in Our Roads," Daily Mail, 1/17/67, p. 2.

from John's newspaper. It was a delicious bit of absurdity, blithely surreal and apropos of, well . . . nothing: *perfect!* In the meantime, they stitched in the "woke up, fell out of bed . . ." sequence that Paul borrowed from another song he'd been fiddling with — "a little party piece of mine" — leaving the rest for improvisation in the studio.

Back at Abbey Road, the Beatles were encouraged by a happy coincidence. The "woke up, fell out of bed . . ." sequence fit into the song exactly at the point where Mal's alarm clock rang! It was almost too good to be true. But they still had twenty-four bars to account for. The best they could hope for was an outrageously long middle eight to materialize.

But the gap whetted Paul's appetite for a grander, more ambitious effort. Sometime during the second day's work, it dawned on him: a big orchestral buildup. "It was a crazy song, anyway," he rationalized. "We could go anywhere with [it]." As he kneaded it for a while, the idea leavened. He envisioned a magnificent instrumental interval, avant-garde in its approach, that produced a spiraling ascent of sound. Explaining it to John, Paul said: "We'll tell the orchestra to start on whatever the lowest note on their instrument is, and to arrive at the highest note on their instrument. But to do it in their own time." The effect would be "something really tumultuous . . . something extremely startling." When he requested that George Martin book a symphony orchestra, however, the producer told him to forget it. The idea appealed to Martin. "But ninety musicians" — the standard symphony configuration — "would be . . . too expensive." Martin already feared that the project was getting away from them. In the past, an evening session was called for seven o'clock *sharp,* with everyone ready to record. Now sessions operated on Beatles Time, which meant that while the staff assembled at seven, Ringo might arrive about 10:45, with the others trickling in before 11:30, in time to grab a cup of coffee or a smoke, maybe catch up with friends, before getting down to work. But — oh, the payoff! All anyone had to do was listen to *Rubber Soul* or *Revolver* as a reminder. Who could argue with that? So, after mulling it over, Martin suggested that *half* an orchestra might serve the same purpose. No one in his right mind would book forty-one musicians — from the prestigious London Philharmonic, no less — to play twenty-four bars of music, but book them he did. Nor did he bat an eye when the Beatles requested that everyone wear evening dress for the occasion.

In the meantime, they set to work on the title song, "Sgt. Pepper's Lonely Hearts Club Band," which Paul wrote, he claimed, "with little or no input from John." With concentration and technical innovation, the track was hustled into shape in a lively two-day marathon, along with a basic reading of "Good Morning, Good Morning," the theme of which John pinched from a Kellogg's Cornflakes commercial.

Each new triumph by the Beatles created an urgent need for fresh material. John and Paul continued to write, both together and apart, delivering "With a Little Help from My Friends" and "Lovely Rita" in the intervening days. Another song was inspired by a "blurry and watery" painting John's four-year-old son, Julian, brought home from nursery school. "The top was all dark blue sky with some very rough-looking stars, [and] green grass along the bottom," Julian recalled years later. Near the corner, he'd drawn a stick-figure girl—presumably his classmate Lucy O'Donnell, identified by her long blond hair. "I showed it to Dad and he said, 'What's that then?'" Julian blurted out the first thing that came into his mind: "That's Lucy in the sky, you know, with diamonds."

The moment Paul learned of it, over cups of steaming tea with John in the breakfast room at Kenwood, he flashed: "Wow, fantastic title!" Perfect for their next song, it was "very trippy" sounding, which meant they could ladle on the psychedelic imagery. John had already begun playing with a few lines inspired by the "Wool and Water" chapter of *Through the Looking Glass,* one of his and Paul's favorite books. "Picture yourself on a boat, on the river . . ." You could go anywhere on the wings of a line like that! They immediately went upstairs and began writing, "swapping psychedelic suggestions," Paul recalled, and "trading words off each other, as we always did." He came up with "cellophane flowers" and "newspaper taxis"; John pitched in with "kaleidoscope eyes." It came together very quickly. The result was sure to please George Martin. First, however, they had to finish "A Day in the Life," which awaited a hot middle passage.

On February 10 the all-male orchestra, in full evening dress, assembled in Abbey Road's Studio One, the cavernous, hangarlike hall near the entrance to the building, dotted with a hundred "ambiophonic" loudspeakers and accommodating up to a thousand musicians, where so many of EMI's legendary symphonies had been recorded. The ghosts of Elgar, Caruso, Menuhin, Heifetz, Casals, Toscanini, Robeson, and Callas were banished to the rafters as the Beatles invaded sacred territory—not in tuxedos, as promised, but tricked out in a wildly flamboyant, neon-rainbow wardrobe and loaded with gag accessories that they distributed to the mortified musicians. The violinists were given red clown noses; their leader, the eminent Erich Gruenberg, fitted with a gorilla's paw on his bow hand. Balloons were attached to the bows of stringed instruments. The brass and woodwind section wore plastic spectacles, with fake noses and funny hats. Badges, bells, and beads were affixed where applicable. John giddily handed out plastic stick-on nipples and fake cigars. "People were running around with sparklers and blowing bubbles through little clay pipes," George Martin recalled. Most of the classical musicians remained bewildered. Many were contemptuous, offended, brimming with hostility. To them, it was an undignified way to behave in the studio. Still, it was a payday, and a good one at that, stretching on and on to accommodate the Beatles' flights of fantasy.

The Beatles also invited a few musical friends of their own stripe, among them Mick Jagger and Marianne Faithfull, Donovan, Brian Jones, Mike Nesmith of the Monkees, Pattie Harrison, two Dutch designers— Simon Posthuma and Marijke Koger, who operated a firm called the Fool that would eventually play a role in another aspect of the Beatles' career— and the Hollies' Graham Nash, all dressed outrageously in flowing robes or waistcoats with long silk scarves and flared pants, all pleasantly stoned, all spectators for the happening that was about to take place.

Once the orchestra was given instructions, the two conductors— George Martin and Paul McCartney, the latter in a red butcher's smock draped over a purple-and-black paisley shirt—led the ensemble through five separate performances, each one a cyclone swirl of rolling, vibrating babel. Martin more aptly termed it an "orchestral orgasm." "It was a re-markable, breathtaking experience," says Ron Richards, who took cover in a corner of the control room and, with head sandwiched between hands, was reported to have cried: "I just can't believe it. . . . I give up!"

But the Beatles were just getting started. All five takes were mixed down onto one track, creating a monster symphonic effect that exceeded everyone's expectations. But the high note that was reached at the end of the sequence just dangled there, unfinished. It needed a coda. But how could anything complement the sound of 205 turbulent instruments? What could, in effect, land the plane with as much panache as the flight? Initially, Martin dusted off one of John's acid fantasies from *Revolver,* when he proposed the sound of four thousand monks chanting accompa-niment to "Tomorrow Never Knows." As nutty as that sounded, Martin thought it might actually work in this case—not four thousand monks, of course, but a chorus of eight or nine people chanting a mantra that could be overdubbed four or five times to create the illusion of thousands. The concept, which everyone responded to eagerly, was ditched after several rehearsals revealed that no one—most of them smokers—could hold the note for more than fifteen or twenty seconds.

Instead, they settled for producing "a gigantic piano chord" that would sustain for just over a minute. The staff rolled three grand pianos into Studio One, including the one reserved exclusively for Daniel Barenboim that was normally kept locked. On the count of four, ten hands—Paul, John, Ringo, Mal Evans, and George Martin—clamped down on an E chord as hard as humanly possible, letting it reverberate, enhanced by some complex technical magic (boldly employing heavy compression and increasing the gain by degrees), right up to the last ounce of fade. It took nine attempts to perfect but was well worth the effort. It was a magnificent—stirring—effect, as conclusive as it was dramatic, capping a dazzling thirty-four-hour arrangement that serves as perhaps the Beatles' outstanding studio performance.

Much has been written over the years analyzing "A Day in the Life," how it expresses John's disillusionment and comments upon the hopelessness of society or redefines the "mythical" Sgt. Pepper's band by interjecting a measure of sobering reality. *Newsweek*'s critic hailed it as the pop version of "The Waste Land." Others singled it out as a case of acid reflux. But, one by one, these grand visions amount to nothing more than personal bias. The song was, after all, recorded before the album concept even took shape, and was written almost as an exercise, lifting random images from the pages of the *Daily Mail* that "got mixed together in a little poetic jumble," according to Paul, so "that [it] sounded nice." No one can argue with the song's beauty or its astonishing power. Moreover, it reveals the Beatles' skill and growing confidence as craftsmen—virtuosos—in the studio. John's vocal, Paul's musical daring, Ringo's exquisite, inimitable drum fills are unparalleled. But whether it is profound remains purely subjective. Instead, "A Day in the Life" shines as one of the most innovative sessions in history, one in which the Beatles experimented with sounds and styles that refined the slapdash recording process into a feat of technical artistry. "I'd love to turn you on . . . ," they had teased, and in the end, it was a promise fulfilled.

George celebrates his twenty-first birthday with a fat stogie, piles of fan mail, and two comely fans.

Clowning with Cassius Clay, whom they met reluctantly in Miami on February 18, 1964, following their performance on The Ed Sullivan Show *and during Clay's training for the title bout against Sonny Liston. Clay insisted he was "the most beautiful" and called the Beatles "worms."*

The face of Beatlemania, October 1965. Outside Buckingham Palace, the police were barely able to contain the fans.

The Beatles spent many afternoons in 1964 locked in Tony Barrow's office, flying through one interview after another.

John and Cynthia arrive at Heathrow Airport in
1964, just prior to their departure for America.

The Lennon estate, Kenwood, during a remodeling.

Paul visits with his father, Jim McCartney, during one of the Beatles' frequent stopovers in Liverpool.

The police had their hands full with overwrought fans outside the Beatles' performances throughout the early sixties. Screaming, swooning, crying, and occasionally fainting were among the nightly rituals that highlighted the mania.

Paul and Jane Asher in 1965, during the early days of their courtship.

John holding a young fan, with Paul and George in Central Park, February 1964.

*George, with Pattie Boyd, soon after they
met on the set of* A Hard Day's Night.

© HULTON-DEUTSCH COLLECTION/CORBIS

*Ringo and Maureen in
1965, greeting the press
after their wedding.*

MIRRORPIX

Following their investiture at Buckingham Palace in June 1965, where they received MBEs from the Queen, the Beatles mask their ambivalence by displaying the medals at a press conference at the Saville Theatre. John later returned his medal.

George and Pattie, celebrating their marriage at Esher Register Office, January 21, 1966.
© Hulton-Deutsch Collection/CORBIS

With Ringo in the hospital, having his tonsils removed, the rest of the Beatles, with Jimmy Nicol now on drums, left for a tour of the Netherlands and later Australia. June 1964.
© Bettmann/CORBIS

Before each recording session, John and Paul would preview their songs for producer George Martin.

TERRY O'NEILL/REX FEATURES

George had already warned off the paparazzi when he blew his cool and launched a drink at photographer Bob Flora in Hollywood. August 1964.

© Bob Flora/
UPI/Bettmann/CORBIS

Sparked by John's comment that the Beatles were more popular than Jesus, young fans in Waycross, Georgia, prepare to burn albums at a bonfire in protest. August 1966.

© Bettmann/CORBIS

*Paul and Mal Evans return
from a holiday in France.
Aboard their return flight, Paul
hit upon the concept for their
new album: salt and pepper—
Sergeant Pepper.*

Paul and Linda Eastman locked eyes early at the press listening party for Sgt.
Pepper's Lonely Hearts Club Band, *at Brian Epstein's flat in May 1967.*

For a brief period, the Apple Boutique wore a forty-foot psychedelic mural painted by the Fool before neighborhood shopkeepers demanded its removal. December 1967.

© HULTON-DEUTSCH
COLLECTION/CORBIS

By 1969, it had come to this: dispassion—along with Yoko Ono—in the recording studio.

MIRRORPIX

Shielded by police officers, Paul and Linda make their way through a throng of fans following their marriage in London. March 1969.

© Bettmann/CORBIS

Visiting with Maharishi Mahesh Yogi in 1967, shortly after his lecture at the Hilton in London.

Mirrorpix

John and Yoko celebrate their impromptu marriage with the Rock of Gibraltar as a dramatic backdrop. March 20, 1969.

Not all the Beatles agreed that Allen Klein should manage them, but they all understood his unique charisma.

PHOTO: JOHN KELLY
CAMERA PRESS (JBA) LONDON

The final concert on the rooftop of Apple Records, as the Beatles, with Billy Preston, perform together—joyously—for the last time. January 30, 1969.

MIRRORPIX

[II]

Even in the midst of this "very productive period," there were muted notes of discontent. Professionally, the Beatles felt the strain of wear and tear on a tightly yoked bond now entering its tenth year. They had been inseparable for the most part, shaping one another's early attitudes toward life, as well as dreams about the future. As boys, they had clung tenaciously to one another—to the Beatles—for stability and even survival, but as men, they were already looking beyond the band in response to individual needs.

George, who suffered through a stretch of extreme growing pains and a preoccupation with all things Indian, found the "assembly[-line] process" of recording overdubs "a bit tiring and a bit boring." To him, the whole Sgt. Pepper business was a turnoff, not so much for its concept, which wasn't all that fascinating, as for the diminishing role he filled in the recording studio. "A lot of the time it ended up with just Paul playing the piano and Ringo keeping the tempo, and we weren't allowed to play as a band so much," he complained, and not unjustly. Certainly there was less for George to do on this album. Guitar parts seemed to have taken a backseat to technical fireworks. Most of the songs he proposed—a miscellany of mantras and ragas—had been rejected by John and Paul. The facade of Beatlemania that had been his pass into John's and Paul's world lost its luster, and now the old sense of alienation that he'd felt in Liverpool and Hamburg was pecking at a nerve.

Whatever restlessness George felt in the studio was compounded by John's personal burden of self-loathing and envy. The destabilizing effects of LSD, coupled with a stagnant marriage and twenty years of snowballing rage, sunk Lennon further and further into an emotional shell. "I was in a real big depression in *Pepper* and I know that Paul wasn't at that time," he recalled. Paul's glaring "confidence," as John saw it, only inflamed his outlook, and as a result, John said, "I was going through murder."

The extent of his anguish is apparent in the volume of photographs that survive as a graphic account of the *Sgt. Pepper* sessions. In picture after picture taken throughout the months at Abbey Road, the sleepless nights begin to show. John looks miserable, achingly sad, his face dissipated from abuse, his eyes as flat and lifeless as a poached carp. Food no longer interested him, probably a condition caused by the drugs that were sustaining him. For hours, sometimes days, he remained transfixed in a cosmic consciousness, either staring at the ceiling like a zombie or giggling into his hands. Cynthia equated John's LSD fixation with "religion" and wrote that, because of the incessant tripping, "it was becoming almost impossible to communicate with [him]." In one respect, she said, his "tensions, bigotry, and bad temper were replaced by understanding and love," but the downside was tragic. During the winter and early spring of 1967, he reached an apogee of drug-taking and self-abuse unparalleled since art college. The nightly scenes when he returned home had lost their intimacy. John was often too spaced out, talking gibberish and behaving much like a child. And he brought home swarms of street freaks "as high as kites," who tripped and drank and passed out in the house, causing havoc chez Lennon.

John's problem, according to Paul, was that he was "stuck out in suburbia, living a middle-class life." It wasn't the John Lennon he knew at all. It was someone else pretending to be John, pretending to be a husband and father in a fake, alien world. The *real* John Lennon was the sharp-tongued bohemian from Liverpool, the guy he knew from art college who enjoyed dancing on the edge, going for broke, not the house husband in the ritzy-titsy Stockbroker Belt, as Weybridge was called, with boring neighbors and a seriously boring wife. Paul knew that wasn't where John was at. And where it left John was plain to him: John was in hell.

———

He had company. Even before the latest round of headaches, Brian had felt threatened by the Beatles' metamorphosis. He had vowed to maintain control over all aspects of their career. But this new direction saw them slipping further from his reach. At the beginning of the year—right after they'd settled into the studio—he had negotiated an extension of the Beatles' contract with EMI. He thought his position would be strengthened by the generally favorable terms and increased royalty rates.* Even with a new deal in place, however, his insecurity mounted. Touring had sustained Brian. He loved the detailed work and traveling with the boys. Hardly a day went by that he didn't bring up the subject of tours, as if to somehow keep the idea of it alive. "I know Brian was convinced they'd go out again," recalls Tony Barrow. "He actually had dates penciled in—they'd start in Glasgow and do Brighton." But Barrow knew better. John and George had been adamant; even the other two had no interest in playing to audiences. Ever.

---

* Having made just pennies an album up to January 1967, their royalty rate ballooned to 10 percent of the album's wholesale price.

Other circumstances indicated to Barrow that Brian had lost control over the Beatles' press functions as well. It was becoming impossible to get any interview or photo session approved, even when it was impressed upon Brian that a prestigious publication had put in a request and was sending Lord So-and-so as its rep. There would be days, maybe weeks, of excuses, hedging, until Brian eventually lost patience and snapped: *"Of course I've been to them. Don't you realize? They've said no."*

When it came to the Beatles, the sad truth was that Brian's role had been reduced to that of a figurehead. Distancing himself even further from the process, Brian moved out of NEMS and took a private, tucked-away office on Albemarle Street, out of which only he and Wendy Hanson operated. He also decided to sell a controlling interest in NEMS to a flashy operator named Robert Stigwood. Like Brian Epstein, Stigwood was among the small, pioneering band of gentleman British impresarios who, beginning in the mid-1960s, built empires by spreading the gospel of rock 'n roll. By 1965, he had already gained prominence as one of the first independent producers and gone broke in the process—twice, in fact, the second time, as Peter Brown points out, with "borrowed money from EMI, knowing he would never be able to pay it back." Nat Weiss sized him up as "a real carnival promoter . . . a man who had two cents [to his name] but could run up a bill." But Brian detected what other music insiders knew and respected, which is that Stigwood had qualities that, in the rock world, superseded fiscal responsibility: fabulous style and taste, not to mention an eagle eye for talent. "Robert seemed like *the* solution to our worries," Peter Brown remembers. "Even though no one came out and said it, Brian was no longer paying attention and couldn't adequately run the company as it was. Suddenly, here was this person who could not only run it effectively but improve on it in the process."

To encourage a deal, Stigwood and his partner, financier David Shaw, whisked Brian off for what has been described as "a dirty weekend" in Paris, an expression that can only be taken to mean attractive young men and wanton sex. Stigwood had already prepared a proposal. "It was quite simple," he recalled. "We'd be joint managing directors together, and he gave me an option . . . for six months. If I paid him half a million pounds [in that time], then the controlling shares . . . would be transferred to me and my company." Half a million pounds seems a ridiculously small amount for a company that, just two years before, was valued at twenty times that. But that was then—when the novelty of Beatlemania was still thrilling, and before the drugs and depression tightened their grip. It wasn't fun anymore. Without much ado, Brian made the deal that was presented to him in Paris, dotting all the i's and crossing the t's that enabled Stigwood and Shaw to move into NEMS right away.

Only one small detail was overlooked: he neglected to tell the Beatles anything about the new arrangement.

Then again, Brian might have outlined the Stigwood deal on a billboard placed outside Abbey Road and the Beatles probably wouldn't have noticed. They were up to their forelocks in recording, cranking out the remaining songs for what would become *Sgt. Pepper's Lonely Hearts Club Band,* and oblivious to the outside world.

In a little over three weeks, they laid down the basic tracks for "Fixing a Hole," "Being for the Benefit of Mr. Kite!" "Good Morning, Good Morning," "Lovely Rita," "Getting Better," and "She's Leaving Home," all songs of which bits and pieces were written during various sessions. The recording staff had never experienced anything like it. Geoff Emerick, the chairman of the board, and Richard Lush, the tape operator, were kept dancing, trying to create the extraordinary effects that caromed around the Beatles' heads. Hardly a note was left intact without dissecting and manipulating its abstract properties. Could a sound be distorted, looped, or played backward? How about speeding up the tape to play havoc with the vocals? (They accomplished just that on "When I'm Sixty-four," satisfying Paul's request to "sound younger . . . and be a teenager again.") Or slowing it down? (On "Lucy in the Sky" the tape was delayed five cycles, which elevated the vocals, then cushioned with tape echo.) And what about orchestration? "She's Leaving Home" gave itself over entirely to a string octet, a harp, and those gentle voices; there wasn't a conventional rock instrument on deck. Nothing was sacred.

One of the most enterprising tracks was "Being for the Benefit of Mr. Kite!" The idea for it came the last week in January 1967 during a break in recording, while the Beatles were filming the promotional films for the "Strawberry Fields Forever"/"Penny Lane" single. It was a clear, bitter cold day, and they were on their way to a restaurant, passing in front of an antiques shop in Sevenoaks, when a poster for an old-fashioned circus— Pablo Fanque's Circus Royal—caught John's eye. Enchanted by circuses as a boy, dazzled by the animals and the costumes—even once flirting with quitting school and "joining up"—he disappeared inside the shop and scarfed up this trophy. It was advertised as "Being for the Benefit of Mr. Kite (late of Wells's Circus)" and promised to be the "Grandest Night of the Season!" "It said the Hendersons would also be there," John recalled. "There would be hoops and horses and someone going through a hogshead of real fire. Then there was Henry the Horse. The band would start at ten to six. All at Bishopsgate." The next week Paul arrived at Weybridge for an afternoon's work and saw the poster on John's living-room wall. "Almost the whole song was written right off this poster," he remembered. "We pretty much took it down word for word and then just made up some little bits and pieces to glue it together."

Writing it, however, was a snap compared with bringing the song to life. John was explicit about the atmospherics: he wanted a "fairground sound," something that toggled his memory of wandering through village fetes, where one could "smell the sawdust" and hear the crowd amid the background racket of the arcade. To George Martin, that conjured up the calliope, and he put out the call for a steam organ. It seemed like a reasonable order, but the cost of renting and programming one was enormous, he discovered, even when it came to his golden boys, the Beatles. Those within financial reason were automatic, not hand-cranked, which sounded fake. Existing recordings seemed like a good alternative, but those he could get his hands on proved useless. Hamstrung, they created their own backing track—"a pumping kind of sound," Martin called it—with a harmonium, various organ overdubs, and a bass harmonica played by the ever-versatile Mal Evans. Over roughly a six-hour marathon, Paul played various keyboards, with Martin pumping the harmonium nonstop until he literally gave out, collapsing on the floor out of exhaustion.

Early session tapes reveal the fairground ambience beginning to take shape, with John contributing "oom-pahpahs" on yet another organ. Nevertheless, on playback it still lacked authenticity. Martin went back to the existing steam organ recordings—variations of John Philip Sousa marches—and transferred the lot of them to tape. "I selected two-minute segments of the taped music," he recalled. Then he enlisted Emerick— "my co-conspirator," as he referred to him—and issued bizarre instructions. "I want you to cut that tape there up into sections that are roughly fifteen inches long. . . . Now, pick them all up and fling them into the air." Geoff did what was asked of him, excited to hear what the randomness provided—"but, amazingly, they came back together in the same order." So they cheated a bit, shuffling the samples, splicing pieces, even turning several upside-down to create a patchwork of one-second segments, and—*voilà!*—a fairgrounds sound materialized, almost uncannily so. More organ was added to lend a more circusy effect, and the backing track was complete. "John was thrilled to bits with it," Martin recalled.

The album grew up and around them. A lot of the joyous mayhem is evident on "Lovely Rita," which Paul had written during a nighttime walk while visiting his brother, Michael, on the Wirral. Its whimsical lyric invited an equally whimsical approach when it came to getting it on tape over a day or two in late February. In four takes, it was more or less intact. But John had one last trick up his sleeve: combs were distributed throughout Studio Two in lieu of instruments, after which Mal was dispatched to the loo for ample lengths of regulation-issue EMI toilet paper (each sheet was stamped PROPERTY OF EMI) to complete the kazoo orchestra. The honky-tonk piano solo, added as an afterthought by George Martin, lifted the exuberant spirit of the song from what John considered its otherwise "boring" subject.

During the recording, Martin's fussy direction provided tremendous downtime during which the Beatles would either rehearse or muck about. Ordinarily John might have doodled in a sketchbook or huddled with Paul, but throughout the prolonged months of working on *Sgt. Pepper,* these languorous stretches were often serviced by drugs. All the Beatles smoked pot in vast quantities; they really *enjoyed* it. But John's intake wasn't so much recreational as it was therapeutic. In the studio, the Beatles' regimen of drugs was fairly limited, although Paul has reported— quite surprisingly—that "the one hard drug used during the making of *Sgt. Pepper* was cocaine." This amounted to a few lines before the sessions: "For *Sgt. Pepper* I used to have a bit of coke and then smoke some grass to balance it out."

Had harder drugs further encroached, they might have seriously impeded the work, but even the buttoned-down Martin maintained that "looking back on it, *Pepper* would never have been formed in exactly that way if the boys hadn't gotten into the drug scene." The album wouldn't have been "quite so flowery," he believed, nor would it have been so intense without LSD. In fact, John told Jann Wenner, the Beatles never dropped acid in the studio. But John quickly corrected his memory, remembering an "accidental trip" toward the tail end of *Sgt. Pepper's*. It happened on March 21, while they were overdubbing the lead and backing vocals on "Getting Better." There was a lull between takes, during which John staunched the boredom with what he thought was a blast of amphetamine. "By mistake this night he had acid," Paul recalled, "and he was on a trip."

It hit John unexpectedly, which played on his paranoia. He felt disoriented, nauseous. Recording continued, but it failed to settle his nerves. "I suddenly got so scared on the mike," he recalled. "I thought I was going cracked." Unsteadily, he climbed the steep staircase to the control room and confronted his producer. "George, I'm not feeling too good," he mumbled. "I'm not focusing on me." One look told Martin that John was distressingly ill. His gaunt face was tightly cinched around the mouth. A hollow-eyed stare obliterated any concentration.

Martin may have exuded common sense, but he knew less than nothing about drugs. In his naïveté, he suggested John get some air—on the *roof*. Fifty feet above the concrete driveway, shivering in the biting air, the two men stood perched on the edge of the studio's flat roof, staring at the stars. John hallucinated wildly. Breathlessly, he filled the night with talk of heavenly brilliance. The aimless gush of his comments surprised George Martin, who by now sensed that John was "wired"; he felt him "swaying gently against my arm . . . [and] resonating away like a human tuning fork." Martin tried to comfort him but sensed the futility of it. Gradually, the paranoia passed. At some point George and Paul "came bursting on to the roof" when they found out where John was, but by that time he was safely out of danger—or at least nowhere near the ledge.

Everyone decided that it would be fruitless to go on. Nothing would be accomplished without John, and he was in no shape to continue. Reluctantly, Martin closed down their session for the night. John had no place to go. His driver wasn't expected for several hours. Cynthia was fast asleep in Weybridge. Since Paul's house was the closest—just around the corner, in fact—it seemed most sensible for the two men to go there to chill out.

Paul's house held its own pitfalls. It demanded a degree of intimacy, which, for all their interaction, had disappeared from their relationship. No one said as much, but acid had driven a larger wedge between them. Paul felt it had intruded upon their careers as well as their extraordinary, productive friendship, whereas John no doubt relied on it to sharpen his self-expression. In some respect, LSD permeated every aspect of their lives, and it affected each of the partners in completely different ways. As they set off and bisected that now-famous zebra crossing outside the studio, John and Paul once again avoided saying anything that either of them might regret. Still, each no doubt felt the implication attached to Paul's good deed. They may have been headed to the same destination, but it was clear to both men that they were on vastly different wavelengths.

Somewhere between Abbey Road and Cavendish Avenue, Paul reached a pivotal decision. "I thought, Maybe this is the moment where I should take a trip with [John]," he recalled. Paul had avoided tripping with the other Beatles. He described himself as "a guy who wasn't keen on getting that weird" because of "a disturbing element to it." As a matter of fact, the prospect terrified him. He later attributed his abstinence to common sense; Paul had great reserves of self-control and an eye on posterity. Even with pot, which was consumed with relish, he felt the reins of responsibility. "I always knew I'd have to keep my shit very well together," he explained. And acid put you squarely in the shit. But unlike the Preludin and pot quagmires the Beatles slogged through as a group, acid had alienated Paul from his mates. They couldn't understand why he wouldn't try it, or why, as they put it, he was "holding out." What was the point? And why did he have to act so high-and-mighty about it? Wasn't he comfortable letting go of it all in their presence? Didn't he trust them? The peer pressure was unrelenting. John needled him endlessly about what a choirboy he'd become, while George, on another spiritual plane altogether, expressed his contempt wordlessly by distancing himself from Paul. From the outset, Paul felt the hostility.

It had become such an issue that late in 1966, against his better judgment, Paul succumbed to the pressure and dropped some acid in the company of Tara Browne. If he was unwilling to take the drug before, his reaction to it leaned more to ambivalence. Overall, he found it quite "spacy," a "very, very deeply emotional experience," ranging in sensations from godliness to depression. Most likely, Paul was too uptight to give it a fair ride.

Whatever the outcome, he'd been in no rush to continue the journey. But now, with John's companionship—just the two of them, alone—it made the prospect more appealing. Deep down, Paul loved John in the way someone loved an elder brother. He knew all of John's faults—many of which frustrated Paul's ambition—but he still looked up to his partner, even courted his attention. John was a loose cannon, but he was the genuine article. His rough edges and fuck-all personality only underscored Paul's pretensions, sparking a contrast that would haunt Paul for the rest of his life. Maybe sharing the experience would help bring them closer.

Into the night, stretching almost until dawn, the two most important songwriters of their generation hallucinated like madmen, staring inscrutably into each other's eyes—"the eye contact thing we used to do," Paul called it—and communing with the unknown. He imagined they "dissolve[d] into each other" and envisioned John as "a king, the absolute Emperor of Eternity." No doubt they'd both drilled deeply into their subconsciouses; a good deal of transference took place. Otherwise, there was a lot of laughter and reminiscing about the past. Nothing was mentioned about their dense tangle of differences. Except for a brief walk in the garden, they hardly budged for about five hours. Still, it was a powerful, emotionally tumultuous five hours, especially for Paul. "It was a very freaky experience," he said, "and I was totally blown away."

[III]

By the third week in April, the Beatles had reached the end of their *Sgt. Pepper's Lonely Hearts Club Band* odyssey. They had logged slightly more than five months in the studio, a staggering, unheard-of amount of time, completely without precedent in the annals of pop recording.* The interminable sessions especially worried their fans, who feared the Beatles' long silence augured some untoward fate.

On the evening of April 21, the band showed up at Abbey Road for what was ostensibly a final salute to the sessions. They gathered in the control room above Studio Two, where George Martin and his engineers were busily remixing the final two songs. Aside from sequencing, there was nothing more for them to do, but the Beatles had insisted on one last laugh.

It had been predetermined that "A Day in the Life" would close the album. There was a finality to the song, effectively bringing the curtain down, that made perfect sense in its placement. But what to do about that climactic piano chord? It just hung there like a last pregnant gasp and, then . . . *scratch, scratch, scratch* . . . the tone arm slid rudely into the record's run-out groove. How annoying! the Beatles grumbled. Wasn't there something they could do to reduce the offensive noise? It remains a mystery who actually proposed filling the groove with gibberish, but the decision to do it was fervent and unanimous. Their reasoning behind it was basically this: if people were too stoned to get up and turn off the record, even if the needle swayed in the groove for a few stagnant hours, the nonsense talk would take on the form of a mantra. Perfect! As Geoff Emerick recalled: "They ran down to the studio floor and we recorded them twice—on each track of a two-track tape. They made funny noises, said

---

* By contrast, the Please Please Me *album wrapped in a spry 585 minutes.*

random things; just nonsense." Only a snippet was chosen—someone saying, "Couldn't really be any other"—which was looped, repeated ad infinitum, and overlapped until it was meaningless. There was nothing artistic about it, it wasn't even earthshaking—except that when listeners who looked for hidden messages in Beatles recordings played it backward, a voice clearly intoned: "We'll fuck you like Superman, we'll fuck you like Superman. . . ."

The gist of the message took the Beatles completely by surprise. "We had certainly not intended to do that," Paul recalled, "but probably when you turn anything backwards it sounds like something . . . if you look hard enough." John Lennon, no shrinking violet, claimed to be "shocked—and delighted." It was even more delicious than his parting contribution: inserting a high-pitched whistle only dogs could hear immediately after the piano chord but before the gibberish began. To John, it seemed only fitting that every dog had its "Day."

Throughout early March, as sessions for *Sgt. Pepper's* accelerated and the album's novel concept edged into focus, the Beatles batted around ideas for a cover that would complement the music. The situation, they agreed, called for something fresh, daring, and grand. Not merely a cardboard slipcase, but something radical: unusual art, psychedelic design, an entertaining sleeve, extra goodies. Perhaps it was necessary to reinvent the entire article, to offer a genuinely new vision of what an album could be.

Before the cover ever materialized, the Beatles hired a fledgling London ad agency, Geer, DuBois, to field and generate ideas. Instantly they set about experimenting with forms. New designs demanded new approaches, new ways of regarding an album. Instead of a one-dimensional surface, they proposed, maybe it should open like a book. That way, it was possible for the Beatles to include sleeve notes to their hearts' content. One of the project coordinators, Gene Mahon, suggested printing the songs' lyrics inside, superimposed over pictures of the Beatles. *Lyrics!* It had never been done. As routine as this practice seems now, the idea was trendsetting and attracted a serious challenge from music publishers, fearing it would cut into their sheet-music sales. Even so, the Beatles persisted. "We wanted the sleeve to be really interesting," Paul insisted. "Everyone agreed."

One thing was for certain: there wouldn't be a standard studio shot of the four mop tops on the cover. Compared with their images on any of the early albums or even *Revolver*'s stark collage, *Sgt. Pepper* demanded a bold departure. Initially, Paul had made pen-and-ink sketches of the Beatles, dressed in Salvation Army–type Lonely Hearts Club Band uniforms, standing in front of framed photographs of their heroes. Another series depicted them being presented to dignitaries on a platform, in front of a garish floral clock. Although generally disdainful of Paul's increasing thirst for control over such details, the other Beatles apparently approved of his design. They also commissioned the Fool, the Dutch design group, to paint an acid-inspired dream landscape for the inside gatefold. The spectacular mural was a mishmash of composition and flamboyance. Several panels of overlapping scenes served up a kaleidoscopic vision of the universe filled with silvery unicorn-like beasts, mystical birds, shamanistic images, peacocks, flowers, rainbows, and, of course, the Beatles, striding out from lush vegetation into a spectral clash of color, all crammed in beneath a comet-streaked sky. It was crude, embarrassingly puerile—and the Beatles loved it.

The arbiter of this material was Robert Fraser, Paul's art dealer and confidant, who had been enlisted as a consultant for the Beatles' album design. Like Victor Waddington and Mateusz Grabowski, Fraser was among the small, daring band of London gallery owners who brought the new wave of modern art to hip, young British collectors. In 1962 Fraser reportedly gave the first show in London of American pop art, and he represented an impressive array of clients, including Claes Oldenberg, Jim Dine, Eduardo Paolozzi (Stuart Sutcliffe's mentor), Richard Hamilton, Colin Self, Harold Cohen, and Bridget Riley. Rock and movie stars alike were drawn not only to his exquisite taste in art but also by his charismatic personal style. A dapper, raffish, irrepressibly arrogant man with a drop-dead smile, he had a showman's panache coupled with a quick, caustic wit and an alluring coterie of friends. He was also a doyen of the fashionable gay drug culture, with a gourmet taste that ran from young boys to heroin. It was a combination that attracted eclectic crowds to his gala openings and his posh flat on Mount Street.

Fraser's involvement with rock stars was nothing new. His best customers, according to gossip, were the Beatles and the Rolling Stones. He sold them dozens of paintings, including most of Paul's René Magritte collection (including *au revoir,* which would become the Beatles' green Apple logo). He provided a relaxed arena where they could learn about modern art and develop an instinct for quality. It was the perfect stimulus for ambitious, newly rich young musicians. With a revealing mix of fondness and admiration, Paul later admitted that, aside from John Lennon, Fraser was "the most formative influence for me."

Fraser took one look at the Fool's slapdash work and, with a flick of the hand, dismissed it as "not good art." It lacked tension. "In years to come, this will be just another psychedelic cover," he told them. "You've had good covers up [un]til now, you've had a high standard. Why don't you ask a fine artist to do it?" At Fraser's insistence, they consulted two of his other clients, photographer Michael Cooper and pop artist Peter Blake.

It stood to reason that they'd find a sidekick in Blake. A devotee of fantasy and abstraction, his fascination with toys and badges played right into the Beatles' wiggy sensibility. He painted to rock music, and what's more, he boasted loose ties to the Liverpool arts scene: in 1963 Blake had won the junior prize at the John Moores competition—the same prize Stuart Sutcliffe won to finance the band's first bass guitar. John had actually seen Blake's winning entry, and when the artist wondered if he'd liked it, John replied as only John would: "No, not very much." Hardly the ring of praise, but Blake appreciated the honesty. Besides, John had gone to several of his exhibitions at the Fraser gallery, in an entourage that included Marlon Brando, Tony Curtis, and the Stones, which delighted him. And Paul appreciated his early work, the famous pinups and the wrestlers.

The Beatles laid out their ideas for *Sgt. Pepper's Lonely Hearts Club Band*. John described their identity as "part German marching band, part military band," and the idea was that they had done a concert. "Perhaps we could do something in a park," he suggested. In Blake's recollection, the crowd concept was his, but most likely he'd been told about Paul's sketches and incorporated them in his design. Sitting in his cozy studio with John, Paul, Brian, and Robert Fraser, he proposed framing the design around a bandstand. A collage seemed like the most expedient way to construct it. "Look, I can make a crowd with photography, cutouts, and waxworks, and so we could have anyone [in it] you really want."

Anyone. It tantalized the Beatles, who loved the prankish quality of it. "Anyone" meant friends or heroes or family or, well, any obscure face that tickled their fancy. And it required no explanation. Let the fans go crazy trying to figure out who was in the crowd—and why. What a hoot it would be!

Blake instructed each of the Beatles, as well as Robert Fraser, to make a list of the people they'd like to include in the crowd. "It was just a broad spectrum of people," George remembered. But his list, of those finally submitted, proved the narrowest: eight Indian holy men, including Babaji, Paramahansa Yogananda, and the Maharishi Mahesh Yogi. Paul went mostly for artsy choices: William Burroughs, Aldous Huxley, Alfred Jarry, Fred Astaire, Aleister Crowley, Groucho Marx, Magritte, and Karl-heinz Stockhausen, as well as an obscure Everton footballer named Dixie Dean, among others. John had little interest in impressing anyone; he wanted to *goose* them, to stir up the ooze. If he felt at all chastened by irate Christians over his now-infamous comments, then starting with Jesus seemed like a "naughty" little choice. Then he requested Hitler—which managed to piss off Paul, who wanted him to take the cover more seri-ously—Gandhi, Nietzsche, Oscar Wilde, H. G. Wells, and, of course, that rascal of rascals, the Marquis de Sade. John threw in his own obscure Liverpool footballer, Albert Stubbins, despite only the vaguest interest in sports. Later, for good measure, he added Edgar Allan Poe and Lewis Carroll.

When Blake collected the names, only Ringo hesitated. "Whatever the others have is fine by me," Ringo replied. "I won't put anyone in."

Robert Fraser contributed Terry Southern, the author of *Candy,* as well as two American artists—Richard Lindner and Wally Berman. "Mine," recalled Blake, "included Dion, one of the very few musicians on the cover . . . the Bowery Boys—Leo Gorcey and Huntz Hall—Lex Barker, the Tarzan [figure], and the waxworks of Sonny Liston, who I was a great fan of. Richard Merkin, the painter, was a friend of mine in New York, so I put him in there, too."

At the last minute, John, to his credit, insisted they include Stuart Sutcliffe.

The legwork was left to Neil Aspinall and Mal Evans, who canvassed the local libraries for photos of the famous crowd. Blake, along with his wife, artist Jann Haworth, made the final selections, blew them up to life-size proportions, and retouched the images before pasting them on a hard-board surface. A set was constructed in Michael Cooper's studio in Chelsea. "We made a rough kind of wooden frame, tacked up all the fig-ures, and stood in the waxworks," Blake recalled. "Built a little platform where the Beatles would then come and stand. I had a drum [skin] painted by a fairground painter [Joe Ephgrave], with the Sgt. Pepper's symbol on it. I also asked [the Beatles] to bring in favorite objects that we might use." The whole thing came together in less than two weeks' time. Aside from Paul's early sketches, there were almost no working drawings. Most of the detail was improvised on the fly. The mock-ups were placed haphazardly, the mementos patched in at will. Even the flowers for the intended floral clock were ordered as if one were sending a dozen roses. As a result, there weren't enough stems to pull it off properly, "so the delivery boy [from Clifton Nurseries] made a guitar with them instead."

In the shadow of Blake's spectacle, the Beatles went to work on their outfits for the cover. It had been decided that a takeoff on soldiers' uniforms would be appropriate. John, whose recent outing in *How I Won the War* gave him some experience in this field, directed his mates to Berman's, the theatrical costumers who had supplied wardrobe and plumage for the movie. "We just chose oddball things from everywhere and put them together," recalled Paul. Color triumphed over substance; anything bright, garish, or remotely psychedelic was given serious consideration. No one worried that anything might clash or offend—and if so, all the better, all the cooler!

Cool—they had always seemed able to define that very term. There was nothing they didn't do naturally that had failed to catch the popular drift: their style of hair, the choice of clothes—from pointy-toed boots to collarless sport coats to loud, flower-print shirts to army jackets—the granny glasses, the handlebar mustaches, everything they touched became vogue. Meanwhile, as individuals, they had become even more handsome than their teenage years indicated, growing into faces that once only suggested the sensuality but now burst into full bloom. The Beatles had always been easy to look at. But in the early days, the spectacle of hair had drawn too much away from their appearance; it made their features less intimate, more like caricature. Now, with *everybody* wearing long hair, they revealed themselves.

None of this was lost on Robert Fraser, whose appreciation of young men rivaled his eye for fine art. On March 30, as the cover photo session transpired, he instructed Michael Cooper to shoot a series of portraits of the Beatles that might be used inside the gatefold. The Beatles were still committed to the Fool's psychedelic design, but they didn't resist the opportunity to sit for Cooper, whose lens captured them in a pose as strong and penetrating as any in their career.

The album, as a package, was almost complete. There were attempts to include a transparent envelope filled "with goodies"—stick-on tattoos, badges, sergeant stripes, and little gifts that would vary from pressing to pressing. But production costs were insurmountable and it would have made the album too bulky and impossible for EMI to ship. In a more practical approach, the Beatles created a less-expensive souvenir cutout kit, with a Sgt. Pepper's Band bass drum, mustaches, and badges that could be slipped into the fold.

As it was, the cover costs alone soared into the stratosphere. A label like EMI usually budgeted anywhere from £25 to £75 for the standard cover photograph, but the bill for *Sgt. Pepper's* topped £2,800. "Joe Lockwood was furious," recalled Fraser, who was called into the EMI chairman's austere chambers to account for the "folly." Glowering like Zeus, he thundered, "I can hire the London Symphony Orchestra for that!"

Lockwood's chief concern, however—and justifiably so—was the label's liability in regard to the cover images. EMI had an international reputation to protect, to say nothing about standards of taste, and as far as he was concerned, that photo of Hitler was out of the question. He also insisted they "take Gandhi out" to avoid any backlash from the enormous overseas market. "If we show Gandhi standing around with Sonny Liston and Diana Dors, they'll never forgive us in India," he said.

Lockwood preferred that the whole cover be scrapped. In an altogether uncharacteristic gesture, Sir Joe had the label's in-house art department tinker with the cover and showed up with it himself, unannounced, on Paul McCartney's doorstep. "We have some problems on this," he reportedly told Paul, handing over the retouched version. "It had the flowers, the drum, the four Beatles—and a big blue sky," recalled Neil Aspinall, who happened to be visiting when Lockwood arrived. "They wiped out all the people [in the crowd] behind [the Beatles] because he was frightened that they might all sue or not want to be on the cover."

Paul refused to buckle, and détente was reached when Lockwood grudgingly approved the original cover, sans Gandhi and Hitler, as long as NEMS got proper permissions, while Paul—with no authority whatsoever—cavalierly agreed to indemnify EMI against any lawsuits arising from the design.

———

Right off the bat, there was friction between Brian and Robert Stigwood over the direction of NEMS. In an effort to get ahold of his life and to concentrate on developing the Saville Theatre, Brian intended to downsize the company's roster. "He certainly couldn't handle them, in his condition," recalls Alistair Taylor. "Brian and I discussed drawing the line at a maximum of six groups, preferably four—the Beatles, Gerry Marsden, Billy [J. Kramer], and Cilla [Black] with Sounds Inc. to back her—but, with Stigwood on board, we went in the opposite direction, *signing* new acts."

Stigwood turned up the promotion of Cream, who were on the verge of breaking wide open, and pursued three or four other acts creating buzz in the London clubs. Then, in March, Brian handed him a letter that changed the course of their relationship. It was from a group in Australia, hoping to interest the Beatles' manager. "I don't deal with this kind of thing," he told Stigwood, expecting him to issue a standard refusal. Instead, Robert took a look at their head shot and "fell in love." They were three siblings who called themselves the Bee Gees—for the Brothers Gibb—and the demo tucked in their press kit sounded incredible.

Stigwood was convinced NEMS could do something with them, but he got no support at all from Brian. "Brian became annoyed when Robert said they would be the next Beatles," recalls Nat Weiss. "As far as he cared, that sealed their fate." But fate had its own way of striking a responsive chord. Stigwood signed the Bee Gees posthaste and decided to originate their record deal in the United States, with Atlantic.

This only magnified Brian's indignation. Perhaps Nat Weiss had been right, fingering Stigwood as a "carnival promoter." But the man seemed to possess a full bag of tricks, which, thus far, had been profitable.

In a style that he copied directly from Brian, Robert decided to launch the Bee Gees in America with a splash—literally—by chartering a yacht, packing it with guests and elegant food, and sailing around Manhattan. It was an elaborate, expensive affair, and Nat Weiss remembers cornering Stigwood during the cruise and asking how he intended to pay for it. "Put it on my personal account," Stigwood replied. The next day Weiss got a call from Brian, who had flown into a rage. "They haven't sold *one* record yet and he's chartered a *yacht!*" he fumed. Weiss told him not to worry. "Robert says he'll put it on his personal account." This only prompted a more ferocious scream: *"He has no personal account!"*

By the time the American visit was over, Brian got his revenge. He described to Weiss Stigwood's preference for good-looking young men but, contrary to Brian's fancy, definitely not hustlers. "Robert likes to be able to win them over," he told the lawyer. Half the pleasure lay in the challenge. "He likes the art of seduction." Brian and Weiss found "the most used-up hustler in New York," hired him, and arranged for an encounter with Stigwood. For months they fed on the story of how "Robert thought he'd seduced someone who could have been available [to anyone] for ten dollars." So spent Brian Epstein his time and efforts.

By May of 1967, says Nat Weiss, "Brian wanted to get rid of Stigwood. He'd already begun proceedings; he had Lord Goodman"—Arnold

Goodman, his personal solicitor — "working . . . to undo all of that." None of this, of course, had the slightest impact on the Beatles. They still had no idea that Brian was even involved with partners, and had they known, they would have certainly disapproved. As it was, they were concentrating on their own album launch, keeping a close check on the progress of the troublesome *Sgt. Pepper's* cover.

For the most part, permissions came smoothly and with expressions of great honor. There were, however, a few snags. Shirley Temple, now an ambassador to the United Nations, wanted to approve the cover first and, barring any objections, receive an autographed copy for her children. In a now-famous response, Mae West expressed her disturbance over an obvious contradiction. "What would *I* be doing in a lonely hearts club?" she wondered. But the Beatles put together a flattering letter to her themselves, which charmed West into granting a release. Leo Gorcey, of the Bowery Boys, wrote back and said he'd be happy to appear on the cover — for a $500 fee. Unwilling to set a precedent, the Beatles refused, "so we had to airbrush him out," Blake recalled. Otherwise, everyone agreed, and the Fates, it seemed, sided with the Beatles: not a single lawsuit would arise from the cover.

For Brian, a crueler fate was yet to come.

[I]

In early April 1967 Paul had slipped in and out of the States to celebrate the twenty-first birthday of Jane Asher, who was touring there in the Bristol Old Vic's production of *Romeo and Juliet*. It had been a whirlwind visit. The few days he spent in San Francisco—showing up at the Fillmore, getting stoned with the Jefferson Airplane, wandering unrecognized into head shops and boutiques—had been among the most carefree in recent months. To Paul, the lure of the Haight's hedonistic hippie scene, entwined with the North Beach beat movement and Ken Kesey's Merry Pranksters, underscored the connection between acid and creativity. The whimsy, self-expression, and romanticism struck him as "golden . . . far-out." Then, in Denver, while shooting some amateur movie footage in a local park, "the idea tumbled together."

Kesey, in 1964, had sploshed spectral ribbons of paint across a beat-up old school bus, loaded it up with like-minded characters, and set out on a now-legendary trip across America, dispensing LSD to the masses. They had filmed the whole riotous, mind-blowing odyssey—later immortalized by Tom Wolfe in *The Electric Kool-Aid Acid Test*—intending to make a documentary movie. Hearing about it again in San Francisco had triggered a childhood memory of Paul's. During the late 1950s, northern councils sponsored "mystery tours" on which kids boarded a chaperoned bus whose ultimate destination was kept secret. "Everyone would spend time guessing where they were going, and this was part of the thrill," he remembered. Couldn't this be updated with a hip, groovy edge? What would happen if the Beatles cobbled the two ideas together? How cool would it be to comb the English countryside in their own private coach, stopping spontaneously in villages and towns to film inspired, nutty sequences? They could write little scenarios, provide an original soundtrack, control the project themselves. It was loaded with possibilities. Before long, he'd imagined it as a surreal sort of mystery tour—no, a *magical* mystery tour, to echo the spirit of the times.

Paul crystallized the idea on the flight back to London. Borrowing paper from a flight attendant, he began framing the project—sketching out dramatic segments and scenes, including the rough draft of a title song. By the time he returned to the studio, on April 20, it was all he could talk about.

Clearly his discussions with the Beatles had an edge of déjà vu. Not even a year earlier, he had worked hard to persuade them to undertake the identity of Sgt. Pepper's band. Now Paul was worked up about another gimmick, and it was all they could do to stay focused. It especially rankled John, who was already exasperated by his partner's slick enthusiasms. "I still felt every now and then that Brian would come in and say, 'It's time to record,' or 'Time to do this,'" John recalled. "And [now] Paul started doing that: 'Now we're going to make a movie. Now we're going to make a record.'"

A feeling crept over John that Paul was somehow trying to dominate the Beatles, which, after all, had been *his* group. Paul had all but taken over the *Sgt. Pepper's* sessions. He contributed so many suggestions for the arrangements, and so fast, so fluently, it was all John could do to keep up with him. It angered him that Paul had come up with the mystery tour concept; he grew peevish, jealous. Why hadn't *he* thought of it first? And yet, admittedly, John "enjoyed the fish and chip quality of [it]," the idea that they'd go out "with a load of freaks" and make a low-budget, tongue-in-cheek film. And even if he hated the idea, he may have been distracted—or too fucked-up—to resist.

It would also help solve the dilemma of what to do with their next film project. It was no secret that after *Help!*, the Beatles had been unable to find a script that captured their fancy. All the ideas submitted were either variations on the Lovable Mop Tops formula, which they despised, or sappy Hollywood retreads. "We didn't see any way of making a similar film of four jolly lads nipping around singing catchy little tunes," said George. "It had to be something that had more meaning."

A magical mystery tour, Paul argued, seemed like the perfect alternative. Because it would be mostly improvised and spontaneous, the Beatles wouldn't have to learn lines. Nor would they truck off to out-of-the-way locations at ungodly early hours, or endure endless waiting on the set.

"Nobody quite knows where they're going. We can take 'em anywhere we want, man!" Paul declared. What's more, they could plan and even direct it themselves.

Paul was convincing enough for the Beatles to finish and record a song or two for the project, right on the heels of their *Sgt. Pepper*'s session. Only four days after they tacked the gibberish and dog whistle onto the end of their forthcoming album, the Beatles headed back into the studio to lay down the basic rhythm track for "Magical Mystery Tour."

According to a music journalist, "McCartney arrived at the studio with only three chords and the opening line of the lyric:" "Roll up! Roll up!—for the Magical Mystery Tour." John and Paul had hit on what was, for them, the perfect bit of wordplay: a phrase that fired up listeners with the keen, romantic cry of circus troupes and carnival barkers rolling their riggings into town—and, a phrase that, to any fan with the slightest streak of hipness, served as a veiled invitation to roll up a joint. It was chock-full of feeble "references to drugs and to trips," Paul recalled. The song was clearly intended as an overture to the mystery tour motif, just as "Sgt. Pepper's Lonely Hearts Club Band" had kicked off an imaginary vaudeville show. But as a gimmick it was stale and sounded forced. Even the fanfare of trumpets felt tired—"the worst kind of musical cliché," writes Tim Riley.

The Beatles worked on polishing "Magical Mystery Tour" over four days at Abbey Road, looping the track with extraneous traffic noise and sound effects from the studio's audio library. When even that failed to lift it off the ground, they added background shouts and layered on echo. What had once provided punch, however, now sounded deliberate, if not heavy-handed. It took every ounce of their imagination to finally finish the song. When the Beatles returned to the studio on May 9, essentially to decide what to do next, it was clear they had run out of steam. The session deteriorated into a disorganized, loopy, seven-hour jam—perhaps due to boredom, perhaps to drugs—nevertheless, a condition that served to stall work on the project for several months.

Obviously, this frustrated Paul, who thrived on the energy crackling in the atmosphere. Even when the Beatles had no commitments, he seldom rested. At the slightest spark, he would flame into action. "We can do this. Then we can do that. And maybe if this falls into place, we can take it there and do . . ." If the rest of them wanted to get stoned and sleep in front of the telly, that was their problem. Fuck the dopeheads! Paul was bursting at the seams with creative energy, and nothing, absolutely nothing, was going to stand in his path.

Somehow he kept things moving long enough to launch yet another session in advance of his mystery tour and several other rapid-fire projects, including a full-length feature cartoon based on the song "Yellow Submarine" and a new single set for summer release. Part of the other Beatles' cooperation may have rested on their curiosity about the studio. For only the second time in their record career, they decided to work outside of Abbey Road, detouring for a night to Olympic Sound, in nearby Barnes. The Stones worked there, as did dozens of the edgy, emerging British bands, where it was said that the studio manager, Keith Grant, ran things at a slam-bang pace. *Fast* was attractive to the Beatles, who were easily bored to begin with; add to that their exacting, exhaustive work on *Sgt. Pepper's,* and a quickie sounded like a splendid proposition.

The Olympic song, itself, was a paste-up job. Based on a news item he'd seen about hippies—the Bay Area's self-proclaimed "beautiful people"—John had been playing around with a lyric called "One of the Beautiful People" that scanned as too convoluted and long-winded on its own. It wasn't going where he wanted it to—that is, until Paul tacked on the lick "baby, you're a rich man" that had floated to the fore in his notebook. Suddenly, as with so many of their collaborations, the Lennon-McCartney team pulled a song out of the scrap heap—or, as John later dismissed it, "a combination of two separate pieces . . . put together and forced into one song"—the whole being spectacularly more than the sum of its parts. With "Baby You're a Rich Man," they had come up with a number whose imagery, if nothing else, captured the blatant hypocrisy of the burgeoning hippie scene.

Working at Olympic was a welcome liberation from the frustrations the Beatles faced during the *Sgt. Pepper's* sessions. There was none of the ponderous, scientific, deliberate approach to sound recording that had paced their recent sessions. No eggheads padded through the control room in identical, starched lab coats, paging through engineering manuals and dog-eared rule books. No one had to be *consulted* before a piece of equipment or technique could be employed. Geoff Emerick, their trusty board man, had the touch—but he was an EMI drone, part of the system, whereas Keith Grant ran his own show from the board. At Olympic, his session *felt* like rock 'n roll.

After laying down the first few takes, several of the Stones showed up to root on the Beatles and lend a hand. Brian Jones tinkered with a spacy oboe effect, Mick Jagger sang a few lines of backup. The whole thing had the feel of an after-hours party. By the time the shindig reached its peak in the postmidnight hours, even John fed off the buzz and grew giddy, expressing his delight by tweaking bits of the lyric. There were numerous aborted takes owing to his frisky, even scandalous, improvisations. He took some wicked shots at Paul, Ringo, and Mick, according to one observer; otherwise, "everyone else was spared."

Not quite everyone. An oblivious victim wasn't mentioned by name, but no interpretation was necessary when John, grinning like a jackal, was unable "to resist singing, on some of the later choruses, 'Baby, you're a rich fag Jew.'"

Rueful of his decision to sell a controlling interest in NEMS, Brian still hadn't told the boys that Robert Stigwood had taken over the day-to-day operations. "He knew he had to confront it," says Peter Brown, "but he couldn't find the right time—or right way." No matter how he presented it, it would seem weak, perhaps even underhanded. Still, by not telling them, Brian was playing a dangerous game; sooner or later the Beatles would find out, at which point there was sure to be a dramatic confrontation. Moreover, they might feel betrayed by the apparent deception. Of course, Brian hoped to invalidate the Stigwood deal before the option came due, making the Beatles' knowledge of it irrelevant. Still, should the strategy backfire, it could damage his relationship with the boys. And he knew it. Paul was already on Brian's back about their intricate financial arrangements, wanting to know, well, *everything*. "He was a real pain in the ass," Brown says. "He always thought he knew best. He was always second-guessing Brian's decisions."

Had he done more than second-guess, Paul might have stumbled into the darkest tunnel, which was the Beatles' personal management contract with NEMS. It was up in October 1967, just a few short months off. After five years at the reins of the greatest show on earth, Brian watched as the date loomed near, and he was terrified—"positively sick"—of being sacked as the Beatles' manager. Brian had certainly taken them to the toppermost of the poppermost, but now that they were there, how much more could he do for them? No dates needed to be booked. No record deals needed negotiating. What, if anything, did they expect from a manager?

As with everything, it came down to money. The Beatles were satisfied, for the most part, by the increases in their new EMI contract, although resentment festered over the remaining careless deals, especially the lopsided music publishing arrangement with Dick James, which was siphoning off hundreds of thousands of pounds, maybe millions, from their coffers. Paul felt strongly that he and John deserved more than a 20 percent share of their copyrights. Why had Brian allowed them to sign away the lion's share of their rights? With so much leverage, why wasn't he able to muscle James into a more equitable arrangement? Paul wasn't the only one asking such questions—George wanted answers, too—but he was the most persistent.

Paul had heard vague rumors about an American accountant named Allen Klein, who had restructured the Rolling Stones' Decca Records contract and won them a $1.25 million signing bonus. "What about us?" he demanded of Brian during a confrontation in a crowded elevator. *What about us?* It was the kind of question Brian dreaded most.

While the paranoia may have been irrational, his fear of Klein wasn't. Brian had taken an immediate disliking to the American the moment he laid eyes on him. They had met in 1964, when Klein was managing Sam Cooke, and it was clear that this was a beast of a different nature. Brian may have liked hustlers, but he didn't like *hustlers,* which Klein clearly was, a "fast-talking, dirty-mouthed man in his early-thirties, sloppily dressed and grossly overweight," as Peter Brown described him in a 1983 memoir. He'd approached Brian on the premise of an opening spot for Cooke on the Beatles' American tour, but once Klein got his foot in the door he cleverly turned the talk to the business of renegotiating the Beatles' EMI contract. Brian, of course, was neither interested nor amused. This cheek— together with Klein's "poaching" of Donovan and the Rolling Stones— earned Brian's bitter enmity. It became Brian's strategy to keep a good distance from such a potentially dangerous adversary, so much so that when Klein bumped into Brian and Nat Weiss at a Cyrkle gig in Palisades Park, Brian refused to shake hands.

No one in the inner circle felt even remotely that the Beatles would cut Brian loose. "At worst, they might have renegotiated his commission, reducing it from twenty-five percent to perhaps fifteen," says Nat Weiss, a believer with particular insight, "and I told Brian this whenever he wrestled with the subject." Nat says that deep down, even Brian believed they would ultimately keep him on—"It's a matter of chemistry," he'd admit— but that, too, would eventually give way to his destructive impulses.

Most days, he couldn't drag himself out of bed before five o'clock in the evening, and often then it was only to stumble downstairs, "fucked-up and all hazy," in pajamas for tea and toast. His personal secretary, Joanne Newfield, "felt that more and more he was having trouble coping." Once, when a phone number he demanded wouldn't go through as a result of Joanne's mistake, "he just went wild," she recalled, hurling a china teapot across the room and striking her. Another time, Joanne misdialed the Grosvenor House and barely dodged the airborne phone. Peter Brown also suffered countless humiliations at Brian's hands. Following a vacation to Acapulco and Mexico City in late February, the two men settled in Brian's usual thirty-fifth floor river-view suite at the Waldorf Towers in New York, where they planned to catch the last performance of Jane Asher's American tour. "One night Peter had been sent out on an errand," recalls Nat Weiss, "and when he came back it was clear he had overspent for something." Brian was presented with a receipt and some change, but it seemed only to aggravate the situation. Suddenly he flung the change in Peter's face and screamed, "You're sacked! Go back to London—and go *economy* class!" Then it got extremely physical. Weiss recalls: "It was really very violent." (Brown did go back to London, but he remained on the NEMS payroll, ever determined to foster Brian's welfare.)

In an effort to reverse, or at least slow, his boss's decline, Brown conspired with their friend John Pritchard, the conductor of the Liverpool Philharmonic Orchestra, to get Brian out of London on weekends, where the go-go lifestyle seemed to be consuming him. Paging through the listings in *Country Life,* they spotted one place in particular, "a rather grand farmhouse" in the next village from Pritchard's, a few miles from Rushlake Green. Brown knew instantly that Brian would love it. Known as Kingsley Hill, it was a handsome, ivy-and-wisteria-covered structure, a few hundred years old, with a small garden and a pond on the property. At £30,000, it was quite reasonable, and Brown had predicted correctly—after one viewing, Brian bought it on the spot. But it did little good.

His drug abuse worse, he became "more irrational, more incoherent." Concluded Robert Stigwood: "You can't count on Brian anymore. He's not in his right mind. The best thing we can do is just ignore him completely."

"Stigwood had Brian written off as though he was dead," says Nat Weiss. Even by Robert's standards, however, it was a little premature.

[II]

May 19, 1967, was launch day: Brian from his quarters at the Priory, where he once again had retreated in yet another failed attempt to reach some equilibrium, and *Sgt. Pepper's Lonely Hearts Club Band* to the London press.* No one had come within a mile of the Beatles since the beginning of the year—the *Daily Mail* complained they had "isolated themselves not only personally, but also musically"—so it was time to put some of the speculation to rest. To commemorate the occasion, a small but "grandiose" party was held at the Chapel Street town house, whose living room had been hastily rearranged to accommodate the handpicked guests. The invitation list was highly selective—a dozen top-tier journalists, a dozen photographers, half as many influential deejays, scattered among a few NEMS insiders and, of course, the Beatles.

Champagne flowed freely as the press awaited the Beatles' grand entrance. They were still upstairs in a photo session brokered by Tony Barrow, held captive while a dozen power-driven cameras clicked away without pause. Normally, photo sessions were excruciating ordeals, stiff and phony, but the Beatles felt comfortable with this outfit. All were familiar faces on the clubby British rock circuit, most of them young, long-haired guys about their age who mixed and socialized after the job was done. All except one, that is.

Linda Eastman was an interloper—an American *and* a woman—but very much a photographer in her own right. She had been twenty-three years old when, two years earlier, she talked her way into a Rolling Stones press party to strike up a conversation with Mick Jagger. Determined to take advantage of the opportunity, "she pulled out an expensive camera," a guest recalls, "and flirted gamely with Mick while reeling off several rolls of film."

The photos became the foundation of her portfolio, featuring rock stars in candid poses. Not many women had broken into this restricted rock photography circle, but Linda had several things going for her. Tall and silvery slim, with a natural milk-and-honey complexion, she was, despite her height, the kind of strikingly pretty girl who nevertheless put guys at ease with a quick grin and easy, outgoing manner. Her bearing impressed: "You knew immediately upon meeting her that she came from privilege," says Nat Weiss, a longtime family friend. "There was something about the way she carried herself and dressed that set her apart from the rabble."

Privilege descended through Linda's father, Lee Eastman, a self-styled New York show-business lawyer and cultural aesthete who mixed just as easily with his bluestocking neighbors as he did with the artists and musicians he represented. Handsome and flamboyant, with an imperious man-

---

* Only Henry Grossman, LIFE's man on the scene, wasn't British.

ner, Eastman had re-created his persona to suit an upward status, changing the family name from Epstein, thus enabling him to maneuver among the Hamptons and country-club set. Songwriter Jerry Leiber, a client and friend, refers to him as "very Waspish, a real anti-Semitic Jew—yachting in Cape Cod, all the mannerisms picked up on the other side of the tracks." To her credit, Linda had none of her dad's pretensions. But she had his ambition and determination.

Linda had launched a career as a rock photographer on her obvious appeal to male musicians. She caught their eye as much as her eye caught their image. Gamboling around the London club scene or backstage at the Fillmore East, the rock gods gravitated to her with appreciable lust. To call Linda a groupie, as the label connotes, demeaned her attractiveness in the equation—the term *groupie* presumes a one-sided exchange that turns on debasement and humiliation—but word of her conquests, professional and otherwise, was legendary. She photographed every major rock star, counting many among them as lovers. Still, throughout her precipitate rise, she continued to tease Nat Weiss that her tastes were of a more specific nature. "She always insisted that she was going to marry Paul McCartney," he recalls, "even before she met him."

Nat maintains that he introduced Paul to Linda at his apartment in New York City, but it is more likely that they met four days before the *Sgt. Pepper's* launch, at a disco in the West End called the Bag o' Nails. Paul had stopped there late one night with Peter Brown, downing a few scotch and Cokes in one of the discreetly hidden alcove tables, while Georgie Fame and the Blue Flames banged through an ear-splitting set. Linda was seated across the room near the stage, squashed in a booth with the Animals, with whom she had worked. During an intermission, Paul cornered her with a corny pickup line, winning him a few hours with her and the singer Lulu back at Cavendish Avenue, discussing art.

Linda, however, had already spent considerable time conspiring to meet her pop crush. A few days earlier she had appealed to Brown, with whom she was somewhat acquainted, for an invitation to the *Sgt. Pepper's* launch. This request was not logical at all. Linda's experience and standing were definite drawbacks (everyone on the guest list was on staff at a major publication), particularly at an event considered "the hottest ticket in town." Almost all of her work had been published in the United States, where photographers were not yet established as cultural names. Technically she did have an assignment, shooting pictures for a paperback book titled

Rock and Other Four Letter Words, but primarily she was in London in an attempt to get her portfolio into the right hands.

One set of hands, in particular, had sticky fingers. Linda had dropped her book off at NEMS, and Peter Brown confessed that he had "stolen a sexy, teasing picture" of Brian Jones out of her portfolio. Fortunately, he felt inclined to barter an invitation to the party in exchange. "Besides," he says, "I thought she was cute and fun, and I thought she'd bring a different perspective to the pictures than all these other guys."

During the afternoon photo shoot, Paul deposited himself majestically in an armchair by the fireplace, sipping champagne and dispensing opinions on everything from art to artificial intelligence, a subject he'd just read about in one of the underground journals he devoured. It was no accident that Linda Eastman veered into his aura. She'd taken a few polite shots of Ringo and George before "zero[ing] in on Paul," who couldn't help but admire her beauty and spunk. Linda had come dressed to kill. Most days she played the typical rock chick, decked out in rumpled jeans and a T-shirt, with little or no makeup and unwashed hair. But today her hair had been carefully blow-dried so that it fell perfectly forward in wing points at her chin. And she was dressed in an expensive double-breasted striped barbershop jacket arranged just so over a sheer black sweater, with a miniskirt that flattered her gorgeous legs. When she squatted down—not so subtly, in what must have been a rehearsed gesture—in front of Paul for an intimate chat, he had trouble keeping his eyes from wandering below-decks. A photograph taken of Paul and Linda during this encounter reveals their powerful attraction. Their heads are less than a foot apart— Linda's tilted slightly, irresistibly, enticing; Paul's chin balanced softly on a clenched hand, a cigarette burning between his fingers; four eyes locked in like radar, in a near-mesmeric stare. Anyone standing nearby "couldn't help but notice that something was happening," according to Tony Barrow, himself a captivated bystander. "This wasn't any stage-door infatuation."

And yet, like any ordinary breathless fan, Linda was soon herded out of the room with the rest of the photographers, leaving Paul reeling in her wake. The Beatles were needed downstairs, on the double, where *Sgt. Pepper's Lonely Hearts Club Band* was already blaring at an unreasonable volume.

The press was astonished when the four men finally appeared on the stairs. They all knew the Beatles rather intimately, having interviewed and mingled with them regularly over the years. But none of them was prepared for the sight he beheld.

John Lennon entered first, dressed in a frilly green flowered shirt and maroon cord trousers, with a sporran cinched at his waist and canary yellow socks. But *was* it John? They weren't sure, at first. Instead of the familiar smirking lad who traded on mischievous delight stood a ghostly figure, gaunt and guarded—one journalist thought he "resembled an animated Victorian watchmaker"—moving clumsily into the room. He "looked haggard, old, ill, and hopelessly addicted to drugs," Ray Coleman reflected. "His eyes were glazed, his speech was slow and slurred." George followed close behind him, grim-faced, fingering one end of a handlebar mustache as though he were worried it might shake loose at any moment. His getup, the centerpiece of which was a maroon velvet jacket, also drew a few open-mouthed stares. Paul, in a striped double-breasted suit with a scarf knotted loosely at his neck, looked to one observer "like someone out of a Scott Fitzgerald novel," and about as affected, while Ringo, bringing up the rear, grinned sheepishly, no doubt because he was embarrassed by the conservative dark suit, white shirt, and perfectly knotted tie that drew an undue amount of attention to him.

"Gentlemen—the Beatles!" Tony Barrow announced to a sea of stunned faces. Local disc jockey Jimmy Saville, who was heard to gasp audibly, did a comical double-take.

The Beatles?

Why, yes, everyone soon realized, it *was* the Beatles, but . . . *What the hell had happened to them?* They looked as though a costume designer had gotten ahold of them for some kind of mystical production. Perhaps, one guest speculated, it was a promo for their next film. Why else would they show up looking like, well, like wizards? *Stoned* wizards, if their eyes were any indication.

"The Beatles live!" Paul shouted, hoisting a glass of champagne in the air.

The guests were mystified by the music as well, which was as strange and exotic as the clothing the Beatles wore. The album played continuously over the several hours that the listen-in stretched on, but, politely or not, no one, aside from a *Melody Maker* columnist, broached a meaningful discussion of the songs. Instead, they seized on a more tangible aspect; twenty-four hours earlier, the BBC had announced that it was banning "A Day in the Life" on the grounds that it "could be considered to have drug-taking implications." "Rubbish!" John snapped in terse response. (He'd obviously missed Paul's point.) There had been so many songs they'd crafted with "drug-taking implications." Leave it to the Beeb to condemn this one.

As Brian sat in a deserted corner of the living room with an ankle balanced on a knee, he couldn't have been happier. But happiness was an anomaly for Brian. He had become disconnected from his own image. Like everything else that year, the party was a painful reminder of his utter insignificance to the Beatles and further proof that he was the disposable part of their success. Nobody would miss him should something fateful come to pass. As if to test this assumption, he slipped out of the flat while the party was still in full swing.

That last week in May, with the album just hours from release, Brian found himself suffering still another emotional setback—once again at the hands of his beloved Beatles. On April 19, the day before their first recording session for *Magical Mystery Tour*, the boys concluded the formation of another business partnership that effectively consolidated their interests as a unit, *minus Brian*. It hadn't been their idea to incorporate (oddly enough, it was *Brian's*), nor were they exploring ways to dissolve their management agreement. This was a tax dodge, short and sweet, to shelter them against Britain's staggering 94 percent bite out of their income. Brian recommended a financial strategy whereby the Beatles would sell 80 percent of themselves to a holding company, giving them a tax-free capital gain, with generous salaries, and the opportunity to charge their personal expenses to the company. Later, perhaps, they could consider taking the new company public. It made perfect sense. Nevertheless, on May 25, when Apple Music Ltd. was formally registered, the actuality of it sent Brian into an emotional tailspin. "He'd decided this was the Beatles' first real step toward ending their relationship with him," recalls Peter Brown, who joined Brian later that evening at Kingsley Hill in Sussex. Nothing Peter said could lift Brian from his despair. Only one group could do that, and they were functioning without him, in London, conducting business that had slipped from his control. There was only one way to reverse that; if he couldn't be in London with the Beatles, then it was time to bring the Beatles to Sussex. They needed to be there, together, with *him*. Instantly, Brian knew what to do. "He wanted to have a housewarming and invited all the Beatles, along with their wives and girlfriends."

To reconcile his own need to foster a "gang's all here spirit," Brian beat the jungle drums, assembling a coterie of friends from the very core of the inner circle—the Beatles' family—guaranteed to amuse him and his favored long-haired guests: Terry Doran, Lionel Bart, Nat Weiss, the Fool, John Pritchard, deejay Kenny Everett, Klaus Voormann, Lulu, Mick Jagger, Marianne Faithfull, Robert Stigwood, Neil and Mal, and even—straight from Los Angeles—Derek Taylor and his very pregnant wife, Joan.

On Sunday, May 28, John, George, Ringo, and their women, along with Terry Doran and the seriously jet-lagged Taylors, traveled together to Sussex in John's brand-new £40,000 Rolls-Royce Phantom V—his so-named gypsy caravan—every inch of whose gleaming black finish had been painted in Day-Glo psychedelic regalia. "A Whiter Shade of Pale" provided the frothy soundtrack, blaring over and over from a turntable installed in the partition separating the passengers from the driver. An atmosphere of dreamlike abandon lingered inside the limo. John and George, who had been up all day and night—"perhaps all week," according to George—in the wake of another LSD trip, wore their new identities unselfconsciously. Draped from head to toe in flowing silks and satins, with braided scarves and strands of beads and amulets strung around their necks, they seemed disengaged from the obligations that pressed upon their public personalities.

Derek Taylor, who'd arrived in a customary white shirt, gray flannel slacks, and a navy blue blazer, was mystified by the Beatles' transformation. The boys embraced—*hugged!*—him, kissed both his cheeks, danced around him like tree nymphs. When Taylor shot back quizzical looks, they would laugh good-naturedly and chime: "*Too much! Too much!*"

Every facet of the visit seemed touched by mirth. It was a gorgeous, sun-drenched day, warm and redolent of summer. "Everyone was getting along beautifully," says Peter Brown. "There was lovely food, lots of good wine, and lots—*lots*—of drugs." A test pressing of *Sgt. Pepper's* played at thunderous volume throughout the day. It was a giddy, gluttonous event, with LSD as the spark plug. "The minute you walked through the door you got dosed," recalls Lionel Bart. "The boys were making the rounds, serving tea out of a china pot that had been generously spiked with acid. The whole party appeared to be tripping like mad; everyone was dancing around to the flame of a candle." The whole atmosphere reminded Cynthia Lennon of "the mad hatter's tea party; everyone was crackers," as far as she could tell. And yet, the temptation to function on John's precious wavelength was too powerful to resist. Perhaps it was time to begin tearing down the wall. According to Cynthia, she decided to go against her better judgment and drop acid along with everyone else. In her memoir, she describes it as a "paralyzing" experience, during which she sank into a hollow-eyed depression, withdrew to a bedroom on the second floor of the house, and contemplated jumping out the window onto the stone driveway below. Instead of being drawn into her husband's grateful embrace, John was furious with her for ruining his drug reverie.*

By midday a conspicuous absence had left Brian disconsolate. Paul was either late or missing in action. Few guests dared mention his absence, but it stood out in galling contrast. A grand piano had been rolled into the freshly painted living room, earmarked for his attention: a place of honor. It was a Liverpool tradition to have a group sing-along at such an event. Paul, at the old gang's request, always played the dutiful accompanist, but about 3:00 he phoned to say that Jane needed a lift home from Heathrow. Sorry, hated to do this, he claimed too matter-of-factly, but they wouldn't be able to attend.

That was all Brian needed. Leave it to Paul to get under his skin. "Wasn't that always the case," he groused. Paul, forever nosy and second-guessing business decisions, always set Brian's teeth on edge, but this went straight to his heart. Everything about his absence seemed personal, like a slap in the face. Brian's mood grew darker and more irrational; his drinking got heavier. It wasn't long before the hand-wringing began. "Paul . . . didn't . . . come," Brian muttered, trying to express his disappointment. His face unbearably wounded, ashen, his eyes filled with tears, he kept repeating it to anyone who would listen. "This day of all days . . . he should have come." Derek Taylor tried to console him, but Brian spun away, bending forlornly over the piano like a spurned lover. "This was to have been for Paul," he sighed in a quivering voice. "Especially for tonight, but he can't come. The only one."

It sucked the life right out of the party, until John and George stepped in to assure him of their love. Their affectionate hugs and the psychedelic fireworks that followed combined to rescue the evening from certain meltdown.

Sgt. Pepper played on in the background. It was the Summer of Love.

---

* Peter Brown reports a similar, though somewhat more sensational, version of these events in The Love You Make. While Cynthia may well have alienated herself from the others, Joan Taylor says she confessed years later that "she hadn't taken anything herself that night but had gone along with everything so that we would be comfortable."

[III]

For all their bluff confidence, the Beatles anguished over public and critical reaction as the release of *Sgt. Pepper's Lonely Hearts Club Band* drew near. "I was downright scared," George Martin admitted, "but not half as worried as the Beatles." The so-called failure of "Strawberry Fields Forever" and "Penny Lane" was still too fresh in everyone's mind. Even though the single had sold well—over 2 million copies worldwide—its chart shortfall was regarded as an omen.

But their worries were groundless. The album's release on June 1 caused an extraordinary sensation, with critics lobbing paragraphs of unprecedented praise. In the *Sunday Times* review, Derek Jewel called *Sgt. Pepper's* "remarkable" and "a tremendous advance even in the increasingly adventurous progress of the Beatles." William Mann went even further in *The Times* daily column: "Any of these songs is more genuinely creative than anything currently to be heard on pop radio stations," he wrote, "but in relation to what other groups have been doing lately *Sgt. Pepper* [sic] is chiefly significant as constructive criticism, a sort of pop music master class examining trends and correcting or tidying up inconsistencies and undisciplined work." Wilfrid Mellers, writing in the *New Statesman*, crawled out on a limb to label their music as "art—and art of an increasingly subtle kind." Where once the critics had described the Beatles and their music in terms befitting cartoon characters, now they scrambled to place them in the pantheon of beloved composers and poets. Since *Revolver,* it seemed, critics had approached the music more seriously, actually analyzing its content instead of treating it like a fad. The fans, too— "They think for themselves, and I don't think we can be accused of underestimating the intelligence of our fans," observed George—were quick to recognize breakthroughs in the Beatles' musical evolution. "Over the last four years Lennon and McCartney have developed into the greatest songwriting team of this century," wrote a follower from Isleworth. "Some of the tracks on the LP are pure poetry and unbelievably advanced in conception." Another, from Llandudno in Wales, complimented "She's Leaving Home" as "one of the most beautiful songs I have ever heard." No ordinary fan but just as effusive in his praise, composer Ned Rorem called it "equal to any song that Schubert ever wrote."

Richard Goldstein, known for his scorched-earth criticism, refused to be swayed by the overwhelming groundswell that followed the album right around the globe. Writing in the *New York Times,* he considered *Sgt. Pepper's* a soft and messy piece of work, a self-conscious record, contrived, and was willing to say what no other critic dared: "Unfortunately, there is no apparent thematic development in the placing of cuts, except for the effective juxtaposition of opposing musical styles. At best, the songs are only vaguely related." (A few months later John concurred, saying: "When you get down to it, it was nothing more than an album called *Sgt. Pepper's* with the tracks stuck together.") The Beatles' usual innovative clarity had shifted sharply out of focus, he argued, owing to their "obsession with production. . . . There is nothing beautiful on *Sgt. Pepper,*" he concluded. "Nothing is real and there is nothing to get hung about."

For all the ink spilled over the album, branding it a cultural and artistic watershed—*Time* gushed that it represented "a historic departure in the progress of music—any music"—one thing was certain: *Sgt. Pepper's Lonely Hearts Club Band* was a runaway bestseller, topping the pace of all previous Beatles albums with a staggering 2,500,000 copies sold in the first three months of its release. For most fans the music had finally become accessible; less yeah-yeah-yeah, more sophistication and cross-rhythms. You could hear it played on practically any station in the world, at practically any time of the day. Deejays considered it the "second renaissance of rock 'n roll," and the Beatles its chief architects. Their old friend Murray the K, who played *Sgt. Pepper's* ad nauseam, until management ordered him to back off, marveled at the way some songs made him realize "they had the pulse of the country," while others demonstrated that "the Beatles were completely in tune with life."

That tune had a somewhat familiar ring to it: a whole new type of Beatlemania had broken out, not powered by screams and swoons as before, but rather a kind of reverence in which every note they played or breath they took was analyzed and dissected for greater meaning. Coincidentally or not, overzealous fans—"the nutters," as Paul referred to them—unscrambled the letters in the title of "Lucy in the Sky with Diamonds" to spell LSD; they concluded that "Fixing a Hole" was a veiled reference to heroin and that Harry the Horse (a character in "Mr. Kite") was a pusher. Pundits extrapolated arcane significance in practically every word—every *effect*—of "A Day in the Life." Essayists and critics devoted columns—*lectures*—to the band's cultural significance. Hard-core journalists referred to the Beatles as "missionaries." Others called them "messengers from beyond rock 'n roll," "progenitors of a Pop avant-garde," avatars. Timothy Leary called them "evolutionary agents sent by God, endowed with mysterious powers to create a new human species."

Paul politely disagreed. "The Beatles weren't the leaders of the generation," he said later, with some distance, "but the spokesmen."

———

Certainly Paul fancied himself in this role. "Even when the others weren't speaking to the press, you could always depend on Paul," says Tony Barrow. "He couldn't resist the opportunity to represent the band in the spotlight. He loved the role; it fed his considerable ego."

He'd pontificate at the drop of a hat, firing off slickly polished sound bites with the cadence of a talk-show personality. "Paul needs an audience," George Martin once observed to great understatement. While Paul considered John "the cock who crowed the loudest," referring, one presumes, to his partner's combative snipes and outbursts, he was more a natural raconteur, a great embellisher; charm oozed from Paul McCartney when in the presence of an attentive ear. On June 19 Paul opened his door to a pair of ITN News reporters, who detoured from what seemed like a standard interview about music into an inquisition about his drug-taking. They were sitting, chatting casually in his garden, when the primary newscaster popped the question. "Paul, how often have you taken LSD?"

There was a hesitation that seemed to last an eternity but ate up no more than a few seconds of airtime, during which Paul thought, "Well, I'm either going to bluff this, or I'm going to tell him the truth." So he answered honestly: "About four times." He added that LSD had changed his life — "After I took it, it opened my eyes," he boasted — and made him "a better, more honest, more tolerant member of society."

The minute it was out of his mouth, Paul must have realized his mistake, because he immediately began to backpedal. "I would like to make it perfectly clear that I do not advocate LSD," he hedged. "I don't want kids running to take it when they hear that I have." An admission of this nature from a personality of his stature might have an adverse effect on young fans, to say nothing of their parents. In Paul's cockeyed logic, that meant the *reporters* had a responsibility not to show the footage. "It's *you* who've got the responsibility!" Paul insisted. "You've got the responsibility not to spread this now. You know, I'm quite prepared to keep it as a very private thing if you will, too. If you shut up about it, I will."

But it was too late. The comments, which were broadcast the next day, unleashed a shitstorm of protest, from government bigwigs to the Reverend Dr. Billy Graham, who seemed less peeved about the dangers of drug-taking than Paul's claim that LSD could give rise to "a religious experience." The tabloids feasted, condemning the Beatles in a united, if shrill and self-righteous, voice. For days, weeks, stories appeared in which politicos expressed their outrage that one of the Beatles had dabbled in drugs. They were shocked—*shocked!*—to learn about the scandalous behavior of no less than an M.B.E. "The press had a field day," George recalled.

Paul's timing couldn't have been worse. Only a few weeks earlier Mick Jagger and Keith Richards had been busted in Sussex for possession of hash, pot, and amphetamines; Paul's art dealer, Robert Fraser, who was arrested along with them, was caught palming twenty-four jacks of heroin. On the same day that *Sgt. Pepper's* was released, John "Hoppy" Hopkins, the founder of *International Times* and a social mate of Paul's, was sentenced to nine months in jail for possession of pot. And Brian Jones was nabbed in a drug sweep while his bandmates faced arraignment.

"No one knew why Paul didn't keep his mouth shut," says Alistair Taylor, voicing an opinion shared by the other three Beatles. They were especially annoyed that he'd focused attention on something they'd been so scrupulously careful to keep private. Acid, which might have been commonplace around Britain's wealthy pop underground, hadn't yet attracted widespread attention among the masses, not even among die-hard rock enthusiasts. "We weren't actually telling anybody about LSD, bar the people who knew us," Ringo recalled, "and [then] Paul decided to come out and tell people." George also considered it a breach of group etiquette, explaining: "I thought Paul should have been quiet about it—I wish he hadn't said anything, because it made everything messy."

Messy—and annoying, considering that for a year and a half John, George, and Ringo had been unable to persuade Paul to join them in dropping acid, "and then," as George fumed, "one day he's on the television talking all about it." It was all over the media: Paul McCartney, the Beatles' acid authority! For John, it was another instance of Paul's stealing his thunder.

In his haste to head off another imbroglio, Brian stood up to the press, choosing to defend Paul's rash comments by adding his own voice to the fanfare, admitting that he, too, had taken LSD and saw nothing wrong with it. A few days later he even repeated the remarks in an interview with

Melody Maker, foolishly minimizing the risks of taking acid, adding: "I think LSD helped me to know myself better, and I think it helped me to become less bad tempered." This was clearly not what the press and Beatles fans had bargained for.

Then, just as quickly as the uproar started, it stopped dead in its tracks, thanks to an event that spun the drug business into the shadows and restored the Beatles' reputations as beloved minstrel spirits. Several months earlier the BBC1 television channel had approached Brian about helping out with a project the network had planned for June 25 to test its new Early Bird communication satellites. Via a live broadcast, they intended, for the first time, to link thirty-one television networks around the globe. An estimated 300 million people could conceivably watch the same show. Called *Our World,* it was designed to allow each of the participating countries a five-minute segment in which to feature material or an act that represented its culture. And, of course, what could be more British than the Beatles?

It's not as hard to figure out why Brian volunteered the Beatles as it is why they agreed to cooperate. They'd just finished five months of intensive work on *Sgt. Pepper's Lonely Hearts Club Band* and were earnestly preoccupied with its promotion. What's more, they were expected to contribute a song for the broadcast. It stood to reason that, because of complicated special effects, they could not perform anything from the new album. And an ancient yeah-yeah-yeah song was out of the question; they'd moved well beyond that image as a band. That meant writing something new for the program, which seemed like a crushing task.

Surprisingly, they didn't balk. Paul had been working on a song anyway—"Hello Goodbye"—that he put up for consideration. At the same time, John brought in "All You Need Is Love," which, according to George Martin, "seemed to fit with the overall concept of the program." The show's producers had issued only one instruction: "keep it simple so that viewers across the globe will understand." Tony Barrow recalled how John sat at the piano and previewed the song slowly, playing it in an almost dirgelike fashion for his mates, after which George leaned toward Paul and muttered: "Well, it's certainly repetitive." The Beatles demo'ed John's song at Olympic Sound and thus made a unanimous decision.

As the broadcast drew near, however, they realized that performing it live, without a safety net, was far too risky. Since the Beatles' first few hurried recording sessions at the beginning of their career, they'd become used to taking their sweet time in the studio, overdubbing and correcting mistakes, stretching vocals, massaging guitar licks, tweaking everything with electronics. Nothing was left to chance anymore. The Beatles hadn't performed as a band in almost a year. There was no telling how they'd sound au naturel. "We must do some preparation for this," George Martin told them. "We can't just go in front of 350 million people without some work."

A backing track would provide an insurance policy. But, unexpectedly, it was rejected by the show's organizers. The idea of the live satellite broadcast, they reminded Martin, was to demonstrate how spontaneous performances were transmitted around the globe. A backing track violated the spirit of the event. But Martin knew what he couldn't dare say: that the Beatles worked casually, by trial and error, often bumping about until he provided firm direction. They weren't prima donnas, but they were in the neighborhood, and thanks to drugs, there was unpredictability to consider. Martin strongly defended using a prerecorded track and urged NEMS to "make it a strict condition upon which the group's appearance would depend," which a designated liaison eventually did. Ordinarily this kind of tactic might have produced a standoff at the BBC, but as time had grown short and the Beatles were already featured prominently in ads for the show, the producers had no choice but to accept.

The recording, as one might expect, grew progressively more complex, with layers of atmospheric and experimental sounds ladled over an otherwise languid rhythm track, the mongrel construction made impossibly more convoluted by stitching a few bars of "La Marseillaise" onto the opening. A harpsichord drifted in and out between plinks on a banjo, pulls on a string bass, bows across a violin (played by George Harrison, of all people), and other oddball effects. Just to make sure no stone was left unturned, a thirteen-piece orchestra filed in one night to weave samples of one of Bach's Brandenburg Concertos, "Greensleeves," and "In the Mood" into the fade. So much for spontaneity. Five days and fifty-eight takes later, a "basic" track was approved.

What had once promised viewers a glimpse of the Beatles during a standard recording session had evolved into a production of epic proportions. Once they'd committed themselves to appearing, once they'd gotten *involved*, it became necessary to stage a spectacular event befitting their spectacular mystique. Heaven forbid the public perceive the Beatles' recording session as merely *routine!* That wouldn't do. So, on the eve of the broadcast, Tony Bramwell was dispatched to the London club circuit with instructions to hunt down famous friends willing to "drop in" on the session. At the Scotch of St. James, Bramwell drafted Eric Clapton; Mick

Jagger and Marianne Faithfull at the Bag o' Nails; Keith Moon and Graham Nash at the Speakeasy; Gary Leeds, one of the Walker Brothers, at the Cromwellian. "Everyone I asked jumped at the chance," he recalls. "In fact, most called it a night early, in order to put together a wardrobe."

"By 7pm [on June 25], the studio appeared to be in chaos," Tony Barrow reported. Studio One, the big hangarlike facility at Abbey Road, was crammed with "flower-waving crowds of Beautiful People," who were oblivious to the battalion of sound technicians and camera operators struggling to put the final touches on the historic transmission. One can only imagine the difficulty they had in adjusting the contrast for the cameras: to complement the carnival atmosphere, the guests were dressed to the nines in flamboyant, brightly colored costumes that clashed with the inflated latex globes and vivid balloons floating above the fixtures. Giant displays of exotic flowers radiated against the garish backdrop. The Beatles themselves gave off a fuzzy flush in their Technicolor garb: Paul, looking debonair in a double-breasted white sport coat draped over a shirt he had hand-colored the night before; George, decked out in an orange paisley jacket whose design and texture resembled an Aubusson carpet; Ringo, swathed cosmically in a silk, suede, and fake-fur outfit designed by the Fool that looked left over from the Crusades. "It was so bloody heavy," he recalled. "I had all this beading on, and it weighed a ton." Only John, doleful and glassy-eyed, turned up in a smart-looking banker's dark pin-striped suit that seemed as outrageous for its elegance as for its posting on John Lennon.

In all the turmoil, between miscues and mischief, the Beatles performed "All You Need Is Love" to the world without a hint of disorganization. They sat perched on barstools placed directly in front of the guests, appearing as cool as only the Beatles could look under such hothouse circumstances. John, Paul, and George seemed impervious to the do-or-die situation, synching their voices beautifully, perfectly, to the backing track. The prerecorded music no longer mattered—if it ever did. Remembered chiefly for its stripped-down, monotonous chorus, the song's verses were nevertheless quite a mouthful for John, who spit them out on camera as though they were child's play. "*There'snothin-youcandothatcan'tbedone . . .*" It sounded effortless, done in one Hail Mary take, much the way he'd fired off "Twist and Shout" four and a half years earlier: rock-steady and right on. For all the technical effects John had come to rely on for vocal support, none were needed to show off his extraordinary range that night. It was all right there, in the pocket, just where it had always been.

John relaxed visibly as the song cruised into its extended fade. "La Marseillaise" drew a ceremonial reprise, giving way to "In the Mood" and "Greensleeves," as planned. But John, who had tinkered in rehearsal with a fragment of "She'll Be Coming 'Round the Mountain," suddenly chimed in with a few bars of an old standby that no one—probably not even John—had anticipated. At a juncture in the action, he sang out: "She loves you, yeah, yeah, yeah . . . ," in an inspired bit of self-parody: perfect!

It touched off a festive reaction in the studio. Balloons and confetti rained down from the ceiling, as five men draped in sandwich boards proclaiming "All You Need Is Love" in four languages paraded across the floor in front of the grinning Beatles. Mike McCartney launched a series of cue cards, instructing viewers to "Smile" and "Laf Now." Another, scrawled hastily by his cousin Anne Danher, brandished the mysterious communiqué: "Come back, Milly! All is forgiven!"—a message to Paul's aunt, on vacation in Australia, who, it was feared, might not return to Liverpool.

With the kind of exposure the song had received, the Beatles were left with little choice other than to release "All You Need Is Love" as a single. Most of the work had already been done. A few overdubs were added to polish the track; Ringo contributed an introductory drum roll, and John, never satisfied with the way he sounded, insisted on patching his splendid vocal. Otherwise, it was ready to be remixed and mastered the next day, and it was shipped a week later as the Beatles' fifteenth single.

Curiously, no single was ever released from *Sgt. Pepper's Lonely Hearts Club Band*. The Beatles had already given that album everything they had and decided that, once again, it was time for them to move on.

[IV]

Brian Epstein had been "too out of sorts" to attend the "All You Need" broadcast. Left to his own devices, Brian languished in seclusion, "zonked," as one employee put it, "either drunk or on drugs." There was no key role in it for him and therefore no emotional upside, nothing for him to grab hold of with which to lift himself out of the funk. Even though he busied himself with ongoing productions at the Saville Theatre (where, on one amazing bill in early June, he presented the Jimi Hendrix Experience, Denny Laine, the Chiffons, and Procol Harum), the sinister warp of moodiness was too strong for him to escape.

Once again Brian tried to blow out the cobwebs by throwing a party at his Kingsley Hill estate. While the affair was meant to lift his spirits, sources indicate that Brian intended to meet with the Beatles before the other guests arrived so that he could tell them about his relationship with Robert Stigwood. With only a few weeks remaining before Stigwood's option came due, he worried that it would appear as though he had deceived them.

It was not to be. After a number of wildly productive months and a reinvented image, the Beatles decided to reinvent Brian's party as a full-fledged acid blowout. Their tripping, which had always been dependent on the drug's available supply, suddenly knew no bounds, thanks largely to John. He had figured out how to tap the mother lode—the source of the purest LSD ever made, courtesy of the legendary chemist Stanley Owsley, whose lab operated out of San Francisco. Buying it was no problem; John had the money and agreed to pay top dollar for a lifetime supply. The problem was smuggling it into Great Britain. With the help of a few film freelancers, he commissioned a cameraman named Steve Sanders to film the Monterey Pop Festival, over the June 17 weekend. It didn't matter that the festival's film rights had long been sold to ABC-TV. When Derek Taylor reminded John of that fact, John didn't demur. The film wasn't intended for distribution, he explained, but for his own private viewing. He might have enjoyed watching it, too, had there ever been film in the canister, but that wasn't John's motive. Instead, the crew's equipment was used to conceal the acid.

Over the next three weeks, under the influence of the especially potent blotter acid, the Beatles seemed locked on a course of reckless hedonism. First they traveled to Greece, under the clutches at the time of a despotic military junta, for the purpose of buying a cluster of islands in the Aegean, where they could live and record communally, in splendid isolation. "The idea was that you'd have four houses with tunnels connecting them to a central dome," Neil Aspinall recalled. The scenic space in between would be filled with meditation posts, recording and painting studios, a go-kart track, and a private landing strip. Neil would also be provided for on the island, along with the usual suspects: Brian Epstein, Mal Evans, Terry Doran, Derek Taylor, and their families. According to several well-placed insiders, this was the brainstorm of Alexis Mardas, the son of a major in the Greek secret police, who had recently ingratiated himself into the Beatles' circle by beguiling them with stories of his mind-boggling inventions. Magic Alex, as John dubbed him, was working as a television repairman when he met the Beatles. Nevertheless, he possessed a powerful imagination and masterly gift for sweet talk.

"Alex wasn't magic at all," George admitted, "but John thought he had something and he became friendly with us." Alex immediately produced his signature artifact, a box decorated with lights that flashed in an irregular fashion. What was it? What did it do? Whatever you wanted, he replied in the spirit of cosmic coolness. John, spaced out on acid, found the box fascinating; he could stare at it for hours. He introduced Alex to Paul and others as his "new guru," shrugging in response to their questions about his powers.

Taking advantage of John's susceptible condition and deepest anxieties, Alex concocted other mystical enthusiasms designed to tantalize his new disciple. He was working on a telephone, he said, that responded to voice recognition and identified incoming callers. There was a substance he was secretly developing that would enable him to build a force field around their homes, another that prevented anyone from rear-ending a car, an X-ray camera, invisible beams, wallpaper speakers. "Magic Alex invented invisible paint," according to Ringo, who marveled at each fantastic brainstorm. He also encouraged a practice he called "trepanning," which involved having a hole drilled in one's head. "Magic Alex said that if we had it done our inner third eye would be able to see, and we'd get cosmic instantly."

Drugs or no drugs, the Beatles had to suspect that they were being taken for a ride, especially when Alex requisitioned the V-12 engines from George's Ferrari and John's Rolls so that he could build a flying saucer. Paul claimed that they were onto Alex early but still enjoyed hearing his interesting ideas. "We didn't really call anyone's bluff," he said, "it would have been a bit too aggressive. So we just let him get on with it."

For the Beatles, the trip was sun-filled and joyous, but the Greek Islands were not, in fact, deemed residence-worthy. Between the rocky slip of a coastline, intermittent severe thunderstorms, and the boredom that set in as soon as the acid wore off, the thought of homesteading never came up. Even so, they instructed their accountants to purchase the islands anyway, paying £95,000, plus a 25 percent premium, which was taken off their hands a few months later for a modest profit. They would not always be so lucky.

For the Maharishi Mahesh Yogi, the Summer of Love was a perfect platform for his ministry of mind expansion, receptiveness, spiritual and sensual fulfillment, self-awareness, intercommunication, tranquillity, knowledge, and brotherhood. The celestial glitter of his spidery face was plastered on walls throughout the London Underground, promoting a treatise on meditation, *The Science of Being and the Art of Living,* and his extraordinary image, a whispery, slight, but impressionable presence, figured prominently in television news stories. The media couldn't resist the guru's eccentric appearance or the oft-perceived flakiness of his spiritual message, extolling love, peace, and eternal happiness. To a skeptical audience of Brits, he came off like a sideshow freak, but as the new sensibilities and surface hedonism of 1967 gained acceptance, his message offered an inspirational refuge from the libertine excess.

Aside from the magnetic personality who captivated young audiences, precious little is known about his background. Born in 1911—"my earthly age is of no importance," he answered in response to questions about his birth—he was the son of an Indian revenue officer who studied Sanskrit and Hindu scriptures with Guru Dev. Later he fell under the spell of another guru, the founder of the Spiritual Regeneration Movement, whose purpose, like many of these mystical followings, was an attempt to combine ancient Eastern religious beliefs with the search for inner truth and wisdom. Spiritual Regeneration instructed people in the discipline of Transcendental Meditation, "a method of quickly and easily reaching a spiritual state."

In 1945 Mahesh (*Maharishi* means "great saint" and was an honorific adopted much later) began a solitary meditation in the Himalaya that lasted for thirteen years, after which he set off on a faith-healing crusade designed to take him seven times around the globe. In the process, he attracted widespread attention from the elderly, as well as the curious, the infirm, and other lost souls to whom Spiritual Regeneration was an attractive pursuit. Mahesh brilliantly and shrewdly cultivated these followers. Lectures, conferences, and retreats became a staple of his transglobal tours. A man of immense charisma, he was a natural performer, energetic and riveting, who could transform crowds of the unfulfilled, the suffering, the troubled, or the alienated with simple aphorisms that struck home. Borrowing liberally from the Bhagavad Gita, he popularized traditional Indian teachings, interlacing them with plainly applied self-help therapies that were elementary in their appeal.

Despite the embarrassing criticism from more traditional Hindu teachers and a predilection for publicity and fund-raising—followers were required to donate the equivalent of a week's salary to the ministry, which ran contrary to the basic Hindu principles of free instruction—the Spiritual Regeneration Movement grew into a worldwide organization, with a luxurious, air-conditioned ashram situated on a fifteen-acre estate in Rishikesh, in the foothills of the Himalaya. There were already meditation centers in more than fifty countries, with the London office attracting more new followers than it was able to process.

The three Beatles (Ringo was visiting Maureen in the hospital, where she had just given birth to their second son) were among nearly a thousand earnest freethinkers who listened to the Maharishi's message on August 24 in a ballroom at the Hilton, overlooking Hyde Park. Years later George explained that they "were looking to reestablish that which was within." George was feeling especially restless following a dispiriting trip to San Francisco, during which he decried the drug-besotted hippies he encountered there as "hypocrites" and "bums," leading him to a startling renunciation of LSD. "After having such an intense period of growing up and so much success in the Beatles and realizing that this wasn't the answer to everything, the question came: 'What is it all about?'" Similarly, Paul would recall how he was "looking for something to fill some kind of hole." He acknowledged feeling "a little bit of emptiness" in his soul, "a lack of spiritual fulfillment." Much of it he blamed on "seeing all this stuff on acid," as well as rampant stardom. "And the next step was to try to find a meaning for it all."

Despite the institutional setting, complete with a cordon of body-guards in three-piece suits and a gallery of doting blue-haired dowagers, the Beatles were clearly entranced by the Maharishi. He was an extraordinary sight to behold: an elfin, bronze-skinned holy man draped in an immaculate white dhoti, positioned in front of acres of soothing lemony yellow curtains. A picture of contentment, he sat cross-legged on a deer-skin mat strewn with flowers and, between arpeggios of an irrepressible giggle, offered to clarify anyone's experiences.

To young men who constantly struggled with their individuality—toward the public, toward their roles as Beatles, toward one another, and toward themselves—Maharishi advised them "to look within in order to find peace." Happiness, he said, serves the purpose of creation. Using the flower as an analogy, with the sap the source of its energy, he explained how it was possible to transcend the relative states of their consciousness—in effect bypassing the intellect—to draw the sap upward. "He said that by meditating, you can go down your stem and . . . reach the field of nutrients, which he called the pool of cosmic consciousness, which was all bliss-ful and all beautiful," Paul recalled.

For George, who had already devoted himself to the practice of yoga and the study of Eastern philosophies, the Maharishi provided him with a practical approach "to further the experience of meditation." Even Paul, a natural skeptic, "thought he made a lot of sense." But it was John, more than anyone, who emerged from the lecture a changed man. Having laid off acid that night, he still bore the look of someone so far gone that it seemed an impossible state without chemicals. "It takes time to come down to earth after an experience like this," he told a reporter on his way out of the Hilton.

In fact, John, along with the others, was gearing up for an unimaginable trip.

[I]

On the afternoon of Friday, August 25, 1967, the platforms and waiting rooms of Euston Station were jammed with travelers of all sizes and ages. It was a hot, suffocating day and the pitiful excuse for air-conditioning gave off only sticky whiffs of dampness, raising the temperature in that human pressure cooker to an ungodly swelter. To make matters worse, trains were insufferably late. Every few minutes the same emotionless voice crackled over the public address system, trying to convince the ornery mass that salvation was only minutes away, but nobody, not even a conductor, was willing to believe it.

Then the unexpected proclaimed itself. A fretful clustering had developed near one of the side entrances. A phalanx of bodies sliced smoothly through the crowd, a maneuver sudden and effortless, coinciding with a unanimous murmur—*Ooh!*—from those nearby. Bursts of recognition, heavy with excitement, echoed through the hall: *The Beatles!* Impossible. Not in public, certainly not in a common rush-hour train station. Wide-eyed passengers converged from all directions, determined to get a better look at the men traveling by themselves, dragging luggage and elbowing their way toward the distant Platform 8.

The night before, during their introduction to the Maharishi, an invitation was extended to the Beatles to attend a Transcendental Meditation seminar he was giving at University College that weekend. A midnight message was left for Ringo, who hastily arranged to sneak away from Maureen, with her blessing. Brian was also invited, John making the call himself.

As far as Brian was concerned, meditation was the last thing he wanted to participate in that weekend. He was desperate, if anything, to raise a little hell. For the past ten days, his mother had been a houseguest at the Chapel Street flat. She'd moved in with Brian immediately following

Harry's sudden death in July, and together, mother and son endeavored to put their lives back on track. In the opinion of Brian's chauffeur, Bryan Barrett: "It was the best damn thing that ever happened to him." Queenie woke him early each morning and they discussed their daily plans over breakfast. Then, Brian dressed in a suit and, for the first time in ages, put in long days at the office. There was no prowling about after sundown, no multidrug highballs. Evenings were spent quietly in each other's company. They were very attentive, very content. "Each night, I drove them to dinner, and often to the theater," says Barrett. "He was like the old Eppy again, sharp, focused, and in control."

It was a good thing, too, because there was a lot on the company drawing board. There was the "Magical Mystery Tour" project that Paul was still hounding about; another Beatles single to schedule with EMI (it would be "Hello Goodbye"); the Stigwood/Shaw deal to untangle; a staging of three short comedies by novelist Saul Bellow in which Brian had invested $14,000; and more—much more. "That very weekend," says Tony Barrow, "he'd finally gotten confirmation from the BBC that Cilla Black would host her own major TV series, which was quite extraordinary, and he was in the process of trying to get hold of her to relate the news." Meanwhile, Brian and Nat Weiss were preparing to release an album by lanky folk heartthrob Eric Andersen, as well as signing Harry Nilsson to a recording contract. And there were plans for a trip to Toronto, where Brian was seriously entertaining an offer to host a weekly television show. But right now Brian wanted some action, and to that end he invited Peter Brown and Geoffrey Ellis to Kingsley Hill, where they planned to meet, according to Brown, "four or five young, amusing guys to distract us for the weekend."

As expected, it was a mob scene at Euston Station. The Beatles had arrived in their chauffeur-driven cars and those inconspicuous psychedelic clothes they favored. In addition to Cynthia, Jane, Pattie, and her sister, Jenny, they'd cobbled together an entourage that included Mick Jagger, Marianne Faithfull, and Donovan. And just in case they felt unnoticed or out of place, thirty or forty reporters had converged on the party as they made their way to the train.

Somehow as they raced along the platform, Cynthia fell behind the others a step or two. "I was struggling . . . with the hand baggage, trying to keep up," she remembered in a subsequent interview. "In front of me, the others leapt on the train. I moved forward, arms full, to follow them, when suddenly a policeman was barring my path." Stammering, she identified herself as Cynthia Lennon, but he'd already turned back a dozen other Cynthia Lennons.

Ahead of her, oblivious, John swung himself jauntily up onto the train. A long blast on the whistle drowned out Cynthia's cries as the heavily laden train chugged forward, out of the station.

Inside, the Beatles bundled into a parlor car adjacent to a first-class compartment containing the Maharishi, who sat lotuslike, in statuesque repose, on a mat strewn with flowers. George drew the blinds and lit incense, while the others, tense yet exhilarated, filled the overhead rack with baggage and got settled. As everyone found seats, it dawned on John that Cynthia was missing.

Frantic, he wrenched open a window and leaned halfway out of the train, squinting to find her in the dispersing crowd. Cynthia could barely make out the words as her husband's pleadings were swallowed by the train's roar. "Tell him to let you on!" John shouted. "Tell him you're with us!" But it was already too late. They were too far apart, without any chance of the train coming to a stop. Peter Brown put an arm around an inconsolable Cynthia Lennon as the caboose disappeared in the distance. He assured her that she could hitch a ride to Bangor with Neil Aspinall, who was driving north later that evening. But Cynthia knew in her heart that though she'd eventually rejoin the gang, her train had finally pulled out of the station.

———

An expanse of concrete and sun-bleached brick, surrounded by acres of lawn, the University College—or Normal, as it was known—spread across a leafy fringe of Bangor like an abandoned sanitorium. As the school was currently on holiday, the Beatles and their mates were quartered in one of the empty nondescript dormitories, a far cry from the luxurious suites they'd occupied on tour for the past few years. "It suddenly felt as if we were back in school again," recalled Marianne Faithfull, who shared the others' excitement about the unglamorous atmosphere.

The freedom they felt was exquisite. There were no handlers, no press, no fans, no obligations. That night, in a show of solidarity, the entire entourage went to a local Chinese restaurant for dinner, where, unrecognized by the staff, they talked with real gusto about the protocols of meditation and the significance of receiving a mantra. No one really knew what to expect, and perhaps to combat the feeling of the unknown, they grew catty and made snickering references to their eccentric Indian guru. "There were already some misgivings being aired about the Maharishi," Faithfull recalled. "We'd heard from Barry Miles that the word in India was that [he] was suspected of certain financial improprieties and sexual peccadilloes, and also an obsession with fireworks."

The following morning everyone was introduced to the seminar's cross section of participants, of which there were nearly three hundred—most of them strangers—as well as to the resident staff instructors. The initial sessions were devoted to the basics of meditation, which, for inveterate movers and shakers, was a difficult concept to absorb. "You just sit there and let your mind go," John explained in his characteristic stripped-down style. Of course, for John, who dropped acid, then zoned out for hours in front of the television, that might have been a snap, but Paul found it difficult to concentrate. His head was cluttered with too many ideas and projects that competed with the spiritual process. "You spend all your first few days just trying to stop your mind dealing with your social calendar," he recalled.

Everything changed, however, after they received a mantra, the mystical form of incantation that guides a meditator, "like a prescription," to a higher level of spiritual consciousness. The password or phrase was conveyed in a private ceremony on Saturday afternoon, during which the Maharishi encouraged all students to "immerse themselves completely in the energy of the soul, to make contact with it and establish a fathomless level of consciousness." Except for a few handicapped cases, all participants took off their shoes and entered a fragrant, candlelit room, where they deposited a few stems of flowers at the guru's slippered feet. After a brief Hindu prayer was intoned, the Maharishi whispered a handpicked mantra in the disciple's ear, along with advice that he or she was never to share it with anyone. "It has been specially chosen to harmonize with your personal vibration," he said. Weeks later, after the novelty had worn off, Mal Evans divulged that his mantra was *I-ing*, at which point everyone discovered they'd been given the same word.

After a casual lunch on Sunday, the famous friends bounded in and out of one another's dorm rooms, expressing their views with cautious fascination and looking for corroboration. No one was sure what to make of it all, but they were surely onto something important. John couldn't resist comparing the Maharishi's message to inhaling a potent drug for which "you get a sniff and you're hooked." Even Mick Jagger, who was a very bright, sensible, and extremely cautious young man, viewed the seminar with an enthusiastically arched eyebrow. Suggestions were made to invite Keith Richards and Brian Jones.

About three o'clock, in the hallway, the infernal pay phone started to ring. Again. No one paid it any attention, thinking it would eventually stop. After an interminably long and noisy stretch, however, Jane Asher excused herself to answer it.

"Jane," the voice on the other end said, "it's Peter Brown. Could you find Paul and put him on the phone?"

Peter Brown: The last thing Paul wanted that day was to speak with anyone from NEMS, but if there was Beatles business that needed immediate attention, then he was the only one suited to take care of it. As it turned out, however, this was business of the kind that even Paul was incapable of processing.

———

Brian had so looked forward to the weekend *"divertissement"* that he skipped the Beatles' send-off to Wales and headed straight for Sussex in his precious Bentley convertible. There were too many last-minute details that required his attention—an alluring dinner menu, drugs, recreation, discreet sleeping arrangements. The invitees were young, rugged East Londoners and naive, which intrigued him. Things could get rough, which intrigued him even more, although it would be difficult explaining that to Geoffrey Ellis, who, by Peter Brown's definition, was "something of a tight ass." But when the boys canceled at the last minute, Brian lapsed into one of his depressions. Peter says he could tell instantly upon his arrival that Brian was in a "dark mood." He was "drinking and stoned, very disappointed that there wasn't going to be any action." Even so, they all sat down to a very civilized dinner, a leg of lamb and root vegetables, served by the staff. "Many bottles of wine" were consumed, along with brandy after the meal. It didn't take long until the three men found themselves "sitting there, looking at each other with boredom." About ten, after calling around London trying to drum up other action, Brian announced that he was going for a drive. "Don't worry about me," Brian assured them. "Go to bed. I'll see you in the morning."

· Brown suspects that Brian drove back to London, stopped off at home, made a few calls, then cruised around the city's usual gay haunts. He obviously found something to amuse him, because on Saturday he didn't wake up until after five in the afternoon. "Brian called us just after that,"

Brown recalls. "Clearly, he'd just woken up, because the sleeping pills, those infernal Tuinals, were still in his system and he was slurring his words."

"I'm sorry for fucking up the weekend," he apologized. "I'll try and come back later."

Brown, sensing that Brian wasn't in any condition to drive, suggested that he take the train—a forty-minute trip to Lewes Station, where someone on the staff would pick him up. But Brian never showed up—and never called.

On Sunday, Brian's housekeepers—Antonio and Maria Garcia—grew concerned that the Bentley, which had been parked at the curb late Friday evening upon its return from Kingsley Hill, hadn't been moved. They called Joanne Newfield, who thought nothing of the matter. "It wasn't unusual for Brian to go in his room and stay there and take some pills and . . . check out for twenty-four hours," she thought. Indulgently, she told them not to worry and thanked them for the call. After lunch with her mother, however, Joanne decided to drive over to Chapel Street "just to make sure that everything was okay."

When she arrived, about twelve-thirty, the house was immaculate and still. There were no telltale signs of an orgy or a rowdy boys' party. Joanne summoned Antonio from the basement staff quarters; together, they went upstairs and knocked on Brian's bedroom door: no answer. That wasn't unusual, either, but when Joanne couldn't rouse her boss on the intercom, she became alarmed. The intercom was in the phone, but you didn't have to lift the receiver to speak into it. Even when Brian was completely out of it, he usually managed a few choice words. Apologetic to a fault, Joanne called Kingsley Hill and eventually reached Peter Brown, who had gone to the Merry Harrier pub in Cabbage for a drink before lunch.

"I'm going to have [Antonio] break the doors down," Joanne sighed.

Brown, however, pleaded with her to wait. They'd broken down doors before, which only made Brian furious. Instead, he suggested that she contact Brian's doctor, Norman Cowan, whose specialty was keeping these indiscretions quiet. But Cowan was away for the weekend, so she called Peter's doctor, John Gallway, a young gay man who would know how to deal with Brian once they got him up and around.

Throughout the unendurable wait for Gallway's arrival, Joanne and Antonio continued to beat on Brian's door. Joanne also called Alistair Taylor, who only half an hour earlier had gotten off a plane from California, where, at Brian's instructions, he'd gone to walk Cream through a visa problem at the American embassy. Frantic, she explained how Brian refused to answer his door. Taylor, a veteran of two previous suicide false alarms, felt no misgiving. (Once, in 1966, Brian had called him "to say goodbye." A heartsick Taylor rushed right over, only to find him sitting up in bed, reading, with an annoyed look on his face: "What do *you* want?") "So? What's new?" he responded now to Joanne. Alistair assured her there was nothing to worry about, but Joanne begged him to hurry over. "Oh, Joanne, I've been flying all night!" Besides, he'd "drank the Pan Am 707 dry on the flight back" with Cream, he was out of uniform (in sandals, a denim shirt, and jeans), and he lived in Clapham, a neighborhood quite a ways out of town. Still, there was something in her voice that disturbed him. "All right," he relented. "As soon as I can get a cab."

John Gallway arrived at Chapel Street at 2:45, a few minutes before Alistair, and spoke on the phone briefly with Peter Brown, who decided it was time to break down the door. Gallway and Antonio put their shoulders into the task. Alistair Taylor rushed up the stairs just as he "heard the door give."

"Just wait outside," Gallway advised Joanne as he entered the darkened chamber, but Joanne didn't want to wait and stood inside the doorway of the outer dressing room, holding her breath. Directly in front of her, she could see Brian's tiny pajamaed figure in shadow, lying eerily on his side. Blood streamed from his nose. Nothing stirred; the room was perfectly still. As Joanne remembered it, Gallway examined Brian for a few minutes — although he probably didn't take more than a few seconds — and when he turned back to her she noticed that all the blood had drained out of his face.

"Is there any brandy in the house?" he asked Antonio. "I think we should all go down to the study and have some brandy."

Gallway walked past Joanne, who was rigid, "in total shock," and picked up the phone receiver, which was dangling off a table. "He's lying on the bed," the doctor told Peter Brown, "and he's gone."

Alistair Taylor walked slowly into Brian's room and lightly, mournfully, touched Brian on the shoulder while Antonio's wife, Maria, sobbed in the hall. Afterward, everyone assembled in the study to gather their thoughts. "It was some time before we called the police," Joanne remembered, "because we wanted to make sure that things were okay in the house—that there were no substances for them to find." They combed through Brian's study, tidying up this and that, and waited for David Jacobs, Brian's lawyer, who was already on his way, via fast train, from Brighton.

Alistair said: "We've got to get hold of Clive before Queenie hears about this on the radio." But no one answered the phone at Clive's house. In the interim, the doorbell rang. Thinking it was the police, Taylor answered without looking through the peephole and came face-to-face with Mike Housego of the *Daily Sketch*. "What are you doing here on a Sunday?" the reporter wondered. "Oh, you know what Brian's like," Taylor responded too quickly. He looked past Housego and wondered whether the garage door was shut or if he could see the Bentley in its space. "Oh, that's a bit weird," said Housego. "We heard he's ill." "*Nooooo!* He's fine. He's got a bit of a headache. That's why he's gone out."

A few minutes later another reporter called. The police must have passed the word to them, Taylor figured, making it more urgent than ever to contact Clive Epstein. "This is going to break," he told Joanne. "The press aren't stupid. If Queenie hears it over the air, we are in trouble."

He finally reached Clive at home and broke the news. "There's been an accident," Alistair remembers telling him. "Oh—not . . . not Brian," his brother stammered. "Is it bad?" Alistair hesitated. "Clive, he's dead." Clive Epstein's reaction was unforgettable. "There was a big scream—a horrendous scream. I'll never forget it to my dying day." Joanne Newfield could hear it over the line, from across the room.

———

Peter Brown and Geoffrey Ellis left Kingsley Hill immediately for London, with stolid Geoffrey behind the wheel, racing the car like a madman along the Eastbourne Road. First, however, Brown had placed a call to David Jacobs at his country house in Hove—it was presumed that Jacobs would know how best to deal with the police—then followed it with the call to Bangor. "The Beatles had to be told before anyone else, and I didn't want them to be told by the press," Brown recalls. "They had to be protected. The press knew where they were; there were photographers in Bangor. I thought they should all come back to their guarded situations in London as soon as possible."

"I'm sorry, but I'm afraid I've got bad news," Brown told Paul when he came on the phone. "Brian has died." Brown thought Paul's reaction to the news of Brian's death was "noncommittal" but says, "Then I suppose he was stunned. Paul never said how terrible a blow it was or how sorry he felt. It must have been confusing, following, as it did, two days of purging the spirit of material energy." The boys had known little or nothing about the state of Brian's health or the extent of his emotional unraveling. Later, at a hastily arranged press conference on the Bangor campus, Paul managed to express the group's reaction: "This is a terrible shock. I am terribly upset." But in the "confusion and disbelief" that followed the phone call, there was only numbness.

What could they do? Who would they turn to for advice? For the moment, Paul recalled, the Beatles "traipsed off to the Maharishi," who was holding court in his inner sanctum amid piles of wilting flowers. "Our friend's dead," they told him. "How do we handle this?" Because Hindu theology dictates that mortals not focus on death but in the transcendence of the spirit—the soul's moving on to another plane—the Maharishi disdained any comments about Brian's physical death. Instead, as Ringo remembered, he advised them not to try holding on to Brian, "to love him and let him go," so that his soul could continue on its upward journey. "You have to grieve for him and love him, and now you send him on his way."

John put it into layman's terms when he faced a crush of agitated reporters sometime later that afternoon. "Well, Brian is just passing into the next phase," he told the stunned press corps, which had never heard such mumbo jumbo. "His spirit is still around and always will be. It's a physical memory we have of him, and as men we will build on that memory." But deep down, John remembered thinking: "We were in trouble then." True, Brian's business edge had been dulled badly by his drug addiction and demons. But he still provided some glue and, in a scene increasingly populated with Magic Alex types and vampires, he could provide some ballast. John admitted feeling "scared" about the Beatles' ability to function, to remain together as a group, without Epstein's instinct and finesse. Indeed, as soon as the news of his death had struck home, John thought, "We've fuckin' had it."

———

Eventually, the press descended on Chapel Street like jackals. Alistair Taylor, dog-tired and "in shock," remembers staying long enough to "fend off the first wave." He refused to let anyone in, but finally even Taylor couldn't handle the relentless crowd on the sidewalk. "There was nothing more I could do," he recalls. Slipping out the back, he went around the corner to a pub whose name he cannot recall. Mike Housego was at a table by the window, nursing a pint. "And I poured my heart out to Mike.

Everything I ever felt about Brian came pouring out. *Everything!*" The reporter just sat and listened, without taking out his notepad. Finally, Alistair asked: "Are you going to print all that, Mike?" Housego shook his head mournfully. "I never asked you to talk," he said softly. "That's not an interview, mate." And not a word of it has ever appeared.

Nothing about the death had been heard backstage at the Saville Theatre, where at 7:30 that night the latest entry of "Brian Epstein Presents . . ." was playing before a packed house. Jimi Hendrix was headlining, with the Crazy World of Arthur Brown and Keith West's Tomorrow as the opening acts, and collectively the combos were burning up the place—literally. Arthur Brown had been electrifying crowds by setting his hair on fire during his finale. And as for the headliner, there was no shortage of excitement.

"We did the first show, which was really great," recalls Tony Bramwell, "but I noticed that Brian hadn't taken his box yet." He'd usually sit in the royal box with friends, and between sets he'd make a rather grand entrance to have drinks with the artists at a bar at the side of the stage.

They were just about to start the second performance and were letting the audience in when there was a phone call backstage saying that Brian had been found dead. "We thought it wouldn't be right to carry on with the show," Bramwell says with typical understatement, "so Eric Burdon, who had stopped by to watch Jimi, went out into the street and told the crowd that the show was canceled, Brian Epstein was dead." Brian's name was up there on the marquee. He'd been a fixture on such shows as *Juke Box Jury* and *Desert Island Discs,* a recognizable part of the scene. In no small way, he'd revitalized the British pop music scene, giving rock 'n roll its most identifiable sound since Elvis Presley hit the turntables. All of this registered as the news of his death rippled along the line outside. Tony Bramwell says the crowd's collective response was palpable. "The kids put their heads down and walked off in absolute silence."

All evidence indicates an accidental overdose. His bedroom door had been locked from the inside, and pages of correspondence and amateur poetry lay scattered about the floor. The police recovered seventeen bottles of assorted pills in the bedroom, plus a residue of brandy shellacked the bowl of a crystal snifter found on his night table. "I believe it was an accident," George Harrison concluded. "In those days everybody was topping themselves accidentally by taking uppers and/or amphetamine and alcohol—

loads of whiskey or brandy and uppers . . . and that's the kind of thing that Brian did." Paul, who heard the rumors of "very sinister circumstances," also believed "it was a drink-and-sleeping-pills overdose."* Suicide— threatened before—seemed out of the question. Says Alistair Taylor vehe- mently, "His father, Harry, had died only six weeks before, and Brian would never have done that to Queenie—not in a million years, no matter how down he was. It just wasn't in the man."

What *was* in the man, however, was enough of a substance called carbrital to kill a small horse. Norman Cowan had prescribed the drug on two occasions for Brian, along with Librium and Tryptizol, issuing large amounts of pills, he told the coroner, "because he was off on holiday and Epstein needed drugs to tide him over." It was impossible not to be suspi- cious, and the authorities were. "Our main concern was to convince the coroner that it was an overdose and not a suicide," recalls Peter Brown, who starred in the witness box at the inquest on the morning of September 9, 1967. Brown and Norman Cowan also planned "very carefully" to claim Brian's body immediately upon delivery of the official verdict and have the funeral the same day. To avoid a media circus in Liverpool, they had arranged to transport the enameled black coffin there directly by limousine and to bury Brian before sunset, as Jewish custom dictates, before the press expected the funeral to have taken place. Everyone else would come by train, except for the Beatles, who had been asked not to attend for fear they would attract a large crowd. Brian Epstein was all of thirty-two years old. On a lovely summer night, he finally got the one thing that had always eluded him: eternal peace.

[II]

In the days immediately following Brian's death, various factions began as- sembling to wrest control of his music empire. "There was a big power grab," recalls Alistair Taylor, who watched the action raptly from the side- lines. "The infighting was awful. Vic Lewis, Robert Stigwood, Peter Brown—the knives were out. Everybody wanted control of the Beatles."

Incongruously, Brian had left no will designating an heir, but his chair- man's share of NEMS legally passed to Clive Epstein, who, according to most observers, wasn't equipped to run the company. It was clear that Brian

---

* *Of all the people interviewed for this book, not one suggested otherwise.*

had wanted Stigwood and his partner, David Shaw, out of the picture and had begun proceedings to ensure against their proposed takeover of NEMS.

In the ensuing mad scramble for control, no one bothered to consult the Beatles about replacing Brian Epstein. Incredible as it might seem, Stigwood had never even met the band. "In fact, the Beatles were shocked to learn that Brian had planned to sell NEMS," Brown recalled. This was the first they'd heard that their management situation was in play—and they weren't happy, to say the least, about the prospect.

On Friday, September 1, 1967, only four days after Brian Epstein died, Paul rounded up the Beatles for a meeting at his house to jump-start his plans for a Magical Mystery Tour. When the others pulled up in front of Cavendish Avenue, late in the afternoon, Paul was waiting for them at the front door with his sheepdog, Martha, panting by his side. "Let's go upstairs to the music room," he said. "There is something we should get to without delay."

He wasn't kidding when he said "without delay." Despite lacking a concrete plan, a crew, or even a basic script, he wanted to begin filming *Magical Mystery Tour* right away, that very week. The Beatles had flirted with leaving for India over the weekend in order to pursue their study of Transcendental Meditation, but Paul convinced them that it was more critical to consolidate their business interests and to keep the band visible. No one had the foggiest idea of what their legal and financial obligations were, he argued. "They didn't know where any of the money was," Neil Aspinall recalled, "they didn't have a single contract for anything with Brian, not with a record company, not with a film company—Brian had them all." And they had no idea where he kept them. What is more, they only had a beggar's stake in NEMS, leaving them dependent, for the time being, on the business decisions of others. "It didn't make them vulnerable," Neil insisted, "but it did make them realize that they had to get it together. . . . [T]hey needed an office and an organization of their own."

Paul's *Mystery Tour* scenario was achingly simplistic. It was diagrammed on a single sheet of paper he'd first shown to Brian Epstein back in May. The entire blueprint was contained in a circle divided into eight segments labeled as follows:

1. Commercial introduction. Get on the coach. Courier introduces.
2. Coach people meet each other / (Song, Fool On The Hill?)
3. marathon—laboratory sequence.

4. smiling face. LUNCH. mangoes, tropical (magician)
5. and 6: Dreams.
7. Stripper & band.
8. Song.
END.

There was no more to it than that; everything else—the look and feel of the project—existed entirely in Paul's head. "John had spent an afternoon in his swimming pool thinking up ideas for the script," an insider reported; otherwise, it was going to be improvised on the fly.

At least a Magical Mystery Tour dealt with elements they were capable of putting to use. Music, for one. Every film needed a soundtrack, especially one that necessitated the Beatles' lip-syncing to certain sequences. There was already a title song in the can, as well as "Your Mother Should Know" and "The Fool on the Hill," which Paul had written while visiting his father in March, during the *Sgt. Pepper's* sessions. He had a fat reserve of songs in his arsenal—John has said as many as twenty, but that is most likely an exaggeration. As John recalled, "[Paul] said, 'Well, here's a segment, you write a little piece for that.'" That put tremendous pressure on John to contribute, a task he wrestled with over that pulpy, hot weekend. However, when the Beatles entered Studio Two on Tuesday evening, ready to roll, it was evident that John had come up with a killer.

"I Am the Walrus" is pure Lennon fantasy, written, he claimed, over the course of two acid trips. The lyric is based on Lewis Carroll's "The Walrus and the Carpenter" from *Through the Looking-Glass*, which John considered "a beautiful poem," although he pleaded ignorance when it came to the political undertones in the narrative. What fascinated John was the mazy wordplay of the original piece, which he used to form his own literary pretzels twisting around a cloud of psychedelic imagery. "Corporation teeshirt, stupid bloody Tuesday man . . ." "Crablocker fishwife pornographic priestess . . ." "The words don't mean a lot," he admitted; they are mostly nonsense, having no more substance than the mantra "Goo Goo Goo Joob" that rounds out the chorus. Of all the imagery, only "I am the eggman" has a basis in personal experience, a reference to a 1966 orgy he attended with Eric Burdon, who earned the nickname for breaking raw eggs on girls during sex.

The session itself was chaotic—George Martin graded it as "organized chaos . . . but also disorganized chaos"—because of the haste in which it was arranged and the prevailing influence of drugs. In many ways the basic rhythm track evolved like any other, beginning with electric piano and drums, then adding overdubs of bass and more drums to support the ever-shifting arrangement. John also laid the vocal in with relative ease, so that by the end of Wednesday's session they had a complete, if unspectacular, version in the can.

There it languished until almost a month later, when the song got a dressing unlike any other in the Beatles' repertoire. John had been listening to—and studying—an acetate of "Walrus" throughout the interim and under a smorgasbord of substances. At that point it was too basic and straightforward, especially for a lyric he considered "so weird." They needed to give it a proper arrangement—*proper,* of course, being a euphemism for weirder than weird.

At first, the Beatles' experiments with a mellotron had little effect on the track other than to produce some spooky, surrealistic textures. But as time wore on, they began to layer on instruments—eight violins, four cellos, a contrabass clarinet, and three horns—building dense levels of overdubs. Take followed take. By playing notes at the bottom end of the scale, they found they could stretch the tones even further. The bizarre sounds began to overlap and curdle until it was hard to distinguish their identities. They did the same thing with voices. The Mike Sammes Singers, an almost comically white-bread commercial chorale, was hired and put through a series of vocal gymnastics. Eight men and women accustomed to doing light television themes and folk songs chanted, "Ho-ho-ho, he-he-he, ha-ha-ha," and, "Oompah, oompah, stick it up your jumper," along with shrill whooping noises. The pièce de résistance, however, came at John's giddy direction: a ludicrous refrain that droned on behind George Martin's orchestration: "Everybody's got one, everybody's got one . . ." (later corrupted by so-called Beatles experts to be "Everybody smoke pot, everybody smoke pot . . .").

Martin, who bristled at the musical hodgepodge, decided to let the Beatles "have their heads" on the session. "Some of the sounds weren't very good," he recalled. "Some were brilliant, but some were bloody awful." The Beatles, however, were clearly pleased.

Even though Martin and the boys had edited and remixed the twenty-five takes of "I Am the Walrus" into a final sizzling master, John delivered the coup de grâce to the performance. While they were mastering the edit, he turned on a radio in the control booth and tuned in a live BBC production of *King Lear,* with John Gielgud in the title role. That was all his overactive imagination needed to hear. In the moments that followed, they mixed lines directly from the broadcast—Act IV, Scene VI—into the track, creating the familiar sound of nighttime radio in an already furiously overloaded song.

"The Fool on the Hill," by contrast, evolved in a stunningly straightforward way. Written back in March, days before finishing "With a Little Help from My Friends," Paul drew unknowingly on personal feelings about social hermits like the Maharishi, whom he had not met at the time. "It was this idea of a fool on the hill, a guru in a cave, I was attracted to," he recalled. Years earlier he'd heard the tale about a recluse in an Italian hill town who had missed World War II, and that may have sparked the title. But one night in Liverpool Paul conjured up the lonely image and wrote what is arguably one of his finest and most beautiful compositions.

Unlike "I Am the Walrus," nothing in the arrangement is cluttered with effects. Paul's plaintive, handsomely controlled vocal matches his lonely piano accompaniment in sentiments that never strayed far from those on an early demo. Only the organ and a flute meander obliquely around the melody in an irregular groaning pattern, playing off the piano figure and giving the production an unpredictably cautious lift.

Throughout the recording of the soundtrack, production began on the *Magical Mystery Tour* film, which proceeded in a predictably haphazard manner. Other than Paul, no one had given it much thought, and even he was shooting from the hip. "We literally made it up as we went," he recalled. There was no real cast to speak of, no featured roles to fill. Faces were the important thing; the Beatles wanted *characters,* eccentrics who would look and perform in an outrageous way. Only John made a specific casting request: he insisted on hiring Nat Jackley, an old-style music hall comedian whom he had always admired, as well as a couple of midgets. ("John would always want a midget or two around," Ringo noted.) The rest of the troupe was filled in by rooting through *Spotlight,* a legitimate casting magazine—fat actors, busty women, grotesque-looking contortionists—and inviting along Victor Spinetti, who had appeared in their other films. Neil and Mal hired the actors, then located a sixty-two-seat bus, an old yellow job on which they painted the *Magical Mystery Tour* logo, which Paul had designed.

The caravan took off for the West Country just after noon on September 11, 1967, leaving from Allsop Place, a service road behind the Baker Street tube station, which had been the starting point for all the early rock 'n roll coach tours. On board were thirty-three actors, four cameramen, a soundman, a technical adviser, the four Beatles Fan Club secretaries, and an entourage of friends, with Paul McCartney acting as tour guide and emcee.

It would be useless to highlight each stopover on the *Magical Mystery Tour*. For the most part, it was a mess—five days of chaotic, incoherent shooting on location, in and around Surrey and Devon, with visits to the Cornish beaches on the Atlantic coast and Somerset. "We would get off the bus: 'Let's stop here,' and go and do this and that," Ringo recalled. "Then we'd put the music to it." Occasionally it worked, but often they were beset by technical and logistical problems that undermined their efforts. What's more, the tour was hardly magical or even a mystery, inasmuch as the bus was trailed everywhere by a convoy of twenty or so cars filled with press, fans, and media hangers-on who blockaded roads and snarled traffic. Fed up, an apoplectic John Lennon leaped off the bus and ripped the banners off the sides.

The Beatles had intended to spend another week filming sequences on a set at Shepperton Studios, outside the city, but in their haste to get under way they'd forgotten to book stage time there or anywhere else. Every soundstage within fifty miles was already reserved, many of them by Stanley Kubrick, who was in production making *2001: A Space Odyssey,* and it took some clever improvising by a NEMS functionary to hire the empty hangars at West Malling Air Station in Kent, a deserted base used by the U.S. Air Force in World War II, for filming the interior sequences.

Eventually, the Beatles had enough footage to string together an hour's worth of film, but everyone involved with the project knew this wouldn't turn out to be one of their masterpieces. Paul had taken over the direction after three separate cameramen botched the job. "It was strictly amateur time," says Peter Brown, who watched with mounting dread as £40,000 of bills began piling up at NEMS. "If Brian had been alive, he would have pulled it into some kind of professional shape—or talked the Beatles out of it. But without him, Paul was not to be appeased."

Back at NEMS, it was clear that no one was minding the store. NEMS needed someone savvy, someone who lived and breathed the music business to take over the reins—and fast. But who? The lineup of prospects was a misbegotten bunch.

Peter Brown was basically Brian's "social secretary" and, along with Alistair Taylor, considered a "Liverpool lad" and therefore not sophisticated enough to stand nose-to-nose with the London jackals. The same with Neil Aspinall, who, as the Beatles' point man, was perhaps the obvious choice to take over. But even George Martin thought Neil lacked "sufficient clout" and, applying typical British prejudice, "was out of his class" in dealing with the genteel executives who ran major record labels.

During the first week of the *Magical Mystery Tour,* Stigwood took matters into his own hands. He marched into Peter Brown's office and ordered him to arrange a meeting with the Beatles so that he could present them with his credentials and discuss the future of the management company. The second week in September, while the Beatles were in Hayward's Heath, he staged his showdown, over lunch in the hotel that doubled as the film company's production office.

On one side of a table, the suits—Robert Stigwood, David Shaw, Clive Epstein, and Peter Brown—sat shoulder to shoulder, with grave faces and guilty eyes. Across two plates piled with sandwiches, facing them like a jury, were the Beatles and Neil Aspinall, arms folded across their chests. Stigwood, who was a charming and effusive man, explained how prior to Brian's death there had been a vacuum at their management company and how he had been running it successfully for the past six months. Clive, shifting culpably in his chair, nodded approval. "Now that Brian isn't here," he said, "I'm the natural successor and I want to take over the operation."

The Beatles sat passively through Stigwood's presentation, the smoke from their four cigarettes clouding the cramped space. Their eyes gave nothing away. Finally, John allowed his face to convey confusion and distaste, saying: "We don't know you. Why would we do this?" Paul didn't give Robert time to respond. "First of all, we don't have a clue about what's been going on. But it doesn't really matter because it's not our business. We've got our own people to look after us, otherwise we don't need anything else." They weren't interested in a manager at the moment, Paul said. Stigwood could go on managing NEMS' interests if Clive so chose, but that had nothing to do with the Beatles.

Despite the cool reception, Stigwood continued to press his point. Why not let things run their course? he wondered. *Because,* John reminded him, *NEMS was built on the Beatles' success,* not on Cream or the Bee Gees. If Stigwood wanted to discuss their continued involvement, they might consider remaining with the company—they *might*—but not, in any case, by holding a minority participation. The percentages would have to be reversed, giving the Beatles a controlling 51 percent interest. Stigwood, however, wouldn't hear of it. He remembered mentally tabulating the bags of money flowing out of NEMS, much of it wasted on Magic

Alex, and thought: "A joint company doesn't work unless I can control it and say, 'There's not a hundred thousand pounds to spend this week.'"

Stigwood needed control, the Beatles craved complete freedom—neither was willing to give an inch. Of course, Brian's unsecured 70 percent stake in NEMS raised the possibility of a hostile takeover. Such action was never threatened per se, although elements in the heated exchange gave the impression that it might be considered, prompting the Beatles to issue a public statement. "They would be willing to put money into NEMS if there was any question of a takeover from an outsider," a spokesman told *NME*. "The Beatles will not withdraw their shares from NEMS. Things will go on just as before."

After a bit of back-and-forth, Stigwood agreed to disassociate himself from NEMS, taking Cream, the Bee Gees, and a few other assets with him as the foundation of a new company, the Robert Stigwood Organization, that would grow into a multimedia empire; the rest of the roster, such as it was, for the moment remained under Clive Epstein's languid control, with Vic Lewis at the helm. (Later, Stigwood would claim, "We shook hands, and I don't think we've ever had a cross word about it." At the time, however, he demanded a £25,000 buyout to leave quietly, which, according to Ringo, "was a very reasonable price" to pay for their freedom.)

After all this time, the Beatles were finally on their own, finally free to make every decision as they alone saw fit.

[III]

Throughout the fall of 1967, while Britain waged an all-out assault on conformity, the Beatles hastened to consolidate their interests. The longtime holding company, Beatles Ltd., was officially renamed Apple Music Ltd., after which seven subsidiaries were formed: Apricot Investments Ltd., Blackberry Investments Ltd., Cornflower Investments Ltd., Daffodil Investments Ltd., Edelweiss Investments Ltd., Foxglove Investments Ltd., and Greengage Investments Ltd., each capitalized with a substantial financial endowment. Money was no problem. "There was an enormous sum of money—well over a million pounds—that had been accumulated by EMI while the new contract was being negotiated," recalls Peter Brown. "The Beatles received twenty-five percent of that—and *that* was the money that set up Apple."

Paul always maintained that Apple was so named for the first school-book phrase that children learn: A is for Apple. An apple conveyed an un-deceptively simple and pure image. Its nature was uncompromising, essential, vital. But like the apple in the Bible, it proved a sinfully irre-sistible temptation, and once the Beatles had bitten into it, there was noth-ing they could do to stop their expulsion from Eden.

Originally the company—a glorified tax shelter—was intended as a real estate operation. Clive Epstein and Harry Pinsker, NEMS' principal financial adviser, devised an ambitious land and retail trading venture, which, of course, held no appeal for the Beatles. Without the benefit of a similar tax scheme, however, they were into Inland Revenue for 86 percent of the pie. "So we'd sit around the boardroom, kicking ideas around," re-calls Alistair Taylor, who had been appointed to the newly reshuffled NEMS executive board after Brian's death. "But every time we came up with something and presented it to the boys, it was: 'You're joking! Bollocks to that!'" The board initially proposed opening a chain of record shops called Apple, but "selling records was dismissed as too commercial for the Beatles." Another idea came from Clive Epstein. "He wanted to set up a chain of card shops—picture cards, Christmas cards, and invitations whose inscriptions would be written by the Beatles themselves," Taylor explains. It seemed to the other board members like a "revolutionary" concept, a sure franchise, and the Beatles were called in for approval. Clive even commissioned a few pasteup cards for their inspection. The Beatles passed them around, turned them over, inside out, upside down. There was an embarrassing silence, followed by John's blunt verdict: "How fucking boring!"

All this showed the Beatles how seriously out of touch the NEMS board was when it came to representing their interests. "You can just imag-ine the Beatles with a string of retail fucking shoe shops," John fumed. "[T]hat was the way they thought."

No, if there was going to be an Apple, it wasn't going to be run by the suits but by the Beatles. After all, they'd just made a movie on their own. They knew a good deal about the recording process. Paul fancied himself a pretty good businessman. They had a secret resource—Magic Alex—and a cache of fabulous songs. Why shouldn't they pool their creative resources and run their own company? "We're just going to do—*everything!*" John told Pete Shotton during a visit soon after the card shop fiasco. "We'll have electronics, we'll have clothes, we'll have publishing, we'll have music.

We're going to be talent spotters and have new talent." Shotton says there was none of the wholesale cynicism that routinely crabbed John's opinions. "He was *very* excited about the Apple idea."

And the excitement was infectious. Terry Doran, Brian's old Liverpool friend, was enlisted to run Apple Music Publishing and manage new bands, a business he knew virtually nothing about. George got involved with launching a string of discotheques, beginning with the flagship establishment in New York. Paul opened discussions with Mick Jagger about the Beatles and Stones forming a partnership to open their own recording studio, with the possibility of starting up a joint label. Magic Alex was commissioned, at a salary of £40 a week and 10 percent of the profits, to patent and begin producing his wacky inventions under an Apple Electronics subsidiary.

First, however, Apple opened a clothing company. The Beatles were delighted by the idea of having their own boutique full of "groovy clothes." At least, as John pointed out, the merchandise would be "something that we'd want, that we'd like to buy." If the Beatles had learned anything from success, from superstardom, it was the extent of their tremendous influence. Fans watched them like hawks: how they talked and looked, what they said and wore, became as important as what they sang. The popularity of long hair alone testified to the impact of the Beatles' style. By Paul's own admission, they were already "dressing in such interesting clothes," most of which had been created by the Fool. If they set the Fool up in business, they were liable to make a fortune.

Of course, the Beatles already had a fortune, which meant they could concentrate less on profits and more on sharing the wealth. Money wasn't everything, they insisted; money was a trap. Money had a way of compromising true creativity. Nor did they want to come off as a bunch of hip tycoons. "The aim of the company isn't a stack of gold teeth in the bank," John said. "We've done that bit. It's more of a trick to see . . . if we can create things and sell them without charging three times our cost." A variety of concepts for the new company were kicked around. John liked Paul's initial idea to "sell everything white." But in the end, the style of clothes would be left entirely up to the Fool. The Beatles' only concern was that the store be "a beautiful place where beautiful people can buy beautiful things."

Early in 1967, as part of a long-term investment, the Beatles had purchased a cute little three-story building zoned for commercial use, at 94 Baker Street, on the corner of Paddington. It was the perfect location for a hip new venture—a few steps off Oxford Street, where it might be considered too mainstream and slick, but close enough to attract steady pedestrian traffic; in other words: shabby chic. The top floor provided suitable space for Apple's corporate offices, such as they were, with accommodating proximity so that the Beatles could keep their fingers in what was going on downstairs.

While the matter of place was settled, however, people close to the Beatles were becoming increasingly unsettled by the Fool. Right off the bat, the designers raised concerns with Harry Pinsker by demanding an employment contract with a signing bonus of £40,000. Pinsker, a relatively conservative accountant who held the Beatles' purse strings, recounted being "horrified" by the payment and advised his clients to reconsider what he felt to be a superfluous expense. The Beatles, however, couldn't be bothered. "Give it to them," Pinsker was told, effectively opening the floodgates.

The Fool passed themselves off as the picture of countercultural perfection, a trio of pale-faced, exquisite sylphs, with more self-possession than Sybil. Their everyday wardrobe could have been lifted out of an Edwardian costume spectacle. According to a description in the *New York Times,* "they wear gypsy headdresses, at least ten necklaces between them, bells, tight pants, boots, 16th-century-looking jerkins, long, full-sleeved blouses and low belts of satin around the hips." The image they cultivated, from their public face to all the workmanship that went into their designs, right down to the embroidery accenting their clothing, "splashed with stars and moons," gave the appearance that they were touched by poetry.

But their true gift was cunning. Like Magic Alex, they dazzled the Beatles with hippie double-talk about spiritual bliss, how the boutique would "have an image of naturel"; it would approximate "a paradise" whose guiding principle wasn't based on "bread" but rather "love" and "turning people on." Stoned and starry-eyed, that was all the Beatles needed to hear. John, besotted by the peace-and-love vibe, urged Pete Shotton to get involved with the project. "You should move to London and run it," Shotton remembers John telling him. "Run it—run Apple." To Shotton, whose experience was managing a supermarket John had bought him, it seemed like a demotion. But Shotton says he misunderstood; John was offering him "the whole thing"—the whole Apple pie. "I couldn't do that," he protested, shaken by the offer, but John remained adamant. "Come on," he insisted, "it's just a joke. We're only spending money, having a laugh. Nobody knows what to do, so just have a go at it."

Ultimately, Shotton turned the day-to-day operation of the supermarket over to his mother and joined the Apple alliance. His first assignment—

getting the Apple Boutique off the ground—gave him an eye-opening view of the cock-up he was inheriting. When he arrived at Baker Street, the scene reminded him of an asylum. "Everybody was smoking dope and taking acid," Shotton recalls. "So, to them, anything could be done, anything was possible." Magic Alex was even commissioned, at considerable expense, to provide an artificial sun that would light up the sky over the boutique. There was a lot of loose talk about being ready for the holidays. The Beatles squinted dizzily at the calendar and picked a date out of the air—November 2. "We'll open then," they decided. *Just five weeks off!* Shotton says he tried to convince them that more time was needed; there were so many details that had to be worked out and arranged for, to say nothing of stocking the shelves with clothing and trinkets. None of this, however, deterred the Beatles from announcing the grand opening to the press. It would be ready, they assured Pete. Somehow these things always took care of themselves.

But as late as October 5, the entire shop still had to be renovated. "It was a shithole," Shotton remembers, "an absolute mess."

Meanwhile, the Fool requisitioned expense money for a ten-day trip to Morocco, ostensibly to buy fabric and jewelry, but in reality as an excuse for "eating majoun and smoking hashish." When the Fool got to work, they were carried away with extravagance; their clothing line cost more to produce than Coco Chanel's latest collection. Silks, velvets, tapestries, and brocades from every international fashion capital were incorporated into their not-so-ready-to-wear line. "The clothes looked more like fancy-dress costumes than anything one could wear day to day," wrote an observer. "[C]ourt jester crossed with harlequin crossed with Peter Pan, rainbow colors, zig-zag hems . . . ballet tights and operatic coats for flower children." It was a dollhouse array of ill-conceived outfits—pretty to look at but completely impractical. "We had to find people to *make* these clothes," recalls Pete Shotton, "and when we finally did, the clothes were shit." Seams burst open, sleeves didn't quite match, sizes never reconciled. Simon Posthuma, the chief Fool, further demanded that the labels for his creations be woven from pure silk. "I did some calculations and figured out that the labels would actually cost more to produce than the items of clothing, so I put my foot down." But John overruled him. "It's a different form of art," he lectured Pete. "Besides, it doesn't matter whether we make money or not. If the labels make that much of a statement, we should have them. Let it go."

Pressure started to mount as the opening neared, and the date had to be pushed back—to early December, at least. But there had to be some kind of trade-off, something tangible, something that the press and public could *see* that more or less justified the delay.

No problem. Over the weekend of November 10–12, while the Beatles were preoccupied with filming a video of their new single, "Hello Goodbye," the Fool set about painting the shop's ancient white brick facade, erecting a scaffolding and draping it with oilcloth so that the work could be done in secrecy. "They refused to tell any of us what it was going to look like," recalls Alistair Taylor. No one, other than the art students hired to execute the design, was permitted to peek at the work in progress. Even the Beatles were warded off like overeager children. "When the time finally came to unveil it, we all gathered in the street. The tarpaulin dropped dramatically, and underneath was the most incredible psychedelic mural covering this beautiful little building, with a two-story genie and stars and moons and fairies and what have you. *Oh my!* We were absolutely *gobsmacked*. It was fabulous! People leaned out of buildings and buses to get a good look. And any car that turned into the street nearly smacked into the one in front of it that had also stopped to stare."

"The painting was gorgeous," Paul said, echoing an opinion shared by the rest of the Beatles and most of the public. Citywide, the Apple Boutique mural was a huge conversation piece. London had never seen anything like it. People came from every district to get a closer look, clogging the sidewalk outside the shop, tying up traffic. It became as popular a tourist attraction as any of the traditional sights. But the City of Westminster's planning commission, whose official permission to paint the facade had been required but seemingly ignored, was less than enthused. "It wasn't long before we heard from their solicitors, saying we had to restore the building to its original appearance," Taylor recalls. Three weeks of overheated legal wrangling ensued until, ultimately, the mural was painted out by the Fool.

Inside, the shop was in no less of a muddle. A layout, with sections and aisles, was needed to give the interior some symmetry, but its style was the subject of constant contention. "There was no direction, no focal point," Pete Shotton remembers. "Paul wanted dividers up. Then John would come in and say, 'Why in the hell are we cutting people off from each other?' and he'd have the dividers ripped out." It went back and forth like that for days, building up and ripping out, until the dispute had less to do with style than with ego. It mirrored their bickering over the music: each of the two Beatles wanted to put his own stamp on the boutique, each suspicious and jealous of the other's contribution. Unable to take sides in the matter, Shotton struggled, ineffectually, to please both John and Paul. "They needed someone strong, someone like Brian, to say no, and I wasn't the one who could do it. . . . I only ever wanted to be friends with them."

The Apple Boutique finally opened—without dividers—on December 7, 1967. A by-invitation-only gala was slated for 8:16 P.M. (one of John's affectations), with a fashion show scheduled at "8:46 sharp." Neither Paul nor Ringo attended—Paul being on vacation with Jane Asher at High Park, an isolated farm he'd purchased in the Scottish moors, and Ringo, off in Rome, putting in a cameo appearance as Emmanuel the gardener in the screen adaptation of *Candy*. Nor was there an artificial sun, its inventor, Magic Alex, pleading a lack of adequate "energy."

What they lacked in solar power, however, was made up by gate-crashers lighting in the doorway and storming the gates. "It was a mess," Taylor says, "a glorious mess. The worse things got, the more pleased everyone seemed. No one minded the crushing crowds or the confusion. Shoplifting was completely overlooked; it was regarded as a kind of benevolence, hippie philanthropy."

John and George may have been satisfied with the economics—but they weren't amused by the opening-night festivities. Unexpectedly there had been an outbreak of screaming, pushing, and shoving when they arrived. It reminded them of Beatlemania, smaller in scale and more concentrated perhaps, yet another mutant form of it. Their uneasiness continued to deepen afterward, over a "tense dinner" with their wives and Derek Taylor, who had arrived from the States especially to attend the gala. Questions kept surfacing about what they'd gotten themselves into.

If they couldn't free themselves from the grip of crazy celebrity, they wondered, was there ever any hope of restoring some normalcy to their lives? That had been the intention when they stopped touring, the underlying purpose of Transcendental Meditation, the restructuring of Apple. Now John and George began to wonder if any escape was possible.

———

If there was one constant the Beatles could rely on, it was record sales. The day after the boutique opened, when everything seemed so topsy-turvy again, EMI released a six-song EP (tucked inside a small book) that served as the soundtrack for *Magical Mystery Tour*. Overall, the music was anything but spectacular; only "I Am the Walrus" and "The Fool on the Hill" measured up to the Beatles' unique standards. Whispers of dissatisfaction murmured through the underground ranks. Knocks like "trivial" and "soft" accompanied reviews. There was even a plot, some claimed, to derail its airplay. In response to a petition by two housewives accusing the BBC of disseminating a "propaganda of disbelief, doubt, and dirt," the radio station's Tory watchdog, Lord Hill, banned "I Am the Walrus," objecting to the line "Boy, you've been a dirty girl, you've let your knickers down." It was a feeble excuse to make headlines off the Beatles' backs; there was nothing indecent about *Magical Mystery Tour,* other than perhaps its uninspired musical quality. However, while critics expressed reservations about the unusual package, the fans were hardly underwhelmed, with 450,000 advance orders and another 300,000 copies in the pipeline by the launch.

Coincidentally, Capitol Records announced that American sales of "Hello Goodbye" had reached the million mark on the same day, giving the Beatles a boost against drastic losses at the Apple Boutique. "There was plenty of stock," recalls Peter Brown, "but no stock control. No one knew where anything was; people were stealing things left and right, much of it by the interminably stoned young staff." Dressing rooms accommodated any shopper who set out to stash something under his clothes or in a bag. No questions asked. Invariably, more things were stolen from the Apple Boutique than were purchased. "It was *disastrous* from start to finish," says Alistair Taylor, who roamed the aisles each day on his way upstairs to the office. Concludes Peter Brown, "*Anyone* who touched *anything* fucked it up with great skill. It was a mess, it was—*disastrous.*"

In the midst of this retail train wreck, another disaster loomed. On December 16 Paul gathered the Beatles and their friends to screen the final cut of *Magical Mystery Tour.* It was a fifty-odd-minute crazy quilt of scenes—"formless, disconnected, disjointed and amateurish," according to its critics—cut and pasted together without the slightest regard for narrative. "There was no plot," Paul admitted, ". . . [d]eliberately so." But his bluff that its essence was "magical" carried no weight. "Nobody had the vaguest idea what it was about," according to Neil Aspinall. There was a lot of chair-shuffling and nervous coughing throughout the seemingly endless screening, during which several people excused themselves, ostensibly to use the loo, and never came back. "It looked awful and it was a disaster," recalled George Martin, who watched it stupefied, in openmouthed horror, as others seated around him decried it as "pretentious and overblown." Afterward, John told Ray Coleman it was "the most expensive home movie ever," which, intended as a boast or not, wasn't too far off the mark.

The Beatles had dropped roughly £40,000 on *Magical Mystery Tour*—

up to that point. Most of the negative expense, if not more, they hoped to recoup from an exhibitor. But who in their right mind would pick up the tab for such a sorry spectacle? Not a cinema chain; it was too short a mess to qualify as a feature. Peter Brown, who "thought it was dreadful," had been enlisted by Paul to help sell it. Initially, in November, they pitched it to the BBC and ITV as a Christmas holiday special, and he says the BBC "were drooling at the mouths at the very idea of it until they got a look at the finished product." ITV passed, on the premise of a scheduling problem. Paul Fox, the head of BBC1, recalled: "I saw it four times before I began to understand it." He admitted that "there were large parts that were unprofessional" but felt "there were also moments of drama and poignancy, which [he] found quite fascinating." Ultimately, it came down to the Beatles, as sure a draw as anything on TV. Even considering the extravagant mess on the screen, Fox "thought it was worth showing."

Brown, however, didn't share his opinion. He worried about the blow it would certainly deal the Beatles' unblemished reputation and urged Paul to reconsider. "After the lackluster response from the BBC," he says, "I tried to suggest writing off the £40,000 and moving on. But Paul didn't know it was a mess and insisted on making the deal." The BBC agreed to show it twice—in black and white on Boxing Day and again in color on January 5—for the paltry fee of £9,000. Rather than appear insulted, Paul insisted that money was never the issue. "Sod it," he thought, "that's not really the important thing." It was a well-known fact that Boxing Day TV audiences were the largest of the year. The coverage they'd get would be unprecedented. As Paul envisioned it, close to 20 million viewers who had eaten "too much turkey and sherry" would sit around living rooms throughout Britain waiting for the "plum pudding special": the Beatles in *Magical Mystery Tour.*

Unfortunately, in this case, all they'd get was more turkey, and it was no surprise that the critics knocked the stuffing out of it. "Appalling!" the *Daily Mail* harrumphed. "It was worse than terrible." James Green, who covered TV for the *Evening News,* stammered over suitably damning adjectives, advising readers to "take your pick from the words: rubbish, piffle, chaotic, flop, tasteless, nonsense, emptiness, and appalling." Accordingly, the *Daily Mirror* chose "rubbish . . . piffle . . . nonsense!" The *Daily Express* limited its slurs to "blatant rubbish" and said, "The whole boring saga confirmed a long held suspicion . . . that the Beatles . . . have made so much money that they can apparently afford to be contemptuous of the public." Punishment was demanded of the culprits. "Whoever authorized the showing of the film on BBC1," wrote the *Daily Sketch,* "should be condemned to a year squatting at the feet of the Maharishi Mahesh Yogi."

But Paul had other things on his mind. During the holiday, "perhaps slightly to [his] own surprise," he gathered the family together and announced his engagement to Jane.

[I]

Throughout the first ten years of the Beatles saga, women knew their place. A fan screamed, wept, engaged in some heavy personal fantasy, and, on the off chance of a close encounter, flung herself recklessly in the general vicinity of one of the Beatles, hoping at the very least for a reciprocal smile. A lucky bird might even get to spend the night. But for a girlfriend or a wife, the role was severe. They were at best a prop in the grand scenario; at worst, a handicap. Aside from creature comforts, which were glorious, the disadvantages of pairing with one of the band outweighed the benefits. For one thing, there was no room for a woman in that crowded spotlight. They gave up whatever individuality they had to support the boys' careers and, as such, were swallowed whole by the monster Beatlemania.

The Beatles were an unconditionally exclusive fraternity — one for all and all for one. Cynthia Lennon, envious of their rapport, called it "a marriage of four minds . . . [that] were always in harmony." *Always* may be too strong a word, but on those occasions when it became necessary to close ranks, the Beatles formed an airtight bond that knew no equivalent; there was nothing and no one capable of infiltrating the core group. Neil and Mal gained entry — at times — but that only made their slavish devotion and loyalty more painful. Perhaps those two more than anyone recognized the boundaries of real friendship; after twenty-hour days that might begin with driving hours on end, then lifting heavy equipment and running what some might view as demeaning errands, a word, even a look, often reminded them exactly who they were and left them outside looking in, just like everyone else.

The Beatles' women, on the other hand, never got that close. Decisions were routinely made without their input. Their opinions were seldom, if ever, sought. It was unthinkable that a project dreamed up and green-lighted by one of the Beatles, even something as significant as Apple, would be referred to the women for comment. "When it came down to business," says Alistair Taylor, "the girls were usually the last to be told."

The same rules pertained to the music. John and Paul might preview a nascent song they'd just written for Cynthia or Jane, but other than a rare special occasion—like the "All You Need Is Love" broadcast—women were barred. No woman had ever been invited into the studio and, as far as can be determined, none had asked. In Paul's view, the studio was sacrosanct, the Beatles' relationship to it like "four miners who go down the pit"—and "[y]ou don't need women down the pit, do you?"

On those nights when the Beatles finished work at a respectable hour, they'd head home to change, collect the girls, and go back out to one of the clubs, where they'd squeeze into a private banquette that functioned as a sort of clubhouse. Conversation revolved entirely around the musicians and their lives. If the women talked at all, it was among themselves. Occasionally one of the Beatles might spot a friend and disappear for the rest of the night—just wander off without a word—leaving his companion to arrange her own way home, no matter how late the hour. Other times one of the girls might sit in the backseat of a limo for a ridiculous stretch of time, waiting until the last fucked-up straggler had paid his respects.

Yet those kinds of sacrifices were made without complaint. In part, of course, this was because it had never been any other way. The Beatles had chosen women—Cynthia, Jane, Maureen, and Pattie—who accepted their offbeat way of life and were willing to put up with the rigors that the role required, without defiance, resentment, or asking too many questions. Nowhere in the Beatles saga do characters appear more selfless. The women surprised even one another by the extent of their thoughtfulness and TLC. Cynthia, who conducted her mornings in monklike silence so that John could sleep until two in the afternoon, marveled at how Maureen pampered Ringo through those all-night recording marathons. "Instead of going to bed," Cyn recalled, "she would wait up until he came home and serve him a wonderful roast dinner, even if it happened to be five in the morning." Jane once remarked to a friend how she admired Pattie for filling the house with incense each day, ready for George's arrival.

And nowhere in the Beatles saga are characters more forgiving. During the boys' long tenure in the spotlight, the women dealt capably with every curveball that was thrown at them. They'd been through the craziness and idol worship, the marijuana and the LSD, the meditation and the mystery tour. They'd dealt with the fickle, heartless press that robbed their families of any privacy. They'd stayed home alone, rattling around their empty mansions during those long tours and even longer recording sessions, dealing with the isolation that stardom imposed. They'd heard the rumors of infidelities and waved them away like smoke. They put aside all personal ambition because they were the Beatles' women, and those were the rules.

But after ten years, the rules were about to change.

Of all the plum roles that had come her way, the Subservient Beatles Woman was the only one Jane Asher refused to play.

She had been only seventeen years old when, five years before, Paul McCartney had literally moved into her life as a housemate and a lover, youthful and innocent, perhaps, but hardly naive. Assuming her rightful place in the Beatles' entourage was never difficult for Jane. "There was something about the way she behaved that put everyone at ease," says a friend. "Although she was posh, you never got the sense she was pretentious or insincere."

And yet, she had too much going for her to take a backseat to anyone, much less her mate. From the beginning, Paul had a hard time keeping up with her. Jane's diary, which she lived by, was a clutter of fascinating appointments and social commitments. "I was amazed by the diary," Paul admitted. "I've never known people who stuffed so much into a day." There were auditions, meetings with television and movie producers, vocal lessons, acting classes, fittings, gallery debuts, screenings, recitals, opening nights. Paul was also impressed that "Jane knew people in the country," which he considered a "rather upper-class thing."

"Paul was clearly in awe of her," says Peter Brown. "He liked the whole package; it was his ticket in." But after a time—and well before 1968—Paul found his own foothold in this once-alien world. He was an internationally known figure, sought after as much by strangely dressed freaks as he was by distinguished diplomats and intellectuals. From the banks of the Mersey to the mansions on the Thames, there wasn't a social circle in which he couldn't form a connection. If anything, Jane now had trouble keeping up with him. Jane was unfamiliar with the work of de Chirico, de Kooning, or Magritte, to say nothing of William Burroughs, Luciano Berio, Antonioni, or the Fugs. And what of the characters involved in the underground who shared Paul's idealistic sympathies? She had no reason to be keenly aware of their issues and schemes, nor did she have a working knowledge of their subversive politics. And Jane hated the drug scene.

"Jane confided in me enough to say that Paul wanted her to become the little woman at home with the kiddies," Cynthia wrote. Another reliable observer says Jane had "clearly decided that she was setting her own terms on how she conducted her career." There were to be no cop-outs, no compromises, no backseats taken to pop stars.

At the time of their engagement, things were already "very tense" between Paul and Jane, according to Marianne Faithfull, who thought their relationship was more "like an act" than a romance. Peter Brown's characterization of it as "a companionship" seems more generous, although not entirely on the mark. Still, they had weathered several ups and downs, including Jane's "traumatic" confession that she intended to leave Paul for a boyfriend in Bristol. They'd gotten past that—but just barely. As far as marriage went, Paul "could not get her to name the day." However, there was something about making the relationship official, so to speak, that seemed to take the pressure off and allowed them to get on with other things. For Paul and Jane, engagement postponed engagement.

Although no one else knew it—not even Paul, George, or Ringo—John Lennon found himself wrestling with similar emotional issues.

For the past few months, there had been a sea change in his life. First, his father, Freddie, reappeared after a three-year hiatus, this time in the company of a nineteen-year-old student named Pauline Jones, whom he would eventually marry. They spent several weeks as guests at Kenwood, John and Freddie struggling to come to terms with their lifelong estrangement. Various sources indicate that it was a difficult, if not contentious, reunion, hardly the reconciliation either man might have hoped for. John was always on the go, "never available" for his father, to say nothing of his own wife, who, Jones observed, "had begun to establish a social life of her own."

Much of John's erratic behavior can be attributed to a situation that threatened to shatter his household routine. Much to his own surprise, he had become infatuated with another woman. She had edged into the picture in late November, following a private seminar with the Maharishi in a London suburb that the Lennons had attended with Pete Shotton and his wife, Beth. As the two couples were leaving the guru's guesthouse, a tiny raven-haired woman, clad head to toe in black, appeared out of the shadows and asked John for a lift back to the city. Shotton recalls that he treated "this stranger" with the kind of "tactful attention" a pop star would give a favored fan. John shifted uneasily from foot to foot—Cynthia noticed that a look of "pure shock" crossed her husband's face—then said, "This is Yoko. Do you mind if she comes back with us?"

Yoko Ono had been "particularly persistent" in her pursuit of John Lennon since their first meeting at her Indica Gallery show in 1966. Over the course of several months thereafter, she had tried unsuccessfully to get his attention, first standing at the gates to Kenwood among the horde of groveling fans and haunting the steps outside the Apple offices, in the hope of a "chance" encounter. She once gained admittance to Kenwood for the purpose of calling a taxi, then planted a ring by the phone, necessitating a return visit. Cynthia recalled that afterward, "there were a lot of phone calls [at home] from Yoko, and John also received a constant flow of letters from her," none of which aroused Cynthia's suspicion—or his, so it seems. "John read them and left them lying around," Cynthia said. She took Yoko for another of the endless would-be artists who approached John for assistance, seeking a personal endorsement or money.

Somewhere along the line, John's attitude toward Yoko Ono changed. Whether it was caused by the end of touring, the shock of Brian's death, or the effects of meditation, it is hard to determine. A more likely reason suggests that the excessive boredom of his marriage finally prevailed. But between November 1967 and January 1968, something piqued his interest in Yoko. Cynthia sensed that change and said that she confronted John about Yoko, but he dismissed her curiosity with genuine indifference. "She's crackers, she's just a weirdo artist," he replied. "Don't worry about it." Nor was there anything to be gleaned from a volume of her poems, *Grapefruit,* lying on John's night table. Even after the number of letters and calls increased, he insisted: "She's another nutter wanting money for all that avant garde bullshit."

But by January that avant-garde bullshit had an impressive price. John sent Yoko to see Pete Shotton at Apple about underwriting one of her myriad projects. In an office above the boutique, she told Pete, "I want two thousand pounds." Pete was staggered by the request. It was "an enormous amount of money," he says, and the magnitude of it took him completely by surprise. Recovering, he asked her what she wanted it for. Only Yoko Ono could have explained a concept as loopy as the one she called "Half-a-Wind," a roomful of everyday objects, mostly furniture and appliances—"all beautifully cut in half and all painted white," as John later described it. Shotton was flabbergasted by the description. "I'll have to talk to somebody about this, Yoko," he says he told her. "I can't give you two thousand pounds to cut furniture up." Yoko flashed an inscrutable smile and told him "it was metaphysical."

"In the beginning, all those screwy ideas of hers amused him," says Peter Brown, "then they intrigued him—and then much more." "She did a thing called 'Dance Event,' where different cards kept coming through the door every day saying, 'Breathe' and 'Dance' and 'Watch all the lights until dawn,'" John explained to Jann Wenner in a 1970 interview, "and they upset me or made me happy, depending on how I felt." And much of *Grapefruit* he found infuriating, scattered with outrageous instructional "pieces," such as "Use your blood to paint. Keep painting until you faint. Keep painting until you die." John, who loved nothing more than to whip up controversy, saw a kindred spirit in Yoko. She refused to play by anyone's rules. Yes, there was the "avant-garde crap" that she perpetrated as art, but she was unlike any other woman he'd ever met, a real challenge to figure out. She *excited* him.

The whole idea of having a secret friend with limitless potential excited John. He believed he had finally met a woman who was not interested in his fame, a woman who insisted that her art and ideas were as important as his own. It was intense—not at all like a one-night stand with a dolly bird, not even sexual. "After Yoko and I met, I didn't realize I was in love with her," John recalled. The attraction was purely intellectual, purely creative, a powerful conflux of like-minded rebels. Their talk, in a series of clandestine nighttime calls, was charged with an electric intimacy that warranted something stronger, deeper, *more* intense.

The trouble was, he was married. And so, it turned out, was she.

[II]

In fact, Yoko had been married for almost half of her young life. She was born on February 18, 1933, into a spectacularly prosperous Japanese family descended from samurai that was as wealthy and influential as, say, the Rockefellers in the United States. Her father, Eisuke, a Christian financier proficient in English and French who headed an institution that would eventually merge with the Bank of Japan, moved his family to America on two separate occasions—once in 1936 and again in 1940, not all that long before the Japanese attack on Pearl Harbor. Those short tenures in the States provided Yoko with perhaps her most formative impressions; from a pampered and sheltered Long Island compound, she developed a fluency in

English and was profoundly influenced by American culture. But the experience was short-lived. World War II almost finished off the Onos. Eisuke was abruptly posted to the bank's satellite office in Japanese-occupied Hanoi, while Yoko, with her mother, brother, and baby sister, remained in Tokyo. Yoko attended the prestigious Gakushuin School, where she was tutored in all phases of Western culture until the escalating bombings eventually drove her family into the countryside, to a worn-out little farming village near Karuizawa, in the south.

It was a lonely and disorienting episode for such a proud, imperious family. The sense of isolation—of being cut off from their lifestyle—was overwhelming. From the moment they arrived, late in March 1945, there was open resentment toward their rarefied ways. They were treated like outsiders by their own people, taken advantage of and plundered. Yoko's mother, Isoko, was forced to sell her possessions for food and shelter. According to one biographer, things got so bad that "they actually went begging from door to door."

But except for those ten months in exile, where she lived among starving peasants, Yoko never suffered from privation. Throughout her childhood, she was raised in a bubble of sumptuous privilege, groomed by a team of servants for enlightenment and social status. Nothing was ever denied her; and after the war, there was no limit to the special treatment she received—ballet lessons, piano instruction, private tutoring, etiquette. Most overindulged Japanese girls raised in such a royal manner became, in the tightly regulated atmosphere of rebuilding, duty-bound to leisure, but Yoko Ono was not destined for anything so conventional. She had always been a curious young woman; now, as her curiosity became subject to maturity, it took on a more ambitious nature. Yoko returned to Gakushuin, concentrating in writing, poetry, and music, and in 1951 enrolled in Gakushuin University, where she intended to matriculate as the first female philosophy major. Ironically, her own mother planted the seeds of rebellion. "She used to tell me that even a woman could become a diplomat or prime minister if she was as bright as I," Yoko reflected in an interview with a Japanese journalist. "She also said that I should not be so foolish as to get married or that I should not be foolish enough to have children."

Rebellious to a fault, Yoko did both.

In 1952 Yoko's father was repatriated from Indonesia and rewarded with another American posting, this one more important and permanent than the previous sojourns. The Bank of Japan handed him its New York branch office, which was leading the way in underwriting the rebuilding of Tokyo. Soon after Eisuke's transfer, Yoko joined the family in America, resuming her studies in 1953 at Sarah Lawrence College, whose campus wasn't far from her home in suburban Scarsdale. There were no majors or grades given at the college, freeing its small body of creative students to express themselves independently. Yoko impressed teachers and classmates as being a "particularly adept" writer of short stories and shone with brilliance, it was said, in music theory. But neither felt right. "See, I was writing poetry and [doing] music and painting, and none of that satisfied me," she told *Rolling Stone* in a 1975 interview. "I knew that the medium was wrong. Whenever I wrote a poem, they said it was too long, it was like a short story; and a short story was like a poem. I felt that I was a misfit in every medium." She was looking for "an additional act," she said, something that allowed her to adequately express her art in a way that existed outside the box.

The answer lay only twenty-five miles away, in New York City. The postwar blinders had come off Manhattan's creative community, and the best minds of every discipline were mixing media as though they were martinis. Great concoctions burbled up from the imaginative wilds, and from this crucible lively scenes developed. The most attractive to Yoko Ono was the avant-garde. The avant-garde was like rocket fuel: you could go anywhere with it, even into outer space.

No shrinking violent, she took right off, staging her own events, or *pieces,* as she preferred to call them, in what would become a characteristically kooky way. Her debut piece, "Painting to Be Stepped On," instructed participants to lay a sheet of blank canvas on the ground and to walk on it; another—"Pea Piece"—involved dropping frozen peas at random places throughout the course of a day, like Hansel and Gretel. Her pieces became more outrageous—and annoyingly adolescent—as figures on the avant-garde scene began to take notice.

And notice they did, in cosmetic ways as well. During her freshman year at Sarah Lawrence, Yoko's clothes looked almost deliberately chosen to make her appear more Western, as if they'd been borrowed from an Asian version of *Blackboard Jungle.* By the time she hit Greenwich Village, however, Yoko had refined her look, giving herself a more severe, almost spooky twist: a baggy black sweater thrown over a black leotard, with her long black hair brushed out and frizzed below the waist. Tall women carried off the pose with sinuous grace. But Yoko, who was tiny and not particularly trim, looked like a character lifted out of one of Charles Addams's cartoons. Although her features were Oriental and her complexion a burnished gold, she was not an exotic woman, and this only added to the overall ethereal effect. Not that Yoko seemed to care one way or the other. If her appearance happened to put people off, she would fix them with either a blank stare or an enigmatic, Mona Lisa smile.

One admirer who caught the right impression of that smile was Toshi Ichiyanagi, a standout piano student at Juilliard—a true prodigy, in fact, whose entry into the avant-garde scene was primed by his progressive master, Vincent Persichetti, the man credited with grooming Philip Glass and Steve Reich. Toshi shared Yoko's passion for John Cage's experimental work, and together they launched themselves into the enthusiastic circle of artists and performers that revolved around the form. In the spring of 1956 she dropped out of Sarah Lawrence and moved into a cold-water flat in SoHo with Toshi, thus rerouting the direction of her life.

New York in the late 1950s and early 1960s was a breeding ground of young militants pursuing revolutionary visions of how modern music and art should be produced. John Cage and Arnold Schönberg had ushered in a fertile avant-garde scene that now included Judith Malina and Julian Beck, Andy Warhol, Robert Morris, Diane Wakoski, Paul Morrissey, and dozens of other artists (many later breaking away to launch the pop art movement), all of whom seemed to reflect one another's intensity.

In the thick of this creative ferment, Yoko encountered two men who would have a far greater effect on her life than her first two husbands combined: La Monte Young, the *enfant terrible extraordinaire* of conceptual art, a man of such enormous visionary talent that serious musicians still discuss his legendary performances the way chess masters dissect classic openings; and George Maciunas, an "eccentric's eccentric," whose uptown art gallery not only launched Yoko Ono but also Fluxus, the experimental movement of renegade artists devoted to demolishing artistic conventions by "promoting living art, anti-art" and what its manifesto referred to as a "non-art reality." Together and separately, they staged a series of events (known as "happenings") in New York lofts and walk-ups that stretched over many years and stood the underground art scene on its head. La Monte Young composed several-hour-long pieces whose entire score consisted of two notes for the cello, two droning notes that were supposed to create their own energy, while collaborators made chalk drawings on the floor around him. As Albert Goldman noted: "Long before Jimi Hendrix set light to his guitar, LaMonte Young ignited a violin on stage." Another piece called for the release of a handful of butterflies. Maciunas, on the other hand, was a card-carrying provocateur (although some preferred the term *con artist*). Nothing delighted him more than coaxing a wicked laugh from the viewer of some outrageous project or stunt perpetrated in the name of Fluxus: sacks filled with paper while a band played military marches, poems filled entirely with nonsense syllables, collages assembled from the detritus of local odd-lot shops.

For Yoko Ono, both mentors fulfilled the visions and images that had been caroming around her head. She took both men for lovers, separating from Toshi, who proved to be, in Yoko's words, "very kind" in regard to a string of affairs she engaged in throughout their marriage. It is difficult to know the extent of their understanding. Friends have referred to it as "an open marriage" or "partnership," but in any regard the arrangement had clearly run its course. In early 1961, after Toshi returned to Tokyo, Yoko devoted every waking moment to launching her career, pushing full steam ahead under the guidance of her mentors.

On November 24, 1961, Yoko staged her first uptown performance at the Carnegie Recital Hall, an intimate theater above the renowned concert house, which featured works in progress by artists who were either on their way up or on their way down. Yoko's "opera," as she billed it, was so strange and unexpected that it had the odd effect of confirming neither direction. One movement in particular caught the slender audience unawares. Entitled "A Grapefruit in the World of Park," it was performed in darkness as well as near silence so that listeners, as she explained afterward, "would start to feel the environment and tension and people's vibrations." At one point, two men tied together, with empty cans and bottles strewn around them, wriggled their way from one end of the stage to the other. "I wanted the sound of people perspiring in it, too, so I had all the dancers wear contact microphones, and the instructions were to bring out very heavy boxes and take them back across the stage, and while they were doing that, they were perspiring a little. There was one guy who was asthmatic, and it was fantastic." Mostly outraged concertgoers exiting the hall were overheard venting their indignation at the crazy experience.

There were other similar performances in New York, one more infuriating than the next, but audiences showed little interest in Yoko's work, the critics even less. Hardly any serious writers wasted ink on a review.

Frustrated by their reaction (or rather, lack thereof), she returned to Tokyo in 1963, where much of the avant-garde community had rallied around her husband, Toshi Ichiyanagi.

But there was no sign of encouragement and no one in Tokyo to inspire her. For months on end she languished in solitude, in a sterile eleventh-floor high-rise, contemplating suicide. Her intention was to escape, to loose the chains of boredom at any cost. On more than one occasion, Yoko's reckless gesture toward an open window forced Toshi to restrain her from plunging to her death. For reasons that are unclear, Yoko had unchecked access to a prescription for sleeping pills and the requisite overdose nearly delivered the coup de grâce. Yoko woke up in a sanitorium, where she was confined for several weeks. It was during this time that Yoko met Tony Cox, a small-time hustler with an art background, who rescued her from her depression and set out to make her a star.

In the course of their tempestuous romance, there was one remaining hitch: she still had not resolved the situation with Toshi. Further complications arose when Yoko discovered she was pregnant. This was not the first time; in the past, Yoko's form of birth control was abortion, of which there were many. "In New York I was always having abortions," she told *Esquire* in a 1970 article, "because I was too neurotic to take precautions." But Cox persuaded her to have the baby and to marry him. "Tony and the doctors frightened me into thinking that I could not safely have another abortion," she recalled. Some suspected that Yoko's pregnancy provided a safety net for Tony Cox, a solution to plaguing visa problems, which marriage and a child would resolve. "Tony got her pregnant to stay in Japan," a close friend insisted.

On August 3, 1963, Yoko gave birth to a girl they named Kyoko Chan. If having Kyoko was intended to bring stability to Yoko and Tony's relationship, it couldn't have been a more wrongheaded decision. The newlyweds were living in a minuscule one-room flat in Shibuya, a neighborhood of mostly artists, musicians, and writers, where a baby only intensified the couple's sense of isolation. How could one create and perform with a newborn infant demanding so much attention? It hadn't been much of a marriage to begin with, and before long, Yoko, an indifferent mother, could not cope. Instead, she buried herself in writing and performing new pieces, including the self-publication of *Grapefruit,* the book of whimsical poems she later gave John as a calling card.

Throughout the spring and summer of 1964, Yoko staged a series of events in Tokyo and Kyoto that traded on her cockamamie instructional scenarios. One, appropriately titled "Sweep Piece," was a four-hour performance during which the audience watched a janitor sweep out the entire theater, stroke by stroke. Another, "Touch Piece," lasting from dusk to dawn, instructed participants to do nothing more than touch their neighbors. Yoko's most provocative piece during this period, performed at the Sogetsu Art Center in Tokyo, was "Cut Piece," in which she appeared on stage in a fetching black dress and invited members of the audience, one by one, to approach and snip away at her clothing with a pair of large scissors. There was always some reluctance from people to participate in a potentially humiliating and grotesque to-do, but eventually one spectator would timidly volunteer—even if it was Tony, appearing as a shill—setting off a group reflex ultimately resulting in near nudity.

Proper recognition as a concept artist was still a long way off, but the Japanese audiences' volatile reaction convinced Yoko that she could not stay in Japan if she expected to attract serious attention. If there were to be additional acts to the Yoko Ono Show, she had to be ready to take it on the road. Yoko landed in New York alone in November 1964, without Tony and Kyoko, the first move in what was effectively a trial separation. Over the next six months Yoko launched an all-out assault, diving right into this mutant gene pool. She staged event after event through 1965, many under the guidance of Tony Cox, who had returned to her side and resumed his promotional crusade.

It was during this go-go period that Yoko performed the pivotal piece that would jump-start her career. In the corner of a gallery located in the Judson Memorial Church in lower Manhattan, where she lived with Kyoko, Yoko performed "Stone Piece," in which she crawled into a large cloth bag, either alone or with Cox, took off her clothes, and engaged in some form of sex. Other times, she would sit, solitary, for hours, moving occasionally, and then only slightly, to provoke the interest of passersby who gathered to watch. "Inside there might be a lot going on," she explained coyly. "Or maybe nothing's going on." Everything depended on the imagination. A critic from *Cue* called it "hypnotically dreamlike," which was only one of many ways the piece affected viewers.

While it didn't bring fame, as Yoko had hoped, something almost as attractive materialized from the Judson Church show: an invitation to participate in a symposium in London called "Destruction in Art," organized by movers and shakers in the avant-garde scene there. Thanks to Tony's resilient advance work, she arrived trailing a paper storm of frothy reviews, many of them written to order by her dutifully calculating husband.

Her performance at "Destruction in Art," on September 28, 1966, already a hotbed of expectation, caused a minor sensation. Appearing before a packed crowd of enthusiasts, Yoko performed both her "Cut" and "bag" pieces, finishing with a number in which she instructed the audience to shout out the first words that came to mind for a period of five minutes.

The London papers were nearly as enthusiastic as the boosters at the symposium, which saluted her pieces with prolonged worshipful applause. The art critic for the *Financial Times* called Yoko's performance "uplifting," and a reviewer for the *Daily Telegraph* called her performance an "elevated conclusion" to an otherwise "dreadful" symposium. Barry Miles, partner with Peter Asher and John Dunbar in the recently opened Indica Bookshop, had seen the performance that night and invited Yoko to showcase an exhibit entirely of her choosing in the basement gallery. The offer, as Miles presented it, was too good to pass up, and it paid off in spades when John Lennon walked in the door.

[III]

Yoko was drawn both to John and to the girth of his bankbook, which could endow her career. Many newcomers to her London entourage recall Yoko and Tony actively seeking a well-situated backer for their projects. "A Beatle," several remember, and according to a close friend: "She said, half-laughingly, 'I'd like to marry John Lennon.'"

John was genuinely intrigued by the odd combination of exoticism and absurdity that Yoko projected, but admitted being "intimidated" by her as well. The way she carried herself, as though nothing could derail her from her mission, was for John the most powerful turn-on. One of his strongest impressions from the start was not of Yoko's work, which he considered "far out," but of her loose, liberated manner, which made him realize she was "somebody that you could go and get pissed with, and to have exactly the same relationship as any mate in Liverpool." It "bowled me over," he acknowledged. He'd never known a woman so much like himself.

———

Apple was still in its critical infancy and required whatever part of John's attention he could muster. In January 1968 the Beatles opened offices at 95 Wigmore Street, an eight-story high-rise around the corner from EMI, and began staffing it with friends and cronies. The old Liverpool gang

(Derek Taylor referred to them as "the old courtiers")—Peter Brown, Geoffrey Ellis, Alistair Taylor, Terry Doran, and Tony Bramwell—were brought over from NEMS; Derek Taylor agreed to return as Apple's press officer; and Peter Asher, Jane's talented brother, launched an A&R department dedicated to recording new talent. John was also collaborating on a short play based on material from his two books, *In His Own Write* and *A Spaniard in the Works,* that no less an august temple than Britain's National Theatre planned to stage in June. And to top it off, before the Beatles left for India, they intended to squeeze in a session to record a new single.

The session, which began on February 3 and meandered over the next eight days, actually produced four sides, the most memorable being "Lady Madonna," which was earmarked from the start as the group's next—and final Parlophone—single. Paul had written it almost entirely himself, as "a tribute to women," he said, although his images of women collide and contradict one another faster than the chitter-chatter of a Greek chorus. Nevertheless, the song returned the Beatles to a more straightforward rock 'n roll structure than they had practiced in the past few years, "not outright rock," according to Paul (Ringo referred to it as "rockswing"), "but it's that kind of thing." The opening barrelhouse piano riff was lifted, Paul has since admitted, from Humphrey Lyttelton's "Bad Penny Blues," a minor hit released in 1956 and produced by none other than George Martin. The vocal, however, took its origins from a different source. "[The song] reminded me of Fats Domino," Paul explained, "so I started singing a Fats Domino impression. It took my voice to a very odd place." Odd, yet familiar to early rock 'n roll fans. Gone were the obliqueness and wearisome effects of the previous two albums. Gone, too, were the umpteen overdubs that made the Beatles' songs impossible to duplicate in concert. "Lady Madonna," for all its power, was basically recorded in a day—the old-fashioned way—with a chorus of saxophones added as an afterthought later in the week.

The "Lady Madonna" sessions included "Hey Bulldog," another pared-down rocker, as well as the music for "Across the Universe" and George's Indian-style spiritual, "The Inner Light." It was becoming increasingly clear that if the Beatles were to find their focus again, they had to play together, as opposed to piece together takes; they had to let 'er rip. For a while Paul endeavored to provide the necessary spark, but after eight days of cheerleading, the Beatles ran out of steam. "I think . . . we were all a bit exhausted, spiritually," he recalled. "We'd been the Beatles, which was marvelous . . . but I think generally there was a feeling of: 'Yeah, well, it's great to be famous, it's great to be rich—but what's it all for?'" The music was the glue that had held it all together, but the music, like their individual lives, was moving in every direction at once. "So we were inquiring into all sorts of various things . . . and after we thought about it all, we went out to Rishikesh."

The plan was to spend three months, from February 15 through April 25, 1968, in Rishikesh, Uttar Pradesh, India, to study Transcendental Meditation and self-realization at Maharishi Mahesh Yogi's ashram. The three wives—Cynthia, Pattie, and Maureen—would accompany the boys, as would Jane Asher, but as early as February, John schemed to have Yoko included in the entourage. "I was gonna take her," he said later in an interview with *Rolling Stone*. It seemed like a good idea at the time to have her around, a convenient way to get to know her better. Ultimately, however, he "lost [his] nerve, because I was going to take [Cynthia] and Yoko, and I didn't know how to work it."

The Maharishi's ashram was a new concept in the Hindu spiritual world. Throughout the region of Uttar Pradesh, wizened holy men, called *sadhus,* sought enlightenment from the Bhagavad Gita in a setting of utter, natural simplicity, strolling barefoot beside the sacred Ganges or meditating in half-lit solitary caves. There were no organized activities other than total commitment to their spiritual pursuit. But the Maharishi's retreat was unique: part temple, part commercial venture. Set within a fenced-in compound on a hillside overlooking the Ganges, the ashram resembled a Himalayan Club Med, with a central courtyard surrounded by six concrete lean-tos, called *puri* (Paul optimistically referred to them as "chalets"; Cynthia, "barracks"), where disciples redefined their place in the universe from a warren of tiny, unheated cells. There was a glass-walled dining area and a terraced lecture hall interconnected by gravel paths, a swimming pool, a heliport, even plans for an airfield, all at the nominal rate of $400 for the three-month stay.

It was the answer to the Beatles' prayers. "We were really getting away from everything," John recalled—the craziness, the drugs, the fame, the inexorable grind. On February 16, after weeks of shuffling an unusually concentrated workload, he and George, along with their wives and Pattie's sister Jenny, left the material world, crossed five time zones, and headed toward the plains in the dense valley between the Himalaya and Delhi. The overland journey from the airport—by taxi, Jeep, and donkey—covered 150 miles and took more than four hours. On a particularly forbidding stretch of road, the weary Beatles party looked out both sides of their car and saw only soft, treacherous cliffs, with no guardrail—and no conceivable access. It took them several minutes to realize that they'd have to continue on foot. "There [was] quite a heavy flow of water coming out of the Himalayas," George remembered, "and we had to cross the river by a big swing suspension bridge" outfitted with a hand-lettered sign warning NO CAMELS OR ELEPHANTS. The Beatles had visited India before—stopping to shop on their way back from the Philippines—but they'd never experienced it from this side of the tracks. A colony of lepers begged on the banks of the Ganges, as dusky-faced monks waded, naked, into the murky current. Sacred cows lazed on the riverbed, monkeys leaped from tree to tree. As one wide-eyed Westerner wrote: "It was a collision of magnificence and wretchedness."

Paul and Ringo followed three days later, along with Neil Aspinall, arriving at the Academy of Transcendental Meditation, where they joined their friends and sixty other students waiting to channel their full potential.

For the next ten days everyone wandered the six-acre retreat, spending long hours absorbed in quiet, thoughtful meditation and listening to the Maharishi's twice-daily instructional lectures, fine-tuning the spiritual fork. A powerful camaraderie developed among the reverent group. After a communal breakfast, they saw one another only occasionally during the day. Meditation, at the Maharishi's suggestion, should last for twelve-hour stretches, with short breaks, but once the Beatles got settled, the formula was markedly reversed, with twenty-minute segments of meditation aimed at breaking up the interplay. Instead, time was made for talking, reading, and lazing in the sun. The actress Mia Farrow, who had matriculated some weeks earlier, at the beginning of the term, recalled experiencing an initial regret at the boys' noisy presence, feeling that it disrupted the commune's focus. "Nevertheless," she later wrote in her 1997 memoir, "with their cheerful chatter and guitars and singing, the new arrivals brought an element of 'normalcy' to the ashram—a sort of contemporary reality, which at first seemed jarringly out of place."

That is not to say that the Beatles did not take TM seriously. George, of course, had been an instant convert, devoting long, intensely pensive hours to the contemplative process even before leaving England, but John, more than anyone, threw himself wholeheartedly into the practice. "I was meditating about eight hours a day," he recalled in a 1974 interview. Cynthia, who admitted being surprised by his discipline, said, "To John, nothing else mattered. He spent literally days in deep meditation." As for the ashram itself, she thought "John and George were [finally] in their element. They threw themselves totally into the Maharishi's teachings, were happy, relaxed and above all had found a peace of mind that had been denied them for so long." Even Ringo, whose tolerance for introspection was considerably lower than his mates', formed an impression that was more agreeable than expected. "It was pretty exciting," he recalled years later. "We were in a very spiritual place."

Only Paul viewed this new enthusiasm with characteristic rationality. "It was quite nice," he thought at the time, like "sitting in front of a nice coal fire that's just sort of glowing." Other times he would say, "It was almost magical." There were instances when Paul allowed the magic to take control of him, like during a midafternoon meditation when he felt "like a feather over a warm hot-air pipe" during which he was "suspended" in midair. But more and more, he had "trouble keeping [his] mind clear," he said, "because the minute you clear it, a thought comes in and says, 'What are we gonna do about our next record?'"

Paul couldn't let it rest, not even in India, not even during afternoon sunbathing with the others on the banks of the Ganges. There was always a guitar within reach, always a few sheets of paper nearby on which to scribble the outline of a lyric or a few nascent lines. Paul wrote like mad in Rishikesh—but truth be told, so did John. ("Regardless of what I was supposed to be doing, I did write some of my best songs while I was there," he recalled.) They threw themselves into their music and began meeting clandestinely in the afternoons in each other's rooms—occasionally with Donovan, who showed up unexpectedly, in pursuit of Pattie's sister—playing acoustic guitars and "having an illegal cigarette." In all, they completed nearly forty compositions; John wrote "Julia," "The Continuing Story of Bungalow Bill," "Mean Mr. Mustard," "Jealous Guy" (originally entitled "I'm Just a Child of Nature"), "Across the Universe," "Cry Baby Cry," "Polythene Pam," "Yer Blues," and "I'm So Tired," while Paul tackled "Rocky Raccoon," "Wild Honey Pie," "I Will," "Mother Nature's Son," and "Back in the U.S.S.R.," the latter an homage to his boyhood idol Chuck Berry.

Often in the evenings the Maharishi led his young followers on excursions to Dehra Dun, the nearest village. There, in a series of dilapidated tents where local tailors sat cross-legged on mats operating ancient sewing machines, the Beatles had outfits made—the loose-fitting, gauzy shirts and wide pajama bottoms, along with saris, that were traditional Indian garb—or shopped for souvenirs. They explored the open-air markets and came to rely on two or three local cafés, including Nagoli's, a restaurant that served perspiring beakers of "forbidden" wine. On one occasion, when a traveling cinema arrived in the village square, everyone trooped down from the meditation center along a dusty jungle path, swinging lanterns in the fading twilight. For some reason Paul had brought his guitar, and as they descended through the steep overgrowth, he serenaded the party with bits of a new song he'd been working on. *"Desmond has a barrow in the marketplace . . . ,"* he sang gaily over the thrash of footsteps. The piece focused on a Yoruba phrase that he'd picked up from Jimmy Scott, a conga player and familiar figure on the London club scene. "Every time we met," Paul recalled, "he'd say 'Ob la di ob la da, life goes on, bra,'" and the expression stuck in his head.

In India, songs came to the Beatles in the most mundane of ways. "Bungalow Bill" was written after two meditators, a middle-aged American woman and her teenage son, broke camp to go on safari—"to go shoot a few poor tigers," as John facetiously put it—then returned to their *puri,* adjacent to the Maharishi's, in order to commune with God. "Across the Universe" borrowed the expression of greeting that TM disciples exchanged when they encountered one another on one of the paths: *Jai Guru Dev,* or "long live Guru Dev," in tribute to the Maharishi's personal swami.

For most of the prolonged stay, Prudence Farrow, Mia's emotionally fragile younger sister, remained locked in her tiny room, meditating as if her life depended on it. She failed to appear for meals or even the nightly question-and-answer sessions with the Maharishi. "Prudence meditated and hibernated," Ringo recalled. "We saw her twice in the two weeks I was there. Everyone would be banging on the door: 'Are you still alive?'"

Eventually, her meditation grew deeper and more extreme. "She went completely mental," John recalled. "If she'd been in the West, they would have put her away." Being as it was the East, however, they sent in the Beatles. George and John had been selected as Prudence's "team buddies," a designation comparable to court jesters, appointed to rescue her from a near-catatonic state. "One night when I was meditating, George and John came into my room with their guitars, singing 'Ob la di ob la da,'" she told her sister, Mia, although it seems unlikely they'd play one of Paul's songs. "Another time John, Paul, and George came in singing 'Sgt. Pepper's Lonely Hearts Club Band,' the whole song!"

How Prudence responded to the gesture is not recorded, except that the boys "got her out of the house." And for John, the experience provided inspiration: using a finger-picking technique he learned from Donovan, the structure for "Dear Prudence" was in place before the night was out.

By now, between them, Paul and John had written enough good songs for two or three albums. "I came up with calling the next album *Umbrella*," Paul recalled, "an umbrella over the whole thing." *An umbrella!* That was all George had to hear. "We're not fucking here to do the next album," he snarled at Paul, "we're here to meditate!" But for Paul, the new repertoire emerging was already part of a masterful aural palette, the songs beginning to overlap and interweave. No doubt the body of an album was taking shape in his mind. He was satisfied with his own substantial output and thought several of John's—notably "Across the Universe" and "Bungalow Bill"—were among his partner's "great songs."

For Ringo, the urge to see his two children became overpowering, and after two weeks he and Maureen decided they'd had enough of the academy. Besides, Maureen had a phobia of the fist-size insects that taxied through their room, and Ringo, still tormented by childhood gastrointestinal problems, couldn't handle the spicy curries used to season the food. What was an intense emotional experience to most of the Maharishi's students was, from Ringo's outlook, "very much like a holiday." But like any good holiday, the time had come to bid it farewell.

Ringo's decision posed something of a public relations nightmare for the Maharishi. Since devoting themselves to his teachings, the Beatles had emerged as his unofficial ambassadors to the world; how would it look to the media, assembled outside the academy's gates, when Ringo walked out early, with his suitcases? Almost immediately after announcing his departure, Ringo came under intense pressure to reconsider. Perceptive to a fault, the Maharishi must have also sensed he was losing his grip on Paul McCartney and Jane Asher. In Peter Brown's estimation, "Paul and Jane were much too sophisticated for [the Maharishi's] mystical gibberish." Paul was obviously never as committed to TM in the way that John and George were, never one to expect "some huge spiritual lift-off."

After a month in Rishikesh, Paul was eyeing an exit strategy that had been in place before he'd left London, but he was concerned that George and John "might never come back."

"John took meditation very seriously," Cynthia recalled. His approach to it brought with it a remarkable transformation; he seemed happier, certainly healthier, now that drugs and hard liquor were out of the picture. But Cynthia was beginning to suspect the Maharishi's sweeping power over John: suspicion that there was some sort of mind control involved to wrest her husband away from his career. "He seemed very isolated and would spend days on end with the Maharishi, emerging bleary-eyed and not wanting to communicate with me or anyone. . . . He went so deeply within himself through meditation that he separated himself from everything."

It didn't occur to Cynthia at the time that John was struggling to separate himself from her. He'd moved into a separate bedroom, hardly exchanging a word with her, even in private moments. Knowing that John despised confrontations with her, Cynthia chose to ignore the bad vibes. "Something had gone very wrong between John and me," Cynthia concluded. "It was as if a brick wall had gone up between us."

It wasn't brick, but paper: a flurry of postcards sent by Yoko Ono were arriving in India almost every day. John rose early and stole away to collect them at the postal drop near the dining hall—another glaring sign because, as Cynthia well knew, John hardly ever got up early. But the postcards were like catnip; he couldn't resist getting the next one to see what kind of cosmic mischief Yoko had cooked up. "I'm a cloud," she scrawled on one, "watch for me in the sky." Others echoed her loopy instructional poems from *Grapefruit*. "I got so excited about her letters," John recalled, ". . . and from India, I'd started thinking of her as a woman, not just an intellectual woman." Yoko Ono, not the Maharishi, had taken control of John's mind.

Paul and Jane decamped on March 24, 1968, a month and a half ahead of schedule. John and George, convinced that enlightenment still lay within reach, pressed ahead in the next stages of their spiritual development on the path to perfection. Although deeply impressed with the strength and insight of the Maharishi's wisdom, John continued to struggle with his own demons. He had certainly tried—tried hard—but the thicket in his skull was too thick to clear. Feeling miserable, John longed for a playmate (George had grown annoyingly introspective), someone to help him blow off a little steam. There are various accounts of the way Magic Alex Mardas appeared in India. Some say John "missed his company" and sent for him. Others maintain Alex came on his own "because he didn't approve of the Beatles' meditating, and he wanted John back." No matter how he materialized or the real reason that he went, all agree that everything unraveled soon after Alex arrived.

Alex didn't share his benefactor's passion for the idyllic ashram. He was "appalled" by the accommodations and quickly pegged the Maharishi as a controlling, holy hoax. It didn't suit Alex's scheme that someone could have more influence over John than he did, and from the outset he looked for a way to regain the upper hand. Somehow, during the course of long walks through the woods, John revealed to Alex that the Beatles intended to tithe a huge chunk of their income to the guru's Swiss bank account. Shortly afterward Alex told the others that the Maharishi was, among other transgressions, *supposedly* having sex with one of his disciples, a young American nurse. The veracity of his claim has never been proved. In her memoir Mia Farrow intimates that the Maharishi *might have* come on to her, but then acknowledges she may have been disoriented and misinterpreted the "advance": it may have been nothing more than the traditional embrace given by a holy man after meditation. The Maharishi, she said, had never shown anything but consideration and respect toward his guests. Paul, upon hearing the charges, also said: "I think it was completely untrue." But George and John were crushed by the accusation. They'd put great faith in the Maharishi, given themselves over completely to his ministry. Faced with these circumstances, they were shaken—and angry. George was indignant. The Maharishi had become his spiritual mentor; thanks in no small part to his holiness, George had managed "to plug into the divine energy and raise [his] state of consciousness," evolving in ways even he'd never imagined were possible. Now this threw everything into a spin. George and John went back and forth all night, arguing heatedly: was it true, or not? Throughout their soul-searching, Alex continued to pour it on, tossing in excoriating details to inflame their doubt. There was really no way the beleaguered guru could defend himself in this situation. The more Alex talked, the more guilty—and despicable—the Maharishi seemed. Eventually George's faith buckled ever so slightly. "When George started thinking it might be true," John said, "I thought, 'Well, it must be true, because if George is doubting him, there must be something in it.'"

Finally, John and George made the decision to leave the ashram. It had to be immediately, Alex insisted; otherwise, the Maharishi might send down some "black magic" upon them. When they awoke early the next morning, cars were already waiting outside the compound gates. Alex had gone into Dehra Dun at the crack of dawn to hire several drivers to take the Beatles to Delhi. The last thing he wanted was for the Maharishi to have an opportunity to talk John and George into staying.

Jenny Boyd, who reluctantly left with her sister and brother-in-law, remembered seeing the Maharishi standing helplessly, looking small and quite forlorn, at the gates to the ashram, as they all filed past with their luggage. *"Wait,"* she recalled him pleading. *"Talk to me."*

It seemed pointless for them to hash out the accusations with the Maharishi. He would only deny them. And George was already feeling ashamed about the way they were leaving things. He already suspected they'd been set up by Alexis Mardas. (Though Peter Brown insists that some months later "John told me he knew for a fact that Maharishi had fucked that young girl.") *Why?* the Maharishi repeatedly implored. A wave of belligerence swept over John, who responded: "If you're so cosmically conscious, as you claim, then you should know why we're leaving."

With those words, the two remaining Beatles walked out of the ashram at Rishikesh—and out of the Maharishi Mahesh Yogi's life forever.

But John Lennon was not finished with the Maharishi. On the way back to Delhi, in a bruised little car that kept breaking down every few miles, he began work on a vengeful song titled "Maharishi." He sang it for George after a long stretch of downtime in which the car developed a flat tire and the driver disappeared, ostensibly to seek out a spare. It had a pungent, assertive melody that gave form to inexplicable feelings. *"Maharishi, what have you done . . ."* George understood where it came from but was appalled by the undisguised lyric. "You can't say that, it's ridiculous," he warned John. There was no reason why the Beatles should give the Maharishi a public flogging. It would ruin the man, George argued. It was completely inappropriate, nothing he wanted to be associated with. Instead, George proposed that John replace the Maharishi's name with Sexy Sadie. Disappointed at first, John tried rearranging the names and laughed at the absurdity. Sexy Sadie—it *was* pretty funny, he admitted; it would be their private joke. *"Sexy Sadie, what have you done . . ."*

Although John clearly intended the song to distract him from the sorry events of the past twenty-four hours, as well as the obvious marriage difficulties, his attention began to drift as they arrived at the Delhi airport. He was already brooding over issues that would have to be addressed once they got home. George had said his good-byes in the car; he and Pattie were headed south, to Madras, for two weeks, where he planned to make an appearance in a documentary film about Ravi Shankar. And now, without George's mediating influence, the tension between John and Cynthia filled the interminable silences.

By the time the plane took off for London, John could endure it no more. He began drinking scotch and Coke—his first hard liquor in several months. And the liquor loosened his tongue in ways not even he had foreseen. Confessions poured forth: John decided to reveal ten years' worth of infidelities, every squalid fuck he'd experienced on the road, including but not limited to intimate friends of theirs. Cynthia didn't want to hear about it; however, John insisted. "But you've got to bloody hear it, Cyn," he was reported to have said. Protests were useless. Nothing Cynthia said, no amount of tears, could staunch the flow of indiscretions. Joan Baez, Ida Holly, Maureen Cleave—John ticked off the names as if they were Beatles songs. No opportunity to inflict pain, no matter how insignificant, went unseized. Liverpool, Hamburg, London, America, Australia, Japan, France—he claimed to have screwed his way around the globe. Hundreds, *thousands*, of girls; he'd lost count a long time ago. It was a cruel, horrible way to put his wife on notice, but John, in his rage, saw no other way of doing it. Later Cynthia wrote: "I never dreamed that he had been unfaithful to me during our married life," but that denial is so much blather. Whatever the case, she undoubtedly understood the indiscreet confession: her marriage, as everyone else knew, was teetering on the edge of collapse. Still, she swallowed her outrage and continued to play the dutiful wife. As if to underscore his disaffection, two weeks after they returned home, John sent Cynthia on a fateful vacation to Greece.

[IV]

Readers who leafed through the London dailies on the morning of April 20, 1968, stopped paging as they came upon a peculiar-looking advertisement. It was so outlandish, so *un-British,* that it was impossible to ignore. Most people who saw it and read through the copy couldn't help but grin abstractedly as they realized who was behind the shenanigan. THIS MAN HAS TALENT, the banner read. Underneath it sat a bespectacled little busker in a pegged suit and bowler hat (Alistair Taylor, pressed into the role over strong objections) with a bass drum strapped to his back, a harmonica poised at his mouth, a litter of instruments, a reel-to-reel tape recorder, a washboard, and other musical paraphernalia scattered around his feet, bent over a guitar and singing into a microphone: a one-man band. "One day he sang his songs to a tape recorder (borrowed from a man next door)," the ad continued. "In his neatest handwriting he wrote an explanatory note (giving his name and address) and, remembering to enclose a picture of himself, sent the tape, letter, and photograph to *apple music,* 94 Baker Street, London, W.1. If you were thinking of doing the same thing yourself—do it now! **This man now owns a Bentley!**"

It had the Beatles' fingerprints all over it. Only two weeks after arriving back from India, they launched Apple with their customary fireworks, in a way that would demand instant worldwide attention. They had kicked around ideas for over a week, trying to decide how to best express the company's philosophy and make the proper splash at the same time. "We want to help people, but without doing it like a charity," explained Paul, whose brainstorm produced the ad. "We're in the happy position of not needing any more money, so for the first time the bosses aren't in it for a profit. If you come to me and say, 'I've had such-and-such a dream,' I'll say to you: 'Go away and do it.'" Apple would cut a check to underwrite the project, just like that.

This announcement touched off a gold rush. The promise of a blank check *and* the Beatles was too much for anyone to resist, whether they had talent or not. "Overnight, we were swamped with calls and kids who wandered in, demanding an audition," says Alistair Taylor. "Everyone tried to get through the door in the next couple of weeks." Worthy artists made their pitch—but so did schemers and crackpots. George, the resident skeptic, called it "madness" and was not too far off the mark. "By the time I came back [from India]," he recalled, "they'd opened the offices in Wigmore Street. I went in . . . and there were rooms full of lunatics, people throwing *I Ching* [John had hired a fortune-teller named Caleb who advised him on business matters based on the readings] and all kinds of hangers-on trying to get a gig." Through it all, the spirit of peace and love abounded—a spirit dedicated to the notion that what goes around comes around. Kids wearing loose-fitting flowered shirts and wide bell-bottoms, with strings of beads around their neck, were camped out, smoking dope and grooving on the vibes. It all seemed positively blissful, but their ultimate objective only betrayed the greed and sloth emblematic of the hippie movement. Everyone's heart was in the right place, George supposed, but "basically, it was chaos."

In fact, among the Beatles, Apple was anything but a collective affair. George, by choice, "had very little to do" with the company. "I hate it," he confided to Derek Taylor on his first day back from India. He'd considered it a "ridiculous" idea from the start and kept himself otherwise preoccupied, scoring a small independent film called *Wonderwall* and communing with the spiritual world. As for Ringo, business wasn't his forte. He was happy to be included in the creative sessions, but as for decision making, whatever the others wanted was fine by Rings. "Paul, for the longest time, *was* Apple," says Peter Brown. "It was his baby. He was coming in every day, and decisions were made by either Neil or me going to him and say-ing, 'Do you approve?' 'Yes.' Okay, it was done. Paul oversaw everything, from building the offices to designing the layouts." Technically, George and John were also directors of the company and, therefore, necessary to any major decisions, but Brown, as much as possible, avoided getting ei-ther one of them involved. "John wouldn't give me an answer," he says, "and George would give me a runaround."

For several months the structure established at Apple was the structure Paul devised. And for the most part, it was a pretty efficient and effective one. The company was run like Decca and EMI, but more relaxed and com-munal, which is how all record companies were run thereafter. Paul had the young staff hopping—one employee said that "he'd stay there all day and he'd go around checking on things, little weird things, like was there toilet paper in the bathrooms"—but feeling that they were an essential part of the show. Without John hanging over his shoulder, Paul had complete control.

Which only made things worse for John. By all accounts, John had hit an all-time low. "John was in a rage because God had forsaken him," George recalled. "Then he went and completely reversed himself. He turned from being positive to being totally negative." According to Pete Shotton, who was spending time with John at Weybridge, there was an overriding feel-ing of humiliation—from the Maharishi, from the Apple Boutique sham-bles, from his deteriorating marriage, from what he felt was his shrinking position in the Beatles. "He was more fucked up than I'd even seen him," Shotton remembers. "It seemed like everything was going to the dogs. He'd been desperately grasping [at] straws, as far as I was concerned, and there wasn't even a straw there." The nonstop drug-taking had left John hollowed-out. Stoned and cranky during his brief outings to the Apple of-fice, he growled at the inexperienced young staff, firing off obscenities at the most insignificant provocation. Otherwise, he just checked out. At a London party on April 18 for the launch of Bell Records, an independent pop label, John arrived already higher than a kite and drank so much champagne that he passed out at the table and had to be carried to his car.

Something had to give. It came as a welcome relief that John and Paul, along with Neil Aspinall, planned a quick trip to New York on May 11, where several press events had been scheduled to announce Apple Records in the States. Friends agreed that getting John away might do him a world of good; being alone, with just Paul to steady him, might have a calming in-fluence. But Paul was grappling with his own set of anxieties. "We wanted a grand launch," Paul said, "but I had a strange feeling and was very nervous." Drugs, he later admitted, may have been at the root of his problem; there was a lot of dope-smoking before takeoff and even during the transatlantic flight. But Jane Asher also helped spike Paul's mood. The grudging engagement between Beatle and actress had been ticklish at best. But since traveling together in India and a subsequent ten-day trip to Scotland, Jane's eccentricities rankled. Paul was having serious second thoughts about the relationship, which had reached a kind of critical, now-or-never stage.

Between John's attitude and Paul's paranoia, the Beatles were a PR nightmare. "It was a mad, bad week in New York," recalled Derek Taylor, who met the two Beatles there to chaperone a round of press conferences, followed by interviews. Taylor had fashioned himself into a debonair drug aficionado since the Beatles first dosed him at Brian Epstein's housewarming party, and now he and John gorged themselves on speed and a "mild and extremely benign hallucinogen" called Purple Holiday, courtesy of their New York chauffeur. The effect of it came through in the interviews. John was gallingly withdrawn and dismissive, Paul unusually distracted — which made them come off as two rich, snooty rock stars peddling another product.

Once two major press conferences and a television appearance were stumblingly completed, John and Paul headed to yet another press party. There the Beatles worked the room, performing their duties with élan. At one point Paul noticed a woman taking photographs of the crowd. In fact, he'd seen her earlier that afternoon, at the Americana function, where she'd also caught his eye. He remembered her from Brian's house, when she'd squatted at his feet and shot two rolls of close-ups, and the allure he experienced then hadn't abated.

"He said, 'We're leaving, give me your number,'" Linda Eastman recalled, "and I remember writing it on a check." By the time she got home that night, he'd already called. There was no time for a drink or an informal walk. He and John were leaving the next afternoon, which made the rest of their schedule airtight. Instead, he invited her to join them in a limo for the ride out to the airport. "There was something awfully steamy going on in that car," recalls Nat Weiss, another passenger to Kennedy, "a lot of heavy checking out, a lot of body heat. It was palpable; you could feel it." There had always been hordes of available women about, but this was the first time, according to Weiss, that he sensed something more than a quick hustle. "Paul's whole demeanor—that cocky defensive shield he wore like armor—melted away and, for a moment, he seemed fairly human."

Despite later claims that he "didn't think she was particularly attractive" and "[a] bit too tweedy," John couldn't have been surprised by Paul's interest in Linda Eastman. She was certainly his type—blond, "high-breasted and extremely attractive," a bit aloof—and she had a pedigree that impressed. He also knew Paul's relationship with Jane Asher was flagging. The irony of it couldn't have been lost on John that he and Paul—increasingly different in so many ways—were on the same timetable with regard to their changing relationships.

On the plane ride home, they talked about Ron Kass, a man they'd met in New York. Kass had been the top executive for Liberty Records in Europe, serving at the company's outpost in Switzerland, and he'd come highly recommended by people at Capitol. "He was a fairly hip person, and very sophisticated," recalls Peter Brown, "he'd been around. The key for us, however, was that he was an American who lived in Europe and understood the international complications of the music business." After Paul and John had given Kass the once-over, the decision was made to provide him with the tools necessary to launch Apple Records. Anyone who thought the Beatles would relinquish creative control to an outsider was, however, seriously mistaken. This very point was demonstrated immediately upon their return, when Paul dined with Twiggy Lawson, who urged him to check out the recent winner of the talent-discovery TV show, *Opportunity Knocks,* a seventeen-year-old chanteuse named Mary Hopkin. Paul tuned in the next week to watch the girl defend the title and was enchanted by her voice. Besides, he recalled, "she looked very pretty, young girl, blonde, long hair, so I thought, Okay. Quite right. We should sign her for Apple, maybe make an interesting record with her."

That was the way the process would work at Apple: see it, hear it, sign it. There would be none of the drawn-out, arduous auditions that had disappointed the Beatles in the early sixties, none of the nitsy policy battles with label functionaries and bean counters. Auditions were "a drag," as the boys saw them. Record executives—"a drag." Mazy contracts—"a serious drag." Expedience became the highest priority. In fact, no sooner had Peter Asher come on board at the end of May than he officially signed Apple's first outside artist, a lanky, twenty-year-old folkie named James Taylor. "He is an American song writer and singer who is extremely good," Asher explained with typical understatement, in a June 1 memo to Ron Kass. "We intend to start recording him 20th June. . . . He is ready to discuss contracts and things as soon as you are." An introduction, a recording date, contract discussions—that was Apple expedience in all its glory.

George, too, was busy with his own Apple project: recording an album with northern guitar swordsman Jackie Lomax, with whom he had developed an enthusiastic relationship. A lot of theorizing about music, about *playing*, went into their daily rehearsals, long unconscious jams exploring new interpretations and techniques. Paul, a prodigious innovator in his own right, might have satisfied George's hunger when it came to musicianship, but Paul had never given him the time of day; like an unfulfilling marriage, George had to get it from someone else. "It all came as a shock, with the freedom Apple brought, when the Beatles started playing with other musicians and finding out what other people did," recalls Tony Bramwell. "They had never played with anyone [outside of the other Beatles], they'd never jammed. When George prepared his Jackie Lomax record, he suddenly found himself playing with other musicians—and *loved* it. He discovered there was another world outside of the Beatles, and it eventually drove a wedge between the boys."

Not that by now animus or infighting would require a great deal of effort. Record production, movies, music publishing, clothing boutiques, electronics . . . "They could never agree on *anything*," Bramwell says. "Ego started becoming more important than success. John automatically blackballed any of Paul's suggestions, Paul killed George's, George rejected John's. I can't remember one decision that was unanimous or even near-unanimous." Even their forthcoming recording sessions for a new album, drawn from the "tons of songs" written in Rishikesh, produced fresh tensions, riven with indecision. Each of the Beatles' chief writers—John, Paul, and more recently George—lobbied fiercely for his personal efforts, extra-sensitive that one of the others' might upstage his individual contributions. "The Beatles were getting real tense with each other," said John, who pegged Paul and George as being "resentful" with regard to his songs.

The resentment might have been coming from a different place. With his marital problems still unsettled and Cynthia gallivanting around Greece, drugs continued to govern John's fitful moods. He dosed himself continuously with LSD, tweaking its random effect with any spare pills he happened to find lying around the house. In the right company, it plunged John into a deep, unfathomable trance that altered between indecipherable rambling and deadpan silences. At Weybridge, into which Pete Shotton had moved in order to keep his friend company, he stayed up nights, tripping and battling wave after wave of incendiary rage. One night, after the usual snack of hallucinogens, Shotton says he noticed John moving his arms around very slowly in a circle. "I said, 'What are you doing?'" recalls Pete, "but John couldn't explain it. He said, 'I can't stop. There's something making me do this. I can't help myself.'" Tears followed, uncontrollable rivers of tears, intermingled with hideous laughter. When Shotton tried to comfort him, John resisted. "I'm not crying," he insisted peevishly, wiping his eyes with the back of a hand. Suddenly John declared that he was Jesus Christ, back from the grave. "He was convinced of it," Pete recalls, "saying . . . 'This is it, *at last*—I know who I am.'" The next day the Messiah convened an emergency meeting at Apple to announce his identity to the other Beatles. Unimpressed, they said: "Yeah, all right then. What shall we do now?" After someone suggested lunch, the matter was dropped.

That night at Weybridge, in the middle of another drug-induced reverie, the TV flickered off, whereupon John, already chastened and in a self-abasing mood, asked Pete if it was okay if he invited a woman to the house. Shotton, who had no intention of staying up another night with his friend, was relieved. "Well, I think I'll call up Yoko," John said.

"Yoko Ono?" Shotton was dumbfounded. He'd seen her around, as something of a mysterious figure on the periphery of the Beatles' entourage, but never saw John raise so much as an eyebrow in her direction. "I didn't know that you fancied her. You never said anything about her."

"I don't know if I fancy her," John replied, "but there is something about her that I like."

Yoko arrived at Weybridge in a taxi sometime before midnight. Things got off to an embarrassingly slow start for two untimid, headstrong souls. "She and John were like two nervous birds," Shotton recalls. They sat in the dimly lit parlor, on the opposite end of a couch, hands folded awkwardly in their laps in the manner of suitors in an arranged marriage. Shotton, unable to make "heads or tails" of their clumsy conversation, excused himself and went to bed. Eventually, John led Yoko upstairs to his studio, where, amid stacks of record albums and toys, sat two reel-to-reel tape recorders on which he'd first sketched out many of the Beatles' hits. "I played her all the tapes that I'd made, all this far-out stuff, some comedy stuff, and some electronic music," John told *Rolling Stone* in 1970. It was such a crazy-quilt collection of material, much like a recorded journal of random thoughts strung together like mismatched beads. Some were leftover tape loops from *Sgt. Pepper's,* some based on Spike Milligan antics; a few dated back to the early Beatles era—those that had survived the aftermath of drug-induced tantrums. The flaky irregularity of it fascinated a conceptualist like Yoko, who slipped right into the spirit of the tapes. "She was suitably impressed," he recalled, "and then she said, 'Well, let's make one ourselves.'"

"We improvised for many hours," Yoko remembered. "He used the two tape recorders and put through them any sounds that came into his hands. . . . I sat down and did the voice." In high-pitched, almost painful wailing, Yoko contributed the kind of jarring vocals that reminded listeners of "the babel inside an insane asylum." They worked steadily through the night, improvising and overdubbing, but especially "enjoying the uncertainty of how it would all turn out." The free-form, impressionistic structure was exhilarating, the momentum a turn-on building all night to a certain feverish conclusion. "It was dawn when we finished," John recalled, "and then we made love at dawn. It was very beautiful."

During the early-morning reverie, John was overcome by the intensity of the whirlwind encounter. "I had no doubt I'd met The One," he recalled. "Yoko and I were on the same wavelength right from the start, right from that first night. That first night convinced me I'd have to end my marriage to Cyn."

John encountered Shotton in the kitchen early the next morning. Shotton says that John acted edgy and distant during a breakfast of hard-boiled eggs. It was clear that he was "shellshocked" by the inevitability of the night's events and the ultimate conclusion he'd reached. Shotton asked how things had gone with Yoko, and John "just looked at me with a dead, blank stare." Finally, John told him: "We've been up all night. Will you do us a favor, Pete? Will you find me a house?"

"You've already got a house," he told John. "You're sitting in it."

"No, I want another house. I want to go and live with Yoko."

"John, you've spent *one night* with her," he argued, "one fucking night!"

But John was not to be deterred. "Pete, this is what I've been waiting for. All. My. Life. I don't give a fuck about the Beatles. I don't give a fuck about the money. I don't give a fuck about the fame. I don't give a fuck about *anything*. I'm going to go and live with Yoko, even if it means living in a tent with her. I'm going—and I don't give a fuck.

"I have just fallen in love—probably for the first time in my life. I can't bear to be apart from her. In fact, I want to go back up [stairs] in case she has an accident—or escapes through the window." And with that, he turned and dashed from the room.

"John had been feeling dead inside for so long," recalls Shotton. "Now, at last, he saw the chance to be reborn."

And Yoko had acquired an additional act.

[I]

"The question they all ask is—have they gone off their heads?" That was the eye-popping headline above Don Short's long-awaited feature about the Beatles in a summer issue of *Melody Maker,* and not an unfair topic at that, considering the stories swirling around John, Paul, George, and Ringo. Opening a boutique and meditating with the Maharishi Mahesh Yogi had given the press and fans plenty to fret about. *Magical Mystery Tour* had provided the first signs of their fallibility. Now each new report out of Apple made the Beatles seem harebrained, if not mad. Except for George's coy reference to "a hectic recording scene," there was hardly any mention of plans for another album on par with *Sgt. Pepper's Lonely Hearts Club Band,* which remained a fixture in the charts a year after its release. No new Beatles film was slated for production, no concert in the works. "It seemed to many of us who followed their exploits that the Beatles had lost their focus," recalls Short.

An Apple press release announcing the May 23 opening of a second boutique caught even the most stalwart Beatles watchers by surprise. It was no secret to anyone that the original shop on Baker Street was a colossal bust. Peter Brown maintains that "the Beatles were embarrassed by the dreadful place." So, who in their right minds, one might ask, would repeat that mistake? To this day, no one seems to have an answer. The most that can be ascertained is that by now they did whatever they liked on impulse, regardless of the cost or consequences. In this case, the impulse was for brightly colored handmade suits that couldn't be had off the rack. Throughout 1967 and most of 1968, the Beatles and their entourage were VIP customers at John Crittle's ultrahip, eponymous tailor shop in New Kings Road. "We bought a few things from him," George recalled at the time, "and the next thing I knew, we owned the place!" Apple bankrolled

51 percent of Crittle's new line, took over his pricey lease, and transformed the shop into Apple Tailoring (Civil and Theatrical), which bore their imprimatur.

Owning another boutique, however, wasn't enough to contain the folly. Paul insisted they produce "de-mob" suits, a double-breasted pinstripe number modeled on the demobilization suits given to former soldiers after the war so that they could return to the workplace in appropriate attire. He was "absolutely fascinated" by the outfit and was convinced they would catch on, wearing them himself to help promote the line. But the public was hostile and appalled. So were John and George when the suits piled up in a basement storage room. John's attitude toward money was indifference, if not disdain—"I had to give it away or lose it," he liked to say—but his attitude toward *Paul's* money-losing schemes steamed his glasses. For him, it wasn't so much the money as it was Paul's "headtrip," his wholesale decision making, hogging the spotlight and calling the shots, while George chafed at the extraordinary waste of funds. It infuriated George that John and Paul "blew millions" of pounds on rubbish, income in which he and Ringo had a rightful share, and it served as a lesson, he said, to discourage anyone from contemplating a partnership.

Even as their accountants panicked at the indiscriminate outlays, the Beatles were shelling out generous advances to scores of strangers who had responded to Paul and John's invitation for an Apple grant. There was no effort whatsoever to cut back expenses, no attempt to conserve chunks of income that might provide them with a reasonable nest egg should the bubble finally burst. By the time any one of them raised an eyebrow, it was already too late. After they appeared on *The Tonight Show* in New York, "tens of thousands" of requests arrived daily begging for monetary support. "Suddenly Apple was a free-for-all," George recalled, with "every weirdo in the country"—in *many* countries—turning up in the Apple foyer, demanding an audition or the opportunity to present some screwy scheme. "Any numbskull could walk in and say, 'Hey, I've got a *great* idea,'" says Alistair Taylor, "and the Beatles would get out the checkbook. 'How much do you need?'"

Everyone came to Wigmore Street seeking a handout. And when Wigmore got too overrun with beggars and schemers, the Beatles simply bought a larger place, plunking down nearly $1.5 million for an eighteenth-century building on Savile Row, the former base of entertainment magnate Jack Hylton, to serve as headquarters for "the chaos."

"I remember going round there when we were thinking of buying it, and the basement was fantastic," recalled George. "There was a huge fire-place and oak beams. . . . We thought, 'This is great! We'll be down here writing and making records.'" In addition to their new record and film companies, their electronics division and merchandising, their sumptuous dining room and private offices, the Beatles saw the opportunity to build a state-of-the-art recording studio where Hylton's private screening room once operated. Why should they put up with the logjam at Abbey Road? Or its antiquated consoles? The seeds of discontent had already been sown. According to George Martin, "Magic Alex said that EMI was no good, and he could build a much better studio." Everyone, including Martin, agreed that the four-track system they'd used for *Sgt. Pepper's* was prehistoric. It was being updated to a bulky eight-track configuration, but Alex promised to deliver a whopping *seventy-two*. All it took, he said, was an infusion of the Beatles' funds.

With Alex at work on this latest knickknack, the Beatles pumped money into several other projects, beginning with Apple Films. No sooner had Denis O'Dell arrived to head the motion picture division than an am-bitious slate of films was announced for immediate production. The pace was furious for such a start-up. O'Dell, who had worked with Stanley Kubrick and Richard Lester, brought with him a Julio Cortázar short story called "The Jam," which John Barry was poised to adapt, then soon after hired Nicolas Roeg to direct a script called "Walkabout," set in Australia. Negotiations had also been completed for the purchase of another script, "Some Gorgeous Accident," based on a popular novel by James Kennaway. There were preliminary discussions about using the Beatles' own 16mm footage for a documentary feature about the Maharishi. And John was tin-kering with writing a screenplay based on his books, *A Spaniard in the Works* and *In His Own Write*.

A more immediate concern of Apple's new film division would be the upcoming full-length cartoon feature, *Yellow Submarine*. The Beatles had played virtually no part in its production, aside from contributing a mix of four original songs to the soundtrack. As far back as 1965 Brian Epstein had dealt away the rights to their animated images to an American pro-ducer backed by King Features, which put out a series of approximately sixty rather charming cartoons based on the Beatles and their songs. It seemed like a marginal matter at the time, a low-level licensing deal (while netting them a high-grade 50 percent of the profits), like other assets in the NEMS portfolio. But buried in the deal was Brian's promise for cooperation on a feature film, along with the Beatles' personal endorsement, which, seemingly negligible at the time, became more valuable as each month passed.

It didn't take King Features long to call in its chit. After seeing the results of the cartoon series, the producers submitted a succession of proposals for a snappy vehicle that combined the Beatles' droll personalities with "Fantasia-like" animation. They'd even hired Roger McGough, a Liverpool poet and bandmate of Mike McCartney's,* to contribute sly, Scouse-like dialogue and in-jokes. But for all the attempts at appeasing him, Brian had not been reassured. He knew the Beatles would hate the whole idea of a cartoon. "He dreaded going to them with it and asking for their involvement," recalls Tony Barrow, "and so, in typical fashion, he dodged the project for as long as was humanly possible, making himself and the Beatles unavailable."

In the meantime, the producers cobbled together a story based loosely on the Beatles' *Sgt. Pepper's* alter egos, laced with hip, karmic dialogue and acid-soaked imagery, and hired actors to imitate the boys' voices. The Beatles themselves were the most superfluous component. "We only had one or two meetings maximum with them," George recalled, "[B]asically there was very little involvement from us." The entire movie was completed with little or no awareness from the Beatles. Even the commitment to provide a soundtrack, which they decided to honor in deference to Brian, was regarded like an albatross. "Their reaction was: 'OK, we've got to supply them with these bloody songs, but we're not going to fall over backwards providing them,'" recalled George Martin. "'[W]e'll give them whatever we think is all right.'" And that is all they did, the bare minimum, ponying up "All Together Now," "Only a Northern Song," "It's All Too Much," and "Hey Bulldog," which, in the scheme of things, were basically throwaways. But now, with Brian dead and the movie out of their control, the Beatles still had to contend with the clatter surrounding its release.

Yellow Submarine had its premiere at the London Pavilion on July 17, 1968, with the fans' reception around Piccadilly Circus exploding into a scene reminiscent of Beatlemania. Thousands of people flooded the garishly lit esplanade, shrieking as the Beatles and their guests arrived in a whirlwind of old-fashioned excitement. With few exceptions, the critical reception was equally enthusiastic. The *Daily Telegraph* hailed the film as "brilliantly inventive" and urged audiences of all ages to give it a whirl,

---

* *They recorded for Parlophone as the Scaffold.*

seconded by the *Christian Science Monitor,* which praised its strong "visual imagination" and "romantic emotion." "The film packs more stimulation, sly art-references and pure joy into ninety minutes than a mile of exhibitions of op and pop and all the mod cons," rhapsodized the *Observer.* Even the Beatles had to admit it was loaded with charm. Ringo, who crooned the main theme, naturally "loved *Yellow Submarine,*" while George, normally the slowest of the four to warm to such a contrivance, flat-out "liked the film," and said, "I think it's a classic."

The strongest reaction to it came from the *Daily Mail.* Trudi Pacter, the paper's crackerjack entertainment columnist, reproached the Beatles for blowing so far off course. "The Beatles stubbornly continue to experiment," Pacter complained, which seemed the real focus of her displeasure. There was a commingling of too many new elements, too many deviations from the simple, happy formula that had amused the world for so long through the Beatles' clever wit and joyous songs. Every week, every *day,* seemed to bring a new announcement from the Beatles of another fabulous project outside of their traditional province. The fans needed to know that they weren't being patronized, they needed something familiar to grab onto, some validation of their faith. They needed to know that there was music in the mix.

[II]

On May 30 the Beatles met at George's house to discuss the next album. Unlike their previous launches, there was a surplus of material to choose from—the luxurious outpouring of songs written in India, as well as several that had been completed in the intervening months. For most of the afternoon they demo'ed the songs, spitting them out like table talk, almost impressionistically, on a reel-to-reel tape recorder. There were twenty-three in all—seven by Paul, eleven by John, and five by George—with others in the hopper, waiting to be reshaped.

Listening to them played back convinced the Beatles they had something powerful to build on. The songs were bolder and more emotional, though less self-conscious, than *Revolver* and *Sgt. Pepper's.* And yet, there was clearly something uneven in their collective tone, something that seemed to pit the songs *against* one another in rhythmic apposition, as if to keep the next phase of the recording process from turning into a rote exercise. "They have a different feel about them," John reflected in glorious understatement, perhaps mocking the jarring irregularity of the material.

The new repertoire, almost to a song, had lost its collaborative aspect. They were individual efforts—John's songs, Paul's songs, George's songs, written alone—and bore few of the familiar qualities that identified them as *Beatles* songs. That wasn't to say they were less accomplished or any less interesting; nor did it say they wouldn't record them as a group, with the same kind of interplay vital to other sessions. But it was a clear indication that each of the writers had evolved in different, aggressively distinctive ways; they were more confident about their work and, therefore, were less willing to compromise.

It also meant that the writing process would forgo the critical feedback—the suggestion of a phrase, a few bars, or a middle eight—that helped shape a Lennon-McCartney song in the past. One of the key ingredients unique to John and Paul's partnership was their reliance on and trust in each other to fine-tune, or, as John described it, "just finish off the tail ends" of each composition. Even with songs that were written almost entirely by one person, some last-minute advice would polish it to perfection. That give-and-take had been instrumental to their success from the very beginning. But now, as Paul pointed out, "it meant that I'd hear some of the songs for the first time when [John] came to the studio, whereas in the past we checked them with each other."

Even though he no longer depended on it, Paul regretted the loss of John's influence, blaming the intensifying emotional crisis in his partner's life for the breach. Over a few weeks in May John's affair with Yoko Ono had all but thrown his life into complete upheaval. After that first encounter John stumbled through the early days of summer in what he described as "my love cloud," admitting, when it came to Yoko, he'd "never known love like this before." It must have been as unnerving as it was exhilarating. He managed to fill those scattered weeks with mundane Apple business but became too distracted, too rocked by the constant clash of emotions. John later claimed that every time he was in Yoko's company "my head would go off like I was on an acid trip." One "sniff" of her potent mojo and he "was hooked," he said, mixing drugs and metaphors in equal measure. "She was the ultimate trip."

For John, the very heat of this relationship only underscored his disaffection for Cynthia. Finally, on the afternoon of May 22, a situation developed that would speed things toward the end. Cynthia decided to return from her vacation in Greece a day earlier than anticipated and, during a stopover in Rome, attempted to call John so that he would expect her. It did not faze her that no one answered at Kenwood; John could be any number of places, possibly asleep or possibly stoned. But when Cynthia arrived at the house about four in the afternoon, she was surprised to find the lights ablaze and the door open. That was odd, she thought. Someone should have been around to greet her—the housekeeper or the gardener—but the place seemed deserted and "eerily silent." With Jenny Boyd and Magic Alex trailing noisily behind, Cynthia wandered through the warren of neglected downstairs rooms, calling to John. Receiving no reply, she bounded into the sun-drenched breakfast room and stopped dead in the doorway. "John and Yoko, wearing nothing but matching purple dressing gowns, turned to look at me," she recalled.* Curled comfortably into a scarlet-cushioned settee, John didn't so much as bat an eye at his wife's unexpected appearance. He calmly put down a mug of tea, stubbed out a cigarette, and said, "Oh, hi."

Struggling to maintain her composure, Cynthia began to babble uncontrollably about the trip back to England. "I had this great idea," she rattled on. "We had breakfast in Greece, lunch in Rome, and Jenny and Alex thought it would be great if we all went out to dinner in London to carry on the whole holiday. Are you coming?"

John, staring expressionlessly at her, replied: "No, thanks."

Panic-stricken, Cynthia held her ground, holding out hope for a last-minute compromise, something that might at least temporarily salvage their marriage. She'd always been willing in the past to ignore his infidelities. It was the ultimate act of love. For John, however, there was no going back. Finally a line had been drawn. *"You bastard!"* Cynthia cried, and darted out of the room.

Cynthia spent the next few days "in complete shock," camped out at Jenny Boyd's flat. But one night in that desperate, wounded span, either out of anger or revenge, she slept with Magic Alex. "She knew it was a mistake the moment it happened," says Peter Brown, "especially with Alex, whom she'd never trusted, nor even liked." If Cynthia believed there was any chance of a reconciliation with John, this indiscretion ended it forever. Alex had John's ear, and Cynthia knew it.

Whatever her reasoning, Cynthia remained determined to see the

---

* In other accounts, she described them as a green-and-white-striped gown and black silk kimono.

marriage through. Convinced that John still needed her, she returned to Kenwood, mollified by his apparent denial that anything improper had occurred. "For a while, everything was wonderful," she recalled. "We could speak more openly and honestly with each other, and there really was a glimmer of light at the end of the tunnel."

But the tunnel was short, and the light soon faded. Within weeks their life together had disintegrated into a revolving state of solicitude and withdrawal, resignation and despondence. Following a stretch when John became disturbingly incommunicative, Cynthia packed once again, escaping on still another vacation to Pesaro, Italy, with her mother, Julian, and a favorite aunt and uncle. It was there, returning at dawn after an uninhibited night "on the town," that she encountered "a very agitated" Magic Alex, pacing along the sidewalk outside the Cruiser Hotel. Over breakfast, Alex confessed that he was there as John's emissary, to demand a divorce on grounds of adultery. Embarrassed but unfaltering, Alex admitted that he'd agreed to be named corespondent and to testify in any proceedings.

Cynthia may have been "absolutely devastated" by the slimy tactic, but she could not have been entirely unprepared for it. A few days earlier, while recuperating from a bout of tonsillitis, she'd opened an Italian newspaper to a picture of John and Yoko, arm in arm, attending the June 18 premiere of *In His Own Write* at London's Old Vic. "I knew when I saw the picture that that was *it*," Cynthia told Ray Coleman. John would never have taken Yoko public, she concluded, if he wasn't ready to file for divorce. He knew the press would pounce all over their appearance together — and he was obviously prepared for the consequences. But he wasn't prepared for the outcry.

John had been planning for some time to step out in public with Yoko. The groundwork for it had already been laid at the Apple Tailoring launch party on May 22, at which she was introduced as his date. "They were like two nervous lovebirds," says Alistair Taylor, recalling how Yoko clung coyly to John's arm that evening as they paraded through the shop, "but it upset those of us who had known Cynthia from the beginning." Most of the old Liverpool contingent avoided them out of embarrassment. If the other Beatles experienced any uneasiness with this development, they kept it to themselves; nothing, as far as it is known, was ever said about it for the record. What John did in his personal life, especially with other women, was John's business; none of the Beatles made those kind of judgments about one another. Only Derek Taylor, whose "loyalty to and affection for

Cynthia Lennon" were unconditional, had the courage to confront John about Yoko. A few days after the party, the two men had lunch at a Japanese restaurant in London, where Taylor, fearful of an imminent media backlash, was barely able to contain his outrage. *Do you have any idea what you are doing?* he wondered. "As your friend and press officer, it is my duty to inform you that despite *my* sealed lips anything you say will be taken down and blown up and broadcast to a waiting world. Not to mention Cyn, Julian, Mrs. Powell, and other loved ones." John warned Derek to mind his own business, indicating that from now on things were going to be different in his life. "So that *is* it—you and Yoko?" Taylor wondered. "Yes," John replied coolly. "That's it."

The turning point occurred a month later at the Old Vic, where the press was lying in ambush. "Word had circulated through the channels that John's marriage was over," recalls Don Short, "and everyone was waiting for the chance to uncover it. This was it." When John got out of his limo, clutching Yoko's tiny hand, flashbulbs lit up the sky and an indignant outcry erupted, the hostility of which caught him by surprise. *"Where's your wife? Where's Cynthia?"* reporters shouted over one another. A look of panic crossed John's face as he fought his way through the crowd. "Who is this?" they demanded. "What happened to your wife, John?"

"I don't know!" he blurted angrily, but it did nothing to staunch the controversy.

If the press and fans were predictably outraged by Yoko's appearance, public opinion was nothing compared with the difficulties it stirred at Apple. The Beatles were days away from beginning work on an important new album, and suddenly domestic issues, not music, had become the group's primary focus. Naturally, everyone's concern was for John's immediate welfare. He had become homeless in the ensuing uproar, having moved out of Kenwood in order to be with Yoko, and needed a place to crash. But where? Hotels were out of the question because of the swarming press. Ringo's old flat at Montagu Square, once the hideaway of Jimi Hendrix, was currently occupied by Cynthia's hostile mother. Brian's place in Chapel Street, as well as the country estate, had been sold. The prospects for a superstar were surprisingly small. Not surprisingly, Paul McCartney rushed in to provide John with instant refuge.

"Paul, in his usual way, tried to be the nice guy and was open-minded about John's weird choice," says Brown. "He invited them to stay at [his house in] Cavendish Avenue for a while." The day after Cynthia's return, they moved into the second-floor guest bedroom and made themselves at home. "But the problem was that Yoko wasn't a very warm person—not even able to say thank you in response to anything Paul did for them. And he went miles out of his way to make them feel welcome, being a nice guy. So that didn't last very long."

Feeling unwanted—and fed up with what they perceived as Paul's insincerity—John and Yoko moved into Peter Brown's flat, which was in the midst of being repainted, then stayed with Neil Aspinall for a week until they brokered a solution: Cynthia could remain in Kenwood for the time being, as long as she agreed to take her mother with her. John and Yoko wanted the basement flat in Montagu Square for themselves. The place was perfect—centrally located, with a nifty escape hatch (Ringo had installed a rear window over the kitchen sink, which led into an unseen alleyway), and dark. The latter condition, as it happened, was most essential to their needs: wearied by itinerancy and the accumulation of tension around them, John and Yoko had begun a chilling dependence on heroin.

Paul assumed that his hospitality would have a therapeutic effect on John and Yoko, that they would enjoy a carefree, homey stay and start off life together on the right romantic foot. Instead, they spent almost all their time at Cavendish camped out on his couch, watching television and staring vacantly into each other's eyes—activities, that, according to Barry Miles, made "Paul [feel] uncomfortable." Miles put much of the blame on "their drug use [which] made communication difficult," but attributed it to smoking weed and "eating hash cookies that Yoko baked."

Paul, however, knew different. "[John] was getting into harder drugs than we'd been into," he recalled, crediting it to a sinister liaison with the junkie art dealer Robert Fraser, who'd only recently gained his release from prison on a drug charge. It was Fraser, according to Paul, who introduced John to heroin before the Beatles left for India, and he'd begun sniffing it with Yoko soon after their return. The residual effects both troubled and "disappointed" Paul, as well as the other Beatles. Outwardly, the drug manifested itself, he said, in John's "adversity and . . . craziness," but the underlying influence had also crept insidiously into the songs.

It was evident right off the bat, when on May 30, 1968, the Beatles began work on the new album. The first song they tackled was John's indecisive but audacious, bluesy "Revolution," which kicked things off in tantalizingly chaotic fashion. Eventually, three versions of the song would find its way into release, but the foundation of this track set the tone for the contradictory rhetoric that followed.

"Revolution" may have sprung from the anger and disillusionment that fractured mainstream society in 1968, but it was written in the peaceful splendor of Rishikesh, which, as John later noted, wrapped a "'God will save us' feeling about it." In the days just preceding the recording, however, the news was full of the student rebellion and subsequent strikes in Paris. John put little faith in the outcome of student violence. His vision was utopian; he didn't believe in *overthrowing* governments; he wanted to *revitalize* them, to change the world peacefully by forcing blissful smiles onto the faces of bureaucrats and ideologues who wielded the power. The way to best serve that, said John, was through talk, through communication, by putting faith in the people. "I really thought that love would save us all." But Paris was on his mind as he entered the studio.

The Beatles recorded an initial eighteen takes of "Revolution" in a blistering ten-hour session that stretched from the afternoon of May 30 well into the night. In its original version, the song swung into a smoldering, bluesy groove that built gradually and coasted into a fade after about five minutes of upbeat jam. On the last take, however, the Beatles let it all hang out. There was more of an edge to John's performance, which signaled the rest of the group to stay alert. They knew the score: anytime a vocal turned hot, there was magic to be mined. And John sounded torrid. He hit all the phrases with particularly sly accents. As the arrangement drew to the usual close, John shifted gears and all hell broke loose, punctuated by fractured chords and strings of shrill violent feedback, with mournful screams riding up over the runaway passage. If the additional six-minute free-form jam was meant to convey the sound of revolution, as he said, it succeeded, thanks to the tumultuous explosion of sound. The squall picked up speed from its own momentum, and the Beatles tore forward for ten minutes, until John shouted: "OK, I've had enough!"

The first part, the blues, became known as "Revolution No. 1." (The rest of it was lopped off and used as the groundwork for what would become the inscrutable blockbuster, "Revolution No. 9.") Honest but conceptually clumsy, the song was never intended as a galvanizing anthem for the radical New Left. "He doesn't really get off the fence in it," Paul said much later. Clearly, John grappled with his position. The next day he took a pencil to it, trying to sharpen his central theme, rewriting the song right up until it was put on tape. Even then he appeared uncomfortable with the point of view. During rehearsals, a studio technician observed John struggling with the lyric—"hedging his bets," as Paul described it—tweaking crucial phrases each pass he made through the verse. "He seemed to be particularly focused on one specific line, testing it again and again with alternative endings." Perched atop a barstool, curled closely over his guitar, John sang, "When you talk about destruction / Don't you know that you can count me out," following it with ". . . you can count me in." Out . . . in . . . out . . . in . . . "I don't think he was sure which way he felt about it at the time," Paul recalled, and on the album version they covered all bases: singing "out" *and* "in."

Throughout each successive take, Yoko Ono sat "perversely" by John's side. "It was fairly shocking," recalls Alan Brown, a technical engineer who had begun working at Abbey Road only a few weeks earlier. Even though Brown was relatively new on the scene, he knew the golden rule: outsiders were prohibited from entering the studio when the Beatles were recording. The boys themselves never allowed visitors to watch them work. *Never!* Even Brian Epstein and Dick James had entered at their own risk and stayed only long enough to conduct some piece of vital business.

Now, suddenly, Yoko had landed in the thick of things. She "just moved in," according to George, who was not at all pleased. "John brought her into the control room . . . at the start of the 'White Album' sessions," said Geoff Emerick. "He quickly introduced her to everyone and that was it. She was always by his side after that."

Yoko's appearance in the studio functioned as a declaration of war. John knew the bombshell he'd drop by pulling such an aggressive stunt, and he seemed perfectly willing to light the fuse. The look on his face "dared the others" to say the wrong word. He almost longed for the opportunity to stage a showdown. Of course, at that very moment, someone should have stood up to him. Someone should have taken John aside and ordered him to get his act together. Someone should have demanded that Yoko leave the studio immediately. Someone should have laid down the law. Incredibly, however, no one did a thing. The other Beatles pretended that nothing unusual had occurred. Inside, they seethed and cut one another tense glances, furious at the intrusion but reluctant to confront John.

Why did they refuse to defend their sanctuary? Why did they shrink from such a petty schoolyard challenge? The Beatles, like everyone else, were caught in the undertow of John's addiction. They were shaken and terrorized by his volcanic mood swings. He had become more irrational, more hostile toward his mates, erupting unpredictably and without provocation in violent rages. He was always on edge. Of course, the more explosive John became, the more careful the Beatles were to avoid setting him off and the harder they had to stretch to look the other way. During a rehearsal at George's house, he swept a tape recorder off the table, sending their work scattering in every direction. Even Paul was unable to bring him under control with a well-placed comment. The emotional ups and downs were simply too difficult for them to fight.

As John waded deeper into the junk, his bond with Yoko strengthened. There wasn't anywhere he went that she didn't follow. If John entered the control room to speak with George Martin, Yoko accompanied him. If he huddled with Paul regarding a song or arrangement, Yoko joined the discussion. Whenever Neil arrived to review personal group business, Yoko sat among them. Studio grunts watched in amazement as she followed John into the bathroom.

What's more, she refused to remain a spectator. From the very first session of the new album, Yoko made it clear that she intended to *participate*, hijacking John's mike during the long "Revolution" jam and moaning or uttering some mumbo jumbo, like "you become naked." The other Beatles had good reason to be pissed off. To them, this behavior violated their unwritten pact. They had put up with John's hair-trigger tantrums, his drug "talk about fixes and monkeys," his increasingly strange and fragmented songs, and his hallucinations. But by allowing Yoko Ono to interrupt their session, he had crossed the line. "[The studio] was where *we* were together, and that's why we worked so well," Ringo explained. "We were all trying to be cool and not mention it, but inside we were all feeling it and talking in corners."

A sticky tension quickly developed in the studio. The Beatles barreled through forty hours of work on "Revolution," trying to overlook the intrusion, but Yoko made herself difficult to ignore. Wherever they turned, she was in their face. On "Revolution No. 9," which meandered on for days while John tinkered with sound effects, Paul remembered: "Yoko was there for the whole thing and she made decisions about which loops to use." She listened to playbacks and critiqued their work. She instructed George Martin to discard takes that everyone else thought were acceptable. Even while the Beatles recorded "Don't Pass Me By" and "Blackbird," John and Yoko remained locked away in Studio Two, experimenting with more loops for "Revolution No. 9."

"Blackbird" was built on a lilting passage from a Bach bourrée that George and Colin Manley had taught Paul at Liverpool Institute. "I bastardized it," he admits of his earnest recitation, "but it was the basis of how I wrote 'Blackbird,' the voicing of the notes . . . [with] the B string open and the bass G." Its placement on the record may have suggested a group decision, but the song was anything but an all-out Beatles effort. George and Ringo weren't even in the studio, having flown off to the States for a brief visit.

It was only a matter of time before tensions boiled over. Paul tiptoed around John and Yoko like a guarded diplomat, but he was clearly disgusted. Wanting nothing more than to work on the music, Paul spent half the time at EMI deferring to the couple's head games. Finally, the second week in June, he gave John a piece of his mind. Given their rivalry, the others must have been surprised that it took him so long. "I could hear them going at it in the hall," recalls an EMI employee who had stopped in his tracks, "and it was terrifying. Paul was positively *livid,* accusing John of being reckless, childish, sabotaging the group." But the more Paul fumed, it seemed, the less John responded. "It wasn't making the least bit of an impression."

John thought he did his best to appease the others, but his hostility was impossible to contain. He decided that by ignoring Yoko, they'd insulted her. It infuriated him that the Beatles refused to welcome her as they would any other musician. "She came in and she would expect to perform with them, like you would with any group," John argued. But when she tried to jam with them, "there would be a sort of coldness about it." That was putting it mildly! Referring to the deep freeze toward Yoko that followed, he later said, "Why should she take that kind of shit from those people?"

But Yoko only brought to the surface resentments that had been brewing among *those people* for the past year. John couldn't stand Paul's crowd-pleasing attitude, nor his insistence on doing things a certain way—*his* way. He was "fed up [with] being sideman for Paul." The type of music he wanted to play was being obliterated by the kind of "cop out" material Paul was churning out for the masses. And Paul, of course, was tired of dealing with a drug addict who was more interested in staring blankly at the television set than in making records.

Just when a showdown seemed inevitable, Paul left on a weeklong visit to the United States, where he planned to promote the Apple agenda at a Capitol Records sales conference. On June 21 he flew to Los Angeles with Ivan Vaughan and Tony Bramwell, while John and Yoko edited "Revolution No. 9" and launched the basic track for "Everybody's Got Something to Hide Except Me and My Monkey." It would not be the last time that maintaining peace necessitated separating John and Paul from each other by different continents.

[III]

In Los Angeles, Paul issued a proclamation that took EMI by surprise. "From now on," he told the stunned audience of adoring execs, "our records will be released on the Apple label." That was news to the Capitol crew, who regarded the Beatles as their star attraction. Convinced of the Beatles' Midas touch, the American label was eager to tap into the promising Apple pipeline.

With Apple at their disposal, assuring them of financial success, the Beatles decided they no longer needed anyone else. In June they had Ron Kass notify EMI that henceforth they would be releasing their own records and expected the company to handle distribution. Sir Joe Lockwood was more annoyed than opposed. Recognizing the Beatles' valuable association with EMI, he became a reluctant ally. He'd allow it for Europe, as long as the group's Capitol identity remained intact. The American label depended heavily on the Beatles' star power as a magnet to attract top talent, and EMI was not about to let them out of the Capitol contract without a fight. But Ron Kass held trump. "Finally, he just told EMI to forget it—that Apple intended to sign a distribution deal in America with another label, at which point they withdrew the demand and agreed to a worldwide arrangement."

In the age when any establishment intervention—"kneeling before the big men," as John put it—was viewed as an affront, the appearance of sticking it to the old ruling class was a satisfying one. Paul certainly felt vindicated after his Capitol address. Despite the sobering message, he was still embraced by the audience, who besieged him for autographs and pictures throughout the short visit. The personal triumph was no less gratifying. During the convention, he'd acted like a businessman, not a rock star. When pressed for facts and figures, he had the right responses. Ron Kass may have worked the crowd, presenting the image of a label head that everyone required, but it was Paul who discussed the intricacies of the deals and the Beatles' goals for Apple.

Paul celebrated by retiring to a bungalow in the Beverly Hills Hotel, where, according to a pointless account in *The Love You Make,* he spent the remainder of the weekend ping-ponging between rooms while servicing two young women. The details of his escapade aren't important, other than that it ended prematurely when a third woman appeared on the scene. Casually, very casually, Paul had invited Linda Eastman out to L.A. that week, promising nothing more than "I'm here if you show up." He didn't act surprised that she turned up as much as how cool and unfazed she was by the crazy scene. "The moment Linda arrived that was *it*, as far as other girls were concerned," says Tony Bramwell, who was barricaded in an adjoining room, enjoying his own randy frolic. "Paul was drawn to her in a completely relaxed way. It was a mood I'd never seen him in before."

"[I'd] always found Linda a very fascinating woman," Paul says now, upon reflection, but at the time, the vibe she gave off packed a powerful punch. She acted more "like a mate," he thought, which paralleled John's first take on Yoko. There was nothing coy about her, none of the wrestling that went on with the other "birds." Nor was she hung up about drugs, rock 'n roll, or even her career, unlike Jane Asher. What he liked best about Linda, Paul recalls, was her take-it-as-it-comes attitude toward life. "We both played the field. . . . We both had quite a few relationships." Linda appeared able to take the larking, to say nothing of his ego, in stride. When a very pretty TV star knocked on his hotel door to declare her undying love, Linda "seemed amused," rather than intimidated. It was a relief from the proprieties that Jane required.

Over the next day or two, Paul and Linda exchanged a wealth of personal information. "Her family was the most academic family on the planet," Paul says, impressed by the firepower of their diplomas. "Her dad, Lee, got a scholarship to Harvard . . . and her brother, John, went to Stanford." Even if Linda didn't attend Smith, as was traditional for the Eastman women, the University of Arizona sounded to Paul like "a very good school."

Their brief encounter was too short to seal the deal. Afterward, stopping at JFK to drop off Linda on his way back to London, Paul intimated they would be seeing more of each other. But he made no promises. Jane still loomed large in his life, if not in his heart. They'd gone through so much together, and she was a lovely girl. But the demands of her work were ceaseless and Paul viewed them ungratefully. Once again she had left on what seemed like an open-ended tour, "abandoning him" for much of the summer. There were plenty of distractions; Paul had never restrained himself when it came to meaningless affairs. But he was getting tired of meaningless and envied John and Ringo their children.

Julian, especially, had been on his mind. Paul "felt particularly sorry" for the boy, who was sandwiched between warring parents. Julian was "a fragile little kid" to begin with, wounded and insecure but touchingly luminous when Paul came to visit. How wonderful it would be, he thought, to give the boy's spirits a lift.

A week or two after returning, Paul decided to drive out to Kenwood to see Cynthia and Julian. This took some cheek—he wasn't certain how John would interpret the gesture—but he decided it was the decent thing to do. Cynthia had been cut off very quickly from the Beatles' family, a victim of what one insider called "the Law of the Husband." "I thought it was a bit much for [her and Julian] suddenly to be *personae non gratae* and out of my life," Paul recalled. Cynthia had been involved from the beginning, even before the Beatles odyssey, when he and Dot Rhone made up half of another fearless foursome. There was something heartbreakingly tragic about erasing her from the scene. Not waiting around for anyone's approval, Paul jumped in his Aston Martin and drove out to Weybridge to "try to cheer them up."

The route from Cavendish Avenue to Kenwood took about an hour in all, during which Paul passed the time singing, improvising a lyric to serve as "a hopeful message for Julian": "Hey Jools—don't make it bad, take a sad song and make it better . . ." His voice glided over the tune, a poignant, wavering melody that draws the listener below its gentle surface like a lullaby. Nothing in his recent repertoire was as openly tender and genuinely stirring.

Paul, being Paul, knew instantly he'd hit upon the pot of gold. The whole rainbow of magical musical elements had fallen right into place. Throughout his visit with Cynthia and Julian, the tune kept turning over in his head, and by the time he returned home he was ready to put on the finishing touches.

Paul tied the song up neatly in one sitting, changing Jools to Jude, after one of the characters in *Oklahoma!*, whose name had the right ring. In his enthusiasm, he rushed to play "Hey Jude" for John and Yoko, who had arrived upstairs in his music room as it all came together. The couple, stoned and sullen, were not so easily impressed, but John later acknowledged the song as "one of [Paul's] masterpieces." His account, however, differs as to what the lyric really means. "He said it was written about Julian, my child," John told *Playboy* in the days preceding his death, "[b]ut I always heard it as a song to me. If you think about it, Yoko's just come into the picture [and] . . . the words 'go out and get her'—subconsciously he was saying, Go ahead, leave me."

Of course, to paraphrase Freud, sometimes a lullaby is just a lullaby. Whatever the case, "Hey Jude" was thrust into the queue of great material still waiting to be recorded. Unlike with the songs written in India, the Beatles held it aside, knowing it was destined to be a single. In fact, they had been looking for the perfect two sides to single out before the album was finished. John was holding out for "Revolution," which he felt was more relevant for its political content and a statement the group needed to make. But "Revolution" had developed problems in the studio, and the group was still on the fence about making it the A-side.

"Hey Jude," on the other hand, sounded like an obvious choice. The Beatles began recording it on July 29, 1968, after receiving a last-minute polish by Paul and John. Instead of settling into Abbey Road, as was customary, they took it to Trident Studios, an independent, thoroughly modern eight-track facility in Soho, where George and Paul were simultaneously producing other Apple artists.

The scenery, however, was the only thing that changed. Paul's decision to instruct the other Beatles to play "Hey Jude" exactly how he wanted it to sound raised the resentments of the previous session to the boiling point. John clenched his teeth while George sizzled with anger. During the verses, George had answered every line by playing a riff mimicking Paul's vocal. As a flourish, it was tired and weakened by overkill, but instead of finessing a potentially delicate situation, Paul, in his bone-dry schoolmaster voice, snapped, "No, George . . . You come in on the second chorus maybe. . . ." He might have slapped George as well for all the hostility it created. Ron Richards, who observed countless Beatles sessions, notes that Paul was "oblivious to anyone else's feelings in the studio." He was determined to make the most exciting record possible, no matter what the emotional cost, "especially," Richards says, "when it came to his own songs."

John was better equipped to deal with Paul's business because of the impregnability of his own success, but for George it stung—and doubly so—from years of mistreatment and insecurity. He'd been spending mornings down the hall, producing "Sour Milk Sea," a single he'd written for Jackie Lomax, and even had the structure for a new song, "Something," pretty much down. And while it was no "Hey Jude," the Beatles only days earlier had finished laying down a demo of "While My Guitar Gently Weeps," which is as close to brilliance as George ever got. No, George had come a long way since that evening he played "Raunchy" on the upper level of a Liverpool bus, and he'd had about all the bullshit he was going to take from Paul McCartney—and he told him that, in not so many words.

This was becoming a familiar scene as the sessions for the album grew more complicated—and intense. Hardly a day went by when one of the Beatles—*or more*—wasn't at one of the other's throats. The pitch of antagonism in the studio ran about as high as a Yoko Ono vocal. Feelings were extremely raw and fragile owing to no small amount of outside stimuli. First and foremost there was Yoko's unspeakable presence to deal with, along with John's zombielike regard for her. No matter what they said over the years as a show of unity or to soothe injured feelings, Paul, George, and Ringo absolutely *hated* Yoko's intrusion. It went against everything they had decided as a group, and it grew worse with each passing day. Each time Yoko walked through the door, she felt more entitled to be there and to offer unwanted opinions about the quality of the music. And those opinions, rattled off in a flat, terse delivery, grated like fingernails on a chalkboard. They weren't intended to be constructive. A malevolent omnivore, Yoko lobbed critical bombs at the Beatles with an impudence that never lost its power to rankle. "Beatles do this . . ." "Beatles do that . . ." Every time she interrupted, it sent a chill through the studio that "made the other Beatles self-conscious and inhibited their musical spontaneity." It was hard for them to work with the hostility she put out. "There was a definite vibe," George recalled, "and that's what bothered me. It was a weird vibe."

Later, the recording process became even more splintered. "I remember having three studios operating at the same time," George recalled. "Paul was doing some overdubs in one. John was in another, and I was recording some horns . . . in a third." It was impossible to produce the songs the same way as before. "For the first time, I had to split myself three ways," George Martin said, "because at any one time we were recording in different studios." Instead of supervising the sessions, "looking after what both the engineer and the artist were doing" and maintaining "control over what the finished product sounded like," he merely bounced between rooms, trying to keep everything from dissolving into chaos.

With the focus running in such contrary directions, friction was inevitable. Tempers flared whenever one of the Beatles didn't get his way or disapproved of one of the other's favorite songs. Paul, especially, fumed over what he perceived to be John's obsession with "Revolution No. 9," a self-indulgent concoction that evoked his earlier home tapes, and was "dead set against putting such a mess on a Beatles album." Similarly, John made no secret that he always felt "hurt when Paul would knock something off without involving" the rest of the band. In an interview later on, he singled out "Why Don't We Do It in the Road" to make his point, saying, "[Paul] even recorded it by himself in another room." By the time John heard the song, it was already a finished track: "Him drumming, him playing the piano, him singing."

George was equally expressive, often repeating, almost verbatim, previous complaints. Publicly he would always deny envying John's and Paul's success, but he felt ignored by them, dismissed as a lightweight, relegated to sloppy seconds. His discontent burned hotter after the Beatles recorded "While My Guitar Gently Weeps," on August 16. They ran through fourteen takes in a dusk-to-dawn session, none of which had the right feel for George. Listening to the playback, it seemed that "there was such a lack of enthusiasm," that John and Paul were just going through the motions. "They weren't taking it seriously," he recalled, "and I don't think they were even playing on it," or, at least, playing up to speed. Even George Martin noticed how during George's song, "the others would join in, a little more reluctantly than they used to." It didn't seem fair, considering the classic it was destined to become. Couldn't they admit he'd written a "pretty good" song? What did he have to do to get their attention?

To his credit, George's form of rebellion was entirely creative.

Two weeks later, on his way to the studio from Sussex, scheduled to give the song another shot, he was explaining to Eric Clapton how something radical was needed to light a fire under the Beatles. "We were in George's car, driving in London," Clapton remembered, "and he said, 'Do you want to come and play on this record?'" It was an astonishing invitation. The Beatles had used plenty of session musicians on other albums, but no one capable of upstaging them, certainly never a rock 'n roll virtuoso on the level of Eric Clapton. Clapton hesitated, unsure of what to do. He knew the other Beatles "wouldn't like it," but George brushed aside his reservations. "It's nothing to do with them," he insisted. "It's my song, and I'd like you to play on it."

Before anyone had a chance to object, Clapton was already in Studio Two, strapping on his Les Paul guitar and listening to the rhythm track mixed down from their work on the sixteenth. The song was pretty much there, creating an effortless, affecting groove, but it lacked a dramatic device to liberate the emotional tension that is never far from George's caged expression. Clapton's poignant guitar riff provided everything it needed. The way it weeps and moans, held in check by Eric's incisive phrasing, creates the longing that gives the song its emotional center. George's vocal couldn't have been more enchanting as he squeezes the mournful lyric of all its desperation, until by the end, he seems to be just barely hanging on, just riding atop the surging guitar as it works to strangle his overlapping cries.

"I was recording not a band of four, but three fellows who had three accompanists each time," recalled George Martin. Martin was an artist in his own right, a diligent arranger and a perfectionist whose new job description, as babysitter to the Beatles, held no real attraction. There was no longer much "producing" involved, at least not in the traditional sense, nothing that offered any artistic challenge. Martin wasn't even enamored of the material they'd chosen to record, feeling the songs themselves needed a good pruning, "because some of them weren't great." Finally, he took his assistant, Chris Thomas, aside and said, "I'm going on holiday. You take over the Beatles for a little while."

If George Martin's departure was an admission of redundancy, Geoff Emerick's was an omen of darkness. The rising tide of tension among the Beatles had taken its toll on Emerick, a gentle, affable man who worked the sound board as diligently and precisely as a surgeon. Their sniping, however, had worn him down to a nub. The whole caustic opera, with new installments every day, was playing clearly through his headphones. And despite a stellar cast, it was no treat. They were "really arguing amongst themselves and swearing at each other," Emerick recalled. "The expletives were really flying." Besides, trying to keep up with them in any practical sense was exhausting. He'd no sooner adjust a level or balance before being summoned to another studio for some other task. There was no continuity to his work, no way to get a handle on the music.

Emerick's patience finally ran out during the recording of "Ob-La-Di, Ob-La-Da," which had turned into a technical nightmare, taking more than ten days to complete. Everything the Beatles played sounded too tight, too ungovernable. It seemed impossible to capture the playfulness of the lyric. As such, the arrangement collapsed into a mishmash of styles. Key signatures were changed routinely, effects were layered on—then removed. Paul continuously wiped the tape of his vocal to try another approach. None of the Beatles were happy with the song, and as their frustration mounted, so, too, did their tempers, erupting in blistering arguments that caused collateral damage. On July 15, during a remix of several takes, Emerick recalled, "Paul was re-recording the vocal again and George Martin made some remark about how he should be lilting into the half-beat," when Paul, building up a rage all afternoon long, snapped his head toward the booth and sneered: "Well, you come down and sing it."

Emerick was disgusted. He idolized George Martin and, like everyone else at Abbey Road, deferred to his level judgment with great, unflagging respect. Talking to him as Paul had done was unacceptable, even from one of the Beatles. The next day, while John was laying down the rhythm track for "Cry Baby Cry," Emerick leaned toward Martin and said, "Look, I've had enough. I want to leave. I don't want to know anymore."

Incidents like their in-fighting and Geoff Emerick's sudden exit signaled the most disheartening development of all: even in the midst of such creative accomplishment, the Beatles' rock-solid support structure was crumbling.

While in the studio, preoccupied with making music, the Beatles tended to block out the outside world; the process of grinding out an album, song by song, track by track, was intense enough. But with the cumulative buildup of tension and the cracks in their personal lives, it was all they could do to concentrate, leaving their business affairs largely in the hands of an inexperienced Apple staff. Without a strong manager at the helm, an enterprise that once ran smoothly now ran amok. There were no checks or balances imposed at Apple, nothing that answered the question, Who is in control?

The Savile Row office was nothing more than an asylum, with the inmates running the works. "None of us had any experience," recalls Alistair Taylor, "so we were basically making it up as we went along." For a while the company's destiny was determined solely by the way Caleb threw the *I Ching*. Eventually one of the Beatles came to his senses and sacked the Apple oracle, at which point everyone on staff just did as he or she pleased.

The offices were decorated indiscriminately and at extraordinary expense. Antiques, designer furniture, imported tapestries, chandeliers, state-of-the-art equipment and gadgets—all sorts of fabulous perks—were delivered at the whim of an employee. Two attractive young women with some Cordon Bleu training were hired as in-house chefs, with the larder stocked to rival a two-star French restaurant. "We invited people to Apple for business lunches," recalls Peter Brown, whose vast, well-appointed office doubled as the corporate dining room, thus necessitating his presence at every meal. Sumptuous four-course feasts would be laid out on his octagonal rosewood desk, accompanied by vintage wines unearthed from the company's private cellar. The liquor bill alone could endow a small university.

Derek Taylor accounted for half of that bill. Taylor had set himself up on the third floor of the town house in what was ostensibly the Apple Press Office. A born raconteur, wonderfully eccentric and with an irresistible, ingratiating demeanor, Derek welcomed any and all to his sanctum with effusive Cyrenaic hospitality. Since returning to London, he had undergone an extreme personality makeover that left his former colleagues scratching their heads. A suave, companionable gentleman had become the apostle of intemperance. Since being dosed by George Harrison, Derek had acquired a sweet tooth for drugs that knew no limits. Acid, hash, grass, peyote, cannabis resin, speed, cocaine—whatever he could get his hands on was devoured with rapacious glee. Not since Robert Fraser had London encountered a more epicurean figure.

The extent of the fun, however, was in the eye of the beholder. One day, the Beatles might revel in the debauchery—"John wouldn't rest until every last kid on the staff was happily stoned," according to Tony Bramwell; another day, they would explode over the misconduct of a squint-eyed secretary. One day, Paul would face the press to explain that Apple's benevolence extended far and wide, saying, "We really want to help people," while eight weeks later he'd exclude cripples who were "not necessarily having a hard time of it, and even if they were having a hard time of it—it's their hard time." One day, Paul ordered partitions to be erected to make the secretaries more productive; another day, George grabbed a hammer and "smashed down an entire eight-by-three-foot panel, showering Sylvia," a part-time secretary, "with plaster and wood and nails." One day, the Beatles "were a mother's dream," recalls Alistair Taylor, "stopping by everyone's desk, being fun-loving lads, and firing up spirits, in general"; another day, "they'd be at everyone's throats, creating fear and mistrust." Gone was the communal spirit that had sparked the original inspiration for Apple. Gone was the concept "to make business fun." In its place was the slow, steady buildup of pressures and creative tensions inherent in an earnest, but extremely hip, million-pound corporation.

The company was still riddled by "chaos," Paul acknowledged in an interview given later that summer, but he wrote it off to the cost of starting up a revolutionary new business venture that would ultimately give them total artistic freedom. All the missteps, all the expense and confusion, even the "foolish disregard," as Derek Taylor called it in an open letter to his bosses, could be attributed to their inexperience as businessmen, but he remained convinced, as did the other Beatles, that they'd "get it together" and succeed. "I mean, all that can happen is that we lose all our money, which I don't mind one bit," Paul explained, in a tone that strained for sincerity. Except that he did mind it—a *lot*. And so did John, George, and Ringo.

[IV]

On Saturday, July 27, the Beatles, along with Yoko Ono, met in the offices at Wigmore Street and decided they'd had enough; it was time to close the Apple Boutique.

But how could they do it and manage to save face? A big going-out-of-business sale? That was too tacky, they argued. It wasn't in the spirit of Apple's hippie manifesto. Besides, as George bluntly put it, they didn't want to be "mistaken for little Jewish businessmen, getting £5,000 out of closing down." To preserve the edge of philanthropy that was germane to Apple, a more radical scheme was plotted. According to John, "Yoko came up with the idea of giving all the Apple stuff away"*; however, others who attended the meeting insist it originated with John and Paul. No matter, everyone aside from Derek Taylor loved the idea. A giveaway! There was only about £10,000 worth of stuff left in the shop. That seemed like a small price to pay for what John considered such "a good happening."

Paul immediately sat down with Derek and fired off a press release explaining the closing. "Originally, the shops were intended to be something else," he admitted, "but they just became like all the boutiques in London. . . . Our main business is entertainment. . . . Apple is mainly concerned with fun, not frocks. . . . Well, the answer is that it was much funnier to give things away."

Once the decision was made, the course of action was clear. On Wednesday, July 30, the store would open punctually at 9:00 A.M. and everything inside would be free. But to be fair, the Beatles called first dibs on the leftover merchandise. "The night before, we all went in and took what we wanted," John recalled, having grabbed a few tasty T-shirts for himself off a lopsided rack. Paul claimed "a smashing raincoat," while Ringo and Maureen took "loads of shirts and jackets." "It was great," John gloated, "it was like robbing." In all, the boys proved to be pretty considerate, choosing only a handful of items they could use. It was Yoko, however, who scored the biggest haul.

"Yoko revealed a greedy side we hadn't seen," recalls Peter Brown, who watched from the sidelines throughout the giveaway. "The night before, without telling John, she came along in the Rolls and filled vast garbage bags full of the clothes before the sale—and before even the Beatles made their selections."

---

* In a subsequent Rolling Stone interview, he asks Yoko: "Was it my idea or yours?"

The official opening touched off, predictably, what one observer called a "semi-riot." "Hundreds of people" stampeded the shop, climbing over displays and one another's backs to grab anything they could get their hands on. "It reminded me of the running of the bulls at Pamplona," recalls Alistair Taylor, who stood off to the side, bristling at how the Beatles regarded the scene as "just a bloody giggle." The shop was an all-out disaster area. "Once the news got around," reported the *Daily Mail,* "hundreds [more] people flocked to the shop, not only teenagers, but middle-aged women and taxi drivers." Ringo remembered seeing "people . . . coming with wheelbarrows," although this was certainly an exaggeration. Nevertheless, "it brought out the worst in people," recalled Derek Taylor. "I thought it was one of the ugliest things I had ever heard of. . . . It was awful and vulgar."

Once Apple Retail* was dissolved, the Beatles could turn their attention back to music. There was much on the agenda besides the new album, which still needed tending to, the most noteworthy being Apple Records' first official release on August 16. The label itself was a hive of activity, with its dynamic staff—as well as the Beatles—assembling the makings of a diverse roster. Since April, Ron Kass and Peter Asher had worked hard, aggressively signing the kind of artists who would bring the label instant cachet. Asher, displaying an extremely talented ear that would sound out hits for the next several decades, had already produced James Taylor's debut single, "Carolina on My Mind," which warranted a full album treatment. Another promising single, "Maybe Tomorrow," by the Iveys—later to be renamed Badfinger—was in the can. George was far enough along in his session with Jackie Lomax to devote time to working on a single for soul favorite Doris Troy. It was all humming along with proficiency.

For the first official release, however, the Beatles had selected four singles—"Our First Four"—they earmarked to make the biggest splash. One in particular, on which Paul seemed to have struck gold, was his project with Welsh talent-discovery Mary Hopkin, "Those Were the Days." He'd been carrying the tune around in his head for several years, having heard an amateur cabaret act sing it on stage at the Blue Angel in Berkeley Square. It was a nostalgic tune of Russian Gypsy origin, far from the archetypical rock 'n roll formula, with a catchy, addictive melody that smacked of a crossover hit. The name of the act eluded him, but a call to the club led Paul to Gene Raskin, an American architect who had written the lyric with his wife, Francesca.

---

* Also referred to as Apple Merchandising.

Paul was a perfect fit for "Those Were the Days." It resonated with all the rinky-tink pub and music hall kitsch he'd flirted with for years, in songs such as "When I'm Sixty-four," "Your Mother Should Know," and, later, "Honey Pie." There was a corny familiarity about it, something that made it suitable for wedding parties, sandwiched between "That's Amore" and "Hava Nagila." Paul knew a hit when he heard one, and he knew exactly what to do with it. Convinced that it was a smash, Paul originally tried to persuade the Moody Blues to record it, without luck. Then in India he went to work on Donovan, who had nearly given it a whirl, but ultimately Hopkin got it.

The version Paul cut with Mary Hopkin would go on to sell 3 million copies in its first few months in release. Later that summer Paul produced a second single for Apple's "First Four," conducting the Black Dyke Mills Band, a famous northern brass ensemble, in the performance of a "jaunty martial" piece called "Thingumybob,"* which *NME* deemed "ideal material for half-time music at football marches." Once again Paul had the framework for it already worked out in his head. "I wanted a really different sound," he recalled, "so we went out[side] and played it on the street," giving the production a "lovely [effect], with very dead, trumpety-sounding coronets."

Even though "Thingumybob" wasn't an obvious pop hit, it brought a nice balance to Apple's roster. George contributed the Jackie Lomax single, "Sour Milk Sea," to flesh out the "First Four," but the showcase of the label's launch was strictly all Beatles. Despite the nicely conceived, eclectic mix of songs on the debut roster, neither Mary Hopkin, Jackie Lomax, nor the Black Dyke Mills Band could match the impact of "Hey Jude." Its melody is a gorgeous collage of genuinely stirring rhythmic passages woven around an inlay of heartwarming emotions: hope, optimism, faith, strength, encouragement, affection. The lyric is loaded with empathy, and Paul's soulful performance establishes a mood of haunting tenderness that swells at the top of each successive line.

As a three-minute song, "Hey Jude" is a tour de force. But while recording the song, something strange happened. Instead of cruising into the standard fade, as the last verse drew to an end, Paul locked onto the word *better* and, riding it up the register, launched a full-throttle chorale that transforms the buildup into an anthemlike extravaganza. Four minutes later, the Beatles are still going strong, with the vocals shrieking and

---

* *The theme from a British TV sitcom of the same name.*

leaping about to the accompaniment of a thirty-six-piece orchestra. "It wasn't intended to go on that long at the end," Paul recalled in a memoir, "but I was having such fun ad-libbing."

The feeling was contagious. "It felt good recording it," Ringo recalled. The Beatles took it into Trident Studios, where sessions with James Taylor, Jackie Lomax, and Mary Hopkin were ongoing, and a party spirit spilled into the icy atmosphere. "We put it down a couple of times—trying to get it right—and it just clicked." It was a dazzling, remarkable recording and, at seven minutes, eleven seconds, the longest pop single ever released. There were plenty of other songs that equaled "Hey Jude" in melody and inventiveness: "A Day in the Life," with its forceful, orchestrated turbulence embroidered around a commentary of modern-day despair—one of the incomparable highlights of the Beatles' career; the surrealistic "Strawberry Fields Forever" with its fathomless layers of riddles and wordplay; "Eleanor Rigby," tragic and lushly dramatic, with its elaborate string quartet sawing through the suds. But nothing was as ravishing or instantly accessible as "Hey Jude," and it enchanted listeners, who made it the largest-selling Beatles record of all time, with a reign of nine weeks at the top of the charts.

For Beatles fans everywhere, "Hey Jude" was further proof that the band was still in top form. Far from dwindling into caricature or esoterica, far from sounding tired or monotonous, they were pushing into exciting new dimensions, evolving but remaining accessible to their audience. But the fans wanted more—and soon. Too much time had passed between the ambrosial *Sgt. Pepper's* and a serious follow-up. Even George Martin, usually tight-lipped on such matters, expressed his impatience with the Beatles' progress, accusing them of taking "all the time in the world" when it came to the ongoing album sessions. They seemed unfocused to him, even undisciplined. Nor was there much cohesion. Paul recorded "Mother Nature's Son" one night after the other Beatles had gone home, not even bothering to run through it for John, as had always been the custom; George's "Not Guilty" was scrapped after more than a hundred futile takes; a discordant, impromptu number of John's (cowritten, he said, with Magic Alex, although more likely Yoko) called "What's the New Mary Jane" so offended Paul that he refused to play on it; George was absent when they recorded "I Will." There was none of the camaraderie or team spirit that contributed to their earlier successes. During the bleakest days, engineers and technicians found themselves abruptly dismissed, told to "go for a walk" or to "go have a cup of tea" while the Beatles attempted to resolve their differences.

Finally, on August 22, sensing that "the whole thing was going down," Ringo threw his hands up and walked out, effectively quitting the group. The in-fighting had finally gotten to him. Everywhere he turned, he encountered the same crude, belligerent exchanges. The ongoing party that had been the Beatles' recording sessions had turned cruel and forbidding. "I couldn't take it anymore," Ringo said upon reflection. "There was no magic, and the relationships were terrible." Ringo had known all along that he wasn't part of the Beatles' exalted brain trust, but he was upset, he said, about the way he'd been treated, ignored until the band was ready for him to play. He told the others that he "felt like an outsider." He felt unappreciated, "unloved and out of it." He had bottomed out.

Convinced that he wouldn't be missed, Ringo took his family to Sardinia for a vacation on Peter Sellers's yacht. The band tried carrying on without him, recording a blistering version of "Back in the U.S.S.R.," but it took all three of them to patch together a composite drum track that suffered from being too mannered. They sorely missed Ringo's "feel and soul," his intuitive fills, which established the beat and kept the rhythm in check. He never got much credit, but his drumming had become a kind of center of gravity for the songs, just as Ringo's droll deadpan helped anchor the band. From the beginning, he'd been the missing piece of the puzzle, and it didn't take long for the Beatles to appreciate his absence.

A week later a telegram arrived at Ringo's Mediterranean beach retreat, begging him to return to the studio. Needing no further invitation, he reached Abbey Road on September 9, in time to participate in an uproarious remake of "Helter Skelter," Paul's attempt at making "the most raucous . . . loudest," dirtiest-sounding track possible, which had originally run on for an epic twenty-seven minutes. The Beatles' goal was to pare down the cacophony to a sleek four minutes. In a studio crowded with perfectionists, it was not an easy task. They threw everything they had at the mikes to make the song "louder and dirtier"—distortion, feedback, echo, tape hiss, howls. John attempted to play the saxophone in a duet with Mal Evans, equally unproficient on the trumpet. Paul's savage vocal, with backup from John and George, kept the Vu meters redlined throughout the deafening onslaught. All the while, they kept pressing Ringo to "just beat the shit out of the drums, just kill them," as he windmilled his arms around the kit. According to an engineer on the scene, he "drummed as if his life depended on it." After a particularly ferocious eighteenth take, Ringo flung his sticks across the room and shouted: *"I've got blisters on my fingers!"* which provided the perfect ending to such an imperfect song.

The Beatles' goal, according to John, had always been to put out a double album. He, George, and Paul had written "so much material" in India that to do otherwise would have meant scrapping too many good songs. Besides, over the four months in the studio, they'd added to their already impressive new repertoire with "Glass Onion," "Birthday," "Savoy Truffle," "Martha My Dear," "Helter Skelter," "Cry Baby Cry," and "Happiness Is a Warm Gun." There were also various versions of "Revolution" being considered. But hardly anyone aside from symphony orchestras and opera companies had ever released a two-record set. It was too expensive for a label to produce that much original material, let alone to pay writers' royalties for so many songs. Bob Dylan had managed to pull it off on *Blonde on Blonde,* but he was a force to be reckoned with, an exception even to the exception.

In addition, George Martin had been dead set against a double album since the subject arose back in April. "I thought we should probably have made a very, very good single album, rather than a double," he later recalled. Ringo also thought a double album was extravagant, preferring its release as two single records, while George viewed the thirty-one songs as being "a bit heavy," the four sides "a mistake."

But this was said in hindsight, with the ring of the cash registers still echoing and nothing at stake. But in October 1968, after five months of hard work on the emotionally charged project, there was a consensus among the Beatles that the complete set was "definitely rocking," and they turned their attention to choosing a suitably rocking cover.

Like the records it contained, the breakthrough album cover was a masterpiece of Beatles ingenuity. Paul decided to revisit Robert Fraser, whose insight during the *Sgt. Pepper's* concept proved particularly instrumental. Fraser, he knew, represented Richard Hamilton, the motivating force behind the pop art movement and no slouch when it came to audacious design. It was Hamilton who proposed calling the album "something as utterly simple" as *The Beatles* and packaging it in a "prissy" all-white cover, with nothing more than an embossed title. Hamilton also contributed the idea of including a squared-off poster in the form of a collage containing family photos of each of the Beatles. As a last, unique touch, Hamilton persuaded them to stamp a number on each album to create the impression of a limited edition. The Beatles liked it so much that they forced EMI to retool its assembly line in order to print consecutive numbers on the covers.

The release of *The Beatles*—known forever afterward as the White Album—on November 22, 1968 (exactly five years after *With the Beatles* appeared), was regarded in most quarters as an international event, certainly "the most important musical event of the year," as the *Times* (London) expressed it in a column that morning. Except for the news that Yoko had miscarried the night before, nothing upstaged its long-awaited appearance. The rush to buy the new record was so great and unprecedented that EMI had considered rationing its initial shipment of 250,000 copies so that supplies would be spread evenly among retailers until more could be pressed. Not surprisingly, the entire run was sold out within hours of its release, with those lucky enough to snag a precious copy scouring Richard Hamilton's minimalist cover for clues, as if it might contain some hidden message in the absence of conventional design.

The press, most of which received copies early that morning by special messenger, responded with fitful delirium. "It isn't revolutionary and won't change the face of music, but . . . [i]t is beyond comparison," argued the *Record Mirror*'s ambivalent critic. "Skill and sophistication abound," declared *Newsweek*, "but so does a faltering sense of taste and purpose." Nik Cohn, writing in the *New York Times,* called *The Beatles* "boring beyond belief" and denounced "more than half the songs [as] profound mediocrities," while elsewhere in the newspaper's pages, Richard Goldstein, who had infamously blasted the beloved *Sgt. Pepper's,* hailed the White Album as "a major success," proclaiming it "so vast in its scope, so intimate in its details, and so skillful in its approach that even the flaws add to its flavor." There was such an extravagance of music on those four sides, so many sprawling themes and styles to sift through, so much energy and vigor in the grooves, that taken as a whole, the album stymied critics as to how it figured in the Beatles' canon. THE BRILLIANT, THE BAD, AND THE UGLY, headlined *NME,* whose editor, the usually rapturous Alan Smith, described "Revolution No. 9" as "a pretentious piece of old codswallop . . . a piece of idiot immaturity and a blotch on their own unquestioned talent as well as the album. For most of the rest," Smith concluded, "God Bless You, Beatles!"

Though the White Album was a somewhat controversial recording, it was nowhere as controversial as what was yet to come. Only one week later, on November 29, Apple released an experimental album by John and Yoko, a composite of their recorded hijinks that first blissful night at Kenwood, called *Unfinished Music No. 1: Two Virgins*. On the front and back covers John and Yoko posed stark naked. "It was a bombshell," recalls Tony Bramwell, who responded to John's request for help with the jacket photo. Bramwell had no idea what he was in for when he arrived at the Montagu Square flat on an afternoon in early November. "John intended to take the picture himself, but about all he could do with that camera was press the shutter. So I adjusted everything for him, worked out the lighting, showed him how to use the 'delayed action' feature, and then left."

For John, the shock value of these dramatic shots of him and Yoko au naturel seemed worth the uneasiness it produced and "the howl that went up." Nothing excited him as much as upsetting the status quo. He'd originally planned to issue the record as a solo vehicle for Yoko, accompanied by a nude shot of her on the cover "because," he said, "her work is naked, basically simple and childlike and truthful." But once they came up with the "two virgins" concept, he was determined to appear in it with her.

Their pose, arranged rather hastily by John, was a grainy, unglamourous image of them standing in front of an unmade platform bed, his arm draped protectively around Yoko's shoulders. There is nothing erotic about the picture; neither of their bodies is particularly attractive or appealing. There is no come-on in their slack, trancelike stares, nor anything to suggest a postcoital lassitude. "What we did purposely is not to have a pretty photograph, not to have it lighted so that we looked sexy or good," John insisted. "We used the straightest, most unflattering picture just to show that we were human."

For John, it was yet another shot aimed at an uptight establishment and a chance to instigate more flak among the other Beatles, who had seen more than enough of Yoko Ono, with or without clothes. He was still steamed over what he perceived as their open hostility toward Yoko, the way "they all sat there, with their wives, like a fucking jury, and judged [her]." Well, he'd take his revenge where he could get it.

Paul remembered John showing him the cover and being "slightly shocked" by the nudity, but Ringo, following his initial embarrassment, turned to John in exasperation and said, "Ah, come on, John. You're doing all this stuff and it may be cool for you, but you know we all have to answer . . . for it." How, he wondered, was this going to affect the Beatles' image as musicians? How were they supposed to explain it to the fans? And not just the cover photo, but the so-called music on the record. "Ringo and Paul hated every last note on that album," says Peter Brown, who admits doing his share to stall the project as long as he could. Mostly everyone agreed there wasn't a redeemable measure on it; it was "a collection of bizarre sounds and effects . . . neither surprising nor important musically," a complete put-on. The kids who bought it, thinking that somehow the Beatles were involved, were sure to feel ripped off.

No one other than John wanted to put it out, but he insisted. Referring to Apple's current lineup, he pointed to the others' pet projects—Paul with Mary Hopkin and the Black Dyke Mills Band, George with Jackie Lomax—as examples of the label's artistic freedom. They had even signed a classical artist, John Tavener. According to John, he had intended all along to produce an album with Yoko and demanded they accept *Two Virgins* as his contribution.

Sir Joseph Lockwood made EMI's position perfectly clear: the company would press the album but had no intention of distributing it (*Two Virgins* was eventually released in London on Track Records, and in the United States by Tetragrammaton). The weekly music magazines—*Disc, Melody Maker,* and *NME*—refused to run ads for it, citing the ages of their impressionable young readers. And the Beatles' accounting firm, Bryce Hammer, resigned in protest over the cover. But the antagonism that *Two Virgins* aroused gave new impetus to John's conviction that the Beatles had become passé and were, moreover, useless to him. As he saw it, the band was content to continue making more Beatles records, content to hone their image as the lovable lads from Liverpool, content to go on treating one another as if they were indispensable friends. And worse: just content. The "togetherness had gone. . . . [R]ound about *Sgt. Pepper's* it was wearing off," John recalled. "There was no longer any spark." As far as creativity was concerned, it seemed that they were headed in opposite directions. He had nothing left to give them. The collaboration with Paul was over, as was his marriage. The Beatles' music no longer intrigued him. Yoko offered John a way out, a way to liberate himself from the stagnation, as well as a radically different perspective. "I decided to leave the group when I decided that I could no longer get anything out of the Beatles. And here was someone who could turn me on to a million things." Yoko represented his ultimate rejection of the Beatles—a rejection that John had been entertaining for some time. With Yoko there to stimulate him, John said, "the boys became of no interest whatsoever, other than they were like old friends." From that moment on, he told Ray Coleman, "It was 'Goodbye to the boys in the band!'"

[I]

After six years' work, for the most part of which you have been at the very top of the music world, in which you have given pleasure to countless millions throughout every country where records are played, what have you got to show for it? . . . Your personal finances are a mess. Apple is a mess. . . ."

Thus began a five-page letter of resignation sent to each of the Beatles on October 23, 1968, by Stephen Maltz, their young and levelheaded in-house accountant. It was a nervy piece of criticism, a blistering indictment of their business practices, which he said had been carelessly conducted almost from the day Apple opened its doors. The company was "a debacle," Maltz avowed, a mosaic of disarray and incompetence. There was so much waste, so much unscrupulous recordkeeping, so much outright *stealing*, that it was a wonder there was anything left in the till for operating expenses.

Throughout the months that followed, troubling details about the Beatles' finances began to emerge. Because of payment cycles snafued by byzantine accounting procedures and slipshod deals, the Beatles had earned virtually nothing in 1968, a "pitiful £78,000." That would not even begin to cover their personal expenses, which had no restrictions. "The deal among the Beatles was: you just charged what you need," according to Peter Brown, who rubber-stamped their vouchers. "The boys used to get cash every week, as they needed it, plus their bills would just be paid for by the accountants, no questions asked." Meanwhile, everyone borrowed against a seemingly bottomless Apple loan account. "John was the biggest spender; he had no sense of money at all. Ringo was next: houses, cars, toys, presents for Maureen." Maltz tried repeatedly to warn them about the enormous tax bite that required ratepayers in the Beatles' bracket to earn almost £120,000 for every £10,000 they spent. What he didn't tell them was that the often disgraceful way they behaved made them a target for criminal investigation.

The final straw came a few days before Maltz's resignation, on October 18, when John and Yoko were busted for possession. It was a seedy, shameful affair at the Montagu Square flat, with a dozen police swarming in windows and doors to search for illegal drugs. John, who had been tipped off before the raid, thanks to a call from Don Short, scoured the place from top to bottom, "flushing handfuls of pills down the toilet," according to Pete Shotton, and madly "hoovering the carpets because Jimi Hendrix and Ringo had lived there." But John was no match for the dogs that sniffed out marijuana residue in a binocular case on the mantel and in a rolling machine stashed in the bathroom. The press had a field day, snapping roll after roll of photos as John and Yoko, looking nervous and disheveled, were marched outside to a paddy wagon idling at the curb.

If the bust signified anything, it demonstrated that the press and police had finally taken off the gloves. Until now, according to Ray Connolly, who was the *Evening Standard*'s pop columnist, the Beatles had been lionized by the press. "It was a measure of their popularity that no bad word was ever written about them in the daily papers," he says. "It was an unspoken contract. The press was rooting for them—and protecting them." Connolly included. He recalls visiting with John one afternoon at the Harrow Road Clinic, a few days before Yoko's miscarriage. "Suddenly, a character called Michael X turned up, a real bad guy [who was later hanged for his part in a murder]. He opened this huge suitcase and took out enough grass to turn on the entire city of Westminster. Now, I'm a member of the press. Do I ever mention it? No, nor would John expect me to. That was the deal at the time." And an exclusive deal, if contingencies were any indication. The Stones were routinely hounded by the press and police, as were other rock bands with a bad-boy image. "Never the Beatles. They were considered untouchable, by the police also. No one wanted to spoil the party."

But that phase of the party, it seemed, was over. John's outrageous public affair, Yoko's out-of-wedlock miscarriage, the scandalous *Two Virgins* cover, even the escapades with the Maharishi—for respectable fans, it was too much to accept. They could deal with John's outbursts, his rebellious nature, his opinions about the war. But with Yoko, apparently, he had crossed the line. No one knew better than John how grim the situation had become. Toward the end of the year, he told friends that everyone— the press, the police, even the fans—"were out to get" him. Convinced that the bust "was a frame-up," he worried that the authorities would relentlessly pursue him from now on, destroying his reverie with Yoko.

As the volatile year 1968 drew to a close, the prevailing mood among the Beatles was both melancholy and uncertain. The complexion of the band had changed, it was in upheaval. The boys' relationship to one another was being drastically realigned. Even their personal issues demanded a break with the past.

On November 8 John's divorce from Cynthia was finalized by the courts.* Earlier, in June, Paul ended his five-year relationship with Jane Asher in much the same fashion that John had dispatched his wife. That summer, with their engagement more or less in limbo, both Paul and Jane sensed that things were going nowhere. Like the Beatles, they'd changed and grown in opposite directions. Paul, especially, knew it had to end. But—how? Who would initiate the break? Ultimately, as was custom, Paul just forced her hand.

As soon as Jane went on tour with the Bristol Old Vic, it was virtually inevitable that he would find, if only temporarily, a replacement. Everyone at Apple detected the familiar symptoms. "When Paul got bored," says Peter Brown, "his dick got twitchy." It was dispiriting coming home from the studio each day to an empty house. He craved some kind of nurturing, some intimacy. In the meantime, Paul entertained himself with an American girl who'd arrived on Apple's doorstep seeking help to finance a screenplay and wound up, instead, with one of the Beatles. Through early June they were seen around town together, dining at restaurants or camped out at one of the clubs. "It wasn't anything serious," says Alistair Taylor, who heard enough of the office gossip to appreciate the situation, "just the usual distraction with a pretty bird." But when Jane arrived home unexpectedly and discovered Paul and the girl in bed together, that was the line in the sand. The relationship was "broken off, finished," as she described it on a popular TV chat show.

No sooner had Jane removed her things from Cavendish Avenue than Paul's interest in Linda began to heat up. In September, Paul invited her to London as the Beatles were putting the finishing touches on the White Album. Then, after the record had been delivered to EMI, they flew to New York together, where the courtship turned serious—and seriously fun. "I loved [it in] New York," he recalls, brimful with lasting memories of those weeks. "Linda had a cool little flat on Lexington and Eighty-

---

* Cynthia settled for £100,000 and custody of their son, Julian.

third . . . and we'd go around a lot." Unlike those surreal New York experiences during Beatlemania, when he was a prisoner in the Plaza and the Delmonico, they trolled the city streets unnoticed, whirling in and out of local galleries and clubs in an effort to take it all in. New York in October was even more magical than he'd remembered. For Paul, life began and ended on those city streets. Together, he and Linda explored every neighborhood, from Chinatown to Harlem, where Paul lingered in local record shops disguised in army-navy surplus and "a big beard, like Ratso out of *Midnight Cowboy*." In a way, it was the culmination of a dream. These were among the rare times when he was absolutely relaxed, in a place he considered the music capital of the world. "Linda eventually took me to the Apollo," Paul recalls. "We just went on our own, took a cab." It was one of those chaotic Wednesday-night talent free-for-alls with Billy Stewart headlining, and they rooted for a soulful little girl in a gray dress who lit up the jaded crowd.

One night, wandering through Chinatown, a feeling crept up on Paul without warning. "Linda was showing me around," he recalls, "and we passed a sign that said, 'Come in now and get a Buddhist wedding.'" He drew a breath and without giving it much thought said, "C'mon, Linda— what about it?" The traffic, the street sounds, the buzz of voices, her heartbeat—everything stopped. He was *serious*, she gathered. Paul McCartney was asking her to marry him, *right now*. He watched as she ran through a whole laundry list of emotions, grinned broadly, and said, "No, no! I *can't* do that."

Later, Paul insisted that he'd only been kidding, but she wasn't so sure of that. And neither was he.

In any case, something important had taken hold that week, something that opened a window onto the future. Paul had fallen deeply in love with Linda Eastman: "her womanliness"; her daughter, Heather (from a brief marriage); her extended family; her "slight rebelliousness"; her seemingly normal life—the whole package. She turned him on in so many ways. She was organized, but in a relaxed way, as opposed to Jane's more rigid manner. There was no pretense, none of the uncertainty. Everything just felt right.

One unusually cool and crisp October afternoon, after a serene stroll shopping on the Upper East Side, Paul suggested to Linda that she and Heather return to London with him—permanently. It was Linda's nature to be spontaneous, but even she had to admit this was fairly extreme. It meant packing up everything she had and moving from a comfortable home. She dreaded leaving New York. "It was great living how I lived [there]," she said, recalling how it felt less "restrained" in New York than in stately England. Her career was in New York, as well as her family, her friends.

By November 1, with their time together rapidly expiring, Linda decided with startling swiftness. She took Paul up on his offer and moved into his house on Cavendish Avenue. A month later the obstacles were ancient history. Prior to leaving for a weeklong holiday to Portugal, Linda discovered she was pregnant and felt "amused" that important decisions were being made naturally for them.

Finally, on a sunny, windswept beach in the Algarve, straining to be heard above the surf as it crashed against the rocky shore, Paul confirmed the rumors for a gathering of short-sleeved reporters that, indeed, he'd fallen in love with an American girl. What he did not tell them was that it was more than a run-of-the-mill rock 'n roll romance. In fact, they had already decided to get married.

The White Album sold faster than any of their previous records (in the United States alone, Capitol had shipped 3.5 million copies to record stores, which were still having trouble keeping it in stock). But as Maltz had warned the Beatles, Apple was draining their resources at a distressingly swift rate. There was nothing coming in from the company's dormant subdivisions: Apple Films, Apple Electronics, Apple Publishing, and Apple Merchandising. The record company struck early gold, but expenses far outpaced future profits. And as far as underwriting dreams went, not a single investment—and there were several hundred—produced so much as a bankable fantasy. "Apple wasn't being run," Ringo said, "it was being run into the ground."

It was time to take some aggressive, remedial measures. But with nerves from the White Album sessions still badly frayed, none of the Beatles felt like making plans for the future. They were exhausted by the constant bickering, by the demands on them to be productive, by having to justify themselves to the public. For the first time in memory, they couldn't even bear to spend Christmas together.

The hang-up, the Beatles agreed, had less to do with music than with their plunging business interests. It infuriated them that the people who worked for them, their loyal entourage—Peter Brown, Alistair Taylor, and Derek Taylor, among others—"were all just living and drinking and eating like fuckin' Rome." They were disgusted at the situation and at themselves for letting it degenerate into such an appalling mess. John remained convinced that Apple did not have to rake in vast profits to function as a viable enterprise, but, as he told *Disc and Music Echo,* "if it carries on like this, all of us will be broke in the next six months." By his calculations, Apple was costing the Beatles £18,000 or £20,000 a week. The company, he said, was sinking fast. "Somehow," he said, "[we] needed a firm hand to stop it."

John had already consulted the basset-hound-eyed, jowly, and irascible Lord Beeching, an old-school industrialist who had helped reorganize—some say wreck—Britain's ailing railway system, in the hope of bringing him on to streamline Apple's sagging fortunes. But Beeching's initial enthusiasm was short-lived after a few days spent examining the company's books. Offering only a few words of advice, Beeching warned John to "stick to music." The Beatles also, according to Peter Brown, courted a handful of unlikely merchant-banking heavyweights—John dismissed them collectively as "animals"—none of whom materialized as saviors.

Fortunately for the Beatles, Linda Eastman had the inside track on a more-than-suitable candidate. Her father, Lee, specialized in international copyright law and represented a slew of important music publishing catalogues, among other prestigious clients. With his son, John, he ran one of the glitziest entertainment law firms in New York, Eastman and Eastman, with the power and resources to stabilize the Beatles' affairs. The Eastmans had impeccable credentials and knew the industry front to back, extending into every area of the arts. Lee himself was a force to be reckoned with. Like his future son-in-law, he was an extraordinarily cagey man. He was fond of saying, "I'm just a country lawyer," to reassure those who just met him that he wasn't as slick as he appeared. "But you always knew the moment he entered a room that he was a tough character and in total control," says Peter Brown, "which underscored the fact that he had a brilliant legal mind."

Lee's mistake—and a critical one, as it turned out—was sending his son, John, to lay the groundwork. A recent NYU law school graduate, John dressed informally, in the everyday college uniform of light blue oxford shirt, chinos, and loafers, with a personality to match. "He was this nice-looking all-American kind of guy, very Kennedyesque," recalls Brown, "a preppy, chirpy person roughly about our age." What Eastman proposed was a series of simple guidelines: get rid of all the distractions—the side businesses, like electronics and film—and concentrate on building a music empire, for which they'd already shown great skill. He parroted his father's cardinal rule: do everything you can to control your copyrights and manage your own publishing company. Today, that philosophy is standard practice for most self-sufficient rock artists, but at the time it was fairly revolutionary and undertaken at considerable risk. It meant buying out Dick James and the Epstein family, which controlled Brian's share through NEMS. And while they were at it, Eastman advised them to buy NEMS as well, which collected the Beatles' record royalties from EMI, pocketing 25 percent off the top. Clive Epstein, desperately in need of cash to pay Brian's estate taxes and weary of the day-to-day headaches involved with NEMS' operation, had been dangling the company out to potential investors as a way of gauging its worth. He'd already been offered in the area of £800,000 from Triumph Investment Trust, one of London's preeminent merchant-banking firms. Eastman proposed the Beatles pay 1 million pounds for NEMS, which EMI agreed to lend them against future royalties.

The Beatles liked what they heard, and engaged John Eastman's services as their general counsel, giving him the green light to open negotiations on the propositions he outlined. John, however, remained leery. He didn't want to be coddled and cultivated by Joe College. And, truthfully, he suspected that the Eastmans would give Paul an unfair advantage over him. Nevertheless, John agreed to go along with the others, if only because he wasn't "presented with a real alternative." At the time, John Eastman was the only game in town. But that, too, was about to change.

[II]

Nothing defined the Beatles' discord as clearly as a business meeting among the four musicians that took place toward the end of 1968 in the conference room at Apple. On one side of the yacht-size rosewood table, George, Paul, and Ringo sat puffing impatiently on cigarettes. Across the way, facing them like legal adversaries, sat John and Yoko, characteristically smug and disapproving.

During the process of reviewing report after report of the company's blunders, Paul, attempting to stem the rising tempers, made an incredible suggestion.

"I think we should get back on the road," he said, "small band, go and do the clubs. Let's get back to square one and remember what we're all about."

There was an agonizing stretch of silence while everyone, shifting nervously in his chair, waited to hear John's response. He sat there impassively, glancing at Yoko, their heavily lidded eyes darting back and forth in some wordless exchange, until, at long last, he said: "I think you're daft. I wasn't going to tell you, but I'm breaking the group up. It feels good. It feels like a divorce."

This little firecracker hit the other Beatles with megaton force. They had weathered the strained feelings during the White Album sessions, although, admittedly, a vestige of resentment still lingered. They had survived the intrusion of Yoko and her destructive airs. It seemed as though they were on the right track when it came to cutting away Apple's soft spots. But breaking up the Beatles had never crossed their minds. Paul recalled: "Our jaws dropped. . . . No one quite knew what to say." They all had their differences, he insisted, but the Beatles were larger than any one of their individual gripes. They were a household name in every free country in the world. It was necessary for them to put aside personal issues. They owed it to one another to do what was best for the group.

Paul's cheerleading only made John more indignant. John didn't have a sentimental bone in his body when it came to the Beatles. Their financial interests were one thing, but nostalgia—nostalgia for "the good ol' days"—repulsed him. It was so typical of Paul to try to hold the group together, to organize projects, to paint rosy pictures, and to search for easy solutions, like magical mystery tours—or *playing clubs!*—to make their personal problems disappear. There was no way John wanted to be involved in any more Beatles escapades. The energy was gone, the magic, the motivation. He and Yoko had been all over this already. No, no, no—he wasn't interested anymore! The group was over as far as he was concerned.

They went back and forth like that for another hour, and eventually John backed down. He agreed to "give it a couple of months" so that they could work out some kind of strategy and to keep an open mind about the group in general. Everyone recognized how bound together they were by business interests. It was more crucial than ever that they remain unified financially and do something that improved their erratic cash flow. Again and again, Paul hammered away at doing some kind of concert—perhaps to air as a TV special. It would bring them instant income, as well as promote their records. Even though privately he had no intention of remaining one of the Beatles, John expressed a willingness, however grudgingly, to participate in such a performance. Part of it may have been a result of seeing Elvis Presley's recent "Singer Special," in which he appeared on TV with a stripped-down band, singing in front of a live audience. "The thing I miss most," John recalled later, "is just sitting down with a group and playing." He hated to admit it, but he'd rather enjoyed shooting a promotional film for "Hey Jude" on September 4, in which they'd played in front of a live audience at Twickenham Studios. If the others insisted, he'd go along with them.

George, however, "scoffed at" the idea of going back onstage. He'd had all he was going to take of the screaming and jelly babies. After Candlestick Park in 1966, that was it, as far as George was concerned. But Paul was adamant. He kept reminiscing about what a great live band the Beatles were. People had forgotten how hot their shows had been in Hamburg, how tight they were as musicians and as friends—and how much fun they'd had bashing about night after night. Beatlemania had killed that part of it for them. And yet, Paul believed they could recapture some of the earlier excitement by going back onstage. If they could no longer communicate as friends, then maybe they could do it as musicians. "I'd hoped that by playing like this in live performance," he said, ". . . everything would sort itself out."

By the end of 1968, he began circulating stories to the press that it was "virtually absolutely definite" that the Beatles would perform together again about Christmas. But come Christmas, plans to hold the concert were shelved until after the New Year. "It will definitely be free," Paul announced, "and we may now do the show in a television studio." But a television studio sounded so exclusive, too contrived. The thrill was gone.

Frantically, the Beatles scrambled to salvage the situation. To pull the show off at all, it would have to be even more spectacular than promised. Everything from the ridiculous to the sublime was proposed: a spontaneous appearance at a provincial pub, perhaps, or a rave-up in an exotic location. "I think the original idea was . . . to pick some songs, pick a location, and record [an] album of the songs in a concert," George recalled. Paul suggested they "go on an ocean liner and get away from the world," but that sounded too hoity-toity and rendered them inaccessible to fans. Michael Lindsay-Hogg, who had directed the "Hey Jude" clip, offered another possibility: a Roman amphitheater in Libya. This appealed to the Beatles' sense of grandeur and allure. They even envisioned a scenario in which a tribe of Bedouins arrive at the empty arena, followed by people of all nationalities who fill up the seats in a powerful display of brotherhood. But that, too, along with an outdoor extravaganza at the Hollywood Bowl in Los Angeles, was scotched by George as "being very expensive and insane."

The search for a proper venue was growing increasingly desperate. Banking on the fact that a suitable location would materialize, the Beatles began rehearsing at Twickenham Studios on January 2, 1969, with a film crew shooting enough candid footage in case they wanted to include it as part of a future television documentary. "The idea was that you'd see the Beatles rehearsing, jamming, getting their act together, and then finally performing somewhere in a big end-of-show concert," Paul recalled.

Whether out of haste or oversight, Twickenham proved a horrible decision. For one thing, it was too much of a hike for the Beatles and wedged them in a perpetual traffic nightmare around the London airport. For another, the soundstage in January was cold and damp; it was horribly impersonal, like "a big barn," according to Ringo. It wasn't conducive to making music—it didn't have the right feel. The climate inside the studio turned even frostier the moment they began running down songs. Paul, as usual, attempted to run the show, which angered the others, who began dragging their feet in response. "To be fair, no one had much enthusiasm for this idea," says an observer, "but Paul was determined to motivate them, which made him come off as controlling and bossy." For everyone concerned, it had disastrous consequences.

By the second week of rehearsals, tensions were at an all-time high. A "general disenchantment" had come to pass, no thanks to the circumstances and the two 16mm cameras buzzing like mosquitoes just near their heads. At the best of times, Ringo and George acted bored, but there were moments punctuated by outrage and contempt. Paul, despite considerable cajoling, could not get John to concentrate. Yoko was all over him, distracting him with kisses whenever possible or whispering in his ear. By John's own admission, he was "stoned all the time . . . on H" and "just didn't give a shit." After all, how could he get behind something that seemed so patently insincere? The music sucked; having not jammed in such a long time, the Beatles were rusty and out of sync. Their conversation was stilted. It disturbed him that they were "going to try and create something phony."

Once again, it was rapidly shaping up as a Paul McCartney project. He was directing the cameramen, choosing the songs, blocking the arrangements as if they were classical scores. He worked frantically trying to fire up enthusiasm. But the way he controlled every aspect didn't allow anyone else to contribute. "We put down a few tracks, but nobody was in[to] it at all," John said.

George, especially, found it "stifling." He had been growing frustrated and disillusioned with the interactions of the group for some time. As usual, the songs he'd written were being ignored. But nothing galled him more than his loss of creativity as a musician. George felt he absorbed more than the others what an insufferable dictator Paul had become, instructing him exactly what to play, as well as how and when to play it, indifferent to his or anyone else's input. John would simply tell Paul to fuck off, but so far George was not up to the task. "I had always let him have his own way," he recalled, "even when this meant that songs, which I had composed, were not being recorded." In fact, on the last few albums, he'd played as a relative sideman for Paul, a role he cited as being particularly "painful." He'd been promised that playing "live," so to speak, would eliminate such heavy-handedness. But by the second week of rehearsals, Paul was cracking the whip and George's patience had gone.

On January 10 there was a tense and hostile morning session during which Paul badgered George about how to play a simple guitar solo. George glared at him, lighting a cigarette in the interim while the anger and frustration building over the past ten days finally boiled to the surface. "Look, I'll play whatever you want me to play, or I won't play at all," he grunted between clenched teeth. "Whatever it is that'll please you, I'll do it!" Later, on the lunch break, the two Beatles squared off in the studio canteen. George had taken enough shit and refused to continue recording in the same manner. It was too degrading, too painful. Paul, as usual, dismissed his grievances as "petty." As their tempers rose, the movie cameras moved in for close-ups, right in their faces, filming the miserable confrontation as though part of a soap opera. "What am I doing here?" George wondered. All the niggling directions—play it slower, come in sooner, hit it harder— seemed suddenly unbearable. He fought the futility of it with rage. "I'm not doing this anymore. I'm out of here." He packed up his guitar, snapping the case shut with sharp, angry blows. "That's it," he said, struggling into his jacket and heading toward the door, "see you 'round the clubs."

When the recording session resumed that afternoon, sans George Harrison, the remaining three Beatles started to jam, a really violent, off-key bashing meant to take the edge off their frustration. The intensity of it was impossible to ignore. They pummeled and tore at their instruments as never before. Ferocious strains of feedback and distortion surged through the damp soundstage. "Our reaction was really, really interesting at the time," Ringo noted. How else could they process all that had happened? Was it realistic to expect them to produce meaningful music without George? Yoko didn't wait for an invitation to fill the void. She immediately laid claim to George's chair and blue cushion. Looking quite pleased with the ominous events, flashing a fierce, tenacious smile, she jumped into the smoky spotlight, clutching the mike with both hands and screeching into it like a wounded animal. Reflexively, the high-strung musicians turned up the heat. For the moment, the Beatles served as her chastened backup band. Some bystanders stared in disbelief. The others, especially Paul and Ringo, may have missed the implication of Yoko's grand triumph, but they understood her well enough to know that it had nothing to do with music.

George did not return at all that Friday, or the next day. Paul and Ringo expressed concern that he was calling it quits, whereas John suffered no such sympathy. "I think if George doesn't come back by Monday or Tuesday," he told Michael Lindsay-Hogg, "we'll ask Eric Clapton to play. Eric would be pleased. . . . [H]e'd have enough scope to play the guitar. The point is, George leaves and do we want to carry on the Beatles? I certainly do." When Lindsay-Hogg suggested they explain George's absence by saying he was sick, John only hardened his position. "If he leaves, he leaves, you know. . . . If he doesn't come back by Tuesday, we get Clapton. . . . We should go on as if nothing's happened."

On Sunday, January 12, all four Beatles met at Ringo's house to discuss the apparent impasse. It was essential, they all decided, to bury the hatchet. Halfway through their talk, however, negotiations broke down and George stomped out, slamming the door as he left. A few hours later he was in the car, heading to Liverpool for a visit.

At first, the rest of the Beatles tried to shrug it off as a passing emotional outburst, throwing themselves dutifully into another round of rehearsals. But by Tuesday, things had reached a critical stage. Paul, unsure of what they should do, dismissed the film crew "as a matter of policy." It was pointless for them to continue without George. In a heated five-hour meeting the next day, at the Savile Row offices, George laid down the terms for his return. If they wanted him to finish the record, they'd have to abandon all plans for a live concert and leave Twickenham. He had no intention of participating in either fiasco.

Without much choice, the other Beatles caved in to his demands. Logistics for the concert had become too much trouble anyway, and they agreed that Twickenham wasn't working out as expected. But they dreaded returning to Abbey Road. The punishing White Album sessions were too fresh in their mind. They'd felt like prisoners there during those contentious five months. A new record required new, upbeat surroundings, some place different, some place with no history of conflict, a fresh slate where the Beatles could concentrate on doing what they did best: making music. But where? Every studio in the city was booked through the spring.

The right studio—the only studio, in John's opinion—was their own, the one Magic Alex was building for them in the basement of Apple. Wasn't that, after all, what they had commissioned it for? Besides, it would be like working at home. They wouldn't have to travel; their staff was right upstairs; they could keep an eye on the business. The suggestion must have sounded like an ideal solution. Typically, no one questioned its feasibility. After talking it over with about as much detail as they'd give to, say, ordering dinner, the matter was settled. On January 20, with a week off to get everything in order, they would begin recording a new album in a place that not only felt like home but bore the family name: Apple Studios.

But Apple Studios, as it turned out, was nothing more than a name. Alex's seventy-two-track marvel was, in George's words, "the biggest disaster of all time." The place was a shambles, with all of Alex's wildest schemes woven into the loose, laid-back fabric of Apple's tapestry. Somehow, seventy-two tracks had dwindled down to a neat, sweet sixteen—twice the number available at Abbey Road—patched together by a dense thicket of wires that snaked across the floor. The accompanying speakers were nailed haphazardly to the walls. "We bought some huge computers from British Aerospace . . . and put them in my barn," recalled Ringo, ". . . but they never left that barn" and were eventually sold for scrap. According to George Martin's AIR studio manager, "the mixing console was made of bits of wood and an old oscilloscope. It looked like the control panel of a B-52 bomber." The building's ancient heating system, conveniently located in a closet next door, rumbled through the walls, no doubt to complement the "very nasty twitter" from the air-conditioning unit. There was no sound-proofing, and Alex had somehow forgotten to invent the invisible sonic screen that he promised would replace the trusty old studio baffles needed to prevent sound leakage into the mikes.

When George Martin arrived to inspect the facilities, he was stunned by the condition of the studios. "They were hopeless," he declared, traipsing from room to room as though inspecting a recent bomb site. "In fact, Magic Alex, for all his technical expertise, had forgotten to put any holes in the wall between the studio and control room," which made it impossible to run the necessary electrical cables for the recording equipment.

Despite Alex's epic failure, the Beatles seemed more determined than ever to utilize their own studio. "You'd better put some equipment in, then," they instructed Martin, who, always eager to indulge them, borrowed a pair of mobile four-track mixing consoles from EMI and installed them in Apple's basement.

The proposed album itself was another matter. For the purpose of focus and vitality, the Beatles decided to scrap the twenty-nine hours of tape recorded at Twickenham and start from scratch. Even with the benefit of the rehearsals, the Beatles were still experimenting with concepts, trying to hit on an interesting approach that would provide the necessary edge. This much they knew: it had to be stripped down and largely spontaneous to give the illusion of a live performance without terrorizing the band. And more than ever they endeavored to delve into their past to get the old magic back, the long-suppressed authentic sound of rock 'n roll. Emphasizing that point for George Martin, John warned rudely: "I don't want any of your production shit. We want this to be an honest album." Martin, who was offended by the implication, managed to hold his tongue. With no idea how to proceed—"I assumed *all* their albums had been honest," he quipped wryly—he merely asked John to describe their idea of an honest album and was told: "I don't want any editing. I don't want any overdubbing. It's got to be like it is. We just record the song and that's it."

Martin's role was tenuous enough without imposing more restrictions. Insecure about their future and eager to appear in control of it, the Beatles now sought to distance themselves from anyone tethered to the past. There was a growing suspicion among the four musicians that members of the old entourage were living off them, not only financially but creatively as well. This rap could hardly be applied to George Martin, who earned practically nothing from their records, nor sought to capitalize on their fame. But they feared that his ever-growing celebrity as their producer was creating a false impression about his contribution to their success. Recently John had grumbled to the press that Martin was more or less a cipher and argued against "all those rumors that he actually was the brains behind the Beatles." It also enraged him that Martin filled up the *Yellow Submarine* album with bland instrumental interludes—John dismissed them as "terrible shit"—that were composed for orchestra. And later he complained to *Rolling Stone* about people, "a bit like Martin, who think they made us." As a result, Paul invited überproducer Glyn Johns, who had worked with the Stones, the Who, the Kinks, and Traffic, to "assist" as a balance engineer during the new sessions, a maneuver that drove

Martin ignominiously to the sidelines. If he was stung or humiliated, Martin refused to let it show, although it is clear that he was absent for many of the sessions, either by necessity or by choice.

Recording began in earnest on January 22, 1969, and rolled on for nearly a week in a knockabout fashion. A series of bluesy, impromptu jams paced the daily sessions, with the Beatles running through a lineup of old Liverpool and Hamburg standbys that reverberated through the halls. They played "Save the Last Dance for Me," "Bye Bye Love," "Shake, Rattle and Roll," "Kansas City," "Blue Suede Shoes," "Miss Ann," "Lawdy Miss Clawdy," "You've Really Got a Hold on Me," "Tracks of My Tears," and "Not Fade Away," all of which received a thoroughly modern update. The interaction was far more animated than it had been earlier in the month. Part of the upbeat atmosphere could be attributed to the studio's feeling like an informal clubhouse. "The facilities at Apple were great," Ringo recalled. "It was so comfortable and it was ours, like home."

As the week progressed, their rising outlooks coalesced into an album. Paul and John both brought in a fair number of original songs that ignited the Beatles to play tighter and harder. "Get Back" was an obvious crowd-pleaser, a "kickass track," in Ringo's estimation, that presented itself as a shuffle but ultimately demolished the form with accented rhythmic jabs and reversals that charge the groove with irrepressible force. Paul had written most of the melody the week before, during breaks at Twickenham. The playfulness of it immediately attracted John's interest, and he collaborated on the words, seizing on the rising racial hostility in England between Pakistani immigrants and the National Front. Behind the good-timey boogie of licks and leaps lies a spikey little lyric as barbed as any of the Beatles' sharp asides. One line—"Don't dig no Pakistani taking all the people's jobs"—was deemed too hot, while an abandoned third verse, especially, caught the inflammatory mood:

Meanwhile back at home too many Pakistanis
Living in a council flat
Candidate Macmillan tell me what your plan is
Won't you tell me where it's at

It was a good piece of social parody, but Paul and John worried it would be misconstrued and used to paint the Beatles as racists. After 1970 most of John's songs, in particular, would bristle with topical references, but for now their artistic energies were directed elsewhere.

Another of Paul's contributions, the spare, engaging "Two of Us," set up another duet with John, and although it was a paean to Linda Eastman, the boys' perfectly balanced harmonies, with voices wrapped around each other like security blankets, established a disarming performance that recalls the synergy of earlier albums.

There seemed to be a renewed sense of teamwork in the friendlier setting. But as the week wore on, as competition revived and the stakes were raised, egos collided anew. Yoko's interference continued to make a bad situation worse. More than ever, according to George, she was putting out "negative vibes." Between the Beatles' takes, John withdrew further from the group fold, whispering in studio corners with Yoko, missing cues, often not showing up on time for a session and refusing to apologize for it. His mood vacillated wildly between the wittiness of previous occasions and the dark self-doubts fed and fueled by Yoko. Throughout the recording he was increasingly nervous and apprehensive. "It was a very tense period," Paul recalled. He attributed much of John's erratic behavior to heroin use "and all the accompanying paranoias." In vastly different interviews about the period, both Paul and George used the identical phrase to describe the situation, saying John was "out on a limb," dangling dangerously above the abyss, headed for a certain fall. "Don't Let Me Down," Paul believed, was "a genuine plea . . . a genuine cry for help." (In fact, John said, "That's me singing about Yoko.") With his painfully thin frame, gaunt face, stringy, unkempt hair, and bloodshot eyes, John looked demonic, like a zombie had claimed his tormented soul. He needed help—just not from the Beatles; he wouldn't accept their assistance, it was out of the question. "I don't think he wanted much to be hanging out with us," George explained, "and I think Yoko was pushing him out of the band."

Of that, there seems little doubt. For someone who desired more interaction with the Beatles, Yoko acted resentful, even scornful toward them. She found the band to be "very childish." As different as it seemed to mainstream ears, to her there was nothing daring about it, and she hooked right into John's own lingering doubts about his creative powers and self-fulfillment.

For months he'd been questioning the limits of his potential, wondering how much he'd sacrificed by blending into a group. Though John continued to participate in group decisions and record with the Beatles, their sound was something he "didn't believe in" anymore. He was just going through the motions, "just [doing] it like a job," he explained. Musically, he was "fed up with the same old shit." He felt constrained by the simplicity and limited format of the pop song. Somehow, he'd abandoned the element of risk. Yoko may not have been much of a musician, but she had the scene down cold and knew what to say in order to discredit it in his eyes. She told John exactly what he wanted to hear: that he was a genius, "better than Picasso"; the others were "insecure"; they weren't "sophisticated, intellectually"; they were dead, artistically; they were holding him back. What, she wanted to know, was he going to do *next*?

Not since Elvis Presley had anyone held such power over John—but Yoko, unlike a symbol, was in a position to use it. "Yoko had him under her spell," recalls Tony Bramwell. "She was always in his ear, telling him what to do, how to sing. If she couldn't get into the act, she was certainly going to influence it through John." Out of these discussions, many of them in the studio, many of them while high on a dangerous drug, John's antipathy toward the Beatles solidified.

John quickly changed the atmosphere in the studio. Once again the Beatles started banging heads; "they started picking on each other," according to John, or rather, picking one another apart. All of them, except perhaps Ringo, belittled the others' suggestions, complaining about someone's contribution—"You're not playing that right" or "That doesn't go there"—blaming one another for the failings of a song. "I started to feel it wasn't a good idea to *have* ideas," Paul recalled, although he certainly did his share to inflame the situation.

George tried to defuse the explosive tension by bringing in a guest musician, the way he'd done with Eric Clapton on "While My Guitar Gently Weeps." On January 19 he and Clapton had gone to a Ray Charles concert at the Festival Hall and recognized a young musician sent out to warm up the crowd. George hadn't seen Billy Preston since Hamburg, when he was a sixteen-year-old wunderkind in Little Richard's backup band. The Beatles had always been fond of Billy. George knew they'd get a kick out of seeing him again, so he invited Billy to sit in with them at Apple Studios the following day.

What George thought he was doing is impossible to say. He may have been hoping Billy's presence would help generate some civility or at least "offset the vibes," the negative vibes, that had been directed at him. Then again, he'd listened to the lethargic playbacks from their first few efforts and no doubt figured Billy's keyboard might light up the band. Hoping to redirect the Beatles' focus and sharpen their lackluster performance, Martin rolled Billy right into their work on "Get Back," which seemed to mobilize the detached elements with a playful complement of electric piano figures, bringing a whole new energy to the song. Ringo appreciated how, when Billy joined the session, "the bullshit went out the window"; otherwise, he felt there was little upside to bringing him into the recording process. Paul welcomed the contribution—at first. He thought Billy "played great" and helped stabilize, however temporarily, his crumbling relationship with John. "It was like having a guest in the house," he explained, "someone you put your best manners on for. . . . It might have helped us all behave better with one another on the sessions." But as with any guest, as time wore on, Paul felt Preston overstayed his welcome. Billy turned up at the studio day after day, participating in everything from the direction of the music to deciding where, or even whether, they would stage a concert. Paul found this intrusion "a little bit puzzling," to say nothing of presumptuous. Sitting in with the Beatles was one thing; *joining* them was another. Although many had claimed the title—Brian Epstein, George Martin, and Murray the K, to name a few—there was no room in the band for a "fifth Beatle." Paul felt the same way when John had suggested replacing George with Eric Clapton; he never would have agreed to it— *never*. The Beatles had a legacy to protect. As far as he cared, they were—and always would be—John, Paul, George, and Ringo.

By the end of January, working together on the project had become completely unmanageable. During lunch at Apple on January 29, the Beatles, along with Glyn Johns and Michael Lindsay-Hogg, sat around the well-appointed conference table, debating how to finish the film, when the discussion turned to the office's resident charm. In the course of conversation, Ringo mentioned that there was a wonderful open roof they intended to turn into a garden. "Oh, that's fantastic," Johns remembered saying. Catching Lindsay-Hogg's eye, he said, "I have an idea. We should go up and look at this roof."

The roof, as it turned out, held the answer to all their problems. It became obvious from the minute they climbed the stairs. The unanimous opinion: "What a great idea it would be to play on the roof—play to the whole of the West End." The Beatles could give a concert from the comfort of their own building, without any of the hassle that usually bogged down such affairs. They wouldn't have to deal with promoters, tickets, security, fans, press, jelly babies—nothing. Just head upstairs, plug in the instruments, and let 'er rip. Brilliant. "Nobody had ever done that," George recalled, "so it would be interesting to see what happened when we started playing up there."

The whole thing was to be very spontaneous, a secret. Not even the

Apple staff was given advance warning. The next morning, a cold, cloud-streaked day, Mal and Neil set up the Beatles' equipment while the film crew, working with a stripped-down unit, staked out territory along the outer retaining walls. The Beatles, along with Billy Preston, Yoko, and Linda, assembled in the basement, going over material. Not since the live broadcast for "All You Need Is Love" had they felt as excited—or more like a band.

Just before noon the haze burned off unexpectedly, the clouds rolled back, and the sun broke through. Before the first song, a breathless version of "Get Back," had even ended, the music had attracted a small lunchtime crowd of onlookers, and word began to circulate that the Beatles—the beloved Beatles, who hadn't entertained in England for more than three years—were playing in public. People working in the surrounding build-ings, mostly a district of tailors and haberdashers, felt the music before they heard it. Windows rattled, floors shook, and a symphony of horns blared from the caravan of traffic that had drawn to a standstill along Savile Row. All around, neighbors rushed into the street or raced to their own roofs to see what all the racket was about.

One interested establishment was the Savile Row police station, only three hundred yards off, at the bottom of the street. Manning a bank of four phones, they'd fielded endless irate complaints since the first notes blared through the streets. A confrontation was inevitable. Shortly after 1:15 the fireworks started. The Beatles had just run through "One After 909" when two uniformed policemen strolled into Apple's reception area and requested that the music be lowered. Mal Evans greeted them, steering the conversation toward one side of the room. "The Beatles had arranged for a camera to be hidden in a booth in the reception area for exactly such a situation," recalls Jack Oliver, who worked in the press office. "Mal wanted to make sure it picked up all the action."

If they'd expected a raid or something comparable, it was a disap-pointment. The police were friendly but insistent: "Honestly, the music has got to go down, or there's going to be some arrests," they avowed. No one was being threatened, they assured Mal. "But can you please turn it down? Can you turn it off, please? Thank you."

Please and thank you—what a colossal letdown. Ringo was especially crestfallen. "When [the police] came up, I was playing away and I thought, 'Oh, great. I hope they drag me off,'" he recalled. Ringo fantasized about being physically restrained "because we were being filmed and it would have looked really great, kicking the cymbals and everything." No such luck, but they still achieved their purpose by having the police interrupt the concert. The Beatles against the establishment: it would look great on film.

"I'd like to say thanks on behalf of the group and ourselves," John mugged into the camera, "and I hope we passed the audition."

Even though the concert was cut short, the Beatles managed to play just enough material to cover a full performance. In a little under forty minutes, they ran through "Get Back" several times, as well as "Don't Let Me Down," "I've Got a Feeling," "One After 909," "I Dig a Pony," and a brief, whimsical version of "God Save the Queen." "With a bit of doctoring, we'll be good," Lindsay-Hogg assured them.

Still, George was incensed that the police had the temerity to legislate the playing of music. "If anybody wants to sing and play on their roof, what's the law say as to why you can't do that?" he wondered.

John responded decisively, "Disturbing the peace." But his answer, even though convincing, resonated with ambiguity.

[III]

As Apple's financial fabric unraveled, so, too, did the delicate peace that for all these months had kept the Beatles from self-destructing.

John's comments to *Disc*—that the Beatles would "be broke in six months"—undid the first knot. Whether it was true or not, Paul felt that their privacy had been breached, and he tore into *Disc*'s gentle columnist Ray Coleman for his role in disseminating potentially harmful information. "You know this is a small and young company, just trying to get along," he roared at Coleman in front of a dozen openmouthed Apple employees outside of Ron Kass's office. "And you know John always shoots his mouth off. It's not that bad. We've got a few problems, but they'll be sorted out." The diminutive Coleman, who was on the verge of tears, hugged the wall as Paul, for whom he had great respect, continued the dressing-down. "I'm surprised it was you—we thought we had a few friends in the press we could trust."

Paul's determination to keep their financial difficulties out of the papers was providential. Within hours of reading John's remarks, a tough little scorpion named Allen Klein attacked the phones in an attempt to contact John about handling the Beatles' assets. Klein, who managed the

Rolling Stones, the Kinks, Bobby Vinton, Herman's Hermits, and Donovan, had been circling the Beatles for years, just waiting for the opportunity to pounce. Klein, at the time a sharp-mouthed thirty-eight-year-old dynamo from Newark, New Jersey, who spoke with an almost comical truck driver brogue and bore "a distant resemblance to Buddy Hackett," had spent part of his childhood in a Jewish orphanage before learning to survive on the streets by his wits. He taught himself the essentials necessary to be an accountant, earning a degree by attending night classes at Upsala College, and began an apprenticeship in the New York entertainment industry, where he became known for rooting through record-company ledgers in search of unpaid royalties. In the process, he unearthed a gold mine: because of the slipshod nature of the way records were kept, every audit revealed discrepancies. He wasted no time in impressing Bobby Darin with his sleuthing tactics. In 1962, at a party celebrating Darin's unprecedented deal with Capitol Records, Klein introduced himself to the singer and handed him a check for $100,000. According to legend, Darin stared puzzlingly at the check and asked what it was for. "For nothing," Klein supposedly replied, delighted with the impression he'd left. Two years later he performed the same feat at RCA for Sam Cooke, solidifying his reputation among artists as a financial gunslinger.

With the Beatles, Klein's timing was impeccable. He'd met John once before and only in passing, in December 1968, at the taping of the ill-fated "Rolling Stones Rock and Roll Circus" TV special. The Stones' manager interrupted a noisy transatlantic phone call to introduce himself with unusual gentility. When Klein mentioned that he was also an accountant, John pulled a face and joked how he did not "want to end up broke, like Mickey Rooney." The look that came over Klein "was orgasmic," said one observer. "To him, John's words seemed fraught with some extraordinary personal message." But it seemed impossible for him to gain entrée; the layers of protection around the Beatles were airtight. No matter how Klein tried to make contact, he was rebuffed at every juncture.

In his exuberant biography, *Fifty Years Adrift*, Derek Taylor admitted giving Allen Klein the introduction he longed for so that the Beatles "could determine whether the reputed coldness of his methods outweighed his undoubted capacity for securing the greatest deals for his clients." On the evening of January 28, two days before the Beatles' roof concert at Savile Row, John and Yoko met Allen Klein in the lavish Harlequin Suite at the Dorchester Hotel, where they formed a mutual, if snakebit, admiration society. Despite the fact that John and Allen, both extremely headstrong and volatile individuals, acted "very nervous . . . nervous as shit," they were immediately drawn to each other for a multitude of reasons. If John Eastman came off as being suave and pretentious, Allen Klein was his polar opposite—ordinary, almost boorish, a real salt-of-the-earth type—in fact, not so much salt as salty, lacing his conversation with ripe, juicy expletives. Forget about uptight preppie attire; Klein was dressed less than casually, in a baggy sweater over blue jeans and beat-up old sneakers. After Brian Epstein's sartorial refinement, John thought this was almost too good to be true. Later, John would call Klein "the only businessman I've met who isn't gray right through his eyes to his soul," and that about nailed his instant attraction. Klein was colorful. More than colorful: the man was gaudy, positively kaleidoscopic. "One of the . . . things that impressed me about Allen—and obviously it was a kind of flattery as well," John said, "he went through all the old songs we'd written and he really knew which stuff I'd written." Klein wasn't the average myopic manager, with a single fix on the bottom line. Music informed every move he made.

"I knew right away he was the man for us," John recalled. Even after the meeting John could barely contain his enthusiasm. "I wrote to Sir Joseph Lockwood that night. I said: 'Dear Sir Joe: From now on Allen Klein handles all my stuff.'"*

It might have helped matters if John had discussed his selection with the other Beatles first, but John was angry, emotional, impulsive. His decision wasn't based on what was good for the Beatles; it was personal and intuitive: him against Paul, rock 'n roll against pop, "a human being" against "an animal."

Besides, Yoko had weighed in. Klein had reeled Yoko carefully into the negotiations, soliciting her views and listening with rapt attention. Furthermore, he promised that Apple would support Yoko's experimental film projects and persuade United Artists to distribute them, sweetening the deal with a million-dollar advance. A day or two later, when Paul confronted John about selecting Allen Klein as his manager, John sheepishly admitted it was more her decision than his, saying, "Well, he's the only one Yoko liked."

---

* *Actually, the letter read: "Dear Sir Joe: I've asked Allen Klein to look after my things. Please give him any information he wants and full cooperation. Love, [signed: John Lennon]."*

That sounded more like a convenient dodge, except for one thing: Yoko was clearly pulling John's strings. Since they became an item, at her insistence John never strayed more than a few inches from her side. Everything he did, everything he said, filtered through her for approval. There was no resistance on his part, primarily because of what she gave him—confidence and control—and because he was so clearly damaged by drugs and his past. No one was going to derail her grand design, especially now that she had a weapon like John Lennon in her arsenal. John was her insurance policy, her safeguard. He gave her instant credibility as a media star.

Now she also had Allen Klein. A man like Klein wouldn't back down to the McCartney-Eastman alliance. Indeed, he'd enjoy wresting John from the grasp of those smoothies, those "big-headed uptight people" (John's description), and kicking some ass in the process. And Klein would aid in her crusade against Paul. No matter how Yoko might deny it, Paul remained her lone nemesis, her obstacle to claiming complete control over John. Paul was the one responsible for holding the Beatles together, for lashing John to that frothy pop confection, "all that Beatle stuff," as she called it. From the outset, she convinced herself that Paul wanted her out of the picture. "Paul began complaining that I was sitting too close to them when they were recording," Yoko said, "and that I should be in the background." *The background!* Never. Paul discouraged her from attending business meetings with the other Beatles. Never. He demeaned and insulted her, scoffed at her style of art. She would destroy him. She had to.

As far as Paul knew, the Eastmans seemed like a shoo-in to represent Apple. They'd even begun negotiations with Clive Epstein about purchasing a majority interest in NEMS. John's unconscionable act of maneuvering behind his back smacked of something insidious, something personal. Whether he realized it or not, it had Yoko's fingerprints all over it. Maintaining his cool, Paul agreed with the others to at least meet with Allen Klein and to keep an open mind, but in fact he had no intention of aligning himself with such a tawdry figure. Paul got around, he'd heard the scuttlebutt; he was familiar with Klein's reputation and wanted no part of it.

George and Ringo, on the other hand, were intrigued. They liked Klein's straight talk, his unconventional appearance, his painless solutions to their problems. "Because we were all from Liverpool, we favored people who were street people," George said, free of irony. Despite Allen's ritzy Dorchester suite and chauffeured limousine, George felt "Lee Eastman was more of a class-conscious type of person. As John was going with Klein, it was much easier if we went with him, too."

Paul opposed Klein's intervention, confident that the group's democratic stopgap would prevail on his behalf. In the past, a one-for-all, all-for-one policy would have scotched the deal. But when the smoke cleared and the votes were tallied, it was three against one for the first time in eleven years. Without much choice, Paul gave in. He agreed to grant Klein authority to perform an audit on the Beatles' behalf, delving into every financial arrangement they had, as long as the Eastmans were appointed as their general counsel. It was a compromise of sorts, but ultimately pointless. The fox had gained the keys to the henhouse, and on February 3, 1969, Allen Klein moved into the Apple offices, where he proceeded to secure his berth for a long, eventful stay.

———

For the most part, the audit of the Beatles' finances produced fairly unastonishing results. The sorry shape of their business affairs was already a known quantity. Klein quickly deduced they'd been "fucked around by everybody." The terms of their contract with EMI were grossly inadequate, leaving them enslaved to the record label for another ten years; the management agreement allowed NEMS to continue collecting 25 percent of the Beatles' royalties for the next seven years, even though the company no longer performed any significant service; dreadful merchandising deals had cost the Beatles a small fortune; and Apple, while profiting somewhat as a boutique record label, was still hemorrhaging money—hundreds of thousands of pounds—on myriad useless salaries and expenses.

On the surface, this scenario may have seemed like a nightmare, but none of these handicaps presented Allen Klein with sleepless nights. With time, he could perform whatever surgery was necessary to correct or renegotiate each disadvantage. The record sales for the White Album were through the roof (it remained the top-selling album in Britain throughout most of the winter); some basic belt-tightening would put the Beatles' finances back on solid ground. The audit did, however, turn up one ticklish spot. In the process of examining John and Paul's publishing deal with Dick James, Klein discovered that Paul, unbeknownst to John, had been quietly buying shares of Northern Songs for his portfolio.

On the surface it seemed harmless. "What better way to invest our money than in ourselves?" Paul offered unctuously, sidestepping the real issue: that he and John were supposed to be equal partners. But if Paul was impervious to the disclosure, his collaborator and partner was not. John regarded it as out-and-out treachery, underhanded, a covert attempt to

wrest control of their copyrights. No matter how Paul justified it, "it belied his innocence and honesty," says Peter Brown, who had been ordered
by Paul to purchase the additional shares. Brown knew John wasn't being
told—and foresaw the inevitable outcome. "They confronted each other in
the office, where John flew into a rage. At one point, I thought he was actually going to hit Paul, but he managed to calm himself down before
really laying into him. 'You're a fucking arsehole! You pretend to be this
honest and straightforward guy—and you're not!'"

Try though he might, Paul didn't deny it. It would have just added
more fuel to an already roaring fire. Besides, there were other serious flare-
ups that required more diplomacy.

The most important concern was their precarious management situation. No one was steering the listing ship. And at times it seemed as though
the Eastmans and Allen Klein were working at cross-purposes. The
Beatles knew it was time to harness their cocaptains. "Let's get them both
together," George recalled saying, and at that time it must have sounded
like a reasonable suggestion. But the powwow itself was more like Waterloo.
Bloodthirsty and bellicose, both factions squared off in Klein's Dorchester
suite, erupting with accusations and expletives. Reaching a consensus no
longer mattered—if it ever had. First of all, John had brought Yoko, who
had no business attending the meeting. Then Allen went to work, picking
apart all of the Eastmans' proposals as though they were nonsense. No
pretense was made of respect or civility. According to Peter Brown, he dismissed their idea to buy NEMS as "a piece of crap" and ridiculed John
Eastman as "a fool" and "a shithead," implying in his most patronizing voice
that only a dilettante would act so feebly for his clients. Eastman, under
fire, derided Klein as "a perfect asshole."

A week later, in an attempt to salvage Paul's position, Lee Eastman
flew to London to confront Klein himself, but John and his bodyguard
were ready for him. John's list of grievances against Eastman, both real and
imagined, had reached new heights of rancor. He had had enough of what
he perceived to be Eastman's "class snobbery." He refused to associate, he
said, with someone who "despises me because of what I am and what I
look like," who thinks "I'm some kind of guy who got struck lucky, a pal
of Paul's." But nothing grated on John's nerves more than hearing "a char-
latan" like Eastman say, "I can't tell you how much I've admired your
work, John," because beneath the smooth tone it had the ring of phoniness. He wasn't about to let some flashy New York lawyer, some "middle-
class pig" who had no instinct for rock 'n roll, exert power over him or,

worse, "con" him with lofty references to Kafka (Eastman apparently referred to the Beatles' recording deal as being Kafkaesque), Picasso, and de Kooning. John had learned from Neil Aspinall that Lee Eastman had changed the family name from Epstein, and he convinced Allen they should address him as such throughout the meeting. All that afternoon John picked at the name, dripping acid when he pronounced it, as if it were an open wound. "How Lee kept his cool was beyond me," recalls Peter Brown, in whose office they met. "Even Yoko, who wasn't supposed to be there, called him Epstein, daring him to respond."

Joining in, Klein continued to taunt Eastman in other ways, "interrupting everything he said with a string of the most disgusting four-letter words he could tick off his tongue." As soon as Klein took a breath, Yoko barreled in, challenging Eastman's judgment and assailing him for condescending to John. "Will you please stop insulting my husband," she snarled. "Don't call my husband stupid." Lee Eastman sat on his hands while his fury mounted, but the tag-team effect took its toll. The whole meeting had been a trap, he concluded. Klein had deliberately baited him, attempting to humiliate him. Unable to take another word of abuse, he finally snapped. He leaped to his feet, exploding in righteous indignation, and tore into the snickering accountant. "You are a rodent," he roared, "the lowest scum on earth!"

Unwittingly, of course, he had played right into John's hands. "We hadn't been in there more than a few minutes when Lee Eastman was having something like an epileptic fit and screaming at Allen," he told *Rolling Stone,* liberally editing the facts to shape his argument. "He had a fuckin' fit. . . . This was supposed to be the guy who was taking over the multi-million-dollar corporation. . . . I wouldn't let Eastman near me. I wouldn't let a fuckin' animal like that who has a mind like that near me." One can only imagine how he described it for Ringo and George, but whatever the case, it served to ice John's position. Eastman was out; Allen Klein was their man.

The Beatles may have found a captain for Apple, at last, but he was at the helm of a slowly sinking ship.

[I]

Though the Beatles had dodged questions about the bubble bursting ever since they first landed in America, they couldn't help but feel the pressure mounting toward the inevitable, ugly bang. By March 1969, John, Paul, George, and Ringo knew the end was near. Months of bickering had steadily dispirited them. The last-ditch, desperate effort to carry on as a group only estranged them further and brought their squabbles more visibly into the open. To ease the tension, they each became involved in personal projects: John and Yoko finished production of an avant-garde film for Austrian TV titled *Rape;* Paul attempted to jump-start Mary Hopkin's anemic career; Ringo accepted a role opposite Peter Sellers in the film adaptation of Terry Southern's send-up *The Magic Christian;* George recorded a solo album, *Electronic Sounds,* at his home and groomed Billy Preston for stardom. But still, they behaved as itinerant Beatles, clinging to the legacy as one might a security blanket until they summoned the means to resolve their differences—or the courage to go their separate ways.

No one was prepared when rumors of Paul's marriage to Linda Eastman began circulating around London. On March 11, a day in advance of the ceremony, Paul leaked word of it to the press before even telling the other Beatles about his plans.* Except for a brief rendezvous at Abbey Road, the four mates hadn't seen one another in weeks. John, Ringo, and George might have been surprised by the sudden announcement, but none was shocked that he wasn't invited to attend. "Why should we be asked to help

---

* *Ray Connolly of the* Evening Standard *recalls that Paul cornered him at Apple, winked, and said: "If you don't tell anybody, I'll tell you all about it."*

Paul celebrate," George wondered, "when we're not even on speaking terms?" Besides, the last thing any of them wanted was to be part of a media circus.

Marrying off the "last bachelor among the Beatles" was big news, and despite appeals that "Paul and Linda want it simple" and a cold, driving rainstorm, nothing kept the fans from staging a crazy mob scene. Indeed, the wedding resembled a page torn from the Beatlemania scrapbook. On the morning of March 12, a few minutes before ten, an ashen-faced Linda, clutching her daughter, Heather, by the arm, "plunged through a mob of weeping teenagers" outside the Marylebone Registry while Paul waved and threw purple-wrapped candies into the crowd, inciting a mad scramble for souvenirs. John, who had expressed "surprise" at the marriage, found the scene stage-managed. "It was just Paul being Paul," he told Peter Brown, "playing to the crowd."

Unknown to Paul, George spent the wedding day lounging in Derek Taylor's office at Apple, where he was paged around 5:00 by his wife, Pattie. There was a team of police at their home, she reported, tossing the place in preparation for a drug bust. They had already found a hefty chunk of hash stowed in a box on the mantel. (George insisted that the police had planted it.) Some grass would later turn up as well. (This was his private stash.) In any case, there was going to be an arrest, and when it came it would vie with Paul's wedding for the morning headlines.

Pete Shotton, who lived nearby, was at Esher when George, dressed in a flamboyant yellow suit, arrived in a stretch limousine with Taylor and a lawyer. The indiscriminate atmosphere in the parlor resembled nothing if not "a party." Several cops were slouched in armchairs with their feet propped up, watching television. Others drank coffee and thumbed through George's record collection, while a police dog clad in a beet-red neckerchief nosed through the bedroom closets. George scanned the scene with a sweep of his head, at which point his eyes went blank. Shotton had seen George riled up before, often, and he could be mean. But this was different. "I'd never seen George so angry in my life," Shotton recalls. "He came into the house—and went *berserk*." He would have told the police where his dope was stashed, but they seemed more interested in playing out the bust, as though it, too, were being stage-managed—which, in a way, it was: even the press had been tipped off to chronicle their handiwork. When a photographer popped out of the front hedge, that was the final straw. "George chased him murderously around the garden," recalls Shotton, who couldn't help laughing at the improbable scene. "George was chasing him; the police were chasing George. It was like something out of the Keystone Kops." Leaping over garden ornaments and bushes, George kept shouting: "I'll kill you! I'll fucking kill you!" Later, being led away by Derek Taylor, he pointed at a reporter and yelled: "The fox has its lair, the bird has its nest. *This is my fucking house!*"

By mid-March the Beatles' escapades commanded an unprecedented amount of ink. Just five days after Paul married Linda, Peter Brown took a call in his hotel room in Amsterdam, where he had gone for the weekend to hear John Pritchard conduct the philharmonic. John Lennon was on the phone, with a discernible swell in his voice. "Why don't you stay there," John suggested. "Yoko and I will come over and get married."

"John made it clear that he didn't want to get married like Paul [had]," Brown recalls. "That is, he did not want crowds; they wanted to get married quietly." But Brown delivered bad news: Holland, like most countries, required a two-week minimum residency. According to the (London) *Times,* England was also out of the question because of "difficulties over Yoko's citizenship" and her recent divorce from Tony Cox. They'd even tried getting married on a cross-Channel ferry, but their car broke down in Basingstoke on the breakneck drive to Southampton, and they were forced to turn back. What were the lovebirds to do?

Brown put Apple's lawyers on the question and discovered that the only place without a residency requirement was Gibraltar, which, as a British possession, recognized John as a citizen. *Gibraltar?* All anyone knew was that it was a *rock.* But if John and Yoko turned up there bearing the proper papers, they would be married in whatever fashion—and speed—was requested.

Brown arranged for them to fly to Paris, where Alistair Taylor met them with the papers and "a load of money." On Tuesday, March 20, John and Yoko arrived in Gibraltar at 8:30 in the morning and were immediately spotted by other tourists. They'd made no effort at all to be inconspicuous, let alone subtle. "Yoko stood out like a sore thumb, dressed in this funny, white knitted miniskirt outfit, with a floppy white hat," says Brown, who met them at the plane. John, who appeared to be *very* nervous, wore a long white corduroy jacket over a white polo sweater, white trousers, and sneakers. "You had to be blind to miss them."

Despite the distraction, John found the setting "beautiful," a flat, open harbor view surrounded by an expanse of turquoise water. He had little time, however, to take in the colony's attractions. In a little under an hour, they swore out affidavits, bought a special license, and were immediately married by the registrar at the British consulate before returning directly to the airport.

Even in a location as remote as Gibraltar, there were already photographers surrounding the plane. "Intellectually, we didn't believe in getting married," John told them. "But one doesn't love someone just intellectually. For two people, marriage still has the edge over just living together." Everyone scrambled aboard for the flight back to Paris, where John and Yoko planned to relax for a few days. Springtime in Paris—it sounded so romantic to the small entourage, who envisioned a traditional, old-fashioned honeymoon. But John and Yoko weren't traditional by any stretch of the imagination. "We had our honeymoon *before* we got married," John explained. No, they had something else up their sleeve, something calculated, something more intriguing.

—————

Before John had left for Paris, he huddled with Allen Klein in an attempt to "rationalize" the situation at Apple. Klein determined that everyone on the payroll was riding what John referred to as the "gravy train," even Neil and Mal, who "were living like kings . . . like fucking emperors," thanks to the Beatles' deep pockets. After much prodding, Peter Brown turned over the employee records to Klein and pleaded for leniency, but to no avail. Many of those in the first wave to be fired were obvious choices. Magic Alex got the early thumb along with Denis O'Dell, whose film division lay dormant; Tony Bramwell; the chefs; and much of the extraneous staff. But the number one name on Klein's hit list raised a few eyebrows: Alistair Taylor. "He'd been with us since 1962," says Brown, who'd been appointed as Klein's hatchet man. "He was an honorable employee through all those years, Paul's gofer, his mate. Whenever any of the boys needed something done, Alistair always saw to it." Brown trembled as he delivered the news. "It was terrible, terrible. Having to do this was the worst," he recalls. Taylor received a "generous" severance: three months' pay as well as rent toward his flat, but he had to leave the premises at once. It was a cruel finale for the man who'd accompanied Brian Epstein to the Cavern on the day he first saw the Beatles. Crueler still was the scene that followed. Shocked and indignant, Alistair called Paul at his home to commiserate and say good-bye. "But Paul refused to come to the phone," he recalls. "Nothing in my life ever hurt as much as that."

When the next list of victims was issued, Ron Kass's name appeared at the top. "Firing Ron—a nice, honorable, successful international record executive—was the only way for Allen to take control of the company," according to Peter Brown. But it wasn't that easy to simply sack a man like Kass, whose contract and reputation stood in the way. So Klein resorted to an old accountant's trick of questioning an expense of Ron's, making it appear as though something improper had transpired, when in fact there was a perfectly reasonable explanation. In this case, it was a company check made out to Kass for cash, which had been advanced to Neil Aspinall in America. Once Klein cast it in doubt, however, there was too much stigma involved. Not even the Beatles would come to his rescue.

Brown was ordered to oust Peter Asher as well. Since the days of Paul's residency at his parents' house, Peter had made quite a name for himself, first as half of the hit-making duo Peter and Gordon, then more recently developing talent as Apple's chief A&R man. After producing James Taylor's debut, Asher was in great demand, with a dozen acts vying for his services. But to Allen Klein, this power was intimidating. Asher, who went on to become one of the most successful producers in the music business, refused to give Klein the satisfaction of sacking him, and resigned.

At the time of the Apple staff liquidation, John Lennon had been staging a seven-day bed-in for peace in the Presidential Suite at the Amsterdam Hilton, ostensibly "as a protest against violence everywhere," though anyone who knew John and Yoko understood that this was mostly an opportunity for them to capture the world's headlines and promote their recent marriage, which appeared grotesque to the public eye.

The couple, convinced they'd be prevented from having a proper private honeymoon, decided to turn the tables on the annoying press and stage the postmarriage function as an international event. "Instead of fighting it," as John explained, "we joined it," choosing "to make maximum use of" the interest for their own purposes. Up to sixty newsmen at a time gained access to their bedroom any time of the day or night, as long as John and Yoko could lobby for a personal cause. A "plea for peace," they believed, was the perfect attention-grabber.

The entire affair was (to the disappointment of the tabloids) tame enough for TV, a tranquilizing prime-time family spectacle, with John and Yoko dressed in neatly pressed pajamas, delivering messages filled with nonviolence and antiwar rhetoric. The room itself was a testament to flaky innocence, decorated with crude hand-painted signs that proclaimed

"Grow Your Hair," "Stay in Bed," "John Loves Yoko," "Hair Peace." Their aphorisms, delivered like gospel, were printed in boldface, including a new standby of John's that found favor among the columnists: "Give peace a chance." It was part demonstration, part sideshow, wrapped in the guise of Yoko's self-indulgent performance art.

As to what had motivated him to begin preaching peace, all John could say was that "it's no good working for money, and there's nothing else to do but work—so working for peace is an objective." But the real motivation may have simply been that John and Yoko craved attention. They loved using the media to stir up controversy, loved the way it painted them as incorrigible rebels, loved the exasperated reactions, loved the power it gave them. "It came at a perfect time in his life," John's biographer Ray Coleman would write, "with the Beatles at a crossroads." Peace—and its power "to force people to re-act"—gave him another imposing vehicle, another public platform from which to reshape and sharpen his image. "We are trying to make Christ's message contemporary," John told an open-mouthed audience at one of the Amsterdam press conferences. "What would He have done if He had advertisements, records, films, TV, and newspapers? Well, the miracle today is communications. So let's use it!"

[II]

At Apple, each week, each day, it seemed, brought new and unexpected departures, along with division consolidations: Apple Retail was shut down, as was Apple Electronics, Apple Films, Apple Publishing, and other offshoots that produced little or no income.

Yet, with so many hands still in the pot, there were too many things that could go wrong—many of which did. On the heels of Allen Klein's remarks that buying NEMS was inadvisable, John Eastman, in his overzealousness as the Beatles' legal counsel, wrote to Clive Epstein in an attempt to stall the negotiations:

> As you know, Mr. Allen Klein is doing an audit of the Beatles' affairs, *vis-à-vis* NEMS and Nemperor Holdings Ltd. When this has been completed I suggest we meet to discuss the results of Mr. Klein's audit as well as the propriety of the negotiations surrounding the nine-year agreement between E.M.I., the Beatles, and NEMS.

Propriety: Clive took the word as an outrageous slap in the face. A principled, moral man, he was indignant that anyone might imply that NEMS, an Epstein family company, had acted in bad faith. Rather than engage in a potentially ugly dispute, he promptly sold his 70 percent of the company to Triumph Investment Trust, giving it the right to pocket 25 percent of the Beatles' record royalties, as well as a 4.5 percent interest in Northern Songs.

The Beatles had reason to be infuriated. As they had hoped, owning NEMS would have given them complete control of their financial interests and access to a much larger chunk of their income. The million pounds that NEMS was prepared to accept from Apple was a pittance compared with what the Beatles would have collected over the next seven years. Besides, the sale put their careers in the hands of a faceless, ruthless corporation whose only interest was the bottom line.

Klein attempted to strong-arm Triumph's managing director, Leonard Richenberg, into selling the company back to the Beatles on reasonable terms. If not, he warned, they intended to have NEMS make good on large sums of money supposedly owed the Beatles for performances over the past ten years. No exact figure was established, according to Richenberg, but it was suggested that NEMS owed the Beatles far more than the company could ever hope to collect.

Richenberg, however, called Klein's bluff. He kicked Allen out of his office and refused to meet with the Beatles as long as their acting manager was involved in the negotiations. For his part, Klein answered him threat for threat. He notified EMI in writing that from that time forth, the label was to pay the Beatles' own merchant bankers "all royalties payable by you directly or indirectly to Beatles and Co. or Apple Corps." Otherwise, it was implied, the Beatles would fulfill the remainder of their recording contract by singing various versions of "God Save the Queen." With more than £1.3 million of royalties owed the Beatles, the company was damned no matter who it sided with. The whole sordid matter was referred to the courts.

The next theater of battle developed on the music publishing front. On March 28, during the Amsterdam bed-in, John opened the newspaper to discover that Dick James and his partner, Charles Silver, were selling their controlling interest in Northern Songs to ATV, the entertainment empire owned by Lew Grade, for roughly £1.2 million. John felt ambushed. He knew their songs effectively belonged to a publicly held corporation, which meant they were somewhere out there in the ozone, somewhere beyond his control, but he hadn't expected a betrayal from what should have been a devoted ally, a grateful ally. The Beatles *made* Dick James. His entire mini-empire was established on their northern backs.

John's ire grew steadily as he absorbed the full meaning of the article until by nightfall he was fuming. "I won't sell!" he bellowed to an audience of tickled journalists. "These are my shares and my songs and I want to keep a bit of the end product." But what about his partner? reporters wanted to know. Shouldn't he consult the reluctant Mr. McCartney for his view of the deal? John remonstrated. "I don't have to ring Paul. I know damn well he feels the same as I do."

The Beatles felt James had ripped them off. They hated him—and now this. James should have offered Northern Songs to the Beatles at the same price. But he was poised for the quick hit. He was afraid of the Beatles—afraid of their eccentricity, afraid of their instability, afraid of their unpredictability and increasingly weird behavior. He was also tired of taking the Beatles' abuse, which had grown harsher since Brian's death. Their behavior, too much of a liability, put his investment at risk, providing even more justification for the sale.

John Eastman spoke for everyone at Apple when he called James "a bastard." The Beatles were determined not to let Northern Songs slip away. But how to do battle with the Herculean ATV? There was one clever solution: have the Beatles declared "a national treasure": under those conditions, they should be protected by statute. Hoping to win such designation, they appealed to a group of London city institutions heavily invested in Northern Songs for control of their blocks of shares. It was a wild long shot—but successful. When combined with the Beatles' own holdings, these pledged shares, totaling about 14 percent, would give them majority interest in the company and a chance at genuine recovery. But as agreements were being signed, John grew suspicious—or paranoid—of his benefactors in the business establishment, whom he proceeded to denounce in the press. "I'm not going to be fucked around by men in suits, sitting on their fat arses in the city," he fumed. It was a bizarre outburst, and in a somewhat stunned response the shares were promptly withdrawn, thus torpedoing the deal.

Throughout April and early May, the war for Northern Songs raged on between the Beatles, ATV, and a consortium of investors who rushed into the deal at the last minute, hoping to play spoiler. Meanwhile, the Beatles had their hands full on other fronts. There was still internal conflict over who would handle their business affairs—Allen Klein or the Eastmans—and hostilities between all the parties escalated as the legal consequences sharpened.

John, George, and Ringo were adamant: Klein was their man; Paul was just as adamant: anyone but Klein. "Paul was getting more and more uptight until [he] wouldn't speak to us," John recalled. He told the other three: "Speak to my lawyer. I don't want to speak about business anymore," which John interpreted as "I'm going to drag my feet and try and fuck you."

"We had great arguments with Paul," Ringo remembered, but none that compared with a confrontation that ultimately determined Klein's fate.

On the night of May 9, 1969, the Beatles were booked into Olympic Sound for a recording session that had been ongoing since mid-April. In the midst of such protracted turmoil, the band managed to agree that making music helped clear the atmosphere, and they were laying down basic tracks for what would eventually become *Abbey Road.* Since the beginning, they had loosely structured "I Want You (She's So Heavy)," "Oh! Darling," "Octopus's Garden," "Something," and "You Never Give Me Your Money," all of which would be reworked throughout the summer. On this night, however, they were due to polish the forthcoming *Get Back* LP under George Martin's direction when Paul was confronted with an ultimatum. John, Ringo, and George wanted his signature on Klein's three-year management contract—*right away.* Klein was outside, waiting for it to be hand delivered.

In essence, Paul had already agreed to the representation, but he hated like hell to formalize it. Now the contract, rolled loosely in his hand, made it official. He couldn't do it; he couldn't put his name on it. The fee to Klein—20 percent across the board—was too rich, Paul told them. "He'll take fifteen percent." This last-minute obstacle enraged the other Beatles. "You're just stalling," they complained. Paul insisted: "No, I'm working for us. We're a big act—the Beatles. He'll take fifteen percent."

They went back and forth over the percentages, neither side budging from its position, until Paul threw up his hands. It was growing late, a Friday evening. "We could easily do this on Monday. Let's do our session instead," he proposed. The others wouldn't hear of it. Voices were raised, threats leveled. The hotter tempers got, the further Paul withdrew. Finally, he'd heard enough: he was waiting until Monday, at which time his lawyer would be present. For the others, that was it. "Oh, fuck off!" they bellowed, before storming out of the studio.

———

Over the next several weeks the Beatles not only aggressively pushed for a solution that would give them control of the company but, clearly acting with their merchant banker's blessing, waged a public campaign against ATV, asking undecided shareholders to reject the conglomerate's offer. John and Paul, realizing that they were vulnerable to the takeover, appeared almost daily in the press, where, to build public support, they painted themselves as helpless victims of corporate rapacity. They promised to fight on, to turn back the repugnant opposition, the haters of music and all that was good.

The Beatles raised the stakes by pledging their own shares in the company, as well as those held by Pattie Harrison, and Suba Films (a division of Apple that had produced *A Hard Day's Night, Help!,* and *Yellow Submarine*), as collateral against a loan from Henry Ansbacher and Company strong enough to beat back ATV's bid. Even Allen Klein stepped up, adding his 145,000 shares of MGM stock to the war chest. It was a powerful countermeasure—John referred to their gambit as playing "Monopoly with real money."

But on the advice of John Eastman, who felt "there was no point in putting out cash to get control of the company," Paul refused to commit his shares as part of the collateral package, touching off what one source called "a monumental row." Paul obviously assumed—Eastman had probably led him to assume—that ATV would ultimately reconsider its position, give up, and sell its 35 percent stake to the Beatles rather than risk losing Paul's and John's services. In any case, Paul believed that no matter what happened, there would always be plenty of income from those songs regardless of ownership; so secure was he in this belief that he hadn't even consulted John before pulling the plug. It was a tremendous mistake. He came off as disunited, antagonistic, and high-handed. John's, George's, and Ringo's patience had just about run out. Despite their entreaties, Paul continued to refuse to sign the agreement with Allen Klein. And now he'd bailed out on them with ATV.

"Paul actually stopped coming into the office," recalls Peter Brown. "Once Klein took charge, it soured things for Paul and, for a time, even the others wanted nothing to do with him." John and Yoko saw it as an opening and rushed to fill the void, demanding "the best office in the building," the room Ron Kass had recently vacated. The once-elegant space, decorated in an array of expensive white Italian furniture, white television console, and an oversize chrome-and-leather desk, became the headquarters for their new venture, Bag Productions, formed exclusively to promote an exuberant line of John and Yoko vehicles. The building became an "ever-changing John and Yoko exhibition." The couple plunged ahead, launching one crazy project after another, hoping to make up in shock value for what they lacked in direction.

For their first press conference in Vienna, John and Yoko lay obscured inside a large white sack, singing and humming, promoting a process they called "total communication." A second album of experimental recordings — *Unfinished Music No. 2: Life with the Lions* — was released with another controversial cover (grainy photos depicting Yoko's hospital stay on one side, their drug arraignment on the other); aside from the usual discordant gibberish, one track contained a four-minute segment of the heartbeat of the baby Yoko miscarried. Derek Taylor, in classic understatement, described their behavior as "very fast living in the mad lane." They filmed hours of self-indulgent documentaries, gobbled down drugs, staged loony press conferences (usually to announce a scheme whose "premise" was ostensibly to promote world peace but wound up promoting a Yoko Ono happening), and scheduled more bed-ins. John jabbered incessantly in a thickening Liverpool brogue, but incoherently, like a lunatic, and his appearance reflected it; he looked gaunt, sickly, from the heroin he ingested, his hair long, unkempt, and stringy. *Variety* reported that two producers were pursuing him to star in a thirteen-part television series, *Jesus of Nazareth,* a report later discredited, though he certainly looked the part. (Months later he actually was approached by Andrew Lloyd Webber and Tim Rice to play the title role in *Jesus Christ Superstar,* but they lost their interest when he said: "If I do it, I would want Yoko Ono to play Mary.") Loyal fans, to say nothing of his closest friends, found him bizarre. "I don't know what people think of John at the moment," Ringo said, puzzled. "Maureen was in Liverpool and I know a lot of people there are saying that he has gone a bit crazy. . . . [T]hey think he has gone off his head."

In Barry Miles's biography, *Paul McCartney: Many Years from Now,* Paul attributes much of John's behavior to the heroin and "paranoia," which he believed was covered up well by John's so-called genius. But the paranoia didn't lead to the antics. Within days after the first bed-in, John announced their next move, Acorns for Peace: sending envelopes "containing two acorns to the head of state of every country in the world" so they could plant trees instead of bombs. Later in the year they would take over billboards in eleven world cities, declaring "The War Is Over." Then, on April 22 John assembled a small gathering of friends and reporters on the roof of Savile Row and officially changed his middle name from Winston, which he hated, to Ono. Yoko insisted that it was politically motivated, based on a conversation they had after their wedding. "How would *you* like it if you had to change your name upon marriage to Mr. John Ono?" she demanded of him. Admitting it was "unfair," John declared: "I do not feel patriotic enough to keep the name [Winston, after Churchill]. I am John Ono Lennon."

John was having so much fun stirring up trouble, manipulating the press with Yoko, that nothing, not even money and legal hassles, was important enough to distract him. Occasionally, when Allen Klein managed to corral his attention, John dealt with matters that affected the Beatles' well-being; once, at a point when the negotiations for control of Northern Songs were going down the tubes, he even attended regular meetings with his Liverpool bandmates. But they belonged to the past, and he rarely socialized with them anymore.

As the Beatles stumbled toward summer, there was still no consensus on a manager, and the prospects for hammering out an agreement—any agreement—seemed bleak. Even so, Allen Klein negotiated a new long-term contract with EMI that gave the Beatles an impressive 25 percent royalty on their albums, paid directly to Apple. With this commitment from the label and infused with newfound enthusiasm, Paul persuaded the others to return to Abbey Road to continue work on a new studio album.

Whether John, George, and Ringo were inclined to record with Paul, they recognized the importance of putting some product in the pipeline. The tapes from earlier in the year that would eventually become *Let It Be* languished in the can, abandoned, a victim of haste and sloppy execution. "[They] were so lousy and so bad," according to John—"twenty-nine hours of tape . . . twenty takes of everything"—that "none of us would go near them. . . . None of us could face remixing them; it was [a] terrifying [prospect]." "It was laying [sic] dormant and so we decided, 'Let's make a *good* album again,'" George recalled.

A good album. He obviously meant with carefully crafted songs and diligent production, both hallmarks of the Beatles' legacy. Either of those conditions, however, would require a top-flight producer—or a referee. Paul phoned George Martin to inquire whether he'd be available, or even willing, to make a Beatles album "like we used to." The request, although routine, caught Martin off guard. Considering the way they were arguing, to say nothing of the way he'd been ignominiously shunted aside for the *Let It Be* sessions, Martin assumed he'd worked his last with the Beatles.

Still, no one excited, challenged, or delivered for him like the boys. Would he do it? Indeed, in a heartbeat, but . . . "Only if you let me produce it the way we used to," he told Paul. John also had to agree, he insisted, but Paul assured him their decision was unanimous.

John was actually psyched to record. When the vast snarl of red tape that had been occupying so much of the past five months finally began to unravel, the drive to make music was so fierce that he couldn't wait for the other Beatles. Yoko had exhorted him repeatedly to "get it down," arguing that he didn't need Paul, George, or Ringo to validate his talent. He was brimming with material, real edgy stuff. Pages of lyrics were strewn conspicuously on a coffee table in his house, their imaginative stanzas and middle eights a constant reminder of his personal output. But Yoko was only partly right. In a pinch, John still relied on Paul to polish a song with potential, as he had with "The Ballad of John and Yoko," which he'd written while on his honeymoon in Paris. On the evening of April 14 only Paul was available (George was in the States; Ringo was preoccupied filming *The Magic Christian*), and ready to rock, the two estranged mates, working like master craftsmen, recorded and mixed the entire song in a fast-paced, productive seven-hour session at Abbey Road. John handled all guitar parts, while Paul filled out the rhythm track, adding piano, bass, and drums, and the two men harmonized beautifully on the chorus, as though they'd been doing it all their lives (which, of course, they had), in a way that truly exemplified *Beatlesque*.

John had also recorded the anthemic "Give Peace a Chance" in a makeshift hotel-room studio staged at a bed-in for peace in Montreal. His original plan had been to get to the United States, where an entourage consisting of Yoko, Ringo, Maureen, Derek Taylor, and his wife, Joan, Terry Southern, Peter Sellers, and Denis O'Dell would pull off a doozy of a press event intended to protest the Vietnam War. On May 16, however, as they were about to set sail from Southampton on the newly christened *QE2*, John was turned back at dock, having been denied an entry visa by U.S. Customs as an "inadmissible immigrant" based on his drug conviction in December. Declassified internal FBI memos reveal that J. Edgar Hoover had long had his eye on John, as had Richard Nixon and a number of American conservative bureaucrats who feared the Beatles' influence in their vocal opposition to the war. This was their petty revenge.

Now John approached the forthcoming session with great enthusiasm. To a music journalist, during a rare moment of détente, he confessed that songwriting was "something that gets in your blood" and forced him to put aside old conflicts. "I think I could probably write about thirty songs a day," he bragged in the course of the interview. "As it is, I probably average about twelve a night. Paul, too—he's mad on it. . . . I've got things going around in my head right now, and as soon as I leave here I'm going round to Paul's place and we'll sit down and start [to] work."

In fact, he was taking Paul the rudiments of "Because," which he'd sketched out only earlier that afternoon. As for his inspiration: "Yoko was playing some classical bit [on the piano], and I said, 'play that backwards,' and we had a tune." According to Paul, he recognized the melody's debt to Beethoven's *Moonlight Sonata*, identifying Yoko's influence from lyrical themes lifted "straight out of *Grapefruit.*" Even so, it was a gorgeous reinterpretation—"one of the most beautiful things we've ever done," George recalled—with three-part harmonies that were as sweet and tight as anything the Beatles ever attempted.

Throughout May and into July they blazed through most of the album's basic tracks. Beginning with George's masterpiece, "Something," the Beatles laid the groundwork for an intensely stirring romantic ballad that would challenge "Yesterday" and "Michelle" as one of the most recognizable songs they ever produced. In John's opinion, George's songwriting "wasn't in the same league [as his and Paul's] for a long time," but that opinion changed after "Something." Even George Martin admitted being "surprised that George had it in him." There was a sense of structure they could no longer overlook, an instinct for atmosphere and emotion that was absent in his earlier songs. *Time,* in its review, called "Something" simply "the best song on the album." Paul, delivering a somewhat backhanded compliment, felt it "came out of left field," but he was struck by its "very beautiful melody" and suggested releasing it as a single.

It was an odd segue into "You Never Give Me Your Money," which Paul wrote, he said, "lambasting Allen Klein's attitude toward [the Beatles]: no money, just funny paper, all promises, and it never works out." The song was written immediately after *Let It Be* finished filming, when Paul's emotions were at their most brittle, and as such, the lyric is infused with stinging bitterness. "Golden Slumbers/Carry That Weight" was another acid-tipped barb aimed in Klein's direction and came next, although it was drawn from a nursery rhyme by a seventeenth-century playwright, Thomas Dekker, whom Paul discovered in a songbook belonging to his new stepsister, Ruth:*

---

* *Jim McCartney had remarried in 1965.*

Golden slumbers kiss your eyes / Smiles awake when you rise,
Sleep pretty wantons do not cry / And I will sing a lullaby.

"I liked the words so much," Paul recalled. "I thought it was very restful, a very beautiful lullaby, but I couldn't read the melody, not being able to read music. So I just took the words and wrote my own music." By contrasting it against "Carry That Weight," he sewed a quiet fury into its lining. Only the tone of the song had changed, not the context of his feelings. He remained furious at his mates, oppressed by the "heavy" atmosphere Klein had brought upon Apple.

John was curiously missing throughout the sessions for the caprice ("Golden Slumbers" and "Carry That Weight" were recorded as one song). On July 1, while on a cross-country vacation in Scotland with Yoko, Julian, and Kyoko, he drove his white Austin Maxi off a road into a steeply graded ditch. "He was driving for the first time in his life," recalled his cousin Stanley Parkes, who had entertained the entourage for a few blissful days in Edinburgh just prior to the accident. Stanley fretted over seeing John behind the wheel, knowing from experience how he "wasn't a competent driver at all." John was headed north, to visit a spectacular glacial bay situated in the Highlands at the Kyle of Tongue, via a weave of roads that Parkes considered dangerous under ideal conditions. A myopic, happily stoned Beatle spelled catastrophe from the outset. He warned John before leaving: "Remember, you're on single-track roads up here. Be very, very careful." But John wasn't listening. Stubbornly, he waved Stanley off. "Oh, I know. Okay, okay." But rounding a jagged bend near Golspie, John encountered another car head-on. "I didn't know what to do," he explained from a bed at Lawson Memorial Hospital, where he was taken after the incident, "so I just let go of the steering wheel," sending the car careening over an embankment and nearly demolishing it. Miraculously, no one was killed, but John required seventeen stitches to close a facial wound, with Yoko and Kyoko suffering similar, if slightly less severe, injuries. Julian, who was traumatized and in shock, recuperated at his aunt Elizabeth's house in Durness.

When the last of the bloody wreckage was recovered, John and Yoko had it shipped to their new home, a spectacular seventy-four-acre estate outside Ascot called Tittenhurst Park, where it was mounted as sculpture outside their living-room window. Ostensibly, as Yoko explained, it served as "a tribute to [their] survival." Everyone knew it also functioned as a warning: John Lennon, under no circumstances, should ever again be permitted to touch the steering wheel of a car.

———

John must have grown impatient—out of the mix again—as the sessions at Abbey Road continued apace in his absence. It went without saying that Paul was back in the captain's seat, George and Ringo playing at his infuriating whim. Precious tape was being spent immortalizing *McCartney songs.* Curses! There was no time to waste in reclaiming his rightful piece of the new album.

On July 6 John and Yoko boarded a chartered helicopter on the hospital's front lawn and flew directly back to London. The next day he reported bright and early at Studio Two, where the rest of the Beatles gathered to work on a seminal recording.

In his absence, George Harrison had been on fire. "I think that until now, until this year, our songs have been better than George's," Paul admitted to John during a break. "Now this year his songs are at least as good as ours." George insisted he "didn't care if [Paul] liked them or not"—all their arrogance and self-complacency seemed suddenly, annoyingly, meaningless. "Here Comes the Sun," which George wrote while meandering around the garden of Eric Clapton's house one gorgeous afternoon in June, increased his currency. No lightweight throwaway, on the order of "Blue Jay Way" or "You Like Me Too Much," it held its own against the Lennon and McCartney songs already on the album, standing out from the pack for its wispy, rolling simplicity and irregular guitar lick that seems to stutter behind the vocal: "Sun, sun, sun—here it comes."

With John's reappearance in the studio came Yoko, back at his side, ever conspicuous as an intruder; however, this time there was an even more offensive twist. Yoko was pregnant again, with strict orders from her doctor to remain in bed while recovering from the car crash. In a characteristically aggravating gesture, she had Harrods deliver a double bed to the studio and instructed an EMI electrician to suspend a microphone above her head that would adequately furnish her comments to the band.

"The three of us didn't quite get it," Paul recalled. Yoko lounged in the bed, reading or knitting, impervious to their scowls, while the Beatles pressed on, tackling a song of John's that he'd completed upon returning from Scotland. "'Come together' was an expression that Tim Leary had come up with for" his mock presidential campaign, John recalled, noting his failed attempt at writing a stump song around the slogan. Later, long after the 1968 election, an idea came to him built around the catchy phrase. He also borrowed liberally from an early Chuck Berry tune, "You Can't Catch Me," recycling one of the master's trademark lines: "Here comes old flat-top." John acknowledged the debt when Paul called him on it during a run-through. It was too obvious; they had to spin it in a different direction, both agreed. "Let's slow it down with a swampy bass-and-drums vibe," Paul suggested, contributing that "querying bass line" that sets an identifying groove.

In an inspired, if eerie, touch, John leaned into the mike and delivered a breathy accent that sounded like *"shoooook"* against the downbeat, repeating the effect at the bridge tying each bar together. Paul must have tried from the beginning to mask the sound with his bass, knowing they'd catch hell if a careful listener caught on—because at the end of each line, John sang the phrase *"shoot me!"* Geoff Emerick, who'd only just returned as the Beatles' engineer, noted how they were up to their old shenanigans. "On the finished record, you can really only hear the word 'shoot,'" he said, explaining how "the bass guitar note falls where the 'me' is."

"Shoot me!" The taunt was indicative of the way John was feeling at the time. If Yoko helped reinforce his contempt for Paul, the heroin made their differences more irrational. Convinced that Paul was stealing his thunder, if not his soul, John fought his resentment with numbness. In John's eyes, any attempt to function as "a group thing . . . really means more Paul." *Abbey Road,* he concluded, was a perfect example, merely Paul's way of producing "something slick to preserve the myth." Not only that, he despised Paul his self-importance, dismissed his shameless indulgences with the press, and deeply resented what he called "those airs."

John's fury made everything harder. As engineer Phil McDonald recalled: "People would be walking out, banging instruments down, not turning up on time and keeping the others waiting three or four hours, then blaming each other for not having rehearsed or not having played their bit right." Yet even though relations among the boys were "getting fairly dodgy," as Paul recalled, the music remained sharp and daring "even though this undercurrent was going on." The band worked intently throughout the summer of 1969, utilizing every available hour, if not every square inch, in the warren of EMI studios. They crisscrossed regularly between Studios One, Two, and Three, like the cast of a British drawing-room comedy, where different phases of the recording process were simultaneously under way, often communicating with one another or the engineers by walkie-talkie to coordinate the proceedings. "There was a great sort of theater to it," recalled one of the resident technicians, who watched in amazement as the Beatles conducted their tour de force. Not content with just the limited studio facilities, they also took over isolated offices and storage areas where special effects, by remote linkup, were produced.

For example, in Room 43, at the top of a second-floor staircase, they had stashed a cumbersome futuristic-looking machine called a *synthesizer*—"a fantastic toy," as someone close to them described it—which George attempted to program, laboring over it like a demented scientist. The size of a small truck, with "hundreds of jackplugs and two keyboards," it had taken him months of fiddling with the apparatus just to get it switched on. "There wasn't [even] an instruction manual," George recalled, frustrated by his initial inability to get any music out of it. But eventually they figured it out, and the Beatles were the first popular group to record with a synthesizer, incorporating it into the solo on "Maxwell's Silver Hammer" and the instrumental track of "Because." John also used it to create a deliberate white-noise effect during the last three minutes of "I Want You (She's So Heavy)," a jarring little surprise, which he added to disrupt the final version.

By August 8, with the battle still raging around them, the Beatles had completed most of the basic tracks for the album and decided, almost on the spur of the moment, to shoot a photograph for its cover. They had originally contemplated calling the album *Everest,* after the brand of cigarettes that Geoff Emerick smoked. It was typically vague, much like *Rubber Soul* or *Revolver,* typically catchy, typically Beatlesque. That title became so fixed, according to engineer John Kurlander, that by July "someone mentioned the possibility of the four of them taking a private plane over the foothills of Mount Everest to shoot the cover photograph." When they finally came to their senses, however, it was decided to simplify matters completely: "just go outside, take the photo there, call the LP *Abbey Road* and have done with it." *Abbey Road:* it was perfect, a tribute to the studio where they had made almost all their incredible music. On a sheet of white typing paper, Paul roughed out a few sketches that he thought might be appropriate: just an understated picture of the four of them, walking along the crossing in the road outside the studio. None of the other Beatles objected. Even John obliged without the usual huffy debate, and sometime after ten o'clock that Friday morning, they marched companionably onto the street to shoot the now-famous cover photo.

As Paul recalled, "it was a very hot day." All of the Beatles, except George, had worn suits for the occasion, which they regretted in a matter of minutes, courtesy of the brutal overhead sun and the soaring humidity. Iain Macmillan, the photographer, intent on grabbing the shot as quickly as possible, lined them up in the most eye-pleasing order: John, "all leonine" in a resplendent white suit and tennis shoes at the head of the pack; Ringo, dressed funereally, in black tails, just behind him; Paul, wearing navy blue and an open-necked oxford shirt trailing in third place; and George, looking very much like a prisoner from a work-release program in a blue jean outfit, bringing up the rear. John, impatient as ever, urged the process forward. "Come on, hurry up now, keep in step," he muttered, thinking, "Let's get out of here. We're meant to be recording, not posing for Beatle pictures." But there were obstacles, most notably a yellow Volkswagen—a *Beetle,* of all things—parked at the curb in the middle of the shot. "It had been left there by someone on holiday," Macmillan recalled. "A policeman tried to move it away for us, but he couldn't." The VW would stay, along with three other bystanders who had drifted into the scene.

Finally, with all the distractions and everyone's patience growing thin, they lined up for a final take, as Macmillan climbed a ladder in the middle of the street. At the last minute, Paul kicked off his sandals and rejoined the procession. "Barefoot, nice warm day, I didn't feel like wearing shoes," he remembered. Accordingly, he lit a cigarette and carried it at his side.

The ordeal was over after six quick shots, but the scene that morning would linger for posterity. Aside from being perhaps the most famous cover shot ever taken, it inspired a bizarre episode—*another* bizarre episode—in the extraordinary Beatles saga.

When *Abbey Road* was released on September 26, 1969, it touched off a feeding frenzy unusual even for Beatles albums. While the record itself received only lukewarm praise—*Newsweek,* for example, called it "a pleasant but unadventurous collection of basically low-voltage numbers," while the *New York Times* considered it "sincere" but "rather dull"—fans swept up copies at a rate that surpassed all precedent. In Britain, advance orders topped out at 190,000 copies, breaking all previous records for an LP, while in the States the album went gold even before its release. There was no indication that the fans were losing interest; if anything, the Beatles' popularity seemed to be exploring new heights. Their fame had begun to feed on itself. Having survived a tumultuous seven years that won them legendary status, they stood poised to cross into a new decade riding an improbable wave of success.

As always, with the success came the madness. On Friday, October 10, a Detroit disc jockey named Russ Gibb went on the air at WKNR-FM and astonished his listeners with news that Paul McCartney was dead. In fact, he had been dead for several years, Gibb insisted, since at least November 1966, when "at 5 o'clock on a rainswept morning . . . [Paul] was out for a spin in his Aston-Martin; the car crashed and the Beatle was killed." How did he know this? Gibb reached this incredible conclusion after reading a review of *Abbey Road* by a University of Michigan student named Fred LaBour in which elaborate clues were presented as proof that Paul had died and was replaced by a stand-in. The *Abbey Road* cover alone provides rich evidence. On it, Gibb argued, Ringo is dressed in a mortician's outfit, while Paul walks behind him, barefoot, in the manner of a corpse prepared for burial in Italy. In fact, the picture itself resembles a funeral procession. The Volkswagen's license plate was another tip-off: it reads 28 IF, suggesting that Paul would be twenty-eight *if* he had lived. (That the plate's number was 281 F didn't daunt this conspiracy theory.) There was more. On the back cover photo of *Magical Mystery Tour,* Paul wears a black carnation, while John, George, and Ringo wear red ones; meanwhile, Paul is dressed in black, the other Beatles in white; inside the album, a picture reveals Paul, in costume as a soldier, standing above a sign that proclaims "I Was You." This particularly convinced Gibb, who recalled a Paul McCartney look-alike contest two years earlier in which a contestant named William Campbell was chosen the winner. No doubt with a little plastic surgery and minimal makeup, the imposture was completed.

Gibb's announcement touched off rumors that swept across the country. Every commercial radio station, joined by an army of impetuous college deejays, jumped on the story, sending hundreds of thousands of distraught fans scrambling to scour their Beatles records for clues. As if anyone needed more evidence, there was plenty to be found in the grooves. For instance, if "Strawberry Fields Forever" is played at 45 rpm instead of 33⅓, probers claimed that John sings the words "I buried Paul." On the White Album, if the drone "number nine, number nine" is taped and played in reverse, they heard a voice saying, "Turn me on, dead man, turn me on, dead man." Others who played the entire track of "Revolution No. 9" in reverse identified it as the sound of a horrifying traffic accident (although the same could be said of the original track), with a voice crying, "Get me out, get me out!" And still others, listening to the regular version, heard "He hit a pole! We better get him to see a surgeon. [*scream*] So anyhow, he went to see a dentist instead. They gave him a pair of teeth that weren't any good at all so—[*a car horn blares*]." A disc jockey at WNEW-FM in New York even picked up some moaning in the silent groove between "I'm So Tired" and "Blackbird," and when it was reversed he supposedly heard John declaring: "Paul is dead. Miss him. Miss him. Miss him."

Paul is dead. The phrase became a slogan as familiar as almost any tune on *Abbey Road.* TV anchors hammered away at it; so did all the major newspapers. *Paul is dead.* It made good copy, despite vehement denials issued by the dearly departed himself. "I'm alive and well and concerned about the rumors of my death," he told the Associated Press, standing large as life on his doorstep ten days after the story broke. "But if I were dead, I'd be the last to know." It also boosted the Beatles' catalogue sales, with "millions of youthful fans straining ears and eyes for signs of Paul's purported passing [on]...album jackets." *Sgt. Pepper's* reappeared at number 124 in the American charts, with *Magical Mystery Tour* close behind, at 146. And *Abbey Road* continued to outsell its competition by a million units.

While *Paul is dead* brought the Beatles all kinds of financial rewards, for the subject in question it soon became "a bloody nuisance." He couldn't go anywhere or do anything without some busybody making a federal case out of it. "Can you spread it around that I am just an ordinary person and want to live in peace?" he pleaded with a *LIFE* correspondent who tracked him down in the flesh at his farm in Scotland. "For the record: Paul is *not* dead.

"But the Beatle thing," he admitted, "is over."

[III]

In late August 1969, John, Paul, George, and Ringo sold their remaining shares in NEMS Enterprises, officially ending all ties to the company they had joined in January 1962. Then, on September 25 they finally lost the yearlong battle with ATV for control of their Northern Songs catalogue; Paul and John held on to about 30 percent of their songs, but the takeover signaled that the identity they had fought so dearly to preserve was slipping from their hands. Impatient to divest themselves of the equity, they sold their remaining shares in Northern Songs to a reluctant ATV board based on Lew Grade's recommendation that "the songs in Northern will live on forever."

With Northern Songs off the table, John, reeling from shock, finally expressed his wish to leave the Beatles. "I told Allen I was leaving" in September, he explained, but Klein warned him against announcing it publicly. "He didn't want me to tell Paul even." But telling Paul was the least of his worries. On the verge of negotiating a new contract with EMI designed to give the Beatles a larger cut of the wholesale price of record sales, Klein wanted nothing to rock the boat. Any outburst from John would surely threaten that deal. Klein had already failed in his attempts to buy back NEMS and gain control of Northern Songs, as promised. It would justify his worth to the Beatles—and, more important, to Paul, his lone adversary—to close the EMI agreement fast and without a hitch.

John may have held off any announcement of a breakup as a favor to Klein, but his actions spoke louder than words. If he couldn't leave the Beatles outright, he'd simply form another band. Accepting an invitation to perform at the Toronto Rock 'n Roll Revival Festival on September 13 alongside "all the great rockers" who had influenced the Beatles—Chuck Berry, Little Richard, Jerry Lee Lewis, Gene Vincent, and Bo Diddley—John cobbled together a group of sidemen that included Klaus Voormann, Eric Clapton, and Alan White and set out for Canada as the Plastic Ono Band. It didn't matter that they hadn't even rehearsed together. Everyone knew the old standards he'd selected: "Blue Suede Shoes," "Dizzy Miss Lizzie," and "Money," along with fairly straightforward rockers like "Yer Blues." There was also a new song he'd just written called "Cold Turkey." "We tried to rehearse on the plane," John recalled, "but it was impossible." Over the Atlantic, he and Clapton huddled in the galley behind the last row of seats, attempting to go over key signatures and arrangements. Clapton remembered: "We picked out chords on the guitar, which you couldn't hear because we had nowhere to plug in, and, of course, Alan didn't have his drums on the plane with him." It also didn't help matters that both John and Clapton were strung out, fighting off waves of nausea from withdrawal symptoms.

The show itself, although workmanlike—Clapton generously referred to it as "a glorified jam session"—was significant if for no other reason than John's own stunning observation: "It was the first gig I have played since the Beatles stopped doing live performances in 1966." Three years away from the stage! It seemed preposterous, inconceivable. There was nothing quite as satisfying, for John Lennon, as playing rock 'n roll in front of a live audience. Although terrified before going onstage—eyewitnesses report him being "really uptight, edgy, and nervous," and John said, "I just threw up for hours until I went on"—he felt liberated, turned on by the experience. "I can't remember when I had such a good time," he exclaimed. "I don't care who I have to play with, I'm going back to playing rock on stage!"

Be that as it may, he didn't intend to play with any of the Beatles again. On the way back to London, he reiterated his desire to leave the group, going so far as to announce it on the plane to a stunned, if disbelieving, entourage. In separate conversations with Klaus Voormann and Eric Clapton, John confided his plans privately and offered them roles in his new group. The two musicians, perhaps out of uncertainty, chose not to reveal this fact to anyone else. But once back in London, John couldn't slow his momentum. He had to tell the other Beatles. But how? His assistant, Anthony Fawcett, recalled in a memoir that "it was not an easy decision. . . . I watched him agonize for days over it—irritable, chain-smoking, and impossible to be around, skulking in his bedroom, losing himself in sleep or drugging himself with television." Clearly John was conflicted, alternately loathing the group identity and trying to preserve its vaunted existence. The thought of pulling the plug on the Beatles for good terrified him.

In October, during a meeting at the Apple offices at which the Beatles had gathered to sign their new Capitol Records contract, John and Paul went head-to-head over an offer for a TV special. Paul pressed to accept it; John flatly refused. Neither man would give an inch; as their tempers flared, John broke the angry impasse with an unexpected outburst, blurting out his intention to seek a divorce. According to John, Paul, extremely distressed, asked, "What do you mean?" to which he responded: "I mean the group is over. I'm leaving."

The others, for the most part, may have written this off to another of John's overheated threats. George admitted dismissing it as bluster at the time. "*Everybody* had tried to leave" the band at one time or another, he recalled, "so it was nothing new." But John believed "they knew it was for real—unlike Ringo and George's previous threats to leave." Recalled Paul, "Everyone blanched except John, who colored a little, and said, 'It's rather exciting. It's like I remember telling Cynthia I wanted a divorce.'"

Moments after the blowout, a colleague working downstairs in his private office recalled how "John burst into the room, red in the face and fuming with rage. 'That's it—it's all over!' he shouted." It seemed long overdue, but so damn incredible, so final.

And in a way, as Ringo noted, it felt like "a relief." The way he recalled it, "we knew it was [a] good [decision]," interpreting John's dismissal favorably to mean leaving the Beatles intact as a corporate entity, while breaking up the band. The constant sniping and infighting among "the lads" had disturbed Ringo's gentle soul. But still the breakup was "traumatic," and he spent time immediately after the climactic meeting sitting in his garden, "wondering what the hell to do with [his] life." George, on the other hand, wasted no time in regret. "I wanted out myself," he recalled. "I could see a much better time ahead being by myself, away from the band. It had ceased to be fun, and it was time to get out of it."

To Paul's relief, he and Allen Klein persuaded John not to announce the breakup of the Beatles publicly. Klein, having only just gotten his hands on the Beatles, stood to lose the sweet flow of cash they were about to put into the pipeline. It had taken him a long time, longer than anyone realized, to gain control of their empire. A breakup now would throw their affairs into chaos and ultimately derail his management agenda. As for Paul, his entire world, "since I'd been seventeen," he acknowledged, had been wrapped up in the group. He had so much invested in it, emotionally and personally. He loved the music they made, loved the recognition and adulation. And privately he held out hope that John would eventually come around. Announcing that the Beatles had broken up added too much of an obstacle. John knew Paul was trying to buy more time, but for whatever it was worth, John agreed to keep the breakup private. Nothing, however, altered his decision.

Whether or not Paul felt encouraged by John's compromise, he was deeply disturbed by subsequent events. In the days that followed, everyone went his own way, which only heightened the feeling that the Beatles had indeed disbanded. He lapsed into a depression—"a withdrawal," he called it in retrospect—that swung between two emotional extremes. Some days he really missed the band, the guys and their horseplay, but there were also times he despised them. "Anger, deep, deep anger sets in," he recalled, ". . . with yourself, number one, and with everything in the world, number two." He felt cheated, abused. "And justifiably so because I was being screwed by my mates."

It must have seemed like it at the time. The other Beatles had betrayed him, Paul concluded, abandoned the dream they had shared. There was nothing he could do to restore their enthusiasm. The others seemed determined to go their own ways. For a few weeks they avoided one another, convinced that it was necessary to ending the nagging dependency. Any business was left to the accountants and lawyers. But Paul's life and his work were inextricably bound, and it was impossible to separate himself from the Beatles. He tried everything to distract himself from the overwhelming loss. There was a line of artists vying for his production skills. He listened to their tapes, even met with Mary Hopkin and Badfinger to discuss other projects. But nothing seemed to capture his immediate interest. He couldn't even get himself out of bed in the morning. "Then, if I did get up, I had a drink," he recalled. "Straight out of bed." He felt inadequate, empty, convinced that "I'd outlived my usefulness." The Beatles had given his life meaning. As he felt the anchor uproot and drift away, his aimlessness knew no bounds. After three weeks of bumping around between the house and the office in a daze, he grabbed Linda and Heather and headed to the farm in Scotland.

This sudden retreat did nothing to staunch the rumors of Paul's death, which were still swirling in the press and expounded on by a legion of conspiracy theorists determined to prove the grand hoax. Nor did it solve his own deepening malaise. The emptiness and anger continued to consume him. At some point his anger turned to despair. He spent hours, days, weeks, trying to make sense of the breakup, lashing out at anyone who attempted to draw him out of the funk. When he could motivate himself at all, instead of writing music, he spent long hours outside "just planting trees" or helping Linda renovate the old farmhouse, making it suitable for a family.

It never occurred to Paul just how much he missed John. More than anyone else, John had been his friend for ten years, to say nothing of his collaborator, his sidekick, his shadow. Not only had they played music together, they'd hung out together, dreamed together, fucked together, become famous together. Grown up together. "We were each other's intimates," he acquiesced. By the barest accounts, the relationship had given him "security, warmth, humor, wit, money, fame. . . ." At first Paul held out hope that the separation was temporary, admitting that "nobody"—especially himself—"quite knew if it was just one of John's little flings and that maybe he was going to feel the pinch in a week's time and say, 'I was only kidding.'" But as the weeks, then months, ticked away, Paul finally realized it wasn't a joke. Convinced that John was now abandoning him, increasingly jealous of his relationship with Yoko—and Allen Klein—Paul atoned for the loss with anger. He was angry at the Beatles, but even angrier at John. It took another six months for him to admit the extent of his heartbreak. "John's in love with Yoko," Paul confessed to a reporter from the *Evening Standard,* "and he's no longer in love with the other three of us." But for all intents and purposes, he might as well have been talking about himself.

Without John, Paul finally admitted, the Beatles were indeed a thing of the past. That did not mean that their music wouldn't endure, that it wouldn't resonate; however, the band as they knew it was finished. The immensity of it flattened him like a speeding car.

Then, one day just after Christmas in 1969, Paul emerged from the foggy wreck. He had a Studer four-track installed at his house in St. John's Wood and, in an attempt to "get it together," began doing the only thing he knew how to: making a new record. Only this time, he was making it by himself.

As far as Paul knew, even as he began this novel adventure, the other three Beatles had already moved on to other projects that expressed their new-found independence. Ringo segued from his brief self-doubt right into making an album of standards—"songs Ringo likes and his parents love," according to an Apple press release—called *Sentimental Journey* with the assistance of George Martin, while George produced records on Apple for Billy Preston and Doris Troy. In his spare time, George even played a few dates as part of Delaney and Bonnie's funk band, shuffling onstage anonymously and without fanfare, which rekindled his enthusiasm for performing. There were no expectations other than playing music that really rocked—and, better yet, no screaming, ducking, police escorts, helicopters, and running for one's life. The experience proved so satisfying that it led George to admit: "I'd like to do it with the Beatles, but not on the old scale, that's the only drag." His preference, he said, would be to model it loosely on "Delaney and Bonnie, with . . . a few more singers and a few trumpets, saxes, organ, and all that."

John was another story altogether. By late fall his and Yoko's life together had become a traveling carnival of put-ons and misbehavior, rhetoric, and activism. No opportunity to grab headlines, no matter how inane or scandalous, went unexplored. After Yoko suffered yet another miscarriage that nearly took her life, the couple went on a tear of public misadventure that stretched out into the following year. To set the scene, they staged a four-hour retrospective of their self-produced films at London's Institute of Contemporary Arts. Under cover of darkness, a "frequently perplexed audience" watched unending footage from *Two Virgins, John and Yoko's*

Honeymoon, Rape, and *Self-Portrait,* the latter of which featured John "smiling beatifically while bird, traffic, and airline noises are heard on the soundtrack." A week later they announced plans to help fund and launch the *Peace,* a 570-ton Dutch freighter converted into a pirate radio station that was to anchor outside the territorial waters of Israel and Egypt, from where it would broadcast news, political commentary, and music. And following that, they released *The Wedding Album,* a lavishly decorated box set of mementos from their marriage ceremony along with an LP that contained one whole side of John and Yoko screaming each other's name.

It didn't stop there. Despite John's concerns that the Beatles were going broke, he gave away Dor Inis, an island off County Mayo in Ireland that he bought as an investment in 1966, offering it free to a group of "dropouts and nonconformists" called the London Street Commune. He and Yoko "donated" tens of thousands of pounds to the Black House, the London headquarters of the militant black power movement, via his drug dealer Michael X.

Then, in perhaps the most unexpected and bizarre twist, John sent his chauffeur, Les Anthony, to Buckingham Palace to return his Order of the British Empire to the Queen, accompanied by a flippant note typed on Bag Productions stationery that read: "I am returning the M.B.E. in protest against Britain's involvement in the Nigeria-Biafra thing, against our support of America in Vietnam, and against 'Cold Turkey' slipping down the charts." British citizens were outraged by his gesture, which they considered a public relations gimmick at the most, and at the very least, disrespectful. A diabolical-looking picture of John and Yoko, smugly holding an identical letter sent to Prime Minister Wilson that appeared in every major newspaper the next day, only boosted public scorn. John told a BBC correspondent that he'd been "mulling it over for a few years." In an eerily delivered rejoinder, he muttered: "Really shouldn't have taken it. Felt I had sold out. I must get rid of it. I kept saying, 'I must get rid of it.' So I did. Wanted to get rid of it by 1970 anyway." He said he had been waiting for "an event to tie up with it," and while he sided with neither Nigeria nor Biafra, he was "beginning to be ashamed of being British."

By saying that, John had finally crossed the line. Even George Harrison admitted the public now viewed John as "a lunatic or something." If he wasn't off his rocker, as many suspected, he had lost their unconditional respect. The *Daily Mirror* went so far as to name John "Clown of the Year" for 1969.

In January 1970 John recorded a new Plastic Ono Band single, "Instant Karma," with Phil Spector overseeing the production. An all-out rocker with a great hook and sharp percussive accents playing against John's raw, agitated vocal, Spector layered it with his trademark "wall of sound" to give the track a heavy, haunting swell, then "mixed [it] instantly," practically on the spot, so as not to lose the incredible energy. It was a powerful piece of music-making straight out of John's Cavern and Kaiserkeller handbag, which to his ears sounded "fantastic . . . like there were fifty people playing." It was honest, thrashing, concussive rock 'n roll. In fact, it was exactly the sound he'd described to George Martin when they set out to record *Let It Be*.

Perhaps there was still hope for that as well. John's enthusiasm over the single led Allen Klein to hire Spector to remix the tapes of *Let It Be*. "None of us could face remixing them," John recalled. They'd been moldering in the can, untouched, for almost a year. Letting Spector have a pass at them, "to tidy up some of the tracks," so to speak, might salvage the abandoned session. George and Ringo voiced no objection, and since Paul hadn't signed the management agreement, they saw no reason to seek his approval. In fact, Paul knew nothing about it until a remixed test pressing of "The Long and Winding Road," which Allen Klein chose as the first single, arrived at his house along with a note from Klein explaining that the changes were necessary. "I couldn't believe it," Paul told Ray Connolly in an interview published shortly thereafter in the *Evening Standard*. It was the same acoustic track he'd written and sung on, but "with harps, horns, an orchestra, and women's choir added." Someone had come in and tampered with his music—the first time *that* had ever happened.

Paul was offended by it and enraged, not only by the remix but that it had been done behind his back. He threatened to sue Klein until John Eastman advised him that it was pointless. To make matters worse, Paul was informed in a handwritten memo from John and George that his solo album, which had been given an April 17 release date, would have to be pushed back to June 4 to make room for *Let It Be* and its accompanying documentary film, which United Artists was releasing the following month. "It's stupid for Apple to put out two big albums within 7 days of each other," they wrote him, "so we sent a letter to EMI telling them to hold your release date. . . . It's nothing personal."

Nothing personal!

That did it, that was the last straw, according to Paul. "From my point of view, I was getting done in," he recalled. "All the decisions were now three against one." Instead of complying, however, instead of following the idea of "majority rules," he dug in his heels. He would not agree, insisting that Apple hold to the original plan.

The other Beatles tried to ameliorate the situation in a series of frantic phone calls, but it was hopeless. "I had an understanding," Paul insisted, refusing to budge off the mark. He even called Joe Lockwood at EMI to complain that he was being sabotaged. On every side, it seemed, they had reached an impasse. Klein convinced the others that Paul's solo album would confuse the public and dilute the impact of *Let It Be*, and perhaps he was right. Either way, they weren't about to let that happen. Finally, as the release date loomed, Paul offered an alternative way out of the mess. He called George, in his capacity as an officer of the company, and said, "I want to get off the label." Replied George: "You'll stay on the fucking label. Hare Krishna." And he hung up.

Still, it didn't end there. With the release date now only weeks away, the others decided they had to confront Paul directly in an effort to change his mind. One of them was recruited to go ring his doorbell and reach a compromise. "Unfortunately, it was Ringo," Paul recalled. The gentlest of the Beatles, the only one who never uttered a bad word about his bandmates, who genuinely loved the others and wanted only their love in return, Ringo appeared at Cavendish Avenue with a letter from the group. "We want you to put your release date back, it's for the good of the group," he told Paul, who went blind with rage. Paul finally snapped and in an interview a week later said, "I called him everything under the sun." He gave poor Ringo a royal tongue-lashing, backing him helplessly against a wall and shaking a finger in his face as all the bitterness and frustration came hurling out. Paul has said in subsequent interviews that it almost came to blows—"it was near enough," he admitted—but just before things reached that point, he came to his senses and simply threw Ringo out.

An alternative offer, although generous, put Paul in an untenable position: in order to release his solo album first, the Beatles insisted he sign the management contract. He flat-out refused. Finally, Ringo threw up his hands in surrender. George Harrison, perhaps out of frustration, also relented. He persuaded the others to let Paul have his way. But overall, George stuck to his belief that Paul "was just trying to grab a bit of the momentum," much as he'd always done. He was just being Paul, an egomaniac, out for himself.

By the end of April 1970, everyone knew it was all over. The only unresolved issue was: Who would spill the beans? Who would go public first?
John, more than anyone, had already distanced himself from the Beatles,
and he'd told friends that he'd left the group for good. As far as he cared,
"there was no common goal anymore," nothing to keep him tied to the
past. But for whatever reason, he chose not to announce it to the press.

Paul, however, couldn't resist. Peter Brown was pressing Paul to do
some selective interviews for the launch of his new solo album, to no avail.
Paul was bitter, despondent. He wasn't in any mood to put a good face on
the Beatles' breakup and he didn't want to face the press with anything but
his best. He couldn't bear to answer the same nagging question: Are you
happy? Even hearing it, he admitted, "almost made me cry." In lieu of interviews, Brown suggested an old Brian Epstein tactic: a homemade ques-
tionnaire. He'd pose a series of mundane questions that Paul could answer,
with some forethought and at his leisure.

Of course, Paul went him one better: they would include it along with
the album's liner notes, as an insert, perhaps, in copies that were sent out
for review. Little did Brown suspect what Paul was really up to.

Q: Do you foresee a time when Lennon-McCartney becomes an active
songwriting partnership again?

A: No.

Q: Have you plans for live appearances with the Beatles?

A: No.

Q: Is your break with the Beatles temporary or permanent, due to personal differences or musical ones?

A: Personal differences, business differences, but most of all because I
have a better time with my family. Temporary or permanent? I don't
know.

Q: Are you planning a new album or single with the Beatles?

A: No.

Q: Do you miss the Beatles and George Martin? Was there a moment,
e.g. when you thought, "Wish Ringo was here for this break?"

A: No.

The *Daily Mirror* headline shot around the world: PAUL LEAVES THE
BEATLES. Newspapers everywhere quickly picked up the story. "Beatle Paul
McCartney confirmed today that he has broken with the Beatles—but 'did
not know' if it was temporary or permanent.' . . . He said he was not in

contact with manager Alan [sic] Klein 'and he does not represent me in any way.'" The rest of the article used everything Paul provided in his "questions and answers" survey to defend the breakup.

What did John have to say about this? Connolly rang him for comment about three the next afternoon, when he finally awoke, and filled him in on the events. "He was cross about it," Connolly remembers. He had no idea Paul was going public and was furious that he had been scooped. "Oh, Christ," John swore, "he gets all the credit for it!"

For an instant, Paul's announcement brought everything to a standstill. A lucid stillness filled the void. The music fell silent. All the tension melted away, the demands of unimaginable superstardom ceased. For the moment, the world as they knew it stopped spinning, seemed perfectly at peace. As the Beatles, they had been to the toppermost of the poppermost. They had encountered the crowds, heard the screams, felt the love. *Saw the light.* In a brief and shining interval, they had lived a dream that no Liverpool lad could imagine—a magical, fabulous dream, like out of a fairy tale. An unforgettable dream. "It was wonderful and it's over," John affirmed to all those waiting for a sign. "And so, dear friends, you'll just have to carry on. The Dream Is Over."

But the legend of the Beatles had only just begun.

There would be the release of *Let It Be,* in all its suffocated Phil Spector production, and then one after another Beatles re-release—red albums, blue albums, rock albums, movie albums, number ones and studio tapes, all massive sellers, all exposing not just old fans but new ones to the magic and the myth. There would be solo careers with hits and misses, crass duets (Paul) and graying all-star supergroups (Ringo and George). There would be huge stadiums of fans cheering Wings, Paul's post-Beatles group, and strollers in Manhattan's Central Park who would smile as John and Yoko passed them by, as if the most normal thing in the world was one of the Beatles at ease. There would be a December night in 1980 when a man walked up to John and shot him in the chest, ending his life. There would be the night, nineteen years later, when an intruder broke into George's home and stabbed him, then the Tuesday in November 2001, when George succumbed to cancer, the cigarettes catching up to him before the jelly babies. Ringo's ex, Maureen, died of cancer in 1996; Paul's "Lovely Linda" would die of cancer, too, in 1998. But not all was ashen. There would be babies born to Beatles, to Beatles fans, millions of people who lived their lives to a soundtrack crafted by four Scouse boys who had either grown up or passed along. And the story changed as the players aged. Paul was no longer Paul—he was Sir Paul, knighted by the Queen in 1997. John was no longer John—he was Saint John, an archetype to angry young rock 'n rollers everywhere. George was no longer a third wheel— he was George Harrison, an artist in his own right and a humanitarian who organized benefit concerts to feed the poor and change the world, *something* and then some. And Ringo—well, he was still Ringo. Always would be. Sure, he had married a former Bond girl, and his son had become the drummer he feared he would, but otherwise, life remained full of simple pleasures. The sickly boy who had almost died so many times had outlived two of his bandmates and so many others in this story. Lives begun together ended apart, as happens everywhere, even in pop songs. But the Beatles were no longer just boys who had played rock 'n roll. They had been mere babes when it all happened; when the band split, McCartney was all of twenty-nine years old; John and Ringo, thirty; and George, twenty-seven. But on reflection, on the radio, on vinyl and cassette and CD, they became not kids, not a band, not anything like anything else. The Beatles. A vastness of talent, of charm, of genius, incomprehensible, an ocean like the one four boys once looked out upon, peering west from the hills of Liverpool. And from them, a flood of song and love and pain and beauty, a flood that cascaded out of the Cavern and Hamburg and London town, into the world, a flow that pushed aside what had come before, that cleansed and battered and in the end nourished. Water.

ACKNOWLEDGMENTS

No one suspected that the two years set aside to research and write this book would ultimately stretch into seven. Throughout the often rugged, always solitary process, I was the beneficiary of the kindness of many people whose assistance and encouragement are responsible for the outcome, and they deserve to share the credit—though none of the criticism—for its content.

The book grew out of a profile commissioned by the *New York Times Magazine* (and eventually published in the newspaper's Arts and Leisure section), which has always been the preeminent showcase for a journalist's work, or as the Beatles might put it: the toppermost of the poppermost. In addition, the paper's morgue and files served as an essential resource, as well as the blueprint for an accurate chronology. And yet, none of it compared with the enormous reference bonanza provided by the *Times'* longtime columnist and resident Beatles expert, Allan Kozinn, whose archives could endow a small museum. His unassuming expertise, to say nothing of his extreme generosity, proved invaluable throughout the writing of this book. All of this was reinforced by various libraries, museums, and their staffs, including the British Library Newspaper Library, the Picton Library in Liverpool, the Business Information Library (U.K.), British Information Services (New York), the Birmingham Chamber of Commerce and Industry (U.K., Rachel Neale), the Liverpool Record Office (Bob Jones), the *Liverpool Echo*, Liverpool Library & Information Services, the Press Association Library (U.K., John Davey), the Victoria and Albert Museum (London), and Wilton Library in Connecticut.

I am indebted to the British Tourist Authority, British Rail (Pat Titley), British Airways, and United Airlines (particularly Cathy Ladd Rodgers) for their kind assistance. I also wish to thank Maria Jefferies for providing access to the *Melody Maker* and *NME* files, Helena Farrington at Pentagram Design (London), Sarah Lazin, Mark Lewisohn, Hans Olof

Gottfridsson (author of a prodigious volume on the Beatles in Hamburg), David Jones of the *Daily Mail*, Spencer Leigh, the late Sarah Calkins, Denny Somac, Trevor Cajio of *Now Dig This*, Annie Bowman at *Hello!*, Barry Rillera, Terry O'Neill, Karen Durbin, the staff at EMI Studios/ Abbey Road, Helter Skelter (London), and especially Eddie Sutton and Jeff Gmelch, who have always set aside a few millimeters of the Strand's "eight miles of books" to aid my research

I am grateful to everyone in Liverpool and London who opened their doors—and hearts—to share extraordinary recollections. Those who agreed to be interviewed for the book are cited in the notes; however, a few deserve special mention. They include historian J. Quentin Hughes, who guided me through four hundred years of local history, in addition to the details of his intimate, albeit embattled, friendship with Arthur Ballard; Joan Murray, for her thorough research of Everton; Mark Julius, the City of Liverpool's director of Housing and Consumer Services, for patiently answering endless questions about Allerton, Speke, Woolton, Childwall, and the Dingle; W. J. Newton of the Liverpool Cotton Association, Ltd.; Shelagh Johnson of the Beatles Museum; Richard Corbett, MEP, Liverpool; Tony and Mary Kenny for their vivid recollection of Litherland; Fred O'Brien of Northern Design; Cavern City Tours; the wild and woolly Adelphi Hotel; and the guys behind the counter at the Beatles Shop.

Archives are a biographer's most invaluable resource, and I was granted access to several exceptional collections. I wish to thank Scotty Meade for sharing the interviews conducted for his lovely *Abbey Road* documentary; Jere Herzenberg and Jane Krupp, the executors of Albert Goldman's estate, for providing dozens of taped interviews assembled for his book *The Lives of John Lennon;* Bill Harry, whose attic full of Beatles memorabilia rivaled the almost fifty hours of personal stories he shared (but not quite), not to mention his expert guided tour of Liverpool; Larry Kane, for making the large collection of his interviews with the Beatles—as well as himself—available; the creative staff of the BBC's wonderful series *Arena*—most notably Anthony Wall, Diana Mansfield, Debby Geller, and Alison Willett—who assisted my research consistently over the years and provided hundreds of pages of transcripts from their masterful "Brian Epstein" documentary; and especially the irrepressible Jonathon Green, author of two stellar works on the sixties culture—*Days in the Life* and *All Dressed Up*—for permitting me to examine and quote from his interviews, raid his fabulous book collection, crash at his flat, badger him incessantly for definitions of British slang, and revel in his enduring friendship. For that, I am gobsmacked and dead chuffed.

In fact, friendships were tested time and again over the years, especially those beset by the excuse "Sorry, can't—I'm writing." Throughout the seemingly endless ordeal, I was enriched by the kindness of devoted friends whose patience, understanding, and support kept the essential elements in balance. My deepest gratitude goes to my dearest friends Angie and Sandy D'Amato, who have shared so many laughs as well as their lives with me, and to Laura Schneider, Robert Spector, Lindsay Maracotta, Yak Lubowsky, Sue and Stanley Schneider, Rob Harris, Everett Potter, Phyllis and Craig Hauenstein, Steve Manz, and Mark Bittman, all of whom checked in often and never questioned the depths to which I had sunk. The same goes for David and Maria Feld, who kept me well fed and in stitches. I'd also like to thank my parents for their loving support; my beautiful daughter, Lily, throughout whose young life she has only known "Dad and his Beatles biography"; as well as Janet and Ken Kretchmer.

Among the many people to whom I am indebted, I must thank Tally Gentry, whose research was of great assistance; Neal Gabler, for exchanging war stories; Jim and Michelle Ford, in whose good hands Lily often resided so that I could work through weekends; and my great friends at Pace: Nancy Oakley, Mickey McLean, Brian Cook, and especially Duncan Christy, whose friendship and generous support will never be taken for granted. Meanwhile, no words can express my appreciation for Sloan Harris, my friend and agent, whose indispensable advice, candor, and encouragement steered me through treacherous terrain and whose faith in me never wavered. The folks at Little, Brown went to extraordinary lengths to support this book, even when it seemed prudent to do otherwise. Michael Pietsch always believed in the Beatles' story—always! And when the grinding pressures as publisher prevented him from editing the manuscript, he left me in the very capable hands of Geoff Shandler. Geoff's keen and laborious edit gave the book shape, sharpened its focus, refined my voice, and endeavored to salvage the yeah, yeah, yeah. For the endless hours he devoted to this book, I shall be forever grateful. I also appreciate the invaluable editorial assistance of Junie Dahn. My sincere thanks to Mario Pulice for a lovely book cover—make that *two* lovely covers—and to Steve Lamont for meticulous—actually, heroic—copyediting.

Special thanks also go to Barbara Witt, whose 1964 school notebook provided the lovely endpapers.

Lastly, I would like to pay tribute to the remarkable individuals I met throughout the course of my research, and to those who are no longer with us. I shall especially miss George Harrison (won't we all!), Derek Taylor, Bob Wooler, Alistair Taylor, Johnny "Guitar" Byrne, Colin Manley, Lionel Bart, Eric Griffiths, Henry Henroid, Walter Shenson, and my dear friend and role model, Timothy White, who encouraged me to write, gave me my first assignment, and reminded me time and again, through his writing and example, how easy it was to bring honor and dignity to rock 'n roll.

Friends, family, colleagues, sources—in my life, I've loved them all.

Bob Spitz, 2005

One of the drawbacks in preparing a definitive biography of the Beatles is the stunning lack of reliable source material. Most of the nearly 500 volumes that make up their canon lack proper citations, and even in those remarkable cases where sources are offered, the accuracy remains suspect. Either memories were vague, tales were recycled, facts went unchecked, or circumstances were fabricated or obscured—sometimes by prejudiced eye-witnesses, other times to protect the innocent. For better or worse, misinformation has always been a key element of the Beatles' legend.

The extent of the misinformation owes much to Napoleon's claim that "history is a set of lies agreed upon." That became clear to me when beginning the research for this book. During an interview with Paul McCartney, he explained how nearly forty years ago the Beatles agreed on a "version of the facts" that would serve as their story, and they stuck to—and embroidered upon—it ever since. Paul told me "about 65 percent" of their "official biography, *The Beatles*—written in 1967, by journalist Hunter Davies—is accurate. (Referring to the book in a lengthy 1970 interview with Jann Wenner, John Lennon said: "It was bullshit . . . my auntie [Mimi] knocked all the truth bits from my childhood and my mother out. . . . I wanted a real book to come out, but we all had wives and didn't want to hurt their feelings.") What's more, all of it has been told and retold so many times that even McCartney is no longer certain where the truth begins and ends—one of the reasons, no doubt, that the wonderful *Anthology* is often referred to as *Mythology*. In any case, the "official Beatles biography" is not only loaded with misstatements and lovely little fairy tales, but inaccuracies: misspelled names, incorrect dates, confused locations—and wide, gaping holes.

Even so, I have relied upon the Davies book to support some of my own research. The oral histories provided in it by the four Beatles—their offhand remarks, as well as their quirky versions of long-forgotten events—

are nevertheless poignant and provide the only vivid (and fascinating) accounts of certain escapades. To the extent that I have incorporated quotes from that book into this biography, be assured that they were scrutinized for accuracy or chosen because they contain a personal reflection that was unassailable for its honesty. Lastly, let it be said that for many of the book's participants — George Harrison's parents; John's aunt Mimi and his father, Freddie; Ringo's mother; Millie Best; and other secondary, supporting characters — the Davies book stands as their only testimony to this remarkable story.

Among other books mentioned in the notes are examples that are either hagiographic or downright silly but nevertheless contain an important interview or anecdote that could not be ignored. For instance, Gareth Pawlowski's *How They Became the Beatles* is one fan's moon-eyed excursion to his idols' birthplace, but it contains an agreement detailing the specific terms of a Larry Parnes engagement, as well as conspicuously revealing photographs. Cynthia Lennon's autobiography, *A Twist of Lennon,* mangles facts as well as dates (she even gets the year of her marriage to John wrong!) while offering personal, affecting reflections that are historically valuable. Still other books are infuriating for their damnable oversight. Keith Badman's *The Beatles: Off the Record* contains one of the most comprehensive compendiums of the band's interviews — with nary a citation. The same goes for *The Beatles: An Oral History,* by David Pritchard and Alan Lysaght, which contains a wealth of revealing interviews. *Where did they come from?* In every case in which information from these books has been used, I relied on seven years of my own durable research, as well as the biographer's intuition — and ear — in determining a source's authenticity.

I was fortunate to work from an amazing archive of magazine and newspaper articles collected and collated by Allan Kozinn, the eminent *New York Times* music columnist and Beatles authority. These papers include most of the *Times'* files, even articles from the morgue that had been "killed" for space considerations, as well as other essential journals from around the world. Among them were most of the articles from *Melody Maker* and *New Musical Express,* both of which reported weekly and extensively on the Beatles' adventures. In the course of my research, however, it was disclosed that many of the Beatles' quotes in those articles — later incorporated into *Anthology* — came via telephone interviews in which Neil Aspinall or Mal Evans masqueraded as John or Paul and, thus, should be taken with a grain of salt. Whenever possible, the quotes in this book came from articles containing eyewitness accounts or those in which it was clear that one of the Beatles was actually in a room with the journalist.

As far as an accurate chronology goes, newspapers served to document the comings and goings of the Beatles; otherwise, I depended on Mark Lewisohn's various listings, including *The Beatles Live!*, *The Beatles: 25 Years in the Life*, *Recording Sessions*, and *The Complete Beatles Chronicle*.

A note about a particular resource deserves further explanation. In the notes that follow, I often credit the Albert Goldman Archives (AGA), which are quite an extensive series of taped interviews for Goldman's controversial—and discredited—biography, *The Lives of John Lennon*. For all his foibles as a writer (and they were many, and legendary), Albert was a dear and trusted friend, who I remained close to until his untimely death. Even so, I found his biography of John unreadable, as well as irresponsible, and told him so. When I decided to write this book, however, I sought out his executors and purchased copies of the taped interviews he conducted for *Lives*. That acquisition turned out to be shocking, revealing, and incredibly rewarding. As far as anyone can determine, Albert never bothered to transcribe the tapes, taking only what he blithely referred to as "the good parts"—those pull quotes that would prove sensational—for his manuscript. Much of the information he chose to ignore, however, was extraordinary in detail, not at all like anything in his book or that we had heard before. Interviews with John's cousins Stanley Parkes and Leila Harvey provided intimate information about the Stanleys, the Smiths, and a boy they described as lovable and gregarious. Barbara Baker's lurid account of their sexual exploits upstaged the poignant recollections about John's and Paul's early songwriting sessions that were left out of the Goldman book. *The Lives of John Lennon* speaks for itself; I hope the material I used from Albert's research adds substance to my account and brings honor to his efforts as a scholar—and to the Beatles' amazing story.

The most important resource for this book was the hundreds of interviews I conducted with the Beatles' family members, friends, fellow performers, and colleagues who provided new, firsthand information and colored in essential details of all the old anecdotes that had become part of the Beatles' myth. Of course, some sources have told their stories so often—and at Beatles conventions, where they are paid a fee for appearing— that they have become rote and are generally unreliable. But scores of these people had never been interviewed before, and the information they provided has helped form a portrait of the Beatles that is both fascinating and substantially different from all previous accounts. Each of their contributions is cited in the notes by name and date, with additional information included where necessary.

PROLOGUE

3　Description of Litherland: Author interviews with Tony Kenny, 2/8/98; Johnny Byrne, 10/8/97; and Tony and Mary Kenny, 4/21/98.

3　The four boys, riding . . . like astronauts: Author interview with Chas Newby, 5/21/98.

5　"We thought we were the best": Sheff, *Playboy Interviews*, p. 62.

5　The word around town: "There was [no band] worse than the Beatles." Author interview with Ray Ennis, 10/1/97. "Although the Beatles had charisma, you couldn't say they were good." Author interview with Sam Leach, 10/6/97.

6　"We sure didn't know them": Author interview with Howie Casey, 10/27/97.

6　"They were so bad": Ted "Kingsize" Taylor, 9/2/85, AGA.

6　Paul McCartney had squandered: Alan Durband, quoted in Salewicz, *McCartney*, p. 69.

6　George Harrison, who regarded school: "George did go back and sit, but he failed everything." Author interview with Arthur Kelly, 1/10/98.

6　Thrilled by performing, Pete Best: Best & Doncaster, *Beatle!*, p. 13.

6　"a gang of scruffs": "We looked like a gang." Paul McCartney in Shepherd, *True Story of the Beatles*, p. 52.

7　"They're fantastic": Author interview with Bob Wooler, 10/30/97.

8　Litherland had a great many shops: Author interview with Don Andrew, 10/4/97.

10　But before he got their name out: "I remember Wooler telling us to begin as soon as the curtains opened, but Paul started singing 'Long Tall Sally' before . . ." Author interview with Chas Newby, 5/21/98.

10　The band's physical appearance: "We went and bought these leather jackets [together]. . . . We all bought cowboy boots as well. Mine and John's were Twin Eagles." Author interview with Johnny Byrne, 10/8/97.

11　"I'd never seen any band look like this": Author interview with Dave Foreshaw, 10/31/97. Bob Wooler says: "The overriding feeling was, 'Who the hell are they?'" Author interview with Bob Wooler, 10/30/97.

11　"It was just so different": Author interview with Billy J. Kramer, 12/16/97.

12　"get your knickers down!": Salewicz, *McCartney*, p. 104; confirmed by Chas Newby in author interview, 5/21/98.

CHAPTER 1: A PROPER UPBRINGING

15　"Gateway to the British Empire": *Encyclopaedia Britannica*.

15　"Scousers": Author interview with Quentin Hughes, 10/3/97; first citation of *scouse* in Oxford English Dictionary, dated 1945. But Jonathon Green dates nautical use to the nineteenth century, author interview with Jonathan Green, 7/3/98.

16　"Scousers have a fierce . . . patriotism": Author interview with Bill Harry, 8/2/97.

16　"stout little ships": W. F. Machin, "A Short History of Liverpool Cotton Market" (typescript, 1957), p. 2.

16　an elaborate Grecian influence: Picton, *Architectural History of Liverpool*, p. 65.

16　the richest city in Britain: Author interview with Quentin Hughes, 10/3/97.

17　"surpasses the pyramid of Cheops": Picton, *Memorials of Liverpool*, p. 660.

18　"a real old sea sailor": Stanley Parkes, 2/3/85, AGA.

19　Julia, nicknamed Judy: "Everybody called her Judy." Leila Harvey, 10/84, AGA.

19　Their first child was a boy: Stanley Parkes, 2/3/85, AGA.

19　Penny Lane: "Penny Lane is not only a street, it's a district." Sheff, *Playboy Interviews*, p. 130.

19　"Those women were fantastic": Ibid., p. 136.

19   "She was born with a keen sense": Stanley Parkes, 2/3/85, AGA.

19   "She had a great sense": Author interview with Pete Shotton, 1/19/98.

20   "I had no intention of getting married": Mimi Smith, AGA (undated).

20   "Grandfather made it impossible": Stanley Parkes, 2/3/85, AGA.

20   "That's long enough!": Ibid.

20   Julia, George Stanley's favorite: "Judy was his favorite." Leila Harvey, 10/84, AGA.

21   "perfect profile": Davies, *Beatles,* p. 6.

21   "I soon forgot my father": Ibid., p. 12.

21   "They wanted nothing to do with him": Leila Harvey, 10/84, AGA.

21   "we knew he would be no use": Davies, *Beatles,* p. 6.

21   "very intelligent . . . a clever boy": Stanley Parkes, 2/3/85, AGA.

21   "Anywhere Freddie turned up": Ibid.

22   "As I walked past her": Davies, *Beatles,* p. 5.

22   "she would get a joke": Stanley Parkes, 2/3/85, AGA.

22   Men ogled her: "Everybody would wink at her, but she laughed, she enjoyed it." Leila Harvey, 10/84, AGA.

22   "Judy was very feminine": Ibid.

23   Instead of working: "He and Julia used to take me out for long walks in the park." Stanley Parkes, 2/3/85, AGA.

23   allegedly at George Stanley's behest: Goldman, *Lives of John Lennon,* p. 29.

23   Entire neighborhoods . . . "just *gone*": Author interview with Quentin Hughes, 10/3/97.

24   but Freddie was gone: Author interview with Charles Lennon, 10/2/97.

24   "Mrs. Lennon has just had a boy": Coleman, *Lennon,* p. 24.

24   "I was dodging in doorways": Davies, *Beatles,* p. 25.

25   "Mary would, on occasion": Stanley Parkes, 2/3/85, AGA.

25   "she would have always had a fellow": Leila Harvey, 10/84, AGA.

25   "pain . . . of not being wanted": John Lennon, 1971 interview, in *Anthology,* p. 7.

25   "I said to her, there's a war on": Davies, *Beatles,* p. 8.

26   he set out on the *Sammex:* Goldman, *Lives of John Lennon,* p. 30.

26   "She claimed that she was raped": Author interview with Charles Lennon, 10/2/97.

27   "she was told quite categorically": Leila Harvey, 10/84, AGA.

27   "She was a beautiful baby": Anne Cadwallader, 9/84, AGA.

27   a Norwegian Salvation Army captain: Ibid.

28   "would always wink at [Julia]": Leila Harvey, 10/84, AGA.

28   Spiv: "So we, as kids, just named him Spiv . . . and it stuck": Stanley Parkes, 2/3/85, AGA.

28   "a nervous cough and . . . thinning . . . hair": John Lennon, 1979 interview, in *Anthology,* p. 10.

28   "He was certainly earning good money": Stanley Parkes, 1/19/85, AGA.

28   "He had a very short fuse": Author interview with Nigel Walley, 3/11/98.

28   "my mother came to see us": John Lennon, 1967 interview, in *Anthology,* p. 10.

28   "It confused him": Albert Goldman, from handwritten notes, 1985.

28   "Oh, for heaven's sake": Leila Harvey, 2/4/85, AGA.

29   "You are not fit": Ibid., 10/84.

29   "disagree with the way she was living": Stanley Parkes, 2/3/85, AGA.

29   "A little bit of tea": Leila Harvey, 10/84, AGA.

29   John's unofficial guardian: "She said she couldn't refuse." Davies, *Beatles,* p. 8.

29   "intending never to come back": Ibid.

29   five years of indifference: "Of not being wanted," John Lennon, 1971 interview, in *Anthology,* p. 7.

29   "She said no": Davies, *Beatles,* pp. 8–9.

30   "He had to decide": Ibid., p. 9.

30 a decision "was forced" on Julia: "It was Mimi and Julia's father that demanded Julia give John up." Leila Harvey, 2/3/85, AGA.

30 "My mother . . . couldn't cope": Sheff, *Playboy Interviews*, p. 136.

30 "a proper upbringing": "Mary would be strict and give him a proper upbringing." Stanley Parkes, 2/3/85, AGA.

30 no-nonsense, if "difficult," housewife: "Mary can be quite difficult." Leila Harvey, 10/84, AGA.

30 "Mimi was a sensible, dignified lady": Ibid.

31 "merciless disciplinarian": Author interview with Pete Shotton, 1/19/98.

31 "she *wanted* John": Leila Harvey, 10/84, AGA.

31 *Wind in the Willows:* "It was passed from me to Leila, from Leila to John." Stanley Parkes, 2/3/85, AGA.

31 Mimi's morning room was always filled: Ibid.

31 "a quiet and jolly man": Stanley Parkes, 1/19/85, AGA.

31 "Uncle George absolutely adored John": Leila Harvey, 10/84, AGA.

32 "I had no time": Coleman, *Lennon*, p. 27.

32 Mimi shelved "twenty volumes": Ibid., p. 26.

32 "My mother had a .22": Stanley Parkes, 2/3/85, AGA.

33 "fit in": "Anyone who had anything didn't fit in." John Lennon, 1969 interview, in *Anthology*, p. 9.

33 "in a trance for twenty years": John Lennon, 1980 interview, in *Anthology*, p. 9.

33 "very deprived": Wenner, *Lennon Remembers*, p. 166.

33 "This image of me being the orphan": Sheff, *Playboy Interviews*, p. 136.

CHAPTER 2: THE MESSIAH ARRIVES

34 "There was always a bad reception": Author interview with Colin Manley, 10/2/97.

34 He was known to "behave distractedly": Account of Lennon's ritual, author interview with Pete Shotton, 1/19/98.

35 "That's the music that brought me": John Lennon, 1975 interview, in *Anthology*, p. 11.

36 "We savored the pleasure": Author interview with Pete Shotton, 1/19/98.

36 "It was the first indication": Author interview with Nigel Walley, 3/7/98.

37 Earlier in the year: Author interview with Eric Griffiths, 7/16/98.

38 "with the thick lads": Davies, *Beatles*, p. 17.

38 "but eventually . . . he just drifted off": Author interview with Rod Davis, 9/30/97.

38 "I was obviously very musical": Davies, *Beatles*, p. 18.

39 Having given up any pretense: "We'd given up all hope by that stage." Author interview with Pete Shotton, 7/16/98.

40 "Daily Howl"/Ivan Vaughan: "Ivan started the Daily Howl much earlier at the Institute, as a number of sheets just clipped together. Later, when John got involved, some of it would be his, but we always saw it in Ivan's handwriting." Author interview with Don Andrew, 10/4/97.

40 "He was his own man": Ibid.

40 "It was so smooth": Author interview with Pete Shotton, 1/19/98.

41 Radio Luxembourg had played: Radio Luxembourg archives.

41 "When I heard it . . . it was the end": John Lennon, 1971 interview, in *Anthology*, p. 11.

41 "Nothing really affected me": Davies, *Beatles*, p. 19.

41 "Heartbreak Hotel" "was the most exciting thing": Author interview with Pete Shotton, 1/19/98.

41 "That was him": Paul McCartney in *Anthology*, p. 22.

41 The uniform, in particular: Description of teddy boy chic drawn from Steele-Perkins & Smith, *The Teds*, pp. 3–5.

42   born Tommy Hicks: Actually, Larry Parnes had seen Steele perform three months earlier at a small supper club called the Gyre and Gimble. Rogan, *Starmakers & Svengalis*, p. 23.

42   "he had enormous presence": Melly, *Revolt Into Style*, p. 26.

44   the influence of country-and-western music: "Country-and-western was so popular here because of the connection through the American sailors." Author interview with Don Andrew, 10/4/97.

44   "the Nashville of the North": "Because it was the biggest [source] in Europe for country music." Author interview with Bill Harry, 8/1/97.

44   It wasn't long before: Liverpool City Council, Leisure Services Directorate.

44   "Rock 'n roll was beyond": Author interview with Eric Griffiths, 7/16/98.

45   Even before he got a guitar: "He would stand in front of his bedroom mirror with the guitar pretending to be that man Elvis Presley." Goldman, *Lives of John Lennon*, p. 63; also author interview with Pete Shotton, 7/10/98.

45   She wouldn't hear of it: "Her attitude was that guitar playing and rock 'n roll was really nasty stuff. It was dirty music, just below her." Author interview with Pete Shotton, 1/19/98.

45   "Perhaps next year": Ibid., 1/18/98.

45   "guaranteed not to split": Davies, *Beatles*, p. 20; also Coleman, *Lennon*, p. 57.

45   "It was a bit crummy": John Lennon, 1963 interview, in *Anthology*, p. 11.

CHAPTER 3: MUSCLE AND SINEW

47   "began chatting about music in earnest": Author interview with Eric Griffiths, 7/16/98.

48   "she retuned our guitar strings": Ibid.

48   "tuned the bottom three strings": Author interview with Rod Davis, 9/30/97.

48   "It took me about two years": John Lennon, 1971 interview, in *Anthology*, p. 11.

48   Fats Domino's first hit: Whitburn, *Billboard Book of Top 40 Hits*, p. 91.

48   Hunter Davies maintains: It wasn't released on the Brunswick label until May. Ward, *Rock of Ages*, pp. 153–54.

49   "John was a born performer": Author interview with Eric Griffiths, 7/16/98.

49   "Should we start a band": Author interview with Pete Shotton, 1/19/98.

49   "Don't be silly—I can't play": "I have no musical genes. It was a joke to me." Ibid.

50   Bessie . . . contributed a washboard: Author interview with Pete Shotton, 7/10/98.

50   "I took it to school": Author interview with Rod Davis, 9/30/97.

51   Right away, Lennon took control: "He was the front man and basically what he said went." Ibid.

51   "I remember being very impressed": Author interview with Nigel Walley, 3/7/98.

52   they gathered at Mendips: "We were in John's house . . . so we had a mini-brainstorm." Author interview with Eric Griffiths, 7/16/98.

53   defection of Bill Smith: "Bill Smith didn't turn up for rehearsals, so [he] discharged himself [from the group]." Ibid.

53   "liberated" the tea-chest bass: "We did break into Bill Smith's kitchen." Author interview with Pete Shotton, 7/16/98.

53   A rarity in Liverpool: "It was pretty rare for someone to have a full set of drums." Author interview with Colin Hanton, 10/6/97.

54   "I didn't know the first thing": Author interview with Nigel Walley, 3/7/98.

54   Business cards: Author interview with Charles Roberts, 7/25/98.

54   "The tea-chest bass and my drums": Author interview with Colin Hanton, 10/6/97.

55   "Julia was unlike anyone": Author interview with Rod Davis, 9/30/97.

55   "She had loads of records": Author interview with Pete Shotton, 1/19/98.

55   "In fact, we discovered Gene Vincent": Author interview with Eric Griffiths, 7/16/98.

56   "They once came and played": Author interview with Mike Rice, 7/27/98.

56   By John's own admission: "John used to say how much an audience meant to him; it made him feel like this wasn't just a lark." Author interview with Eric Griffiths, 7/16/98.

56   *contest/"no pay"*: "We entered all the contests where you never got paid." Author interview with Johnny Byrne, 10/8/97.

57   "People actually preferred the theater": Author interview with Bill Harry, 8/4/97.

57   "They had a coach": Author interview with Rod Davis, 9/30/97.

58   "This is an unusual situation": Author interview with Bill Harry, 8/4/97.

58   "We were robbed": Author interview with Colin Hanton, 10/6/97.

58   "We got a lesson in showmanship": Author interview with Rod Davis, 9/30/97.

58   "I was just drifting": John Lennon, 1965 interview, in *Anthology*, p. 12.

59   "who was crazy for jazz": "It was owned by Alan Sytner, who was crazy for jazz." Author interview with Ray Ennis, 10/1/97.

59   Called the Cavern: Harry, *Encyclopedia of Beatles People*, p. 310.

59   Since its official launch: Lewisohn, *Chronicle*, p. 14.

59   "sophisticated skiffle": "We played what one guy called sophisticated stiffle, which was traditional jazz and blues with a jazzy rhythm section." Author interview with Ray Ennis, 10/1/97.

59   "Can you bring them down": Author interview with Nigel Walley, 3/7/98.

60   "as though we were playing the Palladium": Author interview with Pete Shotton, 1/19/98.

60   "a slight tension": Author interview with Rod Davis, 9/30/97.

61   "John was very witty": Author interview with Nigel Walley, 3/7/98.

61   a Quarry Bank school dance: "The Quarry Men played for at least one school dance. People would be doing quick-steps to the George Edwards Band, but they would jive in the intervals." Author interview with Rod Davis, 7/22/98.

62   "the jungle": Wenner, *Lennon Remembers*, p. 100.

62   His legwork eventually led: Author interview with Pete Shotton, 7/11/98.

62   "[Mike] said he's got this record": Goldman, *Lives of John Lennon*, p. 63.

63   "some things just didn't click": "I'm not even sure that John was as much of an Elvis fan as everyone makes him out to be." Author interview with Eric Griffiths, 7/16/98.

63   "We started doing even more numbers": "John was quite taken with Elvis. For a while, it was all he was interested in." Author interview with Colin Hanton, 10/6/97.

63   "would-be intellectual" clientele: Author interview with Rod Davis, 9/30/97.

63   "Rock and roll is a monstrous threat": *Melody Maker*, 5/5/56.

63   "By this time, John thought": Author interview with Pete Shotton, 1/19/98.

64   "What do you think you're doing?": Author interview with Rod Davis, 9/30/97.

65   "Cut out the bloody rock": This has been reported in almost every version of the Beatles' story and was confirmed in author interviews with Rod Davis, Colin Hanton, and Pete Shotton.

66   "The sound of it got to me": Author interview with Pete Shotton, 1/19/98.

CHAPTER 4: THE SHOWMAN

68   Jet plane travel idled: Author interview with Robin Morgan, 6/18/97.

68   "Indeed, let us be frank": *The Times* (London), 7/21/57.

68   "slave to fate": Donne, Holy Sonnets, no. 10, 1.9 (1612).

68   "There was neither an affiliation": Author interview with Quentin Hughes, 10/3/97.

69   "one of nature's true gentlemen": M. McCartney, *Thank U Very Much* (unnumbered).

69   terrace house at 3 Solva: *Kelly's Directories,* 1905–39.

69   the Margaret Street Baths: Author interview with Joan Murray, 1/6/99.

70   "a place to aspire to": Author interview with Marie Crawford, 1/5/99.

70   "a suburb of which Liverpool": Picton, *Architectural History of Liverpool,* p. 59.

70   "a healthy place to live": Liverpool Housing Authority.

70   "never really excelled": Author interview with Kate Robbins, 1/11/98.

70   "Joe put all his faith": Ibid.

71   "the donkey work"—running along: Author interview with William Newton, 10/31/97.

71   Joe loved opera: M. McCartney, *Thank U Very Much* (unnumbered).

71   He had a brittle, choppy style: Author interview with Shelagh Johnson, 10/29/97.

71   "My father learned his music": Miles, *Paul McCartney*, p. 23.

72   "the swingman of Solva Street": M. McCartney, *Thank U Very Much*; confirmed by author interview with Kate Robbins, 1/11/98.

72   "rakish" black facecloths: Salewicz, *McCartney*, p. 10.

72   "Eloise": Author interview with Kate Robbins, 1/12/98.

72   "a born salesman": Author interview with William Newton, 10/31/97.

73   she spoke "posh": Miles, *Paul McCartney*, pp. 6, 10.

73   she enrolled in a three-year general program: Author interview with Myfanwy Butler, 12/18/98.

73   "Mary was so career-conscious": Author interview with Dill Mohin, 12/16/98.

73   "We were so immersed": "We simply loved our careers. No one had time to consider families." Author interview with Myfanwy Butler, 12/18/98.

73   "wasn't at all musical": Author interview with Dill Mohin, 12/16/98.

73   "utterly charming and uncomplicated": Ibid.

74   Rose was a witch: Author interview with John Mohin, 12/12/98.

74   "Mary went to nursing school": Author interview with Dill Mohin, 12/16/98.

74   the Royal Cotton Commission: Author interview with William Newton, 10/31/97.

74   "Medical personnel were being recruited": Author interview with Quentin Hughes, 10/3/97.

75   It was the "austere side": "Uncle Jim had two sides to him . . . a pretending-to-be-austere side, and then winking at you, as if [to say], 'I don't really mean it.'" Author interview with Kate Robbins, 1/11/98.

75   Ungrudgingly, Jim labored there: Author interview with Dill Mohin, 12/16/98.

75   at Town Hall on April 8, 1941: City of Liverpool, Registrar of Births, Deaths & Marriages, Personnel and Administrative Directorate.

75   On June 18, 1942: Ibid.

75   "teardrop eyes, high forehead": Author interview with Shelagh Johnson, 10/29/97.

76   lime from nearby mass graves: Salewicz, *McCartney*, p. 14.

76   "Everton . . . was a place to leave": Author interview with Shelagh Johnson, 10/29/97.

76   "drab part": Author interview with Dill Mohin, 12/16/98.

76   The building . . . [was] decent enough: Ibid.

77   "much like the parish priest": Author interview with Shelagh Johnson, 10/29/97.

77   a deadly cigarette habit: "Both my parents smoked." Miles, *Paul McCartney*, p. 35.

77   Fairway Street: Author interview with Shelagh Johnson, 10/29/97.

78   "The rot had set in": Author interview with William Newton, 10/31/97.

78   Jim's salary: "If Jim could take home £6 at the end of a hard week's work, he was doing well." Salewicz, *McCartney*, p. 19; higher figure as a result of research conducted at Liverpool Cotton Association, 10/30/97.

78   They'd "never be wealthy": Author interview with Dill Mohin, 12/16/97.

78   "asked [her bosses] for a move": Ibid.

78   "a new model town": Author interview with Mark Julius, Liverpool Corporation, Housing Services, 11/4/97.

78   Speke functioned as a one-class: Author interview with Quentin Hughes, 10/3/97.

79   "we were always on the edge": Miles, *Paul McCartney*, p. 5.

79   "Oh, I've been poorly": Author interview with Dill Mohin, 12/16/97.

80   "duly bashed": M. McCartney, *Thank U Very Much* (unnumbered).

80   "Jim and Mary never smacked the boys": Author interview with Dill Mohin, 12/16/97.

80   "The McCartney boys were like a circus": Author interview with John Mohin, 12/12/97.

80   "followed him like a puppy": Ibid.
80   "charm the skin off a snake": Author interview with Kate Robbins, 1/12/98.
81   In photographs: M. McCartney, *Thank U Very Much* (unnumbered).
81   "quiet diplomacy": Davies, *Beatles*, p. 24.
81   "super spy": Miles, *Paul McCartney*, p. 10.
81   "This is where my love": Ibid.
82   "He was a great conversationalist": Author interview with John Mohin, 12/12/97.
82   "He was very into crosswords": Miles, *Paul McCartney*, p. 12.
82   "Mary was very keen": Author interview with Dill Mohin, 12/16/97.
82   model curriculum: Salewicz, *McCartney*, p. 25.
82   In Paul's class: Joseph Williams Primary School records.
83   "It was too big a cutoff": Author interview with Paul McCartney, 3/21/97.
83   Founded . . . in 1825: Liverpool Institute handbook, 1958.
83   "a gentleman's school": Author interview with Colin Manley, 10/3/97.
83   twenty of the fifty-two faculty members: Ibid.
83   school motto: Liverpool Institute archives.
83   On Monday, September 8: Ibid.
83   Liverpool Institute uniform: Description confirmed by Colin Manley, 10/3/97.
83   Nearly a thousand boys: Author interview with Don Andrew, 10/4/97.
83   "We were *eleven*": Author interview with Colin Manley, 10/3/97.
83   "The first year, I was pretty lost": Author interview with Paul McCartney, 3/21/97.
84   "He had a real talent": Author interview with Don Andrew, 10/4/97.
84   "I always [made] my own Christmas cards": Author interview with Paul McCartney, 3/21/97.
84   "work on these massive, great canvases": Ibid.
84   students never "stayed with art": Author interview with Don Andrew, 10/4/97.
84   "that *they* paint and *we* don't": Author interview with Paul McCartney, 3/21/97.
85   "I remember walking along the art room": Author interview with Don Andrew, 10/4/97.
85   "reasonably academic": Author interview with Paul McCartney, 3/21/97.
85   "had a lot of music in him": Ibid.
85   "sing-along stuff": "My main roots are in sing-along stuff, like 'When the Red, Red Robin Comes Bob-bob-bobbin' Along' and 'Carolina Moon.'" Leigh, *Speaking Words of Wisdom*, p. 6.
85   "Greensleeves" and "Let Me Go Lover": BBC archives.
85   "very northern": Miles, *Paul McCartney*, p. 24.
86   "We made the mistake": Davies, *Beatles*, p. 29.
86   Paul considered it "a revelation": Paul McCartney in *Anthology*, p. 22.
87   Zenith guitar: *Anthology* (video), part 1.
87   "The minute he got that guitar": Davies, *Beatles*, p. 31.
87   "have a little go": "My mom, Bett, who is left-handed and played guitar, used to babysit [Paul]. She had a ukulele and would say, 'Come on, have a little go.'" Author interview with Kate Robbins, 1/11/98.
88   "all rather inexact": Miles, *Paul McCartney*, p. 21.
88   "Physically, she wasn't able": Author interview with Dill Mohin, 12/16/97.
88   "I always thought of the area": Author interview with Dot Rhone Becker, 11/19/98.
90   "there was blood on the sheets": Miles, *Paul McCartney*, p. 20.
90   "The big shock in my teenage years": Paul McCartney in *Anthology*, p. 19.
91   "I was determined not to let it affect": Ibid.
91   "There was no one better suited": Author interview with Kate Robbins, 1/11/98.

CHAPTER 5: A SIMPLE TWIST OF FETE

93   The boys were understandably ecstatic: "We were quite proud to be involved. We were the only skiffle band, and it was the first time one was featured." Author interview with Rod Davis, 9/30/97.

93   "the biggest social event": "Half the village took part in it, and the other half went to watch." Author interview with Colin Hanton, 10/16/97.

93   The band clambered onto a flatbed truck: St. Peter's Garden Fete program, 1957; descriptions also from author interviews with Rod Davis, Eric Griffiths, Nigel Walley, Colin Hanton, Pete Shotton.

94   Sally Wright/Susan Dixon: Liverpool *Echo,* 7/7/57; *Liverpool Weekly News,* 7/10/57.

94   "John packed it in": Author interview with Colin Hanton, 10/16/97.

94   literally dozens of such stalls: O'Donnell, *Day John Met Paul,* p. 87; and "You could throw hoops over things, there would be cake stalls, lemonade." Author interview with Rod Davis, 9/30/97.

94   "John wasn't drinking": Author interview with Colin Hanton, 10/6/97; also author interviews with Eric Griffiths, 7/16/98; Pete Shotton, 1/19/98; and Nigel Walley, 3/11/98.

94   David Birch: David Birch, 3/85, AGA.

95   "a simple soul": "The vicar was a simple soul . . . a really nice guy." Author interview with Pete Shotton, 1/19/98.

95   "The singing got raunchier": Author interview with Nigel Walley, 3/11/98.

95   "It was the first day I did 'Be-Bop-A-Lula'": John Lennon, 1975 interview, in *Anthology,* p. 12.

95   "Come Go with Me": Norman, *Shout!,* p. 43.

95   "I couldn't take my eyes off him": Coleman, *Lennon,* p. 65.

95   Shortly before they were finished: "I remember it as clear as day. They were standing below us, stage left . . . Ivan and Paul." Author interviews with Eric Griffiths, 7/16/98, and Pete Shotton, 1/19/98.

95   Afterward, in the Scout hut: Author interview with Colin Hanton, 10/6/97.

95   "a bit of a stony atmosphere": Len Garry, "The Quarrymen [sic]: Eric, Colin, Rod, John, Pete, and Len," *Q,* 3/95, p. 55.

96   "notoriously wary of strangers": Ibid.

96   a white sport coat: Miles, *Paul McCartney,* pp. 26–27.

96   "He played with a cool . . . touch": Author interview with Nigel Walley, 3/11/98.

96   "Right off, I could see": Author interview with Pete Shotton, 1/19/98.

96   It impressed John: Rod Davis, in "The Quarrymen," *Q,* 3/95, p. 55.

97   "It was uncanny": Author interview with Eric Griffiths, 7/16/98.

97   "Afterwards . . . John and Paul circled each other": Author interview with Colin Hanton, 10/6/97.

97   "I half thought to myself": Davies, *Beatles,* p. 33.

97   "What did you think of that kid": Author interview with Pete Shotton, 1/19/98.

98   "The whole point of grammar school": Author interview with Rod Davis, 7/22/98.

98   He was "disappointed": Davies, *Beatles,* p. 18.

98   "Paul had made a huge impression": Author interview with Pete Shotton, 1/19/98.

99   "Was it better to have a guy": Wenner, *Lennon Remembers,* p. 160.

99   Ivan Vaughan solved part of the problem: "Pete Shotton seems to believe that he asked Paul to join the band, but that is not true. I know for a fact that Ivan asked him several days before that, at the institute, before school let out. Then they told Pete, who talked to John." Author interview with Nigel Walley, 11/30/98.

99   "John was very laid-back": Author interview with Pete Shotton, 1/19/98.

99   Scout camp/Butlins: Miles, *Paul McCartney,* p. 29.

99   "Rod took everything too seriously": Author interview with Nigel Walley, 11/30/98.

100   "He asked me if I could . . . play drums": Author interview with Rod Davis, 7/22/98.

100   John and Nigel Walley procured: Author interview with Nigel Walley, 3/11/98.

100 No nephew of hers: Mimi Smith, AGA (undated).
100 Pobjoy recommended: Coleman, *Lennon,* p. 68; and Davies, *Beatles,* p. 47.
100 John had gone there for an interview: Davies, *Beatles,* p. 47.
100 Ballard's exploits: Author interview with Quentin Hughes, 10/3/97.
101 "Arthur could see right through John": Author interview with Helen Anderson, 11/4/97.
101 And yet, on a deeper level: "The painting teacher liked me, he got me in." Davies, *Beatles,* p. 47. "Arthur felt there was talent there." Author interview with Quentin Hughes, 10/3/97.
101 When Mimi received the . . . acceptance letter: Mimi Smith, AGA (undated).
101 "I was [going] there": Davies, *Beatles,* p. 47.
101 "a rather nasty little boy": Barbara Baker, 8/84, AGA.
102 "So I learned [the chords] upside down": John Lennon, 1980 interview, in *Anthology,* p. 12.
103 "Paul was a showman": Author interview with Pete Shotton, 1/19/98.
103 "To us, they were all dilettantes": Author interview with Bill Harry, 8/1/97.
103 stuck out "like a sore thumb": Author interview with Jonathan Hague, 5/21/98.
103 baby-blue Edwardian jacket: Author interviews with Ann Mason, 10/8/97, and Bill Harry, 8/1/97.
103–104 "There was total and utter freedom": Author interview with Helen Anderson, 11/4/97.
104 "intimidating air"/"so over the top": Author interview with Ann Mason, 10/8/97.
104 "I imitated Teddy boys": John Lennon, 1973 interview, in *Anthology,* p. 13.
104 "He was quite a sight": Author interview with Ann Mason, 10/8/97.
104 "Ah—*he's* the unconventional one": Author interview with Bill Harry, 8/1/97.
105 "marvelous art portfolio": Author interview with Helen Anderson, 11/4/97.
105 he had no Scouse accent: Author interview with Bill Harry, 8/1/97.
105 "More often than not": Bill Harry interview with Pauline Sutcliffe (audio), undated.
105 "Stuart was obsessed with Kierkegaard": Author interview with Bill Harry, 8/3/97.
106 If anyone was more conspicuous than John: Author interview with Ann Mason, 10/8/97.
106 "stand the system on its head": Author interview with Helen Anderson, 11/4/97.
106 "do as you please" policy: Ibid.
106 "John was absolutely untalented": Author interview with Jonathan Hague, 5/21/98.
107 John's cartoons: Author interview with Bill Harry, 8/2/97.
107 "besotted" with Cézanne: Rod Murray, 12/84, AGA.
107 "He was painting like the American painters": Ibid.
107 "very aggressive . . . with dark, moody colors": Author interview with Helen Anderson, 11/4/97.
107 "I remember John being dragged out of class": Author interview with Jonathan Hague, 5/21/98.
108 New Clubmoor Hall: Lewisohn, *Chronicle,* p. 15.
108 "a posh neighborhood": Author interview with Nigel Walley, 11/30/98.
108 "They started talking about white jackets": Author interview with Colin Hanton, 10/6/97.
108 "practicing relentlessly": Author interview with Charles Roberts, 7/25/98.
109 "At first we were embarrassed": Author interview with Colin Hanton, 10/6/97.
109 "You could have your ass kicked": Author interview with Mike Rice, 7/27/98.
110 "The bus station was literally": Author interview with Eric Griffiths, 7/16/98.
110 Out from under Mimi's watchful eye: "We'd go up to John's room and we'd sit on the bed and play records." Miles, *Paul McCartney,* p. 46.
110 "We spent hours just listening": Shepherd, *True Story of the Beatles,* p. 16.
111 "very diverse little record collection": Miles, *Paul McCartney,* p. 81.

111 "have [had] quite as an identifiable voice": John Lennon in WNEW-FM radio interview, 2/13/75.

111 "They were on the same indefinite path": Author interview with Eric Griffiths, 7/16/98.

111 "The band quickly *became* John and Paul": Author interview with Colin Hanton, 10/6/97.

112 "the only claim he had": Author interview with Howie Casey, 11/27/97.

112 "a particularly attractive character": Miles, *Paul McCartney*, p. 46.

112 "After a while, they'd finish each other's sentences": Author interview with Eric Griffiths, 7/16/98.

112 "The rest of us hadn't a clue": Author interview with Colin Hanton, 10/6/97.

113 "John and Paul were inseparable": Author interview with Charles Roberts, 7/25/98.

114 "He had a way of just banging out": Author interview with Eric Griffiths, 7/16/98.

CHAPTER 6: THE MISSING LINKS

115 "We could barely switch chords": Author interview with Arthur Kelly, 1/10/98.

115 "blended in with the scenery": Author interview with Tony Bramwell, 8/6/97.

115–16 "a quieter, more taciturn": Iain Taylor in Pritchard & Lysaght, *The Beatles*, p. 26.

117 "They'd yell at each other": Author interview with Arthur Kelly, 1/11/98.

119 a "blood": Ibid.

119 "a refugee from a Tarzan": Ibid.

120 "being dictated to"/"schizophrenic jerk[s]": Davies, *Beatles*, p. 38.

120 "From about the age of thirteen": Author interview with Arthur Kelly, 1/10/98.

120 Music in some form: Louise Harrison in Pritchard & Lysaght, *The Beatles*, p. 17.

120 "shocked" a visitor: Author interview with Arthur Kelly, 1/10/98.

120 splendid rosewood gramophone: Pritchard & Lysaght, *The Beatles*, p. 17.

120 "loads and loads of records": Davies, *Beatles*, p. 18.

120 Ted Heath and Hoagy Carmichael: Giuliano, *Dark Horse*, pp. 16–17.

120 "just seemed made for me": Davies, *Beatles*, p. 42.

120 Sitting in the front mezzanine: Irene Harrison in G. Harrison & D. Taylor, *I, Me, Mine*, p. 26.

120 Later, fanzine writers: Harry, *Ultimate Beatles Encyclopedia*, p. 204.

121 "By the end of the afternoon": Author interview with Arthur Kelly, 1/10/98.

121 "a crappy old piece": Ibid.

121 the unlikely price of £3 10s.: *Anthology* (video), part 1.

121 "put it away in the cupboard": Davies, *Beatles*, p. 42.

122 "a bloke who lived round the corner": Author interview with Arthur Kelly, 1/10/98.

122 "nicked off an American group": Ibid.

122 decorated with gnomes: George Harrison in Giuliano, *Dark Horse*, p. 19.

122 British Legion gig: Author interview with Arthur Kelly, 1/11/98.

123 "Although George delivered meat": Author interview with Tony Bramwell, 8/6/97.

123 Stealing records at Lewis's: Author interview with Arthur Kelly, 1/11/98.

123 "He knew how to color": Author interview with Colin Manley, 10/2/97.

124 Smokers Corner: Author interview with Arthur Kelly, 1/10/98.

125 "I'd met Paul on the bus": George Harrison in *Anthology*, p. 27.

125 Paul mentioned to his protégé: Lewisohn, *Chronicle*, p. 16.

125 He had traveled alone: Author interview with Eric Griffiths, 7/16/98.

125 The so-called official version: Davies, *Beatles*, p. 44.

125 "Charlie McBain wouldn't have permitted": Author interview with Colin Hanton, 10/6/97.

126 Caldwell raised enough money: Author interview with Iris Caldwell Fenton, 9/30/97.

126 Marjorie Thompson's mother: Author interview with Johnny Byrne, 10/7/97.

126   "It was a dump": Author interview with Colin Hanton, 10/6/97.
126   Ultraviolet skeletons: Author interview with Iris Caldwell Fenton, 9/30/97.
126   a wall fan pumped: Gottfridsson, *From Cavern to Star-Club*, p. 58.
126   first kisses: Author interview with Iris Caldwell Fenton, 9/30/97.
126   Hofner Senator: Gottfridsson, *From Cavern to Star-Club*, p. 58.
126   "He was a very tiny teddy boy": Author interview with Colin Hanton, 10/6/97.
126   "The lads were very impressed": Author interview with Eric Griffiths, 7/16/98.
127   "George was just too young": Davies, *Beatles,* pp. 44–45.
127   "I don't know what I felt": George Harrison in *Anthology,* p. 29.
127   "George idolized John": Author interview with Arthur Kelly, 1/10/98.
128   Griff "took it badly": Author interview with Eric Griffiths, 7/16/98.
128   "I said to him, 'Don't feel so bad'": Author interview with Colin Hanton, 10/6/97.
128   Len Garry: Garry, *John, Paul & Me,* p. 191.
128   "like cracking code": Author interview with Arthur Kelly, 1/10/98.

CHAPTER 7: A GOOD LITTLE SIDESHOW

129   "nothing but a Wham-O": *Who Put the Bomp,* 1971.
129   Kelly, McBain, et al.: Author interview with Bill Harry, 8/1/97.
129   Most wore matching suits: Author interview with Howie Casey, 10/27/97.
130   "John refused to behave": Author interview with Nigel Walley, 10/30/98.
130   "student joint": Author interview with Adrian Barber, 10/4/97.
130   These bands, which became the vanguard: Author interview with Bill Harry, 8/1/97.
130   "I Lost My Little Girl": "I must have played it to John when we met." Miles, *Paul McCartney,* p. 34.
130   John was . . . "floored": Author interview with Pete Shotton, 1/19/98.
131   "You can't be that hungry twice": Sheff, *Playboy Interviews,* p. 120.
131   "Don't copy the swimming teacher": Riley, *Tell Me Why,* p. 17.
131   "idols": Paul McCartney in Somach, *Ticket to Ride,* p. 145.
131   "I'd be Phil": Ibid.
132   "That's where I picked up": Author interview with Eric Griffiths, 7/16/98.
132   "We sat around for an entire afternoon": Author interview with Arthur Kelly, 1/10/98.
132   "People these days take it for granted": Paul McCartney in *Anthology,* p. 22.
132   "John and I started to write": Ibid.
132   The McCartney parlor: Barbara Baker, 8/84, AGA.
133   "playing into each other's noses": Sheff, *Playboy Interviews,* p. 129.
133   They would begin by scrawling: Davies, *Beatles,* p. 57; Miles, *Paul McCartney,* p. 36.
133   "anything [they] came up with": Miles, *Paul McCartney,* p. 36.
133   "We were just writing songs": Sheff, *Playboy Interviews,* p. 129.
133   "Lyrics didn't really count": Ibid., p. 119.
133   "It was great," Paul recalled: Paul McCartney in *Anthology,* p. 23.
133   Their first collaborative efforts: Miles, *Paul McCartney,* p. 36.
133   "I Call Your Name": Ibid., p. 46.
134   "most of them written under two or three hours": Author interview with Paul McCartney, 3/27/97.
135   "It was always good practice": Ibid.
135   Slouched on the furniture: Barbara Baker, 8/84, AGA; author interview with Nigel Walley, 10/30/98.
135   "We'd do some good rhythm": Miles, *Paul McCartney,* p. 36.
135   the occasional stolen afternoons: "My dad would probably finish at five and be home by about six. That meant we had from two until about five." Ibid., p. 34.
135   Weekends were reserved: Author interview with Nigel Walley, 10/30/98.
135   "Something special was growing": Author interview with Colin Hanton, 10/6/97.

135 To augment their time together: Author interviews with Arthur Kelly, 1/10/98; Helen Anderson, 11/4/97; Ann Mason, 10/8/97.

136 "sneaking out": Author interview with Ann Mason, 10/8/97.

136 They craved John's camaraderie: Author interview with Arthur Kelly, 1/10/98; also Miles, *Paul McCartney*, p. 46.

136 "lovely little boys": Author interview with Helen Anderson, 11/4/97.

136 Each day, he met his friends: Author interview with Bill Harry, 8/2/97.

136 beans on toast, with tea: Author interview with Arthur Kelly, 1/10/98.

136 "you could smoke there": Ibid.

136 "whip out a pack": Ibid.

136 Johnnie Crosby: Author interviews with Helen Anderson, 11/4/97, and Ann Mason, 10/8/97.

136 "wonderful honey-blond hair": Author interview with Helen Anderson, 11/4/97.

136 "swanning about and drooling": Author interview with Arthur Kelly, 1/10/98.

136 "Hey, John? Have you had *her* yet?": Ibid.

136 "A student's having sex": Author interview with Ann Mason, 10/8/97.

137 "too afraid of getting pregnant": Barbara Baker, 8/84, AGA.

137 "proposing to [Barb]": Ibid.

137 Despite Baker's belief: Author interview with Pete Shotton, 1/19/98, and confidential source.

137 The institute had a long-standing practice: Author interview with Don Andrew, 10/4/97.

137 "the noise of an electric guitar": Ibid.

138 "such a right swine": Author interview with Colin Manley, 10/3/97.

138 "It was fantastic": Ibid.

138 "We couldn't even get near the door": Author interview with Don Andrew, 10/4/97.

138 "just filling in time": Ibid.

138 "They began playing in the . . . canteen": Author interview with Bill Harry, 8/1/97.

138 "With no backing to speak of": Author interview with Helen Anderson, 11/4/97.

139 "We'd share sandwiches": Ibid.

139 "Most people had a perilous relationship": Author interview with Helen Anderson, 11/4/97.

139 Ye Cracke/*Who Farted?*: Author interview with Bill Harry, 8/2/97.

139 "John had an awful lot of intensity": Arthur Ballard, 2/84, AGA.

140 "very conservative" director: Author interview with Jonathan Hague, 5/21/98.

140 "wallpaper": Wenner, *Lennon Remembers,* p. 164.

140 "I was different": Ibid., p. 166.

140 "All they had was information": Ibid., p. 164.

CHAPTER 8: THE COLLEGE BAND

141 "professional tape and disc recording service": From letterhead, P. F. Phillips Studios, given to author.

141 rambling, redbrick: Author interview with Colin Hanton, 10/6/97.

141 "a theatrical flat": Carole Higgens (Phillips's daughter) in Gottfridsson, *From Cavern to Star-Club,* p. 27.

141 George first heard of the studio: Author interview with Johnny Byrne, 10/8/97.

141 recorded . . . "Butterfly" there in June of 1957: John Lowe in Gottfridsson, *From Cavern to Star-Club,* p. 28.

141 As arranged beforehand, they'd met: Ibid., p. 46.

142 "That'll Be the Day": *Anthology* (audio), disc 1.

142 A rainstorm materialized: Gottfridsson, *From Cavern to Star-Club,* p. 46.

142 "a naffy old man": Author interview with Colin Hanton, 10/6/97.

142 3s. 6d. each: Percy Phillips in *Liverpool Echo,* 12/24/77.

142 "go straight to vinyl": Author interview with Colin Hanton, 10/6/97.

142 John, rather ingeniously, suggested: Ibid.
142 transposed it to the B-string: Author interview with Arthur Kelly, 1/10/98.
143 "Then, out of the blue": Author interview with Colin Hanton, 10/6/97.
143 "For seventeen and six": "I clearly remember him getting hot under the collar." John Lowe in Gottfridsson, *From Cavern to Star-Club*, p. 47.
143 "When we got the record": Paul McCartney in *Anthology*, p. 23.
143 "Charlie got it played daily": Author interview with Colin Hanton, 10/6/97.
144 "week after week went by": Author interview with Nigel Walley, 3/11/98.
144 by Paul's own admission: Author interview with Paul McCartney, 3/21/97.
144 St. Barnabas Hall: Barbara Baker, 8/84, AGA.
144 "with a smile that lit up the room": Author interview with Colin Hanton, 10/6/97.
144 "She couldn't stop moving": Barbara Baker, 8/84, AGA.
145 Mimi "laying down the law": Leila Harvey, 10/84, AGA.
145 She implored her elder sister: Barbara Baker, 8/84, AGA; also Stanley Parkes, 1/19/85, AGA.
145 "He was always very open": Stanley Parkes, 1/19/85, AGA.
145 "I'd gone around to John's": Author interview with Nigel Walley, 3/7/98.
146–47 "we both went white": Davies, *Beatles*, p. 48.
147 "That's really fucked everything!": Ibid.
147 "He didn't say anything": Barbara Baker, 8/84, AGA.
147 "Now we were both in this": Miles, *Paul McCartney*, p. 49.
147 "For months [afterward], John": Author interview with Nigel Walley, 3/7/98.
148 "went out of him forever": Author interview with Pete Shotton, 7/16/98.
148 "a girlfriend-boyfriend relationship": Ibid., 1/19/98.
148 "I lost [my mother] twice": Sheff, *Playboy Interviews*, p. 137.
148 he didn't go visit his cousin: Stanley Parkes, 1/19/85, AGA.
148 Paul provided the basic structure: There are conflicting accounts. For McCartney's, see Miles, *Paul McCartney*, p. 36; for Lennon's, see *Hit Parader*. "'Love Me Do' is Paul's song. He wrote it when he was a teenager." Sheff, *Playboy Interviews*, p. 129.
148 "P.S. I Love You": Miles, *Paul McCartney*, p. 38.
149 in a room at Ye Cracke: Author interview with Jonathan Hague, 5/21/98.
149 John was "very entertaining": Rod Murray, 12/84, AGA.
149 "some blokes . . . prancing about": Ian Sharpe, 8/84, AGA.
149 "John could just as easily": Author interview with Pete Shotton, 1/19/98.
149 "crowded, informal affairs": Author interview with Bill Harry, 8/2/97.
150 "inner bunch"/"anchorman": Author interview with Colin Hanton, 10/6/97.
150 where Julia Lennon had once danced: Stanley Parkes, 1/25/85, AGA.
150 As Nigel Walley had explained it: Author interview with Nigel Walley, 11/30/98.
150 "Aside from George": Author interview with Colin Hanton, 10/6/97.
150 "By the time we had to go on": George Harrison in *Anthology*, p. 31.

CHAPTER 9: CHALK AND CHEESE

151 "peroxide-blond hair": Author interview with Iris Caldwell Fenton, 9/10/97.
151 "stripping down to a tiny bikini": Ibid.
151 "He would do *anything*": Author interview with Ray Ennis, 10/1/97.
151 "because it had excellent pulling power": Author interview with Iris Caldwell Fenton, 9/10/97.
152 "When the lights came up": Author interview with Howie Casey, 10/27/97.
152 "big beat dances": *Liverpool Echo* (repeated ads).
152 "I told him he was too young": Author interview with Johnny Byrne, 10/8/97.
152 Mostly, they just rehearsed: Giuliano, *Dark Horse*, p. 23.
152 "working-men's clubs": Ken Brown in Pritchard & Lysaght, *The Beatles*, p. 21.
153 "By December, he was completely out of control": Author interview with Jonathan Hague, 5/21/98.

153   "Most of his antics": Author interview with Ann Mason, 10/8/97.

153   "he was embarrassingly rude": Author interview with Helen Anderson, 11/4/97.

154   "scruffy, dangerous-looking": "Cynthia Lennon: In Her Own Words," *Hello!*, 4/30/94.

154   "outrageous . . . a rough sort": Ibid.

155   Rodney Begg: Author interview with confidential source.

155   "It was a skill that required": *Hello!*, 4/30/94.

155   "vague friendship between them": Author interview with Bill Harry, 8/3/97.

155   "into [a] blond bombshell": Author interview with Helen Anderson, 11/4/97.

156   "madly in love": *Hello!*, 4/30/94.

156   "He had found someone": Author interview with Jonathan Hague, 5/21/98.

156   "Even as a child, she was easygoing": Author interview with Helen Anderson, 11/4/97.

156   "bohernia": Author interview with Bill Harry, 8/2/97.

156   "When she took a shine to him": Author interview with Ann Mason, 10/8/97.

157   she would duck into "the ladies' loo": Ibid.

158   "It was like all the places": Author interview with Beryl Williams, 11/2/97.

159   "in a Greek joint": Williams, "The Liverpool Scene" (unpublished manuscript).

159   "submit for his certificate": Author interview with Helen Anderson, 11/4/97.

159   "everybody chipped bits of paintings": Rod Murray, 12/84, AGA.

CHAPTER 10: MOONDOGS AND ENGLISHMEN

160   little "whacker": "Mimi always said he had a low-Liverpool voice, a real whacker," Davies, *Beatles*, p. 45.

160   "Cyn and I would be going": Wenner, *Playboy Interviews*, p. 126.

160   "[George] would hurriedly catch up": C. Lennon, *A Twist*, p. 26.

160   "didn't hold a candle to John and Paul": Author interview with Bill Harry, 8/4/97.

160   Ruth Morrison: Ibid.

160   she disclosed . . . a new coffee bar: Guiliano, *Dark Horse*, p. 23; Pritchard & Lysaght, *The Beatles*, p. 21.

161   The house at 8 Hayman's Green: Bill Harry interview with Pete Best, 3/96.

161   Ken was more than familiar: "Ken Brown, one of my friends from the Collegiate, my grammar school . . ." Best & Harry, *Best Years*, p. 21.

161   "I went round to see her": Ken Brown in Pritchard & Lysaght, *The Beatles*, p. 21.

161   a steady buzz built: Best & Harry, *Best Years*, p. 18.

161   lights were put in: Pete Best in Pritchard & Lysaght, *The Beatles*, p. 20.

162   "the perfect house" Author interview with Johnny Byrne, 10/8/97.

162   "shoulder to shoulder": Mona Best in Pritchard & Lysaght, *The Beatles*, p. 23.

162   "Among the songs we performed": Ken Brown in ibid., p. 21.

162   a princely £3: Leigh, *Drummed Out!*, p. 10.

162   "None of us dreamed": Author interview with Colin Manley, 10/3/97.

162   "just about hear the band": Author interview with Bill Harry, 8/4/97.

163   "It was a good idea": Author interview with Arthur Kelly, 1/10/98.

163   "Girls were the main reason": Author interview with Paul McCartney, 3/21/97.

163   Bubbles: Author interview with Dot Rhone Becker, 11/19/98.

163   "It must have been all over my face": Ibid.

164   "the fantastic scenes outside": Best & Doncaster, *Beatle!*, p. 22.

164   the club fees and five-pence admission: "Membership was fixed at half a crown a year (12½ pence) plus a shilling (5 pence) admission fee at the door." Ibid., p. 20.

164   Despite the constant crush: Author interview with Bill Harry, 8/4/97.

164   "They didn't have much": Mona Best in Pritchard & Lysaght, *The Beatles*, p. 23.

165   "an immensely likeable guy": Best & Harry, *Best Years*, p. 25.

165   "Mo decided to pay [Ken]": Ibid.

165 "went ballistic": Author interview with Bill Harry, 8/4/97.
165 "She kept Ken's fifteen bob": Best & Doncaster, *Beatle!*, p. 22.
165 "Right, that's it, then!": Ken Brown in Pritchard & Lysaght, *The Beatles*, p. 23.
165 "back into the business": Best & Doncaster, *Beatle!*, p. 23.
165 "pencils, and later drumsticks": Ibid.
165 "knock beats out": Best & Harry, *Best Years*, p. 24.
166 "Stuart was his last hope": Author interview with Bill Harry, 8/2/97.
166 remembered being "fascinated": "Cynthia Lennon: In Her Own Words," *Hello!*, 7/7/94.
166 "Here with no one watching": Ibid.
166 "Stuart wore tinted glasses": Author interview with Bill Harry, 8/2/97.
166 "[H]e had a lot of innovative": Rod Murray, 12/84, AGA.
166 "a tiddler": "Cynthia Lennon: In Her Own Words," *Hello!*, 5/7/94.
166 "Stuart was not . . . outwardly forceful": Rod Murray, 12/84, AGA.
166 "a tremendous energy and intensity": *Hello!*, 5/7/94.
167 Whatever "milk money": Bill Harry interview with Pauline Sutcliffe (audio), undated.
167 "Stuart never let on": Author interview with Bill Harry, 8/2/97.
167 "John did all the things": Millie Sutcliffe in Pritchard & Lysaght, *The Beatles*, pp. 24–25.
167 The incipient taste was enshrined: Author interview with Bill Harry, 8/2/97.
167 Bratby or . . . de Stael: Bill Harry interview with Pauline Sutcliffe (audio), undated.
167 "kipping in [Stuart's] room": Author interview with Bill Harry, 8/7/97.
168 a "monumental painting": Rod Murray, 12/84, AGA.
168 "real resonance": Ibid.
168 Stuart was ecstatic: Bill Harry interview with Pauline Sutcliffe (audio), undated.
169 he'd "failed everything": Author interview with Arthur Kelly, 1/10/98.
169 "It is very difficult": Ibid.
169 "some old fellow chundering on": Davies, *Beatles,* p. 40.
169 "His parents were fairly easygoing": Author interview with Arthur Kelly, 1/10/98.
170 "singing brilliantly": Ibid.
170 "We got there in the morning": Author interview with Ray Ennis, 10/1/97.
171 "old tatty piece of junk": Ibid.
171 "besotted with each other": Author interview with Bill Harry, 8/7/97.
171 "Paul was furious": Author interview with Dot Rhone Becker, 11/19/98.
172 Hillary Mansions: Rod Murray, 12/84, AGA.
172 "ridiculously expensive": Ibid.
172 Lucretius's *On the Nature of the Universe:* Alan Sharpe, AGA (undated).
173 cemetery in the Anglican cathedral: Bill Harry interview with Pauline Sutcliffe (audio), undated.
173 "Now [that] you've got all this money": Ibid.
174 According to one version, his father: Norman, *Shout!*, p. 64.
174 In fact, using a bit of creative financing: Bill Harry interview with Pauline Sutcliffe (audio), undated.
174 "What the bloody hell": Author interview with Bill Harry, 8/2/97.

CHAPTER 11: HIT THE ROAD: JAC
175 "just thinking about what a good name": Davies, *Beatles,* p. 64.
175 Stuart might have suggested beetles: Ibid., introduction to second edition.
175 "to make it look like beat music": Ibid., p. 64.
175 "John and Stuart came out": Author interview with Paul McCartney, 3/21/97.
176 The only gig to speak of: Author interview with Dot Rhone Becker, 11/19/98.
176 Eddie Cochran and Gene Vincent . . . Liverpool Empire: Author interview with Bill Harry, 8/4/97; Lewisohn, *Chronicle,* p. 18; author interview with Hal Carter, 8/14/97.

176   "They knew that to get any attention": Author interview with Bill Harry, 8/4/97.

176   The Student Union had a discretionary fund: Rod Murray, 12/84, AGA.

177   "troubled"/"distraction": Author interview with Quentin Hughes, 10/3/97.

177   "Oh, the skin has come off": Author interview with Bill Harry, 8/4/97.

177   "Art students were inclined to drop in": Author interview with Beryl Williams, 11/2/97.

177   "They'd go into a great big huddle": Williams, "Liverpool Scene," p. 69.

177   "sort of musical revolution": Ibid., p. 42.

178   "I began to realise the implications": Ibid., p. 44.

178   "In most cases, what attracted Larry": Author interview with Hal Carter, 8/14/97.

178   Parnes had a cluster of glittery stars: Clayson, *Beat Merchants,* p. 40; Lewisohn, *Chronicle,* p. 18.

178   "Larry was on tour": Author interview with Hal Carter, 8/14/97.

178   "immediately fell in love": Ibid.

178   "high cheekbones and restless eyes": Clayson, *Beat Merchants,* p. 41.

178   "a very elegant dresser"/"*schmatte* business": Author interview with Hal Carter, 8/14/97.

179   "fee of about £500": Williams, "Liverpool Scene," p. 45.

179   The show was scheduled for May 3: Lewisohn, *Chronicle,* p. 18.

179   "the tragic death of Eddie Cochran": Williams, "Liverpool Scene," p. 47.

179   Details of Cochran's death: Ward, *Rock of Ages,* p. 223.

179   He flushed with guilt: "Momentarily, I was stupefied, then selfish thoughts intruded. I'd been robbed of my two top stars." Williams, "Liverpool Scene," p. 47.

179   To fill the gaping hole: Lewisohn, *Chronicle,* p. 19.

179   "Everyone who was anyone": Author interview with Bill Harry, 8/7/97.

180   "a seminal event": Author interview with Adrian Barber, 10/4/97.

180   "It was [the type of] voice": Ibid., 8/4/97.

181   "he had convinced Lennon": Ibid., 10/4/97.

181   he was willing to do almost anything: Norman, *Shout!,* p. 74.

181   He also had a day job: Harry, *Ultimate Beatles Encyclopedia,* p. 471.

181   "Tommy Moore was a pro": Author interview with Adrian Barber, 10/4/97.

181   "Cathy's Clown": Norman, *Shout!,* p. 73.

182   following the Stadium concert: "After the show, we all retired to the Jacaranda." Williams, "Liverpool Scene," p. 57.

182   if Williams represented these bands: Ibid., p. 58.

182   "But you *must* have a drummer": Ibid., p. 61.

182   Cass was "the prophet": Ibid., p. 44.

182   "For these two periods": Pawlowski, *How They Became,* p. 12.

183   The audition had been scheduled: Lewisohn, *Chronicle,* p. 19.

183   Allan Williams had taken a lease: Author interview with Beryl Williams, 11/2/97.

183   He'd decided to rename it: "I'd seen that smashing film, *The Blue Angel,* and I'd thought, 'What a marvellous [sic] name.'" Williams, "Liverpool Scene," p. 143.

184   "They blew in, rough and tumble": Author interview with Howie Casey, 10/27/97.

184   "sat stone-faced": Ibid.

184   John Lennon pressed Billy Fury for an autograph: Pawlowski, *How They Became,* p. 15 (photo).

185   "Johnny did and played": Author interview with Adrian Barber, 10/4/97.

185   Only a few pictures . . . exist: The entire set, taken by Cheniston Roland, appears in Pawlowski, *How They Became,* pp. 13–22.

185   "I thought the boys in front were great": Norman, *Shout!,* p. 76.

186   in "a most off-putting style": Williams, "Liverpool Scene," p. 66.

186   "Quite suddenly," Allan Williams recalled: Ibid., p. 121.

186   When Williams brought them the offer: Millie Sutcliffe recalled: "[Stuart] was quite upset, really heartbroken, and he said, 'Mother, I think I've let the boys down.'" Pritchard & Lysaght, *The Beatles,* p. 31.

186   "Forget it, Stu": Ibid.

187   the astounding sum of £90: Lewisohn, *Chronicle,* p. 19.

187   George and Tommy took time off: Compiled from numerous sources, including Norman, Pawlowski, Williams, and Salewicz, *McCartney.*

187   The problem of equipment: Author interview with Bill Harry, 8/3/97.

187   Stuart de Stael: Paul McCartney in *Anthology,* p. 44.

187   Paul Ramon: "I thought it sounded really glamorous, sort of Valentinoish." Davies, *Beatles,* p. 65.

188   Details of the Beatles' train ride: Author interview with Hal Carter, 8/14/97.

188–89   Johnny Gentle's background: "I made my guitar before I went out to sea." Author interview with John Askew, 8/15/97.

189   "The crowd was lovely": Ibid.

189   "They weren't the normal bunch of kids": Author interview with Hal Carter, 8/14/97.

190   "pulled out all the stops": Author interview with John Askew, 8/15/97.

191   "Don't worry about us": Ibid.

192   "You listen to me, mate": Ibid.

192   "flying crates and beer bottles": Author interview with Bill Harry, 8/7/97.

193   "Hully Gully": "Every time we did 'Hully Gully' there would be a fight." George Harrison in *Anthology,* p. 53.

193   "He was injured": Bill Harry interview with Pauline Sutcliffe (audio), undated.

193   defection of Tommy Moore: "I'd had enough of them all—especially Lennon." Norman, *Shout!,* p. 78.

194   New Cabaret Artistes: Author interview with Bill Harry, 8/4/97.

194   "a moonlight flit": Author interview with Beryl Williams, 11/2/97.

194   the "dusky troupe": Williams, "Liverpool Scene, p. 82.

195   "come to Germany and stay": Author interview with Beryl Williams, 11/1/97.

195   "Hamburg fascinated me": Williams, "Liverpool Scene," p. 86.

196   they had changed the spelling: Lewisohn, *Chronicle,* p. 28.

196   "dreadfully crummy": Williams, "Liverpool Scene," p. 88.

196   "the manager of a very famous rock 'n roll group": Ibid.

196   "the Smoke": "We always referred to London as 'the Smoke.'" Author interview with Bill Harry, 8/3/97.

197   "He was always thinking on his feet": Author interview with Howie Casey, 10/27/97.

197   "What a coincidence!": Williams, "Liverpool Scene," p. 90.

198   "He was *the star*": Author interview with Adrian Barber, 10/4/97.

198   "He was unpredictable": Author interview with Gibson Kemp, 8/12/97.

198   "Tony was extremely well endowed": Author interview with Adrian Barber, 10/4/97.

198   "[Koschmider] made us an offer": Author interview with Howie Casey, 10/27/97.

199   "When somebody didn't pay": Author interview with Adrian Barber, 10/4/97.

199   "Limper was the leader": Ibid.

199–200   "you had to chase and work at British girls": Author interview with Ray Ennis, 10/1/97.

200   "We were going to *marry* those girls": Author interview with Howie Casey, 10/27/97.

200   "ruin the scene": Ibid.

CHAPTER 12: BAPTISM BY FIRE

201   "pissing rain": Author interview with Johnny Byrne, 10/8/97.

202   "like a funeral parlor": Ibid.

202   he offered the gig to Rory Storm: Ibid.

202 "Allan was having plenty": Author interview with Bill Harry, 8/1/97.

202 "sort of a crappy group": Allan Williams in Pritchard & Lysaght, *The Beatles*, p. 42.

202 "reporters from the *Empire News*": Rod Murray, 8/84, AGA.

203 Rod Jones: Ibid.

203 "Come on, let's go have a look": Ibid.

203 "They got newspapers": Author interview with Bill Harry, 8/1/97.

203 THIS IS THE BEATNIK HORROR: *Sunday People*, 7/3/60.

203 caught the attention of the . . . residents association: Rod Murray, 8/84, AGA.

203 "to suck up to the press": Author interview with Bill Harry, 8/1/97.

203 "I wasn't altogether happy": Williams, "Liverpool Scene," p. 82.

203 George . . . had remained in touch: Best & Doncaster, *Beatle!*, p. 28.

204 "real pounding rock 'n roll drummer": Harry Prytherch in Leigh, *Drummed Out!*, p. 43.

204 Best told one interviewer: "My mother took a phone call from Paul McCartney. He said that they had an offer to go to Germany and needed a drummer." Leigh, *Let's Go Down the Cavern*, p. 37.

204 "I'd always liked them": Davies, *Beatles*, p. 70.

204 "He was absent too much": Author interview with Helen Anderson, 11/4/97.

204 "feared the worst": Coleman, *Lennon*, p. 116.

205 Over Jim's objections: "My dad's catch phrase was always get a job first . . . a serious job." Mike McCartney in Pritchard & Lysaght, *The Beatles*, p. 38.

205 "I didn't want to go back": Davies, *Beatles*, p. 72.

205 "buy . . . lots of things": M. McCartney, *Thank U Very Much* (unnumbered).

205 Paul invited Allan Williams: "To stamp the seal of approval on things, Paul brought Alan [sic] Williams to the house." Ibid.

205 "a respectable and kind person": Bill Harry interview with Pauline Sutcliffe (audio), undated.

205 "Allan didn't entirely tell . . . the whole truth": Ibid.

206 They'd arrived at dusk: Williams, "Liverpool Scene," p. 84.

207 "mile of sin": *Insight Guides: Germany*, p. 290.

207 "It was an 'anything goes' kind of place": Author interview with Adrian Barber, 2/29/00.

208 "was depressing": Best & Harry, *Best Years*, p. 45.

208 By contract, the Beatles: Lewisohn, *Chronicle*, p. 24 (photo).

208 "You can't imagine the work": Author interview with Ray Ennis, 10/1/97.

209 "were . . . far too deadpan": Williams, "Liverpool Scene," p. 93.

209 "the sexiest music of all": Riley, *Tell Me Why*, p. 59.

209 "C'mon, boys . . . make a show": Lewisohn, *Chronicle*, p. 23, and reported variously in almost every book written about the Beatles, including Miles, Coleman, Davies, Best & Harry, and *Anthology*.

210 "powerhouse music": Best & Harry, *Best Years*, p. 47.

210 "After a few weeks": Author interview with Johnny Byrne, 10/8/97.

210 "possible to pass the whole night": Jürgen Vollmer, 12/84, AGA.

210 "Eating wasn't part of the equation": Author interview with Howie Casey, 10/27/97.

210 "baptism by fire": Author interview with Bill Harry, 8/4/97.

211 "filthy, dirty, and disgusting": Author interview with Howie Casey, 10/27/97.

211 "the black holes of Calcutta": Pete Best in Pritchard & Lysaght, *The Beatles*, p. 50.

211 "It was freezing cold": Author interview with Johnny Byrne, 10/8/97.

213 "We used to work the hell out of it": Miles, *Paul McCartney*, p. 59.

213 Rosa Hoffman: "Mutti's real name was Rosa Hoffman. She was born on April 21, 1900, and died March 15, 1988." Letter, Erich Weber to Bill Harry, 6/21/97.

214 "We thought they were a pretty scruffy bunch": Author interview with Howie Casey, 10/27/97.

214 "Crank it up, Pete": Best & Harry, *Best Years*, p. 50.

214 the "most absurd request": Author interview with John Frankland, 10/6/97.

215 "Mr. Showmanship": Author interview with Bob Wooler, 10/30/97.

215 "crumby": "Rory Storm and the Hurricanes came out here the other week, and they are crumby." Letter, George Harrison to Arthur Kelly (undated).

215 "*und* the Beatles": poster, belonging to Johnny Byrne; also John Lowe in Gottfridsson, *From Cavern to Star-Club*, p. 54 (photo).

215 By all accounts, they were paid more: Clayson, *Straight Man*, p. 38.

215 "blow these guys off the stage": Best & Harry, *Best Years*, p. 53.

216 Vi Caldwell . . . kept Paul in cigarettes: Author interview with Iris Caldwell Fenton, 9/10/97.

216 "the prettiest girl": Author interview with Bill Harry, 8/5/97.

216 "Every night was another . . . jam": Author interview with Johnny Byrne, 10/8/97.

216–17 "It was such an incredible number": Ibid.

217 "I pay five men!": Ibid.

217 "There was a stunned": Best & Harry, *Best Years*, p. 78.

217 "the guy tried to climb up": Author interview with Gibson Kemp, 8/12/97.

217 "like winning the lottery": Author interview with John Frankland, 10/6/97.

218 "he fixed [them] up": Author interview with Howie Casey, 10/27/97.

218 "German customers would say": Best & Harry, *Best Years*, p. 78.

218 mobsters "would come in late at night": Miles, *Paul McCartney*, p. 66.

218 "they were so exhausted": Lewisohn, *Chronicle*, p. 23.

218 "Once you had a few beers": Author interview with Ray Ennis, 10/1/97.

219 "gobbled them down": Miles, *Paul McCartney*, p. 66.

219 "eating Prellie sandwiches": Letter, George Harrison to Arthur Kelly (undated).

219 "was dodgy . . . you could get a little too wired": Miles, *Paul McCartney*, p. 67.

219 "We tried any number of crazy things": Author interview with Johnny Byrne, 10/8/97.

220 "like a waterbed": Ibid.

220 "high-class call girls": Best & Harry, *Best Years*, p. 74.

221 "Nobody really looked at the stage": Jürgen Vollmer, 12/84, AGA.

221 "rockers": "The rockers were exactly like the Beatles—rough." Ibid.

221 Eventually, during a break: Norman, *Shout!*, p. 97.

221 In fact, Stuart had spotted all three: "They wandered into the club about a week ago and seated themselves at a table near the band, where I soon became aware of them." Letter, Stuart Sutcliffe to Susan Williams, 10/60.

221 "typical bohemians": Ibid.

221 The three, it turned out: "Stuart, we knew immediately, was one of us." Jürgen Vollmer, 12/84, AGA.

221 "The minute she walked into a room": Author interview with Bill Harry, 8/5/97.

222 Neither outwardly personable: "Astrid was always . . . unsocial, she was always a loner." Jürgen Vollmer, 8/84, AGA.

222 "She had a tremendous feel": Author interview with Gibson Kemp, 8/12/97.

222 "I had never met anybody like them": Letter, Stuart Sutcliffe to Susan Williams, 10/60.

222 "My impression was that Stuart": Jürgen Vollmer, 12/84, AGA.

222 "exis": "'Exis,' that's what I called them." Davies, *Beatles*, p. 83.

223 "totally and immediately fascinated": Jürgen Vollmer, 8/82, AGA.

223 "It was like a merry-go-round": Astrid Kirchherr in Pritchard & Lysaght, *The Beatles*, p. 48.

223 der Dom: Norman, *Shout!*, p. 97.

224 "Cocteau phase": Jürgen Vollmer, 8/82, AGA.

226 He proved more than capable: "What They Played," Lewisohn, *Chronicle*, pp. 361–65.

226 "a very charming image": Jürgen Vollmer, 8/82, AGA.

226 "I was always practical": Miles, *Paul McCartney*, p. 65.

226   "weak link": Ibid.

226   "I have definitely decided to pack in": Letter, Stuart Sutcliffe to Susan Williams, 10/60.

227   "He was always kidding": Jürgen Vollmer, 8/82, AGA.

227   "But he just seemed to take it": Author interview with Bill Harry, 8/2/97.

227   occupied by a peep show: Lewisohn, *Chronicle*, p. 23.

227   Sheridan's repertoire: Author interview with Johnny Frankland, 10/6/97.

228   "He would play solos": Author interview with Johnny Byrne, 10/8/97.

228   "He'd get guitar diarrhea": Author interview with Gibson Kemp, 8/12/97.

228   "In the end": Author interview with Johnny Byrne, 10/8/97.

229   "We suddenly realized": Best & Harry, *Best Years,* p. 82.

229   along with a clause that forbade: Author interview with Johnny Byrne, 10/8/97.

229   Eckhorn recognized: "They came to me. . . . I liked them and offered them a contract." Davies, *Beatles,* p. 87.

229   He terminated the Beatles' contract: Lewisohn, *Chronicle,* p. 24.

229   The band was required to make an announcement: Miles, *Paul McCartney,* p. 70.

229   "So I had to leave": Davies, *Beatles,* p. 87.

230   "This gave us just enough light": Best & Harry, *Best Years,* p. 82.

230   "attempting to burn down": Ibid., p. 83.

231   "felt ashamed": Davies, *Beatles,* p. 89.

CHAPTER 13: A REVELATION TO BEHOLD

232   A week before Christmas: "Oddly, it was George and I who made the first moves, running around town in search of venues to play." Best & Doncaster, *Beatle!,* p. 81.

232   "disgruntled and very angry": C. Lennon, *A Twist,* p. 52.

232   Williams was in no mood: "There's nothing I can do for you at the moment," he told them. "I'm up to my eyes in trouble." Williams, "Liverpool Scene," p. 113.

233   "job for life"/"drinking heavily": Author interview with Bob Wooler, 10/30/97.

234   "She was always there": Best & Doncaster, *Beatle!,* p. 81.

234   "She gave them the kind of work": Author interview with Bob Wooler, 10/30/97.

234   The Seniors had played there: Davies, *Beatles,* p. 91.

234   "a revelation to behold": Author interview with Bill Harry, 8/4/97.

234   "and had the nerve to play": John Cochrane in Leigh, *Drummed Out!,* p. 19.

234   "We'd been pussyfooting": Pat Clusky in ibid.

235   "were utterly, *utterly* devastated": Bill Harry interview with Pauline Sutcliffe (audio), undated.

235   He had written before Christmas: Ibid.

235   "He didn't seem keen": Letter, Stuart Sutcliffe to Pauline Sutcliffe, 12/24/60.

235   "anybody would be taking her son": Bill Harry interview with Pauline Sutcliffe (audio), undated.

235   "picking on him": Davies, *Beatles,* p. 98.

235   "Come home sooner": Letter, George Harrison to Stuart Sutcliffe, 12/16/60.

235   Without a bass: Gottfridsson, *From Cavern to Star-Club,* p. 64.

236   "put Liverpool on the map": Ray McFall in Leigh, *Let's Go Down the Cavern,* p. 26.

236   "doing the jazzy-type stuff": Author interview with Ray Ennis, 10/1/97.

236   An ersatz ventilation pipe: Leigh, *Let's Go Down to the Cavern,* p. 24.

237   "The Cavern was a shithole": Author interview with Adrian Barber, 10/4/97.

237   "At first, it was difficult to breathe": Author interview with Bob Wooler, 10/30/97.

239   "It was as if they'd gone": Author interview with Dot Rhone Becker, 11/19/98.

239   "Lovely lovely lovely . . . Cyn": *Hello!,* 5/7/94.

240   "John was a flirt": Ibid.

240   For months, Peter Eckhorn: Miles, *Paul McCartney,* pp. 74–75.

240   Pete Best worked the same: Best & Doncaster, *Beatle!,* p. 89.

240 Impervious to his parents' dismay: "They were going to be together and that was that, whether we liked it or not." Bill Harry interview with Pauline Sutcliffe (audio), undated.

240 In January he had been beaten: Millie Sutcliffe in Pritchard & Lysaght, *The Beatles*, pp. 60–61; Best & Harry, *Best Years*, p. 92.

240 John also broke: Best & Harry, *Best Years*, p. 92; Aspinall, *Rave*, 1966; also "John dived to Stuart's defense and got his finger broken in the process." *Hello!*, 5/7/94.

241 "We'd listen to both sides": Best & Harry, *Best Years*, p. 99.

241 they "clubbed together": "NEMS had fantastic listening booths. They'd take a stack of records in there and if someone really loved one . . ." Author interview with Gibson Kemp, 8/12/97.

241 "If someone got out of line": Author interview with Adrian Barber, 8/4/97.

242 "He liked us backing him": Best & Harry, *Best Years*, p. 106.

242 *powsas:* C. Lennon, *A Twist*, p. 57.

242 "Here's something to keep": Best & Doncaster, *Beatle!*, p. 95.

242 "in letters from Germany": Bill Harry interview with Pauline Sutcliffe (audio), undated.

243 "It was loose": Author interview with Beryl Williams, 11/2/97.

244 "[It] struck me as being": Williams, "Liverpool Scene," p. 123.

244 Stuart's follow-up letter: Ibid.

244 "he wasn't disappointed": Author interview with Beryl Williams, 11/2/97.

244 "It was loud": Jürgen Vollmer, 8/82, AGA.

245 "In my art school": Astrid Kirchherr in Pritchard & Lysaght, *The Beatles*, p. 67.

245 Out of ignorance: "This was going too far, we all thought. . . ." Best & Doncaster, *Beatle!*, p. 94; Davies, *Beatles*, p. 103.

245 "The pills and booze": C. Lennon, *A Twist*, p. 55.

245 "he seemed more grown-up": Author interview with Dot Rhone Becker, 11/19/98.

246 John took Cynthia: C. Lennon, *A Twist*, p. 54.

246 "She sounded as though she could": Ibid., p. 55.

246 Astrid and John . . . held hands: "We would hold hands occasionally, but he would find it hard even to do that." Astrid Kirchherr in Coleman, *Lennon*, p. 129.

246 Paul and Dot bunked: "We had our own bedroom. I don't remember seeing much of Rosa." Author interview with Dot Rhone Becker, 11/19/98.

247 "with such a wallop": Best & Doncaster, *Beatle!*, p. 103.

247 "They beat the shit out of each other": Author interview with confidential source.

247 "It was the beginning of the end": Best & Doncaster, *Beatle!*, p. 103.

248 "he was only lending it": Paul McCartney in Pritchard & Lysaght, *The Beatles*, p. 70.

248 a gold band: Author interview with Dot Rhone Becker, 11/19/98.

249 "like lepers": Author interview with Ray Ennis, 10/1/97.

249 Tommy Kent: Gottfridsson, *From Cavern to Star-Club*, p. 68.

249 "He said we were the best": *Liverpool Echo*, 2/20/96.

249 Kaempfert's response was polite: "He certainly showed little excitement at what we were doing." Best & Doncaster, *Beatle!*, p. 104.

249 The Beatles were stunned: Best & Harry, *Best Years*, p. 108.

250 It was a sticky piece: "It was presented as: 'That is the deal you're going to get.'" Ibid.

250 "What the hell": Ibid.

250 along with George's instrumental: Pete Best in Pritchard & Lysaght, *The Beatles*, p. 71.

250 "represented something new": "They were a new invention in those days." Karl Hinze in Gottfridsson, *From Cavern to Star-Club*, p. 83.

CHAPTER 14: MR. X

252 the 500 Limited bus: Author interview with Bob Wooler, 10/30/97.

252 "Look at this. I've just received it": Pritchard & Lysaght, *The Beatles*, p. 73.

252 "Mein Herz ist bei dir nur": Polydor, no. NH 24673; English release date: BBC, *Arena* archives.

252 "Up until then": Author interview with Bob Wooler, 10/30/97.

252 "Let me play it tonight": Ibid.

253 "Go and tell him to get fucking well stuffed": Ibid.

254 "There was only one record store": Pritchard & Lysaght, *The Beatles*, p. 73.

254 In a datebook he carried: Personal diary of Brian Epstein, 1949; courtesy of Bryan Barrett.

254 "lived for Beethoven, Mozart": Author interview with Alistair Taylor, 1/17/98.

254 a collection of the Brandenburg Concertos: "My mother gave them to me when I was nineteen, for my birthday." *Desert Island Discs,* 11/30/64.

254 "The closest Brian ever got": Author interview with Peter Brown, 12/3/97.

254 He was born on September 19, 1934: Stella Epstein Cantor, *Arena* archives.

256 "She knew what it meant to be a lady": Author interview with Rex Makin, 11/1/97.

256 "Tell me, Auntie": Stella Epstein Cantor, *Arena* archives.

256 "Queenie treated him as an equal": Author interview with Rex Makin, 11/1/97.

257 "one of those out-of-sorts boys": Epstein, *Cellarful*, p. 25.

257 "problem child": "When my mother, distressed and weeping, pleaded with the headmaster that I should be given another term, he replied, 'Madam, we have no room for your problem child.'" From Brian Epstein's handwritten journal, 1957.

257 "It was at this school": Ibid.

258 "benevolent academies": "They solved [my school problem] . . . by sending me to one of those benevolent academies where failures are welcomed. . . ." Epstein, *Cellarful,* p. 29.

258 "I tried very hard": Brian Epstein's datebook, 1949.

258 A portfolio of eight drawings: Brian Epstein, portfolio, courtesy of Bryan Barrett.

258 Harry . . . "went up the pole": Stella Epstein Cantor, *Arena* archives.

258 it "was impossible"/"it would be stupid": Brian Epstein's handwritten journal, 1957, p. 6.

258 "In a rage of temper": Ibid.

259 "reported for duty": Epstein, *Cellarful,* p. 31.

259 "a keen interest in display work": "I worked well and had some new ideas." Brian Epstein, handwritten journal, 1957, p. 6.

259 The window sets he redressed: "I placed chairs in the windows with their backs to the window shoppers." Epstein, *Cellarful,* p. 33.

259 Isaac was neither amused: Author interview with Rex Makin, 11/1/97.

260 "latent homosexuality": "It is possible even then I may have been able to settle down after all that had happened, remaining, as I did, unaware of my latent homosexuality." Brian Epstein, handwritten journal, 1957, p. 6.

260 "Within the first few weeks": Ibid.

260 "confused": "My mind was confused and my nervous system weakened." Ibid., p. 7.

260 About the same time, he was robbed: Ibid., pp. 7–8.

260 In his autobiography, Brian invents: Epstein, *Cellarful*, p. 36.

260 "on medical grounds": Ibid., p. 37.

261 "homosexual life and its various rendezvous": Brian Epstein, handwritten journal, 1957, p. 8.

261 "My life became a succession": Ibid.

261 At twenty-one, he was appointed: Ibid., p. 9.

261 Without any warning, he packed: Ibid., p. 8.

261 "I confessed everything": Ibid., p. 9.

261 Incredible as it may seem, Brian impressed: Norman, *Shout!,* p. 131.

261 Peter O'Toole, Albert Finney: Brian Epstein, handwritten journal, 1957, p. 7.

261 His own class boasted: Epstein, *Cellarful,* p. 40.

262 "the narcissism . . . and the detachment": Ibid.

262   "a second male lead": Norman, *Shout!,* p. 131.

262   Loneliness was partly to blame: "Living alone in London I felt acute frustration and loneliness." Brian Epstein, handwritten journal, 1957, p. 5.

262   On the evening of April 17: Ibid., p. 11.

262   "mind went in great fear": Ibid.

262   "[And] after a few minutes": Ibid., p. 14.

262   Miraculously, a family solicitor: Author interview with Rex Makin, 11/1/97.

262   This time, he got involved with: Ibid.

262   "They arranged for a drop": Ibid.

263   "he was oblivious": Author interview with Peter Brown, 12/9/97.

264   "My girlfriend and I": Author interview with Mike Rice, 7/27/98.

264   "the most important record outlet": Author interview with Alistair Taylor, 1/17/98.

264   "There was really no radio": Author interview with Peter Brown, 12/9/97.

264   A grainy picture of Gene Vincent: *Mersey Beat,* 7/6/61.

265   He split the cover price: Author interview with Bill Harry, 8/4/97.

265   "He looked extremely smart": Ibid., 8/2/97.

265   "I can't understand it": Ibid.

265   BEATLES SIGN RECORDING CONTRACT!: *Mersey Beat,* 7/20/61.

265   "This is actually in *Liverpool?*": Author interview with Bill Harry, 8/2/97.

265   "Record Releases by Brian Epstein": *Mersey Beat,* 8/3/61. "He became our record reviewer." Author interview with Bill Harry, 8/2/97.

265   "What about these Beatles?": Ibid.

266   Legend has it that Brian: Epstein, *Cellarful,* p. 43.

266   "The name 'Beatle' meant": Ibid.

266   "He would have had to have been blind": Author interview with Bill Harry, 8/2/97.

266   "Do you remember that record": Author interview with Alistair Taylor, 1/17/98.

266   "The Beatles are at the Cavern": Author interview with Bill Harry, 8/2/97.

267   A letter from Stuart had indicated: Jürgen Vollmer, 8/82, AGA.

267   "I showed them all the places": Ibid.

267   "We both detested pop": Author interview with Alistair Taylor, 1/17/98.

268   "hovering around the counter": Author interview with Bob Wooler, 10/30/97.

268   "Then, I'm sorry to have to tell you": Ibid.

268   They knew who he was: Davies, *Beatles,* p. 125.

268   "And what brings Mr. Epstein": Ibid.

268   "We just popped in": Author interview with Alistair Taylor, 1/17/98.

269   "absolutely awful"/"remarkable": Ibid.

269   "Do you think I should manage them?": Ibid.

CHAPTER 15: A GIGANTIC LEAP OF FAITH

270   "delicious-sounding" names: Author interview with Bill Harry, 8/2/97.

270   Names of Liverpool bands: Leigh, *Let's Go Down the Cavern,* dedication page; and *Mersey Beat,* various issues, 7/6/61–2/13/64.

270   Slightly over three hundred . . . bands: Author interview with Bob Wooler, 10/30/97.

270   Bands played what they wanted: Author interview with Howie Casey, 10/27/97.

271   Brian was "besotted": Author interview with Alistair Taylor, 1/17/98.

271   "John, especially": Author interview with Peter Brown, 12/9/97.

271   "with all the pride of a peacock": Author interview with Bob Wooler, 10/30/97.

272   "for a chat": Epstein, *Cellarful,* p. 48.

272   "never know what made [him] say": Ibid.

272   On December 3, 1961: Lewisohn, *Chronicle,* p. 35; Epstein, *Cellarful,* p. 49.

272   "rattled on the glass": Author interview with Bob Wooler, 10/30/97.

272   "This is me dad": Davies, *Beatles,* p. 126; confirmed by Bob Wooler in author interview, 10/30/97.

272   "Apparently quite a number of people want it": Davies, *Beatles,* p. 126.

273   "he was picking his words very carefully": Best & Doncaster, *Beatle!*, p. 127.

273   "Certainly there were several things": Ibid.

273   "they were delighted that a proper businessman": *Hello!*, 5/14/94.

274   Paul . . . "was more ambitious": Author interview with Dot Rhone Becker, 11/19/98.

274   wiles of "a Jewboy": Author interview with Bill Harry, 8/2/97.

274   "The novelty" would eventually wear off: Davies, *Beatles*, p. 129.

274   "They were as unruly a bunch": Author interview with Bob Wooler, 10/30/97.

274   "thieves": Brown & Gaines, *Love You Make*, p. 68.

274   "a right load of layabouts": Leigh, *Drummed Out!*, p. 28.

274   "I wouldn't touch 'em": Williams, "Liverpool Scene"; Lewisohn, *Chronicle*, p. 35.

275   "there was an immediate bond": Author interview with Peter Brown, 12/3/97.

275   same compatible relationship with Andrew Lloyd Webber: Ibid.

275   "Presumably I looked as if I were . . . perfectly normal": Ibid.

275   "a very unhappy man": Ibid.

275   "Money was the deciding factor": Author interview with Peter Brown, 12/9/97.

276   "he'd discovered a gold mine": Author interview with Rex Makin, 11/1/97.

276   "Harry was indignant": Ibid.

276   "the Beatles would be bigger": "He assured my parents and me that they would be bigger than Elvis Presley." Clive Epstein in Coleman, *Lennon*, p. 158; also author interview with Alistair Taylor, 1/17/98.

276   if Queenie wasn't any more optimistic: Author interview with Peter Brown, 12/3/97.

276   Besides, she knew how stubborn Brian was: Brown & Gaines, *Love You Make*, p. 67.

276   "Okay, you're on": Best & Doncaster, *Beatle!*, p. 130.

276–77   "Right, then, Brian—manage us": Norman, *Shout!*, p. 140.

277   Stuart wasn't expected to return: Bill Harry interview with Pauline Sutcliffe (audio), undated.

277   Both Beatles had kept up a . . . correspondence: Author interview with Bill Harry, 8/7/97.

277   "a restlessness about life": Coleman, *Lennon*, p. 159.

277   "clearly distressed—bizarre": Bill Harry interview with Pauline Sutcliffe (audio), undated.

278   "Stuart looked absolutely god-awful": Author interview with Bill Harry, 8/5/97.

278   "there was no supporting evidence": Bill Harry interview with Pauline Sutcliffe (audio), undated.

278   "Stuart fell over": Rod Murray, 8/82, AGA.

278   A grant had come through: "[He] got a tremendous grant . . . from the German government on Paolozzi's recommendation." Millie Sutcliffe in Pritchard & Lysaght, *The Beatles*, p. 92.

278   "but not both": Ibid.

278   but writing stories and poems: Astrid Kirchherr in Pritchard & Lysaght, *The Beatles*, p. 91.

279   "good sense to keep away from": Bill Harry interview with Pauline Sutcliffe (audio), undated.

279   "to smarten them up": Author interview with Alistair Taylor, 1/17/98.

279   Leather and jeans were fine for the Cavern: "He claimed that no one in the world of entertainment outside our present environment would tolerate our slovenly look." Best & Doncaster, *Beatle!*, p. 133.

280   Brian expected everyone to show up on time: Coleman, *Lennon*, p. 157.

280   "Brian believed that would be very good for us": Miles, *Paul McCartney*, p. 96.

280   "Paul was Mr. Show Business": Author interview with Bill Harry, 8/9/97.

281   "a nice old ballroom": Author interview with Sam Leach, 10/6/97.

281   "Where are we going, boys?": *Anthology*, vol. 1.

CHAPTER 16: THE ROAD TO LONDON

282 A graduate of the Merchant Taylors' School: Leigh, *Drummed Out!*, p. 31.

282 Barrow not only spoke the language: *Liverpool Echo*, 1959–61.

282 "a schoolboy": Author interview with Tony Barrow, 10/31/97.

282 Each week, before placing the NEMS record order: Author interview with Peter Brown, 12/9/97.

283 "I have this fabulous group": Author interview with Tony Barrow, 10/31/97.

283 "instantly impressive": Ibid.

284 "bright lights": Author interview with Richard Rowe Jr., 8/19/97.

284 Brian was "very taken" with Smith: Author interview with Alistair Taylor, 1/17/98.

284 After a rousing lunchtime session: Best & Harry, *Best Years*, p. 137.

285 "Right," Smith said without any ado: Author interview with Alistair Taylor, 1/17/98.

285 "ill humor": Author interview with Dot Rhone Becker, 11/19/98.

285 "very late" the next morning: Pete Best in Leigh, *Drummed Out!*, p. 31.

286 "He was frothing at the mouth": Best & Harry, *Best Years*, p. 137.

286 He'd been out late at a party: Lewisohn, *Chronicle*, p. 52.

286 studios were "freezing cold": Author interview with Tony Barrow, 10/31/97.

286 "ill at ease": Lewisohn, *Chronicle*, p. 52.

286 "[He] believed that the way to impress Mike Smith": Norman, *Shout!*, p. 143.

286 "all these weird novelty things": Letter, John Lennon to Tony Barrow, 12/63; also: *Beatles Book Monthly*, 1/83, p. 7.

286 "We thought hard about the material": Pete Best in Leigh, *Drummed Out!*, p. 90.

286 "fairly silly repertoire": Miles, *Paul McCartney*, p. 89.

287 their performance was flat: Decca audition tape, 1/1/62.

287 too many "pretty" numbers: "Decca didn't want all that pretty-pretty kind of number." Letter, John Lennon to Tony Barrow, 12/63; also: *Beatles Book Monthly*, 1/83, p. 7.

287 work had been "productive": Best & Harry, *Best Years*, p. 139.

287 "Can't see any problems": Ibid.

287 Brian surprised them by ordering: Norman, *Shout!*, p. 144.

287 "What a great way to start 1962": Best & Harry, *Best Years*, p. 139.

288 "best group in Liverpool": *Mersey Beat*, 1/4/62.

288 "He was always on the phone to Polydor": Author interview with Alistair Taylor, 1/17/98.

288 "It became hard, right off the bat": Author interview with Peter Brown, 12/3/97.

288 "Whatever you do . . . don't tell Daddy": Author interview with Alistair Taylor, 1/17/98.

289 "Nine times out of ten": Author interview with Colin Manley, 10/3/97.

289 "Shut yer fucking yap!": Author interview with Bob Wooler, 10/30/97.

289 "rude photos": Author interview with Bill Harry, 8/5/97.

290 "We always stayed out of their way": Author interview with Dot Rhone Becker, 1/19/98.

290 Brian repeated his foremost goal: Letter from R. N. White to Brian Epstein, 12/7/61.

291 "Whilst we appreciate the talents": Ibid., 12/14/61.

291 "amazing record collection": "He sent to America for some of it but acquired the best stuff on the black market." Author interview with Richard Rowe Jr., 8/19/97.

292 "No, Mike, it's impossible": Dick Rowe in Pritchard & Lysaght, *The Beatles*, p. 88.

292 "Liverpool could have been in Greenland": Ibid.

292 "He had very substantial accounts": Author interview with Peter Brown, 12/3/97.

292 "thought it was awful": Author interview with Alistair Taylor, 1/17/98.

292 Philips also passed: Letter from E. J. Harvey to Brian Epstein, 2/11/62.

293 "It appears that we are cursed": Author interview with Peter Brown, 12/8/97.

293 "The people at Decca didn't like the boys' sound": Dick Rowe in Pritchard & Lysaght, *The Beatles*, p. 90.

294   "You couldn't get in": Ibid., p. 89.

294   "You have a good record business": Ibid., p. 90.

294   "completely shattered": *Beatles Book Monthly*, 11/82, p. 32.

295   "Now, who hasn't [already] got a group": Related by Kim Bennett, assistant to Sid Coleman, *Beatles Book Monthly*, 5/69, p. 8.

296   HMV and Columbia got the heavy hitters: Martin, *All You Need*, p. 83.

296   "It was the bastard child": Author interview with Colin Manley, 10/2/97.

296   "a lot of traditional Scottish bands": Author interview with Ron Richards, 12/29/97.

296   Martin would have "to do something" bold: Martin, *All You Need*, p. 84.

296   "between the cracks": Ibid.

297   "We had gone from being known as a sad little company": Author interview with Ron Richards, 12/29/97.

297–98   "so soft the engineers had . . . difficulty": Ibid.

298   "not to be so clever": Letter, John Lennon to Tony Barrow, *Beatles Book Monthly*, 1/83, p. 7.

298   "Right. Try Embassy": Epstein, *Cellarful*, p. 58.

298   "Brian Epstein decided that everyone": Leigh, *Let's Go Down the Cavern*, p. 59.

299   He was "embarrassed": Pete Best in Leigh, *Drummed Out!*, p. 26.

299   "Almost since he joined": Author interview with Bill Harry, 8/1/97.

299   "If one of the others got more applause": Author interview with Bob Wooler, 10/30/97.

299   A poster for *The Outlaw:* Leigh, *Drummed Out!*, p. 26.

299   "He was the only Beatle I mentioned": Author interview with Bob Wooler, 10/30/97.

299   "That had always been Paul's role": Author interview with Bill Harry, 8/2/97.

300   "brilliant"/"they were going to conquer the world": George Martin, *Arena* archives.

300   "had seen it all before": Ibid.

300   "He . . . expressed surprise": Martin, *All You Need*, p. 122.

301   "unswerving devotion": George Martin, *Arena* archives.

301   "a big hype": Martin, *All You Need*, p. 122.

301   "very mediocre": Ibid.

301   "You know, I really can't judge": George Martin, *Arena* archives.

301   "Brian's investment in the band": Author interview with Alistair Taylor, 1/17/98.

301   "Brian was too captivated": Author interview with Peter Brown, 12/3/97.

301   By February, he was taking amphetamines: Author interview with Alistair Taylor, 1/17/98.

302   "Brian didn't want to go to gigs": Author interview with Peter Brown, 12/3/97.

302   "with his hair combed forward": Author interview with Bill Harry, 8/2/97.

302   "We'd heard Brian was queer": Miles, *Paul McCartney*, p. 88.

302   "They always knew he was a queen": Author interview with Peter Brown, 12/3/97.

302   "I see that new Dirk Bogarde film": Author interview with Bob Wooler, 10/30/97.

302   "Within forty-eight hours": Ian Sharp, 8/84, AGA.

CHAPTER 17: DO THE RIGHT THING

304   "The Beatles were home in Hamburg": Author interview with Adrian Barber, 10/4/97.

304   An omen presented itself: "I had German measles so I went a day later than the other guys. . . ." George Harrison in *Anthology*, p. 69.

304   "Where's Stu?": Best & Doncaster, *Beatle!*, p. 150.

304   "Oh, what's the matter?": Coleman, *Lennon*, p. 162.

305   "a bomb going off in his head": "Millie told me it was like a bomb. . . ." Author interview with Bill Harry, 8/7/97.

305   "he was going blind": "Millie told me that she'd got a letter from Stuart, who said he was afraid he was going blind." Author interview with Bill Harry, 8/2/97.

305   Other times, she struggled to hold him down: Norman, *Shout!*, p. 149.

305   According to one account, he'd blacked out: Ibid.

305 On April 10: Lewisohn, *Chronicle*, p. 56.

305 "He has to go to the hospital": Coleman, *Lennon*, p. 162.

306 No one that close in age had died: "Not many of our contemporaries had died." Paul McCartney in *Anthology*, p. 69.

306 "a real shock": Ibid.

306 "looked up to Stu": "I depended on him to tell me the truth." John Lennon, 1967 interview, in *Anthology*, p. 69.

306 Even Astrid insisted that they go on: "[S]he did, indeed, go to the Star Club when the Beatles opened there on 13 April." Coleman, *Lennon*, p. 163.

306 The rest of the bill featured: *Beatles Book Monthly*, 1/83, p. 19.

306 "without [his] approval you did not work": Author interview with Adrian Barber, 10/4/97.

306 "spoke English with a typical German . . . accent": Ted "Kingsize" Taylor, 9/2/85, AGA.

306 "ruthless" pit bull: Ibid.

306 "an immense, cavernous rock 'n roll cathedral": Author interview with Adrian Barber, 10/4/97.

307 "twistin' base": "News from Germany," *Mersey Beat*, 5/3/62.

307 The Beatles took one look: "The Star-Club was great." Paul McCartney in *Anthology*, p. 69; "a big place and fantastic." George Harrison in ibid.

307 "the first real theatrical setting": Author interview with Adrian Barber, 10/4/97.

307 "There was a fucking curtain": Ibid.

307 "The beatings he gave to people": Author interview with Ray Ennis, 10/1/97.

307 the missing three fingers: "When you shook hands with him, he only had a finger and thumb on his right hand. The rest had been cut off." Author interview with Bill Harry, 8/5/97.

307 He doted on them: "He always spoke English very grammatically." Ibid.

307 "Horst made sure we were protected": Author interview with Tony Crane, 10/7/97.

308 "gave [them] immunity": Author interview with Ray Ennis, 10/1/97.

308 "Manfred's Home for Itinerant Scousers": Author interview with Bill Harry, 8/5/97.

308 "roughly 850 to 1,000 people": Don Arden in Pritchard & Lysaght, *The Beatles*, p. 93.

308 "a step up": Coleman, *Lennon*, p. 163.

309 Only one of his songs, "You Better Move On": Whitburn, *Billboard Book of Top 10 Hits*.

309 "We wanted to [sound] like Arthur Alexander": Liner notes, *The Ultimate Arthur Alexander*, Razor & Tie RE 2014.

309 "He opened the barn door": Author interview with Adrian Barber, 2/29/00.

310 John Lennon managed to fuel his rage: "During that trip in Hamburg, John was certainly often wild." Gerry Marsden in Coleman, *Lennon*, p. 164.

310 He'd begun blowing off steam: Horst Fascher in Coleman, *Lennon*, p. 163.

310 "foamed at the mouth": Author interview with Ray Ennis, 10/1/97.

310 "all people [were] basically shit": Author interview with Adrian Barber, 10/4/97.

310 "And all of us just stood there": Gerry Marsden in Coleman, *Lennon*, p. 169.

310 "a trend [for musicians] to bounce around": Ibid.

310 "Hey, remember the war?": Ibid.

310 "a little bit mad": Ibid., p. 164.

310 "*out of my fucking mind*": John Lennon, 1972 interview, in *Anthology*, p. 78.

310 "let loose like maniacs": Author interview with Colin Manley, 10/2/97.

311 a "shabby little . . . bedsit": *Hello!*, 5/7/94.

311 "Imagine having her there all the time": Letter to Cynthia Lennon, 4/62.

311 "The pressure was really getting to him": Author interview with Alistair Taylor, 1/17/98.

312 CONGRATULATIONS BOYS: Lewisohn, *Chronicle*, p. 56.

312 HAVE SECURED CONTRACT: Ibid., p. 55 (picture).

312   None of the Beatles had been forewarned: "It was only Brian telling us we were going to make it and George." John Lennon, 1972 interview, in *Anthology*, p. 68.

312   By way of celebration: Best & Doncaster, *Beatle!*, p. 159.

312   Unable to make ends meet: C. Lennon, *A Twist*, p. 61.

313   "they played tick with hatchets": Author interview with Dave Foreshaw, 10/3/97.

313   "money had run out": C. Lennon, *A Twist*, p. 70.

313   "period got later and later": "Cynthia Lennon: In Her Own Words," *Hello!*, 5/21/94.

313   "The horror of it": "Cynthia Lennon: In Her Own Words," *Hello!*, 5/14/94.

313   Bursting with shame: "For awhile I tried to ignore the problem. The difficulties were almost too great to contemplate." Ibid.

313   "crummy" meals: Author interview with Dot Rhone Becker, 11/19/98.

314   took the stairs "two at a time": *Hello!*, 5/14/94.

314   "As the words sunk in": Ibid.

314   "I thought it would be goodbye": Davies, *Beatles*, p. 153.

315   Resignedly, he proposed: "There's only one thing for it, Cyn, we'll have to get married." C. Lennon, *A Twist*, p. 73; "I was a bit shocked when Cynthia told me, but I said, 'Yes, we'll have to get married.'" John Lennon in Davies, *Beatles*, p. 153.

315   "John didn't share much": Author interview with Bill Harry, 8/5/97.

315   "was [their] last chance": "According to Brian, it was very much a case of like— 'okay, this is your last chance.'" Pete Best, *Abbey Road* transcripts, 2/19/97.

315   "Where's the recording studio?": Ibid.

315   "It's a house!": Ibid.

315   It had originated in 1831: Southall, *Abbey Road*, p. 14.

316   the world's first "purpose- (or custom-) built" studio: Spitz, "The Long and Winding Abbey Road," *Sky*, 9/97, p. 53.

316   The fundamentals of stereo: Author interview with Alan Brown, 6/23/97.

316   "stepping into . . . another world": Pete Best, *Abbey Road* transcripts, 2/19/97.

316   "Coming into Abbey Road": Paul McCartney in Southall, *Abbey Road*, p. 130.

316   "corner suite": *Sky*, 9/97, p. 56.

316   "We were nervous": Pete Best, *Abbey Road* transcripts, 2/19/97.

316   "Look at the size of this place!": Ibid.

317   "it was love at first sight": Martin, *All You Need*, p. 122.

317   "wasn't terribly impressed": Author interview with Ron Richards, 12/27/97.

317   John had patterned it after: "It was my attempt at writing a Roy Orbison song. . . . I heard Roy Orbison sing 'Only the Lonely' or something. That's where the song came from." Sheff, *Playboy Interviews*, pp. 142–43.

318   "They didn't impress me at all": Southall, *Abbey Road*, p. 81.

318   George Martin shared their reservations: "Frankly, they didn't impress me, least of all their own songs." Martin, *All You Need*, p. 123.

318   "They were rotten composers": Ibid.

318   "Their own stuff wasn't any good": George Martin, *Arena* archives.

318   "suitable material": Martin, *All You Need*, p. 123.

318   "embellish[ing] the sound": Norman Smith in Southall, *Abbey Road*, p. 81.

318   "the drummer was no good": Author interview with Ron Richards, 12/27/97.

319   "During that one conversation": Dowlding, *Beatlesongs*, p. 35.

319   refer the band to a venereologist: Author interview with Rex Makin, 11/1/97.

320   "[Paul] was trying to be good about it": Author interview with Dot Rhone Becker, 11/19/98.

320   Jim McCartney . . . "was delighted": Ibid.

320   Between the Parlophone audition: Lewisohn, *Chronicle*, pp. 70–71.

320   "the Eppy-center": Author interview with Tony Barrow, 10/31/97.

320   Everyone was crammed: Author interview with Beryl Williams, 10/7/97.

320   "He was very meticulous": Author interview with Frieda Kelly Norris, 10/5/97.

321   "We'd talk in his office": Author interview with Bob Wooler, 10/30/97.

322   "Sometimes he'd rub his hands": Ibid.

322   "It was an amazing scene": Author interview with Bill Harry, 8/1/97.

CHAPTER 18: STARR TIME

324   "reminded him of a German concentration camp": Author interview with Johnny Byrne, 10/8/97.

324   "boring" image: "We had our original names at Butlins. Rory said, 'It doesn't sound good, it sounds boring.'" Ibid.

324   The only group member who balked: "Ringo was a bit reluctant to do that." Ibid.

324   one of the city's fleetest dancers: "His dancing used to amaze us." Ibid.

324   "Rings": "In Liverpool, I was still wearing a lot of rings, and people were starting to say, "Hey, Rings!"" Ringo Starr in *Anthology*, p. 39.

324   an effort to amend it to Johnny Ringo: Clayson, *Ringo Starr: Straight Man or Joker* (hereinafter, *Straight Man*), p. 34.

324   "Ritch wasn't that interested": Author interview with J. Byrne, 10/8/97.

324   "Starr was a natural": *Melody Maker*, 11/14/64.

325   "He was an excellent drummer": Author interview with Adrian Barber, 10/4/97.

325   "There was a feeling we all had": G. Harrison & D. Taylor, *I, Me, Mine*, p. 33.

326   "always made for the drums": Richie Galvin in Leigh, *Drummed Out!*, p. 56.

326   "Paul was showing Pete": Ibid.

326   it was no secret that the other Beatles resented Mona: Clayson, *Straight Man*, p. 56.

326   "Mona was an attractive, strong . . . woman": Author interview with Bill Harry, 8/4/97.

326   "she could also be a harridan": Leigh, *Drummed Out!*, p. 67.

326   "If she said it was Sunday": Richie Galvin in ibid.

326   "didn't want her interference": Bill Harry in Clayson, *Straight Man*, p. 56.

326   Kingsize Taylor's band, on tour: Clayson, *Straight Man*, p. 54.

326   "Teddy wrote to Ringo": Leigh, *Drummed Out!*, p. 44.

327   "the lifestyle . . . was ideal": Author interview with Johnny Byrne, 10/8/97.

327   "fabulous . . . the best place": Ringo Starr in *Anthology*, p. 39.

327   "But Ringo was . . . ruthless": Author interview with Johnny Byrne, 10/8/97.

329   "Is it possible for us to talk later?": Author interview with Bob Wooler, 10/31/97.

329   "his face looked scared": Davies, *Beatles*, p. 137.

330   "found Brian in a very uneasy mood": Best & Doncaster, *Beatle!*, p. 166.

330   "hedged a little": Epstein, *Cellarful*, p. 69.

330   "Pete, I have some bad news": Best & Harry, *Best Years*, p. 157.

330   "in a state of shock": Ibid., p. 159.

330   "Why?": Best & Doncaster, *Beatle!*, p. 166.

330   And neither did George Martin: "George Martin had not been too happy about Pete Best's drumming." Epstein, *Cellarful*, p. 68.

330   "The lads don't want you": Pete Best in Leigh, *Drummed Out!*, p. 41.

330   "my mind was in a turmoil": Best & Doncaster, *Beatle!*, p. 166.

330   "stab in the back": Ibid.

330   Brian offered to form another group: "I suggested many alternatives. That he could be the nucleus of a group that I would form, that he could be fitted into one of my existing groups. . . ." Epstein, *Cellarful*, p. 69.

331   "What's happened?": Best & Doncaster, *Beatle!*, p. 166.

331   Pete was stunned: "The fact that they weren't at my dismissal hurt me a lot more than the fact that Brian told me that I wasn't a Beatle any longer." Leigh, *Drummed Out!*, p. 49.

331   Where were the Beatles?: John said, "We were cowards when we sacked him." Davies, *Beatles*, p. 140.

331   "disgusted": Best & Doncaster, *Beatle!*, p. 167.

331 Throughout his residency there: Author interview with Bill and Virginia Harry, Johnny Byrne; also Leigh, *Drummed Out!*, pp. 36–37.

331 The birth certificate: City of Liverpool, Legal Services, Registrar of Births.

331 It was all Pete could do: Best & Doncaster, *Beatle!*, p. 167.

331 "I'm not going to the gig": Best & Harry, *Best Years*, p. 159.

331 "Once I was home": Best & Doncaster, *Beatle!*, p. 167.

331 "I never felt sorry": Ringo Starr in *Anthology*, p. 72.

332 "ordinary, poor": Ringo Starr in *Anthology*, p. 33.

332 "He was not a barefoot, ragged child": Author interview with Marie Crawford, 11/1/97.

332 "really rough": Ringo Starr in *Anthology*, p. 34.

332 "artisan working class": Author interview with Quentin Hughes, 10/3/97.

332 "Most of us were brought up there": Author interview with Marie Crawford, 11/1/97.

332 "palatial": Ringo Starr in *Anthology*, p. 33.

332 "the cherry on top": Author interview with Marie Crawford, 11/1/97.

333 Big Ritchie: Clayson, *Straight Man*, p. 1.

334 "no real memories of dad": Ringo Starr in *Anthology*, p. 33.

334 "filled me up with all the things": *Beatles Book Monthly*, 12/86.

334 Richard provided support: Norman, *Shout!*, p. 160.

335 "You kept your head down": Author interview with Adrian Barber, 10/4/97.

336 told by his doctors to prepare for the worst: "They told my mother three times that I'd be dead in the morning." Ringo Starr in *Anthology*, p. 34.

337 "was very lucky to survive": Ibid.

337 "doted on him": Author interview with Marie Crawford, 11/1/97.

338 "cotton bobbins to hit": Ringo Starr in *Anthology*, p. 36.

339 "Someday, I'm going to play": Author interview with Marie Crawford, 11/1/97.

339 never went back to school: "I never went back to school after 13." Ringo Starr in *Anthology*, p. 36.

339 "biscuit tins": Ibid.

339 "He was a really sweet guy": Ibid., p. 35.

339–40 Harry had access to all the luxuries: Author interview with Marie Crawford, 11/1/97.

340 "great gentleness": Ringo Starr in *Anthology*, p. 37.

340 "because they give you suits": Ibid., p. 36.

341 "But it was a great gang": Author interview with Roy Trafford, 11/3/97.

343 "We knew him pretty well": Author interview with Johnny Byrne, 10/8/97.

343 Ritchie borrowed £46: Ringo Starr in *Anthology*, p. 36.

343 "lapped" pigskin: Clayson, *Straight Man*, p. 23.

344 "had about three lessons": Ringo Starr in *Anthology*, p. 37.

344 Ritchie was influenced: "I went through modern jazz—Chico Hamilton, Yusef Lateef, people like that." *Melody Maker*, 8/7/71.

344 "a bubble of personality": Author interview with Iris Caldwell Fenton, 9/10/97.

344 "who liked to take care of the other guys": Ibid.

345 "He always loved his rings": Author interview with Marie Crawford, 11/1/97.

345 "was nominally of the Orange lodge": Ibid.

345 "to say [he] was actually *something*": Ringo Starr in *Anthology*, p. 38.

345 "It was a difficult decision": Author interview with Johnny Byrne, 10/8/97.

346 "Why not?": Author interview with Roy Trafford, 11/3/97.

CHAPTER 19: A TOUCH OF THE BARNUM & BAILEY

347 "We felt sorry for him": Author interview with Ray Ennis, 10/1/97.

347 "I felt sorry for the lads": Author interview with Colin Manley, 10/2/97.

347 "From the time the doors opened": Author interview with Bob Wooler, 10/30/97.

348 "very solid beat": Paul McCartney in *Anthology*, p. 72.

348 "Ringo didn't try and direct the beat": Author interview with Adrian Barber, 10/4/97.

348 "it had all been settled": Author interview with Dot Rhone Becker, 11/19/98.

348 "a bizarre affair": *Hello!*, 5/14/94.

348 Fortunately, Brian sent a car: Ibid.

348 "was never even told": Ringo Starr in *Anthology*, p. 73.

348 John waited until the last minute: "I went the day before to tell Mimi." John Lennon, 1965 interview, in *Anthology,* p. 73.

349 "a fucking pad": Author interview with Peter Brown, 12/3/97.

349 "We actually did a gig that night": George Harrison in *Anthology,* p. 73.

349 "the only one thinking about the future": Cynthia Lennon in Coleman, *Lennon,* p. 176.

350 Bruce Welch of the Shadows: *Abbey Road* archives.

350 "intimidating": Author interview with Ray Ennis, 10/1/97.

350 "a very strong engineering discipline": Author interview with Alan Brown, 6/23/97.

350 "You had to polish your shoes": Geoff Emerick, *Abbey Road* archives.

350 "a right time to speak to artists": Martin Benge, *Abbey Road* archives.

350 "had to know your place": Ibid.

350 "blissfully unaware": Southall, *Abbey Road,* p. 78.

351 the Beatles rehearsed six songs: Norman Smith in Pritchard & Lysaght, *The Beatles,* p. 105.

351 "any evidence of what was to come": George Martin in Southall, *Abbey Road,* p. 81.

351 "it might have made a good 'B' side": George Martin in Pritchard & Lysaght, *The Beatles,* p. 104.

351 "Do it!": Paul McCartney in ibid., p. 104.

352 "We just don't want this kind of song": Paul McCartney in Lewisohn, *Sessions,* p. 7.

352 "Ringo at that point": Paul McCartney in *Anthology,* p. 76.

352 "he didn't have quite enough push": Norman Smith in Pritchard & Lysaght, *The Beatles,* p. 106.

352 "Ringo had a lot more zest": Author interview with Ron Richards, 12/27/97.

352 "probably the top session drummer": Author interview with Ron Richards, 1/8/98.

353 Ringo was stunned: "I was devastated that George Martin had his doubts about me." Ringo Starr in *Anthology,* p. 76.

353 "I knew he could play the beat": Author interview with Ron Richards, 12/27/97.

353 "but he was not pleased": Ibid.

353 "It didn't call for any drumnastics": *Goldmine,* no. 425, p. 40.

353 Martin called it "much too dreary": George Martin in *Arena* archives and in Lewisohn, *Sessions,* p. 20.

353 "work out some tight harmonies": George Martin in Lewisohn, *Sessions.*

354 "undesirable" image: George Harrison in *Anthology,* p. 73.

354 "open doors": "It did open doors for us." Paul McCartney, *Arena* archives.

354 He'd blame the outfits on Paul: "So Brian put us in neat suits and shirts and Paul was right behind him." Wenner, *Lennon Remembers.*

354 quite "gladly": George Harrison in *Anthology,* p. 73.

354 "Hey, listen, Cavernites": Author interview with Bob Wooler, 10/30/97.

354 "an extra two hundred kids": Ibid.

355 It was Brian, not the Beatles: "Brian was furious—he was livid. He complained to Ray, and Ray must have been very contrite." Ibid.

355 "He'd been picking my brains": Author interview with Tony Barrow, 10/31/97.

355 "John . . . likes the colour black": EMI press release accompanying demo disc of "Love Me Do," 10/62.

356 "It was a hell of a job": Author interview with Ron Richards, 12/27/97.

357   Even Parlophone was chagrined: Ibid.
357   EMI did buy time: Lewisohn, *Chronicle*, p. 80.
357   Jimmy Saville . . . was "unimpressed": Author interview with Tony Barrow, 10/31/97.
357   "wasn't at all that thrilled": Author interview with Dot Rhone Becker, 12/19/98.
358   "Brian bought boxes": Author interview with Alistair Taylor, 1/17/98. "They bought many boxes of records. That's how they got it into the charts." Author interview with Ron Richards, 12/27/97.
358   "EMI never gave us any budget": Author interview with Ron Richards, 12/27/97.
358   "When you can write material": Martin, *All You Need*, p. 129.
358   "We've revamped it": Ibid., p. 130.
360   "He spent all day": Author interview with Frieda Kelly Norris, 10/5/97.
361   he met promoter Sam Leach: Author interview with Sam Leach, 10/6/97.
361   "Sam had a habit of not paying groups": Author interview with Bob Wooler, 10/30/97.
362   "Even before the Beatles exploded": Author interview with Peter Brown, 12/3/98.
362   "the Beatles had really hit the big time": Lewisohn, *Chronicle*, p. 82.
362   "When I saw them on the stage": Author interview with Frieda Kelly Norris, 10/5/97.
363   "Immediately . . . the kids started screaming": Author interview with Tony Barrow, 10/31/97.
363   "Everyone had said, 'You'll never make [it]'": Miles, *Paul McCartney*, p. 97.
363   "take a look up North": Author interview with Bill Harry, 8/9/97.
363   Alistair Taylor, who left NEMS that November: Author interview with Alistair Taylor, 1/17/98.
363   "No one ever mentioned London": Author interview with Tony Bramwell, 8/6/97.
363   "His own press officer": Author interview with Tony Barrow, 10/31/97.
363   "did virtually nothing": Martin, *All You Need*, p. 127.
364   Though it placed at forty-nine: *Record Mirror*, 11/22/62.
364   "a riff": Norman, *Shout!*, p. 171.
365   "Dick said, 'Why don't we sign . . .'": George Martin, *Arena* archives.
365   "a slave deal": Paul McCartney, ibid.
365   "Dick James's entire empire": Author interview with Paul McCartney, 3/21/97.
365   Northern Songs to acquire Lenmac Enterprises: Harry, *Ultimate Beatles Encyclopedia*, p. 339.

CHAPTER 20: DEAD CHUFFED

366   *Thank Your Lucky Stars:* Taped 1/13/63 at ATV's Birmingham Studios for ABC, ATV archives.
366   the spots were all "mimed": Author interview with Kenny Lynch, 1/16/98.
367   "To those of us in England": Author interview with Ray Connolly, 8/7/97.
367   Radio Luxembourg had added it: "You've Please—Pleased Us," *NME*, 1/2/63.
367   And sensing some ground gained: Author interview with Frieda Kelly Norris, 10/5/97.
367   "Things were going so well": Author interview with Tony Bramwell, 8/8/97.
368   "probably fancied the lad": Author interview with Alistair Taylor, 1/17/98.
368   "I was just a wild card": Author interview with Billy J. Kramer, 12/16/97.
369   "Whenever word spread": Author interview with Frieda Kelly Norris, 10/5/97.
369   Harry Epstein wasn't pleased: "Mr. Epstein was very upset about it. He made Brian make other plans." Ibid.
369   "I'll ask Bob Wooler": Author interview with Bob Wooler, 10/30/97.
369   "The Beatles made little or no impression": Author interview with Kenny Lynch, 1/16/98.
370   happy "just to get out of Liverpool": Davies, *Beatles*, p. 171.
370   "the audience repeatedly called for them": "An Improved Helen!" *NME*, 2/8/63.

371 the cast album for *Beyond the Fringe:* "George and I went up to Edinburgh and sat under the stage for three nights recording *Beyond the Fringe."* Author interview with Ron Richards, 12/29/97.

371 Instead, Martin prepared a list: "I knew their repertoire from the Cavern . . . and said, 'Right, what you're going to do now . . . is play me this selection of things I've chosen.'" Martin, *All You Need,* p. 130.

372 sessions ran "strictly to time": Author interview with Martin Benge, 3/98.

372 "[His] voice was pretty shot": Norman Smith in Pritchard & Lysaght, *The Beatles,* p. 119.

372 "the sound of the Beatles singing": "What I tried to do was to create the live pop group on tape." Ibid., p. 118.

373 They cut "There's a Place": "[Paul] was the owner of the soundtrack album of Leonard Bernstein's *West Side Story,* which is where the title phrase came from." Miles, *Paul McCartney,* p. 95.

373 Paul had written down in the van: "I did this song going home in a car one night." *Beatles Book Monthly,* 8/83, p. 6.

373 the second line was "useless": Ibid.

373 Sitting on the living-room floor: M. McCartney, *Thank U Very Much* (picture), pages unnumbered.

373 they ran through the alphabet: "We went through the alphabet: between clean, lean, mean." Miles, *Paul McCartney,* p. 93.

374 a galloping bass line: "I played exactly the same notes as he did and it fitted our number perfectly." Paul McCartney in *Beat Instrumental.*

374 "for a pie and a pint": Richard Langham in Lewisohn, *Sessions,* p. 24.

374 "We couldn't believe it": Ibid.

374 a "hack song": Miles, *Paul McCartney,* p. 95.

375 "They just put their heads down": "Brian was so proud of them. He told me they worked their asses off." Author interview with Peter Brown, 12/9/97.

375 "someone suggested they do 'Twist and Shout'": Lewisohn, *Sessions,* p. 26.

375 "A real larynx-tearer": George Martin in *Anthology,* p. 93.

376 Everyone knew they'd have to get it: "It's not an easy number for any vocalist to sing, but we had to get it in one take." Norman Smith in Pritchard & Lysaght, *The Beatles,* p. 119.

376 "got it in one": "I was ready to jump up and down when I heard them singing that." Richard Langham in Lewisohn, *Sessions,* p. 26.

377 "dead chuffed": "As it happens, we were very happy with the result—or to put it more eloquently, dead chuffed!" *NME,* 4/19/63.

377 "to give the boys some air": Author interview with Bob Wooler, 10/30/97.

377 This was a trick they had practiced: "I used to see them backstage, practicing shaking their heads—on a count." Author interview with Kenny Lynch, 1/16/98.

377 "Just a few weeks before": Author interview with Colin Manley, 10/2/97.

377 drawing the biggest queue: "The queue outside on Mathew Street was amazing, larger than any I'd ever seen. The kids had been there all day, maybe all night." Author interview with Bob Wooler, 10/30/97.

378 "a small piece of motorway": Ringo Starr in *Anthology,* p. 83.

378 The *NME* Top Thirty: *NME,* 2/20/63.

379 Since breaking up with Dot Rhone: "I'd go out with Frank, who would give me a pound for the taxi home. But Paul would meet me, and we'd have the pound to spend." Author interview with Iris Caldwell Fenton, 9/30/97.

379 "was berserk over [Iris]": Author interview with Bill Harry, 8/4/97.

379 *Disc,* on the other hand: *Disc,* 2/23/63.

379 The bus was "a drag": "No one liked it." Author interview with Kenny Lynch, 1/16/98.

380 Before the opening bars: "We all got loud. Everyone was cheering." Ibid.

CHAPTER 21: THE JUNGLE DRUMS

383 "Britain's top vocal-instrumental group": *Melody Maker*, 4/13/63.

383 *"We want the Beatles!":* "All one of us had to do was go out there and they'd be screaming, 'We want the Beatles!'" Author interview with Kenny Lynch, 1/16/98.

383 "all the people coming to the show": George Harrison in *Anthology*, p. 90.

383 "have a walk through the streets": Author interview with Kenny Lynch, 1/16/98.

384 "in the dressing-rooms": Coleman, *Lennon*, p. 195.

384 the guesthouses: "The night staff were terrible—poor people." Ringo Starr in *Anthology*, p. 86.

384 "It was always a bore": Ibid., p. 90.

385 To fulfill an urgent request: "I asked them for another song as good as 'Please, Please Me,' and they brought me one." Martin, *All You Need*, p. 131.

385 "Thank You Little Girl": "We'd already written 'Thank You Girl.'" John Lennon in *Melody Maker*, 4/19/63.

385 just "fooling around" on the guitar: Ibid.

385 The new tune came quickly: Talking about "From Me to You," Paul said: "We have such a fairly easy job thinking up tunes." *NME*, 5/10/63.

385 "It went to a surprising place": Paul McCartney in Miles, *Paul McCartney*, p. 149.

385 "Paul and I had been talking": John Lennon in *NME*, 5/10/63.

385 "very direct and personal": "There was a little trick we developed early on . . . which was to put I, Me, or You in it, so it was very direct and personal." Paul McCartney in Miles, *Paul McCartney*, p. 148.

385 "people can identify . . . with it": Paul McCartney in *NME*, 5/10/63.

385 "From Me to You" was finished: "Before that journey was over, we'd completed the lyric, everything." John Lennon in *NME*, 4/19/63.

386 Why not sing the intro?: Author interview with Ron Richards, 12/29/97.

387 Brian shared their dream: "Brian Epstein was putting pressure on George [Martin], who, in turn, was giving me a hard time." Author interview with Roland Rennie, 8/7/97.

387 The stumbling block . . . Capitol: "When EMI bought Capitol, or bought the major position in Capitol, we had an agreement between us—that [with] any of EMI's English artists . . . we had the right of first refusal, and the same in reverse." Alan Livingston, *Arena* archives.

387 "The idea was that [Capitol]": Author interview with Roland Rennie, 8/7/97.

387 "didn't even hear the first Beatles record": Alan Livingston, *Arena* archives.

387 the Beatles were "nothing": "He said, 'Alan, they're a bunch of long-haired kids, they're nothing, forget it.'" Ibid.

387 "a jazz man": "Of course, the A&R guy . . . was a jazz man . . . who couldn't see pop records anyway." Paul White in ibid., p. 141.

388 "I wasn't going to call [Dave] Dexter": Author interview with Paul Marshall, 8/28/97.

389 "fell right to the bottom": "I released the record about a month and a half after the English did and it fell right to the bottom." Paul White in Pritchard & Lysaght, *The Beatles*, p. 137.

389 *NME* broke the story: "The Beatles, yet to have a major British hit . . . have been snapped up for America by Vee Jay." *NME*, 1/25/63.

390 Then, in the February 8 issue: *NME*, 2/8/63.

390 a small follow-up in *Melody*: "American star Roy Orbison is set for a three-week British tour." *Melody Maker*, 3/23/63.

390 clocked somewhere around E: "He had refined his voice into a crystal instrument with which he can hit his E above high C." Dalton & Kaye, *Rock 100*, p. 30.

390 always speed to fall back on: "Roy, who toured with Johnny Cash . . . was also devoted to speed and sleeping pills." Amburn, *Dark Star*, p. 67.

390 A stone staircase swept up: Description of building—author interview with Shelagh Johnson, 10/29/97.

391 "Eppy's Epitorium": Author interview with Frieda Kelly Norris, 10/5/97.

391 "there are three groups in Liverpool": John Lennon in *Hit Parade*, 4/63.

391 music "scene that could only find its counterpart": "The Beat Boys!" *Melody Maker*, 3/23/63.

392 "idolized him": "She only had the one son, and she idolized him." Author interview with Frieda Kelly Norris, 10/5/97.

392 "Elsie felt they were taking him": Author interview with Marie Crawford, 11/1/97.

392 the Harrisons and Jim McCartney "were thrilled": Author interview with Bill Harry, 8/5/97.

392 Friends close to Louise Harrison: "Mrs. Harrison enjoyed it all." Author interview with Frieda Kelly Norris, 10/5/97.

392 "She followed the Beatles as avidly": Author interview with Arthur Kelly, 1/10/98.

392 "Jim was probably the Beatles' biggest fan": Author interview with Bill Harry, 8/5/97.

392 "showing blood": "She was showing blood, and the doctor told her she had to go to bed." Author interview with Dot Rhone Becker, 11/19/98.

393 "drank whiskey after whiskey": "He insisted we drink whiskey after . . ." Paddy Delaney in Badman, *Off the Record*, p. 54.

393 a tall, "spunky" seventeen-year-old: Author interview with Virginia Harry, 8/10/97.

393 they'd been hanging out together: "We didn't know that Cyn was pregnant at the time." Author interview with Bill Harry, 8/10/97.

394 Even *with the Beatles*: Goldman, *Lives of John Lennon*, p. 135.

394 "He had no shame": Author interview with Bill Harry, 8/10/97.

394 Had it been a girl: "We'd already decided that if the baby was a girl she would be called Julia." *Hello!*, 5/14/94.

394 "triumphant at the news": Coleman, *Lennon*, p. 171.

394 "over-sensitive"/"moody": *Hello!*, 5/14/94.

394 carping about Cynthia's "willfulness": Author interview with Dot Rhone Becker, 11/19/98.

394 "a perverse pleasure": Author interview with Bill Harry, 8/7/97.

394 "didn't even emerge from upstairs": Coleman, *Lennon*, p. 180.

394 John turned up two days: Lewisohn, *Chronicle*, pp. 106–7.

394 Julian and Cynthia were still in the hospital: Coleman, *Lennon*, p. 171.

395 "Who's going to be a famous little rocker": C. Lennon, *A Twist*, p. 87.

395 "bloody marvelous": Ibid.

395 "a miracle": *Hello!*, 5/14/94.

395 Brian had insisted that John keep the marriage a secret: "It was wholly down to paranoia on Brian's part about the private lives of his artists." Author interview with Tony Barrow, 10/31/97.

395 Cynthia may have suppressed: "I saw the whole thing in a flash and I realized there and then that I'd have to close my mind to the situation or my relationship with John would be impossible." *Hello!*, 5/21/94.

395 John "was beginning to feel trapped": C. Lennon, *A Twist*, p. 87.

396 "But he never talked about Julian": Author interview with Bill Harry, 8/10/97.

396 "Once the Beatles hit the pop charts": Author interview with Johnny Byrne, 11/3/97.

396 "plenty of sparkle": "Beatles Sparkle Again," *NME*, 4/12/63.

396 "so-so melody": *Melody Maker*, 4/13/63.

396 "came crashing": *NME*, 4/19/63.

396 sales hit 200,000 copies: "Beatles Back with a Bang!" *Melody Maker*, 4/20/63.

396 "By now, the Beatle legend": Melly, *Revolt Into Style*, p. 63.

397 "The Beatles could take it to the Americans": "Beatles—One Out for Week," *Melody Maker*, 3/16/63.

397 "Latest visitors from America": "Screams Acclaim Beatles, Montez, Roe," *NME*, 3/15/63.

397 "A couple of records in the charts": Melly, *Revolt Into Style*, p. 68.

398 "They acted that way": Author interview with Tony Barrow, 10/31/97.

398 "It was my chore": Melly, *Revolt Into Style*, p. 69.

398 evicted Gerry Marsden from his perch: "Top Thirty," *NME*, 4/24/63.

398 "highlight of the pop music year": "Now 4 Extra Acts at NME Poll Concert," *NME*, 4/19/63.

399 "more like that of a father": Author interview with Tony Bramwell, 8/8/97.

399 "Clive took one look": "George once told me a very revealing story." Author interview with Bob Wooler, 10/30/97.

401 "He was in love with me": Sheff, *Playboy Interviews*, p. 76.

401 "wanted to know if [she] objected": C. Lennon, *A Twist*, pp. 87–88.

401 She was "hurt": "I concealed my hurt and envy and gave him my blessing." Ibid., p. 88.

401 "what a bastard": John Lennon, 1970 interview, in *Anthology*, p. 98.

401 "stayed in the sun too long": George Harrison in *Anthology*, p. 98.

402 "nothing would stand in his way": Author interview with Bob Wooler, 10/30/97.

402 "a smart cookie": Paul McCartney in *Anthology*, p. 98.

402 "Paris of Spain": Hans Christian Andersen, 1862.

402 "Where else may I have a gin": Brian Epstein, private journal, 10/5/60.

403 "My God, how he ranted": Author interview with Bob Wooler, 10/30/97.

403 "I watched Brian picking up boys": John Lennon, 1970 interview, in *Anthology*, p. 98.

404 "It was almost a love affair": Ibid.

404 "[John] and Brian had sex": Goldman, *Lives of John Lennon*, p. 140.

404 "I let [Brian] toss me off": Shotton, *John Lennon in My Life*, p. 73.

404 "John lay there, tentative": "Brian and John undressed in silence." Brown & Gaines, *Love You Make*, p. 94.

404 "something to build on": Author interview with Peter Brown, 12/8/97.

404 "the homosexual thing": Paul McCartney in *Anthology*, p. 98.

CHAPTER 22: KINGS OF THE JUNGLE

406 "really had my backside kicked": Dick Rowe in Pritchard & Lysaght, *The Beatles*, p. 122.

407 "almost as good as our Roadrunners": Author interview with Bill Harry, 8/8/97.

407 He took the next train back: "Well, I left him right on the spot, went down to London . . . and drove to Richmond": Dick Rowe in Pritchard & Lysaght, *The Beatles*, pp. 122–23.

407 Gomelsky invited the boys: Wyman, *Stone Alone*, p. 127.

407 "full-bodied R&B" band: Hotchner, *Blown Away*, p. 91.

408 "Keith and Brian—wow!": "I knew then that the Stones were great." Ringo Starr in *Anthology*, p. 101.

408 both boys did nothing all day: Ian Stewart in Hotchner, *Blown Away*, p. 78.

408 "a little bit more radical": John Lennon, 1974 interview in *Anthology*, p. 101.

409 "a cozy little setup": Author interview with Tony Barrow, 10/31/97.

410 "the ins and outs of a dog's dinner": Author interview with Frieda Kelly Norris, 10/5/97.

410 "utter nonsense": Mimi Smith, AGA (undated).

410 "Ritchie came in [the office]": Author interview with Frieda Kelly Norris, 10/5/97.

410 Barrow also invented a national secretary: Norman, *Shout!*, p. 182.

412 "the world's worst chain-smoker": Tony Barrow, "The Girls They Like," *Beatles Book Monthly*, 6/83, p. 8.

412 "undercover existence": C. Lennon, *A Twist*, p. 94.

412 "For up to eighteen months": Author interview with Tony Barrow, 10/31/97.

412 "We still can't mention your marriage": Ibid.

412 One journalist . . . "browsed through the pile": *Beatles Book Monthly*, 6/83, pp. 8–9.

413   "a flop": Paul McCartney in *Anthology*, p. 115.

413   *Cash Box* pounced on it: *Cash Box*, 6/28/63.

413   "it was patently unfair": George Martin, *Arena* archives.

414   "I was considered a traitor": Ibid.

414   Parlophone exercised its option: EMI memorandum from L. G. Wood, 5/28/63.

414   Finally, on June 18: Brian Epstein's journal.

415   John was descending into a black funk: Author interview with Pete Shotton, 1/19/98.

415   "out of my mind with drink": John Lennon, 1972 interview, in *Anthology*, p. 98.

415   "sinking a fair bit of booze": Tony Barrow, "What a Party," *Beatles Book Monthly*, 7/83, p. 6.

415   "Bob has a sarcastic note": Author interview with Bill Harry, 8/2/97.

415   "Come on, John, tell me": McCabe & Schonfeld, *John Lennon: For the Record*, p. 94.

415   "tightly closed fists": *Beatles Book Monthly*, 7/83, p. 6.

415   "Bob was holding his hands": Author interview with Billy J. Kramer, 12/16/97.

415   "I was beating the shit out of him": John Lennon, 1972 interview, in *Anthology*, p. 98.

416   Cynthia, who "was freaking out": Author interview with Billy J. Kramer, 12/16/97.

416   "He arrived with a black eye": Author interview with Rex Makin, 11/1/97.

416   "For my trouble": Author interview with Bob Wooler, 10/30/97.

416   "I first called John in Liverpool": Author interview with Tony Barrow, 10/31/97.

416   BEATLE IN BRAWL: *Daily Mirror*, 6/21/63.

417   "racing up and down the country": "Backstage (and Elsewhere) with the Beatles, Dakotas,"*NME*, 7/26/63.

417   "girls were plucked": "Fans Invade Homes but Boys Love 'Em!" *NME*, 6/21/63.

417   "nearly five thousand fans": *Melody Maker*, 7/27/63.

417   The boys had to climb a scaffolding: "Beatles Paris Date, as EP Makes History," *NME*, 7/26/63.

418   Publicly, the Beatles laughed it off: Melly, *Revolt Into Style*, p. 70.

418   "like persistent termites": *NME*, 7/26/63.

418   "Wave the Union Jack!": *NME*, 7/5/63.

419   "It's terrible," John complained: "I wouldn't buy it." "Beatles Blast Own Hit Disc!" *NME*, 6/22/63.

419   sold an astonishing 150,000 copies: "We had orders for 40,000 within a half-hour." "Beatles Blast Off!" *Melody Maker*, 7/20/63.

419   first EP ever to enter the Top Ten: "Survey by Derek Johnson," *NME*, 8/2/63.

419   "Bad to Me": "Billy J. Kramer—So Much Melody," *NME*, 7/19/63.

419   "Tip of My Tongue": Released on Piccadilly no. 7N 35137, *NME*, 8/2/63.

419   "answering song": "I'd planned an 'answering song.'" Paul McCartney in *Anthology*, p. 96.

420   a "crummy idea": Ibid.

420   "brilliant . . . one of the most vital [songs]": George Martin in Pritchard & Lysaght, *The Beatles*, p. 125.

420   "Oh my God, what a lyric!": Lewisohn, *Sessions*, p. 32.

421   "No one played it": Author interview with Paul Marshall, 8/28/97.

421   "stone-cold dead": Dave Dexter, Pritchard & Lysaght, *The Beatles*, p. 134.

421   "They didn't pay anything": Author interview with Roland Rennie, 8/7/97.

421   "Sometimes, you know, I feel": "Close Up on a Beatle: Paul McCartney," *NME*, 10/7/63.

422   "Beatles fever": *Melody Maker*, 10/26/63.

422   "a staggering 235,000 copies": *NME*, 8/16/63.

422   "sitting round a big fire": "There's nothing better, for me, than a bit of peace and quiet." "Close Up on a Beatle: George Harrison," *NME*, 8/16/63.

422   "I'm not really interested in sport": *NME*, 8/9/63.

423   Ringo "didn't have a large vocal range": Paul McCartney in Miles, *Paul McCartney*, p. 148.

423   "If he couldn't mentally picture": Ibid., p. 152.

423   The boys had been on the way: "We'd go to his office and window shop on the way." Miles, *Paul McCartney*, p. 154.

423   "Mecca": "It was where all the guitar shops were." Paul McCartney in *Anthology*, p. 101.

423   "Well, Ringo's got this track": Ibid.

423   "a throwaway": "We weren't going to give them anything great, right?" Sheff, *Playboy Interviews*, p. 145.

423   They played what they had: Wyman, *Stone Alone*, p. 150.

424   "So Paul and I just went off": Sheff, *Playboy Interviews*, p. 145.

424   "Can I have that song?": Author interview with Billy J. Kramer, 12/16/97.

424   "their act [was] fast": *Boyfriend*, 10/63.

425   "We were like kings": John Lennon, 1974 interview, in *Anthology*, p. 101.

425   "This is it! London!": Miles, *Paul McCartney*, p. 120.

CHAPTER 23: SO THIS IS BEATLEMANIA

426   "there was nothing bigger": Ringo Starr in *Anthology*, p. 102.

426   "My mum, Annie": Author interview with Marie Crawford, 11/1/97.

427   "various decoy routes": Author interview with Tony Barrow, 10/31/97.

427   BEATLEMANIA!: *Daily Mirror*, 10/14/63.

428   "Screaming girls launched themselves": "Siege of the Beatles," *Daily Herald*, 10/14/63.

428   "It was *exactly* the story": Author interview with Don Short, 8/11/63.

428   "impropriety": "I said there had been no impropriety in this association. To my very deep regret I have to admit that this was not true." Letter from John Profumo to Harold Macmillan, 6/4/63.

429   "considerable sexual license": "Even during the Victorian high noon, the upper and upper-middle classes had always allowed themselves considerable sexual license." Melly, *Revolt Into Style*, p. 37.

429   "All over Britain . . . incredible scenes": "This Week's Beatlemania," *Melody Maker*, 11/2/63.

429   "hundreds slept in the streets": Ibid.

429   "midnight panic": "It's really here . . . BEATLEMANIA," *Sunday People*, 11/27/63, p. 1.

429   girls "fainted—and got hurt": "And 50 policemen were struggling to control the singing, screaming crowd." Ibid.

430   "Thousands of girls battled": "60 Teenagers Hurt in Cinema Stampede," *Sunday People*, 11/3/63.

430   "thousands[,] of screaming fans": Davies, *Beatles*, p. 182.

430   By coincidence, "the commotion": "We couldn't believe all the commotion at Heathrow Airport when we arrived." Ed Sullivan in Pritchard & Lysaght, *The Beatles*, p. 140.

430–31 Sullivan had some idea: "Instead of paying the $5,000 that had been asked originally, [Sullivan] was forced to ante up $50,000." Goldman, *Elvis*, p. 203.

431   Cliff Richard . . . had "died": Davies, *Beatles*, p. 192.

431   "He was fourteenth on the bill": John Lennon, 1967 interview, in *Anthology*, p. 116.

431   "We prefer to wait": *Melody Maker*, 6/15/63.

431   "a fuckin' shitty pop movie": Wenner, *Lennon Remembers*, p. 79.

431   during his first meeting with the Beatles: "We piled into a cab and went to EMI Studios, where we gathered in an empty office." Walter Shenson, 4/84, AGA.

431   "Oh, I don't know": "I met with them; John was the spokesman." Author interview with Walter Shenson, 4/22/99.

431 "I really found myself": Ibid.
432 "I'll do it for *nothing!*": Ibid.
432 "We laid out the terms": Ibid.
432 "He was talking percentages of *record albums*": Walter Shenson, 4/84, AGA.
433 "He wanted to see a script": "I was dreading the day that someone finally said, 'What are you going to make?'" Ibid.
433 "the most banal nonsense": Author interview with Walter Shenson, 4/22/99.
433 "And Brian came up with": Wenner, *Lennon Remembers*, p. 79.
433 Shenson was appalled: "I said, 'Why Alun Owen?'" Walter Shenson, 4/84, AGA.
433 "I think it should be an exaggerated": Author interview with Walter Shenson, 4/22/99.
433 "They were nervous": Author interview with Tony Barrow, 10/31/97.
434 BEATLES ROCK THE ROYALS: *Daily Express*, 10/5/63, p. 1.
434–35 "it was impossible to go home": Ringo Starr in *Anthology*, p. 109.
435 "Overflowing ashtrays": Braun, *Love Me Do*, p. 52.
435 "It was such a buzz": George Harrison in *Anthology*, p. 109.
435 "There was no homeliness": Miles, *Paul McCartney*, p. 103.
435 "obligatory period of post-war austerity": Wheen, *The Sixties*, p. 14.
436 "So many factors commingled": Green, *Days in the Life*, p. viii.
436 "It seemed great to me": Miles, *Paul McCartney*, p. 115.
437 Although by no means an intellectual: Author interview with Lionel Bart, 1/16/98.
437 "an intuitive brightness": "Now I'm bright enough but mine is an intuitive brightness." Miles, *Paul McCartney*, p. 106.
437 "Coming in from the provinces": Green, *Days in the Life*, p. 48.
437 "Every man who ever met Jane": Author interview with Alistair Taylor, 1/17/98.
437 a pale, creamy complexion: "Her mass of Titian-coloured hair cascaded around her face and shoulders, her pale complexion." C. Lennon, *A Twist*, p. 121.
437 "We thought she was blonde": Paul McCartney in *Anthology*, p. 110.
438 "She was smart and sexy": Author interview with Peter Brown, 12/8/97.
438 "something about seeing them together": Author interview with Tony Barrow, 10/31/97.
438 "Both of them came with plenty": Author interview with John Dunbar, 1/13/98.
438 every night "out and about": "They were always together." Ibid.
439 "It was really like culture shock": Miles, *Paul McCartney*, p. 106.
439 "For a young guy": Ibid.
440 "I invited the whole industry": Walter Hofer, 3/83, AGA.
440 "a good TV attraction": Ed Sullivan in Pritchard & Lysaght, *The Beatles*, p. 140.
440 "plus five round-trip": Ibid.
441 "to get over this hurdle": Author interview with Roland Rennie, 8/7/97.
441 "But L.G. wasn't asking anymore": Author interview with Paul Marshall, 8/28/97.
441 According to a 1997 interview: "For whatever reason, I said, 'Okay.'" Alan Livingston, *Arena* archives.
442 700,000 copies: "Advance orders for the disc . . ." *NME*, 11/3/63.
442 Even at Capitol: "For an artist that had a following, you might press twenty-five, fifty thousand." Alan Livingston, *Arena* archives.
443 "After a while," Bernstein recalled: Spitz, *The Making of Superstars*, p. 190.
444 "Girls are fainting": "Beatsville," *Melody Maker*, 11/9/63.
444 "rampaging fans": Lewisohn, *25 Years in the Life*, p. 29.
444 "Getting them inside": "Beatsville," *Melody Maker*, 11/9/63.
444 In Sunderland: "The Beatles manage their escape from the Sunderland Theater," Braun, *Love Me Do*, p. 43.
444 George Martin arrived backstage: Author interview with Alistair Taylor, 1/17/98.
446 "a great album": "Here They Come Again—Stand By for New Records," *Melody Maker*, 11/23/63.

446   "a knockout": "Beatles Tell the Secrets Behind Their Golden Tracks," *NME*, 11/15/63.

446   "The second album was slightly better": George Harrison in *Anthology*, p. 107.

446   It was influenced, John recalled: "He described [it] as 'me trying to do a Smokey Robinson.'" Miles, *Paul McCartney*, p. 148.

446   "We were all very interested in American music": Paul McCartney in *Anthology*, p. 107.

446   "one of the all-time great poets": Wenner, *Lennon Remembers*, p. 168.

447   Paul "sounded like a woman": George Harrison in Braun, *Love Me Do*, p. 49.

447   "a failed attempt at a single": Miles, *Paul McCartney*, p. 83.

447   something "artistic": "*With the Beatles* is the first [album cover] where we thought, 'Hey, let's get artistic.'" George Harrison in *Anthology*, p. 107.

447   Freeman posed the Beatles: Freeman, *Yesterday: The Beatles*, p. 8.

448   "shockingly humorless": "Certainly EMI were strongly opposed to its use." Miles, *Paul McCartney*, p. 157.

448   "it would damage their image": Author interview with Tony Barrow, 10/31/97.

448   "I'd never seen anything like it": Author interview with Peter Brown, 12/8/97.

448   On that first day alone: *NME*, 11/29/63.

449   The Cavern sponsored the chartered excursion: "We had about 30 Cavernites on that plane." Author interview with Bob Wooler, 10/30/97.

450   By the last week in November: *Record Retailer*, 11/28/63.

450   The next week "She Loves You": *Disc*, 11/30/63.

450   *NME*'s album chart: "Best Selling LPs in Britain," *NME*, 12/4/63.

451   "the switchboard just went totally wild": "Carroll James Remembers," *Beatlefan*, April-May 1984, pp. 8–9.

451   "There came a time": Author interview with Tony Barrow, 10/31/97.

452   "the craziest Xmas greeting": *NME*, 12/6/63.

452   "Thank you, Ringo": *The Beatles Christmas Record*, Official Beatles Fan Club, 12/63.

452   "Somebody asked us": Ibid.

452   "I started getting jelly babies": *Disc*, April 1964.

452   "it felt dangerous": "It was like being in a zoo on stage!" Ringo Starr in *Anthology*, p. 106.

452   "gone *right off* jelly babies!": *The Beatles Christmas Record*, 1963.

453   "on the cusp of showbiz": Miles, *Paul McCartney*, p. 135.

453   "genuine": In Michael Braun's *Love Me Do*, Paul observes: "Quite a few people mention the word genuine" to describe the Beatles. "Which we're not," John responds (p. 32).

453   "a resident show": Author interview with Peter Yolland, 1/12/98.

453   Delfont suggested he accept: D. Taylor, *Fifty Years*, p. 101.

453   "drive him crackers": Ibid., p. 102.

453   "a shambles, just chaos": Author interview with Alistair Taylor, 1/17/98.

454   "quite revolutionary": Author interview with Tony Barrow, 10/31/97.

454   "When I left Liverpool": John Lennon, 1971 interview, in *Anthology*, p. 109.

454   "brand-new Jaguar XK-E": Author interview with Frieda Kelly Norris, 10/5/97.

455   "My idea was to make the Beatles": Author interview with Peter Yolland, 1/14/98.

456   "I used to wake up": Author interview with Nigel Walley, 3/7/98.

456   "They're not *listening*": Author interview with Pete Shotton, 1/19/98.

CHAPTER 24: ONCE UPON A TIME IN AMERICA

457   Pan Am Flight 101: Pan American Airways flight logs.

457   "been over the moon": C. Lennon, *A Twist*, p. 103.

457   a crowd of four thousand: "Four thousand girls ... had arrived at London Airport." Braun, *Love Me Do*, p. 90.

457   "boom[ed] out over the public address system": *New York Times*, 2/6/64.

457   new pleated mohair suits: "Beatles New Suits for USA," *NME*, 2/7/64.

457   "nothing like it": Paul McCartney in Badman, *Off the Record*, 2/6/64, p. 78.

458   "In Liverpool, when you stood": Fawcett, *John Lennon: One Day at a Time*, p. 115.

458   "with a mess of ideas": Mimi Smith, AGA (undated).

458   "he thought we were winners": George Harrison in Badman, *Off the Record*, p. 78.

458   Since just after takeoff: "Every half hour the stewardesses on the plane would carry a product to Epstein, who would then write a polite, 'No' to the manufacturer." Nora Ephron, "Enter the Beatles," *New York Post*, 2/9/64.

459   "Going to the States was a big step": Davies, *Beatles*, p. 195.

459   Paul was also overheard: Braun, *Love Me Do*, p. 91.

459   "The pilot had rang ahead": Paul McCartney in *Anthology*, p. 116.

459   Shouts—whoops and cheers: "Just listen to that, fellers!" C. Lennon, *A Twist*, p. 105.

459   All day they had been urging listeners: *Melody Maker*, 2/15/64.

459   "Not even for kings": "3,000 Fans Greet British Beatles," *New York Times*, 2/8/64, p. 25.

459   "some punches were exchanged": "Beatles In, Town Knows It," *Daily News*, 2/8/64, p. 14.

459   "As far as I can tell": Giuliano, *Dark Horse*, p. 47.

460   "We had heard that our records were selling": George Harrison in Badman, *Off the Record*, p. 79.

460   "All right then": Braun, *Love Me Do*, p. 94.

460   "Will you sing something": Beatles Press Conference, transcript, 2/7/64.

461   "contagious . . . Beatle wit": *New York Times*, 2/8/64, p. 49.

461   "Hey, I dig your hat": George Harrison in Badman, *Off the Record*, p. 79, and in Pritchard & Lysaght, *The Beatles*, p. 149.

462   "The Beatles are coming": Murray Kaufman in Pritchard & Lysaght, *The Beatles*, p. 146.

462   "Who *are* you?": Badman, *Off the Record*, p. 80.

462   "the Beatles were lifted": Ephron, "Enter the Beatles," *New York Post*, 2/9/64, p. 27.

462   "I remember . . . getting into the limo": Paul McCartney in *Anthology*, p. 116.

463   It came as quite a shock: "The Plaza management was petrified." Braun, *Love Me Do*, p. 96.

463   Exhausted from their flight: *The Beatles: Their First American Visit* (video), 1991.

463   "We wanted to hear the music": John Lennon, 1964 interview, in *Anthology*, p. 119.

463   "We phoned every radio [station]": "Epstein had to stop us." Ibid.

463   "This is the Beatles' station!": WINS-AM archives, 2/7–8/64.

464   "[He] was as mad as a hatter": Ringo Starr in *Anthology*, p. 119.

464   George's temperature: "Beatles Prepare for Their Debut," *New York Times*, 2/9/64.

464   Wendy Hanson: "Capitol called me from Los Angeles and said, 'Can you please get us an English secretary. We need someone for Epstein. We want to impress him.'" Wendy Hanson, 11/27/83, AGA.

464   "a rather nouveau-riche family": Ibid.

465   "trolled with a bunch": Nicky Byrne, 2/84, AGA.

465   A sculptor in London: *NME*, 4/3/64.

465   "Brian's made a terrible mess": Nicky Byrne, 2/84, AGA.

466   By the time Brian arrived: "When it dawned on Brian what had happened, it started to make him physically ill." Braun, *Love Me Do*, p. 129.

466   "smoking night and day": "Bootleggers Trying to Capture a Share of Success," *New York Times*, 2/17/64, p. 20.

466   "Seltaeb was . . . in a business": Walter Hofer, 3/83, AGA.

466   "all sorts of gear": Nicky Byrne, 2/84, AGA.

467   "cruise past the Apollo": Author interview with Paul McCartney, 5/27/97.

467   the label's pressing plants: Dave Dexter in Pritchard & Lysaght, *The Beatles*, p. 155.

467   Otherwise, Meggs put himself: *New York Times*, 2/17/64, p. 20.

467   "vintage Coca-Cola": Braun, *Love Me Do*, p. 103.

468   "asking dumb questions": R. Spector, *Be My Baby*, p. 77.

468   John and George quickly developed serious crushes: Ibid., p. 72.

469   There was no chance of that: "Thank you for your recent request for tickets . . . and [we] are very sorry to tell you that so many ticket requests already have been received that we are unable to send you any at this time." Letter, CBS TV Network, Ticket Bureau, CBS archives.

469   "It's from Elvis!": "America Gets the Beatle Bug from John, Paul, Ringo & George," *NME*, 2/14/64.

469   "these youngsters from Liverpool": *The Ed Sullivan Show*, 2/23/64, CBS archives.

470   "We weren't happy": Paul McCartney in Badman, *Off the Record*, p. 82.

471   "Finally," George recalled: George Harrison in ibid.

471   "just stopped by to get a look": WWDC radio interview, Carroll James, 2/11/64.

471   "having a row": Wendy Hanson, 11/27/83, AGA.

471   "he sung rounds": Ibid.

471   "Now, yesterday and today": *The Ed Sullivan Show*, 2/9/64, CBS archives.

472   "crazy girls, who were going bananas": Goldman, *Lives of John Lennon*, p. 159.

473   "a record, according to the A. C. Nielsen Company": "Sullivan Show Scores," *New York Times*, 2/11/64.

473   "a fad": "The Beatles and Their Audience," *New York Times*, 2/10/64.

473   "false modal frames": Ibid.

473   "seemed downright conservative": *Washington Post*, 2/10/64.

473   "Visually they are a nightmare": *Newsweek*, 2/11/64.

473   BEATLES BOMB ON TV: *New York Herald Tribune*, 2/10/64.

474   "fucking soft": Braun, *Love Me Do*, p. 109.

474   "If everybody really liked us": John Lennon, 1964 interview, in *Anthology*, p. 120.

474   "vicious attack": "He considered the reviews a vicious attack." Brian Sommerville, 7/3/84, AGA.

474   "Before Epstein came here": Braun, *Love Me Do*, p. 114.

474   Ostensibly, the conference was called: "Next morning we had another press conference when the news was released that we'd signed to make 3 films." *The Beatles in America* (pamphlet; no copyright page or numbering).

474   "false modal frames": Beatles press conference transcript, 2/10/64.

476   Three opening acts: "We had Tommy Roe and that groovy group the Chiffons." *The Beatles in America.*

476   Murray the K showed up: "I broadcast my entire show from the Beatles' dressing room." Murray Kaufman in Pritchard & Lysaght, *The Beatles*, p. 152.

476   In most theaters-in-the-round: "Because it was an ice rink, there was no way to come up from under the stage." Carroll James, "Fab Four on the Radio," *Beatlefan*, April-May 1984, p. 9.

476   So Harry Lynn: "Harry Lynn said to me, 'Your job is to keep everybody diverted.'" Ibid.

476   "The reaction was so overwhelming": Paul McCartney, radio interview, 2/11/64, also cited in Goldman, *Lives of John Lennon*, p. 160.

476   "an obstacle course": Goldman, *Lives of John Lennon*, p. 160.

476   "went berserk": "The crowd went berserk with delight." "America Gets the Beatle Bug," *NME*, 2/14/64.

477   "All the Beatlemania ingredients": Ibid.

477   "That night, we were . . . pelted": George Harrison in Badman, *Off the Record*, p. 85.

477   "the ring-side seem like Omaha Beach": Braun, *Love Me Do*, p. 119.

477   "Ringo, in particular": Goldman, *Lives of John Lennon*, p. 160.

477   "the acoustics were terrible": George Harrison in *Grandstand* interview, BBC-TV, 2/22/64.

477   "They could have ripped me apart": "We've Got 'Em Luv, and It's All Gear," *LIFE,* 2/17/64, p. 34.

477   "What an audience!": Braun, *Love Me Do,* p. 130.

477   "champagne party and masked": British embassy invitation.

477   This was precisely the kind of function: "We always try to get out of those crap things." George Harrison in Badman, *Off the Record,* p. 85.

478   as the boys made their entrance: "The whole ballroom of dancers sort of swirled around us when we came in." *The Beatles in America.*

478   "So, what do you do?": *NME,* 2/14/64.

478   "full quota of chinless wonders": Martin, *All You Need,* p. 162.

478   "like something in a zoo": Ringo Starr in Badman, *Off the Record,* p. 85.

478   "exchange pleasantries": Brian Sommerville, 7/3/84, AGA.

478   "slightly drunk woman": Braun, *Love Me Do,* p. 122.

478   But as the raffle presentation wound down: *Daily Express,* 2/13/64.

478   "What the hell do you think": Ringo Starr in *Anthology,* p. 120.

478   "This lot here": *Daily Express,* 2/13/64.

478   John started for the door: Louise Harrison in Badman, *Off the Record,* p. 86.

478   "They were very sad": Harry Benson in ibid.

479   "some giant three-ring": George Martin in *Anthology,* p. 155.

479   "The only place we ever got any peace": George Harrison in ibid.

479   "simply another theater": Brian Sommerville, 7/3/84, AGA.

480   By February 3, a deal had been struck: "I have spoken to Sid Bernstein . . . and Brian Epstein . . . have both agreed . . ." Letter, Brown Meggs to Carnegie Hall, 2/3/64.

480   American Federation of Musicians: *NME,* 2/14/64.

480   "Yells and shouts": "The Night Carnegie Hall Went Berserk," *Melody Maker,* 2/22/64.

480   "looked the audience sternly": *New York Times,* 2/13/64.

481   "thumping, twanging rhythms": "2,900 Voice Chorus Joins the Beatles," *New York Times,* 2/13/64.

481   "They are worth listening to": "Hiram's Report," *New Yorker,* 2/22/64, p. 23.

481   "I hear they write": "Plaque and Luncheon Celebrate a 50th Birthday for ASCAP," *New York Times,* 2/14/64.

481   "Miami was like paradise": Paul McCartney in *Anthology,* p. 120.

481   "bathing beauties": *The Beatles in America.*

481   "Beatle Central": Rayl, *Beatles '64,* p. 51.

481   "cozzies": "Get your cozzies on!" Paul McCartney in ibid., p. 123.

481   "It was a big time": "Miami was incredible." Miles, *Paul McCartney,* p. 162.

482   "rock 'n roll gods": Ringo Starr in *Anthology,* p. 123.

482   Mau Mau Lounge: "The boys went to the Mau Mau Lounge . . . and were knocked out by the Coasters." *Melody Maker,* 2/22/64, p. 11.

482   "the most brilliant place": Ringo Starr in *Anthology,* p. 120.

482   But the relaxed, unfettered lifestyle: "Even when we go swimming . . . the fans toss autograph books at us." *The Beatles in America.*

482   stashed in the back: Norman, *Shout!,* p. 230.

482   borrowed from one of the local . . . affiliates: "We told Brian we wanted a pool, and the guy from the record company had one." Paul McCartney in *Anthology,* p. 123.

482   On the rare days: *NME,* 2/21/64.

482   By February 15: *Billboard,* 2/15/64.

482   Columnist Nat Hentoff: "Gold Drain," *NME,* 2/21/64.

483   Paul felt compelled: "I think Clay is going to win." Rayl, *Beatles '64,* p. 53.

483   "It was a big publicity thing": George Harrison in *Anthology,* p. 123.

483   "who could talk at the rate of": Mailer, *The Fight,* p. 13.

483   "Get a load of them Beatles": "The Beatles and Clay Spar a Fast Roundelay," *New York Times,* 2/19/64.

483 "Where the fuck's Clay?": Remnick, *King of the World*, p. 158.
483 "Hello there, Beatles!": *New York Times*, 2/19/64.
484 "didn't know who they were": Hauser, *Muhammed Ali: His Life and Times*, p. 63.
484 "insisted on having fun": Mailer, *The Fight*, p. 11.
484 "Get down . . . worms": Harry Benson in Badman, *Off the Record*, p. 87.
484 "with his gloved hand": Rayl, *Beatles '64*, p. 53.
484 Poem: "Clay recited a topical epic." *New York Times*, 2/19/64.
484 "with great reluctance": Mailer, *The Fight*, p. 75.
484 "Clay mesmerized them": Harry Benson in Badman, *Off the Record*, p. 87.
485 "Vied you do that?": Hoffman, *With the Beatles*, p. 118.

CHAPTER 25: TOMORROW NEVER KNOWS

486 More than one reporter: Press conference, Heathrow Airport, 2/22/64, Beatles interview. Project.
486 "healthy and British": *New York Times*, 2/23/64.
486 "flattered": Ibid.
486 "Earning all these dollars": George Harrison in *Grandstand* interview, BBC-TV, 2/22/64.
487 the $253,000 check: Rayl, *Beatles '64*, p. 54.
487 *Barclays Bank Review*: *New York Times*, 3/2/64.
487 The U.S. market was flooded with singles: Dusty Springfield at number 15, Dave Clark Five at number 33, Searchers at number 80. *Cashbox*, 2/24/64.
487 "With this transition": *History of British Rock Vol. 3* sleeve notes, Sire Records, 1975.
487 *Big Night Out:* "In addition to sketches, they will sing five songs." *NME*, 2/28/64.
487 Ringo . . . flying home: Lewisohn, *25 Years in the Life*, p. 40.
488 Most of the numbers were slated: "Some—for the soundtrack—were required before the film went into production." Lewisohn, *Sessions*, p. 39.
488 "we knew they were good": Miles, *Paul McCartney*, p. 163.
488 A version of "Can't Buy Me Love": Ibid., p. 162.
488 "It was the first ballad": Ibid., p. 122.
488 "I think it was John": Dick James in Badman, *Off the Record*, p. 90.
488–89 "the middle eight is mine": Miles, *Paul McCartney*, p. 123.
489 "tired and depressed": "But on Tuesday evening, George was tired and depressed." *NME*, 2/28/64.
489 Grudgingly, he'd devoted an hour: D. Taylor, *Fifty Years*, p. 110.
489 *Daily Express* . . . front-page news: *Daily Express*, 2/26/64, p. 1.
489 Dick James . . . cuff links: Lewisoh, *Sessions*, p. 40 (illustration).
489 a gorgeous Rolex: "I am still wearing the watch that I was given by Mr. Epstein." George Harrison in *Anthology*, p. 134.
489 "a black New York girl-group song": Sheff, *Playboy Interviews*, pp. 204–5.
489 It was John's first attempt: MacDonald, *Revolution in the Head*, p. 86.
489 The symmetry of their voices: "recorded—at their request—together on one microphone." Lewisohn, *Sessions*, p. 40.
489 "dripping with chords": *NME*, 2/1/64.
489 "a bit of a formula song": Miles, *Paul McCartney*, p. 163.
490 "The Beatles didn't get totally immersed": George Martin in *Anthology*, p. 124.
490 "We don't stop until we're confident": "People Behind the Beatles," *NME*, 3/6/64.
490 With time to spare: "By the time we did *A Hard Day's Night* we would certainly put the basic track down and do the vocals afterward." George Martin in *Anthology*, p. 124.
490 George had begun to experiment: "For the first time ever on record, I play a twelve-string guitar." *NME*, 2/13/64.
490 an instrument so new: "Harrison's was only the second of these instruments to be made." MacDonald, *Revolution in the Head*, p. 85n.

491   The plan was to keep everything simple: Alun Owen in Badman, *Off the Record*, p. 92.

491   "The director knew we couldn't act": John Lennon, 1964 interview, in *Anthology*, p. 129.

491   "the Beatles fell right into it": Author interview with Walter Shenson, 4/22/99.

491   "high-speed pseudodocumentary": Ward, *Rock of Ages*, p. 278.

491   "disarming and refreshing": Yule, *Man Who Framed the Beatles*, p. 7.

491   "little jokes, the sarcasm": "Alun picked up a lot of little things about us." Paul McCartney in *Anthology*, p. 128.

491   "We *were* like that": John Lennon, 1970 interview, in *Anthology*, p. 128.

491   an ungodly hour: "Getting up early . . . wasn't our best talent." Ringo Starr in *Anthology*, p. 128.

491   "the lads never touched the script": *Beatlefan*, February-March 1985, p. 12.

491   "frantically": "We read [the script] frantically in the car." "A Frank Talk by the Boys," *NME*, 3/27/64.

492   "You never knew": Victor Spinetti in Pritchard & Lysaght, *The Beatles*, p. 165.

492   "We'd make things up": Ringo Starr in *Anthology*, p. 129.

492   "Dick just went on shooting": Victor Spinetti in *Beatlefan*, February-March 1985, pp. 12–13.

492   most of which Paul had written: Miles, *Paul McCartney*, p. 111.

492   "too soft": Author interview with Billy J. Kramer, 12/16/97.

492–93   "I could talk to him": Miles, *Paul McCartney*, p. 113.

493   "Their bedrooms were next door": Author interview with John Dunbar, 1/13/98.

493   "the laboratories": Pearce Marchbank in Green, *Days in the Life*, pp. 32–33.

493   "Somehow it wasn't to do": Paul McCartney in ibid., p. 46.

493   1.7 million copies: *NME*, 3/13/64.

493   "Well, here it is!": "Single Reviews," *NME*, 3/13/64.

494   scores of singles: "Yes! You Can Hold My Hand" by the Beatlettes, "Beatle Fever" by Brett and Terry, "The Beatle Dance" by Ernie Maresca, "The Boy with the Beatle Haircut" by the Swans, "A Beatle I Want to Be" by Sonny Curtis, "The Beatles" by the Buddies, "We Love You Beatles" by the Carefrees.

494   A start-up label, Top Six: *NME*, 1/31/64.

494   Even Decca, at the behest: "Decca Signs Ex-Beatle," ibid.

494   The original demo tape: "I told Jay Lasker 'I need those tapes back,' and Vee-Jay could never find them. 'You know how it is. . . .'" Author interview with Roland Rennie, 8/7/97.

494   Brian pleaded with EMI: "Cap Throws Block vs. Veejay's [sic] Beatles," *Variety*, 2/12/64.

495   "Tell Me If You Can": "We've recorded a composition that Paul McCartney and I wrote." *NME*, 3/20/64.

495   "Brian didn't get very good deals": George Harrison in *Anthology*, p. 98.

495   "wasn't astute enough" Paul McCartney in ibid.

495   "long-term slave contracts": Ibid.

495   "We had fifty times as many offers": Rayl, *Beatles '64*, p. 55.

495   a minimum guarantee of $20,000: Author interview with Sid Bernstein, 1977.

495   "no fewer than one hundred": Standardized GAC contract for the Beatles, 5/64.

496   sold forty thousand copies: *New York Times*, 4/6/64.

496   "scrappy": "The drawings were very scrappy because I'm heavy-handed." John Lennon, 1964 interview, in *Anthology*, p. 134.

496   "There's nothing deep in it": Ibid.

496   descendent of the *Daily Howl*: "It started back in my school days. When I was about fourteen." *NME*, 3/27/64.

496   "gobbledegook": "I used to hide my real emotions in gobbledegook." John Lennon, 1964 interview, in *Anthology*, p. 134.

496 "cultural earthquake": Green, *Days in the Life*, viii.

496 "a laugh a minute": *Public Ear*, BBC, 3/22/64.

496 "worth the attention": *Times Literary Supplement*, 3/25/64.

496 Carl-Alan award: *NME* (ceremony photo), 3/27/64.

497 Record sales were astronomical: *Billboard*'s "Hot 100," 4/11/64.

497 Everyone at NEMS was posted there: "He came into the office at Argyll Street." Brian Sommerville, 7/4/83, AGA.

497 "I stuck out my hand": From a recollection reprinted ad infinitum over the years, but probably originally from an account in the magazine *Tit Bits*, 1965.

497 "You can't turn your back": Brian Sommerville, AGA.

497 "He turned up after I was famous": John Lennon, 1972 interview, in *Anthology*, p. 180.

498 "It was casting a sprat": Author interview with Don Short, 8/11/97.

499 "Whenever fashions changed": C. Lennon, *A Twist*, p. 117.

499 Much later, Twiggy: "Twiggy told me much later she copied Pattie." Author interview with Peter Brown, 12/12/97.

499 "When we started filming": Pattie Boyd in Davies, *Beatles*, p. 201.

499 "semi-engaged": "Pattie . . . declined [George's] offer." Giuliano, *Dark Horse*, p. 62.

499 "confident about [his] relationship": Eric Swayne in Badman, *Off the Record*, p. 96.

500 "Cyn and I had to dress": Pattie Boyd in Davies, *Beatles*, p. 202.

500 "It was all so romantic": Ringo Starr in *Anthology*, p. 128.

500 UA, which never even saw: Walter Shenson, 4/84, AGA.

500 "There was something Ringo said": Miles, *Paul McCartney*, p. 164.

500 "abusing the English language": Author interview with Walter Shenson, 4/22/99.

500 "Ringo would always say": George Harrison in *Anthology*, p. 130.

501 "I was just talking": Ringo Starr in *Grandstand* interview, BBC-TV, 2/22/64.

501 John promptly wrote it down: "John always used to write them down." Ringo Starr in *Anthology*, p. 130.

501 "Ringoism": Sheff, *Playboy Interviews*, p. 148.

501 "We've just got our title!": Author interview with Walter Shenson, 4/22/99.

501 "I'm afraid we're going to need a song": Ibid.

501 They had already shot: "We filmed the scene where all the fans run into the train station." Paul McCartney in *Anthology*, p. 129.

502 The "strident" chord: "The 'strident' chord was the perfect launch." George Martin in Lewisohn, *Sessions*, p. 43.

502 "because I couldn't reach the notes": Sheff, *Playboy Interviews*, p. 148.

502 "in the world of commerce": D. Taylor, *Fifty Years*, p. 20.

502 "There are only a few journalists": Author interview with Tony Barrow, 10/31/97.

502 "painted a new rainbow": D. Taylor, *Fifty Years*, p. 86.

503 "He's one of those people": John Lennon, 1964 interview, in *Anthology*, p. 140.

503 "fact-gathering expedition": "We were allowing ourselves five days . . . for a fact-gathering expedition." D. Taylor, *Fifty Years*, p. 116.

503 "I *am* homosexual": Ibid., p. 117.

503 "my personal assistant": Ibid.

503 "The entire office took to him": Author interview with Tony Bramwell, 8/8/97.

504 "a potboiler": Derek Taylor in *Anthology*, p. 115.

504 *Queer Jew:* Coleman, *Lennon*, p. 203.

504 "My early days at NEMS": D. Taylor, *Fifty Years*, p. 144.

504 "The heat was immediately on": Ibid., p. 142.

CHAPTER 26: IN THE EYE OF A HURRICANE

505 His throat was especially sore: "My throat was so sore. . . . I was a smoker in those days, too." Ringo Starr in *Anthology*, p. 139.

505 "didn't like it one bit": "I got quite a fright when I saw Ringo sink to his knees." Neil Aspinall in Badman, *Off the Record*, p. 101.

505 "Imagine, the Beatles": George Harrison in Badman, *Off the Record*, p. 101.

505 postponed immediately: "I don't want to do the tour without Ringo." George Harrison in D. Taylor, *Fifty Years*, p. 146.

505 "Brian argued with us": Paul McCartney in Badman, *Off the Record*, p. 101.

506 "bullied by Brian Epstein": George Harrison in D. Taylor, *Fifty Years*, p. 146.

506 "It might have looked": *NME*, 6/12/64.

506 "Humpity-Dumpity": *NME*, 5/15/64 (advertisement).

506 There are various versions: "Brian called me and I went down to his office." *Beatlefan*, Oct.-Nov. 1984, p. 22. "It was EMI asking if I could come down to the studio." Baker, *Beatles Down Under*, p. 19. "The phone rang. It was George Martin." Badman, *Off the Record*, p. 102.

506 "I nearly shit": *Beatlefan*, Sept.-Oct. 1994, p. 12.

506 "mischief and carrying on": Ibid.

506 "Wherever we went": Wenner, *Lennon Remembers*, pp. 84–86.

506 "his head was a balloon": *Beatlefan*, Sept.-Oct. 1994, p. 13.

507 "the most relaxing and happy": C. Lennon, *A Twist*, p. 127.

507 "happy families time": Ibid., p. 128.

507 "in the eye of a hurricane": Solt & Egan, *Imagine*, p. 63.

507 "He played well": Paul McCartney in *Anthology*, p. 139.

507 "the Four Fabs": D. Taylor, *Fifty Years*, p. 146.

507 "at least 100,000 cheering": *NME*, 5/12/64.

507 "Fuck off, yer bald old crip!": D. Taylor, *Fifty Years*, p. 149.

508 CHILD DYING: Ibid., p. 147.

508 "We'd been sitting": George Harrison in *Anthology*, p. 139.

508 Fierce crosswinds: Baker, *Down Under*, p. 24.

508 "back of a flat-bed": Neil Aspinall in *Anthology*, p. 140.

509 "the J. F. Kennedy position": George Harrison in D. Taylor, *Fifty Years*, p. 159.

509 "you might get shot": John Lennon, Adelaide press conference, 6/12/64.

509 "It was like a heroes' welcome": Paul McCartney in *Anthology*, p. 140.

509 "a bitterly cold day": *Variety*, 6/24/64.

509 "nearly twice as many": *New York Times*, 6/13/64.

509 "horrendous": Ringo Starr in *Anthology*, p. 140.

509 "madness we had not seen": D. Taylor, *Fifty Years*, p. 161.

510 the girls fainting: "Hundreds of youngsters fainted and . . . sustained minor injuries." *New York Times*, 6/13/64.

510 "screamed so hard": Ibid.

510 "frightening, chaotic": Baker, *Down Under*, p. 57.

511 Description of premiere: Miles, *Paul McCartney*, p. 132.

511 "behaved like delighted": Author interview with Walter Shenson, 4/22/99.

511 "off-beat": "Off-Beat Film on Beatles," *The Times* (London), 7/8/64.

511 "exercise in anarchy": *Sunday Times*, 7/12/64.

511 "delightfully loony": *Daily Express*, 7/8/64.

511 "a whale of a comedy": "The Four Beatles in 'A Hard Day's Night,'" *New York Times*, 8/12/64.

511 "I dug *A Hard Day's Night*": John Lennon, 1970 interview, in *Anthology*, p. 128.

511 "We knew it was better": Ibid., p. 129.

511 "not as good as James Bond": John Lennon, Liverpool interview, 7/10/64.

511 the movie opened to critical success: *NME*, 7/10/64.

512 "with a record 160 prints": "On the British Movie Scene," *New York Times*, 8/2/64.

512 "would gross at least a million": *NME*, 7/10/64.

512 "That's the stuff!": "Beatles Still Love to Play Jokes," *NME*, 7/17/64.

512   "It was extraordinary": "They were absolutely terrified." *Sunday Times* (special Beatles issue), 1983.

512   "[Friends] kept coming down": Press reception transcript, Liverpool, 7/10/64.

512   "one or two little rumors": Paul McCartney in *Anthology*, p. 144.

512   Paul had settled a paternity claim: Goldman, *Lives of John Lennon*, p. 150.

512   "with astonishing nonchalance": D. Taylor, *Fifty Years*, p. 179.

513   "Being local heroes": John Lennon, 1967 interview, in *Anthology*, p. 144.

513   their "own people": Paul McCartney in *Anthology*, p. 144.

513   "Miles away from Speke": *Sunday Times* (special Beatles issue), 1983.

513   "Did you ever imagine": Press conference with Gerald Harrison, 7/10/64.

513   "You want to get some teeth": D. Taylor, *Fifty Years*, p. 181.

514   a 1:30 A.M. flight: Lewisohn, *Chronicle*, p. 165.

514   "really weird characters": C. Lennon, *A Twist*, p. 114.

514   "People were ringing": Author interview with Nigel Walley, 3/11/98.

514   "select": C. Lennon, *A Twist*, p. 114.

515   "They were the hardest-working entertainers": Author interview with Ray Ennis, 10/1/97.

516   "By the time we were getting drunk": D. Taylor, *Fifty Years*, p. 183.

516   she'd suffered a nervous collapse: "Last Monday she went to a hospital with cuts on her arms." *New York Times*, 7/25/64.

516   "Aw, *fuck off*": George Harrison in D. Taylor, *Fifty Years*, p. 183.

516   "very edgy and nervous": Ibid.

516   "was the epitome of great talent": Author interview with Tony Barrow, 10/31/97.

516   "a send-off": Author interview with Ken Partridge, 1/18/98.

517   "He tried hard to conceal": Ibid.

518   "It had a disastrous effect": Author interview with Peter Brown, 12/9/97.

518   "He was always putting pills": Author interview with Billy J. Kramer, 12/16/97.

518   "Brian was far too uptight": Author interview with Ken Partridge, 1/18/98.

519   "on jukeboxes in a hundred thousand joints": *Kansas City Times*, 10/18/64, p. 1.

519   "America was now very aware": Neil Aspinall in *Anthology*, p. 146.

520   "and now it was perceived": Rayl, *Beatles '64*, p. 66.

520   "Communist . . . pact": "Beatlemania Analyzed," *Seattle Times*, 8/22/64.

520   "It scares you": *Los Angeles Times*, 8/19/64.

520   "I saw two girls": "We Couldn't Get into Beatlesville!" *NME*, 8/21/64.

520   "No sooner had the Beatles moved": Walter Hofer, 3/83, AGA.

520   "total madness": Author interview with Larry Kane, 12/24/97.

520   "Security was just awful": Ibid.

521   "exasperated sheriff's deputies": "Youngsters Swarm Over Hotel," *Las Vegas Review-Journal* (story and photo caption), 8/20/64.

521   "pinned in their dressing room": "Beatles Bat It Out for Seattle," *Seattle Post-Intelligencer*, 8/22/64.

521   "a frozen T-bone": Author interview with Art Schreiber, 3/3/98.

521   "dull-sounding big beat": *Vancouver Sun*, 8/24/64.

521   "screaming, weeping ecstasy": *Seattle Post-Intelligencer*, 8/22/64.

521   "It felt like an earthquake": Author interview with Larry Kane, 12/24/97.

522   "They were real players": Author interview with Bill Medley, 5/7/98.

522   "we don't want [the fans] quiet": John Lennon, 1966 interview, in *Anthology*, p. 150.

522   "vibrated like crazy": Author interview with Art Schreiber, 3/3/98.

522   "After a few days of circling": Author interview with Larry Kane, 12/24/97.

522   "Lennon was a fiend": Author interview with Art Schreiber, 3/3/98.

523   George put it, "rattle": "Pop stars shouldn't rattle their audience." George Harrison in *Anthology*, p. 145.

523   "We were being asked about it": John Lennon, 1972 interview, in *Anthology*, p. 145.

523   "We couldn't help ourselves": John Lennon from 1968 and 1972 interviews in *Anthology*, p. 145.

523   "It was all perfectly respectable": D. Taylor, *Fifty Years*, p. 198.

524   "Mal knocked on my door": Author interview with Larry Kane, 3/15/02.

524   the Beatles steered clear: ". . . but no one caught anything." *Seattle Post-Intelligencer*, 8/22/64.

524   A makeshift barricade: Author interview with lobby manager, Edgewater Hotel, 9/4/97.

524   Girls were eventually discovered: *Seattle Post-Intelligencer*, 8/22/64.

524   Later the Beatles learned: "Ringo told me they did it, and how they were all very proud of it." Author interview with Larry Kane, 12/24/97.

524   "explosive situation": *Variety*, 9/9/64.

524   "to jam up against": *Vancouver Sun*, 8/24/64.

524   "If you don't stop": Paul McCartney, from a bootleg recording, Empire Stadium, 8/22/64.

524   "It was pretty scary": Author interview with Chris Hutchins, 8/6/97.

525   "Dozens of fans stormed": *NME*, 9/4/64.

525   In Boston on September 12: *Boston Globe*, 9/13/64.

525   "The police were truly awful": D. Taylor, *Fifty Years*, p. 224.

525   "surged toward the stage": "Police Hard Put to Quell Charge of Beatle Fans," *Cleveland Plain Dealer*, 9/16/64.

525   "as did a brass railing": "Ohio Girls Rush Beatles and Police Interrupt Show," *New York Times*, 9/16/64.

525   "Sit down, sit down": "Bye Bye Beatles Fans, Police Sigh," *Cleveland Press*, 8/15/64.

525   "hurricane of boos": *Cleveland Plain Dealer*, 8/16/64.

526   "It touched off a kind of screaming": Author interview with Art Schreiber, 3/3/98.

526   Several windows were shattered: *Cleveland Plain Dealer*, 8/16/64.

526   The police were reluctant: "The Beatles, now dressed again and not at all pleased at having to push on, did return and Cleveland got its concert." D. Taylor, *Fifty Years*, p. 227.

526   "Welcome to you in the trees!": Audiotape, Hollywood Bowl, 8/23/64.

526   "a gorgeous California night": Author interview with Larry Kane, 12/24/97.

526   A lot of importance: "It seemed so important and everybody was saying things." John Lennon, 1964 interview, in *Anthology*, 150.

526   "They were great as a live band": George Martin in *Anthology*, p. 150.

527   "not much of the mop-haired": "Beatle Fans—Hollywood Bowl Chapter," *Los Angeles Times*, 8/24/64.

527   "almost too well behaved": John Lennon in Jim Steck interview (audio), 8/25/64.

527   "best-looking" starlets: David Gerber in Rayl, *Beatles '64*, p. 100.

527   "very casual": Author interview with Larry Kane, 12/24/97.

528   "We saw a couple of film stars": John Lennon, 1966 interview, in *Anthology*, p. 150.

528   "was a very expensive": George Harrison in D. Taylor, *Fifty Years*, p. 203.

528   "about eight feet tall": Ibid., p. 150.

528   Ringo, who came dressed: "I had a poncho and two toy guns." Ringo Starr in *Anthology*, p. 150.

529   "I wish we had real guns": *NME*, 10/11/64.

529   Bobby Darin and Sandra Dee: "John was receiving visitors like Bobby Darin and Sandra Dee." Ibid.

529   "harangued and hassled": Derek Taylor in Rayl, *Beatles '64*, p. 108.

530   "absolute privacy": D. Taylor, *Fifty Years*, p. 204.

530   "It was bad from the get-go": Author interview with Larry Kane, 3/8/02.

530   "Beatlemania [was] in full frenzy": D. Taylor, *Fifty Years*, p. 204.

530   "the whole of Hollywood paparazzi": George Harrison in *Anthology*, p. 150.

530   "Tell him to drop his camera": John Lennon, 1964 interview, in ibid., p. 153.

530   The next day, predictably: "Beatles Leave L.A. Gasping," *Los Angeles Herald Examiner,* 8/24/64.

530   In Baltimore: Rayl, *Beatles '64,* p. 194.

530   "That was horrendous": George Harrison in D. Taylor, *Fifty Years,* p. 204.

531   But at the old Muhlbach: Author interview with Art Schreiber, 3/3/98.

531   "Older women would come up": Ibid.

531   "After most shows, you couldn't": Wendy Hanson, 11/27/83, AGA.

532   "The Beatles *hated* that": Author interview with Tony Barrow, 10/31/97.

532   "reminded him of Brigitte Bardot": Author interview with Art Schreiber, 3/3/98.

532   "This is it!": Rayl, *Beatles '64,* p. 123.

532   the city hit them: "The Beatles reeled." D. Taylor, *Fifty Years,* p. 207.

532   The Plaza Hotel now knew: "They stayed at the Delmonico because Ed Sullivan lived there and could get them a suite." Sid Bernstein, from notes for Spitz, *Making of Superstars.*

533   But when their limo pulled: "Beatles Reach Town: It's Fan, Fan, Fantastic," *New York Post,* 8/29/64.

533   "a screaming success": "Concentration of Screaming Teen-Agers [sic] Noted at Hotel," *New York Times,* 8/29/64.

533   Paul had discovered him first: "We loved him and had done [so] since his first album which I'd had in Liverpool." Miles, *Paul McCartney,* p. 187.

533   "And for the rest of our three weeks": John Lennon, 1964 interview, in *Anthology,* p. 114.

533   "one of the most memorable": George Harrison in ibid., p. 112.

534   "I'm sure this kind of thing": Paul McCartney in ibid., p. 158.

534   "I'd started thinking about": John Lennon, 1970 interview, in ibid., p. 158.

534   "He made us feel": White, *Rock Lives,* p. 199.

534   "I think it was Dylan": John Lennon, 1970 interview, in *Anthology,* p. 158.

535   "When I met Dylan": John Lennon, 1971 interview, in ibid.

535   "How about something . . . organic?": Rayl, *Beatles '64,* p. 134.

535   "We first got marijuana": George Harrison in *Anthology,* p. 158.

535   "But what about your song": Miles, *Paul McCartney,* p. 187. John says: "Bob Dylan had heard one of our records where we said, 'I can hide,' and he understood, 'I get high.'" John Lennon, 1969 interview, in *Anthology,* p. 158.

535   "a skinny American joint": Miles, *Paul McCartney,* p. 188.

535   "my official taster": Rayl, *Beatles '64,* p. 135.

535   As Paul recounted: Miles, *Paul McCartney,* p. 188.

536   "We were just legless": D. Taylor, *Fifty Years,* p. 212.

536   "he'd been up there": Rayl, *Beatles '64,* p. 135.

536   "It may not seem the least bit": Miles, *Paul McCartney,* p. 189.

536   "Get it down, Mal": D. Taylor, *Fifty Years,* p. 212.

536   "He kept answering our phone": John Lennon, 1969 interview, in *Anthology,* p. 158.

CHAPTER 27: LENNON AND MCCARTNEY TO THE RESCUE

537   "I'll probably open": Beatles press conference, Cow Palace, San Francisco, 8/19/64.

537    $5.8 million in U.S. rentals: United Artists, six-week rentals accounting.

537   By October 1964, EMI: "Sidelights: Profit Is Spelled with a Beatle," *New York Times,* 10/25/64.

537   "largely due to Beatle [sic] records": *Time,* 10/2/64, p. 112.

538   *Variety* also reported: "Epstein Values 1/4 Beatles Slice at $4,000,000," *Variety,* 11/11/64.

538   Now he turned down $10 million: Ibid.

538   "this one in color": *Disc,* 9/26/64.

538   It seemed ridiculous to try: "A lot of it was . . . thinking this was the way things were done if the record company needs another album." Neil Aspinall in *Anthology*, p. 161.

538   "a lousy period": John Lennon, 1964 interview, in *Anthology*, p. 160.

538   "Basically," Paul explained: Paul McCartney in ibid., p. 159.

538   "the moon and June stuff": *Melody Maker*, 2/1/64.

539   "We got more and more free": Paul McCartney in *Anthology*, p. 160.

539   "version of 'Silhouettes'": Sheff, *Playboy Interviews*, p. 147.

539   "too way out": John Lennon in *Melody Maker*, 2/1/64.

539   "[wouldn't] know quite what to make": Miles, *Paul McCartney*, p. 175.

539   "No one was allowed to record": Author interview with Tony Crane, 10/7/97.

540   "The ideas were there": Ringo Starr in *Anthology*, p. 159.

540   "played live so often": George Harrison in ibid., p. 160.

540   "kick things around": "We'd go up to a little room, get our guitars out and kick things around." Ibid., p. 159.

540   "It was like a little blessing": Miles, *Paul McCartney*, p. 174.

540   "was never a good song": Sheff, *Playboy Interviews*, p. 148.

540   "a typical happy": "Beatles Next Album," *NME*, 11/13/64.

541   one of his favorite records: John Lennon, 1974 interview, in *Anthology*, p. 160.

541   "I told [the other Beatles]": "Secrets of the House of Lennon," *NME*, 12/4/64.

541   "lousy"/"sounded like an 'A' side": "I said to Ringo, 'I've written this song but it's lousy.'" Ibid.

541   "a real gas": *NME*, 11/27/64.

541   "We were just about to walk away": Miles, *Paul McCartney*, p. 172.

542   "the first feedback": Sheff, *Playboy Interviews*, p. 147.

542   "We finally took over": John Lennon, 1973 interview, in *Anthology*, p. 193.

543   "all the deals were bad": George Harrison in ibid., p. 290.

543   There was also the lingering suspicion: "There were stories of the Seltaeb people living very high off the hog in America . . . and at the same time not accounting and not paying to NEMS." Geoffrey Ellis, *Arena* archives.

543   "a major ripoff": "It had become apparent to him in London that this was just a major ripoff." Author interview with Nat Weiss, 1/28/98.

543–44   "Seltaeb was not accounting properly": Geoffrey Ellis, *Arena* archives.

544   J. C. Penney and Woolworth's: "Woolworth's returned $40 million worth of merchandise. Penney's $28 million." Nicky Byrne, 2/84, AGA.

544   "The reality is that the Beatles": Author interview with Nat Weiss, 1/28/98.

545   "a Mecca for the Mods": Hewison, *Too Much*, p. 71.

545   "I can remember going down Carnaby": Author interview with Ray Connolly, 8/7/97.

545   "I can't overpitch this": Cohn, *Today There Are No Gentlemen*, p. 67.

545   "popocracy": Melly, *Revolt Into Style*, p. 74.

546   "It was a shouty, lively scene": Miles, *Paul McCartney*, p. 133.

546   "It was the pub": Ibid.

546   "golden boy": "I was kind of a golden boy at this point." Author interview with Lionel Bart, 1/16/98.

547   "Everyone who came in": Author interview with Colin Manley, 10/2/97.

547   "I've sold myself to the devil": Coleman, *Lennon*, p. 256.

548   "Cynthia wanted to settle John down": Miles, *Paul McCartney*, p. 167.

548   There wasn't an ounce of love lost: "She absolutely hated John." Author interview with Ken Partridge, 1/18/98.

548   "It was catastrophic for Cynthia": Author interview with Tony Bramwell, 8/6/97.

548   They had bought a new Rolls-Royce: "Neither of us had passed our driving tests." C. Lennon, *A Twist*, p. 119.

548   "I would frequently spend weeks": Ibid., p. 122.

548 "sick and sleepy": Ibid., p. 131.

549 "George was the worst runaround": Author interview with Peter Brown, 12/12/97.

549 "wasn't married to Jane": Miles, *Paul McCartney*, p. 143.

549 "I got around quite a lot": Ibid., p. 142.

549 "He was well jealous": Ibid., p. 143.

550 "very impressed by . . . the clarity": Ibid., p. 125.

550 "rubbing-up"/"They were on the way out": Ibid., p. 127.

550 "the feebleness of the show": "Beatles' Act Great—But Not the Show," *NME*, 1/1/65.

550 "Obviously this show": "Time Out for the Beatles," *NME*, 1/22/65.

550 "In the second sketch": *NME*, 1/1/65.

551 "a mad story": George Harrison, *Beatles Book Monthly*, 5/65, p. 9.

551 "smoking marijuana for breakfast": *Beatlefan*, Nov.-Dec. 1966.

551 "Dick Lester knew": Ringo Starr in *Anthology*, p. 169.

551 "In a poll": "Closeup: Beatle Drummer," *New York Post*, 2/11/64.

551 "I Love Ringo" badges: Clayson, *Straight Man*, p. 85.

551 "In the States, I know": *Melody Maker*, 11/14/64.

551 how "amazed" he was: "George was amazed." John Lennon, *NME*, 2/19/65.

551 It was a hasty, intimate affair: "The following day George and I had a meeting . . . and after it Brian Epstein told us 'officially' in his car." "Ringo as a Married Man—By John Lennon," *NME*, 2/19/65.

551 "going to wear radishes": "Beatles' Ringo Wed Quietly in London," *New York Times*, 2/12/65.

552 RICH WED EARLY: Paul McCartney in Pritchard & Lysaght, *The Beatles*, p. 190.

552 "Maureen hated the spotlight": Author interview with Roy Trafford, 11/3/97.

552 "We went to the Ad Lib": Author interview with Marie Crawford, 11/1/97.

552 "He's the marrying kind": *NME*, 2/19/65.

552 "No matter what the consequences": "Will Wedding Bells Break Up the Beatles?" *New York Sunday News*, 3/15/64, p. 4.

552 John and Paul had written: Miles, *Paul McCartney*, p. 193.

552 "twelve guitars": Coleman, *Lennon*, p. 236.

552 "had about ten . . . all linked": Wenner, *Lennon Remembers*, p. 128.

553 "We made a game of it": Author interview with Paul McCartney, 3/21/97.

553 "It was a slightly new sound": Wenner, *Lennon Remembers*, p. 106.

553 "Resentfulness, or love": Sheff, *Playboy Interviews*, p. 149.

553 "the way Ringo played": Ibid., p. 165.

553 "We sat down and wrote it together": Miles, *Paul McCartney*, p. 193.

553 "John and I don't work": *New York Herald Tribune*, 12/26/65, p. 26.

554 John brought in most of: Miles, *Paul McCartney*, pp. 194–95.

554 "lyrical melodies dressed": Riley, *Tell Me Why*, p. 20.

554 "impatient"/"real optimistic": Sheff, *Playboy Interviews*, p. 150.

554 "just basically John doing Dylan": Okun, *The Compleat Beatles*, vol. 2, p. 32.

554 "He was paranoid about": George Harrison in *Anthology*, p. 173.

554 "He's a good P.R. man": Wenner, *Lennon Remembers*, p. 61.

555 "He could charm the Queen's profile": Author interview with Bob Wooler, 10/30/97.

555 "We were different": Sheff, *Playboy Interviews*, p. 121.

555 "deep depressions": Ibid., p. 150.

555 "I was fat and depressed": Ibid.

555 "He was feeling a bit constricted": Paul McCartney in *Anthology*, p. 171.

555 "retrospectively": George Harrison in *Anthology*, p. 173.

555 "to complete it": Miles, *Paul McCartney*, p. 199.

555 "non-stop" frivolous: Neil Aspinall in *Anthology*, p. 161.

556 "rather secretively": Paul McCartney in ibid., p. 181.

556 "astonished": "Beatles Astonished by Queen's Award; Other Britons, Too," *New York Times*, 6/13/65.

556 "The M.B.E., barely a notch above": Author interview with Jonathon Green, 8/14/01.

557 "great commercial advantage": "Furor Over Beatles," *New York Times*, 6/20/65.

557 "doubtful if Queen Elizabeth": Ibid.

557 "I was embarrassed": Davies, *Beatles*, p. 207.

557 "It seems that the road": *The Sun* (London), 6/14/65.

557 "irate": "Donald Zec was irate." Author interview with Tony Barrow, 10/30/97.

557 "In the name of all": *Daily Mirror*, 6/14/65.

557 Only the *Daily Telegraph*: *Daily Telegraph*, 6/13/65.

557 "I am so disgusted": "Two British Heroes Protest Award of Honors to Beatles," *New York Times*, 6/16/65.

557 Colonel George Wagg: "Mopheads, M.B.E.," *Newsweek*, 6/15/65, p. 38.

557 while another disgruntled war hero: *New York Times*, 6/20/65.

557 "superior authority's wish": "Irked by Award to Beatles, Canadian Returns Medal," *New York Times*, 6/15/65.

558 "a strange uptempo thing": Miles, *Paul McCartney*, p. 200.

558 "Auntie Gin's Theme": MacDonald, *Revolution in the Head*, p. 123.

558 "dragging you forward": Miles, *Paul McCartney*, p. 200.

558 "larynx-tearing": Lewisohn, *Sessions*, p. 59.

559 Ringo had already recorded: "He recorded it but they didn't think it had worked out very well." Alf Bicknell in Leigh, *Speaking Words of Wisdom*, p. 38.

559 "as simply as possible": George Martin in *Beatlefan*, no. 86, p. 15.

559 "remarkably controlled": Coleman, *Yesterday & Today*, p. 43.

559 "woke up one morning": Paul McCartney in *Anthology*, p. 175.

559 "very nice"/"a nick": Coleman, *Yesterday & Today*, p. 6.

559 "it was all there": Gambaccini, *In His Own Words*, pp. 17–19.

560 "It was fairly mystical": Coleman, *Yesterday & Today*, p. 7.

560 "He hummed it several times": Author interview with Lionel Bart, 1/16/98.

560 "This one, I was convinced": Coleman, *Yesterday & Today*, p. 6.

561 "Jane was sleeping": Miles, *Paul McCartney*, p. 204.

561 "He said straightaway": Coleman, *Yesterday & Today*, p. 18.

562 "I objected to it": George Martin in Pritchard & Lysaght, *The Beatles*, p. 192.

562 "We tried ways of doing it": Leigh, *Speaking Words of Wisdom*, p. 39.

562 "What about having a string accompaniment": George Martin in Pritchard & Lysaght, *The Beatles*, p. 192.

562 "Mantovani"/"syrupy stuff": Ibid.

562 "It sounded a little too gypsy-like": Coleman, *Yesterday & Today*, p. 45.

563 "No, whatever we do": George Martin in *Anthology*, p. 175.

CHAPTER 28: INTO THE COSMIC CONSCIOUSNESS

565 "We've had LSD": George Harrison in *Anthology*, p. 177.

565 This acid . . . had a distinguished provenance: Goldman, *Lives of John Lennon*, pp. 195–96.

565 They got seated and ordered: Author interview with Gibson Kemp, 8/12/97.

565 "Suddenly I felt the most incredible feeling": George Harrison in *Anthology*, p. 177.

566 "half crazy": "I remember Pattie, half playfully but also half crazy, trying to smash a shop window." Ibid.

566 "We didn't know what was going on": Wenner, *Lennon Remembers*, p. 73.

566 "We were all screaming": Ibid.

566 Ringo, who was waiting: Ringo Starr in *Anthology*, p. 178.

566 "It was just terrifying": Wenner, *Lennon Remembers*, p. 74.

566 "a light bulb": George Harrison in *Anthology*, p. 179.

567 party with "some kids": Author interview with Nat Weiss, 1/28/98.

568 "He loved the danger": "I used to go gambling with Brian." Author interview with Ken Partridge, 1/18/98.

568 "He was a heavy gambler": Author interview with Terry Doran, 8/13/97.

568 Toting Francis Bacon along: Author interview with Lionel Bart, 1/16/98; also Lionel Bart, *Arena* archives.

568 "watched him drop $17,000": Author interview with Nat Weiss, 1/28/98.

568 "I remember Brian putting his Dunhill": Miles, *Paul McCartney*, p. 131.

569 "the guy asked Brian": Author interview with Lionel Bart, 1/16/98.

569 "great purple bruises": Author interview with Alistair Taylor, 1/17/98.

569 "You're not going to believe this": Author interview with Ken Partridge, 1/18/98.

569 "he came back with some hunk": Author interview with Terry Doran, 8/13/97.

569 "a fantastic character": Author interview with Don Black, 1/18/98.

569 "Norman Weiss . . . rang Brian": Author interview with Vic Lewis, 1/20/98.

570 "took on"/"were crumbling": Author interview with Tony Bramwell, 8/6/97.

570 "Instantly, it gave them size": Author interview with Don Black, 1/18/98.

570 "run the office": Geoffrey Ellis, 5/83, AGA.

570 "glorified office boy": Author interview with Alistair Taylor, 1/17/98.

570 *The Lucy Show:* Author interview with Don Black, 1/18/98.

571 "We were only trying to play": George Harrison in *Anthology*, p. 143.

571 "the shrine at Lourdes": Author interview with Nat Weiss, 1/28/98.

571 "Crippled people were constantly": Ringo Starr in *Anthology*, p. 142.

571–72 "he had a habit of putting": Paul McCartney in *Anthology*, p. 142.

572 "These lads have become": "Beatles Blamed," *NME*, 7/30/65.

572 "I used to be": Ibid.

572 "definitely not tour Britain": "Beatles Plan to Take Long Holiday," *NME*, 8/6/65.

572 "100 minutes"/"unfunny": "'HELP!'—But It's Just in Fun," *NME*, 7/30/65.

573 "We need less exposure": "John Lennon Slams the Critics," *NME*, 8/6/65.

573 "the Beatles had inspired": "The Beatles Will Make the Scene Here Again, but the Scene Has Changed," *New York Times*, 8/11/65, p. 40.

573 "Things were changing": Paul McCartney in *Anthology*, p. 193.

574 Little did they know: "Prisoners on Floor 33," *NME*, 8/20/65.

574 "happy hysteria": "British Long-Hairs in City to Begin 3rd Tour of U.S.," *New York Times*, 8/14/65.

575 "farcical affairs": Lewisohn, *The Beatles Live!*, p. 185 (caption).

575 Governor's Suite: "They were in the Governor's Suite." Author interview with Nat Weiss, 1/28/98.

575 "unfit to sing in public": *NME*, 8/20/65.

575 "sensed that something strange": Spector, *Be My Baby*, p. 78.

575–76 "It was alarming how hard-shelled": Author interview with Larry Kane, 12/24/97.

576 Chris Hutchins remembers sitting: *NME*, 8/20/65.

576 "Four hours of constant rehearsals": Author interview with Chris Hutchins, 8/6/97.

576 "one of the most amazing cities": Larry Kane interview, "The Beatles at Shea Stadium," 8/13/65.

576 "For the boys": Author interview with Tony Barrow, 10/31/97.

577 "It was terrifying at first": George Harrison in Badman, *Off the Record*, p. 169.

577 "I was caught up": Geoffrey Ellis, 5/83, AGA.

577 "It [was] organized": Bob Whitaker in Badman, *Off the Record*, p. 168.

577 Ed Sullivan, who was filming: Author interview with Larry Kane, 12/24/97.

577 "It seemed like millions": Paul McCartney in *Anthology*, p. 186.

577 "Their immature lungs produced": "Shrieks of 55,000 Accompany Beatles," *New York Times*, 8/16/65.

577 "a dozen jets taking off": Chris Hutchins in *NME*, 8/20/65.

577 "It's frightening": Ibid.

577–78 "the pulsation of the electric guitars": *New York Times*, 8/16/65.

578   "not a minute more": Author interview with Nat Weiss, 1/28/98.

578   "It was ridiculous!": John Lennon, 1965 interview, in Badman, *Off the Record*, p. 169.

578   During two numbers: "I wasn't sure what key I was in in two numbers." *NME*, 8/20/65.

578   "You can see it in the film": John Lennon, 1970 interview, in Badman, *Off the Record*, p. 170.

578   "shattered all existing": *Variety*, 8/18/65.

578   "$100 a second": "The Singers at Shea—$100 a Second," *New York Journal-American*, 8/15/65, p. 4.

578   "It happens every time": "I Watched Them Facing Death!" *NME*, 8/27/65.

578   "Flames were shooting out": Author interview with Larry Kane, 12/24/97.

579   "sat silently, with fixed": *NME*, 8/27/65.

579   Ringo, "pale-faced": Ibid.

579   "Beatles, women, and children": Ibid.

580   "we couldn't relate to them": George Harrison in *Anthology*, p. 190.

580   But Ringo was game: "We were all on acid." Roger McGuinn in Badman, *Off the Record*, p. 175.

580   "We were all ripped": Author interview with Peter Fonda, 7/14/99.

580   "The Beatles actually enjoyed": Author interview with Tony Barrow, 10/31/97.

580   "great feeling": "I got in the swimming pool and it was a great feeling." George Harrison in *Anthology*, p. 190.

580   "He said, 'You know, man'": Author interview with Peter Fonda, 7/14/99.

581   "a bit wasted": "Peter Fonda seemed to us to be a bit wasted." Paul McCartney in *Anthology*, p. 190.

581   "they could not be responsible": *NME*, 8/27/65.

581   "Keen to preserve their artists' prestige": "Elvis and Beatles!" ibid.

581   "laughing . . . all in hysterics": George Harrison in *Anthology*, p. 191.

581   partly from nerves: "It was very exciting and we were all nervous as hell," John Lennon, 1976 interview, in *Anthology*, p. 191.

582   "It was hero worship": Paul McCartney in ibid.

582   "If you guys are just gonna": Hutchins and Thompson, *Elvis Meets the Beatles*, p. 86.

582   "the other Cilla": Ibid.

582   "We all plugged in": John Lennon, 1976 interview, in *Anthology*, p. 191.

583   "It was a load of rubbish": *NME*, 9/3/65.

583   a bit too "wild": John Lennon, 1965 interview, in *Anthology*, p. 187.

583   Before the show, Wendy Hanson: Wendy Hanson, 11/27/83, AGA.

583   "the dreadful crush of fans": "Paul was worried by the dreadful crush of fans." Author interview with Tony Barrow, 10/31/97.

583   "Calm down!" Paul screamed: *Time*, 9/10/65.

583   Paul even stopped the show: "Grand Finale," *Newsweek*, 9/10/65.

583   "At one point I glanced down": Author interview with Tony Barrow, 10/31/97.

583   "We survived": *Newsweek*, 9/10/65.

584   uninspired covers: *NME*, 10/29/65.

584   "a little smasher": *Time*, 9/10/65.

584   "I won't let Zak": Lewisohn, *25 Years in the Life*, p. 67.

584   EMI insisted on the date: "John and Paul . . . had to force themselves to come up with more than a dozen new songs." Lewisohn, *Sessions*, p. 63.

584   The only song ready was "Wait": Miles, *Paul McCartney*, p. 278.

584   "being bored": "Paul McCartney as Songwriter," *Herald Tribune*, 12/26/65, p. 26.

584   "You can't be singing 15-year-old songs": "Bards of Pop," *Newsweek*, 3/24/66, p. 103.

584 "We were expanding": Ringo Starr in *Anthology,* p. 194.
584 "We were suddenly hearing": George Harrison in ibid.
584 They were all still influenced: "The sort of people we were listening to then were on Stax and Motown, black, American, mainly." Paul McCartney in ibid., p. 198.
585 "a very bitter little story": "Tales of Abbey Road," *Beatlefan,* no. 86, p. 16.
585 John claimed he based the narrative: "It was about an affair I was having." Sheff, *Playboy Interviews,* pp. 150–51.
585 "[John] had this first stanza": Miles, *Paul McCartney,* p. 270.
586 "one of the stickiest": Paul McCartney in *Anthology,* p. 194.
586 "the lyrics were disastrous": Miles, *Paul McCartney,* p. 269.
586 "crap"/"too soft": *Newsweek,* 3/24/66.
586 "like the line from 'Respect'": George Harrison in *Anthology,* p. 194.
586 "spent five hours that morning": Sheff, *Playboy Interviews,* p. 163.
586 "I thought of myself": John Lennon, 1967 interview, in *Anthology,* p. 196.
586 "I think . . . it was about the state": Miles, *Paul McCartney,* p. 272.
587 "*that* girl—the one": John Lennon, 1970 interview, in *Anthology,* p. 196.
587 "I had a complete set": Sheff, *Playboy Interviews,* p. 151.
587 But by the time he was finished: "I wrote it all down, and it was so boring." Coleman, *Lennon,* p. 299.
587 "filling out the rest": Miles, *Paul McCartney,* p. 277.
588 "two speeding trains": Author interview with John Dunbar, 1/13/98.
588 "feel comfortable": Miles, *Paul McCartney,* p. 264.
588 "Jane's star was rising": Author interview with Tony Barrow, 10/31/97.
588 "being disillusioned": Miles, *Paul McCartney,* p. 276.
588 "It's a question of value": *Herald Tribune,* 12/26/65.
588 "D'you remember that French": Miles, *Paul McCartney,* p. 273.
588 Chet Atkins–type: Ibid.
589 "I had been listening to Nina": Sheff, *Playboy Interviews,* p. 116.
589 "I was in the studio": George Martin, *Arena* archives.
589 "Thank you, very much": Martin, *All You Need,* p. 183.
589 "a shock to the recording": "Beatles' Martin in Disc Deal," *NME,* 8/20/65.
590 "For the first time we began to think": Lewisohn, *Sessions,* p. 69.
590 "The studio itself was full": George Harrison in *Anthology,* p. 196.
590 "a mind-blower": Ringo Starr in ibid., p. 197.
590 "He'd come up with amazing technical things": John Lennon, 1975 interview, in ibid., p. 197.
590 "They were incredibly inquisitive": George Martin, *Abbey Road* archives, 9/23/96.
591 "something baroque-sounding": Ibid.
591 "just manipulations of the resources": George Martin in Pritchard & Lysaght, *The Beatles,* p. 200.
591 "This was the departure record": Ringo Starr in *Anthology,* p. 194.
591 "Whilst projecting [them]": Freeman, *Yesterday,* p. 5.
592 "Well, you know they're good": Paul McCartney in *Anthology,* p. 193.

CHAPTER 29: JUST SORT OF A FREAK SHOW
595 "*Rubber Soul* broke everything": Author interview with Steve Winwood, 6/16/97.
595 "Bards of Pop": *Newsweek,* 3/24/66, p. 102.
595 "a fine mass placebo": *New York Times,* 2/10/64.
595 "dated stuff": *New York Times,* 1/4/64.
595 a seriously stoned Peter: "Sellers was totally off his head on pot most of the time." *Mojo,* 11/95, p. 49.
595 *The Music of Lennon and McCartney:* Grenada Television archives.
596 "a strong hold on each other": *Woman,* 12/7/69.

596 "all the daily newspapers": Shotton, *John Lennon in My Life*, p. 101.

596 At night, he languished: "The Lennon Interview," *NME*, 3/11/66, p. 3.

596 "Nothing made him happier": Author interview with Ken Partridge, 1/18/98.

597 "People are saying things": *New York Times Magazine*, 7/3/66, p. 13.

597 "It was a very free, formless time": Miles, *Paul McCartney*, p. 218.

597 "wrecked"/"all these crazy ideas": Ibid., p. 234.

597 "taken out of circulation": "George Pities Paul," *NME*, 1/28/66.

598 "have a fiddle around": Paul McCartney in *Anthology*, p. 208.

598 "Ola Na Tungee": Donovan in Badman, *Off the Record*, p. 227.

598 "Often you just block songs out": Miles, *Paul McCartney*, p. 269.

598 "Dazzie-de-da-zu": Paul McCartney in *Anthology*, p. 208.

598 "those words just fell out": Miles, *Paul McCartney*, p. 282.

598 Eleanor Bron: "I liked the name Eleanor." Paul McCartney in *Anthology*, p. 208.

598 "John had a fling": Miles, *Paul McCartney*, p. 283.

598 Jane perform at the Old Vic: She was appearing in *The Happiest Days of Your Life*. Old Vic (Bristol) archives.

598 except for the title: Miles, *Paul McCartney*, p. 288.

599 "The Americans seemed to be": Norman Smith, Pritchard & Lysaght, *The Beatles*, p. 202.

599 "What EMI did for them": George Martin, *Arena* archives.

599 "look over the recording studios": "Beatles for Memphis!" *NME*, 4/8/66.

600 "the Beatles just recorded whenever": Southall, *Abbey Road*, p. 97.

600 Paul recalled that the seed: Miles, *Paul McCartney*, p. 229.

600 "Whenever in doubt": Leary, *The Psychedelic Experience*, p. 14.

600 "I did it just like he said": Sheff, *Playboy Interviews*.

601 "was all on the chord of C": Paul McCartney in *Anthology*, p. 210.

601 Martin "didn't flinch": Miles, *Paul McCartney*, p. 291.

601 "rather interesting": Paul McCartney in *Anthology*, p. 210.

601 "We worked very hard": Paul McCartney in Pritchard & Lysaght, *The Beatles*, p. 209.

601 "It went round and round": George Martin in ibid., p. 209.

601 "little symphonies": Miles, *Paul McCartney*, p. 291.

601 Martin "listen[ed] to them at various speeds": George Martin in *Anthology*, p. 210.

601 "He wanted his voice": Ibid., p. 211.

602 "we suspend him from a rope": Lewisohn, *Sessions*, p. 72.

602 "By putting his voice through that": George Martin in *Anthology*, p. 211.

602 "It meant actually breaking": Lewisohn, *Sessions*, p. 72.

602 Stoned—which they were: "Quite a bit of marijuana was being smoked." Neil Aspinall in *Anthology*, p. 212.

602 "The group encouraged us": *Mojo*, 1/96, p. 70.

603 "thousands of monks chanting": John Lennon, 1967 interview, in *Anthology*, p. 211.

603 "knocked out": Martin, *All You Need*, p. 156.

603 "Well, John," Martin replied: Ibid.

603 "a very acoustic number": Lewisohn, *Sessions*, p. 72.

603 "It was a song about pot": Paul McCartney in *Anthology*, p. 209.

603 not about acid: "It actually describes his experience taking acid." Sheff, *Playboy Interviews*, p. 153.

603 written to a great extent: Miles, *Paul McCartney*, p. 290.

604 John and George repeating: Lewisohn, *Sessions*, p. 72.

604 "a definite jazz feel": Peter Coe in ibid., p. 79.

604 "the mikes . . . right down": Ibid.

604 to launch it into orbit: "You'll really be hearing six trumpets in that coda." Les Condon in Pritchard & Lysaght, *The Beatles*, p. 212.

604   "heavier" rock 'n roll: "Paperback Writer had a heavier sound than some earlier work." George Martin in *Anthology*, p. 212.

604   "a guitar lick on a fuzzy, loud guitar": Sheff, *Playboy Interviews*, p. 151.

604   The only special effect: Lewisohn, *Sessions*, p. 74.

604   was "a co-effort": Miles, *Paul McCartney*, p. 280.

604   "couldn't get a backing track": Paul McCartney in *Anthology*, p. 212.

604   "big, ponderous, thunderous": Miles, *Paul McCartney*, p. 280.

605   The Beatles were halfway through: George Harrison in *Anthology*, p. 213.

605   "I got home from the studio": Sheff, *Playboy Interviews*, p. 167.

605   "The Beatles weren't quite sure": George Martin in Badman, *Off the Record*, p. 208.

605   "While they were out having a break": George Martin, *Arena* archives.

605   "And that was awful": Ibid.

605   "We were really starting to find ourselves": Ringo Starr in *Anthology*, p. 212.

606   "We [wanted] to do something different": John Lennon, 1974 interview, in *Anthology*, p. 205.

606   "was a bit of a surrealist": Ibid.

606   "he, as an outsider": "Meat in Money," *Record Collector*, 10/94, p. 20.

607   "We were supposed to be sort of angels": John Lennon, 1974 interview, in *Anthology*, p. 204.

607   "gross . . . and stupid": George Harrison in ibid.

607   "It's their comment on war": Alan Livingston, *Arena* archives.

607   "we thought it was stunning": Paul McCartney in *Anthology*, p. 204.

607   "They absolutely insist": Alan Livingston, *Arena* archives.

607   Unfortunately for Capitol: "Over a half-a-million or so known to have been pressed." "Meat in Money," *Record Collector*, 10/94, p. 25.

608   "the album cover is being discarded": Letter from Ron Tepper, 6/14/66.

608   "I especially pushed for it": John Lennon, 1974 interview, in *Anthology*, p. 205.

608   "We weren't against a little shock": Paul McCartney in ibid., p. 204.

608   Clive Davis, who "thought the Beatles had peaked": "That is a fact. . . . We were at Columbia and someone brought in the album cover with the dolls and meat . . . and Clive couldn't deal with it." Author interview with Nat Weiss, 1/28/98.

608   "awful-looking picture of us": John Lennon, 1974 interview, in *Anthology*, p. 205.

609   "succumbed to pressure from fans": "Beatles—Vintage '66: The Fan's-Eye View," *Melody Maker*, 6/25/66.

609   "It was too much trouble": George Harrison in *Anthology*, p. 214.

609   "Musically, we're only just starting": *Melody Maker*, 6/25/66.

609   Brian had promised them: Author interview with Tony Barrow, 10/31/97.

609   "I don't think we even thought of": Ringo Starr in *Anthology*, p. 214.

610   On June 16, 1966, Vic Lewis: "Vic Lewis to Tokyo," *NME*, 6/10/66.

610   "But by 1966": Barrow, "Manila: July 1966," p. 2.

610   "And the drugs made things much worse": Author interview with Peter Brown, 12/3/97.

610   uppers and Tuinal: Brown & Gaines, *Love You Make*, p. 181.

610   "a garden-variety hustler": Author interview with Nat Weiss, 1/28/98.

610   "I went over [to Brian's flat]": Author interview with Ken Partridge, 1/18/98.

611   "If you show up again": Author interview with Nat Weiss, 1/28/98.

611   "sweetest, most special plaything": Author interview with Ken Partridge, 1/18/98.

611   "a new British sound": Paul McCartney in Badman, *Off the Record*, p. 222.

611   "sharp, incisive jolts": Riley, *Tell Me Why*, p. 183.

611   "studio-*verité*": MacDonald, *Revolution in the Head*, p. 160.

611   "I had discovered I was paying": George Harrison in *Anthology*, p. 206.

611   "righteous indignation": Paul McCartney in ibid., p. 207.

611 "threw in a few one-liners": John Lennon, 1968 interview, in Badman, *Off the Record,* p. 223.

612 the full symphonic treatment: "This time there were eight [musicians]—a double string quartet." Lewisohn, *Sessions,* p. 77.

612 The song is an elegant ballad: "I was in Switzerland . . . and ended up in a little bathroom in a Swiss chalet writing 'For No One.'" Paul McCartney in *Anthology,* p. 207.

612 gentle wisecracks: "There were funny little grammatical jokes we used to play." Miles, *Paul McCartney,* p. 287.

612 "chains, ship's bells, hand bells": Geoff Emerick in Lewisohn, *Sessions,* p. 81.

612 "They had a whole crowd": Ibid.

613 *Abracadabra:* Miles, *Paul McCartney,* p. 269.

613 "Let's just call it *Rock 'n Roll Hits*": "They Love 'Em—Ja! Ja! Ja!" *Melody Maker,* 7/2/66.

613 John came up with *Beatles on Safari:* "Triumphant Return!" *Beatles Book Monthly,* 8/66, p. 7.

613 Paul put it up for consideration: "Paul thought of *Revolver,* and we hadn't thought of anything better." Ringo Starr in Badman, *Off the Record,* p. 221.

613 the same one that had transported Queen Elizabeth: "It was the train that was used when the royal party toured Germany." George Harrison in *Anthology,* p. 215.

613 "We all knew each other": Author interview with Peter Brown, 12/9/97.

613 "the brutality started to show": *Melody Maker,* 7/2/66.

614 Every one of them was looking forward: "They were excited to get back to Hamburg." Author interview with Peter Brown, 12/9/97.

614 "[they'd] got famous in the meantime": Paul McCartney in *Anthology,* p. 215.

614 "How about Bettina": "Beatles Return to Hamburg," *NME,* 7/2/66.

614 "[A] lot of old ghosts materialized": George Harrison in *Anthology,* p. 215.

614 "the best present I've had": "Beatles Return to Hamburg," *NME,* 7/2/66.

615 "What kind of questions are these?": Beatles press conference, Hamburg, 6/26/66.

615 "soft questions": "You look too old to ask soft questions like that," John snapped at a reporter in Japan. Tokyo press conference, 6/30/66.

615 "Christianity will go": *London Evening Standard,* 3/4/66.

615 The article was picked up on April 13: "Our Fearless Correspondent," *San Francisco Chronicle,* 4/13/66.

616 "The trouble with government": "Lennon on Elections," *Disc,* 4/2/66.

616 Uh-oh, the reporter thought: "The press was still protecting the Beatles." Author interview with Tony Barrow, 10/31/97.

616 "As far as these hooligans were concerned": Author interview with Vic Lewis, 1/20/98.

616 George Harrison had been forewarned: "I remember when George was in Germany he got a letter saying . . ." George Martin in *Anthology,* p. 216.

616 And a steady stream of letters flowed: Author interview with Tony Bramwell, 9/8/97.

617 "We always had to deal with these nuts": Author interview with Peter Brown, 12/9/97.

617 "was turned into an armed camp": Brown & Gaines, *Love You Make,* p. 202.

617 "All the other bedrooms": Author interview with Vic Lewis, 1/20/98.

617 "We were locked up": Paul McCartney in *Anthology,* p. 215.

617 "It was their first time": Author interview with Peter Brown, 12/9/97.

617 Especially with Brian and Brown: "I met a guy at the pool" and "I picked up a Japanese boy and brought him back [to the hotel]." Both ibid.

617–18 "yellow shirts and natty bottle-green suits": Paul McCartney in *Anthology,* p. 216.

618 "like a military maneuver": George Harrison in ibid.

618 "The drive was absolutely eerie": Author interview with Vic Lewis, 1/20/98.

618   "The audience was very subdued": Ringo Starr in *Anthology,* p. 216.

618   "There were one or two screamers": Brown & Gaines, *Love You Make,* p. 203.

618   "I couldn't believe what I was seeing": *Mojo,* 1/96, p. 54.

619   "Those little briefcases": Neil Aspinall in *Anthology,* p. 217.

619   "Our bags were on the runway": George Harrison in ibid.

619   "You fucking idiot!": Author interview with Vic Lewis, 1/20/98.

619   Tony Barrow thinks it was "unlikely": Author interview with Tony Barrow, 10/31/97. Also "I doubt if he even read it thoroughly or ever noticed the crucial suggestion that the Beatles might 'call in on [Imelda Marcos].'" Barrow, "Manila: July 1966," p. 9.

619   Peter Brown has a distinct recollection: "It was in Japan that we got the invitation to the palace. It came from Tony, and Brian's answer was 'regret.'" Author interview with Peter Brown, 12/9/97.

620   "President Marcos, the First Lady, and the three": *Manila Sunday Times,* 7/3/66.

620   "This is not a request": Author interview with Vic Lewis, 1/20/98.

620   "in the interest of diplomacy": "He told us . . . I recommend that you go." Author interview with Peter Brown, 12/9/97.

621   "Well, we were fucking *right*": Ibid.

621   "organized troublemakers": "This left our stationary cars at the mercy of organized troublemakers." Barrow, "Manila: July 1966," p. 15.

621   "Drive on! Go through the people": Author interview with Vic Lewis, 1/20/98.

622   "Your fee is taxed": Ibid.

622   "Oh, dear!" he thought: Paul McCartney in *Anthology,* p. 220.

622   "things started to get really weird": Ringo Starr in ibid.

622   "The passageway was lined": Author interview with Peter Brown, 12/9/97.

622   "Nobody would give us a ride": George Harrison in *Anthology,* p. 220.

623   "The atmosphere was scary": Barrow, "Manila: July 1966," p. 17.

623   "We were shitting ourselves": Author interview with Peter Brown, 12/9/97.

623   "I didn't fancy the chances": Barrow, "Manila: July 1966," p. 18.

623   "I really felt the boys could be killed": Author interview with Vic Lewis, 1/20/98.

623   "We were all carrying amplifiers": George Harrison in *Anthology,* p. 220.

623   "an abusive crowd and police": Author interview with Peter Brown, 12/9/97.

623   "they started spitting": Ringo Starr in *Anthology,* p. 220.

623   "When they started on us": "Lennon: I Thought I Was Going to Get Hurt," *Disc & Music Echo,* 7/16/66.

623–24   "You treat like ordinary passenger!": John Lennon, 1966 interview, in *Anthology,* p. 220.

624   "was Brian's cock-up": John Lennon, 1972 interview, in ibid. And "we didn't feel it was our cock-up." Paul McCartney in ibid.

624   "seizing with tension": Author interview with Peter Brown, 12/9/97.

625   Lewis was concerned: "Vic wanted to make sure he got the $17,000." Author interview with Nat Weiss, 1/28/98.

625   "It was just sort of a freak show": John Lennon, 1969 interview, in *Anthology,* p. 229.

625   "Who fucking needs this?": "It was in Delhi that the Beatles started discussing not touring anymore. It was 'Who fucking needs this?'" Author interview with Peter Brown, 12/9/97.

625   "four waxwork dummies": I reckon we could send out four waxwork dummies." John Lennon, 1966 interview, in *Anthology,* p. 229.

625   "I prefer to be out of the public eye": *Melody Maker,* 6/25/66.

625   "And they decided then and there": Neil Aspinall in *Anthology,* p. 229.

625   "It wasn't like the boys": Author interview with Tony Barrow, 10/31/97.

626   "You'd better get on top of this": Wendy Hanson, 11/27/84, AGA.

CHAPTER 30: A STORM IN A TEACUP

627   blasphemous: "We Love John and God!" *Melody Maker,* 8/19/66.

627   "Beatle Burnings": *Anthology,* p. 224 (illustration).

627   "so it's no sweat off us": Miles, *Paul McCartney,* p. 294.

627   KZEE . . . "damned their songs": *Time,* 8/12/66, p. 38.

628   a Baptist minister in Cleveland: Pritchard & Lysaght, *The Beatles,* p. 218.

628   "joining stations . . . in Massachusetts": "Beatles Manager Here to Quell Storm Over Remarks on Jesus," *New York Times,* 8/6/66.

628   "We were being told": Author interview with Tony Barrow, 10/31/97; "There were threats that John would be shot." Author interview with Alistair Taylor, 1/17/98.

628   "didn't really take it too seriously": Miles, *Paul McCartney,* p. 293.

628   "a storm in a teacup": "Are the Beatles Safe in America?" *NME,* 8/12/66.

628   "The moment he got in the car": Author interview with Nat Weiss, 1/28/98.

628   "were taken completely out of context": Ibid.

628   "He did not mean to boast": Press release, Maureen Cleave, 8/8/66.

628   Brian "request[ed] emphatically no [further] comment": Telegram from Brian Epstein to Wendy Hanson, 8/5/66.

629   "were having a field day": George Harrison in *Anthology,* p. 225.

629   "I'd forgotten [all about it]": John Lennon, 1966 interview in *Anthology,* p. 225.

629   "Tell them to get stuffed": Coleman, *Lennon,* p. 313.

629   "It went back and forth": Author interview with Nat Weiss, 1/28/98.

630   "One thing seems certain": "Beatles Create a New Nursery Rhyme," *NME,* 7/29/66, p. 3.

630   "The 100 Greatest Albums": *Mojo,* 1/96, p. 70.

631   "scaling of new musical peaks": "1966 Band on the Run," *Q,* pp. 86–87.

631   "We're not trying to pass off as kids": John Lennon, 1966 interview, in *Anthology,* p. 229.

631   *NME* reported . . . nine shipped: *NME,* 7/29/66; and "More Beatles LP Covers," 8/12/66.

631   "And so Brian . . . kept asking": Ringo Starr in *Anthology,* p. 226.

632   "We were nervous": Author interview with Tony Barrow, 8/30/97.

632   "feared the Beatles might be assassinated": Coleman, *Lennon,* p. 314.

632   "I'll do anything": Ibid.

632   "never seen John so nervous": Paul McCartney in *Anthology,* p. 226.

632   "If I'd have said, 'Television'": Beatles press conference, Chicago, 8/11/66.

633   "quite prepared to let the Lennon affair": "Stern Reply to Lennon Knocker," *NME,* 8/19/66.

634   In Cleveland, especially: "3000 Fans Rush Stage, Force Beatles to Retreat," *Cleveland Plain Dealer,* 8/15/66.

634   "given the order": Bess Coleman, *Teen Life,* 9/66.

634   "By the time we got to Memphis": Author interview with Tony Barrow, 8/31/97.

634   "Brian was very nervous": Author interview with Nat Weiss, 1/28/98.

634   "If we cancel one": "I heard Paul tell him . . ." Author interview with Tony Barrow, 8/31/97.

634   "the flight from Boston to Memphis": Tashian, *Ticket,* p. 65.

634   "So this is where all the Christians come from": "I was sitting next to John and Paul. John looked out the window and said . . ." Author interview with Nat Weiss, 1/28/98.

634   "Send John out first": *TeenSet,* 9/66.

635   "Driving into Memphis": Tashian, *Ticket,* p. 133.

635   "I will never forget . . . we pulled": Miles, *Paul McCartney,* p. 294.

635   "The Beatles smiled through it all": *Commercial Appeal* (Memphis), 8/20/66.

635   "Everyone started to relax": "On Tour with the Beatles," *TeenSet,* 9/66.

635   "when he heard [the blast]": Ibid.

635 Two teenagers had lobbed: "Bang Joins Shrieks in Beatle Show," *Commercial Appeal* (Memphis), 8/20/66.

636 "It was clear from the start": Author interview with Lionel Bart, 1/16/98.

636 "I've noticed that George": "American Eye-View," *Melody Maker*, 8/27/66.

636 "It had been four years of legging": George Harrison in *Anthology*, p. 229.

636 "Nobody was listening": Ringo Starr in *Anthology*, p. 227.

636 "was fed up playing": Ibid., p. 229.

636 Conditions were so pitiful: "I remember Ringo's drums moving around, and he would get up and move them back." Tashian, *Ticket*, p. 70.

637 "I didn't want to tour": John Lennon, 1980 interview, in *Anthology*, p. 228.

637 "the music was dead": Wenner, *Lennon Remembers*, p. 46.

637 It rained before showtime: "It started pouring just before showtime." "Double-Header with the Beatles," *Cincinnati Post and Times-Star*, 8/22/66.

637 "They'd brought in the electricity": George Harrison in *Anthology*, p. 227.

637 "It was really scary": "The promoter was so cheap he only put a canvas canopy over the stage." Author interview with Nat Weiss, 1/28/98.

637 "the only gig we ever missed": George Harrison in *Anthology*, p. 227.

637 "a couple bits of corrugated iron": Miles, *Paul McCartney*, p. 294.

637 "There were sparks flying": Tashian, *Ticket*, p. 134.

637 "to pull it whenever the first person": Ibid.

638 "We were sliding around": Paul McCartney in *Anthology*, p. 227.

638 Even Paul admitted he'd had enough: "Oh, God, who needs this?" Miles, *Paul McCartney*, p. 294.

638 "had become spiritually rather empty": Ibid., p. 249.

638 "We didn't make a formal announcement": Ringo Starr in *Anthology*, p. 229.

638 "Good news . . . Diz is here": Author interview with Nat Weiss, 1/28/98.

639 "half a dozen or so billets-doux": Brown & Gaines, *Love You Make*, p. 215.

639 "a suicidal depression": Author interview with Nat Weiss, 1/29/98.

639 "It was not the sort of night": Author interview with Tony Barrow, 10/31/97.

639 with 25,000 die-hard Beatles fans: "Beatles' Closing Concert on Coast Attracts 25,000," *New York Times*, 8/31/66.

639 "being jolted from head to toe": Tashian, *Ticket*, p. 118.

639 "sounding like clouds bursting": "Remembering the Night the Beatles Played Candlestick," *San Francisco Chronicle*, 8/29/86, p. 23.

639 "totally familiar studio recorded versions": "Beatles Strike Out at Ball Park," *San Francisco Examiner*, 8/30/66.

640 "John and Paul say exactly": Author interview with Tony Barrow, 8/31/97.

640 "a puppet show": *San Francisco Chronicle*, 8/29/86, p. 23.

640 "I was thinking, 'This is going to be'": George Harrison in *Anthology*, p. 229.

640 "Right—that's it": Author interview with Tony Barrow, 8/31/97.

640 "Is Beatlemania Dead?": *Time*, 9/2/66.

640 Derek Taylor, writing: *Melody Maker*, 11/26/66.

640 "impact . . . and mythology": "The Beatles Break," *Sunday Times*, 11/13/66.

641 "hanging around": "And as anybody knows about film work, there's a lot of hanging around." Sheff, *Playboy Interviews*, p. 130.

641 "He loathed the endless waiting": Coleman, *Lennon*, p. 320.

641 "It was pretty damn boring": John Lennon in Badman, *Off the Record*, p. 251.

641 "He used to sit cross-legged": Michael Crawford in ibid., p. 250.

641 "conjuring up a hazy impressionistic": Martin, *Summer of Love*, p. 14.

641 "psychoanalysis set to music": John Lennon, 1970 interview, in *Anthology*, p. 231.

642 "an old Victorian house": Sheff, *Playboy Interviews*, pp. 131–32.

642 "It [provided] an escape": Miles, *Paul McCartney*, p. 307.

642 "There was something about the place": Goldman, *Lives of John Lennon*, p. 255.

642 "I took the name . . . as an image": Sheff, *Playboy Interviews*, p. 131.

642   "travel incognito, disguised": Miles, *Paul McCartney,* p. 295.

642   "to ease the pressure": Ibid., p. 296.

643   "Let's not be ourselves": Ibid., p. 303.

643   "put some distance between": Sheff, *Playboy Interviews,* p. 166.

643   "We would be Sgt. Pepper's band": Paul McCartney in *Anthology,* p. 241.

644   "I had gone through so many trips": George Harrison in ibid.

644   "You've got to be connected spiritually": Author interview with Arthur Kelly, 1/10/98.

644   "feeling would begin to vibrate": "Soon this feeling would begin to vibrate right through me and started getting bigger and bigger and faster and faster." Giuliano, *Dark Horse,* p. 92.

644   "hung out with him": Ringo Starr in *Anthology,* p. 231.

644   "he offered to give me some instruction": Giuliano, *Dark Horse,* p. 93.

645   "how to sit and hold the sitar": George Harrison in *Anthology,* p. 233.

645   Shankar's "disciple": "George had not come as a Beatle but as my disciple." Shankar, *My Music, My Life.*

645   "Sometimes [George] would play": Giuliano, *Dark Horse,* p. 95.

645   "harmonizing with a greater power": Ibid., p. 93.

645   "by various holy men": George Harrison in *Anthology,* p. 233.

645   "Ravi and the sitar were excuses": Ibid.

646   "blood money": "Just give him his blood money." Brown & Gaines, *Love You Make,* p. 216.

646   "Don't do anything else": Author interview with Nat Weiss, 1/28/98.

646   "just indulging himself": Author interview with Peter Brown; *Arena* archives.

646   "morbid," often incoherent: Brown & Gaines, *Love You Make,* p. 217.

646   "Nothing I said or did": Author interview with Peter Brown, 12/9/97.

647   The collapse, when it eventually came: "I didn't see it coming." Ibid.

647   "I stayed in the library": Ibid., 12/2/97.

647   "a foolish accident": Brown & Gaines, *Love You Make,* p. 217.

647   "I can't deal with this anymore": Peter Brown, *Arena* archives.

648   "But none of us, however shortsighted": Author interview with Nat Weiss, 1/28/98.

648   "You must be *mad!*": Author interview with Ken Partridge, 1/18/98.

648   "He wanted to be Ziegfeld": Author interview with Don Black, 1/18/98.

648   "terrible" musical: Ibid.

649   "During the week, we had Gilbert and Sullivan": Author interview with Tony Bramwell, 8/6/97.

649   an ominous melancholy: "When John came back, he was in a serious funk." Author interview with Tony Barrow, 10/31/97.

649   "There was so much going on": Author interview with John Dunbar, 1/13/98.

649   The future of the Beatles: "At some time or other that's when I really started considering life without the Beatles—what would it be?" John Lennon, 1980 interview, in *Anthology,* p. 231.

649   "There were all those Chelsea people": Green, *Days in the Life,* p. 76.

650   "We never had a painting as such": Aitken, *The Young Meteors.*

650   to "liberate art as a commodity": Author interview with John Dunbar, 1/13/98.

650   "a real happening": "I told him it would be a real happening." Ibid.

650   "I thought, 'Hmm,' you know, 'sex'": John Lennon, 1980 interview, in *Anthology,* p. 235.

650   "Well, watching telly": Green, *Days in the Life,* p. 79.

651   "I was in a highly unshaved . . . state": John Lennon, 1980 interview, in *Anthology,* p. 235.

651   sat in the car for "some time": Les Anthony, 3/87, AGA.

651   "bullshit and phony": Peter McCabe interview, 7/71, AGA.

651   "When he came in, it was like": Author interview with John Dunbar, 1/13/98.

651 "flittering around like crazy": Sheff, *Playboy Interviews*, p. 86.

651 "*mirror to see your behind*": *Unfinished Paintings and Objects*, Indica Gallery catalogue.

651 "Is this stuff for real?": Author interview with John Dunbar, 1/13/98.

651 "This is a joke": Sheff, *Playboy Interviews*, p. 86.

652 "It looked like a black canvas": Wenner, *Lennon Remembers*, pp. 173–74.

652 "You take a magnifying glass": Peter McCabe interview, 7/71.

652 "I argued strongly": Author interview with John Dunbar, 1/13/98.

653 "Okay, you can hammer": Sheff, *Playboy Interviews*, p. 88.

653 "I'll give you an imaginary": Coleman, *Lennon*, p. 327.

653 "My God," she thought: Peter McCabe interview, 7/71.

653 "John was a fun drug-taker": Author interview with Terry Doran, 8/13/97.

653 "first high-voltage superblues group": Dalton & Kaye, *Rock 100*, p. 122.

653 "Show business will vibrate": "Beach Boys Beat Beatles," *NME*, 12/3/66.

654 "We're all four fans": "Paul and Ringo Talk about the Beatles," *NME*, 12/31/66.

654 "This idea of jealousy": Ibid.

654 pure "rubbish": Ibid.

654 "two of the Beatles had approached": *Sunday Telegraph*, 11/18/66.

654 "I think we were itching to get going": Paul McCartney in *Anthology*, p. 237.

654 "it was absolutely lovely": George Martin interview, 12/5/80, in Okun, *The Compleat Beatles*, p. 40.

654 "I was spellbound": Martin, *Summer of Love*, pp. 13–14.

655 Martin cursed himself: "Oh, how I wish I had caught that very first run-through on tape and released it!" Ibid., p. 14.

655 which took over forty-five hours: Lewisohn, *Sessions*, pp. 87–90.

655 "about 80% separately written": Ringo Starr in *Anthology*, p. 237.

655 "creative rivalry": Martin, *Summer of Love*, p. 70.

655 "were often answering each other's songs": Miles, *Paul McCartney*, p. 307.

655 "John and I would often meet": Ibid.

655 "in the middle of the roundabout": Lyric fragment from "Penny Lane."

655 its euphonious name: "He'd been toying with the idea of writing a song called 'Penny Lane' because he liked the poetry of the name." Lewisohn, *Sessions*, p. 91.

655 "painted in an exploding psychedelic": Miles, *Paul McCartney*, p. 259.

655 "more like a play": Paul McCartney in *Anthology*, p. 237.

655 "The lyrics were all based": Ibid.

656 "a small collection of gems": Martin, *Summer of Love*, p. 26.

656 "rooty-tooty variety": Miles, *Paul McCartney*, p. 319.

656 Beatles performed at the Cavern: Lewisohn, *Sessions*, p. 89.

656 "a bit of a shock": George Harrison in *Anthology*, p. 239.

656 "an old trap": Ibid.

657 "Quiet honestly," he admitted: "Most Way-Out Beatles Ever," *NME*, 2/11/67.

657 "the Beatles have developed into": "Other Noises, Other Notes," *Time*, 3/3/67.

657 "The people who have bought our records": John Lennon, 1967 interview, in *Anthology*, p. 241.

CHAPTER 31: A VERY FREAKY EXPERIENCE

658 "cheerful music for dope smokers": Ward, *Rock of Ages*, p. 330.

659 the Beatles' "playground": "They loved the whole process of recording: the studio was a playground." Martin, *Summer of Love*, p. 68.

659 "every trick brought out": George Martin in *Anthology*, p. 242.

660 "because he wanted to sound like Elvis": Martin, *Summer of Love*, p. 53.

660 "dry, deadpan voice": Ibid., p. 55.

660 "I noticed two stories": Sheff, *Playboy Interviews*, p. 155.

660 "The verse about the politician": Miles, *Paul McCartney*, p. 324.

660 "funny . . . little references": George Martin in Pritchard & Lysaght, *The Beatles*, p. 241.

661 "a little party piece": Paul McCartney in *Anthology*, p. 247.

661 "It was a crazy song": Ibid.

661 "We'll tell the orchestra": Ibid.

661 "something really tumultuous": Martin, *Summer of Love*, p. 53.

661 "But ninety musicians": Ibid., p. 56.

661 "with little or no input": Miles, *Paul McCartney*, p. 310.

662 the theme of which John pinched: Sheff, *Playboy Interviews*, p. 155.

662 "The top was all dark": Julian Lennon in Pritchard & Lysaght, *The Beatles*, p. 238.

662 "Wow, fantastic title!": Miles, *Paul McCartney*, p. 311.

662 "very trippy": Ibid., p. 312.

662 John had already begun playing: "The imagery was Alice in the boat." Sheff, *Playboy Interviews*, p. 154.

662 "swapping psychedelic suggestions": Paul McCartney in *Anthology*, p. 242.

662 "trading words off each other": Miles, *Paul McCartney*, p. 312.

663 "People were running around": Martin, *Summer of Love*, p. 58.

663 "orchestral orgasm": Ibid., p. 60.

663 "It was . . . remarkable": Author interview with Ron Richards, 12/29/97.

663 "I just can't believe it": Lewisohn, *Sessions*, p. 96.

664 "a gigantic piano chord": Martin, *Summer of Love*, p. 61.

664 Daniel Barenboim's piano: Miles, *Paul McCartney*, p. 321.

664 It took nine attempts: Lewisohn, *Sessions*, p. 99.

664 *Newsweek*'s critic: Jack Kroll, "The Beatles' *Waste Land*," *Newsweek*.

664 "got mixed together": Paul McCartney in *Anthology*, p. 247.

665 "very productive period": *Mojo*, 11/95, p. 84.

665 "assembly[-line] process": George Harrison in *Anthology*, p. 242.

665 "I was in a real big depression": Interview with Barry Miles.

665 Food no longer interested him: "John said he wasn't eating much and was on a vegetarian diet." Coleman, *Lennon*, p. 334.

666 "it was becoming almost impossible": C. Lennon, *A Twist*, p. 142.

666 "tensions, bigotry, and bad temper": Ibid.

666 "I know Brian was convinced": Author interview with Tony Barrow, 10/31/97.

667 gone broke in the process: "Here was a man who had been bankrupt twice." Author interview with Nat Weiss, 1/28/98.

667 "borrowed money from EMI": Author interview with Peter Brown, 12/9/97.

667 "It was quite simple": Robert Stigwood, *Arena* archives.

668 "sound younger . . . and be a teenager": Martin, *Summer of Love*, p. 35.

668 "joining up": "Once, he told me he thought of joining up. But I'm sure it was another boyhood thing." Author interview with Pete Shotton, 7/16/98.

669 "It said the Hendersons": John Lennon, 1967 interview, in *Anthology*, p. 243.

669 "Almost the whole song was written": Miles, *Paul McCartney*, p. 318.

669 wanted a "fairground sound": "The fairground sound, suggested by John . . ." Ibid.

669 "smell the sawdust": Lewisohn, *Sessions*, p. 99.

669 "a pumping kind of sound": Martin, *Summer of Love*, p. 91.

669 "I selected two-minute segments": Ibid.

669 "but, amazingly, they came back": Lewisohn, *Sessions*, p. 99.

670 "John was thrilled to bits": Martin, *Summer of Love*, p. 91.

670 Paul had written during a nighttime walk: Miles, *Paul McCartney*, p. 320.

670 "the one hard drug used": Ibid., p. 383.

670 "I used to have a bit of coke": Ibid., p. 384.

670 "looking back on it, *Pepper*": Coleman, *Lennon*, p. 335.

670 John told Jann Wenner: "I never took it in the studio." Wenner, *Lennon Remembers*, p. 76.

670   "accidental trip": Miles, *Paul McCartney,* p. 385.

670   "By mistake this night": Ibid., p. 382.

671   "I suddenly got so scared": Wenner, *Lennon Remembers,* p. 76.

671   "George, I'm not feeling too good": Martin, *Summer of Love,* p. 109.

671   "swaying gently against my arm": Ibid.

672   "I thought, Maybe this is the moment": Miles, *Paul McCartney,* p. 382.

672   "a guy who wasn't keen": Ibid., p. 381.

672   "I always knew I'd have to keep": Ibid., p. 185.

672   "spacy"/"very, very deeply emotional experience": Ibid., pp. 380–81.

673   "It was a very freaky experience": Ibid., p. 383.

673   "They ran down to the studio": Lewisohn, *Sessions,* p. 109.

674   "Couldn't really be any other": Miles, *Paul McCartney,* p. 332.

674   "We had certainly not intended": Ibid., pp. 332–33.

674   "We wanted the sleeve": Paul McCartney in *Anthology,* p. 248.

675   His best customers: Hewison, *Too Much,* p. 70.

676   "the most formative influence": Miles, *Paul McCartney,* p. 243.

676   "not good art": "He said, 'It's not good art.'" Paul McCartney in *Anthology,* p. 248.

676   "In years to come": Peter Blake, 8/83, AGA.

676   "No, not very much": Ibid.

676   "It was just a broad spectrum": George Harrison in *Anthology,* p. 252.

677   "naughty" little choice: "That was John's sense of humor. There had been the Christ controversy . . . so I think it was just John being naughty again." Peter Blake in Pritchard & Lysaght, *The Beatles,* p. 245.

677   Hitler—which managed to piss off Paul: "I didn't agree with it, but he was just trying to be far-out really." Paul McCartney in ibid.

677   "Whatever the others have": Ringo Starr in Pritchard & Lysaght, *The Beatles,* p. 244; Peter Blake, 8/83, AGA.

677   The legwork was left: ". . . so Mal and I went to all the different libraries." Neil Aspinall in *Anthology,* p. 248.

677   "We made a rough kind of wooden frame": Peter Blake, 8/83, AGA.

678   "so the delivery boy": Miles, *Paul McCartney,* p. 344.

678   "We just chose oddball things": Paul McCartney in *Anthology,* p. 248.

678   "with goodies": "So we wanted to pack it with goodies." Miles, *Paul McCartney,* p. 340.

678   But production costs rendered: "It was a packaging problem." Peter Blake in Pritchard & Lysaght, *The Beatles,* p. 245.

679   "Joe Lockwood was furious": Robert Fraser, AGA (undated).

679   that photo of Hitler: "Hitler is a definite no." Martin, *Summer of Love,* p. 118.

679   "take Gandhi out": Norman, *Shout!,* p. 291.

679   "We have some problems": Miles, *Paul McCartney,* p. 338.

679   "It had the flowers": Neil Aspinall in *Anthology,* p. 248.

679   friction between Brian and Robert Stigwood: "Brian had become disillusioned with Stigwood." Author interview with Nat Weiss, 1/28/98.

679   "He certainly couldn't handle them": Author interview with Alistair Taylor, 1/17/98.

680   "fell in love": "Robert fell in love with them, especially with Barry Gibb." Author interview with Peter Brown, 12/10/97.

680   "Brian became annoyed": Author interview with Nat Weiss, 1/28/98.

681   Shirley Temple . . . wanted to approve: *Anthology,* p. 251.

681   "What would *I* be doing": Peter Blake, 8/83, AGA.

CHAPTER 32: THE SUMMER OF LOVE

682   getting stoned with the Jefferson: "We went over to their place, smoking pot." Author interview with Nat Weiss, 1/28/98.

682   "golden . . . far-out": Paul McCartney in *Anthology,* p. 254.

682   "the idea tumbled together": Miles, *Paul McCartney*, p. 350.

682   "Everyone would spend time": Ibid.

683   "I still felt every now and then": John Lennon in *Anthology*, p. 272.

683   "enjoyed the fish and chip quality": Fawcett, *John Lennon: One Day at a Time*, p. 92.

683   "We didn't see any way": George Harrison in *Anthology*, p. 272.

684   "Nobody quite knows": Miles, *Paul McCartney*, p. 353.

684   "McCartney arrived at the studio": MacDonald, *Revolution in the Head*, p. 203.

684   "references to drugs": Miles, *Paul McCartney*, p. 353.

684   "the worst kind of musical cliché": Riley, *Tell Me Why*, p. 237.

684   When the Beatles returned: Lewisohn, *Sessions*, p. 111.

685   "a combination of two separate": Sheff, *Playboy Interviews*, p. 155.

686   unable "to resist singing": MacDonald, *Revolution in the Head*, p. 206.

686   "He knew he had to confront it": Author interview with Peter Brown, 12/10/97.

686   "positively sick": Ibid.

687   Paul felt strongly: He considered the Dick James deal "draconian." Miles, *Paul McCartney*, p. 146.

687   "What about us?": "Yeah, well Klein got the Stones a million and a quarter, didn't he?" Brown & Gaines, *Love You Make*, p. 248.

687   "fast-talking, dirty-mouthed": Ibid., p. 247.

687   Brian refused to shake hands: Author interview with Nat Weiss, 1/28/98.

687   "fucked-up and all hazy": ". . . which is what those pill do to you . . ." Author interview with Peter Brown, 12/9/97.

687   "felt that more and more": Joanne Newfield Petersen, *Arena* archives.

688   "One night Peter had been": Author interview with Nat Weiss, 1/28/98.

688   "a rather grand farmhouse": Author interview with Peter Brown, 12/9/97.

688   "more irrational, more incoherent": Robert Stigwood, *Arena* archives.

689   "isolated themselves, not only": *Daily Mail*, 5/12/67.

689   a small but "grandiose" party: "It was done in a very grandiose way." Author interview with Peter Brown, 12/10/97.

690   "very Waspish, a real anti-Semitic Jew": Author interview with Jerry Leiber, 7/11/95.

690   "She always insisted": Author interview with Nat Weiss, 1/28/98.

690   it is more likely that they met: "The night I met Linda I was at the Bag o' Nails," Miles, *Paul McCartney*, p. 432.

690   "the hottest ticket in town": Martin, *Summer of Love*, p. 152.

691   "Besides . . . I thought she was cute": Author interview with Peter Brown, 12/10/97.

691   "zero[ing] in on Paul": Brown & Gaines, *Love You Make*, p. 247.

691   "couldn't help but notice": Author interview with Tony Barrow, 10/31/97.

692   "resembled an animated Victorian": *Melody Maker*, 5/27/67.

692   "looked haggard, old": Coleman, *Lennon*, p. 334.

692   "like someone out of a Scott Fitzgerald novel": *Melody Maker*, 5/27/67.

692   "could be considered to have drug-taking implications": BBC press release, 5/17/67.

693   "He'd decided this": Author interview with Peter Brown, 12/10/97.

694   "perhaps all week": "We picked Derek and Joan up after an all-night (or all week) . . . LSD trip." George Harrison in D. Taylor, *Fifty Years*, p. 298.

694   "Everyone was getting along": Author interview with Peter Brown, 12/9/97.

694   "The minute you walked through": Author interview with Lionel Bart, 1/16/98.

694   "the mad hatter's tea party": C. Lennon, *A Twist*, p. 145.

695   Peter Brown reports: Brown & Gaines, *Love You Make*, p. 255.

695   "she hadn't taken anything": D. Taylor, *Fifty Years*, p. 301.

695   "Wasn't that always the case": Author interview with Peter Brown, 12/10/97.

695   "Paul . . . didn't . . . come": Brown & Gaines, *Love You Make*, p. 254.

695   "This was to have been for Paul": D. Taylor, *Fifty Years*, p. 300.

696 "I was downright scared": Martin, *Summer of Love*, p. 151.

696 "remarkable"/"tremendous advance": *Sunday Times*, 6/3/67.

696 "Any of these songs": *The Times* (London), 6/4/67.

696 "They think for themselves": *NME*, 5/27/67.

696 "Over the last four years": "From Us to You," *NME*, 6/10/67.

696 "equal to any song": "The Messengers," *Time*, 9/22/67, p. 122.

697 "Unfortunately, there is no apparent": "We still Need the Beatles, But . . . ," *New York Times*, 6/18/67.

697 "a historic departure": *Time*, 9/22/67, p. 128.

697 a staggering 2,500,000 copies: sales figures from *Melody Maker*, 6/10/67.

697 "second renaissance": Red Robinson in Pritchard & Lysaght, *The Beatles*, p. 246.

697 "they had the pulse": Murray the K in ibid.

697 "the nutters": Miles, *Paul McCartney*, p. 332.

697 "missionaries": *New York Times Magazine*, 5/7/67.

697–98 "messengers from beyond": "The Messengers," *Time*, 9/22/67, p. 128.

698 "progenitors of a Pop": *New York Times*, 6/18/67.

698 "The Beatles weren't the leaders": Paul McCartney in *Anthology*, p. 253.

698 "Even when the others weren't": Author interview with Tony Barrow, 10/31/97.

698 "Paul needs an audience": Davies, *Beatles*, p. 280.

698 "the cock who crowed": Ibid., p. 370.

698 "I'm either going to bluff": Paul McCartney in *Anthology*, p. 255.

698 "About four times": ITN footage, printed transcript, 6/19/67.

699 "The press had a field day": George Harrison in *Anthology*, p. 255.

699 "No one knew why Paul": Author interview with Alistair Taylor, 1/18/98.

699 "We weren't actually telling anybody": Ringo Starr in *Anthology*, p. 255.

699 "I thought Paul should": George Harrison in ibid.

700 "I think LSD helped": *Melody Maker*, 6/23/67.

700 Several months earlier, the BBC-1: "Beatles-World TV," *NME*, 5/27/67.

700 Paul had been working on: George Martin in Pritchard & Lysaght, *The Beatles*, p. 251.

700 "seemed to fit with the overall concept": Ibid.

700 "keep it simple": Lewisohn, *Sessions*, p. 116.

700 "Well, it's certainly repetitive": "All You Need Is Love," *Beatles Book Monthly*, 7/87, p. 4.

701 "We must do some preparation": George Martin in Pritchard & Lysaght, *The Beatles*, p. 251.

701 "make it a strict condition": *Beatles Book Monthly*, 7/87, p. 5.

701 on the eve of the broadcast: "I went off in the evening to find guests for the next day." Tony Bramwell in Badman, *Off the Record*, p. 292.

702 "Everyone I asked jumped": Author interview with Tony Bramwell, 8/8/97.

702 "By 7pm [on June 25]": *Beatles Book Monthly*, 7/87, p. 7.

702 "It was so bloody heavy": Ringo Starr in *Anthology*, p. 257.

703 "too out of sorts": Author interview with Peter Brown, 12/10/97.

703 "zonked": Bryan Barrett, *Arena* archives.

703 on one amazing bill in early June: Lewisohn, *25 Years in the Life*, p. 91.

704 "The idea was that you'd have": Neil Aspinall in *Anthology*, p. 258.

704 According to several well-placed insiders: Author interview with Alistair Taylor, 1/18/98; also author interviews with Peter Brown, 12/12/97, and John Dunbar, 1/13/98.

704 the son of a major: Goldman, *Lives of John Lennon*, p. 295.

704 Magic Alex, as John dubbed him: "This is my new guru, Magic Alex." Miles, *Paul McCartney*, p. 374.

705 "Alex wasn't magic": George Harrison in *Anthology*, p. 258.

705 "Magic Alex invented invisible paint": Ringo Starr in ibid., p. 290.
705 "We didn't really call anyone's bluff": Miles, *Paul McCartney*, p. 375.
705 paying £95,000: Brown & Gaines, *Love You Make*, p. 261.
706 "my earthly age": "The Guru," *Newsweek*, 12/18/67, p. 67.
706 Later he fell under the spell: Miles, *Paul McCartney*, p. 402.
706 "a method of quickly and easily": Davies, *Beatles*, p. 232.
707 Ringo was visiting Maureen: "At that time, Maureen was in hospital having Jason and I was visiting." Ringo Starr in *Anthology*, p. 260.
707 "After having such an intense": George Harrison in *Anthology*, p. 263.
707 "a little bit of emptiness": Miles, *Paul McCartney*, p. 400.
707 "He said that by meditating": Ibid., pp. 401–2.
708 "to further the experience": George Harrison in *Anthology*, p. 262.
708 "thought he made a lot": Paul McCartney in ibid., p. 260.
708 "It takes time to come down": John Lennon in Badman, *Off the Record*, p. 301.

CHAPTER 33: FROM BAD TO WORSE

709 Brian was also invited: "Brian was going to come at some point . . . he was going to join us there." Paul McCartney, *Arena* archives.
709 John making the call himself: "John called Brian late that night." Author interview with Peter Brown, 12/10/97.
710 "It was the best damn thing": Author interview with Bryan Barrett, 1/9/98.
710 a staging of three short comedies: "3 Bellow Plays Are Precipitated," *New York Times*, 3/8/66.
710 "That very weekend": Author interview with Tony Barrow, 10/31/97.
710 "four or five young . . . guys": Author interview with Peter Brown, 12/10/97.
710 "I was struggling": "Cynthia Lennon: In Her Own Words," *Hello!*, 5/28/94.
711 George drew the blinds: Davies, *Beatles*, p. 231.
711 "Tell him to let you on!": C. Lennon, *A Twist*, p. 147.
711 Peter Brown put an arm: "I put her into Neil's car." Author interview with Peter Brown, 12/10/97.
712 "You just sit there": John Lennon, 1967 interview, in *Anthology*, p. 261.
712 "like a prescription": George Harrison in ibid., p. 263.
712 "It has been specifically chosen": Author interview with Pete Shotton, 1/19/98.
712 Mal Evans divulged that his mantra: "We found out we all had the same word." Ibid.
712 "you get a sniff": John Lennon, 1968 interview, in *Anthology*, p. 261.
713 "*divertissement*": Brown & Gaines, *Love You Make*, p. 268.
713 "something of a tight ass": Author interview with Peter Brown, 12/10/97.
713 "Many bottles of wine": Brown & Gaines, *Love You Make*, p. 268.
714 "Clearly, he'd just woken up": "He said that he had gone to bed late and take [sic] quite a number of sleeping pills." Peter Brown, H. M. Coroner's Report, B. S. Epstein, 9/9/67.
714 "It wasn't unusual for Brian": Joanne Newfield Petersen, *Arena* archives.
715 "So? What's new?": Author interview with Alistair Taylor, 1/17/98.
715 John Gallway arrived: time determined by H. M. Coroner's Report, 9/9/67.
715 Blood streamed from his nose: Inspector George Howlett in ibid.
715 "Is there any brandy": Joanne Newfield Petersen, *Arena* archives.
715 "He's lying on the bed": Author interview with Peter Brown, 12/10/97.
716 "We've got to get hold of Clive": Author interview with Alistair Taylor, 1/17/98.
716 "The Beatles had to be told": Author interview with Peter Brown, 12/10/97.
717 "This is a terrible shock": Press conference transcript, Bangor, Wales, 8/27/67.
717 "confusion and disbelief": Ringo Starr in *Anthology*, p. 264.
717 "traipsed off to the Maharishi": Paul McCartney, *Arena* archives.
717 "Our friend's dead": Ibid.
717 "to love him and let him go": Ringo Starr in *Anthology*, p. 264.

717   "Well, Brian is just passing": Press conference transcript, Bangor, Wales, 8/27/67.

717   "We've fuckin' had it": Wenner, *Lennon Remembers,* p. 52.

718   "We did the first show": Author interview with Tony Bramwell, 8/6/97.

718   "I believe it was an accident": George Harrison in *Anthology,* p. 265.

719   "very sinister circumstances": Paul McCartney in ibid.

719   "His father, Harry": Author interview with Alistair Taylor, 1/17/98.

719   "Our main concern": Author interview with Peter Brown, 12/10/97.

719   the Beatles, who had been asked: "The Beatles were asked to stay away." Brown & Gaines, *Love You Make,* p. 273.

719   "There was a big power grab": Author interview with Alistair Taylor, 1/17/98.

719   Brian had left no will: "He died in August without making a will." *Daily Sketch,* 1/6/68, p. 7.

720   "the Beatles were shocked": Brown & Gaines, *Love You Make,* p. 275.

720   The Beatles had flirted: Lewisohn, *Chronicle,* p. 261.

720   "They didn't know where any of the money": Neil Aspinall in *Anthology,* p. 268.

720   *Mystery Tour* segments 1 through 8: Miles, *Paul McCartney,* p. 358.

721   "John had spent an afternoon": Ibid., p. 356.

721   John has said as many as twenty: "He'd already written *twenty* songs." Sheff, *Playboy Interviews,* p. 157.

721   "[Paul] said, 'Well, here's a segment'": Wenner, *Lennon Remembers,* p. 54.

721   written, he claimed: Sheff, *Playboy Interviews,* p. 156.

721   "a beautiful poem": Ibid.

721   "The words don't mean a lot": "What a Groove It Is Growing Older, Says John Lennon," *Disc and Music Echo,* 12/16/67.

721   only "I am the eggman": Burdon, *I Used to Be an Animal but I'm All Right Now,* p. 139.

721   "organized chaos": Lewisohn, *Sessions,* p. 122.

722   beginning with electric piano: "In the studio, we began with electric piano and Ringo's drums." John Lennon in Pritchard & Lysaght, *The Beatles,* p. 257.

722   "so weird": John Lennon, 1974 interview, in *Anthology,* p. 273.

722   eight violins, four cellos: Lewisohn, *Sessions,* p. 127.

722   "have their heads": Ibid., p. 122.

722   The Beatles, however, were clearly pleased: "It was a fascinating session. That was John's baby, great one, a really good one." Miles, *Paul McCartney,* p. 357.

723   "It was this idea of a fool": Ibid., p. 365.

723   "We literally made it up": Ibid., p. 360.

723   "John would always want a midget": Ringo Starr in *Anthology,* p. 272.

724   "We would get off the bus": Ibid.

724   Brian's "social secretary": Author interview with Nat Weiss, 1/28/98.

725   Neil lacked "sufficient clout": George Martin in *Anthology,* p. 268.

725   "was out of his class": Martin, *All You Need,* p. 171.

725   On one side of a table: Details provided by author interview with Peter Brown, 12/10/97.

726   "A joint company doesn't work": Robert Stigwood, *Arena* archives.

726   "They would be willing to put money": "Clive Epstein—New NEMS Boss," *NME,* 9/9/67.

726   "We shook hands": Ibid.

726   "was a very reasonable price": Ringo Starr in *Anthology,* p. 268.

726   seven subsidiaries were formed: Lewisohn, *25 Years in the Life,* pp. 97–98.

726   "There was an enormous sum": Author interview with Peter Brown, 12/10/97.

727   Clive Epstein and Harry Pinsker: "I suggested to the boys that they buy freehold property and go into retail trading." *Observer,* 9/1/68, p. 12.

727   "So we'd sit around the boardroom": Author interview with Alistair Taylor, 1/17/98.

727   "selling records was dismissed": Brown & Gaines, *Love You Make,* p. 280.

727 "How fucking boring!": Author interview with Alistair Taylor, 1/17/98.

727 "You can just imagine": McCabe & Schonfeld, *John Lennon: For the Record*, p. 103.

727 "We're just going to do": Author interview with Pete Shotton, 1/19/98.

728 George got involved with: "Mime Ban Hits Beatles Clip," *NME*, 12/2/67.

728 Paul opened discussions: "Stones Play It Cool on Possible Beatles Tie-Up," *NME*, 10/21/67.

728 Magic Alex was commissioned: Miles, *Paul McCartney*, p. 442.

728 "groovy clothes": McCabe & Schonfeld, *John Lennon: For the Record*, p. 105.

728 "something that we'd want": Ibid., p. 103.

728 "dressing in such interesting clothes": Miles, *Paul McCartney*, p. 443.

728 "The aim of the company": "A Is for Apple," *Observer*, 9/1/68, p. 7.

728 "sell everything white": "Paul came up with a nice idea, which was 'Let's sell everything white.'" John Lennon, 1970 interview, in *Anthology*, p. 270.

728 "a beautiful place": NEMS press release, 10/3/67.

729 "horrified"/"Give it to them": Harry Pinsker in Badman, *Off the Record*, p. 329.

729 "they wear gypsy headdresses": *New York Times*, 11/21/67.

729 "have an image of naturel": *Sunday Times*, 11/5/67.

729 "You should move to London": Author interview with Pete Shotton, 1/19/98.

730 "eating majoun and smoking hashish": Miles, *Paul McCartney*, p. 444.

730 "the clothes looked more like": Ibid., p. 445.

731 "They refused to tell": Author interview with Alistair Taylor, 1/17/98.

731 "The painting was gorgeous": Paul McCartney in *Anthology*, p. 270.

731 But the City of Westminster's: "The Fool . . . decided to ignore officialdom." Miles, *Paul McCartney*, p. 445.

731 "There was no direction": Author interview with Pete Shotton, 1/19/98.

732 "It was a mess": Author interview with Alistair Taylor, 1/17/98.

732 It reminded them of Beatlemania: "Many of the old fears returned. This, again, was Beatlemania." D. Taylor, *Fifty Years*, p. 322.

733 with 450,000 advance orders: "Beatles 'Magic' Disc-book Held Up," *NME*, 12/9/67.

733 "There was plenty of stock": Author interview with Peter Brown, 12/10/97.

733 "It was *disastrous*": Author interview with Alistair Taylor, 1/17/98.

733 "There was no plot": *Daily Mail*, 12/28/67.

733 "Nobody had the vaguest": McCabe & Schonfeld, *Apple to the Core*, p. 94.

733 "It looked awful": George Martin in *Anthology*, p. 274.

733 "the most expensive home movie": Coleman, *John Lennon*, p. 362.

734 "thought it was dreadful": Author interview with Peter Brown, 12/10/97.

734 "I saw it four times": Paul Fox in Badman, *Off the Record*, p. 335.

734 for the paltry fee of £9,000: "Fox offered him the derisory sum of £9,000." Miles, *Paul McCartney*, p. 366.

734 "Sod it," he thought: Ibid., p. 367.

734 "Appalling!": *Daily Mail*, 12/26/67.

734 "It was worse than terrible": *Evening News*, 12/26/67.

734 "rubbish . . . piffle": *Daily Mirror*, 12/26/67.

734 "blatant rubbish": *Daily Express*, 12/26/67.

734–35 "Whoever authorized the showing": *Daily Sketch*, 12/26/67.

735 "perhaps slightly to [his] own surprise": Miles, *Paul McCartney*, p. 440.

CHAPTER 34: AN ADDITIONAL ACT

736 "a marriage of four minds": C. Lennon, *A Twist*, p. 134.

737 "When it came down to business": Author interview with Alistair Taylor, 1/17/98.

737 "four miners who go down": Paul McCartney in *Anthology*, p. 110.

737 "Instead of going to bed": C. Lennon, *A Twist*, p. 134.

738 "There was something about the way": Author interview with Alistair Taylor, 1/17/98.

738 "I was amazed by the diary": Miles, *Paul McCartney*, p. 115.
738 "Jane knew people in the country": Ibid., p. 120.
738 "Paul was clearly in awe": Author interview with Peter Brown, 12/10/97.
739 "Jane confided in me": C. Lennon, *A Twist*, p. 133.
739 Jane had "clearly decided": Author interview with Peter Brown, 12/10/97.
739 "very tense": Miles, *Paul McCartney*, p. 453.
739 Jane's "traumatic" confession: Ibid., p. 452.
739 Paul "could not get her to name the day": Brown & Gaines, *Love You Make*, p. 240.
739 "never available": Goldman, *Lives of John Lennon*, p. 290.
739 "this stranger": Author interview with Pete Shotton, 1/19/98.
740 "pure shock": Coleman, *Lennon*, p. 336.
740 Yoko had been "particularly persistent": *Hello!*, 5/28/94.
740 She once gained admittance: Coleman, *Lennon*, pp. 335–36.
740 "there were a lot of phone calls": Ibid.
740 "She's crackers": Ibid., p. 336.
740 "I want two thousand pounds": Author interview with Pete Shotton, 1/19/98.
740 "all beautifully cut in half": Wenner, *Lennon Remembers*, p. 175.
741 "In the beginning, all those screwy ideas": Author interview with Peter Brown, 12/10/97.
741 "She did a thing called 'Dance Event'": Wenner, *Lennon Remembers*, p. 175.
741 "Use your blood to paint": Ono, *Grapefruit*, pages unnumbered.
741 "avant-garde crap": Coleman, *Lennon*, p. 345.
741 descended from samurai: Hopkins, *Yoko Ono*, p. 6.
742 "they actually went begging": Ibid., p. 10.
744 Vincent Persichetti: Goldman, *Lives of John Lennon*, p. 214.
744 "promoting living art": Fluxus manifesto, 1962, from *Fluxus, etc.*
745 "Long before Jimi Hendrix": Goldman, *Lives of John Lennon*, p. 217.
745 Yoko's "opera": from the program, Carnegie Recital Hall, 11/24/61.
745 "would start to feel the environment": Hopkins, *Yoko Ono*, p. 29.
746 "I was always having abortions": *Esquire*, May 1970.
746 "Tony and the doctors": Goldman, *Lives of John Lennon*, p. 226.
746 "Tony got her pregnant": Hopkins, *Yoko Ono*, p. 36.
747 "Inside there might be a lot": Sheff, *Playboy Interviews*, p. 91.
747 "hypnotically dreamlike": *Cue*, 3/24/65.
748 Yoko's performance "uplifting": *Financial Times*, 9/26/66.
748 "She said, half-laughingly": Hopkins, *Yoko Ono*, p. 58.
748 "far out": "Her work is far out." Wenner, *Lennon Remembers*, p. 172.
748 she was "somebody that you could go": McCabe & Schonfeld, *John Lennon: For the Record*, p. 55.
749 "a tribute to women": Miles, *Paul McCartney*, p. 449.
749 "not outright rock": "Rock Flavour to Next Beatles' Single," *NME*, 2/17/68.
749 "rockswing": "Ringo Talks," *NME*, 3/23/68.
749 The opening barrelhouse piano: "I asked him if it was from 'Bad Penny Blues,' and he said it was based [on that]." Author interview with Ray Connolly, 8/17/97.
749 "[The song] reminded me": Miles, *Paul McCartney*, p. 449.
749 "I think . . . we were all": Paul McCartney in *Anthology*, p. 281.
750 "I was gonna take her": McCabe & Schonfeld, *John Lennon: For the Record*, p. 55.
750 "barracks": "It was cold and wet, and the complex . . . resembled a barracks." *Hello!*, 5/28/94.
750 nominal rate of $400: "Beatles' Guru Is Turning Them into Gurus," *New York Times*, 2/23/68.
750 "We were really getting away": John Lennon, 1974 interview, in *Anthology*, p. 281.
751 "There [was] quite a heavy flow": George Harrison in ibid.
751 "It was a collision": Farrow, *What Falls Away*, p. 132.

751 Meditation . . . should last for: *Melody Maker,* 3/9/68.

751 "Nevertheless," she later wrote: Farrow, *What Falls Away,* p. 137.

751 "I was meditating about eight hours": John Lennon, 1974 interview, in *Anthology,* p. 283.

751 "To John, nothing else mattered": C. Lennon, *A Twist,* p. 155.

752 "It was pretty exciting": Ringo Starr in *Anthology,* p. 281.

752 "It was quite nice": Miles, *Paul McCartney,* p. 413.

752 "It was almost magical": Paul McCartney in *Anthology,* p. 283.

752 "like a feather over": Miles, *Paul McCartney,* p. 414.

752 "Regardless of what": John Lennon, 1971 interview, in *Anthology,* p. 283.

752 an homage to his boyhood idol: "'Back in the U.S.S.R.' was my take-off of Chuck Berry's 'Back in the USA.'" Miles, *Paul McCartney,* p. 422.

752 There, in a series of dilapidated tents: *Hello!,* 5/28/94.

753 "Every time we met": Miles, *Paul McCartney,* p. 419.

753 "to go shoot a few poor tigers": Sheff, *Playboy Interviews,* p. 168.

753 "Prudence meditated and hibernated": Ringo Starr in *Anthology,* p. 284.

753 "She went completely mental": Sheff, *Playboy Interviews,* p. 168.

753 George and John had been selected: Farrow, *What Falls Away,* p. 139.

753 "got her out of the house": Sheff, *Playboy Interviews,* p. 168.

753 using a finger-picking technique: "I introduced John to a finger-picking style. . . . With this style he wrote 'Julia' and 'Dear Prudence.'" Donovan in Badman, *Off the Record,* p. 341.

754 "Umbrella": Miles, *Paul McCartney,* p. 421.

754 "We're not fucking here": Ibid., p. 420.

754 Besides, Maureen had a phobia: "He couldn't stand the food and his wife couldn't stand the flies." Paul McCartney in *Anthology,* p. 284.

754 "very much like a holiday": *Melody Maker,* 3/9/68.

754 "Paul and Jane were much too sophisticated": Brown & Gaines, *Love You Make,* p. 286.

754 "some huge spiritual lift-off": Miles, *Paul McCartney,* p. 409.

754 "John took meditation": Coleman, *Lennon,* p. 341.

755 "Something had gone very wrong": *Hello!,* 5/28/94.

755 "I'm a cloud": Fawcett, *John Lennon: One Day at a Time,* p. 33.

755 John "missed his company": "Alex was summoned to Rishikesh by John." Brown & Gaines, *Love You Make,* p. 287.

755 "because he didn't approve": Miles, *Paul McCartney,* p. 427.

755 "appalled" by the accommodations: Brown & Gaines, *Love You Make,* p. 287.

756 Maharishi *might have* come on to her: Farrow, *What Falls Away,* p. 141.

756 "I think it was completely untrue": Miles, *Paul McCartney,* p. 429.

756 "to plug into the divine": George Harrison in Badman, *Off the Record,* p. 341.

756 "When George started thinking": Wenner, *Lennon Remembers,* pp. 55–56.

756 "Wait," she recalled: Miles, *Paul McCartney,* p. 428.

757 "John told me he knew": Author interview with Peter Brown, 12/10/97.

757 "If you're so cosmically conscious": Variations of this response have been reported in Wenner, *Lennon Remembers;* Brown & Gaines, *Love You Make;* C. Lennon, *A Twist;* and Jenny Boyd's account in Miles, *Paul McCartney.*

757 "You can't say that": George Harrison in *Anthology,* p. 286.

757 an appearance in a documentary: "30 New Beatle Tracks," *NME,* 4/20/68.

758 "But you've got to bloody hear it": Brown & Gaines, *Love You Make,* p. 291. Cynthia confirms this in *Hello!,* 5/28/94.

758 "I never dreamed": C. Lennon, *A Twist,* p. 163.

759 "We want to help people": *The Tonight Show,* 5/15/68.

759 whose brainstorm produced: "He came up with the idea for the ad in my house." Author interview with Alistair Taylor, 1/17/98.

759 "Overnight, we were swamped": Ibid.

759 "By the time I came back": George Harrison in *Anthology*, p. 287.

759 George . . . "had very little to do": Ibid.

759 "I hate it": D. Taylor, *Fifty Years*, p. 330.

759 "Paul, for the longest time": Author interview with Peter Brown, 12/10/97.

760 "he'd stay there all day": McCabe & Schonfeld, *Apple to the Core*, p. 102.

760 "John was in a rage": D. Taylor, *Fifty Years*, p. 330.

760 "He was more fucked up": Author interview with Pete Shotton, 7/10/98.

760 "It seemed like everything": Ibid., 1/19/98.

760 At a London party: Author interview with a confidential source.

760 "We wanted a grand launch": Paul McCartney in *Anthology*, p. 287.

761 "It was a mad, bad week": D. Taylor, *Fifty Years*, p. 327.

761 "mild and extremely benign hallucinogen": Ibid., p. 329.

761 "He said, 'We're leaving'": Miles, *Paul McCartney*, p. 450.

761 "There was something awfully steamy": Author interview with Nat Weiss, 1/28/98.

761–62 "didn't think she was particularly attractive": McCabe & Schonfeld, *John Lennon: For the Record*, p. 24.

762 "high-breasted": D. Taylor, *Fifty Years*, p. 329.

762 "He was a fairly hip person": Author interview with Peter Brown, 12/12/97.

762 "she looked very pretty": Miles, *Paul McCartney*, p. 454.

762 "He is an American song writer": Memo duplicated in D. Taylor, *Fifty Years*, p. 326.

763 "It all came as a shock": Author interview with Tony Bramwell, 8/6/97.

763 "tons of songs": Sheff, *Playboy Interviews*, p. 160.

763 "The Beatles were getting real tense": Ibid.

763 "I said, 'What are you doing?'" Author interview with Pete Shotton, 1/19/98.

764 "I played her all the tapes": Wenner, *Lennon Remembers*, p. 176.

764 "We improvised for many hours": Coleman, *Lennon*, p. 344.

765 "the babel inside an insane asylum": Author interview with Terry Doran, 8/13/97.

765 "enjoying the uncertainty": Coleman, *Lennon*, p. 344.

765 "It was dawn": Wenner, *Lennon Remembers*, p. 176.

765 "I had no doubt": Coleman, *Lennon*, pp. 344–45.

765 "shellshocked": Author interview with Pete Shotton, 1/19/98.

CHAPTER 35: GOOD-BYE TO THE BOYS IN THE BAND!

766 "The question they all ask": *Melody Maker*, 9/3/68.

766 "a hectic recording scene": "Beatles George Today," *NME*, 6/1/68.

766 "It seemed to many of us": Author interview with Don Short, 8/11/97.

766 "the Beatles were embarrassed": Author interview with Peter Brown, 12/10/97.

766 "We bought a few things": *NME*, 6/1/68.

767 He was "absolutely fascinated": "He wore several of them himself." Author interview with Peter Brown, 12/12/97.

767 "I had to give it away": John Lennon, undated interview, in *Anthology*, p. 290.

767 John and Paul "blew millions": George Harrison in ibid.

767 "tens of thousands" of requests: Brown & Gaines, *Love You Make*, p. 313.

767 "Suddenly Apple was a free-for-all": George Harrison in *Anthology*, p. 290.

767 "Any numbskull could walk in": Author interview with Alistair Taylor, 1/17/98.

767 "I remember going round": George Harrison in *Anthology*, p. 318.

768 "Magic Alex said that EMI": George Martin in ibid.

768 "The Jam"/"Walkabout": "Beatles Broaden Role in Business," *New York Times*, 5/15/68.

768 "Some Gorgeous Accident": *The Times* (London), 4/26/68.

768 There were preliminary discussions: "Beatles Maharishi Documentary Film," *NME*, 3/9/68.

768 a high-grade 50 percent: "The Story of *Yellow Submarine*," *Beatles Book Monthly*, 9/93, pp. 5–11.

769 "He dreaded going to them": Author interview with Tony Barrow, 10/31/97.

769 "We only had one or two": George Harrison in *Anthology*, p. 292.

769 "Their reaction was: 'OK'": Martin, *All You Need*, p. 226.

769 "brilliantly inventive": *Daily Telegraph*, 7/19/68.

770 strong "visual imagination": "Tati and the Beatles New Films in London," *Christian Science Monitor*, 8/3/68.

770 "The film packs more": "Lessons at the Movies," *Observer*, 7/28/68.

770 Ringo . . . "loved *Yellow Submarine*": Ringo Starr in *Anthology*, p. 292.

770 "I think it's a classic": George Harrison in ibid.

770 "The Beatles stubbornly continue": *Daily Mail*, 12/29/67.

771 "They have a different feel": "Interview: John Lennon," *Rolling Stone*, 11/23/68.

771 "just finish off the tail": McCabe & Schonfeld, *John Lennon: For the Record*, p. 119.

771 "it meant that I'd hear": Miles, *Paul McCartney*, p. 487.

771 Paul regretted the loss: "Because John [was divorcing] Cynthia and had gone off with Yoko . . ." Ibid.

771 "my love cloud": Wenner, *Lennon Remembers*, p. 106.

771 "never known love like this": John Lennon, 1968 interview, in *Anthology*, p. 301.

771 "my head would go off": McCabe & Schonfeld, *John Lennon: For the Record*, p. 56.

771 "She was the ultimate trip": Sheff, *Playboy Interviews*.

772 "eerily silent": Coleman, *Lennon*, p. 345.

772 "John and Yoko, wearing nothing": *Hello!*, 5/28/94.

772 "in complete shock": Ibid.

772 But one night in that desperate: Brown & Gaines, *Love You Make*, p. 293.

772 "She knew it was a mistake": Author interview with Peter Brown, 12/12/97.

773 "For a while, everything": C. Lennon, *A Twist*, p. 168.

773 "a very agitated" Magic Alex: Ibid., p. 169.

773 "absolutely devastated": *Hello!*, 5/28/94.

773 "I knew when I saw the picture": Coleman, *Lennon*, p. 350.

773 The groundwork for it: Lewisohn, *25 Years in the Life*, p. 104.

773 "They were like two nervous": Author interview with Alistair Taylor, 1/17/98.

773–74 "loyalty to and affection for Cynthia": D. Taylor, *Fifty Years*, p. 347.

774 "As your friend and press officer": Ibid., p. 340.

774 "Word had circulated": Author interview with Don Short, 8/11/97.

774 *"Where's your wife?":* Author interview with Peter Brown, 12/12/97.

774 "Who is this?": D. Taylor, *Fifty Years*, p. 340.

774 "What happened to your wife": Brown & Gaines, *Love You Make*, p. 297.

774 "Paul, in his usual way": Author interview with Peter Brown, 12/12/97.

775 Ringo had installed a rear window: Author interview with Ken Partridge, 1/18/98.

775 made "Paul [feel] uncomfortable": "Paul felt uncomfortable around John and Yoko." Miles, *Paul McCartney*, p. 486.

775 "[John] was getting into harder drugs": Ibid.

775 John's "adversity and . . . craziness": Ibid., p. 487.

776 "'God will save us'": Wenner, *Lennon Remembers*, p. 131.

776 "I really thought that love": Ibid., p. 132.

776 "He doesn't really get off the fence": Miles, *Paul McCartney*, p. 484.

777 "He seemed to be particularly focused": Author interview with Alan Brown, 5/18/97.

777 Yoko Ono sat "perversely": Coleman, *Lennon*, p. 363.

777 "It was fairly shocking": Author interview with Alan Brown, 5/18/97.

777 She "just moved in": George Harrison in *Anthology*, p. 308.

777 "John brought her into the control room": Lewisohn, *Sessions*, p. 135.

777 "dared the others": Author interview with Alan Brown, 5/18/97.

778 Studio grunts watched: Author interview with Martin Benge, 5/18/97.

778   "talk about fixes and monkeys": Miles, *Paul McCartney*, p. 486.

778   "[The studio] was where *we* were together": Ringo Starr in *Anthology*, p. 308.

778   "Yoko was there": Miles, *Paul McCartney*, p. 484.

778   "I bastardized it": Author interview with Paul McCartney, 3/21/97.

779   "I could hear them": Author interview with Alan Brown, 5/18/97.

779   "She came in and she would expect": Wenner, *Lennon Remembers*, p. 69.

779   "fed up [with] being sideman": Ibid., p. 49.

779   "cop out": Ibid.

780   "Finally, he just told EMI": Author interview with Peter Brown, 12/12/97.

780   Paul celebrated: Brown & Gaines, *Love You Make*, pp. 304–5.

780   "I'm here if you show up": Miles, *Paul McCartney*, p. 451.

781   "The moment Linda arrived": Author interview with Tony Bramwell, 8/6/97.

781   "[I'd] always found Linda": Author interview with Paul McCartney, 3/21/97.

781   Linda "seemed amused": Author interview with Tony Bramwell, 8/6/97.

781   "Her family was the most academic": Author interview with Paul McCartney, 3/21/97.

781   Paul "felt particularly sorry": Paul McCartney in *Anthology*, p. 297.

781   Julian was "a fragile little": Author interview with Alistair Taylor, 1/17/98.

782   "the Law of the Husband": Author interview with Peter Brown, 12/10/97.

782   "I thought it was a bit much": Miles, *Paul McCartney*, p. 465.

782   "try to cheer them up": Paul McCartney in *Anthology*, p. 297.

782   "a hopeful message for Julian": Ibid.

782   "one of [Paul's] masterpieces": Sheff, *Playboy Interviews*, p. 157.

783   John was holding out: "I wanted to put it out as a single." Wenner, *Lennon Remembers*, p. 131.

783   "No, George . . . You come in": Miles, *Paul McCartney*, p. 467.

783   "oblivious to anyone else's feelings": Author interview with Ron Richards, 12/29/97.

783   even had the structure for . . . "Something": While recording "Piggies," George played "Something" for Chris Thomas, George Martin's assistant. Pritchard & Lysaght, *The Beatles*, p. 265.

784   "made the other Beatles self-conscious": Miles, *Paul McCartney*, p. 492.

784   "There was a definite vibe": George Harrison in *Anthology*, p. 308.

784   "I remember having three studios": Ibid., p. 305.

784   "For the first time, I had to split myself": George Martin in ibid.

784   "looking after what both": Martin, *All You Need*, p. 132.

784   "dead set against putting such a mess": Author interview with Ron Richards, 12/29/97.

784   "[Paul] even recorded it": Sheff, *Playboy Interviews*, p. 160.

785   "there was such a lack of enthusiasm": George Harrison in Badman, *Off the Record*, p. 391.

785   "They weren't taking it seriously": George Harrison in *Anthology*, p. 306.

785   "the others would join in": George Martin in Pritchard & Lysaght, *The Beatles*, p. 263.

785   "We were in George's car": Eric Clapton in Badman, *Off the Record*, p. 391.

785   "I was recording not a band": George Martin in Pritchard & Lysaght, *The Beatles*, p. 263.

786   "because some of them weren't great": George Martin in *Anthology*, p. 305.

786   "I'm going on holiday": George Martin in Pritchard & Lysaght, *The Beatles*, p. 264.

786   "really arguing amongst themselves": Lewisohn, *Sessions*, p. 143.

786   "Paul was re-recording the vocal": Ibid.

787   "None of us had any experience": Author interview with Alistair Taylor, 1/17/98.

787   For a while the company's destiny: "We went through a period when we weren't allowed to do anything before someone threw the *I Ching.*" Alistair Taylor in Pritchard & Lysaght, *The Beatles*, p. 273.

787   "We invited people to Apple": Author interview with Peter Brown, 12/10/97.

788 "John wouldn't rest": Author interview with Tony Bramwell, 8/6/97.
788 "We really want to help people": New York press conference transcript, 5/14/68.
788 "not necessarily having a hard time": "Beatles' Loose Habit of Recording," *NME*, 8/17/68.
788 "smashed down an entire . . . panel": D. Taylor, *Fifty Years*, p. 348.
788 Beatles "were a mother's dream": Author interview with Alistair Taylor, 1/17/98.
788 "to make business fun": Ibid.
788 "foolish disregard": Letter, Derek Taylor to the Beatles, 7/26/68.
789 "mistaken for little Jewish businessmen": George Harrison in Badman, *Off the Record*, p. 375.
789 "Yoko came up with the idea": McCabe & Schonfeld, *John Lennon: For the Record*, p. 106.
789 such "a good happening": Wenner, *Lennon Remembers*, p. 59.
789 "Originally, the shops were intended": Beatles press release, issued 7/29/68.
789 "The night before, we all went in": McCabe & Schonfeld, *John Lennon: For the Record*, p. 106.
789 "a smashing raincoat": Paul McCartney in Badman, *Off the Record*, p. 375.
789 "loads of shirts and jackets": Ringo Starr in *Anthology*, p. 296.
789 "It was great": McCabe & Schonfeld, *John Lennon: For the Record*, p. 106.
789 "Yoko revealed a greedy side": Author interview with Peter Brown, 12/10/97.
790 "Hundreds of people" stampeded: *Daily Mail*, 8/1/68.
790 "the bulls at Pamplona": Author interview with Alistair Taylor, 1/17/98.
790 "people . . . coming with wheelbarrows": Ringo Starr in *Anthology*, p. 296.
790 "it brought out the worst": D. Taylor, *As Time Goes By*, p. 143.
791 The version Paul cut with Mary: "He originally tried to get the Moody Blues or Donovan to record it." Badman, *Off the Record*, p. 351.
791 "ideal material for half-time": *NME*, 8/31/68.
791 "I wanted a really different sound": Paul McCartney in *Anthology*, p. 289.
792 "It wasn't intended": Miles, *Paul McCartney*, p. 466.
792 "It felt good recording it": Ringo Starr in *Anthology*, p. 297.
792 the largest-selling Beatles record: *Billboard* research department files.
792 "all the time in the world": "Danger—Beatles at Work," *Saturday Review*, 10/12/68, p. 64.
792 Paul recorded "Mother Nature's Son": Lewisohn, *Sessions*, p. 147.
792 so offended Paul that he refused: Author interview with Ron Richards, 12/29/97.
793 "the whole thing was going down": Ringo Starr in *Anthology*, p. 312.
793 "unloved and out of it": Ibid., p. 311.
793 Ringo's "feel and soul": Paul McCartney in ibid.
793 "the most raucous": Miles, *Paul McCartney*, p. 488.
794 "drummed as if his life": Lewisohn, *Sessions*, p. 154.
794 The Beatles' goal, according to John: "We made the double white album because it was going to be a double album forever." John Lennon, 1970 interview, in Badman, *Off the Record*, pp. 391–92.
794 "I thought we should probably have made": George Martin in *Anthology*, p. 305.
794 "a bit heavy": "I think, in a way, it was a mistake doing four sides." George Harrison in Badman, *Off the Record*, p. 388.
794 "definitely rocking": John Lennon in ibid.
794 "something as utterly simple": "Beatles 'Live' by Paul," *NME*, 10/12/68.
794 "prissy" all-white cover: "I would be inclined to do a very prissy thing, almost like a limited edition." Richard Hamilton in Cooper, *Blinds and Shutters*.
795 "the most important musical": *The Times* (London), 11/22/68.
795 EMI had considered rationing: Syndicated news report, 11/21/68.
795 "boring beyond belief": "A Briton Blasts the Beatles," *New York Times*, 12/15/68, p. 8.

795   "a major success": "The Beatles: Inspired Groovers," *New York Times*, 12/8/68, pp. 33–37.

795   THE BRILLIANT, THE BAD, AND THE UGLY: *NME*, 11/9/68.

796   "It was a bombshell": Author interview with Tony Bramwell, 8/7/98.

796   "the howl that went up": John Lennon, 1969 interview, in Badman, *Off the Record*, p. 399.

796   "because . . . her work is naked": Fawcett, *John Lennon: One Day at a Time*, p. 40.

796   "What we did purposely": John Lennon, 1974 interview, in *Anthology*, p. 302.

796   "they all sat there": Wenner, *Lennon Remembers*, p. 67.

796   "slightly shocked": Paul McCartney in *Anthology*, p. 302.

796   "Ah, come on, John": Ringo Starr in *Anthology*, p. 302.

796   "Ringo and Paul hated": Author interview with Peter Brown, 12/12/97.

797   "a collection of bizarre sounds": Coleman, *Lennon*, p. 374.

797   *Disc, Melody Maker*, and *NME*: DiLello, *Longest Cocktail Party*, pp. 63–64.

797   The "togetherness had gone": McCabe & Schonfeld, *John Lennon: For the Record*, p. 58.

797   "I decided to leave": Wenner, *Lennon Remembers*, p. 69.

797   "the boys became of no interest": Sheff, *Playboy Interviews*, p. 41.

797   "'Goodbye to the boys'": Coleman, *Lennon*, p. 354.

CHAPTER 36: DISTURBING THE PEACE

798   "After six years' work": Letter from Stephen Maltz, 10/23/68.

798   "a pitiful £78,000": Goldman, *Lives of John Lennon*, p. 337.

798   "The deal among the Beatles": Author interview with Peter Brown, 12/10/97.

799   John, who had been tipped: "Don Short . . . had warned him": Coleman, *Lennon*, p. 368; also confirmed in author interview with Don Short, 8/11/97.

799   "flushing handfuls of pills": Author interview with Pete Shotton, 1/19/98.

799   "It was a measure of their popularity": Author interview with Ray Connolly, 8/7/97.

800   the bust "was a frame-up": Coleman, *Lennon*, p. 368.

800   On November 8 John's divorce: "John Lennon Divorced," *New York Times*, 11/9/68.

800   "When Paul got bored": Author interview with Peter Brown, 12/10/97.

800   "It wasn't anything serious": Author interview with Alistair Taylor, 1/17/98.

800   "broken off, finished,": *Dee Time*, BBC-TV, 7/20/68.

800   "I loved [it in] New York": Author interview with Paul McCartney, 3/21/97.

801   "Linda was showing me around": Ibid.

801   "her womanliness"/"slight rebelliousness": Miles, *Paul McCartney*, p. 517.

802   "It was great living": Ibid., p. 521.

802   Capitol had shipped 3.5 million copies: "Apple's Full of Sauce," *Washington Post*, 12/29/68.

802   "Apple wasn't being run": Ringo Starr in *Anthology*, p. 324.

802   "were all just living and drinking": Wenner, *Lennon Remembers*, p. 155.

803   "if it carries on": *Disc and Music Echo*, 1/18/69.

803   £18,000 or £20,000: Wenner, *Lennon Remembers*, p. 155.

803   "Somehow . . . [we] needed a firm": John Lennon, 1971 interview, in *Anthology*, p. 324.

803   "stick to music": Miles, *Paul McCartney*, p. 543.

803   The Beatles also . . . courted: Author interview with Peter Brown, 12/12/97.

803   collectively as "animals": Wenner, *Lennon Remembers*, p. 146.

804   "I think we should get back": Coleman, *Lennon*, p. 372.

805   "Our jaws dropped": Ibid., pp. 373–74.

805   "give it a couple of months": Ibid., p. 374.

806   "The thing I miss most": John Lennon, 1972 interview, in *Anthology*, p. 322.

806 George, however, "scoffed at" the idea: Miles, *Paul McCartney*, p. 528.

806 "I'd hoped that by playing": Paul McCartney in *Anthology*, p. 322.

806 "virtually absolutely definite": "Beatles 'Live' by Paul," *NME*, 10/12/68.

806 "It will definitely be free": "Beatles Holed-Up, Ringo Movie," *NME*, 12/7/68.

806 "I think the original idea": George Harrison in *Anthology*, p. 315.

806 "go on an ocean liner": Paul McCartney in ibid.

806 "being very expensive and insane": Norman, *Shout!*, p. 357.

807 "The idea was that you'd see": Paul McCartney in *Anthology*, p. 315.

807 "a big barn": Ringo Starr in ibid., p. 318.

807 "To be fair, no one had much enthusiasm": Author interview with Peter Brown, 12/12/97.

807 "stoned all the time": Wenner, *Lennon Remembers*, p. 118.

807 "going to try and create": John Lennon, 1976 interview, in *Anthology*, p. 317.

807 "We put down a few tracks": Wenner, *Lennon Remembers*, p. 118.

807 George . . . found it "stifling": George Harrison in *Anthology*, p. 316.

808 "I had always let him": George Harrison in Badman, *Off the Record*, p. 411.

808 "Look, I'll play whatever": George Harrison in *Let It Be* (film).

808 "What am I doing here?": George Harrison in *Anthology*, p. 316.

808 "That's it . . . see you 'round": George Harrison in *Let It Be* (film), 1969.

808 "Our reaction was really": Ringo Starr in *Anthology*, p. 316.

809 "I think if George doesn't come back": John Lennon in *Let It Be* (film); also in Badman, *Off the Record*, p. 412.

810 "the biggest disaster": D. Taylor, *Fifty Years*, p. 358.

810 "We bought some huge computers": Ringo Starr in *Anthology*, p. 291.

810 "the mixing console was made": Lewisohn, *Sessions*, p. 164.

810 "very nasty twitter": Martin, *All You Need*, p. 174.

810 "They were hopeless": George Martin in *Anthology*, p. 318.

811 "You'd better put some equipment in": Martin, *All You Need*, p. 173.

811 mobile four-track mixing consoles: Miles, *Paul McCartney*, p. 533.

811 "I don't want any of your production": George Martin in *Anthology*, p. 317.

811 "all those rumors": McCabe & Schonfeld, *John Lennon: For the Record*, p. 80.

811 "terrible shit": Ibid., p. 81.

811 "a bit like Martin": Wenner, *Lennon Remembers*, p. 62.

812 "The facilities at Apple": Ringo Starr in *Anthology*, p. 318.

812 Meanwhile back at home: "Get Back" lyrics, *Abbey Road* demo.

813 putting out "negative vibes": George Harrison in *Anthology*, p. 316.

813 "It was a very tense period": Miles, *Paul McCartney*, p. 535.

813 "a genuine plea": Ibid., pp. 535–36.

813 "That's me singing about Yoko": Sheff, *Playboy Interviews*, p. 172.

813 "I don't think he wanted much": George Harrison in *Anthology*, p. 316.

813 the band to be "very childish": McCabe & Schonfeld, *John Lennon: For the Record*, p. 59.

813 he "didn't believe in": "I don't know when I realized I was putting down all these things I didn't believe in." Wenner, *Lennon Remembers*, p. 31.

813 "just [doing] it like a job": Ibid., p. 51.

813 "fed up with the same old shit": Ibid., p. 69.

813 He felt constrained: "We were limiting our capacity to write and perform by having it fit into some kind of format." John Lennon, 1971 interview, in *Anthology*, p. 317.

814 "better than Picasso" Coleman, *Lennon*, p. 430.

814 the others were "insecure": McCabe & Schonfeld, *John Lennon: For the Record*, p. 47.

814 "sophisticated, intellectually": Ibid., p. 52.

814 "Yoko had him under": Author interview with Tony Bramwell, 8/8/97.

814 "they started picking on": John Lennon, 1976 interview, in *Anthology*, p. 317.

814 "I started to feel it wasn't": Paul McCartney in *Anthology*, p. 316.

814 "offset the vibes": George Harrison in Badman, *Off the Record,* p. 415.

815 "the bullshit went out the window": Ringo Starr in *Anthology,* p. 318.

815 his crumbling relationship with John: "John was with Yoko full time, and our relationship was beginning to crumble." Miles, *Paul McCartney,* p. 538.

815 "It was like having a guest": Paul McCartney in *Anthology,* pp. 318–19.

815 Billy turned up at the studio: "We were trying to figure out where we could have a concert." Billy Preston in Badman, *Off the Record,* p. 416.

815 "a little bit puzzling": Paul McCartney in *Anthology,* p. 319.

815 "Oh, that's fantastic": John Lennon in Pritchard & Lysaght, *The Beatles,* p. 278.

815 "Nobody had ever done that": George Harrison, in *Anthology,* p. 321.

816 "The Beatles had arranged for a camera": Author interview with Jack Oliver, 10/28/99.

816 "Honestly, the music has got": *Let It Be* (film), 1969.

816 "When [the police] came up": Ringo Starr in *Anthology,* p. 321.

817 "If anybody wants to sing": George Harrison in *Let It Be* (film), 1969.

817 "You know this is a small": Coleman, *Lennon,* pp. 370–71.

818 "a distant resemblance to Buddy Hackett": Goldman, *Lives of John Lennon,* p. 328.

818 He'd met John once before: "I met him at the *Rock and Roll Circus,*" Wenner, *Lennon Remembers,* p. 142.

818 "broke, like Mickey Rooney": Coleman, *Lennon,* p. 376.

818 In his exuberant autobiography: D. Taylor, *Fifty Years,* p. 366.

819 "nervous as shit": Wenner, *Lennon Remembers,* p. 144.

819 "the only businessman I've met": John Lennon, 1969 interview, in *Anthology,* p. 324.

819 "One of the . . . things": McCabe & Schonfeld, *John Lennon: For the Record,* p. 42.

819 "I knew right away": McCabe & Schonfeld, *Apple to the Core,* p. 123.

819 Actually, the letter read: Letter, John Lennon to Sir Joseph Lockwood, in *Anthology,* p. 324.

819 "a human being"/"an animal": Wenner, *Lennon Remembers,* pp. 146–48.

819 a million-dollar advance: "A figure that John repeated to me in the office the next day with pride." Brown & Gaines, *Love You Make,* p. 333.

819 "the only one Yoko liked": Paul McCartney in *Anthology,* p. 324.

820 "big-headed uptight people": Wenner, *Lennon Remembers,* p. 67.

820 Paul was the one responsible: "They all thought Paul was the one who was going to hold it all together." McCabe & Schonfeld, *John Lennon: For the Record,* p. 72.

820 "all that Beatle stuff": Wenner, *Lennon Remembers,* p. 138.

820 "Paul began complaining": McCabe & Schonfeld, *John Lennon: For the Record,* p. 27.

820 Paul discouraged her from attending: Ibid.

820 "Because we were all from Liverpool": George Harrison in *Anthology,* p. 325.

821 "fucked around by everybody": McCabe & Schonfeld, *Apple to the Core,* p. 149.

821 it remained the top-selling album: *Melody Maker, NME* charts.

822 "it belied his innocence and honesty": Author interview with Peter Brown, 12/12/97.

822 "Let's get them both together": George Harrison in *Anthology,* p. 324.

822 "a piece of crap": Brown & Gaines, *Love You Make,* p. 334.

822 "I can't tell you how much I've admired": McCabe & Schonfeld, *John Lennon: For the Record,* p. 150.

823 John had learned from Neil: Wenner, *Lennon Remembers,* p. 148.

823 "How Lee kept his cool": Author interview with Peter Brown, 12/12/97.

823 "interrupting everything he said": Brown & Gaines, *Love You Make,* p. 335.

823 "Will you please stop insulting my husband": Wenner, *Lennon Remembers,* p. 152.

CHAPTER 37: AND IN THE END . . .

824 "If you don't tell anybody": Author interview with Ray Connolly, 8/7/97.

824 "Why should we be asked": Author interview with Pete Shotton, 1/19/98.

825 "last bachelor among the Beatles": "Beatles McCartney Planning to Marry," *New York Times,* 3/12/69.

825 "Paul and Linda want it simple": Apple press release 3/11/69.

825 "plunged through a mob": "McCartney Marries, Teen-Age Fans Weep," *New York Times*, 3/13/69.

825 John . . . expressed "surprise": "I was very surprised with Linda. I wouldn't have been surprised if he'd married Jane Asher." McCabe & Schonfeld, *John Lennon: For the Record*, p. 31.

825 "It was just Paul being Paul": Author interview with Peter Brown, 12/12/97.

825 "I'd never seen George so angry": Author interview with Pete Shotton, 1/19/98.

826 "Why don't you stay there": Author interview with Peter Brown, 12/12/97.

826 "a load of money": "I had, in fact, taken a load of money for them." Alistair Taylor in Badman, *Off the Record*, p. 429.

827 "Intellectually, we didn't believe": Coleman, *Lennon*, p. 393.

827 "rationalize" the situation at Apple: Miles, *Paul McCartney*, p. 545.

827 "gravy train": McCabe & Schonfeld, *John Lennon: For the Record*, p. 66.

827 "were living like kings": Ibid., p. 79.

827 "He'd been with us since 1962": Author interview with Peter Brown, 12/12/97.

827 "But Paul refused": Author interview with Alistair Taylor, 1/17/98.

828 In this case . . . a company check: Miles, *Paul McCartney*, p. 546.

828 Asher . . . refused to give Klein: "He wasn't going to take that shit from anybody." Author interview with Jack Oliver, 10/28/99.

828 "as a protest against violence": "The Lennons Bed Down for Nonviolence," *New York Daily News*, 3/26/69.

828 "Instead of fighting it": "Sgt. Pepper Makes a Pitch for Peace," *Los Angeles*, 6/15/69, p. 14.

828 A "plea for peace": "It is a plea for peace among people." *New York Daily News*, 3/26/69.

829 part demonstration, part sideshow: "Everybody has their bags, and this is ours," he told a reporter. "John's and Yoko's Peace Gimmicks Do Make Sense," *NME*, 3/12/69.

829 "it's no good working for money": *Los Angeles*, 6/15/69.

829 "It came at a perfect time": Coleman, *Lennon*, p. 397.

829 "We are trying to make Christ's message": Amsterdam press conference, 3/23/69.

829 "As you know, Mr. Allen Klein": Letter, made part of *Paul McCartney v. John Lennon, George Harrison, Richard Starkey, and Apple Corps., Ltd.*, English High Court of Justice, Chancery Division, 1971.

830 He kicked Allen out: "Did I tell him to get lost? No, I put it in slightly stronger terms." McCabe & Schonfeld, *Apple to the Core*, p. 127.

830 "all royalties payable": Letter from the Beatles to EMI, 3/3/69.

831 "I won't sell!": *Evening Standard*, 3/29/69.

831 John Eastman spoke for everyone: "I told him he was a bastard." McCabe & Schonfeld, *Apple to the Core*, p. 154.

831 totaling about 14 percent: "The Beatles Besieged," *Time*, 5/30/69.

831 "I'm not going to be fucked around": McCabe & Schonfeld, *Apple to the Core*, p. 155.

832 "Paul was getting more and more uptight": Wenner, *Lennon Remembers*, p. 154.

832 "We had great arguments": Ringo Starr in *Anthology*, p. 326.

832 "He'll take fifteen percent": Miles, *Paul McCartney*, p. 548; also in *Anthology*, p. 326.

833 "Monopoly with real money": "Song Company of Beatles Resists a Take-Over Bid," *New York Times*, 5/17/69.

833 "a monumental row": McCabe & Schonfeld, *Apple to the Core*, p. 159.

833 It was a tremendous mistake: "I thought Paul had made a terrible miscalculation." Author interview with Nat Weiss, 1/28/98.

833   "Paul actually stopped coming": Author interview with Peter Brown, 12/12/97.

834   "total communication": "This is an example of total communication." John Lennon press conference, Sacher Hotel, Austria, 3/31/69.

834   "very fast living": D. Taylor, *Fifty Years,* p. 367.

834   *Variety* reported: Story syndicated in *Go,* 4/4/69, p. 10.

834   *Jesus Christ Superstar:* "Lennon Asked to Portray Christ," *New York Times,* 12/4/69.

834   "I don't know what people think": *NME,* 3/29/69.

834   "paranoia": "One of the things people don't know about John is that a lot of his genius was a cover-up for his paranoia." Miles, *Paul McCartney,* p. 552.

834   "containing two acorns": John Lennon press conference, 3/28/69.

834   Then, on April 22: "Now It's John Ono Lennon," *New York Times,* 4/23/69.

835   "How would *you* like it": Coleman, *Lennon,* p. 390.

835   "[They] were so lousy": John Lennon, 1971 interview, in *Anthology,* p. 350.

835   "twenty-nine hours of tape": Wenner, *Lennon Remembers,* p. 120.

835   "It was laying [sic] dormant": George Harrison in *Anthology,* p. 337.

835   a Beatles album "like we used to": Miles, *Paul McCartney,* p. 551.

836   "Only if you let me produce it": George Martin in *Anthology,* p. 337.

836   His original plan had been: D. Taylor, *Fifty Years,* p. 367.

836   "inadmissible immigrant": "John Lennon Seeks a Visa to Visit U.S.," *New York Times,* 5/16/69.

836   Declassified internal FBI memos: Wiener, *Come Together,* p. 85.

837   "I think I could probably write": *NME,* 5/3/69, p. 3.

837   In fact, he was taking Paul: "I've just written a song called 'Because.'" Ibid.

837   "straight out of *Grapefruit*": Miles, *Paul McCartney,* p. 555.

837   "one of the most beautiful things": "Abbey Road Heading for Fame," *Washington Post,* 10/5/69.

837   George's masterpiece, "Something": "I thought it was George's greatest track." Paul McCartney in *Anthology,* p. 340.

837   "wasn't in the same league": John Lennon, 1974 interview, in ibid.

837   "surprised that George had it in him": George Martin in ibid., p. 340.

837   "came out of left field": Paul McCartney in ibid.

837   "lambasting Allen Klein's attitude": Miles, *Paul McCartney,* p. 556.

838   "Golden slumbers kiss your eyes": Dekker, "Golden Slumbers," *The Pleasant Company of Old Fortunatus,* 1603.

838   "I liked the words": Miles, *Paul McCartney,* pp. 557–58.

838   "He was driving for the first time": Stanley Parkes, 1/19/85, AGA.

838   John required seventeen stitches: Lewisohn, *25 Years in the Life,* pp. 120–21.

838   "a tribute to [their] survival": Author interview with Peter Brown, 12/12/97.

838   Everyone knew it also functioned: Les Anthony, 5/85, AGA.

839   "I think that until now": Fawcett, *John Lennon: One Day at a Time,* p. 96.

839   which George wrote while meandering: "It was written on a nice sunny day in Eric Clapton's garden." "Abbey Road Heading for Fame," *Washington Post,* 10/5/69.

839   "The three of us didn't quite get it": Miles, *Paul McCartney,* p. 552.

839   "'Come together' was an expression": Sheff, *Playboy Interviews,* p. 170.

840   John acknowledged the debt: Miles, *Paul McCartney,* p. 553.

840   "Let's slow it down": Paul McCartney in *Anthology,* p. 339.

840   "querying bass line": Riley, *Tell Me Why,* p. 312.

840   "On the finished record": Lewisohn, *Sessions,* p. 181.

840   "a group thing": McCabe & Schonfeld, *John Lennon: For the Record,* p. 23.

840   "something slick to preserve the myth": Goldman, *Lives of John Lennon,* pp. 353–54.

840   "People would be walking out": Lewisohn, *Sessions,* p. 193.

840   "getting fairly dodgy": Paul McCartney in *Anthology,* p. 340.

841   "There was a great sort of theater": Author interview with Alan Brown, 3/28/97.

841   "a fantastic toy": Author interview with Alistair Taylor, 1/17/98.

841   "hundreds of jackplugs": George Harrison in *Anthology,* p. 340.

841   *Everest:* Paul McCartney in ibid., p. 337.

841   "someone mentioned the possibility": Lewisohn, *Sessions,* p. 193.

841   "just go outside": Ibid.

842   "it was a very hot day": Paul McCartney in *Anthology,* p. 341.

842   "all leonine": *Rolling Stone,* record review, *Abbey Road,* 11/15/69.

842   "Come on, hurry up": John Lennon, undated interview, in *Anthology,* p. 342.

842   "It had been left there": Iain Macmillan in Badman, *Off the Record,* p. 459.

842   "Barefoot, nice warm day": Ibid.

842   "a pleasant but unadventurous": "Beatles in the Web," *Newsweek,* 10/20/69.

842   "sincere"/"rather dull": "Abbey Road by Beatles Marked by Moderation," *New York Times,* 10/4/69.

842   In Britain, advance orders: "George's 'Abbey Road' Track as Beatles' New U.S. Single," *NME,* 9/27/69.

843   "at 5 o'clock on a rainswept": *Newsweek,* 11/3/69, p. 62.

843   Fred LaBour: "This fantastic death wish seems to have been stimulated by a University of Michigan undergraduate named Fred LaBour." "No, No, No, Paul McCartney Is Not Dead," *New York Times,* 11/2/69.

843   Others who played the entire: "The Magical McCartney Mystery," *LIFE,* 11/7/69, p. 104.

844   "I'm alive and well": "Paul Makes It Clear: 'I Feel Fine,'" Associated Press wire story, 10/23/69.

844   "millions of youthful fans": *Newsweek,* 11/3/69.

844   *Sgt. Pepper's* reappeared: *Billboard,* 11/2/69.

844   "Can you spread it around": "The Magical McCartney Mystery," *LIFE,* 11/7/69, p. 105.

844   Then, on September 25: "Beatles Lose Fight for Control of Firm," *New York Times,* 10/27/69.

845   "I told Allen I was leaving": Wenner, *Lennon Remembers,* p. 60.

845   alongside "all the great rockers": John Lennon, 1969 interview in *Anthology,* p. 347.

845   Everyone knew the old standards: "I've played all these numbers before . . . so I know them." Eric Clapton, *NME,* 12/20/69.

846   "can't remember when I had such a good time": "John Lennon Finds Worm in Beatles' Apple," *Variety,* 10/26/69.

846   In separate conversations: "I told Eric Clapton and Klaus that I was leaving." Wenner, *Lennon Remembers,* p. 60.

846   "it was not an easy decision": Fawcett, *John Lennon: One Day at a Time,* p. 101.

846   "What do you mean?": Wenner, *Lennon Remembers,* p. 60.

846   "*Everybody* had tried to leave": George Harrison in *Anthology,* p. 348.

846   "they knew it was for real": John Lennon, 1978 interview, in *Anthology,* p. 348.

846   "Everyone blanched except John": Miles, *Paul McCartney,* p. 561.

846   "John burst into the room": Fawcett, *John Lennon: One Day at a Time,* p. 101.

847   it felt like "a relief": Ringo Starr in *Anthology,* p. 348.

847   "we knew it was [a] good [decision]": Ibid., p. 347.

847   "I wanted out myself": George Harrison in ibid.

847   To Paul's relief: "Paul and Allen said they were glad I wasn't going to announce it." Wenner, *Lennon Remembers,* p. 61.

847   "since I'd been seventeen": Paul McCartney in *Anthology,* p. 349.

848   "Then, if I did get up": Miles, *Paul McCartney,* pp. 568–69.

848   "We were each other's intimates": Ibid., p. 566.

848   "nobody . . . quite knew": Paul McCartney in *Anthology,* p. 349.

848   "John's in love with Yoko": *Evening Standard,* 4/70; author interview with Ray Connolly, 8/7/97.

849   "songs Ringo likes": Apple Records press release, reported in "Ringo May Be Guesting," *NME,* 11/8/69.

849   "I'd like to do it with the Beatles": *NME,* 12/20/69.

849   "frequently perplexed audience": "John and Yoko Films," *Washington Post,* 10/26/69.

850   *Peace: NME,* 11/8/69.

850   gave away Dor Inis: "Hippies to Look Over Island Offered to Them by a Beatle," *New York Times,* 11/14/69.

850   his drug dealer Michael X: "The time Yoko was in hospital, I sat with her all Saturday afternoon. . . . Michael X turns up with this big suitcase full of grass, which he gave to John." Author interview with Ray Connolly, 8/7/97.

850   "mulling it over": BBC interview, 11/27/69.

850   "a lunatic or something": "Why Put Down What We're Doing?" *NME,* 11/22/69.

850   "Clown of the Year": *Daily Mirror,* 12/18/69.

851   "mixed [it] instantly": George Harrison in *Anthology,* p. 350.

851   "fantastic . . . like there were fifty people": Goldman, *Lives of John Lennon,* p. 370.

851   "None of us could face remixing": John Lennon, 1971 interview, in *Anthology,* p. 350.

851   "to tidy up some of the tracks": *Evening Standard,* 4/21/70.

851   He threatened to sue Klein: Miles, *Paul McCartney,* p. 576.

851   "It's stupid for Apple": Memo, John Lennon and George Harrison, 3/5/70.

851   "From my point of view": Paul McCartney in *Anthology,* p. 351.

852   He even called Joe Lockwood: "I'm being sabotaged, Sir Joe." Brown & Gaines, *Love You Make,* p. 365.

852   "I want to get off the label": Miles, *Paul McCartney,* p. 570.

852   "Unfortunately, it was Ringo": Paul McCartney in *Anthology,* p. 351.

852   "We want you to put your release date": Miles, *Paul McCartney,* p. 573.

852   "I called him everything under the sun": *Evening Standard,* 4/21/70.

852   "it was near enough": Paul McCartney in *Anthology,* p. 351.

853   "there was no common goal": John Lennon, 1971 interview, in *Anthology,* p. 352.

853   "almost made me cry": Miles, *Paul McCartney,* p. 572.

853   "Beatle Paul McCartney confirmed today": *Aberdeen Evening Express,* 4/10/70.

854   "He was cross": Author interview with Ray Connolly, 8/7/97.

854   "It was wonderful and it's over": John Lennon, undated interview, in *Anthology,* p. 352.

BIBLIOGRAPHY

BOOKS

Aitkin, Jonathan. *The Young Meteors.* New York: Atheneum, 1967.

Aldridge, Alan, ed. *The Beatles Illustrated Lyrics.* New York: Delacorte, 1969.

Amburn, Ellis. *Dark Star: The Roy Orbison Story.* London: New English Library, 1990.

Andrews, Ben, and Jodi Summers. *Confessions of Rock Groups.* New York: S.p.i. Books, 1994.

Anthony, Gene. *The Summer of Love.* London: Celestial, 1980.

Aughton, Peter. *Liverpool: A People's History.* Preston (England): Carnegie, 1990.

Badman, Keith. *The Beatles After the Breakup, 1970–2000.* London: Omnibus, 1999.

——. *The Beatles: Off the Record.* London: Omnibus, 2000.

Baines, T. *The Port and Town of Liverpool.* Liverpool: 1860.

Baird, Julia, with Geoffrey Giuliano. *John Lennon: My Brother.* London: Grafton, 1988.

Baker, Glenn. *The Beatles Down Under: The 1964 Australia and New Zealand Tour.* Sydney: Glebe, Wild and Woolley, 1982.

Balfour, Victoria. *Rock Wives.* New York: William Morrow, 1986.

Barnes, Richard. *Mods!* London: Eel Pie, 1979.

Barrow, Tony. *Meet the Beatles.* Manchester (England): World Distributors, 1963.

Beatles, The. *The Beatles Anthology.* San Francisco: Chronicle, 2000.

Beckman, Dieter, and Klaus Martens. *Star Club.* Hamburg: Rowohlt, 1980.

Bedford, Carol. *Waiting for the Beatles: An Apple Scruff's Story.* Blandford (England): Poole, 1984.

Benson, Harry. *The Beatles in the Beginning.* Edinburgh: Mainstream, 1993.

Bentley, James. *The Blue Guide: Germany.* New York: W. W. Norton, 1987.

Berman, Marshall. *The Politics of Authenticity.* New York: Atheneum, 1970.

Bernard, Barbara. *Fashion in the 60s.* London: Academy Editions, 1978.

Best, Pete, and Patrick Doncaster. *Beatle! The Pete Best Story.* London: Plexus, 1985.

Best, Pete, and Bill Harry. *The Best Years of the Beatles!* London: Headline, 1997.

Black, Johnny. *The Beatles Complete.* London: HMV, 1988.

Blake, John. *All You Needed Was Love.* London: Hamlyn, 1981.

Bockris, Victor. *Keith Richards: The Biography.* London: Hutchinson, 1992.

Brake, Mike. *The Sociology of Youth Culture and Youth Subcultures: Sex and Drugs and Rock 'n Roll.* London: Routledge & Kegan Paul, 1980.

Braun, Michael. *Love Me Do: The Beatles' Progress.* London: Penguin, 1964.

Bresler, Fenton. *Who Killed John Lennon?* New York: St. Martin's, 1989.

Brown, Peter, and Steven Gaines. *The Love You Make.* New York: McGraw-Hill, 1983.

Burdon, Eric. *I Used to Be an Animal but I'm All Right Now.* London: Faber & Faber, 1986.

Burke, John. *The Beatles in Their First Fab Film! A Hard Day's Night.* London: Pan, 1964.

Butterworth, Eric, and David Weir, eds. *The Sociology of Modern Britain.* London: Fontana, 1976.

Calvocoressi, Peter. *The British Experience, 1945–75.* London: Bodley Head, 1978.

Campbell, Colin, and Allan Murphy. *Things We Said Today: The Complete Lyrics and a Concordance to the Beatles' Songs, 1962–1970.* Ann Arbor: Pierian, 1980.

Caron, Sandra. *Alma Cogan: A Memoir.* London: Bloomsbury, 1991.

Carr, Roy, and Tony Tyler. *The Beatles: An Illustrated Record.* New York: Tribune, 1978.

Chandler, George. *Liverpool.* London: B. T. Batsford, 1957.

Channon, Howard. *Portrait of Liverpool.* Liverpool: Robert Hale, 1970.

Christgau, Robert. *Any Old Way You Choose It.* New York: Penguin, 1973.

Clark, Dick. *Rock, Roll & Remember.* New York: Popular Library, 1978.

Clayson, Alan. *The Beat Merchants: The Origins, History, Impact and Rock Legacy of the 1960s British Pop Groups.* London: Blandford, 1995.

——. *George Harrison: The Quiet One.* London: Sidgwick & Jackson, 1989.

——. *Ringo Starr: Straight Man or Joker.* New York: Paragon, 1991.

Clayson, Alan, and Pauline Sutcliffe. *Backbeat: Stuart Sutcliffe, the Lost Beatle.* London: Pan, 1994.

Cohen, Stanley. *Folk Devils and Moral Panics: The Creation of the Mods and Rockers.* London: MacGibbon & Kee, 1972.

Cohn, Nic. *Today There Are No Gentlemen.* London: Weidenfeld and Nicholson, 1971.

——. *A WopBopaLooBop A LopBamBoom: Pop from the Beginning.* London: Paladrin, 1970.

Coleman, Ray. *Brian Epstein: The Man Who Made the Beatles.* London: Viking, 1989.

——. *Lennon.* New York: McGraw-Hill, 1984.

——. *McCartney: Yesterday and Today.* London: Boxtree, 1995.

Connolly, Ray. *In the Sixties.* London: Pavilion, 1995.

——. *Stardust Memories: Talking About My Generation.* London: Pavilion, 1983.

Cooper, Michael. *Blinds & Shutters.* Guildford (England): Genesis, 1990.

Cordling, Robert, Shelli Jankowski-Smith, and E. J. Laino, eds. *In My Life: Encounters with the Beatles.* New York: Fromm International, 1988.

Cosham, Ralph. *The Beatles at Carnegie Hall.* London: Panther, 1964.

Cott, Jonathan, and David Dalton. *The Beatles Get Back.* London: Apple, 1969.

Cowan, Philip. *Behind the Beatles' Songs.* London: Polytantric, 1978.

Dalton, David, and Lenny Kaye. *Rock 100.* New York: Grosset & Dunlap, 1977.

David, Edward, ed. *The Beatles Book.* New York: Cowles, 1968.

Davies, Hunter. *The Beatles.* 2d rev. ed. New York: Norton, 1996.

Davies, Peter. *Arthur Ballard: Liverpool Artist and Teacher.* Abertillery (England): Old Bakehouse, 1996.

Dean, Johnny. *The Beatles Book.* London: Beat Pub., 1996.

DeCurtis, Anthony, and James Henke, eds. *The Rolling Stone Illustrated History of Rock 'n Roll.* New York: Random House, 1992.

Delano, Julia. *The Beatles Album.* London: Grange, 1991.

Dellar, Fred. *NME Guide to Rock Cinema.* London: Hamlyn, 1981.

Dickstein, Morris. *Gates of Eden: American Culture in the Sixties.* New York: Basic Books, 1977.

DiLello, Richard. *The Longest Cocktail Party.* New York: Playboy, 1972.

Doggett, Peter. *Classic Rock Albums: Abbey Road/Let It Be/The Beatles.* New York: Schirmer, 1998.

Doncaster, Patrick. *Tribute to John Lennon.* London: Mirror Books, 1980.

Doney, Malcolm. *Lennon and McCartney.* London: Midas, 1981.

Dowlding, William J. *Beatlesongs.* New York: Simon & Schuster, 1989.

Ebon, Martin, ed. *Maharishi: The Guru.* New York: Signet, 1968.

Elson, Howard. *McCartney: Songwriter.* London: W. H. Allen, 1986.

Epstein, Brian. *A Cellarful of Noise.* London: Souvenir Press, 1964.

Evans, Mike, and Ron Jones. *In the Footsteps of the Beatles.* Liverpool: Merseyside Council, 1981.

Everett, Walter. *The Beatles as Musicians: The Quarry Men through Rubber Soul.* New York: Oxford University Press, 2001.

——. *The Beatles as Musicians: Revolver through the Anthology.* New York: Oxford University Press, 1999.

Ewen, David. *American Popular Songs: From the Revolutionary War to the Present.* New York: Random House, 1966.

Fantoni, Barry, and Karl Dallas. *Swinging London: A Guide to Where the Action Is.* London: Stanmore, 1967.

Farrow, Mia. *What Falls Away.* New York: Doubleday, 1997.

Fawcett, Anthony. *John Lennon: One Day at a Time.* New York: Grove, 1976.

Finnis, Rob. *The Phil Spector Story.* London: Rockon, 1975.

Flippo, Chet. *McCartney: The Biography.* London: Sidgwick & Jackson, 1988.

Fong-Torres, Ben, ed. *The Rolling Stone Rock 'n Roll Reader.* New York: Bantam, 1974.

Foot, Paul. *The Politics of Harold Wilson.* London: Penguin, 1968.

Freeman, Robert. *The Beatles in America.* London: Mirror Books, 1964.

——. *The Beatles: A Private View.* London: Pyramid, 1990.

——. *Yesterday: Photographs of the Beatles.* London: Weidenfeld & Nicholson, 1983.

Friede, Goldie. *The Beatles A to Z.* New York: Methuen, 1980.

Friedman, Rick. *The Beatles: Words Without Music.* New York: Grosset & Dunlap, 1968.

Frith, Simon. *Sound Effects: Youth, Leisure, and the Politics of Rock 'n Roll.* New York: Pantheon, 1981.

Frith, Simon, and Andrew Goodwin, eds. *On Record: Rock, Pop, and the Written Word.* New York: Pantheon, 1990.

Fulpen, H. V. *The Beatles: An Illustrated Diary.* London: Plexus, 1982.

Gambaccini, Paul. *Paul McCartney: In His Own Words.* London: Flash, 1976.

Garbarini, Vic, Brian Cullman, and Barbara Graustark. *Strawberry Fields Forever.* New York: Bantam, 1980.

Garry, Len. *John, Paul & Me Before the Beatles: The True Story of the Very Early Days.* London: Collector's Guide, 1997.

Gillett, Charlie, ed. *Rock File.* London: New English Library, 1972.

Gitlin, Todd. *The Sixties: Years of Hope, Days of Rage.* New York: Bantam, 1987.

Giuliano, Geoffrey. *The Beatles: A Celebration.* London: Sidgwick & Jackson, 1986.

——. *Blackbird: The Life and Times of Paul McCartney.* New York: Dutton, 1991.

——. *Dark Horse: The Secret Life of George Harrison.* London: Pan, 1991.

——. *The Lost Beatles Interviews.* New York: Dutton, 1994.

Giuliano, Geoffrey, and Vrnda Devi. *Glass Onion: The Beatles in Their Own Words.* New York: Da Capo, 1995.

Goldman, Albert. *Elvis.* New York: McGraw-Hill, 1981.

——. *The Lives of John Lennon.* New York: William Morrow, 1988.

Goldsmith, Martin. *The Beatles Come to America.* New York: Wiley & Sons, 2003.

Goldstein, Richard. *Goldstein's Greatest Hits.* Englewood Cliffs, N.J.: Prentice-Hall, 1970.

Goldthorpe, John H. *Social Mobility and Class Structure in Modern Britain.* London: Clarendon Press, 1980.

Gottfridsson, Hans Olof. *The Beatles: From Cavern to Star-Club.* Stockholm: Premium Publishing, 1997.

Green, Jonathon. *All Dressed Up: The Sixties and the Counterculture.* London: Jonathan Cape, 1998.

——. *Days in the Life.* London: Heinemann, 1988.

——. *It: Sex Since the Sixties.* London: Secker & Warburg, 1993.

Grove, Martin. *Beatle Madness.* New York: Manor, 1978.

Hall, Stuart, and Tony Jefferson, eds. *Resistance Through Rituals: Youth Subculture in Post-War Britain.* London: Hutchinson, 1970.

Hamilton, Richard. *Collected Words.* London: Thames & Hudson, 1982.

Harrison, George, with Derek Taylor. *I, Me, Mine.* New York: Simon & Schuster, 1980.

Harry, Bill. *The Beatles Who's Who.* London: Aurum, 1982.

——. *The Book of Beatle Lists.* London: Omnibus, 1977.

——. *The Book of Lennon.* London: Aurum, 1984.

——. *The Encyclopedia of Beatles People.* London: Blandford, 1997.

——. *The McCartney File.* London: Virgin, 1986.

——. *Paperback Writers: An Illustrated Bibliography.* London: Virgin, 1984.

——. *The Ultimate Beatles Encyclopedia.* New York: Hyperion, 1992.

Harry, Bill, ed. *Mersey Beat: The Beginnings of the Beatles.* London: Omnibus, 1977.

Hauser, Thomas. *Muhammed Ali: His Life and Times.* New York: Simon & Schuster, 1993.

Hebdige, Dick. *Subculture: The Meaning of Style.* London: Methuen, 1979.

Henri, Adrian. *Environments and Happenings.* London: Thames & Hudson, 1974.

Hertsgaard, Mark. *A Day in the Life: The Music and Artistry of the Beatles.* New York: Macmillan, 1995.

Hewison, Robert. *Too Much: Art and Society in the Sixties—1960–1975.* London: Methuen, 1986.

Hignet, Sean. *A Picture to Hang on the Wall.* London: Michael Joseph, 1966.

Hoffman, Dezo. *With the Beatles.* London: Omnibus, 1982.

Hoggart, Richard. *The Uses of Literacy.* London: Chatto & Windus, 1957.

Holloway, David, ed. *The Sixties: A Chronicle of a Decade.* New York: Simon & Schuster, 1992.

Hopkins, Jerry. *Yoko Ono.* New York: Macmillan, 1986.

Hotchner, A. E. *Blown Away: The Rolling Stones and the Death of the Sixties.* New York: Simon & Schuster, 1990.

Howlett, Kevin. *The Beatles at the Beeb: The Story of Their Radio Career.* London: BBC, 1982.

Hughes, Quentin. *Liverpool.* London: Studio Vista, 1969.

Hutchins, Chris, and Peter Thompson. *Elvis Meets the Beatles.* London: Gryphon, 1994.

Hutchinson, Roger. *High Sixties: The Summers of Riot and Love.* Edinburgh: Mainstream, 1992.

Ironside, Virginia. *Chelsea Bird.* London: Secker & Warburg, 1964.

——. *Janey.* London: Michael Joseph, 1973.

Jenkins, Richard. "Is Britain Civilized?" Chapter 9 from *The Labour Case.* London: Penguin, 1959.

Kane, Larry. *Ticket to Ride.* Scranton, Pa.: Running Press, 2003.

Kelly, Michael B. *The Beatle Myth: The British Invasion of American Popular Music.* London: McFarland, 1991.

Kirchherr, Astrid, and Klaus Voormann. *Hamburg Days.* Guildford (England): Genesis, 1999.

Klein, Joe. *Woody Guthrie: A Life.* New York: Knopf, 1980.

Kozinn, Allan. *The Beatles.* London: Phaidon Press, 1995.

Laing, David. *The Sound of Our Time.* New York: Quadrangle, 1969.

Larkin, Rochelle. *The Beatles: Yesterday, Today, Tomorrow.* New York: Scholastic, 1977.

Larson, Bob. *Hippies, Hindus, and Rock & Roll.* Illinois: Creation, 1972.

Leary, Timothy, and Richard Alpert. *The Psychedelic Experience.* New Hyde Park, N.Y.: University Books, 1964.

Leigh, Spencer. *Baby, That Is Rock and Roll: American Pop, 1954–1963.* Folkestone (England): Finbarr International, 2001.

——. *The Best of Fellas: The Story of Bob Wooler.* Liverpool: Drivegreen Publications, 2002.

——. *Drummed Out! The Sacking of Pete Best.* London: Northdown, 1998.

Leigh, Spencer, ed. *Speaking Words of Wisdom: Reflections on the Beatles.* Liverpool: Cavern City Tours, 1991.

Leigh, Spencer, and Peter Frame. *Let's Go Down the Cavern.* London: Hutchinson, 1984.

Lennon, Cynthia. *A Twist of Lennon.* London: Star, 1978.

Lennon, John. *In His Own Write.* London: Jonathan Cape, 1964.

——. *Skywriting by Word of Mouth.* New York: Harper & Row, 1986.

——. *A Spaniard in the Works.* London: Jonathan Cape, 1965.

Lennon, Pauline. *Daddy Come Home.* New York: HarperCollins, 1990.

Levin, Bernard. *The Pendulum Years: Britain and the Sixties.* London: Jonathan Cape, 1970.

Lewisohn, Mark. *The Beatles Day by Day.* New York: Harmony, 1990.

——. *The Beatles Live!* London: Pavilion, 1986.

——. *The Beatles: Recording Sessions.* New York: Harmony, 1988.

——. *The Beatles: 25 Years in the Life, A Chronology: 1962–1987.* London: Sidgwick & Jackson, 1987.

——. *The Complete Beatles Chronicle.* New York: Harmony, 1992.

Lobenthal, Joel. *Radical Rags: Fashion in the Sixties.* New York: Abbeville, 1990.

Lucie-Smith, Edward. *The Liverpool Scene.* London: Donald Carroll, 1967.

MacDonald, Ian. *Revolution in the Head: The Beatles' Records and the Sixties.* London: Fourth Estate, 1994.

Mailer, Norman. *The Fight.* Boston: Little, Brown and Company, 1975.

Marcus, Griel. *Rock and Roll Will Stand.* Boston: Beacon Press, 1969.

Martin, George. *All You Need Is Ears.* New York: St. Martin's, 1979.

——. *Summer of Love: The Making of Sgt. Pepper.* London: Macmillan, 1994.

Martin, George, ed. *Making Music.* London: Pan, 1983.

Marwick, Arthur. *British Society Since 1945.* London: Pelican, 1982.

——. *Class: Image and Reality.* London: Collins, 1980.

Masters, Brian. *The Swinging Sixties.* London: Constable, 1985.

McCabe, Peter, and Robert D. Schonfeld. *Apple to the Core: The Unmaking of the Beatles.* London: Brian & O'Keefe, 1972.

——. *John Lennon: For the Record.* New York: Bantam, 1984.

McCartney, Linda. *Linda McCartney's Sixties.* London: Pyramid, 1992.

——. *Linda's Pictures.* New York: Ballantine, 1977.

McCartney, Mike. *Thank U Very Much: Mike McCartney's Family Album.* London: Barker, 1981.

McCormick, William H. *The Modern Book of Ships.* London: A. & C. Black, 1936.

McDevitt, Chas. *Skiffle—The Definitive Inside Story.* London: Robson Books, 1994.

McKie, David, and Chris Cook, eds. *The Decade of Disillusion: British Politics in the 1960s.* New York: Macmillan, 1972.

Mellor, David. *The Sixties Art Scene in London.* London: Phaidon, 1993.

Mellors, Wilfred. *Twilight of the Gods.* New York: Viking, 1974.

Melly, George. *Owning Up.* London: Weidenfeld & Nicholson, 1965.

——. *Revolt Into Style: The Pop Arts in Britain.* London: Allen Lane, 1970.

Miles, Barry. *Paul McCartney: Many Years from Now.* New York: Henry Holt, 1997.

Miles, Barry, ed. *Beatles in Their Own Words.* London: W. H. Allen, 1978.

——. *John Lennon in His Own Words.* London: Omnibus, 1980.

Mitchell, Carolyn Lee. *All Our Loving: A Beatle Fan's Memoir.* London: Robson, 1988.

Morley, Deirdre. *Look Liverpool: Images of a Great Seaport.* Liverpool: Light Impressions, 1985.

Musgrove, Frank. *Youth and the Social Order.* London: Routledge & Kegan Paul, 1964.

Naha, Ed, ed. *The Beatles Forever.* New York: O'Quinn Studios, 1980.

Napier-Bell, Simon. *You Don't Have to Say You Love Me.* London: New English Library, 1982.

Neaverson, Bob. *The Beatles Movies.* London: Cassell, 1997.

Neises, Charles, ed. *The Beatles Reader.* Ann Arbor: Pierian, 1984.

Neville, Richard. *Play Power.* London: Jonathan Cape, 1970.

Nimmervoll, Ed, and Euan Thorburn, eds. *100 Beatle Facts.* Sydney: J. Albert, 1977.

Noble, Trevor. *Modern Britain: Structure and Change.* London: Batsford, 1975.

Norman, Phillip. *Shout!* New York: Simon & Schuster, 1981.

Nuttall, Jeff. *Bomb Culture.* London: MacGibbon & Kee, 1968.

Obst, Linda, ed. *The Sixties.* New York: Rolling Stone Press, 1977.

O'Connor, Freddy. *Liverpool: It All Came Tumbling Down*. Liverpool: Brunswick, 1984.

O'Donnell, Jim. *The Day John Met Paul*. New York: Hall of Fame, 1994.

O'Grady, Terence J. *The Beatles: A Musical Evolution*. Boston: Twayne, 1983.

Okun, Milton, ed. *The Compleat Beatles*. New York: Bantam, 1981.

Oldham, Andrew Loog. *Stoned: A Memoir of London in the 1960s*. New York: St. Martin's, 2000.

Ono, Yoko. *Grapefruit*. Bellport, N.Y.: Wunternaum Press, 1964.

——. *John Lennon: Summer of 1980*. New York: Perigee, 1983.

Ornstein, Edward, and C. Austin Nunn. *The Marketing Leisure*. London: Associated, Business, 1980.

Pascall, Jeremy, ed. *The Fabulous Story of John, Paul, George, and Ringo*. London: Octopus, 1975.

Pawlowski, Gareth. *How They Became the Beatles: A Definitive History of the Early Years, 1960–1964*. New York: E. P. Dutton, 1989.

Perry, Helen. *The Human Be-In*. London: Allen Lane, 1968.

Picton, J. A. *Architectural History of Liverpool*. Liverpool: privately printed, 1858.

——. *Memorials of Liverpool, Historical and Topographical*. London: Longman, Green, 1875.

——. *Views in Modern Liverpool*. Liverpool: Marples, 1864.

Poirier, Richard. *The Performing Self*. New York: Oxford University Press, 1971.

Pym, Bridget. *Pressure Groups and the Permissive Society*. London: David & Charles, 1974.

Quant, Mary. *Quant by Quant*. London: Cassell, 1966.

Raison, Timothy, ed. *Youth in New Society*. London: Rupert Hart-Davis, 1966.

Rayl, A. J. S. *Beatles '64: A Hard Day's Night in America*. London: Sidgwick & Jackson, 1989.

Rehwagen, Thomas, and Thorsten Schmidt. *Mach Schau: Die Beatles in Hamburg*. Braunschweig: EinfallReich, 1992.

Reich, Charles. *The Greening of America*. New York: Random House, 1970.

Reilly, C. H. *Some Liverpool Streets and Buildings in 1921*. Liverpool: Livery Daily Post & Mercury, 1921.

Reinhart, Charles. *You Can't Do That! Beatles Bootlegs and Novelty Records*. Ann Arbor: Pierian, 1981.

Remnick, David. *King of the World*. New York: Random House, 1998.

Riley, Tim. *Tell Me Why: The Beatles Album by Album Song by Song*. New York: Knopf, 1988.

Roberts, Kenneth. *Leisure*. London: Longman, 1981.

Rogan, Johnny. *Starmakers & Svengalis: The History of British Pop Management*. London: Macdonald, 1988.

Rolling Stone, Editors of. *The Age of Paranoia*. New York: Pocket Books, 1972.

——. *The Ballad of John and Yoko*. New York: Doubleday, 1982.

——. *The Rolling Stone Interviews*. New York: Paperback Library, 1971.

——. *The Rolling Stone Record Reviews*. New York: Pocket Books, 1971.

——. *Rolling Stone Rock Almanac*. New York: Collier, 1983.

Roszak, Theodore. *The Making of a Counter Culture*. New York: Doubleday, 1969.

Russell, Jeff. *The Beatles: Album File and Complete Discography*. London: Blandford, 1989.

Salewicz, Chris. *McCartney*. New York: St. Martin's, 1986.

Saimaru, Nishi F. *John Lennon: A Family Album*. Tokyo: Fly Communications, 1982.

Sampson, Anthony. *Anatomy of Britain*. London: Hodder & Stoughton, 1962.

Sanchez, Tony. *Up and Down with the Rolling Stones*. New York: William Morrow, 1979.

Scaduto, Anthony. *Bob Dylan: An Intimate Biography*. New York: Grosset & Dunlap, 1971.

Schaffner, Nicholas. *The Beatles Forever*. Rev. ed. New York: McGraw-Hill, 1978.

——. *The British Invasion*. New York: McGraw-Hill, 1982.

Schaumberg, Ron. *Growing Up with the Beatles*. New York: Pyramid, 1976.

Schultheiss, Tom. *A Day in the Life: The Beatles Day-by-Day.* Ann Arbor: Pierian, 1980.

Schumann, Bettina, ed. *Insight Guides: Germany.* Boston: Houghton Mifflin, 1996.

Schwartz, Francie. *Body Count.* San Francisco: Straight Arrow, 1972.

Shankar, Ravi. *My Music, My Life.* New York: Simon & Schuster, 1968.

Sheff, David, and G. Barry Golson, eds. *The Playboy Interviews with John Lennon and Yoko Ono.* New York: Playboy Press, 1981.

Shepherd, Billy [Peter Jones]. *The True Story of the Beatles.* New York: Bantam, 1964.

Shevy, Sandra. *The Other Side of Lennon.* London: Sidgwick & Jackson, 1990.

Shipper, Mark. *Paperback Writer.* London: New English Library, 1978.

Shotton, Pete, and Nicholas Schaffner. *John Lennon in My Life.* New York: Stein and Day, 1983.

Sinyard, Neil. *The Films of Richard Lester.* London: Croom Helm, 1985.

Slater, Philip E. *The Pursuit of Loneliness.* Boston: Beacon Press, 1970.

Solt, Andrew, and Sam Egan. *Imagine: John Lennon.* New York: Macmillan, 1988.

Somach, Denny, and Kathleen and Kevin Gunn. *Ticket to Ride.* New York: Quill, 1989.

Somach, Denny, and Ken Sharp. *Meet the Beatles . . . Again!* Havertown, Pa.: Musicom International, 1995.

Southall, Brian. *Abbey Road: The Story of the World's Most Famous Recording Studio.* Cambridge (England): Stevens, 1982.

Spector, Ronnie, with Vince Waldron. *Be My Baby.* New York: Harmony, 1990.

Spence, Helen. *The Beatles Forever.* London: Colour Library, 1981.

Spencer, Terence. *It Was Thirty Years Ago Today.* London: Bloomsbury, 1994.

Spitz, Bob. *Dylan: A Biography.* New York: McGraw-Hill, 1989.

——. *The Making of Superstars.* New York: Doubleday, 1978.

Spizer, Bruce. *The Beatles Are Coming! The Birth of Beatlemania in America.* New Orleans: 498 Productions, 2003.

Stannard, Neville. *The Beatles: A History of the Beatles on Record: The Long and Winding Road.* Vol. 1. London: Virgin, 1982.

——. *The Beatles: A History of the Beatles on Record: Working Class Heroes.* Vol. 2. London: Virgin, 1983.

Steele-Perkins, Chris, and Richard Smith. *The Teds.* London: Traveling Light/Exit, 1987.

Stewart, Tony, ed. *Cool Cats: 25 Years of Rock 'n Roll Style.* London: Eel Pie, 1981.

Stone, Steve, ed. *John Lennon: All You Need Is Love.* New York: Marjam, 1980.

Sulpy, Doug, and Ray Schweighardt. *Get Back: The Unauthorized Chronicle of the Beatles' Let It Be Disaster.* New York: St. Martin's, 1997.

Sutcliffe, Pauline, and Kay Williams. *Stuart–the Life and Art of Stuart Sutcliffe.* London: Genesis, 1995.

Swenson, John. *The John Lennon Story.* New York: Leisure, 1981.

Tashian, Barry. *Ticket to Ride: The Extraordinary Diary of the Beatles' Last Tour.* Nashville: Dowling Press, 1997.

Taylor, Alistair. *Yesterday: The Beatles Remembered.* London: Sidgwick & Jackson, 1988.

Taylor, Derek. *As Time Goes By: Living in the Sixties.* San Francisco: Straight Arrow, 1973.

——. *Fifty Years Adrift.* London: Genesis, 1984.

——. *It Was Twenty Years Ago Today.* New York: Bantam, 1987.

Terry, Carol. *Here, There, and Everywhere: The Beatles First International Bibliography.* Ann Arbor: Pierian, 1990.

Thompson, Phil. *The Best of Cellars: The Story of the World Famous Cavern Club.* Liverpool: Bluecoat, 1994.

Thomson, Elizabeth, and David Gutman. *The Lennon Companion.* New York: Macmillan, 1987.

Tremlett, George. *The Alvin Stardust Story.* London: Futura, 1976.

——. *The John Lennon Story.* London: Futura, 1976.

——. *The Paul McCartney Story.* London: Futura, 1975.

——. *Rock Gold: The Music Millionaires.* London: Unwin Hyman, 1990.

Turner, Steve. *A Hard Day's Write: The Stories Behind Every Beatles Song.* London: Carlton, 1994.

Twiggy. *Twiggy.* London: Hart-Davis, 1975.

Walgren, Mark. *The Beatles on Record.* New York: Simon & Schuster, 1982.

Ward, Ed, Geoffrey Stokes, and Ken Tucker. *Rock of Ages: The Rolling Stone History of Rock & Roll.* New York: Rolling Stone Press, 1985.

Welch, Chris. *Paul McCartney: The Definitive Biography.* London: Proteus, 1984.

Wenner, Jann. *Lennon Remembers.* New York: Fawcett, 1971.

Whale, Derek. *Lost Villages of Liverpool.* Liverpool: Stephenson & Sons, 1978.

Wheen, Francis. *The Sixties: A Fresh Look at the Decade of Change.* London: Century, 1982.

Whitaker, Bob. *The Unseen Beatles.* London: Octopus, 1991.

Whitburn, Joel. *The Billboard Book of Top 40 Hits.* New York: Billboard Publications, 1983.

White, Charles. *The Life and Times of Little Richard.* London: Pan, 1984.

White, Timothy. *Rock Lives: Profiles and Interviews.* New York: Henry Holt, 1990.

Whittington-Egan, Richard. *Liverpool Colonnade.* Liverpool: Philip, Son & Nephew, 1955.

Widgery, David. *The Left in Britain, 1956–1968.* London: Penguin, 1976.

Wiener, Jon. *Come Together: John Lennon in His Time.* New York: Random House, 1984.

Willett, John. *Art in a City.* London: Methuen, 1967.

Williams, Allan, and William Marshall. *The Man Who Gave the Beatles Away.* London: Coronet, 1975.

Williams, Richard. *Out of His Head: The Sound of Phil Spector.* New York: Outerbridge & Lazard, 1972.

Willis, Paul. *Profane Culture.* London: Routledge & Kegan Paul, 1978.

Winn, John C. *Way Beyond Compare: The Beatles' Recorded Legacy, Vol. 1—1957–1965.* Sharon, Vt.: Multiplus, 2003.

——. *That Magic Feeling: The Beatles' Recorded Legacy, Vol. 2—1966–1970.* Sharon, Vt.: Multiplus, 2004.

Woffinden, Bob. *The Beatles Apart.* New York: Proteus, 1971.

Wyman, Bill, and Ray Coleman. *Stone Alone: The Story of a Rock 'n Roll Band.* New York: Viking, 1990.

Yule, Andrew. *The Man Who Framed the Beatles.* New York: Donald I. Fine, 1994.

Zint, Günter. *Grosse Freihei 39t.* Munich: Wilhelm Heyne, 1987.

PAMPHLETS, FANZINES, AND CATALOGS

"Brian Epstein Presents THE BEATLES Christmas Show." Souvenir program. December 1965.

Beatles Book Monthly, The. August 1963 through July 1987, all volumes.

Beatlefan, issues 1–89.

Beatles Unlimited (Dutch magazine).

"Cenario Area Profile Report" for Litherland, Liverpool, 1960.

"Fab Four on Tour!" Press accounts of the 1964 American concert tour prepared by Musicom International for promotional use.

"Fluxus, Etc." Cranbrook Academy of Art Museum. Michigan, 1981.

Leach, Sam. *Follow the Merseybeat Road: With the Beatles.* Liverpool: Eden Pub., 1983, 1992.

Legman, G. *The Fake Revolt.* New York: Breaking Point, 1967.

Liverpool Institute Green Book, 1958.

Machin, W. F. *A Short History of the Liverpool Cotton Market.* Liverpool: Liverpool Cotton Assn.

UNPUBLISHED SOURCES

Barrow, Tony. "Manila: July 1966." Typescript.

——. "California, 1965." Typescript.

Bennett, B., C. Crickmay, and N. S. Sturrock. Report on Central and Lime Street Stations."
    Typescript. University of Liverpool, 1963.
Brooks, N. Gough, and J. Ritchie. "Warehouses in Liverpool." Typescript. University of
    Liverpool, 1961.
Harry, Bill. "Mersey Beat: The Book." Proposal for unpublished manuscript, 1997.
King, M. J. "Commercial Architecture in Liverpool, 1750–1900." Typescript. University of
    Liverpool, 1963.
Leach, Sam. "Some of My Beatles Memories." Typescript, 1993.
Murray, Joan, "The Irish in Liverpool." Unpublished manuscript, 1984.
Williams, Allan. "The Liverpool Scene from the Inside." Unpublished manuscript, 1965.
Yolland, Peter. "The Beatles Christmas Show, 1963." Typescript, 1963.
——. "Another Beatle's [sic] Christmas Show, 1964/5." Typescript, 1965.

LETTERS AND PERSONAL CORRESPONDENCE
To John Mohin, from Raghnall O'Floinn, Assistant Keeper, Irish Antiquities Division,
    National Museum of Ireland, 11/16/89, details of Mohin family history.
To Bill Harry, from Jonathan Hague, details of art school days with John Lennon.
To Arthur Kelly, from George Harrison, 1962, details of working in Hamburg.
To Bill Harry, from Erich Weber, Unna, Germany, 6/21/97, details of Rosa "Mutti"
    Hoffman's birth and death.
Brian Epstein's personal diaries, 1946–60. Courtesy of Bryan Barrett.
Brian Epstein's journal, 1957. Courtesy of Bryan Barrett.
Brian Epstein's dress designs. Courtesy of Bryan Barrett.
Brian Epstein's letters, poetry, and memorandums. Courtesy of Bryan Barrett.
Architectural renderings for John and Cynthia Lennon's house, Weybridge. Courtesy of
    Ken Partridge.

AUDIO/SPOKEN WORD
"John, Paul & Me: Len Garry & Pete Shotton Tour Liverpool and 'Mendips,'" 1997, GCP
    Ltd.
"The Beatles in Their Own Words: A Rocumentary," by Geoffrey Giuliano, Laserlight
    Digital
"The Beatles: Not a Second Time," 1992, Cicadellic Records, Dallas, TX
"The Fab Four on Tour: Larry Kane with the Beatles on Their 1965 American Tour." 1996,
    Dynamic Images
Murray the K Interview—WINS Radio
Capitol Records Interview
KPPC/WBCN/WLS—interviews with George Harrison
KQV Interview with George Harrison
Scott Muni interview with John Lennon and Yoko Ono
Art Schreiber's interviews (1–12) with Ringo, John, George, Derek Taylor, Paul, and fans
Jerry G's interviews with all of the Beatles, and separately with Ringo, George, and Paul
Pop Goes the Bulldog
Carroll James (WWDC)—How "I Want to Hold Your Hand" Became a Hit
WNET interview with John Lennon and Paul McCartney, 5/15/68
Ken Douglas interviews 1 and 2
Monty Lister interview, 10/27/62
Non-Stop Pop, 8/63
Dibbs Mather interview, 12/10/63
AFM interview, Paris, 1/24/64
First album open-end interview, 1964
Fred Robbins interview, 2/7/64
WQAM, Miami, 2/64
Murray the K interviews, 2/64

Washington, D.C., interview, 2/64

Telephone interview, Miami, 1964

Public Ear, 3/22/64

Saturday Club chat, 4/4/64

Larry Kane interview, Las Vegas Convention Center, 8/20/64

Seattle press conference, Seattle Coliseum, 8/21/64

Jim Steck interview, Reginald Owens Mansion, Los Angeles, 8/25/64 and 8/26/64

Larry Kane interview, Delmonico Hotel, New York, 8/28/64

Jacksonville, FL, 9/11/64

Press conference, 1965

Dieter Broer interview, London (undated)

Murray the K interview with George Harrison, re: Pattie Boyd

Wink Martindale interview, KFWB, 1964

Beatles second album open-end interview, 4/64

Tom Clay interview, 1964

Vancouver interview, 8/22/64

Seattle interview, 8/21/64

Beatles press conferences: Indianapolis, Cincinnati

Wilfred D'Ath interview with John Lennon, 6/15/65

Paul McCartney interview re: *Help!*, 1965

"A Midsummer Night's Dream" Sketch (Around the Beatles), 4/28/64

"If I Fell" and sketch ("Big Night Out"), 7/19/64

Radio Luxembourg interviews with George, John, Ringo, and Paul, 4/65

Eamonn Andrews interviews, parts 1 and 2, 4/11/65

Tim Lodge interview, "Sound of the Stars," 3/25/66

Interview with Paul McCartney, *The David Frost Show,* 12/27/67

Radio Luxembourg interview with Paul re: the White Album, 11/20/68

Radio Luxembourg interview with John re: *Abbey Road,* 9/69

Murray the K interview with George, 8/67

Everett Denning interview with the Beatles, 6/6/68

Beatles tour coverage by Bess Coleman: Chicago, 8/12/66; Boston, with Ringo, 8/18/66;
    with George, 8/18/66; with John and Paul, 8/18/66; Cincinnati, 8/20/66; Memphis,
    8/19/66; Cleveland, 8/14/66; Memphis, with John and Paul, 8/19/66; Philadelphia, with
    Ringo, 8/16/66; Toronto, 8/17/66; with George Harrison, 8/17/66; St. Louis, 8/21/66

Bruce Morrow interview, WABC, New York, 8/22/66

WMCA, New York coverage, 8/22/66

WMCA, New York, Beatles press conference, 8/22/66

BBC, "The Lennon-McCartney Songbook," 8/29/66

Saturday Club 400, 6/9/66

Beatles coverage, Chicago, 8/12/66

Capitol Teen Set, with John and Paul, 8/65

BBC, Beatles in New York, 8/24/65

"Beatles Abroad," BBC, 25 separate broadcasts, including music and interviews,
    8/30/65

Apple press conference, New York, John and Paul, 5/13/68

Newsfront, John and Paul, 5/14/68

Tonight Show, John and Paul, 5/14/68

David Frost Presents, Paul with Mary Hopkin, 10/9/68

Light and Local, BBC, with Paul, 5/69

Kid Jensen interview with Ringo re: *Abbey Road,* 9/26/69

"Is Paul McCartney Dead?" WNEW-FM, New York, 11/69

George Harrison interview re: meditation, 1970

George Harrison interview re: Beatles breakup, 1970

Howard Smith interview, WPLJ-FM, New York with John and Yoko, 1/23/72

INTERVIEWS FROM OTHER SOURCES

BBC, *Arena:* interviews for "Brian Epstein"
BBC archives: Beatles radio appearances, 1963–69
Albert Goldman Archives: interviews for *The Lives of John Lennon*
Green, Jonathon: interviews with Derek Taylor, Paul McCartney, John Dunbar
Harry, Bill: interviews with Pauline Sutcliffe; interviews with Pete Best for *The Best Years of the Beatles*
Meade, Scott: interviews for *The Abbey Road Story*
Samuels, Leslie: Paul McCartney and George Harrison interviewed at their homes, July 1967
Wenner, Jann: interviews for *Lennon Remembers* (unedited)

VIDEO

Abbey Road Story, The, EPL Pictures, 1996
A Hard Day's Night (CD-ROM, early uncut version), 1964, Voyager Co.
All You Need Is Cash, BBC-TV, Channel 4
Arena: The Strange Story of Joe Meek, BBC-TV, 1994
Arena: "Brian Epstein," BBC-TV, 1999
Beat City
Beatles Anthology, The, Apple Corps Ltd., Capitol Video, 1996
Lennon and McCartney with Larry Kane, New York, 5/16/68
Mersey Sound, The, BBC-TV, 1964
The Story of Mersey Beat, MGM/UA Home Video, 1986
The Beatles: The First U.S. Visit, Apple/MPL Home Video, 1964, 1990
The Beatles in Washington, D.C., Passport Video, 2003
Beatles Around the World, Entertainment Properties, 2003
Four Complete Historic Ed Sullivan Shows Featuring the Beatles, Sofa Entertainment, 2003
Sound of a City, Rank Cinema Series, 1964
Who Put the Beat in Merseybeat?, 1966
You Can't Do That: The Making of "A Hard Day's Night," VCI, 1994

INTERNET SOURCES

http://mapage.noos.fr/beatlesarchives/index.htm
www.beatlefan.com
www.beatlesite.com
www.macca-central.com
www.mplcommunications.com/mccartney
www.rarebeatles.com
www.pcug.org.au/~jhenry (George Martin)

DISCOGRAPHY

U.S. SINGLES

"My Bonnie" / "The Saints." April 23, 1962. Decca 31382 (Tony Sheridan and the Beat Brothers)

"Please Please Me" / "Ask Me Why." February 25, 1963. Vee Jay VJ 498

"From Me to You" / "Thank You Girl." May 27, 1963. Vee Jay VJ 522

"She Loves You" / "I'll Get You." September 16, 1963. Swan 4152

"I Want to Hold Your Hand" / "I Saw Her Standing There." December 26, 1963. Capitol 5112

"Please Please Me" / "From Me to You." January 30, 1964. Vee Jay VJ 581

"Twist and Shout" / "There's a Place." March 2, 1964. Tollie 9001

"Can't Buy Me Love" / "You Can't Do That." March 16, 1964. Capitol 5150

"Do You Want to Know a Secret" / "Thank You Girl." March 23, 1964. Vee Jay VJ 587

"Love Me Do" / "P.S. I Love You." April 27, 1964. Tollie 9008

"Sie Liebt Dich" / "I'll Get You." May 21, 1964. Swan 4182

"A Hard Day's Night" / "I Should Have Known Better." July 13, 1964. Capitol 5222

"I'll Cry Instead" / "I'm Happy Just to Dance with You." July 20, 1964. Capitol 5234

"And I Love Her" / "If I Fell." July 20, 1964. Capitol 5235

"Matchbox" / "Slow Down." August 24, 1964. Capitol 5255

"I Feel Fine" / "She's a Woman." November 23, 1964. Capitol 5327

"Eight Days a Week" / "I Don't Want to Spoil the Party." February 15, 1965. Capitol 5371

"Ticket to Ride" / "Yes It Is." April 19, 1965. Capitol 5407

"Help!" / "I'm Down." July 19, 1965. Capitol 5476

"Yesterday" / "Act Naturally." September 13, 1965. Capitol 5498

"Day Tripper" / "We Can Work It Out." December 6, 1965. Capitol 5555

"Nowhere Man" / "What Goes On." February 21, 1966. Capitol 5587

"Paperback Writer" / "Rain." May 30, 1966. Capitol 5651

"Eleanor Rigby" / "Yellow Submarine." August 8, 1966. Capitol 5715

"Strawberry Fields Forever" / "Penny Lane." February 13, 1967. Capitol 5810

"All You Need Is Love" / "Baby You're a Rich Man." July 17, 1967. Capitol 5964

"Hello Goodbye" / "I Am the Walrus." November 27, 1967. Capitol 2056

"Lady Madonna" / "The Inner Light." March 18, 1968. Capitol 2138

"Hey Jude" / "Revolution." August 26, 1968. Apple 2276

"Get Back" / "Don't Let Me Down." May 5, 1969. Apple 2490

"The Ballad of John and Yoko" / "Old Brown Shoe." June 4, 1969. Apple 2531

"Something" / "Come Together." October 6, 1969. Apple 2654

"Let It Be" / "You Know My Name (Look Up the Number)." March 11, 1970. Apple 2764

"The Long and Winding Road" / "For You Blue." May 11, 1970. Apple 2832

U.S. ALBUMS

Introducing the Beatles. July 22, 1963. Vee Jay VJLP 1062 (mono), SR 1062 (stereo)
A: "I Saw Her Standing There" "Misery" "Anna (Go to Him)" "Chains" "Boys" "Love Me Do"
B: "P.S. I Love You" "Baby It's You" "Do You Want to Know a Secret" "A Taste of Honey" "There's a Place" "Twist and Shout"

Meet the Beatles. January 20, 1964. Capitol T-2047 (mono), ST-2047 (stereo)
A: "I Want to Hold Your Hand" "I Saw Her Standing There" "This Boy" "It Won't Be Long" "All I've Got to Do" "All My Loving"
B: "Don't Bother Me" "Little Child" "Till There Was You" "Hold Me Tight" "I Wanna Be Your Man" "Not a Second Time"

The Beatles Second Album. April 10, 1964. Capitol T-2080 (mono), ST-2080 (stereo)
A: "Roll Over Beethoven" "Thank You Girl" "You Really Got a Hold on Me" "Devil in Her Heart" "Money (That's What I Want)" "You Can't Do That"
B: "Long Tall Sally" "I Call Your Name" "Please Mr. Postman" "I'll Get You" "She Loves You"

A Hard Day's Night. June 26, 1964. United Artists UA 6366 (mono), UAS 6366 (stereo)
A: "A Hard Day's Night" "Tell Me Why" "I'll Cry Instead" "I'm Happy Just to Dance with You" (two instrumentals by George Martin & Orchestra)
B: "I Should Have Known Better" "If I Fell" "And I Love Her" "Can't Buy Me Love" (two instrumentals by George Martin & Orchestra)

Something New. July 20, 1964. Capitol T-2108 (mono), ST-2108 (stereo)
A: "I'll Cry Instead" "Things We Said Today" "Any Time at All" "When I Get Home" "Slow Down" "Matchbox"
B: "Tell Me Why" "And I Love Her" "I'm Happy Just to Dance with You" "If I Fell" "Komm, Gib Mir Deine Hand"

The Beatles Story. November 23, 1964. Capitol TBO-2222 (mono), STBO-2222 (stereo)
A: Interviews, excerpts from "I Want to Hold Your Hand" "Slow Down" "This Boy"
B: Interviews, excerpts from "You Can't Do That" "If I Fell" "And I Love Her"
C: Interviews, excerpts from "A Hard Day's Night" "And I Love Her"
D: Interviews, excerpts from "Twist and Shout" "Things We Said Today" "I'm Happy Just to Dance with You" "Little Child" "Long Tall Sally" "She Loves You" "Boys"

Beatles '65. December 15, 1964. Capitol T-2228 (mono), ST-2228 (stereo)
A: "No Reply" "I'm a Loser" "Baby's in Black" "Rock and Roll Music" "I'll Follow the Sun" "Mr. Moonlight"
B: "Honey Don't" "I'll Be Back" "She's a Woman" "I Feel Fine" "Everybody's Trying to Be My Baby"

The Early Beatles. March 22, 1965. Capitol T-2309 (mono), ST-2309 (stereo)
A: "Love Me Do" "Twist and Shout" "Anna (Go to Him)" "Chains" "Boys" "Ask Me Why"
B: "Please Please Me" "P.S. I Love You" "Baby It's You" "A Taste of Honey" "Do You Want to Know a Secret"

Beatles VI. June 14, 1965. Capitol T-2358 (mono), ST-2358 (stereo)
A: "Kansas City" "Eight Days a Week" "You Like Me Too Much" "Bad Boy" "I Don't Want to Spoil the Party" "Words of Love"
B: "What You're Doing" "Yes It Is" "Dizzy Miss Lizzie" "Tell Me What You See" "Every Little Thing"

Help! August 13, 1965. Capitol MAS-2386 (mono), SMAS-2386 (stereo)
A: "Help!" "The Night Before" "You've Got to Hide Your Love Away" "I Need You" (three instrumentals by George Martin & Orchestra)
B: "Another Girl" "Ticket to Ride" "You're Going to Lose That Girl" (three instrumentals by George Martin & Orchestra)

Rubber Soul. December 6, 1965. Capitol T-2442 (mono), ST-2442 (stereo)
A: "I've Just Seen a Face" "Norwegian Wood (This Bird Has Flown)" "You Won't See Me" "Think for Yourself" "The Word" "Michelle"

B: "It's Only Love" "Girl" "I'm Looking Through You" "In My Life" "Wait" "Run for Your Life"

Yesterday . . . And Today. June 20, 1966. Capitol T-2553 (mono), ST-2553 (stereo)

A: "Drive My Car" "I'm Only Sleeping" "Nowhere Man" "Dr. Robert" "Yesterday" "Act Naturally"

B: "And Your Bird Can Sing" "If I Needed Someone" "We Can Work It Out" "What Goes On?" "Day Tripper"

Revolver. August 8, 1966. Capitol T-2576 (mono), ST-2576 (stereo)

A: "Taxman" "Eleanor Rigby" "Love You To" "Here, There and Everywhere" "Yellow Submarine" "She Said, She Said"

B: "Good Day Sunshine" "For No One" "I Want to Tell You" "Got to Get You into My Life" "Tomorrow Never Knows"

Sgt. Pepper's Lonely Hearts Club Band. June 2, 1967. Capitol MAS-2653 (mono), SMAS-2653 (stereo)

A: "Sgt. Pepper's Lonely Hearts Club Band" "With a Little Help from My Friends" "Lucy in the Sky with Diamonds" "Getting Better" "Fixing a Hole" "She's Leaving Home" "Being for the Benefit of Mr. Kite!"

B: "Within You Without You" "When I'm Sixty-four" "Lovely Rita" "Good Morning, Good Morning" "Sgt. Pepper's Lonely Hearts Club Band (reprise)" "A Day in the Life"

Magical Mystery Tour. November 27, 1967. Capitol MAL-2835 (mono), SMAL-2835 (stereo)

A: "Magical Mystery Tour" "The Fool on the Hill" "Flying" "Blue Jay Way" "Your Mother Should Know" "I Am the Walrus"

B: "Hello Goodbye" "Strawberry Fields Forever" "Penny Lane" "Baby You're a Rich Man" "All You Need Is Love"

The Beatles (White Album). November 25, 1968. Apple SO-383 (stereo only)

A: "Back in the U.S.S.R." "Dear Prudence" "Glass Onion" "Ob-La-Di, Ob-La-Da" "Wild Honey Pie" "The Continuing Story of Bungalow Bill" "While My Guitar Gently Weeps" "Happiness Is a Warm Gun"

B: "Martha My Dear" "I'm So Tired" "Blackbird" "Piggies" "Rocky Raccoon" "Don't Pass Me By" "Why Don't We Do It In the Road" "I Will" "Julia"

C: "Birthday" "Yer Blues" "Mother Nature's Son" "Everybody's Got Something to Hide Except Me and My Monkey" "Sexy Sadie" "Helter Skelter" "Long, Long, Long"

D: "Revolution I" "Honey Pie" "Savoy Truffle" "Cry Baby Cry" "Revolution 9" "Good Night"

Yellow Submarine. January 13, 1969. Apple SW-153 (stereo only)

A: "Yellow Submarine" "Only a Northern Song" "All Together Now" "Hey Bulldog" "It's All Too Much" "All You Need Is Love"

B: Seven instrumentals by the George Martin Orchestra

Abbey Road. October 1, 1969. Apple SO-383 (stereo only)

A: "Come Together" "Something" "Maxwell's Silver Hammer" "Oh! Darling" "Octopus's Garden" "I Want You (She's So Heavy)"

B: "Here Comes the Sun" "Because" "You Never Give Me Your Money" "Sun King" "Mean Mr. Mustard" "Polythene Pam" "She Came in Through the Bathroom Window" "Golden Slumbers" "Carry That Weight" "The End" "Her Majesty"

Hey Jude. February 26, 1970. Apple SW-385 (stereo only)

A: "Can't Buy Me Love" "I Should Have Known Better" "Paperback Writer" "Rain" "Lady Madonna" "Revolution"

B: "Hey Jude" "Old Brown Shoe" "Don't Let Me Down" "The Ballad of John and Yoko"

Let It Be. May 18, 1970. Apple AR-34001 (stereo only)

A: "Two of Us" "I Dig a Pony" "Across the Universe" "I Me Mine" "Dig It" "Let It Be" "Maggie Mae"

B: "I've Got a Feeling" "One After 909" "The Long and Winding Road" "For You Blue" "Get Back"

ABOUT THE AUTHOR

Bob Spitz has represented the careers of Bruce Springsteen and Elton John. He is also the author of the books *The Making of Superstars, Barefoot in Babylon, Dylan: A Biography*, and *Shoot Out the Lights*, as well as of the screenplay *Silent Victim*. His articles appear regularly in the *New York Times Magazine, GQ, Condé Nast Traveler, Men's Journal, In Style, Esquire, Sky*, and the *Washington Post*. He lives in Connecticut and can be reached at thebeatles@bobspitz.com.